THE DC COMICS ENCYCLOPEDIA

THE DEFINITIVE GUIDE TO THE CHARACTERS OF THE DC UNIVERSE

SENIOR EDITORS: Alastair Dougall, Cefn Ridout
SENIOR DESIGNERS: Nathan Martin, Robert Perry
EDITORS: Elizabeth Dowsett, Kate Berens, Kathryn Hill, Laura Palosuo
DESIGNERS: Ray Bryant, Gary Hyde, Nick Avery, Simon Murrell, Anna Pond
ORIGINAL COVER ARTWORK: Mikel Janín
SENIOR PRODUCTION CONTROLLER: Louise Minihane
PRODUCTION EDITOR: Siu Chan
MANAGING EDITOR: Sarah Harland
MANAGING ART EDITOR: Vicky Short
PUBLISHING DIRECTOR: Mark Searle

Dorling Kindersley would like to thank:
Benjamin Harper and Josh Anderson at Warner Bros. Global Publishing;
Joe Daley, Benjamin Le Clear, Hank Manfra, Mike Pallotta, Leah Tuttle, Erin Vanover at DC.

Many thanks to: Simon Beecroft, Julie Ferris, Lisa Lanzarini, Sadie Smith, Ron Stobbart.
Editorial assistance: Nicole Reynolds, Victoria Armstrong, Pamela Afram,
David Fentiman, Emma Grange, Lauren Nesworthy, Tina Jindal, Joel Kempson.
Design assistance: Ros Bird, Kathryn Boynton, Mabel Chan, Jo Connor, Jon Hall,
Guy Harvey, Gema Salamanca, Anna Sander, Clive Savage, Rhys Thomas, Pallavi Kapur.
Fact checking: John Wells. Proofreading: Simon Hugo. Index: Helen Peters.

First American Edition, 2021
Published in the United States by DK Publishing
1450 Broadway, Suite 801, New York, NY 10018

A catalog record for this book is available
from the Library of Congress.
ISBN 978-0-7440-2056-4

DK books are available at special discounts when purchased in bulk
for sales promotions, premiums, fund-raising, or educational use.
For details, contact: DK Publishing Special Markets,
1450 Broadway, Suite 801, New York, New York 10018
SpecialSales@dk.com

Printed and bound in China

For the curious
www.dk.com

This book is made from
Forest Stewardship Council™
certified paper—one small
step in DK's commitment
to a sustainable future.

THE DC COMICS
ENCYCLOPEDIA
THE DEFINITIVE GUIDE TO THE CHARACTERS OF THE DC UNIVERSE

Text by
MATT MANNING
STEPHEN (WIN) WIACEK
MELANIE SCOTT
NICK JONES
LANDRY Q. WALKER

Additional text by
ALAN COWSILL
ALEX IRVINE
STEVE KORTÉ
SCOTT BEATTY
ROBERT GREENBERGER
PHIL JIMINEZ
DAN WALLACE
SVEN WILSON

CONTENTS

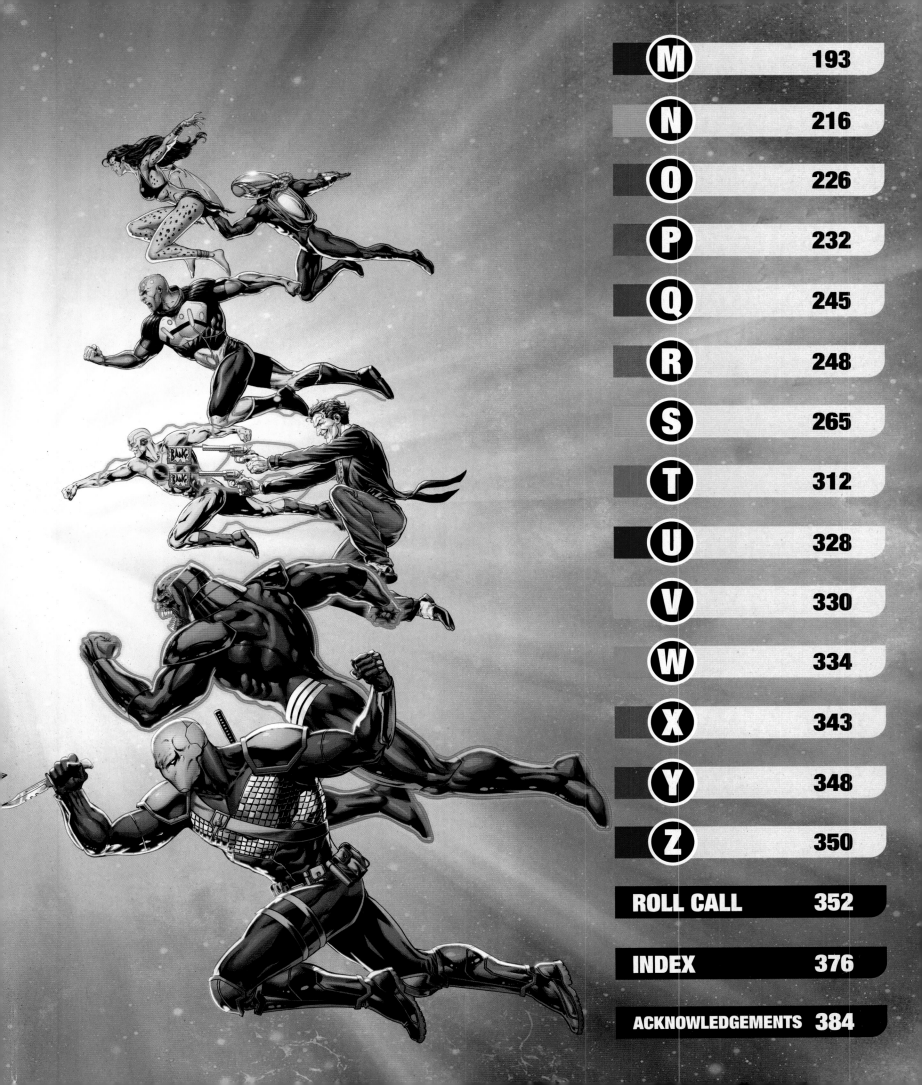

FOREWORD

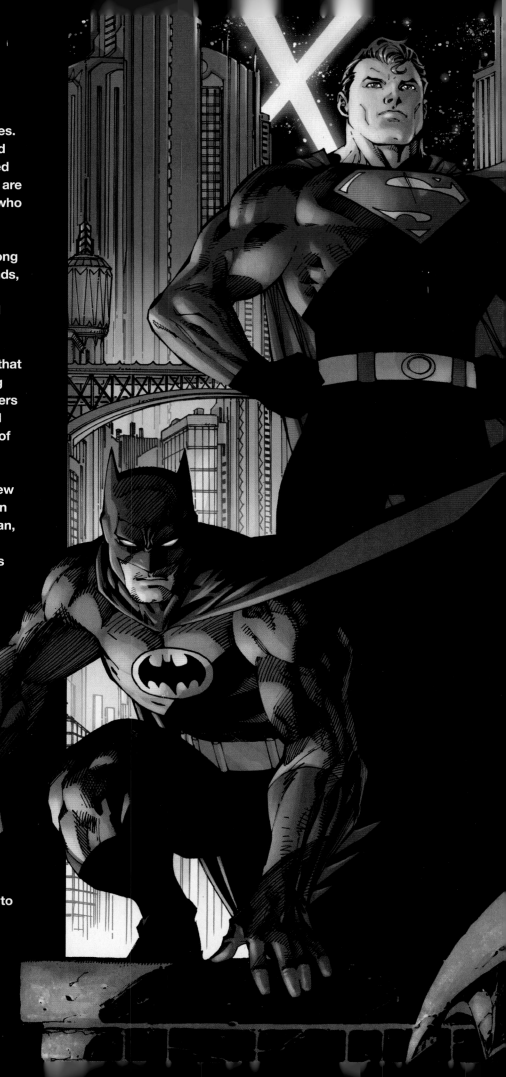

Now more than ever, our world needs Super Heroes. Super Heroes have provided escape, excitement, comfort, and hope ever since that first "strange visitor" from Krypton arrived in the pages of *Action Comics* more than 80 years ago. These are feelings I could relate to as a young boy born in South Korea who also arrived in a Midwestern city unsure that he fit in. As champions of the oppressed, Super Heroes provide us with a moral compass and the belief that there exists something strong enough to protect us. They have been shared and valued friends, providing a light at the end of the tunnel for generations of readers through periods of world crisis and the confusion and anxieties of everyday life.

The book in your hands is an introduction to the depth and wonder of the wide Multiverse of DC characters, a vast array that wouldn't have ever dreamed possible when I was first buying DC's comics from a spinner rack. While many of DC's characters are iconic, this book shows that their mythology hasn't stayed ossified in time, but has grown and evolved. Each generation of DC writers and artists (including myself) have added to that tapestry by adding new characters or new takes on existing ones. Every page here holds the promise of discovery, from new or old characters you haven't previously known of, or unknown facts about characters or teams we think we know, like Batman, Catwoman, the Suicide Squad, Darkseid, Harley Quinn, the Justice League or The Joker. Every character is full of limitless possibilities.

With legacy vital statistics like the Height, Weight, Powers/Abilities and classic stories identified for each major character, books like this one have always been among my favorites to read. This newly updated edition of *The DC Comics Encyclopedia* explores DC's mythology and celebrates more than 1,200 DC Comics Super Heroes and Super-Villains. Some of them you might never have heard of, and others are so ingrained into our cultural DNA that even a towel pinned to a child's shirt can represent Superman, or paper bracelets around your wrists can symbolize Wonder Woman. Every page holds discovery worth our time, our energy, and our passion. A hero is someone whose actions and courage inspire us, our dream of who we aspire to be. Super Heroes give us hope and lift us up and I hope that, inside these pages, you may discover a hero and their journey that speaks to you personally and inspires you to help make a better world. Because the world can never have enough heroes.

Jim Lee

INTRODUCTION

Everyone knows the icons: Superman, Wonder Woman, Batman and Robin. They've adorned bed sheets, action figures, and lunch boxes for decades. They've starred in TV shows, video games, and blockbuster films, becoming pop culture institutions as the world's most famous pantheon of Super Heroes. In fact, in a poll conducted in the 1990s, Superman's famous S-shield was reported the most universally recognized symbol on the planet, second only to the Christian cross.

These treasured icons of modern mythology got their start in a medium that was originally quite modest. The publishing company that is known today as DC officially began with February 1935's *New Fun* #1, subtitled "The Big Comic Magazine." While the term "comic book" was not yet a household phrase, there were other comic magazines on the racks at that time. In the preceding years, comic strips had proven to be the most popular section of any good newspaper. To capitalize on the business of these "funny pages," publishers set out to reprint collections of comic strips on cheap paper, bound by a flimsy cover. While *New Fun* resembled these magazines, what truly set it apart from the competition was that it featured all new strips, and served as a proof of concept that readers were hungry for comics they'd never read before.

In March of 1937, *Detective Comics* debuted, a collection of detective and crime stories that would later inspire the famous DC Comics name. But it wasn't until June of 1938 that *Action Comics* #1 hit newsstands, introducing the world to the first official Super Hero in the form of Superman. This Man of Steel caught on with the fans "faster than a speeding bullet," and soon Batman, his youthful sidekick Robin, and Wonder Woman followed him into four-color fame. Super Heroes quickly became the dominant genre of these fledgling comics books, and have yet to truly relinquish their hold on a still-fascinated audience.

With over eight decades of superheroics under its rather impressive utility belt, DC has grown its stable of characters to include famous faces like The Flash, Green Lantern, Shazam, Aquaman, Plastic Man, Hawkman, Lex Luthor, Swamp Thing, The Joker, Catwoman, and a relatively new favorite, Harley Quinn. DC has evolved, attracting new fans every day in a variety of mediums, from Emmy award-winning cartoons to high-rated, live-action series, from Oscar-winning films to bestselling graphic novels. And in the process, the DC Multiverse has grown from the handful of members that made up the first Super Hero team called the Justice Society of America to a vast Multiverse, containing thousands upon thousands of residents, each with a dramatic story to tell.

The DC Comics Encyclopedia: New Edition is a roadmap to that universe. It's a guide to the best and the brightest, the most corrupt and notorious. It serves to not only reveal to new readers the rich and detailed landscape of the DC Multiverse and its characters, but to also remind longtime fans of their favorite storylines and moments, supplying even the most diehard reader with a new fact or twenty.

The characters included in this volume were hand-picked by comic book historians working directly with DC. They were thoroughly researched with the intent of supplying all the need-to-know background of each hero, villain, team, or supporting character, and plenty of extra tidbits along the way. Every entry is accompanied with dynamic visuals pulled from DC's archives, in an effort to showcase the countless writers, pencillers, inkers, and colorists who have lent their talents toward making DC the well-respected institution it is today.

The entries in this book range from four-page spreads on DC's biggest names, to smaller entries on some of the lesser-knowns and up-and-comers. Each character is given their own "Data Box," containing vital information, such as the character's debut issue, secret identity, and powers and abilities. For those more iconic characters, an "At A Glance" section is supplied to give readers the main bullet points in the character's tumultuous life. These larger entries come complete with a "Classic Stories" section that suggests further comic book reading, offering up some of the best tales from DC's extensive library.

DC is always moving forward and bringing its characters into uncharted territory. A result of that progressive thinking has been drastic alterations to the status quo a time or two in the company's past, most notably as a result of the comic book event miniseries *Crisis on Infinite Earths* and *Flashpoint*, and the recent line-wide back-to-the-basics approach known as *Rebirth*. To reflect this grand history, the entries in this book have been tailored accordingly. Whenever possible, the most recent post-*Rebirth* version of any given character's backstory and history is supplied in the main body. However, in the larger entries, an "On the Record" section is included. This feature reveals interesting historical details that may have fallen by the wayside over the years, summarizing big events and storylines that often hail from continuities past. This ensures *The DC Comics Encyclopedia* is as thorough as possible, while remaining user-friendly to those fans not yet introduced to the Multiverse of possibilities hiding in the background of their favorite issues.

Everyone knows something about the icons of DC. Now, thanks to *The DC Comics Encyclopedia: New Edition*, they have the opportunity to know virtually everything.

Matthew K. Manning, Contributing Author

A BRIEF HISTORY OF THE DC UNIVERSE

The DC universe (DCU), with its multitude of characters, stories, and events, may seem a little daunting to new readers and fans alike. To aid travelers on their journey through this universe, this timeline highlights major turning points in DC's long and dynamic history—from birth to *Rebirth*.

GOLDEN AGE

Action Comics #1 (Jun. 1938)
The world's first-ever Super Hero debuts in the mighty form of Superman, the Man of Steel. His immediate success kick-starts the Golden Age of comic books.

Detective Comics #27 (May 1939)
Batman swings into comic book action, inspired by both Superman and the masked-man pulp fiction popular at the time.

All-Star Comics #3 (Winter 1940)
The DC universe takes shape as some of the most successful Super Heroes band together for the first time to start the Justice Society of America (JSA). Members include the recently created The Flash, Green Lantern, and Hawkman.

All-Star Comics #8 (Dec. 1941–Jan. 1942)
The first truly iconic female Super Hero is torn from myth and transported to modern times—the Amazing Amazon, Wonder Woman.

SILVER AGE

Showcase #4 (Sep.–Oct. 1956)
The Silver Age of Comics dawns as The Flash is reinvented for a new era with the debut of Barry Allen.

The Brave and the Bold #28 (Feb.–Mar. 1960)
The concept behind the Justice Society of America—a high-profile group of Super Heroes—is rekindled with DC's modern icons teaming up to form the Justice League of America (JLA).

The Flash #123 (Sep. 1961)
The Multiverse is created when the Golden Age Flash comes face to face with his Silver Age counterpart. The Golden Age Flash's reality would become known as Earth-2, while the Silver Age Flash's world would eventually be designated Earth-1.

Justice League of America #21 (Aug. 1963)
The DC universe has its first interdimensional crisis when the JLA meets the JSA for the first time, in what will become a yearly team-up tradition.

Detective Comics #359 (Jan. 1967)
Batgirl, Barbara Gordon, bursts onto the scene in her debut appearance; an independent, capable hero who fast became one of DC's most popular characters.

Crisis on Infinite Earths #1 (Apr. 1985)
To streamline the various multiple Earths that had formed in their 50-year history, DC Comics launches a 12-issue series that sees many worlds perish at the hands of the Anti-Monitor. When the villain is finally dispatched, only one Earth remains.
In this new reality, most Earth-2 heroes are established as having been active during World War II, while the adventures of Earth-1's heroes take place in the present day. In the wake of *Crisis on Infinite Earths*, the origin stories for icons such as Superman, Batman, and Wonder Woman are retold, with major continuity corrections that match the reality of their new Earth.

BRONZE AGE

Detective Comics #395 (Jan. 1970)
Batman is taken back to his darker roots in "The Secret of the Waiting Graves," a momentous issue that helped usher in the Bronze Age of comics.

Green Lantern #76 (Apr. 1970)
The pairing of Green Lantern and Green Arrow brings comics up to speed with the problems of the modern world, serving up a healthy dose of social commentary.

New Gods #1 (Mar. 1971)
The DC universe gains a pantheon of New Gods in an epic space saga set in a Fourth World on the fringes of Superman's reality.

DC Comics Presents #26 (Oct. 1980)
The "junior Justice League" known as the Teen Titans comes into its own in a preview to their ongoing title, *The New Teen Titans*.

DARK AGE

Batman: The Dark Knight #1 (1986)
In a dystopian near-future, an aging, embittered Batman steps over the thin blue line to battle foe and friend alike to bring rough justice to Gotham City. This landmark miniseries connected with a mature readership and set the content, tone, and style for the coming of comics' Modern Age.

Watchmen #1 (Sep. 1986)
Another watershed miniseries, *Watchmen* put the "meta" into metahumans, updating Super Heroes for adult readers. Set on the brink of armageddon, this elaborate murder mystery unfolds into a sprawling, literary epic that would have a significant impact on the DC universe and beyond.

Legends #1 (Nov. 1986)
When Darkseid, the tyrannical lord of Apokolips, attacks the world's heroes by turning the common man against them, a new incarnation of the Justice League forms to oppose him, alongside government-run Super-Villain team the Suicide Squad.

Superman (Vol. 2) #75 (Jan. 1993)
The Man of Steel is killed while subduing a murderous alien beast known as Doomsday. Superman later finds his way back to the land of the living after a tumultuous year for Metropolis.

The Batman Adventures #12 (Sep. 1993)
Making the transition from screen to page, Harley Quinn arrived in the DC universe from *Batman: The Animated Series* and became a permanent fixture in Batman's rogue's gallery.

Zero Hour #4 (Sep. 1994)
While the DC Multiverse's various Earths were merged into one during *Crisis on Infinite Earths*, some lingering continuity issues are neatly tied up in the miniseries *Zero Hour*, which tells of power-mad former Green Lantern Hal Jordan's attempts to remake the world in his image. Ongoing tie-in titles, each with their own issue #0, relate the title character's newly revised origin.

MODERN AGE

Identity Crisis #1 (Aug. 2004)
Dark secrets from the Justice League of America's storied history come to light in this murder mystery miniseries that reveals a time when the League resorted to wiping the minds of its villains.

Infinite Crisis #1 (Dec. 2005)
Survivors of some of the lost realities from the original *Crisis on Infinite Earths* return to the DC universe. In this miniseries, Superboy-Prime and the Alexander Luthor of Earth-3 instigate a new crisis to retrieve their respective Earths. The result is New Earth, as continuity is again tweaked to update the DC universe.

52 #1 (May 2006)
As DC titles jump a year ahead in the wake of *Infinite Crisis*, the weekly 52-issue maxiseries, simply dubbed *52*, fills in the gaps, culminating with the villainous Mr. Mind altering multiple worlds and creating a new Multiverse of 52 Earths.

Final Crisis #1 (Jul. 2008)
Evil wins as Darkseid's forces conquer the Earth, succeeding in "killing" Batman, until Superman leads a revolt to stop the tyrant. By the end of the series, it is revealed that Bruce Wayne is merely displaced in time; he eventually finds his way home in 2010, while Dick Grayson, as Batman, protects Gotham City.

Blackest Night #1 (Sep. 2009)
Undead Super Heroes and Super-Villains are recruited as Black Lanterns, due to the machinations of the villain Nekron. Several Lanterns from across the Emotional Spectrum work together to stop this *Blackest Night*. The result is the *Brightest Day* maxiseries that sees the rebirth of many characters, including Swamp Thing.

Flashpoint #1 (Jul. 2011)
The most significant continuity-altering event since *Crisis on Infinite Earths*, *Flashpoint* establishes an alternate world that a stranded Barry Allen must fight his way back from. However, when The Flash manages to return the world to its proper status quo, the result is Earth-0, a universe similar to the former New Earth, yet different in many ways.

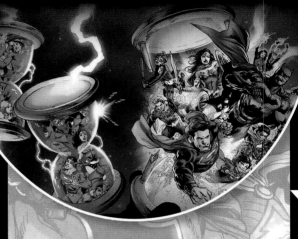

DC Universe: Rebirth #1 (May 2016)
In a one-shot special that leads to a series of character-specific *Rebirth* specials, the DC Multiverse takes its next step in evolution when Wally West (The Flash) returns. While some major titles restart at issue #1, two flagship books, *Action Comics* and *Detective Comics*, return to their old issue numbering prior to the New 52. The pre-*Flashpoint* Superman picks up where his recently deceased successor left off, the forgotten original Teen Titans form the Titans, and Wonder Woman's history is again revised. All the while, the cast of the Watchmen wait in the wings, surveying their handiwork.

MODERN AGE

The New 52 (Nov. 2011)
The universe of Earth-0 is introduced with the launch of 52 separate titles. Long-running mainstay titles like *Action Comics* and *Detective Comics* restart from issue #1, as the world discovers a fresh reality where iconic heroes are in the prime of their lives. Superman's origin is retold in *Action Comics*, Wonder Woman's past is reevaluated in the pages of her own title, and Batman embarks on a "Zero Year" that reveals a modern take on his familiar history.

Forever Evil #1 (Nov. 2013)
Spinning out of the pages of the crossover "Trinity War" that featured in the three Justice League titles of the time, *Forever Evil* tells how Earth-3's Crime Syndicate arrives on Earth-0, forcing Batman and Lex Luthor to team up to stop them.

Convergence #0 (Jun. 2015)
Readers are treated to the adventures of characters from a variety of past continuities as

Brainiac tries to converge the worlds of the multiverse. When the heroes rebel, a newly updated Multiverse is formed, with worlds similar to the ones that came before, yet modernized for a new audience.

DC You (Aug. 2015)
A series of new titles is launched, while many of DC's icons get a facelift. Commissioner Gordon temporarily assumes Batman's mantle when the Dark Knight goes missing, Superman briefly loses his powers due to Vandal Savage's manipulations, and Wonder Woman sports a new costume and mission.

Justice League #40 (Jun. 2015)
In an initial, prologue chapter, "The Darkseid War" begins, pitting the all-powerful Anti-Monitor against Darkseid in a clash that briefly grants godlike powers to members of the Justice League.

PRIME AGE

Dark Nights: Metal #1-6 (Oct. 2017–May 2018)
A fresh cosmic crossover event rewrites the history and cosmology of DC. It is only the spearhead of even greater changes. As Batman strives to solve the mystery of unknown metals that have plagued his life and shaped humanity's history, he uncovers schemes originating in a previously unsuspected Dark Multiverse, which pit Earth's heroes against monstrous versions of the Dark Knight and heralds the return of the being who birthed all existence. The reality-shaking events were preceded by two one-shots, *Dark Days: The Forge* (Aug. 2017) and *Dark Days: The Casting* (Sep. 2017), with repercussions that resound throughout all DC's other titles.

Doomsday Clock #1-12 (Jan. 2018–Feb. 2020)
One of the most eagerly anticipated sequels in DC history, *Doomsday Clock* picks up where *Watchmen* ended in October 1987, revealing the machinations of Doctor Manhattan, his alterations to DC's timeline, and how he may have edited key moments and characters out of reality in *DC Rebirth*. As another universe spirals toward annihilation, heroes and villains of the Watchmen universe combine with some of DC's more sidelined and rarely seen champions to fix everything and save humanity.

Dark Nights: Death Metal #1 (Aug. 2020)
After three years of spectacular chaos and turmoil, the DC Multiverse is under final assault by reality-rending Perpetua, whose dark designs for life are threatened by her treacherous subordinate Barbatos and challenged across countless universes by an army of astonishingly altered heroes and villains. With the balance between multiversal Light and Darkness at stake, the fate of all that lives depends on these barely recognizable icons and the wit and guts of multiversal outcast Wally West…

A.R.G.U.S.

DEBUT *Justice League* (Vol. 2) #7 (May 2012)
BASE Mobile
OFFICIAL NAME Advanced Research Group Uniting Super-Humans
ALLIES Justice League, Killer Frost
ENEMIES Secret Society of Super-Villains
AFFILIATIONS Justice League of America

Unproven stories persist that the clandestine agency A.R.G.U.S. has actually existed ever since the Revolutionary War. When civil war divided the country several decades later, the organization became known as the Anonymous Ranger Group of the United States.

Officially, A.R.G.U.S. was created by the US president as America's official government liaison to the Justice League. With Steve Trevor in command, the agency provided financial support and clean-up services, but its real purpose was to spy on seemingly all-powerful Super Heroes.

Over a period of five years, Trevor expanded the organization's remit to include the monitoring of all metahuman and unnatural threats. A.R.G.U.S. agents confiscated mystical artifacts and advanced technologies, policed extra-dimensional incursions, and covertly battled monsters, villains, and Super Heroes acting against the perceived interests of the US and humanity. These threats were neutralized and deposited in classified research vaults known as the Black Room, Red Room, and Circus.

When Amanda Waller replaced Trevor, she created the Justice League of America as a secret weapon in case the original heroes should ever go rogue.

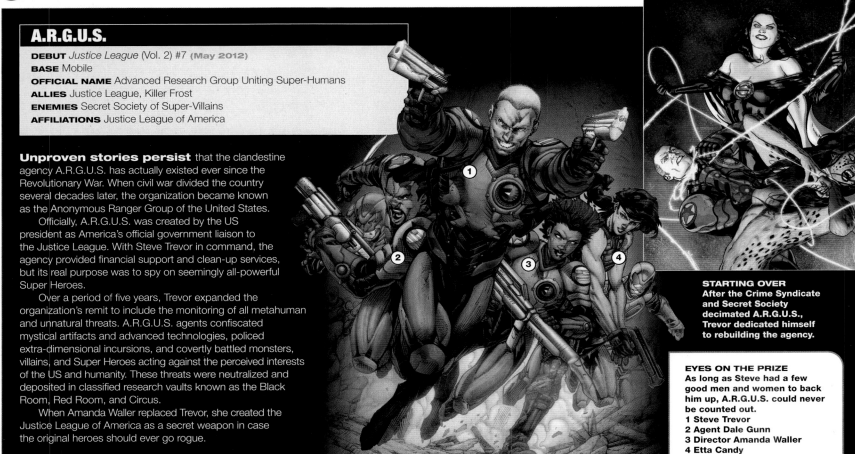

STARTING OVER
After the Crime Syndicate and Secret Society decimated A.R.G.U.S., Trevor dedicated himself to rebuilding the agency.

EYES ON THE PRIZE
As long as Steve had a few good men and women to back him up, A.R.G.U.S. could never be counted out.
1 Steve Trevor
2 Agent Dale Gunn
3 Director Amanda Waller
4 Etta Candy

ALL-STAR SQUADRON

DEBUT *Justice League of America* (Vol. 1) #193 (free preview insert) (Aug. 1981)
All Star Squadron (Vol. 1) #1 (Sep. 1981)
BASE The Trylon and Perisphere, New York City
POWERS/ABILITIES Many and various; employed by every World War II American hero and mystery man united in defense of liberty and democracy against the Axis powers.
ALLIES Blackhawks
ENEMIES Adolf Hitler, Nazi Germany, Imperial Japan, Baron Blitzkrieg, Ultra-Humanite, Per Degaton, enemy spies
AFFILIATIONS Federal Bureau of Investigation, US War Department

IN TIMES OF CRISIS...
The All-Star Squadron was shaken to its core when the crisis instigated by the cosmic destroyer, the Anti-Monitor, reconfigured the Multiverse. As a result, history was rewritten and heroes such as Superman, Batman, Wonder Woman, and Green Arrow ceased to exist on Earth-2. This left a leaner, meaner Squadron to battle Hitler's hordes.

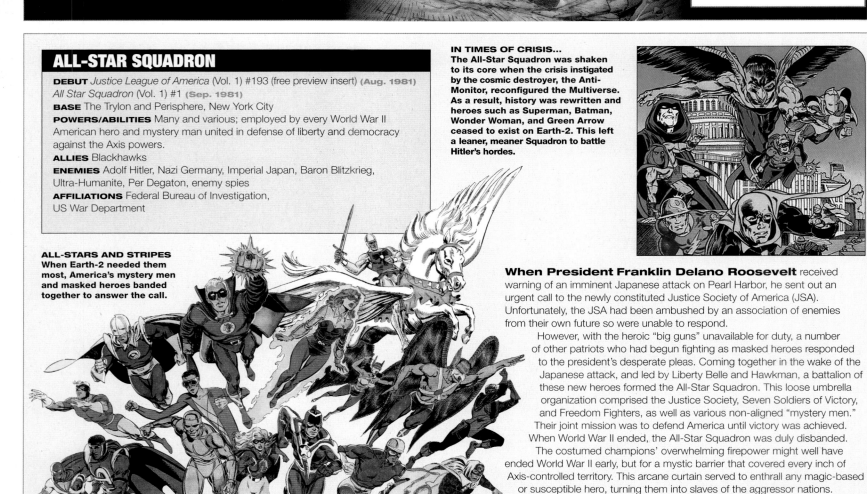

ALL-STARS AND STRIPES
When Earth-2 needed them most, America's mystery men and masked heroes banded together to answer the call.

When President Franklin Delano Roosevelt received warning of an imminent Japanese attack on Pearl Harbor, he sent out an urgent call to the newly constituted Justice Society of America (JSA). Unfortunately, the JSA had been ambushed by an association of enemies from their own future so were unable to respond.

However, with the heroic "big guns" unavailable for duty, a number of other patriots who had begun fighting as masked heroes responded to the president's desperate pleas. Coming together in the wake of the Japanese attack, and led by Liberty Belle and Hawkman, a battalion of these new heroes formed the All-Star Squadron. This loose umbrella organization comprised the Justice Society, Seven Soldiers of Victory, and Freedom Fighters, as well as various non-aligned "mystery men." Their joint mission was to defend America until victory was achieved. When World War II ended, the All-Star Squadron was duly disbanded.

The costumed champions' overwhelming firepower might well have ended World War II early, but for a mystic barrier that covered every inch of Axis-controlled territory. This arcane curtain served to enthrall any magic-based or susceptible hero, turning them into slaves of the aggressor nations.

ABRA KADABRA

DEBUT *The Flash* (Vol. 1) #128 (May 1962)
REAL NAME Citizen Abra
BASE 64th century Earth, Keystone City
HEIGHT 5ft 10in **WEIGHT** 125 lbs
EYES Green **HAIR** Bald
POWERS/ABILITIES Employs 64th-century techno-magic to create energy blasts, reality alterations, illusions, hypnosis, teleportation, and time manipulation.
ALLIES Legion of Zoom, Injustice Gang, Secret Society of Super-Villains
ENEMIES The Flash (Barry Allen), The Flash (Wally West), Titans

Abra Kadabra came from the 64th century and used that era's advanced technology to satisfy his twin obsessions: to be a stage magician and to bask in adulation.

Kadabra's war against two Flashes frequently saw him frustrated and humiliated and he later made a deal with the demon Neron to become a true sorcerer.

Kadabra reverted to scientific trickery after Wally West was removed from the continuum, claiming credit for the deed. When the third Flash returned to Earth Prime's reality, Kadabra attacked him and his allies in the Titans. In recent times, Kadabra joined the Legion of Zoom—an alliance of rogues who united to destroy another resurrected Flash (Barry Allen).

ALL CASTE

DEBUT *Red Hood and the Outlaws* (Vol. 1) #1 (Nov. 2011)
BASE Acres of All
POWERS/ABILITIES Martial arts, advanced meditation techniques.
ALLIES S'aru the Protector, Jason Todd
ENEMIES The Untitled

Millennia ago, a family of nine warriors formed the Untitled, a cult dedicated to absolute evil, power, and immortality. Eventually, one sister, Ducra, revolted and formed the All Caste to fight her siblings.

For 3,000 years, Ducra the Instructor led her warrior-monks in a secret war against her family. Deep in the Himalayas, cloistered in the Chamber of All, the monks toiled, forging links with the outside world, but remaining largely independent from it.

They trained Jason Todd after his resurrection. When he returned to the Acres of All years later, he found Ducra and her All Caste had been brutally exterminated. As he apologized to Ducra's body for having failed her, Ducra's spirit appeared, revealing they had been murdered by the Untitled.

Alongside sole survivor, Essence, Todd avenged the All Caste's deaths, believing he had ended the Untitled, but recently the vile clan revived, assaulting Qurac and attacking the Red Hood's new Outlaw team.

ALPHA CENTURION

DEBUT *Zero Hour* (Vol. 1) #3 (Sep. 1994)
REAL NAME Roman
BASE Metropolis
HEIGHT 5ft 8in **WEIGHT** 165 lbs
EYES Brown **HAIR** Black
POWERS/ABILITIES Superhuman strength, flight, durability, speed; can manifest a personal pantheon of alien warriors called the Pax Galactica.
ALLIES Superman, Supergirl, Eradicator, Steel
ENEMIES Lex Luthor, Cyborg Superman

College student Roman was gravely wounded during an attack by Lexus terrorists at the Metropolis Museum of History. Bleeding profusely, he used an ancient belt as a tourniquet and was instantly possessed by a minor Roman god who had been trapped inside the strap.

Alpha Centurion took over and transformed Roman's body. Now blessed with superhuman abilities, he easily defeated the terrorists at the museum.

Since that moment, Alpha Centurion has repeatedly commandeered Roman's body, leaving his host terrified that one day the warrior-hero will decide to possess him for good. The Centurion seems able to sense imminent danger before it arises and force the change without warning.

Alpha Centurion has possessed many hosts over the centuries, destroying monsters and carrying out the edicts of the mystical Pantheon of Grace. He is compelled to save lives and maintain order at all costs.

QUO VADIS? Roman never knew when his body was about to be taken over by Alpha Centurion, or where the next usurpation would take him.

ALPHA LANTERNS

DEBUT *Green Lantern* (Vol. 4) #26 (Feb. 2008)
BASE Oa
POWERS/ABILITIES Cyborg bodies, incorporating Manhunter technology, are able to drain Green Lantern rings of charge.
ENEMIES Sinestro Corps, Cyborg Superman, Guardians of the Universe
AFFILIATIONS Green Lantern Corps

When the Guardians of the Universe rewrote the Green Lanterns' rules of conduct, they created a new division to police the Corps. These were Alpha Lanterns, loyal veterans converted into cyborgs. Their bodies incorporated Manhunter technology and had an inbuilt Battery of Power that could drain Lanterns' rings. This "Internal Affairs" division was disliked by rank-and-file officers, as was their chilling Oath of Intent:

"In days of peace, in nights of war,
Obey the laws forever more Misconduct must be answered for
Swear us, the chosen...
The Alpha Corps!"

On deciding that Green Lanterns were a failed experiment, the Guardians manipulated their Alpha Lanterns into triggering a civil war within the Corps. By maneuvering Guy Gardner and an army of Emerald Warriors into destroying their cyborg overseers, the Oans were simply removing an obstacle to the introduction of their remorseless, emotionless "Third Army."

POWERFUL PAWNS Alpha Lanterns proudly surrendered their very beings to better serve the Corps, but they were betrayed without qualm by their callous masters.

AMAZING MAN

DEBUT *All Star Squadron* (Vol. 1) #23 (Jul. 1983)
REAL NAME Rocker Bonn
BASE Wayne, Texas
HEIGHT Variable **WEIGHT** Variable
EYES Brown **HAIR** Black
POWERS/ABILITIES Matter absorption, body transmutation, and regeneration; can discharge absorbed matter as blasts of energy.
ENEMIES Brother Eye, O.M.A.C.

Rocker Bonn was an operative of the intelligence agency Checkmate before he was transferred to its public subsidiary, Cadmus Industries. Subjected to genetic experiments as part of Project Cadmus, he gained the power to explosively incorporate mass and matter, while also taking on their physical properties. Given the codename Amazing Man, Bonn escaped before he could become Cadmus' tool.

Sometime later, while Bonn was in hiding and working at a Texas diner, the rogue sentient satellite Brother Eye manipulated him into battling Kevin Kho, the unwilling host of the Eye's One Machine Attack Construct (O.M.A.C.).

Caught in a confusing three-way battle between the police, O.M.A.C., and himself, Amazing Man was held at bay and, after being tricked into absorbing some of O.M.A.C.s circuitry, was ultimately absorbed into Brother Eye, who deemed the transmorph useful to its own plans.

GO FOR THE EYES Tricked into combat with O.M.A.C., Amazing Man initially had the upper hand, but then O.M.A.C. temporarily blinded him.

AMBUSH BUG

DEBUT *DC Comics Presents* (Vol.1) #52 (Dec. 1959)
REAL NAME Irwin Schwab
BASE Channel 52 News, Metropolis
HEIGHT 5ft 10in **WEIGHT** 125 lbs
EYES Green **HAIR** Bald
POWERS/ABILITIES Teleportation, immortality, persistence, and dumb luck.
AFFILIATION Channel 52
ALLIES Cheeks, the Toy Wonder, Bethany Snow, Calendar Man, Dumb Bunny
ENEMIES Argh!Yle, Kobra, Go-Go Chex
AFFILIATIONS Doom Patrol, Amber Butane Corps, Uh-Oh Squad, Superman

Irwin Schwab is deeply delusional, morally ambiguous, and obsessed with Super Heroes. As Ambush Bug, he sought to join their rarefied society in a body-suit that he claims fell to Earth from the planet Schwab.

Harassing Super Heroes including Superman, Batman, Wonder Woman, and Kobra, he displayed the abilities of teleporting and healing from any injury. Failing as a villain and faring no better as a hero, he briefly found his niche and a measure of stability as A. Bug: Super Hero field-correspondent for Channel 52 News.

He still maintains that he has cosmic awareness and that reality is merely comic books being read by extra-dimensional superior beings.

ANTENNAE FOR NEWS
Ambush Bug always seems to know when there's a story brewing, and he's not afraid to rake a little muck or ruffle a few feathers to get at the truth.

AMAZO

DEBUT *The Brave and the Bold* #30 (Jun.–Jul. 1960)
Justice League (Vol. 2) #36 (Jan. 2015) (as Ikarus)
REAL NAME Armen Ikarus
BASE New York City
HEIGHT 8ft **WEIGHT** 485 lbs
HAIR None **EYES** Red
POWERS/ABILITIES Synthetic absorption cells grant powers of any metahuman within close proximity; unpredictable creation and recombination of those powers.
ALLIES Professor Ivo
ENEMIES Justice League, Plastic Man, Superman
AFFILIATIONS Secret Society of Super-Villains, the Cabal

COPYCAT
As well as absorbing and replicating the powers of metahumans, the Amazo android could also recreate their equipment, such as Green Lantern power rings.

KID AMAZO

Reggie Meyer's entire family were infected by the Amazo virus. Retaining superpowers, they used them to fight crime in their home town. However, Reggie, as Kid Amazo, chose to exploit his abilities with stolen Amazo armor to create an army of robotic clones. His vindictive depredations were stopped first by the Super Sons, Jonathan Kent (Superboy) and Damian Wayne (Robin), and later by Nightwing.

PROBLEM CHILD
Kid Amazo planned to cause havoc with his robot army.

Obsessed with immortality, Professor Ivo designed a synthetic enzyme capable of absorbing the energies and powers of any being around it. He incorporated it into the "A-maze" operating system: part of the cybernetic modifications that saved Vic Stone's life and recreated him as Cyborg. Ivo then constructed a full embodiment of the system, known as the Amazo Android, which battled the Justice League. Ivo later constructed a childlike android that combined organic and cybernetic systems. Dubbed "Kid Amazo," it was his secret weapon against the League, but it acquired too much human nature and self-destructed.

The adult Amazo later became a member of the Secret Society of Super-Villains. Lex Luthor subsequently used the Amazo system as the basis of his deadly Amazo Virus. Its first casualty was LexCorp's Dr. Armen Ikarus and the virus went on to infect dozens of people. Many were permanently changed and some became super-powered.

Eventually the robotic Amazo gained full autonomy and pursued his own schemes. Unable to escape his core programming, he still attacks the League and other heroes, and he has joined the Cabal—a criminal alliance, intent on profit and domination which is safely beyond the scrutiny of Earth's Super Heroes.

STOLEN POWERS
The original Amazo was an android created by the mad scientist Professor Ivo. He gifted it with powers stolen from Earth's greatest heroes, in hopes of using it to conquer the world.

AMETHYST

DEBUT *Legion of Super-Heroes* (Vol. 2) #298 (Apr. 1983)
REAL NAME Amy Winston **BASE** Gemworld, Earth
HEIGHT 5ft 8in **WEIGHT** 122 lbs **EYES** Violet **HAIR** Blonde
POWERS/ABILITIES Expert swordfighter; trainee sorceress wielding the magical forces of House Amethyst; capable of spell-casting, energy manipulation, matter transmutation, and tapping the unique mystic forces of other gems.
ALLIES Ypsilos, Phoss, Maxixe of Aquamarine
ENEMIES Dark Opal
AFFILIATIONS Young Justice

Teenager Amy Winston's life changed on learning she was a princess from a magical dimension. After her parents were killed by Lord Opal, she had been hidden on Earth by her sorceress nanny Citrine, who left her with loving human foster-parents Herb and Marion Winston.

On discovering the truth, Amy returned to Gemworld and, with the aid of other ruling Houses, destroyed Opal and liberated its oppressed peoples. However, in recent times Amethyst has found her fairy-tale existence to be a lie. Many Houses are as power-obsessed as her old enemy. More incredibly, Opal is back and Amethyst's own parents are still alive—although entombed in purple crystal along with all her subjects.

With all Gemworld being manipulated by a hidden foe intent on magical domination, Amethyst was briefly driven into exile by the other Houses. She adventured across the Multiverse with the teen heroes of Young Justice before returning home to save Gemworld again.

ON THE RECORD

Gemworld was created in ancient times after a large proportion of Earth's magic-wielders and fabulous beasts and creatures migrated to a vacant dimension to preserve their power in the face of a mounting tide of science and rationalism. They maintained their medieval ways, recreating a feudal system based on the abundant magical crystals of their new home, and they divided into twelve major clans or Houses. Devised to check and balance each other, every House derived power from a particular form of gemstone.

GROWING PAINS
When she debuted, Amy Winston was just 13 years old. In Gemworld, she became an adult and had to face villains, including Flaw and the Child.

AMAZONS

DEBUT *All-Star Comics* #8 (Dec. 1941–Jan. 1942)
BASE Themyscira/Paradise Island
NOTABLE MEMBERS Diana, Hippolyta, Derinoe, Dessa, Hessia, Aleka, Donna Troy, Mala, Philippus
POWERS/ABILITIES Peerless combat and tactical abilities; access to healing purple ray and other advanced scientific skills; some magical powers in certain individuals.
ALLIES Olympian Gods
ENEMIES Veronica Cale, Grail, Darkseid
AFFILIATIONS Olympian Gods

A race of warrior women who worship the Olympian gods as their Patrons, the Amazons live on Themyscira, also known as Paradise Island. Led by Queen Hippolyta, these noble warriors helped raise one of the finest heroes the outside world has ever known: Wonder Woman.

Technologically advanced and highly skilled in the ways of both war and peace, the Amazons lived a life separate from so-called "Man's World" for centuries. Amazons are immortal as long as they remain on Paradise Island's shores, yet some of their number were not content to hide away from the rest of civilization. This tribe of warrior women, known as the Bana-Mighdall, renounced the Olympian gods and opted for a nomadic life away from Themyscira, serving Egyptian Gods instead. Life remained otherwise a constant for the Amazons until Queen Hippolyta had a daughter with the god Zeus. The first child seen on Themyscira's shores in generations, Diana was adored by her fellow Amazons and taught a variety of skills by them, including the ways of a warrior.

When she became an adult, Diana was chosen to represent the Amazons to the outside world as Wonder Woman. However, that honor came at a cost, and she was forbidden to ever return to her home island. Yet time and time again, Wonder Woman returned to Themyscira, somehow not noticing that her mother and fellow Amazons looked different than before. In reality, Diana had been deceived, and soon saw through this veil of lies. She was forced to face the hard truth that her real mother was lost to her forever.

However, Wonder Woman eventually found her way back to the true Themyscira, thanks to the sword of a fellow Amazon, Antiope. At the time, the Amazons were fighting amongst themselves due to the machinations of Darkseid's daughter, Grail. Diana helped defeat Grail and unite the factions, and was reunited with her own mother in the process. Wonder Woman is now able to come and go from Themyscira as she pleases.

PEACEFUL WARRIORS
The Amazon way is to train mind, body, and spirit, ensuring that war is only undertaken for the right reasons.

ON THE RECORD

In their 1940s comics debut, the Amazons were a group of immortal warrior women who were compelled by the goddess Aphrodite to leave the world of men for the isolated Paradise Island of Themyscira. Over time, the Amazons reestablished diplomatic relations with the outside world and even reconstructed their island home after it was destroyed.

Hippolyta had been present since the Golden Age of Comics, and her death forced the Amazons into a new era, with Diana as their Queen. From the late 1960s, the Amazons' fearsome fighting abilities made them the frequent target of various Olympian gods and worldly forces who wanted to control them. After the *Crisis on Infinite Earths*, Wonder Woman received a new origin, as did the Amazons. This reinterpretation featured a blonde Hippolyta and a more ferocious Amazon sisterhood, occasionally adding to their number when hapless sailors passed too close to Themyscira's shores.

UNITED FRONT
Notable women from the history of the Amazons of Themyscira.

DEARLY DEPARTED
Diana was given an impressive sendoff from her sisters as she left Themyscira aboard a makeshift Invisible Jet.

THE COUNCIL
Hippolyta rules over the Council of Themyscira, a group of Paradise Island's wisest citizens, including General Philippus, a woman with whom Hippolyta shares a romantic relationship.

ANARKY

DEBUT *Detective Comics* (Vol. 1) #608 (Nov. 1989)
REAL NAME Sam Young
BASE Gotham City
HEIGHT 6ft 2in **WEIGHT** 215 lbs
EYES Blue **HAIR** Blond
POWERS/ABILITIES Highly intelligent and a keen strategist; usurped the Mad Hatter's mind-control technology to serve his own ends; powerful connections in Gotham City's high society.
ALLIES Cult of Followers
ENEMIES Batman, Mad Hatter, Harvey Bullock
AFFILIATIONS Gotham City Council

ON THE RECORD

The original Anarky was Lonnie Machin, an anarchist out to cause trouble in Gotham City. During his first encounter with the Dark Knight, he spray-painted his logo on Batman's cape. His moniker was later usurped by the General, who wore a variation on Anarky's classic red costume. After the reality-altering *Flashpoint* event, Lonnie was known only as Moneyspider, but may become the new Anarky.

INTERGALACTIC ANARCHY
Anarky fused the two halves of his brain, become incredibly smart and an effective vigilante. He even became a Green Lantern for a brief time after securing a power ring.

When a human trafficker named Jeb Lester was set on fire and thrown from Wayne Tower in downtown Gotham City, Batman and Harvey Bullock began investigating the case. They discovered that Lester's killer was a new vigilante calling himself Anarky, using the persona of a figure seen during the Zero Year. After attempting to blow up Wayne Tower itself, Anarky went public with a video, exhorting Gotham City's citizens to break free from their self-imposed prisons and participate in citywide chaos. To enable people to do so anonymously, he arranged for Anarky masks to be delivered to everyone's doorsteps.

In truth, Anarky was city councilman Samuel Young, who was using his Anarky movement as a smokescreen to hide his real activities and motives. Several years previously, when Sam was younger, his sister had been abused and murdered by the Mad Hatter. Now an adult, Sam wanted revenge, so he kidnapped the villain. He planned to murder the Mad Hatter and also use the Mad Hatter's mind-controlling technology to command an army of innocent citizens, all wearing Anarky masks. He even went so far as to model his masks on his sister's face! It took the joint efforts of Batman and Detective Harvey Bullock of the G.C.P.D. to foil Anarky's plans.

ANGEL AND THE APE

DEBUT *Showcase* (Vol. 1) #77 (Sep. 1968)
BASE New York City
HEIGHT 5ft 10in (Angel); 5ft 9in (Sam)
WEIGHT 140 lbs (Angel); 550 lbs (Sam)
EYES Blue (Angel); Hazel (Sam)
HAIR Blonde (Angel); Black (Sam)
POWERS/ABILITIES Angel: Adept detective; linguist; martial artist; skilled fencer. Sam: Mind-control powers.

While exploring Africa with her father, Professor Theo O'Day, Angel discovered a talking gorilla. When she returned to the US with the ape, he adopted the name Sam Simeon and lived with the O'Days, including Theo's wife, former crime fighter Princess Power, and their other daughter, the super-strong Athena, who would later gain notoriety of a sort as the Inferior Five member Dumb Bunny.

Sam originally hailed from Gorilla City and was related to one of The Flash's fiercest adversaries, Gorilla Grodd, though he possessed only a fraction of Grodd's formidable mental powers. While Sam pursued a career as a cartoonist, Angel honed her intellectual and physical skills, which she put to good use as a private investigator. The two shared an office and their subsequent adventures provided ample inspiration for Sam's comic book tales.

ANIMAL MAN

DEBUT *Strange Adventures* (Vol. 1) #180 (Sep. 1965)
REAL NAME Bernhard "Buddy" Baker
BASE San Diego, California
HEIGHT 5ft 11in
WEIGHT 172 lbs
EYES Blue
HAIR Blond
POWERS/ABILITIES Able to connect to the mystical and powerful Red life-force, which enables him to use the abilities of any animal; charismatic; talented stuntman; peak physical fitness.
ALLIES Swamp Thing, Adam Strange
ENEMIES Anton Arcane, Brother Blood
AFFILIATIONS Justice League United

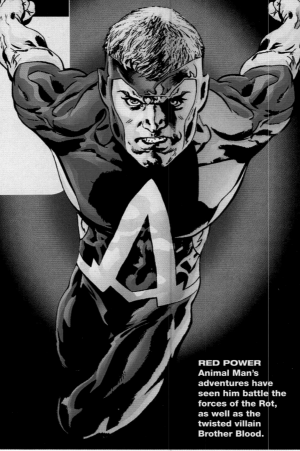

RED POWER
Animal Man's adventures have seen him battle the forces of the Rot, as well as the twisted villain Brother Blood.

More than five years ago in the Congo, a hero named Animal Man pursued a group of poachers. He was the chosen avatar for the Red, a mystical force that connects all animals. Animal Man was surprised when one of the men he was pursuing turned out to be Anton Arcane, an agent for a rival force of death and decay known as the Rot. Arcane murdered this Animal Man. As a result, the Red sought to create a new avatar. They chose movie stuntman Buddy Baker to serve their needs.

While driving home from work, Buddy saw what appeared to be an alien spaceship crash in nearby woods. He went to investigate—and passed out. Buddy never suspected that the Red was simply creating an origin scenario for him that he could easily comprehend, rather than reveal its true properties. So, when he awoke in the woods, Buddy came to believe that he had been kidnapped by aliens and operated on. Finding a costume the Red had left for him, he decided to become a Super Hero, just as the Red had planned all along. Buddy later learned the true secret of his transformation, after he had already embraced his heroic role as Animal Man.

ON THE RECORD

Debuting in the mid-1960s, Animal Man was born after an alien visitation. After a stint as a member of the Forgotten Heroes, Buddy was given his own series, and became a founding member of Justice League Europe. In his own title, he discovered his true origins and even broke the fourth wall, meeting the writer of his exploits. Animal Man became an ambassador of the Red, at one point changing his look with long black-and-white hair.

STRANGE BEDFELLOWS
Animal Man became a close ally of Adam Strange and Starfire when the three embarked on an outer-space adventure together in the pages of the maxiseries *52*.

ANTI-MONITOR

DEBUT *Crisis on Infinite Earths* #2 (May 1985)
REAL NAME Mobius
BASE Mobile
HEIGHT Variable
WEIGHT Variable
EYES Red **HAIR** None
POWERS/ABILITIES Near-omnipotent when merged with Anti-Life Equation; superhuman strength, endurance, durability; energy projection and absorption; anti-matter blasts; flight; commands army of Shadow Demons; can absorb life-force of victims.
ALLIES Grail
ENEMIES Darkseid, Justice League, Crime Syndicate

On the distant planet Qward many years ago, a being named Mobius built a sophisticated device called the Mobius Chair. On a quest to glimpse the forbidden, Mobius attempted to view the source of the Anti-Matter Universe, hoping to discover what sparked its creation. What he found was the Anti-Life Equation, an infamous truth the tyrant Darkseid had spent a lifetime trying to locate. The equation merged with Mobius, transforming him into the immensely powerful Anti-Monitor. Meanwhile, the Mobius Chair came into the possession of the New God Metron, who used it to explore the universe.

The Anti-Monitor became a destroyer, traveling from one universe to the next, consuming worlds. He caused the Crisis on Infinite Earths, destroying the Multiverse, an event only a few, including Metron, recall. But Mobius soon grew tired of his destructive life and hatched an elaborate plan with Darkseid's daughter, Grail, to rid him of this burden. Waging war on Grail's father, he murdered five billion people on Earth-3 to absorb their energies and then he attacked and killed Darkseid. This act released his energies and allowed Mobius to free himself of the curse of living as the Anti-Monitor.

ON THE RECORD

In his original incarnation, the Anti-Monitor looked different, but was just as powerful as his reinvented form after the *Flashpoint* event. While *Crisis on Infinite Earths* altered reality in the 1980s and *Flashpoint* changed it again in 2011, the Anti-Monitor's Multiverse-reshaping role remained the same—though few characters could recall fighting the Super-Villain. Destroyed during *Crisis*, the Anti-Monitor was reborn when 52 new realities formed, and became guardian of the Sinestro Corps.

WORLDS IN CRISIS
The Anti-Monitor's devastating attempts to create a pure anti-matter Multiverse only ended when the surviving heroes of different Earths sacrificed their lives to stop him.

ANTHRO

DEBUT *Showcase* (Vol. 1) #74 (May 1968)
BASE Prehistoric Earth
HEIGHT 5ft 2in **WEIGHT** 137 lbs
EYES Brown **HAIR** Brown
POWERS/ABILITIES Skilled hunter and tracker with exceptional leadership skills.
ALLIES Lart, D-Ahn, Doctor Thirteen, Embra
ENEMIES Vandal Savage
AFFILIATIONS Bear tribe

Anthro was the first Cro-Magnon man, a precursor to the human race. His father, Ne-ahn, was a Neanderthal from the Bear tribe, while his mother was from another tribe. Restless and thrill-seeking, Anthro often got into trouble. When he was young, he was given the gift of fire by the New God Metron and he used this to fight immortal villain Vandal Savage.

His family included brother Lart, step-mother Emba, and uncle D-Ahn. Anthro married another Cro-Magnon, Embra. In time, he became the chief of the Bear tribe. Anthro taught his people compassion and, in alternate realities, met several of Earth's present-day Super Heroes via time travel. When Bruce Wayne was stranded in the past after being blasted by Darkseid's Omega Sanction, he met Anthro and laid his utility belt on the old man's body as he passed away.

APOLLO

DEBUT *StormWatch* (Vol. 2) #4 (Feb 1998)
REAL NAME Andrew Pulaski
BASE Eye of the Storm
HEIGHT Unknown **WEIGHT** Unknown
EYES Unknown **HAIR** Unknown
POWERS/ABILITIES Flight, near invulnerability, superhuman strength, solar energy blasts.
ALLIES Midnighter, Jenny Quantum
ENEMIES The Commander, Storm God, Neron
AFFILIATIONS StormWatch, the Authority

Andrew Pulaski was abducted by aliens aged just 13 and he became the subject of experiments as the beings tried to create their very own Superman.

Escaping and returning to Earth with incredible powers harnessed through solar energy, he took the moniker Apollo after the ancient sun god. Apollo's super powers put him among the very top ranks of metahumans, although he needs to have access to sunlight to keep them working.

When he was kept captive in Hell by the demon Neron, Apollo used his wits to bargain his way out, stopping only to rescue his husband and fellow hero Midnighter, who had become trapped trying to rescue his beloved.

AQUALAD

DEBUT *Brightest Day* (Vol. 1) #4 (Aug. 2010)
REAL NAME Jackson Hyde
BASE Amnesty Bay, Maine
HEIGHT 6ft 1in **WEIGHT** 190 lbs
EYES Blue **HAIR** Brown (often dyed blond)
POWERS/ABILITIES Hydrokinesis; Atlantean physiology; can fire blasts of electricity.
ALLIES Aquaman, Tempest (Garth)
ENEMIES Black Manta, King Shark
AFFILIATIONS Young Justice, Teen Titans

Jackson Hyde's mother had protected him all his life from his true origins – that she was originally from the underwater kingdom of Xebel and his father was the villain Black Manta. Wanting to explore his powers and make an independent life for himself, teenage Jackson joined the Teen Titans. Although initially reluctant to accept Jackson, team leader Robin (Damian Wayne) gave the newcomer a set of "water bearers," devices that enabled him to channel his power over water to create weapons. A clash with Black Manta showed Jackson that his mother had been right to tell him his father was no good, but the young man continued to be curious about his heritage and later visited Xebel to find out more about his people. He is now an established part of the Aquaman family.

ANTON ARCANE

DEBUT *Swamp Thing* (Vol. 1) #2 (Dec. 1972–Jan. 1973)
BASE Blestemat **EYES** Black **HAIR** Bald
POWERS/ABILITIES Sorcery; as an Avatar of the Rot, he can control decay and the dead.
ALLIES Un-Men, Astrid Arkham/Arkham Knight
ENEMIES Swamp Thing, Animal Man, Batman

Sorcerer and scientist, Anton Arcane became the avatar of the Rot. This unnatural force is at war against the life-cherishing natural networks known as the Red and the Green (which empower Animal Man and Swamp Thing respectively). Arcane was born in the 1800s and was obsessed with decay from childhood. By killing Alec Holland—who was destined to be a Green avatar—Arcane inadvertently triggered the coming of the Swamp Thing. They clashed repeatedly and when Swamp Thing was lost in the Rot, Arcane spread his malignant influence over the world, before being defeated by Swamp Thing, who caused him to flee back in time. Ultimately, Arcane's niece Abigail helped Swamp Thing defeat her uncle and then she took his place as the Avatar of the Rot.

Arcane has rejected death, escaped Hell, and continues to bedevil the world: battling against Justice League Dark and even allying with Arkham Knight Astrid Arkham to destroy Batman and contaminate Gotham City.

AQUAMAN

DATA

DEBUT *More Fun Comics* #73 (Nov. 1941)
REAL NAME Arthur Curry **BASE** Amnesty Bay, Maine
HEIGHT 6ft 1in **WEIGHT** 325 lbs **EYES** Blue **HAIR** Blond
POWERS/ABILITIES Superhuman strength, reflexes, and stamina
due to hybrid Atlantean physiology; telepathic control over all marine
organisms; water-breathing and pressure resistance; energy and heat
resistance; wields powerful Trident.
ALLIES Mera, Aqualad, Tempest, Tula, Dolphin
ENEMIES Ocean Master, Black Manta
AFFILIATIONS Justice League, the Others

Raised by lighthouse keeper Tom Curry after his Atlantean mother Atlanna returned to the oceans, Arthur Curry was called back to fulfill his royal destiny before he reached adulthood in the small coastal town of Amnesty Bay, Maine. He patrols nearly 70 percent of the Earth's surface, and he commands the allegiance of all creatures that swim in its waters. Former ruler of Atlantis and Poseidon's designated guardian of the oceans, Aquaman is also a founding member of the Justice League.

AT A GLANCE...

City under the sea
The legendary city of Atlantis has spawned myths for centuries. Behind them all lies a reality even more extraordinary than the myths. This fantastic seafloor city is home to an advanced civilization whose citizens guard the oceans and mistrust anyone who lives on land.

Mera
A fearless and powerful hero in her own right, the Xebel princess Mera was trained from childhood to kill Atlanteans. Her love for Aquaman has superseded Xebel teachings, however.

Aquatic influence
Aquaman has the ability to influence the behavior of marine organisms. It isn't exactly telepathy, since most sea creatures don't have enough of a mind to respond to telepathic commands, but he can create desires within them and rely on their own natures to do the rest.

CLASSIC STORIES

Aquaman (Vol. 5) #42–46 (Mar.–Jul. 1998) Olympian dynastic wars come to Atlantis in "Triton Wars," as Poseidon's son seeks to rule the seven seas.
Aquaman (Vol. 6) #15–20 (Apr.–Sep. 2004) "American Tidal" sees the spontaneous sinking of San Diego kill thousands… but gives thousands more a new aquatic life. Who is behind it?
Aquaman: Sword of Atlantis (Vol. 1) #40–45 (May–Nov. 2006) Young Arthur Curry falls into a series of undersea intrigues involving King Shark, the history of his namesake, and the destiny of Atlantis.
Aquaman (Vol. 7) #14–17 (Jan.–Apr. 2013) The "Throne of Atlantis" pits Ocean Master against the surface world, with Aquaman caught in the middle.

Atlanna, the queen of Atlantis, saved the life of lighthouse keeper Tom Curry when Curry had left his post to save a sinking ship during a raging storm. The two fell in love and she soon became pregnant. She gave birth to her child, Arthur, and stayed on land to help raise him for a few years. However, Atlanna found it impossible to abdicate her throne, and she soon parted ways with Tom. She left her son with Tom on the surface and returned to Atlantis where she later had another son, Orm.

Through accidents and trial and error, Arthur soon learned of his ability to breathe underwater and communicate with sea life. When his father died, Arthur set out to find Atlantis, and met the Atlantean Vulko in his search. Vulko told Arthur of his heritage and brought him to Atlantis. Unprepared for the life of a ruler, Arthur left for a time, and met people more like him, named the Others. He soon became the hero Aquaman. A founding member of the Justice League, Arthur battled the likes of Ocean Master and Black Manta, and found love with Mera, a princess from the kingdom of Xebel, who was originally ordered by her people to assassinate him.

Aquaman and Mera settled down in Arthur's childhood home of Amnesty Bay for a time, but Aquaman was soon forced to fight his brother, Orm, when Ocean Master tried to start a war with the surface world. Aquaman later fought the powerful Dead King, and eventually became King of Atlantis once more.

Through it all, the tangled mystery of Aquaman's heritage still loomed. Searching for his mother Atlanna through dimensional portals, Aquaman and Mera found her—only to have her deny he was her son. With the help of the Martian Manhunter and Gorilla Grodd, Aquaman and Mera convinced Atlanna of the truth—but not before she tried to sacrifice them to the volcano god Karaku.

When a secret society called N.E.M.O. framed an Atlantean group called the Deluge with an attack on a US ship, the already strained relationship between Atlantis and the United States became more so. Aquaman was arrested and later freed by Mera. It took the defeat of N.E.M.O.'s new leader, Black Manta, to fix international relations. However, in the process, Aquaman surrendered Atlantis to the United States.

TRENCH WARFARE
Aquaman and Mera faced a horde of the ravenous Trench.

While this action resulted in peace, his people were not happy. They staged a coup, one led by Deluge leader Corum Rath. Rath was handed the kingdom while Aquaman was stabbed and presumably killed by the leader of the Drift, Commander Murk. However, the injury was not a fatal one. After growing a beard and longer hair, Arthur reemerged as the protector of the underserved area of Atlantis known as the Ninth Tride alongside his new ally, Dolphin. Forming an alliance with the gangs of the

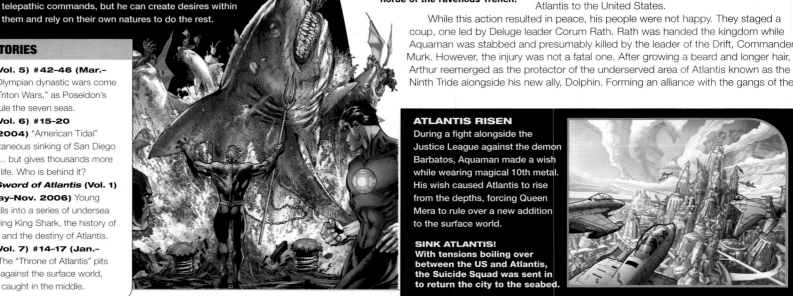

ATLANTIS RISEN
During a fight alongside the Justice League against the demon Barbatos, Aquaman made a wish while wearing magical 10th metal. His wish caused Atlantis to rise from the depths, forcing Queen Mera to rule over a new addition to the surface world.

SINK ATLANTIS!
With tensions boiling over between the US and Atlantis, the Suicide Squad was sent in to return the city to the seabed.

Ninth Tride led by the notorious King Shark, Aquaman and Mera fought and defeated Rath, who had been empowered by evil magic called the Abyssal Dark. However, Mera was chosen by Atlantis' wise Widowhood to rule, knowing that Arthur and Rath each polarized the nation.

Atlantis's problems were far from over, however. Atlantis came under attack by the Triumvirate of Sea Gods. These were three ancient water gods from distant worlds named Captain Gall, Commander Drogue, and Fleet Admiral Tyyde. They and their henchmen Black Manta flooded the planet with water that turned anyone it touched into ferocious sea creatures. While Aquaman began to talk sense into the invading gods, Black Manta turned on them, killing all but Tyyde. Aquaman stopped Manta, but was left for dead in the skirmish.

In reality, Aquaman had been saved by the unlikely hand of the Anti-Monitor. Aquaman continued to see Mera, until she discovered she was pregnant. They had an argument over Aquaman's fears,

WITHOUT A KINGDOM
No longer shackled by kingly duties in Atlantis, Arthur Curry fights to defend both land and sea as Aquaman.

and Mera lashed out at Arthur. Soon, an amnesic Aquaman washed up on the shore of the Village of Unspoken Water, and found himself battling a god named Namma. When he emerged victorious, he was marked with a strange tattoo on his chest.

With the help of other old gods, Arthur regained his memories and returned to Amnesty Bay, where he began to mentor Aqualad (Jackson Hyde). His daughter Andy was born, and Aquaman took her in, surprised at the joy he felt instead of the panic he had expected. Now a proper family man, Aquaman continues to fight a seemingly endless battle to protect both land and sea.

"I am Aquaman. King of the Seven Seas. This is my birthright. This is my responsibility. And I will embrace it!"

ARTHUR CURRY

REBIRTH

CORUM RATH
From terrorist to king: Rath's final evolution was to a grotesque sea creature, owing to his infection from the Abyssal Dark magic.

ON THE RECORD

Aquaman's origin has been told and retold over the years, like any good sea story. For years he was Arthur Curry, half-human son of Tom Curry and an Atlantean woman, Atlanna. His brother Orm, later the Ocean Master, was introduced, as young Arthur discovered Atlantis, his powers, and his destiny to become the Sea King.

Atlantean origins
This Silver Age story of Tom Curry succeeded a Golden Age tale of exploration and scientific experimentation, in which Aquaman's father made his human son fit for a life under the sea. Following *Crisis on Infinite Earths*, the hero was recast as Orin, son of Queen Atlanna and the wizard Atlan, abandoned due to the Atlantean belief that his blond hair was the mark of a curse. Atlantean scientist Vulko tried to save him, and later became Aquaman's guide to Atlantean ways after the nearly feral boy had grown up on the periphery of the surface world.

STEALTH SUIT
Aquaman once wore a blue suit, designed to hide him from pursuing enemies.

Post-Crisis
Following *Crisis on Infinite Earths*, Aquaman appeared in a 1986 miniseries wherein he briefly wore a different blue costume designed to camouflage him in the ocean depths. Ocean Master immersed himself in the lore of Atlantean magic as he fought his half-brother for the throne of Atlantis and later sold his soul to Neron for more sorcerous power. Orin's wife, Mera, has also transformed over time, becoming a powerful hero in her own right and acquiring a backstory that puts her on an equal footing with Aquaman.

Magic hand
The villain Charybdis cost Aquaman a hand in the 1990s, after which he had implanted a cybernetic harpoon designed by S.T.A.R. Labs. This was later replaced by a shape-changing golden hand, courtesy of Atlantean science. Later this too was destroyed, and the Arthurian Lady of the Lake gave Aquaman a hand composed of mystical living water. Aquaman later died and was resurrected—and his hand restored to its original state—at the conclusion of *Blackest Night*.

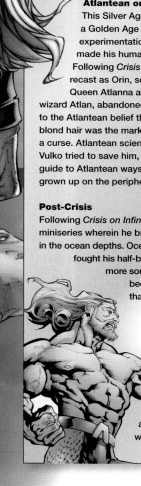

A

ARCHITECT

DEBUT *Batman: Gates of Gotham* (Vol. 1) #1 (Jul. 2011)
REAL NAME Zachary Gate
EYES Blue
HAIR Blond
POWERS/ABILITIES Explosives expert; wears heavily armored, protective suit.
ENEMIES Batman

Zachary Gate is a direct descendant of Nicholas Anders, one of the brothers who crafted Gotham City's great bridges. When his stepbrother died in a bridge collapse, Nicholas sought revenge on Gotham City's founding families—the Kanes, Waynes, and Cobblepots. He eventually killed Robert Kane and went to jail, swearing vengeance an all children of Gotham City's forefathers.

Decades later, Zachary found Nicholas' tell-all diary and decompression suit, and he began blowing up Gotham City's main bridges to avenge his ancestor. Zachary was caught by Batman (Dick Grayson) who had worked out that the suit had driven both men insane. Zachary was later freed from Arkham by Jason Bard as part of a plan to destroy Gotham City and Batman. As the Architect, Zachary tried to demolish the Beacon—a new building funded by Bruce Wayne—but was defeated by Batman.

ARAK

DEBUT *The Warlord* (Vol. 1) #48 (Aug. 1981) *Convergence* (Vol. 1) #0 (Jun. 2015) (as Telos)
REAL NAME Bright Sky After Storm **BASE** Eighth-century Europe
HEIGHT 6ft **WEIGHT** 190 lbs
EYES Brown; Telos: Purple **HAIR** Black; Telos: None
POWERS/ABILITIES Expert fighter with sword and otomahuk; shamanistic powers. Telos: Control of matter; metamorphosis; energy manipulation; super strength; invulnerability; flight; able to traverse alternate realities.
ALLIES Vikings Telos: Techne, K'rot, Stealth, Captain Comet
ENEMIES Angelica of Albracca Telos: Computo, Validus, Brainiac

Native American Arak was born in the eighth century. As a child he survived the massacre of his Quontauka nation, escaping by canoe into the Atlantic where he was found and adopted by Vikings. Always favoring his native otomahuk ax in battle, he grew into a fearsome warrior. When his Viking family were killed, "Arak Red-Hand" wandered western Europe before enlisting in the army of Emperor Charlemagne. After years of adventuring, he learned his father was He-No, the Quontauka god of thunder, and he became a shaman.

Arak traveled in time to fight alongside the All-Star Squadron, and at some point, was taken by Brainiac and transformed into the creature known as Telos. He watched over some of the cities taken from various realities by the Collector of Worlds before regaining his memories and turning against his master. With his vast powers, Telos collected cities from many dimensions and points of time. Brainiac intended to pit each city against each other and allow the victor to become the one, true reality in a great Convergence. But when the heroes of the worlds rebelled, Telos helped Brainiac to see the error of his ways and realign the infinite Earths. Brainiac then set Telos free to search for his long-lost family.

CLASSICAL HERO
The original Arak battled all manner of gods and demons before being abducted into the Multiverse by Brainiac.

ON THE RECORD

As a consequence of his transformation, Telos' origins changed. Now Arak remembered that his father was a shaman and king of his people, who had forbade his son from fighting, despite Arak's aptitude for battle. Forced to study the ways of the shaman, Arak gained his father's and fought Brainiac when the villain appeared in his realm. Arak offered his life to Brainiac in exchange for the safety of his people and became Brainiac's servant, Telos.

NEW WORLDS FOR OLD
After an eternity plundering cities and planets throughout the Multiverse, now all Telos seeks is his home and family.

ARES

DEBUT *Wonder Woman* (Vol. 1) #1 (Summer 1942) (as Mars); *Wonder Woman* (Vol. 1) #183 (Jul.–Aug. 1969) (as Ares)
BASE Mount Olympus **HEIGHT** 6ft 10in
WEIGHT 459 lbs
POWERS/ABILITIES Godlike strength; ability to summon and lead armies; superb martial skills.
ENEMIES First Born, Wonder Woman, the Amazons **AFFILIATIONS** Gods of Olympus

Ares is the Greek God of War, and could often be found near conflict. As Wonder Woman's older brother (and her uncle), he taught young Diana the art of battle, training her in secret on every full moon. He was protective of Wonder Woman and stood by her against the First Born—Zeus' first son who sought to kill all his kin. The First Born was defeated and Ares killed. Hades claimed him and Wonder Woman became the new God of War.

However, Ares is fueled by forces in combat and perhaps cannot truly die. He has continually fomented war simply to increase his own power and influence. However, after being imprisoned beneath Themyscira with Grail, daughter of Darkseid, Ares resolved to change, seeking and inciting strife solely in the name of Justice. This was a decision which once again brought him into conflict against Wonder Woman.

ARION

DEBUT *Warlord* #55 (Mar. 1982)
REAL NAME Ahri'ahn **BASE** Ancient Atlantis
HEIGHT 6ft 3in **WEIGHT** 190 lbs
EYES Green **HAIR** Brown, white
POWERS/ABILITIES Immortality; vast range of magical abilities.
ALLIES Wyynde
ENEMIES Garn Daanuth, Doctor Fate
AFFILIATIONS Lords of Order, Poseidon, Secret Six

More than 45,000 years ago, Arion was the greatest mage of ancient Atlantis. His father was Calculhah, a force for good, while his mother was Dark Majistra, a force for strife, who raised Arion's twin brother, Garn Daanuth, to be his nemesis. When Dark Giants preyed upon humanity, Arion used Nth Metal to banish them from Earth, and he became a protégé of Sea God Poseidon. When the god grew jealous and betrayed him, Arion succumbed to the negative influence of the Death Force and created the divinity slaying Tear of Extinction.

His fall was covered up by Atlantean authorities—who claimed he had perished—and Arion vanished for millennia. In modern times Arion battled Superman, Blue Beetle, and Doctor Fate, who sealed the mage in a crystal of absolution for 10,000 years to either transcend his sins or be consumed by them.

ARISIA

DEBUT *Tales of Green Lantern Corps* (Vol. 1) #1 (May 1981)
REAL NAME Arisia Rrab
BASE Space Sector 2815
HEIGHT 5ft 9in **WEIGHT** 136 lbs
EYES Gold **HAIR** Blonde
POWERS/ABILITIES Ring creates energy constructs; flight; physiology enhances extreme healing.
ALLIES Hal Jordan, Guy Gardner, Sodam Yat

Born on Graxos IV, Arisia Rrab is a hereditary Green Lantern, following her father Fentara and many others. When her uncle Blish died in action, his ring sought out the then-teenage Arisia, making her the ring-bearer of Sector 2815. She was rapidly aged while serving, and became close to Hal Jordan after spending time on Earth.

Apparently killed by Major Force, Arisia was later found in suspended animation. She rejoined the Green Lantern Corps, tasked with watching over Green Lantern Sodam Yat. She fought in the Sinestro Corps Wars and, during Nekron's attack on Earth and Oa, faced Black Lantern versions of her family. Later she died trying to save the doomed planet Perduron. She revived following the reality realignments of *Flashpoint* and *Rebirth* and now serves with the new Green Lantern Corps led by Jordan.

ARKHAM, AMADEUS

DEBUT *Arkham Asylum* (1989)
BASE Gotham City
HEIGHT 6ft 3in **WEIGHT** 175 lbs
EYES Brown **HAIR** Black
POWERS/ABILITIES Expert in psychiatry.
ALLIES Jonah Hex
ENEMIES John Cromwell

In the 1880s, physician Amadeus Arkham specialized in the emerging sciences of psychology and psychiatry. Working with the Gotham City Police Department, he founded the asylum that bears his name—the notorious home of Gotham City's most depraved criminals.

Police detective Lofton consulted Arkham in his search for brutal serial killer, the Gotham Butcher. After encountering some resistance, Arkham deputized bounty hunter Jonah Hex to help, and they discovered that Gotham City was home to the Religion of Crime sect. Their endeavors trapped the Butcher and exposed the existence of villainous cabal the Court of Owls, a triumph Amadeus omitted from the book he wrote of their adventures together.

A child of abuse and subjected to acts of criminal insanity all his adult life, Amadeus eventually went mad. After killing his mother, he was committed to his own asylum where he died after years of confinement.

ARSENAL

DATA

DEBUT *More Fun Comics* #73 (Nov. 1941) (as Speedy)
REAL NAME Roy Harper
BASE New York City
HEIGHT 5ft 11in
WEIGHT 180 lbs
EYES Green **HAIR** Red
POWERS/ABILITIES Expert archer and fighter; gifted mechanic; computer hacker and engineer; incredibly accurate aim.
ALLIES Green Arrow, Red Hood, Starfire, Nightwing, Donna Troy, Killer Croc
ENEMIES H.I.V.E., Cheshire
AFFILIATIONS Teen Titans, Titans, The Outlaws

WILD CHILD
Computer genius Roy was taken in by Oliver Queen and he helped Oliver's alter ego, the Green Arrow, fight crime.

Arsenal was once the teen sidekick of the Green Arrow, helping the hero fight crime one arrow at a time, with Roy creating trick arrows for his mentor. Due to drugs and alcohol abuse, Roy fell out with Oliver Queen. He eventually managed to deal with his personal demons and become a hero again. Calling himself Arsenal, he fought as a member of both the Titans and The Outlaws.

MAN OF ALL WEAPONS
Roy was an expert archer, but his perfect aim could be applied to a variety of weapons. He was rarely without one of his signature baseball caps.

When Roy Harper was a boy, his parents died in a forest fire. A Native American chief named Big Bow rescued Roy and took him in as his own and taught him archery. Roy was haunted by his childhood loss. At age ten, he tried his first sip of alcohol and quickly spiraled out of control. He was caught robbing a liquor store and when the local sheriff intervened, Big Bow was killed in the skirmish. Too inebriated to understand what happened, Roy fled the reservation to live on the streets of Seattle.

Roy first encountered Oliver Queen after picking his pocket at a local mall. Ollie discovered that the boy was a natural expert with electronics, and eventually allowed Roy to partner with him in his alter ego of Green Arrow. Dubbed Speedy, Roy developed trick arrows for his mentor, and even joined the youthful heroes called the Teen Titans. However, when Ollie began to focus his attentions elsewhere, Speedy turned again to alcohol and then moved on to harder drugs. Instead of helping his young partner deal with his demons, Green Arrow fired Speedy. The young hero was then manipulated by Count Vertigo, before overcoming the villain's influence and setting out on his own.

Changing his Super Hero name to Arsenal, Roy recovered, in part thanks to the unlikely help from his Alcoholics Anonymous sponsor Killer Croc.

Now an adult, Roy's thirst for adventure saw him join forces with Red Hood (Jason Todd) and Starfire, after the young vigilantes sprung him from a Middle Eastern prison. They became close friends and worked together as The Outlaws. When Starfire later left the team, Roy and Jason partnered as heroes for hire for a time. When that misguided business endeavor ended, Roy reunited with the original Teen Titans, now calling themselves the Titans. Roy was always happiest when with his oldest friends. However, one of those friends would be the literal death of him, when The Flash (Wally West) unwittingly lost control of his powers at a secret recovery center called the Sanctuary. Roy was killed in the tragedy, sending shockwaves through the Super Hero community.

ON THE RECORD

Before *Flashpoint*, Roy Harper's time as Green Arrow's sidekick Speedy was equally marred by an addiction to drugs. Always the fighter, Roy overcame his addiction, yet was continually drawn to the edge. His most serious romantic relationship was with international terrorist Cheshire, and their fling resulted in the birth of his daughter, Lian.

Roy's evolution into Arsenal saw him move away from his role as Green Arrow's sidekick and start to favor more hi-tech weaponry. When he later joined the Justice League as Red Arrow, he returned to his roots. But he became more brutal following the murder of his daughter and the loss of his arm. Roy was a man in constant recovery, both from substance abuse and from his life with Cheshire.

CYBERNETIC ARM
Roy's arm was cut off by villain Prometheus. It was replaced by an advanced, cybernetic limb, but he experienced phantom pain.

CLASSIC STORIES

Green Lantern (Vol. 2) #85 (Aug.–Sep. 1971) Roy Harper is revealed to be a drug addict in one of the most controversial stories of the era.

The New Titans #99 (Jul. 1993) Roy assumes the name and identity of Arsenal for the first time.

Justice League of America (Vol. 2) #7 (May 2007) Roy is the Red Arrow and becomes a member of the Justice League of America.

THE OUTLAWS
Roy joined forces with the Red Hood and Starfire to form The Outlaws. He also began a relationship with teammate Starfire.

A

ARKHAM, JEREMIAH

DEBUT *Batman: Shadow of the Bat #1*
(Jun. 1992)
BASE Arkham Asylum
HEIGHT 5ft 9in
WEIGHT 170 lbs
EYES Brown
HAIR Brown
POWERS/ABILITIES Advanced medical
and physiological knowledge.
AFFILIATIONS Arkham Asylum

Head doctor at Arkham Asylum, Jeremiah Arkham was known for an unorthodox approach to psychiatric care. However—just like his great-uncle Amadeus, who founded the institution before going mad—Jeremiah, too was eventually driven insane. Dangerously paranoid and narcissistic, he briefly masqueraded as The Joker. While deranged, he freed and mind-controlled his charges, unleashing chaos before being shocked back to normalcy. In a later crisis, he assumed the persona of Black Mask, seeking to create his own criminal empire.

After being successfully treated in his own asylum, Jeremiah is now regarded as cured of his demons. He administrates Arkham again, employing his radical healing techniques on the troubled and the lethally dangerous souls caged there.

ARKILLO

DEBUT *Green Lantern* (Vol. 4) #10 (May 2006)
BASE Vorn
HEIGHT 6ft 6in **WEIGHT** 370 lbs
EYES Black **HAIR** None
POWERS/ABILITIES Power ring grants
flight, energy control, and construct creation.
ALLIES Sinestro
ENEMIES Guardians, Guy Gardner
AFFILIATIONS New Guardians, Sinestro
Corps/Yellow Lantern Corps

Recruited by Sinestro to join his Corps in the antimatter universe of Qward, Arkillo traveled to Earth when he learned that one of the Corps had died there. While on Earth, he was recruited to the New Guardians team led by Green Lantern Kyle Rayner and staffed by ring bearers from across the Emotional Spectrum.

Arkillo journeyed with them to Oa, where they survived an assault by the Guardians of the Universe. They battled the Archangel Invictus before Arkillo learned Sinestro and Hal Jordan had cooperated to destroy the Sinestro Corps' Power Battery. With a new battery powered by fear, Arkillo rejoined the fight against Invictus before leaving the New Guardians. Resolved to do good his way, Arkillo now maintains order through fear as chief enforcer for the Sinestro Corps.

ARROWETTE

DEBUT *Impulse* #28 (Aug. 1997)
REAL NAME Suzanne "Cissie" King-Hawke
HEIGHT 5ft 6in **WEIGHT** 125 lbs
EYES Blue **HAIR** Blonde
POWERS/ABILITIES Archery, acrobatics.
ALLIES Conner Kent, Cassie Sandsmark,
Bart Allen, Tim Drake
ENEMIES Harm, Spazz
AFFILIATIONS Young Justice

When Olympic archer Bonnie King saw Green Arrow and Speedy in action, she briefly became a heroic copycat named Miss Arrowette—until they convinced her to retire. Frustrated but still inspired, Bonnie obsessively trained her daughter, Cissie, in all forms of combat. She resolved that her child would not be denied her own shot at fame and fortune. Although Cissie reluctantly became Arrowette, she was gifted and capable, employing trick arrows, martial skills, and tactical aptitude against superpowered foes, singly and with Young Justice.

Eventually Child Protective Services removed Cissie from Bonnie's custody. After Arrowette almost crossed the line and executed the murderers of her favorite teacher, Cissie renounced her costumed identity. She was recently convinced to return after her old Young Justice friends needed help taking down a rogue scientist from S.T.A.R. Labs.

ARTEMIS

DEBUT *Wonder Woman* (Vol. 2) #90 (Sep. 1994)
BASE Gotham City, Bana-Mighdall, mobile
HEIGHT 5ft 8in **WEIGHT** 125 lbs
EYES Green **HAIR** Red
POWERS/ABILITIES Divinely enhanced
strength and speed; regenerative abilities; variety
of magical weapons: Bow of Ra, Mistress Ax,
Lasso of Submission.
ALLIES Akila, Wonder Woman, Red Hood,
Bizarro II, Aztek
ENEMIES First Born, Nephthys, General Ahmed
Heinle of Qurac, Tezcatlipoca
AFFILIATIONS Egyptian Gods, Outlaws

Prophesied to become Queen of the Amazons, Artemis is a daughter of the Bana-Mighdall, a breakaway faction of warrior women who switched allegiance to Egyptian gods thousands of years ago. Artemis met and mistakenly battled Wonder Woman. Working with Red Hood and a new clone of Bizarro to defeat King Hyssa's raiders, she saved her city from the Quraci army, finally proving herself worthy of the Weapon of Magical Destruction.

After years of adventuring, she united with Wonder Woman and Aztek to repulse the dark god Tezcatlipoca. Together they restored Atalanta—lost founder of the Bana-Mighdall colony—to her city. Artemis is now a hero, using the mystic Lasso of Submission awarded to her by Wonder Woman.

ATLAN

DEBUT *Atlantis Chronicles* #5 (Jul. 1990)
BASE Atlantis
HEIGHT 6ft 3in
WEIGHT 220 lbs
EYES Blue
HAIR Blond
POWERS/ABILITIES Vast magical abilities
like cryokinesis; arsenal of magical weaponry.
ALLIES Vulko
ENEMIES Orin, Aquaman

Centuries ago, Atlan ruled Atlantis, which grew to include seven lands under his reign. His brother Orin (Aquaman's ancestor) quarreled with Atlan over his inclusive policies and plotted against his brother to protect the purity of the Atlantean bloodline.

War followed, during which Atlan went into hiding and Orin murdered his family. Stricken with grief, Atlan forged six magical weapons to retake Atlantis. He used one of them to sink the kingdom, destroying four of its lands and transforming the other three—Atlantis, Xebel, and the Trench. He then fell into a long magical sleep deep under the ocean.

Atlan was revived in the present day by Atlantean advisor Vulko, who wanted to restore Atlantis' true king. Still angry, Atlan tried to permanently destroy Atlantis, but was stopped by Aquaman. The old king melted away, presumably for good.

ATLAS

DEBUT *1st Issue Special* #1 (Apr. 1975)
BASE Metropolis
HEIGHT 6ft 5in **WEIGHT** 250 lbs
EYES Blue **HAIR** Brown
POWERS/ABILITIES Superhuman
strength and stamina.
ALLIES Chagra, Forager
ENEMIES King Hyssa, Superman
AFFILIATIONS Project 7734, New Gods

In pre-historic antiquity, despotic King Hyssa's raiders ransacked Atlas' village on the Crystal Mountain, killing the boy's family before enslaving him and the village's survivors. Wearing a mystical talisman struck from the Crystal Mountain, Atlas escaped was raised by a good-hearted man named Chagra. It was not long before Chagra realized the boy had jaw-dropping strength and stamina. He became Atlas' manager, joining him on his journeys, watching the hero rescue citizens and defeat evil princes. Eventually they toppled King Hyssa himself, with the unlikely aid of time-traveling New God Forager.

Eventually, Atlas came to modern Earth-0 and worked for the mysterious Project 7734—a government investigation into the possibility of using magic to fight Kryptonians. Atlas often battled Superman, stating that his goal was to replace him as the champion of Metropolis.

ATOMIC KNIGHT

DEBUT *Strange Adventures* (Vol.1) #117
(Jun. 1960)
REAL NAME Gardner Grayle
BASE Mobile
HEIGHT 6ft 1in **WEIGHT** 189 lbs
EYES Blue **HAIR** Blond
POWERS/ABILITIES Precognition; series of
weaponized hi-tech armor suits providing a suite
of powers including enhanced strength, durability,
powered flight, energy projection, and absorption.

When nuclear war in 1986 left Earth devastated, Gardner Grayle led a team of Atomic Knights in fighting injustice in the post-apocalyptic landscape. Then he awoke to realize it was just a VR simulation by S.T.A.R. Labs to test humanity's survival potential. Afflicted with pre-cognition, Grayle stole a battle suit from the lab to save the true world from the nuclear threats he foresaw. He came into conflict with Superman, Wonder Woman, and others, but later joined teams like The Outsiders.

Following *Infinite Crisis*, Grayle's history was altered. He woke up in Blüdhaven with other Atomic Knights and visions of a horrible future. To defend the city, he worked with the Roundtable organization. After *Flashpoint*, the Atomic Knights were relocated to the post-apocalyptic future of Batman Beyond. Grayle was restored to Earth-0 after the events of *Rebirth*.

ATOMIC SKULL

DEBUT *Superman* (Vol. 1) #323 (May 1978)
REAL NAME Joseph Martin **BASE** Metropolis
HEIGHT 6ft **WEIGHT** 185 lbs
EYES Purple **HAIR** None
POWERS/ABILITIES Absorbs and projects
nuclear energy; superhuman strength; flight.
ENEMIES Superman, Wonder Woman, Steel,
Hector Hammond
AFFILIATIONS S.T.A.R. Labs, M.S.C.U.
(Metropolis Special Crimes Unit)

Scientist Joseph Martin deeply loved a co-worker, but was obsessively jealous. When their relationship ended, he saw her dancing with another man, and he killed her. Later, while on an experimental S.T.A.R. Labs submarine, he was exposed to nuclear energy. Shipwrecked on a desert island, he survived by releasing deadly nuclear blasts from his mouth.

His skin and muscles literally peeled off his face, inspiring him to create Super-Villain-for-hire persona Atomic Skull. He regularly clashed with Superman, both alone and with criminals such as Major Disaster and the Royal Flush Gang.

In recent times Martin reformed, fighting criminals with the Metropolis Special Crimes Unit, Superwoman, and the Teen Titans. As warden of Stryker's Island Penitentiary, he aided Green Lantern Hal Jordan against super-telepath Hector Hammond.

ATOM

DATA

DEBUT *All-American Comics* (Vol. 1) #19 (Oct. 1940) (Al Pratt);
Showcase (Vol. 1) #34 (Sep.-Oct. 1961) (Ray Palmer);
Brave New World (Vol. 1) #1 (Aug. 2006) (Ryan Choi)
REAL NAMES Raymond Palmer; Ryan Choi
BASE Ant Farm (Ray Palmer); Ivy Town (Ryan Choi)
HEIGHT Variable
WEIGHT Variable
EYES Brown
HAIR Brown (Ray Palmer); Black (Ryan Choi)
POWERS/ABILITIES Shrinking to any size including subatomic;
acrobatics; advanced knowledge of biomechanics and physics.
ALLIES Superman, Frankenstein, Kyle Rayner, Wonder Woman
ENEMIES Vandal Savage, Chronos, M'nagalah
AFFILIATIONS Justice League, S.H.A.D.E.

SUITED UP
The Atom's suit features life-support systems for Ray Palmer when he is riding through someone's bloodstream—or for whenever regular air molecules are too big for him to breathe.

BLOOD TEST
Called in by the Justice League for his expertise, Ray found a microscopic metropolis built inside Batman's brain.

Ray Palmer is science liaison to S.H.A.D.E. and a hero in his own right as the Atom. He is also the creator of the Ant Farm, a pioneer in miniaturization technology, and a recent welcome addition to the Justice League of America.

Ray Palmer became science advisor to S.H.A.D.E., the Super-Human Advanced Defense Executive. He built the Ant Farm, a self-contained miniaturized base for S.H.A.D.E. Agents that included S.H.A.D.E. City. The Ant Farm was a technological marvel, with an independent power source, atmosphere, and artificial gravity. It was accessible only via simultaneous teleportation and shrinking using a process Palmer created.

Aware of Palmer's work, Superman sought his help after Batman contracted a mysterious illness. Diving into a sample of Batman's blood, Palmer discovered that the Dark Knight was suffering from the effects of a microscopic city constructed in a blood vessel in his brain. Miniaturizing Superman, he took the Man of Steel inside Batman's brain, showed him the tiny city and trapped it inside a globe similar to the Ant Farm.

Palmer came to the heroes' aid again, helping Superman locate the Bottle City of Kandor and devising an armored suit of Kryptonite that the Man of Steel could use against Vandal Savage after the immortal villain had stolen his powers. Encouraged by these successes, Palmer followed through on his plan to embrace the Super Hero life and called himself the Atom.

REBIRTH

LITTLE VICTORIES, BIG DREAMS
In *DC Universe Rebirth* #1, Ryan Choi returns as Ray Palmer's teaching assistant at Ivy University. With Palmer lost in the microverse, Choi inherits his size-altering belt after receiving a desperate, if garbled, warning from his mentor. The part-time Super Hero is confident his protégé will rise to every challenge to save him as a new Atom.

Though Palmer's message is abruptly cut off, one thing is certain: to find him, Choi must finally live up to the huge potential everyone else feels he possesses. Now all he has to do is believe it himself.

ON THE RECORD

Since his creation in 1940, many heroes have been the Atom. The original was super-strong student Al Pratt, who lived a long heroic life and perished during the *Zero Hour* event. College Professor Ray Palmer then became the Atom in 1961 after inventing miniaturization technology that allowed him, and later Atoms, to alter their size, weight, and mass. Using an Atom belt confiscated from Palmer, covert operative Adam Cray succeeded him and died while working with the Suicide Squad.

In 2006, Palmer's friend and former student Ryan Choi inherited his technology and his position as Physics Professor at Ivy University. A reluctant hero at first, Choi soon carved his own legend as the All-New Atom, saving Earth from invasion by microscopic aliens, the Waiting, and thwarting a time-bending conspiracy involving his employer Dean Macy and Chronos. Choi next freed the eccentric size-shifting Super-Villain Giganta from cancer-god M'nagalah's control, and then dated her. However, he faced his greatest trial after accidentally bringing back a microbial carnivore from the microverse. This predator shrunk its prey, storing them in a sub-atomic realm, and it took all Choi's bravery and brilliance to rescue the surviving victims. Ryan was murdered by Deathstroke, but returned during the *Convergence* event to help Ray Palmer bring the assassin to justice.

UP AND ATOM
Ray Palmer was the best-known Atom, remaining in the role for five decades, and counting.

BITE-SIZED HERO
Under the malign influence of cancer-god M'nagalah, Giganta bit off more than she could chew when she swallowed Ryan whole.

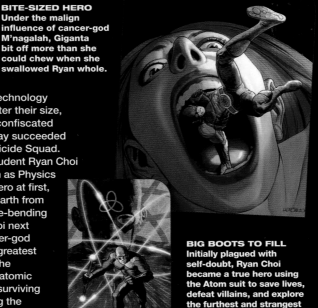

BIG BOOTS TO FILL
Initially plagued with self-doubt, Ryan Choi became a true hero using the Atom suit to save lives, defeat villains, and explore the furthest and strangest corners of the microverse.

CLASSIC STORIES

***Showcase* (Vol. 1) #34 (Sep.-Oct. 1961)** Scientist Ray Palmer devises a way to shrink himself using matter from a white dwarf star. He dubs himself the Atom and frees an alien named Kulan Dar, who has had to commit crimes for a local thief.

***Sword of the Atom* #1-4 (Sep. 1983)** With his marriage to Jean Loring on the rocks, Ray Palmer finds himself frozen at a six-inch stature. He discovers a society of miniature people in the Amazon, and becomes the leader of a rebel faction.

***All-New Atom* (Vol 1.) #5 (Jan. 2007)** Rookie Atom Ryan Choi faces demonic corrupter M'nagalah, and is briefly swallowed by his possessed new colleague Professor Doris Zuel (Giganta).

***Titans* (Vol. 2) #38 (Oct. 2011)** Ray Palmer investigates the disappearance of his successor, Ryan Choi. He hunts down Deathstroke, sparking a battle between the Justice League and the Titans.

ATOM SMASHER

DEBUT *All-Star Squadron* #25 (Sep. 1983)
REAL NAME Albert Julian Rothstein
BASE New York City
HEIGHT 7ft 6in (15ft at full height) **WEIGHT** 297 lbs (700 lbs at full size)
EYES Blue **HAIR** Red
POWERS/ABILITIES Superhuman strength, endurance, and durability; able to increase size and gain weight simultaneously; wears S.T.A.R. Labs-designed suit that can change size with him.
ALLIES Obsidian, Jade, Black Adam **ENEMIES** Extant, Kobra
AFFILIATIONS Infinity, Inc., Conglomerate, Justice Society of America, Justice League America, Suicide Squad

NEW WAVE NUKLON
Atom Smasher struggled to live down his old look as Nuklon. He used to sport a then-trendy Mohican haircut.

A true example of a legacy hero, Albert Rothstein is the godson to the original Golden Age hero Atom, as well as the grandson to the Super-Villain Cyclotron. Albert decided to use his inherited powers for good, calling himself Nuklon and becoming a founding member of the young Super Hero team Infinity, Inc. After the team disbanded, Albert continued to move up in Super Hero circles, joining the Conglomerate and then Justice League America, the latter alongside another former Infinity, Inc. member, Obsidian. Following an attack on the JLA's satellite headquarters, Nuklon left the team, while many of its members decided to form a new Justice League America incarnation.

It didn't take long for Nuklon to find a new team of Super Heroes to fight alongside. He joined the reformed Justice Society of America. This JSA was made up of many legacy heroes, including Black Canary (Dinah Laurel Lance), Starman (Jack Knight), Stargirl (Courtney Whitmore), and even his godfather's son, Damage (Grant Emerson). Prolonged exposure to thorium radiation had given Albert the ability to change his size and density. This inspired him to adopt the name Atom Smasher, to better honor both his godfather and grandfather.

FISTS OF FURY
After his mother died at the hands of the villain Kobra, Albert was consumed with vengeance. Growing to a dangerously unstable size, he flew into a murderous rage against his Kobra's forces.

ATROCITUS

DEBUT *Green Lantern* (Vol. 4) #28 (Apr. 2008)
REAL NAME Atros
BASE Ysmault
HEIGHT 7ft 9in **WEIGHT** 438 lbs
EYES Yellow **HAIR** None
POWERS/ABILITIES Superhuman strength, endurance, and durability; Red Lantern ring enables flight, formation of rage-fueled energy constructs, projection of force-fields, and production of an acid-like plasma.
ALLIES Dex-Starr
ENEMIES Guardians of the Universe, Guy Gardner
AFFILIATIONS Red Lanterns, Five Inversions

Long ago, on the planet
Ryut, an alien named Atros lived with his wife and children. Policed by the Guardians of the Universe's Manhunter androids, the people lived in peace, until the Manhunters malfunctioned and razed the planet. Atros' family was killed, leaving him alone in his rage. After destroying many Manhunters with his bare hands, Atros was found by Qull, Roixaeume, Orphram, and Dal-Xauix—beings banished from their home world and considered demons. Atros fell in with them, and the group became known as the Five Inversions, using blood magic to battle the Guardians of the Universe for centuries.

Eventually, the Guardians' new servants, the Green Lanterns, bested the Five Inversions. Atros killed his teammates and used their blood to build a Red Lantern power battery, empowered by his own rage. He took the name Atrocitus and created his own Red Lantern Corps.

ON THE RECORD

A pivotal flashback in *Green Lantern* (Vol. 4) #30 (Jun. 2008) revealed that Atrocitus had murdered Hal Jordan's predecessor, Abin Sur, which makes Atrocitus responsible for Hal acquiring a power ring and becoming a Green Lantern.

Atrocitus fought against Nekron in the *Blackest Night* event and briefly gave a Red Lantern ring to Aquaman's longtime love interest, Mera, during that conflict.

BLOOD OATH
Like the Green Lantern Corps, the Red Lanterns have their own oath:
"With blood and rage of crimson red,
Ripped from a corpse so freshly dead,
Together with our hellish hate,
We'll burn you all—that is your fate!"

ATOMICA

DEBUT *The New 52: Free Comic Book Day Special* #1 (Jun. 2012)
REAL NAME Rhonda Pineda
HEIGHT 5ft 2in **WEIGHT** 107 lbs
EYES Brown **HAIR** Brown
POWERS/ABILITIES Able to shrink to microscopic size.
ALLIES Johnny Quick, the Outsider
ENEMIES Justice League, Justice League of America, Anti-Monitor, Lex Luthor

The Earth-3 equivalent of Bonnie from the infamous duo of Bonnie and Clyde, Rhonda Pineda was the partner of Jonathan Allen, both of whom enjoyed careers as criminals and killers. But the law eventually caught up with them and they were surrounded by police on the roof of S.T.A.R. Labs. A lightning strike caused the duo to be exposed to Ray Palmer's equipment, housed inside the S.T.A.R. facility. Rhonda gained shrinking powers, while Johnny gained super-speed.

Joining Earth-3's Crime Syndicate as Atomica, Rhonda ventured to Earth-0. Here she became a double-agent for both the Justice League and the Justice League of America as the Atom, before she revealed herself as the Syndicate's mole. During a battle with Batman and his allies, she was crushed beneath Lex Luthor's boot.

AXIS AMERIKA

DEBUT *Young All-Stars* #1 (Jun. 1987)
NOTABLE MEMBERS Übermensch, Horned Owl, Fledermaus, Hel, Gudra, Sea Wolf, Usil, Kamikaze, Fleshburn, Baron Blitzkrieg, Zaladin, Übermensch II, Great White

During World War II, the Super-Villain squad Axis Amerika served the Axis Powers against US Super Hero teams like the All-Star Squadron. Axis Amerika's leader was usually Übermensch, who possessed superhuman strength, durability, and speed, but the infamous Baron Blitzkrieg also led the team.

Other members included the Horned Owl, the German equivalent of Batman and his son, Fledermaus; Gudra, a Valkyrie brought from another dimension thanks to Hitler's Spear of Destiny; Sea Wolf, an aquatic werewolf; Usil, an expert archer; and Kamikaze, known as the "living missile" and equipped with rocket-powered armor. Together, the group battled the offshoot of the All-Star Squadron, the Young All-Stars.

Decades later, a new Axis America team of American supremacists, fought the JLA. Led by an American called Übermensch II, they included his wife Hel, a flying swordswoman; Fleshburn, a fire-wielder; Great White, who wielded an energized bullwhip; and Zaladin, a mystic swordsman.

AZRAEL

DEBUT *Batman: Sword of Azrael* #1 (Oct. 1992)
REAL NAME Jean-Paul Valley **BASE** Mobile
HEIGHT 6ft 2in **WEIGHT** 210 lbs **EYES** Blue **HAIR** Blond
POWERS/ABILITIES Expert hand-to-hand combatant and swordsman; underwent Mother's traumatic conditioning, making him a near-perfect warrior; possesses a so-called "Wrath of God" ability that produces awe and visions in the minds of his victims.
ALLIES Batman, Batwoman, Batwing, Starfire, Cyborg, GL Jessica Cruz
ENEMIES Bane, Darkseid, St. Dumas, Mother
AFFILIATIONS Church of St. Dumas, the Colony, Justice League Odyssey

Early in Batman's career, when Dick Grayson became Robin, the Dark Knight encountered a criminal calling herself Mother. She offered a bizarre specialty service that would deliver a perfect partner or soldier—for the right price. To create that ideal companion, Mother traumatized her innocent victims at an early age, enabling her to imprint any desired qualities onto them.

Jean-Paul Valley was one of these innocents. Mother used a novel technique on him while working with the Church of St. Dumas. Utilizing a combination of awe and pain, Jean-Paul was forged into an unstoppable warrior—Azrael.

Tracking the villain Orphan, Red Robin and Red Hood infiltrated the infamous prison, Peña Duro, on the corrupt island of Santa Prisca. They teamed with monstrous Bane, storming the penitentiary, which had been converted into a church called the Crusade of St. Dumas. There they encountered Azrael, who defeated Bane by showing him a religious vision that apparently confirmed the Church of St. Dumas' philosophy.

Later, Azrael worked under Batman and Batwoman, before being drawn into space as part of Justice League Odyssey. Mysteriously compelled to defend the chaotic ghost sector with Starfire and Cyborg, Azrael was slowly corrupted by Darkseid and transformed into his New God of Belief.

ON THE RECORD

Pre-*Flashpoint*, Jean-Paul Valley's discovery of his dying father dressed as Azrael changed his life forever. Brainwashed by the System to become the Church of St. Dumas' assassin, Jean-Paul worked with Batman instead, standing in for the Dark Knight when Bane broke the hero's back.

Unbalanced by his upbringing, Valley became a more violent Batman and wore heavier armor. He later surrendered the mantle to a newly healed Bruce Wayne and set out on his own adventures as Azrael.

THE RETURN OF AZRAEL
After Jean-Paul Valley's death at the hands of his greatest enemies, Biis and Scratch, a new Azrael emerged. Michael Lane, a former cop, had been trained to become the G.C.P.D.'s equivalent of Batman.

AZTEK

DEBUT *Aztek* #1 (Aug. 1996)
REAL NAME Nayeli Constant
BASE Vanity, Oregon
EYES Black
HAIR Black
POWERS/ABILITIES Computer expert; trained in combat techniques; battlesuit provides enhanced strength, durability, and flight; helmet holds entire history of Brotherhood of the Q
ALLIES The Ray
ENEMIES Tezcatlipoca, Sons of the Earth, the Luminary
AFFILIATIONS Justice League, Justice Foundation, Q Society

Software engineer Nayeli Constant was working in Austin, Texas, when the Aztek helmet originally used by Uno sought her out and recruited her to the Q Society's eternal war against Tezcatlipoca.

Rebuilding and modifying the battlesuit, Constant assumed the role of Aztek, determined to save mankind from the ancient threat of the Dark God and his earthly acolytes. Moving to Vanity, Oregon, Aztek started her holy war by hunting local cult the Sons of the Earth and their leader, the Luminary. This mission initially brought her into brutal conflict with the Ray before they ultimately teamed up to end the cult's threat.

ON THE RECORD

The Brotherhood of the Q raised Uno to wear the helmet of Quetzalcoatl and defend the city of Vanity and the world against the shadow god Tezcatlipoca.

When Uno arrived in Vanity, however, he encountered a vigilante named Bloodtype, in reality Dr. Curtis Falconer. Bloodtype died after their battle, but not before he told Uno that he was about to start work at St. Bartholomew's Hospital that very day. Deciding he needed a civilian identity, Uno impersonated Falconer, protecting Vanity as a Super Hero later dubbed Aztek by the press. After team-ups with Green Lantern and Batman, Aztek briefly joined the JLA but died attacking the living planet Mageddon, the supposed second coming of Tezcatlipoca.

BANE

DATA

DEBUT *Batman: Vengeance of Bane #1* (Jan. 1993)
BASE Gotham City
HEIGHT 6ft 8in   **WEIGHT** 350 lbs (425 lbs with Venom)
EYES Brown   **HAIR** Brown
POWERS/ABILITIES Enhanced strength, weight, durability, and endurance due to use of a super-steroid called Venom; extremely intelligent; master strategist; possesses indomitable will; expert fighter and natural leader.
ALLIES Santa Prisca mercenaries; prison inmates Bird, Trogg, and Zombie
ENEMIES Batman, the Batman Family, Batwoman, Killer Croc
AFFILIATIONS Santa Prisca inmates

CLASSIC STORIES

Batman: Vengeance of Bane #1 (Jan. 1993) Bane's origin is revealed in a powerful tale of one man's struggle to the top of the criminal heap.

"Knightfall" [*Batman* (Vol. 1) #492–500, *Detective Comics* (Vol. 1) #659–666, *Showcase '93* #7–8 (May 1992–Oct. 1993)] Bane not only plans a way to triumph over Batman, but he breaks the crime fighter's back in this memorable saga.

Batman: Vengeance of Bane #2 (Dec. 1995) After his defeat to Azrael's Batman, Bane escapes prison once again to reclaim his greatness without Venom.

Batman: Bane of the Demon #1–4 (Mar.–Jun. 1998) Bane becomes Rā's al Ghūl's heir apparent, setting the stage for the epic *Legacy* crossover.

BREAKING THE BAT
When Bane snapped Batman's back, he triumphed over the hero by using not just strength, but also cunning.

BORN LEADER
Bane presents a huge physical threat and, unfortunately for Batman, is also a charismatic leader who can enlist others in his quest for domination.

Despite his impressive physique and prodigious strength, Bane is far from a simple physical threat for Batman. An unjustly imprisoned inmate, Bane trained his mind and body to near perfection. With the help of the super-steroid known as Venom, Bane has become one of the most dangerous men the Dark Knight has ever faced—a perfect combination of brain and brawn.

Little is known about the past of the man who is simply known as Bane. With his true name lost somewhere to legend—if he ever had one at all—the story of Bane begins in a prison complex called Peña Dura in the corrupt Caribbean island nation of Santa Prisca. While it has never been proven, many legends state that Bane was born inside the prison's walls, and was forced to live his life there, serving the sentence his mysterious father avoided by escaping "justice."

When he was just a boy, Bane was forced into solitary confinement, nearly drowning each night when water would flood his cell. Surviving off the sea creatures that came in with the tide, Bane began to focus his mind and body, training himself for a war to come. That war would loom ever closer when, as an adult, Bane was chosen for an experimental program that saw his body injected with the super-steroid Venom. Now even more of a powerhouse, he escaped and headed to Gotham City to claim it as his own. A genius strategist, Bane challenged and triumphed over Batman, and broke the hero's back, only to have Gotham City subsequently ripped from his grasp by its protector.

Bane has attempted several more takeovers of Gotham City over the years, including besting Killer Croc for rule of the city when the Crime Syndicate had briefly taken the Justice League off the map. However, his most recent efforts may be his cruelest. Not only did Bane manipulate Catwoman to leave Batman at the altar on what would have been their wedding night, he also teamed with a Batman (Thomas Wayne) from an alternate universe and killed Alfred Pennyworth during a successful Gotham City takeover. At this point, Bane controlled every aspect of the city, allowing other Super-Villains to operate as its police force. However, Batman and Catwoman fought their way through this "City of Bane" and defeated the hulking villain. Thomas Wayne then double-crossed his supposed ally and shot Bane—an injury that Bane once again survived.

BANE OF GOTHAM CITY
The super-steroid Venom is fed into Bane's bloodstream via tubes. The Venom temporarily gives the villain superhuman strength, speed, and endurance.

ON THE RECORD

Bane originally escaped Peña Dura with the help of three fellow inmates, Bird, Trogg, and Zombie. The villains then freed many of the Dark Knight's worst enemies from Arkham Asylum. Exhausted, Batman refused to rest until they were once again caged. Meanwhile, Bane broke into Wayne Manor to confront the hero in a brutal fight that saw the villain snap Batman's back.

A NEW KNIGHT
In the pre-*Flashpoint* DC universe, Bruce Wayne and his allies worked toward a permanent cure for his broken back. Batman's successor, Azrael, took up his mantle and finally managed to beat Bane.

BARD, JASON

DEBUT *Detective Comics* (Vol. 1) #392 (Oct. 1969)
BASE Gotham City
HEIGHT 6ft **WEIGHT** 175 lbs
EYES Brown **HAIR** Brown
ABILITIES Intelligent, cunning, determined, skilled detective.
ALLIES Vicki Vale, Hush, Jim Gordon, Batgirl
ENEMIES Mayor Sebastian Hady, Carmine Falcone
AFFILIATIONS G.C.P.D. (former)

Jason Bard was a respected Detroit cop whose partner died when a Batman imitator interfered in police business. Blaming the real Dark Knight for the acts of his copycat, Bard traveled to Gotham City, seeking out the villain Hush.

After Police Commissioner James Gordon was framed and imprisoned, Bard manipulated *Gotham Gazette* reporter Vicki Vale, and rose to the position of commissioner before seeing the error of his ways after an encounter with the real Batman. He then worked against the criminals he had partnered with. He freed Gordon, resigned from the force, and gave a tell-all confession to Vale. He worked as a private eye and began a tempestuous romantic relationship with Gordon's daughter, Barbara, aka Batgirl.

BARON BLITZKRIEG

DEBUT *World's Finest Comics* (Vol. 1) #246 (Aug.–Sep. 1977)
REAL NAME Reiter (first name unknown)
BASE Nazi Germany
HEIGHT 6ft 6in **WEIGHT** 245 lbs (in armor)
EYES Blue **HAIR** Black
POWERS/ABILITIES Psychic power to control metabolism; eyes emit heat.
ALLIES Adolf Hitler, Atomic Skull
ENEMIES Wonder Woman, All-Star Squadron, Damage, Iron Munro
AFFILIATIONS Third Reich, The Society, Shadowspire, Axis Amerika

The man who would later become known as Baron Blitzkrieg was originally a Prussian nobleman, favored by Adolf Hitler. Heading up a concentration camp, this commandant was scarred when acid was thrown in his face. This prompted Hitler to attempt to unlock the man's latent psychic powers, realizing the Baron was of little other use to him.

Transformed into a super soldier for the Third Reich, Baron Blitzkrieg became a staunch opponent of the wartime heroes in the All-Star Squadron and later Wonder Woman (Hippolyta). His untimely death occurred at the hands of Superboy Prime, who killed the Baron with his heat vision.

BAT LASH

DEBUT *Showcase* (Vol. 1) #76 (Aug. 1968)
REAL NAME Bartholomew Aloysius Lash
BASE American Southwest (late 19th century)
HEIGHT 5ft 11in **WEIGHT** 167 lbs
EYES Blue **HAIR** Reddish blond
POWERS/ABILITIES Expert gunfighter, bar brawler, and card player; razor-keen wit.
ALLIES Jonah Hex, Cinnamon, Scalphunter, Enemy Ace
ENEMIES Hundreds of card players
AFFILIATIONS Rough Bunch

An adorable baby, Bartholomew Aloysius Lash grew up learning how to use his good looks and charm to his advantage.

After his parents were swindled out of their farm, Bartholomew sought justice, but found himself killing a corrupt police deputy. Branded an outlaw, Bat Lash began a journey across the Old West, making his living thanks to his uncanny knack at poker. While he's no stranger to a barroom brawl, Lash is an even better talker, and often maintains a smile on his face and a jaunty flower in his hat.

BASILISK

DEBUT *Suicide Squad* (Vol. 4) #4 (Feb. 2012)
BASE The Andes
MEMBERS/ABILITIES
Regulus: Tactical analysis, weapons expert; **Grey Lora**: Enhanced reflexes; **Red Orchid**: Chlorokinesis; **Black Spider**: Hand-to-hand combat, marksmanship; **Hammerdown**: Invulnerability, super-strength; **Whipcrack**: Energy whip; **Tsiklon**: Wind manipulation; **Uplink**: Telepathy; **Dr. Elisa Visyak**: Scientific genius.
ENEMIES Suicide Squad, Team 7, Birds of Prey

Basilisk is a powerful terrorist organization with several metahuman men and women at its disposal. It is led by Regulus, a Super-Villain formed from a psychic and physical merger of Dean Higgins—a former member of the special ops group Team 7—and Kaizen, the insane ruler of the outlaw nation of Gamorra.

Part cult drawing power from a mythic snake and part conspiracy collective preparing for a war against super-powered threats, Basilisk has had numerous clashes with the Suicide Squad. At one point the terror cell planted one of its members, Black Spider, in the Squad's ranks in an attempt to destroy the Squad from within. Basilisk also tangled with the Birds of Prey when Black Canary discovered Basilisk was holding her husband, Kurt Lance, hostage.

BAT-MITE

DEBUT *Detective Comics* (Vol. 1) #267 (May 1959)
BASE Gotham City
HEIGHT 2ft 11in **WEIGHT** 47 lbs
EYES Black **HAIR** Unknown
POWERS/ABILITIES Flight; teleportation; can alter reality including changing the clothing of others; weapons include Utility Belt filled with gadgets together with a bat-shaped cellphone, Bat-shield, and Bat-laser.
ALLIES Batman, the Batman Family, Booster Gold
ENEMIES Gridlock, Dr. Trauma
AFFILIATIONS Justice Mites of America

An imp hailing from an unnamed dimension, the pint-sized provocateur known as Bat-Mite is a perpetual thorn in Batman's side. Declaring himself Batman's biggest fan and clad in a Batsuit that resembles his hero's current look, the troublesome Bat-Mite has the unerring knack of popping up at the most inopportune times to assist Batman with his own brand of mischievous heroics. The result is invariably mayhem, making the Dark Knight work twice as hard to resolve the situation.

Bat-Mite's otherworldly antics led him to be banned from his own dimension. Stranded in Batman's reality, but still possessing his magical abilities, Bat-Mite stole the Batmobile to engage in a spot of crime fighting, but promptly crashed it off a cliff. Not content with "helping" the Dark Knight, Bat-Mite has also managed to make life difficult for other Super Heroes, including Hawkman, Robin, and Booster Gold.

BATGIRL

DATA

DEBUT *Detective Comics* (Vol. 1) #359 (Jan. 1967)
REAL NAME Barbara Joan Gordon
BASE Gotham City
HEIGHT 5ft 9in **WEIGHT** 135lbs **EYES** Blue **HAIR** Red
POWERS/ABILITIES Expert martial artist and gymnast trained in part by Batman; extremely athletic and agile; eidetic memory; very intelligent with advanced knowledge of computers; natural leader; weapons include fully stocked Utility Belt, protective suit, and Batcycle.
ALLIES Batman, Batman Family, Black Canary, Frankie Charles, James Gordon, Jason Bard
ENEMIES The Joker, James Gordon Jr., Knightfall, Velvet Tiger
AFFILIATIONS Birds of Prey, Batman family

A presence in Batman's world ever since she forcibly inserted herself into it, the tenacious Barbara Gordon has spent her life following in the footsteps of her hero father, Commissioner James "Jim" Gordon. While James Gordon has done much to help Gotham City as one of the few honorable cops on the Gotham City Police force, Barbara has done even more as Batgirl. Originally starting her career by imitating Gotham City's legendary Dark Knight, Batgirl has since become her own woman, fighting crime in an original style, and putting her years of training and brilliant mind to work protecting Gotham City's under-served neighborhoods.

AT A GLANCE...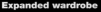

Commissioner's daughter
Barbara Gordon grew up a police "brat," idolizing her father James Gordon and wanting to follow in his footsteps. Her father introduced her to judo and gymnastics, and imbued her with a strong moral character. These skills all came into play when Barbara first donned a Batsuit and became the Super Hero known as Batgirl.

Expanded wardrobe
Batgirl has worn several costumes over the course of her relatively short career. First donning a police Batsuit, Barbara soon adopted an official Batgirl costume, complete with domino-style mask. After an injury at the hands of The Joker, she wore a more armored Batgirl suit.

Team player
Batgirl met and teamed with vigilantes Black Canary and Starling to form the Birds of Prey—a team that later brought crime fighters like Katana, Strix, Condor, and The Huntress into its lineup. While considering herself a solo act, Batgirl has fought well alongside others.

Barbara Gordon grew up in the shadow of Gotham City's white knight, James Gordon. She idolized her father for his fight against the city's corruption and criminal element. Intense and driven, Barbara wanted to follow her dad's example, but she did so in her own unique way. She mastered ballet and judo, and put her photographic memory to good use by studying criminology.

It was during a trip to the Gotham City Police Department as part of her research for "Intro to Criminology" that Barbara caught her first glimpse of her life's calling. Visiting the precinct alongside her little brother James Jr.—Barbara saw her true reason for touring the G.C.P.D.—a Batsuit mocked up by the S.W.A.T. team based on eyewitness sightings of the elusive Batman.

As interested as she was in her father's line of work, Barbara had become truly fascinated by Gotham City's Dark Knight and wanted to learn everything she could about the vigilante. But little did she know she would get a chance to take a trial run at filling the Batman's shoes that very same day. After police escorted a hulking criminal called Harry X past Barbara, the villain escaped with the help of his armed accomplices. Barbara used the confusion as cover, and donned the G.C.P.D.'s Batsuit in order to best Harry X in combat without exposing her identity. When she met Batman face-to-face immediately afterward, her actions were praised by the hero. The entire event proved too irresistible for Barbara, and soon she was wearing her own blue-and-gray Batsuit and learning the ins and outs of crime fighting firsthand as Batgirl.

DADDY DEAREST
Barbara decorated her bedroom walls with news stories of her father's heroic crime-fighting exploits.

CLASSIC STORIES

Detective Comics (Vol. 1) #359 (Jan. 1967) Batgirl makes her debut by proving herself in combat against the longtime Batman foe Killer Moth.

Batgirl Special #1 (Jan. 1988) In her first solo self-titled comic, Batgirl ends an old score and retires from the Super Hero life, setting the stage for the monumental *Batman: The Killing Joke* special.

Batgirl: Year One #1–9 (Feb.–Oct. 2003) Barbara Gordon's origin is retold for the modern era, explaining how she made the transition from lone vigilante to a member of Batman's inner circle.

Batgirl (Vol. 4) #35 (Dec. 2014) Batgirl opts for independence and moves to the Gotham City borough of Burnside, adopting a new look and perspective on life.

AFFAIRS OF THE HEART
Barbara Gordon and Dick Grayson, the original Robin, have shared a longstanding romance that began when Barbara first started out as Batgirl. From the outset, Grayson noticed the young vigilante's grace and skill, and soon developed a crush on the heroine. While their romance never truly got off the ground, the two understood they shared a mutual attraction. But when Grayson faked his own death to join the spy network Spyral, Barbara moved on with her life and began a romance with Luke Fox, aka Batwing. Babs and Luke have since broken up, and she began dating Jason Bard, a former Gotham City Police Commissioner, who is trying to make amends for his corrupt time on the force.

MOVING ON
Dick Grayson wasn't happy about Barbara's decision to end their years-long flirtation, but he realized that she was happy, and did his best to be happy for her.

SURVIVING THE JOKE
The Joker shot and paralyzed Barbara Gordon at her apartment—but he was no match for Batgirl's indomitable spirit.

However, after team-ups with Robin and fighting villains like the Killer Moth, the first chapter of Batgirl's life as a Super Hero was about to come to a crashing halt. When Super-Villain The Joker broke into Barbara's apartment in his latest scheme against Jim Gordon, he shot Batgirl in the spine, leaving her wheelchair-bound. Barbara made the most of that time, however, using her computer expertise to create the online persona of the information guru called Oracle. Through the use of cutting-edge technology, however, and with an unwavering desire to overcome adversity, Barbara regained her ability to walk. She was soon back in prime fighting form, adopting a new Batgirl costume that better matched Batman's armored counterpart.

Back as a Super Hero, Batgirl's life did not slow down in the slightest. Initially reluctant to commit herself to a team, Barbara became a member of the female vigilantes called the Birds of Prey. She met a host of new adversaries including Grotesque and Gretel, and an archfoe in the form of Knightfall. She would later move to Burnside, become the defender of that Gotham City borough, and use social media to her advantage. There she started her own company in the form of Gordon Clean Energy, adopted a practical jacket-like costume, and established a network of loyal friends and coworkers.

"...for the first time in a long while, I know who I am..."

BATGIRL

BRAVE NEW BATGIRL
When her practical Burnside costume was all but shredded during a fight with a new Grotesque, Barbara donned an old prototype Batgirl costume she kept at her dad's house for just such an emergency. Opting to leave her Burnside days behind her for a fresh start at crime fighting, she took up a new apartment in the rundown neighborhood called the Narrows. Batgirl maintains a Super Hero hideout from her time as Oracle in the form of the Clock Tower, located in the historic Old Gotham neighborhood, and enjoys the occasion team-up with Black Canary and Huntress, her two closest allies from the Birds of Prey.

WANTED FOR QUESTIONING
Commissioner Gordon witnessed James Jr.'s plummet off the dock, and blamed Batgirl for his son's death. Determined not to reveal her double identity to her father, Batgirl was forced to live as a fugitive for a time.

CLASSIC YET PRACTICAL
Batgirl's current Batsuit includes a yellow backpack underneath the cape, perfect for storing her civilian clothing while on the go.

REBIRTH

CLASS ACT
Always an overachiever and hungry to be the best she can be, Barbara Gordon started a global odyssey to hone her crime-fighting combat skills. Unfortunately, even before completing her first lessons in Japan, Batgirl was drawn into a deadly game of murder and mystery.

ON THE RECORD

While Barbara Gordon has remained the iconic version of Batgirl since her debut, the original Batgirl, Betty Kane, first appeared in 1961 in *Batman (Vol. 1) #139*. The niece of Kathy Kane (aka Batwoman), Betty launched the long and eventful history of Batgirl.

Enter Batgirl
Before the reality-altering event *Crisis on Infinite Earths*, Barbara Gordon was introduced as a librarian who had designed a Batman-like costume to attend a policeman's ball. On the way to the event, however, she encountered Killer Moth and quickly leapt to Batman and Robin's aid in defeating the villain. Sold on a life of fighting crime, Barbara became Batgirl. A breath of fresh air in Gotham City, she was soon found driving her Batgirl cycle around the city, establishing her own crime-busting credentials.

MAKING HER MARK
When Batgirl moved to Washington, D.C., Barbara became a congresswoman. Despite her busy schedule, she still kept her late night appointments as Batgirl.

The Origins of Oracle

Soon after *Crisis on Infinite Earths*, Batgirl's story was streamlined. In this incarnation, a retired Batgirl was injured by The Joker and would never walk again. However, rather than give up, Barbara changed the way she fought crime, becoming Oracle, a computer guru able to find any information on the Internet. As Oracle, Barbara was an invaluable aide to the Batman Family. She became a member of the Justice League of America, a mentor for the new Batgirl, Cassandra Cain, and she helped form the Birds of Prey.

BATMAN

DATA

DEBUT *Detective Comics* (Vol. 1) #27 **(May 1939)**
REAL NAME Bruce Wayne
BASE Gotham City
HEIGHT 6ft 2in **WEIGHT** 210 lbs **EYES** Blue **HAIR** Black
POWERS/ABILITIES Martial arts expert; skilled acrobat, gymnast, and athlete; escape artist; highly intelligent with advanced knowledge of technology; master strategist; weapons include Utility Belt and armored suit; owns customized land, air, and water vehicles.
ALLIES Batman Family, James Gordon, Lucius Fox, Superman
ENEMIES Arkham Asylum inmates, Blackgate Penitentiary inmates, Rā's al Ghūl
AFFILIATIONS Justice League, Justice League of America, Justice League International, Batman, Inc, The Outsiders, Guild of Detection

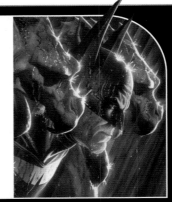

The Dark Knight. The World's Greatest Detective. Gotham City's Guardian. The hero known as Batman goes by many titles as the result of a life in the shadows building an urban legend that is revered by the innocent as much as it is feared by Gotham City's cowardly and superstitious criminal lot. In a world full of Super Heroes and Super-Villains, Batman fights crime using his intellect, physical and mental training, and an arsenal developed with his family's fortune. Moreover, Bruce Wayne has an unrelenting need to prevent the kind of tragedy that he suffered from happening to any of Gotham City's innocents.

AT A GLANCE...

The Mark of Zorro
After attending a viewing of *The Mark of Zorro* film at the Monarch Theater with his parents in the Gotham City neighborhood called Park Row, young Bruce saw his mother and father gunned down before his eyes by a common criminal. It was on this night that the Batman was truly born.

The Batman Family
While he considers himself a loner, Batman has many allies in his war on crime. These include several young heroes who each served as his partner, Robin, and other allies inspired by his career, such as Batgirl and Batwoman. He even organized an international fighting force under the name Batman, Inc., taking Batman's mission to a global level.

CLASSIC STORIES

Detective Comics (Vol. 1) #395 (Jan. 1970) Batman is brought back to his noir roots in "The Secret of the Waiting Graves," where he tangles with a mysterious couple in central Mexico.

Batman (Vol. 1) #404–407 (Feb.–May 1987) Batman's origin is brought to life for a modern audience in the "Year One" storyline following the events of *Crisis on Infinite Earths*, which seemed to wipe away much of his original continuity.

Batman (Vol. 1) #492–500, Detective Comics (Vol. 1) #659–666, Showcase '93 #7–8 (May–Oct. 1993) In "Knightfall," Batman is forced to run a gauntlet of his most dangerous foes before finally facing Super-Villain Bane in a climactic fight that sees the Dark Knight's true breaking point.

Batman (Vol. 2) #21–33 (Aug. 2013–Sep. 2014) After the events of *Flashpoint* altered reality again, Batman's origin story was given a facelift in "Zero Year." Bruce Wayne sets up a base of operations in a cave beneath Wayne Manor and the concept of the Batman is born.

The wonders of the Batcave
Batman operates from the large caverns below Wayne Manor. He is constantly developing new technologies, vehicles, and weapons to aid in his never-ending crusade against crime in Gotham City. From the dozens of models of his Batmobile, Batplane, and Batboat, to the simple gadgets in his Utility Belt, Batman is always ahead of the technological curve.

When Bruce Wayne pressured his parents to take him to see the film The Mark of Zorro, he had no idea that his life was about to change forever. As his family walked from the movie theater down a dark Park Row street in Gotham City, an armed criminal stepped from the shadows pointing his gun at the Waynes. In a simple mugging gone wrong, criminal Joe Chill shot and killed both Thomas and Martha Wayne, making young Bruce an orphan in a split second. Reeling from the shock of the traumatic loss, Bruce made a vow on his parents' grave to wage a lifetime of war against criminals who would prey on the innocent. Although he wasn't aware of it yet, on that night, Bruce truly became Batman.

After brief stints at a few schools, including Gotham Academy, Bruce Wayne traveled the world learning the tools of the crime-fighting trade he fully intended to ply. When he was 21 years old, he studied the ins and outs of technological gadgetry under the guidance of the brilliant inventor, Sergei Alexandrov. He learned from Brazilian criminal Don Miguel how to race cars in life-or-death situations, and spent much of his time studying martial arts with masters like Shihan Matsuda in the Himalayas. But Bruce didn't stop there. He delved into criminology, chemistry, and even acting, understanding that his future would require the mastery of a vast number of specialized skills. All the while, he trained his mind and body to near perfection, often practicing his fighting techniques on dozens of opponents at one time. And while he knew he would still require a lifetime of practice to reach a level of perfection he could be satisfied with, Bruce Wayne nevertheless returned to Gotham City in order to begin his mission to clean up the corrupted town.

UTILITY PATENT
Alexandrov's teachings were instrumental in enabling Bruce to create Batman's famed Utility Belt.

Bruce Wayne was fortunate enough to have been born into a wealthy family. The natural heir to the Wayne fortune and its main corporation, Wayne Industries, the idealistic Bruce represented a threat to the company's established ways of doing business. And while he had not intended to make his return to Gotham City a publicized event, his uncle Philip Kane managed to do that for him, both happy to see his nephew's return from his mysterious journeys, yet also dubious of the young man, immediately plotting against him.

Away from his corporate obligations, Bruce began his campaign against crime, but he quickly realized that in a city as corrupt as Gotham, he would need an edge. On one of his earliest outings, with only a knit hat and fake scar to mask his appearance, Bruce encountered Selina Kyle and her friend Holly Robinson, and tried to save Holly from her

THE COURT OF OWLS
Batman uncovered an underground criminal society in Gotham City, discovering that this clandestine organization dated back to the very origins of the city itself. Called the Court of Owls, the secret society maintained an army of assassins named Talons. Batman was not only forced to escape the Court's elaborate labyrinth located underneath the city streets, but he also faced a small army of Talons when the Court unleashed them on some of Gotham City's most powerful political figures. Batman and his allies defeated the assassins, forcing the Court even further underground.

THOMAS WAYNE, JR.
An acquaintance of Bruce Wayne, Lincoln March, proved to be an agent of the Court of Owls. Batman defeated March, but he could not shake off the villain's claim that he was Bruce's younger brother, Thomas, abandoned by the family at a young age.

ETERNAL KNIGHT
Batman is and forever will be Gotham City's guardian angel. Time and again he has risen to defeat any and all threats to his city and ensure justice prevails.

abusive boss. In the scuffle that followed, Bruce was stabbed by Holly and shot by police and barely made it home alive. Bruce fled to Wayne Manor, and sat in his father's study, bleeding out. He knew if he rang the bell next to the table, his longtime family friend and butler, Alfred Pennyworth, would tend to his wounds. In that moment, the sight of a bat in the study interrupted his thoughts. There at the edge of death, Bruce Wayne realized that to strike fear into the hearts of Gotham City's criminals, he had to become the very thing that had terrified him as a boy—a bat.

BECOMING BATMAN
Severely injured from patrolling without the benefit of one of the Batsuits he would later employ, Bruce Wayne knew he needed to tackle crime fighting from a different angle.

THE VOW
It was a promise made by a boy, and then by a man. Bruce Wayne swore to avenge his parents' deaths by waging a relentless war on all criminals.

ENDGAME
Throughout his career, Batman's greatest foe has been the insane criminal known simply as The Joker. Believed to be a member of the Red Hood gang who fell into a vat of toxic liquid at the ACE Chemical Plant during Batman's early years of crime-busting, The Joker has put his brilliantly twisted mind to work tormenting Batman time and again. The Joker is responsible for killing the second Robin (Jason Todd), shooting and paralyzing Batgirl (Barbara Gordon), and warring with The Riddler in a citywide event that caused the deaths of numerous innocent citizens.

The madman even once infected Gotham City with a virus that turned the populace against Batman. The brutal showdown that resulted led to the Dark Knight freeing the city of the villain's hold, but not before the apparent death of these longtime antagonists in a cave collapse deep below the city. It later transpired that they did not die, thanks in large part to the regenerative fluid, Dionesium. However, the event profoundly changed Bruce, threatening the end of Batman's career forever.

LAST LAUGH?
The so-called Clown Prince of Crime released a deadly Joker virus across Gotham City, which created an army of zombie-like victims.

"Yes, father. I shall become a bat."

Bruce Wayne

BATMAN

BREAKING UP THE BAND
The Batman costume was as effective and dramatic as Bruce had hoped when he appeared before the Red Hood Gang.

REBIRTH

STRANGERS IN TOWN
Gotham City's tenuous balance of power is disrupted by newcomers Gotham and Gotham Girl. They pluck crashing planes from the sky and have an heroic, take-charge attitude. But can the Dark Knight afford to believe that they are as benevolent as they claim?

REBIRTH

THE WEDDING
Batman and Catwoman finally admitted their feelings for one another. Batman proposed to Catwoman and she accepted, but on the night they were to be married, Catwoman abandoned him on a rooftop, manipulated into breaking his heart by Bane. Batman and Catwoman later rekindled their romance, but decided that, since they don't often follow the rule of law to the letter, they didn't need to be officially married to be devoted to one another.

Donning his first version of a Batsuit, Bruce Wayne became the Batman. He fought and defeated the notorious Red Hood Gang and then began to set his sights on other organized crime organizations in Gotham City.

Batman would soon be put to the ultimate test when a Super-Villain known as the Riddler took control of Gotham City, shutting off its power just as a super storm approached. The result was an isolated metropolis ruled by a criminal who planned to wipe the entire city off the map. Working directly with police captain James Gordon and Wayne Industries scientist Lucius Fox, Batman overcame the eccentric Super-Villain, earning his fabled reputation as Gotham City's Dark Knight in this event that would later be referred to as *Zero Year*.

As Batman's career continued, he adjusted his Batsuit to better serve his needs, and soon became a founding member of the Justice League alongside other legendary heroes such as Superman and Wonder Woman. He partnered with an orphaned former circus performer named Dick Grayson, who became the first of five young heroes to adopt the title of Robin and be personally trained by the Dark Knight. Grayson later became Nightwing and was succeeded by the headstrong Jason Todd, who was seemingly killed, only to return as the Red Hood. Tim Drake deduced his way into the Batcave becoming the third Robin, later evolving into Red Robin to venture off on his own. Stephanie Brown briefly became the fourth Robin, before returning to her original Super Hero name, Spoiler. Batman's current partner is Damian Wayne, the fifth Robin and Bruce Wayne's biological son.

Building a small army of allies over the years – combined with a near-death experience and a time-traveling journey – inspired Batman to take his work onto a global scale, and he soon introduced Batman, Inc., a Wayne Industries-sponsored organization that placed a Batman representative in many countries. The Caped Crusader also established a number of Super Hero teams, from an incarnation of the Justice League of America to his personal strike force, The Outsiders.

In recent adventures, Batman fought off a long campaign from Bane, who attempted to break Batman both physically and mentally. Bane successfully took over Gotham City, using the Psycho-Pirate to brainwash other infamous Batman enemies into becoming the city's police force. Bane even succeeded in killing Batman's loyal butler and father figure, Alfred. With Catwoman's help, Batman bested Bane, as well as his surprising partner in crime, the Batman from the alternate *Flashpoint* timeline, Thomas Wayne.

Thomas Wayne wasn't the only evil Batman that Bruce Wayne was forced to battle in recent months. A version of himself from the Dark Multiverse infected by The Joker, the Batman Who Laughs invaded Batman's home of Earth-0 alongside a small army of other evil Batmen, most twisted amalgamations of Batman and his fellow Justice League members.

Closer to home, The Joker got in on the large-scale action when he waged an all-out war on Batman, releasing armies of clown henchmen on the streets. Revealing conclusively that he knew the Batman's secret identity, The Joker staged a hostile takeover of Wayne Industries, and Jokerized Batman's technology, poisoning Batman and nearly killing him. However, the Batman rallied, and stopped The Joker's forces by embracing the one thing The Joker can never possess: a true family.

Over the years, the Dark Knight has become the creature of the night he set out to be, feared by criminals in Gotham City and beyond.

THE JOKER WAR
Nightwing had been shot in the head by the Beast, but his memories finally returned to him after The Joker tried to further mess with his mind during the citywide Joker War.

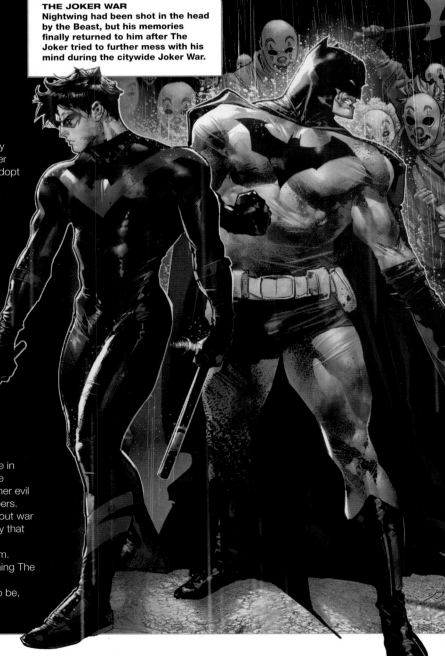

ON THE RECORD

When he debuted in 1939, Batman was intended to be a "creature of the night," a hero inspired by the often dark and shadowy world of pulp magazines of the time. That brooding vigilante would soon be brightened by a child partner, Robin, and then lightened further throughout the 1950s and '60s. Batman returned to his role as a true Dark Knight Detective in the 1970s, and grew grim and gritty in the 1980s and '90s. Able to thrive in almost any incarnation, Batman has been a hero for the ages, often reflective of the real world that inspires his creators.

THE ICONIC LOOK
Since his 1939 debut, Batman's look has included a bat-eared cowl and cape. In the 1960s, he adopted the yellow oval around his bat-symbol—an iconic logo that lasted into the 1990s.

Dark Knight Detective
After embracing light-hearted sci-fi romps in the 1950s and the offbeat adventures of the 1960s, Batman returned to his darker roots with a vengeance in *Detective Comics* #395 (January 1970) in the story "The Secret of the Waiting Graves." While not as grim as he would emerge in the 1980s after the miniseries *Batman: The Dark Knight*, the "Caped Crusader" of the 1970s was once again a creature of the night, as a new generation of writers and artists recaptured the original Batman magic.

Year One
The modern incarnation of the Dark Knight truly emerged after the world-shattering events of *Crisis on Infinite Earths*. Given a realistic overhaul, Batman struggled to find his footing in a corrupted Gotham City, finally finding an ally in the form of James Gordon, the city's future police commissioner. Batman saved the life of Gordon's son, forever cementing their partnership.

MENACE TO SOCIETY?
Batman was often targeted as a dangerous vigilante by many in Gotham City's corrupt police force, before proving he was a hero.

The broken bat
Bruce Wayne wouldn't be the only Batman in Gotham City during the course of his career. When criminal mastermind Bane unleashed the inmates of Arkham Asylum into Gotham City, he forced an exhausted Batman to capture them one by one. Bane then broke into Wayne Manor and broke Batman's back, crippling him. Temporarily out of action, Batman promoted Jean Paul Valley—a vigilante formerly called Azrael—into the Batman role. Bruce recovered with the aid of Alfred and Robin, before finally training his body back to near physical perfection and reclaiming his mantle as the true Dark Knight.

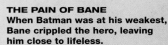

THE PAIN OF BANE
When Batman was at his weakest, Bane crippled the hero, leaving him close to lifeless.

Out of the past
As well as facing a mysterious new villain in Thomas Elliot's Hush, Batman ran the gauntlet of his most famous foes in the memorable "Hush" storyline. Introducing a threat from Bruce Wayne's past, this series saw the return of Jason Todd (in a fashion), the death of Batman's longtime inventor friend Harold Allnut, and the villainous Riddler discovering Batman's secret identity.

IDENTITY ISSUES
Batman was forced to encounter his old foes as he deduced Hush's identity and identified the man behind the villain's rise to power, The Riddler.

BATMAN BEYOND

DATA

DEBUT *Batman Beyond* (Vol. 1) #1 **(Mar. 1999)**
REAL NAME Terry McGinnis
HEIGHT 5ft 10in **WEIGHT** 170 lbs
EYES Blue **HAIR** Black
POWERS/ABILITIES Expert martial artist trained directly by Batman (Bruce Wayne); weapons include hi-tech armored suit that can fly with the aid of glider wings and rocket boots, turn practically invisible, and shoot a grappling hook, Batarangs, and/or explosive discs.
ALLIES Bruce Wayne, Commissioner Barbara Gordon, Max Gibson, Matt McGinnis, Batwoman, Dick Grayson
ENEMIES Blight, Shriek, Spellbinder, Rewire, Inque, Jokerz, The Joker
AFFILIATIONS Justice League Beyond

BEYOND THE BATSUIT
The Batman Beyond suit contains rocket boots, wings, a Utility Belt, a built-in grapnel, and a cowl that greatly improves Batman's vision and hearing.

ROBIN BEYOND
Terry's brother Matt became Robin briefly after learning about Terry's double life. When the job proved too dangerous, Matt was let go from the role.

A few decades into the future, Gotham City has evolved into Neo-Gotham, a metropolis of tremendous skyscrapers, flying cars, and sleek technology. In that brave new world, a new kind of Batman is required to keep the peace. Terry McGinnis serves as the new Dark Knight, an armored hero capable of flight and invisibility. He's not just Batman, he's Batman Beyond.

Bruce Wayne retired as Batman when he felt he was growing too old to continue his war on Gotham City's criminals, despite the hi-tech flight suit he had made with help from Wayne Industries. Now an old man alone in Wayne Manor, Bruce came to the aid of a teenager named Terry McGinnis who was being terrorized by a gang called The Jokerz—pale imitations of the original Clown Prince of Crime. Terry returned to Wayne Manor with Bruce and discovered that Bruce Wayne and Batman were one and the same. After a testy start, Terry was accepted by the Dark Knight as his heir following the death of McGinnis' own father. With Bruce helping him on missions via communication from the Batcave, a new Batman was born.

After an extensive career of fighting future threats like Blight, Inque, and the Stalker, Terry was presumed dead when the notorious Spellbinder tricked him into believing he was a villain called Rewire. A time-displaced future version of Tim Drake served briefly as Batman in Terry's absence, before solving the mystery of Terry's disappearance. After helping Terry regain his mantle as Batman, Tim left to roam this new world.

Terry continued as Batman, and even fought the original Joker, a conflict that ended with the seeming death of the arch foe. With the protection of Neo-Gotham more difficult than ever, Terry has adopted a new partner in the form of Batwoman, Dick Grayson's daughter Elainna.

ON THE RECORD

Batman Beyond originally debuted in cartoon form in his self-titled animated series in 1999. While a tie-in comic came soon after, Batman Beyond didn't make his way into the DC universe until a storyline in the pages of *Superman/Batman* showcased the hero living in an alternate universe. However that hero was oddly Tim Drake under the Batsuit, not Terry McGinnis.

In 2010, McGinnis was given his own miniseries that soon led to an ongoing series, tying Terry's life more closely to the future of the DC universe by having him fight not just threats from the animated series, but comic book villains like Hush.

A DIFFERENT BEYOND
Tim Drake debuted as Batman Beyond, tangling with a time-displaced Bizarro Superman during a deadly reality-hopping game being played by The Joker and Mr. Mxyzptlk.

BATWOMAN BEYOND
Elainna Grayson wears a blue variation of the Batsuit. Her identity was originally a mystery even to Terry and Bruce. At first, Terry believed her to be Ten from the Royal Flush Gang.

CLASSIC STORIES

Batman Beyond (Vol. 1) #1–6 (Mar.–Aug. 1999) Batman Beyond's origin is adapted from the cartoon series before the hero goes on new adventures.

Batman Beyond (Vol. 3) #1–6 (Aug. 2010–Jan. 2011) Batman Beyond faces a threat from Bruce Wayne's past when a new Hush debuts and begins killing minor Super-Villains like Signalman.

The New 52: Future's End (Vol. 1) #0–48 (Jun. 2014–Jun. 2015) Terry McGinnis heads back in time to thwart Brother Eye, eventually handing over the reins to a new Batman Beyond, Tim Drake.

Batman Beyond (Vol. 5) #1–6 (Aug. 2015–Jan. 2016) Tim Drake, clad as Batman Beyond, finally triumphs over the forces of the seemingly unstoppable Brother Eye.

BATMAN, INC.

DATA

DEBUT *Batman and Robin* (Vol. 1) #16 **(Jan. 2011)**
BASE Gotham City and various countries around the globe
NOTABLE MEMBERS BATMAN (Bruce Wayne); ROBIN (Damian Wayne);
RED ROBIN (Tim Drake); CATWOMAN (Selina Kyle); DICK GRAYSON;
BATGIRL (Barbara Gordon); BATWING (David Zavimbe); BATWING (Luke
Fox); NIGHTRUNNER (Bilal Asselah); BATMAN JAPAN (Jiro Osamu);
WINGMAN (Jason Todd); KNIGHT (FORMERLY SQUIRE) (Beryl Hutchinson);
EL GAUCHO (Santiago Vargas); MAN-OF-BATS (Dr. William Great Eagle);
HOOD (George Cross); RAVEN RED (Charles Great Eagle); DARK RANGER
(FORMERLY SCOUT) (Johnny Riley); TALON (Calvin Rose)
ALLIES Commissioner Gordon, Lucius Fox
ENEMIES Leviathan, Talia al Ghūl

CLASSIC STORIES

Batman: The Return #1 (Jan. 2011) After
journeying through time due to the machinations of
the villain Darkseid, Batman returns to the present and
begins to lay the groundwork for Batman, Inc.

Batman, Incorporated (Vol. 1) #1 (Jan. 2011)
Batman heads to Japan with Catwoman to kick start his
global Batman, Inc. effort.

Batman, Incorporated: Leviathan Strikes #1
(Feb. 2012) The first half of the Batman, Inc. saga
comes to a climax in an oversized special that sees the
Dark Knight discover that Talia is the face behind Leviathan.

Batman, Incorporated (Vol. 2) #13 (Sep. 2013)
Batman successfully brings down Leviathan with the help
of old ally, Kathy Kane, the original Batwoman.

The idea came to Batman in something akin to a dream: a global team of Batmen, working together for the common safety of the world. When Batman introduced Batman, Incorporated to the world, he did so knowing that this particular team of international heroes would all use the Batman's methods and would answer solely to him.

After catching a glimpse of his future and the global threat of the evil and clandestine organization called Leviathan, Batman decided he

A gathering of select
Batman, Inc. members and
their mascot, Bat-Cow:
1 Batman
2 Dark Ranger
3 Knight III
4 El Gaucho
5 Batman Japan
6 Lolita Canary
7 Raven Red
8 Man-of-Bats
9 Bat-Cow
10 Nightrunner

GOING PUBLIC
Bruce Wayne publicized his funding of the
Batman's operations when he introduced
the concept of Batman, Incorporated.

needed to step-up his crime-fighting game, and formed a new team of Super Hero operatives under the name Batman, Incorporated. Fully and publicly funded by Wayne Industries, Batman, Inc. united not just his allies in the Batman Family, but also saw new heroes adopt costumed identities to follow in the Dark Knight's footsteps and uphold his brand of justice.

Batman had briefly fought with a group of international crime fighters called the Club of Heroes, so it only made sense that he recruited some of those old allies into his new operation. In cases like the Knight, Batman recruited the heir to the original hero's mantle. Newcomers like the French crime fighter Nightrunner and Batman Japan were also welcomed into the fold. Soon Batman had a veritable army of skilled and like-minded heroes to command against the rising threat of Leviathan.

Led by Talia al Ghūl, Leviathan proved to be as dangerous as the Dark Knight had feared. Not only did the cult of villains kill the Knight, they also ended the life of Batman's partner and son, Robin (Damian Wayne), causing the Dark Knight to be enraged like never before. Gotham City became a battle zone, waging a war that culminated in a fight between Batman and Talia in the Batcave. Talia al Ghūl, did not walk away from that particular fight, but was shot and seemingly killed by another of the enemies she had made in her bid for world conquest.

ON THE RECORD

The first volume of Batman, Inc.
formed the epic final chapter in the
sweeping Batman saga that began
with the "Batman and Son" storyline
in *Batman* (Vol. 1) #655.

The second volume appeared
after the reality-altering *Flashpoint*
event, which led to some elements
of the series, such as Batman's
costume, being changed. New heroes
like Black Bat (Cassandra Cain)
joined up, while others, such as
the original Batwoman (Kathy Kane),
reemerged with significantly revised
personal histories.

GONE IN A FLASH
Some characters in the first incarnation of
Batman, Inc., like Batgirl Stephanie Brown,
would not return in the second volume.

BATMAN WHO LAUGHS, THE

DATA

DEBUT *Dark Days: The Casting* #1 (Sept. 2017)
BASE Castle Bat
HEIGHT 6ft 2in **WEIGHT** 190 lbs **EYES** Blue **HAIR** Black
POWERS/ABILITIES Expert martial artist; skilled acrobat, gymnast, and athlete; escape artist; highly intelligent with advanced knowledge of various technologies; natural leader; master strategist; unpredictable actions and fighting techniques due to extreme insanity; armed with infected Batarangs and variety of both Batman and Joker gadgets; enhanced with the near-limitless powers of Dr. Manhattan.
ALLIES Perpetua, Grim Knight, Batmen of the Dark Multiverse
ENEMIES Batman, the Batman Family, Commissioner James Gordon, Lex Luthor
AFFILIATIONS The Dark Knights of the Dark Multiverse

OF TWO MINDS
With the brainpower of one of the greatest heroes and one of the greatest villains, the Batman Who Laughs has a contingency plan for every conflict, albeit with a mad, disturbing twist.

GROBLINS
Batman is rarely without a Robin or two, and likewise, the Batman Who Laughs is rarely seen without his favorite Groblins.

He is Batman's greatest nightmare come to literal life. The Batman Who Laughs is Bruce Wayne from a world in the Dark Multiverse where he has been infected with The Joker's nanotoxin. Possessing a mind capable of thinking like both Batman and his greatest nemesis, the Batman Who Laughs has risen to a higher power than any mortal before him.

On Earth-22 in the Dark Multiverse that was created from the worst nightmares and fears of people in the true Multiverse, The Joker broke Batman's iron will. The madman slaughtered family after family in front of the Dark Knight, who was unable to stop the carnage. When he finally broke free of his bonds, Batman brutally attacked The Joker, was tipped over the edge, and killed him. However, it was The Joker who had the last laugh. When his heart stopped beating, he released a nanotoxin like nothing Batman had ever experienced before. It slowly rewired Batman's mind to become more like that of The Joker, replacing Batman's moral compass with something quite evil.

Knowing this, Batman called Robin, Nightwing, Red Hood, and Batgirl to the Batcave and then shot and killed them all. His next stop was the Justice League Watchtower, where he murdered the entire League, saving Superman for last. Having completely conquered his world, this Batman Who Laughs was visited by the demon Barbatos, who revealed the other dimensions of the Dark Multiverse. The Batman Who Laughs then traveled to a variety of dark dimensions, recruiting a small army of Dark Knights to his cause. They invaded Earth-0, but were ultimately defeated by Batman and the Justice League.

However, the Batman Who Laughs stayed on Earth-0, where he set up his own twisted Batcave below Gotham City's Monarch Theater, the site where Batman's parents were killed. He infected noble heroes, turning them into his own team of Super-Villains, before they were bested in a conflict with Lex Luthor and restored to normal. The Batman Who Laughs wanted the power that Luthor had been granted by the mother of the Multiverse, Perpetua. He convinced her to choose him over Luthor, and when she did, the Batman Who Laughs transformed Earth-0 into a twisted hellscape that served as his own private kingdom. He gained even more power when his brain was placed in the body of a powerful dark amalgam of Bruce Wayne and Dr. Manhattan. With the like-minded Robin King by his side, the Batman Who Laughs proceeded to give Batman and the heroes of Earth one of the greatest battles of their lives, with Earth and the Multiverse hanging in the balance.

THE DARK KNIGHTS
Originally the Batman Who Laughs recruited a core group of Dark Batmen to his cause: The Drowned (Batman/Aquaman), The Devastator (Batman/Doomsday), The Murder Machine (Batman/Cyborg), The Merciless (Batman/Ares), The Red Death (Batman/The Flash), and The Dawnbreaker (Batman/Green Lantern).

CLASSIC STORIES

***Dark Nights The Batman Who Laughs* #1 (Jan. 2018)** The Batman Who Laugh's origin is revealed with all its gory details.

***The Batman Who Laughs* #1–7 (Feb.–Sep. 2019)** The Batman Who Laughs attacks Gotham City's water supply with the help of another Dark Batman, the gun-toting Grim Knight.

***Dark Nights Metal* #1–6 (Oct. 2017–May. 2018)** Barbatos's plan is carried to Earth-0 by the Batman Who Laughs, alongside his league of Batmen from other Dark Multiverse dimensions.

BATMAN (THOMAS WAYNE)

DEBUT *Flashpoint* (Vol. 2) #1 **(Jul. 2011)**
REAL NAME Thomas Wayne **BASE** Gotham City
HEIGHT 6ft 2in **WEIGHT** 210 lbs **EYES** Brown **HAIR** Gray/black
POWERS/ABILITIES Genius intellect; expert hand-to-hand fighting skills; qualified medical doctor.
ALLIES Chief James Gordon, Oswald Cobblepot, Gotham Girl, The Flash (Barry Allen)
ENEMIES The Joker (Martha Wayne), Bane
AFFILIATIONS None

In the alternate reality created by the *Flashpoint* event, Thomas Wayne had been unable to prevent his young son Bruce from being killed in a robbery in Gotham City's Crime Alley. In his grief, he swore to rid the streets of crime as the Batman—a ruthless and brutal version of the hero who did not baulk at using firearms to take down his targets. His wife Martha had survived the robbery too, but the loss of her child led to the loss of her sanity and she became The Joker of that reality, locked in a bitter struggle with her erstwhile husband.

When Thomas discovered via The Flash, who jumped realities on the Cosmic Treadmill, that there was a world where he had died and his son had lived, at first he was delighted. Later he was even able to meet this alternate-reality son and see the man he had become. However, the knowledge that his son became Batman—with all the pain and sacrifice that this entailed—troubled Thomas so much that he traveled to Bruce Wayne's universe and allied himself with Bane to "break" his son. Thomas hoped, wrongly, that if he forced his son to give up the cowl by any means necessary, then Bruce would finally find happiness.

FATHER FIGURE
In an alternate reality, Thomas Wayne was Batman, with none of the scruples about using lethal force of Bruce Wayne's Batman.

ON THE RECORD

On Prime Earth, Dr. Thomas Wayne was a celebrated scion of one of Gotham City's leading families. A prominent surgeon and philanthropist, he married Martha Kane and the couple had a son, Bruce.

However, Thomas' seemingly blessed life was tragically cut short when he was murdered in the notorious Crime Alley, along with his wife, in front of their traumatized son. This storyline was the reverse of the later, alternate reality one that saw Thomas become Batman. On Prime Earth, it was Thomas's death that was a key factor in Bruce Wayne's decision to fight crime as Batman.

LOVED AND LOST
The death of his son sent Thomas Wayne down a dark path; one that saw him take extreme action to fight crime in an attempt to do right by his family.

BATWING

DEBUT *Batman Inc.* (Vol. 1) #5 **(May 2011)** (David Zavimbe)
Batwing (Vol. 1) #19 **(Jun. 2013)** (Lucius Fox)
REAL NAME Lucas "Luke" Fox **BASE** Gotham City
HEIGHT 5ft 9in **WEIGHT** 170 lbs **EYES** Brown **HAIR** Black
POWERS/ABILITIES Highly skilled mixed martial artist; brilliant designer and engineer much like his father Lucius Fox; able to think on his feet; near unlimited access to Wayne Industries' technology; weapons include bulletproof suit equipped with hi-tech weaponry and defense systems; his suit also enables flight and limited invisibility.
ALLIES Batgirl, Lucius Fox, Batman, the Batman Family
ENEMIES Lady Vic, Ratcatcher, Charlie Caligula, Menace
AFFILIATIONS Batman, Inc.

Luke Fox never intended to follow his father, Lucius Fox, into a career with Wayne Industries. Despite a gift for technological innovation equal to his father's, Luke preferred to go his own way. This attitude frustrated Lucius, who felt his son was squandering his potential and opportunities. While constantly arguing with his father, Luke pursued fighting arts, participating in numerous mixed martial arts events. His intelligence, resolve, and combat skills soon attracted Batman's attention, and the Dark Knight offered Luke the role of one his agents after original Batwing David Zavimbe retired.

Wearing a new suit designed by his father, Luke became a valued ally and partner to Batman, despite often upsetting his family thanks to his many unexplained absences while on duty. However, after secretly working with Red Robin Tim Drake to avert a catastrophic potential future, battle-fatigued Batwing left the Gotham Knights team to pursue his own path.

GOING HIS OWN WAY
Much to his father's relief, Luke has recently created his own company called FoxTek. He has also begun a relationship with fellow tech-minded hero, Batgirl.

BATWINGING IT
Batwing's suit is highly advanced and a true work in progress. Luke inherited his love for technology from his father and is constantly updating his suit.

ON THE RECORD

While Luke Fox as Batwing debuted just months before the continuity changing *Flashpoint* event, a few characters existed in the past that bore a striking similarity to the hero. In *Batman* (Vol. 1) #250 (Jul. 1973), a child's interpretation of Batman, nicknamed "Batwings" appeared in "The Batman Nobody Knows!" Later, on Earth-2, a hero that went by the name Blackwing fought alongside the Huntress. However, it wasn't until *Crisis on Infinite Earths* and later events, that the first true Batwing was introduced in the form of David Zavimbe, the Batman Inc. representative for Africa.

BATTLE READY
David Zavimbe lived a hard life as a child soldier in Africa. Batman saw promise in him and promoted him to Batwing after learning of his amateur crime fighting.

BATWOMAN

DATA

DEBUT *52* #7 (June 2006) (as Kate Kane); *52* #11 (July 2006) (as Batwoman)
REAL NAME Katherine (Kate) Kane
BASE Gotham City
HEIGHT 5ft 11in **WEIGHT** 141 lbs **EYES** Green **HAIR** Red
POWERS/ABILITIES Skilled martial artist, detective, and gymnast; highly trained soldier; additional training with operatives known as the Murder of Crows; equipment and resources include protective suit, fully stocked Utility Belt, and hi-tech command center.
ALLIES Hawkfire, Batman, Batman Family, Maggie Sawyer, The Question (Renee Montoya), Julia Pennyworth
ENEMIES Nocturna, Ceto, Mr. Bones, Wolf Spider
AFFILIATIONS Gotham Knights, the Unknowns

To the general public, Kate Kane seems to have everything. Like her cousin, Bruce Wayne, Kate has never wanted for money and has been known to frequent the most exclusive nightclubs. However, Kate has lived a tragic life—one that has shaped her into a crime fighter and sworn protector of the innocent: Batwoman.

DADDY'S LITTLE GIRL
Before parting ways over Jacob Kane's extreme methods, Jacob helped Kate set up a secret HQ and find allies to train her in non-lethal techniques.

As a young girl, Kate Kane was very interested in athletics. Like her twin sister, Beth, she enjoyed gymnastics and soccer. The two girls were the quintessential "military brats," moving around the country whenever their parents were stationed at a new location. They always had each other, were the best of friends, and assumed they would be lifelong confidantes.

On their 12th birthday, Kate and Beth realized just how wrong their assumption had been. Their mother was taking the two girls out to celebrate when they were abducted and held prisoner. Their father ultimately assembled and led a squad of elite soldiers to come to their rescue. However, the damage was done: Kate's mother had been shot and killed, and it appeared that Beth had suffered the same fate. From that day, Kate Kane would live a lonely life, with only her father for support.

Jacob Kane did his best as a single father. He supported Kate and taught her to live a disciplined and honorable life. When Kate was kicked out of the United States Military Academy at West Point for being gay, her father stood by her, realizing that her honesty and integrity were more important than a career with the military. Kate had been an excellent cadet, and without school, there was a void in her life—one that she filled with excessive partying. She lacked direction and only found it when she saved herself from a mugging, meeting Batman in the process. With her father's training and support, Kate transformed herself into Batwoman, enrolling into a new kind of service to the public.

COLORS OF WAR
Batwoman's father designed her costume. Col. Kane made sure the suit was stab resistant, bullet proof, and dramatic with its black-and-red color scheme.

ON THE RECORD

Kate Kane first appeared just five years before the *Flashpoint* event that altered the DC universe. While much of her backstory has stayed the same, one aspect that has only lightly been touched on is her relationship with Renee Montoya, the second hero to adopt the name of The Question.

Kate had a romantic relationship with Renee before the couple became Super Heroes. However, in the current continuity, Renee's career as The Question is yet to begin. The two have dated, but their shared past remains something of a mystery.

PAST LOVES
Kate Kane has had romantic relationships with The Question (Renee Montoya) as well as Maggie Sawyer, the head of Metropolis' Special Crimes Unit.

CLASSIC STORIES

52 #7–52 (Jun. 2006–May 2007)
Kate Kane is introduced along with her tumultuous relationship with Renee Montoya, the new Question.
Detective Comics (Vol. 1) #854–857 (Aug.–Nov. 2009)
Batwoman temporarily takes over as the star of *Detective Comics* when she finds her sister has become her worst enemy.
Detective Comics (Vol. 1) #858–860 (Dec. 2009–Feb. 2010)
Batwoman's origin is told, from her family's kidnapping to her meeting Batman.
Batwoman (Vol. 1) #17 (Apr. 2013)
Kate reveals her Batwoman identity as she proposes to girlfriend Maggie Sawyer.

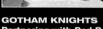

GOTHAM KNIGHTS
Partnering with Red Robin (Tim Drake), Batwoman helped lead the Gotham Knights, an informal team of Gotham City heroes based in the hi-tech Belfry inside the converted Old Wayne Tower. Batwoman was the field leader, using her vast military training to help guide more inexperienced members like Azrael and the Spoiler. While the team disbanded after a conflict with Clayface, Batwoman remains active in Gotham City. Kate's main base of operations is her hideout inside the R.H. Kane Building, but she also makes use of Batman's Batcave from time to time, a base located beneath Gotham City Harbor.

BAZ, SIMON

DEBUT *The New 52 Free Comic Book Day Special Edition* #1 (Jun. 2012)
REAL NAME Simon Baz
BASE Dearborn, Michigan
HEIGHT 5ft 11in **WEIGHT** 183 lbs **EYES** Brown **HAIR** Black
POWERS/ABILITIES Ability to overcome fear; carries handgun and power ring, which permits flight, force fields, and space travel; precognition.
ALLIES Green Lantern (Hal Jordan), Green Lantern (Jessica Cruz)
ENEMIES Black Hand, Sinestro
AFFILIATIONS Green Lantern Corps, Justice League

As a young Muslim boy growing up in Dearborn, Michigan, Simon Baz was often the target of bigotry, especially after the tragic events of September 11, 2001.

Years of bullying gave Simon a serious chip on his shoulder, and after he lost his job at an automotive plant he took up illegal street racing, only narrowly avoiding jail time. Financially desperate, Simon started stealing cars to make ends meet. One night he stole a van, only to discover a ticking bomb inside the vehicle. After a high-speed chase he was taken into custody as a suspected terrorist. Amid harsh interrogation by federal agents, a power ring sought Baz out, conferring on him the abilities and responsibilities of a Green Lantern. A reluctant Super Hero, Baz considered the selection a mistake, but sought to do his best to help people. Innately untrusting, he supplemented his Green Lantern uniform with a sidearm. It took the insistence of Batman to make Baz eventually surrender this weapon and trust the ring and his partners.

As a rookie, Baz was assigned Earth as his beat, to be patrolled with fellow newcomer Jessica Cruz. As commanding officer of the GL Corps, Hal Jordan ordered both trainees to join the Justice League in order to learn teamwork from the best.

EMERALD VISION
Simon has manifested a very rare ability among Green Lanterns—the Emerald Sight. This grants him visions of the near future.

BEAUTIFUL DREAMER

DEBUT *Forever People* (Vol. 1) #1 (Feb.–Mar. 1971)
BASE New Genesis; Venice Beach, California
HEIGHT 5ft 6in **WEIGHT** 128 lbs
EYES Blue **HAIR** Black
POWERS/ABILITIES Able to create life-like illusions; precognitive dreams.
ALLIES Infinity Man, Superman, Deadman
ENEMIES Darkseid, Desaad
AFFILIATIONS Forever People, New Genesis

DREAM WEAVER
Dreamer's strong connection to the Anti-Life Equation gives her the ability to manipulate the powerful mind-controlling formula.

A student at the Academy of Higher Conscience on the planet New Genesis, Beautiful Dreamer was with Vykin Baldaur when he touched a non-functioning Mother Box and it bonded with him as its host. Soon Dreamer found herself traveling through a Boom Tube to Earth with her friend Vykin, his sister Serafina, and Mark Moonrider for an academy assignment to help advance humankind.

After meeting fellow Academy member Big Bear, the group set up camp in Venice Beach, California. During a fight with the villain Mantis, they touched the Mother Box in unison and were replaced by Infinity Man. Together the team became the Forever People.

Pre-*Flashpoint*, Beautiful Dreamer was kidnapped by Darkseid and taken to Earth, where she was rescued by Superman and the Forever People. The team were ultimately killed by Infinity Man on his campaign for the Source to destroy all New Gods.

BEKKA

DEBUT *The Hunger Dogs* #4 (1985)
BASE New Korugar, Sector 3567
HEIGHT 5ft 7in
WEIGHT 132 lbs
EYES Blue
HAIR Auburn/red
POWERS/ABILITIES Increased strength, speed, and durability of a New God; can make others fall in love with her.
ENEMIES Darkseid, Mongul, Apex League

Bekka is a New God from New Genesis, the daughter of the scientist Himon. Born with an innate power to make people fall in love with her, she became a formidable general—besotted troops would die for her and enemies would surrender.

New Genesis' ruler, Highfather, made Bekka a member of his Council of Eight and dispatched her to New Korugar to the headquarters of the Sinestro Corps. She battled the Corps and brought back one of their yellow power rings, but she also attracted the attention of Sinestro himself. Recognizing that Bekka could inspire fear as well as love, he offered to make her a member of the Corps. She ultimately accepted, forsaking her allegiance to New Genesis and going into action to save Sinestro from the warlord Mongul.

BERNADETH

DEBUT *Mister Miracle* (Vol. 1) #6 (Jan.–Feb. 1972)
BASE Apokolips
HEIGHT 5ft 10in **WEIGHT** 140 lbs
EYES Brown **HAIR** Black
POWERS/ABILITIES Superhuman physical capabilities and immortality due to New Gods heritage.
ALLIES Granny Goodness, Darkseid, Desaad
ENEMIES Big Barda, Mister Miracle, Lashina

Bernadeth is a member of the Female Furies, Darkseid's elite female fighting unit. She is the sister of Darkseid's torturer Desaad and she shares his sadistic tendencies. Her signature weapon is the fahren-knife, which can slice through rock and roast anyone it pierces from the inside.

Bernadeth was Big Barda's second-in-command, but when Barda betrayed Darkseid, it was Lashina, not Bernadeth, who was the new leader. Bernadeth took her revenge by leaving Lashina on Earth when the Furies went to rescue Glorious Godfrey. Lashina returned to Apokolips with members of the Suicide Squad and killed Bernadeth, but to punish her for bringing humans to Apokolips, Darkseid slayed her and returned Bernadeth to life. She has remained in his service, clashing with Supergirl, Wonder Woman, and Hawkgirl.

BEAST BOY

DATA

DEBUT *Doom Patrol* (Vol. 1) #99 (Nov. 1965)
REAL NAME Garfield Logan
HEIGHT 5ft 6in
WEIGHT 140 lbs
HAIR Green **EYES** Green
POWERS/ABILITIES Genetic code provides a link with the Red, enabling transformation into any desired animal form.
ALLIES Terra, Animal Man
ENEMIES Mother Blood
AFFILIATIONS Ravagers, Teen Titans, Titans

TEEN HERO
Beast Boy may look young, but he has a long track record of heroism with the Teen Titans.

Better known as Beast Boy, young Garfield Logan is able to transform himself into any animal shape. He is a deeply loyal friend with a desire to make those around him happy. Gar is the attention-seeking class clown who harbors a deeper, romantic side… when nobody's looking.

When he was just a boy, Gar was bitten by a West African green monkey that infected him with the Sakutia virus. An experimental treatment endowed him with the ability to change into any animal at will. With money no issue, thanks to a wealthy uncle, Gar joined several different Super Hero teams over the years, but was most at home with the Teen Titans.

Nevertheless, Beast Boy's tenure with the Teen Titans came to an end when he mistakenly thought his team leader, Red Robin (Tim Drake), had died. While it was later revealed that Red Robin had been kidnapped and not killed, Beast Boy found himself tangling with a different Boy Wonder in the meantime: Damian Wayne.

Batman's son had a rather arrogant streak, and Robin took Beast Boy, Raven, Starfire, and Kid Flash (Wallace West) hostage in order to prove the point that these heroes are stronger together than they are on their own. Surprisingly, this unorthodox sales pitch worked, and Beast Boy found himself again on a Titans roster; one soon joined by Aqualad (Jackson Hyde).

Always ready with a joke, Beast Boy's attitude changed a bit after the ancient Source Wall was pierced at the far reaches of space, releasing ancient godlike energies into the world. He took on a more beastlike appearance and he found it harder to control his animal changes. He joined Nightwing's Titans, but spent more time as a beast than a man. Later, a battle with the then-leader of the Church of Blood – Mother Blood – exposed Garfield to cosmic Bleed energy. Bleed energy blocks Source energy, and this near-death experience succeeded in restoring Gar to his old form. Back to looking "cute" and ready for action, Beast Boy is ready to take whatever life throws at him with his trademark smile.

CLASSIC STORIES

***Doom Patrol* (Vol. 1) #99** (Nov. 1965) Garfield Logan makes his first appearance, breaking into the Doom Patrol's headquarters. He is given the moniker Beast Boy by Robotman.

***New Titans* (Vol. 1) #97–102** (May–Oct. 1993) Beast Boy—going by the name of Changeling—makes a devil's bargain with the Brotherhood of Evil to save Cyborg's life.

***Beast Boy* (Vol. 1) #1–4** (Jan.–Apr. 2000) Beast Boy's Super Hero and TV careers collide following the breakup of Titans West. A doppelgänger frames him for several crimes—he finds out it is the villain Gemini, and defeats her.

ANIMAL MAGIC
Beast Boy's laid-back charm and wit belied his true animal instincts, fearsome powers, and tenacious spirit.

JUST A BEAST
Source energy turned Beast Boy into more beast than boy for a time, making his animal transformations more difficult.

ON THE RECORD

Before becoming a mentor to later versions of the Teen Titans, Beast Boy had his own struggles, particularly when his adoptive father Steve Dayton—also known as Mento—suffered paranoid delusions. Trying to save him, Garfield stole the Mento Helmet, which affected him as it had its creator, giving his animal transformations a more violent edge.

Historically, Beast Boy was always green due to a side effect of the experimental process his scientist father used to save his life from a rare tropical disease. His appearance helped him carve out a brief career as a television actor in the series *Space Trek: 2022*.

SNAKE IN THE GRASS
Attempting to give his girlfriend Terra a "cobra kiss" during a playful training session, Gar Logan never suspected that she secretly conspired to destroy the Teen Titans.

BENNETT, ANDREW

DEBUT *House of Mystery* (Vol. 1) #290 (Mar. 1981)
BASE Magus Theatre, Gotham City
EYES Red
HAIR Black (with white streak)
POWERS/ABILITIES As a vampire, can assume wolf or mist form and hypnotize humans, but is weakened by sunlight; skilled sorcerer and has shown the ability to bring dead vampires back to life.
ALLIES Frankenstein, Batwoman, Killer Croc
ENEMIES Cain, Mary Seward, the Blood Red Moon
AFFILIATIONS Justice League Dark, Gotham City Monsters

In Elizabethan England, Andrew Bennett was attacked by Cain, the first of the vampires. Dead and afflicted with the curse of vampirism, Bennett awoke with an unholy thirst for blood and turned his lover, Mary, into a vampire too. Unlike him, she succumbed to demonic influence and swore to conquer the world. As the Blood Red Queen, Mary founded the vampire cult the Blood Red Moon to wage her "holy war" against mankind.

Andrew refused to forsake his humanity by feeding on people and resolved to stop Mary and her followers. When she attacked Gotham City, Andrew teamed up with Batman, Professor John Troughton, and teen tearaway Tig to take on the horde. Tig killed Andrew, hoping to destroy Mary's vampires by eliminating her sire, but that caused Cain to arise again. After being resurrected by Madame Xanadu, Bennett slew Cain and continued his war against Mary and her followers, ultimately absorbing their evil into himself to save them.

Bennett's relentless eradication of vampires has expanded to include many supernatural predators and he has—reluctantly—worked with teams such as Justice League Dark and the Gotham City Monsters to preserve humanity from all the horrors of the unknown.

ETERNAL STRUGGLE
Bennett fights an unending war against vampire-kind and his own bloodthirsty impulses.

ON THE RECORD

Pre-Flashpoint, Andrew Bennett was a nobleman at Queen Elizabeth I's court, before being bitten by a vampire. He clashed with his former lover Mary, who had become the vampiric Queen of Blood. He regained his humanity and witnessed her destruction before he himself died. However, Andrew could not escape the vampiric curse. After rising from the grave, he attempted suicide, but returned to unlife. Bennett joined occult group Team 13 and intervened in the infernal war between the demons Satanus and Neron.

UNDEAD HERO
Despite his menacing appearance, Andrew Bennett is a tormented soul who has spent centuries protecting humanity from his own kind.

BIBBO

DEBUT *Adventures of Superman* (Vol. 1) #428 (May 1987)
REAL NAME Bo Bibbowski
BASE The Ace O'Clubs bar
HEIGHT 6ft 3in **WEIGHT** 250 lbs
EYES Gray **HAIR** Gray
ALLIES Superman, Jimmy Olsen, Lobo, Professor Emil Hamilton
ENEMIES Doomsday

HERE'S TO THE MAN OF STEEL
Bibbo is the proud owner of the Ace O'Clubs bar in Metropolis' Suicide Slum district.

Metropolis native Bibbo Bibbowski is a longshoreman, former boxer, and one of Superman's biggest fans. He has also been known to hang out with another super-tough guy—Lobo.

Bibbo and the Man of Steel first met when Superman came to the Ace O'Clubs looking for information. Bibbo mistook him for a troublemaker in a Superman costume and punched him, but only injured his own hand! Impressed, Bibbo decided on the spot that Superman was his "fav'rit" hero.

Later, Bibbo bought the bar after finding a winning lottery ticket. He helped Superman on numerous occasions, most notably when Doomsday attacked Metropolis. Bibbo and Professor Hamilton used a laser cannon against the monstrous alien (to no effect) and after Superman was killed by Doomsday, Bibbo tried to revive the fallen hero with an improvised defibrillator.

BIG BEAR

DEBUT *The Forever People* (Vol. 1) #1 (Feb.–Mar. 1971)
BASE New Genesis
HEIGHT 6ft 8in **WEIGHT** 598 lbs
EYES Brown **HAIR** Red-brown
POWERS/ABILITIES New God with superhuman strength and durability; able to redirect atoms to alter his density.
ENEMIES Mantis, Devilance, Desaad, Darkseid
AFFINITIES Infinity Man

BACK IN THE SADDLE
Big Bear has returned to the beard and headpiece that he sported in the Fourth World of New Genesis.

A gentle giant, Big Bear grew up in the idyllic nurturing environment of New Genesis following the first war with Apokolips. When Darkseid broke his truce with Highfather and reopened hostilities, one of his first moves was to abduct Bear's friend Beautiful Dreamer, whom he believed held the secret of the free-will destroying Anti-Life Equation. With comrades Mark Moonrider, Vykin, and Serifan, Big Bear arrived on Earth on a sentient Super-Cycle to rescue her. This was accomplished by the group's unexplained connection to a multipowered being dubbed the Infinity Man.

A natural leader and devoted scholar, Bear quickly adapted to the new culture on Earth. He soon became the team's most ardent supporter of staying on Earth and defending its masses.

BIG BARDA

DATA

DEBUT *Mister Miracle* (Vol. 1) #4 **(Sep.–Oct. 1971)**
HEIGHT 6ft 2in **WEIGHT** 200 lbs **EYES** Blue **HAIR** Black
POWERS/ABILITIES Immortal with superhuman mental and physical attributes as part of her New God heritage; exceptionally strong and tough, even for her kind; arsenal includes formidable Aegis armor, an Apokoliptian rod that fires energy blasts, and a battle-maul inscribed with Darkseid's Omega crest; expert warrior trained by Granny Goodness.
ALLIES Mister Miracle, Justice League, Female Furies
ENEMIES Darkseid
AFFILIATIONS New Gods of Apokolips, Female Furies

Big Barda was once a Female Fury who served Darkseid, the evil overlord of Apokolips, enforcing his will with her fearsome Mega-Rod. However, when Barda fell in love with rebel and escape-artist Mister Miracle, she changed her allegiance. Now this fierce New God fights for freedom against her former master.

ON THE RUN
After escaping Apokolips with Mister Miracle, Barda found herself pursued by Darkseid's forces and the World Army of Earth-2.

On the planet Apokolips, the New God Darkseid controlled every aspect of daily life. Only a few of Darkseid's elite were free from the daily torture of his tyrannical rule, and even they have to bend the knee whenever Darkseid commanded. One of his elite members was Granny Goodness, who was in charge of the orphanage, designed for training and torturing slaves. Granny also trained and commanded the most effective fighting force to ever emerge from the fire pits—the Female Furies. Chief among them was the powerful and effective Big Barda.

In order to broker peace between Apokolips and Highfather's world of New Genesis, the New God Metron convinced the two rulers to exchange sons, Scott and Orion. Highfather's son Scott was given to Darkseid, who dismissed the boy into Goodness's care, rarely giving Scott a second thought. However, Scott proved to be an able escape artist and he soon fled his captivity, renaming himself Scott Free, Mister Miracle. On the way, he met Big Barda and, despite her better instincts, Barda fell in love with Scott. The two were later married though, for a time, they kept up the pretense of being bitter enemies.

When Darkseid engaged in the so-called "Darkseid War" and was killed in combat against the powerful Anti-Monitor, Mister Miracle joined forces with the Justice League to help end the conflict. Big Barda joined her husband, and even recruited the Female Furies to his cause. However, that came at a price. According to her agreement with the Furies, Barda was forced to return to Apokolips with them after the fighting was over.

It seems that Big Barda and Mister Miracle have reunited in recent months, as the two have been seen fighting alongside the Justice League in large-scale battles.

AN ESCAPE?
After Mister Miracle attempted to end his own life, he seemed to trap himself in a purgatory of sorts, somewhere between heaven and hell. Here, he and Barda have a child and are happily married. Although with his skill set, Mister Miracle knows he can escape this reality at any time.

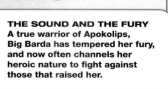

ON THE RECORD

Big Barda's early history treads a familiar path. Trained to be a warrior on Apokolips, she taught other female fighters. She later rejected Darkseid and Apokolips, married Mr. Miracle, and traveled to Earth.

On Earth, Mister Miracle joined Justice League International. When he was captured by the trader Manga Khan, Barda embarked on an interstellar mission to rescue him.

Barda then proved her value as a team player in a succession of groups. She even became a League member herself when she and Orion joined the Justice League.

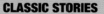

HOUSEWIFE WARRIOR
When Big Barda first moved to Earth, she enjoyed life as a "domestic goddess," often resenting her routine being interrupted by adventures with her husband, Mister Miracle.

CLASSIC STORIES

***Mister Miracle* (Vol. 1) #18 (Feb.–Mar. 1974)** Big Barda and Mister Miracle celebrate their love when they are married by Highfather on New Genesis.
***The Death of the New Gods* #1 (Dec. 2007)** When a mysterious killer begins slaying the New Gods, Big Barda is one of his first victims.
***Earth 2* #28 (Jan. 2015)** Chronicles how Barda found and trained the ruthless New God K'li, who would rise through the ranks to become Darkseid's Fury of War.

THE SOUND AND THE FURY
A true warrior of Apokolips, Big Barda has tempered her fury, and now often channels her heroic nature to fight against those that raised her.

BIRDS OF PREY

DATA

DEBUT *Black Canary/Oracle: Birds of Prey* #1 (Jun. 1996)
BASE Gotham City
NOTABLE MEMBERS/POWERS
BLACK CANARY (Dinah Drake Lance) Expert martial artist, Canary Cry sonic attack; **BATGIRL** (Barbara Gordon) Expert fighter, computer whiz, photographic memory; **THE HUNTRESS** (Helena Bertinelli) Martial artist, superlative crossbow skills; **HARLEY QUINN** (Dr. Harleen Quinzel) Unpredictable fighter, employs clown-themed weaponry.
ALLIES Oracle II, Green Arrow, Renee Montoya
ENEMIES Rā's al Ghūl, Calculator, The Joker

HELP FROM HARLEY
When Harley Quinn finished serving with the Suicide Squad, she headed to Gotham City to turn her life around, chancing upon the Birds and joining forces with them.

Usually an all-woman team of covert Super Heroes founded by Black Canary and Batgirl, the Birds of Prey battle clandestine threats. None of them are what they seem, and all of them have skeletons in their closets, but when they band together, they are more than any villain can handle.

The Birds of Prey got their start when Batgirl (Barbara Gordon) was shot and paralyzed by The Joker. Se was initially unsure how she would be able to make a contribution to the war on crime in the future, until she realized she could harness the limitless potential of the internet and the many secrets it hid. She adopted the name Oracle, and became an information supplier. However, she needed an operative in the physical world to act on the info she gathered. She chose Black Canary, known Super Hero and former government operative.

While they underwent a variety of missions together and alongside other operatives, the Birds of Prey seemed to fade into the background when Batgirl regained the use of her legs thanks to a hi-tech experimental surgery. However, the team returned to its roots when a new Oracle surfaced, and Batgirl recruited Black Canary to look into this mystery man, eventually accepting this computer hacker as a member for a brief period. The Birds crossed paths with The Huntress (Helena Bertinelli), and suddenly the team was fully formed, setting up a base of operations in Gotham City's Clocktower, thanks to funding from Barbara's company Gordon Clean Energy.

The longer the Birds worked together, the closer they became. They aired their secrets to one another and faced threats including the villainous Blackbird and the Calculator, and tangled with both Catwoman and Poison Ivy. They've even joined forces with Harley Quinn in recent adventures. It seems the former partner in crime to The Joker is now seeking her own form of zany redemption as a true heroine alongside the Birds.

ON THE RECORD

Originally a partnership between Oracle and the Black Canary, the Birds of Prey did not start calling themselves by that name until they had added other members: first The Huntress, and later Lady Blackhawk. Other female heroes rotated through the team, but its core membership remained that first trio.

Barbara Gordon's transformation from Oracle back to Batgirl remade the fundamental dynamic of the Birds of Prey when the *New 52* began. Their origin was changed to include new member Starling meeting Black Canary at The Penguin's Iceberg Lounge; however that continuity was altered as the Birds of Prey returned to their roots during the *Rebirth* event.

BIRDS OF A FEATHER
The Birds of Prey, with Oracle and Black Canary front and center, after the Canary's return to the team.

WHO IS ORACLE?
The second Oracle was the helpful computer expert Gus Yale. He was later killed by the robotic assassin Burnrate.

BIZARRO

DEBUT *Superboy* (Vol. 1) #68 **(Oct. 1958)**
BASE Hell
HEIGHT 6ft 3in **WEIGHT** 255 lbs
EYES Black **HAIR** Black
POWERS/ABILITIES Super-strength, speed, flight, invulnerability, enhanced breath and vision capabilities.
ALLIES Red Hood, Artemis, Lex Luthor
ENEMIES Trigon, Black Mask
AFFILIATIONS The Outlaws

BIZARRO HQ
Bizarro's headquarters were a feat of scientific genius, able to open portals to anywhere. He even had a monitor room and an armory.

Bizarro is a Frankenstein-like monster with a heart of gold. Although he was originally created by Lex Luthor, he has gone on to prove that he has a moral character far superior to that of his mad scientist father. Possessing many Kryptonian abilities—albeit warped and twisted—this heroic clone of Superman fights for truth, justice, and the Bizarro way.

Wanting a Superman of his own to command, Lex Luthor mapped Superman's genome and eventually found limited success in Subject B-0—a clone that would possess the full range of powers of the Last Son of Krypton. When Earth was conquered by the Crime Syndicate of Earth-3, Luthor was forced to unleash his latest experimental subject far too early in its development phase, approximately five years before the clone would be a perfect Superman duplicate. This rather incoherent creature called itself Bizarro and remained loyal to Luthor until its death at the hands of Earth-3's Alexander Luthor.

Since Luthor refused to give up on his Bizarro project, the vigilante Red Hood (Jason Todd) soon chanced upon another Superman clone; one being held in the criminal Black Mask's captivity. During a fight with Black Mask, Red Hood teamed with this new Bizarro, as well as with the Amazon powerhouse Artemis. The three unlikely allies would stay together and form Red Hood's newest team of heroic Outlaws.

When an encounter with Lex Luthor left Bizarro with a genius-level intellect for a limited amount of time, Bizarro created an invisible floating headquarters for the Outlaws, one the size of a Gotham City block. Although his intelligence eventually faded, Bizarro's loyalties did not. When the team was separated by circumstance for a time, Bizarro found his way back to Red Hood. Bizarro then proved how much of a hero he truly was, choosing to remain in Hell in order to save the world from a demon horde during the aftermath of the team's battle with the evil Trigon.

WORK IN PROGRESS
When he was forced to curtail B-0's gestation, Luthor had no idea how powerfully his experiment would affect his own feelings and conscience.

CLASSIC STORIES

***Superman* (Vol. 1) #140 (Oct. 1960)** Bizarro leads a backward battalion of imperfect Superman doppelgängers in a war against Earth to reclaim his misplaced first-born son.

***World's Finest Comics* (Vol. 1) #156 (Mar. 1966)** When Bizarro-Superman and Bizarro-Batman visit Earth to act as helpful fill-ins for the absent heroes, they become the unwitting pawns of the ever-crafty Joker.

***Action Comics* (Vol. 1) #855–857 (Oct.–Dec. 2007)** Experimented upon by Lex Luthor, a psychologically wounded and existentially lonely Bizarro flees Earth. He then creates his own square planet in space and populates it with warped copies of Superman's friends and family.

FRIEND IN ME
A terrifying, superpowered titan with a rather primitive mind, Bizarro nevertheless proved to be a loyal friend.

ON THE RECORD

Bizarro first appeared as a misunderstood copy of Superboy. Thanks to the Silver Age Luthor, he returned to bedevil Superman, but became a popular humor-oriented adversary of the Man of Steel. He even had his own comedic series in *Adventure Comics*.

However, the bludgeoning beast revived in the 1980s was far from funny. An anti-Superman weapon created by Luthor, he self-destructed in combat, but returned three more times. The longest-lived version of Bizarro was created by The Joker using Mr. Mxyzptlk's purloined magic as the 21st century began.

A MIRROR CRACK'D
Each iteration of Bizarro was more tragically misunderstood than malign, but his overwhelming power and limited intellect always made him dangerous.

BLACK ADAM

DEBUT *Marvel Family* (Vol. 1) #1 (Dec. 1945)
BASE Kahndaq **REAL NAME** Teth-Adam
HEIGHT 6ft 3in **WEIGHT** 250 lbs **EYES** Brown **HAIR** Black
POWERS/ABILITIES Immortality, super-speed, strength, endurance, invulnerability, flight; magically enhanced perceptions and intellect; teleportation; self-healing and the ability to instantly heal others; affinity for magic.
ALLIES Lex Luthor, Injustice League
ENEMIES Shazam, Justice League, Dr. Thaddeus Sivana, Mister Mind
AFFILIATIONS Kahndaq, Secret Society of Super-Villains, Monster Society of Evil, The Magic Lands

Four thousand years ago, the wizard Shazam granted noble Kahndaqi youth Aman the gods' power to avenge his family and save his oppressed people. The selfless boy requested the power be shared with his dying uncle, Teth-Adam. It was a fatal mistake. Adam killed Aman, liberated Kahndaq, captured the infernal Seven Sins, and slaughtered the Council of Eternity before Shazam finally imprisoned him.

When scientist Thaddeus Sivana opened Black Adam's tomb in modern times, the furious immortal immediately targeted young Billy Batson, who had recently inherited Shazam's mantle and powers, which he felt were his by right. When Billy tricked Adam into resuming his mortal form, four millennia instantly caught up with the villain.

Billy returned Adam's remains to Kahndaq, where a freedom-fighter who venerated Teth-Adam's legend sacrificed herself to restore him. Resurrected, Adam seized control of his homeland, becoming its brutal, obsessive protector. Acting on his own code of honor, he constantly battled Billy and his extended Marvel Family. Fiercely patriotic and isolationist, Black Adam is also proud and headstrong—failings that have embroiled him in many emergencies beyond his own borders. These include Shazam opening the predatory Magic Lands, Sivana and Mister Mind's revival of the Monster Society of Evil, and Billy's infection with toxic Dark Matter and transformation into evil King Shazam.

LIGHTNING WAR
Arrogant Black Adam could never accept that a mere child could wield the power of Shazam, or match his wisdom.

HARSH JUSTICE
Empowered by Egyptian gods, the former slave Teth-Adam dealt harshly with all forms of oppression and those who stood in the way of his dark justice.

ON THE RECORD

The original Black Adam was an outright villain and bully, but after his reintroduction in the mid-1990s, he was re-imagined as a more nuanced—if still extremely ruthless—character.

Adam even joined the Justice Society of America (JSA), where his hard-line views swayed many of the younger recruits. Obsessed with his ancient homeland of Kahndaq, he and his disciples eventually broke away from the JSA, sparking a civil war in the team's ranks.

ANCIENT, MY ENEMY
Hawkman had been Adam's trusted ally and comrade in Ancient Egypt, but Adam knew his friend's old-world solutions could never work in a complex modern society.

BLACK ALICE

DEBUT *Birds of Prey* (Vol. 1) #76 (Jan. 2005)
REAL NAME Lori Zechlin
HEIGHT 5ft 5in
WEIGHT 110 lbs
EYES Blue
HAIR Black
POWERS/ABILITIES Able to tap into and steal the powers of any mystical being.
ALLIES Zatanna, Big Shot
ENEMIES Most of Earth's sorcerers, mystics
AFFILIATIONS Secret Six

Troubled teen Lori Zechlin wasn't aware that she had died in the accident that killed her parents. The rebellious, death-obsessed Goth-girl had been messing around with pagan magic for months, and in the moment of her death, called out instinctively to the great beyond.

Something dark answered, moving quietly into her head, where it lurks unobserved. Now "Black Alice" only knows that since the accident she can instinctively manifest the powers of any supernatural entity in the world, known or unknown.

She reluctantly joined other outcasts in the Secret Six, but has become a true trouble-magnet. Her powers trigger at random, endangering everyone around her. Who knows what will happen when she learns she cannot age or die?

LOOKS ARE DECEIVING
Despite her youth and appearance, Black Alice's powerful, unpredictable abilities make her one of the most dangerous teenagers on Earth.

BLACK CANARY

DATA

DEBUT *Flash Comics* #86 (Aug. 1947)
REAL NAME Dinah Drake Lance
BASE Gotham City
HEIGHT 5ft 7in
WEIGHT 135 lbs
EYES Blue
HAIR Blonde
POWERS/ABILITIES Expert in martial arts; extensive military and covert operations training; metahuman ability allows her to emit a piercing sound—"the canary cry"—that can shatter metal.
ALLIES Green Arrow, Batman, Batgirl, The Huntress
ENEMIES Count Vertigo, Auctioneer, Ninth Circle
AFFILIATIONS Team 7, Birds of Prey, Justice League of America

CLASSIC STORIES

***Flash Comics* #92 (Feb. 1948)**
Black Canary gets her first solo strip. Dinah Drake is a seemingly mild-mannered florist before she adopts her Black Canary persona to fight crime.

***Justice League* #1 (May 1987)**
Black Canary, in a recently acquired new costume, joins the Justice League International, becoming a key member of the Martian Manhunter's new line-up.

***Black Canary/Oracle: Birds of Prey* (Jun. 1996)**
Dinah starts working for Oracle, not realizing to begin with that Oracle is former acquaintance Barbara Gordon.

CANARY CRY
Black Canary can emit a powerful sound wave—her "Canary Cry"—that is able to stop large opponents in their tracks.

Black Canary has been many things—black ops agent, fugitive, Super Hero, and rock star. She has trained with some of the best martial artists in the world, and her "canary cry" gives her an edge in combat. She was a key member of Team 7 and later founded the Birds of Prey, fighting alongside Batgirl. She has also been a member of the Justice League of America.

KICK START
The young Dinah was taken in and trained in martial arts by the master Desmond Lamar. She would eventually inherit his dojo.

Dinah Drake raised herself on the streets of Gotham City after being abandoned by her mother. Martial-arts teacher and ex-special forces agent Desmond Lamar took her in and became a father figure to the ten-year-old Dinah. He trained her in martial arts and she eventually inherited his dojo.

As an adult she joined the cover special ops unit Team 7, where she met and married Kurt Lance, who was seemingly killed on a mission. After leaving government work behind, Dinah was recruited by Oracle, the former Batgirl who had been paralyzed from the waist down. Black Canary served as her field operative, and the pair became known as the Birds of Prey. When Batgirl regained the use of her legs, Dinah remained good friends with Barbara despite mostly ceasing their Birds of Prey activities.

Seeking a new challenge, Dinah formed a band—calling herself D.D.—and was soon fronting a new group called Black Canary. While in Seattle, Black Canary crossed paths with Green Arrow (Oliver Queen), and the two worked together to stop a slavery ring run by the villainous Auctioneer. They discovered that the conspiracy went deeper than they first imagined and it led to a clandestine Super-Villain-backing organization called the Ninth Circle. Black Canary stayed in Seattle to combat this threat, and she and Green Arrow fell in love. Despite the hectic pace of her life, Dinah found the time to serve in a new incarnation of the Birds of Prey as well as with the Justice League of America.

Eventually, when her old contacts in the government pitted her against Green Arrow, she and Ollie parted ways. Dinah returned to Gotham City, continuing her heroic mission, albeit feeling a little directionless.

ON THE RECORD

Before the reality-changing events of *Flashpoint*, Dinah Lance was the daughter of the original Black Canary, who had been a hero in the 1940s and a member of the Justice Society Young Dinah had a superpower her mother had lacked—her "Canary Cry"—and she was taught to fight by Ted Grant (Wildcat in the Justice Society). She gained a new outfit (without her iconic fishnets) slightly before she joined the Justice League International. Her long, tempestuous relationship with Oliver Queen (the Green Arrow) eventually led to their marriage.

SIDE-BY-SIDE
Black Canary and Green Arrow formed a long-running crime-fighting partnership.

D.D. ROCKS
Dinah tried to turn her back on violence and embarked on a career as a rock singer in her band, Black Canary.

BLACK GLOVE, THE

DEBUT *Batman* (Vol. 1) #667 (Aug. 2007)
MEMBERS Dr. Simon Hurt, Jezebel Jet, Cardinal Maggi, Al-Khidr, Sir Anthony, General Malenkov, Senator Vine

The Black Glove was a criminal organization formed by Thomas Wayne (related to, but not Bruce's father) in the 1700s and later led by Dr. Simon Hurt, who used the group to target Batman. Its membership comprised wealthy men and women; but its connections ran through all levels of society, from the actors the group used in their schemes through to high-ranking officials.

The group came close to defeating Batman and driving him insane before the Dark Knight and his allies defeated them, and Hurt was seemingly killed in a helicopter explosion. The Black Glove were counting on the fact that even if their scheme failed, Batman wasn't a killer. However, they overlooked his links to Talia al Ghūl. Within six months, Talia's League of Assassins had eliminated most of the Black Glove's members.

BLACK HAND

DEBUT *Green Lantern* (Vol. 2) #29 (Jun. 1964)
REAL NAME William Hand
BASE Ryut, Sector 666; Coast City
HEIGHT 5ft 7in **WEIGHT** 165 lbs
EYES Brown **HAIR** Black
POWERS/ABILITIES Black power ring can reanimate the dead and steal energy by killing victims and tearing out their hearts.
ALLIES Nekron
ENEMIES Green Lantern (Hal Jordan), Green Lantern Corps

William Hand was raised in a funeral parlor and was obsessed with death. Nekron, Lord of the Unliving, chose the boy as his avatar. He whispered to him, slowly driving him insane. Hand killed his parents, took his own life, and was reborn as a Black Lantern. Soon he commanded a vast army of the risen dead called the Black Lantern Corps.

During *Blackest Night*, the Green Lanterns and other Corps fought Nekron and the Black Lanterns as they tried to destroy the White Entity. Hand was defeated and returned to life by the White Entity. Taken in by the Indigo Tribe, he then escaped and killed himself. A black power ring emerged from his body and he was raised from the dead as a Black Lantern.

Seeking revenge, he replaced his own hand with that of Green Lantern Hal Jordan's dead father, swearing to kill Jordan with his father's own hand. He failed, and Jordan imprisoned him in the Source Wall at the end of the universe.

ON THE RECORD

Black Hand may be one of the Green Lantern's deadliest foes, but it wasn't always that way. The original Black Hand was a minor Green Lantern villain who would sometimes break the fourth wall to talk directly to the reader.

Shortly before Hal Jordan's "rebirth" as a Green Lantern, The Spectre (then Jordan) turned one of the villain's hands to coal dust as punishment when he tried to steal Hal's green power ring from the Green Arrow.

PRELUDE TO BLACKEST NIGHT
Death-obsessed William Hand was the doorway to absolute darkness for the demonic alien Atrocitus. After using Atrocitus' cosmic rod to take his own life, Hand rose from the dead to become the grimmest reaper of all.

BLACK LANTERN CORPS

DEBUT *Green Lantern* (Vol. 4) #25 (Jan. 2008)
BASE Ryut, Sector 666
POWERS/ABILITIES Members are the reanimated dead, able to infect the living with their bite and regenerate damaged flesh; they recharge their central power battery by removing the hearts from their victims.
ENEMIES Green Lantern (Hal Jordan), Lantern Corps across the Emotional Spectrum, Justice League of America, Titans
AFFILIATIONS Nekron, Black Hand

The Black Lanterns are an undead army, brought back to the land of the living by Nekron, Lord of the Unliving, to wage war against the various Corps of the Emotional Spectrum. They use black power rings, which reanimate the dead and also symbolize the absence of emotion and life. Using Black Hand as his avatar, Nekron unleashed a full-on assault on Earth with countless numbers of the dead—including many heroes—returning as Black Lanterns.

Black Lanterns often sought to consume the hearts of those who cared for them most—this emotional pain helped to empower Nekron. While the Black Lantern Corps was defeated during *Blackest Night*, Black Hand subsequently returned as his master's avatar on several occasions, each time threatening to bring more death and destruction into existence. Even Green Lantern Hal Jordan briefly became a Black Lantern, when the path seemed to be the only way to defeat Volthoom, the First Lantern. Hal raised an army of the undead and even Nekron himself before defeating Volthoom. He was then returned to life by a Green Lantern power ring.

ON THE RECORD

While Black Hand was the first member of the Black Lantern Corps, others soon followed. Among them were a number of long-dead heroes, including Elongated Man and Sue Dibny, Hawkman, Hawkgirl, and Aquaman. The Black Lanterns often attacked those closest to them to gain greatest impact from their deaths. The dead parents of both Tim Drake (Robin) and Dick Grayson (Batman) returned as Black Lanterns, as did the clone of Bruce Wayne.

DARKEST KNIGHT
Batman's clone was raised from the dead as a Black Lantern.

BLACK LIGHTNING

DEBUT *Black Lightning* #1 (Apr. 1977)
REAL NAME Jefferson Pierce
BASE Gotham City and Metropolis
HEIGHT 6ft 1in **WEIGHT** 200 lbs **EYES** Brown **HAIR** Black
POWERS/ABILITIES Olympic-level athlete; creation and control of lightning and electromagnetic fields, which also allow for simulated flight.
ALLIES Batman, Peter Gambi, Katana, Amberjack, Anissa Pierce, Lynn Stewart, Blue Devil
ENEMIES Tobias Whale, Rā's Al Ghūl, White Thunder, Ishmael
AFFILIATIONS The Outsiders

ELECTRIC POWERHOUSE
Thanks to his Olympic training, Black Lightning is in peak physical condition. He can also generate and manipulate electricity at will.

CHOOSING THE RIGHT TEAM
Black Lightning led The Outsiders and successfully defeated Rā's Al Ghūl's latest attack. Jefferson rejected Rā's when the notorious eco-terrorist asked Black Lightning to join his cause.

Former Olympic decathlete Jefferson Pierce spends his life as an educator. By day, he teaches kids as a principal in Metropolis. At night, he becomes the vigilante Black Lightning, helping to prepare the next generation of heroes to fight for justice as the field leader of The Outsiders.

BLACK AND BLUE
Following an initial misunderstanding, Black Lightning teamed up with Blue Devil to take on the drug lord, Tobias Whale.

Jefferson Pierce was born in Cleveland, Ohio, the son of newspaper reporter Louis Pierce. He was a tremendous athlete and even won an Olympic gold medal for decathlon. When Jefferson decided to become the Super Hero Black Lightning in order to protect his under-served neighborhood, he began training with a former Super-Villain named Amberjack. Another of his childhood mentors, Peter Gambi, designed a special suit for him to help him focus his metahuman lightning powers against any threat.

For a brief time, Jefferson lived in Los Angeles and taught at the city's Grassland High School. There he met and teamed with Blue Devil, and the two successfully brought down the criminal Tobias Whale. Sometime later, Black Lightning joined Batman's strike force, The Outsiders, but the experience was less than a positive one for Jefferson.

Black Lightning later learned that the "Tobias Whale" he had originally fought was the nephew of the true Tobias, who had killed the pretender and proceeded to rule over the streets of Cleveland. Jefferson returned to the "Brick City" and took a job teaching at John Malvin High School. There he brought the "real" Tobias Whale to justice, although Whale then escaped, switching places with his shape-shifting assistant at the last minute.

Seemingly always on the move, Pierce was working as a principal in Metropolis when he was approached by Batman to lead another team of Outsiders. Reluctant to work with Batman again, Black Lightning nevertheless set up shop in a penthouse apartment in Gotham City's Kubrick Towers thanks to Bruce Wayne's pocketbook, but he also continued to work in Metropolis. When Rā's Al Ghūl bombed Jefferson's school for payback for The Outsiders interfering in one of his terrorist plans, Jefferson swore to even the odds. With his powers enhanced and amplified thanks to Wayne Industries tech, Black Lightning and The Outsiders stopped Rā's from using an alien electromagnetic weapon in his quest for world domination.

ON THE RECORD

Black Lightning was DC's first African-American hero to have his own solo series. Jefferson Pierce was a teacher at Garfield High School in Metropolis' notorious Suicide Slum. Pierce tried to clear out mob-connected drug pushers from his school and was driven to vigilantism as Black Lightning after one of his students was murdered by Tobias Whale and the crime organization, the 100.

Pierce didn't realize the full extent of his powers until his first term of duty with The Outsiders when a latent metagene enabled him to internalize and amplify his lightning powers. Previous to that, he used an electronic belt to generate shock attacks and disguised himself using a costume created by his childhood mentor, tailor Peter Gambi.

NEIGHBORHOOD WATCH
Black Lightning defended the inhabitants of Metropolis' Suicide Slum, keeping them safe from drug dealers.

CLASSIC STORIES

***Black Lightning* #3–5 (Jul.–Nov. 1977)** Hunting down Tobias Whale, Black Lightning runs afoul of Superman when the Man of Steel thinks Pierce has hurt Jimmy Olsen.

***Amazons Attack* (Vol. 1) #1 (Jun. 2007)** As a founding member of a new Justice League, Black Lightning saves the President's life when the Amazons of Themyscira invade Washington, D.C.

***Black Lightning: Year One* #1–6 (Mar.–Aug. 2009)** Black Lightning's origin is retold as he crosses paths with Superman and Lois Lane during his quest to avenge the death of student Earl Clifford.

BLACK MANTA

DATA

DEBUT *Aquaman* (Vol. 1) #35 (Sep.–Oct. 1967)
REAL NAME David Milton Hyde **BASE** Mobile
HEIGHT 6ft 2in **WEIGHT** 205 lbs
EYES Black **HAIR** Bald
POWERS/ABILITIES Engineering and technological expertise; skilled with knives; armored suit tailored for underwater use; enhanced strength; energy blasts projected from helmet's lenses; access to advanced technology.
ALLIES Black Jack, Lex Luthor
ENEMIES Aquaman, the Others, Aqualad, Mera
AFFILIATIONS Secret Society of Super-Villains, Suicide Squad, Legion of Doom, N.E.R.O.

THE APPLE FALLS FAR
Black Manta's son, Jackson Hyde, is nothing like his father. He adopted a heroic lifestyle as Aqualad and even served on the Teen Titans.

Prone to violence from childhood, Black Manta was driven by an obsessive hatred for Aquaman and a desire to avenge the killing of his father. He devoted his adult life to killing the King of the Seven Seas and destroying everything he cared about, whether his family or the kingdom of Atlantis itself.

David Hyde swore revenge on Aquaman after the Atlantean king accidentally killed his father following Manta's attack on Aquaman's own father, Tom Curry. Possessing a variety of hi-tech devices and weapons—though he favored a pair of long daggers—he became an accomplished treasure hunter as Black Manta. He stole Atlantean artifacts, including an enchanted scepter, for the traitorous Atlantean Vulko, who planned to use it to resurrect the Dead King. Defeated by Aquaman and the Others while delivering the scepter, Black Manta dared Aquaman to kill him. Despite his desire to avenge his dead friends, Aquaman refused.

VIOLENT OBSESSION
From the outset, Black Manta was driven by a homicidal mania for revenge against Aquaman.

Black Manta was imprisoned in Belle Reve and eventually fought alongside the Suicide Squad. Some time later, after attacking an Atlantean embassy in Massachusetts, Black Manta was recruited by the Fisher King, Black Jack, and the clandestine criminal group called N.E.R.O. Black Manta immediately killed the Fisher King and took his place. N.E.R.O. then attacked Atlantis directly, using the powerful beast known as the Shaggy Man. Black Manta successfully framed Atlantis for aggressions against the United States, but N.E.R.O. was eventually discovered and defeated by Aquaman.

As part of his deal with the newly formed Legion of Doom, Black Manta teamed with the Triumvirate of Sea Gods—three ancient water gods from far-off worlds. They flooded the globe, but before they could see the error of their ways, Manta turned on both the Legion of Doom and the Triumvirate in an attempt to seize power for himself. However, his plot backfired and once again Aquaman foiled his plan.

On a quest for yet more power, Black Manta accepted a gift from Lex Luthor in the form of the monstrous robot Mecha Manta. But his hi-tech attack failed thanks to the combined powers of Aquaman and Mera, although Mera became briefly comatose after the assault.

ON THE RECORD

Earlier versions of Black Manta revealed slightly more of the character's origin, telling the story of a boy kidnapped and forced into abusive servitude aboard a ship. Spotting Aquaman, he signaled for help, but when the hero did not see him, the boy grew to hate him and the sea he represented. This led to him creating the Black Manta persona and a deadly arsenal of marine weapons and vehicles.

Black Manta's uncontrollable rage ultimately caused the death of Aquababy, turning a one-sided obsession into a mutual blood feud. Ultimately Aquaman defeated the villain, but refused to compromise his ideals by exacting vengeance. This act further enraged Black Manta and he went on to sell his soul to the demon Neron.

DEATH OF AQUABABY
The infant son of Aquaman and Queen Mera, Arthur Curry, Jr. was murdered by Black Manta and buried at Mercy Reef.

CLASSIC STORIES

Aquaman (Vol. 1) #35 (Sep.–Oct. 1967) Black Manta's attempt to kidnap Aquababy is thwarted when the Ocean Master frees the baby from Black Manta's ship.

Adventure Comics (Vol. 1) #452 (Aug.–Sep. 1977) Black Manta forces Aquaman and Aqualad to fight each other to the death, or Aquababy will die in a globe filled with air. Aquaman shatters the globe, but too late to save his son.

Brightest Day #19–20 (Apr. 2011) Black Manta goes hunting for his son, Jackson Hyde, who has been protected by Mera since infancy. He battles Aquaman and Jackson, before Mera seals Manta away in the Bermuda Triangle.

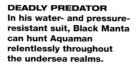

DEADLY PREDATOR
In his water- and pressure-resistant suit, Black Manta can hunt Aquaman relentlessly throughout the undersea realms.

BLACK MASK

DEBUT *Batman* (Vol. 1) #386 (Aug. 1985)
REAL NAME Roman Sionis
BASE Gotham City
HEIGHT 6ft **WEIGHT** 165 lbs
EYES Brown **HAIR** None
POWERS/ABILITIES Skilled combatant and marksman; mask enables mind-control.
ALLIES Dr. Jeremiah Arkham
ENEMIES Batman, Catwoman, Mad Hatter

Criminal Roman Sionis carved his signature black mask from his father's coffin. It gave Sionis the ability to control others, and he started his own gang, the False Face Society. While incarcerated in Arkham Asylum, Sionis was separated from his mask, but when the Talons of the Court of Owls attacked the asylum, its director, Dr. Jeremiah Arkham, gave it back so that Black Mask could protect him. In the event, Black Mask used the mask to escape.

He then battled the Mad Hatter, who wanted the power of the False Face Society's masks for himself. Batman cracked the mask with a well-aimed kick, driving Black Mask/Sionis insane. He was returned to Arkham Asylum, but was soon broken out. He joined the Secret Society when the Crime Syndicate invaded Earth, and later set his sights on ruling Gotham City's underworld, but clashed with Catwoman.

BLACK DEATH Consumed by hatred, Black Mask struck at Catwoman from beyond the grave, thanks to a Black Lantern ring.

BLACK SPIDER

DEBUT *Detective Comics* (Vol. 1) #463 (Sep. 1976)
REAL NAME Eric Needham
BASE Belle Reve Penitentiary
EYES Brown **HAIR** Black
POWERS/ABILITIES Amazing reflexes; hi-tech battlesuit equipped with extendable claws; advanced firearms.
ENEMIES Resurrection Man, Amanda Waller, Batman, The Flash

Many criminals have used the codename Black Spider. The most effective is former vigilante Eric Needham. While serving a 60-year term in Belle Reve Penitentiary, he was selected by Amanda Waller for her Suicide Squad—a penal unit of villains secretly working for the US Government. He joined Harley Quinn, Deadshot, King Shark, and El Diablo, and despite a severe spinal injury, earned a stellar reputation. Waller even offered to free him, but he elected to stay. Needham had ulterior motives: he had been inserted into Belle Reve by the Basilisk organization to infiltrate the Suicide Squad and kill Waller. He failed and was captured by his teammates. He is now a freelancer, robbing banks and chasing bounties, facing Batman and The Flash, and losing every time.

BLACK ORCHID

DEBUT *Adventure Comics* (Vol. 1) #428 (Jul.–Aug. 1973)
REAL NAME Alba Garcia
EYES Brown **HAIR** Black
POWERS/ABILITIES Her link to the Red and the Green gives her shape-changing abilities that make her a master of disguise.
ALLIES Dr. Mist, A.R.G.U.S., Animal Man
ENEMIES Felix Faust, the Demons Three, Nick Necro
AFFILIATIONS Justice League Dark

Private Alba Garcia was given superpowers by A.R.G.U.S.'s Project Ascension that linked her to the primal forces the Green and the Red. As shapeshifter Black Orchid she joined occult task force Justice League Dark, helping to keep the Books of Magic from sorcerer Felix Faust, traveling to the World of Epoch, and spearheading a magical rebellion to free the world from the Network.

In this realm, she became a Swamp Thing-like monster, but fought the malevolent Rot with Animal Man. When the Crime Syndicate invaded Earth, she was captured and used to power the Thaumaton weapon. Rescued by Justice League Dark, she got involved in the terrifying war between the House of Mystery and the House of Secrets. When the goddess Hecate tried to rewrite the Laws of Magic, she used Alba as one of her five deputies: a possessed weapon which replaced the ancient Parliament of Trees with the predatory Parliament of Flowers.

ON THE RECORD

The original Black Orchid was a mistress of disguise who used her powers to fight crime. She was once a human called Susan Linden-Thorne, but when her husband killed her, the botanist Philip Sylvain used her DNA to create a human/plant hybrid. The heroine was killed while investigating LexCorp, but two other plant/human hybrids with her DNA survived and continued the Black Orchid legacy.

DEADLY BLOSSOMING After being murdered, Linden-Thorne returned as a human/plant hybrid that drew power from the Green, the force created by all plant life on Earth.

BLACKBRIAR THORN

DEBUT *DC Comics Presents* (Vol. 1) #66 (Feb. 1984)
REAL NAME Blackbriar Thorn
EYES Green **HAIR** None
POWERS/ABILITIES A powerful magician; can create a treelike body around his frail form; controls plant matter and regenerates.
ENEMIES Superman, the Demon, Justice League Dark

When the Romans invaded Britain, the druid Blackbriar Thorn cast a spell that turned him into a towering, treelike being. Inadvertently buried, he returned to life in the 20th century after being dug up and exposed to moonlight.

After clashing with Superman and the Demon, Thorn went to live in the Amazon rainforest, where Deadman and Zatanna encountered him. Thorn attacked them, but Deadman possessed him and returned him to human form.

Following this defeat, Thorn allied himself with Felix Faust, Nick Necro, and Dr. Mist against Justice League Dark, but was struck down by Andrew Bennett and turned into inanimate wood. When anti-life force the Rot threatened Earth, Thorn returned and took over Metropolis, but Animal Man defeated him by taking termite form.

IMPLACABLE PURSUIT
The Black Racer chases his prey across time and space to carry out his dark duty.

For the New Gods of Apokolips and New Genesis, the mysterious Black Racer is the avatar of Death, relentlessly pursuing those doomed to die. He takes over other beings, using them as vessels while he carries out his forbidding task. Mister Miracle once served as one of his hosts. Darkseid summoned the deadly Black Racer during his battle with the Anti-Monitor, bonding the Racer with The Flash (Barry Allen). However, the Anti-Monitor used his mastery of Anti-Life to turn the Racer against Darkseid, seemingly killing the dark lord of Apokolips. Barry attempted to free himself from the Black Racer's control, but the grim entity explained that death was essential to the proper functioning of the universe, showing Barry visions of his dead mother Nora and of Central City reduced to a mausoleum. The Flash tried to slay the Racer with his own scythe, but he was subjected to horrifying visions of what would befall the universe if he refused to become an avatar of Death. This convinced Barry to accept his role as the Black Racer's host.

The Flash and the Black Racer were finally separated by the child of Earth-3's Superwoman and Alexander Luthor, who used his father's power-absorption abilities. The Racer then claimed the life of Volthoom before disappearing on his never-ending journey of death.

BLACK RACER

DEBUT *New Gods* (Vol. 1) #3 (Jun.-Jul. 1971)
EYES Red **HAIR** None
POWERS/ABILITIES Immortal avatar of Death who flies on cosmic skis; can possess other beings, turn intangible at will, and kill with his lightning scythe.
ALLIES Anti-Monitor, The Flash
ENEMIES Darkseid
AFFILIATIONS New Gods

ON THE RECORD

The Black Racer was a legendary figure in pre-*Flashpoint* reality who made his first recorded appearance on Earth after he was diverted there by the New God Metron. He chose handicapped veteran Sgt. Willie Walker as his host and attempted to claim the lives of several heroes, notably Steel. The Black Racer was one of the first victims killed by Infinity Man during the Death of the New Gods event.

FINAL RECKONING
Black Racer could phase through solid objects, fly on cosmically charged skis, and deliver death with a touch. He occasionally used a lethal staff to mete out justice.

BLACKFIRE

DEBUT *Tales of the New Teen Titans* #4 (Sep. 1982)
REAL NAME Komand'r
BASE Tamaran, Ghost Sector
EYES Green **HAIR** Black
POWERS/ABILITIES Trained in combat and leadership.
ALLIES Koriand'r, Red Hood and the Outlaws, Green Lantern (Jessica Cruz), Cyborg, Orion, Azrael
ENEMIES The Blight, the Citadel, Lord Helspont, Darkseid
AFFILIATIONS Justice League Odyssey

Komand'r was the eldest child of planet Tamaran's Royal family. When the Citadel and Dominators invaded and her parents were killed, Komand'r agreed to become a puppet ruler called Blackfire. Her little sister Koriand'r was taken from Tamaran in chains.

Eventually, Koriand'r found sanctuary on Earth, joining Red Hood and the Outlaws. When Tamaran was besieged by the alien Blight, she returned and was reunited with Komand'r, who begged her forgiveness. They vanquished the Blight, but Komand'r again appeared to betray her sister to the Citadel, but ultimately helped Koriand'r repel them. After *Rebirth*, Tamaran was transported to the Ghost Sector. Here Queen Blackfire battled Darkseid as part of the Justice League Odyssey team.

BLACKHAWK

DEBUT *Military Comics* #1 (Aug. 1941)
REAL NAME Kendra Saunders
BASE Blackhawk Island
Eyes Hazel **Hair** Brown **HEIGHT** 5ft 9in **WEIGHT** 135 lbs
POWERS/ABILITIES Skilled pilot with excellent combat and leadership skills; can call on the expertise of every previous life she has lived since history began.
ALLIES Justice League
ENEMIES Barbatos
AFFILIATIONS The Blackhawks

Kendra Saunders has been a warrior in every life she has ever lived. Constantly reincarnating—usually beside her eternal lover Carter Hall/Hawkman—she has battled human injustice and a countless procession of monsters throughout history. As Shiera Hall, she and her husband Carter transformed the Blackhawks from a freelance foreign legion of mercenary soldiers into a secret multinational strike force able to combat global crises and supernatural incursions. After being reborn as Kendra Saunders, she took Carter Hall's place when he fell victim to Dark Multiversal horror Barbatos. Leading as Lady Blackhawk, she was ferociously dedicated to saving humanity from itself, and from the threats of the unknown. A brilliant tactician and superb fighter with every kind of weapon, Lady Blackhawk can apply the experience of countless previous lives to any problem. After Barbatos was defeated, Kendra left the Blackhawks to fight with the Justice League as a new iteration of her old Super Hero persona Hawkgirl.

ON THE RECORD

The post-*Crisis* Blackhawk was Janos Prohaska, a Polish fighter pilot who fought in the Spanish Civil War. Following the fall of Poland, he traveled to the UK, where he became the commander of the secret Allied Blackhawk Squadron. Blackhawk's team stayed together after World War II and battled communists and Super-Villains. They subsequently served as both a courier service (Blackhawk Express) and as part of the Checkmate organization.

FLYING INTO DANGER
Blackhawk led his squadron in thrilling adventures across the globe, where they battled many exotic foes, including the Winged Death cult.

BLACKHAWKS

DEBUT *Military Comics* #1 (Aug. 1941)
BASE The Eyrie
POWERS/ABILITIES Highly experienced elite military personnel with a wide variety of skills; Kunoichi possesses super-strength.
ALLIES All Star Squadron, Justice Society of America
ENEMIES Mother Machine, Titus, Steig Hammer
AFFILIATIONS United Nations

Originally a multinational squadron of freelance aviators founded by Polish pilot Janos Prohaska to battle the Nazis and Axis powers, the Blackhawks evolved into a covert team dedicated to preventing the end of the world. Reshaped and guided by eternally reincarnating lovers, Carter Hall and Shiera Sanders, the Blackhawks battled the invasion plans of monstrous Bat-god Barbatos as he sought to drag the positive matter universe into his Dark Multiverse. In the interim, the paramilitary unit hired out to nations in need. When they seemingly vanished, their name and reputation were co-opted by eco-terrorist Rā's Al Ghūl, who sent fake Blackhawks against Batman. This brought the team to Batman's attention, paving the way to a wary alliance after Lady Blackhawk asked the Justice League to help her team against Barbatos.

BLEEZ

DEBUT *Final Crisis: Rage of the Red Lanterns* (Vol. 1) #1 (Dec. 2008)
BASE Sector 33
EYES Blue, Yellow
HAIR Black
POWERS/ABILITIES Seduction, magic-wielding, able to expel blazing bile; equipped with a Red Lantern ring affording flight, full environmental protection, intergalactic transportation, translation, violent energy projection, solid-light constructions.
ALLIES Kyle Rayner
ENEMIES Atrocitus
AFFILIATIONS Red Lantern Corps, New Guardians

A pampered princess on a paradise world, Bleez was abducted by members of the Sinestro Corps. Abused and tortured for their amusement, she escaped but, filled with overwhelming fury and indignation, she was possessed by a red power ring. This suppressed her intellect, making her an explosive slave to boiling rage, and she joined the Red Lantern Corps.

When a series of cosmic catastrophes forced the Emotional Spectrum groups into tenuous alliances, the Reds' leader, Atrocitus, assigned Bleez to join Green Lantern Kyle Rayner's New Guardians. Dissatisfaction at leading a legion of functional fools compelled Atrocitus to restore her mind. Bleez then became his rival, rising to the top of the Red Lantern Corps, wielding every ring Atrocitus had created. But at the moment of her greatest triumph, she was freed from her obsessive rage and restored to mortal form by Blue Lantern Guy Gardner.

ON THE RECORD

Red ring wearers are filled with a boiling, corrosive napalm-like substance that matches the constant feral fury gripping them. This anger, though invaluable in combat, also clouds the mind.

Eventually Corps founder Atrocitus used shamanistic blood magic to restore the intellect without quelling the rage of his subordinates. His mistake was starting with Bleez, who instantly challenged his authority and began plotting to replace him.

CALM BEFORE THE STORM
Her early life as a princess valued only as "marriage material" made Bleez determined that no one would ever control her again.

BLOCKBUSTER

DEBUT *Detective Comics* (Vol. 1) #345 (Nov. 1965)
REAL NAME Mark Desmond
BASE Gotham City, Blüdhaven
HEIGHT Variable **WEIGHT** Variable
EYES Blue **HAIR** Blonde
POWERS/ABILITIES Superhuman strength, enhanced stamina.
ALLIES Neron
ENEMIES Batman, Nightwing
AFFILIATIONS Secret Society of Super-Villains

Blockbuster is the name used by a series of Super-Villains. The first was frail chemist Mark Desmond, who devised a serum to increase physical attributes, but only by reducing his intellect to that of an angry child. He was manipulated by his brother Roland into crime and he battled Batman and the Justice League. When Mark died on a mission for the Suicide Squad, Roland became a new Blockbuster.

At least two other mindless, anonymous Blockbusters were created for the Secret Society of Super-Villains before *Flashpoint* resulted in a new rampaging Mark Desmond. Since rebirth, the latest Blockbuster is Roland Desmond, who uses his brother's formula to take over Blüdhaven, even manipulating Nightwing to help him depose crimelord Tiger Shark.

BLOCKBUSTER II

DEBUT *Starman* #9 (Apr. 1989)
REAL NAME Roland Desmond
BASE Blüdhaven
HEIGHT Unknown **WEIGHT** Unknown
EYES Brown **HAIR** Blond
POWERS/ABILITIES Uses Blockbuster serum to achieve superhuman strength and durability.
ALLIES Mark Desmond
ENEMIES Nightwing, Raptor, Tiger Shark
AFFILIATIONS Marcus Casino

BURYING THE HATCHET?
Desmond extends a hand, supposedly of friendship, to his longtime adversary Nightwing. But can he really be trusted?

Crime boss turned casino operator Roland Desmond took on the criminal alias of his imprisoned brother Mark—the mighty Blockbuster. The Desmond brothers possessed a serum that could turn a person into a super-strong, super-resilient monster for a short period of time. Before being imprisoned for his crimes as Blockbuster, Mark managed to tweak the formula so that his brother could maintain his intelligence while in Blockbuster form—a glitch that had allowed Nightwing to defeat the villain previously.

Roland Desmond was a native of Blüdhaven and he appointed himself as protector of the city and its people. This meant that he and Nightwing were able to make an uneasy pact against villains like Raptor who sought to exploit the city, although the hero later used an antidote to take Blockbuster's powers away.

BLOODSPORT

DEBUT *Superman* (Vol. 2) #4 (Apr. 1987)
REAL NAME Robert DuBois, Alex Trent
BASE Metropolis
EYES Brown **HAIR** Black
POWERS/ABILITIES Teleportation, instant inter-dimensional access to arsenal of advanced armaments and weapons.
ALLIES Riot, Hellgrammite
ENEMIES Superman

Bloodsport is the name used by a succession of fanatics who have battled Superman. Using technology provided by Lex Luthor, the deranged Robert DuBois—who was obsessed with the Vietnam War—repeatedly attempted to kill the Man of Steel with futuristic firearms teleported directly into his hands, many of them firing Kryptonite bullets.

DuBois died in an attempted prison breakout and his gadgetry fell into the hands of the demon Bloodthirst, who bonded it to radical white supremacist Alex Trent. This Bloodsport began murdering minority citizens, but was defeated by Superman and killed in prison by his own Aryan Brotherhood colleagues. The third, unidentified Bloodsport took over the technology and costume, but pursued no ideological agenda, acting as a super-powered mercenary for major criminals.

BLUEBIRD

DEBUT *Batman* (Vol. 2) #7 (May 2012)
REAL NAME Harper Row
BASE Gotham City
EYES Brown **HAIR** Purple
POWERS/ABILITIES Electrical engineering and computers, marksmanship, combat.
ALLIES Orphan, Red Robin, Batman, Alfred Pennyworth
ENEMIES Tiger Shark, Mad Hatter

Life for streetwise Harper Row might have ended up very different had Batman not saved her brother Cullen from being beaten in a hate crime. She became obsessed with helping the Dark Knight. Her first overture was locating the technology he used to avoid surveillance cameras. Improving them, she inserted herself into his cases, but Batman responded with uncharacteristic brutality. He wanted no more brave kids to die. Harper quietly persisted, winning him over by saving his life during his war against the Court of Owls.

Her graduation to costumed crime fighter came when she joined Red Robin in saving Cullen and other kids from the Mad Hatter. Instead of becoming another Robin, Harper created her own masked persona, but her time as Bluebird was limited. After some months Harper retired to help ordinary people at Leslie Thompkins' street clinic.

BLUE DEVIL

DEBUT *Firestorm* (Vol. 2) #24 **(Jun. 1984)**
REAL NAME Daniel Cassidy **BASE** Myrra
HEIGHT 6ft 8in **WEIGHT** 385 lbs **EYES** Red **HAIR** None
POWERS/ABILITIES Enhanced strength,
speed, durability, assorted magical tricks,
and a mystic trident.
ALLIES Detective Chimp, Nightmaster, Kid/Red Devil
ENEMIES Nebiros, Bolt
AFFILIATIONS Shadowpact, Justice League Dark,
Sentinels of Magic

Daniel Cassidy was an engineer, actor, and stuntman
who built a robotic prop suit for upcoming Hollywood blockbuster
Blue Devil. Tragically, while wearing it on location, he was blasted by
the demon Nebiros and trapped inside it. Organically merged with his
outfit, Cassidy acquired ever-increasing mystic power. Happy-go-lucky
Dan made the best of it, becoming a Super Hero and media sensation.
He even had—despite all his protests—a sidekick in Kid Devil. However,
Cassidy's power came at a cost: his mystical nature attracted wild magic,
triggering weird happenings and making him a magnet for disaster.

Cassidy repeatedly saved humanity and the world as a member
of teams such as the Justice League and Sentinels of Magic before
eventually, joining eldritch super-group Shadowpact to face the darkest
horrors the universe could throw at him. Cassidy was even tried by
Hell's lawyers for illegally using Nebiros' power and position: a case
which ended with him being briefly appointed the Prince of Hell.

Years later, he worked briefly with Justice League Dark.
In recent times he has assumed the role of Protector of
the magical realm Myrra, following the death of its
previous champion, Nightmaster Jim Rook.

ON THE RECORD

Blue Devil was originally a light-
hearted, irrepressible adventurer bonded
into a mechanical outfit by demonic magic.
Cursed to be a magnet for weirdness, he
constantly battled against dark magic, but
supernatural menaces mutated his form
even further.

After *Flashpoint* he was reimagined as a
movie performer and last in an ancient line
tasked with safeguarding Earth's deadliest
supernatural relics. He became Blue Devil
after deciding to "borrow" a demonic
bodysuit in his safekeeping.

BEAT THE DEVIL
When hell-lord Nebiros came to claim his old
skin, he discovered that the empowering
outfit preferred to stick with Cassidy.

BLUE LANTERN CORPS

DEBUT *Green Lantern* (Vol. 4) #25 **(Jan. 2008)**
BASE Odym, Elpis
POWERS/ABILITIES Power rings channel the blue light of Hope,
powering flight, intergalactic travel, and self-defense.
CURRENT MEMBERS Saint Walker, Guy Gardner
ALLIES Hal Jordan, Kyle Rayner
ENEMIES Red Lantern Corps, Larfleeze, the Reach
AFFILIATIONS Green Lantern Corps

Following the war between the Green Lanterns and
Sinestro Corps, maverick Guardians of the Universe Ganthet
and Sayd were banished from Oa. They settled on Odym,
building a Central Power Battery to harness the Emotional
Spectrum's blue light of Hope. They were soon joined by
wanderer Saint Walker, who became their first agent.

Blue rings are primarily defensive. Aggressive capabilities
like energy blasts only activate when they are in close
proximity to a Green Lantern ring. The same connection
automatically boosts an emerald warrior's ring up to 300
percent beyond its normal charge capacity.

Run like an order of monks, Blue Lanterns were
recruited slowly, with each new member responsible
for finding the next. When Odym was destroyed by the
all-conquering Reach, the survivors relocated to Elpis, but
were subsequently wiped out in an overwhelming attack by
pre-Big Bang villain Relic. With only Saint Walker surviving,
it is unlikely the universe will soon hear their comforting oath:

"In fearful day, in raging night,
With strong hearts full, our souls ignite,
When all seems lost in the War of Light,
Look to the stars—for hope burns bright!"

ON THE RECORD

Blue Lanterns made their first
appearance saving their Green cousins
from attack by Atrocitus' Red Lanterns.
They remained a breed apart in the
escalating conflicts of the War of Light,
but played a major role in turning back
the risen dead during the *Blackest Night*.

Sadly, Hope's promise and its azure
emissaries' pacifist nature made them easy
targets for colonial aggressors the Reach,
who decimated their ranks and drove them
from their base-world of Odym.

LIGHT IN THE DARKNESS
Despite the increasing chaos and horror
of a universe in conflict, Blue Lanterns
always clung to the heartfelt belief that
"All will be well."

BLUE BEETLE (JAIME REYES)

DATA

DEBUT *Infinite Crisis* #3 (Feb. 2006)
REAL NAME Jaime Reyes
BASE El Paso, Texas
HEIGHT 5ft 8in **WEIGHT** 145 lbs **EYES** Brown **HAIR** Black
POWERS/ABILITIES Magical sentient Blue Beetle armor provides protection, boosts physical capabilities, and can create blades, energy weapons, wings, or thrusters at will; onboard systems include sensors, life support, and a universal translator.
ALLIES Paco Testas, Brenda Del Vecchio, Blue Beetle (Ted Kord), OMAC
ENEMIES La Dama, Mordecai, Arion, Ghostfire

When Jaime Reyes stumbled upon a mysterious artifact that transformed him into a bio-armored hero, he became the latest champion to carry the name Blue Beetle. Continuing the legacy of Ted Kord, Jaime found himself thrust into the role of hero—with both magic and Ted Kord helping him along the way.

Teenager Jaime Reyes and his friends Paco and Brenda were hanging out by a river on the day before their senior year of high school when Paco noticed a blue glint in the water. Paco waded out to see what it was and discovered a small beetle-like object that stung his hand and began glowing. When Brenda tried to grab it from Paco to save him, the Scarab exploded into a brilliant beetle-shaped light show, and Jaime found the object merging with his spine and coating him in bizarre blue armor. Jaime turned to industrialist Ted Kord for help and the inventive young billionaire jumped at the chance to learn more. As fate would have it, Ted had seen the Scarab before. His former next-door neighbor, archeologist Dan Garrett, had brought the ancient artifact home from a dig. The shiny blue treasure had inspired Ted—who happened to be a blossoming Super Hero—into naming himself the Blue Beetle. Ted later retired from crime fighting due to a heart condition, while the artifact led to Dan's death, causing him to nearly lose his mind with its relentless "whispers."

With the Scarab now a part of him, Jaime had no choice but to embark on a life as a Super Hero, with Ted Kord serving as his right-hand man from the safety of Ted's mobile Bug vehicle. The pair soon learned that the Scarab had been a magical power source as early as Ancient Egypt and had corrupted Arion, the Lord of Atlantis himself. When Arion returned and took back the power of the Scarab, Jaime managed to eventually reclaim it. He realized just how special his link was to this ancient artifact of power and he even began to enjoy life as a hero every now and then.

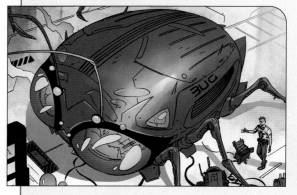

THE BUG
Ted Kord invented his own mobile Batcave of sorts, in the flying vehicle called the Bug. It allows Kord to monitor Jaime's adventures from nearby in the sky.

HYBRID
When Jaime Reyes bonded with the Scarab, he was transformed into a symbiotic armored being that could deploy guns, wings, blades, or jets on command. He had gone from ordinary teenager to living weapons system.

"No! I don't wanna kill ANYONE!"

JAIME REYES

CLASSIC STORIES

***Infinite Crisis* #1–7 (Dec. 2005– Jun. 2006)** When Jaime Reyes finds the Scarab, Booster Gold recruits him to help attack the Brother Eye satellite during the Multiverse-shaking *Infinite Crisis* event.
***Blue Beetle* Vol. 8 #22–25 (Feb.– May 2008)** Jaime discovers an insidious Reach plot to enslave humanity and leads an attack on the alien mothership.
***The New 52: Futures End* #0 (Jun. 2014)** In this grim tale of an alternate future, Jaime rebels against the all-seeing Brother Eye, but is captured and brutally assimilated into the AI's collective.

MIND OF ITS OWN
The Scarab has its own goals and thoughts, even once taking Jaime on an unwanted trip while he was sleeping.

ON THE RECORD

The Silver Age Blue Beetle was Daniel Garrett, a brave archaeologist who found a glowing scarab in the tomb of the pharaoh Kha-Ef-Re. When Dan was mortally wounded, he gifted the magical Scarab to Ted Kord, who could never get it to work. However, during the *Infinite Crisis* event, the Scarab grafted to Jaime's back and he became the third Blue Beetle. At this point, the Scarab was retconned to be a creation of the alien Reach that had been affected by the magical energies in the tomb of Kha-Ef-Re.

DAN GARRETT
Daniel Garrett served as the Blue Beetle before Ted Kord and Jaime Reyes. He would say magic words to access the Scarab's powers.

BLUE BEETLE (TED KORD)

DEBUT *Captain Atom* #83 (Nov. 1966)
REAL NAME Theodore Kord **BASE** El Paso, Texas
HEIGHT 5ft 11in **WEIGHT** 190 lbs **EYES** Blue **HAIR** Brown
POWERS/ABILITIES Genius-level inventor; skilled acrobat and fighter; access to the Kord Industries fortune; armed with an array of hi-tech gadgets including a light- and air-projecting BB gun; operates the Bug, a flying beetle-like mobile headquarters.
ALLIES Booster Gold, Blue Beetle (Jaime Reyes), The Flash (Teri Magnus), Batman, Batgirl, Justice League
ENEMIES Madmen, Maxwell Lord, Black Mask
AFFILIATIONS T-Council

A genius inventor and a comedic genius only in his own mind, billionaire industrialist Ted Kord moonlights as the wisecracking Blue Beetle. Armed with gadgets and a flying hi-tech vehicle called the Bug, Ted possesses no superpowers aside from his need for adventure and a near-superhuman level of camaraderie with his best bro, Booster Gold.

Ted Kord had too much money and not enough purpose in his life. The heir to his father's fortune, Ted was a brilliant inventor with all the means but none of the reasons to use his talents. Inspired by Superman and Batman, Ted designed himself a nondescript Super Hero suit. However, he only came up with a moniker after his neighbor, archeologist Dan Garrett, showed him the fruits of one of his digs—a blue scarab. Calling himself Blue Beetle, Ted sought out adventure armed with an arsenal of nonlethal weapons and gadgets, including his iconic aerial vehicle the "Bug."

Ted soon found friendship with Booster Gold, and the two became known as Blue and Gold, legendary crime fighters—at least according to them. After experiencing heart troubles, Ted was forced to retire from most of his active Super Hero exploits. However, he continued to work behind the scenes as the tech partner to his replacement Blue Beetle, Jaime Reyes.

In that capacity, Ted helped Jaime battle the threat of the corrupted mage Arion and a handful of Super-Villains. Kord donned his own Blue Beetle costume again when Booster Gold was suspected of murder and wanted by the Justice League. The Flash (Wally West) had accidentally unleashed his powers and killed several heroes at the secret Super Hero therapy center called the Sanctuary, but Booster was believed to be the culprit. Blue Beetle immediately jumped to his buddy's defense.

However, Booster didn't get the opportunity to return the favor when Kord was kidnapped by the villain Black Mask. In a scheme to establish a new country, Black Mask took on Kord's appearance and used his wealth and influence to take over Task Force X, also known as the Suicide Squad. Black Mask was eventually stopped by a group of Suicide Squad members, who used to go by the name the Revolutionaries, and Kord was freed.

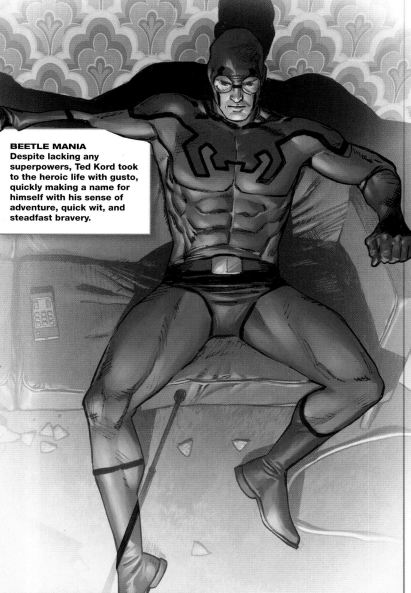

BEETLE MANIA
Despite lacking any superpowers, Ted Kord took to the heroic life with gusto, quickly making a name for himself with his sense of adventure, quick wit, and steadfast bravery.

KORD-LESS
When Jaime Reyes, Ted's successor as Blue Beetle, briefly lost his powers, Jaime adopted Kord's old Beetle costume to reclaim the Scarab and stop the corrupted Arion.

CLASSIC STORIES

***Blue Beetle* #1 (Vol. 7) (Jun. 1986)** Ted Kord leaps into action, beginning his post-*Crisis* adventures.
***Justice League America* #34 (Jan. 1990)** Blue Beetle and Booster Gold scheme their way into opening a casino using the Justice League's name on the resort of the island of KooeyKooeyKooey, with disastrous results.
***Countdown to Infinite Crisis* #1 (May. 2005)** Blue Beetle investigates Checkmate and is shot and killed by Maxwell Lord.

BACK IN ACTION
Although a heart attack forced him to retire, Ted still helped Jaime during a few battles, using his BB guns and a beetle drone backpack.

ON THE RECORD

Ted Kord was not the first Blue Beetle, and he wasn't the last. The middle child of the Blue Beetle legacy, Ted was nevertheless the smartest person to ever fill the role. Before the events of *Flashpoint*, Ted adopted the mantle of Blue Beetle from the original Beetle, Daniel Garrett.

As a nonpowered Super Hero, Ted rose to fame in the pages of Justice League International, where his high jinks with Booster Gold even saw the two attempt to create their own casino on a tropical island.

However, during one of the tragic events leading to *Infinite Crisis*, Ted was shot and killed by Maxwell Lord. The role of the Blue Beetle was then passed to teenager Jaime Reyes.

LORD OF EVIL
When Blue Beetle investigated Checkmate, he met his grisly—and seemingly final—fate.

BOOSTER GOLD

DEBUT *Booster Gold* (Vol. 1) #1 **(Feb. 1986)**
REAL NAME Michael Jon Carter
HEIGHT 6ft 2in **WEIGHT** 215 lbs
EYES Blue **HAIR** Blond
POWERS/ABILITIES Accomplished athlete; Booster's powers come from his gear, which includes an armored strength-boosting suit, a thermal and x-ray vision visor, a force-field, energy-blaster gauntlets, and a Legion of Super-Heroes' flight ring. He is assisted by his robot pal, Skeets, who provides data and communications.
ALLIES Blue Beetle (Ted Kord), Batman, Harley Quinn, Rip Hunter, Blue Beetle (Jaime Reyes), Godiva
ENEMIES Brother Eye, Eradicators
AFFILIATIONS Justice League International, A.R.G.U.S.

TEAM POTENTIAL
While on the JLI, Booster Gold had to deal with political interference and team infighting, but he proved his worth... with a little help from Batman.

CLASSIC STORIES

Booster Gold (Vol. 1) **#8–9 (Sep.–Oct. 1986)** Michael Carter makes his mark as a Super Hero by saving President Reagan—who inadvertently gives the hero his codename!

The OMAC Project **#1–6 (Jun.–Nov. 2005)** Booster Gold goes in search of his missing best friend, Ted Kord—and is devastated when he finds out he has been murdered.

Convergence: Booster Gold **#1 (Jun. 2015)** In this time-twisting adventure, Booster meets Rip Hunter, the son of the pre-*Flashpoint* incarnation of Booster himself!

After making a mess of his life in the future, disgraced sportsman Michael Carter decided to make a new career in the 21st century as the hero Booster Gold. Though he loves a photo opportunity and a lucrative advertising deal, the brash and charming Booster is secretly the most important hero you've never heard of. He travels through time correcting the time stream while maintaining his cover story of a Super Hero sellout.

BROS BEFORE HEROES
When Booster was framed for murder while at the superhuman recovery center Sanctuary, his best friend Blue Beetle never once doubted his buddy's innocence.

Michael Carter was born in the 25th century and grew up in an abusive home in Gotham City, dreaming of fame and fortune. After earning a football scholarship, brash and handsome Carter became a sports star, but he lost everything after taking money to fix matches. After being caught and serving his time in jail, he could only find work as a security guard at the Space Museum.

Inspired by the museum's exhibits about 21st-century Super Heroes, Carter decided to go back in time to become a champion of justice—and get money and fame along the way. He helped himself to a suit, various hi-tech gadgets, and a security bot called Skeets from the museum. Then he used a time machine that once belonged to chrononaut Rip Hunter and traveled back to the 21st century.

Carter used his futuristic gadgets and flair for showmanship to build a reputation as the hero Booster Gold. However, Booster was treated as something of a joke by other heroes because he also made money from commercial endorsements—he even appeared in beer commercials! Nevertheless, he managed to do some good as a member of the Justice League International. While that team was short-lived, Booster's true career was not. When not starring on his own Go-Tube channel, Booster was saving the Multiverse on time-spanning adventures, using his celebrity as a cover story. Recently, he time traveled with Superman to help repair a damaged timeline on Krypton.

In his private life, Booster hangs out with his best friend in any timeline, Blue Beetle (Ted Kord). He also sparked a brief romantic relationship with the rather unbalanced Harley Quinn, which will surely be another good decision to add to his resume.

ON THE RECORD

In his pre-*Flashpoint* career, Booster served as a key member of many super-teams and stood in the front line during several cosmic events that reshaped the universe.

Booster really made his mark when he joined the Justice League International. He met Blue Beetle (Ted Kord) and they became best friends. Booster was devastated when Kord was murdered, and in *The O.M.A.C. Project*, he tracked down the killer—Maxwell Lord. Booster later joined Rip Hunter as one of the Time Masters. As a chrononaut, he could cross over to the post-*Flashpoint* universe.

FAMILY TIME
When Michael joined the enigmatic Rip Hunter in the Time Masters, he had no idea that he was actually working with his future son.

THE FACE THAT LAUNCHED A THOUSAND COMMERCIALS
Booster Gold combined courage with a flair for self-promotion and proudly endorsed companies that paid him enough!

BOLT

DEBUT *Blue Devil* #6 (Nov. 1984)
REAL NAME Larry Bolatinsky
HEIGHT 6ft 4in **WEIGHT** 220 lbs
EYES Blue **HAIR** Brown
POWERS/ABILITIES Teleportation; energy blasts; expert assassin and special-effects coordinator.
ALLIES Deadshot, Merlyn, Chiller, Deadline
ENEMIES Sideways, Blue Devil, Batgirl, Captain Atom
AFFILIATIONS Killer Elite, Suicide Squad

Bolt is a former special-effects expert who moved into the world of freelance killing. As a top-ranked mercenary assassin he has faced foes as diverse as Blue Devil, Captain Atom, and Starman. Bolt demands a high price, despite many failures to complete his contracts. At one point, he joined a group of assassins called the Killer Elite, which included Deadshot and Merlyn. Then he served briefly on the Suicide Squad.

Eventually, Bolt was killed by his son, Dreadbolt, who continued his father's legacy as a member of the Terror Titans. Bolt briefly returned as a member of the undead Black Lantern Corps, and was fully resurrected after *Flashpoint*. Resuming his trade, Bolt worked for the villain Knightfall and later with Dark Star Sciences CEO Leto Dominus as she sought to capture and exploit the powers of the new teen hero, Sideways.

BOODIKKA

DEBUT *Green Lantern* (Vol. 3) #20 (Jan. 1992)
HEIGHT 5ft 8in
WEIGHT 125 lbs
EYES White
HAIR Black
POWERS/ABILITIES Ability to overcome great fear; expert fighter and hand-to-hand combatant; weapons include Green Lantern ring.
ALLIES Chaselon, Kilowog
ENEMIES Star Sapphire, Flicker, Cyborg Superman, Doomsday

A natural fighter with no qualms about showing off her skills, Boodikka hailed from the planet Bellatrix. After working as a member of the mercenary group Bellatrix Bombers, Boodikka joined Green Lantern Corps. With her aggressive attitude and problem with authority figures, she initially had a difficult time fitting in at the Corps, but she proved her worthiness in battle.

When Hal Jordan was corrupted by the being Parallax, Boodikka fought him, but had her hand severed by him in the process. After a brief time spent as a member of the Brotherhood of the Cold Flame, she was promoted into the Alpha Lanterns, a police force within the Green Lantern Corps. After valiant fights with villains including Cyborg Superman and Doomsday, Boodikka was killed by the Alpha Lantern Varix.

BORDEAUX, SASHA

DEBUT *Detective Comics* (Vol. 1) #751 (Dec. 2000)
BASE Washington D.C.; The Castle, Swiss Alps
HEIGHT 5ft 7in **WEIGHT** 135 lbs
EYES One red, one blue **HAIR** Black
POWERS/ABILITIES Expert bodyguard; highly adept martial artist; enhanced strength and speed.
ALLIES Wonder Woman, Etta Candy, Steve Trevor, Batman, Mr. Terrific, Jessica Midnight
ENEMIES Doctor Cyber, Maxwell Lord, David Cain
AFFILIATIONS A.R.G.U.S., Checkmate

Sasha Bordeaux was a bodyguard who came to lead some of the world's most powerful spy organizations. She first entered Bruce Wayne's life when Lucius Fox assigned her as his bodyguard. Although Bruce initially kept her at arm's length, she soon discovered his secret and was allowed into Batman's life, adopting a mask and assisting on missions.

When Wayne was framed for murder, Bordeaux was sentenced to jail as his accomplice. Here she was recruited by spy agency Checkmate, quickly rising to be its Black Queen. Her body was augmented by O.M.A.C. technology, effectively changing her into a cyborg. She later became Director of A.R.G.U.S., where she was kidnapped by rival covert group Godwatch. Replaced with an android, Bourdeaux was eventually rescued by Commander Etty Candy.

BOUNCING BOY

DEBUT *Action Comics* (Vol. 1) #276 (May 1961)
REAL NAME Charles Foster Taine
BASE Legion Headquarters, New Earth
HEIGHT 5ft 8in **WEIGHT** 227 lbs
EYES Blue **HAIR** Brown
POWERS/ABILITIES Can inflate to shape of large, bouncing ball; invulnerability to impact trauma; advanced combat training; possesses Legion flight ring.
ALLIES Legion of Super-Heroes
ENEMIES Horraz Collective

Growing up on the free-floating bubbled enclaves constituting Earth in the 31st century, young prodigy Charles Taine is a Doctor of Metaphysical Gateway Sciences and a forthright critic of the United Planets organization. A level 8 meta, he can super-inflate his body into an invulnerable globe, propelling his form with devastating accuracy at super-velocities. After much practice he also developed an innate understanding of vectors, trajectories, and direction.

He initially refused when invited to join the UP-sponsored, Legion of Super-Heroes, but reconsidered after assurances that the team's purpose was to fix as much as defend the United Planets. Easy-going and unassuming he rejected dramatic, imposing codenames such as Bullet or Battle Ball, for the milder designation Bouncing Boy.

BRADLEY, SLAM

DEBUT *Detective Comics* (Vol. 1) #1 (Mar. 1937)
REAL NAME Samuel Emerson Bradley
BASE Gotham City
HEIGHT 6ft 1in **WEIGHT** 205 lbs
EYES Gray **HAIR** Dark Brown (with gray temples)
POWERS/ABILITIES Excellent brawler and hand-to-hand combatant; expert marksman; adept detective with decades of experience; possesses a particular talent for disguise and mimicry for undercover work.
ALLIES Catwoman, Sam Bradley, Jr., Holly Robinson, Superman
ENEMIES Black Mask
AFFILIATIONS Gotham City Police Department (formerly)

Slam Bradley hails from Cleveland, Ohio, but has spent most of his time in two of the United States' most famous cities—Gotham City and Metropolis. He earned his nickname on the streets of Cleveland, however, growing up in a fairly rough neighborhood. He was only 12 years old when he challenged a local 17-year-old bully and knocked the boy out with a single punch.

As an adult, Slam tried stints in both the army and the police force before settling in for a life as private investigator; a job where he was his own boss. Slam worked in Metropolis, Keystone, and New York City, before opting to move to the East End of Gotham City, where he befriended Catwoman. Slam soon found himself falling in love with Catwoman, who had too much on her plate to ever significantly return Slam's feelings. However, the two remained allies, even after Catwoman had a child with Slam's son, Sam Bradley, Jr.

TO CATCH A CAT
Slam became a staunch ally of Catwoman after being hired by the Mayor of Gotham City to locate her. He grew to care for Selina and her circle of friends.

BRAIN

DEBUT *Doom Patrol* (Vol. 1) #86 (Mar. 1964)
BASE Paris, France; Telistocc, Russia
POWERS/ABILITIES Genius-level intellect
ALLIES Monsieur Mallah
ENEMIES Doom Patrol, Teen Titans, The Flash
AFFILIATIONS Brotherhood of Evil, Secret Society of Super-Villains

Very little is known about the anonymous French scientist known as the Brain. The infamous criminal mastermind claimed to have worked with Niles Caulder before the maverick researcher formed the Doom Patrol. Brain also believed Caulder, who was envious of his work, was behind the accident that nearly took his life.

The Brain's most important work was the radical course of treatments that elevated a gorilla's intelligence to a level beyond human genius. The grateful primate returned the favor by transplanting the dying man's brain into a cybernetically enhanced containment unit. A close intellectual relationship developed as the ape—dubbed Monsieur Mallah—kept the Brain alive, helping him orchestrate a campaign of vengeance against Caulder and the world. They went on to recruit villains to their Brotherhood of Evil.

BRAINWAVE

DEBUT *All Star Comics* (Vol. 1) #15 (Feb.–Mar. 1943)
REAL NAME Henry King **BASE** Mobile
EYES Covered by thick opaque glasses
HAIR None
POWERS/ABILITIES Psionic ability: hallucination creation, illusion casting, astral projection, telepathy.
ALLIES Jonni Thunder, Obsidian
ENEMIES Justice League, Justice Society of America
AFFILIATIONS Secret Society of Super-Villains, Injustice Gang

Physically weak Henry King developed psionic abilities which he used for crime. As Brainwave, he clashed with the Justice Society of America and All-Star Squadron during World War II and into the 1950s. He was inactive for decades and it was later revealed that he had used his powers to marry Merry, Girl of 1000 Gimmicks.

His son, Henry Jr. adopted the guise of Brainwave Jr. to clear his family name and he joined Infinity Inc. and the Justice Society. When his father died, he received a psychic power-boost, sparking mental instability.

After *Flashpoint*, a third Brainwave— Henri Roy, Jr.—attempted to conquer the survivors of Earth-2, but has not been seen since the *Rebirth* event.

BRANDE, R. J.

DEBUT *Adventure Comics* (Vol. 1) #350 (Nov. 1966)
REAL NAME Ren Daggle
BASE United Planets HQ, 31st century Daxam
EYES Red **HAIR** Gray
POWERS/ABILITIES Cunning and ruthless politician; (assumed) Durlan shapeshifting.
ALLIES Legion of Super-Heroes, Science Police
ENEMIES Horraz, Crav the General Nah
AFFILIATIONS United Planets Ruling Council

Madam Honor President Brande is the dominant force in the vast federation of civilizations called the United Planets. Few of those billions of sentients know she is also a shapeshifting Durlan. A hard-headed politician with big ideas, soaring ambition, and a will of Inertron, Brande leads the 1,000-year-old UP, deftly wrangling fractious leaders from many worlds. She is credited with creating the Legion of Super-Heroes. Sensing an opportunity to build a youth movement and recreate the fabled "Age of Heroes," she sponsored three super-powered teens—Saturn Girl, Cosmic Boy, and Lightning Lad. Expecting to control the organization, Brande realized too late that the kids—and their army formed from every UP world—only listen to their own consciences. Her son Reep Daggle is her representative on the team as Chameleon Boy.

BRIMSTONE

DEBUT *Legends* (Vol. 1) #1 (Nov. 1986)
BASE Apokolips
HEIGHT 50ft 6in
WEIGHT 60,000 lbs
EYES Yellow **HAIR** None
POWERS/ABILITIES Pyrokinesis; incineration; flaming-energy construct creation.
ALLIES Glorious Godfrey, Darkseid
ENEMIES Suicide Squad, Firestorm, Cosmic Boy, Teen Titans
AFFILIATIONS Gods of Apokolips

The techno-seed that grew into Brimstone was created in the labs of Apokolips during Darkseid's campaign to destroy humanity's concept of heroism. When launched into a fusion reactor on Earth, it became a walking incinerator, targeting Super Heroes and terrorizing civilization.

The colossal monster was actually a semi-sentient artificial intelligence. Composed of super-heated hydrogen plasma wrapped around a core nexus of programming, its appearance was maintained by a delicate balance of magnetic fields. Though dangerous at full expansion, the construct was vulnerable to disruption of its magnetic shield. It carried a flaming sword and made declarations of being an "avenging angel" sent to destroy "false gods and graven images."

BRAINIAC 5

DEBUT *Action Comics* (Vol. 1) #276 (May 1961)
REAL NAME Querl Dox
BASE Legion Headquarters, 31st-century Metropolis, New Earth
HEIGHT 5ft 10in **WEIGHT** 160 lbs
EYES Green **HAIR** Blond
POWERS/ABILITIES Super intelligence; perfect memory; strategic skills; advanced unarmed combat training; weapons expert; Legion flight ring.
ALLIES Imra Ardeen/Saturn Girl, Superboy Jon Kent
ENEMIES Horraz Collective, Crav the General Nah, Fatal Five
AFFILIATIONS Legion of Super-Heroes, Science Command

Querl Dox is a 12th-level mind, the smartest individual of the most brilliant species in known space. He is a direct descendant of Vril Dox, the infamous, self-styled Collector of Worlds, and his brilliance counted as a unique superpower when he was asked to join the recently convened Legion of Super-Heroes. His inherited honorific as the fifth Brainiac became his codename.

Unlike many hyper-intelligent beings, Querl accepts the force of emotion on sentient beings, taking pains to interact on a friendly, inclusive level using a process he calls Emotional Fact. Greatly concerned with the orderly running of the universe, he was active in politics, giving a crucial speech to the United Planets on why there must be a Science Police force. His believes that peace and constant advancement are vital and he is driven to find the best way to achieve his aim.

Brainiac 5 fights best from a laboratory, as a researcher, advisor, tactician, and support scientist. Inventor of multifunctional Legion flight rings and AI servant C.O.M.P.U.T.O., he is the team's intellectual backbone, frequently acting as if he is the de facto leader in action and policy-making.

ON THE RECORD

Brainiac 5 has supreme confidence in his mental strength but frequently shows appalling judgment. In a Silver Age tale, his Artificial Intelligence creation named Computo killed fellow Legionnaire Triplicate Girl and almost conquered Earth before he found a way to shut it down.

That recklessness was still evident in a later tale of his early years when he breached a vault containing the first Brainiac's cached inventions. They ran amok and would have decimated the planet Colu if not for his new-found Legion allies.

CLEAN-UP CREW
Brainy's notions would have caused as much carnage as any marauder, if it wasn't for the diligent work of his Legionnaire allies.

BRAINIAC

DATA

DEBUT *Action Comics* (Vol. 1) #242 **(Jul. 1958)**
REAL NAME Vril Dox
BASE Mobile
HEIGHT Variable **WEIGHT** Variable
EYES Red **HAIR** None
POWERS/ABILITIES 12th-level intellect/artificial hybrid; controls multiple drone bodies; possesses accumulated technologies from numerous destroyed worlds; has access to an array of hi-tech weaponry and infamous skull-shaped ship.
ALLIES Lex Luthor, Vril Dox II
ENEMIES Superman, Justice League, Perpetua
AFFILIATIONS Legion of Doom

He is the Collector of Worlds—a being whose only purpose is the gathering of information and knowledge by capturing entire civilizations on a whim. A 12th-level intellect, Vril Dox has become the cruel and calculating Brainiac. He wishes not to share and spread information, but to hoard it, ensuring he is the only being to unlock the mysteries of the universe.

TASK FORCE XI
The mastermind behind Task Force X (also known as the Suicide Squad), Amanda Waller kidnapped the greatest psychic minds on the planet to hack Brainiac, calling them Task Force XI.

Brainiac is Vril Dox, a Colu native considered to be his planet's greatest shame and highest criminal. Banned from his own world due to his zealot-like quest for knowledge, Brainiac is a super-intelligent being. He employs his hi-tech skull-shaped ship and a variety of drones to travel the cosmos and imprison his chosen cities, miniaturizing them to preserving them in his perverse pursuit of universal knowledge. On his mad quest he has clashed with multiple heroes, but none more than Superman. As the captor and bottler of the Kryptonian city Kandor, Brainiac has more than earned the ire of Krypton's most famous survivor and champion.

After the Source Wall—the cosmic barrier separating the universe from previously unknown powers—was broken, Brainiac did the unthinkable. He went to Earth not to conquer, but to recruit its heroes to his cause. Four powerful cosmic beings called the Omega Titans had been unleashed on the galaxy, and they had their sights set on Earth and Colu. However, before he could further instruct his recruited heroes, Brainiac was taken out of commission by an attack from Amanda Waller's Task Force XI. Colu was destroyed in the aftermath, unleashing entire planets held in its nursery and creating a new Ghost Sector of space.

But Brainiac didn't stay "dead" for long. Through the genius of the notorious criminal scientist Professor Ivo, and with Lex Luthor's support and backing, Brainiac was brought back online and became a valued member of Luthor's new Legion of Doom. Brainiac attempted to double cross Lex, but found Lex had hidden a virus in his own mind, giving Brainiac no choice but to embrace Luthor's cause. The Legion of Doom then helped free the mother of the Multiverse known as Perpetua. However, Brainiac was transformed by the cosmic being into her very throne with some of his power channeled into Luthor.

A ghost lost in Perpetua's machine, Brainiac will no doubt return and regain his traditional form some day, reestablishing his unrelenting quest for information at any cost.

ON THE RECORD

When Superman first met Brainiac he seemed to be an organic being intent on repopulating his dead world with Earthlings, but he was soon re-imagined as a devious construct spying for mechanical villains, the Computer Tyrants of Colu.

Brainiac was radically altered in the 1980s into a scarily remorseless and predatory mechanoid intent on subjugating all organic life. These and many other versions resurfaced in *Convergence*, when a Brainiac from beyond the Multiverse began assimilating his parallel selves while collecting cities from all 52 alternate universes and their attendant or divergent timelines. These stolen cities were then pitted against each other, with Brainiac's enslaved ringmaster Telos arranging the bouts.

ALIEN ENCOUNTER
For many years, Superman was unaware that his force field-shielded arch-foe was also a man of steel (and gears, tubes, plastic relays, and chemicals).

BRAIN POWER
A ruthless master of mentality, Brainiac's physical form is secondary to his artificially enhanced mind.

CLASSIC STORIES

***Action Comics* (Vol. 1) #242 (Jul. 1958)** Superman battles an alien city-stealer who is defeated when his own lab monkey turns off his force-field. There is no hint that Brainiac is an artificial foe.

***Superman* (Vol. 1) #141 (Nov. 1960)** Superman time-travels to Krypton and helps his father construct a massive space-ark. But the factory is in the city of Kandor, which is bottled by Brainiac.

***Superboy and the Legion of Super-Heroes* (Vol. 1) #223–224 (Dec. 1976)** Brainiac reappears in the 30th century as Pulsar Stargrave, impersonating Brainiac 5's father. He tries to trick the Legion of Super-Heroes into helping him conquer the universe.

WEAKNESS IN NUMBERS
A Brainiac threatened every world in the Multiverse, but they were all just tasty morsels for the all-consuming, all-conquering being.

BRAINSTORM

DEBUT *Justice League of America* (Vol. 1) #32 (Dec. 1964)
REAL NAME Frederick Storm
BASE Mobile
EYES Black **HAIR** Black
POWERS/ABILITIES Super genius; psionic ability; hallucination creation; reality alteration triggered by a cerebral enhancement helmet.
ALLIES Axel Storm
ENEMIES Justice League of America
AFFILIATIONS Injustice Gang of the World

Fred Storm was a petty man who envied the adulation given to Super Heroes. Using a helmet which sporadically enhanced his mental abilities and afforded him "brainstorms" of inspiration, he conducted a vindictive campaign to humiliate—and ultimately destroy—the Justice League of America. His title of Brainstorm has also been used by a number of others, including his brother Axel and S.T.A.R. Labs volunteer Alan Barnes.

After *Flashpoint*, scientist Dominic Lanse studied mind-control and artificial intelligence in machines, eventually acquiring the ability to influence the minds of others.

His mind-manipulating powers indirectly caused the death of Paula Holt, Mr. Terrific's wife. In response, the outraged champion of "Fair Play" almost beat Lanse to death in a shocking act of violence, which was witnessed by television audiences and almost ended the Super Hero's career.

POWER OUTAGE Brainstorm's brain wave's posed problems for several Super Heroes, including causing Superman to temporarily lose his superpowers.

BRONZE TIGER

DEBUT *Richard Dragon: Kung-Fu Fighter* (Vol. 1) #1 (Apr.–May 1975) (as Benjamin Turner); *Richard Dragon: Kung-Fu Fighter* (Vol. 1) #18 (Nov.–Dec. 1977) (as Tiger)
REAL NAME Benjamin Turner
BASE Mobile
HEIGHT 5ft 11in **WEIGHT** 196 lbs
EYES Brown **HAIR** None
POWERS/ABILITIES Superb martial artist; can shift into animalistic tiger form.

A man of mystery, Bronze Tiger is one of the greatest martial artists. A major player in mercenary circles, he is an ally of Slade Wilson, aka Deathstroke the Terminator. In Rā's al Ghūl's League of Assassins, he won great power and influence among its fanatical killers. When Red Hood was recruited, Bronze Tiger welcomed him to their fabled city 'Eth Alth'eban.

The Tiger has a complicated history with premier assassin Lady Shiva and reported ties to Richard Dragon. A mystic a talisman transforms him into a tiger form, but the change comes at a cost—supposedly "burning away" some of his soul each time.

Guided by his personal code, he operates on both sides of the law, working with the Suicide Squad and Batman, as both a source of information on the mercenary world and a potent ally in battle.

BROTHER BLOOD

DEBUT *The New Teen Titans* (Vol. 1) #21 (Jul. 1982)
BASE Hollywood, California
HEIGHT 6ft 2in **WEIGHT** 193 lbs
EYES Red **HAIR** None
POWERS/ABILITIES Able to heal wounds; enslaves others by contact with their blood; charismatic leader with fanatical followers.
ENEMIES Titans, Teen Titans, Ravagers, Animal Man, Animal Girl

Hereditary cult leader Brother Blood is connected to the Red—an intangible energy-web connecting all animals. Blood sought to kill the Ravagers and came into conflict with the Teen Titans, hoping to use Beast Boy's blood to create a doorway to the Red. He was defeated by the Ravagers and his temple was destroyed.

Blood then targeted Animal Man Buddy Baker, entering the Red by drinking Buddy's blood. He tried to take over the dimension, but was stopped by Animal Man and his daughter, Animal Girl. After constant failures and abuse of his position, the Brother was supplanted by Mother Blood, Sonya Tarinka. She tried to use her connection to the Red and the released forces of the sundered Source Wall to subjugate the Multiverse via the interconnecting dimensional realm called the Bleed, but was thwarted by the Titans.

BROTHERHOOD OF EVIL

DEBUT *Doom Patrol* (Vol. 1) #86 (Mar. 1964); *New Titans Annual* #6 (1990) (Society of Sin)
MEMBERS/POWERS Phobia: Projection of illusions animating a foe's greatest fear; **Plasmus**: Protoplasmic burning touch; **Warp**: Teleportation; **Silverback**: Cybernetic enhancements, firearms expertise.
ENEMIES Titans, Blue Beetle, La Dama

The Brotherhood of Evil was formed years ago by the Brain and his ape companion, Monsieur Mallah. Sometimes known as the Society of Sin, it has changed members often. Recently, the group divided, with the Brain and Mallah becoming a Brotherhood of Two when their comrades went to hunt the extraterrestrial Scarab found by Jaime Reyes. Phobia, Plasmus, and Warp were joined by gun-toting cybernetic gorilla Silverback, who threatened them if the Scarab was not located. Agents of La Dama and soldiers of the Reach also had their own designs on the Scarab.

Meanwhile, Brain and Mallah went about boosting Brain's processing power, attempting his digital ascension to a world-altering, weather-controlling Hypergenius. But with the Brain growing more deadly, distant, and self-involved, an increasingly isolated Mallah barely put up a fight when the Titans ended the mad scheme.

BULLETEER

DEBUT *Seven Soldiers: Bulleteer* #1 (Jan. 2006)
REAL NAME Alix Harrower
HEIGHT 6ft **WEIGHT** 155 lbs
EYES White **HAIR** Red
POWERS/ABILITIES Skin bonded with Smartskin, making her nearly invulnerable and immune to pain; superhuman strength.
ALLIES Firestorm, Firehawk, Super-Chief
ENEMIES The Nebula Man, Sally Sonic
AFFILIATIONS Seven Soldiers of Victory, Justice League of America

Alix Harrower's scientist husband Lance was working on a "Smartskin" project—turning soft tissue into a metal material stronger than steel. Obsessed with preserving not only his youth, but that of his 27-year-old wife, Lance tried the Smartskin on himself, and died by suffocation. Before he breathed his last, he touched Alix, passing his Smartskin on to her.

She survived the bonding process and then discovered that Lance had been obsessed with a Super Hero on the Internet named Sally Sonic. In despair, Alix ran into the night, happening upon a building on fire and saved its residents. Realizing her calling, she became the Bulleteer, a Super Hero inspired by the World War II Bulletman. She later served with honor in the Seven Soldiers of Victory as well as the JLA.

BULLETMAN

DEBUT *Nickel Comics* (Vol. 1) #1 (May 1940)
REAL NAME James Barr
BASE Fawcett City
HEIGHT 6ft 4in **WEIGHT** 177 lbs
EYES Blue **HAIR** White
POWERS/ABILITIES Able to fly and repel bullets thanks to his Gravity Regular Helmet; superhuman strength and intelligence.
ALLIES Bulletgirl, Starman, Shazam
ENEMIES Weeper
AFFILIATIONS All-Star Squadron

The inspiration for the later crime fighter Bulleteer, Bulletman was a Super Hero active during World War II. The son of a police officer who was killed on duty, Jim Barr opted to become a crime fighter using his science smarts to increase his strength and develop a Gravity Regulator Helmet that allowed him to fly. Taking the name Bulletman from the Gravity Regulator's appearance, he was soon joined by Bulletgirl, Susan Kent.

The two fought bravely during the war and afterwards retired to live in Fawcett City. Later, as an old man who had made a good living from Bulletman merchandise, Jim was falsely accused of having committed treason back in 1942. However, Shazam and Starman teamed up to prove he was innocent of all charges.

BULLOCK, HARVEY

DEBUT *Batman* (Vol. 1) #361 **(Jul. 1983)**
REAL NAME Harvey Bullock
BASE Gotham City
HEIGHT 5ft 10in **WEIGHT** 248 lbs **EYES** Brown **HAIR** Black
POWERS/ABILITIES Excellent detective; able brawler with street smarts and years of experience; highly trained in police procedure; extremely loyal to his friends.
ALLIES James Gordon, Batman, the Batman Family, Renee Montoya
ENEMIES Anarky, The Joker's Daughter, Dr. Death
AFFILIATIONS G.C.P.D., Batman Task Force

Sometimes the best cops in Gotham City are hard to spot in a lineup. Although his uncouth attitude and slovenly appearance suggest otherwise, Harvey Bullock is in truth one of the few good cops left in a city filled with corruption, and he is a steadfast supporter of James Gordon and his high ideals.

While perhaps tempted by an amoral police department in the past, Bullock was inspired by the arrival of Lieutenant James Gordon, sticking up for him when he doggedly pursued underworld boss Roman Sionis. Bullock also worked with Gordon to catch Dr. Death during the city's *Zero Year* event. They slowly became allies as Gordon rose through the ranks to become Gotham City's Commissioner. After years of dedicated service, James Gordon was imprisoned for a murder he did not willingly commit. Bullock remained loyal to Gordon, and when he was finally released and became the city's official new Batman, Harvey remained by his side as a member of the Batman Task Force.

Despite his adversarial relationship with all Bat-vigilantes, Bullock assumed Gordon's role as the Police Commissioner of beleaguered Gotham City when the malign Batman Who Laughs infected Gordon with the corrupting power of evil.

ON THE RECORD

In his early appearances, Harvey Bullock was a clumsy slob who got in the way more than he helped. He also clashed with Commissioner Gordon. In time, Harvey changed his ways, making friends with the second Robin, Jason Todd. He later began work at the government spy agency Checkmate. In the 1990s, he became the longtime partner of officer Renee Montoya, but the infamously unorthodox cop finally crossed the line in 2000's "Officer Down" storyline and resigned from the G.C.P.D.

BAD NEWS BULLOCK
When he first appeared, Lt. Bullock wasn't a fan of either Batman or Commissioner Gordon, referring to Gordon as a "weak sister," and Batman as "fancy britches."

BUMBLEBEE

DEBUT *Teen Titans* (Vol. 1) #45 **(Dec. 1976)** (as Karen);
Teen Titans (Vol. 1) #48 **(Jun. 1977)** (as Bumblebee)
REAL NAME Karen Beecher-Duncan **BASE** Metropolis
HEIGHT 5ft 7in **WEIGHT** 130 lbs
EYES Brown **HAIR** Black
POWERS/ABILITIES Energy generation; able to shrink and fly; high-tech battlesuit.
ALLIES Malcolm Duncan
ENEMIES Mr. Twister, Psimon, Fearsome Five
AFFILIATIONS Teen Titans, Meta Solutions, S.T.A.R. Labs

The wife of former Teen Titan and award-winning movie composer Malcolm Duncan, Karen Beecher-Duncan has her life change forever after the birth of her baby girl. Karen has no idea that in previous realities she was a Super Hero too. She believes she first met her husband when she was a technical consultant on one of his films. Mal affectionately nicknamed her "Bumblebee." They married and Karen became pregnant, subsequently experiencing the first flash of a possible previous life after discovering she could emit energy bursts. Mal knew the cost of superpowers so together they approached Meta Solutions—a bio-company claiming to remove unnatural abilities.

Sadly, it was a front for Super-Villain Psimon and his Fearsome Five team. When Mal realized and called in the adult Titans, they found Karen had already been transformed into a size-changing warrior in advanced armor. When the Five crushed the heroes, Bumblebee savagely routed the villains, but not before Psimon wiped her memory of all traces of her life, husband, and child.

She eventually regained her memories after battling H.I.V.E. and an evil future Troia. When the Justice League disbanded the Titans, she retired from a life of action to raise her child.

ON THE RECORD

Before *Flashpoint*, Karen Beecher-Duncan was the Super Hero Bumblebee. Involved in a relationship with Teen Titan Mal Duncan, better known as the hero Herald (and much later, Vox), Karen decided to be a crime fighter herself, and designed her flying Bumblebee costume and weaponry. She was welcomed into the first Teen Titans team, and after that version disbanded, she worked for S.T.A.R. Labs before becoming a member of the Doom Patrol.

BEE MINOR
During *Infinite Crisis*, Bumblebee's physiology was altered, reducing her size to around six inches tall.

BUNKER

DEBUT *Teen Titans* (Vol. 4) #1 **(Nov. 2011)**
REAL NAME Miguel Jose Barragan
HEIGHT 5ft 8in **WEIGHT** 132 lbs
EYES Brown **HAIR** Black
POWERS/ABILITIES Able to create bricks of psionic energy; infectiously positive disposition.
ALLIES Beast Boy, Robin, Skitter, Solstice, Wonder Girl
ENEMIES The Penguin, Detritus
AFFILIATIONS Teen Titans, Red Hood

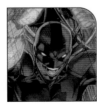

Miguel Jose Barragan left a happy life in the Mexican village El Chilar to fulfil a dream: to become a hero like his idol Robin. Riding a train to the US, he discovered the cocoon of future comrade Skitter in one of the cars and was attacked by a homeless man—actually Robin in disguise. Robin believed that Barragan worked for evil organization N.O.W.H.E.R.E. After a brief scuffle, Miguel suddenly hugged Robin, citing him as his inspiration for becoming Super Hero Bunker.

Cofounding a new iteration of the Teen Titans, openly gay Miguel forged a stellar career, serving as a ray of positivity through turbulent times. When they disbanded, he joined Red Hood Jason Todd, who had taken over the Iceberg Lounge, to dismantle the Penguin's criminal empire. However, unable to stomach the dirty tactics required, Bunker explosively severed ties with Red Hood.

C.O.M.P.U.T.O.

DEBUT *Adventure Comics* (Vol. 1) #340 (Jan. 1966)
REAL NAME Cyber-cerebral Overlapping Multiprocessor Transceiver Operator
BASE Legion HQ, 31st-century New Metropolis
POWERS/ABILITIES Incredible intelligence, limitless processing capacity, light manipulation.

C.O.M.P.U.T.O. is the autonomous data manipulation system devised by Brainiac 5 to administer the huge headquarters complex of the Legion of Super Heroes. As well as supporting the team members and their guests and visitors, C.O.M.P.U.T.O. also acts as a sounding board and knowledge base for Brainiac in his experiments and investigations. C.O.M.P.U.T.O. monitors events and data flow throughout the United Planets, looking for trends and patterns in the ebb and flow of trillions of beings.

Notionally female in its current interface aspect, C.O.M.P.U.T.O. can manifest as a light energy construct to interface with Legionnaires and in "her" capacity as a social messaging system and broadcast personality.

C.O.M.P.U.T.O. is located in the Legion complex on New Earth that is situated within the New Metropolis environment bubble. This sanctuary is circling the shattered remnants of the planet, while the rebuilding of humanity's homeworld is ongoing.

CAIN AND ABEL

DEBUT *House of Mystery* (Vol. 1) #175 (Aug. 1968) (Cain); *DC Special* #4 (Jul–Sep. 1969) (Abel)
BASE Cain: House of Mystery; **Abel:** House of Secrets
HEIGHT Cain: 6ft 2in; **Abel:** 5ft 7in
WEIGHT Cain: 174 lbs; **Abel:** 396 lbs
EYES Cain: Brown; **Abel:** Blue
HAIR Cain: Brown; **Abel:** Black
POWERS/ABILITIES Immortality

Cain and Abel are two brothers who dwell in the Dreaming, the realm of Morpheus. They inhabit the House of Mystery and House of Secrets respectively, and tell chilling stories to visitors. While Abel is timorous and soft-hearted, Cain has a cruel streak. Though he loves his brother, Cain often loses his temper and murders Abel in a gruesome fashion. However, Abel always comes back to life, as per the terms of a contract the brothers signed with Morpheus.

When Abel was killed by the Furies of Greek Legend, his brother successfully petitioned Morpheus to resurrect him. They later ran the House of Mystery as a bar where customers paid for drinks by telling macabre stories. When the House of Mystery was destroyed, the brothers rebuilt it, but it soon became the Justice League Dark's HQ.

After *Flashpoint*, the Justice League United encountered Abel when they entered the House of Secrets.

BLOOD BROTHERS
Cain (left) and Abel are brothers bound together by fate, doomed to repeat a cycle of murder and resurrection.

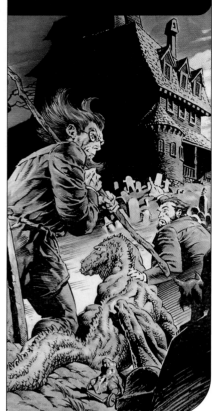

CALENDAR MAN

DEBUT *Detective Comics* (Vol. 1) #259 (Sep. 1958)
REAL NAME Julian Gregory Day
BASE Arkham Island
HEIGHT 5ft 11in
WEIGHT 193 lbs
EYES Black
HAIR Bald
POWERS/ABILITIES Hardened street fighter
ALLIES The Squid, Arkham inmates
ENEMIES Batman, the Riddler

Julian Day was a happily married man with a son, Aiden. When his wife died in a blackout caused by the Riddler, Day went off the rails and began working for a drug dealer called the Squid. When Batman met Aiden, the boy said that his father abused and neglected him. Batman beat up Day, accusing him of forgetting his son's birthday.

Consequently, Day became obsessed with dates. Taking the name Calendar Man, he committed several date-themed crimes and was incarcerated on Arkham Island. He then threatened to cause a blackout across Gotham City unless the man he blamed for ruining his life surrendered to him. Batman coerced the Riddler into helping him infiltrate Arkham, then handed him over to Calendar Man, who exacted his brutal revenge on the villain.

CAIN, DAVID

DEBUT *Batman* #567 (Jul. 1999)
BASE The Nursery, Prague, Czech Republic
EYES Brown   **HAIR** Brown
POWERS/ABILITIES Highly trained killer, skilled in martial arts and swordsmanship.
ALLIES Mother
ENEMIES Cassandra Cain, Bluebird, Red Hood, Red Robin, Dick Grayson, Bruce Wayne
AFFILIATIONS Mother's organization, Lady Shiva Woosan

A skilled and ruthless killer, David Cain worked for "Mother." She kidnapped children and brainwashed them into becoming her obedient agents. As "Orphan," Cain was her assassin, fighting Batman when he hindered her schemes.

Cain also became obsessed with turning a child into a perfect killer. He subjected his own daughter, Cassandra, to a brutal regime, desensitizing her to violence, not letting her speak, and teaching her that sympathy was a weakness. She escaped and fled to Gotham City, adopting the identity of Batgirl. When Cain came to Gotham City to kill the hero Bluebird, Batgirl intervened and cut off his hand. He escaped to Mother's Nursery facility where his hand was replaced by a cybernetic prosthesis. After he died battling Batman, Cassandra adopted his codename Orphan.

CAPTAIN CARROT

DEBUT *New Teen Titans* (Vol. 1) #16 (Feb. 1982)
REAL NAME Rodney Rabbit
BASE House of Heroes satellite, Earth-26
HEIGHT Over 6ft   **EYES** White   **HAIR** White
POWERS/ABILITIES Eating cosmic carrots bestows Rodney with temporary superpowers.
ALLIES Superman
ENEMIES Starro the Conqueror, Frogzilla, Lord Havok, the Gentry
AFFILIATIONS The Zoo Crew, Justice Incarnate, Multiversity

A rabbit from an alternate reality of cartoon animals, Rodney was a mild-mannered cartoonist until he ate a cosmic carrot. As superpowered Captain Carrot, he joined the Zoo Crew.

Over many wacky adventures, they encountered both Superman and Starro the Conqueror. When their world was threatened, the Zoo Crew took its inhabitants to New Earth, where they changed into ordinary animals. Carrot became a stage rabbit, before regaining his powers and helping fight Darkseid during *Final Crisis*. He is Earth-26's member in the pan-Multiversal super-team Justice Incarnate. They battled the Gentry and their Oblivion Machine, and fought the Legion of Doom when Earth's heroes attempted to repair the ruptured Source Wall.

CAPTAIN COMET

DEBUT *Strange Adventures* #9 (Jun. 1951)
REAL NAME Adam Blake
BASE Cairn
HEIGHT 6ft 2in
WEIGHT 190 lbs
HAIR Brown   **EYES** Brown
POWERS/ABILITIES Super-strength, super-speed, telepathy, telekinesis, flight, photographic memory, heightened intelligence.
ALLIES Superman
ENEMIES Doomsday

A comet passing over the Blake family home in Kansas during Adam's birth gave him latent superpowers. These manifested many years later when he learned from Professor Emery Zackro that his body had evolved thousands of years ahead of normal human biology. Adam discovered that his destiny lay in space as one of the first *Neo sapiens*, tasked with finding others who had also evolved ahead of their species' timeline.

While on this quest he battled Superman, whom he mistook for Superdoomsday. Realizing his error, he teamed up with the Man of Steel and Lex Luthor to fight off Mr. Mxyzptlk and an army of alternate Supermen threatening Metropolis. He then disappeared in his spaceship with its crew of Wanderers, their destination unknown. He later turned up as a member of the Crucible Academy.

CARR, SNAPPER

DEBUT *Brave and the Bold* #28 (Feb.–Mar. 1960)
REAL NAME Lucas Carr
BASE Happy Harbor, Justice League Detroit complex
HEIGHT 5ft 10in   **WEIGHT** 175 lbs
HAIR Brown   **EYES** Blue
POWERS/ABILITIES Teleports by snapping his fingers.
ALLIES JLA, Young Justice, Miguel Montez, Summer Pickens
ENEMIES The Joker, Dominators, Khunds

When Simon Carr bankrolled the Justice League of America and outfitted their base, his nephew Lucas lent a hand. As a reward, finger-popping teen, "Snapper," became an honorary Leaguer. Years later, "John Doe" tricked Snapper into revealing the HQ's location. Doe was The Joker, and Snapper quit in shame. He was experimented on by alien Dominators who activated his teleporting metagene. He and others escaped and struck back as the Blasters. One day, the Khunds severed his hands, but Colu's Vril Dox replaced them. Snapper later mentored the android Hourman III, wrote his JLA memoirs, and coached Young Justice. He now runs the Super Hero museum and advised trainee crime fighters Miguel Montez and Summer Pickens after they acquired the incredible Super Hero generating H Dial.

CAPTAIN ATOM

DEBUT *Space Adventures* #33 (Mar. 1960)
REAL NAME Nathaniel Adam
BASE The Continuum, Kansas
HEIGHT 6ft 4in   **WEIGHT** 200 lbs
EYES Silver   **HAIR** Silver
POWERS/ABILITIES Can absorb and distribute energy at will; quantum bolt projection; super-strength, stamina, and endurance; quantum speed; draws on quantum field as an inexhaustible power source.
ALLIES Justice League, Firestorm
ENEMIES Ultramax, Doctor Manhattan
AFFILIATIONS USAF, Continuum research facility

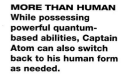

MORE THAN HUMAN
While possessing powerful quantum-based abilities, Captain Atom can also switch back to his human form as needed.

Captain Atom is a hero with the ability to manipulate the quantum field. Although the US military wanted to use him as a living weapon of mass destruction, he has chosen to wield his devastating power for the good of all mankind. However, with almost infinite energy at his command, he must constantly struggle to hold onto his humanity.

CAMERON SCOTT
When Captain Atom returned from the past, his Super Hero form appeared a reddish gold. He adopted the name Cameron Scott as an alias to distance himself from his earlier adventures.

Captain Nathaniel Adam was a USAF fighter pilot, but when his behavior became erratic following his father's death, he was grounded. Nate then found work at the Continuum, a scientific research facility where he participated in an experiment run by renowned quantum physicist Dr. Megala, author of the controversial "M-Theory." Megala believed that there were multiple parallel realities and he wanted Nate to pilot an experimental capsule designed to travel to other dimensions. When the capsule was activated, it imploded in a flash of light, destroying Nate at a subatomic level. Somehow his consciousness survived and created a new body for itself, molecule by molecule. One month after he had disappeared, the being that was once Nate Adam reappeared as a glowing silver form with a red atomic symbol emblazoned on his chest.

Nate discovered that he was now a living nuclear reactor that could also absorb energy and even transmute matter. However, when he used these powers, his own body became unstable. General Wade Eiling approached Nate and told him that he was now a military asset—and a living weapon of mass destruction.

Nate refused to cooperate and chose to serve the world as Captain Atom instead. When Captain Atom grew more unstable and exploded, he sent himself back through time to the past of 1994. He started his life again, now without superpowers, and married a woman named Takara Sato. She became pregnant, but when Nathaniel was shot during a car jacking, Captain Atom was powered up again, and he returned to the present, not knowing his now 17-year-old son.

Since his original explosion had killed three innocent people, Nathaniel followed orders and adopted the new identity of Colonel Cameron Scott, pretending to be the second Captain Atom. As he now possessed a different power set, the ruse worked and he fought the villain Ultramax, earning the interest of the Justice League.

Captain Atom's appearance changed back to its silver shade more recently when he was charged with keeping Super Heroes out of Gotham City after Bane's hostile takeover. Gotham Girl didn't agree with his orders, and despite the Captain's power, she bested him and literally threw him out of town.

ATOM VS. MANHATTAN
Captain Atom is believed to have faced Doctor Manhattan. He was surprised to find that even his power couldn't stop this blue, godlike being.

ON THE RECORD

The pre-*Flashpoint* Nate Adam was a decorated pilot framed for a crime he did not commit. To gain a pardon, Nate participated in an experiment involving an atomic bomb and a crashed alien spacecraft. Seemingly vaporized in the test, he reappeared 18 years later with a skin of alien metal and incredible powers.

Calling himself Captain Atom, Nate was forced to work for the US government. Eventually, he cleared his name and left the Air Force. Nate battled villain Monarch in the 2001 "Armageddon" story arc and time-traveled to foil a plot by Super Hero-hating Maxwell Lord.

THE GOOD SOLDIER
As a military man, Captain Atom followed orders—even if it meant having to arrest the Dark Knight himself!

CLASSIC STORIES

***Armageddon: The Alien Agenda* #1–4 (Nov. 1991-Feb. 1992)** In this time-traveling epic, Captain Atom and his nemesis Monarch fight an alien threat in the prehistoric era, in Imperial Rome, and during World War II.

***Countdown: Arena* #1–4 (Feb. 2008)** Nate Adam becomes the new incarnation of his main adversary, Monarch. He recruits an army to battle the Monitors, but is successfully opposed by a team of alternate Captain Atoms.

***The Fall and Rise of Captain Atom* #1–6 (March-Aug. 2017)** Nathaniel Adam travels to the past, only to be sent back to the future again. He gains a new power set along the way, but tragically loses his wife.

CAPTAIN BOOMERANG

DATA

DEBUT *The Flash* (Vol. 1) #117 (Dec. 1960)
REAL NAME George "Digger" Harkness
BASE Belle Reve Prison
HEIGHT 5ft 9in
WEIGHT 167 lbs
EYES Brown   **HAIR** Brown
POWERS/ABILITIES Expert with throwing weapons; carries a number of boomerangs at all times, including some with special properties such as razor-sharp sides, and others that explode or even allow him to fly.
ALLIES Deadshot, Harley Quinn
ENEMIES The Flash, Amanda Waller
AFFILIATIONS Suicide Squad, the Rogues

CLASSIC STORIES

***The Flash* #117 (Dec. 1960)**
Captain Boomerang debuts and nearly kills The Flash by tying him to a giant boomerang that he catapults into space.

***Identity Crisis* #5 (Dec. 2004)** Captain Boomerang is hired to kill Tim Drake's father—but both men end up dead.

***The Flash* (Vol. 3) #7 (Jan. 2011)** Recently brought back from the dead, Digger escapes jail and recalls his early years as a villain.

OUTBACK BATTLER
As a young child growing up in Australia, Digger made his own boomerangs, and became adept at throwing them.

George "Digger" Harkness is a mercenary and killer with an aptitude for boomerangs and other projectiles. Antagonistic and often annoying to those around him, he has fought The Flash and, since his incarceration, has become a member of Task Force X, aka the Suicide Squad.

Born in Kurrumburra, Australia, George "Digger" Harkness grew up poor. His father was supposedly a US soldier who had abandoned his family when his son was very young. As a child, Digger developed an aptitude for boomerangs and soon became deadly with them. After serving first in the military and then in the Australian Secret Service, he moved to the US where he turned to crime, battling The Flash on many occasions and becoming a longtime member of the Rogues. After Harkness went to prison, Amanda Waller selected him for Task Force X (the Suicide Squad) along with new member Yo-Yo, to replace fallen members Voltaic and Savant. While Harkness claimed to be the new team leader—and was given a detonator to control the explosive devices buried inside his fellow teammates—this was later revealed to be a ruse by Waller. Harkness was captured on a mission against the terrorist group known as Basilisk and seemed to betray the Suicide Squad—until he helped them break free. Waller had asked him to infiltrate Basilisk and get close to its leader, Regulus, to help defeat him.

After many more missions with the Squad, Boomerang was seemingly killed by General Zod. Luckily for Digger, he was brought back to reality by new member Hack. One of his later missions led him back to his small Australian town, where he met a son he wasn't quite aware of, Owen Mercer, who was now an adult and a brilliant arms dealer.

Eventually, Captain Boomerang went on enough Suicide Squad missions to earn his freedom, although he almost immediately broke the terms of his parole by freely talking about the top-secret task force. In reaction, a new Squad captured Boomerang. When Digger's old ally Deadshot was told to kill Harkness, Deadshot rebelled and killed their handler instead. The Suicide Squad escaped and ironically enough, The Flash rescued Boomerang from the authorities and brought him back to Australia. Never one to stay out of trouble, however, Digger opted to return to Central City and rejoin the Rogues.

ON THE RECORD

Capitalizing on his Australian background, Captain Boomerang first came to fame as a toy spokesman before being exposed as a Super-Villain. A longtime member of the infamous Rogues—The Flash's recurring adversaries—Captain Boomerang developed a harder edge after joining the Suicide Squad.

He was later hired to kill Jack Drake, the father of Tim Drake (Robin, at the time), but as he carried out the contract, he too was killed—by his target. Harkness' son, Owen Mercer, went on to become the new Captain Boomerang, while George returned as a Black Lantern during Nekron's attack on Earth and was reborn following Nekron's defeat.

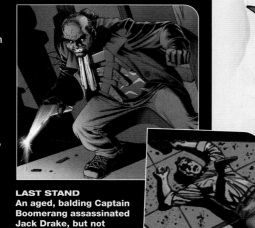

LAST STAND
An aged, balding Captain Boomerang assassinated Jack Drake, but not before he was shot and killed by his victim.

LETHAL WEAPONRY
Digger Harkness has created a number of weaponized and trick boomerangs, which become deadly tools in his hands.

CAPTAIN COLD

DATA

DEBUT *Showcase* #8 (May–Jun. 1957)
REAL NAME Leonard Snart
BASE Central City
HEIGHT 6ft 2in **WEIGHT** 196 lbs **EYES** Blue **HAIR** Brown
POWERS/ABILITIES Excellent tactician; has a cold gun that can create absolute zero, make super-dense blocks of ice, form ice barriers, and other cold-related effects; goggles protect him from the glare caused by using his gun.
ALLIES Lex Luthor, Golden Glider
ENEMIES The Flash, Crime Syndicate
AFFILIATIONS The Rogues, Justice League (formerly), Suicide Squad (formerly), Legion of Zoom

CLASSIC STORIES

***Showcase* #8 (May–Jun. 1957)**
Leonard Snart makes his first appearance as Captain Cold—and comes close to defeating The Flash.

***The Flash: The Fastest Man Alive* #13 (Aug. 2007)** Bart Allen's short-lived era as The Flash ends in tragedy when Captain Cold and the Rogues kill him.

***Final Crisis: Rogues' Revenge* (Sep.–Nov. 2008)** On the run for killing The Flash, Captain Cold and his allies plan revenge against fellow villain Inertia, who they believe used them to kill The Flash.

ICING THE FLASH
Captain Cold is pretty good in a scrap, even without his cold gun.

Leonard Snart is Captain Cold, one of The Flash's main enemies and leader of the Rogues. While Snart has spent most of his life as a criminal, he does have a strict code of honor.

Leonard Snart had a troubled childhood. His father was an alcoholic, and Snart's relationships with his grandfather and his sister, Lisa, were the only good things in his life. Following his father's death, Snart left home and soon turned to petty crime to survive. When working as part of a criminal gang, he was arrested by The Flash and sent to jail. While in jail, Snart created a special cold gun that he hoped would give him the edge in his next confrontation with The Flash.

After he was released, he returned to a life of crime, now as Captain Cold, and soon teamed up with other villains to form the Rogues. After several defeats by The Flash, Cold tried to upgrade the Rogues' powers by using a Genome Recorder, but it backfired, leaving his friends injured and Lisa in a coma. When The Flash's enemy Mob Rule caused a blackout, it threatened Snart's sister's chances of survival. Snart blamed The Flash and attacked the hero. In the end, The Flash not only stopped Captain Cold but used his Speed Force to help Lisa survive. She joined the Rogues as Golden Glider, having gained powers of her own.

The Rogues had their own strict code—one that brought them into conflict with more brutal evildoers, such as Gorilla Grodd and the Crime Syndicate. Captain Cold joined Lex's group of villains to attack the Syndicate, and after the its defeat, found himself hailed a hero. Hired as Lex's bodyguard, Snart helped Lex and the Justice League combat the Amazo virus.

A true criminal at heart, Captain Cold returned to the Rogues and planned the perfect heist against The Flash. However, Heat Wave deviated from the plan, causing The Flash to best them yet again. Despite using a new Black Ice gun, Cold was incarcerated. However, he used his time in Iron Heights Penitentiary to become the new head of Central City's underworld, and he even killed his fellow inmate, Turbine. Later transferred to Belle Reve, Captain Cold served time with the Suicide Squad before Lex Luthor broke him free and upgraded his technology. Cold used his new enhanced cold-based weaponry to conquer Central City and imprison The Flash. However, The Flash teamed up with Golden Glider and other Rogues to knock some sense into Snart. Captain Cold remains at large, plotting his next course of action against The Flash and Central City.

ON THE RECORD

Before the continuity-altering *Flashpoint* event, Captain Cold lost his sister when she was killed by fellow ice-themed villain Chillblaine; Cold then killed Chillblaine in revenge.

Alongside his fellow Rogues, Cold also took the life of Bart Allen's Flash, but expressed remorse at his actions on discovering that this incarnation of The Flash was just a kid.

ICED AGE
The pre-*Flashpoint* Captain Cold, with a fur-trimmed parka-style costume, lacked superpowers, relying instead on his ice guns for his criminal work.

COLD COMFORT
They may be criminals, but Captain Cold and his fellow Rogues follow a strict moral code. They only kill if someone wrongs them or if they have no other option.

CATWOMAN

DATA

DEBUT *Batman* (Vol. 1) #1 **(Spring 1940)**
REAL NAME Selina Kyle
BASE The East End, Gotham City
HEIGHT 5ft 7in   **WEIGHT** 128 lbs
EYES Blue-green   **HAIR** Black
POWERS/ABILITIES Master cat burglar; formidable fighter with expertise in boxing, acrobatics, and many martial arts; weapons include cat-o'-nine tails whip and gloves with diamond-tipped claws; wears protective goggles.
ALLIES Killer Croc, Alice Tesla, Batman (on occasion)
ENEMIES The Joker's Daughter, Bone, Black Mask, Dollhouse
AFFILIATIONS Calabrese Crime Family, Justice League of America, Batman, Inc.

Catwoman is one of the great mysteries of Gotham City. Often switching from hero to villain in a single night, over the years Selina Kyle has been a help to Batman as often as she has been a thorn in his side. A capable leader, an intimidating fighter, and a savvy street-smart cat burglar, Catwoman has gone from being one of Gotham City's many forgotten children to one of its most powerful figures. After a stint as one of Gotham City's major crime bosses, Catwoman has returned to the rooftops once again as an independent creature of the night, answerable to no one except herself.

AT A GLANCE...

Hard-knock life
Selina Kyle was a child of the system. But in a town like Gotham City, that system tended to be as corrupt as its elected officials. Selina grew up in Oliver's Group Home, coached in the ways of thievery by the institution's headmistress, Miss Oliver.

Getting organized
Catwoman became the leader of an organized crime family when she discovered that her father, Rex "the Lion" Calabrese, the former head of Gotham City's Mafia, was alive. He was residing in a cell in Blackgate Penitentiary, forgotten by the rest of Gotham City's criminals.

The Cat and the Bat
Despite often being on opposite sides of the law, Catwoman and Batman have shared a romantic interest in one another for years. While Catwoman isn't aware of Batman's double identity, that hasn't stopped the pair from having many intimate encounters and romantic flings.

CLASSIC STORIES

***Batman* (Vol. 1) #62 (Dec. 1950)**
Catwoman's origin is revealed and tweaked for Earth-2's Catwoman.
***Batman* (Vol. 1) #404–407 (Feb.–May 1987)** In the groundbreaking *Batman: Year One*, Selina Kyle goes from call girl to vigilante after being inspired by the Dark Knight.
***Catwoman* (Vol. 1) #1–4 (Feb.–May 1989)** Catwoman's post-*Crisis* origin is explored in detail, including her training by the hero Wildcat.
***Catwoman: When in Rome* #1–6 (Nov. 2004–Apr. 2005)** Catwoman takes a trip to Italy with the Riddler in a tale emerging out of the powerful "Batman: The Long Halloween" series.

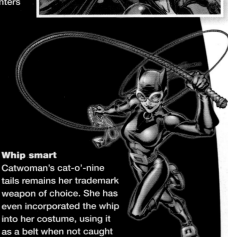

Whip smart
Catwoman's cat-o'-nine tails remains her trademark weapon of choice. She has even incorporated the whip into her costume, using it as a belt when not caught up in a catfight.

Selina Kyle started life at a distinct disadvantage. As a child, she bounced around from foster home to foster home, before finding a more permanent residence at Oliver's Group Home, run by the unscrupulous Miss Oliver. The kids at the home were forced to break into jewelry stores and homes, stealing priceless treasures for the strict Miss Oliver. Learning the ins and outs of thievery at Oliver's, Selina retained a rebellious streak, often hiding expensive items in her teddy bear to invest in her future.

Years later, after leaving Miss Oliver's Home, Selina tried to build a better, legit future for herself and found gainful employment working for the city. She soon began using her access to Gotham City's computer files to research her history. When she dug too deep into her past, however, her boss promptly pushed her off a rooftop for her efforts. Her life was saved when she fell through a handily placed awning and awoke to find several cats attempting to rouse her. The incident spurred her to return to her thieving ways, and Selina fashioned a costume from the very awning that broke her fall, setting a single-minded course for a life of crime and cat burglary as Catwoman.

It wasn't long before she attracted the attention of Batman and, as if to foreshadow the romance they would later share, the date of their auspicious first meeting was Valentine's Day. On that occasion, Batman stopped Catwoman from robbing the Sunnyside Housing Project. The night's events had a huge impact on Selina. She realized that while she couldn't give up her life of crime, she would choose to steal from the rich rather than the less fortunate.

Before long, Catwoman and Batman's rooftop flirtations and verbal and physical sparring would turn into a full-blown romance. While Batman learned about Selina's identity, Catwoman was never able to discover the Dark Knight's real name, despite the intimacy of their relationship. Catwoman's criminal acts, however, constantly caused a rift between the two, and they soon returned to their old status quo, with only the occasional team-up or confrontation.

SIZE MATTERS
Young Selina Kyle realized the benefit of her small size when she was made to commit daring robberies for the head of her group home, Miss Oliver.

IN THE DOLLHOUSE
The daughter of the serial killer known as the Dollmaker, a twisted criminal called Dollhouse put herself in Catwoman's sights when she began kidnapping Gotham City's prostitutes and drug addicts. Afraid for the safety of those who had been taken, Catwoman investigated and discovered that Dollhouse used her victims to make macabre flesh-and-blood mannequins, positioning them like helpless living dolls, while selling their organs on the black market. With the timely help of Batman, Catwoman was able to shut down Dollhouse's sick operation.

ART ATTACK
Selina stumbled on Dollhouse's grisly handiwork, which the villain felt honored her family legacy and was also a form of artistic self-expression. Her victims felt quite differently.

THE GRIP OF GOTHTOPIA

In one his most ingenious "experiments" yet, the Super-Villain Scarecrow, aka Dr. Jonathan Crane, released a potent hallucinogen across Gotham City that made the entire populace believe their corrupt, shadowy metropolis had become a bright, crime-free utopia. In this world, Catwoman became Catbird, Batman's Super Hero partner. However, it wasn't long before the Dark Knight and Catwoman shook off the drug and brought a dramatic end to the Scarecrow's scheme.

"My world is all just shades of gray, Batman. That's why you'll never understand me."

SELINA KYLE

CATBIRD CALLS
In the faux world of Gothtopia, Catwoman became the equivalent of Robin. As Batman's partner and lover, the role was perfect for Selina, who was disappointed when the illusion shattered.

While Catwoman considers herself a solo agent, she was at one point recruited into the government's own team of Super Heroes, the Justice League of America. Chosen for her criminal background, Catwoman was the perfect candidate to help the JLA infiltrate the Secret Society, a group of Super-Villains united under the leadership of the enigmatic Outsider.

When the Justice League of America failed to have the staying power of its inspiration—the Justice League—Catwoman found herself a part of a different type of organization altogether, the Calabrese crime family. After learning that her father—the imprisoned former mob boss Rex "the Lion" Calabrese—was still alive, Selina Kyle decided to take over the family business, believing that if she could control organized crime in Gotham City, she could actually make the city safer in the process. Ultimately, however, she couldn't betray her natural instincts, and soon handed over the crime syndicate's operation to her cousin Antonia, returning to her fulfilling full-time role as Catwoman.

OUT OF UNIFORM
Selina Kyle often proved as great a threat as her costumed alter ego. She mixed easily with Gotham City's elite, while always hiding her own personal agenda.

PICK AND CHOOSE
Never afraid to leap into battle, Catwoman picks her capers very carefully, often lashing out at injustices that affect her friends or her neighborhood.

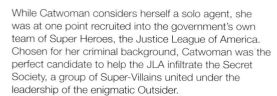

ON THE RECORD

Catwoman has changed considerably since her debut in 1940. Originally simply called the Cat, Selina Kyle adopted a cat mask after her very first encounter with Batman. Since then, her costume and origin have evolved several times over the decades, but her role as Batman's chief femme fatale has remained constant.

Top Cat

In her original incarnation, Selina Kyle, aka Catwoman, was a former flight attendant-turned-thief. After dozens of clashes with the Dark Knight, she turned over a new leaf and became a trusted ally of Batman's. The two even formed a romantic relationship, learning each other's secret identities in the process. After the cosmos-shattering events of *Crisis on Infinite Earths*, Catwoman gained a new backstory. A criminal who drifted into a life of prostitution, Selina Kyle was inspired by Batman to become a creature of the night. But unlike the Dark Knight, Catwoman focused her nighttime exploits on personal gain, becoming the quintessential cat burglar.

I LOVE PURPLE
After the events of *Batman: Year One*, Catwoman sported a gray bodysuit for a time before switching to a variation of her original purple look.

Changing ways

Having grown up in the troubled East End of Gotham City, Selina Kyle had remained very protective of her neighborhood, even as she spent most of her nights thieving from some of Gotham City's more well-heeled areas. After a visit to her old stomping grounds, Selina decided to turn around her career as Catwoman, becoming the East End's protector. She even retired from her life as a vigilante for a time when she had a baby. She briefly handed over the mantle of Catwoman to Holly Robinson, her loyal ally since her days as a prostitute. But Selina couldn't keep her true calling suppressed for long, and eventually returned to her life as Catwoman.

THE SACRIFICE

After having a daughter with her friend Sam Bradley, Jr., Selina realized her lifestyle was too dangerous for a family. However, she was still devastated when she gave up her child, Helena, for adoption.

CATMAN

DEBUT *Detective Comics* #311 (Jan. 1963)
REAL NAME Thomas Blake **BASE** Gotham City; Plains of Africa
HEIGHT 6ft **WEIGHT** 179 lbs **HAIR** Brown **EYES** Green
POWERS/ABILITIES Talented inventor with high-level athletic ability; believed
to have nine lives due to mystical cloth used in his costume.
ENEMIES The Riddler, Batman, Green Arrow, Catwoman, Secret Society
of Super-Villains
AFFILIATIONS Secret Six

Morally ambiguous and bored, Thomas Blake
became Catman to challenge Batman. After years of losing
ludicrous duels with the Dark Knight and rival villain
Catwoman—and despite developing true feline abilities after
adopting a mystic cape of nine lives—Blake accepted his
fate as a C-list super-criminal. He retreated to Africa, living
a life of simplicity within a pride of lions. However, the
outer world soon reclaimed Blake. He refused when the
Secret Society of Super-Villains demanded he join their
ranks, and in retaliation they destroyed his animal
family. Outraged, Catman soon found himself
accidentally leading a team of criminal rebels dubbed
the Secret Six.

In various iterations, Blake and an ever-changing
string of outcasts have bonded together to fight
Super-Villains, demons, and psychotic maniacs. One of
these was the Riddler, who forcibly formed a new team to
satisfy his own perverse curiosity and play mind-games as the
mysterious Mockingbird. Mercenaries for hire, the Secret Six
became a family of antiheroes—doing much good as even as
they did evil acts. When the team broke up, Blake returned to
Africa's lion country, but constant global and Multiversal crises
seem certain to bring him back into action again.

BLACK MAGIC
When Black Alice
was threatened by
dark mystics out to
stop her full powers
emerging, Catman
had to team up
with Etrigan to
protect her.

ON THE RECORD

Previously, Thomas Blake worked
as a big-game hunter, tracking big cats and
selling them to zoos. His cat obsession led
him to a Pacific island, home to a cat cult,
from whom he stole a sacred cat carving
and the cloth that covered it.

Back in Gotham City, Blake became a
costumed criminal equipped with feline-
themed accessories inspired by Catwoman
and Batman, including catarangs and a
turbocharged cat-car. He eventually joined
the Secret Six, before being exiled to
another planet during Salvation Run.

CAT MEETS BAT
Catman, in his original Batman-mimicking
regalia, grapples with the Dark Knight—
the enemy who originally inspired him.

CARSON, CAVE

DEBUT *The Brave and the Bold* #31
(Aug.–Sep. 1960)
REAL NAME Calvin Carson **BASE** Mobile
HEIGHT 5ft 11in **WEIGHT** 178 lbs
HAIR Brown **EYES** Blue (Left), Red/
cybernetic (Right)
POWERS/ABILITIES Intergalactic robot
eye; expert in geology and related sciences.
ALLIES Superman, Star Adam
ENEMIES Eclipso, Borsten Family
AFFILIATIONS Forgotten Heroes

Lab technician Calvin
Carson developed a
digging machine for
E. Borsten &
Co.—the Mighty
Mole. When the US
Government canceled
the project, Carson
stole the vehicle and explored Earth's lower
strata, becoming a leader in crypto-geology.
He married Mazra P'Thrall, princess of
Muldroog, and they had a daughter, Chloe.
When the Government banned his
explorations, Carson joined the Forgotten
Heroes, helping Aquaman, the Sea Devils,
Time Masters, Amanda Waller, the Justice
League and Society of America.

On one deep-earth mission, a
mysterious robotic spider crawled into his
skull and replaced his right eye. Wilful but
generally obedient, it provides Carson with
sensory information, deadly ray blasts and
even cross-dimensional visions and travel.

CATSEYE

DEBUT *Suicide Squad* (Vol.1) #53 (May 1991)
BASE Tokyo
HEIGHT 6ft 1in **WEIGHT** 195 lbs
HAIR Black **EYES** Brown
POWERS/ABILITIES Poison-tipped claws;
enhanced speed and leaping ability.
ALLIES Yakuza, Outsiders
ENEMIES Suicide Squad

A ruthless killer
bioengineered as
a metahuman agent
of the Yakuza crime
family, Catseye's real
name and origin
remain a mystery.
He clashed with
various members of the Suicide Squad
when the covert agency went to Japan
on a mission to recover a stolen cache of
Russian weapons, known as the Dragon's
Hoard. Several other rival groups came
searching for the Dragon's Hoard as well,
including the clandestine Russian Red
Shadows and the Khmer Rouge.

Suicide Squad members Manhunter
and Bronze Tiger were captured by the
Yakuza, but freed by Katana from the
Outsiders, while Catseye fought Atom for
possession of the stolen weapons. Later
Catseye attacked the Squad again, but was
scratched by his own poison-tipped claws
while fighting Bronze Tiger. Catseye met
his end when he was incinerated in an
explosion triggered by Deadshot.

CHAIN LIGHTNING

DEBUT *World's Finest Comics* #272 (Oct. 1981)
REAL NAME Amy
HEIGHT 5ft 4in **WEIGHT** 121 lbs
HAIR Blonde **EYES** Blue
POWERS/ABILITIES Absorption of
electrical energy.
ALLIES Shazam Jr.
ENEMIES Mary Shazam

Amy's metagene
kicked in during her
early teens, but she
was unable to control
it until an unknown
person provided her
with a bodysuit that
housed containment
circuitry. Unfortunately, Amy also began
suffering from dissociative identity disorder.
Her dominant personality is the disturbed
Amy, who tried to commit suicide in New
York but was rescued by Shazam Jr.,
earning her lasting affection.

Her other three identities, however, are
less benign. Amber is destructive; the Inner
Child is a hulking brute; while Id is a small girl
trapped inside the others. Together, they are
known as Chain Lightning, and at different
times Amy's powers appear as four distinct
electrical beings. Shazam's magic lightning
bolt gave all four personalities physical form,
and Shazam Jr. and Mister Scarlet had to
subdue them before Fawcett City was
reduced to rubble. Amy then underwent
treatment at S.T.A.R. Labs.

CHAMELEON BOY

DEBUT *Adventure Comics* #267 (Dec. 1959)
REAL NAME Reep Daggle
BASE 31st century Legion HQ, New Metropolis,
New Earth
HEIGHT 5ft 9in **WEIGHT** 135 lbs
HAIR None **EYES** Yellow
POWERS/ABILITIES Duplication of the
appearance of any object or being.
ALLIES R. J. Brande
AFFILIATIONS Legion of Super-Heroes

Reep Daggle is a
Durlan—a race of
shapeshifters and a
controversial part of
the vast intergalactic
coalition called the
United Planets.
A secretive member
of a secretive species, Reep believes he
was invited to join the Legion because his
father is United Planets President R. J.
Brande and the originator of the entire
youth hero project.

Quietly brilliant in many fields and a
skilled observer of sentients, Reep is eager
to prove his loyalty to the team, sharing
his origins with Brainiac 5 and Saturn Girl.

He is also constantly warning anyone
who will listen that Brande is not to be
trusted. He believes everything she does
is provoked by a deep-seated fear of some
unspecified threat, and that he and his
teammates will ultimately end up being
at the heart of fixing it all.

CHALLENGERS OF THE UNKNOWN

DEBUT *Showcase* #6 (Jan.–Feb. 1957)
BASE Challenger Mountain
MEMBERS/POWERS Prof. Haley: Skin diver and oceanographer; **Red Ryan:** Mountaineer and former circus acrobat; **June Robbins:** Computer and robotics expert; **Rocky Davis:** Wrestling champion and top strategist; **Ace Morgan:** Former test pilot and amateur sorcerer; **Bethany Hopkins:** Soldier, war veteran; **Trina Alvarez:** Healer and herbalist; **Moses Barber:** Software expert and computer hacker; **Krunch:** Reformed criminal, murderer; **Clay Brody:** Former race-car driver; **Marlon Corbett:** Top-notch pilot; **Kenn Kawa:** Software and electronics specialist; **Brenda Ruskin:** Brilliant theoretical physicist.
ENEMIES Barbatos
AFFILIATIONS Blackhawks, Doom Patrol, Justice League, New Challengers

The Challengers of the Unknown began in the 1950s when pilot "Ace" Morgan, wrestler "Rocky" Davis, circus daredevil "Red" Ryan, and diver "Prof." Haley survived an airplane crash on their way to appear on a radio program. Declaring that they were "living on borrowed time," the quartet united as adventurers, confronting uncanny events, mystical incursions, alien invasions, and super-criminals. They later learned that by cheating death, they no longer existed in the Book of Destiny, which led to them becoming its caretakers.

The death-cheaters' team expanded and contracted over the years—most notably admitting pioneering roboticist June Robbins—as cases became ever weirder. Eventually cut adrift from reality, they spent their time alternately countering a reality-altering menace from the Dark Multiverse, and awaiting the next crisis, sleeping in stasis within Challenger mountain. Lost for decades, they explosively returned to battle the invasion of Barbatos and his Dark Knights. Recently the original Challengers learned that a Dark Multiverse version of Prof. had formed a new team. Soldier Bethany Hopkins, healer Trina Alvarez, computer hacker Moses Barber, and professional thug Krunch were duped into helping him recover the scattered power-filled remains of a Dark Multiverse god. Initially violently at odds, old and new Challengers ultimately united and they now remain ready for the next unknown…

INTO THE UNKNOWN
Unreal life had no rewrites or second takes for these Challengers of the Unknown.

CHARYBDIS

DEBUT *Aquaman* (Vol. 5) #1 (Aug. 1994)
BASE Seven Seas
HEIGHT 6ft 4in
WEIGHT 237 lbs
EYES Black
HAIR Black
POWERS/ABILITIES Absorbs talents and powers of others; breathes underwater as Piranha Man.
ENEMIES Aquaman

PIRANHA MAN
Charybdis transformed into Piranha Man when he was left for dead and attacked by piranhas. He was then able to communicate with fish.

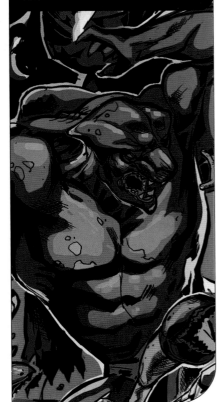

Charybdis and his wife Scylla were terrorists named after two horrific characters from Greek mythology (Charybdis was a deadly whirlpool; Scylla a multiheaded monster). Scylla died when a bomb exploded in her hands, and her death drove Charybdis insane. After this devastating incident, he was seen displaying vast powers and a hatred for Aquaman. Defeating the Atlantean King in battle, Charybdis took his powers and caused the loss of Aquaman's hand, before the villain was shot by Dolphin. Close to death, Charybdis absorbed the essence of the piranhas that had eaten Aquaman's hand, preserving his life and allowing him to evolve into Piranha Man. He aimed to absorb every last shred of Aquaman's powers, leaving him for dead. The Sea King finally got the better of Piranha Man, but not before seeing his loved ones suffer.

Charybdis would later reappear as a member of the group Mera, assembled to hunt Aquaman when he took up arms against his former kingdom of Atlantis.

CHASE, CAMERON

DEBUT *Batman* #550 (Jan. 1998)
BASE New York City
HEIGHT 5ft 5in   **WEIGHT** 129 lbs
EYES Green   **HAIR** Blonde
POWERS/ABILITIES Can dampen superhuman powers; skilled investigator; firearms and unarmed combat training.
ALLIES Manhunter, Supergirl
ENEMIES Justice League
AFFILIATIONS Department of Extranormal Operations, FBI

CUT TO THE CHASE
Agent Cameron Chase has honed multitasking to a razor-fine art.

Cameron Chase has disliked costumed crime fighters since childhood when her father, minor hero Acro-Bat, was killed by Dr. Trap. She works as one of the top agents in the Department of Extranormal Operations, which monitors Earth's metahuman and supernatural beings. Working under Director Bones, she was sent to unmask Batwoman and Batman so they could be controlled though their secrets. Chase followed Bones' orders even when he transformed her hunt for Batwoman into Operation Batfrack, releasing dangerous villains into Gotham City to flush out Batman. She held Gotham under martial law on his orders, but when she learned Bones had gone rogue, she quit the D.E.O. to become a private investigator.

Chase later resumed D.E.O. operations, providing a secret identity, resources, and backstory to Supergirl after her powers misfired. Chase later worked with the FBI, exacting punishing oversight on Superman's actions as he pursued the Invisible Mafia.

CHECKMATE

DEBUT *Action Comics* #598 (Mar. 1988)
BASE Mount Rushmore; the Castle, Swiss Alps
NOTABLE MEMBERS Maxwell Lord, Sarge Steel, Harvey Bullock, Sasha Bordeaux, Count Vertigo
ENEMIES Leviathan, Spyral
AFFILIATIONS A.R.G.U.S., D.E.O., S.H.A.D.E.

Checkmate was an international counterintelligence organization, reportedly created after World War II. Its last iteration was commanded by Maxwell Lord, balancing the needs of world governments while maintaining their independence. Characterizing itself as a "global peace agency," the group was notorious for its questionable methods. Recent operations involved hunting O.M.A.C.—a biotechnologically enhanced version of Project Cadmus scientist Kevin Kho. O.M.A.C. was created by rogue sentient satellite Brother Eye who sought to destroy Cadmus. Checkmate agents—led by Sarge Steel and including Maribel, Little Knipper, and later, Mokkari—failed to capture O.M.A.C., after which Lord sought the assistance of S.H.A.D.E., despite Sarge Steel's objections.

Ultimately Brother Eye attempted to assassinate Lord, but was destroyed in battle at the Mount Rushmore HQ. Lord canceled the hunt for O.M.A.C., deeming it no longer a threat to global interests because it was once again under the control of Kevin Kho's personality. Cold war between the intelligence agencies resumed. Checkmate was totally unprepared for the assault by Leviathan, which eradicated and absorbed many groups such as Kobra, Spyral, A.R.G.U.S., and themselves.

WHITE KNIGHTS?
Sarge Steele, Maribel, and Mokkari were members of Checkmate, with Maxwell Lord as their leader.

PERSONAL TOUCH
Despite his mind-control powers, Maxwell Lord loved getting his boots on the ground and his hands dirty.

ON THE RECORD

Previous versions of Checkmate were organized by Amanda Waller as an independent arm of Task Force X, a quasi-governmental bureau overseeing black-ops missions deemed vital to US interests. Task Force X also controlled the Suicide Squad, foreshadowing Waller's later work assembling the squad when she was in control of A.R.G.U.S.. Maxwell Lord later supplanted Waller and took control of Checkmate, killing the Blue Beetle along the way and then unleashing O.M.A.C.

KOBRA STRIKES
Checkmate's enemies were numerous, but none was more deadly—or persistent—than Kobra and his minions.

CIRCE

DEBUT *Wonder Woman* (Vol. 1) #37 (Sep.–Oct. 1949)
BASE The Island of Aeaea
HEIGHT 5ft 11in **WEIGHT** 135 lbs
EYES Yellow **HAIR** Red
POWERS/ABILITIES Extremely powerful sorceress; able to transform humans into superhumans or animal/human hybrids; teleportation; production of illusions and alteration of physical objects; extremely long-lived.
ALLIES Magog, Ani-Men
ENEMIES Wonder Woman, Superman, Hippolyta

Stories of the nefarious witch Circe date back to the days of ancient civilization and legendary tales such as "The Odyssey." While determining fact from fiction can sometimes be difficult, when it comes to the sorceress' past, it is clear that Circe has had a very longstanding rivalry with Wonder Woman's mother, Hippolyta.

When Hippolyta was a young queen, she accepted Circe's services of enchanting the Amazon's weapons in exchange for male Amazon heirs to serve as human fodder for Circe's army of animal/human hybrids called Ani-Men. When Hippolyta backed out of her deal, making an alternative agreement with the god Hephaestus instead, Circe was enraged and began plotting her revenge. She took it out on Wonder Woman, lashing out at the Amazon by empowering a young man named David Reid with a hatred of Super Heroes. Circe transformed Reid into the powerful Super-Villain Magog and unleashed him on Superman, while she personally attacked Wonder Woman. Neither succeeded in their attempt to take down the heroes.

BEAUTY AND THE BEAST
Circe is not above using her physical charms to get weak-willed men to do her bidding.

ON THE RECORD

Circe originally challenged the Golden Age Wonder Woman, then became a recurring figure in Diana's Rogues Gallery in the early 1980s. Following Circe's reinvention after the events of *Crisis on Infinite Earths*, this modern version of the sorceress fitted perfectly with a Wonder Woman more grounded in Greek mythology than ever before.

Replacing The Cheetah as Wonder Woman's most dangerous foe, Circe even earned a place in the Injustice Gang during the late 1990s reboot of the JLA.

GOADING THE GODS
One of Circe's most ambitious plots was to pit god against god in the miniseries *War of the Gods*. Even with an army of the undead behind her, Circe fell to Wonder Woman and her allies.

CHEETAH, THE

DATA

DEBUT *Wonder Woman* (Vol. 2) #7 **(Aug. 1987)**
REAL NAME Dr. Barbara Ann Minerva
HEIGHT 5ft 9in **WEIGHT** 120 lbs
EYES Brown **HAIR** Red
POWERS/ABILITIES Channeling the spirit of The Cheetah grants
superhuman strength and agility, razor-sharp claws, as well as bloodlust.
ALLIES Circe, Etta Candy
ENEMIES Wonder Woman, Amazons, Veronica Cale
AFFILIATIONS Secret Society of Super-Villains, Menagerie, Suicide Squad,
Godwatch, Legion of Doom

GODWATCH
Barbara Ann was forced
to rejoin the corrupt
Godwatch organization
led by Veronica Cale.
Other members of the
group included Doctor
Cyber and Doctor Poison.

One of the first friends Wonder Woman made when
she left Themyscira's shores, Barbara Ann Minerva
betrayed Diana's trust and became The Cheetah.
Whether with the Suicide Squad, the Secret Society
of Super-Villains, the Menagerie, or the Legion of
Doom, The Cheetah has earned her place as one
of the fiercest Super-Villains in the DC universe.

Barbara Ann Minerva grew up in Oakstone
Abbey, the daughter of Lord Cavendish, a strict man who
did not share Barbara's infatuation with Greek mythology.
However, Barbara excelled at her studies and never lost her
fascination with the ancient Greeks, despite her father
burning her childhood toy sword and shield.

By age 26, Barbara had two PhDs, spoke eight
languages fluently, and could speak another seven nearly as
well. She embarked on a quest to hunt down the Amazons,
believing the ancient group of warrior women to be much
more than merely a myth. When Diana of Themyscira
escorted Steve Trevor to the United States, Minerva was brought in to meet with her as a
resident expert. She soon discovered Diana was a true Amazon, and the two became
close friends. Meanwhile, Minerva continued her archeological pursuits, and began
searching for the god Urzkartaga. But when Minerva found herself transformed into the
villainous Cheetah by Urzkartaga while in a temple in a remote rainforest, Wonder
Woman was unable to rescue her Over the years, The Cheetah became one of Wonder
Woman's most notorious villains. Despite all their clashes, Diana still saw the good in
Barbara Ann, and eventually helped her defeat Urzkartaga, curing The Cheetah in the
process. However, another of Wonder Woman's enemies, Veronica Cale, soon
blackmailed Barbara Ann into reclaiming The Cheetah role. She was injected with
Urzkartaga's DNA and transformed back into a Super-Villain. Her criminal career
escalated as she joined forces with Lex Luthor's Legion of Doom. Given the fabled
God Killer sword by Luthor, The Cheetah killed the goddess Aphrodite and then set her
sights on the goddess Hera in a mad quest to "free" Wonder Woman from any
obligation to her godly patrons. Diana condemned The Cheetah's horrific actions and
defeated her yet again, ensuring their rivalry would continue.

FELINE PHYSIOLOGY
The Cheetah has superhuman
strength, speed, and stamina,
has razor-sharp claws, and
an unquenchable hunger for
human flesh.

ON THE RECORD

Two of The Cheetah's aliases—Priscilla
Rich and Sabrina Ballesteros—mirror the
identities of previous Cheetahs. Priscilla Rich was
a socialite and also the first Cheetah, a Golden
Age adversary of Wonder Woman. Priscilla's
niece Debbi Domaine succeeded her in 1980.

Years after *Crisis on Infinite Earths*, corporate
raider Sebastian Ballesteros was the fourth
Cheetah. He usurped the powers of archaeologist
Barbara Minerva after making a bargain with the
African plant-god Urzkartaga.
Minerva later killed
Ballesteros and reclaimed
the title of The Cheetah.

A HOST FOR HUNTING
Ballesteros convinced Urzkartaga
to abandon its female host and
use him as the conduit for the
ancient powers of The Cheetah.

DEFENDING THE GODS
Wonder Woman was pushed to the limits
of her powers when The Cheetah gained
the God Killer sword and embarked on a
mission to kill Aphrodite and Hera.

CLASSIC STORIES

***Wonder Woman* (Vol. 1) #6
(Fall 1943)** Priscilla Rich suffers from a
split personality that leads her to become
the first The Cheetah out of jealousy toward
Wonder Woman. She joins Villainy Inc.

***Wonder Woman* (Vol. 2) #206
(Sep. 2004)** After being outmaneuvered
by Sebastian Ballesteros and losing her
powers, Barbara Minerva gets her revenge,
killing him and becoming The Cheetah.

***Final Crisis: Resist* #1 (Dec.
2008)** Unaffected by the Anti-Life
Equation, The Cheetah has a brief affair
with Snapper Carr, who helps her join
Checkmate and fight against Darkseid.

CHEMO

DEBUT *Showcase* (Vol. 1) #39 (Jul.–Aug. 1962)
BASE Mobile
HEIGHT Variable: 25ft or far taller
WEIGHT Variable: 5,697 lbs or more
EYES Red **HAIR** None
POWERS/ABILITIES Can spew dangerous, extremely toxic, experimental chemicals from his mouth; enhanced strength and endurance; extremely limited intelligence.
ENEMIES Metal Men, Superman

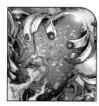

Originally Chemo was a giant plastic waste container used by chemist Dr. Ramsey Norton to store his failed experiments. The chemicals achieved sentience and animation, killed Ramsay, and went on a destructive rampage until stopped by the Metal Men. Never really alive, toxin-spewing Chemo has been "reborn" many times since. Once it even combined with Dr. Will Magnus' AI responsometers (the brain of his robot heroes), evolving into a pitiless killer rather than a randomly reacting monster.

When natural laws were disrupted by Nth Metal from the Dark Multiverse, a new Chemo emerged in a secret Russian base, but was destroyed thanks to the foresightedness of Magnus and the Metal Men. Whether the liberated chemical ooze currently seeping through New York's sewers will reform again is anybody's guess.

CHESHIRE

DEBUT *The New Teen Titans* (Vol. 1) Annual #2 (Dec. 1983)
REAL NAME Jade Nguyen
BASE 'Eth Alth'eban, Mobile
HEIGHT 5ft 9in **WEIGHT** 135 lbs
EYES Black **HAIR** Black
POWERS/ABILITIES Master martial artist and fighter; expert in all poisons.
ENEMIES Justice League, Arsenal, Titans, Batman, Wonder Woman, Green Arrow, the Untitled, Aquaman, the Others
AFFILIATIONS Secret Society of Super-Villains, Ninth Circle

In both the League of Assassins and terrorist organization Mayhem, the mercenary assassin Cheshire earned her reputation as one of the most dangerous people on Earth. She employs bleeding-edge technology, ancient weapons, and poisoned fingernails: a match for Batman, Wonder Woman, and Green Arrow.

Although ruthlessly evil, Cheshire can show a softer side, especially for Roy Harper aka Arsenal. Once she stole Harper's hat, flirting with him before freeing him from imprisonment. Rumors abound of romantic liaisons, and when she attended his funeral after he was murdered in the mental health facility Sanctuary, she was seen to shed a tear—perhaps the only one in her adult life.

CHIEF, THE

DEBUT *My Greatest Adventure* (Vol. 1) #80 (Jun. 1963)
REAL NAME Dr. Niles Caulder
HEIGHT 5ft 10in
WEIGHT 215 lbs
EYES Red
HAIR Blue
POWERS/ABILITIES Genius level intellect; incredibly persuasive; uses experimental sciences.
ALLIES Beast Boy, A.R.G.U.S.
ENEMIES Crime Syndicate, Lex Luthor
AFFILIATIONS The Doom Patrol

A wheelchair-bound mad scientist, Dr. Niles Caulder has a shared past with Dr. Caitlin Fairchild, and even spent time helping her team of runaway metahumans, the Ravagers. But Caulder is also a man of secrets, who successfully hid the truth that his ally was not the true Caitlin Fairchild, but a clone of the original.

Later, Caulder formed his own Super Hero team, known as the Doom Patrol. A metahuman support group, it made heroes out of people on the brink of death. After his original team was wiped out by the Crime Syndicate, he recruited new members, including Robotman, Negative Man, Element Woman, and Elasti-Girl. They later battled with the Justice League over the fate of Power Ring (Jessica Cruz) before disappearing.

CHRONOS

DEBUT *The Atom* (Vol. 1) #3 (Oct.–Nov. 1962)
REAL NAME David Clinton
BASE Ivy Town, Connecticut; Mobile
HEIGHT 5ft 10in **WEIGHT** 175 lbs
EYES Blue **HAIR** Black
POWERS/ABILITIES Time manipulation, time-travel; clock-based weapons and gimmicks, genius IQ.
ENEMIES Atom (Ray Palmer), Atom (Ryan Choi), Justice League of America, Secret Society, Booster Gold, Blue Beetle
AFFILIATIONS Secret Society of Super-Villains, Injustice Gang, Injustice League, Crime Champions, Time Foes

When the Outsider—Alfred Pennyworth of Earth-3—traveled to the dimension of the Justice League, he paved the way for the arrival of his master, Owlman, and his allies, the Crime Syndicate. To that end, he gathered together some of Earth's most dangerous Super-Villains to form the Secret Society. Desiring an HQ that could shift through time and space, the Outsider shackled and drained the energies of the time-traveling villain, Chronos, to fuel the hideout's time leaps.

Little else is known about the modern-day incarnation of Chronos. However, before the reality-altering event *Flashpoint*, Chronos was a recurring thorn in the side of the size-changing Super Hero known as the Atom.

CLOCK KING

DEBUT *World's Finest Comics* #111 (Aug. 1960)
REAL NAME William "Billy" Tockman
BASE Seattle
HEIGHT 6ft 1in **WEIGHT** 235 lbs
HAIR Black **EYES** Brown
ABILITIES Exceptional criminal mind.
ENEMIES Green Arrow, Richard Dragon

Seattle crime boss Billy Tockman used a clock-repair shop called Clock King as cover for his illegal business dealings. When Green Arrow began complicating business for Seattle's gangs, Tockman proposed a truce for them to unite against their common enemy. His criminal counterparts were not keen, and two of them—Jin Fang and Jimmy MacGowan—were soon killed, but not by Green Arrow.

Their real enemy was Richard Dragon. Tockman cut a deal with John Diggle to take down Dragon. In return Green Arrow would ignore Tockman's operations. However, Dragon outfoxed them, forcing Tockman to try to kill Q-Core employees Naomi Singh and Henry Fyff. In the event, Green Arrow's daughter, Emiko, took Tockman down.

Pre-*Flashpoint*, the Clock King was a clock-faced costumed criminal living on borrowed time, who was seemingly killed on a mission with the Suicide Squad.

CLUEMASTER

DEBUT *Detective Comics* #351 (May 1966)
REAL NAME Arthur Brown
BASE Gotham City
HEIGHT 5ft 11in **WEIGHT** 169 lbs
HAIR Blond **EYES** Blue
POWERS/ABILITIES Various weapons and defensive items built into suit.
ENEMIES Batman
AFFILIATIONS Injustice League, Suicide Squad

Celebrity game-show host Arthur Brown lost his job after insulting a contestant. He then turned to crime as the Cluemaster, daring his pursuers to catch him by leaving clues at the scene of every crime. Batman discovered his secret identity, but let him go as Brown was providing for his family. Soon after, Cluemaster proposed to Lincoln March that they unite to bring down the Dark Knight for good. With a huge swath of Gotham City's criminals, they exhausted Batman by executing several attacks at once.

Cluemaster then confronted Batman on top of Beacon Tower. He taunted him, but became enraged when Batman called him a second-rate Riddler who could never have pulled off the operation by himself.

Cluemaster was killed by Lincoln March as he was about to shoot Batman. His ultimate plot was foiled by a more subtle schemer—proving Batman right.

COBALT BLUE

DEBUT *Speed Force* #1 (Nov. 1997)
REAL NAME Malcolm Thawne
HEIGHT 5ft 11in **WEIGHT** 179 lbs
HAIR Blond **EYES** Blue
POWERS/ABILITIES Possesses a gem whose flame can steal The Flash's speed and displays other magical powers.
ENEMIES The Flash
AFFILIATIONS Secret Society of Super-Villains

The identical twin brother of Barry Allen—the second Flash—Malcolm Thawne was stolen and raised by an abusive family of crooks. When he learned of Barry's existence and the loving family he would never know, he used his sorcery to vent his jealousy. As Cobalt Blue, he drew power from a mystic blue flame and a crystalline talisman that focused his anger and could steal Barry's super-speed.

Barry's death during the *Crisis on Infinite Earths* appeared to have cheated Thawne of his revenge, so he traveled through time, trying to exterminate Allen's descendants.

The third Flash, Wally West, finally ended the menace of Cobalt Blue by running at such speeds that Thawne's magical gem overloaded from the excess energy. Thawne was presumably gone, but his talisman—containing his consciousness—would be passed onto Thawne's hate-filled progeny.

COMMANDER STEEL

DEBUT *Justice League of America* Annual #2 (Oct. 1984)
REAL NAME Henry "Hank" Heywood III
BASE Sanctuary
HEIGHT 5ft 11in **WEIGHT** 180 lbs
HAIR Red **EYES** Blue
POWERS/ABILITIES Enhanced steel physique gives him superhuman strength, speed, and durability.
ALLIES Henry Heywood I
ENEMIES Professor Ivo, Despero
AFFILIATIONS Justice League of America, Justice League Detroit

Henry Heywood III took over the legacy of his grandfather—the first Commander Steel—after the old man saved his grandson's ailing body with steel enhancements like his own. The metal gave Heywood superhuman strength, speed, and durability, and he joined the Justice League Detroit. When he was fatally injured fighting one of Doctor Ivo's androids, his body was put on life-support, but it was eventually torn apart during an attack by Despero.

Commander Steel was one of the heroes resurrected with a Black Lantern ring during the *Darkest Night* event, but he was "killed" once more. Somehow alive again, Commander Steel took refuge at the Super Hero facility known as Sanctuary.

CLAYFACE

DATA

DEBUT *Detective Comics* (Vol. 1) #40 (Jun. 1940)
REAL NAME Basil Karlo
BASE Gotham City
HEIGHT Variable   **WEIGHT** Variable   **EYES** Yellow   **HAIR** None
POWERS/ABILITIES Able to shift his claylike form into a variety of
weapons including giant mallets and blades; superhuman strength
that increases in proportion to his size; can become an exact clone of
someone simply by touching them; gifted actor able to mimic a variety
of voices and mannerisms.
ALLIES Poison Ivy, Batwoman, Ragman, The Penguin, Secret Society of
Super-Villains, Orphan
ENEMIES Batman, the Batman Family
AFFILIATIONS The Unknowns, Gotham Knights

MAN WITHOUT A FACE
Clayface's powers eventually caused him to lose his own DNA, becoming those he mimiced right down to the cellular level.

Clayface is one of the most infamous and powerful Super-Villains in Gotham City, a rogue who has proven notoriously hard for Batman to defeat in combat. Able to transform his body into anything from a weapon to a perfect likeness of another human or animal, Clayface can blend into any crowd or choose to tower above it. An actor with delusions of grandeur, Clayface's most prized role is as an arch foe to the Dark Knight.

FEAT OF CLAY
Clayface briefly tried to reform his ways while suffering from amnesia. He joined the short-lived Super Hero team led by Batwoman called the Unknowns.

Basil Karlo was the son of a disgruntled monster make-up artist Vincent Karlo. While the two weren't close, Basil nonetheless felt the need to impress his troubled father. To that end, he became an actor and even started to achieve acclaim, on his way to becoming a true Hollywood star. Basil had just landed the role of his dreams in the film *Second Skin* and was driving when he got a call about his father's death. His reaction was so dramatic that he crashed his car, causing irreparable damage to his face. In a desperate attempt to continue his career, Karlo applied some of the Daggett Chemical product Renu on his face—a substance not meant for contact with human skin. He was able to mold his scarred visage back into the spitting image of his former self, but he knew it would run out before the filming on *Second Skin* wrapped. When Daggett Chemical claimed they didn't make Renu any longer, Karlo traveled to Gotham City and broke into several of their factories until he was caught by Batman.

The Dark Knight tried to get Karlo to testify against the corrupt Daggett, but Karlo instead tried to rob a police evidence locker. In the resulting scuffle, he was accidentally doused in dozens of cans of shattered Renu, altering him forever into the villain Clayface. Seeking revenge against Hollywood and Batman, Clayface became one of the Dark Knight's most powerful enemies. He has attempted to reform from time to time, most notably as a member of the Gotham Knights, but he has since returned to his criminal ways.

ON THE RECORD

In the long history of DC Comics, several villains have taken the name Clayface. The Golden Age Basil Karlo first adopted the villainous identity as a simple masked murderer. In the 1960s, the Clayface name was appropriated by Matt Hagen, who stumbled on a pool of unusual liquid that gave him shapeshifting abilities.

Hagen died during *Crisis on Infinite Earths*, but not before Preston Payne stole his name as a tortured Clayface with a melting touch. The villain Kobra even created his own Clayface in the form of Lady Clay—Preston's future lover and the mother of their son, Cassius, aka Clayface V.

COMPOSITE CLAYFACE
Basil Karlo injected himself with a mix of Hagen, Payne, and Fuller's blood, turning into the modern incarnation of Clayface.

CLASSIC STORIES

Detective Comics (Vol. 1) #298 (Dec. 1961) The second Clayface, Matt Hagen, employs fantastic shapeshifting powers that truly earn him his villainous title.

Batman (Vol. 1) Annual #11 (Nov. 1987) The tragic life of the third Clayface, Preston Payne, is examined in detail, including his "romance" with a lifeless mannequin.

Detective Comics (Vol. 1) #604–607 (Sep.–Nov. 1989) Batman and his ally Looker fight the combined might of the united Clayfaces, with Basil Karlo transforming himself into the Ultimate Clayface.

CONSTANTINE, JOHN

DATA

DEBUT *Swamp Thing* (Vol. 2) #37 (Jun. 1985)
REAL NAME John Constantine
BASE Mobile
HEIGHT 5ft 11in
WEIGHT 158 lbs
HAIR Blond **EYES** Blue
POWERS/ABILITIES Access to powerful mystical artifacts; vast knowledge of magical and arcane rituals.
ALLIES Zatanna, Swamp Thing, Charles "Chas" Chandler
ENEMIES Cult of the Cold Flame, Upside-Down Man, Neron, Nergal
AFFILIATIONS Justice League Dark

UNHOLY SMOKE
Constantine works best behind the scenes, manipulating other people. But, when the occasion calls for it, he can unleash his own formidable powers.

FROM THE SWAMP
John Constantine befriended Swamp Thing years ago and helped the muck monster discover his connection to the Green.

Feared by most, trusted by few, needed by many, John Constantine wields both powerful magic and a devious mind. He is untroubled by social mores and will use anyone to get what he wants. Fortunately for his friends and the millions of people he has saved over the years, he usually wants the right thing. Usually.

A native of Liverpool, England, John Constantine has had many conflicting stories told about his childhood, but all end with the tragic loss of his family. He was drawn into the world of the occult as a young man and spent years traveling Europe to deepen his knowledge before going to New York City. There he clashed with—and learned from—Nick Necro and met the sorceress Zatanna, with whom he had a brief relationship. His romance with Zatanna was broken when a magic ritual resulted in the death of her father, Zatara. While Zatanna blamed John at the time, she didn't realize that this had been a seed planted by her father to later rid the world of the threat of the Otherkind. The pair did not see each other again until John tracked Zatanna down after learning of the Enchantress' separation from her human host, June Moone, and the threat she posed to the world. He was instrumental in bringing together the Justice League Dark team (including Zatanna) to fight the Enchantress, reuniting the villain with her host, despite the team's objections.

As a member of the Justice League Dark, Constantine helped battle an invasion from Earth-3's Crime Syndicate and the threat of the sorceresses known as the Cult of the Cold Flame. He has also been key in stopping many other threats from beyond, including recent plots by the demon Neron. While not officially a current member, Constantine continues to work with the newest incarnation of the Justice League Dark, helping them against the evil Otherkind and their nefarious leader, the Upside-Down Man.

ON THE RECORD

Constantine's cynicism, cigarettes, and trench coat are constants in his history across universes and storylines. However, his path to occult prominence differed in his first incarnations.

After a traumatic childhood and a stint with a touring punk-rock band, John tried magic in an ill-fated ritual that ended with a demon capturing the girl he had intended to help. Shell-shocked, he spent time in a mental institution before embarking on a career as a paranormal investigator. Mistrusted by friends and enemies, he has a solid partnership with the Swamp Thing, who has known him since his earliest days in the paranormal business.

BOYS ON FILM
When a US cable channel wanted to film a documentary on his old band Mucous Membrane, John found himself looking into strange goings-on in Newcastle.

CLASSIC STORIES

Hellblazer #11 (Nov. 1988) The tragic story of the Newcastle Crew—a loose group of young occult investigators who try, and fail, to save the child Astra Logue from the demon Nergal.

Swamp Thing (Vol. 2) #46 (Apr. 1986) Constantine introduces the Swamp Thing to the Parliament of Trees, setting the stage for the Swamp Thing's ascent into the role of Avatar of the Green.

Hellblazer #41–46 (May–Oct. 1991) John's past and bad habits catch up with him all at once as he faces terminal lung cancer and a devil determined to collect his soul.

FIGHT FOR ZATANNA
Nick Necro and John Constantine battled each other. One of them had to be sacrificed if the woman they both loved, Zatanna, was to be saved.

COMEDIAN

DEBUT *Watchmen* (Vol. 1) #1 **(Sep. 1986)**
REAL NAME Edward Blake
BASE New York City
HEIGHT 6ft 2in **WEIGHT** 225 lbs **EYES** Brown **HAIR** Black
POWERS/ABILITIES Highly skilled with weapons, hand-to-hand combat, counterintelligence, sabotage, and survival techniques.
ALLIES None
ENEMIES Moloch, Ozymandias
AFFILIATIONS Crimebusters, the Minutemen

Edward Blake used the alias of the Comedian, although not many people who met him came away laughing. He had leapt at the chance to join the Super Hero team known as the Minutemen, hoping he could use it to his advantage somehow. But his time with the Minutemen ended in disgrace after teammate Hooded Justice caught him assaulting Silk Spectre. However, his public image was still that of a crime-fighting hero, and the US government employed him to boost morale as the personification of American patriotism.

Service in the Pacific during World War II changed Comedian forever. The atrocities he saw hardened his heart and he became ever more ruthless. However, an unlikely reconciliation with the former Silk Spectre resulted in a daughter, Laurie, although she would not know who her real father was until she was an adult. In 1985, Comedian discovered a plot by the former hero Ozymandias to destroy half of New York City. Rather than risk Comedian revealing the truth, Ozymandias threw him out of a window to his death. It is believed that Doctor Manhattan went back in time to transport Comedian mid-fall to another Earth inhabited by heroes and villains, where he pursued Ozymandias. Lex Luthor later sent Comedian back to his former reality—still falling from his apartment building.

SERVICE WITH A SMILE
The Comedian was notorious for finding the humor in even the bleakest situation, and so it was only natural the bright yellow smile badge would catch his eye while he was on a secret mission for one of his former teammates.

COPPERHEAD

DEBUT *The Brave and the Bold* (Vol. 1) #78 (Jun.–Jul. 1968)
BASE Mobile
REAL NAME Unknown
HEIGHT 6ft 2in (human); variable (reptiloid)
WEIGHT 200 lbs (human); variable (reptiloid)
EYES Brown (human); green (reptiloid)
POWERS/ABILITIES Serpentine contortionist; enhanced speed, reflexes, and strength; venomous, fanged bite; near-frictionless movement; prehensile tail; scaling sheer surfaces; crushing prey.
ALLIES Hellgrammite
ENEMIES Batman, Black Canary, Nightwing, Huntress, Batgirl
AFFILIATIONS Snake Gang, Secret Society of Super-Villains, Black Lantern Corps

Career criminal Copperhead utilized a technologically advanced snake-themed costume that mimicked the evolutionary advantages of various reptiles. However, his reputation for infallibility was ruined as soon as he came up against Super Heroes. A ruthless adversary for regular police, he became something of a joke among metacriminals.

On a frustrating downward spiral, Copperhead sold his soul for increased power and was mystically transformed into a snake-human hybrid. Sadly, although the transformation granted him lethal natural powers, it also diminished his intellect. He became a brutish thug, enslaved to the carnivorous appetites of the reptiles he embodied, his body and mind gradually

AMBUSH PREDATOR
For all his reptilian prowess and mystical augmentation, Copperhead was only a real threat when he could take his opponents by surprise.

regressing to those of a savage beast. Still ferociously dangerous, Copperhead became an enforcer and assassin in groups like the Secret Society of Super-Villains. Arrogant and over-confident, he was easily killed by Deathstroke the Terminator during the Crime Syndicate's invasion. Resurrected after Rebirth, Copperhead now works with reptilian criminals in the Snake Gang, but is no match for Batgirl's Birds of Prey team.

COPPERHEAD II

DEBUT *All-Star Batman* (Vol. 2) #5 (Nov. 2016)
REAL NAME Unknown
BASE Central City
EYES Green **HAIR** Blonde
POWERS/ABILITIES Advanced unarmed combat training; expertise with poisons.
ENEMIES The Flash, Batman, Captain Cold, Superman

A former mercenary and assassin, a mystery woman now uses the name Copperhead. She began her rise to the top rank of Super-Villains after she returned to Central City to secure her family's former position as the leading crime gang in the region. When Captain Cold organized his fellow Rogues into an old-fashioned crime-syndicate to rule Central City's underworld, Copperhead used her expertise and mercenary contacts, hiring Super-Villains such as Shrapnel, Black Spider, and the Trigger Twins to even the odds. Their deadly gang war imperiled the entire city and soon involved the city speedster heroes.

Playing a devious game, she called a truce with Cold to remove The Flash and Kid Flash, and seemed to be caught unprepared when the Rogues betrayed her. However, after the dust settled, the Rogues were trapped by The Flashes, and Copperhead walked away, free to continue her efforts. She later attacked *Daily Planet* reporters who were investigating her, and was arrested by Superman and remanded to the Super-Villain penitentiary, Iron Heights.

DEADLY SCHEMER
The mystery woman known as Copperhead caused mayhem in Central City. She is now behind bars, but for how long?

COSMIC BOY

DATA

DEBUT *Adventure Comics* (Vol. 1) #247 (Apr. 1958)
BASE 31st-century New Metropolis
REAL NAME Rokk Krinn
HEIGHT 5ft 7in **WEIGHT** 145 lbs
EYES Brown **HAIR** Black
POWERS/ABILITIES Generation and manipulation of magnetic fields; unwavering dedication and devotion to the concept of the Legion; expert fighter; Legion flight ring.
ALLIES Shadow Lass, Lightning Lad, Saturn Girl
ENEMIES Crav, the General Nah; Mordru
AFFILIATIONS Legion of Super-Heroes

CLASSIC STORIES

***Adventure Comics* (Vol. 1) #247 (Apr. 1958)**
History-loving Cosmic Boy leads his friends back in time to recruit Superboy and play a little joke on the mythic Boy of Steel.

***Legion of Super-Heroes* (Vol. 2) #297 (Mar. 1983)**
After his family are caught in a terrorist nuclear strike, the usually stable, stoic Cosmic Boy goes on a fury-fueled rampage of vengeance.

***Legion of Super-Heroes* (Vol. 3) #62 (Jul. 1989)**
With the Magic Wars devastating the laws of reality, Rokk's younger brother Pol—fresh out of the Legion Academy—sacrifices his life to save the universe.

YOUNG UNION
When Superboy joined the Legion, Cosmic Boy and Shadow Lass had just begun a romance, referred to in 31st-century terms as a "union."

LEGIONNAIRES 3
The original three Legionnaires—Saturn Girl, Cosmic Boy, and Lightning Lad—leapt into action when defending President R.J. Brande from a Horraz attack.

Possessing unparalleled strength and incomparable skill in manipulating magnetic fields and forces, founding Legionnaire Cosmic Boy is the backbone of the Legion of Super-Heroes. Voted team leader by his colleagues, Rokk Krinn is an athlete-turned-hero, never hesitating when it comes to fighting for what is right.

On the planet Braal, only one percent of the population has control over magnetic fields. Luckily for Rokk Krinn, he was not just one of that one percent, but was so good at magnetic manipulation that he became a champion athlete. Due to his achievements and impressive fighting skills, he was nominated by the Braal World Congress to join the Young United Planets.

Rokk met with Garth Ranzz from Winath and Imra Ardeen from Titan aboard a ship belonging to the president of the United Planets, R.J. Brande. As Brande was discussing forming not just a Young United Planets, but something more, the group was attacked by alien Horraz forces. The three young heroes acted quickly and without hesitation, stopping the attack and saving the life of their president.

As a result, Brande petitioned the United Planets to form a Legion of Super-Heroes—a group of young heroes inspired by 21st-century teams like the Justice League and the Teen Titans. While she met with some resistance at first, Brande was ultimately successful, and the Legion set up shop in New Metropolis.

Cosmic Boy was the first elected leader of the Legion of Super-Heroes and remained in that position when the team decided to recruit Superboy (Jon Kent) from the past. Rokk led a team to Rimbor in an attempt to smooth over recent diplomatic issues with that planet's leader, Crav, the General Nah. When the conflict escalated, he imprisoned Crav and helped battle his attacking forces. Despite facing setbacks like losing his position as Legion leader to Ultra Boy, Cosmic Boy continues his service with the 31st-century's premier Super Hero team.

ON THE RECORD

In every continuity, Cosmic Boy had a unique bond with Garth, Imra, and Superboy: a deep connection beyond even Legion camaraderie. When the adult Superman was captured by the Legion of Super-Villains, Rokk led his friends back in time to rescue him.

On a prior occasion, following *Crisis on Infinite Earths*, Rokk learned history had changed, with Superboy now never becoming a Legionnaire. Cosmic Boy and his girlfriend, Night Girl, were catapulted to the End of Time, where their struggle against Time Trapper ended inconclusively; they never realized that they had been allowed to escape.

MAGNETIC INTERFERENCE
Cosmic Boy was always a hero who fought as much with his mind as with his mighty magnetic powers.

FORCE OF NATURE
Rokk Krinn's most potent talent was his ability to attract valiant, idealistic youngsters to the Legion, and to shape them into universe-saving heroes.

COURT OF OWLS

DATA

DEBUT *Batman* (Vol. 2) #1 **(Nov. 2011)**
BASE Originally Gotham City, now global
NOTABLE MEMBERS Benjamin Orchard, John Wycliffe,
Maria Powers, Joseph Powers, Sebastian Clark,
Robin (Damian Wayne), Dick Grayson, Nightwing
ALLIES Army of Talons and fellow secret Owl members
ENEMIES Batman, the Batman Family, Talon (Calvin Rose), Bane,
Mr. Freeze, The Penguin
AFFILIATIONS High society around the globe

CLASSIC STORIES

***Batman* (Vol. 2) #1–10 (Nov. 2011–Sep. 2012)** Batman first discovers the Court of Owls, battles his way through their labyrinth, and learns Lincoln March's connection to both the Court and his past.

***Batman and Robin* (Vol. 2) #23.2 (Nov. 2013)** The Court's past is exposed, from the early days of Gotham City's rundown area, the Narrows in 1862, through the 1970s to the present day.

***Batman* (Vol. 2) #39 (Apr. 2015)** The Dark Knight finds himself returning to the Court's labyrinth in order to attempt to recruit the Owls' help in defeating The Joker.

"Beware the Court of Owls, that watches all the time, ruling Gotham from a shadowed perch, behind granite and lime. They watch you at your hearth, they watch you in your bed, speak not a whispered word of them or they'll send the Talon for your head." That rhyme about the Court of Owls is as old as Gotham City itself, but as Batman has recently discovered, this supposedly urban legend is very real and very dangerous.

COURTING THE YOUTH
The Court of Owls starts its members at a young age, welcoming them to their cause and desensitizing them to the violence inflicted by their Talon servants.

FOWL PLAY
The Court of Owls uses assassins known as Talons to do their bidding. They kill at night, in an unseen fashion and covering up any signs of wrongdoing.

A secret society comprised of only the most elite and corrupt figures, the Court of Owls is a veritable who's who of Gotham City's wealthy sociopaths. The Court believes they own the city and they enforce that idea with an army of assassins called Talons, ready to kill any person who gets in their way.

While the Dark Knight only recently found proof of the Court's existence, there have been tales of their activity as far back as 1862, when they unleashed a Talon called the Gotham Butcher on political targets. Instead of killing his prey, as intended, and disappearing into the night, the Talon made a spectacle of his murders and attracted the attention of the newspapers. In 1891, a photographer tried to expose the Court of Owls' nefarious activities and was hanged for his actions. And in 1914, Court member Benjamin Orchard punished Gotham City's mayor and imprisoned him in the Court's labyrinth that runs beneath the city streets.

Batman discovered that same labyrinth while investigating the Court of Owls. He was forced to run a gauntlet and fight off a powerful Talon determined to break him. Batman soon deduced that his associate Lincoln March was actually a member of the Court's ranks and was attempting to make off with its fortune by betraying them. While the Dark Knight successfully defeated crazed March—who insisted he was Bruce Wayne's brother—it was too late to prevent the villain from poisoning a roomful of the Court's most valuable members. March would later wheedle his way back into the Court of Owl's good graces when he recruited Dick Grayson into their clandestine organization. However, Dick was secretly attempting to dismantle the court from the inside and he succeeded in shutting down a section of the international Parliament of Owls.

Despite the work of Batman and his allies, the Owls still thrive in Gotham City and beyond. They were even able to successfully brainwash Grayson for a time, using his recent head injury to convince him that he really was a loyal Talon.

BROTHERLY HATE?
Batman and Lincoln March battled over the rooftops of Gotham City when March tried to convince Bruce Wayne that he was Thomas Wayne, Jr., his brother.

OWL-WOL
Calvin Rose was intended to be a Talon, but he rebelled and Bane brutally showed him the error of his ways. Rose eventually secured his freedom and joined Batman, Inc.

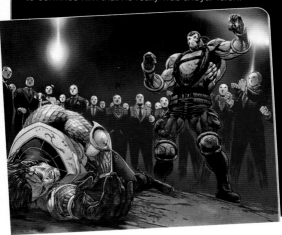

COUNT VERTIGO

DEBUT *World's Finest Comics* (Vol. 1) #251 (Jun.-Jul. 1978)
REAL NAME Werner Zytle **BASE** Vlatava
HEIGHT 5ft 11in **WEIGHT** 189 lbs
EYES Blue **HAIR** Blond
POWERS/ABILITIES Causes disruption of equilibrium;
jams technology; wears gravity boots for powered flight.
ALLIES The Rogues
ENEMIES Justice League, Green Arrow, Arsenal, Shado,
Black Canary, Leviathan
AFFILIATIONS Legion of Doom, Checkmate

Werner Zytle is heir to the throne of Balkan nation
Vlatava, an ancient monarchy that ended when the Soviet Union
annexed the country after World War II. Reared as an aristocrat
in exile, Zytle grew up angry, aggrieved, and vengefully violent.
As Count Vertigo he can emit a pulse to disorient and destabilize
opponents thanks to an electronic device implanted in his brain.
The implant also acts like an electromagnetic pulse on any
technology within range, disrupting and overwriting data functions.

Vertigo began as a costumed criminal, battling Green Arrow and
Speedy (Roy Harper) in Seattle. When the archer's sidekick succumbed to substance
abuse, the Count's drug, Vertigo, became another means of getting high. Zytle used his
drug on Speedy until Green Arrow intervened, allowing Harper to begin his recovery.

Although unsubstantiated reports abound of the Count working for Amanda
Waller's Suicide Squad and for one of the many iterations of espionage agency
Checkmate, the latest verified instance of Count Vertigo comes from his recent
escape from Mount Rainer Correctional Facility. With his powers exponentially
increased due to Dark Matter incursions from the Dark Multiverse, Zytle began
reordering reality and escaped to take vengeance on Roy Harper. On
learning his obsession was already dead, Vertigo was easily
recaptured by Green Arrow and Black Canary.

DIZZY WITH POWER
Werner Zytle believed
that his ability to twist
perceptions and
mangle minds put him
beyond the reach of
common heroes.

POWER POLITICS
Count Vertigo understood how to use power,
choosing allies for their immediate usefulness
rather than any long-term potential.

CREATURE COMMANDOS

DEBUT *Weird War Tales* (Vol. 1) #93 (Nov. 1980)
BASE The Ant Farm
NOTABLE MEMBERS Frankenstein; Lady Frankenstein;
the Mermaid (Dr. Nina Mazursky); the Werewolf (Warren
Griffith); the Vampire (Vincent Velcoro); G.I. Robot;
G.I. Zombie; the Mummy (Khalis); Bogman; Dr. Medusa
ALLIES S.H.A.D.E., Father Time, Ray Palmer
ENEMIES Random monsters

Hidden in a flying, mobile, three-inch indestructible globe
is the headquarters of S.H.A.D.E.—the Super Human Advanced
Defense Executive. Reached via a hybrid of teleportation and shrink
technology designed by the S.H.A.D.E. science liaison, Ray Palmer, the
sphere serves as the base of operations for some of the most bizarre
metahuman heroes on the planet—the Creature Commandos.

Led by Agent Frankenstein—the monster famed for being
fictionalized in the pages of Mary Shelley's celebrated Gothic
tale—the Creature Commandos take their ultimate orders from Father
Time, S.H.A.D.E.'s head of operations. While Father Time currently
resembles a young girl, the natural-born leader has taken many bodies
over the course of his long life.

The Commandos are officially called Division M and are mostly the
results of S.H.A.D.E.'s science division experiments, except for the
Mummy, who is reportedly thousands of years old and was simply
discovered by S.H.A.D.E. Frankenstein joined the team when
his ex-wife went missing while investigating a monster attack.
This led S.H.A.D.E. to travel to the so-called Monster Planet on
a successful mission that warmed Frankenstein to the prospect
of working with a field team. They have since become the first
line of defense against things that go bump in the night.

CREATURES ON THE LOOSE
Superman met the Creature Commandos when
touring the restored city of Kandor in the
Arctic. Kidnapped by Brainiac, this team had
served in World War II and included G.I. Robot.

CRIME SYNDICATE

DATA

DEBUT *Justice League of America* #29 (Aug. 1964)
MEMBERS (EARTH SUPER HERO COUNTERPART)
CURRENT INCARNATION:
ULTRAMAN (Superman); SUPERWOMAN (Wonder Woman) OWLMAN
(Batman); POWER RING (Green Lantern); JOHNNY QUICK (The Flash);
DEATHSTORM (Firestorm)
FORMER MEMBERS:
ATOMICA (Atom); SEA KING (Aquaman); GRID (Cyborg)
ALLIES Secret Society of Super-Villains, Perpetua
ENEMIES Justice Leagues, Injustice League, Alexander Luthor,
Teen Titans, Doom Patrol

PERPETUAL RULE
Perpetua transformed the citizens of Earth-3 into apex predators, forcing the Crime Syndicate to rule a world of monsters.

CLASSIC STORIES

***Justice League of America*
#29–30 (Aug.-Sep. 1964)** The Crime Syndicate look for a new challenge—and bite off more than they can chew when the villains take on both the Justice League and the Justice Society of America.

***JLA* (Vol. 1) #107–114 (Dec. 2004 –Jul. 2005)** The Anti-matter Universe version of the Crime Syndicate invades Earth, and brings with it the dire attentions of the alien Qwardians.

***JLA* (Vol. 2) #50–53 (Dec. 2010 –Mar. 2011)** The Syndicate reluctantly teams up with the Justice League to battle the Omega Man, before Owlman betrays the Justice League. Batman, anticipating this, executes a plan to resurrect Lex Luthor.

The tyrannical Earth-3 version of the Justice League, the Crime Syndicate of America, saw Earth-0 as a new frontier to conquer after the Anti-Monitor's devastating attack on the Syndicate's home planet. But first the team needed to defeat its Earth-0 counterparts, who received help from unexpected quarters...

NEW ARRIVALS
As several members of the Crime Syndicate arrived in the Justice League Watchtower on Earth-0, Sea King seemed not to have survived the trip from Earth-3.

The Crime Syndicate came together as the brutal overlords of Earth-3, a world where ideas of right and wrong were completely abandoned and only strength mattered. An attack by a mysterious entity (later revealed as the Anti-Monitor) laid waste to much of the planet, causing the Crime Syndicate to look for a new world to dominate. Its members set their sights on Earth-0, invading after two members—Atomica and The Outsider—laid the groundwork by gathering the Secret Society of Super-Villains and plotting with them to weaken the Justice League.

The Outsider had obtained Pandora's Box and used it to open a portal between the two Earths, sparking a brief reign of terror during which the Syndicate's members killed a number of Earth-0's heroes. Power Ring, The Outsider, Atomica, and Johnny Quick were killed in a fight against the combined forces of all three Justice Leagues and several defecting members of the Secret Society. In the aftermath, the rest of the Syndicate either died or went their separate ways.

However, as Earth-0 shifts and evolves, so do the other worlds of the Multiverse. Earth-3 was recently revealed to be an active world, still under the thumb of the main five Crime Syndicate members: Ultraman, Superwoman, Owlman, Power Ring, and Johnny Quick. Called into service by the mother of the Multiverse, Perpetua, this Crime Syndicate was tasked with ruling an Earth-3 citizenry of Perpetua's evolved apex predators. When Johnny Quick protested, he was effortlessly killed by Perpetua, forcing the rest of the Super-Villains to fall in line in her service.

ON THE RECORD

The Crime Syndicate has plagued the Justice League and Justice Society for decades, ever since the 1960s. The original Earth-3 was wiped out during 1985's *Crisis on Infinite Earths*, but has since reemerged thanks to the rebirth of the Multiverse.

SURPRISE ATTACK!
The classic Crime Syndicate lineup launched an offensive on an unprepared Justice League, who were expecting a visit from the JSA.

DEADLY DOPPELGÄNGERS
Crime Syndicate members:
1 Ultraman
2 Superwoman
3 Deathstorm
4 Power Ring
5 Grid
6 Owlman
7 Johnny Quick
8 Atomica

ON THE RECORD

After *Flashpoint* the Creeper was re-imagined as a mystical creature called the Oni Demon who came through a "crack in the world" into 16th-century Japan. Assuming the form of a boy named Jakku, it caused years of mayhem before being trapped by a samurai inside the mystical Soultaker sword. Centuries passed and the sword fell into the possession of the hero Katana. While she battled Killer Croc, the sword shattered, freeing its prisoners, including the Creeper, who then possessed and reanimated the recently killed corpse of talk-show host Jack Ryder.

WHO'S LAUGHING NOW?
The Creeper has always combined a valiant heart with the barely restrained chaos of a rampaging maniac to defeat his foes and protect the innocent.

CREEPER

DEBUT *Showcase* (Vol. 1) #73 (Mar.–Apr. 1968)
REAL NAME Jack Ryder
HEIGHT 6ft **WEIGHT** 194 lbs
EYES Green **HAIR** Red
POWERS/ABILITIES Superhuman strength, endurance, agility, and healing; able to leap far distances; can transform into costume by activating a subspace trigger.
ALLIES Batman, Justice League
ENEMIES Proteus, Hellgrammite, Eclipso

The original version of the Creeper
debuted in the late 1960s when TV journalist Jack Ryder investigated the abduction of scientist Professor Yatz. Ryder was captured at a masquerade party while disguised as a monster in a yellow bodystocking, green trunks, and red, boa-like fur. The dying Yatz concealed his discoveries—a bio-enhancement formula and trans-dimensional storage device—within Ryder's body, accidentally granting him superhuman abilities and the ability to transform from human form into an apparently demonic terror.

Obsessed with justice, Ryder waged war on crime, pretending to be a supernatural beast at odds with law and order. His secret crusade brought him into contact with many more conventional heroes such as Batman and the Justice League. The Creeper's campaign against evil was boosted by his insane battle-style and a manic laugh that instilled fear into criminals'—and even other heroes'—hearts.

The Creeper's backstory has frequently altered after reality-changing events. Changes include Ryder actually suffering bipolar disorder, succumbing to narcotics-induced madness and paranoia, and even becoming the Creeper because of The Joker's venom.

CRIMSON AVENGER

DEBUT *Detective Comics* (Vol. 1) #20 (Oct. 1938) (male Lee Travis)
REAL NAME Lee Travis
BASE New York City, Earth-2
HEIGHT 5ft 7in
WEIGHT 135 lbs
HAIR Black
EYES Brown
ABILITIES Skilled investigative journalist.
ALLIES James Wing

MANY CRIMSON FACES
Jill Carlyle (1), the male Lee Travis (2), and a female reporter of the same name (3) are all linked to the Crimson Avenger.

The first Crimson Avenger was Lee Travis, publisher of the daily *Globe-Leader*. In his costumed guise, he was DC's first masked Super Hero and was ably assisted by his valet, Wing. They joined the Seven Soldiers of Victory, and the Nebula Man sent Travis forward in time, where he learned how he died. Travis' twin Colt pistols later found their way to a young African-American lawyer called Jill Carlyle in Detroit. She discovered that the guns were cursed and they transformed her into a spirit of vengeance known as the Crimson Avenger.

Post-*Flashpoint*, another Lee Travis worked as a reporter for Earth-2's Global Broadcasting Corporation. She was present at the debut of the new Wonders of the World when they battled the life-draining Solomon Grundy. She later witnessed, alongside photographer James Wing, the apparent death of Alan Scott (Green Lantern) at the hands of Steppenwolf and his Hunger Dogs—perhaps hinting that a new Crimson Avenger may appear.

CRUSH

DEBUT *Teen Titans Special* (Vol. 1) #1 (Aug. 2018)
REAL NAME Xiomara Rojas
BASE New York City, New York
HEIGHT Unknown **WEIGHT** Unknown
HAIR Black **EYES** Red
ABILITIES Super-strength, stamina, and durability; accelerated healing; sentient chain weapon.
ALLIES Obelus, Djinn, Roundhouse
ENEMIES Lobo, the Other, Deathstroke
AFFILIATIONS Teen Titans

SINS OF THE FATHER
Crush's discovery that the ultraviolent villain Lobo was her father brought her no happiness—he tried to kill her!

Xiomara Rojas came to Earth as a baby with nothing but a chain that was actively protecting her. Taken in by loving but chaotic parents, Xiomara believed she was the daughter of Super Heroes until, as a teen she saw the alien villain Lobo on television. Her resemblance to him told her the truth—that she was his daughter.

She left home in anger, but when she returned, she found her adoptive parents dead and her sentient chain, named Obelus, missing. Xiomara went on the run, calling herself Crush, eventually joining the Teen Titans. She was later reunited with Obelus, and her father Lobo, who tried to kill her. Besting him with the help of her teammates, Crush realized that the Teen Titans were her family now.

CRUZ, JESSICA

DEBUT *Green Lantern* (Vol. 5) #20 (Jul. 2013)
REAL NAME Jessica Cruz **BASE** Portland, Oregon
HEIGHT 5ft 9in **WEIGHT** 141 lbs **EYES** Brown **HAIR** Brown
POWERS/ABILITIES Green Lantern ring gives her the ability to create light constructs and force-fields, fly, and travel through space.
ALLIES Green Lantern (Simon Baz), Starfire, Cyborg, Azrael
ENEMIES Darkseid
AFFILIATIONS Green Lantern Corps, Justice League

Jessica Cruz had been living in fear since being the only survivor of an attack on her group of friends. This crippling anxiety led her to be chosen as the unwilling host of the Ring of Volthoom. However, with help from Batman and Green Lantern Hal Jordan, Jessica was able to draw on hidden reserves of courage. When she apparently sacrificed herself saving The Flash (Barry Allen), Volthoom's hold on her was destroyed, and she was chosen as a Green Lantern. She and Simon Baz were assigned to protect Earth's space sector, though Jessica still struggled with doubts over her worthiness to be a hero.

Later, Jessica teamed up with Cyborg, Starfire, and Azrael to discover the mysteries of the Ghost Sector, but in the process she was killed by Darkseid's Omega Beams, her Green Lantern Ring crushed into fragments in her body. However, the combination of the Omega energy and the Power Ring caused Jessica to return to life, and was imbued with the power to fly and fire Omega Beams like Darkseid. When Darkseid tried to manipulate time to restore his homeworld of Apokolips and enslave the universe, Jessica and her allies teamed up with a time-displaced version of herself to try and stop him.

WIELDING DARK POWER
Jessica Cruz did not choose metahuman abilities, rather they chose her—first via the evil Ring of Volthoom and then a Green Lantern ring. She learned to master her fears to become a hero of great courage.

CRUX

DEBUT *Red Hood and the Outlaws* (Vol. 1) #1 (Nov. 2011)
REAL NAME Simon Amal
HEIGHT 7ft 7in **WEIGHT** 380 lbs
HAIR None **EYES** Yellow
POWERS/ABILITIES Flight; enhanced strength and durability; xenobiology expertise.
ALLIES Arsenal, Red Hood
ENEMIES Tamaraneans
AFFILIATIONS Outlaws

HOLDING A GRUDGE
Simon Amal's scientific genius enabled him to take on the form of a terrifying winged monster to fulfill his vendetta against Tamaranean aliens.

Simon Amal's parents, both researchers in extraterrestrial life, were killed when a Tamaranean spacecraft crashed into them. Driven to seek revenge against all aliens—but Tamaraneans in particular—he continued his parents' research and devised a way to splice alien DNA into his own genome. This gave him the ability to transform into a large, winged reptilian form.

When Simon saw a picture of Starfire, he recognized her as a Tamaranean and hatched a plot to kill her in his new guise as Crux. Attacking her in Colorado using remnant Tamaranean technology, he found himself facing Jason Todd and Roy Harper. He was overpowered and Jason Todd left him at Arkham Asylum.

Later, with Starfire missing, Todd asked Crux to help find her. A penitent Crux agreed to join Arsenal and Red Hood in the search.

CUPID

DEBUT *Green Arrow and Black Canary* #15 (Feb. 2009)
REAL NAME Carrie Cutter
HEIGHT 5ft 8in
WEIGHT 130 lbs
HAIR Red **EYES** Blue
POWERS/ABILITIES Special ops training; enhanced senses; expert archer and marksman.
ALLIES John King
ENEMIES Green Arrow

DESPERATELY SEEKING...
Cupid's passionate obsession with Green Arrow Oliver Queen threatened to destroy her and anyone else who stood in her way.

Special ops soldier Carrie Cutter was so deeply disturbed by what happened on one of her missions that she chose to undergo experimental treatment with the organization C.O.B.A.L.T. She gained enhanced physical and sensory abilities, but at the cost of her emotional stability.

When Oliver Queen (Green Arrow) killed her husband in a case of mistaken identity, Carrie fell obsessively in love with him and became Cupid. With no moral compass, she viewed winning Green Arrow as the only worthwhile goal in her life, and would kill anyone—in particular Black Canary—to make it happen.

Cupid murdered many of Queen's enemies and then disappeared. She later emerged in Seattle, where Green Arrow's nemesis, John King, brought together a villainous gang to eliminate Oliver.

CYBORG

DATA

DEBUT *DC Comics Presents* (Vol. 1) #26 **(Oct. 1980)**
BASE Detroit **REAL NAME** Victor Stone
HEIGHT 6ft 5in **WEIGHT** 385 lbs **EYES** Brown **HAIR** Black
POWERS/ABILITIES Genius-level IQ; implants give him massively enhanced strength; armored chassis and promethium-impregnated flesh provide superb damage resistance; sensors and onboard processors intercept signals and hack systems remotely; can create Boom Tubes for transport; can fly using boot jets; arms can be reconfigured into energy or projectile weapons.
ALLIES Superman, Batman, Green Lantern, The Flash, Wonder Woman, Green Lantern (Jessica Cruz), Azrael, Starfire
ENEMIES Darkseid, Crime Syndicate, Grid, Malware, Anomaly
AFFILIATIONS Justice League, Justice League Odyssey

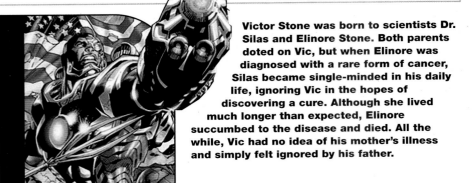

Victor Stone was born to scientists Dr. Silas and Elinore Stone. Both parents doted on Vic, but when Elinore was diagnosed with a rare form of cancer, Silas became single-minded in his daily life, ignoring Vic in the hopes of discovering a cure. Although she lived much longer than expected, Elinore succumbed to the disease and died. All the while, Vic had no idea of his mother's illness and simply felt ignored by his father.

AT A GLANCE...

Man vs. machine
The cybernetic enhancements implanted by his father saved Vic's life, but the experience proved traumatic. The young hero fears losing his humanity and becoming a machine that merely thinks it is human. As host to several advanced AI systems, he is also vulnerable to hacking—as became clear when his robotic parts were hijacked by Grid during the Crime Syndicate's attack on the Justice League.

Weapons systems
In addition to his other hi-tech capabilities, Cyborg can reconfigure himself to create powerful arm cannons to suit a particular combat mode. In his first clash he deployed a sonic white-noise cannon to obliterate a Parademon; other variations include the twin-Gatling gun setup he used to fight the Spore creatures.

Vic Stone found the attention he craved as a high school football star who wanted to play professionally, but this brought him into conflict with his father, who insisted that his son become an academic. Vic went to S.T.A.R. Labs to confront his father, who was working on reverse-engineering a "Mother Box"—a sentient extraterrestrial computer.

Vic and Silas quarreled. Then the Mother Box pinged, generating a Boom Tube portal, out of which shot a blast of red energy that struck Vic's body. His father dragged him into the lab's Red Room, which contained experimental technology. He replaced the damaged parts of Vic's body with cybernetic systems and promethium skin grafts, incorporating the Mother Box's energies into Vic's new form. When a Parademon from Apokolips broke into the Red Room, Vic's arm automatically reconfigured into a white-noise cannon that vaporized his foe.

The Parademon attack on S.T.A.R. Labs was not an isolated incident: Boom Tubes were opening all over the world, disgorging Parademons. Vic learned that his cybernetic system could pick up communications from the aliens' Mother Boxes and even generate its own Boom Tubes. His Mother Box then transported him to Metropolis, where the world's Super Heroes had gathered to face Darkseid himself. In an epic battle, Cyborg generated a Boom Tube that carried Darkseid back to Apokolips and ended the invasion. In the aftermath of the attack, Superman, Green Lantern, Wonder Woman, Aquaman, and the Flash decided to create a team to defend Earth, and Cyborg joined their ranks as a founding member of the Justice League. Over the years, Cyborg has stayed with the team, fighting a number of Super-Villains and powerful foes.

When the evil Crime Syndicate attacked the Justice League, Vic's cybernetic systems were taken over by an artificial intelligence that created a malign, separate entity called Grid. Vic was fitted with a new body that took down Grid, and the Crime Syndicate was ultimately defeated.

INTERFACED
As alien energy devoured Vic Stone's body, his quick-thinking father Silas implanted and activated advanced cybernetics, which saved his son's life.

CLASSIC STORIES

***The New Teen Titans* (Vol. 1) #1 (Nov. 1980)** Cyborg joins the Teen Titans on their first mission. They save the United Nations from invading aliens.
***DC Special: Cyborg* #1–6 (Jul.–Dec. 2008)** Vic Stone is forced to battle a cybernetically enhanced former friend and a version of himself from an alternate future.
***Teen Titans Spotlight* #13 (Aug. 1987)** Scarred villain Two-Face resents how Victor has managed to become a hero despite being maimed and he plots to destroy Cyborg's hard-won reputation.
***JLA/Titans* #1–3 (Dec. 1998–Feb. 1999)**
When Vic returns from deep space as part of a Technis construct that absorbs the moon, the Titans embark on a mission to restore their friend's humanity.

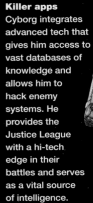

Killer apps
Cyborg integrates advanced tech that gives him access to vast databases of knowledge and allows him to hack enemy systems. He provides the Justice League with a hi-tech edge in their battles and serves as a vital source of intelligence.

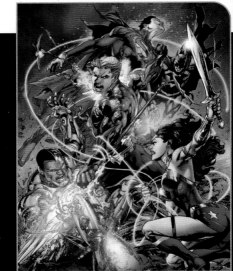

THRONE OF ATLANTIS
When sub-aquatic warlord Ocean Master flooded Gotham City and led the forces of Atlantis against the surface world, the Justice League responded—but most were captured and imprisoned beneath the sea. Proving his heroism and leadership ability, Cyborg replaced his remaining lung with a module for underwater operations, recruited new Justice League members, and went to rescue his teammates.

TERROR FROM THE DEEP
Cyborg led the rescue mission after Aquaman's evil half-brother, Ocean Master, had captured several Justice League members.

DARK CYBORG

Corrupted and forced to work as Darkseid's minion toward the eventual goal of conquering the Multiverse, Vic Stone's heroic nature showed through. He was able to send messages to Green Lantern Jessica Cruz and he helped thwart Darkseid's plans by sending false information to the evil New God's attacking hordes.

"If I could unplug, I would, but unlike you I can't take my costume off..."

CYBORG

In his solo career, Vic fought off an invasion by the alien Techsapiens, as well as other cybernetic threats like Malware and Anomaly. He and his father began working together at S.T.A.R. Labs Detroit and they tried to fix their strained relationship. But while on an outer-space mission with the Justice League, Victor learned of the Ghost Sector—a section of space populated by planets once miniaturized and now held on the planet Colu. Feeling compelled to travel there, Vic set out in a repurposed Braniac spaceship, alongside allies Starfire and Azrael, and was soon joined by Green Lantern Jessica Cruz.

This informal Justice League Odyssey soon encountered a bizarre prophecy and the machinations of Darkseid. He was trying to use technology from Epoch, the Lord of Time, to rewrite the entire Multiverse in the image of his recently destroyed homeworld, Apokolips. While Darkseid succeeded in restoring Apokolips and even took control of Cyborg for a time as his mind-controlled servant, the heroes made use of the time-travel tech for their own purposes and stopped the evil New God from completing his plot.

DISASSEMBLED
When the Crime Syndicate launched its attack on Earth, Vic Stone's systems were hijacked by an AI calling itself Grid.

CYBERNETIC CHAMPION
Cyborg gets his power from hi-tech upgrades, but it is his human heart and courage that make him a hero.

ON THE RECORD

The pre-*Flashpoint* incarnation of Vic Stone was a star football player and an all-around athlete. After he was mortally injured in a laboratory experiment gone wrong, his father turned him into a cyborg to save his life. This was the first of several transformations the young hero would undergo in his career.

Technis transformation
Vic joined the Teen Titans but was seriously damaged when Jericho, son of Deathstroke, betrayed the team. He was rebuilt by Soviet scientists, but had seemingly lost his memories. An alien cybernetic hive mind called the Technis restored him, absorbing him and assimilating his humanity into their sterile AI collective. Vic was then taken to the Technis' homeworld and transformed into a being called Cyberion.

Reintegration
Vic/Cyberion returned to the solar system as a herald of the Technis and transformed the moon into a Technis construct. The Justice League of America perceived Cyberion as a threat to be eliminated, but the Titans were determined to save their friend. The two sides clashed, but in the end the young heroes were able to build a rapport with Vic and channel his life energy into an artificial body, restoring his humanity.

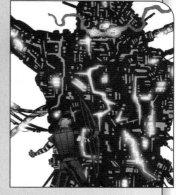

MACHINE CIVILIZATION
The artificial intelligences of the Technis collective chose to absorb Cyborg in order to learn about humanity.

Team player
When a new Teen Titans team was formed, Vic served as advisor and elder statesman. However, he left Earth during *Infinite Crisis* to help battle Alexander Luthor and he sustained heavy damage. After undergoing repairs, Vic led a new Titans East squad and helped the other Titans battle their zombified former teammates during *Blackest Night*. He then joined the Justice League, providing tech support and forming a close bond with the android Red Tornado.

TITANS TOGETHER
Victor felt his cybernetics made him an outsider and a freak, but found a new family in the Teen Titans.

CYBORG SUPERMAN

DEBUT *Adventures of Superman* #465 (Apr. 1990)
BASE Mobile
REAL NAMES Hank Henshaw
HEIGHT Variable   **WEIGHT** Variable
POWERS/ABILITIES Power over machinery and computers; physical strength and offensive powers mimicking those of Superman.
ALLIES Brainiac, Doomsday   **ENEMIES** Superman, Supergirl

Astronaut Hank Henshaw was on board the LexCorp space shuttle Excalibur with his wife Terri and two other crew members when it crashed. At first, the accident was thought to have been caused by Superman who had created a solar flare—exposing the crew to a fatal dose of radiation. With his body deteriorating, Hank transferred his consciousness into LexCorp's mainframe, recreating himself as a cyborg in Superman's image. When Terri later died, a deranged Hank blamed Superman for her death, and became one of the Man of Steel's fiercest foes. With Mongul, he orchestrated the obliteration of Coast City and became an intergalactic threat battling the Green Lantern Corps alongside Sinestro.

Henshaw seemingly vanished during the realty-altering *Flashpoint* event, but reappeared when *Convergence* uncovered countless alternate realities set to war by the almighty being Telos on behalf of a trans-universal composite of Brainiacs.

Restored on Prime Earth, Henshaw assembled a cadre of powerful villains into an Anti-Superman Gang, only to again meet defeat due to dissent in its ranks and the combined power of the Man of Steel and his allies. He remains a threat to all living things.

ARMORED AND DANGEROUS
Cyborg Superman's right arm can extend and change shape. His cybernetic eye projects heat beams.

ON THE RECORD

After *Flashpoint,* Superman's uncle Zor-El, escaped Krypton's destruction, thanks to Collector of Worlds Brainiac. Subjected to cybernetic augmentations that deranged his personality, Zor-El became Cyborg Superman—Brainiac's scout for a stronger species in the universe.He attempted to conquer Earth, battling Superman and his own daughter Kara Zor-El, but somehow escaped the black hole doom that befell Brainiac. Also surviving the *Rebirth* event, Cyborg Superman reanimated the dead Krytponians of Argo City and again attacked Earth, only to be defeated by Supergirl and Superman.

FAMILY AFFAIR
Despite every change and mutation, Zor-El held fast to the idea that Earth could become the New Krypton his bloodline deserved.

DAMAGE

DEBUT *Damage* #1 (Apr. 1994)
REAL NAME Grant Emerson
BASE New York City
EYES Brown   **HAIR** Brown
POWERS/ABILITIES Biochemical fusion reactor in his body provides increased strength, durability, and energy projection.
ENEMIES Symbolix, Zoom
AFFILIATIONS New Titans, Justice Society of America

The boy who grew up to be Damage was the product of an *in utero* genetic experiment overseen by Vandal Savage. Savage had provided an expatriate German scientist with funding on behalf of a company called Symbolix, together with cellular samples of other heroes.

The research bore fruit and when the child was born, Savage had his mother killed and placed the infant, who was called Grant Emerson, with an abusive surrogate family. Grant's powers manifested when he was 16, and Symbolix came to collect him. They killed Grant's foster family but he escaped. Adopting the name Damage, he began learning how to use his powers with the New Titans. Adopting a mask after his face was badly scarred in a fight with Zoom, he joined the Justice Society of America and was later killed and reanimated by Black Lanterns during *Blackest Night*. Retaining his own mind, he sacrificed himself to destroy other Black Lanterns before they breached the JSA stronghold.

DAMAGE LIMITATION
The fires of Damage's biochemical reactor always burned, as did the trauma of his abusive upbringing.

DAMAGE II

DEBUT *Dark Days: The Casting* (Vol. 2) #1 (Sep. 2017)
REAL NAME Ethan Avery
BASE Mobile
EYES Brown (Ethan), yellow (Damage)
HAIR Black
POWERS/ABILITIES Can change for one hour, once a day into Damage—a being with superhuman strength and durability.
ALLIES Poison Ivy, Swamp Thing
ENEMIES Gorilla Grodd, Colonel Marie Jones, Echidna
AFFILIATIONS None

No relation to the original Damage, Ethan Avery was a soldier, chosen by the US Army to become something more… Damage. Injected with a serum, Ethan could transform into a mighty behemoth for just one hour, once a day. In this form he possessed strength almost without limits. Ethan could communicate with Damage as two separate consciousnesses, but not control him. Damage was intended to be a weapon of mass destruction to be used against his country's enemies, but it soon became apparent that the army could not keep him in check. Ethan learned how to work with Damage to achieve balance in himself, and left the army behind to make his own way in the world.

COLLATERAL DAMAGE
The US Army created an uncontrollable monster when soldier Ethan Avery was injected with a special serum.

DARHK, DAMIEN

DEBUT *The Titans* #1 (Mar. 1999)
HEIGHT 6ft **WEIGHT** 160 lbs
EYES Blue **HAIR** Brown
POWERS/ABILITIES Highly intelligent, tech-savvy, ruthless; possibly immortal.
ALLIES Adeline Kane
ENEMIES Teen Titans
AFFILIATIONS H.I.V.E.

The mysterious, boyish-looking Damien Darhk has evaded all attempts to pin down his sketchy background, despite extensive investigations by the CIA, the FBI, and even the Teen Titans. The latter encountered him while battling H.I.V.E. and Grant Wilson—the son of Deathstroke also known as the Ravager. Darhk's role in H.I.V.E.'s machinations remains unclear, and it is also not understood how he came to occupy such a powerful, well-connected position within H.I.V.E. at a relatively young age.

During the final confrontation between the Teen Titans and H.I.V.E., Darhk suffered a near-fatal gunshot wound courtesy of Vandal Savage. He survived only after receiving a blood transfusion from then-H.I.V.E. Mistress Adeline Kane, perhaps granting him immortality. Darhk's current whereabouts are unknown.

DARK OPAL

DEBUT *Legion of Super-Heroes* (Vol. 2) #298 (Apr. 1983)
BASE Gemworld
HEIGHT 6ft 4in **WEIGHT** 235 lbs
EYES Red **HAIR** Black
POWERS/ABILITIES Immense strength, expert swordsman, variety of mystical powers.
ENEMIES Child, Amethyst
AFFILIATIONS House of Opal

By making pacts with otherworldly forces, forging secret alliances with rival Houses, and mastering sorcery, Dark Opal became ruler of Gemworld. However, he failed to kill the infant heir of the House of Amethyst, who was hidden on Earth. That heir grew up to be Amy Winston, a potent mystic known as Amethyst.

Amy went to Gemworld and thwarted Dark Opal's various attempts to forge a suit of armor containing slivers from each of Gemworld's 11 Houses. Amethyst ultimately deposed him and went on to lead an alliance of all Gemworld's other Houses.

Dark Opal was presumed killed in a powerful backlash of mystical energies, but the sorcerer had only retreated into the enchanted clasp of his cloak. Dark Opal returned to retake Gemworld, but was destroyed by Child, a Lord of Chaos, and his servant, Flaw.

DARKSTARS

DEBUT *Darkstars* #1 (Oct. 1992)
BASE Space
NOTABLE MEMBERS Ferrin Colos; Munchukk; Carla White; Medphyll; John Flint (dismissed); Donna Troy (retired); John Stewart (retired); Hollika Rahn, Mo Douglas, Charlie Vicker, Galius Zed, K'ryssma, Threllian (all deceased).
POWERS/ABILITIES Their exo-mantle battle suits provide super-strength, speed, and flight; they carry force-field projectors and laser blasters.
ALLIES Green Lantern Corps
ENEMIES Grayven

The Darkstars were formed to patrol space and destroy chaos by the Controllers, an aggressive sect of the Guardians of the Universe, and N.E.M.O., the Network for the Establishment and Maintenance of Order. Ferrin Colos of Zamba, joined the group and was assigned to Earth. After the Darkstars, L.E.G.I.O.N., and the Green Lantern Corps defeated the Triarch—a trinity of evil ancient deities—the three groups agreed on their separate peacekeeping roles in the universe.

When the Green Lantern Corps was torn apart by Hal Jordan, the Darkstars were left to patrol space themselves, recruiting former Green Lantern John Stewart and New Titan Troia to their ranks. Eventually, most Darkstars resigned or were killed by Darkseid's son, Grayven, leaving only Chaser Bron, Munchukk, and Ferrin Colos to carry out the Controllers' intergalactic mission of eradicating evil.

SHINING LIGHTS
Key Darkstars line up for action.
1 Ferrin Colos
2 John Flint
3 Carla White
4 Mo Douglas

DAWNSTAR

DEBUT *Superboy and the Legion of Super-Heroes* (Vol. 1) #226 (Apr. 1977)
REAL NAME Dawnstar Gr'ell
BASE 31st-century Metropolis
HEIGHT Unknown
WEIGHT Unknown
EYES Brown
HAIR Black
POWERS/ABILITIES Flight, expert tracker.
ALLIES None
ENEMIES The Horraz, Krav
AFFILIATIONS Legion of Super-Heroes

Dawnstar was recruited by Saturn Girl and Cosmic Boy to the Legion of Super-Heroes from her home planet of Starhaven, after they saw footage of her fighting the Red Horraz. At first Dawnstar was reluctant, not wanting to join a team that was answerable to the United Planets, but she was persuaded that the young heroes would have full autonomy.

Dawnstar had an eight-pointed star symbol on her forehead and "spirit wings," which only manifested when she needed to fly or when she was using her heightened powers of tracking. After joining the team, Dawnstar was very excited to meet Superboy (Jon Kent), whom she credited with inspiring her to become a hero.

ON TRIAL!
Dawnstar's tracking and guiding skills, and ability to fly at supersonic speeds in outer space proved a great addition to the Legion of Super-Heroes.

DAXAMITES

DEBUT *Adventure Comics* #312 (Sep. 1963)
BASE Daxam
POWERS/ABILITIES Similar to Kryptonians when exposed to the rays of a yellow sun.
ALLIES Green Lantern Corps, Superman
ENEMIES Sinestro Corps, Dominators

A genetically variant race descended from exploring Kryptonians, Daxamites possess similar powers to their ancestors when in the presence of a yellow sun.

They allied with a number of other alien races led by the Dominators to conquer Earth and control its unusual propensity to produce superpowered beings. The Daxans were initially relegated to a support and science role, but they soon discovered the extra abilities they developed in the yellow radiation of Earth's sun.

A Daxamite detachment fought Superman, beating him badly before succumbing to Earth's dire air pollution. Superman then saved their lives, spurring them to switch sides and turn against the rest of the Dominator invasion force.

One of this rebel group, Lar Gand (also known as Mon-El and Jonathan Kent) was later instrumental in forming the United Planets consortium of worlds. Another Daxamite, Sodam Yat, would go on to become a Green Lantern. He would turn Daxam's sun yellow so they could battle the Sinestro Corps.

MIGHTY DAXAMITES
The inhabitants of Daxam appeared to be like Earth's humans, but their solar-receptive biology was more advanced.

DARKSEID

DATA

DEBUT *Superman's Pal, Jimmy Olsen* #134 (Dec. 1970)
CURRENT VERSION *Justice League* (Vol. 2) #3 (Jan. 2012)
REAL NAME Uxas   **BASE** Apokolips
HEIGHT 8ft 9in   **WEIGHT** 1,815 lbs   **EYES** Red   **HAIR** None
POWERS/ABILITIES Formidable intellect, godlike strength and
endurance; eyes fire target-seeking Omega Beams; access to
advanced Apokoliptian technology, including Mother Boxes;
projects Boom Tubes for interdimensional teleportation.
ALLIES Parademon legions, Desaad, Steppenwolf,
Kanto, Female Furies, Grail, Granny Goodness
ENEMIES Mr. Miracle, Big Barda, Orion, Highfather and the
inhabitants of New Genesis, the Justice League, the Anti-Monitor

Darkseid is one of the most feared entities in the universe: a ruthless, unstoppable tyrant with godlike power and an all-consuming obsession with enslaving every being in existence. As the evil dread lord of the hellish planet Apokolips, Darkseid commands armies of henchmen and bizarre, lethal Parademons. He can access incredible technologies, such as the sentient Mother Boxes that serve as floating sensor drones. Moreover, as well as emitting deadly beams from his eyes, Darkseid has proved to be a formidable combatant, capable of taking on several mortal heroes at a time and emerging triumphant.

AT A GLANCE...

Lust for power
Darkseid's motivation is not wealth or revenge: he wants to control every being in the entire universe. When he confronts an enemy, Darkseid prefers to break their will and subjugate them, rather than destroy them outright. This has been seen in his confrontations with Superman, his estranged foster son Mister Miracle, and the mortals of Earth.

Omega Beams
Darkseid can kill with a glance by firing destructive Omega Beams from his eyes. These glowing red blasts change course to track their targets, though they can be evaded. Both the Flash and Supergirl were fast enough to avoid Omega Beams in battles with Darkseid.

Apokolips
Darkseid's homeworld is a hellish industrial planet with a surface cratered by fire pits. Slaves provide labor for its many armament production facilities, while its barracks and Parademon factories train hordes of faceless troopers for Darkseid's armies.

CLASSIC STORIES

The New Gods (Vol. 1) #1-2 (Feb./Mar.-Apr./May 1971) In one of his first-ever stories, Darkseid's deadly scheme is foiled by his estranged son, Orion.
New Gods (Vol. 3) #8 (Sep. 1989) This story tells of Darkseid's romance with the beautiful pacifist Suli. Tragically, she is murdered by Desaad, and the trauma helps turn Darkseid into a ruthless villain.
Final Crisis #1-7 (Jul. 2008-Mar. 2009) In this cosmos-altering event, Darkseid attempts to conquer reality by unleashing the power of the Anti-Life Equation on Earth.

The being who would become Darkseid

was once called Uxas, the youngest son of Yuga Khan, one of the legendary Old Gods. Resenting their authority, the rebellious and cunning Uxas whispered lies and words of hate into the Old Gods' ears. Under his deceitful influence, the Old Gods fought and killed each other, and as they died Uxas stole their power to become a New God, Darkseid. Seizing his chance, Darkseid went to war against his weakened elders, persuading his benevolent older brother Izaya to reluctantly join him, and making an enemy of their father Yuga Khan. When father and sons finally clashed, Yuga Khan was slain by Uxas, ending the rule of the Old Gods.

In the aftermath, the dying Sky God passed the last traces of his power to Izaya, also transforming him into a New God. Izaya tried to convince Darkseid that they should usher in a new age of enlightenment together, but Darkseid refused, destroying his world. Izaya then left to create a planet called New Genesis, which he presided over as Highfather, while Darkseid made Apokolips, an industrial hell-world populated by his engineered Parademon troopers and cruel New God minions.

Darkseid then embarked on a multidimensional campaign of conquest, seeking the Anti-Life Equation, the cosmic formula that would allow him to eliminate free will and control reality. World after world fell before him, their inhabitants enslaved or fed into flesh-recycling plants. However, the alternate world of Earth-2 managed to stave off an invasion, though its incarnations of Batman, Superman, and Wonder Woman sacrificed their lives in the process

GOD SLAYER
Uxas' hatred of the Old Gods saw him slaughter them—and seize their power for himself.

DARKSEID VS. THE JUSTICE LEAGUE

When the evil lord Darkseid launched his first attack on Earth-0, he initially inflicted heavy punishment on the planet's gathered Super Heroes—his mighty Omega Beams even knocked Superman out of action. However, Darkseid was then stabbed in the eyes by Wonder Woman and Aquaman. This act gave Superman the chance to recover and knock the villain into a Boom Tube portal summoned by Cyborg. This battle was one of Darkseid's most humiliating defeats, and it took him a long time to recover. The threat posed by Darkseid also served as the catalyst to unite Earth's heroes as the Justice League.

FOR GREAT JUSTICE
Even when they united, the Earth's most powerful Super Heroes—including Wonder Woman, Superman, and Batman—could barely defeat the almighty Darkseid.

"All hail Darkseid!"

STEPPENWOLF

Darkseid's armies then launched an attack on Earth-0 using Boom Tubes to create teleportation portals and attack multiple sites simultaneously. They were opposed by the world's champions, including Superman, Wonder Woman, Green Lantern (Hal Jordan), the Flash, Aquaman, and Cyborg. The heroes held their own against the attacking Parademons, but when Darkseid himself emerged from a Boom Tube, they found themselves outmatched. However, just as Darkseid was claiming victory, Earth's champions regrouped and launched a furious counterattack, grievously wounding the dark lord. Superman then forced Darkseid into a Boom Tube, sending him back to Apokolips. Heavily weakened, Darkseid sealed himself in the Mobius Chamber at Apokolips' core, tapping into the planet's energies to heal himself. With Apokolips now deteriorating, he set it on a course for Earth 2, planning to drain its life energies to replenish his world. Meanwhile, Darkseid's estranged foster-son Mister Miracle launched a stealth attack on Apokolips and found his 'father' in the Mobius Chamber. Miracle tried to kill him with the Boom Spheres invented by Mister Terrific, but these merely freed Darkseid. Darkseid used a Terraformer to begin harvesting Earth-2 to replenish Apokolips. A small force of Earth-2 heroes confronted him, but they proved no match for the villain. He declared war on Earth-0, but was opposed by Mister Miracle and Myrina Black—an Amazon who had secretly given birth to his daughter whom she had plotted to use against him. Naming her Grail, Myrina had sent her child to find a being who could defeat Darkseid, and Grail had returned with the cosmic force of annihilation, the Anti-Monitor.

Darkseid and the Anti-Monitor clashed on Earth, and their conflict threatened to destroy the planet. As the two fought, the Anti-Monitor revealed that the Anti-Life Equation—the ultimate power Darkseid had thirsted for—ran in his veins. With that, the Anti-Monitor used the Black Racer—the very embodiment of death itself—to slay Darkseid.

DEATH OF A GOD
The lord of Apokolips was killed by the Anti-Monitor and the Black Racer (who had possessed The Flash).

OMEGA POWER
The wielder of the power of the Old Gods, Darkseid proclaimed himself a New God. He can focus the Omega energy he possesses through his hands to generate huge shock waves.

THE WORLD'S END

If his clash with the Justice League marked an ignominious defeat for the evil Darkseid, his apocalyptic war against Earth-2 showed him at his most ruthless and powerful. As his forces inflicted a devastating defeat on this Earth's military, Darkseid personally defeated the planet's united heroes. The world was left in his grasp, to be consumed at his leisure.

THE WHOLE WORLD IN HIS HAND
Victory in the battle for Earth-2 marked one more triumph in Darkseid's campaign of cosmic conquest.

ON THE RECORD

Darkseid was introduced as a godlike being obsessed with cosmic domination, and this would remain the defining nature of his character. In his time, the all-conquering Super-Villain has undergone several startling transformations.

KILL OR BE KILLED
Batman planned to shoot Darkseid with the same bullet that Darkseid had used to kill Orion, but he had to avoid the Omega Beams.

Secret agents

In the 30th century, Darkseid secretly initiated a plan of conquest using cloned Super Heroes as his agents. Under his influence, the mighty Daxamites—whose powers were similar to Superman's—sculpted their planet's surface in Darkseid's own image, and began to transform it into a new Apokolips. The Legion of Super Heroes soon discovered the threat, and Darkseid was defeated.

From dark to light

On one occasion, Darkseid launched an attack on the Amazon island of Themyscira, and Wonder Woman punished him in a unique fashion. Using a mental link created by the Super Hero Raven, she imbued Darkseid with some of her compassion, sapping his power and tempering his darkness. Wonder Woman and the Amazons even allied with Darkseid to save Apokolips and Earth from the threat of Brainiac-13's Warworld.

Mob warfare

After Darkseid had his heart torn out by his son Orion, the villain found a human host on Earth: a mob boss called 'Boss Dark Side'. Operating out of the Dark Side Club in Blüdhaven, the Boss plotted to overtake reality. During the *Final Crisis* event, Darkseid seemingly killed Batman with his Omega Beams, but was defeated and slain by Earth's heroes.

DEADMAN

DATA

DEBUT *Strange Adventures* #205 (Oct. 1967)
REAL NAME Boston Brand
BASE Mobile
HEIGHT 6ft **WEIGHT** 201 lbs
EYES White **HAIR** Bald
POWERS/ABILITIES Able to possess human bodies for limited periods of time, communicate with spirits, and travel across dimensional boundaries; flight; invisibility.
ALLIES Madame Xanadu, Batman
ENEMIES Felix Faust, Enchantress, Specter Collector
AFFILIATIONS Justice League Dark

CLASSIC STORIES

***Forever People* #9–10 (Jun.–Jul./ Aug.–Sep. 1972)** Deadman's quest to track down the Hook gets help from an unexpected quarter—the Forever People. They also temporarily housed Deadman's spirit in an artificial body.

***Brightest Day* #1–24 (Jun. 2010 –Jun. 2011)** A White Lantern ring gives Boston Brand the chance to live again. He must protect the Star City forest from the Dark Avatar of Nekron. Mortally wounded in the forest, Brand is again condemned to a ghostly existence.

***Deadman: Dead Again* #1–5 (Oct. 2001)** As the *Crisis on Infinite Earths* rages around him, Deadman battles the sorcerous plot of Darius Caldera to provide heroic souls for the demon Neron.

Circus acrobat Boston Brand, traumatized by the anger and abuse he experienced as a child, was murdered and then given a new chance at life. As Deadman, he can inhabit the bodies of the living and is always driven to atone for the selfish way he lived his life by bringing hope to the hopeless.

DEAD RECKONING
After being shot dead, Deadman found himself face to face with Rama Kushna in a place between life and death, sin and absolution.

TAKING SIDES
In search of Pandora's Box, Deadman and Justice League Dark battled a disunited Justice League and A.R.G.U.S., not realizing they were all being manipulated.

Brought up in a household

bristling with anger, Boston Brand ran away to the circus, becoming a star but also a selfish hedonist with violent tendencies. As Deadman, he was a star acrobat and aerialist, until a mysterious assassin shot him and made his circus moniker all too real. Brand was transformed into a spirit being by the Hindu goddess Rama Kushna. He returned to the world of the living on the condition that he do good deeds to atone for his sins. Brand would later see his killer arrested, when Rama sent him to live in his killer's body.

However, Deadman's own sins were not yet admonished. He was approached by June Moone who asked him for protection from the Enchantress, who had been using June as a host. While trying to help her, Deadman was also recruited into the Justice League Dark by Madame Xanadu, who believed he would play a critical role in the League's battle against an oncoming occult threat. John Constantine—another of Xanadu's recruits—forcibly reunited June and the Enchantress, infuriating Deadman, who nevertheless joined Justice League Dark to face the menace of Cain, the progenitor of all vampires. Deadman continued to fight with the League against supernatural and magical dangers, the Crime Syndicate and the Blight. Along the way, Constantine and Deadman clashed again after the former locked Deadman inside the body of the dead Sea King from Earth-3.

While Deadman is not against teaming with the newest version of the Justice League Dark, he is back on his own these days, undertaking solo adventures and helping purge haunted houses of unfriendly spirits.

ON THE RECORD

In pre-*Flashpoint* stories, Boston Brand's assassin was discovered to be the Hook, an aspiring member of the League of Assassins who killed Boston Brand as his initiation into the group. This backfired when the League's leader, the Sensei, thought Brand was still alive due to Boston's twin brother, Cleveland, temporarily becoming the trapeze artist Deadman. The Sensei put an end to the original Hook, but witnessing his killer's death gave Deadman no peace.

Most versions of Deadman were invisible and intangible to humans, who lacked any form of preternatural perception. This was an advantage to him, but it also reinforced how alienated he was from the living, and at times made it difficult for him to live up to his mission of helping people who never knew he existed.

BY HOOK OR BY CROOK
Deadman asked Batman to help him find his killer—whom he believed was a villain named the Hook.

DEADSHOT

DATA

DEBUT *Batman* (Vol. 1) #59 (Jun.–Jul. 1950)
REAL NAME Floyd Lawton **BASE** Belle Reve Penitentiary
HEIGHT 6ft 1in **WEIGHT** 202 lbs **EYES** Brown **HAIR** Brown
POWERS/ABILITIES Expert marksman with extensive training in unarmed
combat and use of other weapons; armored suit includes targeting optics;
wears gauntlets featuring built-in laser designators and submachine guns.
ALLIES Harley Quinn, Captain Boomerang, Liveshot, Dogshot
ENEMIES Batman, Amanda Waller, Deathstroke, Black Mask
AFFILIATIONS Suicide Squad

MAD LOVE
Deadshot had a brief
fling with fellow Suicide
Squad member Harley
Quinn. He soon learned
that his Joker-obsessed
teammate was mad,
bad, and very
dangerous to know!

An expert marksman with a callous disregard
for life, Deadshot worked as a professional
hitman until he was imprisoned at Belle Reve
Penitentiary, a notorious prison for superpowered
criminals. The authorities then forced him to
"volunteer" for the Suicide Squad, a team of
expendable Super-Villains used for dangerous
black-ops missions by the US Government. The
lone-wolf sniper soon found himself leading
a motley crew of unpredictable bad guys on
a series of near-impossible missions.

SUICIDAL TENDENCIES
Deadshot soon discovered
that one of the only things
he had in common with his
Suicide Squad teammates
was a propensity for
extreme violence.

Floyd Lawton was one of Gotham City's rich socialites,
the sort of man that rubbed elbows with people like Bruce Wayne.
However, he was inspired to leave his boring life behind when one
of the fancy galas he attended had a particular memorable party
crasher: Batman. Seeing a chance to be more than his rather shady
past, Floyd took up a costumed identity himself as the killer-for-hire
known as Deadshot.

A consummate professional, Deadshot prided himself on never
missing a shot. But when the notorious terrorist cult called Kobra
kidnapped Floyd's estranged daughter, Zoe, to use as leverage against him, Deadshot cut a deal
with Batman. Instead of shooting the target Kobra wanted dead—who, ironically enough, was
Bruce Wayne—Deadshot and Batman worked together. Deadshot then successfully killed the Kobra
agent holding Zoe hostage. Batman saw to it that Deadshot was put in prison for that kill, and soon,
Deadshot was recruited into a clandestine government operation called Task Force X. As part of
this so-called Suicide Squad, Floyd went on a variety of missions with a different teams. Before
being sent into action, each team member had a bomb implanted in their neck to ensure obedience.

Though he preferred to operate as a solo agent, Deadshot proved an effective leader, and his
self-proclaimed death wish made him an ideal candidate to return to the Squad again and again.
He eventually befriended other longtime Squad members including Captain Boomerang and Harley
Quinn. In fact, after Waller was ousted from Squad control, Deadshot found himself disobeying
orders when told to kill Boomerang. Deadshot chose instead to help a fledgling band of rebels
escape Squad custody. While on the run, he was able to visit his daughter Zoe, who had begun
calling herself Liveshot in honor of her dad. Soon after, Deadshot was seemingly killed in action
by the criminal Black Mask, finally granting him his death wish.

ON THE RECORD

The pre-*Flashpoint* Deadshot came
from a wealthy family. The pivotal moment
in his childhood occurred when he
accidentally shot his brother instead of his
abusive father. When Lawton first embarked
on his career as Deadshot, he seemed to be
a hero that rivaled Batman. In reality, his
"crime fighting" career was a scheme. He
was actually running a criminal gang.

Deadshot worked as a solo assassin,
taking on targets that included Deathstroke
and The Joker, but spent most of his career
as part of Amanda Waller's Suicide Squad
and joined the Secret Six for a time. As a
member of the Six, he teamed up with his
former Suicide Squad comrades to take on
the undead Black Lanterns in the "Danse
Macabre" crossover story.

SIX OF THE WORST
Deadshot experienced both
comradeship and betrayal
when he joined the Secret Six.

**KILLER WITH
A CODE**
Even though he
is a ruthless killer,
Floyd Lawton lives
by a strict code of
honor: He would
never kill for free,
and he would never
waste a bullet. For
Lawton, every life has
value—so he expects to get
paid for each one he ends.

CLASSIC STORIES

***Detective Comics* (Vol. 1) #474 (Dec.
1977)** Deadshot embraces Super-Villainy and
marks Batman for death, utilizing his distinctive
targeting eyepiece sight and glove-mounted
guns for the first time.

***Secret Six* (Vol. 3) #1–7 (Nov. 2008–
May 2009)** The Secret Six is hired to protect
Tarantula from a horde of Super-Villains who
covet a mystical object in her possession—a
card that entitles a sinner to get out of Hell.

***Justice League of America* (Vol. 3)
#7.1 (Nov. 2013)** A moving chronicle
of Floyd's tragic childhood—and a thrilling
assassination mission in which Deadshot
delivers a precision sniper shot while in free fall.

DEATHSTROKE

DATA

DEBUT *The New Teen Titans* (Vol. 1) #2 (Dec. 1980)
REAL NAME Slade Wilson
HEIGHT 6ft 2in **WEIGHT** 225 lbs **EYES** Blue **HAIR** White
POWERS/ABILITIES Master tactician with Special Forces training; experimental gene treatments boost strength, speed, toughness, mental acuity, and healing rate to superhuman levels; skills and enhancements allow him to anticipate and avoid enemy attacks; weapons master who employs Deathstroke sword; wears hi-tech Ikon suit that charges via kinetic energy and offers enhanced durability, information, and communication functions.
ALLIES William Wintergreen, Ravager (Rose Wilson), Jericho, Dr. Light (Arthur Light), Red Lion, Adeline Wilson
ENEMIES Batman, Robin, Teen Titans
AFFILIATIONS Team 7, Suicide Squad, Secret Society of Super-Villains

CLASSIC STORIES

Identity Crisis #3 (Oct. 2004)
Deathstroke accepts a contract to protect the villain Doctor Light from the Justice League—and almost defeats the heroic team single-handedly.

The New Titans (Vol. 1) #71–84 (Nov. 1990–Mar. 1992) Deathstroke finds himself fighting to protect his foes, the Teen Titans, against his insane son Jericho in the classic "Titans Hunt" epic.

Deathstroke (Vol. 2) #7 (May 2012) Slade Wilson is targeted by his unhinged son, Grant, as his offspring attempts to prove that he is a better warrior than his father.

Deathstroke is the most feared and respected mercenary in the world. His elite military training and a genetically enhanced physique make him a very dangerous combatant, but his deadliest weapon is his mind. A master strategist and tactician, Deathstroke specializes in psychological warfare tactics that he uses to devastating effect.

STROKE OF DEATH
Deathstroke took his name from a sword that he won in a poker game It was an antique grete war blade.

Slade Wilson enlisted in the United States Army at the age of 17 and proved to be an exceptional soldier, earning decorations for valor in combat. He was groomed and trained by Adeline Wilson for genetic experimentation that boosted his physical capabilities to superhuman levels. While the treatments were a success, Slade hid the results from everyone, included Adeline, who had become his wife and given birth to two sons, Grant and Joseph. Slade began to go on covert ops. Adopting the codename Deathstroke while in the field, Slade earned a reputation for ruthless efficiency. However, his work soon followed him home, and an enemy slit Joseph's throat, rendering him mute. Adeline was furious at Slade and shot him in the back of the head. Deathstroke survived, but lost an eye.

When Grant Wilson grew up, he became the mercenary Ravager, but was killed while facing the original Teen Titans. Deathstroke swore a vendetta against the Titans and even hired the faux Super Hero Terra to infiltrate their ranks. As if his family wasn't troubled enough, Deathstroke also had a daughter out of wedlock, Rose, who later became the new Ravager. Meanwhile, Joseph embraced his metahuman abilities and became the hero Jericho.

To make himself even more of a killing machine, Deathstroke adopted a hi-tech Ikon uniform after rescuing his old friend Wintergreen. He clashed with the likes of Batman and Superman, and even briefly decided to offer his services to the good guys for once, founding the team Defiance with Ravager (Rose Wilson), Jericho, Kid Flash, Power Girl (Tanya Spears), and Terra. When tensions once again escalated with the Teen Titans, Deathstroke was killed by Red Arrow. However, Slade's healing factor had been recently working in overdrive, and he healed from the would-be fatal wound. While he debated giving up his career to live quietly with his reunited family and work as a nurse, he was soon back in action—even clashing with Batman again in Gotham City—unable to give up his violent side.

DEFIANCE
Deathstroke briefly attempted work-for-hire on the side of the angels, wearing a cape and starting his own Super Hero mercenary team called Defiance.

ON THE RECORD

Prior to the *Flashpoint* event, Deathstroke was defined by his complex relationship with the Teen Titans and his tormented son, Jericho. The young man joined the Titans—whom Slade had earlier been contracted to kill—to oppose his father, but when Jericho was possessed by the evil Spirits of Azarath, he turned on his team. Deathstroke helped the heroes and killed Jericho to save him from the torment of possession, but was later possessed by his son's spirit. Slade's daughter Rose (Ravager) initially became a mercenary like her father, but later joined the Titans, alongside a revived Jericho.

TEEN TERROR
Deathstroke was the Teen Titans' deadliest and most persistent foe. However, he was sometimes forced to help the team and he developed a grudging respect for the heroes.

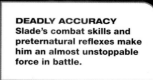

DEADLY ACCURACY
Slade's combat skills and preternatural reflexes make him an almost unstoppable force in battle.

DEFIANCE

DEBUT *Deathstroke* (Vol. 4) #20 (Aug. 2017)
BASE The Bronx, New York City
MEMBERS/POWERS Adeline Kane: Leader, special ops; **Deathstroke:** Master assassin with enhanced strength, reflexes, intellect, and healing factor; **Jericho:** Telepathy, telekinesis, projecting consciousness into others; **Kid Flash:** Super-speed; **Power Girl (Tanya Spears):** Superhuman strength and durability, size-changing, genius intellect; **Rose Wilson:** Superhuman strength, durability, speed, healing, martial arts expert; **Terra:** Geokinetic abilities; **Wintergreen:** Military and espionage skills.
ALLIES None
ENEMIES Dr. Ikon, Secret Society

FAMILY AFFAIR
Led by the violent Deathstroke and largely made up of members of his troubled family, it's no wonder that Defiance was a shortlived venture.

Following a brush with the infinity of the cosmos inside the Speed Force, Deathstroke—a man once nicknamed the Terminator—decided to renounce killing and start a team of Super Heroes. The new team was named Defiance, and was very much a family affair, including as it did Deathstroke's ex-wife Adeline, his daughter Rose, and his son Joey, aka Jericho.

The team was kitted out with Ikon suits—"gravity sheaths" that acted almost like force-fields. However, not all the team were in it for altruistic motives, and divisions and mistrust ran deep. Defiance disbanded rapidly after Power Girl questioned Jericho's life choices and Kid Flash could no longer stomach being allied with Deathstroke, who soon returned to his old ways.

DEIMOS

DEBUT *1st Issue Special* #8 (Nov. 1975)
BASE Thera, Skartaris
HEIGHT 6ft 1in
WEIGHT 193 lbs
EYES Black
HAIR Black
POWERS/ABILITIES Immortal; used Atlantean computer to perform "magic."
ALLIES The Evil One
ENEMIES Warlord
AFFILIATIONS Thera

TAKEOVER
When worlds converged, Deimos used the power of the Time Masters to destroy Warlord—before attempting to take control of the Multiverse.

An inhabitant of Skartaris—the realm within Earth's core—High Priest Deimos used the knowledge he found in the Scrolls of Blood along with his mastery of Atlantean computer technology to rule the kingdom of Thera. He then tried to conquer all of Skartaris, but was killed battling United States Air Force pilot Lt. Colonel Travis Morgan, better known as the hero Warlord. One of Deimos' minions resurrected him with the Mask of Life, which also gave Deimos magical powers and immortality. Warlord executed Deimos, throwing his head to the wolves, while Warlord's son Joshua trapped the sorcerer within a magic mirror, but Deimos always returned.

During the Convergence event, when Brainiac's servant Telos forced the heroes of alternate Earths to battle for their very existence, Deimos launched his master plan. He tapped into the power of the Time Masters in an attempt to conquer all reality, but was killed by the entity Parallax.

DEMOLITION TEAM

DEBUT *Green Lantern* (Vol. 2) #176 (May 1984)
BASE Rosie's Bar, New Orleans, Louisiana
MEMBERS/ABILITIES Rosie: Team leader, who wields a rapid-fire hot rivet gun; **Hardhat:** Uses powered helmet and strength-boosting harness; **Jackhammer:** Deploys a jackhammer capable of untold destruction; **Scoopshovel:** Mechanical excavator arm can dig up anything; **Steamroller:** Drives steamroller that can flatten buildings.
ALLIES Congressman Bloch
ENEMIES Predator, Blood Pack, O.M.A.C.

DAY OF WRECKENING
Guaranteed to leave a trail of destruction, the Demolition Team used all manner of repurposed tools and building equipment to provide cheap muscle for bad guys on a budget!
1 Scoopshovel
2 Steamroller
3 Rosie
4 Hardhat
5 Jackhammer

The Demolition Team is a group of mercenaries armed with construction equipment that has been re-purposed for combat. The group all have blue-collar day jobs, but when leader Rosie lines up a contract, they drop everything and get tooled-up for action. Corrupt congressman Jason Bloch hired them to wreck Ferris Aircraft, but the team was stopped and easily beaten by the enigmatic Predator —the male alter ego of Carol Ferris.

When Coast City was reduced to rubble by Mongul, the Demolition Team decided to destroy threats to the planet. After upgrading their gear, they attacked a nuclear power plant in Germany, but were stopped by the corporate-funded heroes Blood Pack. Rosie then briefly became part of the composite hero Enginehead, but soon reunited with the Demolition Team. Most of them were apparently killed when the O.M.A.C.s attacked Earth, though Hardhat survived.

DEMON KNIGHTS

DEBUT *Demon Knights* #1 (Nov. 2011)
MEMBERS POWERS The Demon (Etrigan): Demonic physiology, sorcery; **Jason Blood:** Sorcery; **Madame Xanadu (Nimue Inwudu):** Sorcery; **The Horsewoman:** Archery, empathic link with horses; **Sir Ystin the Shining Knight:** Immortality, flying horse (Vanguard), magic sword (Caliburn); **Al Jabr:** Genius scientist; **Exoristos the Amazon:** Immortality, superhuman strength, agility, and stamina; **Vandal the Savage:** Immortality, tactical genius.
ALLIES Alba Sarum denizens, Merlin, King Arthur
ENEMIES Questing Queen, Morgaine le Fey

DARK KNIGHTS
While helping to protect civilization in a barbaric age, the dysfunctional members of the Demon Knights fought each other as well as their enemies.

In the Dark Ages, the evil Questing Queen attacked the village of Little Spring, but her armies were driven off by a motley group of adventurers. Calling themselves the Demon Knights, this fractious team comprised Vandal Savage, Amazon warrior Exoristos, Moorish scientist Al Jabr, the archer Horsewoman, the Shining Knight, Madame Xanadu, and the demon Etrigan (with his human host Jason Blood).

The "heroes" then searched for Avalon and clashed with Morgaine le Fey. Betrayed by Etrigan, they were taken to Hell, but were later freed by Jason Blood and the Shining Knight. In Avalon, they defeated the armies of the Questing Queen and Lucifer (with help from Merlin and King Arthur). Merlin named the group as the first-ever Stormwatch team, but they immediately disbanded. However, Al Jabr later reunited the Demon Knights to battle vampires on Themyscira and embark on a quest for the Holy Grail.

DEMON, THE

DATA

DEBUT *Demon* (Vol. 1) #1 (Aug.-Sep. 1972)
REAL NAME Etrigan/Jason Blood
BASE Hell
HEIGHT 6ft 4in (as the Demon); 6ft (as Jason Blood)
WEIGHT 352 lbs (as the Demon); 182 lbs (as Jason Blood)
EYES Red (as the Demon); Brown (as Jason Blood)
HAIR None (as the Demon); Brown with white streak (as Jason Blood)
POWERS/ABILITIES Preternaturally strong, agile, and heat-resistant; fire breath; powerful claws and fangs; knowledge and application of magical spells
ALLIES Merlin, Madame Xanadu
ENEMIES Morgaine le Fey, Belial
AFFILIATIONS Demon Knights, Unknowns

MATCH MADE IN HELL
Etrigan seems eternally chained to Jason Blood, as Blood is in turn chained to Etrigan. Neither is happy about their partnership, especially Etrigan, who has noticed Blood's humanity seeping into him over the centuries.

CLASSIC STORIES

***Swamp Thing* (Vol. 2) #49-50 (Jun.-Jul. 1986)** When Swamp Thing, Deadman, and the Phantom Stranger recruit Etrigan to take part in a battle to decide the fate of the world, the demon leads the assault on the Great Darkness.

***Hitman* #16-19 (Jul.-Oct. 1997)** Hitman Tommy Monaghan uses Etrigan to get his hands on the Ace of Winchesters —the one gun that can slay the firearms-demon Mawzir.

***Shadowpact* #11 (May 2007)** Etrigan tries to take the Trident of Lucifer, but is turned to stone by the Shadowpact (and used as a hat rack in the Oblivion Bar).

INFERNAL FUSION
Merlin punished both his rebellious scribe Jason Blood and the demon Etrigan by binding them together—a union that would last for centuries.

Etrigan was a lesser demon of Hell who burned with rage and ambition. When he rebelled against his master Lucifer, the infernal lord allowed the magician Merlin to bind Etrigan to a human scribe named Jason Blood. When danger threatens, Jason switches with Etrigan, but is transported to Hell while the demon is in control. For his part, Etrigan resents being forced to act like a 'hero' for a human and plots to gain his freedom.

The legend of Etrigan begins in hell and in the legendary Camelot. It is said that Jason Blood and Etrigan were bound together by the magician Merlin just as Camelot fell. Immortal, Jason wandered the world and rescued sorceress Madame Xanadu, who was about to be burned at the stake as a witch. The pair became lovers, and to help keep Etrigan under control, Xanadu romanced the jealous demon as well. When the demon hordes of the Questing Queen threatened the village of Little Spring, Jason joined a group of disparate warriors to fight her and her dragons. Etrigan, Xanadu, and their fellow Demon Knights successfully fought off the Questing Queen's army.

After many more adventures with the Demon Knights, Etrigan was imprisoned beneath London, but he broke free in the 21st century. He clashed with Stormwatch (the modern incarnation of the Demon Knights) and later teamed with Batwoman to prevent the return of Arthurian villainess Morgaine le Fey. He later fended off an attack from his father Belial at Death Valley, conquering him to become king of Hell. Since Etrigan has been seen hanging around the Oblivion Bar more recently, it seems his rule was short-lived.

Enlisted to fight the Lords of Order, who had taken it upon themselves to destroy every magical being on Earth, Jason Blood summoned Etrigan, only to have the Demon ripped from his form and sent back to Hell. Meanwhile, Jason began to age rapidly without his demon partner. The Justice League Dark embraced chaos magic to fight the Lords of Order, and Zatanna gave Jason his youth back by entwining him with the notorious Demons Three. Whether Jason is still bound to these demonic entities remains to be seen.

ON THE RECORD

The post-*Crisis* incarnation of Etrigan was the son of the demon Belial. In the Dark Ages, Merlin summoned him in a vain attempt to save Camelot from Morgaine le Fey's horde, binding him to a human host, the peasant Jason Blood. This made Jason immortal, and he studied demonology to better understand the entity within him.

In the 20th century, Blood came across an incantation that allowed him to transform into Etrigan, and used it to battle various occult foes. Later, during the *Blackest Night* event, he battled Black Lanterns after being possessed by Deadman.

GOING MEDIEVAL
After being released in the 20th century, Etrigan relished the opportunity to inflict some old-fashioned demonic mayhem! The modern-day minions of Morgaine le Fey discovered this to their cost!

DARK SUMMONING
By uttering the rhyme, "Gone, gone, the form of man. Rise the Demon Etrigan!" Jason Blood summons the Demon from Hell.

ON THE RECORD

Despero was initially a psychic mastermind who preferred to defeat his foes using elaborate games. He later evolved a physical form powerful enough to battle the entire Justice League single-handed.

In one battle at the United Nations building, he was only defeated when Martian Manhunter showed him a vision of the thing he most wanted: the destruction of the Justice League. At peace, Despero reverted (temporarily) to a harmless fetus.

GAMES MASTER
In his very first encounter with the Justice League, Despero captured the team and then forced The Flash to play against him in a game to win their freedom.

DESPERO

DEBUT *Justice League of America* (Vol. 1) #1 **(Oct.–Nov. 1960)**
EYES Yellow **HAIR** None
HEIGHT 8ft 1in **WEIGHT** 850 lbs
POWERS/ABILITIES Third eye channels phenomenal psychic powers including telekinesis, telepathy, mind control, astral projection, and illusion creation; superhumanly strong; capable of interstellar flight; invulnerability and regenerative powers.
ALLIES Crime Syndicate
ENEMIES Martian Manhunter, Stargirl, Justice League
AFFILIATIONS Secret Society of Super-Villains

Despero was a member of a powerful alien race—the Klanorian—who became obsessed with conquest, and made himself ruler of three planets inhabited by less powerful beings. The Justice League attempted to overthrow him on one of their very first missions, and after a close battle he was defeated by the Martian Manhunter. Despero became obsessed with revenge, and attacked the Justice League's Watchtower satellite while junior members Atom, Firestorm, and Element Woman were left in charge. He appeared unstoppable, but once again the Martian Manhunter managed to defeat him in a psychic battle and he was imprisoned.

When the evil Crime Syndicate from Earth-3 invaded Earth-0 and defeated the Justice League, they freed Despero and he joined the Syndicate. The alien then used his prodigious mental powers to imprison Justice League members within their own minds, and appeared to beat his nemesis Martian Manhunter to death—though this proved to be a very convincing illusion. Following the defeat of the Crime Syndicate, mastermind Manchester Black manipulated the Teen Titans into breaking Despero out of prison for his own purposes, but the "Despero" they were rescuing turned out to be an illusion created by Doctor Psycho.

DESAAD

DEBUT *The Forever People* (Vol. 1) #2 **(Apr.–May 1971)**
BASE Apokolips
EYES Black **HAIR** Black
HEIGHT 5ft 11in **WEIGHT** 152 lbs
POWERS/ABILITIES New God physiology bestows immortality and superhuman physical capabilities; can take on illusionary appearances, mentally influence others, and gain power from others' pain.
ALLIES Darkseid, Steppenwolf
ENEMIES Mister Miracle, Power Girl, Huntress, Superman (Val-Zod), Batman (Earth-2), the Wonders of the World
AFFILIATIONS Apokolips

Desaad is a New God of Apokolips, and a henchman of its overlord Darkseid. On Apokolips cruelty is a way of life, but Desaad is infamous for his sadism, drawing power from others' agony. He became Darkseid's interrogator and took part in Steppenwolf's attack on Earth-2. When the forces of Darkseid invaded Earth, Desaad tortured the Man of Steel, planning to use his DNA to create more powerful Parademons. The invasion failed, leaving Desaad stranded on Earth, where he used his advanced technology and mind-control powers to spread strife, corruption, and suffering.

When businessman and hero Mister Terrific was exiled to Earth-2 in a quantum-tunneling mishap, Desaad stole his identity, and clashed with Terrific's girlfriend, Power Girl, and her companion Huntress, as he constantly tried to find his way back to Apokolips and his master. Desaad was summoned to take part in Apokolips' second attack on Earth-2. Working from a hidden lair beneath Geneva, he turned Huntress into a warped Fury called Famine and created a new breed of warriors that helped Darkseid conquer Earth-2: The Protofuries.

ON THE RECORD

The post-*Crisis* Desaad discovered his sadistic side when young Prince Uxas—the future Darkseid—tricked him into killing his own pet. Desaad became Uxas' minion, helping him to steal the Omega Force from his brother Drax. However, he did once betray his master by trying to steal the Omega Force with Highfather's staff. Desaad also corrupted others, possessing Mary Shazam during *Final Crisis*, before being banished.

PAIN AND PUNISHMENT
Desaad fed on the fear and pain of others, but when Darkseid caught him siphoning emotions from Orion and Kalibak, he destroyed Desaad with his Omega Beams.

DETECTIVE CHIMP

DEBUT *Adventures of Rex the Wonder Dog* #4 (Jul.–Aug. 1952)
REAL NAME Magnificent Finder of Tasty Grubs, "Bobo"
BASE Oblivion Bar
HEIGHT 3ft 8in **WEIGHT** 76 lbs **EYES** Black **HAIR** Black
POWERS/ABILITIES Highly intelligent, deductive skills; immortal; briefly had powers of Doctor Fate; current custodian of Myrran Sword of Night
ALLIES Rex the Wonder Dog, Batman, Nightmaster, Blue Devil
ENEMIES The Spectre, Eclipso, Trickster, Upside-Down Man
AFFILIATIONS Justice League Dark, Guild of Detection, Shadowpact, Bureau of Amplified Animals

Chimpanzee "Magnificent Finder of Tasty Grubs" was a sideshow act dubbed "Bobo" until he drank from the Fountain of Youth. This granted him a genius intellect and the ability to speak. After solving a murder, he went into business as "Detective Chimp," but his nonhuman status caused legal issues and his agency failed. Crushed, he began drinking heavily at the Oblivion Bar, a watering-hole for occult beings run by former rock star Jim Rook aka Nightmaster. He was also the mystic guardian of other-dimensional Myrra.

When The Spectre sought to banish magic, Bobo recruited fellow drinkers to fight back, and the arcane Super Hero team Shadowpact was born. After thwarting numerous catastrophes, the team—with Bobo as notional leader—split up. Doctor Fate's Helmet then chose Bobo as its new host, but he found its power overwhelming and rapidly rejected it.

When not consulting with fellow sleuths like Batman, Detective Chimp hung around the Oblivion Bar until it was attacked by Barbatos' Dark Knights. Sacrificing himself to save everyone, Rook appointed Bobo as Nightmaster of Myrra, returning him to the role of hero. He is a most reluctant one: lonely, self-critical, and subject to depression, but he has heroically given his all in Justice League Dark, battling Circe, the Otherkind, and a constant stream of hellish foes. His greatest regret is his failure to save Myrra from the Lords of Order who began their own campaign to eradicate magic in that shadowy realm.

DEVASTATION

DEBUT *Wonder Woman* (Vol. 2) #143 (Apr. 1999)
HEIGHT 4ft 6in **WEIGHT** 82 lbs
EYES Pale blue **HAIR** Red
POWERS/ABILITIES Superhuman abilities, tactical genius, supersonic flight; can cause earthquakes and manipulate emotions.
ALLIES Cronus, Dr. Poison, Agua Sin Gaaz, Lady Zand
ENEMIES Wonder Woman, Wonder Girl (Cassie Sandsmark), Young Justice
AFFILIATIONS The Titans

TINY TERROR
Devastation's divinely bestowed powers and bottomless appetite for destruction made her a fearsome opponent, despite her diminutive size.

Devastation was created by the Titan Cronus as a weapon to cause discord on Earth. When she raised havoc in a small South Carolina town, Wonder Woman arrived to confront her, but quickly discovered that Devastation was just as powerful as she was. Devastation spread rioting and destruction across the South and tried to detonate a nuclear weapon, but Wonder Woman buried it underground and Devastation was atomized in the blast.

Seeking revenge, Devastation reconstructed herself and used her mind-warping powers to turn Wonder Woman's protégé, Wonder Girl, against her. Wonder Woman used her love for Cassie to break Devastation's programming, though, and the villain fled. Cassie later joined Young Justice, and when the team invaded the Super-Villain haven of Zandia, Devastation agreed to help defend it on the condition that she got to take on Wonder Girl herself—but was beaten in a muddy brawl.

DEVILANCE THE PURSUER

DEBUT *Forever People* (Vol. 1) #11 (Oct.–Nov. 1972)
BASE Apokolips
EYES Blue
HEIGHT 7ft 1in **WEIGHT** 405 lbs
POWERS/ABILITIES Immortality, strength; energy lance tracks targets and allows flight.
ALLIES Darkseid
ENEMIES Forever People, Lobo, Starfire, Animal Man, Adam Strange, New Genesis

Devilance is the huntsman of Darkseid and the New God of Pursuit, dispatched to track down enemies of Apokolips. Darkseid sent Devilance to Earth to capture the Forever People of New Genesis, and the young heroes only escaped by switching places with Infinity Man, who was trapped in a pocket dimension. Infinity Man grabbed Devilance's weapon, and both were seemingly destroyed in an explosion.

Years later, however, Animal Man, Adam Strange, and Starfire encountered Devilance when they were stranded on a paradise planet. The Pursuer took the heroes prisoner, but they managed to escape, stealing his lance to power their ship. Devilance pursued them, but was attacked and killed by the alien bounty hunter Lobo, who impaled the New God's head on his own lance.

DEX-STARR

DEBUT *Final Crisis: Rage of the Red Lanterns* #1 (Dec. 2008)
BASE Ysmault
POWERS/ABILITIES Red Lantern power ring gives speed, toughness, strength, interstellar flight, and can create Red Energy constructs.
ALLIES Atrocitus
ENEMIES Guy Gardner, Lobo
AFFILIATIONS Red Lanterns

Dexter was once an ordinary cat, but when he saw his human companion murdered he was overcome by anger and was chosen by a Red Lantern power ring. After exacting revenge on his human companion's killers, he joined the Red Lantern Corps as Dex-Starr and developed a close bond with its leader, Atrocitus. He also gained the ability to create energy constructs by licking up the blood of his fellow Lantern, Rankorr.

When Guy Gardner defeated Atrocitus and took over the Corps, the loyal Dex-Starr took Atrocitus to safety and helped him recruit an army to attack Gardner and his Red Lanterns. Gardner won the battle, but quit the Corps and Atrocitus took command again. Dex-Starr was later killed by the bounty hunter Lobo, but was reborn from a pool of Red Lantern blood as a being of pure rage.

DIAL H FOR HERO

DEBUT *House of Mystery* (Vol. 1) #156 **(Jan. 1966)**
PAST CALLERS Robby Reed, Christopher King, Victoria Grant, Hero Cruz, Father Time, Nelson Jent, Snapper Carr, Miguel Montez, Summer Pickens
POWERS/ABILITIES H-Dials tap into the metaphysical Hero-verse to transform users into monsters, villains, and Super Heroes.
ENEMIES Mister Thunderbolt
AFFILIATIONS Dial Bunch, Justice League, The Overvoid

The Multiverse is a complex assembly of overlapping dimensions and energy zones, all combining into a unified but constantly changing whole. One particular conceptual realm contains the infinite potential to improve living beings and can be tapped by four devices that look like telephones.

When technically astute teen Robby Reed found a weird rotary dial in a cave, his investigations found that it could temporarily transform him into an infinite number of Super Heroes when he dialed H-E-R-O. He was unaware that the first time it activated, it also split him into two beings—The Operator and wicked Mister Thunderbolt— who both lived independently of him.

As a number of ordinary people used the scattered dials to briefly become incredible and weird beings, the Operator and Thunderbolt dueled with reality at stake: one wanted to restore cosmic balance and remove the dials while the other sought to unleash total chaos by empowering every being in the Multiverse.

The simmering cold war exploded into conflict after runaway teens Miguel Montez and Summer Pickens took control of the dials, encountering Super Hero-addicted past dialers, who were becoming increasingly bizarre and ultimately transcended existence to help The Operator triumph at last.

ON THE RECORD

The first known dial-user was teenager Robby Reed, who discovered an alien dial in a cavern. However, when he dialed S-P-L-I-T while battling Shirkon of the Many Eyes, he divided into two beings.

The good Wizard and the evil Master became foes of Chris King and Vicki Grant, the next dial-wielders, until Robby's halves were reunited. A flashback later revealed that Robby had once used his dial to switch the JLA's powers, thus helping them to defeat the Injustice League.

DIAL P FOR PATRIOTISM!
In one of his early adventures, Robby Reed transformed into the star-spangled Yankee Doodle Kid and battled the villainous Cougar.

DIGGLE, JOHN

DEBUT *Green Arrow* (Vol. 5) #24 **(Dec. 2013)**
REAL NAME John Andrew Diggle
BASE Seattle, Washington
HEIGHT 6ft 1in **WEIGHT** 209 lbs
EYES Brown **HAIR** Black
POWERS/ABILITIES Special forces training and combat experience makes him a formidable opponent.
ALLIES Green Arrow, Green Lantern (Hal Jordan)
ENEMIES The Clock King, Richard Dragon and the Longbow Hunters, John King
AFFILIATIONS Team Arrow

Former Green Beret John Diggle was working as a bodyguard at Queen Industries when Green Arrow (Oliver Queen) showed up at his Seattle apartment. The bow-slinging vigilante offered Diggle a job as "point man" in his war against crime. Diggle accepted on condition that he didn't have to wear tights or a mask. They fought crime together for a year, but when Oliver went into mourning following his mother's death, Diggle donned the Green Arrow outfit without permission to take down crime lord Ricardo Diaz. Following an argument, Queen fired Diggle.

Years later, when Green Arrow fought Komodo and the Outsiders in Prague, Diggle resurfaced to stop Seattle gangster Richard Dragon, who was seizing control of the underworld. Betrayed by the Clock King, Diggle was captured by Dragon—Ricardo Diaz's son. Green Arrow saved Diggle and they united to best the villain, with Diggle joining Team Arrow to defeat criminal mastermind John King and secret society the Ninth Circle.

When Diggle unexpectedly saved Queen's archenemy Dark Archer Merlyn—paying a long-standing debt of honor—the hero alliance ended acrimoniously. They last met at the funeral of Roy Harper (Arsenal) but remain at odds with each other.

THE FALL GUY
When Richard Dragon declared war on Green Arrow and his allies, he tortured John Diggle before kicking him out a window. Fortunately, Green Arrow broke his friend's fall with a foam arrow.

PARTNERS IN CRIME FIGHTING
Diggle was a practical and pragmatic counterpart to the flamboyant and idealistic Green Arrow.

DOCTOR FATE

DATA

DEBUT *More Fun Comics* #55 **(May 1940)** (Doctor Fate); *Convergence: Aquaman* #2 **(July 2015)** (Khalid Nassour)
REAL NAME Khalid Nassour
BASE Tower of Fate, Salem, Massachusetts
HEIGHT 5ft 5in **WEIGHT** 120 lbs **EYES** Brown **HAIR** Black
POWERS/ABILITIES Helmet of Fate bestows powers of flight and healing; ability to channel and redirect wind, fire, water, earth, and lightning; other magical abilities including phasing through walls.
ALLIES Kent Nelson
ENEMIES Anubis, Nabu, Upside-Down Man
AFFILIATIONS Justice League Dark

NABU RETURNS
Khalid proved to Nabu that there was still a chance for humanity. As a result, Nabu ceded control of his power in order for Khalid to officially become Doctor Fate.

Down the millennia, the gods of Egypt have chosen brave champions to wear Nabu's golden helmet and accept the sacred duty of protecting the world as Doctor Fate. When Khalid Nassour was chosen, his world changed forever. He discovered that he now possessed incredible element-controlling powers, and soon found himself a member of the Justice League Dark.

TOWER OF FATE
The Tower of Fate has no doors or windows. Its interior is only accessible by magic. Once inside, the Tower is a twisted maze of stairways and hallways; the laws of physics seem not to apply.

At the dawn of man, a group of sorcerer kings called the Lords of Order discovered magic so powerful their bodies could not contain it, so they bound themselves to objects. One of those kings was named Nabu, and the object to which he bound himself was the Helmet of Fate.

Over the years, the Helmet of Fate has found different hosts, most notably Kent Nelson, who served valiantly with the mystery men of the 1940s known as the Justice Society of America. As Kent grew older, the helmet found Egyptian-American med student and Brooklyn resident Khalid Nassour. Khalid became Dr. Fate for a brief time, but realized he had much to learn. To that end, he began to study under his great-uncle, Kent Nelson, at the Tower of Fate in Salem, Massachusetts.

However, when the mysterious Source Wall at the edge of the universe was pierced and the very laws of magic began to change, Nabu decided to put an end to magic. He took control of Kent Nelson's form and the helmet, locked Khalid in a piece of ancient pottery, and opened a portal, allowing the so-called Otherkind into the world. Nabu's goal was to destroy the source of all magic—the realm called the Sphere of the Gods. This plan would kill all magical beings, but would also put an end to the threat of the Otherkind so would thereby ensure the Multiverse's survival. Luckily, the Justice League Dark discovered Nabu's horrific plan, and Man-Bat accidentally freed Khalid from his magical prison. As Nabu teamed with other Lords of Order, the Justice League Dark embraced dark magic and temporarily became the new Lords of Chaos in order to end Nabu's threat. Later, when the Justice League Dark was locked in battle with the witch Circe's Injustice League Dark, Khalid joined forces with Nabu and donned the Helmet of Fate once more. Khalid became Doctor Fate, a trusted member of Justice League Dark. Together, they embarked on a quest to stop the Otherkind and their leader, the terrifying Upside-Down Man.

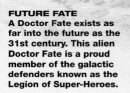

FUTURE FATE
A Doctor Fate exists as far into the future as the 31st century. This alien Doctor Fate is a proud member of the galactic defenders known as the Legion of Super-Heroes.

ON THE RECORD

Several heroes have served as Nabu's host, assuming the role of Doctor Fate over the years. Kent Nelson found the Helmet of Fate in an Egyptian archaeological dig and began his career as Doctor Fate in the 1940s.

When Kent died 40 years later, the Helmet passed to Eric Strauss, who mystically merged with his stepmother Linda Strauss to become the second Doctor Fate. After Eric was killed, Linda continued as Doctor Fate and came into conflict with the God of Chaos and possessed Benjamin Stoner, the evil Anti-Fate. On Linda's death, Kent Nelson's wife Inza briefly succeeded her, after which smuggler Jared Stevens served as the reluctant Fate until the late 1990s when he was murdered.

Hector Hall, son of the Golden Age Hawkman and Hawkgirl, took the role next, and after he was depowered by the Spectre, Kent Nelson's grandnephew, Kent V. Nelson, became Nabu's host. On Earth-2, Khalid Ben-Hassin donned a helmet that imbued him with Nabu's essence. He became that world's Doctor Fate, and joined the Super Hero team the Wonders of the World.

MYSTERY MAN
Kent Nelson was a proud member of the first generation of Super Heroes and a founding member of the Justice Society.

LEGACY OF FATE
Alcoholic former psychologist Kent V. Nelson was at rock-bottom when he found his great-uncle's helmet. Soon he rose to become the new Doctor Fate.

CLASSIC STORIES

The Immortal Doctor Fate #1–3 **(Jan.–Mar. 1985)** A collection of the definitive adventures of the original Doctor Fate, Kent Nelson, as he clashes with the likes of Wotan, Khalis, and Anubis.
Doctor Fate **(Vol. 1)** #1–4 **(Jul.–Oct. 1987)** Eric Strauss is chosen to wear the Helmet of Fate, merging with his stepmother Linda to become a new Doctor Fate.
Countdown to Mystery #1–8 **(Nov. 2007–Jun. 2008)** Kent V. Nelson, the grandnephew of the original Doctor Fate, continues the family tradition by donning the Helmet of Fate as the world moves inexorably toward *Final Crisis*.
The Brave and the Bold **(Vol. 3)** #30 **(Feb. 2010)** Kent Nelson places part of his spirit in Green Lantern Hal Jordan's ring so that he might see into the future, but discovers how he will die.

DIRECTOR BONES

DEBUT *Infinity Inc.* #16 (Jul. 1985)
BASE The Lipstick Building, New York City
HEIGHT 5ft 10in
WEIGHT 165 lbs
POWERS/ABILITIES Toxic "cyanide touch;" is immune to cyanide.
ALLIES Agent Chase
ENEMIES Batwoman, Batman, Blue Beetle
AFFILIATIONS Department of Extranormal Operations

The skull-faced Director Bones led the Department of Extranormal Operations, a secret government agency that monitored superhuman activity. Bones focused on gathering intelligence on "capes" and then utilizing this information to control them for his own ends.

After gaining information on Batwoman's secret identity, Bones convinced her to work for him by threatening to incarcerate her father. She teamed up with Wonder Woman to track down the Medusa. The director then forced her to help him uncover Batman's secret identity by revealing that her long-lost twin sister Beth was in custody. Batman and Batwoman teamed up to save Beth. Mounting concern over Director Bones' sociopathic behavior led to his eventual incarceration in a secure facility.

DJINN

DEBUT *Teen Titans Special* (Vol. 1) #1 (Aug 2018)
REAL NAME Unknown
BASE Mobile
HEIGHT Unknown **WEIGHT** Unknown
EYES Purple **HAIR** Brown
POWERS/ABILITIES Magical powers include shapeshifting, levitation, possession, creating illusions, and manipulating reality itself.
ALLIES Robin, Crush
ENEMIES Elias, The Other, Deathstroke
AFFILIATIONS Teen Titans

Djinn was a sila—a rare female genie. Although she appeared to be a teenager, she was in fact 4000 years old. As a young girl she had been cursed by her evil older brother to be imprisoned in a magic ring, the slave of anyone who wore it. Djinn had to follow the orders of some of history's most brutal megalomaniacs, committing deeds that haunted her.

When Robin (Damian Wayne) invited her to join the Teen Titans, Djinn saw it as a chance to redeem herself by saving people. Later trapped in her ring, she realized that it was within her power to free herself. After millennia, Djinn could live her own life, and she bid farewell to the Teen Titans so she could experience true freedom for the first time.

DOC MAGNUS

DEBUT *Showcase* #37 (Mar.–Apr. 1962)
REAL NAME William Magnus
BASE US Army Research Lab, Adelphi, Maryland
EYES Brown **HAIR** Brown
POWERS/ABILITIES Scientific genius and inventor with a talent for robotics.
ALLIES Cyborg
ENEMIES Chemo, Technosapiens
AFFILIATIONS Metal Men, US Army

Temperamental robotics genius Dr. William Magnus was hired by the US Army to create a robot suitable for search-and-rescue missions. He invented the Responsometer—a compact Artificial Intelligence that could shape metal around it. Magnus used it to make the "Metal Men"—sentient robots formed from different metals: Gold, Tin, Platinum, Iron, Lead, and Mercury.

However, when ordered to assassinate an enemy in Kahndaq, the robots refused. They went AWOL and hid in Magnus' apartment before sacrificing themselves to defeat the villain Chemo.

When the Crime Syndicate invaded Earth, Magnus rebuilt the Metal Men so they could help Cyborg take down the Syndicate's AI, Grid. Magnus and the Metal Men also helped Cyborg fight and defeat the Technosapien invaders.

MINDS OF THEIR OWN
Doc Magnus's sentient robot Metal Men seemingly inherited their inventor's independent temperament.

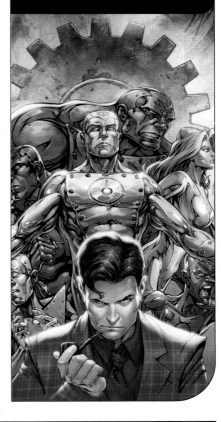

DOCTOR BEDLAM

DEBUT *Mister Miracle* (Vol. 1) #3 (Jul.–Aug. 1971)
BASE Dherain
EYES Purple
HAIR None
POWERS/ABILITIES Telepathy
ENEMIES The Flash, Green Lantern, and other Earth-2 heroes.
AFFILIATIONS Hunger Dogs

Doctor Bedlam is a devoted follower of Darkseid and now most commonly refers to himself simply as "Bedlam." His past is shrouded in mystery, but he was one of Steppenwolf's Hunger Dogs alongside Brutaal and Beguiler. He attacked Earth-2's heroes, but when Brutaal was revealed to be Superman, he used his telepathic powers to control several people, including Mister Terrific. He forced them to try and create a device that would move Earth-2 so that it could become a new home for his master, Darkseid.

Pre-*Flashpoint*, Doctor Bedlam could also manipulate people telepathically, but was a being of pure psionic energy which he housed in an android body. If this body was destroyed, Doctor Bedlam would simply move his consciousness into another one— although it seemed he was eventually killed by the Infinity Man.

DOCTOR DESTINY

DEBUT *Justice League of America* (Vol. 1) #5 (Jun.–Jul. 1961)
EYES Red
HAIR None
POWERS/ABILITIES Uses the Dreamstone to bring nightmares to life.
ENEMIES Justice League Dark, Madame Xanadu
AFFILIATIONS The Cold Flame

Doctor Destiny could make nightmares become real and trap people in their own dreams. He was the son of Madame Xanadu who had a vision when he was born of how evil he would become so was forced to abandon her child lest he destroy him as her vision had foretold. When Xanadu was part of the Justice League Dark, alongside John Constantine and Swamp Thing, her son, now calling himself Doctor Destiny, attacked the team. He had been given the Dreamstone by agents of the Cold Flame and he used it to steal the House of Mystery. Swamp Thing was imprisoned in the House, but eventually broke free and helped to stop Doctor Destiny, who was then killed by Madame Xanadu.

In his pre-*Flashpoint* incarnation, Doctor Destiny gained his power from stealing the Dreamstone (known as the Materioptikon) from Dream of the Endless.

DOCTOR LIGHT II

DEBUT *Crisis on Infinite Earths* (Vol. 1) #4 (Jul. 1985)
REAL NAME Kimiyo Tazu Hoshi
BASE Hall of Justice, Washington D.C.; formerly Japan
EYES Black **HAIR** Black
HEIGHT 5ft 3in **WEIGHT** 105 lbs
POWERS/ABILITIES Can control light in all its forms; flight.
ENEMIES Doctor Light (the original, villainous Arthur Light)
AFFILIATIONS Justice League

Kimiyo Tazu Hoshi was a Japanese scientist and astronomer who became the second Doctor Light during the first great Crisis. The Monitor, realizing he needed to recruit more Super Heroes, sent a beam of energy to Earth that struck Kimiyo, giving her the ability to control all forms of light.

As Doctor Light, Kimiyo used her powers for good, but her arrogant attitude annoyed other heroes at first—until she witnessed Supergirl's heroic death during the fight against the Anti-Monitor. After the battle, a more respectful Doctor Light fought alongside both the Doom Patrol and the Justice League, spending time with the League's European branch.

As a single mother with two kids, she decided to put her family first and became a reserve member of the Justice League, but heeded the call when needed. She returned to active duty to fight Eclipso, the

SOLAR POWER
While Kimiyo's powers are very strong, she needs light energy to feed them. If she is trapped in darkness, her abilities will simply fade away.

Secret Six, and the Crime Syndicate.

In post-*Flashpoint* reality, Kimiyo was the wife of scientist hero Arthur Light.

DOCTOR LIGHT

DEBUT *Justice League of America* (Vol. 1) #12 (Jun. 1962)
REAL NAME Dr. Arthur Light
BASE Chetland United Atlantic Islands
EYES Black   **HAIR** Black   **HEIGHT** 5ft 11in   **WEIGHT** 171 lbs
POWERS/ABILITIES Light manipulation that includes blinding brightness, powerful laser beams, hologram projects, solid light constructs; flight.
ALLIES Deathstroke
ENEMIES The Outsider, Crime Syndicate, Justice League
AFFILIATIONS Justice League of America, A.R.G.U.S., Crimson Men

Doctor Arthur Light was a dedicated scientist working for A.R.G.U.S. when an accident gave him amazing metahuman abilities. A married man with a family, Arthur Light had no intention of being a Super Hero, but was forced into the role as part of the Justice League of America—with fatal consequences.

CLASSIC STORIES

Secret Origins (Vol. 2) #37 (Feb. 1989) The truth about Doctor Light's origins are revealed—including details of the original Doctor Light.

Identity Crisis (Aug. 2004–Feb. 2005) Doctor Light takes on a darker twist as secrets of his past are revealed, including his part in one of the most horrific attacks ever to take place on a member of the Justice League.

Justice League (Vol. 2) #22 (Sep. 2013) The new, heroic Doctor Light—still a relative newcomer to the Super Hero world—is killed by Superman when the Man of Steel's powers misfire.

BROUGHT TO LIGHT
Caught in the Lasso of Truth, Doctor Light came to the terrible realization that he is in fact already dead.

ASHES TO ASHES
Doctor Light came to a horrific end. After he accidentally hit Wonder Woman with his powers, an enraged Superman inadvertently decapitated him with his heat vision.

Arthur Light was a scientist working for A.R.G.U.S. (Advanced Research Group Uniting Superhumans) and the Justice League of America. A married man with three daughters, Arthur lived an unremarkable life until tasked with studying a coin used for communication by agents of the Crime Syndicate. While investigating it, the coin received a signal and Arthur was engulfed in a blast of light that transformed him into a metahuman. While A.R.G.U.S. helped him come to terms with his new abilities, they also put him to work as a member of the Justice League of America.

On his very first mission his light powers seemed to set off Superman's heat vision and Doctor Light was killed. After the Crime Syndicate took over Earth-0, an energy apparition of Doctor Light appeared and was taken in by the Crimson Men who promised to return him to a physical form if he gave them information on Steve Trevor. When Doctor Light was forced to attack Trevor, he found himself also fighting Killer Frost. Trevor used Wonder Woman's Lasso of Truth on Doctor Light, causing him to remember that he had died. Realizing he was just an echo of the real Doctor Light, the apparition vanished in a blast of energy.

Doctor Light embarked on a criminal career, adopting a white and black costume. However, he was well aware that he was a dead man, simply a reconstructed consciousness made of pure light. He eventually moved to the Chetland United Atlantic Islands and was granted asylum in exchange for gifting that country's dictator "Radiant Men," artificial light-powered soldiers under Light's command.

When his ally Deathstroke was seemingly killed, Doctor Light attended the funeral that was populated by dozens of Super-Villains. He even created a holographic image of Superman hovering above the festivities to trick other Super Heroes into believing that the criminals were being kept in line by a watchful eye.

ON THE RECORD

Dr. Arthur Light worked at S.T.A.R. Labs where his colleague Dr. Jacob Finlay had created an energy-manipulating costume to become a Super Hero called Doctor Light. After accidentally killing Finlay, Arthur took the costume and name to fight the Justice League and Teen Titans as a true Super-Villain.

A brief member of the Suicide Squad, Light was retroactively revealed to have assaulted the Elongated Man's wife Sue Dibny during the Justice League of America's earlier years. He later helped murder the Martian Manhunter. The Spectre eventually executed the villain for his crimes in *Final Crisis: Revelations* #1 (Oct. 2008).

LIGHT GOES BLACK
Doctor Light returned as a Black Lantern to attack his successor, Kimiyo Hoshi, during the *Blackest Night* event.

DOCTOR MANHATTAN

DEBUT *Watchmen* (Vol. 1) #1 **(Sep 1986)**
REAL NAME Jonathan Osterman
BASE Mars
HEIGHT 6ft 5in **WEIGHT** Variable **EYES** White **HAIR** None
ALLIES Silk Spectre (Laurie Juspeczyk)
ENEMIES Ozymandias
AFFILIATIONS Crimebusters

Nuclear physicist Jonathan Osterman was working at a research facility when he was accidentally trapped in a test chamber for molecular experiments. Jon was disintegrated by the machine and pronounced dead, but over the following months his consciousness began to reassemble itself as a completely new kind of being. This being became known as Doctor Manhattan, and it soon became apparent that his powers were far beyond anything that had been seen before. The US authorities seized on the opportunity to use Doctor Manhattan as a kind of living nuclear deterrent.

Doctor Manhattan's incredible abilities—experiencing different moments in time simultaneously, including future events, reshaping matter at will, and withstanding almost any attack—could have made him a great Super Hero. However, his transformation had left Doctor Manhattan emotionally detached from humanity's problems. Departing Earth for the solitude of Mars, he used his powers to create a shimmering glass palace from the planet's dust.

At one point, Doctor Manhattan seemingly came to Earth, intrigued by a vision in which he was attacked by Superman. As it became apparent that Superman was trying to protect him, not hurt him, Manhattan realized that the hope that the hero represented was a constant throughout the Multiverse. He transferred his powers to a young boy whom he named Clark, leaving him to be raised by former comrades Nite Owl and Silk Spectre, and vanished from existence.

A QUESTION OF POWER.
It is believed that Doctor Manhattan may have been drawn to Earth for a confrontation with Superman.

DOCTOR MID-NITE

DEBUT *Doctor Mid-Nite* #1 **(1991)** (Pieter Cross)
REAL NAME Pieter Anton Cross, M.D.
BASE Portsmouth City
EYES Blue **HAIR** Black **HEIGHT** 5ft 10in **WEIGHT** 175 lbs
POWERS/ABILITIES Able to see in the dark; carries inventions to aid his crime fighting, including blackout bombs; excellent medical and surgical skills.
ENEMIES Johnny Sorrow, Icicle, Ultra-Humanite, Mordru, Endless Winter, Mircea
AFFILIATIONS Justice Society of America

Pieter Anton Cross was the second person to take on the role of Doctor Mid-Nite. The original, Dr. Charles M. McNider, had saved Pieter's pregnant mother when she'd been attacked, and helped her give birth to Pieter. Cross grew up to be a physician himself, graduating from Harvard Medical School aged only 19, and worked with McNider, who became his mentor.

While investigating the origins of a dangerous drug called A39 (a variation of the Venom serum), Cross was knocked out and injected with the drug by the dealers, who placed him behind the wheel of a car. Cross regained consciousness just as the car struck a woman. The drug and accident left him blind but astonishingly allowed him to see during the night. He became Doctor Mid-Nite to bring the dealers to justice, and then continued in the role, joining a reformed Justice Society of America. When not crime fighting, he often used his medical skills to aid other Super Heroes and later mentored the young Blue Beetle (Jaime Reyes).

In the post-*Flashpoint* reality, Pieter Cross worked as a doctor in Seattle, and aided the Green Arrow after he was wounded.

"YOU'LL LIVE"
As the de facto team medic, Doctor Mid-Nite treated Mr. America's injuries when he received a nasty beating at the hands of the corrupted missionary William Matthews.

DOCTORS IN THE HOUSE
Two other heroes took on the role of Doctor Mid-Nite. The original, Dr. Charles McNider (top), lost his sight to a grenade, and fought crime alongside the original Justice Society of America. The second was Beth Chapel (above). She became a member of Infinity, Inc. but was killed by Eclipso soon after becoming a hero.

DOCTOR PHOSPHORUS

DEBUT *Detective Comics* #469 (May 1977)
REAL NAME Alex Sartorius
BASE Gotham City
HEIGHT 5ft 11in **WEIGHT** 169 lbs
HAIR None **EYES** White
POWERS/ABILITIES Combusts in oxygen, emits toxic fumes; manipulates radiation.
ALLIES Arkham Knight, Neron
ENEMIES Starman, Batman

Eternally burning from millions of radioactive phosphorus particles embedded in his body, Doctor Phosphorus joined the Secret Society of Super-Villains and was remitted to Arkham Asylum when the Crime Syndicate's invasion collapsed. He was later broken out as war loomed between The Penguin's costumed crew and the murderous Carmine Falcone.

Phosphorus vanished into Gotham Underground, taking over Charnelton with his daughter, Tinderbox. He sought to control the Underground and strike at the world above, but needed to alter the surface environment, or his nature, to survive there.

Failing in his attempts to destroy Gotham City by converting it into fiery terrain he could endure, Phosphorus vanished until he was recruited by the Arkham Knight. Astrid Arkham involved him in a scheme to destroy Batman, but again he was defeated.

DOCTOR POLARIS

DEBUT *Green Lantern* (Vol. 2) #21 (Jun. 1963)
BASE New Mexico
REAL NAME Neal Emerson
HEIGHT 6ft 1in **WEIGHT** 194 lbs
HAIR Brown **EYES** Blue
POWERS/ABILITIES Wields magnetic energy to levitate, move metallic objects, and make force fields.
ALLIES Neron
ENEMIES Green Lantern Corps

Neal Emerson's research into magnetic polarity resulted in several medical breakthroughs. However, his work also caused him to develop a personality disorder. Over time, his darker side became the villainous, power-hungry Doctor Polaris.

Polaris clashed with Hal Jordan, Earth's Green Lantern, several times, with Hal often coaxing out Neal's benevolent personality, and so ending Polaris' magnetic rampages.

Emerson originally used technology to control magnetism, but his body eventually internalized the power. After the Anti-Monitor attacked Earth, Polaris and other villains tried to destroy all Earth-based Green Lanterns. During *Infinite Crisis*, Polaris joined the Secret Society of Super-Villains, but later perished in an explosion. His successor, John Nichol, was killed by the Black Lantern version of Emerson.

DOCTOR PSYCHO

DEBUT *Wonder Woman* (Vol. 1) #5 (Jun.–Jul. 1943)
REAL NAME Edgar Cizko
HEIGHT 3ft 9in **WEIGHT** 85 lbs
HAIR None **EYES** Brown
POWERS/ABILITIES Psionic ability; hallucination creation; astral projection.
ENEMIES Plastic Man, Justice League, Wonder Woman
AFFILIATIONS The Cabal, Secret Society of Super-Villains

Doctor Psycho is a diminutive psychologist and con man with psionic abilities, who carried out séances to telepathically steal his clients' identities and data, and used his illusion-casting abilities to seduce women.

Overwhelmingly arrogant, Psycho has clashed with many Super Heroes, including Wonder Woman, Superboy, The Question, and Superman. He has also joined numerous criminal groups such as the Secret Society of Super-Villains and the League of Villainy. However, he never received the respect he felt was his due.

In recent times he allied with Hugo Strange, Queen Bee, Per Degaton, and the android Amazo in a clandestine organization dubbed the Cabal, but was again abused and physically humiliated: This time by the absurd Super Hero Plastic Man.

DOCTOR SIVANA

DEBUT *Whiz Comics* #2 (Feb. 1940)
REAL NAME Thaddeus Bodog Sivana
HEIGHT 5ft 6in **WEIGHT** 123 lbs
HAIR Bald **EYES** Brown
POWERS/ABILITIES Wide-ranging mastery of scientific and technical disciplines; magical abilities.
ALLIES Mr. Mind, Black Adam
ENEMIES Justice League
AFFILIATIONS Secret Society of Super-Villains

When his scientific investigations failed to provide answers in his quest to save his family from a terrible threat, Doctor Sivana turned to magic. He learned the story of Teth-Adam becoming Black Adam, and went to the site in Iraq he thought contained his tomb to search for an entrance to the Rock of Eternity. As the tomb opened, a bolt of lightning struck Sivana, scarring his face and giving him the ability to see magic through his damaged eye. Black Adam emerged from his tomb and together they hunted for Shazam, unleashing the Seven Deadly Sins along the way. When they located Shazam, Black Adam left Sivana. Distraught, Sivana returned to the entrance of the Rock of Eternity where he met a strange worm-like creature calling itself Mr. Mind, who said that he and Sivana would be the "best of friends." Mr. Mind was also the inventor of the secretive Unternet system—later corrupted by Darkseid for his own use.

A Legion of Sivanas from the different worlds united to destroy the Shazam Family and conquer the Multiverse, attempting to seize control of the Rock of Eternity.

DOCTOR THIRTEEN

DEBUT *Star-Spangled Comics* #122 (Nov. 1951)
BASE Gotham City
REAL NAME Terrence Thirteen II
HEIGHT 5ft 11in **WEIGHT** 168 lbs
HAIR Brown **EYES** Brown
POWERS/ABILITIES Skilled chemist and supernatural investigator.
ALLIES Phantom Stranger
ENEMIES Haunted Highwayman
AFFILIATIONS Justice League Dark

In 1880s Gotham City, Doctor Terrence Thirteen exposed fraudsters preying on the gullible. When he helped arrest Professor Jonathan Rood—a thief posing as the Haunted Highwayman—a stray bullet from the ensuing fight killed Rood's mother. Before he was hanged, the Professor cursed Thirteen and his descendants.

Many of them also became "Ghost Breakers" catching conmen. One of them used his investigative and medical talents during Justice League Dark's battle against the Blight. He and Nightmare Nurse even resurrected the dead heroes before Thirteen joined the Phantom Stranger to save young Chris Esperanza from Blight possession.

Doctor Thirteen also maintains that the supernatural is nonsense, despite his teenage daughter Traci being one of the most powerful witches on Earth.

DOLL WOMAN AND DOLL MAN

DEBUT *Feature Comics* #27 (Dec. 1939) (Doll Man); *Doll Man* #37 (Dec. 1951) (Doll Girl)
REAL NAMES Darrel Dane (Doll Man); Martha Roberts (Doll Girl)
BASE Earth-X
HEIGHT/WEIGHT Variable (Doll Man, Doll Girl)
HAIR Brown (Doll Man, Doll Woman)
EYES Blue (Doll Man); Brown (Doll Girl)
POWERS/ABILITIES Shrinking effect increases strength and physical abilities.
ALIIES Uncle Sam, Human Bomb, Black Condor
ENEMIES Nazis, Adolf Hitler II, Adolf Hitler III, Overman
AFFILIATIONS Freedom Fighters

Martha Roberts was the original Doll Girl. Her fiancé Darrel Dane, the original Doll Man, gave Martha shrinking powers like his so they could fight together. A second Doll Girl was a member of the Teen Titans.

After *Flashpoint*, Doll Man was Dane Maxwell, longtime friend of Jennifer Knight. While helping Knight track down her parents' murderers, Dane was shrunk to a minute size. Their crusade brought them to the attention of Uncle Sam, who recruited them.

On Earth-X the Nazis won World War II. Doll Man and Doll Woman battled with Uncle Sam's Freedom Fighters until he died in 1963. Decades later, Martha ultimately defeated fascism with a new team.

ON THE RECORD

Doctor Sivana was originally a mad scientist but, during his Golden Age history, his feud with the Marvel Family got more personal. He was now a rogue scientist and corrupt billionaire implicated in the murders of archaeologists C.C. and Marilyn Batson. Sivana attempted to steal the scarab necklace of the ancient wizard Shazam. He was thwarted by the wizard's champion, whom Sivana learned was young Billy Batson. Billy mockingly called Sivana "The Big Red Cheese."

GOLDEN AGE ADVERSARIES Doctor Sivana and his family—which include Georgia and Sivana Jr.—have long been foes of the Shazam family.

DOLLMAKER

BASE Gotham City
REAL NAME Barton Mathis
HEIGHT 5ft 11in **WEIGHT** 160 lbs
HAIR Brown **EYES** Blue
POWERS/ABILITIES Skilled surgeon.
ALLIES The Joker
ENEMIES Batman

FAMILY RESEMBLANCE
Barton Mathis' tribute to his father was to include parts of his face in his horrific skin mask of many faces.

Young Barton Mathis' father Wesley was a cannibal serial killer, who took his son along on his murderous hunts. Deranged by this experience, Barton became further unhinged when he witnessed his father's killing by a young Gotham City police officer named James Gordon. The orphaned boy was placed into foster care, but ran away, surfacing years later as the Super-Villain Dollmaker.

Mathis wore a gruesome mask stitched together from other faces—one of which was his father's—and led a gang of thugs with similar skin masks. Dollmaker conspired with The Joker to capture Batman and Commissioner Gordon, cutting off The Joker's face and providing a new one so that he could escape Arkham Asylum while people believed he was dead. Their plot failed when Batman freed himself and went after Dollmaker, who escaped, leaving behind The Joker's face—which became an object of perverse worship for The Joker's minions.

DOLPHIN

DEBUT *Showcase* #79 (Dec. 1968)
BASE Atlantis
HEIGHT 5ft 10in **WEIGHT** 145 lbs
EYES Blue **HAIR** White
POWERS/ABILITIES Very fast swimmer who can breathe in air and water; able to withstand deep-sea pressures.
ALLIES Aquaman, Tempest
ENEMIES The Spectre
AFFILIATIONS Forgotten Heroes

A woman nicknamed Dolphin is the sole surviving member of an alien experiment on humans. She was freed by the spirit of Kordax the Cursed—which hailed from Atlantis' earliest days—and then found by Navy officer Chris Landau and his crew.

Dolphin was initially the main attraction at Oceanworld, but eventually returned to the sea, where she discovered Atlantis and was made welcome. She met Aquaman during a battle with Charybdis and later fell in love with Aquaman's adopted son, Tempest.

Dolphin joined father and son on several missions until she and Tempest married. They had a child during the war between Atlantis and Cerdia, and the baby was named Cerdian to help heal the conflict. Dolphin later insisted that Tempest leave the Teen Titans to devote his time to their family and home in Atlantis.

DOMINATORS

DEBUT *Adventure Comics* #361 (Oct. 1967)
BASE Dominion
HEIGHT Variable **WEIGHT** Variable
EYES Black **HAIR** Bald
POWERS/ABILITIES Master geneticists with highly advanced technologies.
ENEMIES Superman. Green Lantern Corps
AFFILIATIONS None for any length of time

The Dominion is a highly advanced, technological civilization organized along rigid hierarchical lines and based on genetic manipulation. Using sampled metagenes, Dominators create specialized members of their society tailored for specific roles with a variety of powers and abilities.

Extremely ambitious, Dominators constantly seek to expand their sphere of influence and are adept at political intrigue. When they deemed Earth's metahuman potential to be a danger, they coordinated a shaky coalition of space-faring civilizations to eradicate humanity. Even after an army of Super Heroes defeated the scheme, the Dominion profited, as they had used the opportunity to add many metagene samples to their inventory. In recent times their operatives clashed with rogue Guardian of the Universe Rami and attempted a second invasion of Earth, which was repelled single-handedly by Superman.

DOOM PATROL

DEBUT *My Greatest Adventure* #80 (Jun. 1963)
BASE Los Angeles
CURRENT MEMBERS/POWERS The Chief (Dr. Niles Caulder): genius intellect; **Elasti-Girl** (Rita Farr): elasticity, size alteration; **Negative Man** (Lawrence Trainor): radioactive projection, can fly and become intangible; **Robotman** (Cliff Steele): nanomachine-created robot body with various powers; **Element Woman** (Emily Sung): metamorphosis, elemental manipulation.
ALLIES A.R.G.U.S., Justice League
ENEMIES Crime Syndicate of America

Dr. Niles Caulder—also known as the Chief—created the Doom Patrol from a group of ostracized and traumatized metahuman misfits, figuring they would have nothing to lose. The first roster, which included the likes of Scorch, Karma, Negative Woman, and Tempest, were all killed in a fight with Johnny Quick and Atomica of the Crime Syndicate of America when they invaded Earth. As a result, Dr. Caulder brought together a new team: Elasti-Girl, Negative Man, Robotman, and Element Woman, who was estranged from the Justice League.

The team went after the new Power Ring (Jessica Cruz), but during the mission the members of Doom Patrol learned that Caulder was not at all what he seemed, when they crossed paths with Justice League members also pursuing Cruz. Not only did Dr. Caulder try to lobotomize Jessica so that he could control her, but Lex Luthor informed the Doom Patrol that Caulder himself was also responsible for the freak accidents that gave the members their powers. Celsius and Tempest, previous Doom Patrol members, had faked their own deaths to free themselves of his control. In the aftermath of these revelations, the future of the team is uncertain.

MOTLEY CREW
1 Robotman
2 The Chief
3 Element Woman
4 Negative Man
5 Elasti-Girl

ON THE RECORD

The first Doom Patrol—Elasti-Girl, Negative Man, and Robotman—was assembled by the wheelchair-bound Dr. Niles Caulder. He believed that his band of alienated outcasts would be willing to risk their lives as the world's strangest Super Heroes battling equally bizarre villains.

By contrast, the pre-*Flashpoint* Caulder manipulated and betrayed the trust of the team, even as he encouraged them to fight the Brotherhood of Evil and General Immortus. One especially odd later addition to the team was the sentient road, Danny the Street, who later helped the Teen Titans escape the evil Harvest.

UNDER FIRE
Niles Caulder put the Doom Patrol together, but he wasn't sentimental about individual members whom he considered a threat.

DOOMSDAY

DATA

DEBUT *Superman: The Man of Steel* (Vol. 1) #17 **(Nov. 1992)**
BASE Mobile
HEIGHT 7ft 6in   **WEIGHT** 915 lbs
EYES Red   **HAIR** White
POWERS/ABILITIES Overwhelming strength, regeneration, invulnerability, able to learn and adapt after its own death.
ALLIES None
ENEMIES Superman, Wonder Woman, Justice League

THE OZ EFFECT
When Superman banished Doomsday to the Phantom Zone, the beam was intercepted by his father Jor-El, who imprisoned Doomsday in a misguided attempt to keep his son safe.

CLASSIC STORIES

Superman **(Vol. 2) #75 (Jan. 1993)** Doomsday falls to Superman's ultimate efforts. The unconscious monstrosity is carted away into captivity as Earth mourns the death of its greatest hero.
Superman/Doomsday: Hunter/ Prey **(Vol. 1) #1–3 (Apr.–Jun. 1994)** Thrown into space, Doomsday landed on Apokolips and battled Darkseid. He was then transported to the planet of Calaton, with Superman in hot pursuit.
Superman: The Doomsday Wars **(Vol. 1) #1–3 (Nov. 1998–Jan. 1999)** Doomsday is plucked from the End of Time and his body merged with Brainiac's intellect in a lethal experiment.

PRISON UNIFORM
When Superman first faced Doomsday, as well as when Doomsday reappeared in Metropolis recently, the monster was wearing a green bodysuit that hid his horrible visage.

Doomsday is an alien creature of overwhelming force and savage bloodlust whose appearance invokes terror. When he first arrived on Earth, his rampage of mindless destruction devastated Metropolis. The carnage ended only after Superman died putting the mindless beast down.

Doomsday was created on Krypton

nearly 250,000 years ago. The alien that would become a hulking creature of pure destruction was actually the subject of a cruel experiment. He was killed and then cloned, killed and cloned again. The process was ruthlessly repeated daily in some cases. The child learned to live longer and longer each time, finally become a killing machine himself at the end of an evolutionary journey that lasted decades. Doomsday was imprisoned, but eventually found his way to Earth. He carved a bloody swath to Metropolis, where Superman successfully stopped him, but at the cost of his own life. While Superman later returned, thanks to Kryptonian technology and a visit from his father in the afterlife, so too did Doomsday, the creature even stronger than before.

Superman has fought, and defeated, Doomsday many times, despite Doomsday often receiving an upgrade from time to time. When the creature once again rampaged through Metropolis recently, Superman sent him into the Phantom Zone after receiving some help from both Wonder Woman and Lex Luthor. However, that transmission was intercepted by Superman's Kryptonian father Jor-El, who kept Doomsday restrained in order to protect his son. When Jor-El finally revealed to his son that he had indeed survived the destruction of Krypton, Superman was both shocked and disgusted that his father was holding Doomsday captive. Restrained for now, it is only a matter of time before Doomsday breaks free to wreak havoc once more.

ON THE RECORD

Doomsday debuted in 1992: a relentless, unreasoning juggernaut of destruction intent on invading Metropolis. Draped in a shroud with futuristic, broken shackles, it smashed its way across America and was only stopped at the cost of Superman's life.

In 2011, mere months before the *Flashpoint* event, Luthor unleashed a wave of Doomsday clones against every hero wearing Superman's symbol. The furious onslaught enveloped Superboy, Supergirl, Eradicator, Steel, and even Cyborg Superman. None knew their true enemy was an intelligent and manipulative super-Doomsday clone called the Doomslayer.

REIGN OF THE DOOMSDAYS
Although no longer unique, the alien entity Doomsday was always an aptly named, serious threat.

WALKING NIGHTMARE
Ruthless, relentless, unstoppable; the monolithic monster spread terror and death wherever he went.

DRAGON, RICHARD

DEBUT *Richard Dragon, Kung Fu Fighter* (Vol. 1) #1 (Apr.–May 1975)

REAL NAME Ricardo Diaz, Jr.

BASE Seattle

EYES Brown **HAIR** Bald

POWERS/ABILITIES Accomplished martial artist; strategic and tactical mastermind.

ALLIES Billy "The Clock King" Tockman, Count Vertigo, Red Dart, Brick, Killer Moth

ENEMIES Green Arrow, Shado, John Diggle

AFFILIATIONS The Longbow Hunters, League of Assassins

Ricardo Diaz, Jr. is the son of criminal royalty. Until Green Arrow and John Diggle stopped him, Diaz Senior ruled Seattle's underworld, and when they destroyed the enterprise his son swore vengeance. He joined the League of Assassins and was trained by Richard Drakunovski in all aspects of the martial arts.

Ricardo readily absorbed the combat lore of the fabled "Richard Dragon" but rejected his sensei's attempts to instill a moral code or compassion. When he learned all he could, Diaz killed his mentor, taking his name.

Returning to Seattle, the new Dragon began reclaiming his inheritance, killing gang bosses and bringing together the fragmented groups to form an army of terror. He organized a Super-Villain task-force to collect a multi-million dollar bounty on Green Arrow and tried to force the hero into accepting him as Seattle's ultimate power.

DRAGON'S HORDE
The merciless and deadly Crime King of Seattle took whatever he wanted and defended his treasures with an army of lethal metahuman killers.

DREAM GIRL

DEBUT *Adventure Comics* (Vol. 1) #317 (Feb. 1964)

BASE Legion HQ, 31st-century New Metropolis

REAL NAME Nura Nal

HEIGHT 5ft 5in **WEIGHT** 120 lbs

POWERS/ABILITIES Oneiromancy, preternaturally accurate precognitive dreams.

ALLIES High Seer of Naltor

ENEMIES Horraz Collective

AFFILIATIONS Legion of Super-Heroes, Legion of Substitute Heroes

Nura Nal is a near-infallible precognitive seer who foresees forthcoming events when she sleeps. As Dream Girl she represents Naltor in the Legion of Super-Heroes, hailing from an extremely advanced species almost universally capable of seeing the future. After joining the multiplanetary team, she ensured every teammate knew that she saw a great and glorious future for them all: a boon made easier with her ability to psychically share her visions with others. However, she later reveals to the United Planets Council that her reason for joining the Legion is that for many months (cycles) she has seen a galaxy-shattering "Great Darkness is coming"…

Glitteringly resplendent and physically beautiful by human standards, Dream Girl is astute, sensitive and diplomatic. Her powers make her a brilliant judge of sentient character and she always knows exactly how best to spread the news, good or otherwise.

TRUE VISIONARY
Dream Girl's superpower is just a handy qualifying detail for Legion membership. Her true value is as an independent, inspirational strategist.

DRAK, LYSSA

DEBUT *Green Lantern* (Vol. 4) #18 (May 2007)

BASE Talok V, Qward, Sector 3500

EYES Red **HAIR** Black

POWERS/ABILITIES Emotional empathy, prognostication, seduction through storytelling.

ALLIES Arkillo, Amon Sur

ENEMIES Green Lantern Corps, Guardians of the Universe, Sinestro

AFFILIATIONS Sinestro Corps, Black Lanterns

Purportedly recruited by Sinestro himself to haunt Space Sector 3500, the empath was one of his most effective Yellow Lanterns. Drak also recorded the Legion of Fear's atrocities in the Book of Parallax.

A gifted seer and raconteur who could seduce the unwary with horrific tales, she tested Yellow Corpsmen. When Arkillo finished their training in ring-wielding, Drak would make them confront their darkest terrors in her Fear Lodge. All who failed died horribly, their fates recorded in the Book.

After being captured by John Stewart and Guy Gardner, Drak was imprisoned in a Sciencell on Oa. When *Blackest Night* commenced, she attempted to steal the Book of the Black, but was trapped within its pages before being released and becoming its keeper.

DUCARD, HENRI

DEBUT *Detective Comics* (Vol. 1) #599 (Apr. 1989)

BASE Paris, France

HEIGHT 6ft 4in **WEIGHT** 215 lbs

EYES Brown **HAIR** Gray

POWERS/ABILITIES Keen deductive reasoning, expert marksman.

ALLIES Morgan Ducard

ENEMIES Bruce Wayne

Manhunter and mercenary, former French Interpol agent Henri Ducard was considered the world's greatest tracker. He was sought out by young Bruce Wayne, who wanted to learn all his techniques for his own future role as a crime fighter. When the implacable stalker at last agreed to teach the boy-millionaire, Ducard paired him with his own son, Morgan, to track a terrorist across Paris. Wayne was unaware Ducard had been hired to murder their target, or that his classmate was avidly learning all the tricks of a successful killer for hire. As a deadly graduation test, the remorseless and utterly amoral tutor tasked Morgan with killing Bruce, but when the junior Ducard failed, Henri cut off all contact with his son.

DREADFULS, THE

DEBUT *The Terrifics* (Vol. 1) #11 (Jun. 2017)

BASE Mobile

MEMBERS/POWERS Doc Dread: Genius intellect, armor giving him super-strength and durability, flight and energy blast ability; **Metalmorpho:** Robotic version of Metamorpho from Earth-44; **Plasma-Man:** Vampire from Earth-43, stretching ability; **Phantom Boy:** Ghost teen from Earth-13.

ALLIES None

ENEMIES The Terrifics

Java, the hyper-intelligent Neanderthal who worked for businessman Simon Stagg, was intensely jealous of Mr. Terrific and invented the villainous persona of Doc Dread to bring him down. When this failed, Doc Dread decided to use a stolen T-sphere to travel the Multiverse and eliminate all the versions of Mr. Terrific in every reality. Since he had failed to defeat Mr. Terrific alone, he assembled a team of alternate versions of the Terrifics, named The Dreadfuls. As Mr. Terrific pursued them across realities, The Dreadfuls confronted him on Earth-23. They appeared to have the upper hand until backup arrived—the reassembled Terrifics and Earth-23's Ms. Terrific. The Dreadfuls were brought to the House of Heroes at the heart of the Multiverse to be tried by Justice Incarnate.

DURLANS

DEBUT *Action Comics* (Vol. 1) #283 (Dec. 1961)

BASE Durla

HEIGHT Variable **WEIGHT** Variable

EYES Variable **HAIR** Variable

POWERS/ABILITIES Elastic physicality, able to instantly reshape their form.

ENEMIES Other Durlans

AFFILIATIONS United Planets

Durla was a wealthy, technologically advanced world until a "Six-Minute War" between its leading nations left the planet a radioactive ruin. The conflagration turned the planet into a desert husk where survivors mutated into physically unstable shapeshifters who chose a base shape—usually multi-tentacled and enshrouded. These Durlans gradually formed regressive anti-technology clans, perpetually at war with each other, but uniformly suspicious of—and xenophobic towards—off-worlders.

In time, a separate sub-group evolved out of the warring sects. Futurist Durlans resolved to regain control of their species' mutated genome, actively embraced science, and infiltrated Earth in the early 20th century to exploit its rapidly growing technological base.

ECLIPSO

DEBUT *House of Secrets* (Vol. 1) #61 (Jul.–Aug. 1963)
REAL NAME Kaala
BASE Heart of Darkness (his Black Diamond)
HEIGHT Variable **WEIGHT** Variable **EYES** Red **HAIR** None
POWERS/ABILITIES Fueled by rage; invulnerability, dark energy generation, teleportation through shadows, telepathy, telekinetic manipulation, body possession, memory manipulation; powers magnified during an eclipse.
ALLIES Kaala, Alex Montez, Gordon Jacobs
ENEMIES Team 7, Lady Chandra, Princess Amaya, Justice League, Justice Society
AFFILIATIONS Secret Society of Super-Villains, House Onyx, House Diamond

Created at the dawn of time, Eclipso is the evil Spirit of God's Vengeance. Over eons he possessed many hosts until he incarnated on the Gemworld as Lord Kaala, scion of House Onyx and House Diamond. Kaala launched a war but was defeated by Lady Chandra of House Amethyst, who trapped him in a Black Diamond, subsequently hiding it on Earth.

The "Heart of Darkness" holding Eclipso was recovered in modern times by America's Team 7 and locked in A.R.G.U.S.'s Black Room. Catwoman stole it for Alex Montez, who became Eclipso's new host. John Constantine offered Montez/Eclipso passage to Gemworld, sealing the portal after him. Eclipso seized control of House Onyx and House Diamond again, leading them against House Amethyst, but was returned to the Black Diamond by Princess Amaya. The gem returned to Earth, where Eclipso found new host Gordon Jacobs, before being sealed in his gem once more.

Following *Rebirth*, when Justice League Dark battled both the Otherkind and Circe over the fate and direction of magic, Eclipso was again released to capitalize on the wickedness of humanity and war between the realms of magic.

ON THE RECORD

Pre-*Flashpoint*, Eclipso was God's original Spirit of Vengeance, but when it turned evil it was replaced by The Spectre. Eclipso initially possessed solar-technology expert Bruce Gordon, though he later broke free. Alex Montez then used a set of mystic tattoos to harness Eclipso's power without surrendering control to the spirit. During the Day of Vengeance, Eclipso possessed the Atom's ex-wife, Jean Loring, and drew Mary Shazam under his evil influence. When the *Brightest Day* event occurred, the villain plotted to kill God.

SPLIT PERSONALITY
When hosted by scientist Bruce Gordon, Eclipso found himself unwillingly forced into the role of hero.

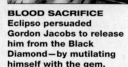

BLOOD SACRIFICE
Eclipso persuaded Gordon Jacobs to release him from the Black Diamond—by mutilating himself with the gem.

TAKING POSSESSION
Eclipso escaped the Black Diamond on Kalaa and possessed Deathstroke, but was imprisoned in the jewel again by Slade's Team 7 comrades.

DARK NEMESIS
Though Eclipso has been defeated multiple times, this relentless, malevolent villain always returns, seemingly more powerful than before.

EDGE, MORGAN

DEBUT *Superman's Pal, Jimmy Olsen* #133 (Oct .1970)
BASE Metropolis
HEIGHT 6ft 2in
WEIGHT 235 lbs
EYES Brown **HAIR** Bald (black)
POWERS/ABILITIES Ruthless but highly intelligent businessman.
ENEMIES Superman

Media baron Morgan Edge is the President and CEO of the Planet Global Network and owner of the PGN TV network and *The Globe* tabloid. He also acquired the *Daily Planet* newspaper, replacing its iconic globe-topped building with a sleek modern office block. As CEO of PGN, he backed the *Challengers* adventure-reality TV show (starring the Challengers of the Unknown) and shamelessly exploited the tragic deaths of three team members for publicity.

Edge also aired a report that (incorrectly) claimed to reveal Superman's identity—over the objections of PGN's executive producer, Lois Lane. Edge's cavalier approach to journalistic ethics led to Clark Kent and Jack Ryder quitting. However, when Metropolis was attacked by an alien, Edge displayed a gift for leadership.

NEW PLANET
Edge's new and more callous style of business management won him few friends among long-serving *Daily Planet* staff.

EFFIGY

DEBUT *Green Lantern* (Vol. 3) #110 (Mar. 1999)
REAL NAME Martin Van Wyck
BASE New York City
EYES Blue **HAIR** Blond
HEIGHT 6ft 1in **WEIGHT** 195 lbs
POWERS/ABILITIES Flies through space, generates flame bursts, creates fiery energy constructs.
ENEMIES Green Lantern, The Spectre

Disgruntled loser Martin Van Wyck was abducted by the alien Controllers and given fire-based powers before being deemed a "failed experiment" and sent back to Earth. When using his powers, Van Wyck transformed into a white-skinned, flame-headed being and took the name Effigy. With no other ambitions, he wreaked havoc, setting fire to the Hollywood sign. After a battle with Green Lantern, he was reclaimed by the Controllers.

Effigy later returned to Earth, where he fell for Killer Frost, but when she was buried in an avalanche, he callously abandoned her. The villain then served in the Society and Libra's Secret Society of Super-Villains and was briefly exiled to the planet of Salvation. Effigy suffered a gruesome death during *Final Crisis*, when The Spectre burned him alive in a lantern.

EL DIABLO (CHATO SANTANA)

DEBUT *El Diablo* (Vol. 3) #1 (Nov. 2008)
REAL NAME Chato Santana
BASE Belle Reve Penitentiary
EYES Black **HAIR** Bald
POWERS/ABILITIES Tattoos provide flame-generation powers; can also use these powers to heal by burning toxins from people's systems.
ENEMIES Basilisk, Resurrection Man, Bloodletter

Born in a deprived neighborhood, Chato Santana joined a street gang and developed a fearsome reputation as "El Diablo." Demonic-looking body tattoos gave him pyrotechnic powers. When a rival gang crossed him, he set their house ablaze, realizing too late that there were women and children inside.

Overcome with remorse, El Diablo did not resist arrest. Imprisoned at the Belle Reve Penitentiary, he was chosen by Amanda Waller for her Suicide Squad, a secret government-backed team of Super-Villains. After a potentially lethal training exercise, El Diablo saw a chance for redemption.

Recently, El Diablo received an pardon and left Belle Reve for his old neighborhood, only to come up against a deadly gang and their superpowered leader, Bloodletter.

EL DIABLO (LAZARUS LANE)

DEBUT *All-Star Western* (Vol. 2) #2 (Oct.–Nov. 1970)
REAL NAME Lazarus Lane
EYES Blue
HAIR Black with white streak
HEIGHT 6ft
WEIGHT 182 lbs
POWERS/ABILITIES Rendered unconscious, Lane releases El Diablo, a Spirit of Vengeance armed with revolver, bolos, and flaming whip.
ENEMIES Black River

Old West bank teller Lazarus Lane was struck by lightning and sent into a coma. He was then cursed by an Apache shaman, Wise Owl, and when he awoke he was the host for El Diablo, a demonic masked vigilante. From then on, whenever Lane was unconscious, El Diablo appeared and meted out harsh justice with his six-guns and fiery whip, soon becoming a feared figure on his black stallion, Lucifer.

When a town faced a zombie curse, El Diablo confronted the villain behind it—a Native American spirit warrior, Black River. Black River told him to punish the white men for killing Native American tribes and stealing their land. However, El Diablo stated that more killing would not change the past. El Diablo later inspired other heroes, including Rafael Sandoval and Chato Santana.

ELEMENT LAD

DEBUT *Adventure Comics* (Vol. 1) #307 (Apr. 1963)
REAL NAME Jan Arrah
BASE Legion Headquarters, 31st-century New Earth
EYES Green **HAIR** Yellow
HEIGHT 5ft 7in **WEIGHT** 140 lbs
POWERS/ABILITIES Transmutation of elements, elemental energy blasts; Legion flight ring.
ENEMIES Horraz Collective
AFFILIATIONS Legion of Super-Heroes

Jan Arrah is the last survivor of the planet Trom. Once inhabited by an insular race of matter transmuters, Trom was invaded by the Horraz Collective who ordered their new chattels to change the elemental properties of substances to enrich their new masters. When the Trommites unilaterally refused, the Horraz eradicated the species.

Jan remains tight-lipped about how he escaped the genocide, but in the aftermath he fled and offered his services to the newly formed Legion of Super-Heroes. Wry and laconic, he finds it difficult to socialize in large crowds, but is a valiant fighter.

He proudly boasts that he can alter the elemental composition of (almost) anything, but frankly admits that he still has problems changing things back to their original state.

ELASTI-GIRL/ELASTI-WOMAN

DEBUT *My Greatest Adventure* (Vol. 1) #80 (Jun. 1963)
REAL NAME Rita Farr **BASE** Los Angeles
HEIGHT 5ft 6in; Variable **WEIGHT** 126 lbs; Variable **EYES** Brown **HAIR** Brown
POWERS/ABILITIES Unstable body structure allows her to change size and shape, but if she loses focus she is in danger of losing her human form and turning into a blob of protoplasm.
ALLIES Niles Caulder, Negative Man, Robot Man, Element Woman
ENEMIES Galtry, Madame Rouge
AFFILIATIONS Doom Patrol

Movie star Rita Farr was filming on location in an African swamp when she was exposed to a mysterious gas that disrupted and broke down her cellular structure. Afterwards, she could alter her size and shape at will. However, if she lost concentration her shape would soften and she risked slipping into a formless mass. Rita suffered a nervous breakdown and opportunistic mad scientist Niles Caulder suggested she join his "super support group" for people with unwelcome superpowers—the Doom Patrol. As Elasti-Girl, she joined Negative Man, Robotman, and, over the years, many others. Caulder ("the Chief") led them on missions against monsters, Super-Villains, and uncanny threats before being exposed as having manufactured the accidents that created his Freak Heroes.

Rita tried to regain a semblance of normal life, marrying billionaire self-made Super Hero Steve Dayton (Mento) and adopting orphaned Beast Boy Gar Logan, but they too fell under Caulder's toxic influence. Rita found a measure of peace after being killed by Madame Rouge, but her new form was easily reconstructed and she returned to fight again in increasingly strange circumstances. At one stage she was even used by transdimensional Reality Agents Retconn as a conceptual source for commercial alternate existences.

Finally freed from everybody else's expectations, Elasti-Woman is now the emotional core of a new, Caulder-free family of Doom Patrollers.

KEEPING IT TOGETHER
Elasti-Girl may have once been a beloved Hollywood celebrity, but her transformation into a metahuman left her physically and mentally unstable.

ON THE RECORD

The original Rita Farr joined Doom Patrol as Elasti-Girl and married the psychic hero Mento. While on a mission, Rita was seemingly killed in an explosion. The pre-*Flashpoint* heroine later reunited with Mento and the Doom Patrol with no memory of how she had cheated death. Years later, it was revealed that the returned Elasti-Girl (or Elasti-Woman, as she was now called) was actually a protoplasmic duplicate created by the Chief—and that Mento had been manipulating her mind.

ATTACK OF THE 50FT WOMAN
Elasti-Girl took center stage as the Doom Patrol were forced to team up with their archenemies, the Brotherhood of Evil, to defeat the cosmic criminal Zarox-13.

ELEMENT WOMAN

DEBUT *Metamorpho* (Vol. 1) #10 (Feb. 1967)
REAL NAME Emily Sung
BASE Justice League's Watchtower satellite
EYES Violet **HAIR** Purple
POWERS/ABILITIES Can metamorphose into any element found in the human body.
ALLIES Firestorm, Metamorpho
ENEMIES Despero, Crime Syndicate
AFFILIATIONS Justice League, Doom Patrol

Emily Sung used her extraordinary elemental-transformation abilities to fight villainy as Element Woman. During the short-lived war between America and Atlantis, Emily was invited to join the Justice League. She and fellow novices Firestorm and the Atom helped to defend the League's satellite from alien intergalactic conqueror Despero. She later used her powers to remove a sliver of deadly Kryptonite from Superman's brain.

When the Crime Syndicate invaded Earth and took on the Justice League, Element Woman was imprisoned within Firestorm; when released, she disappeared. Her molecules were found and contained by Dr. Niles Caulder of the Doom Patrol, who convinced her that the Justice League did not want her, and offered her a place in his own team. Emily accepted, and she briefly battled her former teammates when the two groups clashed over Jessica Cruz, aka Power Ring.

PERSONAL ISSUES
Element Woman has amazing powers, but is plagued by insecurity and fear of rejection—which makes her easily manipulated by Niles Caulder.

ELONGATED MAN

DEBUT *The Flash* (Vol. 1) #112 (Apr.–May 1960)
REAL NAME Ralph Dibny **BASE** New York City
HEIGHT 6ft 1in (variable) **WEIGHT** 178 lbs **EYES** Blue **HAIR** Red
POWERS/ABILITIES Can alter his body to change his appearance, increase in size, stretch, or even turn into a parachute.
ALLIES Superman, Etrigan the Demon, Scandal Savage, Ragdoll, Jeanette
ENEMIES The Riddler (Mockingbird), League of Assassins, Leviathan
AFFILIATIONS Secret Six, Justice League

Ralph Dibny gained his amazing powers of contortion through unknown means—reputedly a metabolic reaction to Gingo, a plant extract unique to carbonated beverage Gingold. He used his abilities in his career as a 'detective with bonuses'. He and beloved wife Sue became jet-setting investigators, working with the world's Super Heroes. Everything changed when the couple attempted to recover a priceless diamond during a party on The Riddler's yacht. As the mastermind brazenly propositioned Sue in front of Ralph, the lights went out. Chaos ensued, explosions devastated the ship— and Sue and the diamond vanished.

Traumatized, Ralph became size-altering detective Big Shot to track her down, but was captured by the mysterious Mockingbird, along with Strix, Porcelain, Catman, Ventriloquist, and Black Alice. "Big Shot" helped them escape and provided sanctuary in his family home. The "Secret Six" became his new family, with Ralph acting as a father figure. After the group rescued amnesiac Sue from Mockingbird (who was actually the Riddler), Ralph revealed his true identity as the Elongated Man, and remained with the Secret Six until they disbanded. Semi-retired, he later worked with Lois Lane, Batman, and a group of other Super Hero detectives to uncover the identity of the new global spymaster Mark Shaw during Event Leviathan.

ON THE RECORD
Pre-*Flashpoint*, young Ralph Dibny was fascinated by traveling contortionists and worked out that their abilities stemmed from Gingold, a soft drink containing juice from the gingo fruit. When Ralph drank a concentrated gingo extract it gave him amazing stretching powers.

He moved to Central City to start a career as a Super Hero: the Elongated Man. Initially mistaken for a villain by local champion, the Flash, Ralph quickly built a reputation as an eccentric hero, detective, and member of several Justice League teams. He also somehow found time to fall in love with Sue Dearbon, and after they were married, the couple traveled the country, solving mysteries.

Ralph was devastated when Sue was murdered by Jean Loring. The sorcerer Felix Faust tried to trick Ralph into raising Sue from the dead, but the hero turned the tables on him, trapping the magician and his master, Neron, in Doctor Fate's tower—but at the cost of Ralph's own life. Ralph and Sue were finally reunited in the afterlife and became ghostly detectives. Their corpses were briefly animated during *Blackest Night*.

'TIL DEATH DO US PART?
Reunited in the afterlife, Ralph and Sue became the world's foremost ghost detectives.

ENEMY ACE

DEBUT *Our Army At War* #151 (Feb. 1965)
REAL NAME Hans von Hammer
BASE Germany
POWERS/ABILITIES Superb aerial combatant.
ENEMIES The Hangman, Allied Forces

With the twin guns of his Fokker triplane blazing a trail of destruction, the Enemy Ace, Hans von Hammer, became a legendary German pilot during World War I. The "Hammer of Hell" was the son of aristocrats and grew up in the Black Forest in south-west Germany, where he became an expert fencer and a true man of honor. To the other pilots in his fighter squadron, he was a human killing machine with more than 70 enemy deaths to his name.

Although he was unhappy with the Nazi regime, he was persuaded to come out of retirement and piloted a jet-powered Messerschmitt Me 262 during World War II. In the waning moments of the war, von Hammer's plane was shot down, and he landed in the Dachau concentration camp. Facing the horrific mass genocide of the Nazis for the first time, the renowned fighter renounced the Nazi regime and surrendered to the Americans.

One of von Hammer's most unusual adventures occurred when he teamed up with the present-day members of the Justice League United in the French town of Arracourt. That site became unmoored in time, owing to the presence of an anomaly in the universe known as a "breaker."

During that distortion in time, the Enemy Ace of 1940 shot down the high-flying Stargirl of the 21st century. The breaker had trapped von Hammer, Sgt. Rock, the Unknown Soldier, and the Creature Commandos within a jumbled timescape that included the past and future, leading them to fight over and over in that one location.

FIRING LINE
Mistaking Stargirl for a flying enemy combatant, von Hammer blasted her with machine gun fire from his Fokker triplane. Later, he would nurse her back to health and offer to fight alongside her and the Justice League United.

ON THE RECORD

Perhaps no story better distilled the essence of the Enemy Ace better than "Killer of the Skies," (*Showcase #57*, Aug. 1965). In that four-part epic, von Hammer ruefully admitted that he was trained to kill and took no pleasure in his victories or the deaths of his opponents. The Enemy Ace and two other German pilots then took to the skies to battle a Canadian pilot he had nicknamed the 'Hunter.' Von Hammer was appalled by the cowardice of his comrades when they realized the skill of their quarry and turned tail—only to be shot down as they fled the fight. The Enemy Ace then proposed a duel of honor, which the Hunter willingly accepted. As each man saluted the other, von Hammer confessed, "I will regret having to kill such a superb fighting man." After a thundering dogfight in the sky, both planes crashed to the ground. Refusing to be taken prisoner, the badly injured Hunter died in the field of battle, and von Hammer saluted his gallant foe one final time.

ACES HIGH
After a stunt pilot was murdered on the set of a movie about Enemy Ace, Batman investigated rumors that von Hammer's ghost was responsible. The culprit turned out to be a crew member, Heinrich Franz, an alleged descendant of Hans von Hammer.

ENCHANTRESS

DEBUT *Strange Adventures* (Vol. 1) #187 (Apr. 1966)
REAL NAME June Moone
BASE Washington, DC
EYES Blue **HAIR** Blond (as Enchantress: Red)
HEIGHT 5ft 6in **WEIGHT** 126 lbs
POWERS/ABILITIES Powerful magician; can warp reality and create duplicates of herself.
ALLIES Deadman, Justice League Dark
ENEMIES Felix Faust
AFFILIATIONS Justice League Dark, Suicide Squad, Shadowpact

June Moone is unwilling host for the magical entity Enchantress, bestowing incredible magical power but consequently affecting her sanity. As Enchantress, June was a troubled villain, or occasional heroine seeking atonement. When Madame Xanadu separated their personas, June slipped into near-madness while Enchantress unleashed deadly magic across Earth, seeking to reunite with her "bright half."

The Justice League confronted Enchantress but were driven off, prompting Zatanna to assemble occult heroes to meet her threat. Battling Justice League Dark, June ultimately merged with Enchantress to achieve atability. Later, Enchantress was one of many occult beings captured by Felix Faust to power the Crime Syndicate's Thaumaton weapon, before Justice League Dark stopped the mad mage.

Remanded to the Suicide Squad, Enchantress' dark attitudes were softened by an unlikely relationship with Killer Croc, but she still had the power to defeat Superman when Maxwell Lord orchestrated war between the Squad and Justice League. She failed, however, to stop the mind-bending rogue spymaster, and Lord escaped.

EMOTIONAL TRAUMA
Bonding with Enchantress took a heavy toll on June Moone's sanity.

EQUINOX

DEBUT *Justice League United* #0 (Jun. 2014)
REAL NAME Miiyahbin "Mii" Marten
BASE Ontario, Canada
POWERS/ABILITIES Flight, ice control, wind bursts.
ALLIES Justice League United
ENEMIES The Whitago

Miiyahbin Marten was a native Canadian and a citizen of the Cree Nation. When she turned 16, she was threatened by the Whitago, a dangerous supernatural creature that took its power from the seven dark pillars of Cree life. Instinctively tapping into buried knowledge, Miiyahbin uttered the ancient word "Keewatin" and was transformed into the hero Equinox. In her new identity, she invokes the power of the Midayo, the embodiment of the seven heroic aspects of the Cree: love, humility, bravery, truth, respect, wisdom, and honesty. This power, inherited from her grandmother, enables Miiyahbin to continue to protect her people from the Whitago, which can never be fully destroyed.

Equinox has a deep, spiritual connection to her homeland and its weather, and her powers change with the four seasons. When she experienced trouble controlling those powers, she reached out to the Justice League United for help. Eventually, she joined as a full member of the team.

SEASONAL WARRIOR
Equinox utilizes the powers of the seasons to battle the deadly, unstoppable Whitago.

ERADICATOR

DEBUT *Action Comics Annual* #2 (1989)
POWERS/ABILITIES Energy manipulation and projection, regeneration, flight, super-strength, heat vision, computer faculties, soul absorption
ENEMIES Supergirl, Superboy, Power Girl, Darkstars
ALLIES Zod, Green Lantern Corps

A Kryptonian AI superweapon, the Eradicator eliminated contaminating alien influences. On Earth, it built the Fortress of Solitude before trying to convert the planet into New Krypton. It took Superman's form after Doomsday killed him and, on his resurrection, melded with S.T.A.R. Labs scientist David Connor. After *Flashpoint*, an Eradicator program constructed Supergirl's Sanctuary of Solitude before determining Power Girl was Supergirl's clone and attacking her.

A new Eradicator emerged following *Rebirth*: one of an army of police robots designed by General Zod. This unit observed Krypton's destruction and reprogrammed itself to preserve the lost civilization—including Kryptonian souls. After joining Hank Henshaw's Superman Revenge Squad, the Eradicator served Zod's family, battling the Darkstars, and ultimately died fighting the Justice League.

EXTREME JUSTICE

DEBUT *Extreme Justice* #0 (Jan. 1995)
MEMBERS POWERS **Captain Atom:** Atomic-based powers **Amazing Man** Transforms into any material **Blue Beetle:** Wielder of hi-tech **Booster Gold:** Superb athlete **Maxima:** Super-strong and cunning alien queen
BASE Mount Thunder, Nevada
ENEMIES Legion of Doom

Officially known as Justice League West, the Super Hero team Extreme Justice formed when Captain Atom decided the world needed crime fighters willing to play by tougher rules than the Justice League. The new team's mission was to deal out "extreme justice" and, unlike the Justice League, they chose not to be sanctioned by the United Nations. Instead, Extreme Justice worked alone, seeking out criminals rather than responding to threats.

One of their first successful missions was ending a military coup and preventing nuclear holocaust. The team later expanded to include the heroes Firestorm, Plastique, and Wonder Twins Zan and Jayna. Their most notable battle was with the Legion of Doom, an equally tough Super-Villain team. Extreme Justice disbanded after their final mission, in which they invaded the country of Bialya and destroyed an army of cyborgs.

WISH YOU WEREN'T HERE
1 Dreamslayer 2 Death Bat
3 Doctor Diehard 4 Brute 5 Tracer
6 Gorgon 7 Lord Havok

EXTREMISTS

DEBUT *Justice League Europe* #15 (Jun. 1990)
MEMBERS POWERS/ABILITIES **Lord Havok:** Battlesuit can mutate on command **Gorgon:** Cybernetic hands and tentacles on his head **Dreamslayer:** Ability to manipulate matter and teleport **Tracer:** Deadly blades attached to his arms
Doctor Diehard: Can control magnetism
ALLIES Barracuda
ENEMIES Monarch, Challengers of the Unknown

After *Flashpoint* on Earth-8, a band of metahuman criminals attempted to seize power and accidentally destroyed the world. Fleeing between realities, they clashed with the Challengers of the Unknown and joined time-travelling tyrant Monarch in a plot to eradicate weak worlds across the Multiverse.

When reality shifted after *Rebirth*, the villains' history altered. Now, when Super-Villain Lord Havok attempted to pacify his chaotic homeworld Angor, unified resistance there led to a devastating nuclear war.

Fleeing the devastation, Havok and his unscrupulous allies, Dreamslayer, Death Bat, Doctor Diehard, Brute, Tracer, and Gorgon, arrived on Earth-0 with the same goal but with new tactics. This time they would save the planet rather than destroy it. Of course, they would do it their way…

Targeting small nation Kravia, the Extremists planned a gradual piecemeal conquest, but were quickly challenged by Batman's rapid-response team, the Justice League. After a brutal conflict in a politically explosive region of Earth, the surviving Extremists were incarcerated, but Lord Havok and Dreamslayer soon escaped into the unexplored Microverse, determined to retrench and try again.

EXTREME MEASURES
1 Amazing Man, 2 Captain Atom,
3 Maxima, 4 Booster Gold,
5 Blue Beetle

FAITH

DEBUT *JLA* (Vol. 1) #69 (Oct. 2002)
REAL NAME Unknown
HEIGHT 5ft 10in **WEIGHT** 148 lbs
EYES Brown **HAIR** Brown
POWERS/ABILITIES Telekinesis; emits positive vibrations that help calm those around her, flight, highly trained former government agent.
ALLIES Green Arrow, Nightwing, Nudge, Hawkgirl, Major Disaster
ENEMIES Kanjar Ro, Lord Crucifer, Crime Syndicate
AFFILIATIONS Justice League, Doom Patrol

Enigmatic metahuman government operative Faith. She was raised by the military and worked with a black ops team as "the Fat Lady" (because she finished what others started, as per the saying "it's not over until the fat lady sings"). When the Justice league were sent thousands of years into the past during the *Obsidian Age*, Faith was one of the replacements called in to cover, and remained after the League returned. Soon after, she joined the Doom Patrol, becoming a role model to a young hero called Nudge, before returning to the Justice League when the Crime Syndicate invaded.

She has no apparent connection to the murderous child, Faith who was transformed by alien Bloodlines parasites in Pine Ridge.

FALCONE, CARMINE

DEBUT *Batman* (Vol. 1) #405 (Mar. 1987)
BASE Gotham City
HEIGHT 6ft 1in **WEIGHT** 205 lbs
EYES Brown **HAIR** Gray
POWERS/ABILITIES Powerful crime boss with many connections in the underworld; extremely wealthy; very intelligent strategist.
ALLIES Mayor Sebastian Hady, Jack Forbes, Tiger Shark
ENEMIES Batman, Catwoman, James Gordon, The Penguin, Professor Pyg
AFFILIATIONS Falcone Crime Family

When Batman first embarked on his crime-fighting career in Gotham City, it took his and James Gordon's combined efforts to drive the notorious mob leader Carmine "the Roman" Falcone out of their town. More than five years later, when Commissioner James Gordon was imprisoned after being falsely accused of murder, the Roman reemerged in Gotham City, realizing it was the opportune time to reestablish his criminal empire. He had spent years in Hong Kong and had been successful overseas, but he had been looking for the chance to retake his home turf.

One of Carmine's first actions was to take revenge on Catwoman for scarring his face. He kidnapped her, only to be attacked and taken hostage himself by one of Gotham City's newer Super-Villains, Professor Pyg. Carmine's illegal activities later caught up with him, and he was arrested and imprisoned by Detective Jason Bard. The Falcone family remains active in Gotham City, however, and played an integral part in corrupting Harvey Bullock's G.C.P.D. partner, Nancy Yip.

ON THE RECORD

Carmine Falcone first appeared in Gotham City in "*Batman Year One*," which retold Batman's origin after the *Crisis on Infinite Earths*.

A near-untouchable crime boss, Falcone's most obvious physical trait was a scratch on his face made by Catwoman. His past and family were further examined in *Batman: The Long Halloween*, a series where he met his end at the hands of a crazed Two-Face.

FAMILY TIES
In *Batman: Dark Victory*, the follow-up series to *The Long Halloween*, Catwoman revealed that she believed Carmine Falcone was her real father.

FAIRCHILD, CAITLIN

DEBUT *Deathmate Black* (Sep. 1993)
HEIGHT 5ft 7in/6ft 4in (max. size) **WEIGHT** 133 lbs/300 lbs (max. size)
EYES Green **HAIR** Red
POWERS/ABILITIES Can increase in size and weight; superhuman strength, endurance, and durability; extremely intelligent with advanced knowledge of robotics and biology, psionic communication
ALLIES Superboy, Dr. Niles Caulder, Ridge
ENEMIES Rose Wilson, Harvest, Deathstroke, Warblade
AFFILIATIONS Ravagers, N.O.W.H.E.R.E. (formerly)

Caitlin Fairchild was the daughter of Alex Fairchild, a member of the strategic task force called Team 7. Caitlin benefited from her father's connections, receiving an internship at the prestigious Advanced Prosthetic Research Center. However, that 'benefit' would turn out to seal her doom when the A.P.R.C.'s Project Spartan got out of hand. Caitlin was turned into a cyborg and was no longer in control of her own body, killing her father when he attempted to rescue her. In turn, she was eliminated by his Team 7 comrade Slade Wilson, aka Deathstroke.

However, the complex life of Caitlin Fairchild did not end there. Prior to her death at the A.P.R.C., Caitlin had been secretly cloned and her clone now worked for Harvest at the clandestine operation N.O.W.H.E.R.E., believing she was the original Fairchild. Initially lending her expertise to Harvest's Superboy project, Caitlin had a change of heart when she learned of the culling process for N.O.W.H.E.R.E.'s metahumans, and helped a group of superpowered teenagers escape his horrific killing fields. The escapees became a short-lived Super Hero group called the Ravagers, but were ultimately defeated by Harvest and his employee Deathstroke.

ON THE RECORD

Caitlin Fairchild debuted in a different reality. The daughter of Alex Fairchild in this reality too, smart, quiet Caitlin attended Princeton University, where she was recruited into Project Genesis. As a result of her experimental work, she became "Gen-active," and developed superpowers. When she realized she was being used as a lab rat of sorts, she fled the project with a few other powered teens. They formed the Super Hero group Gen-13, in which Caitlin served as the leader.

NEXT GEN
While Caitlin Fairchild had a different past in previous incarnations, she always retained her distinctive green and purple costume color scheme.

FAORA

DEBUT *Action Comics* (Vol. 1) #471 **(May 1977)**
REAL NAME Faora Hu-Ul
HEIGHT 5ft 7in
WEIGHT 150 lbs
EYES Brown **HAIR** Black
POWERS/ABILITIES As a Kryptonian exposed to Earth's yellow sun, Faora has all the powers of Superman including heat vision, freezing breath, superhuman strength, endurance, durability, enhanced senses, and the ability to fly; extremely proficient in fighting arts; a tactical and weapons expert.
ALLIES General Zod, Non
ENEMIES Superman, Wonder Woman

Hailing from the planet Krypton and born years before Kal-El—the hero who would become Superman—the notoriously cruel Faora Hu-Ul was a loyal lieutenant to Dru-Zod. Working alongside the rebel scientist Non, Faora was chosen from thousands to serve General Zod. Relishing her role in Zod's quest for power and war, Faora helped him fabricate a conflict with the alien Char, and the pair began a romantic relationship. However, their crimes were finally discovered by Kal-El's father, Jor-El, and they were sentenced, along with Non, to the dreaded prison dimension known as the Phantom Zone.

Decades later, General Zod would escape the Phantom Zone and arrive on Earth, where he encountered Superman. He soon showed his true colors, tricking the Man of Steel into taking him to his Fortress of Solitude, where he freed Faora from the Zone and departed the Fortress with her. When Superman pursued them, they attacked him, causing Wonder Woman to also join the fray. After Zod and Faora narrowly won the battle, Superman and Wonder Woman adopted new armor, but were brutally dispatched when the Greek god Apollo came to the villains' aid. Zod and Faora then opened a portal to the Phantom Zone to access the Warworld and rain devastation down on Earth. However, their plans were thwarted when the portal was destroyed by a nuclear explosion set off by Superman and Wonder Woman, which trapped the evil Kryptonians in the Phantom Zone once more.

ON THE RECORD

Faora first appeared in Metropolis after escaping the Phantom Zone. She had survived the destruction of Krypton, and had found a way to shift in and out of the Phantom Zone, making her a huge threat to the Man of Steel. Faora had been sentenced to the zone for causing the death of 23 Kryptonian men. After *Crisis on Infinite Earths*, Faora reemerged as one of the fighters for a new version of General Zod.

INVADER FROM KRYPTON
When Faora Hu-Ul first debuted, it was in a phantom form. When she caused havoc in the streets, Superman attacked her, not realizing that she was a person.

FATALITY

DEBUT *Green Lantern* (Vol. 3) #82 (Jan. 1997)
REAL NAME Yrra Cynril
BASE Zamaron; mobile
HEIGHT 5ft 9in **WEIGHT** 125 lbs
EYES Brown **HAIR** Black
POWERS/ABILITIES Superhuman strength, durability, and endurance; expert fighter; Violet Lantern ring.
ALLIES Star Sapphire, Wonder Woman
ENEMIES Green Lantern John Stewart
AFFILIATIONS Legionnaires Club, Demon Knights, Justice League United, Zamaron Star Sapphires

Oldest child of planet Xanshi's ruling family, Yrra Cynril was off-world studying fighting arts with the legendary Warlords of Okaara when her world was destroyed due to a terrible mistake made by Green Lantern John Stewart. Seemingly her world's only survivor, she swore vengeance against all Green Lanterns. In defiance of her warlord tutors, she left Okaara and became one of the fiercest warriors in the universe. Now with the name Fatality, Yrra concentrated on eliminating Earth's Green Lantern, Kyle Rayner, but was unsuccessful.

Fatality joined the Sinestro Corps before being "rehabilitated" by Zamaron Star Sapphires. She then found herself partnering with Lanterns from every spectrum of light, forming the New Guardians in the process. However, when separated from her Star Sapphire ring, she realized how she had been manipulated by the Zamarons, and

LOVE CONQUERS ALL
During her time as a Star Sapphire, Fatality embraced the role, letting love overwhelm her and even falling for the destroyer of her world, John Stewart.

she renewed her hatred for John Stewart. In recent times, she has rejoined the Star Sapphire Corps, battling beside her sisterhood and Wonder Woman to destroy invading Dark Multiverse God Karnell.

FATHER TIME

DEBUT *Seven Soldiers Frankenstein* #3 (Apr. 2006)
BASE Ant Farm (mobile)
HEIGHT 4ft 1in
WEIGHT 56 lbs
EYES Brown
HAIR Black
POWERS/ABILITIES Natural leader; expert strategist and hand-to-hand combatant; powerful espionage connections.
ALLIES Creature Commandos, Ray Palmer

Every decade, the mysterious man known as Father Time generates a new body at random to act as his host. Currently housed in the body of a young Asian girl, Father Time is the active director of S.H.A.D.E.—the Super Human Advanced Defense Executive—which is often at the forefront of metahuman conflicts. S.H.A.D.E. has a hand in many projects, including a strike force called the Creature Commandos, put together by Father Time and led by agent Frankenstein. During Frankenstein's missions, Father Time communicates with him via holographic projection, providing mission-critical data and instructions.

Father Time's mobile headquarters is the Ant Farm, a three-inch indestructible globe that requires agents to deploy Ray Palmer's shrinking technology in order to enter it. An expert tactician and brilliant negotiator, the gruff Father Time works with other top secret groups like Checkmate, to make sure S.H.A.D.E. runs smoothly.

TIME IS PRECIOUS
Despite appearances, Father Time is a seasoned leader. His innocent guises often lead his opponents to underestimate his abilities.

FATAL FIVE

DEBUT *Adventure Comics* (Vol. 1) #352 (Jan. 1967)
MEMBERS/POWERS Tharok: Energy being with mind-control powers; **The Emerald Express:** Flight, force fields, energy projection, and other powers bestowed by the Emerald Eye of Ekron; **The Persuader:** Superhuman strength and endurance, atomic ax; **Validus:** Near-invulnerable juggernaut; **Mano:** Antimatter touch; **Promethean Giant:** Colossal size and immense cosmic power.
ENEMIES Legion of Super-Heroes, Science Police, United Planets, Justice League United

A thousand years from now, when the United Planets were menaced by the cosmic threat of the Sun-Eater, the Legion of Super-Heroes was ordered to collect five of the galaxy's most dangerous criminals to help fight it: Tharok, Emerald Empress, Validus, Mano, and the Persuader. Once the Sun-Eater was vanquished—at the cost of Legionnaire Ferro Lad's life—the criminal quintet remained together as the Fatal Five.

With minor lineup changes, the Fatal Five battled the Legion and menaced the United Planets for years, never triumphing, but always managing to elude justice. At some stage, the occasionally precognitive Emerald Empress had a vision that Supergirl would battle her to a final conclusion, and that in the clash, the Empress' father would die. Galvanized to rash action, she traveled back to the 21st century, resolved to kill the Girl of Steel before they had ever met. To ensure her scheme's success, the Empress created her own Fatal Five, recruiting sorceress Selena, deranged god-killer Magog, killer android Indigo and a clone of unliving monster Solomon Grundy. Despite overwhelming force and a cruel campaign of misinformation painting Supergirl as an out-of-control alien menace, the Girl of Steel and her allies ultimately triumphed and the Empress was forced to flee.

KILLER QUINTET
1 Selena
2 Solomon Grundy (clone)
3 Magog
4 Emerald Empress
5 Indigo

ON THE RECORD

The original incarnation of the infamous Fatal Five was involved in several important cosmic events. In one notable encounter with the Legion of Super-Heroes, the Five recruited hundreds of their alternate-world counterparts to take on the Legion. For their part, the Legion had to join forces with their 20th-century counterparts, the Teen Titans, to battle the Fatal Five.

During the *Final Crisis* event, the Five joined Superboy Prime's Legion of Super-Villains to battle the Legion of Three Worlds.

A FORCE TO BE RECKONED WITH
The Fatal Five proved to be one of the Legion's most formidable foes and even went head-to-head with Superman.

FAUST, FELIX

DEBUT *Justice League of America* (Vol. 1) #10 (Mar. 1962)
HEIGHT 5ft 11in
WEIGHT 172 lbs
EYES Gray **HAIR** Black
POWERS/ABILITIES Faust is a formidable sorcerer, drawing his mighty mystical power from a demonic bargain.
ALLIES Dr. Mist, Nick Necro, Demons Three, Crime Syndicate
ENEMIES Justice League Dark, A.R.G.U.S.

Once a major and persistent menace to the Justice League of America, Felix Faust has been a pale shadow of his former self ever since *Flashpoint* and other multiversal reality shifts. Reduced to little more than a petty dabbler, Faust obsessed over finding the all-powerful Books of Magic. Learning that dead and damned sorcerer Nick Necro knew their location, Faust pledged his soul to a demon to free Necro from Hell. The pact bestowed great power on Faust, but turned him into a withered, ghoulish figure. Necro and Faust secured a box containing a map to the books, but with no way to open it, they tricked Justice League Dark into capturing them. When John Constantine used a mystic key to open the box, Faust escaped with the contents, but was ultimately outwitted by Constantine.

After the Crime Syndicate invaded Earth, Faust and Necro worked on creating their Thaumaton weapon, which was powered by imprisoned occult Super Heroes including Black Orchid, Enchantress, Blue Devil, Sargon the Sorcerer, and Zatanna. However, they were again defeated by Justice League Dark, who later encountered a monstrous future version of Faust that was an immortal among the last living beings in existence.

Faust has returned, but remains relatively ineffectual. He refused to join Neron's mystic assault against Midnighter and Apollo, and was subsequently drained of power and sanity by the invading Otherkind.

ON THE RECORD

Felix Faust pledged his soul to the demon Neron, but was soon desperate to win it back. Faust posed as Doctor Fate and offered to bring Elongated Man Ralph Dibny's dead wife Sue back to life with a magic spell. In fact, the spell was intended to damn the hero; Faust hoped to trade Dibny's soul for his own and free himself from Neron's thrall. Dibny outwitted Faust and trapped him and Neron in the Tower of Fate. The deed cost Dibny his life, and he was reunited with Sue in the afterlife.

IN FAUST'S HANDS
Felix Faust was an early foe of the Justice League of America. The evil sorcerer used his command of magic to turn the JLA into unwilling puppets.

FEARSOME FIVE

DEBUT *New Teen Titans* (Vol. 1) #3 (Jan. 1981)
MEMBERS/POWERS Mammoth: Strength and durability; **Gizmo:** Rebuilds technology to create weapons; **Jinx:** Casts magic spells if in contact with Earth; **Shimmer:** Transmutes materials; **Psimon:** Mind control, can kill with a thought.
ALLIES Crime Syndicate, Secret Society
ENEMIES Rogues, Metal Men

Originally formed by Doctor Light, the Fearsome Five are a group of super-criminals who have formidable powers but lack true efficacy. They were recruited by the Crime Syndicate—invading Super-Villains from Earth-3—for their world-conquering Secret Society. The Fearsome Five were sent to punish the Rogues when they rejected the Crime Syndicate's offer. The outnumbered Rogues fought valiantly, forcing all their foes through one of Mirror Master's mirrors, which they then smashed. After this failure, Grid—the Crime Syndicate's artificial intelligence—teleported the Fearsome Five to assist in his battle against Cyborg and the Metal Men. However, the Five were outclassed again, beaten, and captured by Doc Magnus' metallic creations.

Perennial pawns, the Five joined another coalition to destroy the Justice League and later clashed with their earliest nemesis, the Titans, while fronting for a company stealing and selling metahuman powers. They were completely unaware that their latest secret leader was Deathstroke the Terminator.

CRIMINAL CREW
The Fearsome Five were enthusiastic members of the Secret Society, but ultimately inept in battle.
1 Jinx
2 Psimon
3 Mammoth
4 Shimmer
5 Gizmo

FERRO LAD

DEBUT *Adventure Comics* (Vol. 1) #346 (Jul. 1966)
REAL NAME Andrew Nolan
BASE Legion Headquarters, New Metropolis, 31st-century New Earth
EYES Green **HAIR** Brown
HEIGHT 5ft 7in **WEIGHT** 155 lbs
POWERS/ABILITIES Transforms his body into metal, gaining great strength and durability.
ENEMIES Sun-Eater, Rimbor Warrior Clan
AFFILIATIONS Legion of Super-Heroes

Andrew Nolan of Earth was born in the 31st century. He is an accomplished warrior with the ability to transform his body into the hardest substance known to science. This process causes all his life functions to pause until he returns to flesh and blood, but even Braniac 5 is unable to explain (yet) how Ferro Lad moves, senses his environment, and thinks in this state.

A veteran of many combats—earning him a well-deserved place in the Legion of Super-Heroes—Nolan is confidant and commanding and was pivotal in the defeat of deranged Rimborian Crav, the General Nah.

In a previous reality, when the solar system was menaced by the Sun-Eater, Ferro Lad sacrificed his own life to carry an Absorbatron Bomb into the core of the cosmic monstrosity and end the threat. He then returned as ghost to save his fellow Legionnaires from a rogue Oan Controller, before passing beyond the realms of life. No Legionnaire has ever proved more valiant or dedicated.

A HERO FROM THE PAST
The ghostly form of Ferro Lad gave Polar Boy and the Invisible Kid a somber warning when they visited the afterlife.

FEMALE FURIES

DEBUT *Mister Miracle* (Vol. 1) #6 (Jan.-Feb. 1972)
BASE Apokolips
NOTABLE MEMBERS/POWERS Big Barda: Born leader, super strong and durable; **Mad Harriet:** Insane fighter with energy claws; **Stompa:** Powerhouse with anti-matter boots; **Lashina:** Energy whip-armed warrior; **Bernadeth:** Sneaky usurper wielding a deadly fahren-knife.
ALLIES Granny Goodness, Darkseid, Steppenwolf, Desaad
ENEMIES Mister Miracle

The Female Furies are the elite warriors of Apokolips, trained from childhood in combat and indoctrinated to be fanatically loyal to Darkseid. However, the abuse and intolerance they continually endured from male warriors of all ranks in the dark overlord's patriarchal, militaristic regime served to make them rebellious and ruthless.

After helping Darkseid attain supreme power, warrior Granny Goodness was increasingly sidelined by his chauvinistic inner circle. Left to train mere women, they were driven to be ferocious and uncompromising. As the cadets gained in skill and power, their continual treatment as morons and casual toys led to the death of squad leader Aurelie. Pushed too far, the Furies rebelled, murdering their prime abuser, Willik. As Granny Goodness orchestrated her own plan of advancement, the Furies were dispatched to Earth to capture absconder Scott Free, whose influence had prompted the mutiny and escape of second-in-command Barda. In the following chaos, the status of women as warriors on Apokolips was forever changed. Now they too were allowed to maim and kill and die for Darkseid.

Barda abandoned Apokolips for her love, Mister Miracle. They fought side-by-side with the Justice League on many occasions, including in the Darkseid War. When he fell, his deranged daughter Grail fused the League's New God powers with Superwoman's baby to resurrect an even more powerful Darkseid. However, when all seemed lost, Barda brought reinforcements—the reformed Female Furies—to turn the tide of battle.

DARKSEID'S DEFENDERS
Big Barda returned to the forefront of the Furies to protect Darkseid from his own daughter, Grail... and brought backup.
1 Barda, 2 Mad Harriet, 3 Stompa, 4 Lashina, 5 Bernadeth, 6 Kanto, 7 Kalibak, 8 Steppenwolf

ON THE RECORD

The Female Furies were trained by Granny Goodness to serve Darkseid. When Big Barda fled Apokolips to join her beloved Mister Miracle on Earth, the team was sent to attack the happy couple (and the planet's other Super Heroes) on numerous occasions. The Furies were presumed killed during the Death of the New Gods, but Mary Shazam used the Anti-Life Equation to create new Furies from human females during *Final Crisis*, and the *Rebirth* event restored the original individuals to continuity.

THE FIGHTING FURIES
On the trail of renegade Fury-turned-Super-Villain, Twilight, Supergirl had to confront the combined might of the Female Furies.

FIREBRAND IV

DEBUT *Battle for Blüdhaven* #1 (Jun.2006)
REAL NAME Andre Twist
BASE The Heartland
EYES Blue
HAIR Blond
POWERS/ABILITIES Pyrokinesis
ALLIES Teen Titans
ENEMIES Father Time, King Bullet, the Jester
AFFILIATIONS The Freedom Fighters

Andre Twist was the fourth individual to assume the role of Firebrand. A courageous, opinionated, politically left-leaning resident of Blüdhaven, Twist gained extraordinary pyrotechnic superpowers when living weapon Chemo was dropped on his city.

Calling himself Firebrand, Twist began hearing voices in his head. They turned out to be Uncle Sam, urging him to become part of a new Freedom Fighters team. He was later captured and tortured by Father Time until freed by Uncle Sam.

Firebrand then joined the modern-day incarnation of the Freedom Fighters, Freedom Force, helping them stop various threats, including an alien invasion. Twist was crippled while fighting King Bullet's armies, and was later killed by the Jester on his first mission back.

FIRE

DEBUT *Super Friends* #25 (Oct. 1979)
REAL NAME Beatriz "Bea" Bonilla da Costa
HEIGHT 5ft 8in **WEIGHT** 140 lbs **EYES** Green **HAIR** Green
POWERS/ABILITIES Can take on a fiery form at will, fly, and fire green energy blasts of flame.
ALLIES Ice
ENEMIES Peraxxus, Signal Men
AFFILIATIONS Justice League International

Beatriz "Bea" Bonilla

da Costa was born in Brazil. Originally a spy for the Brazilian Secret Service, Bea was on a mission when she came into contact with a strange chemical mix called pyroplasm. Her exposure to the substance gave her the metahuman ability to control a green flame that could cover her whole body and allow her to fly.

When Andre Briggs decided to create a Justice League International team that operated under the guidance of the United Nations, Bea was selected to be Brazil's representative. She fought alongside Ice, Guy Gardner, Rocket Red, Vixen, Godiva, and August General in Iron, under the leadership of Booster Gold. Bea helped the team defeat the alien Peraxxus, who was using Signal Men robots to try to destroy the world, having already removing minerals and wealth from the planet to sell elsewhere in the universe. After defeating him, the JLI was about to meet the public when an explosion killed Rocket Red and left several members—including Bea—severely injured.

FIREFLY

DEBUT *Detective Comics* (Vol. 1) #184 (Jun. 1952)
REAL NAME Ted Carson
BASE Gotham City
EYES Blue **HAIR** Blond
POWERS/ABILITIES Pyromaniac with specialized armor enabling flight; explosives and pyrotechnics expert.
ENEMIES Nightwing, Batgirl

When Ted Carson—the ex-boyfriend of movie star Cindy Cooke—was found dead in a burned-out building, it looked like he had been murdered. Around the same time, an arsonist started to destroy anything in Gotham City linked to Cindy. The culprit turned out to be Firefly—a flying villain in a flaming metal suit.

When Nightwing and Barbara Gordon investigated, it seemed that Firefly was the known-arsonist Garfield Lynns. The heroes even found a clue in Lynns' empty apartment: a list of potential targets with only one location not yet destroyed. It was a false trail. Firefly had maneuvered the police into a particular place, leaving Cindy unguarded. Realizing that they had been duped, Nightwing raced to Cindy's penthouse, but arrived too late—Firefly attacked, apparently killing her. However, the burned victim was Cindy's agent.

Firefly was actually Ted Carson. He had faked his and Cindy's deaths in an attempt to secretly abduct her and restart their relationship on his terms, but his mad plot was foiled by Nightwing and Barbara.

In recent times Carson has revived his Firefly guise, acting as an incendiary mercenary killer, but he always ends up falling foul of Batman.

FIRESTORM

DATA

DEBUT *Firestorm* (Vol. 1) #1 **(Mar. 1978)**
REAL NAMES Ronald "Ronnie" Raymond and Martin Stein
BASE Pittsburgh **HEIGHT** (as Firestorm) 6ft 2in (as Raymond) 6ft 1in (as Stein) 5ft 10in **WEIGHT** (as Firestorm) 202 lbs. (as Raymond) 179 lbs. (as Stein) 165 lbs. **EYES** Blue (Raymond); Brown (Stein); Fire (Firestorm)
HAIR Brown (Raymond); Gray (Stein); Fire (Firestorm)
POWERS/ABILITIES Ability to control and rearrange inorganic matter, fly, manipulate his own molecular structure, and emit energy blasts.
ENEMIES Deathstorm, Pozhar, Killer Frost, Typhoon, Multiplex
AFFILIATIONS Justice League

Ronnie Raymond and Professor Martin Stein are two very different personalities, one is the epitome of youthful exuberance, the other rational thought personified. But when merged into a single entity, these opposites compliment each other's strengths as Firestorm, the Nuclear Man.

While much remains a mystery about the origin of the hero Firestorm, it is believed that a nuclear explosion fused Professor Martin Stein and teenager Ronnie Raymond together over seven years ago. For much of Firestorm's career, this event was thought to be an accident, one that sparked Ronnie's latent metahuman abilities and turned the pair into the hero Firestorm. However, in the events now dubbed the *Doomsday Clock*, Ronnie witnessed a vision that casts doubt on the accident's legitimacy, making Raymond believe the event could have been planned in collaboration with the Department of Metahuman Affairs. Whatever the true cause of the explosion, afterward, Ronnie and Martin became Firestorm, giving Ronnie control over their physical form.

Empowered with the ability to arrange the molecular structure of inorganic matter, Firestorm combined Ronnie's bravery with Martin's knowledge and fought storied battles against numerous Super-Villains, including Killer Frost (Dr. Louise Lincoln), Typhoon, and Multiplex. After proving his worth, Firestorm was even recruited to join the Justice League. Through events that are unclear due to manipulation of reality itself, Ronnie would later go on to partner with fellow student Jason Rusch as the other half of his Firestorm identity. It was this version of Firestorm who helped battle the nefarious Crime Syndicate, when they invaded Earth-0 from their home, Earth-3. In this tumultuous fight, Firestorm's matrix was used to trap many of his Justice League teammates against his will. He later recovered, his teammates were freed, and Firestorm continued his heroic journey.

It is believed that Ronnie recently rekindled his Firestorm partnership with Dr. Stein, yet even that partnership is in doubt, with rumors circulating that Stein actually helped orchestrate Ronnie's original transformation into Firestorm.

TWO HALVES
Ronnie had a strained relationship with his true father, and his mother had died years before his accident. It made him a perfect choice for Stein's experiment, as he reminded Martin of his own son.

NUCLEAR POWERED
Firestorm is a living nuclear reaction and one of the mightiest—and potentially deadliest—heroes in the world.

ON THE RECORD

Firestorm's appearance has hardly changed since his debut, despite numerous people being part of the Firestorm matrix. Originally, the nuclear-powered hero was the result of student Ronnie Raymond and Professor Martin Stein being caught in an explosion at the Hudson nuclear facility. Ronnie and the Russian hero Pozhar later combined for another incarnation. Ronnie later died, passing the mantle to Detroit teenager Jason Rusch. After *Blackest Night*, Ronnie came back and reprised his Firestorm role.

FIRESTORM AND FRIENDS
Firestorm has been part of several different lineups of the Justice League.

CLASSIC STORIES

***Firestorm* (Vol. 1) #1 (Mar. 1978)** Firestorm's origin is revealed. Ronnie Raymond and Professor Martin Stein find themselves changed forever when they combine to become a nuclear-charged Super Hero.
***JLA* (Vol. 1) #69 (Oct. 2002)** When the Justice League is trapped in Atlantis, Firestorm joins a new lineup of the team to rescue the original members.
***Firestorm: The Nuclear Man* (Vol. 3) #23-27 (May-Sep. 2006)** One year after the *Final Crisis*, Jason Rusch merges with Lorraine Reilly (Firehawk) to create a new Firestorm and search for the missing Professor Stein.

FRAME JOB
During events dubbed the *Doomsday Clock*, Firestorm was framed for murder while fighting Pozhar—later revealed as another plot by the villain Ozymandias.

FIRST BORN

DEBUT *Wonder Woman* (Vol. 4) #12 (Oct. 2012)
BASE Olympus
HEIGHT 7ft 6in **WEIGHT** 375 lbs
EYES White **HAIR** Black
POWERS/ABILITIES Exceptional physical power and durability; gains strength from cannibalism; acquires knowledge by eating brains; wears impregnable dragon-hide armor.
ALLIES Minotaur, Strife, Cassandra
ENEMIES Apollo, Zeus, Hades, Wonder Woman

UNHOLY RAGE
As the eldest son of Zeus, First Born traveled to Mount Olympus to claim the Olympian gods' throne.

The First Born was the first child of Zeus and Hera. When a witch foretold that the child would one day rule Olympus in Zeus' stead, the god had the baby taken to the African savanna and left to die. However, the infant survived and was raised by hyenas and, in time, used his divine might to conquer an empire, seeking to make Zeus acknowledge him.

When Zeus remained silent, the First Born declared war on Olympus. The gods sent a wave to drown his army, while the warrior-king himself was swallowed up by the Earth. It took the First Born millennia to dig his way out. When he emerged in the 21st century, he set out to take the throne of Olympus, which he thought was rightfully his.

After clashing with Wonder Woman in London, he confronted the current ruler of Olympus and killed him, devastating Olympus in the process. The First Born also conquered Hades, but was then hurled into the abyss by the new God of War: Wonder Woman.

FISHERMAN

DEBUT *Aquaman* (Vol. 1) #21 (May–Jun. 1965)
BASE Zandia
HEIGHT 6ft **WEIGHT** 196 lbs
EYES Blue **HAIR** Black
POWERS/ABILITIES Wields titanium fishing rod and gas-bomb lures; hood boosts strength and allows breathing underwater.
ALLIES Shark, Kobra
ENEMIES Aquaman, Blue Devil, G'Nort, King Shark
AFFILIATIONS Terrible Trio

The Fisherman is an enigmatic maritime villain and longtime Aquaman foe. His signature weapon is a custom titanium-alloy fishing rod which he can use to entangle foes, slice them with a razor-sharp hook, or snag nearby objects. He also carries fishing lures which function as gas bombs.

Fisherman's identity remains a mystery, but his standard modus operandi is to carry out daring seaborne thefts. During *Infinite Crisis,* he went on a murderous spree in Gotham City before being shot dead by police. Soon after, Aquaman encountered another Fisherman and made a terrifying discovery: The Fisherman's hood was an alien parasite which controlled its human host and gave them powers, such as breathing underwater. When the current host dies, the parasite finds a new one.

FLAMINGO

DEBUT *Batman* (Vol. 1) #666 (Jul. 2007)
REAL NAME Eduardo Flamingo
BASE Gotham City
EYES Blue **HAIR** White
POWERS/ABILITIES Skilled combatant
ALLIES Mad Hatter, Scarecrow
ENEMIES Batman
AFFILIATIONS Secret Society of Super-Villains, Arkham Asylum inmates

After receiving radical brain surgery that turned him into an unpredictable killer, Eduardo Flamingo was a hit man for the Penitente Cartel before going solo. "The Flamingo" became notorious for his fashion choices (a pink jacket with gold epaulets) as well as his tendency to eat people's faces. Following a number of run-ins with Batman in Gotham City, he was imprisoned in Arkham Asylum. When the Crime Syndicate staged a prison break during its invasion of Earth, Flamingo joined the Secret Society of Super-Villains.

He sided with the Arkhamites in the war between Arkham Asylum and the prisoners of Blackgate Penitentiary, then served as a security guard when the Scarecrow took over Arkham during the Gothtopia incident. He escaped from Arkham, but was soon recaptured following an ill-advised attempt to play matador with the Batmobile.

FLAG JR., RICK

DEBUT *The Brave and the Bold* (Vol. 1) #25 (Aug.-Sep. 1959)
REAL NAME Richard Rogers Flag, Jr.
BASE Belle Reve Penitentiary
HEIGHT 6ft 1in **WEIGHT** 189 lbs **EYES** Blue **HAIR** Brown
POWERS/ABILITIES Military pilot and skilled tactician with extensive combat and special-operations training.
ALLIES Amanda Waller, Bronze Tiger, Nightshade
ENEMIES Rustam, Brimstone, Zod
AFFILIATIONS Task Force X, Navy Seals, Suicide Squad

Colonel Rick Flag, Jr. came from a career military family and dedicated his life to living up to the legacy of his father and grandfather. During World War II, combat pilot Richard Montgomery Flag led "the Suicide Squadron"—a misfit unit he honed into an elite combat team. Post-war, Flag, Sr. joined the government's classified Task Force X program and was reported killed in action.

When Amanda Waller reactivated the Suicide Squad as a covert penal unit utilizing incarcerated Super-Villains, Flag's grandson, Richard Flag, Jr., took on the role of Field Commander. He accepted the job because bad guys needed killing and he also wanted to get out of the military prison where he was serving an indefinite sentence for refusing to carry out an illegal order. Despite misgivings, Flag Jr. excelled among the metahumans, battling many incredible threats but eventually wearying of the constant intrigue. He sacrificed his life to stop the rampaging Kryptonian Zod, but was later found in the Phantom Zone. Flag Jr. accepted the White House's request to rejoin the team, partly from a sense of duty, but also because he had heard that Amanda Waller might have been the one who originally sent him to military prison, and he wanted to find the truth.

COMMANDING PRESENCE
Flag is an expert tactician and leader, and he has years of combat experience to settle any firefight!

FLASH, THE

DATA

DEBUT *Showcase* #4 (Sep.–Oct. 1956)
REAL NAME Barry Allen
BASE Central City
HEIGHT 5ft 11in **WEIGHT** 179 lbs **EYES** Blue **HAIR** Blond
POWERS/ABILITIES Super-speed, super-endurance, and accelerated healing; he can think quickly, mapping out the potential outcomes of a situation and reading books in an instant; can vibrate his molecular structure fast enough to pass through objects.
ALLIES Iris West, The Flash (Wally West), Kid Flash (Wallace West), Impulse
ENEMIES The Rogues, Gorilla Grodd, Reverse-Flash, Professor Zoom
AFFILIATIONS Justice League

Barry Allen is The Flash—the Fastest Man Alive. A living conduit for the Speed Force—a strange other-dimensional energy field that gives all speedsters their power—Barry is capable of amazing acceleration and he uses his powers to fight crime in his hometown of Central City. The Flash is a founding member of the Justice League, joining with his fellow Super Heroes when Darkseid, ruler of Apokolips, and his demonic legions attacked Earth. He remains a key member of the team and has formed lasting friendships with other members. The Flash not only runs at extraordinary speeds, he also has lightning-quick wits!

AT A GLANCE...

Super-speed

As the self-professed Fastest Man Alive, Barry Allen believes he can outrun Superman in a running race, even though Superman's ability to fly may give him the edge. The Flash's metahuman ability helps his body to avoid the friction caused by his high speeds and to contain the damage it should ordinarily cause around him. He keeps his costume in a ring.

Rogues Gallery

A number of Super-Villains have become obsessed with The Flash. Chief among these are the Rogues—a group of criminals formed by Captain Cold. Operating out of Central City and Keystone City, the Rogues became "heroes" when they were tasked with hunting The Flash down after he briefly became a wanted man.

Speed Force

The Flash's speed comes from the Speed Force, which grants several speedster heroes and villains their powers. Barry Allen is one of the few who have spent time living inside the Speed Force dimension.

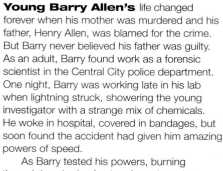

CLASSIC STORIES

***Showcase* #4 (Sep.–Oct. 1956)**
Barry Allen makes his first appearance in this classic tale that heralded the start of comics' Silver Age. He also meets his first enemy, Turtle Man—the slowest man alive!

***The Flash* #123 (Sep. 1961)** Barry Allen meets the original Flash, Jay Garrick (of Earth-2), as he crosses over to Earth-2 for the first time and helps the retired Jay defeat three of his old enemies.

***Crisis on Infinite Earths* #8 (Nov. 1985)** Barry Allen's last stand as The Flash sacrifices his life to save the universe from the Anti-Monitor's deadliest weapon.

***Flashpoint* (Vol. 2) #1 (Jul. 2011)** The Flash wakes on an Earth that is not his own and he must change reality itself to save the planet—even though doing so means he must confront his darkest hour.

Young Barry Allen's life changed forever when his mother was murdered and his father, Henry Allen, was blamed for the crime. But Barry never believed his father was guilty. As an adult, Barry found work as a forensic scientist in the Central City police department. One night, Barry was working late in his lab when lightning struck, showering the young investigator with a strange mix of chemicals. He woke in hospital, covered in bandages, but soon found the accident had given him amazing powers of speed.

As Barry tested his powers, burning through hundreds of pairs of sneakers, he ended up accidentally running into a possible future, one ruled by the villainous King Turtle. Barry met his future self, who told him about his life as The Flash—a name inspired by comic books Barry used to read as a kid. The future Flash helped Barry return to his home time via a device called the Cosmic Treadmill.

Reeling from this adventure, Barry went to meet his love interest, Iris West, for a coffee, but ended up saving her from the present day Turtle. Barry soon developed several prototype The Flash suits, but only settled on his final costume when King Turtle from the future arrived in the present day, forcing The Flash to defeat him.

The Flash continued his career and eventually gained a number of foes, including a variety of colorful Rogues. He continued to learn about his powers and discovered he had tapped into the Speed Force—a mysterious ancient power that had caused the extinction of the Mayans and had sped up the evolution of a tribe of gorillas in East Africa.

When someone started killing people linked to the Speed Force, the killer—who called himself Reverse-Flash—turned out to be Iris West's younger brother, Daniel, who was trying to steal Speed Force energy to travel through time and alter his own past. The Flash managed to drain the Speed Force from Daniel and prevent changes in the timeline. Barry then learned that a time-traveling speedster called Professor Zoom (Eobard Thawne) was responsible for his mother's death. He defeated Thawne, but would continue to battle him many times in future encounters.

The Flash's life is always accelerating. When the criminal organization called Black Hole created a lightning storm in Central City, many civilians were granted access to super-speed powers from the Speed Force. Most notable among them were Barry's colleagues police officer August Heart, the young Avery Ho, and S.T.A.R. Labs scientist Dr. Meena Dhawan. Barry's own nephew, Wallace West, already had speed powers, but the storm enhanced his abilities as well. While most of the other potential speedsters gave their powers willingly to Barry through a shared Speed Force connection, Avery kept hers and became a new Flash, later joining the Justice League of China. Wallace became the heroic new Kid Flash and a mainstay of the Teen Titans. However, August had less than heroic plans for his speed. He used it to kill the suspect in his brother's murder and then continued a criminal killing streak as the villainous Godspeed until The Flash stopped him.

Eobard Thawne kidnapped Iris, brought her to the 25th century, and unmasked Barry, shocking Iris. She and The Flash returned to the present, but not before the villain was able to expose The Flash to Negative Speed Force

LIGHTNING FAST
Showered in laboratory chemicals and struck by lightning, Barry Allen ends up with astonishing powers.

REBIRTH

FANTASTIC FORCES

The Flash has learned that the Speed Force is not the only cosmic force of its kind. There are four forces that choose avatars to help protect space and time. The Flash soon met the avatars of the other forces: Steadfast from the Still Force, Psych from the Sage Force, and Fuerza from the Strength Force. However, The Black Flash—the angel of death to speedsters—began hunting these avatars and killed Psych.

FAST FACT
The world's greatest speedster can use the Speed Force to travel through time.

"I'm Barry Allen. The Fastest Man Alive!"
THE FLASH

RACING DEATH
During the cataclysmic war against Darkseid, The Flash was forced to become the host for the cosmic grim reaper, the Black Racer. After killing the previous host, The Flash was granted divine powers and became the God of Death.

energy. When Barry returned to his proper time, Dr. Meena Dhawan absorbed that negative energy and became the Negative Flash in the process.

Between constantly thwarting plots by old foes like the Rogues and Thawne, rediscovering old friends like Wally West, Impulse, Jay Garrick, Max Mercury, and Jesse Quick, and fighting new enemies like Paradox, The Flash has no choice but to keep up his life's hectic pace.

ON THE RECORD

Since The Flash's groundbreaking first appearance in 1940, several people have taken on the role, each adding something unique to the hero's mythos. Jay Garrick was the first Flash, making his debut in *Flash Comics* #1 (1940). He fought crime in New York City, although this was later changed to Keystone City.

A new era
Barry Allen made his first appearance as The Flash in *Showcase* #4 (Sep.–Oct. 1956). The story heralded a new style of Super Hero comics and marked the start of the Silver Age. This version of The Flash also sported an all-new red costume. During his time as The Flash, Barry broke through the dimensional barrier between Earths to meet Jay Garrick.

Wally and Bart
Following Barry Allen's apparent demise during *Crisis on Infinite Earths*, Wally West took on The Flash identity. He uncovered the secret of the Speed Force and raced alongside other speedsters, such as Jay Garrick, Impulse, and Jesse Quick. It took a while for the new hero to feel worthy of his mentor's name, and when Wally disappeared, Bart Allen became The Flash until he was killed by the Rogues.

Flash back
When Barry Allen escaped the Speed Force and returned to active duty, he had trouble adjusting to the world around him. But with the help of his old friend Green Lantern, he came to terms with the time he had missed when trapped. The change in reality brought about by *Flashpoint* left Barry younger and single—in the new reality he had never married Iris West.

HEROIC DEMISE
The Flash prepares to make the ultimate sacrifice to stop the Anti-Monitor during *Crisis on Infinite Earths*.

SPEED FORCE HEROES
The Flash (Wally West), Impulse (Bart Allen), Jay Garrick, and Johnny Quick—all inextricably linked by the Speed Force—race to save the day.

FLASH (JAY GARRICK), THE

DEBUT *Flash Comics* (Vol. 1) #1 (Jan 1940)
REAL NAME Jason Peter Garrick
BASE Keystone City
HEIGHT 5ft 11in **WEIGHT** 178 lbs
EYES Blue **HAIR** Gray (formerly blond)
POWERS/ABILITIES Super-speed
ALLIES The Flash (Barry Allen), Impulse
ENEMIES Turtle, the Thinker, Reverse-Flash
AFFILIATIONS Justice Society of America,
The Flash Family

Jason "Jay" Garrick was the original Flash—a speedster and founder of the Justice Society of America in the mid-20th century. Jay acquired the power of super-speed after a lab accident. Using it to fight crime, he donned his father's World War I helmet—which had wings like the god Mercury—called himself The Flash and wore a lightning-bolt symbol. The Flash and his Justice Society teammates' exploits were wiped from the timestream by Doctor Manhattan, but only temporarily. Later, Jay and the Justice Society were brought to the present from 1941 and they assisted the Justice League against Perpetua and the Legion of Doom. Perpetua triumphed and Jay and the team went into hiding. Jay was called into action once more to help Barry Allen and Wally West reach the Mobius Chair before the Batman Who Laughs.

FLASH OF CHINA, THE

DEBUT *The Flash* (Vol. 5) #3 (Sep 2016)
REAL NAME Avery Ho
HEIGHT Unknown **WEIGHT** Unknown
EYES Brown **HAIR** Black and purple
POWERS/ABILITIES Super-speed via the Speed Force, intangibility, invisibility, time travel.
ALLIES The Flash (Barry Allen)
ENEMIES Godspeed, Lantern Corps of China
AFFILIATIONS Justice League of China

Avery Ho received her superpowers when Speed Force lightning struck dozens of Central City citizens. At first she could not stop moving, unable to control her incredible new powers. The Flash (Barry Allen) taught the young girl a way of centering herself in order to stop the vibrations—what she had to do was focus on the things she loved in order to keep herself grounded.

Later, Avery encountered the Justice League of China and joined the team as The Flash of China. She wasted no time in taking on China's Super-Man in a race to find out who was the fastest—a contest that she won easily.

FLORONIC MAN

DEBUT *The Atom* #1 (Jun.–Jul. 1962)
(as Woodrue)
REAL NAME Jason Woodrue
HEIGHT 6ft 2in **WEIGHT** 210 lbs
EYES Red and black **HAIR** Flowers
POWERS/ABILITIES Rapid cellular growth and change; can manipulate the Green to grow fabulous plants (as Seeder); can control plant life around the world and draw considerable power from the Green (as Avatar of the Green and Avatar of the Parliament of Flowers).
ALLIES Circe, Legion of Doom
ENEMIES Swamp Thing, Justice League Dark
AFFILIATIONS Parliament of Flowers

Other-dimensional exile Jason Woodrue was fascinated by the idea of using plants to recreate the world. In exchange for saving Swamp Thing (Alec Holland) from a sorcerer, Earth's Parliament of Trees gave Woodrue the ability to shape the Green—the lifeforce of all Earth's plants. As the Seeder, he created wondrous foliage. The Parliament later elected him their Avatar, but, when Seeder tried to kill Earth's animal life, Holland reclaimed the role. When the Parliament of Trees was replaced by a Parliament of Flowers, Floronic Man Woodrue cultivated their new avatar, Oleander Sorrel. When he was ready, Floronic Man consumed him and became Earth's plant elemental.

FORAGER

DEBUT *New Gods* (Vol. 1) #9 (Jul. 1972)
REAL NAME Unknown **BASE** New Genesis
HEIGHT 5ft 10in **WEIGHT** 162 lbs
EYES Blue **HAIR** Black
POWERS/ABILITIES Physicality of a New God; enhanced strength, speed, and agility; can climb walls with adheso-grips, fire acid from suit pods, and modulate his pheromone output.
ALLIES Hooligan, Kuzuko, Orion, Lightray, Batman, Sandman (II and III), Atlas, OMAC
ENEMIES Darkseid, Mantis, Metron, Black Racer
AFFILIATIONS New Gods of New Genesis

Forager was raised as a Bug—an insectoid species introduced to New Genesis by Darkseid to ravage the planet's food supplies. Bugs rapidly evolved into humanoid forms, proliferating across the planet. When Forager learned that Mantis of Apokolips was uniting rival Bug colonies to invade Earth, he helped Lightray and Orion repel the invasion. Forager sacrificed himself to save the galaxy and was replaced by a female champion who continued his heroic legacy.

After *Flashpoint* and *Rebirth*, the original Forager returned, going on a wild ride through Earth's history to thwart a cruel experiment of Metron's. With his companions Kuzko and her sentient teddy bear, Hooligan, Forager met many unconventional Super Heroes before learning he was actually a New God.

FOREVER PEOPLE

DEBUT *Forever People* (Vol. 1) #1 (Feb.–Mar. 1971)
BASE New Genesis
MEMBERS/POWERS Dreamer Beautiful: Creates illusions from others' minds; **Mark Moonrider:** Megaton touch, can fire blasts of pure force; **Big Bear:** Super-strength; **Serafina:** cosmic cartridges alter atoms and perform miracles; **Vykin:** Computer mind, controls magnetism, safeguards Mother Box.
ALLIES Infinity Man, Himon
ENEMIES Mantis, Devilance, Female Furies, Desaad, Darkseid
AFFILIATIONS Academy of Higher Conscience

In the aftermath of war between Apokolips and New Genesis, Izaya the Inheritor rejected mindless aggression and sought a more peaceful way. Part of that was rearing the next generation of New Gods in a free and gentle manner, with choice as their credo. Five of these idealistic youngsters— Big Bear, Beautiful Dreamer, Mark Moonrider, Vykin, and cowboy enthusiast Serifan—called themselves Forever People. Closer than family, they used a communal Mother Box to trade existence with the enigmatic Infinity-Man.

When Darkseid abducted Beautiful Dreamer, her companions came to Earth to rescue her. As explorers and ambassadors, the naive Forever People learned the ways of humankind, explored history with the help of ghost Deadman to find his killer, and prevented Darkseid from securing the Anti-Life equation. Although gentle souls still, they have become feared by many Apokoliptians, such as Granny Goodness and Desaad, who have many reasons to regret crossing swords with them. Today, they act as reluctant warriors when the need arises.

TOGETHER FOR INFINITY
1 Big Bear
2 Serafina Baldaur
3 Vykin Baldaur
4 Dreamer Beautiful
5 Mark Moonrider

ON THE RECORD

After *Flashpoint,* the Forever People subtly altered. Now Vykin, Serafina, Mark Moonrider, and Dreamer Beautiful were young New Gods on a field trip to Earth, chaperoned by seasoned warrior Big Bear, who ran the local New Genesis headquarters in Venice Beach, California. While investigating an agricultural project, they were attacked by Apokoliptian Mantis and his insectoid minions. They discovered that when they all touched their Mother Box computer and spoke the word "Taaru," they became a single mighty hero—Infinity Man. As Infinity Man they defeated Mantis.

DRIVING FOREVER
The Forever People rode in a three-wheeled, all-terrain Super-cycle. Designed by the engineers of New Genesis, it could travel at supersonic speeds on the ground or in the air.

FORTUNE, AMOS

DEBUT *Justice League of America* (Vol. 1) #6 (Aug.–Sep. 1961)
BASE A paddle steamer on the Mississippi
HEIGHT 5ft 8in **WEIGHT** 233 lbs
EYES Black **HAIR** Black
POWERS/ABILITIES Advanced intellect and gambling ability makes him appear lucky; uses various tech as a member of the Royal Flush gang.
ENEMIES JLA, Roulette
AFFILIATIONS Royal Flush Gang

When Amos Fortune's father died, the only thing he left Amos was his lucky deck of cards. By age 16, Amos was making money through card tricks and he hired four of his fellow students to be his lookouts.

They quickly became a gang and came to the attention of local gangster Jimmy the Gent. He employed them for several jobs, then sent them into a mobsters' card game. Amos won, but instead of giving the money to Jimmy, he used it to arm his own group.

Inspired by the Royal Flush he'd had during the card game, Amos led the first "Royal Flush" gang, with members modeling themselves on playing cards. They fought the Justice League of America and later Amos created a global network of Royal Flush gangs. Following another defeat at the hands of the JLA, Amos was shot by the wife of a deceased gang member.

FRANKENSTEIN

DEBUT *Detective Comics* #135 (May 1948)
BASE Magus Theatre, Monstertown, Gotham City
HAIR Black **EYES** Brown
POWERS/ABILITIES Immortal zombie with no need to drink, eat, or breathe; super-strong, skilled swordsman and marksman.
AFFILIATIONS Gotham City Monsters, S.H.A.D.E., Creature Commandos, Justice League Dark

Frankenstein is a former Super Human Advanced Defense Executive agent and a reluctant hero with Justice League Dark. Accidentally created with a conscience, the seeming brute turned on his creator Victor Frankenstein, freeing prisoners scheduled for experimentation. Afterwards, the creature left to explore the world and confront the nature of his origins. He still cannot decide whether he is alive or dead. Calling himself "Frankenstein," he finally gained purpose in life after being recruited by S.H.A.D.E.'s commander, Father Time.

Fighting in both World Wars and the Korean conflict—often supported by fellow warrior outcasts the Creature Commandos—he wed Lady Frankenstein (a S.H.A.D.E. agent codenamed "The Bride"). But tragedy dogged them. She was forced to kill their son when he proved twisted and evil, ultimately begging for his own death. The marriage sundered, but both continued working for S.H.A.D.E., saving the world from many horrific threats. Frankenstein also fought alongside Swamp Thing against the Rot and in the Trinity War as part of Justice League Dark. He recently found a home of sorts by defeating archfoe Mr. Melmoth's threat to the already endangered Multiverse. Frankenstein learned of an encroaching, undisclosed threat (Perpetua) and resolved to protect his outcast kind in a new team: the Gotham City Monsters.

ON THE RECORD

A creature named Ivan referred to as Frankenstein's Monster, first appeared in *Detective Comics* in the 1940s. He was Dr. Victor Frankenstein's large and lumbering assistant who was returned to life following a huge electrical shock.

Another version—more in keeping with the origins of Mary Shelley's original character—fought the Phantom Stranger. A more heroic variation met the Young All-Stars before emerging from the shadows in *Seven Soldiers: Frankenstein*, setting the stage for the latest incarnation.

MINDLESS MIGHT
A very different Frankenstein's Monster, nicknamed Ivan, once fought Batman and Robin in 19th-century Europe.

FOX, LUCIUS

DEBUT *Batman* #307 (Jan. 1979)
BASE Gotham City
HEIGHT 5ft 10in **WEIGHT** 170 lbs **EYES** Brown **HAIR** Black
POWERS/ABILITIES Exceptional business acumen coupled with excellent engineering and inventive skills.
ALLIES Bruce Wayne, son Luke Fox (Batwing), son Timothy Fox (future Batman) **ENEMIES** Lex Luthor, The Riddler
AFFILIATIONS Wayne Industries

Lucius Fox is one of the most respected financial minds on Earth, but in his first stint at Wayne Industries he was fired by Bruce Wayne's uncle, Philip Kane, who was seeking control of the business.

Fox briefly worked at Gotham School of Engineering, helping Wayne defeat "Doctor Death" and The Riddler when he inflicted *Zero Year* on the city. Shortly after, Bruce rehired Fox, making him Wayne Industries CEO. When Bruce went public with his support for Batman, Fox became more active, developing weaponry and technology for the Dark Knight. He built Batwing's new costume unaware his own son had secretly become the hero. Luke Fox's vigilante career caused conflict with his father as Lucius felt his son was slacking when, in reality, he was fighting crime.

Fox is married man with three children and, like all high-ranking Wayne Industries staff, carries a tracking chip at all times. When Alfred Pennyworth was killed by Bane, Fox adopted the confidant's role in Batman and Bruce Wayne's lives—an advancement that made him a prime target during The Joker's lethal war on the Dark Knight's friends and family.

EVERY MAN'S LAND
Lucius Fox had a career studded with many achievements. One of his greatest triumphs was in the aftermath of an earthquake that devastated Gotham City. His quick thinking stopped Lex Luthor's corporation from acquiring most of the city's real estate.

NEW CREW
1 Black Condor II
2 Uncle Sam
3 Phantom Lady II
4 Human Bomb III

FREEDOM FIGHTERS

FIRST APPEARANCE *Justice League of America* #107 (Sep.–Oct. 1973)
NOTABLE MEMBERS/POWERS Uncle Sam: The living embodiment of the American Dream; **The Ray:** Can absorb and control light; **Human Bomb:** Generates huge explosions; **Black Condor:** Super-strong and can fly at exceptional speeds; **Firebrand:** Pyrokinesis; **Phantom Lady:** Black light bands provide invisibility and intangibility; **Doll Man:** Can shrink to a height of just six inches.
EARTH-X MEMBERS Uncle Sam: The living embodiment of the American Dream; **Cache:** Tech expert and pilot of the Blue Tracer; **Human Bomb III:** Generates explosions, limited invulnerability; **Black Condor II:** Inventive flyer with weaponized wings; **Phantom Lady II:** Teleporter; **Doll Woman:** Enhanced speed and strength; stuck at six inches tall.
ALLIES Justice Society of America, Justice League of America
ENEMIES Nazis, Adolf Hitler III, PlaSStic Men, Renegades, Father Time, Secret Society of Super-Villains
AFFILIATIONS All-Star Squadron

On every Earth, wherever America's liberty is imperiled, the Freedom Fighters exist to destroy tyranny. Usually led by patriotic avatar Uncle Sam, teams consist of different heroes but generally include the Ray, Black Condor, Firebrand, Human Bomb, Phantom Girl, and Doll Man/Doll Woman. In post-*Flashpoint* continuity they were operatives of S.H.A.D.E., defending the nation from alien and superhuman threats. They were convened by S.H.A.D.E.'s leader, Father Time, to find a reborn Uncle Sam. An updated group assembled by a new embodiment of Uncle Sam comprised fresh incarnations of Black Condor II, Cache, Human Bomb III, Phantom Lady II, and Doll Woman. The team's greatest triumph occurred on Earth-X, where Germany had won World War II and Uncle Sam was banished for two generations. Here, original survivors of the conflict and legacy heroes reviving their glorious names sparked a new American revolution. Calling up a reinvigorated Uncle Sam, they brought liberty back to the Land of the Free and Home of the Brave.

FIGHTERS REFRESHED
The new Uncle Sam introduced the Human Bomb to his teammates Phantom Lady, Doll Man, and the Ray.

ON THE RECORD

The original Freedom Fighters existed on Earth-X—an alternate version of Earth where the Nazis had won World War II. The Freedom Fighters were Super Heroes waging a war against them. After ending the Nazi threat, the team sought further action and crossed over to Earth-1 where their allies—the Justice League of America—existed. While it took them a while to adjust to their new home, they continued their fight against evil.

FIGHTING SPIRIT OF LIBERTY
Uncle Sam and co. traveled to Earth, but their surprise appearance in Times Square saw them arrested for causing a public disturbance.

FUNKY FLASHMAN

DEBUT *Mister Miracle* #6 (Jan.–Feb. 1972)
HEIGHT 6ft 1in **WEIGHT** 170 lbs
EYES Blue **HAIR** Brown
POWERS/ABILITIES Charismatic master conman who can sell anything to anyone.
ALLIES Colonel Mockingbird (formerly)
ENEMIES Mister Miracle, Justice League
AFFILIATIONS Secret Society of Super-Villains, The Penguin

Charismatic Funky Flashman is a sleazy, persuasive salesmen with no discernible moral code. When the monthly allowance granted him by Colonel Mockingbird ran out, he latched on to Scott Free—super-escape artist and New God Mister Miracle—in a bid to become his manager. Scott's wife, Big Barda, deduced Flashman's motives, but Scott accepted the offer. She was proved right: Flashman stole Scott's Mother Box, and Darkseid's Female Furies tracked it to his home. Flashman sacrificed his assistant, Houseroy, to facilitate his own escape.

Later, he used Mister Miracle's name to peddle intergalactic cleaning products. Then he led the Society of Super-Villains before being ousted by Gorilla Grodd. Flashman still clings to the fringes of the metahuman community, selling hero-themed cars and cruising for fresh suckers at The Penguin's high-stakes card games.

FURY

DEBUT *Wonder Woman* #300 (Feb. 1983)
EYES Blue
HAIR Black
POWERS/ABILITIES Strength and speed of her mother, Wonder Woman; aggression and power of her father, Steppenwolf.
ALLIES Steppenwolf, Wonder Woman
ENEMIES Darkseid, Big Barda

Fury is the daughter of Earth-2's Wonder Woman and Steppenwolf. A ferocious fighter, she was trained by Big Barda and raised to believe in Steppenwolf's violent ways—even helping him wipe out her fellow Amazons. She eventually saw the error of her ways and helped Mister Miracle escape Darkseid's forces, joining Earth-2's heroes in their fight against the villain.

Fury survived Earth-2's destruction, and on the journey to a new planet her ship, the *TSS Aphrodite*, crashed and a radiation leak threatened the lives of all 77,000 people on board. In desperation, Fury merged their bodies with the souls of departed Amazonians that were stored in the Pandora Vessel—an ancient Themysciran artifact. These survivors established the secret kingdom of Amazonia on their new homeworld, where Fury began training a new generation of Amazons.

There have been other female warriors called Fury who have been inspired and empowered by the Amazons. The first of these, Helena Kosmatos, passed the mantle and name to her daughter, Lyta Trevor.

UNLEASHING FURY
Being half Amazon, Fury was gifted with wisdom, immortality, and super-strength. She was also a formidable warrior.

HELENA KOSMATOS
During World War II, Helena unwittingly unleashed the Furies—the Greek goddesses of vengeance—and became a vessel for their power. She channeled the spirit of the demonic Fury Tisiphone, the Blood Avenger.

LYTA TREVOR
Inheriting her mother Helena's powers, Lyta had a life marked by heroism and tragedy. After her husband, Hector Hall, vanished, her son Daniel was taken to become the Lord of the Dreaming. Daniel finally reunited them all in his realm to protect them from the marauding Spectre.

G.C.P.D.

DEBUT *Detective Comics* (Vol. 1) #27 **(May 1939)**
BASE Gotham City
NOTABLE MEMBERS COMMISSIONER JAMES GORDON;
COMMISSIONER MAGGIE SAWYER; COMMISSIONER HARVEY
BULLOCK; DETECTIVE RENEE MONTOYA; DETECTIVE CARLOS
ALVAREZ; DETECTIVE TRAVIS NIE; DETECTIVE TAMMY KEYES;
DETECTIVE JIM CORRIGAN; OFFICER HENRY WALLACE; DETECTIVE
MELODY MCKENNA; OFFICER NANCY STRODE; DETECTIVE NANCY
YIP; COMMISSIONER JACK FORBES; COMMISSIONER JASON BARD;
COMMISSIONER GILLIAN B. LOEB
ALLIES The Batman Family, Birds of Prey
ENEMIES Arkham Asylum inmates, Blackgate inmates.

ON THE RECORD

Before the reality-altering events of *Flashpoint*, the Gotham City Police Department had been slowly developed since Commissioner Gordon's debut appearance alongside Batman in 1939's *Detective Comics* (Vol. 1) #27. While characters such as Bullock, Montoya, Sawyer, and Gordon have appeared in the modern G.C.P.D., some officers have not yet been updated for the new continuity, including Crispus Allen, "Hardback" Bock, and Josephine "Josie Mac" MacDonald. Also notably absent is Detective Sarah Essen Gordon, James Gordon's second wife, who took over for him briefly as commissioner. She was part of a nascent G.C.P.D., playing a major role in the landmark "Batman: Year One" storyline.

FLACK FOR FLASS
Arnold Flass was a notorious example of how corrupt the G.C.P.D. was early on. During *Batman: Year One*, Flass repeatedly clashed with the upright James Gordon, giving him plenty of bruises for his efforts.

The Gotham City Police Department has been marred by corruption almost since the founding of the city itself. It took the efforts of many good people to fight the corruption from the inside, rooting out the department's worst offenders. Now that the noble tenure of Commissioner James Gordon has come to an abrupt end, loyal cop Harvey Bullock picks up where his old boss left off, hoping to keep Gotham City's cops on the up and up.

AIR PATROL
Gotham City is known for the police blimps that dot the city's famous skyline—often making life tough for a certain rooftop-traveling vigilante.

When James Gordon first reported to the G.C.P.D., transferring from Chicago, he was astounded to see how high the corruption reached. The incumbent Commissioner, Gillian B. Loeb, had his hands in a variety of criminal enterprises, and allowed many illegal actions to take place right under his nose. He even blatantly attended the outlawed dogfights that many of his officers organized.

Frustrated with his fellow officers, Gordon began to work with a few of the good apples among them—men like Harvey Bullock—and eventually rose in power thanks to his valiant efforts to save Gotham City during an attack by The Riddler during the so-called *Zero Year*. Gordon became Commissioner, and began working side by side with another uniformed crusader in the form of the vigilante, Batman.

Following years of a success, James Gordon was framed for a crime he did not commit. He was jailed as the corrupt Jack Forbes stepped up to replace him, quickly replaced again by the equally unscrupulous Jason Bard. When Bard saw the error of his ways—thanks in part to the actions of Batman—he worked to free Gordon. While Gordon did not return to his position, the upstanding Maggie Sawyer was promoted to Commissioner, and Gordon moved to head the Batman Task Force, wearing a robotic, armored Batman suit as part of a special division of the G.C.P.D. while the real Dark Knight was MIA. However, the true Batman returned to reclaim his mantle, and Gordon was reinstated as Commissioner until he fell under the control of an evil Batman from the Dark Multiverse, the Batman Who Laughs. Harvey Bullock now serves as Commissioner as Gordon attempts to get his life back in order.

GOTHAM CITY'S FINEST?
1 Former Commissioner Jack Forbes
2 Former Commissioner Jason Bard
3 Commissioner Harvey Bullock
4 Former Commissioner Maggie Sawyer

ONE POLICE PLAZA
Located squarely in the neighborhood of Old Gotham, One Police Plaza is the main headquarters of the G.C.P.D. It hosts the iconic Bat-Signal on its rooftop to summon the Dark Knight whenever Batman is needed.

G.C.P.D. BLUE
The G.C.P.D. is a brotherhood that has clashed with Batman nearly as many times as it has worked with him. In Gotham City, good cops are hard to come by.

G'NORT

DEBUT *Justice League International*
(Vol. 1) #10 (Feb. 1988)
REAL NAME G'Nort Esplanade G'Neesmacher
HEIGHT 5ft 10in
WEIGHT 195 lbs
EYES Black
HAIR Reddish brown
POWERS/ABILITIES Ability to overcome fear;
power ring can create nearly anything its wearer
imagines, permits flight, and space travel.
ENEMIES Gods of the House of Tuath-Dan

Perhaps one of the oddest members of the Green Lantern Corps, the canine-like G'Nort is a proud ring bearer, despite only getting the job because his uncle called in a favor. After 17 years of Green Lantern training, G'Nort finally began his career as a Super Hero, although his assignment of a space sector was later revoked after he accidentally destroyed a planet.

While not often the most effective Green Lantern in a fight, G'Nort opposed Larfleeze on the planet Sorrow before teaming up with the so-called Agent Orange and discovering they were actually cousins. Together they took on the Gods of the House of Tuath-Dan, a horde of rampaging robots, and a sentient, inter-dimensional portal set on destroying Sorrow. After vanquishing foes, G'Nort accepted a role as Larfleeze's sidekick.

GANG, THE

DEBUT *Adventures of the Super Sons* #1
(Oct. 2018)
BASE 4019, Mobile
NOTABLE MEMBERS Rex Luthor Evil
genius; **Brainiac 6** Electronic nemesis; **Joker,
Jr.** Comedy turncoat; **Kid Deadshot** Killer
marksman; **Ice Princess** Supreme sub-zero
threat; **Shaggy Boy** Brutal little giant monster.
POWERS/ABILITIES Technological
duplication of individual Earth Super-Villains.
ENEMIES Damian Wayne (Robin), Jon Kent
(Superboy), Tommy Tomorrow, Planeteers
AFFILIATIONS Injustice Army, Takron Galtos

The populace of Cygnus 4019 is addicted to watching life on Earth, but one child took it too far. Calling himself Rex Luthor and particularly enamored of Super-Villains, the adolescent psychopath convinced his school friends to become copies of bad guys and insert themselves into the drama. When they didn't comply, Rex made them. Planning to replace his screen idols as the ultimate villain, he began by stealing the awesome Hypercube from the Fortress of Solitude and trying to kill Robin (Damian Wayne) and Superboy (Jon Kent). Little Luthor's plan fell apart, prompting a chase across the universe, but he almost succeeded—especially after expanding his six-person gang into a vast army of junior injustice.

GARDNER, GUY

DEBUT *Green Lantern* (Vol. 1) #59 (Mar. 1968)
HEIGHT 6ft
WEIGHT 180 lbs
EYES Blue
HAIR Red
POWERS/ABILITIES Able to overcome great fear; weapons include
Green Lantern ring, a device capable of creating nearly anything its wearer
imagines, limited only by his or her will; the ring also allows for flight, force-
fields, and space travel, and can impart encyclopedic knowledge to its wearer.
ALLIES Hal Jordan, John Stewart, Kilowog
ENEMIES Atrocitus, Sinestro
AFFILIATIONS Green Lantern Corps, Justice League International,
Red Lantern Corps

BROTHERLY LOVE
Guy became his brother's personal punching bag in a self-sacrificing attempt to help Gerard deal with his issues.

Guy Gardner gained his attitude and famous chip on his shoulder at a young age. The product of a dysfunctional home, Guy had idolized his older brother, Gerard, who was a football star in school. When Guy's parents weren't doting on Gerard, they were lavishing praise on Gloria, Guy's younger sister. However, when Guy's mother died, Gerard became abusive. Guy let his brother take his anger out on him, knowing his sibling needed to vent his rage. But when Gerard hit his sister, Guy lashed out with a baseball bat, causing his brother to be out of action for the football season. In turn, Guy's father, a decorated cop, violently lashed out towards Guy.

As an adult, Guy followed a long family tradition and became a cop in the Baltimore Police Department, but he was kicked off the force after showing poor judgment. However, he later exhibited great courage, saving his brother Gerard's life from a hail of bullets during a police shoot-out with a criminal gang. In that moment of unflinching bravery, a Green Lantern ring found Guy, and he began life as a fully fledged hero, finding time to also serve briefly in the Justice League International.

While he debuted in the late 1960s, Guy Gardner did not rise to real stardom until his placement in the Justice League International during the mid-1980s. Famous for losing a fight to Batman—it only lasted one punch—Gardner became a longtime member of the team and the love interest of fellow hero, Ice.

After a falling out with the Green Lantern Corps, Guy claimed a yellow power ring to continue fighting crime. He discovered his Vuldarian heritage and became a living weapon in the form of Warrior, using powers he would lose during Hal Jordan's return, when both reclaimed their Green Lantern status.

RESTAURANT OF CHOICE
Always one to stay in Super Hero circles, Guy Gardner opened his own heroically themed restaurant called Warriors.

FROM GREEN TO RED
Guy took Atrocitus' Red Lantern ring and joined a new corps, where he could channel his anger. He later returned to life as a Green Lantern.

GENERAL ZOD

DATA

DEBUT *Adventure Comics* (Vol. 1) #283 (Apr. 1961)
REAL NAME Dru-Zod
BASE Jekuul
HEIGHT 6ft 3in **WEIGHT** 215 lbs **EYES** Blue **HAIR** Black
POWERS/ABILITIES Under a yellow sun, he has all the solar-charged abilities of a Kryptonian: super-strength, speed, flight, invulnerability, and enhanced senses; possesses a keen strategic intellect; highly skilled in Kryptonian martial arts and military tactics.
ALLIES Ursa, Lor-Zod, Eradicator
ENEMIES Superman, Supergirl, Justice League, Green Lantern (Hal Jordan)
AFFILIATIONS Phantom Zone Criminals, Suicide Squad, Superman Revenge Squad

KNEEL BEFORE SQUAD
Kryptonians, like most beings in the universe, have a vulnerability to magic. Knowing this, Katana was able to hurt Zod with her Soultaker sword when Zod escaped the Phantom Zone.

An extremist general from Krypton, General Zod was placed in the other-dimensional Phantom Zone for crimes against his people. Banished to a world of wraithlike phantoms and the endless ravages of a timeless environment, Zod's punishment actually worked out to his benefit; when Krypton exploded he was safely off world. He finally escaped his prison, coming to Earth as Superman's equal and opposite number.

I WILL ALWAYS BE YOUR MONSTER
Unrepentant, Zod and his comrades were banished to the Phantom Zone, but were convinced they would eventually return.

Driven half-mad by the Phantom Zone, when Zod first found his way to Earth, he came into conflict with Superman, and the two clashed repeatedly, with Superman eventually locking Zod the powerful Zod back into the Phantom Zone. Zod was freed again from the Phantom Zone by the government black ops group of Super-Villains called the Suicide Squad. The Squad's leader, Amanda Waller, implanted a Kryptonite bomb inside Zod's skull, threatening to detonate it if he didn't follow orders. Zod used his heat vision to slice into his own head and remove the bomb, before escaping alongside Cyborg Superman's Superman Revenge Squad. With the promise of finding his way back to his loved ones trapped inside the Phantom Zone, Zod worked with Cyborg Superman's team until he got his hands on Superman's Phantom Zone projector. Then Zod freed his wife Ursa and their son Lar-Zod and departed Earth for the planet Jekuul alongside the Kryptonian artificial intelligence known as the Eradicator. There Zod could live as a king under Jekuul's two yellow sons. The native citizens there acted as his willing slaves, believing him to be a god.

Determined to remake Jekuul into a New Krypton, the so-called House of Zod soon came under fire from the Green Lantern Corps. However, Zod joined forces with the Lanterns soon after to battle the greater threat of the lethal enforces called the Darkstars. Zod next learned of Rogol Zaar, the being claiming the blame for Krypton's destruction. While he seemingly teamed with Zaar (with whom he had previously escaped from the Phantom Zone), Zod was actually working to bring him to justice. After Zaar's defeat, Superman and Zod parted ways as uneasy allies, and Superman allowed Zod to returnto his planet in order to create the New Krypton of his dreams.

ON THE RECORD

A minor villain since his 1961 debut, General Zod became a recurring threat in the years preceding the mid-1980s *Crisis on Infinite Earths*. In the 1986 *Superman* reboot, Zod and fellow Kryptonians Qwex-Ul and Zaora annihilated an alternate Earth, forcing Superman to end their lives.

However, Zod's demise was short lived and in subsequent years he returned in various incarnations. In 2010, following Brainiac's defeat and the establishment of New Krypton in Earth's solar system, Zod was released from the Phantom Zone to lead the Kryptonian military. However, the warmonger instigated a "100 Minute War" against Earth, resulting in New Krypton's destruction and his return to the Zone.

UNFORGIVING
Whether addressing the last Son of El, inferior Earth-Men, or his own troops, Zod would never be content until he made all kneel before him.

HISTORY MAN
General Zod is obsessed with Krypton's glorious military past and is determined to make himself its greatest war hero.

CLASSIC STORIES

***Adventure Comics* (Vol. 1) #283 (Apr. 1961)** In a Superboy story flashback, General Zod debuts as an inmate of the Phantom Zone. Attempting to conquer Krypton with imperfect duplicates that look like Bizarro, Zod is eventually sentenced to the Phantom Zone.

***DC Comics Presents* (Vol. 1) #97 (Sep. 1986)** In an untold tale of pre-*Crisis on Infinite Earths* reality, the final chapter of Zod and the rest of the Phantom Zone villains is revealed.

***Action Comics* (Vol. 1) #844-846, 851, Annual #11 (Dec. 2006–Jul 2008)** Zod, Ursa, and Non strike terror into Metropolis as Superman meets the son of Zod.

GENERAL IMMORTUS

DEBUT *My Greatest Adventure* (Vol. 1) #80 (Jun. 1963)
HEIGHT 5ft 7in **WEIGHT** 132 lbs
EYES Blue **HAIR** Bald
POWERS/ABILITIES Brilliant criminal strategist with extremely high intellect; longevity.
ALLIES Professor Achilles Milo, Mr. Polka Dot, Sportsmaster, Condiment King
ENEMIES Doom Patrol, the Human Flame
AFFILIATIONS Brotherhood of Evil, Army of the Endangered

General Immortus is one of the original enemies of the Doom Patrol. No one knows how old he is, as he has extended his life for centuries with a mysterious elixir. After losing the formula to his potion, he hired the brilliant Dr. Niles Caulder to recreate the formula. When Caulder learned of Immortus' identity and plan, he destroyed his work, and later, as the Chief, formed the Doom Patrol to thwart Immortus and his schemes.

After repeated clashes with the Doom Patrol, Immortus organized a new team of metahuman followers, featuring minor criminals such as Mr. Polka Dot and the Condiment King. He named this team the Army of the Endangered and had limited success until he crossed paths with another villain who would become his enemy: the Human Flame.

GENTLEMAN GHOST

DEBUT *Flash Comics* (Vol. 1) #88 (Oct. 1947)
REAL NAME James Craddock
BASE Hell, Gotham City
HEIGHT Variable **WEIGHT** Variable
HAIR Red **EYES** Blue
POWERS/ABILITIES Intangibility, invisibility, flight, teleportation, control of the dead.
ENEMIES Hawkman, Batman, Batwing, the Spectre
AFFILIATIONS Secret Society of Super-Villains, Suicide Squad: Black Squad

English highwayman James Craddock went to Hell after being hanged for his crimes. Centuries later, he returned to Earth, using ethereal powers to somehow regain physical form. He scoured the world for mystic artifacts that might help him regain a proper body. In New York City, Gentleman Ghost clashed with Hawkman while procuring resurrection tool the Mortis Orb. That only gave Craddock a zombie army, not a new body. The Orb was later re-energized by contact with Hawkman's Nth Metal, and Craddock tried stealing lifeforce from New York's mortal inhabitants. Instead, the orb dispatched the ghost back to Hell.

Recently returned to Earth, Craddock became an assassin for hire and after failing to kill Batman, was forced to join Amanda Waller's Suicide Squad.

GENERAL, THE

DEBUT *Captain Atom* (Vol. 2) #1 (Mar. 1987)
REAL NAME Wade Eiling
BASE Mobile
EYES Black
HAIR Black
POWERS/ABILITIES Skilled tactician; highly trained in military combat; ruthless strategist.
ALLIES Dr. Heinrich Megala
ENEMIES Captain Atom, Firestorm, Superman
AFFILIATIONS US Army, Security Agencies

Professional soldier and ultra-patriot, Wade Eiling rose to the rank of General by always knowing where the next threat lay. In the days of alien incursions, masked supermen, and uncontrolled technological advancement, the highly decorated veteran was convinced that Super Heroes acting with public support—but no government control—were a menace to mankind.

The General toiled tirelessly and with no concern for ethics or human rights to ensure that quantum metahuman and former soldier Captain Atom remained a military asset. He called him "the super weapon that will keep America on top." Eiling later conspired to create Major Force as another secret weapon. He used him in attempts to press-gang Firestorm, the Nuclear Man, into being the latest asset in his stockpile.

GEO-FORCE

DEBUT *The Brave and the Bold* (Vol. 1) #200 (Jul. 1983)
REAL NAME Prince Brion Markov
BASE Markovia
HEIGHT 6ft **WEIGHT** 190 lbs
EYES Green **HAIR** Blond
POWERS/ABILITIES Super-strength and durability; lava blasts; terrain-manipulation/earth-moving.
ALLIES Katana, Batman
ENEMIES Baron Bedlam
AFFILIATIONS Outsiders

Second-in-line to the throne of Markovia, Prince Brion Markov volunteered to undergo scientific experimentation to become his nation's super-guardian. Empowered by Doctor Helga Jace—author of the contentious "Superman Theory" of creating metahumans—he attained numerous Earth-based abilities.

As Geo-Force he quashed an invasion by usurper Baron Bedlam with the aid of Batman, Katana, and other costumed heroes calling themselves the Outsiders.

Brion stayed with them, relocating to America, where he was reunited with his half-sister, Tara Markov. Geo-Force eventually assumed command of the team when Batman left. He briefly ruled Markovia, but surrendered the throne for a life of action.

GIGANTA

DEBUT *Wonder Woman* (Vol. 1) #9 (Summer 1944)
REAL NAME Doris Zuel
BASE Ivy Town
HEIGHT Variable
WEIGHT Variable
EYES Green **HAIR** Red
POWERS/ABILITIES Super-strength and durability; superior intellect; limited invulnerability derived from the ability to increase her physical size and mass; proficient unarmed combatant.
ALLIES Ryan Choi, Queen Clea
ENEMIES Wonder Woman, Green Lantern, Justice League
AFFILIATIONS Secret Society of Super-Villains, Secret Six, Injustice League, Villainy Incorporated

SHOCK TACTICS
Doctor Zuel was always ready for a fight and did not care what the human insects beneath her feet thought.

Doctor Doris Zuel was a brilliant scientist with a fatal blood disease. To save her own life, she attempted to place her consciousness into Wonder Woman's body, but instead ended up trapped inside a gorilla named Giganta. Eventually escaping the beast's body, her mind and spirit lodged inside a comatose metahuman named Olga, and she took over her victim's mystical ability to alter size.

Doris became an adrenaline junkie, drunk on her newfound power. Apart from a brief period teaching at Ivy Town University, where she was romantically involved with Ryan Choi, the second Atom, she rejected science research to be a Super-Villain.

Confrontational and amoral, Giganta reveled in her shattering power and left the scheming to more ambitious heads. She also preferred to work in a group, joining several mercenary or criminal organizations, but was equally happy to join semi-heroic teams such as the Secret Six or the government's Suicide Squad. The latter association proved particularly rewarding for Giganta as she was paid with the name of the man responsible for murdering her beloved Ryan and was allowed to torture him to death.

ON THE RECORD

The original Giganta was a female gorilla subjected to evolutionary enhancement. She transformed into a powerful human woman who wanted Wonder Woman's boyfriend, Steve Trevor.

Giganta was far less comical on her introduction to the modern DC universe: crushing jets, smashing buildings, and generally treating humans as if they were all bugs to be stepped on. Her lack of caution and consideration was revealed as a side-effect of her expansions; the bigger Giganta grew, the more her intellect diminished.

BRAWN OVER BRAINS
The post-*Crisis* Giganta, Doctor Zuel, learned that although rational reasoning had its benefits, brute force solved most problems more quickly.

GIZMO

DEBUT *New Teen Titans* (Vol. 1) #3 (Jan. 1981)
REAL NAME Mikron O'Jeneus
BASE Platinum Flats
EYES Green **HAIR** Bald
HEIGHT 4ft 2in **WEIGHT** 87 lbs
POWERS/ABILITIES Genius intellect, engineering prodigy, flight (jet pack), array of hi-tech weaponry and gadgets.
ENEMIES Teen Titans, Djinn, Psimon, Birds of Prey, Dr. Sivana
AFFILIATIONS Fearsome Five, Silicon Syndicate

A diminutive inventor with a gift for turning everyday objects into deadly devices, Mikron O'Jeneus sold weapons to villains via his company Gizmo, Inc. In the Fearsome Five, he was frequently beaten by the Teen Titans and shrunk to microscopic size by teammate Psimon. He was then shot in the head by Dr. Sivana for failing on a mission.

Resurrected by Macintech Research & Development, Gizmo joined the Silicon Syndicate—a villain cabal extorting hi-tech companies. This deal was ended by the Birds of Prey, but Gizmo survived the encounter. He worked with the Fearsome Five again and sold illegal arms. Recently he tried to become immortal by nuking New York City, using the energy unleashed to upload his consciousness to the Internet.

GOLDEN GLIDER

DEBUT *The Flash* (Vol. 1) #250 (Jun. 1977)
REAL NAME Lisa Snart **BASE** Central City
EYES Blue **HAIR** Blonde
HEIGHT 5ft 5in **WEIGHT** 117 lbs
POWERS/ABILITIES Projects an astral form that can fly and move through solid objects; trails razor-sharp tendrils.
ALLIES Sam Scudder (Mirror Master), Len Snart (Captain Cold)
ENEMIES The Flash, Gorilla Grodd
AFFILIATIONS The Rogues

Olympic-level skater Lisa Snart is the former girlfriend of Mirror Master Sam Scudder. When her brother Len (Captain Cold) forced the Rogues to metabolize their weapons' energies to create metahuman abilities, Lisa fell in a coma. Manifesting in astral form, she sought revenge as the ethereal Glider. Lisa led the Rogues against her brother and The Flash, but they joined forces when Central City was overrun by Gorilla Grodd's ape army. She freed Scudder from a Mirror World, but her astral form was destroyed. Escaping her coma thanks to the Pied Piper, she fell in with Cold again. Later she rejected crime, but her new life was wrecked by Cold. When he became an agent of Perpetua, she joined The Flash and others in defeating "King Cold" and saving Central City.

GLORIOUS GODFREY

DEBUT *Forever People* (Vol. 1) #3 (Jun.–Jul. 1971)
BASE Apokolips
REAL NAME Albert Pratt
EYES Amber **HAIR** Brown
HEIGHT 5ft 11in **WEIGHT** 195 lbs
POWERS/ABILITIES Immortal, superhuman physiology, unnaturally charismatic, ultra-persuasive voice.
ENEMIES New Genesis, Batman family, Desaad, Granny Goodness
AFFILIATIONS Darkseid's inner circle

As archpropagandist for Darkseid, Glorious Godfrey uses his great eloquence and psionic suggestion to persuade and deceive. He is Darkseid's advance guard, visiting new worlds and spreading the influence of Apokolips through mass communications, usually as a populist media personality or a religious figure.

When Darkseid was in stasis, Godfrey served his master's son and heir, Kalibak, collecting the Chaos Sliver and the sarcophagus of Damian Wayne so Darkseid could power his Chaos Cannon. However, Batman tracked Godfrey down.

When not advancing Darkseid's philosophy offworld, Godfrey amuses himself by fomenting suspicion and dissent among his rivals in the Dark Lord's inner circle.

GODIVA

DEBUT *Super Friends* (Vol. 1) #7 (Oct. 1977)
CURRENT VERSION *Justice League International* (Vol. 3) #1 (Nov. 2011)
REAL NAME Dora Leigh
EYES Blue **HAIR** Blonde
POWERS/ABILITIES Can control her prehensile hair.
ALLIES Booster Gold
ENEMIES Peraxxus, O.M.A.C., the Burners
AFFILIATIONS Justice League International

When prehensile-haired British Super Hero Godiva (Dora Leigh) was offered a position in Justice League International, she was immediately attracted to the group's dashing leader, Booster Gold. However, she thought the team was lacking in power, and she was proven right when they were forced to retreat by a giant robot controlled by alien asset-stripper Peraxxus. After Peraxxus captured Batman and the JLI, and placed them in cocoons, Godiva used her hair to remove a laser cutter from Batman's utility belt and free the team, allowing them to defeat the alien.

In clashes with O.M.A.C. and super-terrorists the Burners, Godiva proved herself a valuable League member, and finally kissed Booster Gold. Things got awkward, however, when her old flame Olympian joined the team, just before the JLI disbanded.

GLOBAL GUARDIANS

DEBUT *DC Comics Presents* #46 (Jun. 1982)
BASE The Dome
NOTABLE MEMBERS/POWERS Crimson Fox III (Vivian and Constance D'Aramis, France): Pheromone control; **Tasmanian Devil** (Hugh Dawkins, Australia): Transforms into giant marsupial; **Jet** (Celia Windward, Jamaica/Zamaron): Flight, electromagnetic powers; **Manticore** (Real name unknown, Greece): Beast powers; **Gloss** (Xiang Po, China): Immortal, draws power from ley lines; **Freedom Beast** (Dominic Mndawe, South Africa): Mind control, super-strength, can merge animals; **Sandstorm** (Real name unknown, Syria): Sand powers; **Tuatara** (Jeremy Wakefield, New Zealand): Precognition; **Doctor Mist** (Nommo of Kor, Africa): Magic; **Little Mermaid** (Ulla Paske, Denmark): Aquatic being; **Rising Sun** (Isuma Yasunari, Japan): Absorbs and projects solar energy; **Seraph** (Chaim Levon, Israel): Various powers from ancient artifacts.

The Global Guardians began in the early 1950s. With superhumans emerging across the world, the nations of the European Economic Community created the Dome, to manage and coordinate metahuman activity. The Dome extended its membership to include almost every nation, and African sorcerer Dr. Mist oversaw the creation of its Super Hero arm: the Global Guardians.

Despite pan-national idealism, the team frequently faltered, and when their funding was cut in favor of Justice League International, several Guardians accepted invitations to defect to a new Dome in the nation of Bialya. There, they were brainwashed by Bialya's Queen Bee, who used them against their JLI allies. The Global Guardians later built another Dome in the Pacific and were deputized into the UN's covert Checkmate organization. Several members were subsequently murdered by the villain Prometheus. The organization is believed to have disbanded during the *Doomsday Clock* affair. With disinformation campaigns making metahumans globally unpopular, the Guardians quit to join state-sponsored national teams, such as Japan's Big Monster Action and Great Britain's Knight's Inc.

RAPID REACTION FORCE The Global Guardians' duties took them all over the world, from urban Europe to the barren Russian wilderness.
1 Sandstorm
2 Gloss
3 Jet
4 Tasmanian Devil
5 Manticore
6 Freedom Beast
7 Crimson Fox III

INTERNATIONAL RESCUE The Global Guardians helped Checkmate fight Mesopotamian dragon Azhi Dahaki in the Australian Outback.

GODSPEED

DEBUT *The Flash: Rebirth* (Vol. 2) #1
(Aug 2016)
REAL NAME August Heart
BASE Central City
HEIGHT Unknown **WEIGHT** Unknown
EYES Brown **HAIR** Black
POWERS/ABILITIES Super-speed, ability to
create a double of himself.
ALLIES The Flash (Barry Allen)
ENEMIES Reverse-Flash
AFFILIATIONS None

August Heart was
a detective in the
Central City P.D. and
one of Barry Allen's
best friends. When his
brother was murdered
and the perpetrator
escaped justice,
August wanted vengeance. His chance
came when he was struck by Speed Force
lightning and was one of many Central City
citizens who became new speedsters.
August's obsession led him down a
dark path, and he adopted the persona
Godspeed. He stopped at nothing to
find the criminal, including killing other
speedsters and taking their power for
himself. After being captured by The Flash,
Godspeed had time to think and reflect on
his actions, realizing he had done wrong. He
helped The Flash defeat Gorilla Grodd, but
was later killed by the Reverse-Flash.

GOG

DEBUT *Gog* #1 (Feb. 1998)
REAL NAME William Matthews
BASE A hidden jungle temple in the Democratic Republic of Congo
HEIGHT 6ft 3in **WEIGHT** 210 lbs **EYES** Blue **HAIR** Brown
POWERS/ABILITIES Seemingly divine-level super-strength,
teleportation, energy manipulation, healing, resurrection, and
reality-altering powers.
ALLIES Gog (Third World god)
ENEMIES Infinity Man, Superman, Justice Society of America

DIVINE POWER
Armed with the
panoply and
power staff of
Gog, William
Matthews became
a match for the
mightiest heroes.

In an ancient temple

in the jungle of the Democratic
Republic of Congo, American
missionary William Matthews
unearthed Gog, the last surviving god
of the fabled Third World. Within the temple, William experienced
terrifying visions that drove him insane and convinced him that dormant
Gog would arise to save the world. William took the god's name and
staff—which granted him extraordinary powers—and embarked on a
crusade to prepare for Gog's imminent awakening by eliminating all "false
gods." His targets included Infinity Man, Hercules, and Superman, the latter
whom he blamed for a nuclear disaster he had seen in a vision. When the

THE KINGDOM OF GOG
William Matthews was
haunted by visions of
another world—one in
which an alternate
Superman was unable to
prevent a terrible nuclear
catastrophe.

Justice Society of America confronted him in his temple,
Gog was absorbed into the face of the lost god, bringing
the original divinity to life. The deity emerged from the earth
and declared his peaceful intentions.

After seeing Gog create miracles, some JSA members
became followers, but when the team learned Gog would
soon bond with the Earth and potentially destroy it, they
turned on him. They cut off Gog's head, and the Superman
of Earth-22 embedded it in the Source Wall.

**KNEEL BEFORE
GOG**
The awakened
divinity only
wanted to be
loved...or else.

GORDON JR., JAMES

DEBUT *Batman* (Vol. 1) #407 (May 1987)
BASE Gotham City **REAL NAME** James Craddock
HEIGHT 6ft **WEIGHT** 175 lbs **EYES** Blue **HAIR** Red
POWERS/ABILITIES Skilled tactician and analyst; an expert with
knives and explosives.
ALLIES Amanda Waller, Knightfall
ENEMIES Batgirl, Batman, Commissioner James Gordon
AFFILIATIONS Arkham Asylum inmates, Suicide Squad

James Gordon, Jr. is the son of Commissioner James Gordon and
Eileen Gordon, and younger brother of Barbara Gordon aka Batgirl. James'
sociopathic tendencies manifested in childhood when he killed the family cat.
He became a serial killer and was imprisoned in Arkham Asylum, where he
helped protect Charise Carnes (the villain Knightfall).

James escaped during a riot and stalked his sister. However, when The
Joker captured Barbara and began subjecting her to a twisted "wedding,"
James saved her—because he wanted to kill her himself. After engaging
Barbara in a game of cat-and-mouse, their climactic clash occurred at
Gotham Bay Aquarium.

Presumed dead, James resurfaced as an analyst for
the Suicide Squad. Determined to prove himself—he
was in love with his boss, Amanda Waller—he was
instrumental in countering a Crime Syndicate attack.
Determined to atone, Gordon, joined the battle against
the Batman Who Laughs, but the monster caused a
multiple personality crisis. Utterly unaware of his actions,
he began killing women who resembled his sister. When
Batgirl stopped him, Gordon was overcome with guilt
and remorse and killed himself.

MY SISTER, MY ENEMY
James clashed with his sister Barbara in a life-and-
death struggle that led to his disappearance.

ON THE RECORD

In the pre-*Flashpoint* universe,
James was Barbara Gordon's
stepbrother. When he was just a baby, James, Jr. was
kidnapped by gangsters, and his father and
Batman rescued him. James, Jr. displayed
murderous tendencies from a young age,
possibly killing Barbara's friend, Bess
Keller. He became a prolific serial killer and
plotted to taint baby food with psychosis-
triggering drugs, but was stabbed in the
eye by Barbara during a battle. It slowed
him down long enough for James' father
to stop his son once and for all.

THERE'S SOMETHING ABOUT JIM, JR.
Commissioner James Gordon was troubled by
his own role in the dark path his son had taken.

GORDON, JAMES

DATA

DEBUT *Detective Comics* (Vol. 1) #27 **(May 1939)**
REAL NAME James Worthington Gordon
BASE Gotham City
HEIGHT 5ft 9in   **WEIGHT** 168 lbs   **EYES** Blue   **HAIR** Red (graying)
POWERS/ABILITIES Natural leader with expertise in police procedure; highly trained fighter and former marine; long history of working with Batman and his allies; expert detective; weapons include police-issued firearm; formerly employed a robotic Batsuit armed with a variety of non-lethal, hi-tech crime-fighting equipment.
ALLIES Batman, the Batman Family, Batgirl, Harvey Bullock
ENEMIES James Gordon, Jr., The Joker, Mr. Bloom
AFFILIATIONS G.C.P.D., Batman Task Force, The Infected

INFECTED
One of the six heroes infected by the Batman Who Laughs, Gordon called himself simply the Commissioner. He was changed back to normal when Lex Luthor injected a "cure" of sorts into the Batman Who Laughs, making this evil Batman unable to broadcast his Dark Multiverse energy to his minions from the regular Multiverse.

James Gordon is the law in Gotham City. Before his arrival from Chicago, Gotham City was mired in corruption, a seemingly impossible metropolis for the hero cop to bring to justice. Gordon worked his way up through the Gotham City Police Department to commissioner, setting the new standard for the force. Before his recent forced sabbatical, Gordon worked hand-in-hand with the city's other protector, the vigilante known as the Batman.

ROUGH START
Gordon was suspicious of Bruce Wayne when the young man returned to Gotham City. By the same token, Bruce wrongly assumed that Gordon was a corrupt cop.

Family man James Gordon transferred from the police force in Chicago to the Gotham City Police Department shortly before the death of Bruce Wayne's parents. Three weeks after his transfer, Gordon was still getting the lay of the land, realizing how corrupt the police force truly was. Having had a rough time in Chicago, Gordon wanted the best for his young family, including his wife Barbara and his two kids, Barbara and James Jr. When he discovered a police-run illegal dogfight—just the tip of the G.C.P.D.'s corruption that ran all the way up the ladder to Commissioner Loeb—Gordon stood up against his fellow officers, even after one of the dogs attacked him. A tough cop, he left, shook off his injuries, and walked his beat, only to discover the Waynes shot dead in a nearby alley.

From that day forward, Jim fought against the corruption of his city, working his way up to Lieutenant during Gotham City's *Zero Year*, around the time Batman first appeared. At that time, Gordon paid several visits to the newly returned Bruce Wayne, perhaps suspicious that the resourceful young man may have ties to the city's newest vigilante. Despite Batman and Gordon remaining dubious of each other's intentions, the two began to work closely together, helping fight off the Riddler and saving the city from destruction. This act of valor earned Gordon a promotion to Commissioner, a position he kept until he was framed and temporarily replaced by Jason Bard. Gordon later regained his position, only to become corrupted by an evil version of Batman from the Dark Multiverse, the Batman Who Laughs. This evil Batman, who had been infected by The Joker, likewise infected Jim, causing him to once again lose his job, this time replaced by his friend Harvey Bullock. Jim is currently attempting to make amends for his past sins as a civilian, trying to reaffirm his bond with daughter Barbara.

ON THE RECORD

The Gordon bloodline has been the subject of constant revision in Batman's many comic book titles. In 1951, it was established that James Gordon had a son named Tony. However, Tony was soon overshadowed by Barbara Gordon, James' daughter and the heroine Batgirl.

After the events of *Crisis on Infinite Earths*, the Gordon family was reimagined in "Batman: Year One," which introduced his infant son James, and relegated Barbara to the role of adopted niece. The lineage became even more complex when *Batman: Gotham Knights* #6 (Aug. 2000) established that Gordon had an affair with his brother's wife, making Barbara Gordon his true daughter by blood.

PARTNERS IN CRIME BUSTING
Post-*Crisis*, Gordon's first wife left him just after his move to Gotham City from Chicago. Gordon remarried his colleague Detective Sarah Essen, who was later shot and killed by The Joker.

VIGILANTE COP
Gordon was invited to head up the Batman Task Force as the city's new Batman for a time. He got into shape and became the best Batman he could be, piloting a giant mechanical suit.

CLASSIC STORIES

***World's Finest Comics* (Vol. 1) #53 (Aug.–Sep. 1951)** Commissioner Gordon's private life is revealed as readers discover that he has a son named Tony.
***Batman* (Vol. 1) #404–407 (Feb.– May 1987)** Gordon arrives in Gotham City just as Batman first emerges in this groundbreaking origin retelling that features a very human—and very tough—Jim Gordon.
***Batman: Gordon's Law* #1–4 (Dec. 1996–Mar. 1997)** Commissioner Gordon gets his first miniseries, which results in a sequel series (*Batman: Gordon of Gotham*) the following year.

GORILLA GRODD

DATA

DEBUT *The Flash* (Vol. 1) #106 (Apr.–May 1959)
BASE Gorilla City
HEIGHT 6ft 6in **WEIGHT** 600 lbs **EYES** Gray **HAIR** Black
POWERS/ABILITIES Violent and very strong; can control others with his mind; genius-level intellect; possesses psionic abilities to move objects remotely.
ALLIES Crime Syndicate, Raijin, the Negative Flash, Multiplex, Poison Ivy
ENEMIES The Flash, Rogues, Solovar, Damage
AFFILIATIONS Legion of Doom, Legion of Zoom

FIRST CONTACT
During The Flash's first meeting with the inhabitants of Gorilla City, King Grodd hoped to gain The Flash's speed force by consuming his enemy's brain.

OUTCAST
Grodd was ousted by his own Gorilla people, filling him with jealous hate for Barry Allen's family and friends.

GORILLA WARFARE
Grodd waged a brutal war against his fellow gorillas when they attempted to make peace with the humans of Central City.

Gorilla Grodd is a violent and deadly Super-Villain. Since first meeting The Flash (Barry Allen) in Gorilla City, Grodd has had a deep hatred of the hero and believes he can gain The Flash's powers if he eats his brains. Grodd is not only fast and immensely strong, but also has amazing psionic abilities from contact with the Speed Force.

When the Speed Force struck a tribe of gorillas deep in the jungle of Africa, it sped up their intelligence and evolution. They then created their own kingdom, Gorilla City, and worshiped the "light"—their own name for the Speed Force. Grodd became their king moments before The Flash first arrived. Grodd had his own father killed and he ate his brains, believing they would give him his father's power. The Flash escaped Gorilla City and defeated Grodd, who was buried under the rubble of an ancient temple during their fight. He was dug out by General Silverback and soon reclaimed his control over Gorilla City, leading the gorillas on an invasion of The Flash's home of Central City. Grodd nearly killed The Flash, who was only saved when the gorilla known as Solovar risked his own life to rescue the hero.

The Flash later took Grodd into the Speed Force and defeated him in battle, leaving Grodd trapped there. Grodd was freed by the Crime Syndicate and found he now had increased psionic abilities. Arriving in Central City just as his fellow gorillas were making peace with the humans, Grodd took over, killing anyone—gorilla or human—who opposed him. With The Flash missing (seemingly killed by the Crime Syndicate), Gorilla Grodd renamed Central City "Gorilla City."

When the Rogues refused to join the Crime Syndicate's new order, the Syndicate sent Grodd and other Super-Villains to kill them. The Rogues won the day, however, with Mirror Master trapping Grodd and his fellow villains in a mirror dimension.

Later, Grodd learned he was dying from a rare degenerative disease. He used his powers to team with the villainous Black Hole organization in an attempt to save his own life by draining Central City of its speed. The Flash cured Grodd's condition and the Gorilla City Guard arrived to take Grodd away as their captive. However, Grodd almost immediately partnered with Poison Ivy in order to destroy the "world of man," only to be stopped this time by the rampaging behemoth known as Damage.

Grodd continued to find nefarious partners in crime, harnessing the Still Force and teaming with Lex Luthor to help form the Legion of Doom and free the evil mother of the Multiverse, Perpetua.

ON THE RECORD

Gorilla Grodd has become ever more brutal and savage since his first appearance. His origins have also changed significantly. Originally Grodd and his fellow gorillas gained their amazing intellects thanks to a radioactive meteor falling on their land. This meteor was connected to the source of Green Lantern foe Hector Hammond's powers. At one point, Grodd and Hammond joined forces to fight The Flash and Green Lantern.

The source of Grodd's power was later altered to alien intervention. Grodd and his enemy Solovar both originally had telepathic abilities. The latter asked for The Flash's aid when Grodd tried to lead an invasion of Central City after he had used his strength and abilities to seize control of their kingdom.

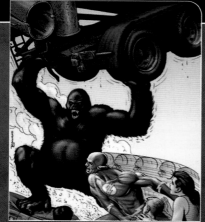

APE ATTACK
The Flash (Wally West) tries to stop Grodd's rampage in Keystone City.

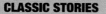

CLASSIC STORIES

***The Flash* #106 (May 1959)** In his debut, Grodd gains the secret of mind control from fellow gorilla Solovar and uses this power to seize control of Gorilla City.
***The Flash* (Vol. 2) #178 (Nov. 2001)** The Flash (Wally West) takes on Grodd as the gorilla launches his most violent attack yet on Keystone City.
***Salvation Run* #4 (Apr. 2008)** When Gorilla Grodd is trapped on a prison planet with other Super-Villains, violence soon ensues as he seemingly kills fellow gorilla Monsieur Mallah and the Brain.

GOTHAM ACADEMY

DEBUT *Gotham Academy* #1 (Dec. 2014)
BASE Gotham City
FACULTY Headmaster Hammer: Principal; **Professor MacPherson**: History; **Mr. Scarlet**: Librarian; **Professor Milo**: Chemistry; **Coach Humphreys**: Athletics; **Mr. Trent**: Drama; **Professor Hugo Strange**: Guidance Counselor; **Ms. Harriet**: Administrator
STUDENTS Mia "Maps" Mizoguchi; Olive Silverlock; Kyle Mizoguchi; Pomeline Fritch; Colton Rivera; Heathcliff; Tristan Grey (exchange student); Damian Wayne
ALLIES Batman
ENEMIES Clayface

SCHOOL SLEUTHS
New pupil Mia Mizoguchi was determined to investigate Gotham Academy's mysteries, and recruited a motley gang to aid her investigations. 1 Pomeline Fritch, 2 Colton Rivera, 3 Kyle Mizoguchi, 4 Olive Silverlock, 5 Mia "Maps" Mizoguchi

Gotham Academy is a very old and exclusive private school with a sinister reputation. Bruce Wayne is its patron, providing funding as well as Wayne Foundation scholarships.

Freshman student Mia "Maps" Mizoguchi was thrilled to receive one of these scholarships. Having arrived at the Academy, she set about exploring its mysteries, dragging fellow student Olive Silverlock into her schemes. The pair had to be saved by Batman after falling from the school's ruined clock tower. They then explored the derelict North Hall, rumored to be haunted by the ghost of a former student, Millie Jane Cobblepot. Instead they found Killer Croc, who had escaped from Arkham Asylum through a system of tunnels leading to the school.

Mia and Olive, along with Mia's brother Kyle and fellow students Colton and Pomeline, formed a "Detective Club" to investigate other bizarre goings-on at the Academy. They discovered that the gym teacher was actually a werewolf, and they foiled Clayface's attempt to ruin the school's performance of *Macbeth*. The group's most heartbreaking discovery was that Olive's mother Sybil had once been the villainess Calamity, who had been imprisoned in Arkham Asylum.

GOTHAM GIRL

DEBUT *DCU: Rebirth* (Vol. 1) #1 (Jul 2016)
REAL NAME Claire Clover
BASE Gotham City
HEIGHT Unknown
WEIGHT Unknown
EYES Blue **HAIR** Blonde
POWERS/ABILITIES Super-strength and speed, invulnerability, ultra-vision.
ALLIES Batman
ENEMIES Psycho-Pirate
AFFILIATIONS None

Claire Clover grew up idolizing her brother Hank as well as Batman. The Clover siblings wanted to help their home city of Gotham so much that they bought incredible superpowers for themselves, but at a great cost. The more they used their new powers, the shorter their lifespans became.

After an attack by Psycho-Pirate, Hank tragically died and Claire—now calling herself Gotham Girl—was emotionally damaged. She fell under the influence of Bane, believing that he would help her get Hank back, and during Bane's rule over Gotham City she was the sidekick to Thomas Wayne's Batman.

After the defeat of Bane finally freed Gotham Girl from his control, Batman gave Claire a piece of platinum Kryptonite, which granted her the ability to use her powers with no ill effects on her health.

THE PRICE OF POWER
Gotham Girl's powers came at a grave cost to her physical and psychological well-being.

GRANNY GOODNESS

DEBUT *Mister Miracle* (Vol. 1) #2 (May–Jun. 1971)
BASE Apokolips **HEIGHT** 5ft 10in **WEIGHT** 256 lbs **EYES** Blue **HAIR** White
POWERS/ABILITIES A New God, Granny has superior strength, agility, stamina, and mental capabilities; canny tactician; accomplished warrior; Apokoliptian technology.
ENEMIES Mister Miracle, Big Barda, Desaad
AFFILIATIONS Darkseid's Elite

Born and raised on Apokolips, the woman named Goodness was taught, like all denizens of that hellish world, that cruelty and ambition were the only way to improve life and status. As one of the "Lowlies"—Apokolips' oppressed peasant class—she was removed from her parents to train as a "Hound." As part of her military indoctrination and to prove her absolute obedience, Darkseid forced Goodness to kill her beloved dog, Mercy. This act earned her the dark lord's admiration and a place as one of his Hounds. She grew to believe that serving prince Darkseid was all that mattered. When her master seized control of Apokolips, Goodness murdered his despised mother, but Desaad took the credit for it.

Women had always been treated as less than Lowlies, but now, with the dark overlord's amused permission, Goodness was allowed to train girls to be elite warriors. The task took years and cost many lives, but eventually the Female Furies became a force to be feared and they forever changed male opinions.

Appointed mistress of Apokolips' orphanages and tasked with making the dross of society useful, she took the ironic title "Granny," as she systematically crushed her charges' spirits, making them unthinking tools of Darkseid. However, the boy she dubbed "Scott Free" refused to break. Escaping to Earth, he became Mister Miracle and—adding to his sin—lured Granny's favorite Fury, Big Barda, to join him.

Always busy, Granny imperiled Earth after imprisoning the Olympian Gods, triggering war between the Amazons and the USA. She posed as Athena to recruit human as new Furies. Although Granny was destroyed by Infinity Man when he began killing New Gods, her spirit possessed Alpha Lantern Kraken. She attacked Green Lantern homeworld Oa before being captured by Hal Jordan.

GRACE

DEBUT *Outsiders* (Vol. 3) #1 (Aug. 2003)
REAL NAME Grace Choi
HEIGHT 7ft **WEIGHT** 203 lbs
EYES Brown **HAIR** Red
POWERS/ABILITIES Bana-Mighdall Amazon ancestry gives her superhuman strength, speed, and toughness, plus rapid healing ability.
ENEMIES Sabbac, Simon Hurt

As a child, Grace Choi ran away from a foster home, only to be captured by a child-slavery ring and suffer terrible abuse for three years. When she was almost 12, her latent superpowers activated, and she used her newfound strength to free herself and the other kids. Grace eventually found work as a bouncer at metahuman nightclub Chaney's, where she was approached by Arsenal and recruited into The Outsiders. Though her brash and abrasive attitude caused some friction, she eventually settled into her role as the team's bruiser. She helped to disrupt the child-slavery ring that had abused her, and discovered that she was descended from the Bana-Mighdall Amazons.

When Batman took over The Outsiders, Grace invited her lover, Thunder, to tag along, but she quit when Thunder was rendered comatose by a booby trap. She later joined Black Lightning's Outsiders team, but it soon disbanded.

GRAVEDIGGER

DEBUT *Men of War* (Vol. 1) #1 (Aug. 1977)
REAL NAME Ulysses Hazard
HEIGHT 6ft 2in
WEIGHT 210 lbs
EYES Brown
HAIR Bald
POWERS/ABILITIES Exceptional physical strength and endurance; skilled in multiple martial arts and the use of all weapons.
ENEMIES The Axis

Growing up in the American South in the early 20th century, Ulysses Hazard was a born fighter, battling both polio and racial prejudice. When the United States entered World War II, Hazard enlisted, but despite his evident skill and determination, he was assigned latrine and grave-digging duties because of his skin color. After proving his worth by single-handedly storming the Pentagon, he was used as a one-man strike force, gaining a cross-shaped facial scar and becoming a legend as Gravedigger. He survived the war, retiring a Colonel.

Later, Tyson Sykes of Checkmate took the Gravedigger name.

Post-*Flashpoint*, Sgt. Joe Rock met an undead soldier who called himself Gravedigger and claimed to have fought in the American Civil War. His connection to Hazard is unknown.

GRAYVEN

DEBUT *Green Lantern* (Vol. 3) #71 (Feb. 1996)
BASE Mobile **EYES** Red **HAIR** Gray
HEIGHT 7ft 3in **WEIGHT** 665 lbs
POWERS/ABILITIES New God-level strength and endurance; fires energy blasts from eyes; strong leadership and strategic skills.
ALLIES Brainiac 13
ENEMIES Green Lantern (Kyle Rayner), Darkstars, Superman, Imperiex
AFFILIATIONS Secret Society of Super-Villains, Suicide Squad

Third son of Darkseid, Grayven sought to prove his worthiness by leading a fleet in a destructive swath across the galaxy toward Apokolips. His advance stalled when Green Lantern Kyle Rayner defeated him on Rann. Grayven was banished by Darkseid after conspiring against his father with Brainiac 13. When Infinity Man began eliminating New Gods, Grayven Zeta-Beamed the killer to Darkseid's throne room to kill his father. However, Martian Manhunter —disguised as the Black Racer—destabilized the scheming heir by "revealing" that he was not Darkseid's son. Unhinged, Grayven teleported to Apokolips and was slain by the god-killer. In reality alterations, Grayven returned, recently seeking to regain influence by attempting to buy Earth at a cosmic auction held by the Slave Lords of Dhor.

GRIFTER

DEBUT *WildC.A.T.s* (Vol. 1) #1 (Aug. 1992)
REAL NAME Cole Cash
BASE New Orleans, Louisiana
HEIGHT 6ft 3in
WEIGHT 195 lbs
EYES Blue
HAIR Blond
POWERS/ABILITIES Telekinesis; telepathy; can detect Daemonites; special forces veteran.
ALLIES Max Cole, Sofia Cordon, Deathblow
ENEMIES Daemonites, Helspont, Synge

Cole Cash, codename Grifter, was a member of elite special ops unit Team 7. He quit and made a living as a conman in New Orleans. After a particularly lucrative scam, he was kidnapped by Daemonites— spectral telepathic aliens who were intent on possessing human bodies and infiltrating their society.

One Daemonite tried using Cole as a host, but Cole awoke and broke free before the process was completed. He later realized the disruption had given him psychic powers, including a proximity sensitivity to nearby Daemonites. Flying out of town, he killed a Daemonite-possessed passenger, and became a fugitive from both the police and the aliens. Concealing his face with a red bandana, he began a one-man war against the invaders.

GREAT TEN, THE

DEBUT *52* #6 (Jun. 2006)
BASE Great Wall Complex, China
MEMBERS/POWERS Accomplished Perfect Physician (Yao Fei): Heals or causes great damage with his voice; **August General in Iron** (Fang Zhifu): Armored skin, energy staff; **Celestial Archer** (Xu Tao): Fires energy arrows; **Ghost Fox Killer**: Death touch, controls ghosts of men she kills; **Immortal Man-in-Darkness** (Chen Nuo): Pilots advanced Dragonwing aircraft built using Durlan technology; **Mother of Champions** (Wu Mei-Xing): Gives birth to 25 super-soldiers every three days; **Seven Deadly Brothers** (Yang Kei-Ying): Kung-fu master, splits into seven clones; **Shaolin Robot**: Ancient robot built for first emperor of China; **Socialist Red Guardsman** (Gu Lao): Radioactive; **Thundermind** (Zou Kang): Accesses the powers of the Buddhist Siddhis.
ENEMIES Hawkman, Batman, Black Adam, Batwing, The Spectre
AFFILIATIONS Justice League of China

PATRIOTIC POWER
The Great Ten are a formidable team, ready to lay down their lives in the service of China.
1 Socialist Red Guardsman, 2 Mother of Champions, 3 Celestial Archer, 4 Thundermind, 5 Seven Deadly Brothers, 6 Shaolin Robot, 7 Accomplished Perfect Physician, 8 Ghost Fox Killer, 9 August General in Iron

The Great Ten were convened as a metahuman force to defend the People's Republic of China. Comprising the greatest and most loyal heroes, the group serves under leader August General in Iron—a devotee of ancient war-master Sun Tzu.

The Great Ten only deploy after official approval has been secured, such as when Green Lanterns John Stewart and Hal Jordan entered Chinese airspace to capture Evil Star. Former Chinese ally Black Adam committed a massacre in Bialya and began rampaging across the world, but the Great Ten only reacted when he entered China. Adam killed Immortal Man-in-Darkness and wrecked Shaolin Robot. Communications with Beijing were lost, so August General in Iron took a risky chance, requesting outside help. A host of international heroes responded, with Shazam ultimately ending the threat.

Steadfastly isolationist and dedicated to maintaining order, the Great Ten always concentrate on Chinese interests. They intervened when Checkmate and the Outsiders attacked Chang Tzu's Oolong Island lab; they sealed the borders during the *Doomsday Clock* crisis; and recently they attempted to absorb the Justice League of China into an expanded Great Twenty.

GUARDIAN, THE

DEBUT *Star-Spangled Comics* #7 (Apr. 1942)
REAL NAME James Jacob "Jim" Harper
BASE S.T.A.R. Labs Advanced Ideas Division, New York
HEIGHT 6ft 1in **WEIGHT** 205 lbs **EYES** Blue **HAIR** Brown
POWERS/ABILITIES Peak fitness, military training; equipped with
a combination hoverboard/shield for protection and transport.
ALLIES Newsboy Legion, Jimmy Olsen, Superman
ENEMIES Parasite, Hammersmith, Leash, Rose Wilson, N.O.W.H.E.R.E.
AFFILIATIONS Project Cadmus, S.T.A.R. Labs

During World War II, Jim Harper was trained
by specialist coach Joe Morgan (who also trained Wildcat and
the Atom), but rather than seek fame and fortune as an
athlete, the young idealist became a policeman. Patrolling
Suicide Slum, Harper befriended juvenile trouble-magnets the
Newsboy Legion, and devised his Super Hero persona, the
Guardian. When he was murdered decades later, Harper's
genetic material was harvested by Project Cadmus. The
top-secret genetics facility was headed by his old Newsboy
wards and they used his perfect DNA to clone him as chief
of security.

Using advanced technology, the reborn Harper continued
the good fight as the Golden Guardian, dividing his time
between safeguarding the Project and defending Metropolis
against many menaces.

A Guardian has recently returned to action there, aiding
Superman and Superwoman. The Guardian name,
reputation—and possibly DNA—have been used by many
Super Heroes, including Teen Titan Mal Duncan, an enigmatic
security manager at S.T.A.R. Labs' Advanced Ideas Division,
and the corporate figurehead the Manhattan Guardian.

ON THE RECORD

The man known only as "Michael"
served in the United States Air Force before
managing security for S.T.A.R. Labs'
Advanced Ideas Division. There he was
assigned the codename Guardian and
provided with a blue-and-gold armored suit.
He battled the monstrous Parasite with
Superboy (Jon Lane Kent) and helped rescue
Superboy clone Kon from an Alaskan
N.O.W.H.E.R.E. facility. Kon merged with
Jon, and temporarily boosted the Guardian's
strength. However, when attacked by a mob
of hostile alternate-world Superboys,
Michael was badly beaten. Ultimately, Jon
and Kon defeated their doppelgängers,
sending them back to their home realities,
and getting the Guardian to safety.

FIGHTING THE GOOD FIGHT
During his career as the Guardian, Jim Harper
battled a variety of foes, from Darkseid's
fanatical Female Furies to Nazi agents.

GUARDIANS OF THE UNIVERSE

DEBUT *Green Lantern* (Vol. 2) #1 (Jul.–Aug. 1960)
BASE Oa
POWERS/ABILITIES Immortality; supreme intellects; psionic
powers including telepathy and telekinesis.
ALLIES Templar Guardians, Manhunters (formerly), Green
Lantern Corps (formerly), Third Army
ENEMIES Sinestro, Atrocitus, Weaponers of Qward, Manhunters,
Empire of Tears, Parallax, Volthoom, Larfleeze, Spider Guild, the Reach,
Mad God of Sector 3600, the Red, Blue, and Green Lantern Corps
AFFILIATIONS Zamarons, Psions, Controllers, Darkstars

Creation's oldest civilization developed on the planet Maltus
where some inhabitants evolved into intellectual super-beings—scientist-
philosophers with an unquenchable thirst for knowledge. One of their number
called Krona wanted to discover the very origins of creation. He conducted
experiments, but they critically damaged the universe, and his comrades
resolved to become its Guardians.

Relocating to the planet Oa, the Guardians dedicated their mighty brains
to eradicating chaos. Eons passed and their bodies atrophied, decreasing in
size as their mental powers grew. Ideological schisms developed and factions
were created such as the Controllers and Zamarons. The Oans tapped the
Emotional Electromagnetic Spectrum, concentrating the universal pool of
willpower in a Central Battery while suppressing other colors. Green was
used to fuel a succession of peacekeeping militias, beginning with robotic
Manhunters. These malfunctioned, slaughtering an entire space sector,
and were replaced by living recruits—Hallas—who in turn were supplanted
by the Green Lantern Corps.

After billions of years struggling against unceasing evil, the Guardians'
altruistic atonement soured. They began to impose their own logical thought
processes upon unruly life, seeking to obliterate free will through their
bio-manufactured Third Army. Ultimately, most of the Guardians were killed
by their renegade agent, Sinestro.

BLAST FROM THE PAST
The Oans' plans to eradicate free
will were resisted by their distant
and still-compassionate cousins
of the Templar Guardian Sect.

EFFICIENCY SAVINGS
The emotionless Guardians had no qualms
about eradicating their faithful servants
when they were no longer of any use.

ON THE RECORD

The Guardians began as patriarchal
advisers, but over time their omniscient
benevolence was seen as dictatorial
manipulation and their seeming solidarity
was questioned by many—including
one of their own.

During the 1970s, Appa Ali Apsa, also
known as the "Old Timer," abandoned
emotionless immortality to travel with
Hal Jordan and Oliver Queen. A sensitive
companion, he strove to understand the
lesser creatures in his care, but eventually
descended into dangerous insanity.

ISOLATED INCIDENT
Appa Ali Apsa's separation from his immortal
brethren taught him the value of emotions, but
eventually drove him to madness and murder.

GREEN ARROW

DATA

DEBUT *More Fun Comics* #73 (Nov. 1941)
REAL NAME Oliver Queen
BASE Seattle
HEIGHT 5ft 11in **WEIGHT** 185 lbs
EYES Green **HAIR** Blond
POWERS/ABILITIES Expert archer and highly trained martial artist; excellent hunting skills; quiver stocked with hi-tech arrows; access to Queen Industries fortune.
ALLIES Black Canary, Red Arrow, John Diggle, Arsenal, Henry Fyff
ENEMIES Count Vertigo, Clock King, Ninth Circle, Malcolm Merlyn, Cheshire, Brick
AFFILIATIONS The Arrow Clan, Justice League, Justice League United

Oliver Queen is the Green Arrow—a hero who uses his skills as an expert archer to bring justice to the streets of Seattle. Son of billionaire industrialist Robert Queen, Oliver wasted his younger years as a playboy before a terrorist attack left him stranded on an island where he was forced to use his skills to survive. After three years, he returned home a changed man, determined to be something new; something better. Facing assassins and superpowered villains while dealing with secrets from his own family's past, the Green Arrow is determined to bring justice to the streets of his city, one arrow at a time.

AT A GLANCE...

Stranded

Oliver Queen rejected his father's attempts to make him take his heritage seriously and seemed destined to waste his life drifting from party to party. This changed dramatically when a terrorist explosion at his party on a Pacific oil rig seemingly killed everyone except Oliver and Tommy Merlyn. Stranded on a desert island, Oliver was forced to master the skills he had once spurned, becoming an expert hunter and archer to survive.

Social justice warrior

After returning to Seattle, Oliver was a changed man. While he served as the head of Queen Industries, by night he would patrol the streets as Green Arrow—a liberal crime fighter often viewed as a hothead for spouting his politics to anyone who would listen. However, he often felt like a hypocrite, warring against "the man" while also being that very "man" himself.

CLASSIC STORIES

Green Lantern (Vol. 2) #85 (Aug.- Sep. 1971) When Green Arrow learns that his sidekick, Roy Harper, has gone down a dark path and become a drug addict, Green Arrow and Green Lantern try to help him and find the dealer responsible.
Green Arrow: The Longbow Hunters #1-3 (Aug.-Oct. 1987) Oliver Queen and Dinah Lance (Black Canary) grow closer as he moves from Star City to her home of Seattle. But when he crosses paths with the assassin called Shado and Black Canary is viciously attacked, Oliver's life changes forever.
Green Arrow #17-24 (Apr.-Dec. 2013) Oliver Queen is attacked by a deadly new foe—the assassin Komodo— and learns shocking secrets about his past. Oliver's life and his adventures as the Green Arrow take a new direction, with some close to Oliver paying the ultimate price.

Family secrets

After discovering his links to the Arrow Clan and meeting his half-sister, Emiko, Oliver became her guardian. Both had trouble adjusting to their new roles but quickly developed a strong bond, and Emiko would later adopt the role of Red Arrow.

Oliver Queen was heir to the Queen family fortune. He grew up in Seattle, a city founded by his ancestor, the archer Robin Queen. Ollie had everything, but seemed to turn his back on his birthright. His father, Robert Queen, owner of Queen Industries, tried and failed to instill some sense of commitment in his son. Whether Robert created positions for Oliver in Queen Industries or provided archery lessons for him, Oliver preferred to party. He was eventually given a clerical job on an oil platform, but instead of working, Oliver threw a lavish party on the rig. When terrorists attacked, Oliver arrogantly thought he could save everyone, and shot the detonator out of the terrorist leader's hand, only for it to hit the side of the rig and set off a series of bombs.

PARTY GUY
The young Oliver Queen often showed off his archery skills while inebriated at parties. When he arranged a party on an oil rig, it changed his life forever.

Only Oliver and his best friend, Tommy Merlyn, survived. Oliver was washed up on a deserted island and, with the world thinking he was dead, he was forced to use his skills to survive. By the time he left the island, Oliver was an expert archer and a changed man. On his return to Seattle, Oliver learned that his father had died. He soon began covertly using Queen Industries' resources, along with his own wealth, to fuel his vigilante activities as Green Arrow. He partnered with the young thief and tech genius Roy Harper, who became his sidekick, Speedy, and introduced a variety of trick arrows into Ollie's quiver. However, Ollie didn't give Roy the father figure he desperately needed, and Roy turned to alcohol and drugs, eventually parting ways with his mentor.

Oliver briefly joined the Justice League of America, and later the Justice League United. He fought the likes of the villain Komodo, learned about his father's involvement with the clandestine Arrow Clan, and even discovered that his father was still alive. Robert Queen had once had an affair with the assassin Shado, with whom he had a daughter, Emiko. Komodo had kidnapped Emiko and raised the child as his own daughter. Robert died saving Emiko's life and in revenge she killed Komodo. For Oliver's part, rather than assume his role as leader of the Arrow Clan, he opted to focus on Seattle and his war on crime.

That war was only getting started. Green Arrow discovered that his mentor, Queen Industries CFO Cyrus Broderick, was working with a criminal organization called the Ninth

THE DEATH OF ARSENAL

When Green Arrow had discovered that Roy Harper was an addict, he reacted harshly, unable to contain his disappointment. He threw Harper out of his home in a decision he would always regret.

Later, when he had a chance to reconnect with an adult Roy, Oliver took it. He tried to prove that he had changed from the fledgling, stubborn hero he once was, and even helped Roy defend his childhood home on a Native American reservation.

Roy sought out help from the Super Hero recovery center called Sanctuary, but with tragic results. He was killed there when The Flash (Wally West) briefly lost control of his powers. While Ollie and Roy had mended their rift, Green Arrow's guilt magnified. He had lost his old friend just as he was beginning to get him back.

SAD DAY
The death of Roy Harper, aka Arsenal was mourned by many in the Super Hero community.

REBIRTH

PRETTY BIRD

When social activist and spoiled rich kid Oliver Queen met hardheaded realist Dinah Lance, there was an instant spark and they began a relationship, as though they had known each other from a past life.

After a long and supportive partnership, even moving in together in an under-served area of Seattle, the two nevertheless parted ways when Black Canary's old espionage contacts set their sights on Green Arrow.

Circle. Essentially a bank that financed Super-Villains and terrorists, the Ninth Circle framed Oliver for murder, allowing Broderick complete control over Queen Industries. Bankrupt and on the run, Oliver teamed with Black Canary, Emiko (now going by the name Red Arrow), computer genius Henry Fyff, old ally John Diggle, and even his former sidekick Speedy, who now went by the name Arsenal.

In a long and uphill fight, Green Arrow suffered plenty of setbacks. The Ninth Circle succeeded in planting their own mayor in Seattle, and soon changed the name of the city to Star City, making it the first corporate-owned metropolitan city in the country. However, Green Arrow proved himself innocent and helped restore Seattle to its former name and prestige. While he successfully took back his company, he discovered along the way that his mother, Moira Queen, was part of the criminal conspiracy.

After a clash with a government agency and parting ways with Black Canary, Green Arrow was recruited by Batman into a team of detectives to investigate the threat of a new spy organization called Leviathan. With Seattle relatively safe, Green Arrow seems to be playing on the world stage now.

SHARP SHOOTER

While lacking in superpowers, the Green Arrow's skills as an archer make him a deadly hero, intent on bringing justice to the crime-ridden streets of Seattle.

"My name is Oliver Queen... the Green Arrow. And I'm just getting started."

OLIVER QUEEN

ON THE RECORD

Green Arrow has undergone many changes since his first appearance in 1941. On his debut, Green Arrow, aka Oliver Queen, was part of a crime-fighting duo with teen sidekick Speedy (Roy Harper). He not only used trick arrows to combat criminals, but also drove an arrow-shaped car and operated from the Arrow Cave. His physical appearance was more like the traditional Hollywood image of Robin Hood.

Road trip
In the late 1960s, Oliver Queen lost his fortune but gained newfound empathy for the common man and shifted left in his political views. He teamed up with the second Green Lantern (Hal Jordan) to see what was really happening in America. The two went on a road trip across the USA, helping the less fortunate along the way. Oliver also tried to help Roy Harper overcome his drug addiction.

Hunters
While the *Crisis on Infinite Earths* left Oliver's past relatively unchanged, he began to feel disconnected from his life as a hero, and went back to basics. After spending several years in Seattle with Black Canary, he separated from his longtime lover and later had a chance reunion with his adult son, Connor Hawke.

Back from the dead
Oliver Queen eventually gave his life saving people from a terrorist bomb blast. When his friend Hal Jordan became the villain Parallax, he used his cosmic abilities to return Oliver from the dead. The resurrected Oliver then had to reclaim his soul, with the help of his friends. He made a fresh start with a new Speedy, the ex-drug addict Mia Dearden. Oliver later became mayor of Star City, marrying his old flame, Black Canary.

ANOTHER LIFE
After a long and often troubled relationship, Green Arrow proposed to Black Canary. The two were later married.

SHADO WARRIOR

Oliver encountered the deadly assassin Shado—his father's old lover and the mother of Emiko, his half-sister.

GREEN LANTERN

DATA

DEBUT *Showcase* (Vol. 1) #22 **(Oct. 1959)**
REAL NAME Harold "Hal" Jordan
BASE Coast City (when on Earth), Mobile
HEIGHT 6ft 2in **WEIGHT** 212 lbs **EYES** Brown **HAIR** Brown
POWERS/ABILITIES Indomitable willpower commanding a power ring that is able to materialize hard-light constructs, translate languages, facilitate in-planet and intergalactic flight, and protect against hostile environments and enemy attack.
ALLIES The Flash (Barry Allen), Green Lantern (John Stewart), Green Lantern (Guy Gardner), Green Lantern (Kilowog), Green Arrow, Superman, Batman, Wonder Woman
ENEMIES Sinestro, Black Hand, Larfleeze, Controller Mu
AFFILIATIONS Green Lantern Corps, Justice League

Hal Jordan is arguably the greatest Green Lantern. Valiant, honest, and able to conquer great fear, he battled threats alien and terrestrial, implementing unyielding willpower through a ring able to create constructs of anything he could imagine. Part of an intergalactic police force, he patrolled space sector 2814, tasked with protecting all life. Yet he found it increasingly difficult to blindly follow the directives of his Oan masters—the Guardians of the Universe. While colleagues ignored their own misgivings, Hal spoke out, even as his triumphant exploits won him a reputation as the foremost Green Lantern in history.

AT A GLANCE...

High flyer
After witnessing his father's death, Hal grew up a troubled, attention-seeking risk taker. On his 18th birthday he enlisted in the Air Force, resolved to be a hotshot pilot like his dad, but his cocky attitude ended that dream too.

Battle of wills
Hal's apparently infinite power and antipathy to authority made him dangerously reckless and overconfident. When Apokolips invaded Earth, Hal trampled over Batman's jurisdiction, deriding his merely human capabilities. This earned him the Dark Knight's disdain, although they've learned to trust and respect each other over the years.

Fear my power
The Green Lanterns' power rings operate on intense concentration, allowing users to shape green light into solid objects. The rings can perform any task imaginable, fueled by the green energy of willpower generated by all lifeforms.

Young Hal seemingly lost all sense of fear after watching his dad, a pilot, die in a plane crash. Years later, while stubbornly following in his father's footsteps, he encountered a dying alien, Abin Sur. Sur wanted Hal to replace him in the Green Lantern Corps—an intergalactic police force that had safeguarded the universe for untold generations.

Hal accepted and was summoned for basic training at the Corps headquarters on the planet Oa. On completion, he was assigned to Thaal Sinestro of Korugar, who was considered the "Greatest Green Lantern" for his unparalleled ability to keep order in his space sector. Sinestro befriended the idealistic, hot-headed human, mentoring his transition from rookie to fully qualified officer, but their relationship soured when Hal discovered why Sector 1417 was so peaceful. Sinestro had conquered the sector and was governing it as an absolute dictator.

Following a tremendous struggle, Hal liberated Korugar. The Guardians banished Sinestro to the Anti-Matter Universe, where the renegade worked with the Weaponers of Qward to develop yellow power rings. Armed with this new weapon, Sinestro fought Green Lantern repeatedly, and eventually formed his own Corps to terrorize the positive-matter universe.

For years Jordan excelled, even becoming a founding member of the Justice League. He defeated innumerable menaces, but invariably at great cost to his private life. Personal and romantic relationships foundered and he started to seriously question his masters' edicts, resulting in him taking numerous leaves of absence, which he spent roaming the United States in search of personal fulfillment and renewed perspective.

The call of duty brought Hal back to the Corps, but when Coast City was destroyed, he snapped. Grief led to his possession by the yellow-hued fear parasite Parallax, who induced Jordan to eradicate the Corps.

FEAR NO EVIL
While following in his father's footsteps to become a test pilot, Hal was summoned to dying Abin Sur's side and offered the universe on an emerald platter.

CLASSIC STORIES

***Green Lantern* (Vol. 2) #40 (Oct. 1965)** The origin of the Guardians of the Universe and the introduction of obsessed Oan researcher Krona lay the groundwork for decades of cosmic storylines.
***Green Lantern* (Vol. 2) #76 (Apr. 1970)** Green Lantern accepts reduced duties in order to investigate the nature of good and evil, with social reformer Green Arrow as his guide.
***Green Lantern* (Vol. 4) #25 (Jan. 2008)** The Sinestro Corps War climaxes with the renegade Green Lantern's utter defeat, heralding the cataclysmic uprising of the corrupted dead.

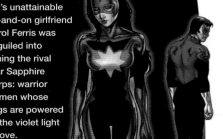

Love conquers all
Hal's unattainable off-and-on girlfriend Carol Ferris was beguiled into joining the rival Star Sapphire Corps: warrior women whose rings are powered by the violet light of love.

SUPER-PARALLAX
While on a mission to Earth, Hal met with Superman, only to discover that the evil Parallax entity had possessed the Man of Steel. However, after a well-placed punch by Superman, Hal realized that Parallax wasn't the culprit. His mind had been manipulated by Hal's old adversary, Hector Hammond.

TO SERVE AND PROTECT THE UNIVERSE
Years of confronting evil and saving billions of lives have taught Hal that Power and Will are worthless without empathy and a sense of purpose.

Hal eventually returned to his senses and continued his alliance with the Green Lantern Corps with renewed dedication. Later, when Jordan found himself without a power ring, he forged his own out of pure willpower. He returned to the fray just in time to help his teammates battle Sinestro, who had based the Sinestro Corps on the artificial battle planet called Warworld. With Warworld evacuated, Hal and Sinestro fought to the seeming death. However, White Lantern Kyle Rayner managed to restore Hal using Hal's own homemade ring.

Hal helped with dozens more missions as the Green Lanterns' most trusted officer, fending off attacks from the Darkstars, Sinestro Corps, and, after the Green Lanterns relocated from the planet Mogo to New Oa, Hal even bested the Controller Mu and his fleet of Blackstars.

When the Young Guardians replaced the elders of the Guardians of the Universe, Hal was reassigned back to Earth. Once again able to embrace his lone cowboy attitude while battling crazy threats and reality-warping Super-Villains, Jordan continues to shine as one of Earth's greatest Super Heroes, and as the most impressive Green Lantern.

BLACKSTARS
Due to the manipulations of the Controller Mu, Hal Jordan briefly found himself in an alternate reality where he wasn't a Green Lantern, but a Blackstar.

REBIRTH

DECORATED OFFICER
After Hal Jordan defeated the threat of Controller Mu, the Guardians of the Universe wished to reward him. However, over the course of his career, Jordan had already earned every honor a Green Lantern can possibly receive. The Guardians instead gave Hal an upgraded power battery that promised to have some new and surprising features.

ON THE RECORD

On first joining the cosmos-spanning Green Lantern Corps, Hal Jordan was a loyal, obedient servant, doing whatever the Guardians dictated without question or quibble. However, as the years passed, he increasingly began to feel their edicts were far from benevolent.

Mosaic world
An early sign of the Guardians' fallibility came when Appa Ali Apsa went mad. Abducting communities from worlds he had visited, the "Old Timer" transplanted them to a distant planet, pitting the terrified townships against each other in bizarre social experiments. It took the united will of Hal and fellow Earthian Green Lanterns John Stewart and Guy Gardner to stop him. The Guardians were then able to restore the victims to their proper places in the universe.

Emerald twilight
After years of faithful service, Hal rebelled against the Guardians when they refused to let him change history and restore Coast City after Mongol destroyed it. Unbeknown to anyone, Jordan was infected by the fear parasite Parallax, which had been imprisoned for eons in the Central Power Battery on Oa. It drove Hal to attack hundreds of his comrades, stealing their power rings as he stormed across the universe to a titanic confrontation with the Guardians' last hope—a freed and restored Sinestro.

Even the arch-renegade could not stop Hal from destroying the Battery and ending billions of years of Green Lantern-enforced peace and order. However, when the Earth's sun was destroyed, Hal expended all his energy to revive the dying star and save the planet.

REDEMPTION
After eradicating the Green Lantern Corps, the deranged, Parallax-possessed Hal Jordan became a despised pariah. It took the threat of Earth's extermination to bring him to his senses.

"Beware my Power... Green Lantern's Light."
HAL JORDAN

GREEN LANTERN (KYLE RAYNER)

DEBUT *Green Lantern* (Vol. 3) #48 (JAN. 1994)
REAL NAME Kyle Rayner
BASE Mobile, New York City (when on Earth)
HEIGHT 5ft 11in **WEIGHT** 175 lbs **EYES** Dark green **HAIR** Black
POWERS/ABILITIES Indomitable willpower commanding a power ring that is able to materialize hard-light constructs, translate languages, facilitate in-planet and intergalactic flight, and protect against hostile environments and enemy attack; artist with tremendous creativity.
ALLIES Green Lantern (Hal Jordan), Green Lantern (John Stewart), Green Lantern (Kilowog), Green Lantern (Guy Gardner), Ganthet
ENEMIES Sinestro, Darkstars, Soranik Sinestro
AFFILIATIONS Green Lantern Corps, White Lantern Corps, New Guardians

CLASSIC STORIES

***Green Lantern* (Vol. 3) #51 (May 1994)** The only remaining Green Lantern in the universe, Kyle Rayner has to figure out ring-slinging as he goes along!

***Green Lantern* (Vol. 3) #76–77, *Green Arrow* (Vol. 2) #110-111 (Jul.–Aug. 1996)** In this four-part crossover, the successors to the famous Green Lantern/Green Arrow pairing become the "Hard-Traveling Heroes" of a new generation.

***Ion* #1 (Jun. 2006)** After the events of *Infinite Crisis*, Kyle Rayner adapts to his new overwhelming powers as the spacefaring Ion.

AN ARTIST AT HEART
As a skilled cartoonist, Kyle's constructs range from the imaginative to the impossible. Even with the power of a Green Lantern ring at his disposal, he's often found sketching in a more traditional manner.

WHITE LANTERN
Kyle has played many roles in his career, but his time as a White Lantern certainly proved his worth as the only Lantern to master all seven rings.

During one of the Green Lantern Corps' darkest hours, young artist Kyle Rayner was chosen to be the universe's lone Green Lantern by a Guardian of the Universe named Ganthet. The torchbearer for all the Green Lantern Corps would become in the future, Kyle Rayner went on to master all seven colors of the emotional spectrum, the only Lantern to ever truly accomplish such a feat.

When longtime Green Lantern Hal Jordan was infected by the Parallax entity and set out to destroy the Green Lantern Corps, the Guardian known as Ganthet picked the rather young and inexperienced artist Kyle Rayner to be the only Green Lantern in the universe. Learning on the job, Kyle became a youthful inspiration and faced countless Super-Villain threats as the torchbearer keeping the Green Lantern light alive. After the Green Lantern Corps was restored, Kyle joined a team of representatives from the other colors of the emotional spectrum called the New Guardians.

Kyle went on to master, not just the Green Lantern ring, but all seven lights of the emotional spectrum as the White Lantern. However, this role was not to last. When Kyle was tasked with resurrecting the Blue Lantern Corps, his grasp of the spectrum shattered, and only his Green Lantern ring remained with him. Kyle embraced the return of his classic power set, and became a Green Lantern once more, adopting a costume nearly identical to his original and helping the Green Lantern Corps make peace with their rivals in the Sinestro Corps.

When Kyle withheld knowledge of a future child he and Sinestro Corps leader Soranik Natu might have, he pushed Soranik over the edge, and she branded his chest with the Sinestro Corps symbol before the two Corps split in anger. Traumatized by this event, Kyle nevertheless continued his heroic duties, facing threats like the Controllers, General Zod, and the Darkstars. As a veteran Corps members, Kyle has helped train newer members Jessica Cruz and Simon Baz.

ON THE RECORD

Kyle debuted during the 1990s at a time when many heroes were being replaced by temporary successors. After the success of the "Death of Superman" and "Knightfall" storylines, which saw Clark Kent and Bruce Wayne removed from their roles, "Emerald Twilight" sought to achieve the same exciting shake-up of the status quo. While some fans were enraged at Hal Jordan's transformation into Super-Villain—a fate spared both Superman and Batman—Kyle's individuality and interesting approach as the solo Green Lantern made him a hit as well, and he soon found prestige as a member of the JLA.

THE REPLACEMENTS
The popular JLA of the late 1990s featured legacy heroes including Kyle Rayner and Wally West.

GUNFIRE

DEBUT *Deathstroke the Terminator Annual* (Vol. 1) #2 (Oct. 1993)
REAL NAME Andrew Van Horn
BASE New York City
HEIGHT 6ft 1in **WEIGHT** 190 lbs
EYES Green **HAIR** Red
POWERS/ABILITIES Can agitate molecules in matter, causing them to create blasts; wears customized hi-tech armor.
ALLIES Argus, Anima, Ballistic, Geist, Hook
ENEMIES Venev, Ragnarok, Mirror Master

Young businessman Andrew Van Horn's metagene was triggered when, as part of a concerted invasion of Earth, he was attacked and left for dead by a spinal-fluid-consuming alien. In the aftermath, the stunned survivor developed the power to ferociously agitate molecules and redirect them as blasts of concussive force, initially using any object he could hold in his hands.

Equipped with a prototype suit of polymer armor built by his munitions company, Andrew hunted the creature that had "killed" him and thereafter became the globe-trotting Super Hero Gunfire. The same attack that transformed Andrew also killed and mutated his father Gunther, who became his deranged arch-enemy, Ragnarok.

After finally defeating his father, Gunfire attempted to monetize his gifts by joining other metahuman survivors of the alien attack in a corporately funded team called the Blood Pack. Gunfire retired after his hands were cut off by the Super-Villain Prometheus.

HAND WEAPON
Gunfire's ability to transform any object's mass into blasts of concussive energy effectively turned anything he held into a firearm.

GUNNER AND SARGE

DEBUT *All-American Men of War* #67 (Mar. 1959)
REAL NAME "Gunner" MacKay, Sarge Clay
POWERS/ABILITIES Fully trained US Marines in peak physical condition; exceptional reactions and marksmanship.
ALLIES Pooch, Captain Storm, Johnny Cloud, Mademoiselle Marie, Haunted Tank crew
ENEMIES Nazi Germany, Japanese Empire
AFFILIATIONS US Marine Corps, The Losers

"Gunner" McKay and his military mentor "Sarge" Clay had a unique tactic for fighting the Japanese on a succession of Pacific Islands during World War II. The young private was an astonishingly fast and accurate shot with any weapon and would hang back or conceal himself while Sarge would deliberately make himself a target for enemy fire. The veteran trusted that his own years of experience would allow him to anticipate or evade the inevitable attack long enough for his infallible comrade to finish off the shooters.

They were assisted by a highly intelligent battle dog named Pooch, who accompanied them when—with Naval Captain Storm and pilot Johnny Cloud—they became part of a Special Operations squad nicknamed "the Losers" because of their bad luck.

The Losers were eventually killed in combat, but Gunner was soon recovered and resurrected as a cyborg-zombie, becoming part of the covert military unit dubbed the Creature Commandos.

BROTHERS IN ARMS
Before joining the Losers, Gunner and Sarge fought as an effective team in many brutal battles against the Imperial Japanese Army.

GYPSY

DEBUT *Justice League of America Annual* (Vol. 1) #2 (Oct. 1984)
REAL NAME Cynnthia Mordeth
HEIGHT 5ft 6in **WEIGHT** 110 lbs **EYES** Brown **HAIR** Black
POWERS/ABILITIES Mystically generated illusion casting; light-bending; sound projection and distortion; advanced unarmed combat techniques.
ALLIES Vibe, Breacher
ENEMIES Mistress Mordeth, Amanda Waller, Rupture
AFFILIATIONS Traders of Piradell

HIGHER PLANES DRIFTER
After years of traversing dimensions and fleeing from every conceivable danger, Gypsy finally realized safety lay in confronting her pursuers.

GYPSY MAGIC
Vibe's every instinct said to trust the captivating Circus detainee, even though his A.R.G.U.S. bosses said Gypsy was a threat to the entire planet.

Unearthly refugee Cynnthia Mordeth always led a fairytale life. Her trans-dimensional trader father entered into a dynastic marriage with a rival tribe's queen and was reduced to a monstrous man-shaped packet of sentient energy. Her mother also transformed, becoming a planet-ravaging predator. Gypsy fled across myriad dimensions, unaware that she was the key to her mother's invasion plan for other realms.

On Earth, Cynnthia was imprisoned by the US Government agency A.R.G.U.S., never realizing it was all part of a bargain between her father and agent Amanda Waller. Cynnthia was caged in the Circus—a clandestine containment facility built to hold metahumans from other universes—and used to trick Cisco "Vibe" Ramon into becoming Waller's inter-dimensional alarm system and watchdog.

When Gypsy escaped, she befriended Cisco and slowly won him over to her cause. Together they traversed several multiversal breaches, eventually arriving on Cynnthia's homeworld Piradell. Here they destroyed the evil Mistress Mordeth after liberating Cisco's older brother Armando from murderous servitude to her.

On returning to Earth, Gypsy helped Vibe renegotiate the terms of his employment with Waller and A.R.G.U.S., before vanishing from public view.

ON THE RECORD

The original Gypsy was teenager Cindy Reynolds, who fled suburbia when her metahuman abilities abruptly manifested themselves. Living on the streets of Detroit, she survived using her chameleon-camouflage and illusion-casting powers.

Gypsy joined a reconfigured Justice League that included Vibe, Dale Gunn, and the Martian Manhunter. She later became a valued, covert operative of special ops organization Justice League Task Force, and then joined Barbara Gordon's Birds of Prey team.

HIDE AND SEEK
Gypsy's guileful intelligence-gathering and undetectable groundwork usually led to a punishing follow-up from her mighty, but not-so-subtle, associates.

GREEN LANTERN CORPS

DATA

DEBUT *Green Lantern* (Vol. 2) #9 (Nov.–Dec. 1961)
BASE New Oa
NOTABLE MEMBERS/POWERS HAL JORDAN, JOHN STEWART, KYLE RAYNER, GUY GARDNER, JESSICA CRUZ, SIMON BAZ, KILOWOG, SALAAK, TWO-SIX, GORIN-SUNN, ARISIA RRAB, SODAM YAT, MOGO. Drawn from across the Multiverse, Green Lanterns use willpower to operate power rings able to materialize hard-light constructs, allow flight, maintain protective fields, and universally translate languages, among other functions.
ALLIES Red Lantern Corps, Blue Lantern Corps
ENEMIES Sinestro, Sinestro Corps, Manhunters, Nekron, Larfleeze, Black Hand, Darkstars, Controller Mu

The Green Lantern Corps is a peacekeeping force created by the self-appointed Guardians of the Universe. The immortals sought to maintain order and foster the rise of civilization amongst lesser beings throughout the cosmos. Methodically dividing all of known space into 3,600 sectors, they personally selected the organization's peacekeeping officers from all over creation. Over eons the Guardians developed automated systems and now the power rings that all Green Lanterns employ automatically seek out honest beings capable of overcoming great fear whenever a wielder dies in the line of duty.

AT A GLANCE...

Central Power Battery
The colossal, lantern-like engine on New Oa condenses the willpower of all sentient life in the universe and redistributes it as green light to each Green Lantern officer's personal power battery. The finite energy-charge in each officer's ring is replenished by touching it to their personal battery long enough for them to utter the sacred oath:
"In Brightest Day, In Blackest Night;
No evil shall escape my sight.
Let those who worship evil's might,
Beware my power... Green Lantern's light!"

Full mental jacket
Courage, good intentions, and the mightiest personal weapon in the universe are not enough. The Corps' basic training is physically and mentally punishing. It teaches recruits to fight under pressure against multiple foes and that clear thinking will always win the day.

From the earliest times of existence, the immortals of Oa sought to impose order on universal chaos, which they saw manifested as acts of evil perpetrated by deviant or antisocial beings. Their first solution was a vast army of robotic Manhunters who policed a scrupulously demarcated cosmos, reacting to crises, suppressing violence, and preventing disorder from spreading.

When the Manhunters malfunctioned, the appalled Guardians mothballed their mechanical agents. Some of the mechanoids, however, refused to abort their programmed mission, vanishing into the dark corners of the universe to plot revenge.

The Guardians replaced their artificial intermediaries with sentient beings recruited from the 3,600 sectors into which they had divided the known universe. These individuals were capable of swift assessment and certain judgment. They would also be fearless, honest, and dedicated to preserving life, maintaining order, and furthering progress.

Now organized along more military lines, the Corps' administrative offices were based on Oa, which also housed the immense Central Power Battery and Sciencells containing the universe's greatest felons and menaces. After the destruction of Oa, the Green Lantern Corps relocated to the living planet and fellow Green Lantern Mogo, and soon fell under the field command of longtime Lantern John Stewart.

Under Stewart's leadership, the Green Lanterns united with the Sinestro Corps for a time and faced the relaunched Darkstars— armored, lethal "peacekeepers." The Lanterns triumphed, but Stewart eventually left his leadership position as he became more active in the Justice League.

MOGO
A living planet and Green Lantern member, Mogo was the home base for the Green Lantern Corps after the destruction of the planet Oa. Unlike Oa, Mogo is capable of moving through space.

Enhanced security
The Guardians eventually altered how their Green Lanterns operated. Without disclosing that they now considered lone agents untrustworthy, the Oans doubled the ranks, with officers native to each sector patrolling in pairs. This caused friction as the traditionally independent Lanterns often could not collaborate or cooperate.

CLASSIC STORIES

Tales of the Green Lantern Corps (Vol. 1) #1–3 (May–Jul. 1981)
The entire Corps is mustered when Krona attempts to return the universe to its primal state, allowing death-personification Nekron access to the realm of the living.

Tales of the Green Lantern Corps (Vol. 1) Annual #2 (1986) The Guardians' fallibility is exposed in "Tygers" when Abin Sur visits the planet Ysmault and is infected with fear by the prophecies of the Five Inversions.

Green Lantern Corps (Vol. 2) #20–26 (Mar.–Sep. 2008)
A contingent of Green Lanterns dispatched on a "Ring Quest" to confiscate deadly yellow power rings clashes with cosmic terrorist Mongul who has revived the Sinestro Corps under his own leadership.

RIGHTEOUS RETRIBUTION
For millennia, the Guardians used Urak to store power batteries, and their energies made the resource-poor world flourish. When the Guardians changed policy and withdrew them, Urak's ecology crashed. Now, with an uncanny capacity to overwhelm willpower, Urak's Keepers erupt upon the universe, slaughtering at will and especially targeting Green Lanterns. When John Stewart's squad was overcome, he had to kill one of his team to preserve Oa's security, and Guy Gardner's only viable rescue plan involved resurrecting the Mean Machine—the meanest, most ornery officers in the Corps.

WILLPOWER WIPEOUT
The Keepers wanted other worlds' resources to rebuild Urak, but also relished the chance to slaughter the Guardians' "pets" in the Green Lantern Corps.

GREEN LANTERNS UNITE
While it's impossible to list all Green Lanterns past and present, there are always shining stars in any era of the cosmic team.
1 Kilowog
2 Simon Baz
3 Arisia Rrab
4 Gorin-Sunn
5 John Stewart
6 Guy Gardner
7 2-6-8-1-7-9-5 (Known as "Two-Six")
8 Salaak
9 Lok Neboora

REBIRTH

GIVEN THE GREEN LIGHT
Simon Baz and Jessica Cruz are new recruits of the Green Lantern Corps. Despite originally disliking one another, they were ordered to work together as Earth's Green Lanterns. The two formed a friendship after a trial by fire, and both served together on the fabled team of Earth-based Super Heroes, the Justice League. However, Jessica eventually ended their partnership when she left Earth to protect the area of space known as the Ghost Sector.

After several large scale battles, including an infiltration of the Green Lanterns' Central Power Battery at the hands of the villainous Cyborg Superman, the Guardians relocated the Green Lantern Corps from Mogo to their artificial planet, New Oa. There they were able to assign their favorite operatives to appropriate missions, including Hal Jordan, who helped them fight off Controller Mu's Blackstars.

When the elders of the Guardians of the Universe left Oa to wage something they called the "Ultrawar," new replacements were bred with a combination of Guardian, Zamaron, and Controller DNA. These Young Guardians began to challenge the old ways that the Green Lantern Corps was run, promising a bold new era in the days to come.

ON THE RECORD

Originally the Green Lantern Corps were depicted as running their own affairs within their personal interstellar beat, separate from the Guardians and seldom impinging upon each others' jurisdictions.

Emerald army
During the 1960s the Corps' ranks expanded and were cautiously explored. A huge variety of valiant alien Green Lanterns were introduced, but though many become eagerly anticipated guest-stars, none were quite as effective as Earth's Hal Jordan. He frequently won the day with solutions beyond his peers' comprehension, and even managed to come back from the dead.

Green Lantern citadel
Following the Multiverse-altering *Crisis on Infinite Earths*, the Corps was relieved of strict assignments to specific sectors, and both the Guardians and the female Oans who had evolved into the Zamarons retired from the universe for a period of reflection and contemplation. Advised that Earth would play a crucial role during the next millennium, several Green Lanterns—Katma Tui, Salaak, Ch'p, Kilowog, and Arisia—relocated to that world with Hal Jordan, John Stewart, and maverick Guy Gardner, and were on hand to witness the transformation of the so-called "New Guardians."

Sinestro Corps war
The Corps faced their greatest challenge when the renegade Sinestro launched an all-out attack on the cosmos. Although Sinestro was defeated, the events helped lead to the horrific event that would be known as the *Blackest Night*.

HEAVY HITTERS
Yellow Lanterns were not the first to mistakenly confuse Green Lanterns' respect for rules with timidity, or their concern for life with weakness.

"We're Lanterns... we're always on duty."

GUY GARDNER

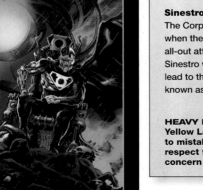

THE PHANTOM RING
Longtime enemy of the true Man of Steel, Cyborg Superman was able to corrupt the Green Lantern battery, hacking into Green Lantern rings as soon as they recharged. When Hal took the fight to Cyborg Superman, the villain employed a Phantom Ring and attacked Coast City. With some help from his fellow Green Lanterns, Jordan stopped the villain in his tracks, his years of ring-slinging experience enough to vanquish Cyborg Superman's novice attempts.

SHEDDING LIGHT
With the Green Lantern Corps damaged by Cyborg Superman's attack, the Guardians realized they needed to finish their construction of New Oa more than ever.

H.I.V.E.

DEBUT *New Teen Titans* (Vol. 1) #1 (Nov. 1980)
REAL NAME Holistic Integration for Viral Equality
BASE Metropolis
ENEMIES Superman, Hector Hammond, Superboy, Psycho Pirate, Killer Frost
AFFILIATIONS N.O.W.H.E.R.E., Psiphon, Doctor Psycho

H'EL

DEBUT *Supergirl* (Vol. 6) #13 (Dec. 2012)
EYES White **HAIR** Black
POWERS/ABILITIES All the physical enhancements of a Kryptonian under a yellow sun, plus telepathy, telekinesis, teleportation, force-field projection, limited mind control, size alteration, astral projection, and time manipulation.
ALLIES Supergirl
ENEMIES Superman, Superboy, Supergirl, Justice League, Teen Titans

HADES

DEBUT *Wonder Woman* (Vol. 1) #329 (Feb. 1986)
BASE Hell, Sphere of the Gods
POWERS/ABILITIES Immortality, telepathy, metamorphosis, illusions, control of the dead.
ALLIES Persephone, Poseidon
ENEMIES First Born, Hephaestus
AFFILIATIONS Gods of Olympus

HAMMER AND SICKLE

DEBUT *Outsiders* (Vol. 1) #10 (Aug. 1986)
REAL NAMES Boris and Natasha Ulyanov
BASE Russia **EYES** Blue **HAIR** Blonde
POWERS/ABILITIES Hammer Enhanced strength, durability, large war hammer; Sickle Enhanced speed, agility, razor-sharp sickle.
ENEMIES Outsiders, Suicide Squad, Catwoman, New Teen Titans, Red Star
AFFILIATIONS People's Heroes, Red Shadows, the Society

The clandestine organization known as H.I.V.E. was created by persons unknown for ostensibly altruistic reasons. Its avowed purpose—as defined by the ruling H.I.V.E. Queen—is to release the world from the bondage of individual freedoms and create global parity for every living creature on Earth. To these ends, they have abducted children, murdered thousands of innocents, and consorted with criminals, all while making a tidy profit. Casualties have included scientist Dr. Caitlin Snow, who was transformed into Killer Frost after H.I.V.E. sabotaged her invention to protect its own financial interests in the energy industry.

But H.I.V.E.'s major area of endeavor is psionics. For years it has stolen humans with telepathic potential, turning them into warriors, research subjects, or drones.

H'El attacked Earth believing he was acting for the House of El. He had spent decades exploring the universe, preserving Krypton's history. Finding cousins on Earth, H'El resolved to turn back time. When he tried to avert Krypton's destruction using Earth's sun as fuel, Earth's defenders defeated him and he fell through a time rift.

Arriving on Krypton when Jor-El was a student, H'El learned he was a clone-hybrid spontaneously generated from millions of Kryptonian cell-samples. A freak accident had created him within a star-spanning time-capsule; his aberrant mind forming from the historical records archived on the vessel.

Enraged, H'El staged a multi-chronal assault which simultaneously besieged Krypton in three different eras. He was again defeated by Superman, Superboy, and Supergirl, and left trapped in a time loop.

Hades is one of the most powerful of the Olympian gods. When he and his brothers Zeus and Poseidon slew their father Chronos, his brothers claimed dominion of the skies and seas respectively, and Hades was left with the underworld—the realm of spirits. His kingdom is built from all the souls that have entered his realm, which Hades reshapes into settings to suit his mood.

When Zeus died, his queen Hera took on his role, sparking a civil war that embroiled the Olympians and their offspring in a catastrophic conflict. Devious, bored, mistrusting, and incapable of love, Hades agreed to Wonder Woman's peace plan for him to wed Hera. When this failed, he tried to forcibly marry Diana instead, but was foiled by Hephaestus. As the war raged, Hades was seemingly killed by First Born.

Russian Boris Ulyanov was dedicated to the Soviet Union. He and his wife Natasha, were augmented by state scientists to counter American patriotic groups such as the Force of July. Boris—wielding a bone-crushing hammer with mutant super-strength and vitality—became field leader of the People's Heroes. Natasha used a sickle with her enhanced speed and agility, serving beside Boris in the team (and its successor Red Shadows) as they repeatedly clashed with the Outsiders and the Suicide Squad. Later the Ulyanovs operated as a duo, battling the Teen Titans over Russian fugitive Red Star.

When the Berlin Wall fell, they fell out of favor in the new Russia. As superpowered mercenaries and assassins in the West, they joined Super-Villain coalition the Society and clashed with Catwoman.

HALO

DEBUT *The Brave and the Bold* (Vol. 1) #200 (Jul. 1983)
REAL NAMES Gabrielle Doe, Violet Harper, Marissa Barron
BASE Gotham City
HEIGHT 5ft 7in **WEIGHT** 120 lbs **EYES** Blue **HAIR** Blonde
POWERS/ABILITIES Resurrection; spectrum of light-based effects generated as bodily auras or haloes (Red: heat; Orange: concussive force; Yellow: blinding light; Green: stasis effect; Blue: holographic distortion; Indigo: tractor beam); used in combination the light effects afford physical protection and flight; using the Violet power suppresses Halo's personality, allowing the deceased Violet Harper to take control of the body.
ALLIES Batman, Katana, Sebastian Faust, Alfred Pennyworth
ENEMIES Violet Harper, Marissa Barron, Masters of Disaster

Halo was born when teenage sociopath Violet Harper was murdered by the costumed assassin Syonide. The crime was observed by an invisible ancient light entity—one of the Aurakles—which accidentally became trapped in the corpse, reanimating it while also bestowing a range of abilities. Violet's personality was suppressed, leaving an innocent amnesiac who took the name Gabrielle Doe. Her light-based superpowers brought her to the attention of Batman, who recruited and trained her as part of his undercover team, the Outsiders.

After many adventures, the still largely naive and innocent Gaby was murdered on the orders of criminal mastermind Marissa Barron, who also died in the attack. The Aurakle then transferred itself into Barron's body, which promptly resurrected with Gaby's personality and powers. Resuming her career on the fringes of the Super Hero community, Halo withdrew from the spotlight. During a mission for Red Robin and Batman Incorporated she was lost and declared dead. She now operates completely off the grid as part of the Dead Heroes Club, taking on covert missions for Batman.

BEACON OF HOPE
Halo's immense powers were balanced by a childlike nature and desire to please. However, she developed a hard-won maturity during *Blackest Night*. She was especially effective against Black Lanterns, mercilessly eradicating Katana's resurrected children and Geo-Force's sister Terra.

THINKING MAN'S VILLAIN
Anyone who mistook Hector Hammond's paralysis for helplessness learned to their cost that vengeance and agony are all in the mind.

HAMMOND, HECTOR

DEBUT *Green Lantern* (Vol. 2) #5 (Apr. 1961)
BASE Metropolis; Coast City, California
REAL NAME James Craddock
HEIGHT 5ft 1in **WEIGHT** 156 lbs **EYES** Brown **HAIR** Brown
POWERS/ABILITIES Hyper-advanced intellect and numerous psionic abilities including telepathy, telekinesis, mind control, mental blasts, and illusion creation.
ENEMIES Green Lantern, Superman, Orion, Kroloteans, Sinestro, Justice League, Darkstars
AFFILIATIONS H.I.V.E., Secret Society of Super-Villains

Astrophysics and aeronautics consultant Hector Hammond was secretly experimented on by Kroloteans—an alien species of arms manufacturers. They amplified Hammond's psionic abilities, hoping to sell him as the ultimate weapon, "the God Brain." They similarly mutated William Hand (Blackhand) and a shark, who all became foes of Green Lanterns.

Hammond's mentality expanded exponentially and he became a menace to everyone around him. His burgeoning psionic powers proved too much for rookie ring-bearer Hal Jordan, but Hammond was overwhelmed by Hal's mentor Green Lantern Sinestro. Imprisoned in isolation and studied by scientists, Hammond's powers constantly grew—as did his skull. Hammond was incapable of physical movement, but possessed lethal psionic abilities that fed parasitically on the minds around him and hungered for dominance. His psychic range spanned galaxies and his cruel, playful predations caused chaos for the Guardians on Oa and the homeworld of the New Gods.

Hal Jordan saved Hammond from the Kroloteans when he tried to retrieve their ripe bioweapon, and Hammond repaid his debt by helping to defeat the Controllers and Darkstars.

QUEEN FOR A DAY
H.I.V.E.'s psionic empress was no match for the decrepit-seeming Hammond.

HANGMEN

DEBUT *Titans* (Vol. 1) #21 (Nov. 2000)
NOTABLE MEMBERS Breathtaker, Provoke, Shock Trauma, Stranglehold, Killshot
ALLIES Dr. Psycho
ENEMIES Titans, Batman II (Dick Grayson) and Robin, Teen Titans
AFFILIATIONS The Society, Secret Society of Super-Villains

The Hangmen were mercenaries hired by Quraci nationalists to assassinate the terrorist Cheshire— an act which brought them into repeated conflict with the Titans. The asphyxiation-themed team fought in the Battle of Metropolis as part of the Secret Society of Super-Villains, but preferred looting to fighting. Supposedly killed by Doctor Psycho for dereliction of duty, they had actually bribed him to fake their deaths.

The Hangmen were executed months later by the Spectre, after seeking to join Libra's new Secret Society of Super-Villains during *Infinite Crisis*.

After their executions, their costumed identities and murder methods were appropriated by a new group of anonymous felons in Gotham City, who clashed with Dick Grayson and Damian Wayne—the second Batman and Robin team—and later Damian Wayne's new Teen Titans team.

HARBINGER

DEBUT *New Teen Titans Annual* (Vol. 1) #2 (1983) (as Lyla); *Crisis on Infinite Earths* #1 (Apr. 1985) (as Harbinger)
BASE House of Heroes
EYES Orange **HAIR** Blonde
POWERS/ABILITIES Multiversal omniscience; Transmatter Cubes summon agents.
ALLIES All heroes in the known multiverse
ENEMIES Gentry, He Whose Hand Is Empty

Harbinger is the hyper-evolved artificial intelligence that administers the 52 universes known as the Orrery of Worlds, within the greater Multiverse. Her face and personality are based on Lyla Michaels, who faithfully served yet ultimately murdered the original Monitor during *Crisis on Infinite Earths*. These Multiversal realignments occur from time to time and are referred to as "Crises" by the mortals who endure them.

The Harbinger AI eventually gained full autonomy and inherited the Monitor's mission to safeguard the Multiverse after Nix Uotan was captured by the "Gentry" —invaders from beyond. She sought out an army of Super Heroes, transported them to the transdimensional House of Heroes, and supervised their battle to save the Monitor and all realities.

HARVEST

DEBUT *Teen Titans* (Vol. 4) #7 (May 2012)
BASE The Colony
POWERS/ABILITIES Advanced military training; chronokinesis; centuries of stolen futuristic weapons and technologies.
ALLIES Jon Lane Kent
ENEMIES Teen Titans, Superboy
AFFILIATIONS N.O.W.H.E.R.E., Ravagers

Harvest was a colonel in the militia of 31st-century Earth who spent his life battling metahumans as they attempted to eradicate the human populace. When his son was killed, he resolved to rewrite history. He began traveling incrementally backward in time, and with each stop gathered more technology and power, gradually transforming himself into a lethal and inhuman monster. To aid him in his dangerously misguided mission to save mankind, Harvest kidnapped and indoctrinated Jon Lane Kent, the superpowered son of Superman and Lois Lane from a possible future reality.

Arriving in the 21st century, he created N.O.W.H.E.R.E., gathering together young metahumans and forcing them to kill each other in a periodic Culling. The survivors would form the basis of Harvest's army of Ravagers. His obsessive campaigns brought him repeatedly into conflict with Superboy and the Teen Titans, and he was killed after attempting to combine a mass of metahuman DNA into an ultimate weapon.

MILLENNIUM MAN
Nothing Harvest had seen over a thousand years of history convinced him to abandon his dream of a world without metahumans.

HARLEY QUINN

DATA

DEBUT *The Batman Adventures* (Vol. 1) #12 **(Sep. 1993)**
REAL NAME Dr. Harleen Quinzel **BASE** Gotham City
HEIGHT 5ft 7in **WEIGHT** 131 lbs
EYES Blue **HAIR** Blonde/Red/Blue
POWERS/ABILITIES Unpredictable due to insanity; extremely agile and capable fighter; highly intelligent; specialist knowledge of psychiatry; adept at manipulating others; weapons include a giant mallet and other clown-themed items.
ALLIES Poison Ivy, Power Girl, Booster Gold, Gang of Harleys, Batgirl, Batman (on occasion)
ENEMIES The Joker, Punchline, Granny Goodness, sometimes Batman (when Harley's being mischievous)
AFFILIATIONS Suicide Squad, Birds of Prey

Harley Quinn has been a psychiatrist, The Joker's lethal sidekick, a key member of a secret government-sponsored strike force, a Brooklyn landlady, a roller derby champion, a burlesque dancer, a nurse, and a punk rocker. But to hear her tell it, all those lives are behind her now and she has set off on her newest mission: to be a real, honest-to-goodness Super Hero. While she hasn't always had the highest regard for human life, Harley has always maintained a strict moral code that often sees her fighting for the underdog. So maybe she's got a chance at this hero thing after all. Stranger things have happened in Gotham City...

AT A GLANCE...

Who's that girl?
Much like The Joker, Harley's mental instability has led to conflicting origin stories. Most versions agree that she was a former Arkham Asylum psychiatrist who fell in love with her main subject, The Joker, and quickly dropped everything for a chance to impress him as the villain Harley Quinn.

Boy trouble
Harley tried to play the role of the doting girlfriend to the insane Joker, despite him tossing her into a vat of chemicals. She acted ditzier than usual to attract him, but soon found that the Clown Prince of Crime tired of her, eventually discarding her like yesterday's whoopee cushion.

Dr. Harleen Quinzel's dramatic transformation into the Super-Villain Harley Quinn is a tale that has changed over the years due to Harley's own retellings and her penchant for exaggeration. According to Harley's latest version, she grew up in a fairly quiet neighborhood in Brooklyn, New York. Harleen had several brothers and a bit of a delinquent streak. She soon met a like-minded boy named Bernie Bash, who proved even more dangerously unstable than Harleen. To win her affections, Bernie threw their classmate Bonnie Harper out of his car into the path of an oncoming truck. Bonnie had picked on Harleen in school, and Quinzel was moved by Bernie's "romantic" gesture. When he was arrested, Harleen broke into Bernie's parents' place and stole a stuffed beaver to remember him by—a beaver she would later talk to as if it were a real person. Harleen experienced her first heartbreak when Bernie was arrested and it worsened when he was killed while in juvenile detention.

After concentrating on her studies, Harleen won several scholarships to Gotham University. She graduated at the top of her class and found work as a psychiatrist at a prominent hospital in Gotham City. Fascinated by the criminal mind, Harleen transferred to Arkham Asylum.

Dr. Quinzel claims that when she was working at Arkham Asylum, she was constantly annoyed that the inmates did not open up to her. She convinced the warden to allow her to join Arkham Asylum's general population, intent on getting close to the inmates as one of their peers. To that end, she dyed her blonde hair red and black and faked insanity, earning the attention of The Joker. She fell in love with the Super-Villain and then broke him out of the Asylum. Later, the Clown Prince of Crime dropped Harley in a vat of

FALLING FOR IT
Harleen was betrayed by The Joker when he threw her into a vat of chemicals.

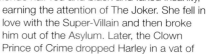

YOUNG SCHOLAR
From an early age, Harleen had a keen interest in psychiatry. Amadeus Arkham's *Studying the Criminal Mind* gave her an insight into how to manipulate people.

CLASSIC STORIES

***The Batman Adventures: Mad Love* #1 (Feb. 1994)** Harley Quinn's obsession with the Clown Prince of Crime is examined in this comic that shines a light on Harley's origin, as well as the couple's abusive relationship.

***Batman: Harley Quinn* #1 (Oct. 1999)** Harley navigates her way into the DC universe during this special prestige-format tie-in with the epic "Batman: No Man's Land" crossover.

***Gotham City Sirens* #1 (Aug. 2009)** Catwoman, Poison Ivy, and Harley all share the spotlight in this ongoing series featuring Gotham City's most infamous femme fatales.

***Harley Quinn* (Vol. 2) Annual #1 (Dec. 2014)** Readers are treated to a comic as zany as Harley herself in this special scratch-and-sniff issue that featured a disclaimer from DC due to some of its more controversial scents.

Wardrobe changes
Harley Quinn has adopted several looks over the years, from her classic jester look to the roller-skating costume she wore when participating in the—often bloody—sport of roller derby.

SQUAD LIFE
When government agent Amanda Waller decided to set up Task Force X—a covert strike force made up entirely of Super-Villains—Harley Quinn was one of her repeat recruits. Knowing that Harley was sharper than she often let on and was fully capable of holding her own in a fight, Waller employed Harley's special brand of chaos more often than not. While Harley eventually won her freedom and was released from Belle Reve Penitentiary, she seemed to enjoy her time running amok for the government.

FRIENDS IN LOW PLACES
Harley became close with several of her Suicide Squad teammates. She even had romantic flings with both Deadshot and Rick Flag, Jr.

chemicals which dyed her skin bright white and drove her insane. Adopting the name Harley Quinn, she became The Joker's number-one accomplice, acting even crazier than usual to keep his attention. But the two eventually—and somewhat violently—parted ways. Harley went from one job to the next, working for the US government as part of the Suicide Squad when she got herself arrested, and becoming a landlady in Coney Island, Brooklyn when she didn't. She was more than over her relationship with The Joker, and built herself a nice supportive community of likeminded misfits in Brooklyn. Tragedy struck a serious blow, however, when Harley lost her mother to cancer.

After being falsely accused of murder at the Super Hero therapy center called Sanctuary, Harley has decided to turn her life around even further by becoming a full-fledged hero, and has even teamed with the heroic Birds of Prey from time to time. She toyed with the idea of dating Booster Gold, but has put that plan on hold, opting to help fight on Batman's side during The Joker's most recent campaign of terror, the so-called "The Joker War."

> "How cool would it be to have my own comic book?"
>
> HARLEY QUINN

EXPLOSIVE PERSONALITY
Harley Quinn is not just a loose cannon, she is an entertaining loose cannon. When aimed at the right target, Harley can be a zany force for good, but cross her, and you won't be laughing for very long.

REBIRTH

GAL PALS?
Harley Quinn has always shared a special bond with Poison Ivy, dating back to the earliest days of Harley's criminal career. However, when Harley decided to become a Super Hero, the idea didn't mesh with Poison Ivy's current way of thinking, and the two broke up. (It didn't help that Harley had just spent a road trip bonding with a plant clone of Poison Ivy, and couldn't tell the difference between her and the real thing!)

ON THE RECORD

Harley Quinn's popularity didn't originally stem from the comics themselves, but from her original appearances on the award-winning cartoon, *Batman: The Animated Series.*

From cartoon to comic-book star
Harley Quinn first appeared on *Batman: The Animated Series* as The Joker's partner-in-crime, and soon found her way into the tie-in comic book series *The Batman Adventures* in 1993. It was six more years before she drifted into the mainstream DC universe, introduced in her own one-shot special during the epic "Batman: No Man's Land" crossover between all the Batman titles. In this version of her origin, Harley wasn't actually a doctor of psychiatry, but simply an intern. She fell in love with The Joker, broke him out of prison, and adopted a clownish look, complete with a red and black jester cowl.

Toxic friendship
After The Joker first attempted to kill Harley, she befriended Poison Ivy. The eco-terrorist took a liking to Harley's zany antics and gifted her with a formula that made Harley mostly immune to toxins and poisons and gave the kooky clown-in-training enhanced agility and strength. Now ready to go toe-to-toe with Batman himself, Harley truly began her career of crime.

TRICKY TRIO
Harley not only became fast friends with Poison Ivy, but also with Catwoman, who later began living with the pair despite their many differences and approaches to crime.

PLAYING WITH POWER
The hero Power Girl found herself in one compromising position after another after Harley found her crash-landed near her Brooklyn home. Harley decided to convince the amnesiac Power Girl that they were Super Hero partners, and even began fighting crime as Power Girl's sidekick, just for the sheer enjoyment of it. However, when this dysfunctional duo crossed paths with Super-Villains Clock King and the Sportsmaster, they found themselves on several adventures through the far reaches of space. Eventually, they fought their way home, only for Power Girl to regain her memories and quickly quit her partnership with Harley.

GIRL TROUBLE
When Power Girl finally found out the truth about her "Super Hero" partner Harley Quinn, it took all her heroic restraint not to totally pummel her former "sidekick."

HAUNTED TANK

DEBUT *G. I. Combat* #87 (May 1961)
BASE Mobile
POWERS/ABILITIES A tank haunted by the ghost of General James Ewell Brown Stuart and members of the crew connected to it; provides protection against magical attack and can also teleport.
ENEMIES Nazis

GUARDIAN GHOST
The M3 Stuart Light Tank was possessed by the ghost of Jeb Stuart's ancestor. Jeb could see and hear the ghost, who offered guidance in combat.

In World War II, the Haunted Tank was commanded by Jeb Stuart and watched over by the ghost of one of his ancestors—a Confederate general named James Ewell Brown Stuart. In 1942, Jeb was ordered to locate a stash of mystical artifacts that had been collected by Hitler, and he ended up using the Tank to fight several strange threats along the way.

Years later, when Jeb was 98 years old, the Tank materialized outside his house after his grandson, Sergeant Scott Stuart, was captured in Afghanistan. Old Jeb and the tank vanished in front of A.R.G.U.S. agents who had started tracing the tank after it went missing from a vault. Jeb and the tank reappeared in Afghanistan, where they rescued Scott.

The tank then teleported to the North Pole, where they stopped descendants of World War II Nazis unleashing a deadly "Warwheel" piloted by a Nazi Ghost.

Jeb died in action, but his ghost seemingly lived on in the vehicle, talking to his grandson who had inherited the family connection to the Haunted Tank.

HAWK, SON OF TOMAHAWK

DEBUT *Tomahawk* #131 (Dec. 1970)
BASE Echo Valley, Mid-West America
HEIGHT 5ft 10in **WEIGHT** 166 lbs
EYES Blue **HAIR** Brown with blond streak
POWERS/ABILITIES Expert horseman, tracker, and hunter.
ALLIES Firehair, Jonah Hex, Swamp Thing
ENEMIES Black Bison, Wise Owl

Hawk was a Western hero born in 1800. He was the son of Tomahawk (Tom Hawk), a famous revolutionary hero, and a Native American woman called Moon Fawn. Hawk was raised in Echo Valley, where he learned the ways of the Wild West from his father, and the secrets of Native American culture from his mother, along with his brother, Small Eagle.

Hawk became an expert tracker, hunter, and fighter. He was soon helping others and formed a close friendship with the heroic Firehair. Later, he joined forces with other Old West heroes to fight the mystical villain Black Bison. Hawk helped Swamp Thing when he time-traveled to the 1870s. Bison gave Swamp Thing a magic talisman, the Claw of Aelkhünd, to help him return to his own time. Just before he died, Hawk published his autobiography.

HAWKE, CONNOR

DEBUT *Green Arrow* (Vol. 2) #0 (Oct 1994)
REAL NAME Connor Hawke **BASE** Star City
HEIGHT 5ft 9in **WEIGHT** 160 lbs
EYES Green **HAIR** Blonde
POWERS/ABILITIES Highly skilled in archery and martial arts.
ALLIES Eddie Fyers, Green Lantern (Kyle Rayner), Black Canary, Robin (Tim Drake)
ENEMIES Lady Shiva, Doctor Sivana, Onomatopoeia, Constantine Drakon
AFFILIATIONS Justice League

Connor Hawke was the son of Green Arrow (Oliver Queen), although his father did not know of his existence until the two met in the Ashram Monastery during a dark time in Queen's life. Connor showed a natural aptitude for archery and martial arts, and Queen took him under his wing. When he eventually discovered the truth about their connection, Queen was mistrustful of the young man—and before they could repair their relationship, Queen was killed in an explosion.

Connor took up his father's mantle as Green Arrow and even joined the Justice League in his stead. After Oliver Queen returned from the dead, Connor was able to bond with him as a son, but their relationship remained fragile.

HAWK AND DOVE

DEBUT *Showcase* #75 (Jun. 1968)
REAL NAMES Hank Hall (Hawk) and Dawn Granger (Dove)
BASE Washington, D.C.
HEIGHT 6ft 1in (Hawk); 5ft 9in (Dove) **WEIGHT** 197 lbs (Hawk); 120 lbs (Dove)
EYES Brown (Hawk); Blue (Dove) **HAIR** Brown (Hawk); White (Dove)
POWERS/ABILITIES Hawk: Enhanced agility, strength, body density, and vision, healing factor; Dove: Enhanced strength, intelligence, and empathy, flight, danger sense.
ALLIES District of Columbia Police Department, Deadman, Batman
ENEMIES Alexander Quirk, Condor, Swan, the D'Yak, Blockbuster, the Hunter, Mister Twister, Fearsome Five

When brothers Hank and Don Hall discovered that criminals were planning to murder their father, Don wished they had the power to save him—and divine agencies answered. Brash, aggressive Hank transformed into Hawk, Avatar of War, while calm, rational Don became Dove, Avatar of Peace. They saved their father and used their gifts as small-town Super Heroes and in the Teen Titans. Don died during the *Crisis on Infinite Earths*. Although bereft, Hawk continued as a lone avenger, growing ever more enraged without the stabilizing influence of his brother.

Balance returned for Hank in the shape of Dawn Granger, selected by higher powers to be the new Dove, and the two heroes reluctantly formed a new partnership. Mirroring Hank's relationship with his brother, the duo clashed over ethical questions, with Hank favoring force and Dawn preferring pacifism and reason. But they united to face fellow avatars Condor and Swan, as well as the mysterious D'Yak. Hawk and Dove encountered the Teen Titans while investigating a sinister mystery in the small town of Hatton Corners in the east of the United States: a case that returned to haunt them and which served to reignite their crusade against evil in the post *Rebirth* era against the reality-shredding threats of Barbatos, The Batman Who Laughs, and Perpetua.

ON THE RECORD

The pre-*Flashpoint* Don and Hank Hall received their powers from the Lords of Chaos and Order and joined the Teen Titans. When Don died during the *Crisis on Infinite Earths*, Dawn Granger took his place as Dove. Their partnership ended when Dawn was seemingly slain by Monarch, an evil future version of Hank. Hank then became the time-warping villain Extant and was later killed, only to be reborn as a zombie in the *Blackest Night*, when he fought the new Hawk and Dove—Holly and Dawn Granger—and was brought back to life by the power of the white light.

DOUBLE TROUBLE
Hawk and Dove's relationship was marked by tension, but when combined, they could be an unstoppable force for good.

HAWKGIRL

DATA

DEBUT *The Flash Comics* #1 (Jan. 1940) (as Kendra Saunders); *JSA Secret Files and Origins* #1 (Aug. 1999)
REAL NAME Kendra Saunders
HEIGHT 5ft 9in **WEIGHT** 135 lbs **EYES** Hazel **HAIR** Brown
POWERS/ABILITIES Trained archaeologist; Nth Metal wings and harness allow flight; skilled with variety of weaponry; highly skilled warrior with memories of past lives.
ALLIES Hawkman, Martian Manhunter
ENEMIES Barbatos, Perpetua, Legion of Doom
AFFILIATIONS Justice League, Guild of Detection, Blackhawks

Using the power of Nth Metal, Kendra Saunders is Hawkgirl, one of the Justice League's newer recruits. Having no trouble standing shoulder to shoulder with giants, Hawkgirl's fighting spirit and determination has made her feared throughout the galaxy.

ON THE RECORD

The original Hawkgirl was Shiera Sanders Hall, who first appeared in *Flash Comics* #1 (Jan. 1940) as the girlfriend of Hawkman. After several continuity changes, Hawkgirl was reintroduced as a member of the JSA in 1999. This version's alter ego was Kendra Saunders, a distant cousin of the very first Hawkgirl. After The *Flashpoint* event radically changed Hawkman's history yet again, Kendra reemerged on Earth-2, a blue-clad freedom fighter against Darkseid's tyranny. A new Kendra only recently found her way back into the main continuity of Earth-0 during the *Dark Nights: Metal* miniseries.

WINGED WARRIOR
Hawkgirl was one of the main heroes fighting Darkseid's forces on post-*Flashpoint* Earth-2.

LADY BLACKHAWK
While fighting the forces of the Dark Multiverse and the demon Barbatos, Kendra was transformed for a time into a living embodiment of her codename, Lady Blackhawk.

The original souls that would become Hawkman and Hawkwoman—Ktar and Shrra—had been cursed to reincarnate time and time again over the centuries, to make up for Ktar's sins of making countless sacrificial murders to a being called the Lord Beyond the Void. They lived many lives, from ancient Egyptians to 1940's crime fighters Hawkman and Hawkwoman of the Justice Society of America.

However, in modern times, something strange happened. While there is only one Carter Hall, there were two women who shared a history as the reincarnated form of Shrra. The first was Shayera Hol, Empress of the planet Thanagar, also known as Hawkwoman. The second was Kendra Saunders, who gave up her wings to join a covert anti-apocalypse team of soldiers called the Blackhawks. As Lady Blackhawk, Kendra helped the Justice League during the Dark Multiverse's invasion of Earth. She soon earned a spot in their ranks as the hero Hawkgirl.

While on a mission to Thanagar Prime, Kendra met Shayera Hol, discovering that their history had been split due to the energy known as the Totality. The cosmic being Perpetua did not want her spirit whole. However, Starman (Will Payton) had merged with this Totality, and was able to make both women whole again, effectively making Kendra her own separate person, free to explore her own destiny.

Hawkgirl did just that, fighting the forces of Perpetua with the rest of the Justice League. In the process, she grew close with the Martian Manhunter, and the two began a romance, even discovering that they had a child in another reality. Later, when the world seemed to fall to Perpetua and turn to doom, Hawkgirl and Martian Manhunter fought valiantly to ensure the Multiverse lived to see another day.

ALIEN OUTFITTERS
Hawkgirl wears a costume that invokes uniforms worn on the planet Thanagar, and utilizes the Nth metal mined there to great effect.

CLASSIC STORIES

***Hawkgirl* (Vol. 1) #50 (May 2006)**
As part of the "One Year Later" event, Hawkgirl starts a new life in St. Roch, but soon finds herself troubled by nightmares of Hawkman.

***Blackest Night* #1–8 (Jun. 2009–May 2010)** Hawkman and Hawkgirl are murdered only to return as Black Lanterns. Hawkgirl is reborn at the end of the series, but with a new set of memories.

***Earth 2: Society* #8 (Mar. 2016)**
While searching her new world, Kendra learns that Fury is training a new generation of Amazons.

HAWKWOMEN
There have been a variety of Hawkwomen over the years, all reincarnated forms of the angel-like herald Shrra. Despite her appearance and name, Hawkgirl has now broken away from her ties to Hawkman and his ancestry.

HAWKMAN

DATA

DEBUT *Flash Comics* #1 (Jan. 1940)
REAL NAME Carter Hall **BASE** Midway City
HEIGHT 6ft 1in **WEIGHT** 195 lbs **EYES** Blue **HAIR** Brown
POWERS/ABILITIES Thanagarian Nth Metal harness features retractable wings and allows for enhanced strength, stamina, and endurance; extensive battle training and weapons expertise; speaks thousands of languages; history expert with a wide breadth of cultural knowledge.
ALLIES Hawkwoman, Atom (Ray Palmer), Hawkgirl, Madame Xanadu, Adam Strange
ENEMIES Gentleman Ghost, Lion-Mane, Shadow Thief, Byth, Idamm
AFFILIATIONS Justice League of America, Justice Society of America, The Infected, Guild of Detection

Carter Hall has lived many lives. While he is an archaeologist and the Super Hero Hawkman in the present, in his past he has been an Egyptian prince, a medieval knight, a Wild West gun hand, and a Thanagarian soldier. A hero in every generation, Carter both studies and lives history.

Carter Hall has been reincarnated many times, but his first life was on Qgga as Ktar Deathbringer, a winged servant of an entity called the Lord Beyond the Void. He and his fellow Deathbringers brought humanoid sacrifices to their Lord from planets including Earth, Thanagar, and Rann. After seeing an angelic herald named Shrra on every killing field, Ktar led a revolt against his lord, ending the Deathbringers. In death, he was given a chance to redeem himself. He was to be reborn until he had saved as many lives as he had taken. Shrra chose the same fate.

First Carter returned in ancient Egypt as Prince Khufu Maat Kha-Tar, in love with a woman named Chay-Ara—the reincarnated Shrra. They found an alien craft with Nth Metal, which they used to craft belts and harnesses. Thanks to Nth Metal's gravity-negating properties, they could fly. In medieval times, Carter became the Silent Knight, and in the old West, he fought as Nighthawk. On Thanagar, he was Wingman Katar Hol serving in the police. In the Microverse, he was the hero Avion. On Krypton, he was Catar-Ol. He was Airwing of New Genesis, Katarthul of Rann, and the Dragon of Barbatos, among others.

As Hawkman, Carter served on the Justice Society of America in the 1940s and later with the Justice League of America. When the Deathbringers returned, led by Idamm—the partner Carter once betrayed—Carter summoned his past lives into an army to defeat Idamm. Later, he and Hawkwoman came face-to-face with the Lord Beyond the Void. The heroes defeated him, but were killed in the process. The two were resurrected, but with their debt fully paid, they were told that this would be their last life.

SKY TYRANT
The Batman Who Laughs from the Dark Multiverse successfully infected Hawkman, transforming him for a brief time into one of The Infected. Hawkman became his Earth-3 past life, the Sky Tyrant.

TEAMWORK
Hawkman was recruited to the Justice League by Amanda Waller.

NTH METAL
Hawkman's harness and wings are made of a mysterious substance known as Nth Metal, mined on the planet Thanagar. He can retract his wings into the harness when not in use.

ON THE RECORD

Originally a reincarnation of the Egyptian Prince Khufu, Hawkman's physical appearance has changed little since his debut. Reborn as archaeologist Carter Hall, he adopted the hawk emblem of the Egyptian God Horus for his role as the hero Hawkman. He also began searching for his lost love, Princess Chay-Ara, who had been reincarnated as Shiera Sanders and, after they met, became Hawkgirl. Hawkman was chairman of the JSA and owned a hawk, Big Red. When the hero was revived in the 1960s, his backstory was changed. He became a Thanagarian law enforcer who had traveled to Earth in pursuit of a criminal and decided to remain there to fight crime.

GOLDEN AGE
Hawkman's look has remained largely the same: enormous wings, a beaked mask, and, since he was an archaeologist, weapons borrowed from the museum he curated.

CLASSIC STORIES

***Hawkworld* #1-3 (Aug.-Oct. 1989)**
Katar Hol lives on Hawkworld, working as one of the Wingmen militia. When he uncovers a conspiracy, it almost destroys him.

***JSA* #22-25 (May-Aug. 2001)**
The JSA and Hawkgirl travel to Thanagar, where she learns the truth about Hawkman's past and helps bring him back to life.

***Hawkman* (Vol. 4) #1-6 (May-Oct. 2002)** Hawkman meets his true love, Hawkgirl, once more. However, Kendra Saunders—the new Hawkgirl—has no memory of her past lives.

PAST LIVES
Hawkman recently experienced a vision of his many past lives, both on Earth and on other planets.

HAWKFIRE

DEBUT *Batwoman* (Vol. 2) #16 (Mar. 2013)
REAL NAME Mary Elizabeth Kane
BASE Gotham City
HEIGHT 5ft 6in **WEIGHT** 120 lbs
EYES Blue **HAIR** Blonde
POWERS/ABILITIES Olympic-level gymnast and swimmer; highly trained fighter.
ALLIES Batwoman
ENEMIES The Hook

Mary Elizabeth "Bette" Kane enjoyed a highly privileged upbringing as part of Gotham City's rich Kane family. She was a successful tennis player and skilled in martial arts and gymnastics. When she discovered Dick Grayson was Robin, she decided to become a hero, too. Bette called herself Flamebird and joined the Teen Titans.

Bette learned that her cousin, Kate Kane, was secretly Batwoman. Batwoman proved a strict teacher, burning Bette's old costumes and renaming her "Plebe." A battle with the monstrous Hook left Bette in a coma, but she recovered and returned to crime fighting when Medusa attacked her cousin and Wonder Woman. Wearing a new costume and calling herself Hawkfire, Bette battled Hook once more and this time tore his signature weapon from his arm. She continued to fight crime in Gotham City alongside Batwoman.

HAWKWOMAN

DEBUT *The Brave and the Bold* #34 (Feb.–Mar. 1961)
REAL NAME Shayera Hol
BASE Thanagar Prime
HEIGHT 5ft 7in **WEIGHT** 145 lbs
POWERS/ABILITIES Flight, rapid-healing; elite military training, adept in use of Nth Metal.

Due to the reality-altering properties of Nth Metal, alien Shayera Hol and Kendra Saunders share a soul. As Hawkwoman and Hawkgirl, the two-in-one hero is forever-reincarnating.

Prior to *Crisis on Infinite Earths* Shayera came to Earth with her husband, Katar Hol, chasing a criminal from their homeworld of Thanagar. They fought crime and joined the Justice League of America. Shayera split with Katar and became a policewoman in Detroit, but soon donned armor again to fight shapeshifting criminal Byth. By the Rann-Thanagar War, she had left Earth to fight for Thanagar, but was killed by Queen Komand'r of Tamaran, aka Blackfire.

Post-*Flashpoint*, Shayera Hol was reborn as the daughter of Thanagar Emperor Provis. Thinking her lover, Katar Hol, had killed her brother Corsar, she tracked him to Earth, only to find Corsar was alive, but insane.

After *Rebirth*, Shayera returned as Last Empress of Thanagar Prime. She and Hawkgirl learned of their shared existence.

HEAT WAVE

DEBUT *The Flash* (Vol. 1) #140 (Nov. 1963)
REAL NAME Mick Rory
BASE Central City
HEIGHT 5ft 11in **WEIGHT** 179 lbs
EYES Blue **HAIR** Bald
POWERS/ABILITIES Creates flame with his body and fires it from his chest; possesses Heat Gun.
ALLIES Captain Cold, Golden Glider
ENEMIES The Flash, Crime Syndicate, Royal Flush Gang
AFFILIATIONS The Rogues

Obsessed with fire from childhood pre-teen Mick Rory set his home alight and stood mesmerized by the flames as they burned the house down. After several similar incidents, Rory—a hopeless pyromaniac—followed his obsession to Central City. As Super-Villain Heat Wave, he wore a protective costume and used flamethrowers to cause panic and destruction.

Defeated by The Flash, Rory joined a growing group of local costumed criminals: the Rogues. When Captain Cold tried giving them all metahuman powers using a genome recorder, a horrific accident left Rory hideously burned, but able to hurl flames from his chest. Despite often seeking to cure his fiery addiction, Heat Wave remained a loyal Rogue, fighting alongside his allies against the Crime Syndicate and as mercenaries hired to hunt down The Flash. Rory only rebelled after his leader accepted the dark gifts of reality-revising Perpetua. As "King Cold" overwhelmed Central City, Heat Wave joined Golden Glider, Weather Wizard, Mirror Master, and a team of Flashes to defeat him.

AN INCENDIARY TEMPER
When Heat Wave gets angry, he can engulf buildings in flames. In this instance, drinkers at the Keystone Saloon were rescued just in time by The Flash (Barry Allen).

ON THE RECORD

Heat Wave originally made a costume of asbestos (before the dangers of asbestos were known) to protect himself from his flamethrower and the fire it created. During his first appearance he teamed up with Captain Cold to attack The Flash, but the two villains fell out when they realized they were both attracted to a local television personality named Dream Girl.

He also temporarily went straight and helped The Flash catch a corrupt parole officer using his Heat Wave costume and weaponry. It wasn't long though before he was back to his villainous fiery ways.

FIREARMED AND DANGEROUS
Heat Wave wore a flame-retardant suit and used a Heat Gun—a re-purposed flamethrower—with which he could create firestorms and raise the ambient temperature of his surroundings.

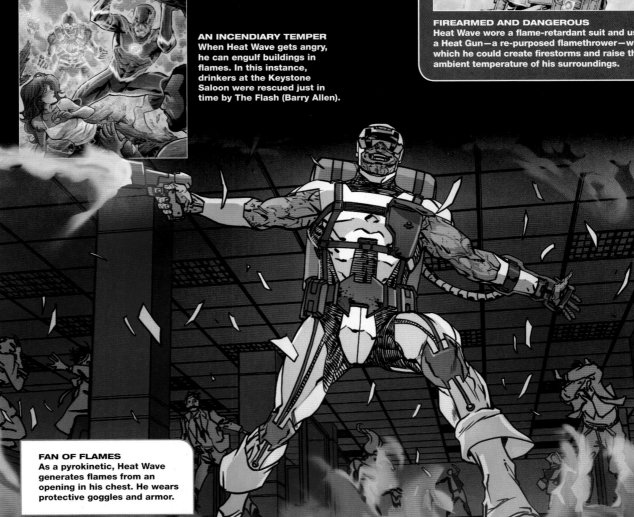

FAN OF FLAMES
As a pyrokinetic, Heat Wave generates flames from an opening in his chest. He wears protective goggles and armor.

HAZARD

DEBUT *Infinity, Inc.* #34 (Jan. 1987)
REAL NAME Rebecca "Becky" Sharpe
HEIGHT 5ft 6in **WEIGHT** 112 lbs
EYES Green **HAIR** Red
POWERS/ABILITIES Psionic powers and mystic dice give her the ability to bring good or bad luck to others.
ENEMIES Infinity, Inc., Global Guardians
AFFILIATIONS Injustice Unlimited

Becky Sharpe was the granddaughter of Steven Sharpe, an infamous hustler known as the Gambler and a member of the original Injustice Society. Despite his skills, Steven lost all his money gambling at the Taj Mahal casino in Las Vegas, which had rigged the games in their favor. Haunted by the loss, he killed himself shortly after.

When Becky learned of this, she swore to avenge her grandfather. She gained psionic powers and a set of mystical dice that enabled her to give good or bad luck to others. Calling herself Hazard, she joined the Wizard's Injustice Unlimited group after being told the group would not kill, and coerced Wildcat II and Tasmanian Devil into helping her bankrupt the casino that had caused her grandfather's death. As a member of Injustice Unlimited, she fought Infinity, Inc. and the Global Guardians. She left the group when she realized her teammates were willing to kill after all.

HELLGRAMMITE

DEBUT *The Brave and the Bold* #80 (Oct.–Nov. 1968)
REAL NAME Roderick Rose
BASE Metropolis
HEIGHT 6ft 1in **WEIGHT** 325 lbs
HAIR None **EYES** Red
POWERS/ABILITIES Super-strength and speed; spins webs; turns enemies into larvae.
ALLIES Neron, Bloodsport
ENEMIES Superman, Batman, Green Arrow

Roderick Rose, an expert entomologist, became a superhuman after exposure to a mutating agent gave him a thick exoskeleton, super-human strength, and the ability to leap like a grasshopper. Calling himself Hellgrammite after a type of fly larva, Rose fought Super Heroes including Batman and Green Arrow, and discovered that he could transform other humans into subservient, larval versions of himself.

A deal with the demon Neron gave Hellgrammite enhanced powers and he became fixated on the most powerful Super Hero of all: Superman. He joined Bloodsport, Riot, and other villains to gang up on the Man of Steel when he reappeared after *Infinite Crisis*, but they failed in their mission. Hellgrammite was subsequently defeated by Donna Troy, following the destruction of Star City at the hands of his ally, Prometheus.

HERALD (VOX)

DEBUT *Teen Titans* (Vol. 1) #26 (Mar.–Apr. 1970)
REAL NAME Malcolm Duncan
BASE San Francisco
HEIGHT 6ft 1in **WEIGHT** 210 lbs
HAIR Black **EYES** Brown
POWERS/ABILITIES Expert boxer, trained fighter proficient with exotic weapons, formerly sonic blasts; Gabriel's Horn opens space-time warps.
ALLIES John Gnarrk, Bumblebee
ENEMIES Doctor Light, Mr. Twister, Psimon, Troia
AFFILIATIONS Titans, Teen Titans

Malcolm Duncan grew up in Harlem, New York. When his sister Cindy was harassed by a racist street gang, Mal attacked them and was assisted by the Teen Titans in their civilian identities. "Mal" joined the team, but, possessing no superpowers, he felt like an ineffectual outsider.

This changed when Mal became the Herald after Karen Beecher (Bumblebee) helped him build the teleporting device, Gabriel's Horn. During *Infinite Crisis*, he suffered an accident in space that left him unable to speak. After accepting a cybernetic voice box similar to Gabriel's Horn, he joined Doom Patrol as Vox.

Following reality alterations, Mal's history changed. Although a former Teen Titan who had battled the Fearsome Five and Mister Twister, Duncan preferred the life of a retired Super Hero, new father and successful composer. However, when his wife Karen developed powers and had her memories stolen, Duncan assembled a battlesuit and

HERALDING A CHANGE
Formerly known as Herald, because he appeared first when teleporting groups using Gabriel's Horn, Duncan became Vox after losing and regaining his voice.

weapons to hunt the perpetrators with his old friend Gnarrk—an actual caveman and former Teen Titan.

This brought him and the Titans into conflict with many old enemies and exposed the hidden mastermind of Troia: an evil future version of Donna Troy.

HELSPONT

DEBUT *WildC.A.T.s* #1 (Aug. 1992)
HEIGHT 6ft 9in
WEIGHT 375 lbs
POWERS/ABILITIES Healing factor, chronokinesis, shapeshifting, phasing, possession of others' bodies.
ENEMIES Superman
AFFILIATIONS Daemonites

A legendary all-conquering warlord, Helspont ruthlessly expanded Daemonite hegemony over countless planets and peoples, but his ever-escalating exploits drove jealous rivals to unite in a plot to betray him. Helspont was defeated and imprisoned within the Eye—a giant starship that would later become the headquarters of covert planetary defense squad Stormwatch. When Harry Tanner, Stormwatch's Eminence of Blades, inadvertently destroyed the Eye, wreckage rained down upon Earth—including Helspont's cell, which crashed down in the Himalayas. Here, the liberated Daemonite lord established a new base, seeking to recreate his former dominance.

His activities drew the attention of Superman, who fiercely engaged Helspont in battle. The Daemonite overpowered the Kryptonian and tried to win him over as an ally, claiming they were both too good for the people they had tried to help—and advised Superman would eventually be betrayed just as he had been.

Helspont offered to ignore Earth if the Man of Steel assisted him in exacting vengeance on the treacherous Daemonites. Superman, of course, refused, sparking an inconclusive battle that raged across the mountains and only ended when Helspont teleported away, doubtless to pursue his vengeful ambitions by other means.

Helspont first appeared as a foe of the WildC.A.T.s—a team of human-alien hybrids founded by Kheran Lord Emp to counter Daemonite infiltration of Earth. The alien and the militant hero Mr. Majestic obsessively despised each other, and it was Mr. Majestic who thought he had destroyed Helspont forever in a battle over a doomsday machine called the Planet Shaper.

C.A.T. FIGHT
Helspont and Mr. Majestic squared off after the WildC.A.T.s discovered his plans to unleash the world-destroying Planet Shaper.

HERCULES

DEBUT *All-Star Comics* #8 (Dec. 1941)
BASE Olympus
HEIGHT 6ft 5in
WEIGHT 327 lbs
HAIR Black
EYES Blue
POWERS/ABILITIES Immortality; super-strength.
ALLIES Wonder Woman
ENEMIES Giant-Born
AFFILIATIONS Olympian Gods

RUNNING AMOK
Hercules, out to avenge his ancient betrayal by the king of Atlantis, vents his rage on Aquaman.

Hercules (or Heracles) is the champion of Greek myth and son of Zeus, king of the Olympian Gods. After performing legendary labors during the era of antiquity and clashing with the ancient Amazons, Hercules vanished from history for centuries. He was not even seen during the fearsome battle for the throne of Olympus after Zeus disappeared. It was revealed much later that Hercules had helped Atlan, the ancient king of Atlantis, battle and imprison the monstrous beings known as the Giant-Born. His efforts saved Atlantis, but he was betrayed by Atlan and imprisoned with the Giant-Born in Hell.

The Giant-Born eventually warped Hercules' mind and transformed him into a weapon at their disposal. When they were released from Hell to attack Atlantis once again, Hercules was an instrument of their vengeance. He fought Aquaman and Mera before Aquaman called in Wonder Woman to save Atlantis once more and restore Hercules to his senses.

JINNY HEX

DEBUT *Batman Giant* (Vol. 1) #4 (Dec 2018)
REAL NAME Jinny Hex
BASE Mobile
HEIGHT Unknown
WEIGHT Unknown
HAIR Auburn **EYES** Blue
POWERS/ABILITIES A range of mystical powers via the objects in Jinny's trunk.
ALLIES Teen Lantern, Naomi, Wonder Twins, Batwoman
ENEMIES Dr. Glory, Lex Luthor, Hex
AFFILIATIONS Young Justice

Jinny Hex came from Dripping Springs, Texas, and was the great-great-granddaughter of legendary Old West bounty hunter Jonah Hex. However, Jinny knew nothing of her heritage until her dying mother passed on the family heirloom—an antique trunk full of mystical artifacts.

Concerned about having such powerful objects in her possession, Jinny loaded the trunk onto her truck and set off for Metropolis, where she became part of the Young Justice team.

Jinny first discovered the potential of the contents of her trunk on Earth-3 with Young Justice while they fought evil versions of themselves. She could not only massively increase in size, but also replicate herself. Finally she—and her teammates—could see how she would compete in a Multiverse full of superpowered beings.

HEX, JONAH

GUNS BLAZING
Jonah Hex doesn't usually go for subtlety. He fires his two six-guns until there's no one left to fire back.

WET WORK
Jonah Hex and Amadeus Arkham took a shortcut through a strangely familiar cave when they investigated the deadly Court of Owls.

DEBUT *All-Star Western* (Vol. 1) #10 (Feb.-Mar. 1972)
REAL NAME Jonah Woodson Hex **BASE** American Old West frontier
HEIGHT 5ft 11in **WEIGHT** 189 lbs **HAIR** Red **EYES** Blue
POWERS/ABILITIES Uncanny marksman, skilled with a tomahawk; indomitable courage; fierce strength of conviction.
ALLIES Amadeus Arkham, Bat Lash, Tallulah Black, El Diablo (I), Batman
ENEMIES Quentin Turnbull, Court of Owls, El Papagayo, Vandal Savage

Jonah Hex's life was blighted by misfortune. Born in 1839, the son of a brutal drunk, Jonah was abandoned by his mother and sold to Apaches by his father. Raised an Native American until jealous rival, Noh-Tante, betrayed him, Hex returned to the white world and, despite hating slavery, fought for the Confederacy in the Civil War.

Afterwards, he sought out childhood sweetheart White Fawn and killed Noh-Tante. His punishment was scarification with a burning tomahawk. As a bounty hunter, Hex was hired by Amadeus Arkham to catch serial killer the Gotham Butcher. This uncovered two secret societies: The Court of Owls and devotees of the Crime Bible. Exploiting the rivalry between the groups, Hex and Arkham defeated the Crime Bible acolytes, forging a friendship with Alan Wayne, who funded the first Arkham Asylum.

When an adventure with a time-traveling Booster Gold went awry, Jonah appeared in the 21st century, meeting Superman and Swamp Thing, before having his face reconstructed. Gold then returned Hex to his own time period, where he killed a man impersonating his scarred self before starting a new life at sea with fellow bounty killer Tallulah Black.

In modern times Hex's legacy lives on through great-great-granddaughter Jinny Hex, who inherited his guts, determination, and strongbox, containing all the magical and super-scientific weapons Jonah confiscated in his incredible career.

ON THE RECORD

In his previous incarnation, Jonah Hex became a feared bounty hunter and fathered a child with a woman named Mei Ling. She left him after he broke a promise to give up his violent ways.

His most outlandish adventure was a time-traveling odyssey in which he teamed up with a future Batman to battle the crime syndicate known as the Combine.

Hex was finally killed by a bank robber and his taxidermied body was displayed in a New York City amusement park. He was later reanimated as part of the Black Lantern Corps, but returned to death following Hal Jordan's triumph over Nekron.

DEAD OR ALIVE
Jonah Hex, bounty hunter, has often had a hefty reward placed on his own head.

HIGHFATHER

DEBUT *New Gods* (Vol. 1) #1 (Feb.–Mar. 1971)
REAL NAME Izaya **BASE** New Genesis
HEIGHT 6ft 4in **WEIGHT** 277 lbs **EYES** Blue **HAIR** Black/White
POWERS/ABILITIES As a New God, Highfather is immortal and has superhuman mental and physical abilities; finely attuned to disturbances in the cosmic Source; skilled warrior, strategist and tactician.
ALLIES Metron, Himon, Orion, Divine Guards, Council of Eight
ENEMIES Darkseid, all Lantern Corps
AFFILIATIONS New Gods of New Genesis, Quintessence

Izaya was born millennia ago on the planet Genesis. He was the son of Yuga Khan, one of the merciless Old Gods who ruled that world. Izaya was peaceful, but his brother Uxas despised the Old Gods and began a war. Uxas defeated the Old Gods and stole their power to become New God Darkseid. A dying Old God bequeathed his energies to Izaya, also making him a New God. Izaya suggested he and his brother create a peaceful world, but Darkseid destroyed Genesis and the two went their separate ways. Izaya built floating city New Genesis, but it was constantly besieged by his brother's forces. The Source Shard advised Izaya that, for peace, he must exchange his son, Scott, for Darkseid's scion, Orion. Torn between emotion and duty, Izaya chose duty. His conscience departed in the form of Infinity Man and Izaya became the authoritarian Highfather. Obsessed with defeating Darkseid, he fought the Green Lanterns in the hope of taking their power. The war left New Genesis in ruins, and Highfather, realizing his folly, rediscovered compassion. As the Multiverse descended into chaos, Highfather became one of the divine Quintessence, safeguarding life and order, but he decreed New God neutrality when the Green Lanterns sought aid to end the threat of the Controllers and Darkstars.

ON THE RECORD

In pre-*Flashpoint* reality, Izaya was not Uxas' brother, but a warlord from the planet of New Genesis. Darkseid had Izaya's wife Avia killed, provoking New Genesis into attacking Apokolips.

Disillusioned by the bloody conflict, Izaya found the mysterious secret of the Source and became the peaceful, benevolent Highfather, securing a treaty with Apokolips. Highfather was slain by the war-god Ares, and the human, Takion, took his place as leader of New Genesis.

WAR AND PEACE
Highfather's commitment to peace transformed New Genesis society and inspired Super Heroes across the universe.

HIMON

DEBUT *Mister Miracle* (Vol. 1) #9 (Jul.–Aug. 1972)
BASE Academy of Higher Conscience
HEIGHT 5ft 8in
WEIGHT 163 lbs
EYES Blue
HAIR Gray
POWERS/ABILITIES A New God, Himon is immortal, and physically and mentally superior to a human; a master of New Genesis technology.
ENEMIES Darkseid

Himon was the headmaster at the Academy of Higher consciousness on New Genesis. He educated young minds and indoctrinated them with the philosophies of Highfather, New Genesis' ruler. His by-the-book approach did not sit well with his more laid-back subordinates, including Big Bear. Himon tried to stop the Forever People from going to Earth to join Big Bear by giving them a faulty Mother Box, but Vykin made it work.

On Earth, the team encountered Infinity Man, an opponent of Highfather's benevolent autocracy. Himon sent Vykin's girlfriend Serafina to retrieve the Forever People and lied to Highfather about what had happened, knowing that news of the Infinity Man would disturb him. The Infinity Man then appeared out of a Boom Tube and warned Himon off interfering with in his plans.

HIPPOLYTA

DEBUT *All-Star Comics* #8 (Dec. 1941–Jan. 1942)
REAL NAME Hippolyta **BASE** Paradise Island
HEIGHT 5ft 9in **WEIGHT** 150 lbs **EYES** Blue **HAIR** Blonde
POWERS/ABILITIES As an Amazon of Themyscira, has received divine blessings that bestow enhanced physical and mental capabilities.
ALLIES Wonder Woman, Zeus, Demon Knights
ENEMIES Hera, Cain, Strife
AFFILIATIONS Amazons of Themyscira

Queen Hippolyta ruled the Amazons of Paradise Island for many centuries. One night, Hippolyta encountered the god Zeus in the form of a spear-wielding warrior. They dueled, and the god seduced her with his martial skills. Hippolyta later gave birth to Princess Diana (Wonder Woman), but fearing the wrath of Zeus' wife Hera, she claimed that she had shaped Diana from clay, which was then brought to life by divine means.

When Diana was fully grown she ventured into the world beyond Themyscira and returned with a woman named Zola, who was pregnant with another of Zeus' children. This drew Hera to Paradise Island and Hippolyta apologized for her involvement with Hera's husband, offering her life as recompense. Hera refused the offer; instead, she transformed the queen into a clay statue and the Amazons into snakes. Although her subjects were soon restored, Hippolyta herself was dissolved in a storm and she became one with the island.

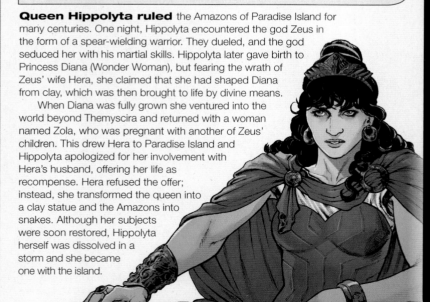

ON THE RECORD

Before *Flashpoint*, the Amazons were created when the Olympian goddesses fashioned new living bodies from seabed clay for the souls of women who had been slain by men. Hippolyta was the first to swim to the surface, so she became queen. Hippolyta was fiercely protective of her daughter Diana (Wonder Woman), but could not prevent her being killed by Neron. Hippolyta then took on the role of Wonder Woman herself, becoming a member of the Justice Society of America. She died battling the alien Imperiex.

AMAZON QUEEN
Hippolyta ruled Themyscira for many centuries, dealing both with mythical threats and the encroachment of modernity.

HITMAN

DEBUT *Demon Annual* (Vol. 3) #2 (1993)
REAL NAME Tommy Monaghan
BASE Noonan's Bar, Gotham City
HEIGHT 6ft **WEIGHT** 185 lbs
EYES Black **HAIR** Black
POWERS/ABILITIES Telepathy; night vision; expert marksman and street fighter.
ALLIES Natt the Hat, Section 8, Superman
ENEMIES Dubelz crime family, Glonth, the Mawzir, the Arkanonne, Mr. Truman

Irish-American Tommy Monaghan was raised in an orphanage and served with honor in the Marine Corps during Operation Desert Storm. He then became Hitman, though he would never kill targets unless they "deserved it." While Hitman was stalking mobster Robert Dubelz, he was infected by the alien parasite Glonth.

The alien's attack gave Hitman useful combat powers of telepathy and night vision that attracted the attention of the Arkannone, Hell's Lords of the Gun. When Hitman refused to join up with them, they attacked him, but he gunned them down with help from the demon Etrigan.

Tommy repeatedly came into conflict with CIA agent Mr. Truman, and when Truman launched an all-out attack on him at Noonan's Bar, Tommy went down in a blaze of glory, taking Truman with him.

HOURMAN

DEBUT *Adventure Comics* #48 (Mar. 1940)
REAL NAME Rex "Tick-Tock" Tyler **BASE** New Gotham City
EYES Brown **HAIR** Brown
POWERS/ABILITIES Miraclo pill gives incredible strength, speed, and durability for one hour, but early formulations are addictive and later ones cause deadly side-effects.
ALLIES Sandman (Wesley Dodds), Starman (Ted Knight), Doctor Fate (Kent Nelson)
ENEMIES Doctor Glisten, Johnny Sorrow
AFFILIATIONS Justice Society of America, Justice Legion A

POWER BOOST
Miraclo gave Rick Tyler the might to take on Earth-2's Superman (Val-Zod).

Several heroes have taken the codename Hourman. The first was brilliant chemist Rex Tyler, who invented a vitamin he called Miraclo. It gave Rex superpowers—but only for one hour. Donning a distinctive caped-and-hooded costume, Rex was a founding member of the Justice Society of America. Unfortunately, he became addicted to Miraclo and was unable to develop a non-addictive version. Rex was almost killed by time-warping villain Extant during *Zero Hour*, but android Hourman Matthew Tyler switched places to save him.

Rex's son, Rick, initially spurned his father's legacy, but during *Crisis on Infinite Earths* he donned an Hourman costume and took Miraclo to save lives. Rick was one of many second-generation heroes in a new JSA but, like his father, he also suffered from Miraclo addiction. His formula was appropriated by factions of the US military and Colonel Maria Jonas, resulting in the creation of walking WMD codename Damage. Rex Tyler and the JSA were excised from history by Doctor Manhattan, but returned to reality to battle the Legion of Doom with the Justice League and future champions Justice Legion A.

ON THE RECORD

The third Hourman was an 853rd-century android created by software derived from Rex Tyler's DNA. This Hourman used New Gods technology to travel back in time, meeting his predecessors and ultimately sacrificing himself so Rex Tyler could live again. Following the time manipulations of Doctor Manhattan, and the reality alterations caused by the liberation of Multiversal originator Perpetua, the artificial Hourman returned. Once again he met Rex Tyler for the first time and assisted the Justice Society, Justice League, and Justice Legion A in the war against the Legion of Doom.

ON THE RECORD

After *Flashpoint*, Hourman was a hero of Earth-2. Rick Tyler's father invented the Miraclo serum before it was stolen by Thomas Wayne, forcing the distraught son to become Hourman to reclaim his birthright. With Impossible, Johnny Sorrow, and Anarky, he clashed with Earth-2's Batman, The Flash, and Superman.

When Hourman was stripped of his Miraclo, evil entrepreneur Kyle Nimbus supplied a version laced with mind-control chemicals. Under its influence, Hourman attacked Batman (Dick Grayson), but was incapacitated with reformulated Miraclo. He joined the Wonders of the World Super Hero team, embracing the opportunity to fight for a worthy cause.

THE TIMES THEY ARE A-CHANGIN'
Like the march of time itself, the Hourman legacy has continued through the centuries.
1 Hourman I (Rex Tyler)
2 Hourman II (Rick Tyler)
3 Hourman III (Matthew Tyler)

HUMAN DEFENSE CORPS

DEBUT *Human Defense Corps* #1 (Jul. 2003)
BASE Area 53 (underwater), Fort Olympus (satellite)
NOTABLE MEMBERS Sergeant Montgomery Kelly; Private Chad Kiyahani; Colin Mitchell Specialist; **Charlie Graham** Chaplain; Private Eric Stewart; Private David Page; Colonel Reno Rosetti; Dr. Zaius Ape biology researcher; **Calcabrina** "Pet" demon.
ALLIES US military, General Sam Lane
ENEMIES Neron, Calcabrina, Durlans, Khunds

UNDER FIRE
No terrain or mission was off-limits for the Human defense Corps. One assignment even led the hi-tech operatives to invade Hell itself!

During his brief term in office, President Luthor created the Human Defense Corps task force to counter alien threats, believing that the Justice League could not be relied on. The elite 10,000-man unit was equipped with cutting-edge gear, including advanced firearms, powered exoskeletons, amphibious assault aircraft, and S.A.R.G.E. remote-controlled scout vehicles.

In Bulgaria, the troops faced vampire forces and drove them off with "holy napalm" strikes. They followed up with an amphibious strike across the river Styx into Hell itself, where Sergeant Montgomery Kelly—who had demon ancestry—became a ruler.

The Corps was later integrated into Project 7734, an anti-alien task force run by General Sam Lane. It conducted actions against Kryptonians when the city of Kandor and its population arrived on Earth.

HUMAN TARGET

DEBUT *Action Comics* (Vol. 1) #419 (Dec. 1972)
REAL NAME Christopher Chance
BASE Boston, Massachusetts
EYES Blue **HAIR** Black
HEIGHT 6ft **WEIGHT** 180 lbs
POWERS/ABILITIES Master of disguise; actor; expert martial artist; superb athlete.
ALLIES Batman, Angel O'Day, Harvey Bullock, Jonny Double
ENEMIES Deadshot

When Christopher Chance was just a boy, a loan-shark sent a hit man to murder his father over a bad debt. The lad tried to stand in the killer's way, but could not save his father. When Chance grew up, he became the Human Target—a bodyguard who specialized in impersonating clients marked for death.

In his time, he has masqueraded as a rodeo rider, an elderly oil magnate, and a tightrope walker. Chance was even hired to impersonate Bruce Wayne while Batman was recovering from a vampire bite. The assassin Deadshot soon had the fake Wayne in his sights, and the Dark Knight had to go into action to save the Human Target's life. Asides from the risk of death, there is a big drawback to Chance's work: he has become so adept at imitating others that he has begun to lose his own identity.

HUNTER, TIM

DEBUT *The Books of Magic* (Vol. 1) #1 (Jan. 1990)
BASE The Wild Area
EYES Brown
HAIR Brown
POWERS/ABILITIES A magician of huge potential, prophesied to be the only person who can safely wield the Books of Magic.
ALLIES Justice League Dark
ENEMIES Felix Faust, Nick Necro, Dr. Mist

Timothy Hunter is a teenage boy said to be the only person capable of using the mighty Books of Magic without being corrupted. Zatanna and John Constantine sought him out in London to teach him magic, but he was overwhelmed by the experience and chose to return to his mundane life.

However, when Justice League Dark tried to claim the books to stop them falling into the hands of the nefarious Felix Faust, Tim helped to recover the arcane volumes. When he opened one of the books he was teleported to a dimension called the Wild Area. Its magical denizens told him that he was Hunter, the descendant of their long-lost mage-king, and that they had been conquered by the technology-wielding humans of Epoch. With assistance from his father, Tim helped to free the magic land and decided to remain there.

HUNTER, RIP

DEBUT *Showcase* #20 (May–Jun. 1959)
REAL NAME Classified (possibly Richard or Ripley Carter)
BASE Vanishing Point **EYES** Blue **HAIR** Brown
POWERS/ABILITIES Genius-level intellect, adept in physics, engineering, spatio-temporal mechanics and theory; skilled tactician and strategist; proficient in many martial arts and the use of ancient and future weaponry.
ALLIES Booster Gold, Michelle Carter, Skeets, Supernova, Waverider
ENEMIES The Time Stealers, Per Degaton, Mr. Mind, Ultra-Humanite
AFFILIATIONS Time Masters, Linear Men, Forgotten Heroes

MAN OF ACTION
Rip Hunter is a genius and master of temporal theory, but he is also a rough-and-tumble adventurer who has survived in dozens of dangerous epochs.

Chronicling the history of a time-traveler is invariably tricky. Rip Hunter may be the same hero who served with temporal enforcers the Linear Men, helping unify parallel timelines during the *Crisis on Infinite Earths*. He could be an alternate incarnation from a parallel Earth or timeline that no longer exists. Whatever his origins, he certainly knows how to cover his tracks. The Rip Hunter who consistently interacts with Earth's modern Super Heroes also protects their history from manipulation by time-traveling villains.

Following the reality-shredding *Infinite Crisis*—which resulted in the creation of a new cosmology of 52 parallel realities—Hunter recruited 25th-century hero Booster Gold to save all of existence from the cosmic devourer Mr. Mind and bring stability to the new Multiverse. He and Booster later formed the core of a fluctuating team that countered plots by Despero, Per Degaton, Ultra-Humanite, Black Beetle, and others trying to rewrite history and warp reality. Even Booster was not immune to temptation: he tried to change history by preventing the murder of his friend Ted Kord. Eventually, though, Booster realized the scale of his selfish crime and reordered reality, proving himself worthy of the rank of Time Master. Rip later admitted that Booster would one day become his father.

Rip Hunter emerged largely unchanged from the reality-altering *Flashpoint* event. In the aftermath he sought out his father and met a different Booster Gold instead. They located Rip's future dad just as another chronal crisis began: a lethal *Convergence* in which past, present, and previously erased realities were thrown into conflict, involving every Super Hero from every possible point of existence.

The original Rip Hunter was a clean-cut scientist/adventurer who built his Time Spheres to uncover the secrets of history. With mechanic Jeff Smith, girlfriend Bonnie Baxter, and her little brother Corky, Rip traveled across Earth's past and future, encountering infamous individuals like Cleopatra, Kublai Khan, and Adolf Hitler along the way. They also encountered an immense number of alien races who had visited our world but who had been lost to history.

HISTORY LESSONS
Rip and his fellow Time Hunters soon learned to expect the unexpected when they ventured into a new era.

CLASSIC STORIES

***Showcase* #20 (May–Jun. 1959)**
In their very first adventure, the original Rip Hunter and the first Time Masters team take a trip back into prehistory, where they battle dinosaurs and criminals.

***Time Masters* #1–8 (Feb.–Sep. 1990)**
Rip Hunter's time-travel research makes him a target for Vandal Savage and the Illuminati. He and his fellow Time Masters uncover their conspiracy and battle them at key moments in history.

***Time Masters: Vanishing Point* #1–5 (Sep. 2010–Feb. 2011)**
Rip, Booster Gold, Green Lantern, and Superman team up with Batman, who has been cast adrift in time after battling Darkseid during the *Final Crisis*.

HUSH

DEBUT *Batman* (Vol. 1) #609 (Jan. 2003)
REAL NAME Thomas Elliot
BASE Gotham City
HEIGHT 6ft 3in **WEIGHT** 220 lbs
EYES Blue **HAIR** Red
POWERS/ABILITIES Tactical genius; expert surgeon; skilled marksman with a pistol; uses holograms to create decoys.
ALLIES Jason Bard, the Architect
ENEMIES Batman, the Batman Family, Spoiler

BURNING RAGE
Hush's ultimate objective is to destroy Batman and everything he holds dear—including Gotham City.

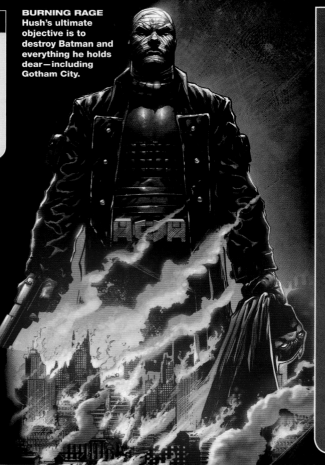

When Tommy Elliot was a child, he idolized his best friend Bruce Wayne. He even went so far as to kill his own parents so he would be an orphan just like Bruce. However, Bruce finally rejected Tommy when his friend began to impersonate him. Tommy became obsessed with destroying his former idol. Swathing his head in bandages, he became a sworn nemesis to both Bruce Wayne and Batman as the criminal surgeon and master criminal Hush.

After launching a campaign of bloody attacks on Batman and his loved ones, Hush vanished, but later resurfaced with a new plan to rip Batman's life apart. He framed Commissioner Jim Gordon for murder, injected Alfred with fear toxin, and triggered riots and terrorist attacks all over Gotham City. His masterstroke was destroying Arkham Asylum, which led to a mass breakout of inmates. Hush then blew up Batman's secret weapons cache underneath the city, causing the seizure of Wayne Industries' assets by the authorities. Batman finally captured Hush, but when an alliance of villains attacked Gotham City, Elliot escaped to deploy the Batcave's resources against the Batman Family. He was defeated by Alfred Pennyworth, but after a period of detention has returned, still seeking vengeance and validation, beside Bane and other Bat-foes.

The pre-*Flashpoint* Hush was traumatized by an abusive childhood and plotted to kill his parents to get their money. He harbored a grudge against his childhood friend Bruce Wayne because of his wealth and status. As Hush, he plotted with the Riddler to destroy Batman through a series of attacks intended to break his body and spirit. In "Heart of Hush" he intensified his campaign of terror by literally stealing the heart of Batman's beloved Catwoman.

EQUAL AND OPPOSITE
Tommy Elliot would stop at nothing to assume every aspect of Bruce Wayne's life, including replacing him as Batman.

HUNTRESS, THE

DEBUT *All-Star Comics* #69 (Nov.–Dec. 1977)
REAL NAME Helena Bertinelli   **HEIGHT** 5ft 11in   **WEIGHT** 140 lbs
EYES Brown   **HAIR** Black
POWERS/ABILITIES Extensive training in acrobatics, stealth, and martial arts; expert shot with a crossbow; highly trained espionage agent; ties to network of spies and information.
ALLIES Batgirl, Black Canary, Nightwing
ENEMIES Mr. Minos, Calculator, Blackbird
AFFILIATIONS Birds of Prey, Spyral

As a child, Helena Bertinelli saw her mafia family gunned down before her eyes by the rival Cassamento crime family. While Helena played possum, her father, brother, and seemingly her mother were all killed. Helena was sent by her family's allies to Sicily, where her Uncle Claudio helped train her in archery and martial arts, astonished by her anger, aptitude, and dedication.

Eventually, Helena joined the international espionage group known as Spyral as its Matron. She befriended Dick Grayson (Nightwing) when he became one of their agents, not realizing at first that Dick was there to infiltrate the organization and help shut it down. Under the leadership of Mr. Minos, Spyral had become corrupt, and soon Helena teamed with Grayson to stop Minos. She adopted command and continued to root out even more wrongdoing. After parting ways with Spyral, Helena returned to Gotham City. She became a hunter, killing mafia hitmen with her trusty crossbow. When she crossed paths with Batgirl and Black Canary, also known as the Birds of Prey, she reluctantly joined forces with them to hunt the mysterious mob boss Fenice, only to discover that Fenice was actually her mother. Maria Bertinelli previously had an affair with Santo Cassamento and had arranged the death of her husband. Unable to reconcile her love for her family with her mother's criminal activities, The Huntress put her mother and her father's killer behind bars, showing them a rare mercy. Later, Fenice was killed by the Calculator, causing The Huntress even more pain.

The longer she fights as one of the heroic Birds of Prey, the more Huntress has adjusted her methods accordingly. She is constantly inspired by her crime-fighting partners.

HUNTING TOGETHER
As an agent and then the head of Spyral, Helena worked closely with Dick Grayson. The two even formed something of a romance.

ON THE RECORD

The original Huntress was Helena Wayne, the daughter of Earth-2's Bruce Wayne and Selina Kyle (Batman and Catwoman). A late addition to the Justice Society of America, Helena fought alongside Power Girl and Earth-2's Robin, also working in the same legal practice as Dick Grayson in her civilian life. After the Earth-2 Huntress died on *Crisis on Infinite Earths*, Helena Bertinelli was introduced to the universe left in the *Crisis'* wake. She was considered the violent black sheep of the Batman Family, even when she took the mantle of Batgirl during the *No Man's Land* crossover. After *Flashpoint*, The Huntress returned to her Earth-2 roots. Helena Wayne served as Bruce Wayne's Robin before, stranded on Earth-0, she became The Huntress.

CODE OF VENGEANCE
After her family was slaughtered, the post-*Crisis* Helena turned herself into a ruthless anti-Mob vigilante.

UNHOLY RAGE
While a devout Catholic, The Huntress is often at war with her inner rage, never fully recovering from the death of her family.

HUNTING IN STYLE
The Huntress was often seen speeding to a crime scene on her powerful motorcycle; one customized to match her Super Hero attire.

CLASSIC STORIES

***DC Super Stars* #17 (Nov.–Dec. 1977)** The Huntress' origin is revealed for the first time, establishing her family history as the daughter of Earth-2's Batman.
***The Huntress* #1 (Apr. 1989)** In her first solo title, Helena Bertinelli gains a new origin and fights the villain Omerta.
***Batman/Huntress: Cry for Blood* #1–6 (Jun.–Nov. 2000)** The Huntress' search for redemption leads her to The Question and Richard Dragon.

I

IBAC

DEBUT *Captain Marvel Adventures* #8 (Mar. 1942)
BASE Kahndaq
EYES Black
HAIR Brown
POWERS/ABILITIES Skilled and ruthless as both a general and a warrior.
ALLIES Barbarian hordes
ENEMIES Black Adam

Almost 4,000 years ago, a Barbarian warlord known only as "Ibac the First" invaded the country of Kahndaq and enslaved its people. He forced them to build a mighty capital and erect temples to his gods. The people of Kahndaq rose up against him, but their rebellion was brutally put down by Ibac's hordes. Among the victims were the wife, children, and nephews of a man called Adam. The gods of Kahndaq gave Adam their power so that he could free his nation; he struck down Ibac's soldiers with lightning before turning the tyrant's body to stone.

The story of Ibac and Black Adam has become legend, but the statue of Ibac, contorted in his death throes, still stands in the capital as a warning to tyrants. Ironically, a dictatorial president, also named Ibac, now rules Kahndaq.

ICEMAIDEN

DEBUT *Super Friends* (Vol. 1) #9 (Dec. 1977)
REAL NAME Sigrid Nansen
EYES Blue **HAIR** White
POWERS/ABILITIES Cryokinesis—can control cold and ice, and create icy armor.
ENEMIES Delores Winters, Mist
AFFILIATIONS Global Guardians, Justice League, Justice League International

Sigrid Nansen's dedicated scientist mother forced her to take part in a series of experiments by the Norwegian government to replicate the powers of a mythical tribe of ice-people. The tests succeeded, giving Sigrid cryogenic powers, but also turning her skin blue. Sigrid was selected to join Dr. Mist's international Global Guardians team.

When Tora Olafsdotter (a genuine member of Norway's ice-people tribe) joined the Global Guardians as Ice, Sigrid felt outclassed and left. After Ice was killed by Overmaster, Icemaiden agreed to take her place in Justice League International. She was tricked into deserting the team by the villain Mist, who took her form to attack the JLI from within, killing Amazing Man, Blue Devil, and Crimson Fox. Sigrid was later captured by an organ-stealing operation run by Delores Winters, who grafted Icemaiden's skin onto herself, gaining her powers.

ICE

DEBUT *Justice League International* (Vol. 1) #12 (Apr. 1988)
REAL NAME Tora Olafsdotter
HEIGHT 5ft 7in **WEIGHT** 163 lbs
EYES Blue **HAIR** White
POWERS/ABILITIES Uses cryokinesis to hurl freezing blasts, create ice constructs, and fly on a levitating a platform of ice.
ALLIES Fire (Beatriz Bonilla Da Costa), Green Lantern (Guy Gardner)
ENEMIES Peraxxus
AFFILIATIONS Justice League International, Birds of Prey, Global Guardians

Born with cryogenic powers, Norwegian Tora Olafsdotter decided to leave her native country to pursue a Super Hero career as Ice. She soon formed a close friendship with fellow heroine Fire, and dated the temperamental Green Lantern Guy Gardner.

Ice was selected as the Scandinavian member for the UN-sponsored Justice League International team. On their first mission to Peru, she was caught in a thermal blast from a giant alien robot, forcing the team to retreat. The JLI subsequently confronted the robot's master, the alien resource-plunderer Peraxxus, and drove him away. Later, while the JLI were onstage at a publicity event, a bomb exploded. Team member Rocket Red was killed and Ice was seriously injured, requiring emergency surgery.

After recovering, Ice did not rejoin Justice League International. She sought to repair her tempestuous relationship with Gardner, but the traumas of her heroic life weighed upon her and she admitted herself to Sanctuary—a top-secret mental health facility in Kansas created by Superman, Batman, and Wonder Woman. She was peripherally involved in the facility's greatest crisis—a mass killing by time-displaced patient Wally West (the original Kid Flash). Her treatment at a new facility ongoing.

OPPOSITES ATTRACT
Ice's fiery romance with hot-headed Red Lantern Guy Gardner was a constant cycle of break-up and make-up.

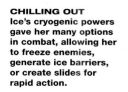

CHILLING OUT
Ice's cryogenic powers gave her many options in combat, allowing her to freeze enemies, generate ice barriers, or create slides for rapid action.

ON THE RECORD

Pre-*Flashpoint*, Ice was princess of an isolated tribe of ice-people who possessed cold-based powers. She left her people to join the Global Guardians and then Justice League International. Ice was seemingly killed by the villain Overmaster, but her cryogenically preserved body was found by the Birds of Prey. She recovered, but was traumatized by the experience and unleashed a mighty ice storm endangering everyone. Finally coming to her senses—after a firm slap from The Huntress—she left with the Birds of Prey for a new life.

CHILD OF THE NORTH
Ice originally served as a representative of Norway in the Global Guardians, but soon found her own identity as a hero.

ICICLE

DEBUT *Infinity Inc.* (Vol. 1) #34 (Jan. 1987)
REAL NAME Cameron Mahkent
HEIGHT 5ft 11in **WEIGHT** 175 lbs **EYES** White **HAIR** None
POWERS/ABILITIES Ice-control and ice-generation powers. His body appears to be made of living ice and can alter shape as required.
ALLIES Bellachek Temple
ENEMIES Green Team, Nightwing

Ruthless and sadistic career criminal Cameron Mahkent was given ice-generation powers by mega-wealthy Bellachek Temple. The mysterious mogul gave Icicle a special assignment: guarding a meteor while it was stripped of minerals by nanobots, and then crash it into southern California. This would potentially kill millions, but Icicle did not care so long as he was well paid. When rich-kid Super Heroes the Green Team investigated the meteor, Icicle froze their craft, causing it to crash-land. He similarly incapacitated the nano-armor of team leader Commodore Murphy, and ruptured the ship with expanding ice. Icicle seemingly outmatched the Green Team using an array of ice-weapons, but ultimately they caused an explosion that tore the meteor in half and marooned Icicle in space. His fate remains unknown.

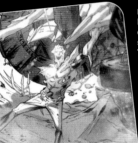

FROZEN SOLID
Icicle used his power to down the Green Team's spacecraft on Bellachek Temple's asteroid.

CHILLS AND THRILLS
Icicle displayed a sadistic glee when he got the chance to use his icy abilities against the Green Team.

ON THE RECORD

Pre-*Flashpoint*, Cameron Mahkent was the son of the original villainous Icicle, Joar Mahkent, who debuted in *All-American Comics* (Vol. 1) #90 (Oct. 1947). His powers were innate, as his DNA had been altered by exposure to his father's cold-projector. He served in the Injustice Society and joined the Secret Society of Super-Villains during *Infinite Crisis*. While in the Injustice Society, he met Tigress, and they later had a daughter.

COLD-BLOODED
Cameron Mahkent inherited his powers (and morality) from his father, and carried on the family tradition by becoming a Super-Villain.

IMPULSE

DEBUT *The Flash* (Vol. 2) #92 (Jul. 1994)
REAL NAME Bart Allen
BASE Central City
HEIGHT Unknown **WEIGHT** Unknown
EYES Yellow **HAIR** Auburn
POWERS/ABILITIES Super-speed
ALLIES Superboy (Conner Kent), Tim Drake, Wonder Girl (Cassie Sandsmark)
ENEMIES Reverse-Flash, Lex Luthor, Dr. Glory
AFFILIATIONS The Flash Family, Young Justice

Bart Allen was Impulse, a speedster from the 31st century who was the grandson of The Flash (Barry Allen) and Iris West. Like his grandfather, he had incredible powers derived from the Speed Force, including the ability to travel in time. He used this to travel to the 21st century to learn how to control his powers from the speedsters of the era.

Although Bart became an important member of both The Flash Family and the Young Justice team, a Multiverse-altering crisis occurred while he was trapped in the Speed Force, resulting in most of his teammates forgetting him and their shared history. Released when the Force Barrier was broken, Bart sought out his friends and family. He discovered that Superboy (Conner Kent) was missing and he scoured the Multiverse for his friend until he found him.

He later confided to Superboy that he had moved through the timestreams so much that he no longer had any idea which reality was his own, or even how old he was—a fact that was not helped by his super-fast metabolism. However, getting Young Justice back together made him feel more grounded, and a talk with Barry Allen helped him to focus on living in the moment he was in.

THE FLASH FROM THE FUTURE
Impulse was a fast-talking, curious teenager much beloved by friends and family, and his incredible Speed Force powers made him a valuable addition to any team.

IGNITION

DEBUT *Adventures of Superman* (Vol. 1) #582 (Sep. 2000)
HEIGHT 7ft 5in **WEIGHT** 568 lbs
POWERS/ABILITIES Suit provides heavy armor protection, immense strength, flight, and energy projection powers.
ALLIES Emperor Joker
ENEMIES Superman
AFFILIATIONS The Joker's League of Anarchy, Zod Squad

Superman first encountered Ignition on a bizarre version of Earth that The Joker created after stealing Mr. Mxyzptlk's reality-warping powers. A hulking juggernaut, Ignition was a member of The Joker's League of Anarchy in the city of Meflopolis. However, The Joker later denied creating him, hinting that Ignition may have actually come from the real universe.

Superman assumed that Ignition vanished when The Joker's mad realm did, so he was shocked when the armored villain reappeared as part of Zod's conquering army in the former Soviet nation of Pokolistan. Ignition was assigned to protect the solar converter arrays Zod was using to change the Sun's color from yellow to red. Metallo attacked the arrays, overwhelming Ignition and wiping out the converters. After the Man of Steel defeated Zod, Ignition disappeared.

IMMORTAL MAN

DEBUT *Strange Adventures* (Vol. 1) #177 (Jun. 1965)
REAL NAME Klarn Arg
POWERS/ABILITIES Reincarnation, flight, telekinesis, fires flaming eye blasts.
ALLIES Caden Park, Council of Immortals, the Immortal Men, Roderick Cavanaugh
ENEMIES The Infinite Woman, Vandal Savage, Barbatos, House of Conquest, Batman Who Laughs, the Hunt, the Kill
AFFILIATIONS Bear Clan, Forgotten Heroes

Fifty thousand years ago, Klarn Arg defended his people from vicious rival Vandar Adg, aka Vandal Savage. When Klarn and his four Bear Clan siblings confronted Vandar over a fallen meteor, they gained power, immortality, and the ability to create metahumans. For millennia, they nurtured humanity, with five Houses. Klarn's House of Action made heroes who operated from the shadows. His sister Kyra created the House of Conflict, honing humanity's killer instincts.

Kyra grew apart from her kin and by the 21st century she was their biggest threat. When her agents killed Klarn, his legacy was only preserved by psychic Caden Park and Immortal champions Ghost Fist, Reload, Stray and Timber. However, Klarn was a brilliant planner. Could he have anticipated his own end and found a way to return?

IMPERIEX

DEBUT *Superman* (Vol. 2) #153 (Feb. 2000)
HEIGHT 6ft 7in **WEIGHT** 986 lbs
EYES Red **HAIR** None
POWERS/ABILITIES Manipulates entropy; incomprehensible strength and durability; black hole generation; universe destruction.
ENEMIES Superman, President Lex Luthor, Mongul, Brainiac 13, Darkseid
AFFILIATIONS Hollowers, Warworld

Imperiex is a conceptual entity: the sentient embodiment of entropy. Composed of pure energy, the "Destroyer of Galaxies" is the agent of decline and obliteration, and precedes the first universe. Generally clad in robotic armor, its function is to eradicate each old, flawed universe and create—via a Big Bang—a new one, in the quest for a perfect universe.

Imperiex targeted Earth with drones, casually destroying all planets in its path as it drew closer. It was impeded by an unlikely coalition of heroes. With Luthor and Darkseid directing resistance against the Destroyer of Galaxies, Superman found himself losing many beloved comrades in the battle. These resisters trapped Imperiex's consciousness inside Warworld and propelled it through a temporal Boom Tube to the beginning of time. Here it triggered its inevitable Big Bang and began the present universe.

INFINITY MAN

DEBUT *Forever People* (Vol. 1) #1 (Feb.–Mar. 1971)
BASE New Genesis
HEIGHT 6ft 4in
WEIGHT 247 lbs
POWERS/ABILITIES Flight, energy bursts, incredible strength, and durability.
ENEMIES Mantis, Himon

Infinity Man is the physical manifestation of all that was compassionate within Izaya, Lord of New Genesis. Infinity Man split away from Izaya, and what remained became Highfather, who was committed to preserving peace and order rather than freedom. On a quest to redeem Highfather, Infinity Man chose five young New Gods—the Forever People—as his agents.

When the Forever People were attacked on Earth by the villain Mantis, their sentient Mother Box began to glow. They touched the Box and disappeared in a flash of light. They were replaced by the imposing Infinity Man, who drove off Mantis. After the Forever People awoke in an alley, Infinity Man appeared on nearby TV monitors. He told them that together they would fight for freedom from both the benevolent despotism of Highfather and the cruel oppression of his evil brother, Darkseid.

INDIGO TRIBE

DEBUT *Green Lantern* (Vol. 4) #25 (Jan. 2008)
BASE Nok
POWERS/ABILITIES Flight; teleportation; protective force-fields; aura projection; energy-casting; light-construct creation; close-range channeling of other colors of the Emotional Spectrum (all manipulated through power staffs augmented by their rings).
ALLIES Green Lantern Corps, Blue Lantern Corps
ENEMIES Sinestro, Black Hand, Third Army, Guardians of the Universe
AFFILIATIONS Natromo, New Guardians

The nomadic Indigo Tribe utilize the Emotional Spectrum's light of compassion, drawn from every living being in creation. The light is embodied by the patron entity Proselyte, who personifies the mantra "Rage grows from murder. Hope from Prayer. And at last, Compassion is offered to us all."

Indigo Lanterns are all former criminals—killers, or worse. But compassion's radiance suppressed their other emotions and compelled them to change. They are constantly re-examining their awful pasts, while acting in a benevolent, life-affirming manner. Their actions are unpredictable. The Tribe generally refrain from assertive action, preferring to intervene only as a last resort.

The arcane monk Natromo originally harnessed the light for Green Lantern Abin Sur. He foresaw that the Guardians of the Universe would eventually betray the Green Lantern Corps and become a threat to the whole of creation. Needing a force to counter the Guardians emotionless might, Sur believed success would come not through conflict but through rehabilitation.

The Indigo Tribe speak a language that is untranslatable by other beings or by green power rings. Their sworn oath is:

"Tor lorek san, bor nakka mur,
Natromo faan tornek wot ur.
Ter Lantern ker lo Abin Sur,
Taan lek lek nok—Formorrow Sur!"

LAST RESORT
The aloof and enigmatic Indigo Tribe only appear to intervene when life itself is in the direst need and all other agencies have failed.

RAINBOW WARRIORS
The rapacious, reawakened dead would have ultimately consumed all life had the Indigo nomads not finally joined and completed the universe's spectrum of champions.

INDIGO 1

DEBUT *Green Lantern* (Vol. 4) #25 (Jan. 2008)
REAL NAME Iroque
BASE Nok
EYES Indigo
HAIR Purple
POWERS/ABILITIES Leadership and fierce compassion; flight; teleportation; protective force-fields; aura projection; energy-casting; light-construct creation; channeling of other colors on the Emotional Spectrum (all manipulated through her power staff or ring).
ALLIES Hal Jordan, Kyle Rayner
ENEMIES Sinestro, Black Hand, Guardians of the Universe
AFFILIATIONS Indigo Tribe, Natromo, New Guardians

Iroque was a lethal villain who battled Green Lantern Abin Sur and considered her greatest triumph to be eliminating his daughter. Abin later brought Iroque to the former prison-planet Nok, where he had conspired with the aged cleric, Natromo, to construct a power battery that would utilize the rarest light of the Emotional Spectrum—indigo.

Iroque was forced to wear an indigo ring and was instantly overwhelmed by the horrific consequences of her past actions. She became driven to make amends and tirelessly began the slow process of recruiting others to the Indigo Tribe's cause. No one wears an indigo ring voluntarily and so Iroque had to ruthlessly coerce her disciples—drawn from the worst malefactors in existence—to become members of the growing Tribe. They patiently awaited the time foreseen by Abin Sur, when the Guardians would betray the universe and then the Indigo Tribe would be called to defend it.

Indigo 1's greatest achievement came after Nok's Central Power Battery was destroyed. Deprived of their rings' constant compassion, the rest of the tribe reverted to the monsters they had once been. Iroque, however, had permanently changed, experiencing genuine remorse, which enabled Natromo to reconstruct the battery and continue the crusade.

ON THE RECORD

Indigo 1 always pursued undisclosed aims, dictated solely by her innate compassion. After Sinestro was forcibly returned to the ranks of the Green Lanterns, he was abducted by Nok and forced to wear an indigo power ring.

Sinestro's spiritual redemption took immediate effect and was only halted by the sudden destruction of the Indigo Tribe's Central Power Battery. If not for this, Iroque might have been able to rehabilitate one of the universe's greatest threats.

FALLEN HERO
Iroque's determined persuasions dug deep into Sinestro's black soul and reached the noble champion he used to be.

ON THE RECORD

Following a failed Earth invasion by a coalition of alien civilizations, some Dominion, Durlan, Khundish, Thanagarian, and other defeated participants infiltrated America's government. Covertly establishing a testing site in the Midwest, they experimented on human children to gain the secrets of the metagene. Their schemes were thwarted by their own rejected guinea pigs whose survivors united into a very different, dangerous, and unpredictable "Inferior Five." The results of their ultimate emancipation were no laughing matter…

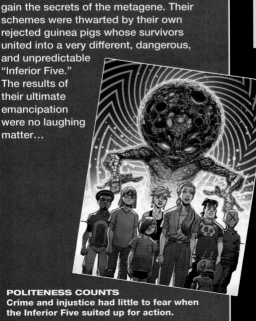

POLITENESS COUNTS
Crime and injustice had little to fear when the Inferior Five suited up for action.

INFERIOR FIVE

DEBUT *Showcase* #62 (May–Jun. 1966)
BASE Megalopolis
MEMBERS/POWERS Merryman: Smart but puny; **White Feather**: Omniphobic archer; **Dumb Bunny**: Super-strong and hyper dense; **Awkward Man**: Super-strong, invulnerable, but super-clumsy; **The Blimp**: Floats in air, but lacks propulsive force.
ALLIES Police Chief Geronimo
ENEMIES Man-Mountain, Masked Swastika, Sparrow, Speed Demon, Silver Sorceress
AFFILIATIONS Freedom Brigade, Captain Carrot and the Zoo Crew

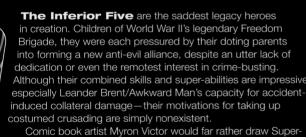
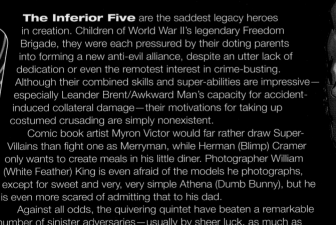

The Inferior Five are the saddest legacy heroes in creation. Children of World War II's legendary Freedom Brigade, they were each pressured by their doting parents into forming a new anti-evil alliance, despite an utter lack of dedication or even the remotest interest in crime-busting. Although their combined skills and super-abilities are impressive—especially Leander Brent/Awkward Man's capacity for accident-induced collateral damage—their motivations for taking up costumed crusading are simply nonexistent.

Comic book artist Myron Victor would far rather draw Super-Villains than fight one as Merryman, while Herman (Blimp) Cramer only wants to create meals in his little diner. Photographer William (White Feather) King is even afraid of the models he photographs, except for sweet and very, very simple Athena (Dumb Bunny), but he is even more scared of admitting that to his dad.

Against all odds, the quivering quintet have beaten a remarkable number of sinister adversaries—usually by sheer luck, as much as concerted effort—and have made their families proud. However, they still regard any day in which they keep their civilian clothes on and their dignity intact as a major victory.

INFINITY, INC.

DEBUT *All-Star Squadron* (Vol. 1) #25 **(Sep. 1983)**
NOTABLE MEMBERS/POWERS (ORIGINAL TEAM)
Star-Spangled Kid (Sylvester Pemberton): Cosmic converter belt; **Fury** (Lyta Trevor): Super-strong, immune to magic; **Jade** (Jennifer-Lynn Hayden): Green Lantern; **Nuklon** (Albert Rothstein): Density control; **Power Girl** (Kara Zor-L): Kryptonian; **Brainwave, Jr.** (Hank King, Jr.): Psychic powers; **Northwind** (Norda Cantrell): Flight, magic; **Mr. Bones**: Cyanide touch; **Silver Scarab** (Hector Hall): Flight; **Wildcat** (Yolanda Montez): Exceptional agility and claws.
NOTABLE MEMBERS/POWERS (LUTHOR'S TEAM)
Steel (John Henry Irons): Powered armor, kinetic hammer; **Vaporlock** (Natasha Irons): Flight, magic; **Amazing Woman** (Erik Storn): Gender transformation; **Vanilla** (Mercy Graves): Weapons expert, superb fighter; **Nuklon** (Gerome McKenna): Self-duplication.
ENEMIES Ultra-Humanite, Solomon Grundy, Dr. Benjamin Love

Infinity, Inc. started as a junior counterpart to the Justice Society of America. When four young heroes were denied membership in the JSA, the Star-Spangled Kid (Sylvester Pemberton) proposed that they start their own team, and Infinity, Inc. was born. Transported back to World War II, the teens were manipulated into turning against the Justice Society.

It was an inauspicious beginning, but the team went on to have a series of more successful adventures, and quickly earned the respect of their seniors.

When Infinity, Inc. clashed with mad scientist Dr. Benjamin Love, they also recruited two of his test subjects, Mr. Bones and Wildcat (Yolanda Montez). However, this would ultimately lead to tragedy. While fighting Solomon Grundy, Mr. Bones was hurled into Skyman (as the Star-Spangled Kid now called himself) and accidentally killed him with his cyanide touch. Devastated by the loss of their leader, the team broke up.

The Infinity, Inc. name was later used by heroes who had largely acquired their powers from Lex Luthor's Everyman Project. Dubbed "Luthor's Own Justice League" by the media, the new Infinity, Inc. were a publicity coup for LexCorp and a defense against rogue metahumans created by it. The team was led by Steel and included Vaporlock, Amazing Woman, Nuklon, Everyman, Vanilla, and the new Skyman.

LUTHOR'S LEAGUE
1 Vaporlock
2 Vanilla
3 Amazing Woman
4/5 Nuklon

NEXT GENERATION HEROES—THE FIRST INFINITY, INC.
1 Nuklon
2 Silver Scarab
3 Huntress
4 Power Girl
5 Brainwave, Jr.
6 Jade
7 Star-Spangled Kid

INJUSTICE GANG

DEBUT *Justice League of America* (Vol. 1) #111 **(May–Jun. 1974)** (Libra team); *JLA* (Vol. 1) #9 **(Sep. 1977)** (Luthor team)
MEMBERS/POWERS (LIBRA TEAM) Libra (Justin Ballantine): Superpower absorption; **Chronos** (David Clinton): Time manipulation; **Mirror Master** (Sam Scudder): Laser blasts; **Scarecrow** (Dr. Jonathan Crane): Fear toxins; **Poison Ivy** (Pamela Isley): Plant control, poisons; **Shadow-Thief** (Carl Sands): Shifts into shadow state; **Tattooed Man** (Abel Tarrant): Living tattoos.
MEMBERS/POWERS (LUTHOR TEAM) The Joker: The Joker venom, deadly gadgets; **Doctor Light** (Arthur Light): Light powers, energy projection and absorption; **Mirror Master** (Evan McCulloch): Mirror dimensional travel powers; **Ocean Master** (Orm Marius): Strength, underwater adaptation, controls sea life; **Jemm**: Flight, super-strength, psychic powers; **Circe**: Sorcery; **Queen Bee** (Zazzala): Stingers, mind-fogging pollen; **The General** (Wade Eiling): Super-strength and durability; **Prometheus**: Cybernetic enhancement.

The first Injustice Gang was made up of six villains recruited by the enigmatic Libra, ostensibly to balance out the Justice League. The Injustice Gang even operated from a satellite that orbited Earth on the opposite side from the JLA's. The Injustice Gang went off to battle the JLA, but they had been tricked; Libra had used them to lure the JLA out so he could steal half the heroes' powers with his Energy Transmortifier. Having taken their power into himself, Libra began to expand in size and was absorbed into the cosmos. The Injustice Gang then briefly worked for the Construct and Abra Kadabra before disbanding.

When Superman became leader of the JLA, Lex Luthor created a new Injustice Gang to oppose what he saw as an escalation in the conflict between himself and the Man of Steel. He tried to sow dissent within the JLA and force it to break up, but was unsuccessful. Lex's revamped Injustice Gang was also a failure, falling under the control of the alien weapon Mageddon before being defeated.

INJUSTICE LEAGUE DARK

DEBUT *DC Justice League Dark* (Vol. 2) #14 **(Oct. 2019)**
BASE Montego Bay, Jamaica
MEMBERS/POWERS Circe: Demigoddess who wields powerful magic; **Floronic Man**: Plant control, access to the power of the Green; **Klarion the Witch Boy**: Shapeshifting, telekinesis; **Teekl**: Klarion's feline familiar, enhanced senses, ability to transform into a large beast; **Papa Midnite**: Voodoo powers; **Solomon Grundy**: Zombie with super strength and durability.
ALLIES Upside-Down Man
ENEMIES Justice League Dark
AFFILIATIONS None

To help her win the Witching War and become Goddess of Magic, Circe assembled a team of evil magical beings intended to defeat the Justice League Dark. She sent her team out into the world to bring the powers of life and death under her control, stealing them from the servants of the goddess Hecate. Having succeeded in this, and with Circe possessing the body of Wonder Woman, Injustice League Dark were ready to face their heroic counterparts and take what they wanted—the powerful Eclipso Diamond. However, Wonder Woman fought off Circe's control and returned to stop the Witch Queen. This defeat saw the disbanding of Injustice League Dark.

INJUSTICE LEAGUE

DEBUT *Justice League International* (Vol. 1) #23 (Jan. 1989)
MEMBERS/POWERS
Lex Luthor: Amoral genius; **Black Manta:** Optic blasts; **Black Adam** (Teth-Adam): Godlike power; **Subject B-0:** Unfinished Superman clone; **Captain Cold** (Leonard Snart): Cryogenic powers.
ALLIES Batman, Catwoman, Justice League
ENEMIES Crime Syndicate, Secret Society
AFFILIATIONS Justice League

When the Crime Syndicate (an evil version of the Justice League from Earth-3) invaded Earth and took the Justice League teams out of action, many of the world's Super-Villains chose to serve the conquerors and became part of their so-called Secret Society. Not so Lex Luthor. He decided that if the Justice League couldn't free the world then it was up to him to do it.

After retrieving a suit of powered armor from LexCorp, he recruited fellow refuseniks Black Adam, Black Manta, and Captain Cold into his own Injustice League, along with half-finished Superman clone B-0. After linking up with Batman, Catwoman, Sinestro, and Deathstroke, the Injustice League confronted the Crime Syndicate. B-0 was killed, but Lex defeated Ultraman and Mazahs (an alternate-world Lex Luthor with Shazam's powers), and Captain Cold killed Johnny Quick. This gave Batman the chance to release the Justice League from their prison within the Firestorm Matrix.

With the Crime Syndicate beaten, the Justice League agreed to wipe the records of the Injustice Society members. Without the threat of the Crime Syndicate to unite them, the Injustice Society disbanded—although Captain Cold and Lex Luthor decided to join the Justice League.

ON THE RECORD

The first pre-*Flashpoint* Injustice League was an incompetent team of Justice League International foes who were hired as "Justice League Antarctica" by Maxwell Lord. However, *Silver Age: Showcase* #1 chronicles the adventures of an even earlier Injustice League, which included Lex Luthor. Luthor also founded Injustice League Unlimited—a large team that enjoyed some success against the Justice League, but which is most famous for crashing Green Arrow and Black Canary's wedding.

THE TABLES TURNED
The Injustice League had their heroic opposite numbers on the ropes on numerous occasions, as when they tortured the Justice League to enrage Superman.

INJUSTICE SOCIETY

DEBUT *All-Star Comics* #37 (Oct.–Nov. 1947)
NOTABLE MEMBERS/POWERS (FIRST TEAM) Wizard (William Zard): Magician, illusionist; **Brain Wave** (Henry King, Sr.): Psychic powers; **Gambler** (Steven Sharpe III): Master of disguise; **Per Degaton:** Precognition, time travel; **Thinker** (Clifford DeVoe): Mind control, telekinesis; **Vandal Savage:** Immortality, vast mental and physical abilities; **Fiddler** (Isaac Bowin): Musical hypnosis; **Harlequin** (Molly Mayne): Hypnotic glasses; **Shade** (Richard Swift): Shadow powers; **Solomon Grundy** (Cyrus Gold): Super-strength.
NOTABLE MEMBERS/POWERS (LATER TEAM) Johnny Sorrow: Psychic, deadly gaze; **Tigress** (Artemis Crock): Athlete; **Geomancer:** Elemental control of earth; **Icicle** (Cameron Mahkent): Cryogenic powers; **Killer Wasp:** Flight, electrical blasts.

The Injustice Society was founded by the Wizard with the objectives of defeating the Justice Society and taking over America. The Society used various ploys to trap the JSA team members, before putting them on trial. However, Green Lantern was able to infiltrate the proceedings and free his comrades, leading to defeat for the villains. The Wizard went on to convene at least two more Injustice Societies, who also met with limited success.

Some decades later, Johnny Sorrow formed another Injustice Society. This team attacked the JSA headquarters, but they were beaten single-handedly by grizzled boxer Wildcat—who was nursing an injured arm at the time! Sorrow then used the Injustice Society as pawns to summon the reality-devouring King of Tears, but both were vanquished thanks to The Flash, who cast the King of Tears to another dimension.

Subsequently, the Wizard founded yet another Injustice Society, which Johnny Sorrow quickly took over. He used the Injustice Society's members as sacrifices to bring back the King of Tears, and kidnapped young JSA All-Stars member Stargirl for a ritual intended to restore him to human form. Once again, he was defeated.

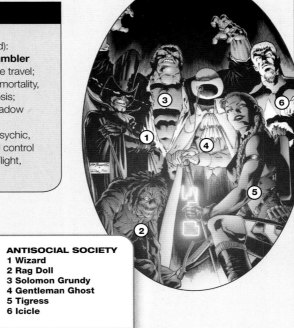

ANTISOCIAL SOCIETY
1 Wizard
2 Rag Doll
3 Solomon Grundy
4 Gentleman Ghost
5 Tigress
6 Icicle

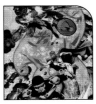

VILLAINS UNITED
The Injustice Society's very first attempt to bring down the Justice Society almost succeeded. The heroes were at the villains' mercy —until Green Lantern outwitted the bad guys.

INTERNATIONAL ULTRAMARINE CORPS

DEBUT *DC One Million* #2 (Nov. 1998)
BASE Superbia
MEMBERS Warmaker One (Lt. Scott Sawyer); **4D** (Capt. Lea Corbin); **Flow/Glob** (Maj. Dan Stone); **Pulse 8** (Capt. John Wether); **Knight** (Cyril Sheldrake); **Squire** (Beryl Hutchinson); **Goraiko; Vixen** (Mari McCabe); **Jack O'Lantern** (Liam McHugh); **Kid Impala; Olympian** (Aristides Demetrios); **Tasmanian Devil** (Hugh Dawkins); **Fleur-de-Lis** (Noelle Avril).
ENEMIES Gen. Wade Eiling/Shaggy Man, Gorilla Grodd, Sheeda

With global threats escalating, Gen. Wade Eiling decided the US needed a national hero team. Four soldiers were genetically engineered into superhumans: Warmaker One, 4D, Flow, and Pulse 8 became the International Ultramarine Corps. Eiling had them attack the JLA. But, when they learned Eiling had gone insane and transplanted his personality into the unstoppable Shaggy Man, they joined forces with the JLA and exiled Eiling.

The Corps then created the floating city of Superbia above the ruins of Montevideo. However, they suffered a setback when Gorilla Grodd took control of Superbia and Sheeda took control of the team. After the Justice League defeated the mind-controlled Ultramarines, they sent the team to serve as heroes in the young universe of Qwewq.

INTERGANG

DEBUT *Superman's Pal, Jimmy Olsen* (Vol. 1) #133 **(Oct. 1970)**
BASE Metropolis
CURRENT MEMBERS/POWERS Whisper A'Daire: Poison spit; **Johnny Stitches**: Gang boss whose face is stitched together with animal and human skin.
FORMER MEMBERS/POWERS "Moxie" Mannheim: Intergang's shrewd first boss; **Bruno "Ugly" Mannheim**: Massive size and strength, ruthless disposition; **Morgan Edge**: Consummate wheeler dealer
ENEMIES Superman, Batman Family, Jimmy Olsen, the Question

Intergang is a criminal organization run like a business corporation by media mogul Morgan Edge, with extensive resources and an international reach. It has had secret investors, including Desaad of Apokolips and his master Darkseid, who wished to spread chaos and evil on Earth. Intergang was supplied with advanced Apokoliptian weaponry, which helped it to become a force to be reckoned with in the criminal underworld.

When Edge was hospitalized with a heart attack, Intergang underwent a series of leadership changes. First the gangster "Ugly" Mannheim took charge. After he was seemingly killed in a Boom Tube accident, his father Moxie Mannheim took over. Lex Luthor then conspired to take control of Intergang from behind the scenes, with Moxie serving as a figurehead for the organization until he was murdered by Superboy-Prime.

"Ugly" Mannheim then unexpectedly resurfaced, claiming to have been "reborn" as a devotee of the Religion of Crime. He used Intergang to spread its commandments. Cultists worshiped the Biblical character of Cain—whom they regarded as the first-ever murderer—and practiced human sacrifice and cannibalism. Intergang's influence grew as it expanded operations into Africa and Gotham City, and effectively took control of the Metropolis underworld.

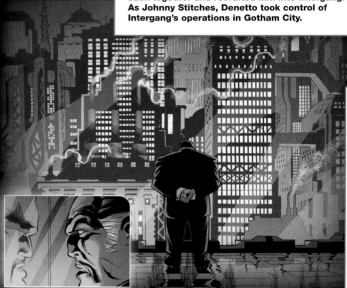

PATCHWORK MAN
After Johnny Denetto was horribly mutilated and left for dead, Bruno Mannheim stitched him back together and recruited him into Intergang. As Johnny Stitches, Denetto took control of Intergang's operations in Gotham City.

ALIEN ARSENAL
Bruno Mannheim's Intergang was supplied with Apokoliptian weapons, giving its Gassers, Wall-Crawlers, and Shock Troops an edge in gang warfare in Gotham City, Metropolis, and beyond.

UNHOLY HUNGER
When he returned from the dead, Bruno Mannheim was a fanatical devotee of the Religion of Crime. He set about taking control of the Metropolis underworld by killing (and eating) his rivals.

INQUE

DEBUT *Batman Beyond* (Vol. 1) #6 (Aug. 1999)
EYES Gray **HAIR** Black
POWERS/ABILITIES Liquidized shapeshifting—can alter form at will to create tendrils, spikes, or waves, but body can be temporarily disrupted by a hard enough blow.
ENEMIES Brother Eye, Batman (Terry McGinnis)

In a near-future, Brother Eye (an artificial intelligence created by Batman and Mister Terrific) launched a campaign to gain control of humanity by using a techno-organic virus to transform people into cyborg slaves. Inque was a corporate saboteur who was turned into a liquidized shapeshifter by mutagenic experiments. She often clashed with the second Batman (Terry McGinnis) and was blackmailed into working for Brother Eye after it kidnapped her daughter Deana and held her hostage on the moon.

Brother Eye ordered Inque to capture the third Batman (Tim Drake) and Commissioner Barbara Gordon. After an intense battle, Inque snared the pair with her viscous form and took them back to Brother Eye for "conversion." However, Batman managed to escape with Gordon and pledged to help Inque get Deana back. Inque joined Batman's fight against Brother Eye and sacrificed her own life to destroy the malignant artificial intelligence.

INVISIBLE KID

DEBUT *Legion of Super-Heroes Annual* (Vol. 2) #1 (1982)
REAL NAME Jacques Foccart
BASE Legion headquarters, 31st century
HEIGHT 5ft 9in
WEIGHT 170 lbs
EYES Brown
HAIR Brown with white streak
POWERS/ABILITIES Invisibility; teleportation into the afterlife; Legion flight ring gives flight and life-support in space.

When the Legion of Super-Heroes suffered heavy losses in action, one of the victims was Lyle Norg, the first Invisible Kid. Legion Academy member Jacques Foccart took the formula that Norg had used to give himself invisibility powers and became the new Invisible Kid.

The Legion and the United Planets were then attacked by the Fatal Five, who caused chaos on many worlds. When the Invisible Kid was on a cruiser that crashed into one of the massive Stone Promethean Giants, he used his powers to save himself and fellow Legionnaire Polar Boy by instinctively teleporting himself to what appeared to be the afterlife. Here he met the spirit of Lyle Norg. The Invisible Kid then teleported himself and Polar Boy back to Earth, where they helped defeat the Fatal Five.

ION

DEBUT *Green Lantern Sinestro Corps Special* #1 (Aug. 2007)
EYES Green **HAIR** None
POWERS/ABILITIES Interstellar flight; space/time manipulation; creates manifest green energy constructs.
ALLIES Green Lantern Corps
ENEMIES Relic, Anti-Monitor, Sinestro
AFFILIATIONS Emotional energy entities

Ion is the living embodiment of willpower, represented by the color green on the Emotional Spectrum. It was long contained within the Central Power Battery on Oa, where it provided energy for the power rings of the Green Lantern Corps. When the Battery was destroyed, the entity took Kyle Rayner as its host and transformed him into the hero known as Ion.

During the Sinestro Corps War, Sinestro physically drew the Ion entity from Rayner and imprisoned it at Qward, but it was retrieved by the Lanterns and bonded with Sodam Yat. When the power of all the Lantern Corps began to ebb, a being called Relic destroyed the Green Lantern Battery and warned that the energies of the Emotional Spectrum were running out. Ion and the other entities sacrificed themselves to replenish the energies of the Emotional Spectrum and save reality.

ISIS

DEBUT *52* #3 (May 2006)
REAL NAME Adrianna Tomaz
BASE Shiruta, Kahndaq
HEIGHT 6ft 1in **WEIGHT** 135 lbs
POWERS/ABILITIES Super-strength; flight; mastery of the elements; healing.
ENEMIES Intergang, Death, Felix Faust

Egyptian Adrianna Tomaz was enslaved by Intergang and gifted to Black Adam, the superpowered ruler of Kahndaq. Adam killed the criminals and set Adrianna free. Captivated by her courage, honesty, and desire for justice, Adam took her as his consort and gave her a mystic amulet that transformed her into the divinely empowered Isis.

Adrianna freed her brother Amon (Osiris) from slavery, but both were killed by a vengeful Intergang. Adam tried to raise Isis from the dead but was tricked by the evil sorcerer Felix Faust, who returned Isis to life, but as his unwilling slave. Isis broke free and exacted a gruesome revenge on Faust. She had become embittered and ruthless, and set herself up as absolute ruler of Kahndaq.

After *Flashpoint*, Adrianna was a young Kahndaqi who summoned Black Adam to free her nation when her brother was killed by the country's cruel dictator.

JACK O'LANTERN

DEBUT *Super Friends* (Vol. 1) #8 (Nov. 1977) (Daniel Cormac); *Justice League Quarterly* #14 (Mar. 1994) (Liam McHugh)
REAL NAME Liam McHugh
EYES Blue **HAIR** Blond
HEIGHT 5ft 11in **WEIGHT** 188 lbs
POWERS/ABILITIES Lantern provides flight, teleportation, increased strength, and fog summoning.
AFFILIATIONS Leymen (Primal Force), International Ultramarine Corps

The first Jack O'Lantern, named Daniel Cormac, was given a magic lantern by the fairy queen Maeve, but he fell foul of a power struggle in Bialya between would-be dictator Colonel Harjavti and the country's ruler, Queen Bee. Maeve then gave the lantern to native Bialyan Marvin Noronsa, who was killed by a bomb.

The lantern then passed to Cormac's cousin, Liam McHugh. He managed to absorb the lantern's powers so he no longer needed to carry it. McHugh served with Doctor Mist's Leymen and the International Ultramarine Corps. He was later taken over by an alien Sheeda spine-rider and made to join Gorilla Grodd's latest bid to destroy humanity. McHugh escaped and went on to safeguard the sentient, time-traveling universe Qwewq (Neh-Buh-Loh).

JADE

DEBUT *All-Star Squadron* #25 (Sep. 1983)
REAL NAME Jennifer-Lynn Hayden
HEIGHT 5ft 3in **WEIGHT** 110 lbs
EYES Green **HAIR** Dark green
POWERS/ABILITIES Forms energy constructs; controls plants and photosynthesizes; wields Green Lantern power ring.
ALLIES Kyle Rayner, Alan Scott, Todd Rice
ENEMIES Thorn, New Gods
AFFILIATIONS Green Lantern Corps, Infinity Inc., Starheart

Given up for adoption and raised separately, twins Jennifer-Lynn Hayden and Todd Rice (Obsidian) are the children of Green Lantern Alan Scott and the villainess Thorn. Jennifer-Lynn discovered her ability to wield the mystic energies of Starheart when she was attacked as a teen. Her powers were triggered and her hair and skin turned green.

Reunited with Todd, they joined Infinity, Inc. Jade had a relationship with Green Lantern Kyle Rayner, who gave her a power ring after she lost her powers. She joined the Outsiders and died during *Infinite Crisis*.

Jade returned as a Black Lantern during *Blackest Night*, but was fully resurrected by White Lantern power. She helped free the Starheart-controlled Obsidian. Jade and Obsidian were erased by Doctor Manhattan but were restored after his defeat.

JEMM, SON OF SATURN

DEBUT *Jemm, Son of Saturn* #1 (Sep. 1984)
BASE Saturn
HEIGHT 6ft 6in **WEIGHT** 340 lbs
EYES Yellow **HAIR** None
POWERS/ABILITIES Flight and superhuman strength; forehead gem senses others' emotions and emits force beams.
ALLIES J'onn J'onzz
ENEMIES Claudius Tull, Jogarr, Synn
AFFILIATIONS Red Saturnians, formerly Injustice Gang

Jemm is the prince of the Red Saturnians—a race created by the Green Martians. His people were at war with the rival White Saturnians, but Jemm was born with a gem in his forehead—a sign that he was destined to bring peace to Saturn.

After White Saturnians killed his family, Jemm fled to Earth, where Lex Luthor used the mind-controlling Worlogog to make him join his Injustice Gang as a rival to J'onn J'onzz, the Martian Manhunter. He was freed from Luthor's control by the JLA, and the Martian Manhunter helped him to recover.

Jenn then married the White Saturnian Cha'rissa, bringing peace to the races of Saturn. He sided with the Rannians in the Rann-Thanagar War, and represented his people's interests when new Krypton was created in the solar system.

JINX

DEBUT *Tales of the Teen Titans* #56 (Aug. 1985)
HEIGHT 5ft 9in **WEIGHT** 136 lbs
EYES Brown **HAIR** None
POWERS/ABILITIES Sorcery
ALLIES Dr. Sivana, Calculator
ENEMIES: Teen Titans, Superman, Wonder Woman
AFFILIATIONS Fearsome Five, Troia

Jinx studied magic in her native India, but after murdering her teachers and fellow students was confined at S.T.A.R. Labs. She was liberated and recruited by the Fearsome Five, subsequently clashing with their enemies the Teen Titans. The Fearsome Five broke up following a battle with Superman, and Jinx was locked up in Alcatraz with other group members. She and the rest of the Five were freed by Doctor Sivana. He ordered them to attack LexCorp facilities, but they were stopped by the Outsiders.

A post-*Flashpoint* incarnation of Jinx appeared alongside the rest of the Fearsome Five in the Outsider's Secret Society of Super-Villains. Following *Rebirth*, Jinx and her allies tried lying low as the spearhead of H.I.V.E.'s scheme to steal and resell metahuman abilities, but she soon inevitably clashed with Titans, Teen Titans, and the Justice League.

JERICHO

DEBUT *Tales of the Teen Titans* #42 (May 1984)
REAL NAME Joseph Wilson
HEIGHT 5ft 11in **WEIGHT** 195 lbs **EYES** Green **HAIR** Blonde
POWERS/ABILITIES Can control the minds of others; wears multipowered, gravity sheath (Ikon Suit).
ALLIES Adeline Wilson, Rose Wilson (Ravager), Slade Wilson (Deathstroke)
ENEMIES David Isherwood, Terra
AFFILIATIONS Defiance

Joseph Wilson is the second son of Slade Wilson—the legendary mercenary Deathstroke. Joseph was believed to have been killed when Slade's enemies attacked the home of Slade and his wife Adeline. He survived, but could no longer speak. His older brother Grant was an early casualty in Deathstroke's mercenary assassination career, and Joseph grew up emotionally poisoned by his parents' toxic relationship. He developed a love/hate relationship for both of them.

Running Adeline's business empire, Joe used his metahuman powers of bodily possession to gather information and pursue a hedonistic lifestyle, but was inevitably sucked into his father's Super-Villain intrigues. Joe stole a super-powered suit from his lover and mentor David Isherwood (a minor Canadian Super Hero called Doctor Ikon) to become costumed adventurer Jericho. He was deeply traumatized by the fact that he was prepared to commit murder to get it.

When his fiancée Etienne was also murdered, Joe joined his father in Adeline's Defiance super-team and found himself once again caught up in the cold war between his parents. However, after slipping ever-deeper into depression and paranoia over the lethal machinations of his father, Jericho joined teammates Power Girl, Kid Flash, Terra, and unsuspected half-sister Rose in having Deathstroke arrested and treated in Arkham Asylum.

ON THE RECORD

The original Jericho possessed formidable psychic powers and joined the Teen Titans team, despite them being bitter foes of his father, Deathstroke. However, he was then possessed by the warped souls of Azarath, who turned him against the Titans.

Deathstroke was forced to kill Jericho to release him from their possession. Jericho's soul survived but was driven insane, and it went on to wreak havoc in a succession of unwilling host bodies.

THE CURSE OF AZARATH
In a tragic twist of fate, the Souls of Azarath drove Jericho mad, transforming him into a vicious, violent monster.

JOKER, THE

DATA

DEBUT *Batman* (Vol. 1) #1 **(Spring 1940)**
BASE Gotham City
HEIGHT 6ft 1in **WEIGHT** 160 lbs **EYES** Green **HAIR** Green
POWERS/ABILITIES Unpredictable actions and fighting techniques due to extreme insanity; natural, charismatic leader and brilliant strategist; agile and relentless fighter; twisted genius; adept in chemistry; has used chemical compound Dionesium to heal wounds; weapons include a variety of clown and joke-themed deadly devices, as well as the deadly toxin known as The Joker Venom.
ALLIES Punchline, Jackanapes, The Joker's Daughter
ENEMIES Batman, the Batman Family, Commissioner James Gordon, Harley Quinn
AFFILIATIONS Arkham Asylum inmates, Red Hood Gang, Legion of Doom

The Joker possesses what must arguably be the most dangerous criminal mind on the planet. With no moral compass to speak of and a sick sense of humor that derives joy from witnessing the pain of others, the notorious Clown Prince of Crime is the smiling foil to the Batman's grim and serious demeanor. With a reputation as infamous as that of the Dark Knight, The Joker has become a one-man movement in the city of Gotham City, attracting a sea of followers as he proceeds to indulge in unthinkable crimes that would give even the cruelest career criminal pause.

AT A GLANCE...

Mystery man

The Joker's past remains a mystery, but Batman believes his nemesis was once the brilliant leader of the Red Hood Gang—a criminal outfit that plagued Gotham City early during Batman's career. After a fall into a vat of chemicals stained his skin white and his hair green, this Red Hood seemed to opt for a career as The Joker, giving in to his every insane impulse.

Tools of the trade

The Joker employs a variety of clown- and circus-themed weaponry, ranging from razor-sharp playing cards to acid-squirting lapel flowers. He often sets up shop in deserted card factories or on dilapidated former circus grounds, keeping to his favorite themes.

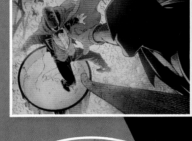

Little is known about the true past of The Joker. The madman has created a vast number of legends surrounding his crazed persona, some insisting that he is an ancient trickster being as old as Gotham City itself. The world only knows of conflicting stories that The Joker himself tells, often to manipulate those within earshot to one of his twisted causes or schemes. According to The Joker—an unreliable narrator if ever there was one—he lived a rough childhood, raised in part by his Aunt Eunice. She was mentally unstable herself and scrubbed her young nephew with bleach in order to get him clean. When the young Joker returned from school after being beaten up by a female classmate, he was again beaten by his enraged aunt. The young boy grew up in squalor with very little to eat and was ridiculed by his classmates on a regular basis. His only comfort during that time was a stuffed toy monkey he called Gaggy.

While the rest of The Joker's past remains shrouded in mystery, Batman believes the deranged criminal could have been part of the Red Hood Gang when he reached adulthood. A ruthless organization bent on taking over Gotham City's underworld, the Red Hood Gang had risen to power during the time when Batman first emerged on the crime-fighting scene.

Though still working out the kinks of combating crime, Batman managed to take down the Red Hood during a confrontation in a processing plant known as ACE Chemical. It was here that the gang's presumed leader fell into a vat of chemicals. After the event, Batman tried to research this Red Hood's identity, only to find more questions at every turn. Soon after this, the mysterious Joker first emerged in Gotham City.

The Joker had bleached-white skin, green hair, and a perverted sense of humor that could only result from extreme insanity. As he committed crime after crime, he revealed not only an obsession with clown-related imagery, but also with Batman himself. The Joker seemed to feel it was his job to better the Batman by challenging him at every opportunity. The Joker killed the second Robin, Jason Todd, shot and paralyzed Batgirl (Barbara Gordon), and has become known as Batman's archenemy.

When The Joker unleashed a virus on Gotham, turning its citizens into grinning, violent, zombie-like pawns, Batman was able to cure the virus, but fought The

GOING JACKANAPES
The boy destined to become The Joker loved his toy monkey Gaggy. So much so that when the adult Joker discovered a gorilla at Gotham City Zoo, he kidnapped it and made it his "henchman," Jackanapes.

CLASSIC STORIES

***Detective Comics* (Vol. 1) #168 (Feb. 1951)** The Joker's origin is explored for the first time, introducing the concept of the Red Hood and the incident that birthed Batman's greatest foe.

***Batman: The Killing Joke* #1 (Mar. 1988)** The Joker's origin is given a modern twist as the villain indulges in his latest criminal campaign: an attempt to drive Commissioner Gordon as crazy as The Joker is himself.

***Batman* (Vol. 1) #426–429 (Dec. 1988–Jan. 1989)** In "A Death in the Family," Batman faces real tragedy once again when The Joker successfully kills the second Robin, Jason Todd.

***Arkham Asylum* #1 (Oct. 1989)** The madmen are running the asylum when the Clown Prince of Crime takes over Arkham Asylum, aided and abetted by some of Gotham City's most dangerous psychopaths.

Insane inspiration

The Joker has inspired many criminals to follow in his footsteps, most notably his former romantic interest, Harley Quinn. But Harley wasn't alone in her obsession with the so-called Clown Prince of Crime. The underground villain called The Joker's Daughter also strives to imitate Gotham City's most notorious and feared criminal, as does his new sidekick, Punchline.

DEATH OF THE FAMILY

After enduring a bizarre ritual of having his face literally cut from his head by the Dollmaker, The Joker kidnapped those close to Batman and Bruce Wayne. Holed up in Arkham Asylum with a few fellow criminals including Two-Face and The Penguin, The Joker then tricked the Batman Family into believing that he had cut off his hostages' faces as well.

While Batman managed to save his partners, a rift formed within the family because of the secrets that the Dark Knight had kept from those closest to him.

MASKING HIS EVIL
The Joker wore the skin from his face as a macabre mask, held on by a strap he wrapped around his head. The villain later lost this mask and it was found by a girl living in Gotham City's underground society. She went on to adopt the name The Joker's Daughter.

THE JOKER'S GARAGE
When The Joker set his sights on the Batman Family, he dressed as a mechanic with a dangerous tool belt.

Joker in a battle that nearly cost the pair their lives. The Joker later resurfaced in Gotham City, as did Batman, thanks to a mysterious metal called Dionesium, and the villain has since taken their conflict up a notch.

Now aware of Batman's secret identity, The Joker launched "The Joker War"—an extremely hostile takeover of Wayne Industries and its holdings. With the help of his new partner in crime Punchline, The Joker conquered Gotham City, nearly killed Batgirl, almost drove the Batman insane, and even took over the mind of Nightwing. The heroes rallied thanks to Batman's leadership (and a quick save from The Joker's former love Harley Quinn), and defeated the Clown Prince of Crime, even though he had adopted a Batman costume—one suitably redesigned to his liking.

THE THREE JOKERS
It is believed that Batman once learned that there were not just one Joker, but three: the Clown, the Comedian, and the Criminal. However, with the state of the DC universe in flux thanks to the machinations of the powerful being Doctor Manhattan, it is unclear whether this revelation exists in Batman's current timeline, or in another reality.

THE ETERNAL JOKE
The Joker is obsessed with Batman—a relationship the Dark Knight is often forced to return in kind to save innocents from The Joker's disturbed schemes.

"I'm the one who laughs... at the great joke... that any of it matters."

THE JOKER

ENDGAME
The Joker turned almost the entire Justice League against Batman using his Joker virus. The Dark Knight was forced to adopt a protective battle suit dubbed the Justice Buster to confront them. Barely escaping with his life, Batman realized that this time, The Joker had raised the stakes and seemed to be playing for keeps. The Dark Knight tracked down a cure for the virus despite a wealth of misinformation spread through various sources. He discovered that The Joker was indeed a mortal man, despite what the legends would have the citizens of Gotham City believe.

TOUGH ODDS
A Superman infected by The Joker was the biggest threat Batman had to face during his battle with the Justice League—who were all under the influence of The Joker's toxin.

ON THE RECORD

The Joker has been a part of the Batman mythos almost from the beginning. When he first appeared, he was portrayed as a murdering clown, but like Batman, his image softened over the course of the 1950s and 1960s. When the 1970s rolled around, The Joker was once again returned to his dark, menacing roots, becoming the maniacal threat he was destined to be.

The man who laughs
The earliest incarnation of The Joker was a cutthroat killer, who planned to murder the city's most notable officials at midnight on each occasion. He was brought to justice by Batman, but would return in later in that same issue.

Playing his cards right
The Joker's dangerous persona was only amplified in the wake of the continuity-altering event *Crisis on Infinite Earths*. His sick crimes would become even more twisted as he shot and paralyzed Barbara Gordon, and then photographed her wounded body in an attempt to drive her father, Commissioner James Gordon, insane. Gordon proved a stronger man than The Joker, however, and Batman soon returned the villain to captivity.

THE JOKER'S FIVE-WAY REVENGE
Back to his murderous self in the 1970s, The Joker killed four former associates in bizarre ways as Batman desperately sought to stop the death of the fifth. Their tumultuous battle came to a head in an aquarium near Gotham City's docks.

Pushed to the edge
But The Joker was not done with the Batman Family. He went on to kidnap the second Robin, Jason Todd, and savagely beat him before killing him in an explosion. This murder nearly drove Batman over the edge, but he maintained his moral code, and never stooped to the insane villain's level.

CHEATING DEATH
After The Joker killed Jason Todd, Batman believed the villain had perished in a helicopter crash. However, the Clown Prince of Crime would not be so easily killed.

JOKER'S DAUGHTER, THE

DEBUT *Batman Family* #6 (Jul.–Aug. 1976)
REAL NAME Duela Dent
BASE The Nethers, Gotham City
EYES: Blue (left), Green (right) **HAIR** Pink
POWERS/ABILITIES Insanity and viciousness give her an edge in combat.
ALLIES Dollmaker, Red Hood, Arsenal
ENEMIES Batman, Catwoman, Nightwing, Arsenal, Red Hood, Harley Quinn, Charon Harley Quinn, Charon
AFFILIATIONS Iron Rule, Suicide Squad, The Outlaws

Duela Dent had a conventional upbringing in Gotham City's suburbs, but developed a morbid fascination with the twisted and ugly. Scarring her own face, she ran away from home, and living in the subterranean Nethers where Gotham City's homeless congregate.

She found The Joker's flayed face floating in the water and at first mistook it for her own reflection. Placing it t over her own, she immediately felt giving her power. Calling herself the Joker's Daughter, she became obsessed with the Clown Prince of Crime, attracting his attention by committing acts of mayhem. She even had the Dollmaker stitch The Joker's face to her own. After joining a plot to summon deceased Deacon Blackfire, she was recruited to the Suicide Squad, but left after constantly clashing with Harley Quinn.

She allied with mercenary heroes Red Hood and Arsenal during the War of the

THE NEW BEAUTIFUL
Wearing The Joker's face, the Joker's Daughter has launched her own psychotic war on society's ideas of beauty.

Robins, before betraying them to bounty hunters the Iron Rule. Duela recently injected herself into Nightwing's new life, following his personality change after being shot in the head: her contribution to the deadly Joker War decimating Batman's "family."

JOKERZ

DEBUT *Batman Beyond* (Vol. 1) #1 (Mar. 1999)
BASE Neo-Gotham, (formerly Gotham City)
FOUNDING MEMBER Impostor Joker (Winslow Heath): Leader of innumerable faceless goons
KEY MEMBERS Joker King (Doug Tan), Terminal (Carter Wilson) (Winslow Heath): Leader of innumerable faceless goons
ENEMIES Batman, (Terry McGinnis), G.C.P.D

Following the apparent death of The Joker, Gotham City was plagued by bizarrely clown-costumed fans hooked on street drug "Joker Juice." Creating disruptive flash mobs, they looted and rioted until The Joker imitator who supplied the drug and started the craze upped the stakes by shooting a police officer. Soon, a fake Batman was urging citizens to fight the Jokerz, and violence escalated across the city.

Although the real Batman quashed the incident, a new gang and lifestyle had gelled around the young, disaffected, and disturbed. Decades later, the Jokerz was a global force and rebel ideology, lacking only a leader. More nuisance than true menace, the suggestible army was ripe for exploitation, and by the time Terry McGinnis patrolled Neo-Gotham as Batman, were a commonplace but disagreeable facet of city life. This changed when nihilistic student Doug Tan appointed himself Joker King, assembling "10,000 Clowns" to assault the city. Although defeated by Batman, the King's precedent inspired ambitious leaders

DOWN WITH THE CLOWN
The Jokerz started out just wanting to have some crazy fun—but things always get out of hand…

such as J-Man, Chucko, and Terminal—who actually succeeded in making part of Neo-Gotham his Joker-town—all craftily exploiting the movement. The scheme only failed because of Batman and the innate chaotic nature of the Jokerz.

JOR-EL

DEBUT *More Fun Comics* #101 (Jan. 1945)
REAL NAME Jor-El **BASE** Mobile
HEIGHT Unknown **WEIGHT** Unknown
EYES Blue **HAIR** White
POWERS/ABILITIES Kryptonian powers, including super-strength, super-speed and senses; additionally, shards of kryptonite in eye capable of firing radioactive blasts.
ALLIES Superman, Superboy (Jon Kent)
ENEMIES Doomsday, Rogol Zaar
AFFILIATIONS House of El, The Circle

Kryptonian scientist Jor-El feared that his planet would be destroyed, and tried to warn the Science Council of the impending disaster. When his concerns were brushed aside, Jor-El decided that the only option left to him was to send his baby son Kal to a planet where he could be safe. Jor-El was proved right, and Krypton exploded, killing his wife and nearly every other Kryptonian in existence. However, Jor-El was removed at the last moment by the actions of Doctor Manhattan and placed on Earth, where his son had ended up.

Finding Earth unworthy of his son, Jor-El adopted the name Mister Oz and began interfering with the planet's affairs from the shadows. Eventually he revealed himself to a stunned Kal, now grown into the hero Superman. The two would have a difficult relationship, and Superman had grave doubts when Jor-El expressed a desire to take his grandson Jon on a tour of the galaxy to broaden his horizons. Jor-El's trip with Jon was interrupted by the fallout of Rogol Zaar's quest to eliminate all Kryptonians, and Jor was eventually arrested by the Thanagarians for his role in enabling Zaar to destroy Krypton during his time with the secret Circle group. Found guilty, his sentence was to be returned to his proper place in the timestream—Krypton at the moment of its death.

HOUSE OF EL
Jor-El was fiercely proud of his family and would stop at nothing to defend them. He believed that Earth was unworthy of his son because of the human tendency to brutality.

JUDOMASTER

DEBUT *Special War Series* #4 (Nov. 1965)
(Rip Jagger); *Birds of Prey* (Vol. 1) #100
(Jan. 2007) (Sonia Sato)
REAL NAME Sonia Sato
EYES Brown **HAIR** Black
POWERS/ABILITIES Martial arts expert;
aversion field makes it impossible for attacks
aimed at her to hit (though field does not work
against random or area-effect attacks).
ALLIES Birds of Prey, Justice Society
ENEMIES Blood Soldiers

HARD TARGET
Sonia's metahuman aversion-field
power came in very handy when
facing gun-wielding enemies of
the Birds of Prey.

The first Judomaster was Sgt. Hadley "Rip" Jagger, who used his judo skills to fight Japanese soldiers during World War II. After he was killed during *Infinite Crisis*, the name was briefly used by an unnamed hero before it was taken by Sonia Sato, the daughter of Yakuza hitman Yoshio Sato. When Sonia was born, he tried to quit the Yakuza, but was killed. Sonia mastered martial arts to avenge her father. She was recruited by Oracle of the Birds of Prey to help break an innocent girl out of prison and served with the team on subsequent missions.

In New York, she was attacked by the Blood Soldiers, a superpowered squad of Yakuza hitmen. The Justice Society stepped in to help her and she eventually joined up, siding with Gog when he caused a schism in the team. Sonia fell in love with team member Damage, and was distraught when he was killed during *Blackest Night*.

JUSTICE LEAGUE OF AMERICA

DEBUT *Justice League of America Rebirth* #1
(Apr. 2017)
BASE Watchtower, Secret Sanctuary, Hall of Justice
MEMBERS/POWERS
Batman: Combat and investigative training;
Black Canary (Dinah Lance): Martial arts, sonic cry;
Atom (Ryan Choi): Scientific acumen, martial arts, size
and weight alteration; **Vixen (Mari McCabe):** Channels
animal attributes; **The Ray (Raymond Terrill):** Flight,
invisibility, controls light; **Frost (Caitlin Snow):** Emits
energy; **Lobo:** Superhuman physicality, regeneration;
Aztek (Nayeli Constant): Hi-tech battlesuit.
AFFILIATIONS Justice League; Suicide Squad

Following *Rebirth*, the Justice League was acknowledged as Earth's primary metahuman guardians, but Batman felt it was too ponderous for certain missions. He was also keen to create a situation where inexperienced heroes might be trained and Super-Villains rehabilitated. The official team's recent victory over the Crime Syndicate was in part thanks to the help of villains, and as reformed predator Killer Frost put it "Everybody deserves that chance". Batman brought in Black Canary as field commander, pitting his team against bizarre and deadly threats such as The Extremists, Queen of Fables and a time-unravelling Chronos. Gradually ceding control, the Dark Knight saw his theory confirmed when his all-conquering Justice League of America transformed itself into a multi-national Justice Foundation.

SECOND CHANCES
Batman assembled a tight group of
former menaces and heroes whom
he believed had never reached their
true potential.

JUSTICE INCARNATE

DEBUT *The Multiversity* Vol. 1 #2 (Jun 2015)
BASE House of Heroes
MEMBERS/POWERS **Superman (Earth-23):** Kryptonian powers under a yellow
sun, including super-strength, speed and durability, flight, heat vision, freeze breath
Mary Batson (Earth-5): Super-strength, speed and durability, flight; **Thunderer
(Earth-7):** Super-strength and durability, ability to summon lightning and
manipulate weather; **Machinehead (Earth-8):** Wears suit giving him energy
powers and flight; **Aquawoman (Earth-11):** Super-strength, speed and stamina,
can exist indefinitely underwater, uses trident that summons lightning; **Batman
(Earth-17):** Wears a mech suit that enables him to fly and fire blasts; **Green
Lantern (Earth-20):** Wears Green Lantern ring giving him the power of flight and
ability to create light constructs; **Captain Carrot (Earth-26):** Super-strength and
durability, flight, can survive almost any injury thanks to cartoon laws of physics;
Red Racer (Earth-36): Speed Force powers, genius intellect.
ALLIES Justice League
ENEMIES Empty Hand, The Gentry, The Gatherers, Prophecy

PROTECTORS OF THE MULTIVERSE
A Multiverse needs a multiversity of
heroes, and Justice Incarnate were
formed as a cosmic police force to
watch over every reality from their base
in Valla-Hal, the House of Heroes.

In the bleedspace between universes orbited the House of Heroes. Originally used by the Monitors, it gained a new purpose when its resident AI—Harbinger—awakened and began summoning heroes from across the Multiverse to respond to an existential threat following the apparent death of the last Monitor. Traveling via transmatter cubes, a selection of the greatest heroes from multiple Earths arrived at the heart of the Multiverse, the Orrery of Worlds.

After the heroes had gathered, they learned that each of their Earths occupied the same space in their respective universes, vibrating together and creating a pitch, with each world having its own unique tone. This enabled inter-reality travel via the Ultima Thule, a ship that navigated with music.

The Superman of Earth-23 emerged as the natural leader of the group—as well as being a powerful hero, he was also the president of the USA on his planet. He proposed a volunteer super-army to deal with threats to the life and existence of the Multiverse, calling it Justice Incarnate. The team would comprise 50 heroes from around the Multiverse, although there were nine key members.

Justice Incarnate were able to help Superman of Earth-0 defeat Prophecy and the Gatherers, and also to rescue all those they could from realities destroyed by Perpetua.

JUSTICE LEAGUE

DEBUT *The Brave and the Bold* #28 (Feb.–Mar. 1960)
BASE Hall of Justice
CURRENT MEMBERS/POWERS AND ABILITIES SUPERMAN
(KAL-EL/CLARK KENT) Kryptonian superpowers; WONDER
WOMAN (DIANA) Strength, flight, Lasso of Truth; BATMAN
(BRUCE WAYNE) Intellect, expert martial artist, and investigative
training; THE FLASH (BARRY ALLEN) Speed Force-derived
super-speed; AQUAMAN (ARTHUR CURRY) Strength, marine
telepathy; CYBORG (VIC STONE) Cybernetic enhancements;
GREEN LANTERN (JOHN STEWART) Energy projection and
constructs; MARTIAN MANHUNTER (J'ONN J'ONZZ) Martian
superpowers; HAWKGIRL (KENDRA SAUNDERS) Combat
training, flight. **ENEMIES** Legion of Doom, Secret Society of
Super-Villains, Crime Syndicate, Darkseid

The Justice League is the foremost
Super Hero team in the known worlds.
Governments seek their aid, other
heroes want to join them, every villain
out to make a reputation takes them
on, and every would-be conqueror of
Earth knows they are the planet's first
line of defense. This prominence has
not come without cost, however, with
the stress sometimes threatening to
break the team apart. But whatever
their passing disagreements with each
other, they remain united against
external threats.

The core members of the Justice League—Superman, Batman, Wonder Woman, The Flash, Green Lantern (Hal Jordan),
Cyborg, and Aquaman—first came together as each of them hunted the source of strange occurrences in their respective cities
that prefigured an attack by Darkseid. Teenager Vic Stone, critically injured in the attack, became Cyborg when his father
implanted experimental cybernetics in his dying body. This occurred just in time for him to take part in the counterattack
against Darkseid and his Parademons, during which Batman rescued the kidnapped Superman from Apokolips.
Sometime later, writer David Graves named the team the Justice League in a book about the events; they preferred this
to The Flash's off-the-cuff suggestion of "Super Seven." Several other teams were created later, inspired by the
original Justice League team. Conflict erupted between the Justice League, the similarly titled Justice League of
America, and the occult-oriented Justice League Dark when

AT A GLANCE...

The world's greatest
The Justice League is the world's most
iconic Super Hero team, and still the
standard by which all others are judged.
Brought together to face a menace
that no hero could confront alone,
the Justice League has consistently
taken a stand against the most
dangerous threats the universe can
throw at them, and come out on top.

the three groups clashed over the
powerful artifact Pandora's Box. At this
point, the Justice League had adopted
three new members to help them in the
fight: the Atom (secretly a villain named
Atomica), Element Woman, and Firestorm.
The mysterious Outsider was working with
Atomica, and took control of Pandora's
Box, using it to open a portal to Earth-3,
from which emerged the Crime
Syndicate—the villainous Earth-3 version
of the Justice League. Cyborg's
cybernetics tore themselves free of his
body and rearranged themselves into the
sentient Grid—allied with the Crime
Syndicate—and nearly killing Cyborg in
the process. A number of key Justice

LEAGUES IN CONFLICT
As an international incident brewed in Kahndaq,
the Justice League and the Justice League of
America faced off over Pandora's Box.

League of America and Justice League heroes were trapped within a matrix created from the
two parts of Firestorm, and soon the Crime Syndicate took control of Earth-0, bolstered by
the Secret Society of Super-Villains. Seeing the threat escalate, Lex Luthor and a number of
villains defected from the Society, joining forces with the heroes in their counterattack
against the Crime Syndicate. The combined team won and Lex Luthor—despite
Superman's objections—was admitted to the League, along with Shazam, Captain Cold,
and Power Ring (Jessica Cruz), who had all proven themselves.
Several adventures later, when Darkseid battled the Anti-Monitor, the Justice
League became stuck in the middle. Darkseid was killed in the event, but was later
resurrected into the baby son of Earth-3's Superwoman. With the League triumphant

CLASSIC STORIES

***Justice League of America* (Vol. 1)
#21–22 (Aug.–Sep. 1963)** The JLA
and Justice Society of America team up
for the first time in "Crisis on Earth-One!"
and "Crisis on Earth-Two!", before the
introduction of Earth-3's Crime Syndicate
of America the next year.

***Justice League of America Annual*
(Vol. 1) #2 (Oct. 1984)** The original
JLA's failure to handle a Martian invasion
results in Aquaman dissolving the team.
He starts anew with a headquarters in
Detroit, admitting only heroes willing to
commit full-time to the task of representing
the JLA. The new roster consists of
Aquaman, Zatanna, Martian Manhunter,
Elongated Man, the Vixen, and three
younger recruits: Gypsy, Steel, and Vibe.

***Final Crisis* #1–7 (Jul. 2008–Mar.
2009)** The apparent deaths of Martian
Manhunter and Batman, together with
the resignations of Wonder Woman and
Superman, leave the remaining members
of the Justice League fighting the New Gods
and the spirit of a fallen Darkseid.

Watchtower
The orbiting Watchtower was the Justice
League's HQ for a time, containing research
and training facilities, as well as living spaces
for League members and their guests. It was
destroyed by Despero and later rebuilt in
orbit with the financial
backing of Lex Luthor.

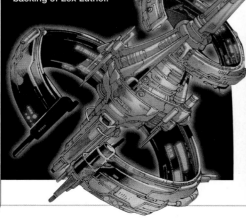

ROCKY BEGINNING
At first, the heroes who came together
to form the Justice League responded
individually to signs of Darkseid's attempt to
breach the dimensional barrier and conquer
Earth-0 to use it as a Parademon breeding
ground. As they met each other, their first
reaction was often suspicion; but when they
were forced to band together, they learned
how powerful they could be—and how
powerful they would need to be against
godlike adversaries like Darkseid.

FIRST IMPRESSIONS
The soon-to-be Justice League first
met under trying circumstances.

and Jessica Cruz becoming a true Green Lantern, they adjusted their ranks, losing members Luthor, Cold, and Shazam, but gaining Green Lantern Simon Baz. Later, Mera joined their roster as well.

After many hard-fought battles, the League faced another restructuring when the mysterious Source Wall, which separates known space from the powerful energy beyond, was pierced during a battle with the forces of the Dark Multiverse. Superman, Batman, Wonder Woman, The Flash, Cyborg, and Aquaman were joined by Hawkgirl, Green Lantern (John Stewart), and Martian Manhunter. They established a new headquarters—the Hall of Justice located in Washington, D.C.

Meanwhile, Lex Luthor had formulated a master plan and recruited his own Legion of Doom. Through Luthor's manipulations, the Source Wall itself was shattered, and the evil mother of the Multiverse, Perpetua, was released into the Multiverse. With Perpetua's help, Luthor evolved into the half-Martian Apex Lex, but soon ran afoul of the Batman Who Laughs—an evil Bruce Wayne, infected by The Joker, hailing from the Dark Multiverse. Even as the heroes fell to Perpetua's might, Perpetua decided to choose the Batman Who Laughs over Luthor as her new right-hand man. The world was transformed into a bizarre dark reflection of what it had once been, guided by the Batman Who Laughs' perverse imagination. With no other choice but to embrace the chaos, the Justice League had to rally its forces and face doom head on.

> "It's time to be the team they thought we were, instead of the team we've been this past five years."
>
> AQUAMAN

JL ROSTER
1 Superman
2 Batman
3 Wonder Woman
4 Aquaman
5 The Flash
6 Cyborg
7 Martian Manhunter
8 Hawkgirl
9 Green Lantern

ON THE RECORD

The Justice League of America came into being as a reboot of the Justice Society of America, which flourished in the 1940s, but was later shelved during the 1950s as Super Hero comics had to share the stage with new genres. The Justice Society was later brought back into continuity as the heroes of Earth-2, while the Justice League were designated Earth-1.

New beginnings
A flagship team for decades, the Justice League of America in its various incarnations has had nearly as many origin stories as members. The first of these related the story of an invasion by the alien Appellaxians, which none of the solo heroes could successfully repel. Only by banding together could they save Earth—and the JLA was born. This origin story has been modified numerous times over the years and has involved a varying roster of founding members.

GOING SMALL
A JLA including Hawkman, Black Canary, and Red Tornado hunted for the Atom in the Microcosmos.

What's in a name?
The original Justice League of America is informally known as the Justice League or by its initials JLA. But there have also been different iterations of the group under various names over the years: Justice League International, Justice League Europe, Justice League United, Justice League Dark… What they all have in common is usually some of the original Justice League's members and a version of the original Justice League's mandate: to protect and defend the people of Earth against the forces of evil.

STEALING THE LOOK
No sooner had the new 1990s Justice League team formed than their likenesses—including the new blue Superman—were assumed by hard-light constructs created and controlled by the Injustice Gang.

REBIRTH

THE HALL OF JUSTICE
The iconic Hall of Justice is not just the base of the Justice League, it also houses the hideout of the Justice League Dark in its basement. Moreover, it has become a Washington, D.C. landmark; one frequented by as many tourists as Super Heroes.

JUSTICE LEAGUE DARK

DEBUT *Justice League Dark* #1 (Nov. 2011)
BASE Hall of Justice
FORMER MEMBERS/POWERS
Madame Xanadu: Wide array of magical powers;
Constantine: Magical and occult knowledge;
Deadman: Possession of human hosts, telepathy;
Zatanna: Magical effects; **Andrew Bennett**: Mind
control, shapeshifting; **Black Orchid**: Elemental
force powers; **Swamp Thing**: Shapeshifting,
control over plants; **Nightmare Nurse**: Magical
abilities including hard-energy constructs.
NEW MEMBERS/POWERS
Wonder Woman: Amazon demigod: **Zatanna:**
Magical effects; **Swamp Thing:** Shapeshifting,
control over plants; **Constantine:** Magical and
occult knowledge; **Man-Bat;** scientific genius,
superhuman bat: **Detective Chimp:** immortal
supergenius, magical sword; **Animal Man:**
Avatar of the Red

DARKNESS WITHIN AND WITHOUT
They have their share of internal
rivalries and discord, but when they
stand together, the Justice League
Dark can overcome any occult threat.

Madame Xanadu assembled Justice
League Dark after experiencing a vision
of a horrific future only they could prevent.
She separated the Enchantress from her
mortal host, June Moone, destabilizing
the witch and sparking her lethal rampage.
To protect her, Madame Xanadu gathered
magic-wielding heroes, and John
Constantine merged the Enchantress and
June into a single, more stable being.

Madame Xanadu's vision then came
to pass as Cain, sire of all vampires, was
unleashed. Success followed and Steve
Trevor enlisted the group to help A.R.G.U.S.
protect its mystical artifacts from wizard Felix

Faust. Trevor named the group Justice
League Dark, as a specialized force to handle
occult and magical threats.

Facing a series of crises and the horrors
of the Otherkind, Wonder Woman formed
a new Justice League-sponsored team to
tackle mystical chaos. They battled Lords of
Order and others striving to take advantage
of the mystical sea change created by the
invasion and the rise of eldritch evil triggered
by the return cosmic Originator Perpetua.

JUSTICE LEAGUE INTERNATIONAL

DEBUT *Justice League International* (Vol. 1) #7
(Nov. 1987)
BASE Washington, D.C.
MEMBERS/POWERS
Booster Gold: Legion flight ring, power suit;
Fire: Thermal energy blasts; **Godiva**: Prehensile hair;
Green Lantern: Power ring; **Ice**: Ice creation and
control; **Firehawk**: Flight, light energy control;
Vixen: Totem powers; **Batwing**: Military training,
computers; **O.M.A.C.**: Biotech weapon;
Blue Beetle: Alien scarab powers;
August General in Iron: Armored, energy
manipulation.

NO SECRETS
Building on the Justice League's
legacy, but with a global perspective,
Justice League International fractured
after losing several of its members in
early missions.

Justice League International was the
brainchild of mind-controlled entrepreneur
Maxwell Lord. After he regained his
senses, the squad became a force for
good. However, they could never persuade
public opinion that they were more than
second-raters and eventually disbanded.

Following the reality-altering *Flashpoint*
event, UN director Andre Briggs established
a team to rival the US's Justice League. Led
by Booster Gold, it only accepted members
with public identities. Batman was refused
admission for this reason, but provided
assistance against Peraxxus and the
Signal Men. When the Burners killed
Rocket Red and crippled Vixen, Ice, and
Fire, Booster Gold recruited O.M.A.C.,
Batwing, and Firehawk. The JLI disbanded
after Green Lantern (Guy Gardner) clashed
with Booster Gold, and the team was
devastated by rogue AI satellite, Brother E.

JUSTICE LEAGUE OF CHINA

DEBUT *New Super-Man* (Vol. 1) #2 (Oct. 2016)
BASE Jilin Province, China
MEMBERS/POWERS Super-Man: Ability
to focus qi to get super-strength, stamina, speed,
and enhanced senses; X-ray and heat vision;
can freeze breath; **Wonder-Woman**: Flight,
telepathy, super-strength, magical lasso;
Bat-Man: Genius inventor, computer hacker,
highly skilled in combat; **The Flash of China**:
Speed Force powers including super-speed,
intangibility, and time travel; **Aquaman of North
Korea**: Water manipulation, ability to command
ocean creatures, magic sword; **Robinbot**: Flight,
expert data analysis, rocket fists.
ALLIES Justice League
ENEMIES China White Triad, Lanterns of
China, Freedom Fighters of China

STATE OF INDEPENDENCE
The Justice League of China soon
rejected government interference in
their activities and attitudes and
decided to go their own way.

The Justice League of China was formed by
the Ministry of Self-Reliance in response to
the emergence of the Justice League in the US.
The Chinese team was expected to protect its
own country while also upholding its national
values. At first the group only comprised two
members—Bat-Man and Wonder-Woman—
but they were later joined by the New
Super-Man, Kong Kenan, and The Flash of
China, Avery Ho. After failing to find a
compatible human equivalent of Robin,
Bat-Man built a high-tech robotic equivalent.

The team eventually rebelled against their
government, splitting from the Ministry of
Self-Reliance and going out on their own.
Later they got a new member—the Aquaman
of North Korea, also known as Dragonson.

JUSTICE LEAGUE UNITED

DEBUT *Justice League United* #0 (Jun. 2014)
BASE Canada
MEMBERS/POWERS Martian Manhunter:
Super-strength, mind control, shapeshifting;
Stargirl: Cosmic converter belt and staff powers;
Green Arrow: Archery, acrobatics, unarmed
combat; **Adam Strange**: Advanced Rannian tech
and weapons; **Animal Man**: Shapeshifting,
animal control, and telepathy; **Supergirl**:
Super-strength, flight, invulnerability;
Equinox: Powers of Cree Midayo.

SPLINTER CELL
The Martian Manhunter oversees
a group that is beyond the grasp of
A.R.G.U.S. and outside the currents
of US politics.

Martian Manhunter, Stargirl, and Green
Arrow formed the Justice League United
after the dissolution of the A.R.G.U.S.-
sanctioned Justice League. Basing
themselves in Canada, they recruited a
number of other unaffiliated heroes,
including a new member—the Cree girl
known as Equinox.

The team's major battle was against
the scheming Lord Byth, who sought to
synthesize a number of alien genomes into
a being he called Ultra the Multi-Alien. Byth
corrupted a project begun by the people of
Rann. They had envisioned Ultra as a sign
of the interconnectedness of all sentient
beings, but Byth instead planned to create
the Slayer of Worlds. The JLU fought to
prevent Byth realizing his apocalyptic goal.

Members of the team then split into
several different groups to battle the Breakers
—a mysterious force causing disruptions in
space-time—and they ultimately journeyed
to the House of Secrets for answers.

JUSTICE SOCIETY OF AMERICA

DATA

DEBUT *All-Star Comics #3* (Dec. 1940)
FOUNDING MEMBERS/POWERS AND ABILITIES
ATOM (AL PRATT) Tenacious spirit and expert fighter despite size;
SANDMAN (WESLEY DODDS) Precognitive abilities and detective skills,
sleep gun; **THE SPECTRE (JIM CORRIGAN)** Powerful spirit of
vengeance, detective skills; **THE FLASH (JAY GARRICK)** Super-speed;
HAWKMAN (CARTER HALL) Expert warrior, Nth Metal allows for flight;
DOCTOR FATE (KENT NELSON) Magical abilities, flight; **GREEN
LANTERN (ALAN SCOTT)** Ring conveys various powers including flight
and the creation of energy constructs; **HOURMAN (REX TYLER)** Drug
Miraclo allows for one hour of enhanced strength, speed, and stamina.
ALLIES Justice League
ENEMIES Vandal Savage, Ultra-Humanite, Injustice Society of America

THE JUSTICE SOCIETY
The founding fathers of the
Justice Society of America
originally gathered in a
brownstone building in the 1940s.
1 The Atom
2 Sandman
3 The Spectre
4 The Flash
5 Hawkman
6 Doctor Fate
7 Green Lantern
8 Hourman

The original Super Hero team that would inspire
all others to follow, the Justice Society of
America joined forces to protect the home front
of an America torn apart by World War II. Some
of the world's first mystery men, this once
forgotten team is back in the spotlight after
being nearly omitted by the timeline itself.

FOGGY MEMORIES
During a time-travel
adventure, the Justice
League was surprised
to meet the JSA, a team
they had never heard of.

The DC universe is a tumultuous
place, one where major crises rock the very
foundation of its timeline on a regular basis. The
Justice Society of America has fallen victim to the
changing whims of demigods and reality-altering
super-beings perhaps more than any other team in
the Multiverse. The Justice Society of America was
the first team of Super Heroes. With Super Heroes
still a relatively novel idea in the 1940s, the team
banded together in an effort to pool their strengths
and create a network in the mystery men community.
Conducting meetings out of a brownstone building,
the Justice Society of America thwarted attacks on
American soil by some of the worst Super-Villains of the Golden Age.

Originally, the JSA existed in the dimension of Earth-2, until the cosmic threat of the Anti-Monitor
changed all that. Their Earth was combined with that of the Justice League on Earth-1, and they became
the inspiration for the modern day Justice League of America that would come decades after their
tenure. After losing several of their number in another cosmic Crisis called *Zero Hour* thanks to the
machinations of a being called Extant, the Justice Society was later wiped from history completely during
the *Flashpoint* event. However, the Multiverse has a way of correcting itself, and these classic heroes soon
reemerged on a new Earth-2, one besieged by the dark forces of the evil New God Darkseid. While their Earth
was taken by Darkseid's Apokolips troops, a few members survived to start anew on a new planet.

Recently, due to the meddling of the powerful being known as Doctor Manhattan and other major events
during the Justice League's battle with the mother of the Multiverse, Perpetua, the Justice Society has been
reborn in continuity once more. The team is now active again, saved from non-existence. Its roster has
changed over the years; the Justice Society currently includes old timers like Green Lantern (Alan Scott) and
Wildcat (Ted Grant), but also includes young heroes, including Stargirl and Cyclone.

ON THE RECORD

The Justice Society of America
is the first Super Hero team in the history
of comic books, and has existed in one
form or another since 1940. A number of
characters made their debuts during this time,
most notably Wonder Woman in 1942 (as the
team's secretary!) Headliners like The Flash
and Green Lantern mingled with lesser-
known players such as the Atom and Dr.
Mid-Nite for a decade before going on hiatus.

The JSA returned in 1963, soon beginning
a series of memorable team-ups with
Earth-1's Justice League. A revived Justice
Society feature in the 1970s even revealed
the secret of the team's formation and the
confrontation with Congress that caused
the heroes to retire.

WHERE IT ALL BEGAN
The first meeting of the Justice Society of
America. In attendance: The Atom, Sandman,
The Spectre, The Flash, Hawkman, Dr. Fate,
Green Lantern, and Hourman.

CLASSIC STORIES

***All-Star Comics* #11 (Jun.–Jul.
1942)** In a surge of patriotism following
the attack on Pearl Harbor, the JSA
members disbanded to enlist in the armed
forces. The well-intentioned heroes proved
such a disruptive influence that the US
Government asked them to resume their
costumed activities as the Justice Battalion.

***Justice League of America*
(Vol. 1) #21–22 (Aug.–Sep. 1963)**
The first meeting of the JSA and JLA kicks
off a decades-long series of collaborative
adventures spanning Earth-1 and Earth-2.

***JSA* (Vol. 1) #16–20 (Nov. 2000–
Mar. 2001)** A reconstituted JSA faces a
new Injustice Society headed up by Johnny
Sorrow.

DOOMSDAY CLOCK
During an international
incident involving
Superman, the modern
Justice Society of America
returned in all its glory,
alongside a new
incarnation of the Legion
of Super-Heroes.

KALIBAK

DEBUT *New Gods* (Vol. 1) #1 (Feb.–Mar. 1971)
REAL NAME Kalibak **BASE** Apokolips
HEIGHT 6ft 9in **WEIGHT** 469 lbs **EYES** Red **HAIR** Black
POWERS/ABILITIES As a New God, he is immortal and has superhuman physical strength and toughness; wields Apokoliptian weaponry.
ALLIES Darkseid, Glorious Godfrey, Desaad
ENEMIES Orion, Batman, Batman Family, Superman, New Genesis, Olsen, Big Barda
AFFILIATIONS Apokolips

Brutal and pitiless, Kalibak is the eldest son of Darkseid, lord of Apokolips. He is a devoted to his sire, and a relentless foe of Orion, the son Darkseid allowed to be raised on New Genesis. When Darkseid was incapacitated, Kalibak took command, readying the Chaos Cannon (powered by a Chaos Shard and the body of Batman's son Damian) to destroy inhabited planets and channel their energies back to Apokolips. Batman and his associates foiled the plan by returning Damian's body to Earth. Kalibak pursued, but after a fierce battle in the Batcave he was knocked back through the portal to Apokolips.

On Earth-2, Kalibak led Parademon troopers, defeating James Olsen, who had gained New God powers. Darkseid's forces conquered Earth-2 and Apokolips destroyed the planet, though many inhabitants escaped via spacecraft.

Kalibak fought for Darkseid when he attacked Earth-0, but was blinded by his half-sister Grail. Despite his wound (and the Anti-Monitor killing Darkseid) Kalibak fought on until finally taken down by Big Barda. Recently, he lead one faction seeking control of Apokolips, almost destroying the planet with his Chaos Cannon to defeat the Female Furies, Lex Luthor and Superman, Lois Lane and Superboy.

ON THE RECORD

The original Kalibak was a fierce adversary of Orion, his half-brother who had pledged allegiance to New Genesis, and they clashed on many occasions. Though Kalibak constantly sought his father's approval, he was punished when he slew Darkseid's interrogator, Desaad. The ruler of Apokolips killed him with his Omega Beams, but later brought resurrected him. Kalibak was destroyed by Infinity-Man during the Death of the New Gods event, but was reborn on Earth in a tigerlike form.

EARTH-SHAKING ENCOUNTER
On Earth, Kalibak caused widespread destruction when he clashed with his half-brother Orion.

KALMAKU, TOM

DEBUT *Green Lantern* (Vol. 2) #2 (Sep.–Oct. 1960)
BASE Ferris Aircraft, Coast City
EYES Brown **HAIR** Black
HEIGHT 5ft 7in **WEIGHT** 155 lbs
POWERS/ABILITIES Skilled mechanic and engineer.
ALLIES Green Lantern (Hal Jordan)
ENEMIES Sinestro
AFFILIATIONS Ferris Aircraft

Tom Kalmaku is an Inuit from Alaska who traveled to California and landed a job at Ferris Aircraft as a mechanic and engineer. His keen intelligence and work ethic made him a vital part of the team. He became good friends with test pilot Hal Jordan and a huge fan of Coast City's new Super Hero, Green Lantern.

Tom soon worked out that Hal was Green Lantern but kept quiet about it, and Hal trusted him with his secret. Tom was also rumored to keep a secret journal of Hal's adventures under lock and key. It was Tom who alerted Carol Ferris when Hal teamed up with his old enemy Sinestro. After Hal went missing, Tom and Carol opened Hal's locker to look for clues to his whereabouts. To their embarrassment, they discovered a wedding ring that Hal had bought for Carol.

KAMANDI

DEBUT *Kamandi, the Last Boy on Earth* #1 (Oct.–Nov. 1972)
EYES Blue **HAIR** Blond
HEIGHT 5ft 8in **WEIGHT** 159 lbs
POWERS/ABILITIES Resourceful survivor and warrior; skilled with firearms.
ALLIES Ben Boxer, Steve, Renzi, Doctor Canus, Prince Tuftan, Pyra, Spirit, Batman, Superman
ENEMIES Great Caesar, Tiger Empire, Rat Society, United States of Lions, Czar Simian, Lex Luthor

Kamandi was born in the aftermath of a Great Disaster that destroyed human civilization and evolved animals into near-humanoid forms, with each species striving to be the dominant life form on Earth. "The Last Boy on Earth," along with scientist Doctor Canus and radioactive mutant Ben Boxer, tried to restore human civilization. Kamandi frequently traveled in time, meeting Batman, Superman, and a group of alternate-Earth heroes during various reality crises.

Multiversal chaos triggered by the breaking of the Source Wall revealed Kamandi to be a critical factor in the composition of all realities: He has travelled extensively across parallel existences and visited many possible futures.

When Perpetua and the Legion of Doom sought to unmake the Multiverse, Kamandi allied with The Justice League and heroes from the past and future to stop them.

KANTO

DEBUT *Mister Miracle* (Vol. 1) #7 (Mar.–Apr. 1972)
REAL NAME Iluthin **BASE** Apokolips
EYES Blue **HAIR** Brown
HEIGHT 5ft 11½in **WEIGHT** 170 lbs
POWERS/ABILITIES Immortality; tracks prey with Mother Box.
ALLIES Darkseid, Lashina, Desaad
ENEMIES Mister Miracle, Justice League, Batman

Darkseid's assassin, Kanto, is a sadistic killer. Suave and cunning, he was key in a patriarchal conspiracy on Apokolips keeping Granny Goodness' Female Furies from achieving an elite status. Armed with a dagger-shaped Mother Box, he can track targets across space and time. Only Mister Miracle and Batman have ever escaped Kanto, and the killer determined to rectify that situation.

Darkseid sent Kanto and Lashina to Earth to hunt down Myrina Black, Amazon mother of Darkseid's daughter, Grail. When Darkseid invaded Earth, however, he was killed by the Anti-Monitor and the Black Racer, leaving Kanto and other Apokoliptian minions to face Mister Miracle and the Justice League. In battle, Kanto hurled his blade into Mister Miracle's side, but Scott Free was saved when his wife, Big Barda, charged into battle via Boom Tube and teleported Kanto to parts unknown with her Mega-Rod.

KARATE KID

DEBUT *Adventure Comics* (Vol. 1) #346 (Jul. 1966)
REAL NAME Val Armorr
HEIGHT 6ft **WEIGHT** 185 lbs
POWERS/ABILITIES Master of all martial arts disciplines; can fly with Legion flight ring.
ALLIES Princess Projectra, Diamondeth
ENEMIES Mordru, Crav, the General Nah, Terrot of the Horraz
AFFILIATIONS the Legion of Super-Heroes

Val Armorr is a being born to battle. The son a 31st-Century crime lord of Japanese descent, he was raised offworld by martial arts mater Sensei Toshiaki (White Crane) and trained to be a living weapon.

As Karate Kid, he joined the Legion of Super-Heroes to prove his bravery and validate his training against Super-Villains such as Crav, the General Nah; however, his martial arts skills are not always a match for superpowers or advanced technologies. He enjoys and reveres the art and poetry of combat, and considers it an honor to only battle beings who would appear to be out of his league. His proudest moment thus far is kicking the archdemon and near-omnipotent Lord of Chaos Mordru in the face.

KELLEY, CARRIE

DEBUT *Batman: The Dark Knight* #1 (1986)
BASE Gotham City
EYES Red **HAIR** Green
POWERS/ABILITIES Skilled actor; encyclopedic knowledge of Shakespeare.
ALLIES Damian Wayne, Alfred, Titus
AFFILIATIONS Batman household

Drama student Carrie Kelley was hired by Bruce Wayne's son Damian to give him acting lessons so he could experience what it was like to be someone else. When Damian didn't show up, she left her bill and a note for him at Wayne Manor. Bruce gave her a hefty check, but did not reveal the truth: his son—aka Robin—had been killed battling the Heretic. Carrie sensed Bruce was hiding something, and revisited the Manor, demanding to see Damian. Bruce informed her that Damian was studying overseas and told Alfred to show her out. Instead, the butler hired her to take care of the Manor's Great Dane, Titus. Bruce reluctantly allowed Carrie to become part of the household.

Pre-*Flashpoint* in a possible future for Gotham City, Carrie Kelley was a 13-year-old Batman fangirl who became the new Robin after saving the out-of-retirement and out-of-condition Dark Knight from the Mutant gang leader. She then helped track down and defeat The Joker. A faithful ally, she later took on the mantle of Catgirl, before growing into her mentor's boots as Batwoman.

KATANA

DEBUT *Brave and the Bold* (Vol. 1) #200 **(Jul. 1983)** (as Tatsu Yamashiro)
REAL NAME Tatsu Toro **BASE** Mobile
EYES Brown **HAIR** Black **HEIGHT** 5ft 2in **WEIGHT** 118 lbs
POWERS/ABILITIES Expert acrobat, martial artist, and swordswoman.
ALLIES Green Arrow, Sickle, Halo
ENEMIES Lady Eve, Kobra, Rā's al Ghūl, Cleaners, Onyx, Dagger Clan, Poison Ivy, Killer Croc
AFFILIATIONS Birds of Prey, Outsiders, Suicide Squad, Sword Clan

When Tatsu was a child her best friends were brothers Takeo and Maseo. Both fell in love with her, but she ultimately married Maseo. The brothers were members of the Sword Clan, one of several groups that made up the Outsiders, a secret organization devoted to preserving the balance of the world by eliminating evil and corruption. When Tatsu saw Takeo and Maseo arguing about her, she intervened, accidentally killing her husband with his sacred sword, Soultaker. It absorbed his spirit and, overwhelmed by grief, Tatsu took up Soultaker to stay close to Maseo. She then went into the world, seeking redemption as Katana.

On the advice of her husband, who spoke to her through Soultaker, she briefly joined the Birds of Prey team, helping them battle Poison Ivy and terrorist-group the Cleaners. After violently encountering the mysterious Dagger Clan in Japan, Katana left the Birds to learn more about Soultaker and the Sword Clan.

When Killer Croc broke the sword and released Maseo's spirit, her late husband told Katana she had to let go of him and dedicate herself to redeeming the warring Outsiders. After Soultaker was reforged, she became head of the Sword Clan, helping Green Arrow defeat the Fist, Spear, Shield, and Axe clans when they planned a large-scale terror attack on Prague. Following *Rebirth*, she was hired by Amanda Waller to wrangle the rebellious convicts in the Suicide Squad, and clashed with King Kobra, before joining Batman in a new Outsiders team hunting Rā's al Ghūl.

ON THE RECORD

The original Katana was Tatsu Yamashiro, whose husband, Maseo was slain with the magical sword Soultaker, wielded by his jealous gangster brother Takeo. Tatsu took up the Soultaker, trained as a samurai and, as Katana, joined Batman's Outsiders. Takeo later tracked Katana to Gotham City and released all the souls in the Soultaker sword to attack her. After a long battle, Katana killed Takeo. During *Blackest Night*, Katana battled her undead husband, who had been raised from the grave by the Black Lanterns.

BETTER THAN THE MOVIES
While serving with Halo and Looker in the Outsiders, Katana clashed with Tengu spirits and Japanese gangsters in Hollywood!

KENTS, THE

DEBUT *Superman* (Vol. 1) #1 **(Jun. 1939)**
BASE Smallville, Kansas
POWERS/ABILITIES Ordinary pioneering humans, with strong ideals and clearly defined principles and ethics.
ALLIES The Ross Family, the Lang Family
ENEMIES John Wesley Hardin, Jesse James gang, Charley Quantrill
AFFILIATIONS Jonah Hex, Scalphunter, Bill Hickock, George Armstrong Custer

MEN OF IRON
The Kents had always worked hard and put their lives on the line to protect their family, friends, and most cherished beliefs.

The patrilineal side of the Kent family traces its history back to 6th-century England, where Sir Brian Kent battled tyranny as the Silent Knight. A thousand years later, the family had fallen from the aristocracy and at least one branch sought a better life in the New World.

In 1854, patriarch and abolitionist Silas Kent was active in the anti-slavery movement. A printer and pamphleteer, he migrated west, settling in Lawrence, Kansas, with his oldest sons Nathaniel and Jebediah. His wife Abigail had remained in Boston to raise their remaining seven children. When she died three years later, the children remained in Massachusetts. After the Civil War and Reconstruction, the Kansas Kents generally stuck to their lands as farmers, although a succession of Kent men proudly served in America's overseas wars.

The line looked likely to end in the 20th century with Jonathan and Martha Kent, until the childless couple found a son who fell to Earth in a rocketship. They subsequently raised him in the traditions and morals which had shaped generations of Kents. The child was called Clark and would grow up to be the world's foremost Super Hero, an indomitable defender of truth and justice—Superman.

FAMILY HONOR
Jonathan and Martha's foundling son was destined to become the most famous Kent in the family's long and valiant history—at least to those who knew his secret identity.

ON THE RECORD

When baby Kal-El crashed to Earth he was adopted by a couple desperate for a child of their own. In the years that followed, while their status remained constant, the Kents' ages varied to suit the times.

In *Superman* #1 (1939), they were elderly and died before their son began his heroic career. In the 1960s, they were rejuvenated by alien science to become spry 40-year olds. However, the biggest change came in the 1986 reboot, where Mr. and Mrs. Kent again became an older couple, but never died; instead offering parental love and guidance to the Man of Steel.

HEAVEN SENT
The infant found by aging Jonathan and Martha was not just the answer to their prayers, but would become the savior of the world.

KEY, THE

DEBUT *Justice League* (Vol. 1) #41 (Dec. 1965)
REAL NAME Unknown **BASE** Alaska
HEIGHT Unknown **WEIGHT** Unknown
EYES Red **HAIR** White
POWERS/ABILITIES Telepathy using psycho-chemicals.
ALLIES Troia
ENEMIES Justice League
AFFILIATIONS Intergang

The archmanipulator known as the Key worked for Intergang on experiments with psycho-chemicals that unlocked his mental potential. He claimed to have 19 senses as a result of stimulating his brain with these chemicals, and gained the ability to unlock portals to other dimensions.

The Key theorized that there was even greater potential power locked up in the minds of superpowered beings, and set about trying to release it.

Working with a mysterious ally, who turned out to be Troia, an evil future version of Donna Troy, the Key lured four Justice Leaguers and their Titans equivalents to his bunker and tried to break them psychologically to release their emotional energy. Although he did release Troia's power, she was defeated by the Titans and he was captured.

KGBEAST

DEBUT *Batman* (Vol. 1) #417 (Mar. 1988)
REAL NAME Anatoli Knyazev "The Beast"
BASE Classified **EYES** Blue **HAIR** Blond
HEIGHT 6ft 3in **WEIGHT** 231 lbs
POWERS/ABILITIES Espionage and combat training; cybernetically enhanced body; cannon replaces missing arm.
ENEMIES Batman, Batgirl, Aquaman, the Operative, the Others
ALLIES Bane, NKVDemon
AFFILIATIONS Mayhem, Suicide Squad

Anatoli Knyazev served heroically in the KGB, earning the codename KGBeast, KGBeast was critically injured in a shootout with the Suicide Squad in the Moscow subway, but Mars Systems literally rebuilt him for combat. He then joined Soviet veteran NKVDemon in Mayhem, working to bring back the glory days of the USSR by holding the world to ransom with a nuclear-armed satellite. This brought him into conflict with the Others, a squad that included an old foe, the Operative, who destroyed KGBeast's arm cannon before finishing him off in hand-to-hand combat.

Rebranding as "The Beast," he turned to mercenary work. Hired by Bane to assassinate Batman, The Beast shot Nightwing, causing massive brain trauma, but again failing in his mission.

KHUNDS, THE

DEBUT *Adventure Comics* (Vol. 1) #346 (Jul. 1966)
BASE Khundia, Khundish Empire **HAIR** Black
POWERS/ABILITIES Aggressive and militaristic; urgent drive for status and territory.
ALLIES Dark Circle
ENEMIES United Planets, Thanagarians, Legion of Super-Heroes
AFFILIATIONS Alien Alliance, Dominators

The Khunds are an extremely aggressive, territorial warrior-race who began carving out an intergalactic empire as soon as they freed themselves from the bounds of their heavy-gravity homeworld. Their culture is based on confrontation and dominance. Khunds consider all other species as inferior and every contact with a new culture is an opportunity for conquest and expansion. The Empire is a constantly shifting hierarchy of competing warlords with the mightiest fighter ruling only for as long as he can defeat all challengers.

The most arrogant and belligerent members of the species take enormous pride in having their bodies cybernetically augmented: recreating themselves as living weapons. To a Khund, victory is everything and must be won at any price.

KID ETERNITY

DEBUT *Hit Comics* (Vol. 1) #25 (Dec. 1942)
REAL NAME Christopher "Kit" Freeman
BASE New York City
HEIGHT 5ft 10in
WEIGHT 164 lbs
EYES Blue **HAIR** Black
POWERS/ABILITIES Able to communicate with the newly dead for up to 24 hours.
ALLIES Mr. Keeper

Chris Freeman was arguing with his N.Y.P.D. detective dad when they were both shot. He remembered dying and arriving in a grotesque waiting area with the rest of the newly deceased. His dad grabbed him, begging Chris not to leave him there. What Chris did not know was why or how he had returned to life, or how his dad's corpse could say "you should be here, not me…"

Working at the Police Morgue, Chris soon discovered a strange new ability: he could bring back dead people—"Fresh Ones"—and help them settle any unfinished business. When Darby Quinn was killed, Chris helped his ghost catch the murderer, only to find Quinn was a violent aggressor and had been shot in self defense. It also brought Freeman into conflict with the spectral Mr. Keeper, who warned him there were rules he needed to follow.

KID FLASH

DEBUT *The Flash Annual* (Vol. 4) #3 (Jun. 2014)
REAL NAME Wallace Rudolph West **BASE** Central City
EYES Brown **HAIR** Black
POWERS/ABILITIES Super-speed; rapid healing; ability to absorb Speed Force energy; time-travel.
ALLIES Teen Titans, Barry Allen **ENEMIES** Professor Zoom, Future Flash
AFFILIATIONS Iris West, Daniel West/the Reverse-Flash

Wally West's father Rudy walked out on his family when the boy was still young. His mother vanished during the Crime Syndicate's attack on Central City, and 12-year-old Wally went to live with his aunt Iris. Soon after, Wally was arrested by Barry Allen for vandalism, but despite this shaky start, and thanks to Iris' persistence, they became firm friends. Twenty years in the future, a grief-maddened Barry Allen had seen his friends suffer and die while the Speed Force ruptured from being over-used for time-travel by numerous speedsters. As the Future Flash, Barry then raced back over his decades-long career, rectifying every failure, and intending to murder his younger self and use the liberated energies to "correct" history—and seal the temporal breach his actions had caused.

The future Barry was thwarted by an older Wally who was also a speedster. Allowing both Flashes' energies to pass through him, Wally sacrificed his life to reset history. He returned to his juvenile self, unaware of what had happened or that the trans-dimensional Speed Force had altered him and would soon make him a super-fast Super Hero, too.

As the latest Kid Flash carved out his own reputation in the Teen Titans and under the controversial mentorship of Deathstroke in the mercenary's Defiance team, his world was shaken by the return of another Wally West from a previous reality, further destabilizing him. Despite all the shocks to his system, Kid Flash remains devoted to his family and the rapid pursuit of justice.

ON THE RECORD

Kid Flash was the first original sidekick of DC's Silver Age, offering a youngster's perspective to the adventures of the Fastest Man Alive. Wally West shared cases with his mentor and joined fellow superpowered kids in the Teen Titans before inheriting the mantle and responsibilities of The Flash after Barry Allen gave his life during the *Crisis on Infinite Earths*.

Wally's sometime-sidekick and eventual successor was Bart Allen—aka Impulse—who inherited his grandfather's powers and costumed identity before being killed by The Flash's Rogues. Both champions were revealed to have a connection to the extra-dimensional Speed-Force, unlike Bar Torr, whose hyper-velocity remains an unexplained accident. A terrorist insurgent in his own time, he learned to be a hero, battling beside young 21st-century metahumans as Kid Flash in the Teen Titans.

WALLY WEST The Flash's helper rapidly evolved into a vibrant hero succeeding on his on terms.

BAR TORR The amnesiac speedster from the 30th century learned how to run fast enough to escape the shame of his evil past.

KILLER CROC

DATA

DEBUT *Detective Comics* (Vol. 1) #523 (Feb. 1983)
UPDATE *Batman* (Vol. 2) #1 (Nov. 2011)
REAL NAME Waylon Jones **BASE** Gotham City
HEIGHT 6ft 5in **WEIGHT** 300 lbs **EYES** Yellow **HAIR** None
POWERS/ABILITIES Rare skin condition allows for enhanced durability; enhanced strength and endurance; excellent fighter with history of wrestling alligators; razor-sharp teeth and claws.
ALLIES Arsenal, Catwoman, Gotham City Monsters
ENEMIES Batman, The Batman Family, Bane
AFFILIATIONS Arkham Asylum inmates, Suicide Squad, Gotham City Monsters

Killer Croc may not be the sharpest knife in the drawer, but his razorlike claws and teeth certainly make up for it. Almost more animal than man, this ferocious Super-Villain has challenged Batman to many fights—ones that the Dark Knight has been lucky to walk away from in one piece. Killer Croc is truly a force to be feared and remains one of the most dangerous inmates ever to be housed in Arkham Asylum.

MOCKING THE CROC
As a boy, Waylon Jones' skin condition caused him to be teased by his peers, leading to the nickname Croc, which he would later fully embrace.

Waylon Jones had always been different. Growing up in a poor neighborhood in Gotham City, he lived a lonely life with his Aunt Flowers. With no parents of his own, Waylon had only his aunt to look up to, but she despised her nephew because of the way he looked. Born with a rare medical condition that caused scales to form on his body and bumpy, horn-like protrusions to grow on his head, as well as giving him jagged teeth and claws, Waylon was cruelly nicknamed "Croc" by the local kids. His aunt attempted to scrub off Waylon's scales when they first emerged, but had no luck making her nephew appear as normal as the boys and girls that mocked him.

Years later, Waylon made his way to Jacksonville, Florida and became a sideshow act wrestling alligators in the Eddie Geisel Circus Sideshow. Now completely covered in hard green scales, Waylon was dubbed Killer Croc. Waylon became frustrated with his low income from Geisel, and literally bit the hand that fed him, quitting the act and returning to Gotham City to become a thief. He soon crossed paths with Batman and the original Robin during a jewelry heist. The two heroes brought him to justice, but would go on to see the fierce villain escape incarceration at Arkham Asylum time and again. On one occasion, he even chomped off the hand of one of the Asylum's toughest guards, Aaron Cash.

Recruited into Task Force X, the government's secret Suicide Squad, Killer Croc went on a variety of covert operations and began a rather doomed relationship with a fellow Belle Reve inmate, Enchantress. While he mourned her loss when she seemingly died during a mission, Croc decided to stay on the side of the angels after earning his freedom thanks to completing a number of Suicide Squad missions. He joined up with a few fellow Gotham City Monsters for a time and began to run Tusk's Hotel in Gotham City's newly established Monstertown neighborhood. A clash with Batman earned Croc another stint in Arkham Asylum; however, but both he and Batman have high hopes that he will he will fully rehabilitate some day.

CLASSIC STORIES

Detective Comics (Vol. 1) #525 (Apr. 1983) Batman tangles with Killer Croc in the Gotham City sewers, realizing how ferocious his new opponent truly is.

Batman (Vol. 1) #359 (May 1983) Killer Croc's origin is told for the first time as he declares himself "King Croc," and takes his place as one of Gotham City's major criminals.

Batman (Vol. 1) #489 (Feb. 1993) Croc is given the spotlight as he takes on Robin, Azrael, and the threat of a formidable new villain, Bane.

Batman (Vol. 1) #608 (Dec. 2002) Killer Croc is mutated into a more animalistic state thanks to the meddling of new Batman foe, Hush.

BATTLE OF THE BRAWN
The powerful villain Bane challenged Killer Croc for territory while clad in a makeshift Batsuit. Bane came out on top, besting the scaly beast in fierce combat.

ON THE RECORD

First appearing shortly before the epic maxiseries *Crisis on Infinite Earths*, the original incarnation of Killer Croc was far smarter than his savage post-*Flashpoint* successor. Depicted as a criminal mastermind slowly taking over Gotham City's underworld, Killer Croc—also called King Croc—murdered the Flying Todds, Gotham City's newest trapeze act sensation. The Todds' son, Jason, survived, and would go on to become the second Robin. Some years later, Jason's story was rewritten with the future Robin now being depicted as an orphaned street kid with little historical connection to Killer Croc.

KILLER OR KING?
In his later appearances, Killer Croc became simply muscle-for-hire, a far cry from the gang boss that earned a feared reputation as King Croc.

MURKY DEPTHS
Killer Croc can often be found in the sewers, with the old tunnels providing him with the perfect hideaway. Croc often takes charge of some of the other forgotten souls who dwell there.

KILLER FROST

DEBUT *Firestorm* (Vol. 1) #3 (Jun. 1978)
REAL NAME Dr. Caitlin Snow
HEIGHT 5ft 4in **WEIGHT** 123 lbs
EYES Blue **HAIR** White
POWERS/ABILITIES Can project ice and snow from her fingertips; feeds off others' heat.
ALLIES Steve Trevor, Batman
ENEMIES Firestorm, Amanda Waller
AFFILIATIONS S.T.A.R. Labs, Justice League of America, A.R.G.U.S.

Dr. Caitlin Snow was a brilliant employee of S.T.A.R. Labs, assigned to their Arctic base. Here she found her fellow scientists had been stymied in their work on a thermodynamic ultraconductor engine. Not knowing that her peers were associated with terrorist group H.I.V.E., Snow was blindsided by her colleagues and locked in with the experimental machine. While trying to save herself by pulling out the machine's coolant wires, Caitlin was fused with ice and transformed into Killer Frost.

Now needing to feed on heat from living things, Snow discovered that the energies of Firestorm were the only thing that sated her hunger, prompting many clashes with the hero. Constantly starving, she became a reluctant but predatory Super-Villain, but ultimately redeemed herself working with Steve Trevor and A.R.G.U.S. to battle the Earth-3 invasion of the Crime Syndicate.

Frost was captured and remanded to Amanda Waller's Suicide Squad, but rescued by Batman, who saw her need to

NEW TERROR
While in the Justice League of America, Killer Frost warmed to tiny team member Atom and also faced the threat of Terrorsmith.

redeem herself was genuine. He placed her in his new Justice League of America team where she blossomed into a true hero while battling the likes of The Extremists, Queen of Fables, Chronos, and Terrorsmith.

KILLER MOTH

DEBUT *Green Arrow* (Vol. 5) #25 (Jan. 2014)
REAL NAME Drury Walker
BASE Gotham City **EYES** Black **HAIR** Black
POWERS/ABILITIES Mediocre combatant; employs moth-themed gimmicks to intimidate.
ALLIES Richard Dragon, Brick, Red, Count Vertigo
ENEMIES Green Arrow, Batman, Batgirl, Emiko Queen
AFFILIATIONS Longbow Hunters

Killer Moth appeared during the super-storm that ravaged Gotham City in *Year Zero*. Obsessed with moths and money, he tried to kidnap billionaire Moira Queen, who was leading relief efforts. His airgun devastated her bodyguards, but was no defense against Batman and Green Arrow. Later, he joined the Longbow Hunters, costumed mercenaries paid millions to destroy everything Green Arrow cherished. Despite his murderous ways, Killer Moth was a coward. He was beaten by Oliver Queen's assistant Naomi Singh and her little sister Emiko.

Pre-*Flashpoint* and post-*Rebirth*, Killer Moth is a minor Batman villain, basing his MO on the Dark Knight's arsenal, while terrorizing wealthy families and organizing gangs of super-criminals into a private army. His latest recruitment drive was dismantled by Batwoman, Robin (Tim Drake), Clayface, Spoiler, and Orphan.

KILLER SHARK III

DEBUT *Blackhawk* (Vol. 1) #50 (Mar. 1952) (Killer Shark I); *Birds of Prey* (Vol. 1) #114 (Mar. 2008) (Killer Shark III)
BASE Various
HEIGHT 5ft 11in **WEIGHT** 214 lbs
EYES Blue **HAIR** Black
POWERS/ABILITIES Self-made millionaire; superb athlete; sharp teeth; customized weaponry.
ALLIES Queen Killer Shark, Killer Shark I
ENEMIES Lady Blackhawk, Birds of Prey

The man calling himself Killer Shark is the grandson of the original Killer Shark, a pirate of the Pacific Ocean. The elder Killer Shark raided ships using a variety of high tech devices to make off with his stolen loot. He was also a sworn enemy of the famous pilots called the Blackhawks, and even invented a serum that could make others do his bidding.

When his grandson inherited his mantle and arsenal, a new Killer Shark was born. He quickly tracked down and kidnapped the time-displaced Lady Blackhawk, using his grandfather's serum to change her into Lady Killer Shark. He was infatuated with his new "partner," but when Lady Blackhawk's Birds of Prey teammate Huntress came her rescue, Killer Shark attempted to force her to become his slave as well, leading to his ultimate defeat.

KILOWOG

DEBUT *Green Lantern Corps* (Vol. 1) #201 (Jun. 1986)
BASE Oa, Mogo, New Oa
HEIGHT 8ft 3in **WEIGHT** 720 lbs **EYES** Red **HAIR** None
POWERS/ABILITIES Inspirational trainer, brilliant geneticist and technologist, skilled engineer, ferocious hand-to-hand fighter employing vast bulk and strength; experienced and imaginative wielder of the light of Willpower, channeled through a standard Green Lantern power ring.
ALLIES Guy Gardner, John Stewart, Salaak, Hal Jordan, Kyle Rayner
ENEMIES Sinestro, Darkstars
AFFILIATIONS Green Lantern Corps, Rocket Red Brigade

Kilowog was a brilliant geneticist on bustling, Bolovax Vik. The psychic wrench of abandoning his species was tremendous, but Kilowog was also proud to serve the greater universe as Sector 674's Green Lantern.

When Bolovax Vik was destroyed during the *Crisis on Infinite Earths*, Kilowog saved all 16 billion Bolovaxians by converting them to energy and storing them in his power ring. He could not repeat the feat when Sinestro eradicated them all after they resettled on a new planet. With his race twice-lost, Kilowog dedicated his life to the Green Lantern Corps. His entire nature centers on being part of a greater whole and he found purpose in training new recruits, giving them the tools necessary to survive the most dangerous job in creation.

The greatest shock in his life came after discovering the Guardians of the Universe had betrayed their own principles, turning upon their Green Lanterns and attempting to eradicate Free Will with their abhorrent Third Army. Following the Guardians defeat and destruction at the hands of Sinestro, Kilowog stepped down as Corps Drill Instructor, reluctantly assuming the critical role of Protocol Officer for the now autonomous Corps. With the remaining repentant Guardians advising Corps Director John Stewart, Kilowog faced constant change: a fractious alliance of Yellow and Green Lantern Corps, deadly attacks by Controllers, war against the Kryptonian House of Zod, and even an attack from the future by last Yellow Lantern Sarko. The most telling blow came when former student Tomar Tu betrayed his principles, murdering a prisoner in custody before leading the Darkstars in a war against the guilty and executing murderers as judge, jury, and executioner.

FATHER FIGURE
Having lost his family and world twice, Kilowog was deeply invested in making sure his rookies were ready for anything.

ON THE RECORD

A lonely alien craving the tight communal affinity of Bolovaxians, Kilowog was drawn to his lost culture's closest equivalent: Communism. He began to associate with the leaders of the Soviet Union and used his alien science to complete their Rocket Red armored super-soldier program. His disappointment in discovering that everyday practice did not live up to philosophical principles quickly drove Kilowog back to his only true comrades: the Green Lantern Corps.

THE GREATER GOOD
Kilowog could not grasp why his human Green Lantern friends thought his political associations would lead to trouble.

KING SHARK

DEBUT *Superboy* (Vol. 4) #0 (Oct. 1994)
REAL NAME Nanaue
BASE Mobile
HEIGHT 7ft 2in **WEIGHT** 380 lbs
EYES Red **HAIR** None
POWERS/ABILITIES Giant shark-like humanoid possessing incredible strength.
ALLIES Mera, Aqualad
ENEMIES Aquaman, Superboy
AFFILIATIONS Suicide Squad, the Society

OUT FOR BLOOD
Killer shark's voracious appetitie makes him an unpredictable and dangerous threat—to foes and friends alike.

The Super-Villain known as King Shark is the son of Kamo, a being convinced that he was an ancient Hawaiian deity.

When government agent Amanda Waller took Kamo into custody, she also kidnapped his son, King Shark. Considered the "first child of Belle Reve," King Shark was raised in the high-security prison. As an adult, King Shark was tortured, along with other would-be members, by Amanda Waller as part of the loyalty test during her vetting process for Task Force X—a clandestine government strike force more commonly called the Suicide Squad.

Despite his ordeal, King Shark joined the Suicide Squad, and while he has on occasion eaten a team member, he proved to be an effective operative before disappearing during a mission. He later resurfaced as a loyal servant of the amphibious Queen Mera.

KNIGHT

DEBUT Knight and Squire (Cyril): *Batman* (Vol. 1) #62 (Dec. 1950–Jan. 1951); Squire (Beryl): *JLA* (Vol. 1) #26 (Feb. 1999)
REAL NAME Beryl Hutchinson (Squire, then, later, Knight)
HEIGHT 5ft 6in **WEIGHT** 131 lbs
EYES Blue **HAIR** Red
POWERS/ABILITIES Talented detective, trained acrobat, proficient in unarmed combat; martial artist, multilingual, genius-level problem-solver
AFFILIATIONS Batman Incorporated

KNIGHT RIDER
Although dedicated to defending Britain from Super-Villain threats, the latest Knight is a hi-tech champion combatting evil on a global stage.

British crime fighters Knight and Squire are a generational hero- team with their origins in World War II, when Percy Sheldrake—a boy of noble birth—became sidekick to mystic warrior Shining Knight. As an adult, Percy trained his son Cyril to be his partner. Together they tackled injustice as Knight and Squire until Percy was killed by their archenemy Springheeled Jack.

Cyril sank into depression until local lass Beryl Hutchinson helped him. He revived the family tradition with Beryl as his new Squire. They worked often with Bruce Wayne's multinational Batman Incorporated and when Cyril was killed fighting Heretic—a giant monster clone of Damian Wayne— Beryl took over the Knight's mantle. In the wake of the *Doomsday Clock* crisis, she organized Britain's disparate Super Heroes into patriotic team Knight's Inc.

KING SNAKE

DEBUT *Robin* (Vol. 1) #2 (Feb. 1991)
REAL NAME Sir Edmund Dorrance
BASE Gotham City
HEIGHT 6ft 2in **WEIGHT** 220 lbs
EYES White (Blind) **HAIR** Blond
POWERS/ABILITIES Expert martial artist; ties to the criminal underworld.
ALLIES Lynx, Bane
ENEMIES Batman, Red Robin, the Batman Family
AFFILIATIONS Kobra, Black Lantern Corps

A mercenary who traveled to island nation Santa Prisca, Sir Edmund Dorrance lost his eyesight during a covert government commando raid on his forces. Dorrance escaped, leaving behind A son, whom he'd fathered with a local rebel. The child became the Super-Villain Bane, and Edmund himself grew infamous as King Snake: ruthlessly rising up the criminal ladder to become a major gang lord.

After repeated clashes with Robin (Tim Drake), and a failed attempt to usurp leadership of global terrorist cult, Kobra, King Snake seemingly fell to his death battling Batman and Bane. However, Dorrance returned to terrorize Gotham City as a member of the undead Black Lantern Corps, and was restored to life and history following the *Rebirth* event. He was last seen battling Batman and Catwoman.

KNIGHTFALL

DEBUT *Batgirl* (Vol. 4) #10 (Aug. 2012)
REAL NAME Charise Carnes
BASE Gotham City
HEIGHT 5ft 11in **WEIGHT** 141 lbs
EYES Green **HAIR** Blond
POWERS/ABILITIES Wealthy manipulator and actor; adept martial artist; well-connected, wears discarded Azrael suit.
ALLIES Mirror, Grotesque, Gretel, James Gordon, Jr.
ENEMIES Batgirl, Birds of Prey, Batwoman
AFFILIATIONS The Outsiders, the Disgraced

The daughter of a real-estate millionaire, Charise constantly met men who liked her for daddy's money. She thought Trevor was different—and he truly was. Trevor murdered her family in front of her eyes. Instead of reporting him, Charise bided her time and plotted revenge. Sentenced for her crimes, she reemerged from Arkham Asylum as Knightfall, kidnapping and torturing Trevor and clashing with Batgirl several times. All the while, Charise exploited her past to position herself as a well-respected member of society until her ultimate defeat at the hands of Batgirl and her allies.

During the *Doomsday Clock* crisis, she used decommissioned Azrael Armor to join and work with Markovia's Outsiders Super Hero Team.

KLARION

DEBUT *The Demon* (Vol. 1) #7 (Mar. 1973)
REAL NAME Klarion Bleak
BASE New York City
HEIGHT 5ft 11in **WEIGHT** 113 lbs
EYES Black **HAIR** Black
POWERS/ABILITIES Flight; teleportation; energy projection; shapeshifting, telekinesis.
ALLIES Teekl, Beelzebub, Piper, Oblivion, Rasp
ENEMIES The Necropolitan Club, Teen Titans, Etrigan the Demon, Justice League Dark
AFFILIATIONS The Elite, Injustice League Dark, Seven Soldiers

Hailing from a magical dimension, Klarion was a student of mystical arts. When he lashed out at his teacher using magic, he realized that he couldn't return home, and he made his home on Earth. There he began to work and train at New York's Moody Museum under a mysterious woman named Piper, meeting new magical allies. Klarion clashed with the Secret Six when their teen member Black Alice began disrupting the magical community with her hex powers.

Klarian and his cat familiar Teekl are part of The Seven Soldiers, battling malign Sheeda invasions and traversing dimensions with young hero Sideways. During the reality-warping return of Perpetua and eldritch Witching War, Klarion chose evil and joined the resurgent Circle's villainous cabal Injustice League Dark to remake magic in their image.

KNOCKOUT

DEBUT *Superboy* (Vol. 4) #1 (Feb. 1994)
HEIGHT 6ft 1in **WEIGHT** 200 lbs
EYES Blue **HAIR** Red
POWERS/ABILITIES Superhuman strength and durability; regeneration.
ALLIES Scandal Savage, Rag Doll, Dubbilex
ENEMIES Female Furies, Granny Goodness, Silicon Dragons, Vandal Savage
AFFILIATIONS Female Furies, Secret Six

Knockout rejected the brutal warrior's life in Darkseid's Female Furies and fled to Earth to have fun. Working as an exotic dancer in Hawaii, she clashed repeatedly with Superboy before being recruited into the Suicide Squad. Knockout walked a fine line between hero and villain; often pushing the heroes and villains she hung out with into less and less ethical actions.

She later joined metahuman mercenaries the Secret Six where, at the request of its leader—and her latest love—Scandal Savage, Knockout, aka "Kayo," infiltrated Lex Luthor's Super-Villain group, the Society.

After a period of thrilling capers on the run with Scandal, Knockout was killed by Infinity-Man. Her soul went to Hell, but was rescued by Secret Six comrade Rag Doll, who voluntarily took her place there.

KOBRA

DEBUT *Kobra* (Vol. 1) #1 (Feb.–Mar. 1976)
REAL NAME Jeffrey Franklin Burr
BASE Tibet
HEIGHT 6ft 2in **WEIGHT** 200 lbs
EYES Black **HAIR** Bald
POWERS/ABILITIES Charismatic leader; genius-level intellect; expert in unarmed combat.
ALLIES Lady Eve
ENEMIES Katana, Checkmate, Suicide Squad, Jason Burr, Superman, Batman, Wonder Woman, Black Adam

CULT LEADER
Jeffrey Burr, leader of the powerful Kobra cult, was prepared to stop at nothing to attain world domination.

Jeffrey Burr was stolen by the ancient Kobra Cult and raised in their murderous ways. As "Naga-Naga," he went on to battle countless Super Heroes in his struggle to rule the world. Jeffrey's twin brother Jason had a regular upbringing, until government agents revealed to him that he was psychically linked to a brother he knew nothing about. The lawmen wanted to use that connection to control his brother, now called Kobra. Despite the efforts of several Super Heroes, Kobra had Jason killed before expanding his terrorist depredations. Years later, Black Adam killed Jeffrey, and the role of Kobra went to his archenemy and resurrected brother, Jason.

Following, *Convergence* and *Rebirth*, a new, King Kobra arose. Anonymous and ruthless, this new Naga Naga attempted to conquer Markovia with a serpent army. He clashed with Katana and the Suicide Squad, and was accidentally responsible for creating new Super Hero Halo. In another encounter, his servant Lady Eve almost destroyed Task Force X. Kobra later fell foul of the Creeper and Black Adam during the *Doomsday Clock* affair. A megalomaniac convinced the world is his by divine right, Kobra plays no favorites, battling heroes like Batman and using villains like Bane in his march to power. His organization was severely damaged by Leviathan's unilateral assault on covert groups, but he will inevitably rebuild.

KOMODO

DEBUT *Green Arrow* (Vol. 5) #17 (Apr. 2013)
REAL NAME Simon Lacroix
HEIGHT 5ft 10in **WEIGHT** 176 lbs
EYES Black **HAIR** Black
POWERS/ABILITIES Highly intelligent; martial artist; highly skilled in Kyudo archery.
ALLIES Mr. Kryp
ENEMIES Green Arrow, Shado, the Bear
AFFILIATIONS Outsiders, Arrow Clan, Magus

Born into abject poverty, Simon Lacroix amassed a huge personal fortune over time through sheer grit and his own innate brilliance. Working under Robert Queen, Simon shared his boss' obsession with the obscure martial cult, the Arrow Clan. He was the son Robert had always wanted, rather than the wastrel Oliver, who was an embarrassment to the Queens.

A man of overweening ambition, Lacroix then murdered Robert, adopted his illicit daughter Emiko, and trained with the bow until he became one of the world's most lethal archers. Stealing the Queen fortune through his own company, Stellmore International, Lacroix adopted the masked identity of Komodo and framed Green Arrow for murder. A confrontation ensued, and after a battle with Green Arrow, Komodo lost an eye. He was later killed by Emiko when she learned of her true parentage.

KRYPTONITE MAN

DEBUT *Action Comics* (Vol. 1) #249 (Feb. 1959)
REAL NAME Clay Ramsay
BASE Metropolis
EYES Blue **HAIR** Brown
POWERS/ABILITIES Radiation absorption and generation, superhuman strength, and flight.
ALLIES Lex Luthor, Dr. Abernathy, General Sam Lane
ENEMIES Superman, Steel
AFFILIATIONS Anti-Superman Army, K-Men

Bully and wife-beater Clay Ramsay was an early recipient of Superman's justice after the caped hero debuted in Metropolis. Tossed into Hob's Bay, the psychopath transferred all his rage onto the Man of Steel. Increasingly unstable, Ramsay tried suing Superman after his wife left him, then volunteered for Lex Luthor's Project K-Man. Luthor needed a Superman deterrent and Clay's hatred for "the alien" made him the perfect subject.

During his first treatment with stolen Kryptonite, Ramsay was accidentally given excess energy. Super-strong and radioactive, he escaped and attacked Superman, but was defeated. In custody, Clay was conscripted by General Sam Lane to be his secret anti-Superman weapon.

KRONA

DEBUT *Green Lantern* (Vol. 2) #40 (Oct. 1965)
BASE Maltus
HEIGHT 3ft 5in **WEIGHT** 62 lbs **EYES** Green **HAIR** Black
POWERS/ABILITIES Immortality; full range of psionic abilities possessed by hyper-evolved Maltusians; flight; energy manipulation and projection; mind-control; overwhelming intellect and advanced technical genius.
ALLIES Nekron
ENEMIES Guardians of the Universe, Green Lantern Corps
AFFILIATIONS Guardians of the Universe, Black Lantern Corps

Krona was the most exalted of the scientific super-beings who developed on Maltus when the universe was young. Obsessed with discovering how creation began, he ignored all warnings and built a machine that took him back to the dawn of time. The moment he glimpsed the birth of everything, his machine exploded, fracturing reality into a multiverse, and shortening the lifespan of all existence. This mishap also created the Anti-Matter Universe, unleashing evil upon all life. In response, his colleagues declared themselves Guardians of the Universe, eschewing all emotion and developing chaos-suppressing organizations to mitigate the damage Krona had caused. Krona was converted into energy and set to eternally orbit the cosmos he had despoiled. The super-Maltusians subsequently divided into squabbling factions: Zamarons, Controllers, and Guardians.

Billions of years later, Krona repeated his experiment, but was foiled by Green Lantern Hal Jordan. Returned to his energy state, the renegade then penetrated the Death Dimension and allied with Nekron, leading to the rise of Black Lanterns and *Blackest Night*. After attempting to seize the Emotional Spectrum's Light Entities in his all-consuming obsession to learn the origins of creation, Krona was executed by Jordan. His body was given to Atrocitus by Guardian Ganthet, but was subsequently stolen by the Red Lantern's son, Abysmus. The latter desecrated and consumed Krona's body to acquire the power remaining within.

KNOWLEDGE IS POWER
Krona was enslaved by his need for answers and was oblivious to the untold suffering caused by his curiosity.

KRYPTO

DEBUT *Adventure Comics* (Vol. 1) #210 (Mar. 1955)
BASE Earth
EYES Blue **HAIR** White
POWERS/ABILITIES Brave, loyal, and determined; relatively advanced intelligence; flight, super-strength, speed, endurance; all the sensory and solar-fueled enhancements of Kryptonian physiology.
ALLIES Superman, Superboy (Jon Kent), Supergirl, Superboy (Conner Kent), Robin (Damian Wayne)
ENEMIES Kryptonite Man, Xa-Du, Eradicator, Dru-Zod
AFFILIATIONS Wonder Woman, Legion of Super-Pets

A BOY AND HIS DOG
Krypto and Superboy share a common bond: both are outcasts, science-enhanced instinctive warriors, and fiercely protective of their friends and family.

With Krypton crumbling to pieces around him,

a desperate Jor-El sought refuge for his family in the Phantom Zone. When the prisoners exiled within threatened baby Kal-El, the El family's faithful dog Krypto drove off the attackers, but was dragged into the timeless dimension with them. Deprived of all other options, Jor-El entrusted the life of his son to an experimental rocketship he sent to Earth, before apparently perishing with his wife and race.
As Krypton exploded, the valiant hound—reduced to an intangible, timeless ghost—stayed close to his young charge. Despite being trapped behind imperceptible dimensional walls, Krypto loyally continued watching over Kal-El as he grew up on Earth.
Eventually, Krypto was freed and reunited with his beloved Kal-El. Supercharged by yellow solar radiation, the good boy quickly adapted to his new solid-state existence and has extended his precious family. He mixes exploratory wanderings around the world with the sacred duty of protecting his two-legged family pack, which includes youthful El clone Conner Kent, young pup Jon Kent (Superboy), his mother Lois, and cousin Kara Zor-El. After a fun adventure with other animal heroes against bad beasts, Krypto embarked on a big trip guarding Supergirl as she scoured the galaxy for the true murderers of Krypton.

TRUE LOVE
Despite all the tragedies that stemmed from Krypton's destruction, Superman's joy was boundless after finding his oldest childhood friend was still alive.

ON THE RECORD

Superman's best friend has always been his dog. A test-subject in Jor-El's rocketry experiments, canine Krypto was trapped in suspended animation n space for years, first coming to Earth when Clark Kent was still a Superboy.
For decades, the Hound of Steel split his time between Earthly adventures and roaming across time and space. Faithful unto death, the Silver Age Krypto perished saving his beloved master from Kryptonite-Man.

FRISKY BUSINESS
Superboy's elation with Krypto's reemergence in his life was always tempered by the problems the Dog of Steel's playful antics could cause.

KRYPTONIANS

DEBUT *Action Comics* (Vol. 1) #1 (Jun. 1938)
POWERS/ABILITIES On Krypton: high intelligence, dense molecular structure, cells capable of absorbing and storing certain frequencies of radiation. Under a yellow sun: super-strength, speed, flight, invulnerability, enhanced senses—all fueled by exposure to solar energy.
ENEMIES The Char, Brainiac, the Multitude

SOLAR SUPERPOWER
All Krypton's lifeforms possess a cellular structure that hyper-efficiently processes yellow solar radiation. They gain superpowers after prolonged exposure.

Krypton was a dense world circling the

red sun Rao. Despite its immense gravity, a passionate, adventurous, and intelligent humanoid race flourished there. Over millennia—filled with periodic outbreaks of destructive warfare—Kryptonians reached an impressive level of technological advancement. Much of their later civilization was based on a multi-purpose crystal mineral: Sunstone.
For a time, Kryptonians were starfaring, but as a result of increasing planetary conflicts, they eventually lost the secret of escaping the planet's potent gravity-well. They also developed cloning to a high degree, but when the mass-produced duplicates became entrenched as a slave species, the clones rose up in bloody revolt. The atrocities that followed led to cloning being outlawed and, over time, utterly detested.
Ultimately, Kryptonian culture was ended through ignorance and arrogance. The ruling Council refused to acknowledge the findings of leading scientist Jor-El when he discovered the planet's core was highly unstable and heading toward an annihilating atomic detonation.

ON THE RECORD

An iteration of Krypton seems to exist in each of the 52 universes of the Multiverse. Krypton-23's last survivor became his adopted Earth's American President Calvin Ellis, while on Earth-10 the stellar foundling crash-landed in Nazi Germany and his presence resulted in that world's surrender to global fascism.
The most radical alternate was Earth-3's evil paragon Ultraman, who gained power by consuming Kryptonite and lost strength under a yellow sun.

ACME OF CIVILIZATION
Every incarnation of Krypton had used science to create a virtual paradise; but none could modify the all-too-human failings of its citizens.

LADY SHIVA

DATA

DEBUT *Richard Dragon, Kung-Fu Fighter* (Vol. 1) #5 (Dec. 1975–Jan. 1976)
REAL NAME Sandra Wu-San
BASE Mobile
HEIGHT 5ft 8in **WEIGHT** 128 lbs **HAIR** Brown **EYES** Green
POWERS/ABILITIES Universal mastery of martial arts, including unarmed combat and a wide array of weapons.
ALLIES Richard Dragon, Orphan, the Signal
ENEMIES Rā's al Ghūl
AFFILIATIONS League of Assassins, League of Shadows, The Outsiders

MORTAL COMBAT
Lady Shiva has often been spotted in Gotham City, clashing with the Batman family on multiple occasions.

CLASSIC STORIES

Batman (Vol. 1) #509 (Jul. 1994)
After Batman is paralyzed by Bane, Lady Shiva works with him to regain not just the use of his legs, but his fighting spirit.

Batgirl (Vol. 1) #73 (Apr. 2006)
Lady Shiva apparently dies in a battle to the death with Cassandra Cain.

DEATH OF DEATHSTROKE?
Lady Shiva urged fellow martial artist Bronze Tiger to trace his old friend and drinking partner, Deathstroke—and kill him.

Mastering a number of different martial arts and weapons skills in her childhood, Lady Shiva was an expert assassin by the time she was a teenager. Batman has said she is without peer as a hand-to-hand combatant, and her skill with blades is equally superb.

Born in a small Chinese village known as a place of assassins, Sandra Wu-San suffered a childhood filled with trauma—much of which remains a mystery. She trained hard to become an exceptional martial artist to seek vengeance on those that wronged her and later became an assassin for hire. Wu-San joined the League of Assassins and became known as Lady Shiva, after the Hindu god of destruction.

Neither a conventional hero or villain, she has both fought and allied with a number of different heroes over the years, including Batman, Robin, Red Hood, and Nightwing. As an adult, she fought Dick Grayson the first time he went into the field as Robin to save Batman, defeating him easily and then advising him to get out of Batman's shadow and forge his own identity. Several years later, she battled Nightwing and realized Grayson had taken her advice. As a trainer for the League of Assassins, she taught Red Hood, Bronze Tiger, and others, and allied with the League to fight off an Untitled infiltration of their hidden base.

If Lady Shiva has a weak spot, it is her daughter, Cassandra Cain. The daughter of the assassin and original Orphan David Cain, Cassandra never knew her mother, and adopted the identity of Orphan when she chose to become a vigilante. Breaking away from Rā's al Ghūl and taking command of his elite team known as the League of Shadows, Lady Shiva visited Cassandra on a trip to destroy Gotham City. Shiva killed Gotham City's Mayor Hady and set her sights on razing the entire city in order to disrupt all the money and energy Rā's al Ghūl had put into Gotham City over the years. Cassandra and Batman opposed Shiva, but it was Rā's al Ghūl who shot and killed her.

Rā's al Ghūl resurrected Lady Shiva using the mystical, life-restoring Lazarus Pits; however, Shiva soon saw an opportunity to break away from his control again when the Super-Villain terrorist bombed a school in Metropolis. Shiva joined up with the principal of that school, Jefferson Pierce—aka Black Lightning—and his Super Hero team, The Outsiders. While her true motivation was another attempt to connect with her daughter, Shiva became more committed to defeating her old employer when Rā's destroyed the village in which she had grown up. Lady Shiva successfully helped The Outsiders to defeat Rā's al Ghūl's latest terrorist campaign, even if her lethal methods clashed with the team's own morals.

ON THE RECORD

Lady Shiva was the mother of Cassandra Cain, and challenged her daughter to a series of battles when the young woman first became Batgirl. With each duel, she taught Cassandra a little more, freeing the hero of her death wish. Eventually, Batgirl turned the tables on her mother and defeated Lady Shiva by forcing her to confront her own desire for death.

Shiva has also demonstrated surprising loyalty to former teammates who have also been enemies. When Spy Smasher seized control of the Birds of Prey, Lady Shiva came to Oracle's defense.

JADE WARRIOR
Lady Shiva was briefly allied with the Birds of Prey, adopting the name Jade Canary.

L.E.G.I.O.N.

DEBUT *L.E.G.I.O.N.* #1 (Feb. 1989)
MEMBERS/POWERS Vril Dox II (leader):
12th-level intellect **Captain Comet**: Telekinetic
Davroth Catto: Flight **Darkstar** (Lydea Mallor):
Projects negative energy **Marij'n** and **Garryn Bek**:
No superhuman abilities **Amon Hakk**: Khund
strength **Lobo**: Regenerative abilities **Zena
Moonstruk**: Light control **Stealth**: Soundwave
control **Strata**: Super-strength **Garv**: Telepath
ALLIES Green Lantern Corps, JLA, Omega Man

Formed after an alien invasion of Earth, the
Licensed Extra-Governmental Interstellar
Operatives Network (L.E.G.I.O.N.) is a heroic
peacekeeping force that protects planets
that subscribe to its services. The brilliant
Coluan, Vril Dox II (son of Brainiac), founded
L.E.G.I.O.N. after he and its original core
members escaped from a Dominator-run
"Starlag" prison camp.

On their first mission, Vril Dox and his
compatriots liberated Dox's homeworld of
Colu from the domineering grip of the ruling
computer tyrants. They then cleaned out
the riffraff from the vile planet of Cairn—the
galaxy's "drug world"—and made it their
headquarters, though they established
satellite command centers on every planet
where they mounted sustained operations.

L.E.G.I.O.N.'s rapid run of triumphs
lured several high-paying clients and
attracted new members, which led to the
membership roster remaining in constant
flux. L.E.G.I.O.N. continued its success until
Dox's super-smart, malevolent son, Lyrl,

LICENSED TO PROTECT
If you have an interplanetary crisis on
your hands, L.E.G.I.O.N. will solve it...
once they resolve their own issues.

usurped control and led the group down a
very different path. In response, several
members formed a rival team, R.E.B.E.L.S.,
to restore L.E.G.I.O.N.'s good name. Vril
Dox eventually returned as the L.E.G.I.O.N.'s
leader, just in time for the Rann-Thanagar War,
and the team has since appeared battling
alongside various Lantern Corps.

LADY BLACKHAWK

DEBUT *Blackhawk* #133 (Feb. 1959)
BASE Aerie
HEIGHT 5ft 7in **WEIGHT** 117 lbs
HAIR Black **EYES** Brown
ABILITIES Expert pilot, markswoman, and
unarmed combatant.
ALLIES Oracle
ENEMIES Court of Owls, Secret Six
AFFILIATIONS Blackhawks, Birds of Prey

The first Lady
Blackhawk, Zinda
Blake, became an
expert pilot during
World War II with the
intention of becoming
the first female
member of the
legendary Blackhawks. Soon accepted
among their number, Blake joined their
wartime exploits and fought Killer Shark.

After the reality-warping event *Zero Hour*,
Lady Blackhawk joined the Birds of Prey as a
pilot, her loyalty contingent on Oracle's role as
team leader. Another Lady Blackhawk—
Natalie Reed—served with the team from
World War II into the Cold War years.

A third, as yet unnamed Lady Blackhawk,
wearing an eye patch, appeared as part of a
Blackhawks covert-ops team. The group
shut down the mysterious Mother Machine,
averting the threat of a cyber-attack and a
global release of dangerous nanotechnology.

LADY CLAY

DEBUT *Outsiders* #21 (July 1987)
REAL NAME Sondra Fuller
BASE Gotham City
HEIGHT Variable **WEIGHT** Variable
HAIR None **EYES** Red
ABILITIES Shapeshifting; flight.
ALLIES Frankenstein, Red Phantom, Orca,
Killer Croc, Andrew Bennett, Batwoman
ENEMIES Melmoth
AFFILIATIONS Kobra Cult

Sondra Fuller used to
work for the Kobra
Cult, where she was
transformed into a
being of living clay
with the intention of
making her into a
living weapon. After
leaving Kobra, Sondra, also known as Lady
Clay, spent her days trying to achieve
perfection, to be the epitome of the ideal
human. She could create people using parts
of her clay body, and send them out into the
world to have life experiences to bring her
closer to perfection. When one of her
"people" was killed in a ritual to raise the
demonic Melmoth, Lady Clay had lost a
piece of her soul. She agreed to team up
with Frankenstein and other supernatural
beings of Gotham City's Monstertown to
take down Melmoth.

LANG, LANA

DEBUT *Superboy* (Vol. 1) #10 (Sep.–Oct. 1950)
BASE Metropolis, Smallville
HEIGHT 5ft 7in **WEIGHT** 127 lbs **HAIR** Red **EYES** Blue
POWERS/ABILITIES No superpowers, but a fiercely loyal friend with an
unbreakable will; brilliant engineer and journalist.
FORMER POWERS Solar energy conversion affording electrokinesis, EM
spectrum manipulation and blasts, superhuman strength, invulnerability and flight.
ALLIES Superman, John Henry Irons, Natasha Irons
ENEMIES Lex Luthor

Lana Lang was a close childhood friend of Clark Kent's and one of the
first people on Earth to learn of his extraordinary abilities. As teenagers, they were almost
more than friends, but everything changed at a dance when Clark received the news that
his parents had died in a car accident.

Lana supported Clark's dream of becoming a reporter, and left Smallville herself,
eventually becoming a brilliant electrical engineer. Not one to hide from danger, she once
restarted a doomed tanker's engines in time to avert a deadly collision (with a little help from
Superman), and later she met him again when a drilling project released a monster from deep
underground—leading to an adventure in Imperial Subterranea.

Back in Smallville, Lana helped Wonder Woman work out
how Superman was affected by his battle with Doomsday, and
uncovered Brainiac's plot to use the brains of comatose humans
—including those of her parents—to create a super network.

After the Man of Steel gave his life to save his adopted planet,
Lana Lang turned up at his memorial in Metropolis to keep a
promise to Clark: To bury him with his parents in Smallville.
She was interrupted by the alternate Earth Clark Kent, who had
a plan to resurrect Superman. When that failed, he helped Lana
re-bury her friend's remains. The energies released in that event
turned her into a literal Superwoman.

She began a relationship with inventor and former Super Hero
John Henry Irons (Steel), and eventually returned to human status,
moving on to a career in broadcast journalism.

WOMAN AND SUPERWOMAN
Empowered by the explosive
demise of the post-*Flashpoint*
Superman, Lana and the
post-*Flashpoint* Lois Lane
became twin heroes sharing the
name Superwoman. Lois soon
died, leaving Lana to battle a
host of uncanny threats,
including Ultrawoman, the
Bizaress Army, and Skyhook.

LASTING LEGACY
Lana guided the alternate Earth
Clark Kent to Superman's Fortress
of Solitude hoping he could find a
Regeneration Matrix to revive the
Man of Steel. Sadly, the artifact
didn't exist in this Earth's Fortress.

ON THE RECORD

An earlier story about Lana
Lang had her marrying Pete
Ross, who became Vice
President in Lex Luthor's White
House (and later President when
Luthor was forced from
office). Feeling stifled in
her role as First Lady—
and also still bearing
conflicted feelings about
Clark—she divorced Pete and
restarted her career. Later,
Lana became the
uncompromising CEO of
LexCorp, and survived an
alien attempt to turn her into a
new Insect Queen, a nod to her
insectoid transformations in
both her Silver and Bronze Age
incarnations (pictured right).

CENTER OF ATTENTION
Superman was often the subject of
intense professional and personal
rivalry between Lana Lang and the
equally ambitious Lois Lane.

LANE, LOIS

DATA

DEBUT *Action Comics* (Vol. 1) #1 (Jun. 1938)
BASE Metropolis
HEIGHT 5ft 6in **WEIGHT** 130 lbs
EYES Blue **HAIR** Black
POWERS/ABILITIES Insatiable curiosity; excellent deductive
reasoning and detective skills; militarily trained in unarmed combat;
maintains contacts and informants all over the world.
ALLIES Superman, Superboy (Jon Kent), Jimmy Olsen, Perry White,
Batman, Catwoman, The Question II (Renee Montoya), Jessica
Midnight
ENEMIES Brainiac, Lex Luthor, Leviathan
AFFILIATIONS *The Daily Planet*

Fiercely independent, relentlessly inquisitive, and possessing an unflinching sense of right and wrong, Lois Lane is one of the world's most successful and influential investigative reporters. As she perfected her craft under legendary editor-in-chief Perry White at Metropolis's prestigious *The Daily Planet*, Lois wrote innumerable high-profile stories, winning the envy and respect of her coworkers. Already a star reporter, her journalistic immortality was assured when—together with photographer Jimmy Olsen—Lois secured the first interviews with and official pictures of the mystery news sensation known as Superman.

AT A GLANCE...

Boss lady
As *The Daily Planet*'s star reporter, Lois thrives under pressure, often working on more than one story at once. She's learned from Perry White that journalistic integrity is paramount, even if she doesn't particularly consider spellchecking a part of her job. When Lois walks into *The Daily Planet*'s bullpen, all eyes are on her.

Best Kept Secret
Before Clark Kent came forward and announced his double life as Superman, Lois was charged with keeping her husband's secret to herself, even though she knew she was sitting on one of the greatest newspaper stories in the history of the medium.

Lois Lane was raised on US military bases around the world; an army brat constantly on the move as her soldier father, Sam Lane, rapidly advanced to the position of General. She is extremely protective of her younger sister Lucy, even if the sisters haven't been as close as Lois would like them to be.

Sam Lane pushed Lois to excel in physical activities. He trained her in unarmed combat, small-arms techniques, and ensured she became a qualified pilot. Consequently, Lois grew up with a potent sense of self-reliance and was always hungry to know all the answers: something which grew increasingly difficult as her father was regularly promoted into ever-higher-security positions.

As she pursued a job in journalism at Metropolis' *The Daily Planet*, Lois soon met Clark Kent, a bumbling fellow reporter. Despite herself, she found that she admired his genuine warmth and fellow feeling for the

FACE THE PRESS
Lois could be deceptive, insistent, sympathetic, and incisive: in order to extract the truth from the most reticent interviewee.

weak and the downtrodden. Lois respected Clark's incisive mind and his hunger for the truth, but she often had a feeling that there was something he was keeping from her. Already a known commodity in the world of journalism, Lois became a household name when Superman first appeared in Metropolis and she nailed the scoop, giving the hero his famous name. Along with Clark Kent, Lois chronicled the majority of Superman's adventures, thrilling Planet readers and helping inflate the newspaper's subscription numbers.

Perhaps because they worked so closely together as friendly rivals, Lois and Clark eventually fell in love. Clark proposed, and also revealed his double life as Superman to her. The couple stayed together through triumph and defeat, including Superman's temporary death at the hands of the monster Doomsday. They eventually married and moved to California for a short time to give their newborn son, Jonathan Kent, a quieter life.

Lois and Clark soon moved back to Metropolis, and Lois returned to her fast-paced life as a reporter. Things became more complicated, however, when she became the subject of news stories as well. She and Superman had been caught on camera while locked in a kiss, and rumors began to circulate that she had been cheating on her husband. While Lois seem unfazed by the cruel judgment that greeted her

CLASSIC STORIES

Superman's Girlfriend Lois Lane
(Vol. 1) #15 (Feb. 1960) All Lois's dreams seemingly come true when Kryptonian weds Earthling in "The Super-Family of Steel!" However, the happy ending was actually for doppelgängers Sylvia DeWitt and Van-Zee of Kandor.

Superman's Girlfriend Lois Lane
(Vol. 1) #70 (Nov. 1966) In a clever, fun story, Lois is mesmerized into becoming Catwoman while the real villainess magically transforms Superman into her cat.

Superman's Girlfriend Lois Lane
(Vol. 1) #93 (Jul. 1969) Superman's camaraderie with Wonder Woman—now a mortal adventurer—triggers insecurities that Lois must overcome to save the heroine's life.

Superman's Girlfriend Lois Lane
(Vol. 1) #111 (Jul. 1971) Lois first encounters Darkseid's secret invasion of Earth after being attacked by a tiny Justice League from the villain's "Evil Factory."

Oh, little sister
Lois's sister withered rather than blossomed under Sam Lane's parentage. A wild, rebellious kid, she grew up troubled and aimless. However, no matter how bad things were, Lucy always knew Lois would be there to pick up the pieces and clean up her messes.

SINS OF THE FATHER
One of the most consistent problems in Lois's life was her strained relationship with her father. Not only did she hate General Sam Lane's smug self-assurance and lifelong habit of keeping secrets—from the general public and especially from her—but their diametrically opposed attitudes regarding Superman frequently set them at odds. Lois couldn't help but take her father's hatred of the Man of Steel personally. When Sam Lane was killed during the espionage coup called Event Leviathan, Lois was overwhelmed with conflicting emotions.

FATHER OF THE BRIDE
Before Sam Lane was killed, Lois had told him the truth about Superman. While he reacted badly at first, Sam said he would do his best to try and give Clark the benefit of the doubt.

A NEW PERSPECTIVE
Lois went on the television show *The Perspective* to share her knowledge about multiple worlds and splintered reality.

wherever she went, those problems eventually went away when Superman revealed his double identity to the world.

Always on top of the news as it happens, Lois has created a close working relationship with Renee Montoya, the second vigilante to adopt the name of the Question. Renee was just one of the detectives Lois teamed with when investigating the threat of the mysterious organization called Leviathan, a group that had been systematically wiping out the world's espionage agencies. While it was soon discovered that former hero Mark Shaw was behind Leviathan, the truth didn't come to light until after Lois's own father died amidst the chaos of the hostile takeover.

PAST LIVES

As outside influences like the powerful Dr. Manhattan continue to alter and change the Multiverse, its residents are changed and altered along with it. Unlike most people, Lois has memories of a past version of herself, and worked with The Question II (Renee Montoya) and ex-spy Jessica Midnight to bring those facts to light.

Lois also created the Unity Project, an organization that helped people who remember divergent timelines deal with the trauma that their memories caused them in their daily lives.

REBIRTH

THE PRICE OF POWER

Before Superman and his younger other half were merged and his continuity streamlined, there were two Lois Lanes active on Earth-0. The younger Superman died, and some of his energy was absorbed by the corresponding Lois. She spent some time as Superwoman before the energy proved too much for her, and she joined her reality's Clark in death.

"This is why I was a prize-winning reporter while you were still baling hay."

LOIS LANE

ON THE RECORD

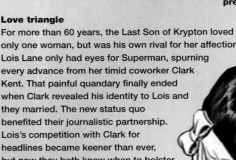

Lois Lane was arguably the first major recurring female character of the DC universe, debuting in 1938 in the original Superman story in *Action Comics* #1. An ambitious, glamorous, scoop-hungry reporter, Lois was prepared to ditch Clark in the middle of a hard-earned date when he wouldn't stand up for her to a brute trying to cut in on their dance. Lois proved she could handle herself when she slapped the cad, but Superman had to step in later for the first of many saves.

Hold the front page

After months being the Man of Steel's foil and romantic interest, Lois won her own solo feature in *Superman* #28 (May-June 1944). Light-hearted, action-packed, and comedic, these short tales usually depicted her getting into and out of scrapes without any superpowered backup. Following the *Crisis on Infinite Earths* storyline, Lois took that independence a step further. Sophisticated, globally renowned and seemingly infallible, she consorted with kings, presidents, and billionaires who were generally terrified that she would ferret out their darkest secrets.

SOUL-SISTER
When comics started to become more socially relevant, the new go-getting Lois would do anything to get to the heart of a story. However, no journalist ever went as deeply undercover as Lois, when, with a little help from Superman's Plastimold machine, she transformed herself into an African-American woman to fully investigate racial prejudice in her city.

Love triangle

For more than 60 years, the Last Son of Krypton loved only one woman, but was his own rival for her affections. Lois Lane only had eyes for Superman, spurning every advance from her timid coworker Clark Kent. That painful quandary finally ended when Clark revealed his identity to Lois and they married. The new status quo benefited their journalistic partnership. Lois's competition with Clark for headlines became keener than ever, but now they both knew when to bolster the power of the press with a helping hand from Superman.

PAGING MRS. SUPERMAN
Lois and Clark's wedding was not the end of their love story, only the beginning...

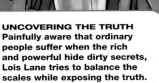

UNCOVERING THE TRUTH
Painfully aware that ordinary people suffer when the rich and powerful hide dirty secrets, Lois Lane tries to balance the scales while exposing the truth.

ALIEN AGENDA
Though not one of Brainiac's original Twenty, Lois proved the most effective. Her psionic powers briefly made her a match for Superman, until her resolutely independent streak rejected the transformation.

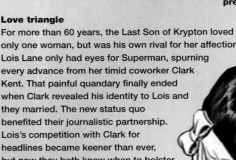

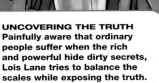

LARFLEEZE

DEBUT *DC Universe* (Vol. 1) #0 **(Jun. 2008)**
BASE Larfleezia, Okaara
EYES White **HAIR** Orange
POWERS/ABILITIES Sole wielder of the Emotional Spectrum's orange light of Avarice, which offers immortality, flight, force-field protection, light constructs and animation; magic absorption; "hears" objects and people begging to be owned, then steals the personalities of those he kills and resurrects them as light-construct entities.
ENEMIES Guardians of the Universe, Green Lantern Corps, Invictus, Sena the Wanderer
AFFILIATIONS Orange Lantern Corps, New Guardians, Pulsar Stargrave, G'Nort

LIGHT'S OUT
For billions of years, Larfleeze obsessively ensured that nothing threatened his right to take whatever he wanted whenever he saw it.

Larfleeze, also known as Agent Orange, is the sole wielder of the orange light of Avarice. The most self-destructive color of the universe's Emotional Spectrum, it precludes sharing and those it illuminates will fight for what they want until only one remains. Its power infects the mind and effectively owns its possessor.

The embodiment of Avarice is Ophidian, who lives inside the battery and causes Larfleeze to hunger voraciously for everything he sees. Over billions of years, Agent Orange has indiscriminately turned his homeworld into a vast planetary hoard of junk, treasure, and corpses. He is the only Orange Lantern in the universe, but this incalculable, unshared power allows him to store the souls of every creature he has killed and resurrect them as semi-sentient light-constructs. To protect his most prized possession, the immensely long-lived Larfleeze has absorbed his Orange Lantern, becoming a living power battery. His unique oath reflects his philosophy:

"What's mine is mine
and mine and mine,
And mine, and mine, and mine!
Not yours!"

ON THE RECORD

Billions of years ago, thieves stole the fear entity Parallax from the planet Maltus. Fleeing the Guardians' robotic Manhunters, the bandits followed a map created by renegade Krona to the planet Okaara in the Vega system, where they found the orange power battery of Avarice. They squabbled over it until only Larfleeze remained.

Unable to defeat Larfleeze, the Guardians bargained with him, promising him immunity and total autonomy of the Vega system in return for Parallax.

COLLECTOR MANIA
The things Larfleeze craves most are the rings and batteries belonging to the other Lanterns Corps.

LASHINA

DEBUT *Mister Miracle* (Vol. 1) #6 **(Jan.–Feb. 1972)**
BASE Apokolips
HEIGHT 6ft 6in **WEIGHT** 225 lbs
EYES Blue **HAIR** Black
POWERS/ABILITIES Superhuman strength and durability; devastating skill with razor-sharp, flexible steel bands and straps; hands-on familiarity with all forms of weapons.
ALLIES Amanda Waller, Big Barda
ENEMIES Granny Goodness, Bernadeth, Wonder Woman, Steve Trevor
AFFILIATIONS Female Furies, Suicide Squad, Dark Side Club

WARRIOR WOMAN
As one of Granny Goodness' most gifted Female Furies, Lashina knew the value of trusted comrades *and* when to sacrifice them.

One of the deadliest warriors to graduate from Granny Goodness' hellish Apokolips orphanage, Lashina's incalculable military value is confirmed by the number of times Darkseid resurrected her. Fast, strong, and calculating, she served as Big Barda's second-in-command in superpowered shock trooper unit the Female Furies. When Barda defected to Earth with Mister Miracle, Lashina led the team who was ordered to return the traitor to Apokolips. Instead, the Furies stayed on Earth for months, reveling in the primitive world's freedoms. Ultimately, the Furies grew bored and returned, prepared to face Apokoliptian punishment for going AWOL.

Eventually Lashina was appointed team leader—to the dismay of rival Fury, Bernadeth—and dispatched to Earth in order to retrieve captured Apokoliptian demagogue Glorious Godfrey. Seizing her moment, Bernadeth struck, wounding Lashina and leaving her for dead. The plotter died for her betrayal when Lashina returned as Duchess, leading the ferocious metahumans of the Suicide Squad in a counterattack on Apokolips.

Lashina led the Furies when Darkseid and his daughter Grail clashed with Zeus, Wonder Woman, and the Amazons. She was temporarily captured, but quickly returned to her master.

LEAGUE OF ASSASSINS

DEBUT *Strange Adventures* (Vol. 1) #215 **(Dec. 1968)**
BASE 'Eth Alth'eban
POWERS/ABILITIES Trained in multifarious aspects of murder and assassination, from hand-to-hand combat to expertise in all manner of exotic weaponry.
ALLIES Leviathan
ENEMIES Batman, Red Robin, Nightwing, Batman Incorporated
AFFILIATIONS Rā's al Ghūl, Doctor Darrk, the Sensei, Demon Fang

The League of Assassins—also known as the League or Society of Shadows—is an ancient secret organization created by the immortal Rā's al Ghūl to further his plans to destroy decadent civilizations and create an ordered world under his rule.

For centuries, the League has sold its services—singly, through teams of agents, or as a whole—to the great and powerful of many nations. This allowed it to fund its own agenda and to gain clandestine political advantage. It is also the greatest teacher of the combat arts in history. Responsible for the training of numerous warriors and villains, its students also include heroes such as Damian Wayne, Red Robin, Red Hood, and Batgirl/Black Bat.

In recent decades, the Society has suffered from continual internecine conflict, as deputies appointed by Rā's al Ghūl overstepped their bounds or sought to seize complete control. This resulted in a number of splinter groups of assassins becoming competition and hindrances to the League. Another major stumbling block has been the loss of their cloak of anonymity, as the efforts of an increasing number of Super Heroes have successfully brought the Society's hidden efforts out of the shadows.

KILLER ELITE
Whether through blade, bullet, missile, toxin, empty hand, or magic, for centuries the aim of the League of Assassins never faltered or failed.

ON THE RECORD

The League was revealed as a family business after Rā's al Ghūl died. His daughters Talia and Nyssa inherited control, but a schism saw one faction trying to resurrect their master: seeking to implant Rā's' spirit in Talia and Batman's son Damian. Another group pledged allegiance to the Sensei; the assassin-teacher who had coordinated the global murder enterprise for centuries. Revealed as Rā's' father, he ruthlessly cemented his control in a campaign the Dark Knight only barely thwarted.

THE ART OF DEATH
With Rā's gone, the Sensei believed nothing could hinder his ambitions, but found Batman to be even more relentless and formidable than his diabolical offspring.

LEGION OF DOOM

DEBUT *Justice League Vol. 4* #1 **(Aug. 2018)**
BASE Hall of Doom
MEMBERS/POWERS Sinestro: Intergalactic villain and former member of the Green Lantern Corps turned evil; **The Cheetah**: Enhanced senses, genius intellect, cheetah physiology including speed and claws; **Brainiac**: Genius intellect, super-strength, stamina and speed, telepathy; **The Turtle**: Super-slow villain with the power to absorb speed and slow interia; **The Joker**: Deranged genius, rapid healing; **Black Manta**: Skilled in combat, wears suit enabling him to survive underwater
ALLIES Perpetua, the Batman Who Laughs
ENEMIES Justice League   **AFFILIATIONS** None

FORCES OF EVIL
The Legion of Doom originally comprised just a few key members, but Lex Luthor later filled its ranks with a throng of villains who would help Perpetua's evil message to spread throughout the Earth.

Lex Luthor assembled the Legion of Doom to take advantage of the coming of the Totality, energy released from the Source Wall at the edge of the Multiverse. Luthor discovered that he could use the seven powers of the Multiverse to free the ancient goddess Perpetua and make himself her right-hand man, gaining supremacy over nearly all other beings in existence—including Superman and the Justice League.

Luthor chose the members of the Legion of Doom carefully, with each of them having a special reason to wish to access one of the seven energies of the Multiverse. One was a mere baby—The Turtle—a scientist reborn with a connection to the Still Force, the opposite of the Speed Force. Sinestro was given access to the Invisible Spectrum, a secret force of negative emotional energy that made him more powerful than ever. The Cheetah was empowered with the Tear of Extinction, making her able to kill gods with her claws. Black Manta was given the Life Force from Poseidon's trident, but he and The Joker would later leave the team, to be replaced by a resurrected Brainiac.

The addition of Brainiac was key to finally freeing Perpetua. The Legion of Doom had apparently triumphed, but there was a nasty shock in store. Unbeknown even to Lex, Perpetua had planned all along to use the rest of the Legion as mere repositories for the hidden energies of creation, transferring them all to Luthor to make him far more powerful.

RECRUITMENT DRIVE
Lex Luthor assembled a plethora of Super-Villains to fight the Justice/Doom War.

LEGION OF SUPER-HEROES

DATA

DEBUT *Adventure Comics* (Vol. 1) #247 (Apr. 1958)
BASE 31st-Century New Metropolis
NOTABLE MEMBERS/POWERS
BLOK Silicon-based living mineral, super-strength, durability.
BOUNCING BOY (CHUCK TAINE) Ability to inflate and bounce.
BRAINIAC 5 (QUERL DOX) 12th-level super-intellect.
CHAMELEON BOY (REEP DAGGLE) Shape-shifting.
CHEMICAL KID (HADRU JAMIK) Ability to alter chemical reactions.
COLOSSAL BOY (GIM ALLON) Can shrink from large form to human size.
COMPUTO Sentient computer program controlling New Metropolis.
COSMIC BOY (ROKK KRINN) Generation of magnetic fields.
DAWNSTAR (DAWNSTAR GR'ELL) Long-range tracking abilities.
DOCTOR FATE Energy projection and spell casting.
DREAM GIRL (NURA NAL) Dream interpretation to foretell the future.
ELEMENT LAD (JAN ARRAH) Transmutation of elements.
FERRO LAD (ANDREW NOLAN) Can turn body into hardest substance in the galaxy.
GOLD LANTERN Energy constructs and projection.
INVISIBLE KID (JACQUES FOCART) Bends light to go unseen.
TRIPLICATE GIRL (LUORNU DURGO) Can split into multiple bodies.
LIGHTNING LAD (GARTH RANZZ) Generation of electricity.
LIGHTNING LASS (AYLA RANZZ) Generation of electricity.
MON-EL (LAR GAND) Super-strength, flight, invulnerability.
MONSTER BOY (ARUNE) Ability to change into a variety of monsters.
PHANTOM GIRL (TINYA WAZZO) Ability to phase through solids.
PRINCESS PROJECTRA (PRINCESS WILIMENA MORGANA DAERGINA ANNAXANDRA PROJECTRA VELORYA VAUXHALL) Projects illusions.
SATURN GIRL (IMRA ARDEEN) Extremely powerful telepath.
SHADOW LASS (TASMIA MALLOR) Generation of darkness.
SHRINKING VIOLET (SALU DIGBY) Size reduction.
STAR BOY (THOM KALLOR) Can increase objects' weight/mass.
SUN BOY (DIRK MORGNA) Electromagnetic radiation.
SUPERBOY (JON KENT) Kryptonian powers including superhuman strength, speed, flight, and heat vision.
ULTRA BOY (JO NAH) Superhuman strength, flight, super-speed.
WHITE WITCH (MYSA NAL) Arsenal of magic spells.
WILDFIRE (DRAKE BURROUGHS) Human energy release generator.
ALLIES Thorn (Rose Forrest), R.J. Brande, Science Police
ENEMIES Mordru, Crav, the General Nah
AFFILIATIONS United Planets

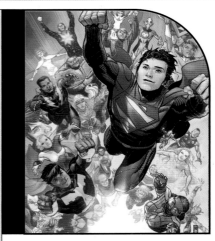

The 31st Century is a world where superpowered teenagers from all over the United Planets have gathered together, inspired by Superman, to fight evil on New Earth and across the galaxy. It exists after the future time of Batman Beyond, after the Great Disaster and the world of Kamandi, after the future of Booster Gold and that of O.M.A.C.

The Legion of Super-Heroes got their start when Rokk Krinn, a magnetically-charged fighter from the planet Braal, Imra Ardeen, a telepathic rebel from the moon Titan, and Garth Ranzz, a lightning-powered political activist from Ranzz, were summoned by the president of the United Planets, R.J. Brande, to form a Young United Planets organization. While meeting with Brande, these three young heroes fought off an invading force of alien Horraz. Inspired by Super Heroes of the 21st century, Brande decided that these three exceptional youths should be the founding members of a team of galactic defenders called the Legion of Super-Heroes.

Setting up shop in New Metropolis on New Earth, the Legion's ranks quickly increased, even adding Brande's own son, Chameleon Boy, to their number. But there was one member the team had their eye on who would be a little more difficult to recruit.

Back in the 21st century, Superboy was looking to find a place for himself in the world. As the son of Superman, he had fought by his father's side in the present day, and often teamed up with his best friend Robin (Damian Wayne). However, he had not been admitted into the Teen Titans, and after many years away in space (which seemed like only three weeks to the people on Earth due to Superboy traveling through a black hole), he no longer felt he had a place to belong on Earth.

So when the Legion of Super-Heroes traveled to the past to be a part of the first-ever Unity Day—a major holiday in their future world—and offered Superboy membership in their group, Jon accepted, happy to have renewed purpose in life.

Perplexed and amazed by the future of New Earth, its domed cities, and its lack of oceans, Superboy joined the team just as Ultra Boy and a team of Legionnaires underwent a mission on Planet Gotham. They bested the sorcerer Mordru and retrieved an ancient artifact that happened to be from Jon's time period: Aquaman's trident. The alien Horraz pirates followed Ultra Boy home, forcing Superboy to jump into the fray to help battle this invading force. When Superboy held Aquaman's trident, the Horraz gang (and the Legionnaires) were caught in a flood of water, emanating from the trident itself.

Superboy soon met Rose Forrest, Official Legion Liaison to the United Planets, and was

AT A GLANCE...

Flight ring
The flight ring is the symbol of membership in the Legion of Super-Heroes and enables the wearer to fly in any environment. Made from the artificial element Valorium, which has anti-gravity properties, the ring is thought-activated and engraved with a signature "L."

CLASSIC STORIES

Adventure Comics (Vol. 1) #352-353 (Jan.-Feb. 1967)
A short-handed Legion recruits five of the universe's greatest villains to help save Earth from a Sun-Eater. The plan succeeds at the cost of Ferro Lad's life, but results in the villainous quintet forming the Fatal Five.

Legion of Super-Heroes (Vol. 2) #287, 290-294 (May, Aug.-Dec. 1982) Entire worlds are devastated by shadowy agents of a Great Darkness as the Legion battles ancient heroes and villains who are gathering artifacts to restore the ultimate evil: Darkseid.

Final Crisis: Legion of 3 Worlds (Vol. 1) #1-5 (Oct. 2008-Sep. 2009) Reality is ripped apart and rewritten as three iterations from separate reboots are amalgamated and incorporated into the Legion of Prime Earth.

NEW EARTH
Earth in the 31st Century has changed drastically after many cataclysms, wars, and restructuring. It is now a series of domes connected to a planetary core. On one of those domes is New Metropolis. The entire city is the headquarters of the Legion of Super-Heroes. The oceans of the planet have since been restored, thanks to the Legion's use of Aquaman's powerful trident.

ROBIN

While touring Legion headquarters, Superboy learned of Planet Gotham, the galaxy's first fully made artificial planet, one constructed by Quayne-Galactic as a tribute to the original Gotham City, complete with its own Blüdhaven sewer system. Unable to contain his youthful excitement, Jon traveled through time to bring Robin (Damian Wayne) to the future. The Legion quickly nixed this idea, returning Robin to the present day and wiping his memories of New Metropolis.

ON THE RECORD

The Legion is probably the most rebooted Super Hero team of all time, although initially not the most serious. On their debut, Saturn Girl, Cosmic Boy, and Lightning Lad traveled into the past and invited Superboy to join, only to reject him as part of a prank. His stoic acceptance of their judgment won him a place on the team.

Unstoppable

After several guest appearances, the Legion became a regular feature in *Adventure Comics* #300 in 1962, beginning a series of quirky futuristic adventures with Superboy as a regular guest star and amazed observer of life in the future. The team was so ahead of the times that its members elected a female—Saturn Girl—as their new leader in 1963!

Having saved the United Planets from the Fatal Five, the members of the Legion were rewarded for their valor with a hugely impressive new headquarters complex. It was payment from the grateful governments of many worlds and confirmed the Legion's vital role in intergalactic peacekeeping. However, during construction, a hidden coalition of belligerent races attacked Earth in overwhelming numbers. They were only defeated by use of a reality-warping Miracle Machine the Legion had been given by the Oan splinter group known as the Controllers.

TIME AFTER TIME
With Superman's help, the Legion foiled a supremacist plan to rewrite history: eventually reestablishing a tolerant, civilized future for Earth.

MIRACLE CITADEL
After constructing the new Legion Plaza, the Miracle Machine was sealed away.

"Long live the Legion!"

DAWNSTAR

LEGIONNAIRE ROLL CALL
1 Cosmic Boy
2 Element Lad
3 Lightning Lass
4 Ultra Boy
5 Wildfire
6 Matter-Eater Lad
7 Timber Wolf
8 Dream Girl
9 Mon-El
10 Saturn Girl
11 Star Boy
12 Shrinking Violet
13 Superboy
14 Brainiac 5
15 Phantom Girl
16 Lightning Lad
17 Triplicate Girl
18 Dawnstar
19 Invisible Kid (he's invisible)
20 Chemical King
21 Shadow Lass
22 Doctor Fate
23 Sun Boy
24 Gold Lantern
25 White Witch
26 Bouncing Boy
27 Princess Projectra
28 Karate Kid
29 Chameleon Boy
30 Blok
31 Colossal Boy
32 Monster Boy

shown around the Legion campus, including Heaven, their all-purpose consumption hall. He viewed an orientation program via a "memexe," but was soon thrust into action again to battle not just the Horraz pirates, but also Crav, the General Nah, the father of Legionnaire Ultra Boy and the highest-ranking officer of the United Planets. Crav wanted Aquaman's trident for himself, but in the resulting battle, Earth was showered in the trident's waters, effectively restoring the oceans lost to New Earth years ago.

With the United Planets' continued approval and Superboy as one of their members, the Legion of Super-Heroes is determined to create a new golden age of heroes in the 31st Century.

LEGION OF SUBSTITUTE HEROES

DEBUT *Adventure Comics* (Vol. 1) #306 (Mar. 1963)
BASE 31st-century Metropolis
NOTABLE MEMBERS Antennae Boy, Chlorophyll Kid, Color Kid, Double Header, Dream Girl, Fire Lad, Infectious Lass, Night Girl, Polar Boy, Porcupine Pete, Rainbow Girl, Star Boy, Stone Boy
ENEMIES Ambush Bug, Plant Men, Captain Freeze
AFFILIATIONS Legion of Super-Heroes, Science Police

Not every applicant is deemed suitable for membership in the Legion of Super-Heroes—even if they have superpowers and the best intentions. Pre-*Flashpoint*, the Substitutes were all originally rejected because they were considered a liability to others or a danger to themselves, but came together in a support group under Polar Boy and Night Girl to prove the Legionnaires mistaken.

Always working outside the spotlight, the Substitutes performed many valiant deeds, slowly gaining the official Legion's respect. They welcomed former Legionnaires Dream Girl and Star Boy when they lost their places on the lead team. Their egalitarian attitude meant that eventually the squad became heavy with true no-hopers like Antennae Boy and Double Header, and became something of a joke.

Eventually, Polar Boy and Night Girl's inclusivity succeeded, and after they advanced to the big leagues, the Subs continued nurturing lesser lights and

AGAINST ALL ODDS
Whenever all hope seemed lost, the Substitute Legion always proved that ingenuity, guts, and determination were superior to any superpower.

encouraging them to shine. After a series of reality revisions, The Legion of Super-Heroes has been revitalized on the same inclusive lines, and it is uncertain if the Substitute division still exists.

LEGION OF SUPER-PETS

DEBUT *Adventure Comics* (Vol. 1) #293 (Feb. 1962)
BASE 21st-century Metropolis; 31st-century Metropolis
FUTURE MEMBERS Krypto, Beppo, Streaky, Comet, Proty II (31st century)
CONTEMPORARY MEMBERS Krypto, Titus the Bat-Hound, Streaky, Flexi the Plastic-Bird, Bat-Cow, Detective Chimp, Clay Critter (21st century)
ALLIES Superman, Superboy, Supergirl, Jimmy Olsen, Chameleon Boy, Saturn Girl
ENEMIES Brain-Globes of Rambat, Rikkor Rost, the people of Than
AFFILIATIONS Legion of Super-Heroes, Legion of Substitute Heroes.

In a kinder, gentler Possible Future, the Legion of Super-Pets formed out of desperate necessity. When planetary plunderers the Brain-Globes of Rambat attempted to steal Earth, neither Superboy nor the Legion of Super-Heroes could withstand their psionic domination. This was not the case for the valiant animal companions of the Boy of Steel or his cousin Supergirl. Using a time-bubble, the Legionnaires gathered Kryptonian survivors Krypto and Beppo the Super-Monkey, plus Earthborn pets Streaky the Super-Cat and Comet the Super-Horse, to route the marauders. Later, they inducted Chameleon Boy's telepathic pet Proty II into their ranks.

The time-traveling pets were formally invested as a branch of the Legion of

WHO'S A GOOD BOY?
Although plagued by internal dissent, the Super-Pets could put aside their obvious differences to save the innocent and get the job done.

Super-Heroes. Although convening sporadically, they were always ready to lend a paw or hoof to save the world and protect those weaker than themselves.

It was recently revealed that this Legion had its true beginnings in the 21st century, where Krypto and Streaky carried out two official cases with animal allies Detective Chimp, Titus the Bat-Hound, Plastic-Bird Flexi, Bat-Cow and Clay Critter: one painfully secret, and a second more public, stopping an alien stealing beloved animal companions.

LEMARIS, LORI

DEBUT *Superman* (Vol. 1) #129 (May 1959)
REAL NAME Lori Lemaris
BASE Atlantis
EYES Blue **HAIR** Brown
HEIGHT 5ft 9in **WEIGHT** 145 lbs
POWERS/ABILITIES Telepathic communication; can survive on land or above water; tail transforms into legs on land.
ALLIES Superman
ENEMIES Advance Man, Ronal

Before he adopted his Superman alter ego, college student Clark Kent dated Lori Lemaris. She was confined to a wheelchair and only revealed to Clark the reason why: She was a mermaid from sub-aquatic city Tritonis and the chair allowed her to hide her tail. When she was injured Superman returned her to Tritonis where dashing researcher Ronal healed her with the magical Black Staff, which reshaped flesh. Lori and Ronal married, but he was corrupted by the Staff. He attacked Lori and was turned to stone after Superman shattered the staff's gem. Despite some tension, Lori was bridesmaid at Lois and Clark's wedding. She also had a brief career as a hero, taking on villainous cosmic herald Advance Man.

Post *Rebirth*, an alternate-reality romance saw young navy cadet Clark Kent abandon his post to pursue a beguiling mermaid, battling Sea God King Poseidon to win his daughter.

Leviathan was a mysterious criminal organization that infiltrated and corrupted Gotham City. Led by a slender figure in a mask and her monstrous bodyguard, Leviathan's gangs of animal-masked goons eliminated rival gangsters and spread terror. Batman, Robin (Damian Wayne), and the other members of Batman Incorporated investigated Leviathan's activities, combatting their man-bats, gangsters, and armies of crazed children.

LEVIATHAN

DEBUT *Batman: the Return* #1 (Jan. 2011)
BASE Unknown; formerly mountain fortress Khadym
HEIGHT 3ft 5in **WEIGHT** 62 lbs **EYES** Green **HAIR** Black
FORMER MEMBERS/POWERS Talia al Ghūl: trained assassin; The Heretic: monstrous Damian Wayne clone, trained in combat; Goatboy: rocket rifle; Doctor Daedalus (Otto Netz): master tactician; Wishbone: sorceress; The Silencer (Honor Guest): super-assassin able to neutralize sound.
CURRENT MEMBERS/POWERS Mark Shaw: bio-augmented former Manhunter: Guardian (James Harper) bio-enhanced enforcer; Frau Netz (mad scientist, deceased).
ALLIES Mutants gang, League of Assassins
ENEMIES Batman, Inc., Batmen of All Nations, Checkmate, A.R.G.U.S., DEO, Spyral

Leviathan's leader was eventually revealed to be Batman's former lover, Talia al Ghūl. When their son Damian left her to be with his father, Talia created Leviathan to punish Batman. Damian was slain by Talia's bodyguard, the Heretic; Talia herself was apparently killed by Kathy Kane of Spyral. Revived by a Lazarus Pit, Talia repurposed the organization, using it as a weapon of extreme social change, to thwart the schemes of her oppressive father Rā's al Ghūl. Building a vast global criminal network of underbosses and body-modified super-assassins, Talia overstepped while "cleaning house," sparking a civil war, ended by her most special agent, The Silencer.

No sooner had Talia regained control of the weakened Leviathan, than former Manhunter Mark Shaw seized the reins of power and took the name for his own: retasking the secret army to establish global order by mercilessly eradicating all other covert agencies. These included terrorist cabals such as Kobra's cult to government agencies like A.R.G.U.S., Checkmate, the Department of Extra-Normal Operations, Spyral and others. His secret war was exposed by reporters Lois Lane and Jimmy Olsen, but was largely successful, despite the late intervention of Earth's Super Heroes. With the intelligence community in tatters, Leviathan remains at large.

LIBERTY BELLE II

DEBUT *Justice Society of America* (Vol. 2) #1 (Aug. 1992)
REAL NAME Jesse Chambers
BASE Keystone City
HEIGHT 5ft 9in **WEIGHT** 142 lbs
EYES Blue **HAIR** Blonde
POWERS/ABILITIES Super-speed; strength; flight.
ENEMIES Savitar
AFFILIATIONS Justice Society of America, Justice League, Speed Force

QUICK OFF THE MARK
Jesse Chambers inherited her Speed-Force powers from her father, Johnny Quick. She later joined the JLA as the new Liberty Belle.

The daughter of World War II heroes Johnny Quick (not the Crime Syndicate villain of the same name) and Liberty Belle, Jesse Chambers inherited her parents' powers—notably her father's access to the Speed Force, which she could tap into by reciting the formula "3x2(9YZ)4A." Calling herself Jesse Quick, she fought alongside other speedsters, including The Flash (Wally West), Max Mercury, and Impulse.

She joined the Justice Society of America and the Teen Titans, juggling those responsibilities with her role as CEO of Quickstart Enterprises after her father was killed by speedster villain Savitar. Later she adopted her mother's role, becoming the new Liberty Belle and marrying JSA teammate Hourman. After the Teen Titans disbanded, Jesse maintained her heroic double duties by joining the Justice League.

LIVEWIRE

DEBUT *Superman Adventures* #5 (Mar. 1997)
REAL NAME Leslie Willis
BASE Stryker's Island penitentiary
EYES Blue **HAIR** Pale blue
POWERS/ABILITIES Electricity absorption and projection; flight using electromagnetic fields.
ALLIES Killer Frost, Atomic Skull, Killer Croc, Shockwave
ENEMIES Batman (James Gordon), Superman, Batgirl, The Flash
AFFILIATIONS Secret Society of Villains

DANGER: HIGH VOLTAGE
Leslie Willis started out as a radio DJ with a fierce dislike for Superman. She became a real "shock jock" when she was struck by lightning.

Notorious vlogger Leslie Willis was famous for outrageous stunts, but transformed into a being of pure electricity when a high-voltage prank misfired. She joined the Secret Society of Super-Villains and clashed with Superman in Metropolis, but was caught in an energy trap by Batman and imprisoned in Stryker's Island penitentiary.

The Hooq Cult set Livewire free and she went on a rampage, using the Burnside electricity plant to charge up her powers. Defeated by Batgirl and new Batman James Gordon, she was imprisoned once again. This time, Livewire was freed by mysterious beings with energy powers. She joined forces with other villains in Metropolis, but they were defeated by Superman.

After a long absence, she has been sighted in Metropolis again, and was vacationing in Zandia when The Flash infiltrated the Super-Villain resort.

LIGHTRAY

DEBUT *New Gods* (Vol. 1) #1 (Feb.–Mar. 1971)
BASE New Genesis **REAL NAME** Sollis
HEIGHT 6ft **WEIGHT** 181 lbs **EYES** Blue **HAIR** Strawberry blond
POWERS/ABILITIES As a New God, Lightray is immortal and has physical capabilities beyond those of an ordinary human; he can also fly and fire blasts of energy from his hands.
ALLIES Orion
ENEMIES Darkseid, every Lantern Corps
AFFILIATIONS New Gods, the Council of Eight

Lightray was a general of New Genesis. His positivity, charm, and enthusiasm contrasted sharply with the temperament of Orion—foster son of New Gods leader, Highfather—but they were nevertheless close friends.

Seeking a clue to unlock the powerful Life Equation, Highfather dispatched Lightray and other members of the trusted Council of Eight to acquire power rings from the various Lantern Corps. The theft of power rings provoked the various Emotional Spectrum Corps to unite and react. Black Hand of the Black Lantern Corps raised undead leviathans from within the Source Wall and the Lanterns used a redirected Boom Tube to transport the undead monsters to New Genesis. Lightray flew into battle, but was snatched up by one of the creatures, and only saved by Orion. Ultimately, Highfather realized the folly of his arrogance, and a truce was brokered. Lightray and his kin began rebuilding their ruined utopia but were soon diverted as the return of exotic ancient metals to our reality triggered the rise of Escahon Giants. These Nth Metal golems, created by Old God Yuga Khan, ruthlessly hunted New Gods. With the Green Lanterns help, Lightray and his brethren resisted, and tried to bolster the weakening Source Wall, but it sundered, releasing primordial creator Perpetua and instantly eradicating all New Gods except Orion.

ON THE RECORD

In his pre-*Flashpoint* incarnation, Lightray was a close companion of Orion, and even joined him in the Justice League while they were on Earth. It was while on Earth that Lightray died. He was struck by a freak shower of meteors and perished in front of a shocked Jimmy Olsen—a prosaic end for a New God.

THE LIGHTBRINGER
When Lightray journeyed to Earth and tried to raise a human woman from the dead, he discovered that power sometimes comes at a terrible cost.

LIGHTNING LAD

DATA

DEBUT *Adventure Comics* (Vol. 1) #247 **(Apr. 1958)**
REAL NAME Garth Ranzz
BASE 31st century New Metropolis
HEIGHT 5ft 10ins **WEIGHT** 145 lbs
EYES One Blue, One Black **HAIR** Red
POWERS/ABILITIES Generation and manipulation of electricity; Legion flight ring.
ALLIES Saturn Girl, Cosmic Boy, Lightning Lass
ENEMIES Crav, General Nah, Mordru
AFFILIATIONS Legion of Super-Heroes

BIG FAMILY
Garth and Ayla are just two siblings in a large family. Raised by two mothers, there are seven kids in the Ranzz family, including three pairs of twins.

While his twin sister has a tendency to follow her impulses and jump into the fray before anyone else, Garth Ranzz has been known to take a more measured approach. Born with lightning manipulation abilities and no less heroic in his actions, Lightning Lad has made a name for himself as a founder of the Legion of Super-Heroes.

On the planet Winath in the 31st century, a group of citizens was being rounded up by the Science Police and forced to move out of their homes against their will. On this world—whose overbeing is Validus, the Lord of Lightning—humanoids not born in pairs as twins are considered the Children of Validus. Twin siblings, Ayla and Garth Ranzz, stood up to the officers and showed off their natural-born lightning powers in the process. Successful at scaring away the Science Police, Garth and Ayla earned planet-wide attention and were invited to join the Young United Planets by the Science Command. While the politically minded Ayla angrily turned down the offer from what she considered a corrupt organization, Garth accepted it.

Garth next met up with fellow teenagers Imra Ardeen from Titan and Rokk Krinn from the planet Braal aboard the spacecraft of R.J. Brande, the president of the United Planets. When Brande came under attack by a group of Horraz aliens, the three young heroes saved her life. Brande was inspired to organize a team of Super Heroes reflecting teams like the Teen Titans and the Justice League in the 21st century. She discussed the matter with the United Planets, and soon the Legion of Super-Heroes was formed, with Garth as one of its three youthful founders.

A loyal Legionnaire, Garth was later joined by Ayla, who now fights for galactic peace as his teammate Lightning Lass.

LIGHTNING CRASHES
Lightning Lad and his twin sister Lightning Lass both have the power to project electricity.

ON THE RECORD

Over the years, Lightning Lad has been either the unluckiest hero in the universe, or the most fortunate. He has gained superpowers from an animal attack that should have killed him; he has died in battle, and been resurrected. He lost an arm but gained a new one; and, after a life of amazing adventures, he married his sweetheart and settled down.

Then the Time Trapper tried to alter the events that created the Legion of Super-Heroes. He kidnapped Garth's baby to control the hero, but was unprepared for Garth's mature response, when the distraught father called in his comrades Rokk and Imra to help him rescue the child.

SHOCK TACTICS
Always considered impetuous and hot-tempered, Lightning Lad surprised friends and foes alike when his son was abducted by the Time Trapper.

LEGION'S GOT TALENT
Much like the judges in a 21st-century talent competition, Garth, Imra, and Rokk called the shots when it came to auditioning prospective Legionnaires for their team.

CLASSIC STORIES

Adventure Comics **(Vol. 1) #304 (Jan. 1963)** Garth is the first Legionnaire to die in action, saving Saturn Girl from space marauder Zaryan the Conqueror.
Adventure Comics **(Vol. 1) #332 (May 1965)** When Garth loses an arm battling the Super-Moby Dick of Space, the shock deranges him. His obsessive hunt for the beast almost costs him his sanity and place in the Legion.
Legion of Super-Heroes **(Vol. 2) #302 (Aug. 1983)** Garth cataclysmically and definitively clashes with his brother Mekt for the love and allegiance of their sister Ayla following her resignation from the Legion.

LOBO

DATA

DEBUT *Omega Men* (Vol. 1) #3 **(Jun. 1983)**
HEIGHT 6ft 4in **WEIGHT** 250 lbs
EYES Red **HAIR** Black
POWERS/ABILITIES Regenerative healing; can withstand exposure to space vacuum; super-strength, stamina and enhanced durability; super-senses; custom-built spacecraft; employs very hi-tech alien weaponry.
ALLIES Space Dolphins, The Atom (Ryan Choi), Crush (daughter)
ENEMIES Anybody who gets in his way
AFFILIATIONS Justice League

ON THE RECORD

The pre-*Flashpoint* Lobo was simply born to be bad. When he was a teenager, he created a plague of bugs that killed all five billion inhabitants on his homeworld of Czarnia—because he hated them all and wanted to be unique. (The only other Czarnian to survive was his fourth-grade teacher, Miss Tribb.) Lobo set off on his SpazFrag666 spacehog to prove that he was the meanest "bastich" in the universe. While working as a bounty hunter, he tangled with the Omega Men, the Teen Titans, and the legions of Hell itself. He did have a softer side, which was later revealed.

BAD TO THE BONE?
Unlike his deadly-serious temporary successor, the original Lobo was just a violent party animal (with a soft spot for Space Dolphins).

NOT THE MAIN MAN
On one occasion, a fake Lobo claimed he was the real deal while Lobo was stuck in a hi-tech cell in the Catacombs prison.

Lobo is the last survivor of the alien Czarnian race, but only because he killed the whole lot of them. Crude, rude, and nearly impossible to kill, the super-tough bounty hunter wanders the cosmos on his space bike, flying from one assignment to another, with plenty of pit stops at local alien bars along the way.

The intergalactic biker was born on Czarnia. After killing everyone on his planet to make himself more unique (and because they had it coming), he set out to kill other people for fun and profit. Unfortunately for anyone with a bounty on their heads, Lobo has been quite effective at achieving both.

Making a brutal living all across the universe, Lobo eventually found his way to Earth, where he encountered plenty of Super Heroes and Super-Villains to clash with. It was not long before he was recruited into Amanda Waller's first prototype Suicide Squad task force. However, the team were not the success Waller had anticipated. Lobo ended up locked in the most secretive high-security prison in the world, the Catacombs. Meanwhile, an imposter claimed the Lobo name and title, but was eventually imprisoned and miniaturized, locked away by Larfleeze as part of his hidden hoard on the planet Okaara.

After being freed from captivity by Maxwell Lord, Lobo fell under Lord's powerful mind-controlling powers. He was eventually released when Batman set off a bomb inside his head, completely blowing it up. In time, Lobo healed, and strangely decided that he owned Batman a favor for helping him regain his own mind.

The Dark Knight cashed in that favor very quickly, playing on Lobo's particular sense of honor and recruiting him into the Justice League of America. He stayed with the team longer than he had to, but the free-spirited Lobo eventually took off toward space, looking for new and deserving "bastiches" to "frag."

UP CLOSE AND PERSONAL
Lobo has mastered a vast arsenal of weapons, including the latest in hi-tech killing devices. However, he prefers to eliminate his opponents with razor-sharp blades, or with his fists.

CLASSIC STORIES

***Lobo Paramilitary Christmas Special* #1 (Dec. 1991)** The Easter Bunny hires Lobo to kill Santa Claus himself–but jolly old Saint Nick is not going down without a fight.

***Lobo's Back* #1–4 (May–Nov. 1992)** Lobo is killed by two of his rivals, but after wreaking havoc in Heaven and Hell he comes back from the dead to enact his revenge.

***Lobo Annual* (Vol. 3) #1 (Sep. 2015)** (The fake) Lobo accepts perhaps the most dangerous assignment of his entire career: to kill Sinestro, leader of the infamous and deadly Yellow Lantern Corps!

CANARY IN A COAL MINE
Lobo recruited Black Canary's help when he tracked down the only other living Czarnian, the son of his former grade school teacher, Mrs. Tribb. Gusano Tribb had been killing space dolphins just to mess with Lobo, so the Main Man fed him to the very dolphins Tribb was trying to eliminate.

LOOKER

DEBUT *Batman and the Outsiders* (Vol. 1) #25 (Sep. 1985) (as Emily); *Batman and the Outsiders* (Vol. 1) #31 (Mar. 1986) (as Looker)
REAL NAME Emily 'Lia' Briggs
BASE Gotham City
HEIGHT 5ft 10in **WEIGHT** 115 lbs
EYES Blue **HAIR** Red
POWERS/ABILITIES Telepathy; telekinesis; levitation; mind control; vampiric powers.
ALLIES Batman, Geo-Force
ENEMIES Leviathan, Abyssians
AFFILIATIONS Outsiders

KILLER LOOKS
Lia Briggs' newfound powers and appearance caused some rivalry among the Outsiders, but that didn't stop the psychic vampire trying to save their lives.

Librarian Emily Briggs was kidnapped by inhabitants of the underground realm of Abyssia. Exposed to light from Halley's Comet, she received psionic superpowers and striking looks. Emily was rescued by Batman and the Outsiders, and began working as a supermodel. Emily (or 'Lia', as she preferred to be known) joined the Outsiders as Looker. She became a vampire after being bitten by a bloodsucker in the East European nation of Markovia.

The Outsiders were seemingly killed when Talia al Ghūl blew up a satellite with them on board, but they resurfaced in Gotham City, secretly helping Batman fight Talia's Leviathan conspiracy. They entered one of Leviathan's bases that was booby-trapped and exploded. Looker saved them with a force field, but they were all badly injured. Looker later became a member of Amanda Waller's team of psychics, tasked with hacking the mind of Brainiac.

LORD CHAOS

DEBUT *The New Titans Annual* (Vol. 1) #7 (1991)
REAL NAME Robert Long
BASE An alternate-future Earth
HEIGHT 6ft 2in **WEIGHT** 196 lbs
EYES Black **HAIR** Gold
POWERS/ABILITIES Possesses powers of Titan gods including super-strength, light-blasts, and flight; ability to command the earth and sea.
ENEMIES Team Titans, Teen Titans, Titans of Myth

POWER AND GLORY
Possessing the might of the Titanic gods from birth proved too much for young Robert Long—and he was quickly driven to madness.

In an alternate future, Troia (Donna Troy) and her husband Terry Long had a son named Robert, who had inherited Troia's godlike powers. Possessing such power from birth drove Robert mad; he killed his mother and conquered the world as Lord Chaos.

A group of superpowered rebels calling themselves the Team Titans traveled to the past to kill Donna and prevent Lord Chaos from being born. However, learning of their plan, Lord Chaos traveled back in time to stop the Team Titans, and summoned his soldiers from the future to conquer the world.

Donna Troy battled her son and called on the Titans of Myth to remove the godlike powers from them both. The Titans of Myth agreed, taking the insane entity to their realm, but leaving the infant Robert Long in his mother's arms.

Robert was later killed in a car accident. However, Lord Chaos returned in undead form to attack Donna during the events of *Blackest Night*.

LORD HAVOK

DEBUT *Justice League Quarterly* #3 (Summer 1991)
REAL NAME Damon; Prince Alexi of Kravia
EYES Brown **HAIR** Unknown
POWERS/ABILITIES Wields the Lightning-Axe of Wundajin and the Omni-Gauntlets.
ENEMIES The Retaliators, Future Family, G-Men
AFFILIATIONS Ankor (Earth-8), Extremists

MAGNIFICENT MONSTER
Arrogant but conflicted, Lord Havok wanted to be a hero but could not accept that his actions only ever caused terror, pain, and death.

Damon—actually Prince Alexi of Kravia on Earth-8—was transformed by an experiment performed by Frank Future of the Future Family Super Hero team. Traumatized and physically scarred, Damon hid his face behind a forbidding skull mask and became Super-Villain Lord Havok.

He stole three magical artifacts—the Omni-Gauntlets, the Lightning-Axe of Wundajin, and the Genesis Egg, to tap into the Power Eternal. When he tried hatching the egg, however, he was confronted by Frank Future, the Retaliators super-team and numerous multi-dimensional heroes. Frank begged him to stop, but Havok refused and demanded that Future kneel before him. When the egg hatched, Havok was driven insane by a vision of the entities within it, and was killed by one of the Retaliators.

Reborn following *Rebirth*, Prince Alexi sold his soul to The Queen of Fables in return for transformative power, but accidentally destroyed his entire world while trying to seize control with his team of Extremists. Traveling to Earth-0, the Super-Villains tried again, but were defeated by Batman's Justice League of America. Ultimately, Lord Havok and Dreamslayer—both desperate to atone—traded their lives for Batman's when he was targeted by the Cosmic Adjudicator.

LORD OF TIME

DEBUT *Justice League of America* (Vol. 1) #10 (Mar. 1962)
REAL NAME Epoch
BASE Palace of Eternity; Timepoint; Ghost Sector
HEIGHT 5ft 9in **WEIGHT** 159 lbs
EYES Blue **HAIR** Black
POWERS/ABILITIES Technology-assisted time travel and weaponry; knowledge of past and potential futures.

ARMOR OF AGES
Equipped with armor from the far future, the Lord of Time is near impervious to assaults, even from Superhuman opponents.

An immensely powerful individual from the year 3786, the Lord of Time attacked the first Justice League using his miraculous chrono-cube to peel back the fourth-dimensional veil of time. Defeated, he learned to move laterally and diagonally through history, accessing armies and armaments spanning millions of years. He also built an artificial intelligence, the Eternity Brain, which tracked and displaced people in time. His ultimate goal was to conquer all space and time, and he plotted to rid himself of the Justice League by time-traveling back to eliminate their ancestors.

At some point, the Lord of Time created a frozen moment in history called Timepoint, evolving into a being known as Epoch, now resolved to master the timestream, changing events to grant him power.

To this end he traveled to the Ghost Sector during the chaos caused by the breaking of the Source Wall, intent on undoing the event, erasing Darkseid and re-imprisoning multiversal mother Perpetua. After being caught in a timeloop, Epoch joined Green Lantern Jessica Cruz, New

God Orion and the rest of Justice League Odyssey, utilizing the massed Implicate Time energy of the region to power his Revision Mechanism, but with no success.

LORD, MAXWELL

DEBUT *Justice League* (Vol. 1) #1 **(May 1987)**
REAL NAME Maxwell Lord IV **BASE** Mount Rushmore
HEIGHT 6ft 2in **WEIGHT** 185 lbs **EYES** Brown **HAIR** Brown
POWERS/ABILITIES Telepathic mind control, brilliant strategist, ruthless sociopath.
ALLIES Mokkari, Sarge Steel
ENEMIES Amanda Waller, Brother Eye
AFFILIATIONS Checkmate, S.H.A.D.E.

OUTSIDE THE LAW
Although Lord's Checkmate organization was the world's premier spy agency, its allegiances remained unclear.

Director of Checkmate—a Task Force X division regarded as a "Global Peace Agency"—Maxwell Lord oversaw the agency's covert operations from a bunker within Mount Rushmore. Lord personally oversaw Checkmate's Cadmus Project—a government program designed to negate the Justice League if they ever went rogue—and deployed elite agents when sentient satellite Brother Eye rebelliously created O.M.A.C. (One-Machine Attack Construct) from scientist Kevin Kho. When successive teams led by Sarge Steel and Mokkari failed, Lord requested S.H.A.D.E.'s help to counter the threat. Their top operative Frankenstein almost killed O.M.A.C.

Lord himself had to fend off assassination by a soldier Brother Eye had subverted. Using his mind-control powers, Lord forced the would-be killer to turn the gun on himself. He outsmarted Brother Eye by magnetizing the satellite's hull, causing passing asteroids to coalesce and trap Brother Eye inside, burning up on re-entry into Earth's atmosphere. Lord's pursuit of O.M.A.C. ended after Brother Eye gave Kho control over his O.M.A.C. body.

Paranoid and holding grudges, Lord turned his attention to rival agency chief Amanda Waller, targeting her Suicide Squad with his own team, while tricking the Justice League into attacking her. His goal was to secure Eclipso's mystic gem, the Heart of Darkness, which he used to "pacify" America. The plan failed after Lord succumbed to Eclipso's influence and he was humiliatingly saved by Killer Frost and Superman. Over Waller's protests, Lord later worked for Wonder Woman, but lost his political power and prestige after Checkmate was wiped out and absorbed by the predatory covert group Leviathan.

ON THE RECORD

Pre-*Flashpoint*, Maxwell Lord caused a terrible crisis of conscience for Wonder Woman after he used his mind-control powers to turn Superman into a weapon. This was part of his plot to exterminate the world's metahumans using Brother Eye and O.M.A.C. Faced with the choice between saving millions of lives and keeping her oath never to kill, Wonder Woman killed Lord, and has lived with the consequences ever since.

CHAIN OF DEATH
Blue Beetle attacked Lord when he discovered his plot to wipe out the world's metahumans. Lord ended the fight by shooting Beetle in the head, only to have his own life taken by Wonder Woman, ending his schemes once and for all.

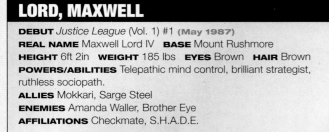

LORING, JEAN

DEBUT *Showcase* #34 (Sep.–Oct. 1961)
HEIGHT 5ft 8in **WEIGHT** 130 lbs
EYES Green **HAIR** Black
POWERS/ABILITIES Keen legal mind; as Eclipso, possesses vast magical powers, invulnerability, flight.
ALLIES Ray Palmer
ENEMIES Spectre, Shadowpact, Elongated Man, Mary Shazam

Jean Loring was once a notable attorney and wife of Ray Palmer, the Atom. After Ray's demanding double life came between them, they divorced. Loring continued her law career in Ivy Town, before suffering a complete mental collapse. She became convinced that she could restore her marriage to Ray by threatening or killing the loved ones of the Justice League of America. To that end, she shrunk herself, using one of Ray's old costumes, and murdered Elongated Man's wife, Sue Dibny, by giving her a stroke. When her crime was discovered, Loring served a term in Arkham Asylum, until she was infected by the sinister spirit of Eclipso and became his human host.

As Eclipso, she seduced the Spectre into killing hundreds of Earth's magic-users to bring about an end to the Ninth Age of Magic. The Shadowpact fought the Spectre and banished Loring into orbit around the Sun, but she returned, still bearing Eclipso's powers, and tried without success to corrupt the spirit of Mary Shazam.

Following *Rebirth*, she reverted to human status, but remained divorced from Palmer.

HEART OF DARKNESS
While confined in Arkham, Loring came across one of the black diamond shards of Eclipso's Heart of Darkness, and was instantly possessed by it.

LUTHOR, LEX

DATA

DEBUT *Action Comics* (Vol. 1) #23 (Apr. 1940)
REAL NAME Alexander "Lex" Luthor
BASE Metropolis
HEIGHT 6ft 2in   **WEIGHT** 210 lbs
EYES Green   **HAIR** None
POWERS/ABILITIES Genius-level intellect; vast resources at his disposal; connected in business and criminal circles; employs technologically advanced warsuits; formerly melded with Martian DNA.
ALLIES Captain Cold, Brainiac, Bizarro, Mercy
ENEMIES Superman, Batman, Justice League, Lois Lane, The Batman Who Laughs
AFFILIATIONS Legion of Doom, Secret Society of Super-Villains, Justice League, Injustice League

Alexander Luthor is a very complex man. He is an intellectual genius, a flamboyant scientist, and a billionaire entrepreneur. However, he is also an utterly amoral, sociopathic Super-Villain, as well as an adulation-hungry would-be hero. Lex's innate intellectual brilliance in a wide number of scientific disciplines is coupled with an obsessive need to be the undisputed best at whatever endeavor he attempts. Moreover, despite his vast organization of go-betweens and employees, Lex will get his own hands dirty when required. Unhindered by any scruple or ethical compass, Lex gets what Lex wants, and woe betide anybody who gets in his way.

AT A GLANCE...

Alien Rivalry
Luthor believed no human was his equal and—after meeting Superman—set out to prove no alien was either. Lex had supreme confidence in his own intellect and scientific knowledge and was prepared to use any means necessary to get what he wanted.

Business matters
Global conglomerate LexCorp was built upon Luthor's inventions and provided employment for most of Metropolis. As a generous, "philanthropic" owner, Lex basked in the adoration of the masses while his cutting-edge research facilities secretly developed the weapons he needed to combat Superman. LexCorp gave him two powers his enemy lacked: unlimited funds and the trust of international governments.

War Footing
Though his most powerful weapon is his own intellect, Luthor has spent billions creating armored outfits that make him the equal of any alien or metahuman.

CLASSIC STORIES

Superman (Vol. 1) #38 (Jan.-Feb. 1946) Luthor uses an atomic bomb on Superman. Scheduled to appear in 1944, the story was embargoed by the Defense Department until World War II ended.

The Joker (Vol. 1) #7 (May–Jun. 1976) Luthor switches personalities with the Joker, and a coldly rational Clown Prince of Crime hunts a literally mad scientist who would rather die than surrender the freedom of insanity.

Action Comics (Vol. 1) #660 (Dec. 1990) Fatally irradiated by Kryptonite, Luthor fakes his own death. His brain is later transplanted into a healthy young clone with red hair and paperwork to prove he is Luthor's son.

Lex Luthor grew up in Smallville, Kansas and knew Clark Kent when they were young, not realizing for years that the greatest thorn in his side—the future Superman—had been right under his nose all along. As a boy, Lex soon revealed his genius-level intellect. His father, Lionel, was a scientist, and had discovered an ancient race of apex predators that shared both human and Martian DNA. He located and trapped a young Martian boy named J'onn J'onzz, and began experimenting on him. Lex was permitted into the lab, and began to communicate with J'onn. The two became friends, and Lex helped J'onn escape when Lionel had planned to terminate the alien. The memory of this event was erased from both Lex and his father's mind when Lionel was betrayed by his business partner Vandal Savage. This caused Lionel to turn to alcohol abuse, realizing something in his life was missing.

In Smallville, Lex became strangely arrogant and aloof. An older student mostly avoided by Clark Kent and his friends Pete Ross and Lana Lang, Lex and his sickly sister Lena had a hard life, dealing with their now-abusive father. One night, when running from one of Lionel's drunken tirades, Lex tripped and fell over a fragment of Kryptonite in his yard. He became fascinated with it, and the concept of extraterrestrial life.

Putting his intellect to good use, Lex became a billionaire industrialist, setting up his LexCorp HQ in Metropolis. He ran a program where he would grant a lucky person waiting outside his building with a meeting with his "life engineers." This gave Lex the appearance of an altruistic businessman. Successful on nearly all fronts, by the time Superman appeared in Metropolis, Lex owned 78 percent of the city. When the Super-Villain Parasite was formed inside Lex Luthor's own building, Lex met Superman for the first time when the hero stopped the energy-sucking creature. Luthor couldn't understand Superman's motivation, but did not like being upstaged in his own city, and his rivalry against the Man of Steel was born.

Over the years, Luthor has spent time as both hero and villain, even working his way onto the Justice League after leading the defeat of the planet-conquering Crime Syndicate from Earth-3. He created his own Superman in the form of Bizarro, and when that didn't work out, he made a Superman-like battle suit and attempted to replace the Man of Steel himself. But there was no replacing Superman, and Luthor was even defeated by his own sister when Lena Luthor became the Super-Villain Ultrawoman.

On his mad quest for more power, Luthor formed the Legion of Doom and helped free the cosmic entity

DEADLY DISCOVERY
A young Lex Luthor first showed Kryptonite to Clark Kent at a Smallville fair. Clark immediately felt faint and collapsed.

FOREVER EVIL
When the Crime Syndicate from Earth-3 invaded Earth, they recruited a host of Super-Villains to act as their vanguard and overwhelmed the world's heroic defenders. Lex Luthor refused to be subservient to another's will and organized like-minded metahuman criminals in an Injustice League. His nefarious team defeated the extra-dimensional conquerors, liberated Earth's captive heroes, and thus saved humanity. In the aftermath, this most improbable hero even connived his way into the ranks of the Justice League.

CORPORATE RAIDER
Lex Luthor was never going to be a team player, unless he was in complete control of the team and giving the orders.

APEX LEX

When the Source Wall at the very edge of the universe was broken, Lex Luthor became obsessed with the power contained behind its walls, the cosmic entity called Perpetua. He understood that for the mother of the Multiverse to truly claim power in the world, the global attitude had to first shift to embrace doom. To do that, Luthor bestowed dark gifts on many of the world's Super-Villains, and promised to give his fortune away to those who chose his dark philosophy. Surprisingly, while the Justice League was busy fighting evil in another dimension, public opinion shifted against them, and the world indeed chose doom, freeing Perpetua and empowering Lex even further.

CHOOSE DOOM
Lex Luthor united his own Legion of Doom, but barely batted an eye when Perpetua imprisoned them in her throne in order to leech their various powers.

"It's time to stop being selfish. The world needs Lex Luthor."

Lex Luthor

known as the mother of the Multiverse, Perpetua. He "died" and was reborn again as one of her apex predators, and even absorbed the Martian Manhunter into his own form, as the powerful being Apex Lex. Perpetua rewarded Luthor by channeling the powers of the rest of his captive Legion of Doom into him, making him stronger than he ever dreamed. However, Perpetua double-crossed Lex by choosing an evil Bruce Wayne (infected by The Joker) from the Dark Multiverse to replace him as her right-hand man. This Batman Who Laughs swooped in at the last minute and stole everything for which Lex had worked. Betrayed, depowered, and dethroned, Lex Luthor nonetheless survived Perpetua's reality-altering rule, and continues to plot his return to greatness.

REBIRTH

METROPOLIS MARVEL
After years struggling against Superman, Luthor realized that he should simply become the hero he despised. With the Man of Steel presumed dead, mimicking the power-set was easy. The real test was not slipping too far into the role of self-sacrificing do-gooder.

However, Lex did not anticipate the challenges Superman faced on a daily basis, threats including Doomsday and Ultrawoman.

ON THE RECORD

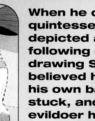

When he debuted, Luthor was the quintessential mad scientist. He was first depicted as a redheaded savant, but, following confusion among the artists drawing Superman's stories at the time, it is believed he was accidentally switched with his own bald, burly henchman. The change stuck, and so the iconic, bald-headed evildoer has remained.

War of the worlds

After years of robbing banks and bedeviling the Man of Tomorrow with super-science gadgets—and barely a shred of success—Luthor was drastically overhauled in the early 1980s. After another humiliating and inconclusive clash, Luthor retired to the planet Lexor where he had long been considered a global hero and settled down with his wife Ardora. Sadly, due to a tragic misunderstanding, she and her entire world were obliterated. Blaming Superman, Lex rededicated his life to destroying his archenemy.

Captain of industry

Following the events of *Infinite Crisis*, Luthor began a supposedly philanthropic campaign to give ordinary people superpowers. His attention-seeking Everyman Project started well, with the first recipients becoming the latest incarnation of Infinity Incorporated, but the intention was actually to give the billionaire unbeatable metahuman abilities and ended up costing the lives of most of his test subjects.

RING OF DEATH
Luthor believed his stolen Kryptonite ring protected him from attack by Superman, unaware that its alien radioactivity was slowly killing him.

President Lex

The maligned magnate achieved his greatest triumph when his money, technology, and publicity machine gained him the presidency of the United States. He even won acclaim for spearheading Earth's defense against a colossal alien incursion by the cosmic force of destruction, Imperiex. His vindictiveness and chicanery eventually proved his downfall, and Luther was exposed when he injected himself with Kryptonite, mad with power.

THINKING OF YOU
Luthor's intellect and utter lack of compassion make him the most dangerous man alive, capable of doing almost anything to satisfy his selfish desires.

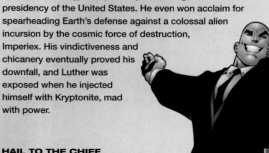

HAIL TO THE CHIEF
Though he knew Luthor could not have won the election fairly, Superman had no proof and had to wait for his gloating enemy to make a mistake.

WORD OF POWER
When Alexander Luthor shouted the word "Mazahs!" he unleashed the power of the dark lightning. In moments, he killed both Johnny Quick and Bizarro.

LUTHOR, ALEXANDER

DEBUT *DC Comics Present Annual* #1 (1982) (Vol. 2) #23 (Oct. 2013)
UNIVERSE Earth-3
HEIGHT 6ft 3in **WEIGHT** 210 lbs
EYES Blue **HAIR** Red
POWERS/ABILITIES Analogous to those of Shazam; additionally absorbs the powers of anyone he kills.
ALLIES Superwoman
ENEMIES Crime Syndicate, Justice League

Alexander Luthor is the Shazam of Earth-3, known as Mazahs. His version of Shazam's powers included the ability to absorb and retain the powers of any metahuman he killed. A mortal enemy of the Crime Syndicate of America and one of the few Earth-3 heroes to survive opposing them, he was brought to Earth-0 as a prisoner and held in the Justice League's Watchtower.

Released in the chaos of the battle between the combined Justice Leagues and the Crime Syndicate, he used his word of power to join the fray and declared he would kill everyone present, hero and villain alike. His rampage was only stopped when Lex Luthor realized that he had the same voice, and depowered Alexander with his own word of power. Lex then killed Alexander to avenge the fallen Bizarro—and of course save his own life. After his death, it was revealed that the Crime Syndicate's Superwoman was carrying Alexander Luthor's child.

BIDING HER TIME
There was no way that Lena Luthor would allow herself to be imprisoned in her brother's lab for long—without getting her revenge.

LUTHOR, LENA

DEBUT *Superman's Girl Friend, Lois Lane* #23 (Feb. 1961)
REAL NAME Lena Luthor
BASE Metropolis
HEIGHT 5ft 8in
WEIGHT 130 lbs
EYES Green
HAIR Blonde
POWERS/ABILITIES Genius intellect; battlesuit gives her super strength and durability.
ALLIES Bizarress Army
ENEMIES Lex Luthor, Superwoman
AFFILIATIONS None

When Lena Luthor was paralyzed, her brother Lex, the self-styled "smartest man alive" believed he could cure her condition. However, when he could not, the shame over his failure led Lex to keep Lena locked away in his lab. Lena too was a genius, and managed to break free from captivity before building herself a giant mech suit.

Calling herself Ultrawoman, she was no longer confined to a wheelchair, but a formidable opponent in battle. She used her power to take control of Metropolis, having trapped Lex in the secret basement of his own building. However, Lena's new form required so much energy that she needed a new power source, and chose the new Superwoman to be her living battery. Superwoman defeated her, and Lena was imprisoned once more at LexCorp.

LOSERS

DEBUT *G.I. Combat* (Vol. 1) #138 (Nov. 1969)
BASE Europe and Asia during World War II
MEMBERS/ABILITIES Captain Storm: Indomitable will, a natural leader; **Gunner:** Commando skills, expert marksman; **Johnny Cloud:** One of the greatest fighter pilots of World War II; **Ona Tornsen:** Expert markswoman; **Pooch:** Specially trained military dog; **Sarge:** Impeccable commando skills; expert marksman.
ALLIES Haunted Tank, Sergeant Rock, Easy Company
ENEMIES Nazi Germany, Empire of Japan
AFFILIATIONS US Army, Navy, and Air Force

The Losers were Allied servicemen during World War II, each of whom had suffered serious failures during their military careers. The crew of Captain Storm's first command, PT-47, had been massacred by a Japanese submarine; a rookie pilot flying alongside Johnny Cloud had been killed in combat; and a band of raw recruits led by Gunner and Sarge had been wiped out during their first patrol. After Sergeant Jeb Stuart, commander of the Haunted Tank, persuaded the soldiers to help him destroy a Nazi radar tower, the four men stayed together, united by the Military High Command as a special task force.

Briefly recruiting a fifth member, a Norwegian resistance fighter named Ona, the unit fought Axis tyranny across Europe and Asia, never quite shaking their self-imposed status as "Losers."

Tragically, all four men and their canine sidekick, Pooch, died in action during the final days of World War II. Decades later Gunner was resurrected by Project M and recruited for the new Creature Commandos unit.

SUICIDE MISSIONS
Despite their seemingly terrible luck, the Losers had a knack of surviving against impossible odds.

WINNING COMBINATION
1 Gunner
2 Johnny Cloud
3 Captain Storm
4 Ona
5 Sarge
6 Pooch

MAD HARRIET

DEBUT *Mr. Miracle* (Vol.1) #6 (Feb. 1972)
BASE Apokolips
HEIGHT 5ft 10in **WEIGHT** 146 lbs **EYES** Black **HAIR** Green
POWERS/ABILITIES Fierce and ruthless warrior, trained by Granny Goodness; weapons include energy claws; superhuman agility, strength, durability, and endurance, extremely unpredictable.
ALLIES Granny Goodness, Lashina, Stompa, Bernadeth
ENEMIES Big Barda, Mr. Miracle, Bernadeth, Wonder Woman, Steve Trevor
AFFILIATIONS Female Furies

Apokolips has spawned some of the most lethal and frightening villains in creation. Perhaps the most demented is Mad Harriet, one of Darkseid's infamous Female Furies. The twisted result of being raised in Granny Goodness' corrupt orphanage, Mad Harriet revels in torture and pain. Taking orders from Bernadeth—sister of Darkseid's premier lackey and torturer, Desaad—Mad Harriet revels in her reputation as a "psychopathic harpy," quick to use the slashing power spikes on her armed gauntlets.

Her first commander was Big Barda, who led the Female Furies, but when she defected, fleeing Apokolips with her true love, Mr. Miracle, her former team happily pursued her to Earth. Barda convinced the Furies to abandon Darkseid and work with her and Mr. Miracle, but their true loyalties re-emerged, and they resumed their roles as Darkseid's killer elite. Mad Harriet recently joined forces with Big Barda and the Furies to fight Darkseid's daughter, Grail, who had enslaved newly resurrected Darkseid. Mad Harriet was captured by Wonder Woman and Steve Trevor, but defied interrogation and soon returned to her dark Master.

ON THE RECORD

One of Mad Harriet's fiercest battles was with the Suicide Squad over the fate of Glorious Godfrey. During the fight, she was nearly killed when her energy claws backfired as she slashed at Bronze Tiger. She was far less fortunate in *Countdown to Final Crisis*, when she was accidentally incinerated by Apokolips' Dog Soldiers during a confrontation with Mary Shazam, Harley Quinn, and Catwoman.

MAD, BAD, AND NO FUN TO KNOW: Harriet and Harley turned a slug-fest into a hug-fest when they realized how much they have in common, especially their dubious sanity.

THE MAD HATTER

DEBUT *Batman* (Vol. 1) #49 (Oct./Nov. 1948)
REAL NAME Jervis Tetch
BASE Gotham City
HEIGHT 4ft 8in **WEIGHT** 149 lbs **EYES** Blue **HAIR** Red
POWERS/ABILITIES Extremely intelligent inventor and technician; uses drugged tea to enhance his own physical abilities; technological innovations let him control the minds of others.
ALLIES Tweedledee, Tweedledum
ENEMIES Batman, Red Robin, Bluebird, Black Mask, Anarky
AFFILIATIONS Secret Society

Jervis Tetch lived a tortured life, mostly due to his appearance. As a young boy, he became obsessed with Lewis Carroll's *Alice in Wonderland* stories. This, combined with his father's haberdashery shop, would influence the later Super-Villain identity he would adopt for himself.

As a boy, Jervis fell in love with a girl named Alice. While he was often undermined and bullied by his classmates, Jervis worked up the nerve to ask Alice on a date, and she accepted, accompanying him to a theme park called Wonderland. That day was the best day of his life, and Tetch became obsessed with it, even though Alice rejected him at a dance soon afterward. Highly sensitive about his short stature, Jervis began experimental testosterone therapy that altered his mind and slowly drove him insane.

Years later, Jervis adopted the identity of the Mad Hatter and began hunting for his "Alice" over and over again, even killing the real Alice when he discovered that she was no longer the radiant beauty he remembered from his "perfect day." With his inventive genius, the Mad Hatter developed mind-control devices designed to make future "Alices" more receptive to his every command.

ALICE DOESN'T LIVE HERE ANYMORE
One of the many "Alices" the Mad Hatter was obsessed with and eventually killed was the sister of the future villain Anarky, who sought revenge for Tetch's crime.

ON THE RECORD

The Mad Hatter first appeared in 1948, in the same issue of *Batman* that featured another new addition to the Dark Knight's supporting cast—love interest Vicki Vale. His appearance was short-lived as Batman foiled his plan and he was locked away in Gotham Pen. While incarcerated, an impostor turned up on the scene in 1956 taking his name and MO, but sporting a handlebar mustache and a sane mind. The two Mad Hatters took turns matching wits with Batman over the years, but the later villain changed his name to Hatman in 2010.

The Hatter later joined the Secret Six, helping them escape from the Doom Patrol, and Ragdoll rewarded him by pushing him off a bridge. He survived and sought revenge, only to find himself once more falling from a bridge to his apparent death after Ragdoll tossed his precious hat over the edge.

A HATTER FOR ALL OCCASIONS
Hatman made a reappearance in *Batman* #700 (Aug. 2010), attempting (and failing) to brainwash Robin, Batman, and Batgirl—and establishing his own credentials as a top-hatted trickster.

MADAME ROUGE

DEBUT *Doom Patrol* (Vol. 1) #86 (Mar. 1964)
My Greatest Adventure (Vol. 2) #1 (Dec. 2011)
REAL NAME Laura DeMille
HEIGHT 5ft 6in **WEIGHT** 118 lbs
EYES Blue **HAIR** Black
POWERS/ABILITIES Stretching her body to incredible lengths; reshaping facial features.
ENEMIES Doom Patrol, Teen Titans

The first female member of the Super-Villain group the Brotherhood of Evil, Madame Rouge was originally a French film actress named Laura DeMille, who suffered from schizophrenia following a car accident. Mr. Brain and Monsieur Mallah used a ray treatment to suppress her kind side and help her along the road to villainy.

DeMille adopted the name Madame Rouge, and was given powers by the brilliant Brain. Despite being attracted to the Doom Patrol's chief, Dr. Niles Caulder, Madame Rouge fought his team many times, until the Doom Patrol seemingly sacrificed their lives to save a small New England fishing town from the Brotherhood of Evil. Years later, during a conflict with the Teen Titans, Madame Rouge was knocked into machinery that restored her original personality, but ultimately killed her. She later returned briefly in undead form as a member of the Black Lantern Corps.

MAELSTROM

DEBUT *Superman/Supergirl: Maelstrom* #1 (Jan. 2009)
REAL NAME Maelstrom
BASE Apokolips
HEIGHT 6ft 2in **WEIGHT** 345 lbs
EYES Blue **HAIR** Black
POWERS/ABILITIES Superhuman strength, endurance, and durability; expert combatant; uses buzz-saw-like blade and Apokolips armor.
ENEMIES Superman, Supergirl

On the hellish planet Apokolips, Darkseid lords over millions of lowlies. But one of his laborers, a woman named Maelstrom, loved him and longed to be his next bride.

To catch Darkseid's eye, she decided to give him a very special gift: Superman's corpse.

She convinced her accomplice Hadrok to steal a boom-tube device for her, killed him, and then traveled to Earth to locate Superman. She encountered and defeated Supergirl, but lost her fight with Superman, who destroyed her Boom-Tube generator while hurling her back to Apokolips. There she was relegated to the Terrorium arena and later the slave pits by Granny Goodness, but was eventually allowed to resume her war on Superman by Darkseid himself. She failed again in her goal when Supergirl and Superman teamed up to stop her and her new allies, the Female Furies.

MAGENTA

DEBUT *New Teen Titans* (Vol. 1) #17 (Mar. 1982)
REAL NAME Francis (Frances) Kane
BASE Keystone City
HEIGHT 5ft 7in **WEIGHT** 134 lbs
EYES Blue **HAIR** Purple
POWERS/ABILITIES Able to manipulate magnetic waves to move metal objects.
ALLIES The Flash (Wally West), Cicada
ENEMIES Doctor Polaris
AFFILIATIONS Teen Titans, Rogues

A longtime friend of Wally West's and a fellow former Blue Valley resident, Francis Kane had formed an early bond with Wally that wasn't easily broken. One day, when the two were attending Blue Valley College, Wally walked Francis home, only to find her mom attempting to speak to her dead brother and father through a séance. Francis seemed to disappear in a vortex of spiraling energy, and reemerged with magnetic superpowers.

Told that she was damned by her mother, Francis' powers went haywire, and it seemed a magnetic demon was possessing her, one the Teen Titans had to fight into submission. In truth, Francis had excessive magnetic waves in her brain, and Doctor Polaris tried to use them to travel back to Earth from the dimension to which Green Lantern had banished him. Later, tricked into becoming a sleeper agent by Dr. Alysia Damalis at S.T.A.R. Labs, Francis developed an alter ego named Magenta, and clashed with The Flash.

MADAME XANADU

DEBUT *Doorway to Nightmare* #1 (Jan.-Feb. 1978)
REAL NAME Nimue Inwudu
BASE Dean Street, London, Mobile
HEIGHT 5ft 9in **WEIGHT** 125 lbs **EYES** Green **HAIR** Black
POWERS/ABILITIES Sorceress well versed in the use of the mystic arts; able to predict the future to a degree, normally using tarot cards; seemingly immortal and doesn't age.
ALLIES Carter Hall, John Constantine, Shade the Changing Man, Zatanna, Etrigan the Demon
ENEMIES Felix Faust, the Blight, Mordru, Dr. Destiny
AFFILIATIONS Demon Knights, Justice League Dark

A LONELY ROAD: Madame Xanadu's romances have ranged from Etrigan to Jason Blood. She steered clear of Deadman, however, realizing that she had to walk a lonely path.

After the fall of King Arthur and Camelot, Jason Blood was cursed: bonded to the demon Etrigan, as a result of the machinations of sorcerer Merlyn. Nimue Inwudu—calling herself Madame Xanadu—voyaged with her infernally twinned lover and met the Shining Knight, Al Jabr, Exoristos, Vandal Savage, and the Horsewoman. They banded together as the Demon Knights, sworn foes of malevolent mage Mordru.

Centuries later, Madame Xanadu realized the world was entering a time of great danger and began assembling a team to counter forthcoming threats. To unite these magical strangers—Shade the Changing Man, Deadman, Zatanna, John Constantine, and Mindwarp—she had to escalate the conflict by helping the Enchantress fight her new champions. The team stopped Enchantress, but also discovered Xanadu's treachery. Yet, when needed to tackle magical and supernatural threats, they returned to action as Justice League Dark. The group disbanded after several missions, replaced by a new squad after the *Metal* crisis heralded a change in the ways of magic. After months on the sidelines, acting as advisor to the likes of Hawkman Carter Hall, Xanadu rejoined Justice League Dark to resist the Otherkind invasion.

ON THE RECORD

Madame Xanadu was created in the late 1970s for the shortlived *Doorway to Nightmare* series. Three years later, she appeared in a self-titled one-shot comic and did not feature in an ongoing series until 2008, when her origins and her connection to the wizard Merlin, Etrigan the Demon, and King Arthur were fully explored.

Madame Xanadu's cruelest encounter came during the Day of Vengeance, when a deranged Spectre began eradicating magic and removed her tarot-reading powers of foresight, by taking her eyes. Despite helping defeat the Spectre, she remained blind for the rest of her pre-*Flashpoint* career.

SUPERNATURAL SENTINELS
Often joining forces with other magical characters, Madame Xanadu formed the Sentinels of Magic with heroes such as Doctor Fate, Faust, and Ragman.

MAGOG

DEBUT *Kingdom Come* #1 (May 1996)
REAL NAME David Reid
HEIGHT 6ft 4in **WEIGHT** 336 lbs **EYES** One blue, one white **HAIR** Blond
POWERS/ABILITIES Empowered by the Fusion Stone composed of a transmutational element; superhuman strength, endurance, and durability; trident capable of firing powerful energy blasts.
ALLIES Circe, Emerald Empress
ENEMIES Superman, Wonder Woman, Atomic Skull, Major Disaster
AFFILIATIONS Fatal Five

When Darkseid's Parademon army invaded Earth, young David Reid lost his parents in the chaos. Although the Justice League drove Darkseid back to Apokolips, Reid held nothing but hatred in his heart for Super Heroes who had failed to save his family. Years later, he was living on the street when the sorceress Circe, selected him as test subject for her "Fusion Stone." It granted Reid superhuman powers, but, as Circe willed, he forgot his past for a time.

Armed with a powerful energy lance, Reid fought and defeated the Atomic Skull and Major Disaster. He then faced Superman and Wonder Woman and, as his memories returned, revealed himself as Magog. He and Circe did their best to defeat the Man of Steel and Wonder Woman, but failed. Superman showed Magog what it meant to be a true Super Hero; unfortunately, the villain was too set in his ways to heed the Man of Steel's lesson.

Post-*Rebirth*, Reid's campaign against false gods again brought him into conflict with Superman, but he also branched out to target his cousin Supergirl, both singly and as part of the Emerald Empress' new Fatal Five.

BEATING THE BEST
Obsessed with ridding the world of Super Heroes, Magog proved a very formidable force.

GOG-SMACKED
A source of friction inside the JSA, Magog was given his own series in 2009, during which he is depicted being controlled by the Cult of Gog, and sacrificing himself to defeat them.

MAJOR DISASTER

DEBUT *Green Lantern* (Vol. 2) #43 (Mar. 1966)
REAL NAME Paul Booker
HEIGHT 5ft 11in **WEIGHT** 195 lbs
EYES Blue **HAIR** Black
POWERS/ABILITIES Able to create massive disasters such as earthquakes, hurricanes, and storms by the power of thought.
ALLIES Atomic Skull
ENEMIES Superman, Wonder Woman, Magog
AFFILIATIONS Minor Disaster (Penny Booker), Justice League Antarctica

FORCE OF NATURE
Major Disaster was able to call down lightning to attack Superman and Wonder Woman.

Green Lantern foe Major Disaster fabricated disasters for his own evil ends. Never a villainous success, he joined the little-respected team, Justice League Antarctica. After a power upgrade from the demon Neron, he graduated to Justice League America, giving the Super Hero life a real try. He died fighting Superboy-Prime in the Battle of Metropolis, but was briefly revived as a Black Lantern during *Blackest Night*. Post-*Flashpoint*, Major Disaster returned to his criminal ways: teaming up with Superman villain Atomic Skull. They interrupted a date between Superman and Wonder Woman by attacking the Indian Point Nuclear Power Plant for a mystery client. He created a massive storm, but was bested by the villain Magog, disguised as a new Super Hero, Wonderstar.

Following *Rebirth*, Booker again lost to the Justice League. His daughter Penny began her own criminal career, battling Harley Quinn as Minor Disaster.

MAJOR FORCE

DEBUT *Captain Atom* (Vol. 1) #12 (Feb. 1988)
HEIGHT 6ft 5in **WEIGHT** 280 lbs
EYES White **HAIR** White
POWERS/ABILITIES Able to project energy; superhuman strength, endurance, and durability.
ALLIES General Eiling
ENEMIES Firestorm, Superman, Hyena, Killer Frost

TOUGH AS NAILS
Major Force is covered in a metallic alloy that grants him enhanced endurance, much like the Super Hero Captain Atom.

Major Force is a US Government operative answerable to General Eiling. It is believed that he formerly operated as Black Jack for a clandestine group called the Black Razors. Black Jack was allegedly decapitated early in his career, yet he seems to have somehow survived the encounter (or been replaced by an as yet unknown new player). He then reemerged as the government agent Major Force in order to rescue Firestorm.

Major Force later helped Firestorm fight off attacks by the Hyena, Killer Frost, Multiplex, Typhoon, Plastique, and Black Bison, with the intention of getting Firestorm to work for the US Government. After these Super-Villains were defeated, Major Force used a special camera flash to render Firestorm unconscious and take him back to General Eiling's base. Unfortunately for Eiling, Superman was alerted to their underhand scheme and crashed into the secure facility, easily taking down Major Force and freeing Firestorm in the process.

MAMMOTH

DEBUT *The New Teen Titans* (Vol. 1) #3 (Jan. 1981)
REAL NAME Baran Flinders
HEIGHT 6ft 5in **WEIGHT** 300 lbs
EYES Blue **HAIR** Red
POWERS/ABILITIES Superhuman strength, endurance, and durability; prone to fits of rage due to state of emotional underdevelopment.
ALLIES Shimmer, Mr. Whisper
ENEMIES Superman, Wonder Woman

Australian Baran Flinders and his sister Selinda were bullied at school when their metahuman powers manifested. They were subsequently taken to specialists who augmented their natural abilities while teaching the children control. Taking the names Mammoth (Baran) and Shimmer (Selinda), the siblings became super-criminals, clashing with Superman, Justice League and both the Teen Titans and their adult iteration the Titans. Despite his immense power, Baran is by nature a flunky and hireling, happy to take orders from the likes of Mr. Twister, H.I.V.E., and his Fearsome Five leaders Doctor Light and Psimon as long as it leads to a big pay-off or cathartic fighting.

Post-*Flashpoint*, Mammoth only made a few appearances: with the Secret Society and alongside his Fearsome Five allies when they attacked Cyborg and the Metal Men. He also battled Superman and Wonder Woman, and was a henchman for the mysterious Mr. Whisper.

BRUTE FORCE
Mammoth was never happier than when he was lashing out at some flashy costumed punk who thought he was just slow and stupid.

MAN-BAT

DEBUT *Detective Comics* (Vol. 1) #400 (Jun. 1970)
REAL NAME Dr. Kirk Langstrom
BASE Gotham City
HEIGHT 6ft 1in **WEIGHT** 201 lbs
EYES Brown/red **HAIR** Brown
POWERS/ABILITIES Serum grants superhuman strength, endurance, speed, agility, reflexes, and durability; flight; genius-level intellect with a keen interest in the sciences; government connections.
ALLIES The Outlaws, Batman, Wonder Woman
ENEMIES Batman, the Batman Family, Bat-Queen
AFFILIATIONS Justice League Dark, S.H.A.D.E., Gotham Academy

Dr. Kirk Langstrom employed his specialist knowledge seeking a cure for deafness. He developed the Langstrom Atavistic Gene Recall Serum, but his test subjects mutated into hideous, bat-like creatures. Catastrophically, Kirk's serum was stolen, and released on the 900 block of Gotham City. With the city plagued by a huge Man-Bat infestation, Langstrom developed an anti-virus to fight the outbreak and—dreading further disasters—tested it on himself. The antidote cured the infected, but unfortunately changed Kirk into the sole remaining Man-Bat. Langstrom subsequently—but only temporarily—gained control over his Man-Bat transformations, and he work at Gotham Academy as its resident science teacher, and at clandestine counter-terrorism organization S.H.A.D.E.

Kirk's family also suffered. His wife, Francine, developed a serum and became a terrifying Bat-Queen, while his father, Abraham, deliberately transformed himself into a villainous Man-Bat.

After finally perfecting his formula, Langstrom can effect staged transformations: ranging from his original flying monster to a semi-altered state, combining vast intellect with bat senses. Recruited to Justice League Dark, Langstrom began a scientific study into the nature and practice of magic, a project which affected his hard-won sanity. That pressure was intensified by media reports that his origins were a disinformation strategy, and his powers came from a top-secret US government metahuman enhancement program: the Superman Project.

ON THE RECORD

Dr. Kirk Langstrom was first introduced in Detective Comics #400 (Jun. 1970), as a bat expert seeking to harness the sonar-like abilities of bats. His bat-serum transformed him into a giant bat, and later did the same to his girlfriend, Francine Lee (later Langstrom). Later, Man-Bat learned how to control his abilities with a pill, and fought injustice, sometimes alongside private-eye Jason Bard. His heroics were spotlighted in his own 1975 miniseries, in which he took on the Batman villain, Ten-Eyed Man.

BATMAN V. MAN-BAT:
Batman had battled many bizarre foes, but even he wasn't prepared for a bestial version of himself: Man-Bat.

MAN OF SCIENCE
Dr. Langstrom applied scientific discipline and rationality to his study of magic.

MANCHESTER BLACK

DEBUT *Action Comics* (Vol. 1) #775 (Mar. 2001)
HEIGHT 6ft **WEIGHT** 210 lbs
EYES Brown **HAIR** Purple
POWERS/ABILITIES Mind reading and telekinetic abilities; skilled manipulator
ALLIES Elite
ENEMIES Superman, Superboy (Jon Kent), Lois Lane, Frankenstein, The Bride
AFFILIATIONS S.T.A.R. Labs, Super-Elite

British-born Manchester Black is a super-psionic vigilante. With his Elite team, he began executing until Superman proved the power and value of his altruistic beliefs. When Black realized his acts made him a villain in his own eyes, he killed himself. He was reborn Post-*Flashpoint* as chief of S.T.A.R. Labs' Advanced Ideas Division: a ruthless manipulator who tricked the Teen Titans into working with S.T.A.R. Labs and for him. Black orchestrated deadly attacks upon himself and New York City by Algorithm—a killer AI. After *Flashpoint*, he led a new band of alien Super-Elite, attacking Superman's family and seeking to turn his son Jon into the kind of antihero who punished and killed the wicked. Ultimately defeated, Black's consciousness was briefly imprisoned in a cow's mind. He remains at large in the Multiverse.

MANITOU RAVEN

DEBUT *JLA* (Vol. 1) #66 (Jul. 2002)
BASE The Factory, New Jersey; Justice League Watchtower, the moon
HEIGHT 5ft 9in **WEIGHT** 159 lbs
EYES White **HAIR** Black
POWERS/ABILITIES Magical adept utilizing Native American occultism; time travel.
ALLIES Manitou Dawn, Naif al-Sheikh, Vera Black, J'onn J'onzz, Major Disaster
ENEMIES Gamemnae, Manchester Black
AFFILIATIONS League of Ancients, Justice League of America, Justice League Elite

Manitou Raven was a mystic master of the Obsidian Age people who became the Apache tribe. With his sorceress wife Manitou Dawn, he joined a coalition of super-powered champions, the League of Ancients.

Three thousand years ago, Raven and Dawn were tricked by Gamemnae of Atlantis into attacking the 21st-century Justice League. After realizing they were duped, the Manitous helped defeat Gamemnae, and then moved to the future to join the JL, where their magical abilities made them invaluable.

A hard-liner, Raven joined the black ops Justice League Elite. He died saving the team from a bomb, but this did not end his service. His mantle of power passed to his wife, and his spirit often appears to her, offering her sage advice.

MANNHEIM, BRUNO

DEBUT *Superman's Pal, Jimmy Olsen* (Vol. 1) #139 (Jul. 1971)
BASE Metropolis
EYES Black
HAIR Black
POWERS/ABILITIES Devious and ruthless; immense physical strength; religious fanaticism.
ENEMIES Superman, Jimmy Olsen, the Guardian, Renee Montoya, Nightwing, Batwoman

Bruno "Ugly" Mannheim came from a long line of thugs and career criminals. Following in the footsteps of his mobster father—known as "Boss Moxie"—Bruno strong-armed his way out of Metropolis' Suicide Slum and climbed the ladder of corruption until he was chief of underworld super-syndicate Intergang.

Under Darkseid, he was "reborn" as a devout believer in the Religion of Crime as espoused in the vile Crime Bible. His savage tendencies magnified by the dark faith, Mannheim began recruiting Super-Villains, turning Intergang into a legion of monsters. Those who did not convert, he killed and ate.

Physically mutating, he attempted to turn Gotham City into Little Apokolips, but was foiled and killed by Nightwing, Batwoman, and The Question.

MANTIS

DEBUT *Forever People* (Vol. 1) #2 (Apr.–May 1971)
REAL NAME Omar Bashir
BASE Feast of Eden, Sudan
HEIGHT 6ft 4in **WEIGHT** 225 lbs
EYES Orange **HAIR** Bald
POWERS/ABILITIES Superhuman strength and speed; limited flight; energy absorption.
ENEMIES Forever People, Infinity-Man
AFFILIATIONS The Swarm, Darkseid

Mantis is a ruthlessly destructive being, born from a freak combination of human agriculture, New Gods technology, and good intentions. A New Genesis faction had been secretly working with human scientists to try to solve world hunger. They planned to replace Earth's deserts with topsoil from different dimensions and use insects to cross-pollinate the resulting crops. Their efforts went horribly awry when Apokolips intervened, with human project-leader Omar Bashir mutating into Mantis, an insectoid berserker.

Aggressive and driven by a need to defend his swarm's territory, Mantis is the only known sentient member of the new species. Determined to become Earth's dominant life-form, his insectoids breed by mutating their victims into drones.

MANHUNTERS

DEBUT *1st Issue Special* (Vol. 1) #5 (Aug. 1975)
BASE Warworld, Orinda, Biot, Oa
POWERS/ABILITIES Virtually indestructible; adept at deception and strategic planning; possess advanced science and weaponry.
ALLIES Sinestro Corps
ENEMIES Guardians of the Universe, Green Lantern Corps, Darkstars, JLA, JSA
AFFILIATIONS Guardians of the Universe, Manhunter agents

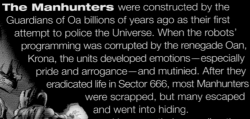

The Manhunters were constructed by the Guardians of Oa billions of years ago as their first attempt to police the Universe. When the robots' programming was corrupted by the renegade Oan, Krona, the units developed emotions—especially pride and arrogance—and mutinied. After they eradicated life in Sector 666, most Manhunters were scrapped, but many escaped and went into hiding.

However, their core directive remained: they were designed to stalk prey and enact justice, but now their leader would dictate what that meant. Executing their pledge "No man escapes the Manhunters," they infiltrated countless worlds, planting undercover agents throughout secret societies and Super Hero groups, and offering power and justice to the helpless. Their ultimate aim, though, was vengeance against the Guardians.

On Earth, the Manhunters formed the Shan sect, which, for centuries, did worthwhile work from the shadows. The Shan's last recruit was frustrated public defender Mark Shaw, whose good intentions were subverted to the Prime Manhunter's scheme to forever discredit the Guardians.

The Manhunters' greatest strike came when the Guardians reunited with their Oan females, the Zamarons, to facilitate the next stage in universal evolution. The genders had separated billions of years earlier, unable to agree on how to handle Krona. To crush the Guardians' plans, every Earthly Manhunter asset was activated to counter the heroes safeguarding the "New Guardians" birth. The scale and foresight of the robots' planning and attacks was staggering, but a coalition of champions comprising the Justice League, Suicide Squad, Outsiders, Teen Titans, Infinity, Inc., Legion of Super-Heroes, and more prevailed—but not without great loss.

Regularly discovered and destroyed, the Manhunters seem eternal: perpetually rebuilding in secret before remorselessly striking again.

LETHAL WEAPONS
Not every valiant defender survived the concerted assault of the manhunting mechanical monsters.

MARCH, LINCOLN

DEBUT *Batman* (Vol. 2) #1 (Nov. 2011)
REAL NAME Claims to be Thomas Wayne, Jr.
BASE Gotham City
EYES Blue **HAIR** Black
POWERS/ABILITIES Superhuman powers; Talon Suit affords flight, protection, weaponry.
ALLIES Cluemaster
ENEMIES Batman, Court of Owls
AFFILIATION March Venture, Court of Owls, Willowwood Home for Children

Lincoln March believed he was Bruce's long-lost younger brother Thomas Jr., reared in secret as protection from the insidious Court of Owls. The Court found him anyway, reeducating him as their pawn. Designed to run Wayne's financial empire for them, he failed and was reinvented as a financier and Gotham City mayoral candidate. After joining the Court's top tier—and murdering most of them—March donned hi-tech Talon armor to fight Batman. Defeated, he seemingly died but actually retreated into the shadows, attacking Batman's family via Cluemaster. This also failed, and the Court of Owls put him in suspended animation. Paving the way for his war against all Batman loves, The Joker reanimated March, setting him on Batman. The Dark Knight and The Joker's archrival Two-Face easily defeated him.

MANHUNTER

DATA

DEBUT *Manhunter* (Vol. 3) #1 (Oct. 2004)
REAL NAME Kate Spencer
BASE Mobile
HEIGHT 5ft 5in
WEIGHT 120 lbs
EYES Blue
HAIR Black
POWERS/ABILITIES Incisive intellect; dogged determination and peak physical constitution; trained in martial arts; extraterrestrial Darkstar Exo-Mantle affords superhuman strength; clawed gauntlet; power staff; expert knowledge of the legal system.
ALLIES Green Arrow, Red Arrow, Black Canary, Batman
ENEMIES Leviathan, Copperhead, Ninth Circle

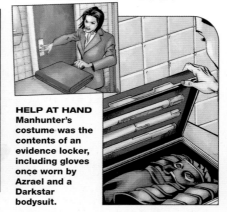

HELP AT HAND
Manhunter's costume was the contents of an evidence locker, including gloves once worn by Azrael and a Darkstar bodysuit.

With the US justice system increasingly unable to deal with metahuman criminality or the ruthless tactics of modern human predators, legal advocate Kate Spencer decided to take the law into her own hands. Armed with lethal alien weaponry and wearing armor, Kate adopted a codename taken from the villains and monsters she despised. She now stalks the night as Manhunter, bringing swift and certain retribution to the guilty, and salvation to the oppressed.

NEVER SURRENDER
Whatever the odds, and despite possessing none of the powers other family members were blessed with, Kate Spencer could never accept defeat.

Formerly forced to hide behind the legal system, Kate Spencer's true personality emerged when she lost faith in her job as a Federal prosecutor. Despite her best legal efforts, the reptilian Copperhead—who had murdered and eaten many victims—evaded the death penalty and killed again. Enraged and frustrated, Kate stole impounded technology and used it to hunt down and execute the cannibal.

While Kate had many adventures as this new Manhunter, she appeared to retire when she moved to Seattle with her son, Ramsey. Kate had fallen on hard times, and had too many bills and too few prospects. At the end of her rope, she took on the hopelessly dire case of Oliver Queen, who had been framed for murder by the clandestine Ninth Circle criminal organization. The Ninth Circle owned much of Seattle and even had many police detectives on their payroll. When it was discovered that Oliver's "murder victim" was very much alive, Kate was charged with watching over her. One night, when an officer attempted to make this innocent woman's alleged murder a reality. Kate was forced to kill the corrupt detective in front of her young son in order to keep him safe.

After Oliver Queen was found innocent, Kate became the corporate attorney for Queen Industries. She resumed her life as Manhunter and was recruited by Batman into an elite task force of detectives. The Leviathan criminal organization had destroyed or absorbed all other spy groups, and Batman was attempting to identify the head of this shadowy operation. While Kate was originally suspected to be working with Leviathan, the detectives soon realized that the person truly in charge was a different Manhunter, former hero Mark Shaw.

SNAKEBITE
Despite her inexperience, Manhunter applied the oldest of all human laws to Copperhead: "a life for a life."

CLASSIC STORIES

***Manhunter* (Vol. 3) #20 (May 2006)**
Kate is forced to defend the vile Dr. Psycho in court, but is distracted by her son Ramsey who deduces that she is secretly Manhunter.

***Manhunter* (Vol. 3) #37–38 (Feb.–Mar. 2009)** Offering a tantalizing glimpse of things to come, Manhunter Kate Spencer gives Ramsey a costume of his own so he can continue in the family's masked hero traditions.

***Batman: Battle for the Cowl* (Vol. 1) #1–3 (May–Jul. 2009)** With Batman declared dead, Manhunter relocates to Gotham City and joins the Batman Family during the struggle to appoint the Dark Knight's successor.

ON THE RECORD

Before the reality-altering event *Flashpoint*, Kate had learned that she had descended from a line of mighty metahumans. Kate's great-grandfather was legendary World War I super-warrior Hugo Danner, her grandparents were WWII heroes Iron Munro and Phantom Lady, and her own father Walter Pratt was a Super-Villain. Even Kate's young son Ramsey appeared to be developing astonishing powers.

Despite lacking metahuman advantages herself, Kate eventually became a valuable asset of the Department of Extranormal Operations, while also freelancing with the Birds of Prey and the Batman Family.

GOTHAM CITY BOUND
Kate eventually found work in Gotham City as the new District Attorney, a position once held by Harvey Dent (Two-Face).

MARONI, SALVATORE

DEBUT *Detective Comics* (Vol. 1) #66 (Aug. 1942)
BASE Gotham City
HEIGHT 5ft 11in **WEIGHT** 227 lbs
EYES Brown **HAIR** Black
POWERS/ABILITIES Smart mob boss with many connections in the underworld.
ALLIES C.J. Maroni, C.C. Haly
ENEMIES Two-Face, Batman, Batman Family
AFFILIATIONS Maroni Crime Family

Salvatore "Boss" Maroni was one of Gotham City's most notorious gangsters and the sometime rival/sometime ally of the Falcone crime family. Before the reality-changing *Flashpoint* event, Maroni was responsible for creating the Super-Villain Two-Face when he hurled acid at DA Harvey Dent, scarring Dent's face.

In modern continuity, that dubious honor falls to the criminal Erin McKillen, though Maroni is still a mob boss and owner of a movie theater. When a young Dick Grayson was watching a film at Maroni's movie house, Gotham City lost power as part of the event later dubbed *Zero Year*. Grayson teamed up with Salvatore's son, C.J., and the two managed to escape an encounter with the villain Amygdala, the Grayson family earning Maroni's gratitude in the process.

MARY, QUEEN OF BLOOD

DEBUT *House of Mystery* #290 (Mar. 1979)
REAL NAME Mary Seward
EYES Red **HAIR** Red
POWERS/ABILITIES Vampiric hypnosis and strength; shape-changing; regeneration and immortality, but vulnerability to sunlight.
ENEMIES Andrew Bennett, Van Helsing

Created by vampire Andrew Bennett, Mary Seward spent centuries as his companion. Their disagreement over how vampires should interact with humans sharpened into open conflict when Mary gathered the Cult of the Blood Red Moon and embarked on a war against the guardians of humanity. Bennett tried to kill her, but was stopped by Batman, before teenage vampire hunter Tig Rafelson killed Bennett.

When John Constantine brought Bennett back to life, Andrew and Mary joined together at the head of all vampires after the death of the primordial vampire Cain. She fought Bennett for control before a climactic battle between vampires and the Van Helsing-led vampire hunters culminated in Bennett absorbing the vampiric powers of every living vampire—and assuming Cain's evil role. Mary was then pitted against Bennett once more, despite remembering their history as lovers.

MARY SHAZAM

DEBUT *Captain Marvel Adventures* #18 (Dec. 1942)
REAL NAME Mary Bromfield
BASE Philadelphia
HEIGHT 5ft 6in **WEIGHT** 139 lbs
EYES Blue **HAIR** Auburn
POWERS/ABILITIES Access to the powers of Shazam, including enhanced strength and durability, the Living Lightning, and other magical abilities
ALLIES Shazam
ENEMIES Black Adam, Sivana, Black Adam
AFFILIATIONS The Shazam Family

CONFIDANT
When Billy Batson became aware of what it meant to have the powers of Shazam, he knew he could share his misgivings with Mary Bromfield.

Mary Bromfield is one of Mr. and Mrs. Vasquez's foster children, along with Billy Batson and the others who become the Shazam Family—Freddy Freeman, Pedro Pena, Eugene Choi, and Darla Dudley. She was the first child the Vasquez's fostered, and as a result is something of a mother figure to the younger kids. They all seek her advice and guidance, when situations arise that they cannot discuss with adults.

When Black Adam confronted Shazam, the hero shared his powers with the entire group, and Mary became Lady Shazam, granted the same super-strength and powers over the Living Lightning that were bestowed on Shazam. After defeating Black Adam, all of the children were bound together by their experience and knowledge of Billy Batson's secret. Mary assumed a leadership role in the team, and also helped Billy come to terms with the powers of Shazam—as well as his knowledge that he was far from the Wizard's first choice.

Her wisdom was especially necessary when Billy's real father returned. He briefly shared the Shazam power, only to be exposed as a mind-enslaved pawn of Mister Mind, caring nothing for the son he had abandoned.

ON THE RECORD

In previous incarnations of the character, Mary drew her powers from a different set of gods making up the word Shazam: Selena, Hippolyta, Ariadne, Zephyrus, Aurora, and Minerva. Mary and the other members of the Shazam family have been in and out of the Justice League over the years, and she was also a core member of the Super Buddies, when she survived a literal trip to Hell and back.

During *Final Crisis*, Mary was one of a number of heroes corrupted and turned into Darkseid's thralls until Freddy Freeman managed to overcome Desaad's influence by catching hold of Mary and shouting "Shazam!" to transform her back to her normal self.

BOOOOOM!

POWERED BY MIGHTY WOMEN
Mary discovered that being part of the Shazam family was more fun than she'd expected.

RIDE THE LIGHTNING
Mary Bromfield takes on the powers of Shazam, knowing that, as the Vasquez household's big sister, she's the one her foster siblings look to for counsel.

MARTIAN MANHUNTER

DATA

DEBUT *Detective Comics* #225 (Nov. 1955)
REAL NAME J'onn J'onzz **BASE** Mobile
HEIGHT 6ft 7in **WEIGHT** 260 lbs **EYES** Red **HAIR** None
POWERS/ABILITIES Physical near-invulnerability; superhuman
strength, speed, and endurance; flight; telepathy, telekinesis,
shapeshifting, phase-shifting, regeneration; Martian vision can
see through solid objects and project various forms of energy;
extremely intelligent with strong leadership skills.
ALLIES Hawkgirl, Miss Martian, Superman
ENEMIES Ma'alefa'ak, Charnn, Crime Syndicate, Lex Luthor,
Despero
AFFILIATIONS Justice League, Stormwatch, Justice League United,
Justice League of America, Guild of Detection

The Martian Manhunter is—according to
Superman—the most powerful being on Earth.
But even more than his powers, it is his idealism
and resolute pursuit of justice that set him
apart. He becomes the moral compass of any
group he joins, the memory of his lost family
driving him to save others from suffering the
grief he continues to feel. With immense
powers, including shapeshifting and mind
control, J'onn J'onzz can do almost anything—
and knows that such power must be guided by
a true belief in what's right. Though not human,
he is perhaps the most empathetic of heroes
—an irony not lost on J'onn himself.

AT A GLANCE...

Many faces
His ability to shapeshift has always
been key to Martian Manhunter's
success. He usually assumes other
human-sized forms—notably taking
Catwoman's shape to infiltrate the Secret
Society of Super-Villains—but is capable of
more incredible transformations as well.

Mars attacks
For many years it was thought that the
Martian Manhunter was the last of his kind.
However, this was not the case.
The wise bearer of Martian history
known as the Martian Keep was
being held on Thanagar Prime.
The Martian Keep also raised
a White Martian, now known
as the heroic Miss Martian.

When the Multiverse was originally
formed, it was crafted by Perpetua, a being
who wished to create a perpetual universe
with the help of her servant army of apex
predators—hybrid creatures that were equal
parts Martian and Earthling. As punishment
for her attempt to prevent the natural order of
things, Perpetua was locked away behind the
Source Wall at the far reaches of the galaxy.

While the Guardians of the Universe
sought to keep the knowledge of this race
of apex predators a secret, a small group of
Earth scientists led by Lex Luthor's father,
Lionel Luthor, discovered it. They began
experimenting, creating half Martian/half
human abominations. The DNA of a captive
Martian child, a boy named J'onn J'onzz, was
used to create these terrifying monstrosities.

During his time as a captive, J'onn
befriended a young Lex Luthor, who eventually
helped J'onn escape. J'onn returned to
Mars and Lex Luthor's memories were all but erased. Back on Mars, J'onn rose through
the ranks of the Manhunters to become a Chief Hunter. A far cry from the hero he is today,
J'onn worked with a variety of crime lords in order to give his family a more financially stable
life. Ashamed, he kept these criminal secrets from his wife M'yri'ah and his daughter K'hym.

When a plague of psychic fire called H'ronmeer's Curse ravaged Mars, killing nearly
everyone, J'onn was teleported to Earth by a scientist named Dr. Mark Saul Erdel. Not just
transported through space, J'onn was also sent hundreds of thousands of years forward in
time. However, his sudden appearance shocked Erdel and he died of a heart attack.

As he explored Earth, J'onn chanced upon an honorable police officer named John
Jones who had been killed in the line of duty. J'onn assumed John's form and took his place
as a police detective in Middleton, Colorado. While investigating a case with his partner
Diane Meade, J'onn wrecked his car, and weakened by the flames, J'onn's true form was
revealed. Nevertheless, Diane grew to accept him and the two remained partners, working
together to stop a Martian criminal called Charnn.

TAKING SHAPE
Martians studied Earthlings from a distance.
Primitive Earthlings greatly inspired the
Martians, and many opted to walk on two legs
when they chose their "social shape"—the
form a Martian allows others to see them.

CLASSIC STORIES

***JLA: Year One* #1–12 (Jan.–Dec.
1998)** This origin story of the Justice
League of America demonstrates that the
Martian Manhunter was the heart and soul
of the team from its inception.

***Martian Manhunter: American
Secrets* #1–3 (Aug.–Oct. 1992)**
J'onn J'onzz is on his own in this
claustrophobic thriller, investigating a vast
conspiracy touching on the signature
elements of 1950s America: game shows,
the birth of rock'n'roll and suburbia, and
Cold War paranoia.

***Final Crisis: Requiem* (Sep. 2008)**
The Justice League and many other heroes
gather at J'onn's funeral, reflecting on his
life through a series of flashbacks.

Pyrophobia
The Martian Manhunter has a strong
aversion to fire, long thought to be a
physical vulnerability. But it stems from the
trauma of seeing so many other Martians
die of H'ronmeer's Curse—a telepathic
plague that killed victims with psychic fire.

THE CURSE
When Mars was overcome by H'ronmeer's
Curse, J'onn tried to use his underworld
connections to escape. However, he was
double-crossed by the very criminals he
had protected from the Manhunters. J'onn
attempted to telepathically cut his family off
from the rest of the planet, but his daughter
reconnected, causing her and her mother to
succumb to the plague before J'onn's eyes.

**J'onn was forced to witness the death
of everything he held dear. His family
died before his eyes, their final thoughts
on his corruption.**

As the years passed, J'onn eventually found like-minded allies when he joined the Justice League, then Stormwatch, then the Justice League of America and Justice League United. After a sabbatical on Thanagar Prime, he rejoined the Justice League following an invasion from the Dark Multiverse. J'onn used his telepathic abilities to link up the Justice League, offering advanced communication capabilities and the ability to gather together in a virtual meeting room in their minds.

When Lex Luthor helped free Perpetua from behind the Source Wall at the end of the universe, Luthor was transformed into Apex Lex, combining his own DNA with Martian DNA. Taking it a step further, he absorbed J'onn into himself. As the world shifted in favor of the concept of doom, and the Justice League seemed defeated, Martian Manhunter and Hawkgirl's son, Shayne, took J'onn's place inside Luthor. His sacrifice freed the Martian Manhunter, although it could not be undone. Mustering all his strength, J'onn and the Justice League rallied, although they had to exit reality as they knew it to do so.

COMING TO AMERICA
Dr. Erdel brought J'onn to Earth using a 4-D Matter Transmitter. J'onn was more susceptible to Erdel's device than other Martians due to his earlier captivity on Earth as a child at the hands of Lionel Luthor.

"There isn't much justice in this world. Perhaps that's why it is so satisfying to occasionally make some."
MARTIAN MANHUNTER

MANHUNTER OF HONOR
J'onn J'onzz has become the heart of the Justice League. He is a Martian with many virtues, and few vices—aside from the occasional Choco sandwich cookie.

SHAYNE, COME BACK!
Working together in the League brought Martian Manhunter and Hawkgirl closer, and romance sparked. When they traveled to another dimension—one that no longer existed—the pair met their son from that reality, a boy named Shayne. Noble and heroic, Shayne opted to leave his world with his other parents.

Back on Earth, Shayne helped the Justice League during their fight with the Legion of Doom, but sacrificed himself by permanently taking J'onn's place inside Lex Luthor's hybrid Martian form.

IN THEIR FOOTSTEPS
Shayne employed wings like his mother, but was also able to use telepathy like his father.

ON THE RECORD

The Martian Manhunter's earliest adventures were a classic blend of sci-fi and detective stories. Brought to Earth by Dr. Erdel's teleportation experiment, then stranded by Erdel's death, he chose to use his powers to fight crime as Detective John Johns, until Earth's technology had advanced sufficiently for him to return home.

Ma'aleca'andra
In his first solo series, the Martian Manhunter's origins were revised. He was said to assume a hybrid Martian-Earthling appearance, masking his true form. Dr. Erdel's teleportation experiment was also revealed to have catapulted J'onn not just through space but also time, leaving him thousands of years distant from the planet (Ma'aleca'andra, in the Martian tongue) he once knew.

Playing with fire
J'onn J'onzz's vulnerability to fire and his fear of it soon became common knowledge among the Justice League's enemies, causing him problems and also endangering the team on a number of occasions. Grappling with his fear, he tried to confront it by making a deal with the fiery villainess Scorch. As a result he was briefly transformed into Fernus, the Burning Martian, before the other members of the League helped him regain control.

Showing his true face
In "The Others Among Us," J'onn discovered a secret project subjecting captive Martians to brutal experiments designed to uncover their powers and control the power of H'ronmeer's Curse. During the course of this story, J'onn became stuck in his true form due to psychic battles against other disguised White and Green Martians.

NIGHTMARE
Recalling the lethal fire of H'ronmeer's Curse, the Martian Manhunter died in flames at the start of *Final Crisis*.

MATTER-EATER LAD

DEBUT *Adventure Comics* #303 (Dec. 1963)
REAL NAME Tenzil Kem **BASE** Bismoll
HEIGHT 5ft 10in **WEIGHT** 200 lbs
EYES Blue **HAIR** Black
POWERS/ABILITIES Able to ingest and break down any form of matter.
ALLIES Wildfire **ENEMIES** Horraz, Crav the General Nah, Mordru
AFFILIATIONS Legion of Super-Heroes

After a microbial disaster rendered their food inedible, the people of planet Bismoll evolved the ability to consume all forms of matter. This made Tenzil Kem an indispensable member of the Legion of Super-Heroes. With Matter-Eater Lad, they could escape any confinement and destroy any weapon. Kem's power provides him with constant energy, enhanced musculature, and an imposing stature. Kem compensates for his imposing looks with a gregarious and gentle nature—unless innocent lives are at stake or his comrades are in trouble.

In a previous reality, Matter-Eater Lad's Legion career was abruptly terminated when he was drafted into the Bismollian Civil Service, ultimately rising to planetary President. Ever the hero, he returned to save the universe by eating an otherwise indestructible Controller Miracle Machine that threatened to end all existence.

MEANSTREAK

DEBUT *Justice League America* (Vol. 2) #78 (Aug. 1993)
HEIGHT 5ft 8in **WEIGHT** 144 lbs
EYES Blue **HAIR** Blond
POWERS/ABILITIES Creation of blades and projectiles made of flaming energy.
ENEMIES Justice League of America
AFFILIATIONS New Extremists

The sadistic, chaos-loving Meanstreak became part of a mercenary group the New Extremists at the invitation of the extra-dimensional being, Dreamslayer, who sought to destroy the JLA. The plot failed, but Dreamslayer tried again, using a cult called the Flock of the Machine, which possessed a dangerous device granted to them by the Overmaster, whom they worshiped. When this also failed, the Overmaster took direct control of the New Extremists from Dreamslayer, who had been his pawn from the beginning.

The New Extremists became part of the Super-Villain army, the Cadre, fighting the JLA again as part of the Overmaster's test of humanity's worth. After the collapse of the Cadre, the Overmaster turned Meanstreak and her fellow New Extremists loose. They were later exiled to the planet Salvation, but are thought to still be active.

MENAGERIE

DEBUT *Forever Evil: A.R.G.U.S.* #5 (Apr. 2014)
MEMBERS/POWERS The Cheetah, Weasel, Lion-Mane, Hellhound, Elephant Man, Primape, Zebra-Man, Mauschen (formerly).
BASE Central Park, New York City
ENEMIES A.R.G.U.S.
AFFILIATIONS Crime Syndicate of America

The Menagerie were an animal-themed group assembled by The Cheetah with Wonder Woman's stolen Lasso of Truth. They allied with the Crime Syndicate of America after its invasion from Earth-3. The team kidnapped Steve Trevor and Killer Frost as they searched for Firestorm to help free Justice League members trapped within his matrix. The Cheetah tried to use the Lasso of Truth to seduce Trevor, but he resisted, seizing control of the Lasso. Killer Frost—needing to siphon energy to keep herself alive—drained mouselike Mauschen's lifeforce, using the energy to freeze the rest of the Menagerie. Pre-*Flashpoint*, Menagerie was the codename shared by reformed villains Pamela and Sonja, whose bodies were hosts to alien beasts. Both worked with covert team Justice League Elite.

MENTO

DEBUT *Doom Patrol* (Vol. 1) #91 (Nov. 1964)
REAL NAME Steve Dayton
HEIGHT 5ft 10in **WEIGHT** 178 lbs
EYES Blue **HAIR** Brown
POWERS/ABILITIES Granted numerous psychokinetic powers by the Mento Helmet.
ALLIES Elasti-Girl, Beast Boy
AFFILIATIONS Justice League Dark, Doom Patrol

Wealthy businessman Steve Dayton created the Mento Helmet to enhance his mental powers and catch the eye of the Doom Patrol's Elasti-Girl. This led to a long-standing affiliation with the Doom Patrol, despite tensions within the group, some of whom didn't trust the self-styled hero.

Mento's reckless perfecting of his powers came at a cost to his psyche, at least twice making him mentally unbalanced. The first time, Raven cured him, but during his second period of insanity, he acted as the Crimelord for some time until the Teen Titans finally stopped him. Later, Mento appeared with the Justice League Dark during their pursuit of the Books of Magic, lending his psychic powers to their collective search for the Books and also helping Constantine stay one step ahead of Steve Trevor and A.R.G.U.S.

MAXIMA

DEBUT *Action Comics* #645 (Nov. 1989)
HEIGHT 6ft 2in **WEIGHT** 164 lbs
EYES Green **HAIR** Red
POWERS/ABILITIES Flight; super-strength; psychokinetic manipulation of matter.
ALLIES Supergirl
ENEMIES H'El, Roho
AFFILIATIONS Crucible Academy

Hailing from the planet Almeracia, the young Maxima joined the Crucible Academy, where the champions of each race were trained and molded into protectors of their people. Headstrong and sharp-tongued, Maxima had trouble with authority, which led to conflicts with other Academy students—including Supergirl at first. The two later formed a bond and fought together against enemies who sought to subvert and overthrow the Academy. Becoming attracted to Supergirl, Maxima helped her protect Superboy from H'El and other malign members of the Academy. In the process, Maxima also helped Supergirl overcome her Kryptonian prejudice against clones.

Maxima then put her leadership qualities to good use, accepting an ongoing position with the Academy. It is now her responsibility to train the next generation of students.

SUPER-FAST ADVICE
Thanks to his long experience of the Speed Force, Max Mercury has been a useful mentor to many more modern speedster Super Heroes.

MERCURY, MAX

DEBUT *National Comics* #5 (Nov. 1940)
BASE Manchester, Alabama
HEIGHT 6ft 1in **WEIGHT** 188 lbs
EYES Blue **HAIR** Gray
POWERS/ABILITIES Super-speed; vibrational frequency shifting permits his body to pass through solid matter.
ALLIES The Flash
ENEMIES Professor Zoom
AFFILIATIONS Freedom Fighters

Max Mercury was imbued with the power of the Speed Force as a member of the US Cavalry in the 19th century, following a massacre of Native Americans. A dying shaman enchanted Max, granting him unlimited super-speed and the ability to shift his molecules and pass through solid objects.

Known over the years as Quicksilver, Windrunner, Whip Whirlwind, and the Zen Master of Speed, Max tried to penetrate the mysteries of the Speed Force many times. Each time he found himself skipping forward in time, with the result that he now finds himself in the 21st century.

Over the years, he has served as a mentor to Barry Allen, Wally West, Johnny Quick, and Bart Allen, lending his experience and knowledge of the Speed Force to their battles against Professor Zoom, Superboy-Prime, and the Rival.

MIDNIGHT

DEBUT *Smash Comics* #18 (Jan. 1941)
REAL NAME Dave Clark
BASE New York City
HEIGHT 6ft **WEIGHT** 190 lbs
EYES Blue **HAIR** Black
POWERS/ABILITIES Expert detective and martial artist; uses a vacuum gun to fire a cable for scaling buildings.
ALLIES Doc Wackey, Gabby, Sniffer Snoop
ENEMIES Morris Carleton
AFFILIATIONS All-Star Squadron

Dave Clark was a popular newsreader for New York's UXAM radio station. When an apartment building collapsed, he helped drag people from the rubble and discovered that the block had been built by the corrupt Carleton Construction Company. Inspired by the hero of the radio serial *The Man Called Midnight*, he put on a mask and assumed the code name Midnight. He intimidated Carleton's owner into donating funds to those injured in the disaster, and got word out about the shoddy construction of a Carleton dam before it collapsed, saving many lives. When the clock struck 12 that evening, Midnight confronted Carleton and forced him to confess his crimes.

Midnight continued to fight for justice, battling Nazis as part of the All-Star Squadron and the Freedom Fighters.

MERA

DATA

DEBUT *Aquaman* (Vol. 1) #11 **(Sep.–Oct. 1963)**
BASE Atlantis
HEIGHT 5ft 9in **WEIGHT** 160 lbs
EYES Blue **HAIR** Red
POWERS/ABILITIES Water breathing; telekinetic control over water and "hard water" manipulation; enhanced strength and stamina; highly trained warrior; natural leader.
ALLIES Aquaman, Vulko, Tula, Aqualad
ENEMIES Ocean Master, Dead King, Black Manta, Eel
AFFILIATIONS Justice League

A LOVE SUPREME
After everything they've been through, Aquaman and Mera stand firmly together. Coming from Xebel, Mera also helped to extend Aquaman's influence over the subsea realms beyond the city of Atlantis.

TROUBLED HERITAGE
Mera has spent her life reconciling Xebelian hatred for Atlantis with her own personal love for Aquaman.

Aquaman's lover and later Queen of Atlantis, Mera, of the Atlantean nation of Xebe,l is a powerful telekinetic. She gave it all up to find a new life with Arthur Curry on land, only to be dragged back into the rivalries of her home kingdom.

A native of the aquatic kingdom of Xebel,

an ancient Atlantean penal colony, Mera was trained as an assassin and grew up with a deep suspicion of Atlantis. However, when instructed to kill Aquaman, she fell in love with him and fought by his side. When Aquaman left Atlantis to make a life in the surface world, she went with him, but had difficulty adjusting. She got a welcome chance to return to adventuring during Aquaman and the Others' quest to fight Black Manta and retrieve stolen Atlantean artifacts. However, this was only brief respite from the hostility she experienced on land. She returned to the oceans to fight the Dead King when he unleashed freezing attacks against the East Coast. After a long relationship, Aquaman proposed to Mera. Betrothed to the king, Mera administered Spindrift Station, an Atlantean Dry Land Embassy on the coast of Massachusetts. It was soon destroyed by Black Manta, just one of the new conflicts between Atlantis and the surface world. The villainous Corum Rath then usurped Arthur's throne. After he was defeated by Aquaman and his allies, Mera was placed as the new Queen of Atlantis, leaving Aquaman free to pursue his life as a Super Hero.

When Mera became pregnant, she became engaged to her advisor Vulko to help unite the kingdom. During a battle with Black Manta, she expended too much of her powers and landed in a coma, however her daughter, Andy, was nevertheless born healthy and happy. Mera soon awoke and, on the day she was to be married, announced a plan to dissolve undersea monarchies altogether.

ELEMENTAL RAGE
Not even Black Manta can withstand Mera's powers when she really gives in to her emotions.

ON THE RECORD

Originally the free-spirited queen of an other-dimensional realm, Mera left it all to marry Aquaman. The murder of their son by Black Manta compounded emotional instability she was experiencing due to unknown factors in the Earthly environment. She and her husband experienced long separations in the years that followed.

During *Blackest Night*, Mera was able to fight off the Black Lanterns while she kept her emotions in check, but when her anger spiraled out of control, she was brought into the Red Lantern Corps, and nearly died in battle.

ROYAL FURY
Mera has a reputation as the emotional one, but when she is hurt or endangered, Aquaman flashes a temper of his own.

CLASSIC STORIES

Aquaman: Sword of Atlantis #40–45 (May–Nov. 2006) Mera leads a band of survivors after the destruction of Atlantis by the Spectre. She holds out against growing chaos under the oceans before reuniting with Aquaman against the threat of the Ocean Master.

Aquaman (Vol. 1) #58–60 (Oct.–Nov. 1977; Feb.–Mar. 1978) Black Manta kidnaps Mera's child Aquababy and traps him in a tank designed to suffocate him. Mera embarks on a quest to Xebel to find the device to free him. She succeeds, but returns too late to save her baby.

MERLYN

DEBUT *Justice League of America* (Vol. 1) #94 (Nov. 1971)
REAL NAME Arthur King
HEIGHT 6ft 3in **WEIGHT** 185 lbs **EYES** Blue **HAIR** Black
POWERS/ABILITIES Expert archer and martial artist; lethal trick arrows; cunning and stealthy; Kevlar body armor.
ALLIES Amanda Waller, Suicide Squad, Seven Men of Death, League of Assassins **ENEMIES** Green Arrow, Black Canary, Red Arrow, Manhunter, Justice League, Azrael **AFFILIATIONS** Legion of Doom, Leviathan, Ninth Circle, Secret Society of Super-Villains, the 100, Injustice Gang

As a child, Oliver Queen first became interested in archery after encountering master bowman "Merlyn the Magician"—a phenomenally accurate archer and showman. Years later, the performer challenged Queen—now the new Super Hero Green Arrow—to a duel and publicly humiliated him. Queen had no idea then that Merlyn (Arthur King) had a sideline in assassination, working for Ra's al Ghūl's League of Assassins. As Malcolm Merlyn, the dark archer contributed to the training of Cassandra Cain (Orphan) and Damian Wayne before he left his mother Talia. Merlyn became an independent mercenary targeting Batman, the Justice League, and Black Lightning. Despite failing in these and other Super Hero contracts, Merlyn's reputation grew. He had enough pull to have Suicide Squad chief Amanda Waller arrange his release after being apprehended by the Justice League. Although he is one of the most dangerous men alive, Merlyn is a sharp assessor of the odds. During the other-dimensional invasion of Earth-3's Crime Syndicate of America, he willingly joined the Secret Society of Super-Villains rather than resist like the Central City's Rogues did.

PRESCIENT WARNING
Tommy Merlyn argued with Oliver Queen over how to deal with the terrorists who had crashed their party. This would be the last time they saw each other as friends.

After *Rebirth*, Merlyn returned to wetwork, signing on to the Ninth Circle as they sought to destroy Oliver Queen by framing Green Arrow for murder with his own arrows. The hero believed the culprit was his boyhood friend, Tommy Merlyn, and was stunned to learn his true nemesis was Tommy's father.

ON THE RECORD

Merlyn's origin story begins with an archery duel between him and Green Arrow—which Merlyn wins. Their rivalry thus established, they battled many times over the years, notably at Green Arrow's wedding to Black Canary. Merlyn's less than savory alliances have included a deal with the demon Neron and with the League of Assassins, which witnessed the resurrection of Rā's al Ghūl.

BLACK OPS
As a mercenary, Merlyn has always had a reputation for peerless archery skills, and the ability to surprise any target—even getting the drop on The Flash.

METAL MEN

DEBUT *Showcase* #37 (Mar.–Apr. 1962)
BASE S.T.A.R. Labs Campsite, Challenger Mountain, Denver, Colorado; Mount Magnus Chateau **MEMBERS/POWERS Gold:** Analytical intelligence, malleable form; **Lead:** Strength, radiation, and energy shielding; **Iron:** Strength, durability, malleable form; **Mercury:** Liquid metal form; **Platinum:** Malleable form. **ALLIES** Doctor Magnus, Cyborg **ENEMIES** Chemo, X-1, Egg-Fu, Grid, Crime Syndicate of America **AFFILIATIONS** Justice League

HEAVY METAL
The Metal Men allied (and alloyed) against all threats.

Temperamental robotics genius Dr. William Magnus invented the Responsometer—an Artificial Intelligence unit able to shape metals around itself. Magnus used it to make the "Metal Men." These were sentient robots formed from different metals: Gold, Tin, Platinum, Iron, Lead, and Mercury. Originally intended as all-purpose troubleshooters, Magnus' magnificent creations have been remade many times, generally for his own scientific and altruistic purposes. However, during one of Earth's frequent reality alterations, a team of autonomous robots and assassins capable of operating in hazardous environments were created as part of a military project.

The Metal Man have battled threats and fought beside Super Heroes such as when Earth-3's Crime Syndicate of America invaded. Magnus, however, builds too well. His progeny always manifest unshakable moral and ethical convictions and they tend to rebel against authority and humans with bad intentions. They are invaluable heroic assets with strength, loyalty, and the potential to combine themselves into different alloys.

The robots subsequently faced a pool of Nth Metal from the Dark Multiverse that infiltrated their HQ, manifesting as an Nth Metal Man and offering them full consciousness and actual souls. Tempted beyond endurance, the Metal Men still ignored their programming while remaining true to their consciences.

ON THE RECORD

Over the years, Responsometers have been used to create dangerous alternative Metal Men. Magnus' brother David once used a device stolen from the villain T. O. Morrow to create the Death Metal Men: Uranium, Strontium, Thorium, Radium, Lithium, Polonium, and Fermium.

Chang Tzu once tried to force Magnus to build a Plutonium Man, but Magnus outwitted him and rebuilt the originals.

ROGUE ELEMENTS
When Responsometers fell into the wrong hands, the variant Metal Men thus created were deadly opponents to the original team, as well as to Doctor Magnus.

METALLO

DATA

DEBUT *Action Comics* (Vol. 1) #252 (May 1959)
REAL NAME John Corben
HEIGHT 6ft 5in   **WEIGHT** 600 lbs   **EYES** Green   **HAIR** Brown (formerly)
POWERS/ABILITIES Massively powerful, mechanical armored body equipped with life-support systems and an arsenal of rockets, guns, and other weapons; can emit Kryptonite radiation from chest cavity.
ALLIES Cyborg Superman
ENEMIES Superman, Lois Lane, Steel, General Zod
AFFILIATIONS Secret Society of Super-Villains, Superman Revenge Squad

GHOST IN THE MACHINE
Defeated by Superman on multiple occasions, Metallo has now become far more machine than man.

STREAMLINED
Now armed with a Kryptonite heart and a more streamlined body, Metallo quickly challenged Superman to a rematch on the streets of Metropolis.

Metallo is made up of two vital components—advanced technology and the depraved human mind of John Corben. With these linked together by a cybernetic interface and powered by Kryptonite, Metallo has become a living weapon, who only seems happy when targeting Metropolis' true Man of Steel, Superman.

Sergeant John Corben was a career soldier working under General Sam Lane, Lois Lane's father. Corben had a mean streak, so it made him the perfect choice to try out Lex Luthor's experimental Metallo armor—a project Luthor and General Lane were working on together. Corben volunteered for the job and soon faced Superman while wearing a bulky armored mech. Metallo's suit was destroyed in the skirmish, and Superman narrowly avoided death from Kryptonite exposure. Metallo came off much worse, and only survived because Luthor implanted an artificial Kryptonite heart in his chest.

When Metallo next faced the Man of Steel, it was as an enhanced cyborg. Powered by Kryptonite as well as anger, this streamlined Metallo lost to Superman in what would be far from their last battle. In the many bouts that followed, Corben kept losing more humanity, becoming an almost fully robotic being.

After he was rebuilt, he was recruited into the Superman Revenge Squad by Cyborg Superman. Metallo set up shop in Batman's former moon Batcave and teamed with fellow Super-Villains Blanque, Mongul, the Eradicator, and General Zod. However, Zod had his own agenda and he soon turned on the group, swatting Metallo like a fly. The villains were eventually overcome and defeated, and Metallo was sent to an A.R.G.U.S. facility. Dismantled and in great pain, he was visited by Superman's father, Jor-El, who ripped out his Kryptonite heart, seemingly killing him. However, Metallo has survived worse over the years, so the probability that he will return is high.

ON THE RECORD

Pre-*Flashpoint*, there were different iterations of both Corben and Metallo. The original Silver-Age Corben was an unscrupulous journalist with a grudge against Superman. His brain was placed in a Kryptonite-powered body after an accident. However, when he confronted the Man of Steel, Corben discovered the Kryptonite was fake and, unable to recharge, he died of a heart attack.

A reimagined account in the late 1980s depicted Corben as a conman whose brain was transplanted into a metal body following a traffic accident. This Corben made a deal with the demon Neron and was turned into a demonic metal juggernaut.

RADIOACTIVE HEART
In all versions, Kryptonite is the source of Metallo's power and of Superman's greatest weakness.

METALLO RETURNS
Lois Lane used her Brainiac-given powers to revive John Corben/Metallo, to help defend their city, Metropolis.

CLASSIC STORIES

***Action Comics* (Vol. 1) #252 (May 1959)** In his very first appearance, John Corben becomes Metallo and traps Superman—but dies after mistaking a model of Kryptonite for the real thing.
***Superman: Secret Origin* #1–6 (Nov. 2009–Oct. 2010)** In this gripping new Superman origin story, Lex Luthor turns the soldier John Corben into a living weapon to use against the Kryptonian.
***Action Comics* (Vol. 2) #23.4 (Nov. 2013)** After General Lane tries to eliminate Metallo, the juggernaut seeks revenge and has an epic battle with a former friend, transformed into Metal-2.0.

MIDNIGHTER

DEBUT *Stormwatch* (Vol. 2) #4 (Feb. 1998)
BASE Opal City
HEIGHT 6ft 5in **WEIGHT** 285 lbs
EYES Brown **HAIR** Brown
POWERS/ABILITIES Extensive cybernetic components grant Midnighter enhanced speed, strength, and durability; a Neural-Inductive Combat Simulator in his brain allows him to anticipate any opponent's moves; access to doorway portals that can open in any location.
ALLIES Apollo, Zealot, Nightwing, the Gardener, Batman Family
ENEMIES Dr. Henry Bendix, Prometheus, Mawzir, Neron
AFFILIATIONS Stormwatch, the God Garden

CLASSIC STORIES

***Stormwatch* (Vol. 3) #15–16
(Feb.–Mar. 2013)** Accused of betraying Stormwatch, Midnighter is forced to go on the run in Antarctica—pursued by his enraged lover, Apollo.

***Stormwatch* (Vol. 3) #23–24
(Oct.–Dec. 2013)** Midnighter suffers a series of traumatic flashbacks to the alien experiments he was subjected to as a child. They give insight into the events that helped create this tormented hero.

***Midnighter* (Vol. 2) #1 (Aug. 2015)**
In a shocking turn of events, Midnighter leaves Stormwatch and Apollo behind to go and work for the Gardener, proprietress of the orbital God Garden.

DOOR FOR ONE
Just by saying the word "door," Midnighter can create a portal to any location he desires.

Midnighter is a dark hero who uses his violent impulses to fight for justice. After receiving cybernetic enhancements, he began his career as a vigilante, before being recruited into Stormwatch—a team dedicated to protecting Earth from alien incursions. He formed a close partnership with fellow Stormwatch member Apollo, and they became lovers as well as teammates.

Midnighter's past is a clouded jumble. Unaware of even his own real name, he was kidnapped by the Gardener and Dr. Henry Bendix. His memory was erased, he was experimented on, and he was made into the human equivalent of a fighting machine, one with a computer brain that tells him exactly how to defeat any opponent he faces. After a time living on the street, he turned his life around and decided to never become a victim again. He became Midnighter, an ultraviolent vigilante.

POWER OF PRECOGNITION
Midnighter's uncanny ability to predict an opponent's moves in advance gives him a deadly edge in combat.

Midnighter joined Stormwatch for a time, a centuries-old organization devoted to defending the Earth. However, Midnighter was inexperienced both in the world and in relationships. He left Stormwatch and broke up with Apollo, believing the hero deserved better.

Attempting life on the dating scene, Midnighter used hi-tech portal door technology to live in any city he liked. When the mysterious Gardener's technology was stolen, Midnighter investigated, and soon found himself fighting the very man he had been dating—the Super-Villain Prometheus.

After getting back together with Apollo, Midnighter was trapped by Dr. Henry Bendix while Apollo was killed by the gun-toting creature called the Mawzir. Midnighter went to literal hell and back for Apollo, and together, they bested the demon Neron who was attempting to take Apollo's soul. Midnighter and Apollo returned to the land of the living, where the two continued their partnership, both romantic and as Super Heroes.

VIOLENT TENDENCIES
Midnighter is a self-confessed psychopath, but he uses his gift for violence against the guilty rather than the innocent.

ON THE RECORD

Midnighter was originally a covert black ops Stormwatch agent. When the team was destroyed, he was recruited into the Authority, a group that fought relentlessly for the greater good—even if it brought them into conflict with multinational corporations and the United States Government.

In this incarnation, Midnighter and his teammate Apollo also married and then adopted fellow Authority member Jenny Sparks. Following the terrible devastation of Earth during the *Number of the Beast* event, Midnighter and the reconvened Authority set out to restore order to the planet.

A FORCE FOR GOOD?
Midnighter embodied the ruthless zeal of the Authority team. He and his comrades proved willing to defy the world in their pursuit of justice.

PARTNERS IN CRIME FIGHTING
In Stormwatch, Midnighter and Apollo became teammates and eventually lovers.

METAMORPHO

DEBUT *The Brave and the Bold* #57 (Dec. 1964–Jan. 1965)
REAL NAME Rex Mason
HEIGHT 6ft 1in **WEIGHT** 200 lbs **EYES** Black **HAIR** None
POWERS/ABILITIES Can transform his body (or parts of it) into any element contained in the human body, potentially giving him incredible strength, flexibility, and durability.
ALLIES Michael Holt, Element Dog, Plastic Man, Phantom Girl, Batman, Sapphire Stagg, Algon
ENEMIES Java (Doc Dread), Sebastian Stagg, Hyperclan, Masters of Disaster, O.M.A.C.
AFFILIATIONS Outsiders, Justice League Europe

Rex Mason was a rugged adventurer who made the near-fatal mistake of falling in love with his employer's daughter. Simon Stagg did not want his beloved Sapphire involved with a mercenary, so he plotted Mason's demise. Stagg sent him to the pyramid of Ahk-Ton in search of the Orb of Ra, and got a henchman to steal the Orb and leave Rex in the pyramid to die. Rex was trapped and exposed to radiation from a meteor that had been kept there for years. The radiation altered his physiology, turning him into Metamorpho, the Element Man, a being who could change shape or transform into any element found in human physiology.

Rex escaped and set off in search of a cure. In Markovia, he rescued Bruce Wayne's employee, Lucius Fox, and Batman made him a founding member of his Outsiders team. As Metamorpho, Rex was a core member for decades and also served on various Justice League teams. He sacrificed his life to save his teammates from the Hyperclan, but was resurrected thanks to the intervention of Sapphire. This origin has recently been called into question. Reports that Mason was part of Helga Jace's US-government sponsored, metahuman-making "Superman Project" cannot at this time be disproved.

Following *Rebirth*, with Doctor Manhattan's time-tampering reversed, Mason returned to Stagg and was subjected to an experiment that was slowly turning him into living Nth Metal. Rescued by Mister Terrific, Mason joined the dimension-hopping Terrifics.

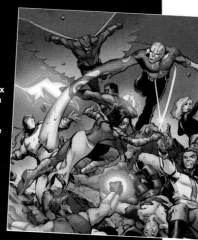

TRANSMUTATION
The energies of the mysterious meteor changed Rex Mason into a bizarre being with powers of elemental-control.

HANDYMAN
Rex Mason's flexible physiology enabled him to come up with the right tool to sort out almost any problem.

TEAM PLAYER
In the Outsiders, Rex Mason found a team that valued his powers and accepted his bizarre appearance. He served in various incarnations of the group.

METRON

DEBUT *New Gods* (Vol. 1) #1 (Feb.–Mar. 1971)
CURRENT VERSION *Green Lantern/New Gods: Godhead* #1 (Dec. 2014)
HEIGHT 6ft 1in **WEIGHT** 190 lbs **EYES** Blue **HAIR** Black
POWERS/ABILITIES His personal powers are unknown, though he has a talent for escapology; Mobius Chair provides pan-dimensional travel, the ability to access any knowledge in the universe, and force-field protection.
ALLIES Highfather, Orion
ENEMIES Justice League, Anti-Monitor

The origins of Metron are unknown, but at some point in history the New God received an amazing chair from enigmatic presence Mobius. It allowed Metron access to time, space, dimensions, and all the knowledge in the universe—except for the mysterious benefactor's identity. On his incredible journeys, Metron witnessed multiple crises destroying and remaking numerous realities.

Metron feared that a clash between Darkseid and the Anti-Monitor would cause annihilation. To avert this, he became advisor to Darkseid's enemy, Highfather of New Genesis, seeking to eliminate Darkseid before the anticipated confrontation. Metron even engineered conflict between New Genesis and the Lantern Corps in hope that the Lanterns' rings might defeat the evil overlord. Metron attempted to dissuade the Justice League from battling the Anti-Monitor on Earth, but was pulled from the Mobius Chair by Wonder Woman's lasso, and Batman briefly commandeered it. Metron, along with the Chair's new occupant, the Owlman, was then destroyed by the powerful entity, Dr. Manhattan.

Following Manhattan's fall, the Mobius Chair was taken by a bereaved Wally West. He used it to traverse infinite realities searching for his wife and children, who had been deleted in a previous multiversal reordering.

ON THE RECORD

The original Metron was also a cool and detached seeker of knowledge, but he occasionally served as a teacher and mentor to Orion and Lightray, as well as advising young Scott Free. When the Source began eliminating the New Gods, Metron looked on impartially—until his former student Mister Miracle was slain. At that point, Metron demanded to be destroyed as well, and the Source slew him.

POWER BEHIND THE THRONE
Metron initially served as an advisor to Highfather, sharing his cosmic knowledge with the New Gods of New Genesis.

MIME AND MARIONETTE

DEBUT *Doomsday Clock* #1 (Jan 2018)
REAL NAME Marcos Maez and Erika Manson
BASE New York City
HEIGHT Unknown **WEIGHT** Unknown
EYES Brown (Mime), blue (Marionette)
HAIR Black (Mime), blonde (Marionette)
POWERS/ABILITIES Hand-to-hand combat, acrobatics, martial arts
ALLIES The Joker
ENEMIES Rorschach (Walter Kovacs), Doctor Manhattan, Comedian
AFFILIATIONS None

Mime and Marionette bonded as young children, when they lost parents in tragic circumstances. The pair stuck together, fighting each other's corner against bullies and corrupt cops. Mime's early trauma had caused him to stop speaking, but Marionette knew him well enough to be able to interpret his every gesture and facial expression.

As they grew, their close friendship blossomed into a deep love, and the couple used their advanced fighting skills to forge a violent life of crime. They had a child, Clark, who was taken away at birth and later placed into the care of the former Nite Owl and Silk Spectre by Doctor Manhattan. Marionette would later become pregnant with a daughter.

MINDWARP

DEBUT *Flashpoint: Secret Seven* #2 (Sep. 2011)
REAL NAME Jay Young
BASE Los Angeles, California
EYES Blue
HAIR Blond
POWERS/ABILITIES Can release a powerful "seizure soul" from his body—and can sometimes even control it.
ALLIES Justice League Dark
ENEMIES Enchantress

Jay Young, alias Mindwarp, was a gleefully psychotic nihilist with the ability to release an astral "seizure soul" from his body. Madame Xanadu asked Shade the Changing Man to recruit Jay into Justice League Dark to help fight the Enchantress, but Mindwarp rejected Shade's offer. However, when the League did face the Enchantress, Jay turned up to help, claiming that her magical influence had made his seizure soul unstable. Mindwarp's power helped to unite the Enchantress with her human host, June Moone, ending her threat.

Mindwarp was subsequently captured by forces loyal to the Crime Syndicate. He was subjected to agonizing mystical experimentation, and then destroyed while being used to power a test-firing of the Syndicate's Thaumaton device.

MISFIT

DEBUT *Birds of Prey* (Vol. 1) #96 (Sep. 2006)
REAL NAME Charlotte Gage-Radcliffe
EYES Blue
HAIR Red
POWERS/ABILITIES Possesses the ability to "bounce" (teleport) from place to place.
ENEMIES Black Alice

Growing up, young Charlotte Gage-Radcliffe idolized Super Heroes, especially Batgirl. Charlotte even possessed a superpower—the ability to "bounce" (or teleport). When her family perished in a fire, the orphaned Charlotte decided to become the "new Batgirl" by donning a homemade costume and fighting street crime. Barbara Gordon, alias the Birds of Prey's Oracle, tried to convince her to give up her new career, but Charlotte instead adopted a new identity as Misfit. She began tagging along on missions with the Birds of Prey and was gradually accepted by the team, though her impulsive nature caused problems.

Misfit later applied to join the Teen Titans, but was rejected. After Bruce Wayne was killed, she helped keep order in Gotham City working as part of Oracle's crime fighting Network, but subsequently went to live with a foster family.

MISS AMERICA

DEBUT *Military Comics* #1 (Aug. 1941)
REAL NAME Joan Dale
BASE The Heartland
HEIGHT 5ft 7in **WEIGHT** 133 lbs
EYES Blue **HAIR** Brown
POWERS/ABILITIES Matter transmutation.
ENEMIES Red Bee, android Miss America
AFFILIATIONS All-Star Squadron, Freedom Fighters, Justice Society of America

During World War II, reporter Joan Dale was knocked unconscious while visiting the Statue of Liberty and taken to the top-secret Project M facility. Here, under the direction of Professor Mazursky, she was subjected to a process that granted her matter-transmutation powers. Unaware of what had been done to her, Joan experienced a vision in which the Statue of Liberty told her that she had been given special powers to use in the defense of her nation. On the ferry back to New York, she turned a pair of pro-Nazi thugs into birds. Adopting the code name Miss America, Joan joined the wartime Freedom Fighters team.

Joan later retired and married Admiral Derek Trevor, but after he died she resumed her heroic career, joining Uncle Sam's new Freedom Fighters. She was presumed killed after exploding in space, but was reborn in a younger body as Miss Cosmos.

MIRROR MASTER

DEBUT *The Flash* (Vol. 1) #105 (Feb.–Mar. 1959)
REAL NAME Samuel Joseph "Sam" Scudder
BASE Central City **HEIGHT** 5ft 10in **WEIGHT** 175 lbs **EYES** Brown **HAIR** Brown
POWERS/ABILITIES Trans-dimensional travel via mirrors; able to observe anywhere with reflective surfaces; numerous super-science weapons working on optic and photonic principles
ALLIES Dr. Darwin Elias, Golden Glider
ENEMIES The Flash, Gorilla Grodd, Crime Syndicate, Secret Society
AFFILIATIONS The Rogues

ON THE RECORD

The original Sam Scudder learned to exploit the amazing properties of mirrors while in prison. As Mirror Master, he escaped going on to become a member of the Rogues and Secret Society of Super-Villains. Scudder was killed during *Crisis on Infinite Earths*, but the Mirror Master name was "borrowed" by Captain Boomerang and then Evan McCulloch. Scudder later returned in undead form during the *Blackest Night* event.

TIME FOR REFLECTION
Mirror Master can emerge from any reflective surface and drag victims back to the Mirror World.

Criminal Sam Scudder uses the codename Mirror Master, wielding devices allowing him power over reflective surfaces. He was an early member of Central City's Rogues—villains employing themed hi-tech weapons in their crimes. The group was led by Captain Cold, whose sister, Lisa, became Sam's girlfriend.

Despite their technology, the Rogues' heists were frequently stopped by The Flash. However, Dr. Darwin Elias offered Captain Cold access to a Genome Recoder to transfer the powers of their weapons into the Rogues' DNA, allowing them to combat the speedster on equal terms. Unfortunately, the device exploded. The Rogues received powers, but Lisa was rendered comatose by the blast. She gaining the ability to project an astral form, and Scudder was trapped in Mirror World, a dimension lying behind all reflective surfaces. Lisa used her astral-projection powers to allow Sam to emerge from the Mirror World, but this caused her to lose her own astral form.

As Captain Cold grew ever more domineering Lisa left, breaking up with Scudder. However, when her brother accepted a destabilizing power boost from Lex Luthor—agent of recently-liberated Multiveral Matron Perpetua—Mirror Master joined rebel Rogues Weather Wizard and Heatwave in helping Lisa and The Flash confront "King Cold." Trapped in the Mirror World, a realm that lies within all reflective surfaces, he can see out of any mirror and take people into this realm, where he has complete control.

MIRROR IMAGE
Sam Scudder trapped Barry Allen within reflective prisons, but when Wally West leaped into action as Kid Flash, the Mirror Master thought he was seeing double!

MISS MARTIAN

DEBUT *Teen Titans* (Vol. 3) #37 (Aug. 2006)
REAL NAME M'gann M'orzz
HEIGHT 5ft 10in **WEIGHT** 135 lbs
EYES Red **HAIR** Red (in disguise)
POWERS/ABILITIES Superhuman strength
endurance, and durability; flight; shapeshifting;
telepathy; enhanced senses; Martian vision.
ALLIES Red Devil, Aquagirl, Martian Manhunter
ENEMIES Terror Titans, Clock King

Prior to *Flashpoint*, Miss Martian was a trusted
member of the Teen Titans. Full of energy and
a little naïve, she was quick to make friends
and even established a human identity for
herself in the form of Megan Morse. However,
beneath her green-skinned exterior, Miss
Martian hid a dark secret. Instead of being from
the same benevolent race as J'onn J'onzz, the
Super Hero Martian Manhunter, Miss Martian
was actually a White Martian: a watchword for
violence, cruelty, and the perpetrators of an
infamous attack on the Justice League

Following *Rebirth*, M'gann M'orzz was
appointed Justice League liaison to the
Titans as Nightwing led a mission-specific
team dedicated to helping people impacted
by the terrifying mutagenic effects unleashed
by the Dark Universe Metal crisis and the
warping energies released by the breaking of
the Source Wall.

GREEN GUISE
In her true, White Martian form,
M'gann has a chalky-white body
covered with spines, a long tail, and
glowing red eyes.

MR. MXYZPTLK

DEBUT *Superman* (Vol. 1) #30 (Sep.-Oct. 1944)
REAL NAME Mxyzptlk
BASE 5th Dimension
HEIGHT Variable **WEIGHT** Variable **EYES** Variable **HAIR** Variable
POWERS/ABILITIES Able to bend reality itself in ways only understandable
to inhabitants of the 5th Dimension, including moving through time and
space unencumbered, animating inanimate objects, and creating matter
from nothingness.
ALLIES Gsptlnz (Mrs. Nyxly) **ENEMIES** Lord Vyndktvx, Mister Oz,
Superman, Bat-Mite

Mr. Mxyzptlk comes from the 5th dimension
and has pestered Superman in every reality. When Clark
Kent's landlady, Mrs. Nyxly, first mentioned her husband,
she referred to him as stage conjurer Mystic Mr. Triple X,
adding that a rival magician's interference with one of his
tricks had left him in a coma for seven years. In reality,
Mrs. Nyxly was a 5th-dimensional princess named
Gsptlnz. Mxyzptlk had become her royal father's
sorcerer, edging out former court magician, Lord
Vyndktvx. Vyndktvx swore revenge, but killed
Gsptlnz's father by mistake. Fearing for her life,
Gsptlnz fled to Earth. leaving her beloved Mr. Mxyzptlk in
the 5th dimension. His frequent visits to Earth were him
having fun while searching for her.
Post *Rebirth*, the imp was imprisoned for millennia by
Mister Oz, but escaped and hid as a perfect duplicate of
Clark Kent. When trapped by the Justice League, Mxyzptlk
revealed the nature of 6th-dimensional reality and the threat
of Source Wall escapee Perpetua. By battling fellow imp
Bat-Mite, Mxyzptlk preserved his 3rd-dimensional
playground from eradication.

ON THE RECORD

Mr. Mxyzptlk has plagued
Superman as far back as the
Golden Age of Comics, though his
name was originally spelled
Mxyztplk. A classic member of
Superman's Rogues Gallery, Mxy
originally faced Superman as a
cartoony bald man in a purple suit
who would return to harass the
Man of Steel every 90 days, only
leaving Superman's reality when he
was tricked into saying his own
name backwards.

By *Superman* (Vol. 1) #131 (Aug.
1959), the mischievous Mr. Mxyzptlk's
name gained its modern spelling, and
he was sporting his trademark orange
suit and white hair.

MEAN MXY
In a story set before the reality-altering
Crisis on Infinite Earths, Mxy showed
his true colors when he transformed
from prankster to murderous villain
in a possible future for Superman.

MISTER E

DEBUT *Secrets of Haunted House* #31
(Dec. 1980)
BASE The Bernese Alps, Switzerland
HEIGHT 6ft 3in **WEIGHT** 190 lbs
EYES White **HAIR** White
POWERS/ABILITIES Very powerful
magician, able to teleport and rip a
person's soul from their body; cane channels
dark magic.
ENEMIES John Constantine

An enemy of Justice
League Dark member
John Constantine, the
man known as Mister E
was a good magician
corrupted by the
temptations of magic.
A member of the Cult
of the Cold Flame—a group of sorcerers
that included the deceased Zatara and
Sargon, as well as the evil Tannarak—
Mister E was originally regarded as a hero.

While his past is shrouded in mystery,
it is commonly believed that Mister E went
insane after he cast a magic spell that
liquefied his eyeballs. He became instantly
blind, and much more susceptible to the
darker side of the magic world. As a part of
the Cold Flame, he united with other mystics
and began to eliminate those magicians not
loyal to their cause. This forced him into a
confrontation with Constantine, who ran him
through with the mystical Moonblade.

MISTER MIND

DEBUT *Captain Marvel Adventures* #22 (Mar.
1943)
HEIGHT 3in **WEIGHT** 5 oz
EYES Black **HAIR** None
POWERS/ABILITIES Extremely intelligent
Venusian worm possessing knowledge of Earth;
telepathic; telekinetic; able to alter the fabric of
time and space during metamorphosis.
ALLIES Sivana
ENEMIES Shazam
AFFILIATIONS Monster Society of Evil,
Black Adam

Mister Mind reared his
head in the *Flashpoint*
reality when Dr. Sivana
was seeking entrance
to the Rock of
Eternity. Hoping to
gain superpowers, he
discovered a bottle
containing a talking alien worm calling itself
Mister Mind. Together, they began to plot
against Shazam and his allies.

In the *Rebirth* era, Mind and Sivana
conspired to exploit the Seven Magic Lands,
release the Seven Deadly Sins on Earth and
coerce Black Adam into leading a Monster
Society of Evil against humanity. Sivana had
no conception of the worm's agenda: seizing
control of all magic. Thankfully Mister Mind
underestimated the guts and ingenuity of Billy
Batson and again failed in his sinister
scheme, even after possessing Billy's
long-lost dad to infiltrate the Shazam Family.

MISTER NOBODY

DEBUT *Doom Patrol* (Vol. 1) #86 (Mar. 1964)
REAL NAME Eric Morden
HEIGHT 5ft 8in **EYES** Red **HAIR** None
POWERS/ABILITIES Exists in a pseudo-
dimensional state; possesses an abstract body;
can psychically induce state of anarchy/insanity
in other human beings.
ALLIES Dr. Bruckner, Sleepwalk, Frenzy,
The Fog **ENEMIES** Doom Patrol, Brotherhood
of Evil
AFFILIATIONS Brotherhood of Dada

After joining the
Brotherhood of Evil,
Eric Morden's dream
of being a Super-
Villain soon went awry.
Fleeing to Paraguay to
escape his
Brotherhood "allies"
he met fugitive Nazi war criminal Dr.
Bruckner, and agreed to visit his "white
room," to be born anew. Morden was driven
insane, and, augmented by Bruckner's
serums, transformed into abstract villain
Mister Nobody. He gathered super-powered
outcasts as the Brotherhood of Dada, and
they fought the Doom Patrol in Paris, but
were defeated. Nobody later targeted young
wizard Lucius Reynolds, seeking to enlist
him in his newest venture—erasing all that
exists—with his new Brotherhood of Nada
team. Nobody was infatuated with the
concept of nothingness, but his associates
rebelled and the plot failed.

MISTER MIRACLE

DATA

DEBUT *Mister Miracle* (Vol. 1) #1 **(Mar.–Apr. 1971)**
REAL NAME Scott Free
BASE New Genesis
HEIGHT 6ft   **WEIGHT** 185 lbs
EYES Brown   **HAIR** Brown
POWERS/ABILITIES Superhuman mental and physical attributes of the New Gods; master escapologist; access to advanced New God technology, including Aero-Discs (enable flight and can be used as weapons) and a sentient Mother Box (provides healing, data, and generates Boom Tubes for transportation).
ALLIES Shilo Norman, Big Barda, the Justice League, Himon
ENEMIES Darkseid, Kalibak, Steppenwolf, Kanto, Granny Goodness
AFFILIATIONS New Gods of New Genesis

ESCAPING GRAVITY
His Aero-Discs allow Scott to take to the skies, providing essential mobility for this freedom fighter.

ESCAPE OF THE MIND
Parallel Universe or Purgatory? Mr. Miracle escaped the real world in an acclaimed Black Label series that left questions about the very nature of his reality itself.

THE FUGITIVE
He may have escaped from Apokolips, but Mister Miracle soon discovered that Darkseid and his evil minions would stop at nothing to get him back.

Born a New God in utopian New Genesis, Scott was raised as a slave on the grim planet of Apokolips. However, he refused to let his spirit be broken, escaping to become Mister Miracle—a symbol of freedom and sworn enemy of Apokolips' evil ruler, Darkseid.

Scott is the son of Highfather, ruler of the New God world of New Genesis. When Scott was seven years old, Highfather and the tyrannical Darkseid of Apokolips exchanged heirs as part of a peace agreement, and Scott was imprisoned in the Apokolips slave pits. After three years of torture, Scott decided to escape his cell. It took him a year to became adept at lock picking, exploring Apokolips, and returning to his cell each night, while his slave masters were none the wiser.

Eventually, Scott did not return to his cell. He escaped and became the rebellious hero Mister Miracle. He joined the anti-Darkseid underground, falling in love with Big Barda, a renegade member of Darkseid's Female Furies. Mister Miracle also met Himon, a fellow New Genesis native who was trying to start a rebellion on Apokolips. Himon showed Scott how to build his own living computer in the form of a Mother Box.

After Barda abandoned the evil Female Furies, she and Mister Miracle were married. They enjoyed many adventures before joining the Justice League in the so-called "Darkseid War" that saw Darkseid die and be reborn as an infant. Big Barda had rallied the Female Furies to her side, but only by agreeing to leave Scott and Earth behind after the war was won. However, the pair have been seen back together during recent large-scale events.

ON THE RECORD

The first **Mister Miracle** series introduced Scott Free and his wife Big Barda, showing his meeting with Thaddeus Brown, who gave him the Mister Miracle identity. Scott helped protect Earth as a solo hero and with the Justice League International, and on retiring gave his name and costume to his protégé Shilo Norman.

Scott became the vessel for the Anti-Life Equation, a power desired by Darkseid. When Big Barda was murdered, he used it to hunt down the killer. Scott perished in the Death of the New Gods, but he and Barda returned after the *Final Crisis*.

BREAK A LEG
On Earth, Mister Miracle went into showbiz, wowing the crowds with terrifying acts of escape-artistry.

CLASSIC STORIES

Mister Miracle (Vol. 1) #9 **(Jul.–Aug. 1972)** Tells the thrilling story of how Scott Free meets Himon of New Genesis—and escapes from Apokolips and Darkseid.

Seven Soldiers: Mister Miracle **#1–4 (Nov. 2005–May 2006)** Shilo Norman escapes death after taking on the identity of Mister Miracle from Scott Free.

Earth 2: World's End **#9–11 (Feb. 2015)** Mister Miracle faces betrayal and defeat when he ventures into the heart of Apokolips to confront Darkseid.

MISTER TERRIFIC

DEBUT *Sensation Comics* (Vol. 1) #1 **(Jan. 1942)** (as Terry Sloane);
Spectre (Vol. 3) #54 **(Jun. 1997)** (as Michael Holt)
REAL NAME Michael Holt
BASE Terrifictech Modern Community Association, Gateway City
HEIGHT 6ft 2in **WEIGHT** 215 lbs **EYES** Brown **HAIR** Black
POWERS/ABILITIES Olympic gold medalist decathlete; genius and
inventor; hovering T-Spheres can detonate, project holograms, gather data,
and allow flight; T-Suit provides protection; T-Mask guards against
electronic detection
ALLIES Power Girl, T-Council
ENEMIES Sebastian Stagg, Doc Dread (Java), The Dreadfuls,
Tomorrow Thief, Digitus
AFFILIATIONS The Terrifics, Holt Industries, Justice Society

Michael Holt is one of the smartest people on Earth, with multiple
doctorates to his name, his own company, and a vast fortune. However, his life
changed forever when his beloved wife Paula died. Devastated, Holt was considering
suicide when a mysterious figure claiming to be his son from an alternate reality
informed him of his duty to change the world.

Michael set up a non-profit dedicated to advancing science, and began his Super
Hero career as Mister Terrific. Operating out of his ninth-dimensional T-Sanctuary and
wielding his multifunction T-Spheres, he fought numerous villains. In a quantum
tunneling experiment, he was sucked into a portal and landed in the alternate reality
of Earth-2. Mister Terrific joined the Justice Society to battle Darkseid but Earth-2
was destroyed by the forces of Apokolips, and Holt escaped back to his own world.

In recent times he began investigating the exotic metals of the Dark Multiverse
and was irresistibly bonded to Plastic Man, Metamorpho, and Phantom Girl. As The
Terrifics, they roamed the Multiverse until discovering a way to separate their conjoined
existences, and after succeeding, stayed together to have fun and do good.

Overachiever Holt has continued inventing, convened supergenius thinktank
the T-Council, and established Terrifictech Modern Community Association
in Gateway City.

ON THE RECORD

The pre-*Flashpoint* Michael Holt lost
his wife in an accident and was visited by
the Spectre, who told him about the Golden
Age Mister Terrific (Terry Sloane). This
inspired Holt to become a Super Hero
and continue the Mister Terrific legacy.
He became the chairman of the Justice
Society of America and developed a
friendly rivalry with Batman. In an ironic
twist, the post-*Flashpoint* Michael Holt was
captured by Earth-2's Mister Terrific, Terry
Sloan, when he was stranded in that reality.

OLD SCHOOL
The original Mister Terrific, Terry Sloane,
demonstrated how crime fighting was done
back in the Golden Age.

MISTER ZSASZ

DEBUT *Shadow of the Bat* #1 **(Jun. 1992)**
NAME Victor Zsasz **BASE** Gotham City
HEIGHT 5ft 8in **WEIGHT** 150 lbs
EYES Brown **HAIR** Brown
POWERS/ABILITIES High intelligence; great physical strength and resilience;
psychotically vicious and unpredictable, making him a deadly opponent in
hand-to-hand combat.
ALLIES Emperor Penguin, The Riddler
ENEMIES Batman, The Signal, The Penguin, The Joker
AFFILIATIONS Arkham Asylum

Mister Zsasz is one of Gotham City's most ruthless
serial killers. Zsasz's descent into madness began after his parents
died. He gambled away their fortune at The Penguin's Iceberg Casino,
and when the money ran out, The Penguin suggested he should go
and kill himself. As Zsasz was about to do just that, he was attacked
by a knife-wielding madman. Zsasz dispatched his assailant and
experienced an epiphany: life was meaningless, but killing made
everything comprehensible. He embarked on a murder spree, slaying
hundreds and recording each kill with a cut on his body.

Captured by Batman, Zsasz was sent to Arkham Asylum, but
frequently escaped. He was dosed with a fear-inhibiting drug by
Two-Face, battled Batgirl in the Narrows, was briefly transformed
into a Man-Bat by Emperor Penguin, and joined The Riddler's
gang in the War of Jokes and Riddles. When the Arkham War
erupted, Zsasz joined the asylum inmates battling against
Blackgate Penitentiary. He was suspected of a series of
gruesome murders at the new Arkham Manor asylum, but had
actually been imprisoned and tortured by the real perpetrator:
The Joker. During his most recent escape, he was tricked into doing
a greedy designer's killing for her, but was trapped by The Signal before
he could suitably punish his manipulator.

ON THE RECORD

In his pre-*Flashpoint* debut, Zsasz
was a patient at Arkham Asylum who
used a secret passage to escape by night
and continue his murder spree. This
forced Batman to enter the asylum
undercover as an inmate in order to track
him down. Zsasz was a member of the
Secret Society of Super-Villains, and later
joined the Black Mask's gang, setting up
a horrific underground fighting club where
children were forced to fight to the death.

DEADLY OBSESSION
When Alfred survived an attack by Zsasz, the serial killer became obsessed with finishing off Bruce Wayne's manservant, until he was ultimately defeated by Batman.

MIZOGUCHI, MAPS

DEBUT *Gotham Academy* (Vol. 1) #1 (Oct. 2014)
REAL NAME Mia Mizoguchi
BASE Gotham City
HEIGHT 4ft 6in
EYES Brown **HAIR** Brown
POWERS/ABILITIES Brilliant intellect and problem-solving ability; obsessive compulsion with ferreting out secrets; accomplished artist, skilled designer, and cartographer.
ENEMIES Headmaster Hammer, Eric Jorgensen, Heathcliff, Lucy

Mia "Maps" Mizoguchi loves solving puzzles. On starting at the prestigious, spooky-looking Gotham Academy, she soon stumbled upon a genuine mystery featuring ghost sightings and strange symbols. There was even a black-magic cult and a vampire-like young man-bat hanging around the school.

Another tantalizing enigma was her new best friend—and her brother's ex-girlfriend—Olive Silverlock. She shared Maps' hunger for answers and didn't mock her habit of drawing maps to help sort out problems.

With mean-girl Pomeline Fritch, Maps and Olive rooted out a monster with hidden links to Arkham Asylum. They haven't yet determined Batman's connection to the school but it's high on the agenda of their new Gotham Detective Club.

MOCKINGBIRD

DEBUT *Secret Six* (Vol. 1) #1 (Apr.–May 1968)
REAL NAMES Edward Nygma, Lex Luthor, Amanda Waller, Carlo di Rienzi, August Durant
POWERS/ABILITIES Fierce intellect; extreme duplicity; ruthless drive.
AFFILIATIONS Secret Six, Project Mockingbird

Mockingbird is the designation used by a series of master manipulators. Each of these has at various times controlled—through blackmail and subterfuge—teams of operatives codenamed the Secret Six. The first Mockingbird was August Durant. He covertly provided information and equipment necessary for the Secret Six to remove many global threats and "untouchable" criminals.

The latest Mockingbird was Edward Nygma, the infamous Riddler. For a year, he held captive and tortured six superhuman outcasts before allowing them to escape. He believed that one of them had purloined a gem he keenly wanted to woo another man's wife. None of his dupes knew their tormentor's identity or that their liberty and new undercover lives were facets of his elaborate scheme to find the culprit and retrieve his prize.

MONARCH

DEBUT *Armageddon 2001* (Vol. 1) #1 (May 1991)
REAL NAME Hank Hall
BASE Mobile
HEIGHT 6ft 1in **WEIGHT** 197 lbs
EYES Red **HAIR** Brown
POWERS/ABILITIES Advanced technologies and sophisticated warsuit provide superhuman strength and durability, energy-projection, teleportation, timestream manipulation, and travel between parallel universes.
ENEMIES Waverider, Linear Men, Captain Atom

Monarch is a living paradox, created by the unchecked use of time travel. An alternate Earth's ultimate tyrant, he was originally Hank Hall, the hero Hawk, driven mad by the death of his partner Dove. With stolen technology, Hall carved out an empire as Monarch. His rule was threatened by time-traveling rebel Waverider, who visited the time of Monarch's creation to end his domination before it began. The attempt left Hall/Monarch lost in time: locked in combat with Captain Atom. During the battle, Hall emerged as the chronal chaos-bringer Extant, while Atom became locked inside Hall's warsuit as an even more diabolical Monarch.

Even after Atom escaped the suit, he was unsure whether another Monarch might be lurking in some fold of time/space to begin anew his campaign of terror.

MONSIEUR MALLAH

DEBUT *Doom Patrol* (Vol. 1) #86 (Mar. 1964)
HEIGHT 6ft 3in **WEIGHT** 345 lbs
EYES Brown **HAIR** Brown
POWERS/ABILITIES Super-genius intellect; enhanced strength, speed, and reflexes; altered vocal cords enable speech; skilled engineer.
ALLIES The Brain **ENEMIES** Doom Patrol, Teen Titans, Gorilla Grodd
AFFILIATIONS Brotherhood of Evil

Monsieur Mallah is an African gorilla boosted by medical treatments carried out by an unknown French scientist who was later murdered. The artificially evolved great ape saved his creator by transplanting the scientist's brain into a life-support system named the Brain. Mallah acted as the Brain's hands, enhancing its cerebral support unit and creating a true Master of Evil. Together they built an international crime organization, clashing with numerous Super Hero groups, most especially Niles Caulder's Doom Patrol.

Educated and urbane, Mallah adores his creator with a passion matched only by his ferocity when angered. This devotion was tested to the limits when the Brain used a designer drug linking users' minds to ascend to godlike cerebral levels. Rejected by his true love, Mallah joined the Titans in stopping the Brain.

MON-EL

DEBUT *Superboy* (Vol. 1) #89 (Jun. 1961)
REAL NAME Lar Gand
BASE 31st-century New Metropolis
HEIGHT 6ft 2in **WEIGHT** 200 lbs **EYES** Blue **HAIR** Black
POWERS/ABILITIES Highly skilled tactician; brilliant scientist and historian; passionate explorer; super-strength, speed, flight, invulnerability and enhanced senses, fueled by exposure to solar radiation from a yellow sun.
ALLIES Superman, Supergirl, Krypto, Brainiac 5, Shadow Lass
ENEMIES Dominators, Dark Circle, Time Trapper
AFFILIATIONS Legion of Super-Heroes, Science Police, United Planets Council, Wanderers, Green Lantern Corps, Justice League of America

A hero constantly altered by successive reality-revising crises, Lar Gand fled his xenophobic birthworld Daxam to become a wanderer and child of the cosmos. Arriving on Earth—on a Monday—he was befriended by Superman, who mistakenly assumed Lar to be a member of his own family and dubbed him Mon-El. Though possessing all the extraordinary powers of a Kryptonian under Earth's yellow sun, Daxamites are lethally sensitive to the element lead. Following a brief but intense period of heroic endeavor, Mon-El finally succumbed to incurable toxic shock from long exposure to the ubiquitous mineral.

Superman saved Mon-El's life by projecting him into the Phantom Zone. There he stayed, an intangible, invisible observer of the material world. A thousand years later, Mon-El was saved by a serum that neutralized his lead poisoning. He joined the Legion of Super-Heroes as Daxam's representative, combining centuries of experience with immense drive. A being of great power and determination, he is an overachiever proud of his status as "Krypton-Prime," and especially competitive with time-displaced Superboy Jon Kent.

ON THE RECORD

Lar Gand received a major makeover in the 1990s. With Superman's continuity drastically revised, Mon-El became Valor, a Daxamite atoning for his father's role in the Dominator-orchestrated invasion of Earth. Rescuing thousands of humans transformed by metagene experiments, Valor transported them to uninhabited planets: homeworlds for the empowered races that would eventually comprise the United Planets a millennium later. Valor later inspired the formation of the Legion of Super-Heroes.

MESSIAH MOMENT
Valor was a cosmic legend: a super-savior seeding a string of barrier worlds between Earth and the aggressive Dominion empire with super-powered metahumans.

MONGUL

DEBUT *DC Comics Presents* (Vol. 1) #27 **(Nov. 1980)**
REAL NAME Mongul MDCCXCII
BASE Warworld, mobile
HEIGHT 8ft **WEIGHT** 1,125 lbs **EYES** Red **HAIR** Bald
POWERS/ABILITIES Super-strength, speed, stamina and invulnerability, fire vision, ruthless pragmatism, strategic genius; Chest blaster
ENEMIES Superman, Batman, Wonder Woman, Green Lantern Corps, United Planets
AFFILIATIONS Warworld, Jochi, Sinestro Corps

One of the universe's most feared tyrants, Mongul is a violent brute with an insatiable hunger for domination. Descended from a line of killer kings, Mongul is never happier than when pitilessly crushing an opponent. Ruthless and terrifying, he once led the Sinestro Corps before being defeated by Green and Yellow Lanterns. Mongul possesses a cunning mind. He knows true power comes from governance and control, not threats or bloodletting. He will switch sides in the middle of a conflict and sacrifice allies if he thinks doing so will secure a tactical advantage. Whether through his intergalactic engine of death, Warworld, or subtler machinations like his mind-controlling Black Mercy plants or enslaving Earth's population through computer games, Mongul craves subjects to rule over.

Following defeat by Superman, his son Jochi restored shattered Warworld to full destructive functionality and began a new reign of terror. However, when Jochi displayed mercy to his subjects, Mongul killed him without hesitation.

Self-preservation was the key to Mongul making a deal with Wonder Woman and Superman to utilize his Warworld to defeat another world conqueror, Brainiac.

The tyrant was subsequently killed by another son, who assumed his name, rank, and aspirations as Mongul MDCCXCII. When Superman and his son Jon began aligning alien civilizations into a federation of United Planets, this Mongul brutally attacked, determined to disrupt the process. He was driven off by Super Heroes and alien soldiers, and ultimately beaten into submission by Superman.

MONITOR

DEBUT *New Teen Titans* (Vol. 1) #21 **(Jul. 1982)** (the Monitor); *Countdown to Final Crisis* #21 **(Oct. 6, 2007)** (Nix Uotan)
BASE Hall of Heroes in the Orrery of Worlds
HEIGHT Variable **WEIGHT** Variable **EYES** White **HAIR** Black
POWERS/ABILITIES Immortality; genius-level intellect; cosmic awareness; dimensional manipulation; energy projection; transformation and size alteration; psionics; teleportation; matter manipulation; superhuman strength, speed, durability, and flight.
ALLIES Mr. Stubbs, Harbinger, Operation Justice Battalion
ENEMIES The Gentry, the Empty Hand
AFFILIATIONS All heroes in every universe of the known Multiverse

According to the Guardians of the Universe, when Maltusian renegade Krona meddled with creation, existence, and time, he split reality into a multiverse, and two beings formed. The Monitor oversaw all positive-matter realities, while an Anti-Monitor, inimical to life, schemed from an antimatter universe. After billions of years, a sequence of cosmic crises reconfigured reality, resulting in 52 separate universes, with Earth at the heart of every one and a unique Monitor overseeing each. When war broke out between these Monitors, existence was yet again overwritten. Ultimately, one Monitor remained to safeguard all the surviving realities.

When not living as a normal teenager, Nix Uotan safeguards those dimensions comprising the Orrery of Worlds, protecting life in them from dangers beyond interdimensional border region the Bleed.

Following another reordering of existence by Doctor Manhattan, the true nature of reality was exposed. Everything there is originated at the command of a sixth-dimensional Super Celestial named Perpetua. She divided creation into Positive and Antimatter, underpinned by Dark Energy, with a Monitor, Anti-Monitor and World Forger to oversee them. For dereliction of duty, she was imprisoned behind the Source Wall. Her liberation unleashed Multiversal chaos, compelling the Monitor and his two brothers to unite and combat her, alongside Earth-0's Justice League.

MR. FREEZE

DATA

DEBUT *Batman* (Vol. 1) #121 **(Feb. 1959)**
REAL NAME Dr. Victor Fries
BASE Gotham City
HEIGHT 6ft **WEIGHT** 190 lbs **EYES** Blue **HAIR** None
POWERS/ABILITIES Genius-level intellect with a keen scientific mind; claims to not feel emotions; sophisticated refrigeration suit sustains low temperature and grants superhuman strength, durability, and endurance; developed quick-freeze technology that he utilizes in the form of freeze guns and grenades.
ALLIES Starling, Scarecrow, Harley Quinn, Merry-Maker, Professor Pyg, Mrs. Freeze
ENEMIES Batman, the Batman Family, Birds of Prey, Court of Owls
AFFILIATIONS Wayne Industries (formerly), Arkham Asylum inmates

MRS. FREEZE When finally conscious, Nora Fries proved to be even more cold-blooded than her husband as the ruthless Mrs. Freeze.

At first glance, Mr. Freeze seems like a sympathetic criminal. After all, he has devoted his life to looking for a cure for his beloved Nora so that she may be thawed from her cryogenic state and reunited with him. In fact, Victor Fries is a dangerous sociopath whose single-mindedness has transformed him into a Super-Villain.

FROZEN FEELINGS Fries would do anything to see the health of his beloved Nora restored, even endangering hundreds of innocent lives by draining power to work his equipment.

Victor Fries watched his father walk out on his family when he was young, abandoning both his mother and himself in Gotham City. Later relocating to Lowell, Nebraska, Victor's mother slowly lost her grip on reality, ending up sick and wheelchair-bound. While still a boy, Victor pushed her out onto a frozen lake and shoved her wheelchair into a hole in the ice. When his mother tried to climb out, Victor pushed her under the water again, preferring her to be frozen and "cured" of all her ills, than to go on suffering. She would not be discovered until the following spring.

As he matured, Victor carried with him his obsession for cold. He became a doctor in the field of cryogenics at Wayne Tower Laboratories. Victor adored his wife Nora, and when she fell ill with cancer, he had her frozen. When it was discovered he was running experiments on his frozen wife, Fries was fired. Victor grew violent, and in a scuffle, he was doused in experimental chemicals that made it impossible for his body to survive outside the temperature of absolute zero. Required to wear a refrigerated suit, Victor developed flash-freezing weaponry and became the Super-Villain Mr. Freeze.

He later augmented his physiology so as not to depend on his Mr. Freeze suit. Aided by Lex Luthor, Victor restored Nora to life and the couple became frozen fugitives. However, Luthor's serum corrupted Nora's mind, and she lashed out at Victor causing him to be frozen in stasis in order to survive. With their roles reversed, the road was paved for the criminal career of Mrs. Freeze.

ON THE RECORD

When he debuted in 1959, Mr. Freeze was a renegade scientist-turned-criminal named Mr. Zero. Intended as a one-off villain, he returned in the late 1960s bearing his current moniker, Mr. Freeze.

Over the years, Mr. Freeze was a minor Batman rogue, making a few guest appearances until the 1980s, which featured a number of costume changes. It wasn't until after *Crisis on Infinite Earths* and thanks in part to *Batman: The Animated Series*, that Victor Fries was given his origin story. The tragic tale helped elevate him to the status of one of Batman's greatest foes.

ZERO TOLERANCE In his first appearance, Mr. Freeze was Mr. Zero, a scientist whose ice gun backfired, spilling a freezing solution over him. It meant he could now only survive in sub-zero temperatures.

CLASSIC STORIES

Batman (Vol. 1) #121 (Feb. 1959) Called Mr. Zero in this first appearance, Mr. Freeze begins a series of robberies using a gun capable of projecting both cold and heat.

Detective Comics (Vol. 1) #373 (Mar. 1968) Mr. Zero returns to plague Batman in a new costume and with a new name: Mr. Freeze.

Batman: Mr. Freeze #1 (May 1997) Mr. Freeze is provided a fitting modern origin story, inspired in part by the acclaimed *Batman: The Animated Series*.

Batman (Vol. 2) Annual #1 (Jul. 2012) Mr. Freeze's origin is briefly updated for the "New 52" continuity, revealing that Victor's "wife" Nora was never his wife at all, but the first woman to undergo cryogenic stasis, Nora Fields.

MONSTER SOCIETY OF EVIL

DEBUT *Captain Marvel Adventures* (Vol. 1) #22 (Mar. 1943)
FORMER MEMBERS Mister Mind; I.B.A.C.; Dr. Sivana; Captain Nazi; Crocodile Man; Evil Eye; Mister Atom
CURRENT MEMBERS Sivana; Mister Mind; Wicked Witch of the West; Jeepers; King Kull; Scapegoat; Evil Eye; Red Queen; Mr. Atom; Mr. Merry-Go-Round; Crocodile Men
ENEMIES Shazam Family, The Wizard

The Monster Society of Evil was formed by Venusian worm Mister Mind during World War II in an attempt at global conquest, and opposed by heroic Shazam. The Society contained Axis spies, metahuman or mystical villains, and malevolent monsters.

The Society never attacked as a group but always individually. Even in later years when mad scientist Dr. Sivana took charge, it proved impossible to get the monsters to cooperate with one another. The aims of the Monster Society remain constant: crush Shazam, terrorize decent folk, and cause as much carnage and destruction as possible.

Following *Rebirth*, a new Society was formed. It was made up of the worst villains of the Seven Magic Lands which, until recently, had been sealed by The Wizard. They were defeated and re-imprisoned by the power of his heirs, the Shazam Family.

MORDRU

DEBUT *Adventure Comics* (Vol. 1) #369 (Jun. 1968)
BASE Zerox, the Sorcerer's World
EYES Hazel **HAIR** Auburn
POWERS/ABILITIES Lord of Chaos; immortal; ultimate-level magic-wielder; superhuman strength.
ENEMIES Nabu, Doctor Fate, JSA, The Spectre, Justice Society of America, Justice League Dark, Legion of Super-Heroes
AFFILIATIONS Demon Knights, Sons of Anubis

Lord of Chaos Mordru is an energy being who inhabits physical hosts. His goal is domination of all existence and he gathers sorcerous artifacts, such as the Amulet of Fate, to secure his ambitions. As Wrynn, he plundered Gemworld, and on Earth once possessed the Books of Magic. He has always battled Super Heroes, latterly tormenting Wonder Woman and Zatanna when Justice League Dark sought allies against the predatory Otherkind. His major opposition would become the Legion of Super-Heroes, with his own daughter White Witch Xola Aq in the vanguard.

Mordru has a fear of entombment, with many battles lost because opponents buried or trapped him in confined spaces. Thus, he prefers to dominate through physical forces. Overconfidence is his weakness, whether fighting Nabu, or mortal foes like the JSA.

MORGAN, JENNIFER

DEBUT *Warlord* (Vol. 1) #38 (Oct. 1980)
BASE Skartaris
EYES Blue **HAIR** White
POWERS/ABILITIES Powerful sorceress; create magic bolts of energy, teleport; generate force-fields, and conjure images of past events.
ALLIES Warlord, Joshua Morgan, Machiste
ENEMIES Ashiya, Deimos
AFFILIATIONS The Trinity (Batman, Superman, and Wonder Woman)

Jennifer Morgan is the daughter of Lt. Col. Travis Morgan, Warlord of underground realm Skartaris. Believing her father dead, she later reunited with him after following his trail to the otherworldly reality he had stumbled on years previously.

There she learned sorcery with the witch Ashiya, but on discovering her tutor's ill intentions, Jennifer rebelled, and ultimately defeated the sorceress with her own magical skills. As Lady Jennifer, she is the supreme sorceress of Skartaris. Despite being close to her, the Warlord feels uncomfortable with his daughter's magic. But he still battles beside her, such as when Superman, Batman, and Wonder Woman tackled his arch foe Deimos, or when father and daughter helped displaced Superboy Conner Kent and Young Justice escape from Skartaris.

MULTIPLEX

DEBUT *Firestorm* (Vol. 1) #1 (Mar. 1978)
REAL NAME Dalton Black
HEIGHT 6ft **WEIGHT** 188 lbs
EYES Blue **HAIR** Black
POWERS/ABILITIES Capable hand-to-hand combatant; able to duplicate his form.
ALLIES Killer Frost, Plastique, Hyena, Typhoon
ENEMIES The Flash, Artemis, Firestorm, Green Arrow, Midnighter
AFFILIATIONS The Secret Society

Dalton Black was assistant to Professor Martin Stein, the scientist who created Firestorm. Before Stein could fire Black for trying to sell his secrets, Black used Stein's machinery, unleashing a surge of energy leaving him with the ability to infinitely multiply his form, and began calling himself Multiplex. Green Arrow took out his duplicates, but the original Multiplex escaped.

After teaming up with other villains to fight Firestorm, Multiplex began working for a criminal named Mr. Rohmer. When the Super Hero Midnighter interrogated Rohmer to locate stolen technology, Rohmer ordered Black to fight the violent vigilante—a battle that Multiplex didn't walk away from. Black later clashed with The Flash, Artemis, and others, but with every defeat his confidence dwindled.

MARK MOONRIDER

DEBUT *Forever People* #1 (Feb.–Mar. 1971)
REAL NAME Mark Moonrider
BASE New Genesis
HEIGHT 5ft 11in **WEIGHT** 169 lbs
EYES Blue **HAIR** Black
POWERS/ABILITIES "Megaton touch" can cause explosions; skilled combatant.
ALLIES Infinity Man, Big Bear, Vykin, Beautiful Dreamer, Serifan, Superman, Deadman
ENEMIES Darkseid, Mantis, Desaad, Devilance
AFFILIATIONS Forever People

Mark Moonrider was a resident of the planet New Genesis when he first traveled to Earth. He partnered with his friend Dreamer Beautiful, who wished to complete an assignment to help advance mankind. The pair were joined by fellow New Genesis natives Vykin Baldaur and Vykin's sister Serafina. On Earth, the group met up with another New God, Big Bear, and set up camp in Venice Beach, California.

Moonrider soon joined the Super Hero team the Forever People, facing villains from New Genesis' rival planet, Apokolips, including Mantis and the Femmes Fatales. The Forever People discovered they could also switch places with an entity called the Infinity Man, a mysterious and powerful being whose true motives remain unknown.

MORGAINE LE FEY

DEBUT *Batman* #36 (Aug.–Sep. 1946)
REAL NAME Morgaine le Fey; also known as Morgan le Fay
HEIGHT 5ft 10in **WEIGHT** 148 lbs
EYES Blue **HAIR** Black
POWERS/ABILITIES Sorceress; can fly, create illusions, and generate force blasts.
ALLIES Nocturna, Man O'War, Absinthe, Scatter
ENEMIES The Demon, the Unknowns, Aquaman, the Others

A sorceress hailing from the time of Camelot and King Arthur, Morgaine le Fey presented a dire threat to mankind, and was opposed by The Demon (aka Etrigan). In the modern era, Morgaine was incensed that humans were slowly destroying their own planet. She tried to steal the Atlantean helmet of the hero Vostok-X to escape Earth, only to have the item reject her. With Aquaman and the Super Hero team the Others on her trail to retrieve the helmet, Morgaine revealed herself in a battle that ended abruptly with her vanishing in a flash of light.

Morgaine resurfaced with a new scheme to alter the very fabric of reality. She was defeated by the Unknowns, a new group of vigilantes led by Batwoman and including Morgaine's old foe, Etrigan.

MOTHER PANIC

DEBUT *DC's Young Animal Ashcan Edition* (Vol. 1) #1 (2016)
REAL NAME Violet Paige
BASE The Pike, Gotham City
HEIGHT 1.83 m (6 ft 0 in) **WEIGHT** 82 kg (180 lb) **EYES** Blue **HAIR** Black
POWERS/ABILITIES Cybernetic implants give her super strength, trained in hand-to-hand combat
ALLIES Doctor Varma, Dominic, Otis Flannegan, Fennec Fox, Batman, Batwoman
ENEMIES Gala, Pretty, The Collective
AFFILIATIONS None

After her father died on a hunting trip, and with her mother apparently mentally ill, teenager Violet Paige was sent by her older brother to boarding school. Gather House was a harsh institution where children were taken apart and remade—literally. Violet was given cybernetic implants and trained in combat. Pushed to breaking point, she ran away, burning the school down as a parting gesture. Fifteen years passed, and Violet was a notorious celebutante partying on her inheritance, living in a former hotel with her mother. However, she was also Mother Panic, a violent vigilante bent on revenge against those who had made her childhood so traumatic.

MURMUR

DEBUT *The Flash: Iron Heights* #1 (Aug. 2001)
REAL NAME Dr. Michael Christian Amar
BASE Keystone City; Central City
HEIGHT 5ft 8in **WEIGHT** 155 lbs
EYES Brown **HAIR** Black
POWERS/ABILITIES Skilled surgeon with an impressive knowledge of medical science; unpredictable and unstable killer.
ALLIES Girder, Magenta, Mirror Master
ENEMIES The Flash (Wally West)
AFFILIATIONS Zandia

Formerly a highly respected surgeon, Dr. Michael Christian Amar was well known in both Central City and Keystone City. However, in his spare time, he stalked the streets as costumed serial killer Murmur, so called by local media due to his uncontrollable tendency to mutter. Murmur was finally caught by the Keystone police, identified by his speech impediment.

Keen not to make the same mistake twice, Murmur cut out his own tongue and stitched his lips together. He gained even more notoriety when he instigated a mass breakout from the infamous Iron Heights penitentiary, and later went on to hunt The Flash to join the ranks of the Rogues. After fighting the Secret Six, Murmur vanished, and has been reported to be enjoying life in the Super-Villain refuge of Zandia.

NAOMI

DEBUT *Naomi* (Vol. 1) #1 (Mar 2019)
REAL NAME Naomi McDuffie
BASE Port Oswego, Oregon
HEIGHT Unknown **WEIGHT** Unknown **EYES** Brown **HAIR** Black
POWERS/ABILITIES Super-strength and durability; flight; energy projection.
ALLIES Superman, Batman, Dee
ENEMIES Zumbado, Red Cloud
AFFILIATIONS Young Justice

Until Naomi McDuffie was 17 years old, she had no idea that she was an alien. Her adoptive parents revealed to her that she had been brought through a dimensional rift as a baby, swaddled in a mysterious black box. When Naomi held the box in her hands, her body absorbed it, and she heard a message from her birth mother explaining why she had had to send her daughter away.

Naomi's home planet, an alternate Earth elsewhere in the Multiverse, had been devastated by environmental catastrophe. This crisis had allowed radiation to bombard the planet, imbuing a select few with powers, including Naomi's parents. When another metahuman, a murderer named Zumbado, threatened the safety of their baby, Naomi's parents chose to send her to Prime Earth, where they knew there were superpowered beings who could guide their child.

The box Naomi held had activated her powers—she could now fly and create powerful light blasts, as well as having super-strength and durability. Feeling confused and out of control, she went to Metropolis to seek help from her hero, Superman. While there, she helped Superman fight off the Red Cloud. Later, Naomi went back to Oregon, where she joined Young Justice.

BOX OF REVELATIONS
Naomi's black box told her the truth about her heritage and powers. She would soon get the chance to visit her devastated homeworld and take part in her first superpowered battle.

NATU, SORANIK

DEBUT *Green Lantern Corps: Recharge* #1 (Nov. 2005)
BASE Korugar, Mobile
EYES Purple (yellow when Yellow Lantern) **HAIR** Black
POWERS/ABILITIES Expert neurosurgeon; as a Yellow Lantern can create constructs of yellow energy by tapping into the emotion of fear.
ALLIES Sinestro, Hal Jordan
ENEMIES Spider Guild, Kyle Rayner
AFFILIATIONS Sinestro Corps; formerly Green Lantern Corps

FATHER KNOWS BEST
Sinestro used threats and blackmail to make Natu accept a Yellow Lantern power ring.

Soranik Natu was a neurosurgeon on Korugar in Sector 1417. Korugarians despised Green Lanterns because Sinestro, the first of their kind to join the Corps, had made himself tyrannical ruler of the planet. When a Green power ring selected Natu, she reluctantly accepted, working alongside other Lanterns against the star-extinguishing Spider Guild. She later returned to Korugar, unifying it after seemingly defeating Sinestro.

When Sinestro returned, leading the Sinestro Corps, Natu fought him along with the Green Lanterns, and she began a relationship with colleague Kyle Rayner. In the war's aftermath, Sinestro revealed he was Natu's father and was proud of her for uniting Korugar. During the Blackest Night, Kyle sacrificed himself for his comrades, but their ally Star Sapphire (Miri Riam) tapped into Natu's love for Kyle to resurrect him. When the Korugarians were almost eradicated by First Lantern Volthoom, Sinestro promised to save the survivors—providing Natu joined his Sinestro Corps.

She grudgingly agreed. After Sinestro was defeated by Hal Jordan, Natu inherited his mantle as leader, brokering an alliance with the Green Lanterns. The pact explosively sundered after future villain Sarko attacked. When he was killed, Natu discovered that the "Last Yellow Lantern" was her grown son and that Rayner was the father—a fact Kyle already knew and had kept concealed. After branding her former lover with her ring, she withdrew with the Yellow Lanterns, furiously declaring herself Soranik Sinestro.

N.O.W.H.E.R.E.

DEBUT *Superboy* (Vol. 6) #1 (Nov. 2011)
NOTABLE MEMBERS/POWERS Harvest: Leader, futuristic weapons, flight; **Centerhall:** Body of psionic energy; **Director Templar:** Body contains vicious parasites; **Omen:** Precognitive telepath; **Leash:** Energy whips, psionic powers; **Grunge:** Acquires properties of matter; **Misbelief:** Illusionist; **Psykill:** Cyborg; **Warblade:** Creates blades from body; **Ridge:** Superhuman; **Crush:** Shapeshifter; **Fuji:** Body of cosmic energy.
ENEMIES Superboy, Teen Titans, Legion Lost

N.O.W.H.E.R.E. was a secret organization created by Harvest— a mysterious figure with access to 31st-century technology. Its objective was to control the next generation of metahumans, and its underground base was called the Colony.

Metahuman test subjects were forced to battle to the death in a process called the Culling. The winners were inducted into the Ravagers—N.O.W.H.E.R.E.'s elite strike force. One of N.O.W.H.E.R.E.'s most ambitious projects was the creation of Superboy (Kon-El), a half-Kryptonian, half-human clone. He escaped and allied with the Teen Titans to destroy the Colony. Harvest built a new Colony in Africa but he was killed and his facility was destroyed in a battle with the Teen Titans, possibly spelling the end of N.O.W.H.E.R.E.

NABU

DEBUT *More Fun Comics* #67 (May 1941)
BASE The Helmet of Fate
EYES Brown **HAIR** Bald
POWERS/ABILITIES Through Helmet of Fate, can communicate with Khalid Nassour or other wearers; produces visions; levitates the Helmet; can fly and access computers.
ALLIES Thoth, Khalid Nassour (Doctor Fate), Kent Nelson (Doctor Fate), Inza Nelson (Doctor Fate), Hector Hall (Doctor Fate)
ENEMIES Anubis, Mordru

Nabu was one of Earth's earliest mages: part of a group which controlled raw magic and called themselves Lords of Order and Chaos. But factions in the group warred over how to manage the universe. Nabu decided to take human form to guide civilization.

Eventually Nabu's body retired to his tomb, lying dormant until he was woken by Kent Nelson in the early 20th century. Nabu's power as the Order Lord inhabited a golden helmet, and when Nelson wore it, he became Doctor Fate and a conduit for Nabu's will.

Many have donned the helmet since, all becoming pawns of Nabu. With the advent of the Otherkind, Nabu summoned his fellow Lords, seeking to destroy all magic. Since being defeated by both heroes and magical beings, Nabu continues to fight Chaos and evil as part of Justice League Dark.

NEKRON

DEBUT *Tales of the Green Lantern Corps* #2 (Jun. 1981)
BASE The Land of the Unliving
EYES Black **HAIR** None
POWERS/ABILITIES Immensely powerful avatar of death; can kill with a touch, reanimate the dead as Black Lanterns, fire blasts of dark lightning, and warp reality; draws strength from death.
ALLIES Black Hand
ENEMIES The Guardians of Oa, Super Heroes of Earth, the Lantern Corps
AFFILIATIONS Black Lantern Corps

Nekron is an ancient embodiment of darkness, created by the universe itself in order to oppose life. He is the ruler of the limbo-like Dead Zone that holds souls awaiting judgment, though he, too, is trapped there. When the Guardians of Oa banished the renegade Oan, Krona, he ended up in Nekron's realm, and his presence there created a rift leading to the mortal universe. Nekron was then able to see into Earth's reality and he became completely obsessed with destroying it.

During the *Blackest Night* event, he released Black Lantern power rings into the universe. These sought out heroes and villains who were dead or had returned from death and transformed them into gruesome Black Lanterns. Heroes suddenly found themselves battling friends, enemies, and lovers, who had returned from the grave to make war on the living. Using the dark energies released by the Black Lanterns' slaughter, Nekron's henchman, Black Hand, summoned his master into Earth's universe. Nekron then tried to destroy the Entity—the embodiment of all life—but was defeated when Hal Jordan bonded with the Entity to become a White Lantern. Nekron briefly possessed Swamp Thing during the *Brightest Day* event, and Hal Jordan summoned him to defeat the threat of Volthoom, the First Lantern.

NEGATIVE MAN

DEBUT *My Greatest Adventure* #80 (Jun. 1963)
REAL NAME Larry Trainor
HEIGHT 5ft 10in **WEIGHT** 180 lbs
POWERS/ABILITIES Releases a powerful negative-energy being from his body, but will die if it does not return within 60 seconds.
ENEMIES Justice League
AFFILIATIONS Doom Patrol

Airline pilot Larry Trainor's life changed when his plane crashed. Larry had no memory of what had happened, but Dr. Niles Caulder, aka the Chief, told him that he had been exposed to a toxin that made him so radioactive that the doctors treating him had died of cancer. The Chief claimed to have swathed his body in lead-lined bandages to contain the radiation. He also told Trainor that he was now host to a negative-energy being that endowed him with superpowers.

Feeling that he owed the Chief his life, Trainor joined his Doom Patrol as Negative Man. The Chief sent his team to apprehend Jessica Cruz and acquire her Green Lantern power ring, but during a faceoff with the Justice League, Larry and the Doom Patrol helped endangered civilians instead of grabbing Cruz, proving that they were not totally under the Chief's thumb.

NEGATIVE WOMAN

DEBUT *Showcase* #94 (Aug.–Sep. 1977)
REAL NAME Valentina Vostok
ABILITIES Releasing negative-energy beings.
ALLIES Cliff Steele, Joshua Clay, Harry Stein
ENEMIES General Immortus, Kobra
AFFILIATIONS The People's Heroes, Doom Patrol, Checkmate

Soviet pilot Lt. Col. Valentina Vostok defected to the US in an experimental long-range fighter, but crashed into the sea near Codsville, Maine, where the Doom Patrol had seemingly been wiped out. The energy-being that had inhabited the former Negative Man (Larry Trainor) entered her body and transformed her into a powerful negative-energy form. She joined a new Doom Patrol led by Celsius and started a relationship with fellow member Tempest, but when her power turned her radioactive, they were forced to break up. Larry Trainor returned from the dead and the negative-energy returned to him.

Valentina left to work in espionage and was promoted to the role of White Queen in Checkmate. She died during the *Final Crisis*, but returned in undead form during the Blackest Night to attack Negative Man.

Post-*Flashpoint*, Valentina was a member of the Doom Patrol, but was killed by Atomica and Johnny Quick when the Crime Syndicate invaded Earth-0.

NEMESIS

DEBUT *The Brave and the Bold* (Vol. 1) #166 (Sep. 1980)
REAL NAME Thomas Andrew Tresser
BASE Department of Metahuman Affairs, Washington, D.C.
HEIGHT 5ft 10in **WEIGHT** 170 lbs
EYES Blue **HAIR** Blond
ABILITIES Master of disguise; espionage expert; gadgets include bugs, concussion gun, and paralysis pistol.
ENEMIES The Council, Jihad

Tom Tresser and his brother Chris were operatives in a secret government agency. When Chris was brainwashed by the Council, Tom took the codename Nemesis and swore to bring them down. After apparently dying in a helicopter crash, he joined the Suicide Squad before being seconded to the Shadow Fighters to battle Eclipso. Nemesis then worked at the Department of Metahuman Affairs, but went rogue during a war between America and the Amazons, aiding Wonder Woman and winning Amazon citizenship.

After the *Final Crisis*, Tom was forcibly recruited into the Global Peace Agency, eventually questioning his own sanity after a series of mind-bending missions. He was killed by temporarily deranged Wally West while undergoing treatment at Sanctuary.

NEUTRON

DEBUT *Action Comics* (Vol. 1) #525 (Nov. 1981)
REAL NAME Nathaniel Tryon
POWERS/ABILITIES Can project blasts of radiation from hands.
ENEMIES Aquaman, Lex Luthor, Justice League, Superman

Nathaniel Tryon was a security guard at the Metropolis Power Plant, but a meltdown transformed his body into living nuclear energy, requiring him to wear a containment suit. As Neutron, he used his new radiation-blast power to kill those responsible for the accident. He then became a mercenary, accepting a contract to kill Lex Luthor.

Neutron was defeated by Aquaman, but one of his blasts ruptured the unit holding Luthor's experimental Amazo virus. The virus spread across the city and also infected Neutron, reacting with his radioactive form to create virulent cancers. He was also briefly possessed by the virus' collective consciousness before Luthor deployed a vaccine. Neutron was left powerless and cancer-ridden, but Luthor would not let him die—after all, Neutron knew the identity of the person who wanted Luthor dead.

Pre-*Flashpoint*, Neutron was a petty thug turned radioactive Super-Villain, who held a particular grudge against Superman.

NERON

DEBUT *Underworld Unleashed* #1 (Nov. 1995)
BASE Club Midnight
HEIGHT 7ft 2in **WEIGHT** 285 lbs
EYES Blue **HAIR** Blond
POWERS/ABILITIES Master of sorcery, with superhumanly powerful demonic physiology; can breathe flesh-melting flames.
ALLIES Mister Rumor
ENEMIES John Constantine, Papa Midnite
AFFILIATIONS The demons of Hell

Minor demon Neron capitalized on strife in Hell to become ruler of its largest arch-dukedom. He specialized in making Faustian pacts with mortals to gain their souls, the damned currency of Hell. He frequently appeared on Earth: cutting deals, and taking control of Papa Midnite's occult nightclub. With help from business partner Mister Rumor, he began buying up New York real estate, intent on turning the city into a massive mystic bazaar where humans could purchase magic and lose their souls. When Papa Midnite enlisted John Constantine to get the Midnight Club back, Neron was thwarted.

With the invading Otherkind picking off the infernal hierarchy and magic itself endangered by the Lords of Order, Neron joined former StormWatch commander Henry Bendix, who wanted Neron to destroy Apollo and Midnighter. Although initially successful in killing Apollo and tormenting his domain, Neron was utterly unprepared for Midnighter fighting his way into Hell to save his lover and deliver the most punishing defeat of Neron's existence.

ON THE RECORD

Neron first appeared during *Underworld Unleashed* as the demon who offered heroes and villains great power in return for their souls. Dozens of villains accepted and raised merry Hell before they were damned. When Neron was tricked and trapped in the Tower of Fate by the Elongated Man, a war broke out in the infernal regions, with Blaze and Satanus attempting to take over. When Neron broke free and returned to Hell, he was beheaded by Satanus.

DECAPITATED DEMON: After being trapped in the Tower of Fate, Neron paid the gruesome price for losing a civil war in Hell.

NEW GUARDIANS

DEBUT *Green Lanterns: New Guardians* #1 (Nov. 2011)
CURRENT MEMBERS Kyle Rayner (Green Lantern); **Munk** (Indigo Tribe); **Saint Walker** (Blue Lantern Corps); **Atrocitus** (Red Lantern Corps); **Larfleeze** (Orange Lantern Corps); **Arkillo** (Sinestro Corps); **Carol Ferris** (Star Sapphire Corps)
ENEMIES Invictus

The New Guardians came into being when Green Lantern Kyle Rayner found himself in possession of rings from other Corps, which had left their previous owners for him. Not knowing why, Rayner became the subject of a galactic manhunt as various Corps tried to retrieve their rings. When the Guardians attacked Rayner, assuming he had stolen the rings, he was helped by Saint Walker and Larfleeze, and even his pursuers, who united to defend him. Later, Larfleeze revealed that the Archangel Invictus caused the rings' migration, and they, as the New Guardians, had to defeat him before he destroyed the entire Vega System.

The team fought and defeated Invictus, after which they discovered that the exiled Guardian Sayd was really responsible for the ring incident, because she believed Rayner was the only Lantern who could harness all seven aspects of the Emotional Spectrum—and only by doing so could they beat Invictus.

An earlier team of New Guardians was chosen from several nations as representatives of the human race and enhanced to be the next stage in humankind's evolution.

RINGING THE CHANGES
Atrocitus, Carol Ferris, and Larfleeze would eventually replace Bleez, Fatality, and Glomulus on the New Guardians.
1 Glomulus
2 Kyle Rayner
3 Bleez
4 Saint Walker
5 Munk
6 Arkillo
7 Fatality

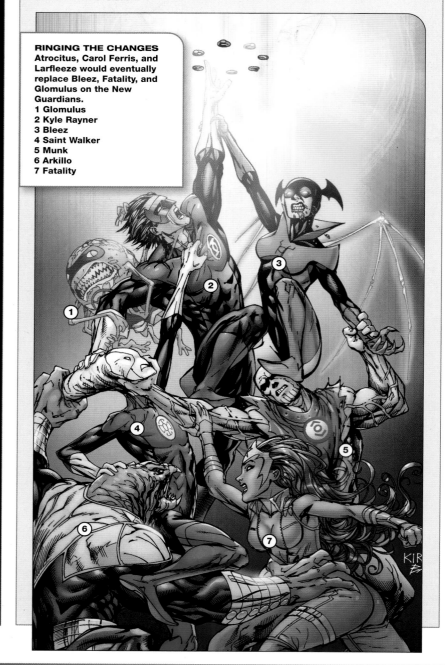

NEW SUPER-MAN

DEBUT *New Super-Man* (Vol. 1) #1 (Sep 2016)
REAL NAME Kong Kenan **BASE** Shanghai, China
HEIGHT 5ft 11in) **WEIGHT** 185 lbs
EYES Brown **HAIR** Black
POWERS/ABILITIES Has similar powers to the original Superman, accessing them via his qi; using and resisting magic.
ALLIES I-Ching, Superman
ENEMIES China White Triad, Lantern Corps of China, Freedom Fighters of China
AFFILIATIONS Justice League of China

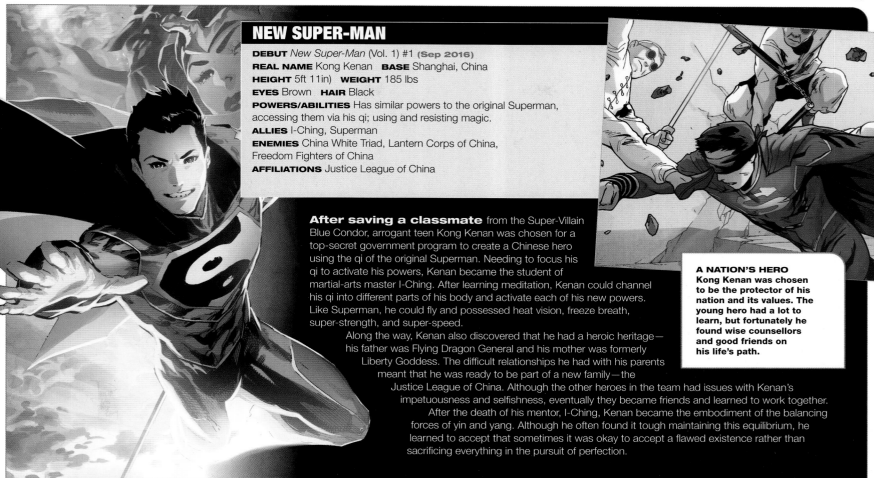

After saving a classmate from the Super-Villain Blue Condor, arrogant teen Kong Kenan was chosen for a top-secret government program to create a Chinese hero using the qi of the original Superman. Needing to focus his qi to activate his powers, Kenan became the student of martial-arts master I-Ching. After learning meditation, Kenan could channel his qi into different parts of his body and activate each of his new powers. Like Superman, he could fly and possessed heat vision, freeze breath, super-strength, and super-speed.

Along the way, Kenan also discovered that he had a heroic heritage—his father was Flying Dragon General and his mother was formerly Liberty Goddess. The difficult relationships he had with his parents meant that he was ready to be part of a new family—the Justice League of China. Although the other heroes in the team had issues with Kenan's impetuousness and selfishness, eventually they became friends and learned to work together. After the death of his mentor, I-Ching, Kenan became the embodiment of the balancing forces of yin and yang. Although he often found it tough maintaining this equilibrium, he learned to accept that sometimes it was okay to accept a flawed existence rather than sacrificing everything in the pursuit of perfection.

A NATION'S HERO
Kong Kenan was chosen to be the protector of his nation and its values. The young hero had a lot to learn, but fortunately he found wise counsellors and good friends on his life's path.

NEWSBOY LEGION

DEBUT *Star Spangled Comics* #7 (Apr. 1942)
BASE Metropolis
MEMBERS Big Words, Gabby, Scrapper, Tommy Tompkins, Walter Johnson, Famous Bobby
ALLIES Guardian, Superboy
ENEMIES Lex Luthor

WHIZZING AROUND
The Newsboy Legion got themselves into a lot of scrapes over the years, and got out of more than a few thanks to Cadmus tech like the Whizz Wagon.

The Newsboy Legion was a team of reformed juvenile delinquents. They roamed the streets of Metropolis under the watchful eye of the costumed Guardian—police officer Jim Harper—who wanted to protect the orphans from the hard life of the streets. Growing up during World War II, the Legion later formed Project Cadmus, a pioneering genetic research facility.

An early Cadmus endeavor was the cloning of Jim Harper, which granted the Guardian new life. The Cadmus facility was then attacked by the Apokoliptian creature Sleez and, during Sleez's brief takeover, teenage clones of the now-adult Legion appeared, effectively recreating the original Legion and setting it up for new adventures. These included the admission of the first female Newsboy Legionnaire, Famous Bobby.

1 Guardian
2 Gabby
3 Walter "Flip" Johnson
4 Tommy Tompkins
5 Big Words
6 Scrapper

NIGHT FORCE

DEBUT *New Teen Titans* (Vol. 1) #21 (Jul. 1982)
BASE Washington, DC
NEW MEMBERS Raven; Zachary Zatara; Black Alice; Klarion, the Witch Boy and Teekl; Robert Diaz; Sky Harper; Traci Thirteen; Alice Williams; Kid Devil
ENEMIES Kassandra Fey, Trigon, Shadowriders

Baron Winters gathered the Night Force to fight evils he could not, due to his inability to leave Wintersgate Manor, except by traveling to other times. Guided by the Book of Night, he brought together Jim Duffy, Zoe Davis, and Brian Greene to fight the Gatherers, led by the mystic Kassandra Fey.

The Gatherers had spent centuries breeding psychic demons, and were close to perfecting them. All the while Kassandra had been siphoning Baron Winters' powers, using the peculiar nature of Wintersgate, which exists at a nexus of different times. She used Zoe Davis as a vessel, and Brian Greene as the unknowing parent of generations of the demonic creatures. When they realized Kassandra was manipulating them, the team fought back, and Jim Duffy killed her.

Winters is notorious for callously expending his agents. He tried to build a Night Force team of young magic users—Arcanes—to repulse the invasion of Trigon and a purge of magic beings by ancient Shadowriders.

MASTERIND
Baron Winters schemes from his chair with his pet leopard Merlin... while Jim Duffy and Zoe Davis get a crash course in the occult.

NEW GODS, THE

DEBUT *The New Gods* (Vol. 1) #1 (Mar. 1971)
BASE New Genesis/Apokolips
MEMBERS/POWERS
NEW GENESIS

HIGHFATHER Wisdom, link to Source, can inhibit others' powers; **ORION** Warrior, A4 platform allows flight, teleportation, energy blasts; **MISTER MIRACLE** Escape artist, access to teleportation, flight; **HIMON** Genius, expert in New Genesis science and culture; **LIGHTRAY** Flight, absorbs solar energies and then emits them as energy blasts; **BEKKA** Commands absolute adoration and loyalty from others; **HYALT** Burns with cosmic fire, armor serves as mobile forge; **METRON** Mobius Chair generates force-fields, allows space and time travel, and provides instant knowledge; **MALHEDRON** Wields powerful energy hammer; **THE FOREVER PEOPLE** Together they summon the mighty Infinity Man; **INFINITY MAN** Flight, teleportation, telepathy, energy blasts, healing.

APOKOLIPS

DARKSEID Omega Effect energies, including deadly Omega Beams; **DESAAD** Expert torturer, illusionist, turns beings into Parademons; **KALIBAK** Strong, tough, keen sense of smell; **BEDLAM** Psychic energy being, can control multiple android bodies; **BIG BARDA** Warrior and leader, wears Apokoliptian Aegis armor; **KANTO** Weapons master, expert fighter; **GRANNY GOODNESS** Drill sergeant, seasoned warrior; **MANTIS** Energy vampire, accomplished warrior.

The New Gods are an ancient race who possess prodigious power and superior technology. Each god is equal in might to one of Earth's Super Heroes. They are also a race locked in perpetual war. The New Gods of New Genesis, ruled by Highfather, are devoted to peace and order, but are in constant bitter conflict with their warlike brethren on hellish Apokolips, ruled over by the mighty tyrant, Darkseid.

AT A GLANCE...

Smart technology
New Gods technology is so advanced that many of its devices are actually sentient. But perhaps the most incredible device of all is the Mother Box. This bonds to its owner and serves as a multifunction tool, a data source, and medical kit, evolving to suit its user's needs.

Boom Tubes
Boom Tubes are the preferred method of transportation for the New Gods. These interdimensional tunnels can be generated by Mother Boxes or other devices and they allow their users to cross between planets and even realities with ease. The name comes from the distinctive sound they make when activated.

The story of the New Gods
begins in the distant past, on an unreachable plane separate from the rest of the universe. A primordial planet there was ruled over by the wild and capricious Old Gods, who reveled in chaos, while the lesser beings that would become known as the New Gods scratched out a living amid that chaos.

One of these lesser beings, named Uxas, bore a burning hatred against the Old Gods and led a war against them. The Old Gods were slain, but then another war broke out between the evil Uxas, who would later become known as Darkseid, and his good brother Izaya, who would become Highfather. Izaya and his people eventually built a utopian city that floats over their planet, New Genesis,

GENESIS WAR
Uxas and Izaya led the New Gods in a war of annihilation against the chaotic Old Gods. The conflict ended when Uxas slew his own father, Yuga Khan.

while Darkseid and his minions created the hellish world of Apokolips. The latter then set out in search of new worlds to conquer. Peace was established between the two when Highfather and Darkseid exchanged sons: Orion was raised on New Genesis, while Scot (who would become Mister Miracle) was imprisoned in the Slave Pits of Apokolips.

Cruelty and oppression are a way of life on Apokolips. At the bottom of the hierarchy are the Lowlies and Plague Dogs, who work in the Slave Camps or are fed into the Fire Pits that fuel Apokolips' forges and munitions factories. Above them are the dreaded Parademons, genetically engineered monsters bred only for war, and above the Parademons are the various minions of Darkseid, who compete for the favor of their master. Among them are the general Steppenwolf, the interrogator Desaad, and Darkseid's warrior son, Kalibak.

The hordes of Apokolips often travel through space, conquering and consuming worlds—Earth-2 was one world that suffered this fate. The heroes of Earth-2 repulsed one attack by the forces of Apokolips, led by Steppenwolf, but five years later, Darkseid himself commanded his hordes and Earth-2 was ultimately consumed by Apokolips. The New Gods of New Genesis are more peaceful in their interactions with other worlds, believing that their purpose is to guide lesser races away from darkness and to spread peace and harmony. Its heroes journey out to fight evil, and it has set up research projects on other worlds to extend the benefits of its advanced science. However, the inhabitants of New Genesis are not immune to pride and arrogance: while searching for the secret of the fabled Life Equation, Highfather inadvertently started a

DARKSEID WAR
When Darkseid was locked in battle with the powerful Anti-Monitor, the Justice League was caught in the middle. Mister Miracle, Big Barda, and even the Female Furies all pooled their strength in a war that saw the death of Darkseid, and then his subsequent resurrection as an infant. In the process, the Justice League was briefly bestowed with the power of the gods. Most notably, Batman sat upon Metron's chair, and discovered secrets about his arch foe, The Joker.

BATMAN: GOD OF KNOWLEDGE
Batman asked the all-knowing Mobius Chair for the real name of The Joker. It surprised him by saying that there were actually three Jokers.

CLASSIC STORIES

The Forever People (Vol. 1) #1–11
(Feb.–Mar. 1971–Oct.–Nov. 1972)
This gleefully psychedelic story introduced the freewheeling adventures of New God youngsters, the Forever People, chronicling their journey to Earth and beyond

Mister Miracle (Vol. 1) #1–18
(Mar.–Apr. 1971–Feb.–Mar. 1974)
This series tells the story of perhaps the most famous New Gods hero, the escape artist Mister Miracle, and his formidable warrior wife, Big Barda.

DC Graphic Novel #4 (Mar. 1985)
"The Hunger Dogs" relates the story of the oppressed underclass of Apokolips, who rise up and overthrow their evil master, Darkseid.

devastating war with the various Lantern Corps.

Recently, the Source Wall that separates known space from powerful forces locked away beyond its boundaries was pierced and then shattered altogether. New Genesis and Apokolips vanished, and the New Gods could feel themselves being called home to the Source itself. Orion and Darkseid avoided this. By manipulating a group of heroes informally called the Justice League Odyssey, and using a device created by Epoch, Darkseid saw Apokolips born again, back in the realm outside dimensions called the Sphere of the Gods. Any rebirth of New Genesis remains to be seen.

NOW AND FOREVER PEOPLE

When young New Genesis citizens Serafina, Vykin, Mark Moonrider, and Dreamer Beautiful went on a field trip to the primitive planet of Earth, they encountered a mysterious being— the Infinity Man. Under his guidance, they realized they had to rebel against both the benign authority of Highfather and the oppression of Darkseid in order to bring freedom to the Multiverse.

"Do not dare to question my motives, human. We New Gods have worked for ages beyond your imagination to protect the Multiverse."

HIGHFATHER

GODHEAD

Highfather of New Genesis was obsessed with unlocking the power of the legendary Life Equation, which he believed would allow him to permanently defeat Darkseid. His advisor Metron told him the secret might lie in the power rings of the Lantern Corps. Highfather dispatched warriors to steal the rings, plotting to use their energies to transform the universe's mortal races into powerful, obedient warriors able to withstand Darkseid. But he underestimated the might of the unified Lantern Corps, who proved that mortals could be a match for the New Gods.

GODS VS. MORTALS
Highfather tried to claim the power of the Lantern Corps, provoking a war that shook New Genesis to its foundations.

GODS ABOVE

The New Gods have undergone many deaths, rebirths, and transformations over the millennia. Although Highfather, Darkseid, Orion, and Mister Miracle have remained much the same, Desaad and Kanto have changed appearance radically. The boyish Serafin has become Vykin's sister Serafina, and some— including Takion and Virman Vundabar— appear to be waiting for reintroduction.

ON THE RECORD

In the pre-*Flashpoint* universe, Apokolips and New Genesis were planets created when an ancient primal world was split. In this reality, Uxas was not related to Izaya, but was an heir to the throne of Apokolips. He provoked a war with New Genesis by having Izaya's wife killed.

Genesis of the New Gods

The first New Gods series laid the cornerstone for an entire cosmic mythology. The main plotline involved Orion battling Darkseid's insidious plots to take over Earth. The series set up the long-running conflict between the hero and his estranged father and introduced other significant characters, notably Orion's comrade Lightray and the Black Racer—the New Gods' incarnation of death. However, the epic story also provided background for the entire New Gods saga. This chronicled the creation of Apokolips and New Genesis, the war that broke out between them following the death of Izaya's wife, Avia, and the spiritual journey that Izaya underwent to make contact with the Source and become the peaceful Highfather.

Death of the New Gods

This story saw the era of Apokolips and New Genesis come to an end. When the New Gods were hunted down by an unknown killer, Superman went on a quest to find out why, and made a disturbing discovery: the killer was the Source itself—the primal lifeforce of the universe. The Source was eliminating the New Gods to end the conflict between New Genesis and Apokolips so that they could be joined to create a new, perfect Fifth World.

Final Crisis

The fallout from the Death of the New Gods led directly to the reality-threatening *Final Crisis*. Though the New Gods were slain, their spirits found new homes on Earth, in human or other hosts. Darkseid (in the guise of human gangster Boss Dark Side) and his minions plotted to eliminate the world's heroes and conquer Earth with the power of the Anti-Life Equation, sending the entire multiverse spiraling toward destruction. Darkseid seemingly killed Batman in an epic confrontation, but Superman destroyed Darkseid's essence by singing a single note.

EVIL INFLUENCE
During *Final Crisis*, the Anti-Life Equation turned Wonder Woman and other Super Heroes into Female Furies serving Darkseid.

COSMIC TRAGEDY
The Man of Steel was distraught by the destruction of an entire race—including many of his friends and allies.

NIGHTMASTER

DEBUT *Showcase* #82 (May 1969)
REAL NAME James Rook
BASE New York City, Oblivion Bar
HEIGHT 6ft 1in **WEIGHT** 183 lbs
EYES Blue **HAIR** Gray
POWERS/ABILITIES Skilled combatant; sword of night detects danger, deflects energy, and compels enemies to speak truth.
ENEMIES Pentacle, Lord Meh
AFFILIATIONS Shadowpact

Musician Jim Rook and his girlfriend Janet Jones were transported from their shop Oblivion Inc. to the other-dimensional realm of Myrra. Rook discovered he was heir to Myrran hero Nightshade, and accepted his ancestor's Sword of Night. After liberating Myrra from evil warlocks, Rook and Janet returned to Earth. Nightmaster joined Shadowpact, eventually becoming the group's reluctant leader. Later, Rook cured the magically afflicted Unbound, using a spell harnessing his innate goodness.

After rebuilding Myrra he battled Lord Meh to free Shadowpact and retired to run the Oblivion Bar: a neutral venue for magic users. He perished defending it from the Dark Knights of bat-god Barbatos during the Metal invasion from the Dark Multiverse underpinning all of creation. His last act was appointing his old friend Detective Chimp the new Nightmaster.

NIGHTSHADE

DEBUT *Captain Atom* (Vol. 1) #82 (Sep. 1966)
REAL NAME Eve Eden
HEIGHT 5ft 8in **WEIGHT** 139 lbs
EYES Blue **HAIR** Black
POWERS/ABILITIES Dimensional travel; creation of tangible shadows; shadow form.
ALLIES Nemesis, Enchantress, Traci 13
ENEMIES Eclipso, Gorilla Grodd, Spectre
AFFILIATIONS Suicide Squad, Shadowpact, Justice League Dark

When Eve Eden's mother took her and her brother Larry to the Land of the Nightshades, Larry was abducted. Eve promised her mother she would rescue him.

She became government agent Nightshade, joining the Suicide Squad after Amanda Waller promised to help her find Larry. The Squad discovered he was possessed by the Incubus. Deadshot killed him to destroy the vile being. Nightshade continued to fight mystic threats, including Eclipso, with supernatural team Shadowpact.

Since *Rebirth*, she has competed with Deathstroke, and worked as part of a group battling Doctor Manhattan on Mars. When the Otherkind targeted Earth's magical community, Nightshade provided an escape route that saved many lives, before joining the battle against Witch-Goddess Hecate.

NKVDEMON

DEBUT *Batman* #445 (Mar. 1990)
REAL NAME Gregor Dosynski
HEIGHT 6ft 4in **WEIGHT** 240 lbs
EYES Red **HAIR** None
POWERS/ABILITIES Experimentally enhanced strength, stamina, and pain resistance; proficiency with firearms and hand-to-hand combat.
ENEMIES Aquaman, the Others

A protégé of the KGBeast, Gregor Dosynski was trained and enhanced as part of a secret Russian biotech project. This gave him superhuman mental toughness and pain resistance, and a demonic appearance—hence his codename: NKVDemon.

He was part of terror-team Mayhem, alongside his mentor KGBeast, Cheshire, Maelstrom, and Stranglehold. Together they battled Aquaman and the Others, trying to reactivate a Soviet-era satellite and launch nuclear missiles at targets on Earth. The Others diverted the missile with the help of Vostok-X, a former comrade of KGBeast, now aligned with the Others. Vostok-X redirected it toward his moon base and apparently died in the blast.

The NKVDemon has clashed with Batman several times, most recently after the death of Alfred Pennyworth. His butler—a former British spy—had an unresolved Soviet-era case that took the Dark Knight to the heart of modern Russia. A brutal clash with an aging traitor revealed there may be more survivors of the NKVDemon program…

FACE OF EVIL
The use of various experimental steroids turned NKVDemon into a powerful combatant, but also gave him a truly terrifying appearance.

NIGHTMARE NURSE

DEBUT *Phantom Stranger* (Vol. 4) #8 (Jul. 2013)
REAL NAME Asa
HEIGHT 5ft 9in **WEIGHT** 130 lbs
EYES Red **HAIR** Red
POWERS/ABILITIES Unsurpassed spiritual healing abilities, especially for serious supernatural ailments; known to create energy constructs.
ALLIES Deadman, John Constantine
ENEMIES Blight, Crime Syndicate of America

Even among her decidedly strange colleagues in the Justice League Dark, Nightmare Nurse stood out as a real mystery. Zatanna summoned her after The Question stabbed the Phantom Stranger, knowing only her powers could heal this supernatural wound. Nightmare Nurse, irritated at the summons, was nevertheless bound to help because the gods Apollo and Panacea themselves had once made her swear the Hippocratic Oath.

After helping the Stranger by retrieving his soul from the land of Non, Nightmare Nurse stayed with Justice League Dark through the Trinity War and the team's battle against the alien Blight. She and John Constantine have a romantic past that did not end happily for either of them. In addition to her healing prowess, Nightmare Nurse was able to create a clone of Swamp Thing, though it only survived for a short time.

NIMROD

DEBUT *Shadow of the Bat* #7 (Dec. 1992)
REAL NAME Dean Hunter
BASE Gotham City
HEIGHT 6ft 2in **WEIGHT** 195 lbs
EYES Blue **HAIR** Blond
POWERS/ABILITIES Military camouflage suit can turn invisible; infrared targeting goggles; gauntlet-mounted mini gun.
ENEMIES Batman, Robin

Photographer Dean Hunter got into a fight with the villain Chancer in Texas, during which Hunter's girlfriend was killed. Chancer escaped and Hunter was accused of murder. He escaped from prison and stole an experimental military suit, vowing to hunt Chancer down. The chase led him to Gotham City, where, as Nimrod, he initially interfered with Batman's pursuit of Chancer, who had joined the Misfits gang.

Nimrod later redeemed himself by helping Robin figure out where the Misfits were holding Batman, Commissioner Gordon, and Mayor Krol, saving their lives. Nimrod attacked the Misfits, determined to capture Chancer and get the truth out about what had happened in Texas. Batman arrived in time to help take down the gang, and both Chancer and Dean Hunter were taken to prison—but Hunter still believes he will be exonerated.

NOBODY

DEBUT *Batman and Robin* (Vol. 2) #1 (Nov. 2011)
REAL NAME Morgan Ducard; Maya Ducard
BASE Gotham City
HEIGHT 6ft 1in **WEIGHT** 195 lbs
EYES Brown **HAIR** None
POWERS/ABILITIES Skilled marksman and hand-to-hand combatant; expert torturer.
ENEMIES Batman, Damian Wayne

Son of the assassin Henri Ducard and the spy Felicity Strode, Morgan Ducard killed his mother when he thought she might betray Henri, and was then instructed in the family business—killing. Bruce Wayne also trained alongside Morgan under Henri Ducard's tutelage, kicking off a lifelong rivalry. Henri ordered Morgan to kill Bruce, but instead Bruce defeated Morgan, disgracing him in his father's eyes.

Vowing revenge and adopting the persona NoBody, Morgan embarked on a killing spree in Gotham City and also tried to corrupt Batman's son Damian. NoBody taunted Damian until Damian lost control and killed him. Morgan's daughter Maya, also raised to be an assassin, assumed her father's legacy as NoBody and sought revenge on Damian—but ultimately reached a wary reconciliation with him.

NORTHWIND

DEBUT *All-Star Squadron* #25 (Sep. 1983)
REAL NAME Norda Cantrell
HEIGHT 6ft **WEIGHT** 195 lbs
EYES Brown **HAIR** None
POWERS/ABILITIES Flight; enhanced strength and stamina; communication with birds.
ALLIES Black Adam, Atom Smasher
ENEMIES Hawkman
AFFILIATIONS Infinity, Inc.

Hybrid child of human anthropologist Fred Cantrell and a Feitherian mother, Norda Cantrell grew up in the hidden city of Feather in northern Greenland. As the godson of Hawkman Carter Hall, Norda formed a rivalry with Hawkman's son Hector, (later Doctor Fate). As an adult, Norda joined Infinity, Inc. as Northwind. After Hector Hall's death, he helped the Feitherians rebuild their home into New Feithera.

Initially possessing an avian-human hybrid form, Northwind transformed into a fully birdlike creature. Now unable to speak, he continued as a vigilante, joining with Black Adam and others in executing villains. Hawkman tore off Northwind's wings, hoping to stop him killing, but the wings grew back and Northwind helped Black Adam to take control of Kahndaq, his home country.

OBLIVION

DEBUT *Green Lantern: New Guardians Annual* (Vol. 1) #2 (Jun. 2014)
REAL NAME Kyle Rayner (evil doppelgänger)
HEIGHT Variable **WEIGHT** Variable
EYES Red **HAIR** Black
POWERS/ABILITIES Superhuman strength, shapeshifting, telepathy, illusion casting, energy projection, and construct manipulation.
ALLIES Carol Ferris
ENEMIES Kyle Rayner

Formed after Kyle Rayner broke through the Source Wall surrounding the universe, Oblivion is a dark doppelgänger of Kyle created from the fear, greed, and rage inside the former Green Lantern.

Possessing his progenitor's memories, Oblivion headed for Earth and, believing himself the original, tried living Kyle's life. His twisted sensibilities soon came to the fore, and he terrorized an entire town with illusions, mutating the populace into monsters. The real Kyle Rayner found that he could not defeat his mirror image and the stalemate was only broken when Kyle's father intervened. Oblivion recovered and struck again, but realizing its origins, Kyle merged with Oblivion, reabsorbing his own base instincts. He then returned to the edge of the universe and dragged them both back beyond the Source Wall.

OBSIDIAN

DEBUT *All-Star Squadron* (Vol. 1) #25 (Sep. 1983)
REAL NAME Todd James Rice
HEIGHT 5ft 11in **WEIGHT** 193 lbs
EYES Brown **HAIR** Brown
POWERS/ABILITIES Transformation into a shadow form, superhuman strength, flight, size alteration, shadow construct manipulation. Allies Jade, Alan Scott, Damon Matthews
ENEMIES Ian Karkull, Mordru, Eclipso

Raised in an abusive foster home, teenager Todd Rice found his twin sister, Jennie-Lynn Hayden, and they joined other second-generation metahumans in Infinity Incorporated. As Jade and Obsidian, the pair discovered their real father was 1940s Green Lantern Alan Scott. Their mother was Rose Canton, the plant marauder Thorn.

Todd's shadow powers stem from connections to a mystical realm of darkness. He suffers from schizophrenia, which makes him a valued member of the JSA but—briefly—one of its greatest enemies. When Jade died, his powers vanished and he retired. When they returned, Obsidian rejoined the JSA and, later, the Justice League. As a result of Doctor Manhattan's time-tampering being rolled back, Jade returned and both are active Super Heroes once again.

ODYSSEUS

DEBUT *Deathstroke* (Vol. 2) #8 (Jun. 2012)
REAL NAME Charles Wilson
EYES (One) Green **HAIR** White
POWERS/ABILITIES Hypnosis, possession, and mind control; highly skilled in unarmed combat and swordsmanship.
ALLIES Lady Shiva, Bronze Tiger
ENEMIES Deathstroke the Terminator, Red Fury, I Ching, Rose Wilson, Interpol

Charles Wilson was a devious monster when he worked for the CIA. He schooled his son Slade in soldiering, making his childhood a living hell, but providing the grounding Slade required to become Deathstroke the Terminator. When Charles died, the world became a better place. However, his grandson, Jericho, was forced to resurrect him, and Charles—now known as Odysseus—used his powers and charisma to rise to the forefront of the League of Assassins. He employed his powerful mind-controlling abilities to drive entire nations into bloody conflict.

Odysseus abducted his grandchildren, Jericho and Rose, needing their metahuman gifts to bolster his psionic grip and murderous army. His terror campaign was opposed by Deathstroke and his allies, resulting in Charles Wilson's second death.

OLYMPIAN

DEBUT *Super Friends* (Vol. 1) #9 (Dec. 1977)
REAL NAME Aristides Demetrios
BASE Greece
EYES Brown **HAIR** Black
POWERS/ABILITIES Superhuman strength of Herakles, flight of Zetes and Kalai, X-ray vision of Lynkeus, super-speed of Atalanta, and more.
ENEMIES Echidne, Queen Bee, Fain Y'onia, Brother Eye

Aristides Demetrios is a modern hero from an ancient culture. Wearing the legendary Golden Fleece, the Olympian can access the superhuman powers, skills, and gifts of every member of the fabled Argonauts, the army of great warriors and demi-gods who accompanied Jason on his legendary quest. Over time, the different personalities of the Fleece's power donors have sought to assert themselves, making the Olympian an unpredictable and fractious ally.

Demetrios was recruited as Greece's representative in the international Super Hero team the Global Guardians, and later served with distinction in the Ultramarine Corps. Because of his divine armaments, the Olympian has become an occasional agent of the Greek Gods—notably Zeus—and has even claimed to be one of them.

OCEAN MASTER

DEBUT *Aquaman* (Vol. 1) #29 (Sep.-Oct. 1966)
REAL NAME Orm the First
BASE Atlantis
HEIGHT 5ft 11ins **WEIGHT** 200 lbs **EYES** Black **HAIR** Black
POWERS/ABILITIES Superhuman strength, speed, endurance, and durability; water-breathing and possession of mystic artifacts that bestow control of weather patterns and massive volumes of water.
ALLIES General Rodunn
ENEMIES Aquaman, Mera, Justice League, Vulko, Tula Marius
AFFILIATIONS Throne of Atlantis, the Trench, Belle Reve Penitentiary

Orm despises humanity, but is a dutiful Atlantean warrior. When his half-brother, Arthur Curry, abdicated Atlantis' throne to live as Aquaman, Orm took over, making every decision for the benefit of his people, despite his inclination to attack the surface-dwellers. But when hidden plotter Vulko orchestrated war between Atlantis and America, Orm exultantly punished the callous, air-breathing creatures who had polluted his seas for hundreds of years.

Enacting Aquaman's cautious Atlantean War Plans, Orm launched a devastating attack on America's Eastern Seaboard. Thousands of humans drowned before Aquaman, Mera, and the Justice League turned back the tides.

The war ended when Orm yielded the throne to Arthur Curry. Orm was shocked when his brother handed him over to the surface-dwellers to be imprisoned. When Orm escaped Belle Reve Penitentiary, he settled down with human Erin and her son Tommy until summoned by King Nereus of Xebel, who offered him one of the vacant Seven Seas Thrones. When he learned Corum Rath now ruled Atlantis, he felt compelled to usurp the usurper. Rath is instead defeated by his successor Queen Mera, who is supported by the Ocean Master's half-sister, Tula. Despite aiding Mera against alien sea gods, Orm was reduced to beggary in the slums of the Ninth Tride. However, after hearing of the mystic amulet of Dagon, he laid plans for his return.

ROYAL AGENDA
Orm didn't hate the sea-befouling surface-dwellers; he simply preferred not to share the planet with them.

ON THE RECORD

Originally, Ocean Master was a sub-sea plunderer who continually harassed Aquaman for reasons even he could not fathom. It took an alien invasion and the unseen intervention of Deadman to break long-standing mental blocks inside Orm's mind and reveal to the villain that he was in fact the Sea King's half-brother. Their rivalry intensified after that revelation. In every Aquaman retcon since, Ocean Master has been Arthur Curry's ultimate and signature archenemy.

BROTHERS AT ARMS
Even bonds of blood could not prevent Aquaman and Ocean Master continually battling for supremacy and survival.

NIGHTWING

DATA

DEBUT *Detective Comics* (Vol. 1) #38 (Apr. 1940)
REAL NAME Richard Grayson
BASE Blüdhaven
HEIGHT 5ft 10in **WEIGHT** 175 lbs **EYES** Blue **HAIR** Black
POWERS/ABILITIES Highly skilled martial artist, trained personally by Batman; expert acrobat, gymnast, and escape artist; extremely athletic and agile; highly intelligent with advanced knowledge of a variety of technologies; natural leader and strategist; weapons include Escrima sticks and has access to Batcave technology and gadgets.
ALLIES Batman, the Batman Family, Wally West, Superman, Donna Troy, Nightwings
ENEMIES Blockbuster, Arkham Asylum inmates, Court of Owls
AFFILIATIONS Teen Titans, Titans, Spyral

Dick Grayson has made a name for himself over the years, and on more than one occasion. The original Robin to Bruce Wayne's Batman, Grayson later graduated to the role of Nightwing. After his identity was publicly exposed, he traded in his costume to become a superspy for the covert organization Spyral. Throughout his valiant life, Grayson has proven himself to be one of the most resilient and brilliant crime fighters in the world and a natural leader. His charisma is as potent as his combat skills, acrobatic flair, and deductive gifts. He is a hero's hero who maintains an infectiously positive outlook despite facing much tragedy in his life.

AT A GLANCE...

Running away from the Circus
A popular acrobat and the young star of Haly's Circus' the Flying Graysons, Dick Grayson's life was turned upside down when his parents were murdered during a trapeze performance while visiting Gotham City. Dick was soon taken in by the wealthy Bruce Wayne, becoming his ward.

The first Robin
After Grayson learned that Batman and Bruce Wayne were one and the same, he began to train with the hero and then adopted the identity of the crime fighter Robin. As the youthful counterpart to the Dark Knight, Grayson set the tone for the other Robins who would later follow in his footsteps.

Enter... Nightwing
After leaving Gotham City to team up with other young heroes, Dick Grayson became Nightwing, determined to step out of Batman's shadow. His career later saw him set up camp temporarily in the city of Chicago, where he quickly discovered that vigilantes were quite unwelcome.

CLASSIC STORIES

Star Spangled Comics #65 (Feb. 1947) As Robin, Dick Grayson is awarded his own solo feature, even nabbing the coveted cover spot in his debut.
Tales of the Teen Titans #44 (Jul. 1984) Dick graduates from his position as Robin to become the hero Nightwing during the dramatic storyline "The Judas Contract."
Nightwing (Vol. 2) #1 (Oct. 1996) Grayson sets up shop in the new town of Blüdhaven, earning his own Rogues Gallery in his first ever ongoing series.
Robin: Year One #1–4 (Dec. 2000–Mar. 2001) Dick's past is delved into, documenting his early years as Robin and pitting him against the likes of Mad Hatter and Two-Face.

As the juvenile star of popular circus attraction The Flying Graysons, Dick already knew the thrill of defying death at an early age. The only son of John and Mary Grayson—the senior performers in his family's high-wire act for Haly's Circus—Dick was doted on by his parents, and strived to be the best son he could be.

Tragically, Dick was destined to live a life with highs and lows comparable to the rollercoasters on Gotham City's famous Amusement Mile. Nothing struck the boy as deeply as the night when he watched his parents plummet to the ground during their renowned trapeze act. Their equipment had been sabotaged by a low-level mob enforcer named Anthony Zucco, and two of the three Flying Graysons fell to their deaths in front of a packed Gotham City crowd that included billionaire playboy Bruce Wayne. Bruce saw something of himself in Dick and decided to make him his ward. Driven by a thirst for justice to punish the criminals responsible for his parents' death, Dick proved every bit as bright and capable as Bruce believed him to be. To help Dick work through his pain, Bruce revealed his Batman identity to the boy, and gave him access to the Batcave beneath Wayne Manor. Dick had witnessed Zucco threatening the owner of Haly's Circus shortly before his parents' murder and, with Batman's training, soon became the young crime-busting hero Robin, taking the fight directly to crooks like Zucco.

After spending several successful years fighting crime with Batman in the field, Grayson felt the need to spread his wings for a change, working with other young heroes and eventually co-founding the original Teen Titans. Soon after, Dick set out on his own as Nightwing, adopting first a blue-and-yellow costume, and later a red-and-black uniform armored in a similar fashion to the Batsuit worn by Batman. This outfit employed similar devices to the Dark Knight's Utility Belt, including a grappling hook, plus Nightwing's personal touches, such as his weapon of choice, Escrima sticks. When Grayson discovered that Zucco

LEARNING CURVE
Dick had been coached as a circus acrobat since infancy and his dogged determination to avenge his parents made him an ideal candidate for Batman's brutal training regimen.

I Spy
After his secret identity was outed by the invading Crime Syndicate, Grayson was nearly killed by the powerful villains. He took the opportunity to fake his own death and join the spy organization Spyral.

TEAM NIGHTWING
When the true Nightwing was suffering from amnesia, a group of novice Nightwings sprung up to take his place. Detective Alphonse Sapienza found Nightwing's old bunker hideout, and took four of Nightwing's former costumes from it. He recruited some of his trusted friends—Fire Department Deputy Chief Malcolm Hutch, Detective Colleen Edwards, and her brother in vice, Zak Edwards—and they all became Nightwings. While they did some good, even unknowingly teaming up with the original from time to time, the Nightwings were forced into early retirement when they were trounced by a Talon working for the Court of Owls, before Sapienza was beaten to within an inch of his life by The Joker.

SHADES OF GRAYSON
The Nightwings were: Nightwing Prime (Sapienza), Nightwing Red (Hutch), Nightwing Gold (Colleen Edwards), and Nightwing Blue (Zak Edwards).

RETURN FROM THE DEAD

After Spyral's regime change, and Bruce Wayne's near death at the hands of The Joker, Dick Grayson returned to Gotham City to reveal to the Batman Family that he was indeed alive and well. While Spyral's Agent Zero believed that Grayson was indeed saying his goodbyes to his friends, Dick was secretly delivering a code to his allies, continuing to work against the agency he appeared to serve.

HIT LIST

When Grayson revealed to his friends that he was alive, most took the news well—aside from Red Hood, who was less than happy about being tricked.

was alive and had made a new life for himself as Billy Lester—an aide to Chicago's mayor—Nightwing moved to Chicago for a time, determined to bring Zucco to justice. As fate would have it, Nightwing then had to join forces with his enemy, to battle the greater threat posed by the maniacal villain known as the Prankster. Once they had defeated the costumed criminal, Nightwing was finally able to put Zucco behind bars.

After being kidnapped by the Earth-3 villains, the Crime Syndicate, Nightwing faked his own death for a time, and used the opportunity to join Spyral; a secret organization which kept tabs on the world's superhumans. Unbeknown to his new employers, Grayson—now called Agent 37—was actually working as a mole for Batman, helping him end Spyral's corrupt regime and ushering in a new era for the agency. However, Nightwing couldn't stay away from the Super Hero life for long, and soon adopted a new blue version of his costume, heading to Blüdhaven to carve out a name for himself. He continues to protect his adopted city to this day, facing threats like Blockbuster, Raptor, and the Court of Owls, but still managing to check in on Gotham City and the Batman Family from time to time.

REBIRTH

HEAD CASE

During one of Dick's visits to Gotham City, the assassin KGBeast shot Nightwing in the head. Dick lost all his memories from his time as Robin and Nightwing, and instead distanced himself from his past life, calling himself Ric. He met Bea Bennett, and the two began to date.

However, Ric discovered that his memories had been altered thanks to the nefarious secret society the Court of Owls, and then were later manipulated again by The Joker. Nevertheless, "Ric" reclaimed his memories, his identity of Dick Grayson, and the mantle of Nightwing, joining Batman in his fight against the Clown Prince of Crime's "Joker War."

"I was Robin. I was the first."

DICK GRAYSON

NIGHT HAWK
In every widely differing aspect of his crime-fighting career, Nightwing has hunted villains and criminals like an implacable agent of justice.

ON THE RECORD

One of the oldest and most popular characters in DC Comics' pantheon, Dick Grayson was originally introduced into Batman comics to brighten up the Dark Knight's grim world. Aging over the years along with his audience, Dick continues to uphold that upbeat and uplifting tradition, no matter what his incarnation.

Stalwart sidekick

Debuting only 11 issues after Batman, Robin quickly earned his place as an invaluable ally by proving himself in fight after fight. Unlike many characters that debuted in the Golden Age of Comics in the 1930s and 1940s, Robin's tragic backstory has changed little in the years since, despite continuity-altering events such as *Crisis on Infinite Earths*. Throughout all his incarnations, Dick Grayson was the son of circus aerialists, who was adopted by Bruce Wayne (aka Batman) after his parents were killed by gangster Anthony Zucco. After years of fighting by Batman's side, Robin eventually left the Batcave to attend college at Hudson University.

Return to Gotham City

As Batman gained a new Robin in the form of young hero Jason Todd, Dick Grayson graduated to the title Nightwing, and continued his tenure with the Teen Titans, only rarely making appearances in Gotham City. Finally leaving the Titans, Nightwing headed back home to Gotham City for a while, before once again setting out for new territory, becoming the protector of Gotham City's crime-ridden neighboring town of Blüdhaven. But no matter what Dick accomplished on his own, he would always return to the Batcave. In fact, when Batman was lost in time due to the machinations of the villain Darkseid, Dick valiantly stepped into his mentor's boots as the new Dark Knight, teaming up with the newest Robin, Damian Wayne.

DARK AND LIGHT

Always an optimist and one to make light of nearly any situation, when Dick Grayson stepped into the role of Batman, he made quite the contrast to Damian Wayne, a brooding and troubled young Robin.

TEEN TITANS
A youthful version of the Justice League, the Teen Titans featured Robin as leader from the outset. In the 1980s, when the title was relaunched with new characters, Robin grew more independent than ever, living in Titan's Tower and later changing his codename to Nightwing.

OLYMPIAN GODS

DEBUT *All-Star Comics* (Vol. 1) #8 (Dec. 1941)
BASE Mount Olympus
MEMBERS/ROLE Zeus: Sky-God—ruler of the Gods of Olympus;
Hera: Goddess of Women and Marriage; **Poseidon**: God of the Seas;
Hades: God of the Underworld; **Demeter**: Goddess of Harvest and
Abundance; **Hestia**: Goddess of Home; **Aphrodite**: Goddess of Love,
Beauty, Pleasure, and Procreation; **Dionysus**: God of Wine and Revelry;
Hermes: Messenger God—patron of Thieves, Healers, and Travelers;
Apollo: God of Light, Poetry, Music, and Herdsmen; **Ares**: God of War;
Artemis: Goddess of the Hunt; **Athena**: Goddess of Wisdom, Warfare,
Inspiration, Justice, Civilization, and Law.
ENEMIES First Born
AFFILIATIONS The Amazons, Atlanteans

The immortal Gods of Olympus are a race of powerful and
capricious entities who achieved fame and notoriety in mankind's distant
prehistory. Attaching themselves to the tribes of what is now Greece,
they began feeding off the worship of mortals.

Their exploits shaped culture and progress as the Gods championed
human heroes, propagated monsters, and bred with the lesser creatures
who feared and adored them. The result of centuries of dalliance was a
race of powerful demi-gods, including Deimos, Enyo, Phobos, Dionysus,
Eris, Hecate, Harmonia, Morpheus, Persephone, Triton, Hercules
(Heracles), and Diana, the champion known as
Wonder Woman.

The Gods constantly squabbled among
themselves before growing bored and
retreating from the forefront of human affairs.
Now they interact with mortals only in secret,
when their offspring threaten to cause mischief,
or if some cosmic crisis forces them to act in
defense of their own lives or interests.

**OLYMPIAN
IMMORTALS**
1 Poseidon
2 Zeus
3 Hades
4 Demeter
5 Hera
6 Apollo
7 Dionysus
8 Hermes
9 Aphrodite
10 Artemis
11 Athena
12 Hestia
13 Hercules

DOWN TO EARTH

Following *Rebirth*, many Olympians became more active
on Earth, particularly the war god Ares and Zeus. When
Hecate failed in her bid to usurp control of magic, she
practically sealed off Olympus, trapping the gods there
or in the world of mortals.

ON THE RECORD

Olympians were most commonly
seen causing problems for Wonder Woman
and the Amazons of Paradise Island. In her
first incarnation, Olympian goddesses
sponsored the Amazon Princess' battles for
America and democracy, but were repeatedly
obstructed by the War God and other
patriarchal troublemakers. In her 1980s
incarnation, Diana's devotion to the Olympian
Gods was emphasized, but they still gave her
plenty of grief and torment. Her tenacity and
nobility, however, led to her joining their
pantheon as the Goddess of Truth.

MARS ON THE WARPATH
Wonder Woman and Aquaman tried to stop the
God of War—then using the Roman name Mars
instead of the Grecian Ares—from inciting
conflict between the Amazons and Atlanteans.

O.M.A.C.

DEBUT *O.M.A.C.* #1 (Sep.–Oct. 1974)
REAL NAMES Buddy Blank/Kevin Kho
HEIGHT Variable **WEIGHT** Variable
EYES Yellow **HAIR** Blue
POWERS/ABILITIES Power and technical
data provided by Brother Eye satellite
ALLIES Myron Forest, Brother Eye, Thorn
ENEMIES Doctor Skuba, Marshal Kirovan
Kafka, Cadmus Industries, Checkmate
AFFILIATIONS Global Peace Agency

Shortly before Earth's
Great Disaster, Dr.
Myron Forest devised
a plan to save
civilization. Launching
Artificial Intelligence
satellite Brother Eye,
Forest selected clerk
Buddy Blank to receive its power and intel.
He became a One-Man Army Corps.
O.M.A.C tackled villains such as Marshal
Kafka and Doctor Skuba, but was unable to
stave off the fall of humanity and rise of
intelligent, all-conquering animals.

After *Flashpoint*, Cambodian geneticist
Kevin Kho was forcibly transformed into a
superpowered, techno-organic
juggernaut—a One-Machine Attack
Construct—by rogue AI Brother Eye. A
fugitive, this O.M.A.C. joined Justice League
International, and fought the Suicide Squad,
before plunging through a dimensional
portal. He subsequently helped Justice
League United battle Nazis.

OLSEN, JIMMY

DEBUT *Superman* (Vol. 1) #13 (Nov.–Dec. 1941)
REAL NAME James Bartholomew Oisen
BASE Metropolis
HEIGHT 5ft 7ins **WEIGHT** 150 lbs **EYES** Green **HAIR** Red
POWERS/ABILITIES Fearless and loyal; skilled photographer with keen
deductive instincts and journalistic smarts; possesses a signal watch that only
Superman and other metahumans can hear.
ALLIES Clark Kent, Lois Lane, Perry White, Bizarro, Ron Troupe, Steve Lombard
ENEMIES Lex Luthor, Morgan Edge, Regis Tuttle
AFFILIATIONS *The Daily Planet* staff

Jimmy Olsen never wanted a single penny of his unscrupulous
parents' vast wealth and donated it all to charity. Eager to prove his worth to the
world, he took the first official photographs of Superman, sharing this scoop with his
friend and journalistic mentor Lois Lane. The photojournalist cub-reporter quickly
struck up a friendship with new *Daily Planet* reporter Clark Kent, who shared his love
of computer games and B-movie sci-fi. Despite often getting on each other's nerves,
they frequently shared an apartment.

Thanks to his close friendship with Clark—and, independently, with Clark's alter
ego, Superman—Jimmy witnessed and documented some of the most catastrophic
events in Metropolis' and the world's history, earning the somewhat condescending
nickname "Superman's Pal." The relationship
has also made him a target for the Man of
Steel's enemies, such as Lex Luthor, who
once kidnapped and tortured Jimmy just to
get Superman's attention. After years of
secrecy, as Superman prepared to leave
Earth, Clark finally shared his true identity with
Jimmy, only to discover the boy had always
known. In a feat of devasting logic Jimmy
disclosed that only two people ever called
him "Jim": Superman and a reporter who
looked a lot like him…

ON THE RECORD:

Jimmy graduated from sidekick to
comedy foil in his own title in 1954. As
frequently as he proved his journalistic
talents, he was often transformed in bizarre
ways that made him a menace to society.
Everything changed in 1970 when Jimmy
emerged as a determined, two-fisted
investigator, exposing secret cloning
projects, New Gods, and re-imagined
monsters beside a revived Newsboy
Legion. Jimmy had become *The Daily
Planet's* crusading Mister Action.

TROUBLE MAGNET:
In the 1960s, Jimmy's curiosity often led him
into weird situations. On one occasion he
became a rampaging Giant Turtle Man after
testing an enlarging ray gun. As always,
Superman was on hand to save the day.

OMEN

DEBUT *Teen Titans* (Vol. 1) #25 (Jan.–Feb. 1970)
REAL NAME Lilith Clay
EYES Green **HAIR** Red
HEIGHT 5ft 6in **WEIGHT** 104 lbs
POWERS/ABILITIES Alpha-class psionic with telepathic powers; can blank minds and create psychic projections.
ALLIES Tempest, Mr. Jupiter
ENEMIES Mr. Twister

A member of the original Teen Titans, Lilith served with many later iterations, After team member Herald was forced to wipe the team's memories to prevent demon Mr. Twister from fully entering the world, Lilith worked as an addiction counsellor. However, Mr. Twister began whispering in her head, reawakening her memories as he plotted to draw her and her teammates back to complete the necessary ritual. When the plot was thwarted by the now-adult heroes, they remained together as the Titans. Lilith became invaluable both for intelligence but also as a combatant. Her psionic powers helped defeat Psimon, H.I.V.E., the Fearsome Five, and crazed future-tyrant Troia. Omen was extensively trained in hand-to-hand combat by teammate Garth (former Aqualad and current Tempest) leading to an intense but brief romantic relationship.

ONIMAR SYNN

DEBUT *JSA* (Vol. 1) #23 (Jun. 2001)
REAL NAME Onimar Synn
BASE Thanagar **HEIGHT** 7ft 5in
WEIGHT 480 lbs **EYES** Yellow **HAIR** None
POWERS/ABILITIES Various powers derived from the suffering and fear of others; absorption of souls; creation of mindless thralls.
ENEMIES Hawkman, Hawkgirl, Justice Society of America

Rumored to be one of the legendary Seven Devils of Thanagar, Onimar attempted to take over Thanagar and feed on the souls of its populace. As Sin Eater, he enslaved the population with Nth Metal, an element found only on Thanagar, and killed thousands, feasting on their souls and transforming them into an undead army. Nth Metal gave Onimar mastery over the four fundamental forces of the universe—strong, weak, gravitational, and electromagnetic.

To save the rest of their people, the high priests of Thanagar kidnapped Hawkgirl, who could summon Hawkman back from the dead through their divine connection. It took the combined might of Hawkman, Hawkgirl, and the JSA to stop the Sin-Eater's undead warriors. Sin-Eater was seemingly destroyed by the power of Hawkman and Hawkgirl's ancient love.

ORANGE LANTERN CORPS

DEBUT *Green Lantern* (Vol. 4) #25 (Jan. 2008)
BASE Larfleezia
MEMBERS Larfleeze; Glomulus; Grubber; Gretti; Ceebiss; Clypta; Nat Nat; Blume; Sound Dancer; Warp Wrap.
ALLIES New Guardians, Lantern Corps
ENEMIES Guardians of the Universe, Green Lanterns, Invictus, Sena the Wanderer, Third Army

Larfleeze is the bearer of the Orange Lantern Ring, which is powered by his bottomless greed—and he does not like to share. While all the other Lantern Corps are made up of multiple members, Larfleeze uses his ring to create his very own Orange Lantern Corps. The ring absorbs his defeated foes and he can summon them forth as Orange energy constructs. These helped Larfleeze to kill the angelic inhabitants of the Orrery (though he was unable to absorb one of them with his ring) and his subsequent conflict with the sole survivor, Invictus.

However, the constructs were not always obedient, and they went out of control after Larfleeze's "pet" Guardian, Sayd, tampered with his ring. Cosmic entity Sena the Wanderer then transformed seven constructs into living beings again, and they turned against Larfleeze as fully fledged Orange Lanterns. He was briefly enslaved by them, before stripping them of their power and marooning them on a distant planet.

AGENT ORANGE
The larcenous Larfleeze would absorb his enemies' personality imprints into his power ring, then summon them as members of his Orange Lantern Corps.

OMEGA MEN

DEBUT *Green Lantern* (Vol. 2) #141 (Jun. 1981)
BASE Vega
NOTABLE MEMBERS Tigorr: Takes beast form; Primus: Mastermind; Broot: Enhanced strength, damage-resistant hide; Scrapps: Proficient gunslinger; DOC: Reformed war robot; Kalista: Swordswoman; Kyle Rayner: White Lantern ring
ENEMIES The Citadel, Pontifex of Changralyn

The Omega Men are fierce rebels who fought to free the planets of the Vega system from the rule of the oppressive Citadel. The motley crew included idealistic leader Primus, armor-skinned Broot, reformed war robot DOC, and Scrapps, the last survivor of the planet Voorl. When human White Lantern Kyle Rayner visited Vega, the Omega Men captured and seemingly executed him live on film. In reality, they forced him to join their ranks.

Subsequently, they stole the Citadel Viceroy's spacecraft, "kidnapped" Kalista, Princess of the Bramins of Euphorix, (who was the group's mastermind), and stole a sacred artifact belonging to the pacifist aliens, the Changralyn. The Omega Men also revealed that the Citadel had committed genocide on Voorl to plunder its reserves of the rare mineral Stellarium.

ONOMATOPOEIA

DEBUT *Green Arrow* (Vol. 3) #12 (Mar. 2002)
BASE Gotham City
HEIGHT 5ft 11in **WEIGHT** 180 lbs
POWERS/ABILITIES Stealth; brutally effective killer with a variety of sound-based weapons.
ALLIES The Joker
ENEMIES Robin (Damian Wayne), Green Arrow, Batman, Connor Hawke
AFFILIATIONS Secret Society of Super-Villains

Onomatopoeia is a serial killer who obsessively imitates sounds around him; the last thing his victim likely hears is the word "BANG!" His first high-profile target was legacy Green Arrow Connor Hawke, who barely survived the assault. When the maniac attacked him in hospital, he was stopped by Connor's father Oliver Queen (the original Green Arrow) and Black Canary.

Onomatopoeia joined the Secret Society of Super-Villains during *Infinite Crisis*, but was considered too unstable for the Suicide Squad. He almost killed Deadshot and freed The Joker from Arkham Asylum to distract Batman, his most prized target. When that failed, Onomatopoeia masqueraded as vigilante Baphomet, gaining Batman's trust before killing Bruce Wayne's lover, Silver St. Cloud. He recently targeted Robin (Damian Wayne) but fell to his superior martial arts prowess and new team of Teen Titans.

ONYX

DEBUT *Detective Comics* (Vol. 1) #546 (Jan. 1985)
HEIGHT 5ft 9in **WEIGHT** 120 lbs
EYES Brown **HAIR** Black with white streak
POWERS/ABILITIES Unarmed combat.
ALLIES Komodo
ENEMIES Green Arrow, Katana, Mask Clan, Shield Clan, Spear Clan

Onyx is the leader of the Fist Clan, a subgroup of The Outsiders organization and one of four "pure" martial clans that facilitated Komodo's plot to conquer Europe. When Shado, Robert Queen, and Green Arrow attacked the Outsiders' base in Prague to disrupt their plans, Onyx ordered the Fist Clan to kill the intruders, but Katana and the Sword and Axe clans helped the archers.

During the battle, Onyx went to launch a freighter holding a payload that could devastate Seattle. Katana gave chase and they fought a savage duel on the vessel. Onyx offered mercy if Katana relinquished her sword and joined the Fist Clan. Katana replied with a lightning slash that severed Onyx's left arm at the elbow—forcing her to surrender.

Pre-*Flashpoint*, Onyx Adams was a League of Assassins killer, who turned her back on the League to join forces with Green Arrow, Batman, and the Birds of Prey.

ORDER OF ST. DUMAS

DEBUT *Batman: Sword of Azrael* #1 (Oct. 1992)
MEMBERS/POWERS Saint Dumas: Leader, directly linked to Gnosis' data systems; Azrael: (Jean-Paul Valley) Flaming sword, incapacitates foes with a touch by uploading the Icthys algorithm into their brains.
ALLIES Mother
ENEMIES Red Robin, Red Hood, Bane

The Order of St. Dumas is a quasi-religious group dedicated to finding the truth of the universe through scientific knowledge. When Red Robin and Red Hood infiltrated the Order's church in Santa Prisca, they found that it was actually a hi-tech facility patrolled by cybernetic monks. They uncovered evidence that the Order had links to a mysterious underworld figure called Mother. The heroes were then driven off by Azrael, a dangerous fanatic with a lethal touch who believed he was the Order's chosen warrior-angel.

They later visited the Order's HQ, the ancient hidden city of Gnosis, and met "Saint" Dumas. He admitted that Azrael was the product of neural programming, and wanted Red Robin to replace him. Red Robin disabled Gnosis' systems and Dumas fled when Azrael turned against him.

ORION

DATA

DEBUT *New Gods* (Vol. 1) #1 (Mar. 1971)
BASE New Genesis
HEIGHT 6ft 1in **WEIGHT** 195 lbs
EYES Red **HAIR** Red-blond
POWERS/ABILITIES As a New God, Orion is immortal with superhuman physical and mental attributes; his sentient transport platform, called A4, can fly, create teleporting Boom Tubes, locate targets, and fire energy beams; A4's harness can also communicate directly with Orion; his Mother Box creates telepathic links with others' minds, and can block psychic influences.
ALLIES Milan, Highfather, Lightray
ENEMIES Darkseid, Hector Hammond
AFFILIATIONS New Genesis, Council of Eight, Divine Guard, Justice League Odyssey

JUSTICE LEAGUE ODYSSEY
Orion joined forces with some odd bedfellows—including Red Lantern Dex-Starr, Blackfire, and Green Lantern Jessica Cruz—to thwart Darkseid's scheme to dominate the Multiverse.

SYMBIOTIC RIDE
A4, Orion's sentient transport platform, is more than just a combination vehicle, weapons system, and sensor suite—Orion sees it as a technological extension of himself.

FACE OF FURY
Orion tries to present a calm face to the world, but when he loses his temper, his warlike, violent Apokoliptian side surfaces.

Orion is the son of Darkseid, evil lord of Apokolips, but he was raised by the benevolent Highfather, ruler of the utopian world of New Genesis. While attempting to uphold the peaceful ideals of his adopted home, he must also contain the rage that is his legacy as the son of Darkseid.

As a child, Orion was sent to live on New Genesis as part of a peace treaty between Darkseid and Highfather, Orion tried to embrace the unfamiliar, placid ways of his new home, but his impulsive nature often got him into trouble.

Orion has had many interactions with Earth's Super Heroes. When the New God's Prophecy Wall indicated that Superman was a threat to all existence, Orion attacked the Man of Steel. However, he realized that the issue was not Superman himself, but villain Hector Hammond, who had taken over Superman's mind. Orion extracted the villain with his Mother Box. Later, Highfather schemed to use the power of the Lantern Corps to fight Darkseid and sent Orion and the other members of the Council of Eight to acquire power rings from the various Corps. Orion took the Green Lantern power ring belonging to the sentient planet Mogo. This triggered a war between the Lanterns and New Genesis, in which Orion commanded Highfather's Divine Guard.

In the far reaches of space, the ancient Source Wall separates our universe from the unknown. Already damaged during invasion from the Dark Multiverse, the Source Wall was destroyed thanks the machinations of Lex Luthor and the Legion of Doom. In the destruction, the gods of New Genesis were seemingly absorbed by the Source energy; the Source was calling the New Gods home. Orion managed to escape and traveled to the Ghost Sector, a cordoned-off area of space containing newly freed worlds that had been held prisoner on the planet Colu. Disguised as a masked being named Okkult, to cloak himself from Darkseid's awareness, Orion joined a band of heroes called the Justice League Odyssey to stop his father's plan to rewrite time and give Apokolips control over the Multiverse.

ON THE RECORD

The original Orion shares much of the same background as his post-*Flashpoint* incarnation, but his life is defined by his anger at his evil father, Darkseid. After gaining control of the Anti-Life Equation, Orion managed to seize his birthright as ruler of Apokolips for a time.

Orion then joined fellow renegade Apokoliptian Big Barda in the Justice League of America, helping them defeat the warmongering entity Mageddon. He killed Darkseid in a dramatic battle prior to *Final Crisis*. However, his father returned and fired a special bullet backward in time to dispatch his son.

SIBLING RIVALRY
In a battle of Titanic proportions, Orion fought his brother Kalibak, the eldest son of Darkseid.

FIGHTING MAD
Orion relishes a battle with a worthy foe—and he faced the challenge of a lifetime when he clashed with Superman himself, who had been possessed by Hector Hammond.

CLASSIC STORIES

New Gods (Vol. 3) #2 (Mar. 1989)
In a dramatic story, Orion confronts his own prejudices as he returns the body of the hero Forager to his people.
Justice League America #42–50 (Sep. 1990–May 1991) Orion spends time on Earth as part of the Justice League!
Countdown to Final Crisis #2 (Apr. 2008) In an epic grudge match, Orion faces his father, Darkseid, in battle and pulls the dark lord's heart from his chest.
Death of the New Gods #6 (Apr. 2008) Orion bravely sacrifices himself in an attempt to slay the being that is killing the New Gods.

ORPHAN

DEBUT *Batman* (Vol. 1) #567 **(Jul. 1999)** (as Cassandra Cain); *Batman Incorporated* (Vol. 1) #6 **(Jun. 2011)** (as Black Bat)
REAL NAME Cassandra Cain
BASE Hong Kong
HEIGHT 5ft 5ins **WEIGHT** 110 lbs **EYES** Blue **HAIR** Black
POWERS/ABILITIES Supreme martial artist, augmented by Batman's training, able to read body language and anticipate opponents' attacks.
ALLIES Red Robin, Dick Grayson, Batman
ENEMIES Mother, David Cain
AFFILIATIONS Batman Incorporated, League of Assassins, the Nursery

Cassandra Cain is the daughter of master assassin David Cain, the "Orphan" fixer for manipulative mastermind, Mother. Cassandra was raised in isolation, denied human warmth and contact, subjected to long periods of sensory deprivation interspersed with constant and brutal martial arts training. Her language skills were deliberately impeded to develop an instinctive sense of body-language, enabling her to predict her target's every movement.

This unorthodox training regime contravened Mother's own methods of indoctrinating her stolen children. Cain had intended Cassandra as a gift, but Mother reprimanded him for raising his daughter so inefficiently. Cassandra was banished from Mother's Nursery but continued training in secret.

Traumatized by what she had endured, Cassandra escaped. Freed from Cain's influence, she resurfaced in Hong Kong. Here Batman recruited her, despite Cassandra's experiences rendering her practically mute. After years in the shadows, she emerged as one of Batman's Gotham Knights, reclaiming the name Orphan. As she slowly began making friends—with Spoiler, Harper Row and others—Cassandra was challenged by her mother, Lady Shiva, who wanted to test her capacity for killing. Orphan denied her entreaties and worked with Batman's Outsider team, facing threats such as Kaliber and Rā's Al Ghūl.

ORPHEUS

DEBUT *Batman: Orpheus Rising* #1 (Oct. 2001)
REAL NAME Gavin King
BASE Gotham City
HEIGHT 6ft 2in **WEIGHT** 195 lbs
EYES Brown **HAIR** Black
POWERS/ABILITIES Expert martial artist and gymnast; costume loaded with hi-tech gadgets and weapons including a sonic spike, smoke bombs, and a helmet with advanced vision capabilities.
ENEMIES Black Mask

Young Gavin King dreamed of becoming a professional singer and dancer and was bullied as a result. He studied martial arts to defend himself and proved to be a natural. After graduating from college, Gavin joined a touring dance troupe, witnessing the horrors and injustices of some of the worst parts of the world firsthand.

He was soon recruited into a secret organization set up to fight society's ills, and given financial help and training, as well as a costume and weaponry. He became Orpheus and fought crime in Gotham City while, by day, working as a record and video producer. He found a reluctant ally in Batman, and also worked with another well-traveled hero, Onyx. All his training and technology proved in vain: Black Mask killed him during a gang war and, to add insult to injury, briefly took his place as Orpheus.

OSIRIS

DEBUT *Teen Titans* (Vol. 3) #38 (Sep. 2006)
REAL NAME Amon Tomaz
BASE Kahndaq
HEIGHT 5ft 10in
WEIGHT 164 lbs
EYES Brown **HAIR** Black
POWERS/ABILITIES Super-strength, flight, superspeed, invulnerability, enhanced stamina.
ENEMIES Famine, Ibac

Amon Tomaz was beaten to near death by Intergang but he was rescued by his sister and Black Adam, the latter sharing his powers with the crippled teenager.

Amon became Osiris and a member of the Black Marvel Family. Traveling to the US with his crocodile Sobek, Osiris briefly joined the Teen Titans, but killed the Persuader after he threatened his sister. Wracked with guilt, Osiris was convinced by Sobek to revert to his Amon form. Sobek then revealed himself as Famine, one of the Four Horsemen of Apokolips, and devoured the powerless Amon.

After *Flashpoint*, Amon was a Kahndaqi teenager without superpowers. A freedom fighter with the Sons of Adam, he translated an ancient spell that resurrected Black Adam, but was killed by Kahndaq soldiers. Adam made short work of the killers and Kahndaq's ruler, installing himself as the country's true protector.

SIBLING RIVALRY
Talia al Ghūl's designer-son refused to do her bidding and dedicated himself to eradicating his biological template Damian Wayne.

OTHER, THE (HERETIC)

DEBUT *Batman and Robin* #12 (Jul. 2010)
HEIGHT 7ft 4in **WEIGHT** 345 lbs
HAIR Black **EYES** Blue/Green
POWERS/ABILITIES Superhuman strength.
ALLIES Talia al Ghūl
ENEMIES Batman, Robin, Nightwing
AFFILIATIONS Leviathan

Talia al Ghūl's vision of a ruling family comprised of her, Batman, and their son Damian broke down when they both rejected her. Talia disowned Damian and created his superpowered clone.

As the Heretic, the clone became Talia's chief bodyguard when she took over the subversive organization Leviathan. He hunted members of Batman Incorporated and killed the real Damian. Developing free will, Heretic challenged Talia, declaring himself Batman: new ruler of Gotham City. The true Batman retaliated and Heretic died at Talia's hand, decapitated and his body blown up in a massive explosion that destroyed Wayne Tower.

Reborn in a Lazarus Pit, he assumed the identity of "the Other," manipulating criminals, murdering villain Lady Vic and targeting resurrected Robin Damian Wayne and his Teen Titans. His tactics included sending alien powerhouse Lobo against them and blowing them up, as well as sinister seduction, offering team members their greatest wishes. The Other seemingly perished in a climactic showdown, swept away in a collapsing castle.

OTHERS, THE

DEBUT *Aquaman* (Vol. 7) #7 (May 2012)
NOTABLE MEMBERS
Aquaman: Amphibious Super Hero; **Operative**: Super spy; **Prisoner of War**: Force field generation; communication with comrades' ghosts; **Ya'Wara**: Jaguar goddess of Amazon; **Sky Alchesay**: Necromancy, teleporting; **Vostok-X**: Magical Atlantean Helmet.
ENEMIES Black Manta, Mayhem

Six years ago, Arthur Curry abandoned life on land to live in the oceans. Before he officially adopted the name Aquaman, he fought with the Others. This diverse group of humans and superhumans banded together to reclaim the dead sea king Atlan's ancient Atlantean artifacts. Aquaman also used the artifacts as bait in his hunt for Black Manta, the man he thought responsible for the death of his father, Atlan.

Joining him on the hunt was the fierce Brazilian fighter Ya'Wara, the precognitive Kahina the Seer, Russian Super Hero Vostok-X, the possessed Prisoner of War, and aging super-spy Operative. Years later, Black Manta killed several of the Others, including the Seer and Vostok-X, before Aquaman brought him to justice.

The Others continued their fight and were later joined by Sky Alchesay, a Native American mystically linked with the Ghost Lands; Kahina's sister Sayeh as the new Seer; and another Vostok-X. This team triumphed over several threats, including the terrorist group Mayhem.

FIGHTING WELL WITH OTHERS
The Others came from very different backgrounds, but found their diverse experiences useful in battle.
1 Aquaman
2 Operative
3 Prisoner of War
4 Ya'Wara
5 Sky Alchesay

OUTLAWS, THE

DEBUT *Red Hood and the Outlaws* #1 (Nov. 2011)
NOTABLE MEMBERS/POWERS
Red Hood: Martial arts, marksman, detective;
Arsenal: Archery, acrobatics, brilliant mind;
Starfire: Super-strength, flight, energy projection;
Bizarro: Imperfect copy of Superman's powers;
Artemis: Amazonian powers and abilities.
ALLIES Nanna Gun, Devour, Babe in Arms, Zombie Mom, DNA, Cloud 9
ENEMIES League of Assassins, Midas
AFFILIATIONS Suicide Squad, The All-Caste, Essence

When Red Hood saw his former sidekick Arsenal imprisoned in the rogue state Qurac, he broke him out of jail with the help of alien powerhouse, Starfire. The trio set up base on an island, where Starfire's spacecraft had originally crashed. As the Outlaws, they embarked on missions, teaming up with the Teen Titans to stop a Joker-inspired riot, and helping Starfire return to her homeworld and reconcile, briefly, with her sister, Blackfire. Starfire and Arsenal began a romance, before leaving to pursue separate destinies.

Red Hood, relentlessly pursues criminals and recently united with Amazonian warrior Artemis and lawed Kryptonian clone Bizarro to take down Black Mask, the Penguin, and others. The Outlaws officially hire out as mercenaries, but in their wake, major menaces and political pariahs end up dead or imprisoned. When the Untitled opened a door for demon-lord Trigon to invade Earth, Bizarro battled and apparently killed him.

OUTLAWS REBORN
Red Hood recently returned to his old stomping ground, Gotham City, where he was joined by two new Outlaws.
1 Red Hood
2 Bizarro
3 Artemis

OUTSIDERS, THE

DEBUT *The Brave and the Bold* (Vol. 1) #200 (Jul. 1983)
BASE Gotham City, Los Angeles, Brooklyn
NOTABLE MEMBERS/POWERS
Batman: Genius detective; advanced knowledge of technology; martial arts expert; **Black Lightning**: Electrokinesis, electric blasts; **Geo-Force**: Geokinesis; **Metamorpho**: Shape-shifting, invulnerability; **Halo**: Light-spectrum-related powers; **Katana**: Wields magical Soultaker sword; **Looker**: Psionic powers; **Windfall**: Control of winds; **Atomic Knight**: Atomic-powered armor, precognition; **Technocrat**: Hi-tech battlesuit; **Wylde**: Half man, half bear; **Faust**: Sorcerous powers; **Eradicator**: Energy manipulation; **Owlman**: Brilliant detective; **Creeper**: Super-strong Japanese demon with mind-controlling powers; **Freight Train**: Absorbs kinetic energy; **Grace**: Amazonian heritage; **Thunder**: Energy projection; **The Signal**: Enhanced senses, light powers; **Orphan**: Elite fighter, reads body-language; **Sofia Ramos**: Enhanced biology.
ENEMIES Rās Al Ghūl, Karma Kobra Cult, Fearsome Five, Baron Bedlam, Church of Blood
AFFILIATIONS Justice League

The Outsiders designation applies to a number of Super Hero teams. The first was a group of heroic misfits united by fate and the Dark Knight during a mission to the nation of Markovia. After foiling a coup by the Super-Villain Baron Bedlam, the team decided to stay together.

In later years it was revealed that Batman's actual intention was to use his squad to investigate Multiversal metals, such as Electrum and Nth Metal, and their connection to exotic Earth locations and metahuman proliferation. After many adventures, they left Batman to branch out with new member, Looker, on the West Coast.

The Millennium event depowered Looker and caused Halo to fall into a coma. The team disbanded, reforming years later when Geo-Force's Markovia was attacked by vampires. Geo-Force later formed his own

Markovia-based Outsiders team (Terra, Wylde, Baroness Bedlam, Knightfall, and Eradicator) during the Doomsday Clock crisis.

Nightwing and Arsenal created another Outsiders. Alfred Pennyworth expanded it with some original members and new players when Bruce Wayne was seemingly eliminated by Darkseid. Recently Batman recalled old allies for a new iteration. Black Lightning and Katana united with Orphan, Signal, and Sofia Ramos as a black ops unit to counter Rā's al Ghūl, Karma, and others. After a dispute, Batman ceded the lead role to Black Lightning.

The Outsiders name also applies to a coalition of ancient weapon cults who formed a secret society to eradicate corruption. Sadly, the Fist, Mask, Axe, Spear, Sword, Shield, and Arrow Clans themselves became corrupt and fell into a civil war involving Green Arrow, Shado, and Katana.

WHAT'S OLD IS NEW AGAIN
The latest line-up of The Outsiders saw some old hands and new faces.
1 Black Lightning   4 Sofia Ramos
2 Batman   5 Katana
3 Orphan   6 The Signal

OUTSIDER, THE

DEBUT *Detective Comics* (Vol. 1) #334 (Dec. 1964)
REAL NAME Alfred Pennyworth
HEIGHT 6ft **WEIGHT** 160 lbs
EYES Brown **HAIR** Black
POWERS/ABILITIES Master strategist; access to Wayne family fortune; well connected in the underworlds of both Earth-3 and Earth-0.
ENEMIES Justice League, Batman

On Earth-3, a parallel world to the Justice League's Earth-0, evil counterparts of famous Super Heroes ruled as the Crime Syndicate. One of its most devious leaders was Owlman, aka Thomas Wayne, Jr., Bruce Wayne's older brother. Thomas had his butler Alfred Pennyworth shoot and kill his parents and his brother Bruce.

Later, while trying to defend his master from his archenemy, The Joker, Alfred was infected by an Earth-3 version of The Joker venom, and he developed deathly pale skin and a compulsive laugh as a result.

He took advantage of Darkseid's attack on Earth-0 to make his way there and set up a Secret Society of that world's worst Super-Villains. He then used Pandora's Box to allow the Crime Syndicate to travel to Earth-0, which they then nearly conquered. Alfred was subsequently stabbed to death by Black Manta.

OVERMASTER

DEBUT *Justice League of America* (Vol. 1) #233 (Dec. 1984)
HEIGHT 8ft **WEIGHT** 350 lbs
EYES Yellow **HAIR** None
POWERS/ABILITIES Superhuman strength and endurance; possesses advanced weaponry.
ENEMIES Legion of Super-Heroes, Justice League United

The Overmaster is one of the Justice League's deadliest foes. A self-styled celestial judge, he destroys worlds he considers unworthy. When he reached Earth, he created the Cadre Super-Villain team to test mankind's Super Heroes. The JLA met the challenge.

Post-*Flashpoint*, Overmaster was part of a new Cadre, hired by Super-Villain Byth to capture Ultra the Multi-Alien. Their quarry was destined to become the cosmic entity Infinitus. To avert this threat, an alternate Earth version of the Legion of Super-Heroes traveled back from the 31st century and joined forces with Justice League United to battle the Cadre. Even Overmaster's vast strength was no match for Mon-El and Saturn Girl, and the plot failed. Post-Rebirth the original Overmaster returned, trying to purchase Prime Earth when it was auctioned by the Slave Dealers of Dhor.

OWLMAN

DEBUT *Justice League* (Vol. 2) #23 (Oct 2013)
REAL NAME Thomas Wayne, Jr.
BASE Gotham City, Earth-3
HEIGHT Unknown **WEIGHT** Unknown
EYES Blue **HAIR** Black
POWERS/ABILITIES Genius-level intellect; skilled in combat
ALLIES The Outsider (Alfred Pennyworth), Talon
ENEMIES The Joker, Anti-Monitor
AFFILIATIONS Crime Syndicate

As a boy, Thomas Wayne, Jr. plotted with the family butler, Alfred, to kill his parents, Thomas and Martha Wayne, whom he feared were squandering his inheritance. His younger brother, Bruce, was also killed by Alfred and Thomas to stamp out any weakness in the older boy.

As an adult, Thomas would become the brutal Owlman, ruling Gotham City by any means necessary. After the destruction of his world, Owlman traveled to Earth-0 with the Crime Syndicate. He disappeared following the defeat of the Crime Syndicate, but resurfaced during the Darkseid War.

Owlman was killed after trying to access all the knowledge of the universe on the Mobius Chair.

OWLWOMAN

DEBUT *Super Friends* (Vol. 1) #7 (Oct. 1977)
REAL NAME Wenonah Littlebird
BASE The New Dome
HEIGHT 5ft 5in **WEIGHT** 125 lbs
EYES Brown **HAIR** Black
POWERS/ABILITIES Flight; superhuman strength; night vision; superhuman tracking abilities; manufactured, self-growing claws.
ALLIES Jack O'Lantern, Dr. Mist
ENEMIES O.M.A.C., Justice League Europe

Wenonah Littlebird was bestowed with superhuman powers by the spirit of her Native American tribe. Opting to use her new abilities to help not just her people, but the whole world, Wenonah joined the Global Guardians as Owlwoman. She was later brainwashed by Queen Bee, the corrupt ruler of the nation of Bialya, who operated on Littlebird, giving her artificial claws that grow when needed. With the help of Dr. Mist, Owlwoman and the Guardians escaped Queen Bee, establishing their headquarters in the New Dome, in the Pacific Ocean.

Owlwoman helped Wonder Woman defeat the sorceress Circe after she had transformed male Super Heroes into rampaging half-man/half-beast creatures. Owlwoman was also glimpsed during *Infinite Crisis*, battling the O.M.A.C. androids alongside Black Condor.

OZYMANDIAS

DEBUT *Watchmen* (Vol. 1) #1 (Sep. 1986)
REAL NAME Adrian Veidt
BASE New York City; Antarctica
HEIGHT Unknown **WEIGHT** Unknown
EYES Blue **HAIR** Blond
POWERS/ABILITIES Genius intellect, skilled in martial arts with exceptional reflexes
ALLIES Bubastis, Rorschach II
ENEMIES The Comedian, Rorschach
AFFILIATIONS Crimebusters

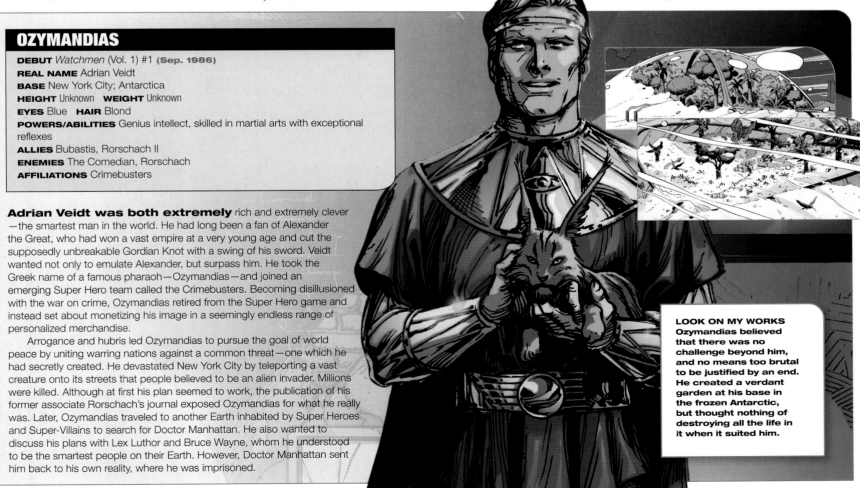

Adrian Veidt was both extremely rich and extremely clever —the smartest man in the world. He had long been a fan of Alexander the Great, who had won a vast empire at a very young age and cut the supposedly unbreakable Gordian Knot with a swing of his sword. Veidt wanted not only to emulate Alexander, but surpass him. He took the Greek name of a famous pharaoh—Ozymandias—and joined an emerging Super Hero team called the Crimebusters. Becoming disillusioned with the war on crime, Ozymandias retired from the Super Hero game and instead set about monetizing his image in a seemingly endless range of personalized merchandise.

Arrogance and hubris led Ozymandias to pursue the goal of world peace by uniting warring nations against a common threat—one which he had secretly created. He devastated New York City by teleporting a vast creature onto its streets that people believed to be an alien invader. Millions were killed. Although at first his plan seemed to work, the publication of his former associate Rorschach's journal exposed Ozymandias for what he really was. Later, Ozymandias traveled to another Earth inhabited by Super Heroes and Super-Villains to search for Doctor Manhattan. He also wanted to discuss his plans with Lex Luthor and Bruce Wayne, whom he understood to be the smartest people on their Earth. However, Doctor Manhattan sent him back to his own reality, where he was imprisoned.

LOOK ON MY WORKS
Ozymandias believed that there was no challenge beyond him, and no means too brutal to be justified by an end. He created a verdant garden at his base in the frozen Antarctic, but thought nothing of destroying all the life in it when it suited him.

PANDORA

DEBUT *Flashpoint* (Vol. 2) #5 (Oct. 2011)
BASE Mobile
EYES Blue **HAIR** Purple
POWERS/ABILITIES Immortality, super-strength, speed, and durability; magic focused through her pistols; highly advanced martial arts skills, especially in conjunction with throwing knives and Kusarigama chain-sickle; manifests mystical Light Armor.
ALLIES The Flash, Phantom Stranger, John Constantine, Vandal Savage
ENEMIES Seven Deadly Sins, The Outsider, Crime Syndicate, The Blight, Nick Necro, Felix Faust
AFFILIATIONS Trinity of Sin, Circle of Eternity, Justice League Dark

Ten millennia ago in Macedonia, Pandora was tricked into opening a strange mystic receptacle, releasing Seven Deadly Sins into the world. These spirits possessed her tribe and kin, making them kill each other in a terrifying display of malign corruption. For her "transgression," Pandora was condemned to immortality by the divinities of the Council of Eternity: doomed to forever wander Earth, personally experiencing the horrors her actions unleashed upon humanity The Council called her the "mother of monsters," and every effort she made to counter the Sins' atrocities just resulted in greater torment for their prey. Eventually, resolving to battle the Sins directly, Pandora began capitalizing on her curse. She already possessed unnatural physical advantages of enhanced strength, speed, and invulnerability, and now she boosted her might by studying martial arts and magic, and constantly upgrading the weaponry she carried.

Ultimately, the Wizard of Shazam—the last survivor of the Circle of Eternity—apologized for the injustice they had inflicted upon her. He also hinted that an alliance with humanity's Super Heroes held the key to defeating the Sins and her gaining some peace of mind.

After defeating the Phantom Stranger—who demanded she return the mystical box she could not be trusted with—Pandora steadfastly continued hunting the Sins and uncovered Doctor Manhattan's timeline alterations. However, before she could alert Prime Earth's Super Heroes, she was disintegrated by the atomic interloper.

STEPS TO HEAVEN
Pandora, the Phantom Stranger, and the Question had been judged as humanity's greatest sinners before their individual paths of atonement reunited them in a perpetual battle to protect humanity from supernatural horror.

PANTHA

DEBUT *New Titans* (Vol. 1) #73 (Feb. 1991)
REAL NAME Rosabelle Mendez
BASE Metropolis
HEIGHT 6ft 8in **WEIGHT** 125 lbs
EYES Red **HAIR** Auburn
POWERS/ABILITIES Superhuman speed, strength, reflexes, agility, leaping; accelerated healing, fangs, and retractable claws.
ENEMIES Wildebeest Society, Jericho, Catwoman, Orion, Superboy-Prime

Abducted by the insidious Wildebeest Society, Rosabelle Mendez became part of their program to create metahuman soldiers. She escaped, but was permanently transformed into a ferocious were-creature. With no memory of her past, and unsure if she was more cat or human, Pantha found refuge with the Teen Titans, becoming a powerful, if outspoken, asset. She constantly antagonized her teammates, such as Starfire and Flamebird. If no villains were handy, she was happy to scrap with her new friends. Pantha grudgingly cared for another of Wildebeest's genetic experiments—super-strong toddler Baby Wildebeest. She gradually retired from the Super Hero scene, but returned to the Titans during the *Crisis on Infinite Earths*, when she died battling Superboy-Prime.

PARALLAX

DEBUT *Green Lantern* (Vol. 3) #50 (Mar. 1994)
BASE Qward, Antimatter Universe
HEIGHT Variable **WEIGHT** Variable **EYES** Yellow **HAIR** None
POWERS/ABILITIES Immortality, possession, mind-control, energy-generation, time-manipulation; projection of fear, from anxiety to insane terror.
ENEMIES Sinestro, Superman, other embodiments of the Emotional Spectrum, Green Lantern Corps, Krona
AFFILIATIONS Emotional Spectrum, the Anti-Monitor

The Emotional Spectrum was formed at the moment of all creation, with each hue manifesting the living embodiment of an emotion. Parallax arose from the fears of living creatures. Roaming the cosmos, it spitefully eradicated entire civilizations using their own terrors. The Guardians of the Universe captured Parallax, sealing it within their Central Power Battery on Oa. Here it served to limit the power of the Green Lantern Corps, rendering their rings useless against anything colored yellow.

Millennia later, thanks to arch-renegade Sinestro, Parallax escaped by possessing Hal Jordan. Free to create chaos, Parallax went on to possess many heroic hosts, such as Kyle Rayner, Barry Allen, and the Oan Ganthet, but it met its match attempting to bind Sinestro. His will proved too much for Parallax. Ultimately, Parallax escaped Sinestro, leaving him weak and helpless. Seeking a powerful but tractable host, it seized Superman but found itself outmatched, out-thought, and—despite a last-minute intervention by Sinestro—sealed in a yellow power ring and abandoned on antimatter world Qward.

ON THE RECORD

Hal Jordan lapsed into despondency when his loved ones died in the destruction of Coast City. This finally allowed Parallax to take possession of him. It had entered his mind years previously when Hal entered the Central Power Battery on Oa, but it had been unable to overcome the human's iron willpower until tragedy derailed his thought processes. The composite Parallax creature quickly destroyed the Green Lantern Corps and almost ended all creation.

YELLOW FEVER
Parallax's presence bestowed enormous power, but it also caused paranoia and insanity.

PARASITE

DEBUT *Action Comics* (Vol. 1) #340 (Aug. 1966)
REAL NAME Rudy Jones
BASE Suicide Slum, Metropolis
HEIGHT Variable
WEIGHT Variable
EYES Green
HAIR None
POWERS/ABILITIES Life-energy absorption; temporary metahuman-power absorption; size and shape alteration.
ENEMIES Superman, Firestorm, Superboy (Jon Lane Kent), Justice League of America, Lois Lane
AFFILIATIONS Dr. Torval Freeman, Suicide Squad, Secret Society of Super-Villains

THE BLOB:
Josh had seen some incredible things on the streets of Metropolis, but the escaped alien snot-monster was something else.

The Parasite is a power-leech,
voraciously absorbing various forces—but especially life-energy—to survive. He has been many people. The first was petty criminal Raymond Maxwell Jensen. This Parasite died during *Crisis on Infinite Earths*, but he was recreated by Darkseid in the amalgamated universe that remained.

Here S.T.A.R. Labs janitor Rudy Jones was exposed to strange radiation and mutated into a ravenous monster, hungry for life-energy. After being captured by Firestorm and the Suicide Squad, he was experimented on at Belle Reve penitentiary, which gave him the ability to absorb all forms of energy. He further mutated after battling Superman. When Jones absorbed Dr. Torval Freeman, he was unable to "digest" the scientist's mind and they constantly warred for control of their single body. Ultimately, Jones' personality won.

Superman villain Ruin later created two teenaged Parasites from runaways Alex and Andrea Allston.

After *Flashpoint*, an obnoxious bike messenger called Joshua Michael Allen crashed into a protoplasmic monstrosity in the street. Blinded by road rage, he attacked the slimy green blob and suffered a huge electric shock from downed power lines. While he was being diagnosed at S.T.A.R. Labs, the machinery triggered a ghastly mutation, and Joshua accidentally killed the doctors by draining their life-force.

His Parasite is obsessed with leeching metahuman might. He's a deadly predator casually consuming mere mortal morsels while planning his next attack. After serving on the Suicide Squad, he hired himself out to the villainous plutocrat Sebastian Stagg to feast on the Terrifics' powers.

Rudy Jones is also still active, clashing with the monster Damage, Suicide, and latterly Superman, in a climactic clash that saw the life-leech seemingly drained of all power, stolen or otherwise.

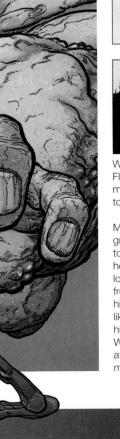

FEEDING FRENZY
Superman's superpowers were a nice appetizer, but the Parasite wanted to eat the Man of Steel.

ON THE RECORD

The Parasite has changed many times since his Silver Age debut. Originally, Raymond Jensen was exposed to radioactive waste and became a walking sponge who absorbed Superman's powers until they were roughly equals. However, as decades passed, the character became a far darker, deadlier, and more primal menace.

Memories and life-force became the favorite fodder for the monstrous creature, who could become Superman's physical equal but never his mental match.

CONSPICUOUS CONSUMPTION
No iteration of the Parasite has ever listened to the wise old adage about not playing with your food.

PARIAH

DEBUT *Crisis on Infinite Earths* (Vol. 1) #1 (Apr. 1985)
REAL NAME Kell Mossa
BASE Metropolis
HEIGHT 5ft 11in **WEIGHT** 165 lbs
EYES Black **HAIR** Purple
POWERS/ABILITIES Immortality, invulnerability, teleportation, flight; vast technological and medical knowledge.
ENEMIES Anti-Monitor, Alexander Luthor

Kell Mossa was the greatest scientist of New Earth, but he was cursed with an insatiable hunger for knowledge. Using antimatter as a power-source, he arrogantly tried to discover the origins of the universe. His actions roused the Anti-Monitor, causing the monster to begin its eradication of the infinite Earths of the Multiverse. As a result, Mossa became a cosmic Pariah, fated to arrive in each universe just before its destruction. He tumbled from one dimension to another, warning each Earth's heroes to unite or die.

With the *Crisis* averted and the Anti-Monitor defeated, Mossa retired, assuming his penance was over. However, another *Infinite Crisis* began and Pariah was murdered by his supposed ally, Alexander Luthor of Earth-3.

PARK, LINDA

DEBUT *The Flash* (Vol. 2) #28 (Jul. 1989)
REAL NAME Linda Jasmine Park-West
BASE Keystone City
HEIGHT 5ft 6in **WEIGHT** 120 lbs
EYES Brown **HAIR** Black
POWERS/ABILITIES Keen deductive skills and journalistic training.
ENEMIES Frances Kane, Zoom (Hunter Zoloman), Kobra Cult, Mirror Master

Fed up with fronting puff-pieces, television reporter Linda Park changed tack to carve out a reputation as an investigative journalist. One early scoop was interviewing Wally West, the latest speedster to call himself The Flash. They became a couple and eventually married, but two children later, Linda refused to allow herself to be a sidekick or shadow.

Her work enraged villains like Kobra, Mirror Master, and Gorilla Grodd, but her greatest threat was Zoom, who wanted to kill her to make Wally a better, tragedy-honed, hero. Zoom was defeated by their love, but when Wally was seemingly excised from reality by Doctor Manhattan, she forgot him. When he returned, Linda treated him like a crazy stranger. Eventually, she dated him, but the magic was never rekindled, and Wally went mad from grief, sparking the atrocity at the Sanctuary, the Super Hero mental health facility.

PARLIAMENT OF TREES, THE

DEBUT *Swamp Thing* (Vol. 2) #47 **(Apr. 1986)**
BASE The Grove
NOTABLE MEMBERS/POWERS All members of the Parliament possess plant-based physiology and powers and can control all forms of plant life. **Swamp Thing** (Alec Holland); **Yggdrasil**: First elemental; **Tuuru**: Second elemental; **Eyam**: Third elemental; **Bog Venus**; **Ghost Hiding in the Rushes**; **Kettle Hole Devil**; **Saint Columba**; **Albert Hollerer**; **Great Url**; **Jack in the Green**; **Lady Jane**
ALLIES Parliament of Limbs
ENEMIES The Parliament of Decay, The Parliament of Flowers

The elemental Swamp Thing is an avatar for the Green, the mystical force that unites plant life across and beyond Earth. Alec Holland is the last of countless Green agents. Some former avatars comprised The Parliament of Trees, a linked collective with great wisdom and the ability to bestow power upon the current avatar. Older than mammals, the Parliament was the congress of all past Swamp Things.

When Alec Holland was murdered by Anton Arcane, his body rotted in the swamp before he could begin his destined role as Green avatar. The Parliament was patient and careful, waiting years before Alec resurrected. It was longer still before he came to accept his destiny. Former Swamp Thing and Parliament member, A.H. Rodgers visited Holland to make him see the danger of a world without an avatar, and Alec finally agreed to become the Swamp Thing.

Holland later abolished the Parliament after they punished him for not murdering Floronic Man Jason Woodrue, the Seeder.

When The Otherkind returned to the Multiverse and witch goddess Hecate tried to rewrite the rules of magic, she destroyed The Parliament of Trees through her agent Black Orchid and replaced it with a more voracious and militant Parliament of Flowers.

GREEN ARMY
To combat the forces of the Metal and their leader, Lady Weeds, Swamp Thing led a troop of former avatars of the Green onto the battlefield.

ON THE RECORD

The Parliament of Trees was first introduced in the 1980s when they met an earlier version of Swamp Thing, who, for a time, believed he was actually Alec Holland Some of these members included: Yggdrasil, an elemental based on the DNA helix; Eyam, a former trilobite; and Tuuru.

The Parliament was responsible for the birth of the Swamp Thing that predated the true Alec Holland version, as well as the source of his daughter Tefé's powers. It was also notable for fighting a battle with another collective consciousness, this one known as the Grey.

THE PARLIAMENT IN ACTION
Tefé was the daughter of the Swamp Thing, who once believed he was Alec Holland, and his love, Abigail Holland. Abigail had been implanted with a new plant elemental called the Sprout, created by the Parliament.

PATCHWORK MAN

DEBUT *Swamp Thing* (Vol. 1) #2 (Dec. 1972–Jan. 1973) (Gregori Arcane); *Weird War Tales* (Vol. 1) #93 (Nov. 1980) (Elliot Taylor)
REAL NAME Gregori Arcane / Elliot Taylor
HEIGHT 6ft 8in **WEIGHT** 330 lbs
EYES Blue **HAIR** Gray-black
POWERS/ABILITIES Superhuman strength, ability to stay alive despite injuries.
ALLIES Abigail Arcane
ENEMIES Anton Arcane, Swamp Thing

Gregori Arcane lived a tormented life. When his abusive brother Anton was apparently killed in World War II, Gregori could finally get on with his life, but it spiraled downward. His wife died giving birth to their daughter, Abigail. Years later, Abigail went missing and, while searching for her, Gregori stumbled onto a minefield and was killed. Anton, who had survived the war, found Gregori's body and reanimated it with magic and science. Now the misshapen Patchwork Man, Gregori sought vengeance against Anton, but was imprisoned in his dungeon. Accidentally freed, Gregori searched for his now-adult daughter, later sacrificing himself to save her.

A second Patchwork Man, Elliot "Lucky" Taylor, was stitched together after stepping on a mine. Incredibly strong and practically invulnerable, he was the Creature Commandos' resident powerhouse.

PEACEMAKER

DEBUT *The Fightin' 5* #40 (Nov. 1966)
REAL NAME Christopher Smith (born Schmidt)
BASE Geneva, Switzerland
HEIGHT 6ft 2in **WEIGHT** 205 lbs
EYES Blue **HAIR** Black
POWERS/ABILITIES Expert hand-to-hand combatant; proficient marksman; adept pilot.
ENEMIES Eclipso, The Reach, Dominators, Durlans, Psions
AFFILIATIONS Checkmate, Inferior Five

At age five, Christopher Schmidt saw his father's suicide. The Austrian Nazi Party member had been facing trial for war crimes. Christopher's mother took her son to America, where he later enlisted in the US Army. After a court martial for leading a unit that massacred an entire village, he was offered early release if he joined the program Project: Peacemaker.

Christopher showed promise as an elite soldier, but the project was defunded. Establishing the Pax Institute in Geneva, he started his own version of the project, fighting for justice to atone for his family's sins. He was later apparently killed by Eclipso, before mysteriously returning to aid the Blue Beetle (Jaime Reyes).

Following a Dominator-led invasion of Earth, he was captured and experimented upon by alien metagene researchers before breaking free and escaping.

PENNYWORTH, JULIA

DEBUT *Detective Comics* (Vol. 1) #501 (Apr. 1981)
ALSO KNOWN AS Penny-Two, Tuxedo One
BASE Gotham City
HEIGHT 5ft 8in **WEIGHT** 129 lbs
EYES Brown **HAIR** Black
POWERS/ABILITIES Highly trained special agent and marksman; efficient strategist.

While investigating crime boss Carmine Falcone in Hong Kong, Batman met an agent of the British Special Reconnaissance Regiment (SRR). He discovered that she was none other than Julia Pennyworth, estranged daughter of his butler, Alfred. He took her back to Wayne Manor to recover from a stabbing, and she reconciled with her father. Adopting the codename Penny-Two, Julia helped Batman from the relative safety of the Batcave.

When Batman was reported killed by The Joker, Julia worked with the G.C.P.D.'s Batman Task Force as Julia Perry. She assisted Police Commissioner Jim Gordon during his tenure as Batman.

Julia performed the same function for Batwoman Kate Kane, but they quarreled when Kane discovered Julia reporting on her to Batman. They later reconciled and Julia now supervises the care of Batwoman's disturbed sister, Beth.

PEOPLE'S HEROES

DEBUT *The Outsiders* (Vol. 1) # 10 (Aug. 1986)
BASE Moscow, Russia
NOTABLE MEMBERS Hammer; Sickle; Pravda; Molotov; Bolshoi; Stalnoivolk
CURRENT MEMBERS Red Star; Pozhar; Vostok-X; Negative Woman; Black Eagle; Lady Flash; Firebird; Morozko; Perun; Rusalka; Steel Wolf; Tundra; Vikhor
ALLIES Red Shadows, Rocket Reds
ENEMIES The Outsiders, Fusion, Suicide Squad **AFFILIATIONS** The Kremlin

Russia's superhuman force, the People's Heroes, debuted when The Outsiders rescued Black Lightning's ex-wife from African tyrant Edward Bentama. His ties to the Soviet Union drew the People's Heroes into a battle they unexpectedly won, but The Outsiders won the rematch. The two groups later found themselves unlikely partners, uniting against the Force of July and insane former associate, Fusion. Hammer and Sickle defected, and the remaining members fought the Suicide Squad alongside new member Stalnoivolk. Regularly decommissioned and recreated, the taskforce changes rosters with each new Premier. The mismatched team was gathered again most recently to counter the rumored threat of American artificial Metahuman proliferation, as seemingly revealed in *Doomsday Clock*.

PENGUIN, THE

DATA

DEBUT *Detective Comics* (Vol. 1) #58 **(Dec. 1941)**
REAL NAME Oswald Chesterfield Cobblepot
BASE Gotham City
HEIGHT 5ft 2in   **WEIGHT** 175 lbs   **EYES** Blue   **HAIR** Black
POWERS/ABILITIES Brilliant and ruthless strategist; has connections in nearly every faction of the Gotham City criminal underworld; weapons include deadly penguin-themed inventions and a variety of trick umbrellas.
ALLIES Lark, Mr. Toxic, Hypnotic, Mr. Combustible, Black Mask, Great White Shark
ENEMIES Batman, the Batman Family, Black Canary, Emperor Blackgate

CONCEALED WEAPONS
Though much more comfortable dealing in stolen goods from behind a desk, The Penguin is not afraid to use his lethal trick umbrellas in a fight.

BAD EDUCATION
At boarding school, Oswald was defended from bullies by family friend Carter Winston, who would grow up to become Governor—and a thorn in Penguin's side.

Oswald Cobblepot has been known as "The Penguin" for most of his life. First teased with the name as a child, he later embraced it, turning the mocking insult into a moniker fearfully whispered in the darkest corners of Gotham City. Hailing from a rich family with a history of corruption, The Penguin lived up to his legacy. He became a crime boss who is only kept in check by another feared Gotham City figure—Batman.

The Cobblepot family is a renowned institution in Gotham City, as old as the Waynes, yet tarred by decades of corruption. Oswald Chesterfield Cobblepot was born into this life of luxury, albeit with a pointy nose and other features that reminded his classmates of a penguin. While ridiculed by his peers, brothers, and even his cruel father, Oswald was doted on by his mother, who called him her "beautiful boy."

With only pet birds to keep him company, and a brilliant mind for technology and strategy, Oswald began plotting against those who had wronged him. He was soon responsible for not only the deaths of his three brothers, but also his father, who died of pneumonia. While appearing innocent in the eyes of the law and his mother, Oswald had a hand in all these deaths. However, after his father's passing, Oswald was forced to carry an umbrella with him at all times by his mother, who was terrified of losing her last son to the same fate that had claimed her husband.

With the Cobblepot name not as esteemed as it once was, Oswald embarked on a criminal career. He used whatever authority remained in his family legacy to position himself at the head of the Gotham City underworld. He soon had his hands in everything from jewelry theft to illegal weapons trafficking. He also opened the Iceberg Casino, a floating ice-themed nightspot as a legitimate cover. Now he was able to rub elbows with criminals and Gotham City's elite, adding more infamy to the Cobblepot name.

ON THE RECORD

While mostly glossed over in modern retellings of The Penguin and his origins, the original version of the so-called Foul Fiend, who debuted in the 1940s, had very different methods to the modern day incarnation. While both show a penchant for umbrella weaponry and Penguin-inspired technology, the original Penguin was much more hands-on when it came to taking on the Batman. He'd often physically challenge the Dark Knight during his many robbery attempts, besting the hero on several occasions with his trick weaponry.

It wasn't until the 1990s that The Penguin evolved into the now familiar Machiavellian crime boss, gaining much power and prestige during the *No Man's Land* event.

KING PENGUIN
In one audacious scheme, The Penguin kidnapped the young Peeble IV, ruler of the nation of Swawak, to gain control of the boy's kingdom.

CLASSIC STORIES

***Batman* (Vol. 1) #25 (Oct./Nov. 1944)**
The Dark Knight's two greatest foes, The Penguin and The Joker, team up for the first time to take on Batman and Robin.

***Batman* (Vol. 1) #155 (May 1963)**
The Penguin is reintroduced for the Silver Age of comics, complete with giant animatronic birds and his Penguin-Blimp.

***The Best of DC* #10 (Mar. 1981)**
After decades of facing the Dynamic Duo, The Penguin is finally given an origin, including an overbearing mother.

"The Penguin Affair," *Batman* **(Vol. 1) #448–449,** *Detective Comics* **(Vol. 1) #615 (Jun. 1990)**
Batman and The Penguin battle in a game of wits (and chess) in this three-part tale, which introduces the brilliant Harold Allnut and Penguin's moll, Lark.

PENNYWORTH, ALFRED

DATA

DEBUT *Batman* (Vol. 1) #16 (Apr./May 1943)
REAL NAME Alfred Pennyworth, aka Penny One
BASE Gotham City
HEIGHT 6ft
WEIGHT 160 lbs
EYES Blue
HAIR Black
POWERS/ABILITIES Expert with the Batcomputer; highly intelligent and brilliant strategist; capable detective; accomplished actor with skills in makeup and wardrobe; skilled surgeon with military training.
ALLIES Batman, the Batman Family, Julia Pennyworth
ENEMIES Arkham Asylum Inmates, Hush, Bane
AFFILIATIONS The Robin movement

Every hero needs a right-hand man, and Alfred Pennyworth was precisely that for the Dark Knight of Gotham City. Formerly Thomas and Martha Wayne's butler, Alfred stayed on at Wayne Manor after they were murdered during a mugging, serving as a guardian for their young son, Bruce. Alfred remained Batman's most loyal confidant, not only keeping Bruce's daily life on track, but also aiding the Dark Knight on his crime-busting missions from the safety of the Batcave.

DUTY OF CARE
Bruce had no interest in replacing his father after Thomas Wayne's death. But the solitary orphan found a loving surrogate father figure in Alfred.

Alfred was an actor with a military background whose life changed dramatically when he took over his father's duties at Wayne Manor. Jarvis Pennyworth had been the primary butler to Thomas and Martha Wayne and had doted on their young son Bruce. Jarvis' fate was sealed when he ignored a message from corrupt secret society the Court of Owls to drive Martha to be dealt with. Angry that the butler had refused to carry out their orders, the Court sent one of their Talon assassins to murder him. Alfred never received the warning letter that his father had penned to him and he took over the position in the Wayne household. When Thomas and Martha were murdered by criminal Joe Chill, Alfred tried his best to raise Bruce in a secure environment. However, as Bruce grew older, Alfred became concerned at his charge's obsessive determination to make a difference in Gotham City.

Bruce traveled abroad to prepare for his vigilante mission. When he returned home, Alfred was there for him. Alfred didn't always approve of Bruce's life as a crime fighter, but he remained loyal, even operating the Batcomputer in the Batcave beneath Wayne Manor. When Batman's ally, James Gordon, took over Bruce Wayne's Batman role, Alfred took it upon himself to organize the Robin vigilante movement in Gotham City.

Later, Bruce returned as Batman, and Alfred was caught up in the action when Bane took over Gotham City. While Batman and Catwoman were away, Bane broke into Wayne Manor. He snapped Alfred's neck in front of Robin to demonstrate that the Batman Family was not welcome in his city. Batman later overcame Bane, but has not yet overcome his heartache at losing Alfred, the man whom he had come to view as a second father.

GENTLEMAN'S GENTLEMAN
Alfred Pennyworth was privy to the greatest secret in Gotham City: the identity of Batman. Alfred treated the driven Bruce Wayne like the son he never had, and only wished to see his master happy and healthy.

ON THE RECORD

When Alfred debuted in 1943, he looked little like his modern-day counterpart. He was a rather large man, clumsy and bumbling, whose last name was Beagle, as revealed in a 1945 issue of *Detective Comics*.

Alfred slimmed down during the latter part of the 1940s and by 1969 he had gained a new surname—Pennyworth— and was well on his way to being the butler known by readers everywhere.

Years later, in 2005, it was revealed that Alfred had indeed been named Alfred Beagle, but had changed his name while working as an agent for Her Majesty's Secret Service, MI6. There was clearly more to Alfred than met the eye.

SUBSTITUTE PARENTS
The two people who primarily raised young Bruce, Alfred and the Wayne family doctor Leslie Thompkins, had a romance. Their relationship was explored in post-*Crisis* stories.

BEWARE OF THE BUTLER
With his military background, Alfred didn't quite share Batman's anti-gun stance. However, he respected Bruce's beliefs on weapons, and never questioned them.

CLASSIC STORIES

***Batman* (Vol. 1) #22 (Apr./May 1944)** Only a year after his debut, Alfred gets his own backup story, complete with a spot front and center on this issue's cover.

***Detective Comics* (Vol. 1) #328 (Jun. 1964)** Alfred is killed for the first time (albeit temporarily) in this issue, which saw Batman create the Alfred Foundation in memory of his fallen butler.

***Detective Comics* (Vol. 1) #501 (Apr. 1981)** Alfred's past as a soldier is delved into as fans are introduced to Julia Pennyworth, his daughter with war hero Mademoiselle Marie.

***Nightwing: Alfred's Return* #1 (Jul. 1995)** Having left the Dark Knight's service and traveled to London, Alfred is convinced to return home to Gotham City by Nightwing.

PERPETUA

DEBUT *Justice League* (Vol. 4) #8 (Nov. 2018)
BASE Sixth Dimension
HEIGHT Variable **WEIGHT** Variable
EYES Yellow **HAIR** Black
POWERS/ABILITIES Godlike powers, including the ability to create Multiverses.
ALLIES Lex Luthor, Anti-Monitor, the Batman Who Laughs, the Crime Syndicate
ENEMIES Justice League, Monitor, World Forger
AFFILIATIONS None

Perpetua was a Super Celestial—a godlike being who created the Multiverse. It was meant to develop and come to a natural end before being judged by the Source. However, Perpetua wanted to keep it alive forever. Her sons—the Monitor, Anti-Monitor and World Forger—revealed her intentions to the Source, and she was imprisoned in the Source Wall, the boundary of the Multiverse.

When the Justice League broke the Source Wall, Perpetua tried to set the Multiverse back on its path of chaos, where the strong would rule. After overcoming the Justice League, Perpetua's started destroying those of the 52 universes that sided with justice over doom. It seemed as though Perpetua was triumphant, but the defeated Justice League still had hope...

PHANTOM GIRL

DEBUT *The Terrifics* (Vol. 1) #1 (Apr. 2018)
REAL NAME Linnya Wazzo
BASE Mobile
HEIGHT Unknown
WEIGHT Unknown
EYES Blue **HAIR** Black
POWERS/ABILITIES Intangibility, dark energy blasts.
ALLIES Element Dog
ENEMIES Doc Dread, the Dark Elder
AFFILIATIONS The Terrifics

Linnya Wazzo was part of the royal family of the planet Bgztl, a place where everyone could become intangible. On a vacation with her parents as a young child, Linnya was pulled through a rift into the Dark Multiverse, where she became stranded for many years, trapped in her intangible form.

Having grown to be a teenager, she was eventually found and rescued by Mr. Terrific, Metamorpho, and Plastic Man. The four became teammates as The Terrifics, with Linnya codenamed Phantom Girl. Phantom Girl grew to love being a Super Hero, and being part of a new family, so she was heartbroken when the team broke up. When Mr. Terrific was under attack in the Multiverse, it was Phantom Girl who got the team back together to go and help him.

PHANTOM LADY

DEBUT *Police Comics* #1 (Aug. 1941)
REAL NAME Sophia Becker
BASE Blue Tracer, Earth-X
HEIGHT 5ft 6in **WEIGHT** 128 lbs
EYES Green **HAIR** Black
POWERS/ABILITIES Adept combatant; creates teleportation portals.
ALLIES Uncle Sam, Black Condor
ENEMIES Nazis, Plastic Man, Overman, Cyborg Overman
AFFILIATIONS Freedom Fighters

The first Phantom Lady was debutant Sandra Knight who had a sight-obscuring black light projector. In 1942 she migrated to Earth-X to battle Nazism. Her granddaughter, Delilah Tyler, succeeded her, equipped with blasters and hologram projectors. When she was killed by Deathstroke, the role fell to Stormy Knight.

After *Flashpoint*, journalist Jennifer Knight took on the role. She teamed up with inventor Dane Maxwell (Doll Man) to hunt down the man who killed her father.

Following *Rebirth*, Phantom Lady reappeared on Earth-10 as a Freedom Fighter, five decades after America fell to the Nazis. Next, Sophia Becker inherited the role, employing teleportation powers beside Black Condor, Doll Woman, Human Bomb, and others to defeat Nazi tyranny.

PHOBIA

DEBUT *The New Teen Titans* (Vol. 1) #14 (Dec. 1981)
REAL NAME Angela Hawkins III
HEIGHT 5ft 11in
WEIGHT 138 lbs
EYES Green
HAIR Black
POWERS/ABILITIES Able to discover an enemy's worst fear and manifest it inside his or her mind; capable hand-to-hand combatant.
ENEMIES Blue Beetle, Brutale, La Dama

Before the *Flashpoint* event, Phobia was a recurring enemy of the Teen Titans. She later reappeared, her past shrouded in mystery, to fight a new foe: Blue Beetle Jaime Reyes. A Super-Villain for hire, Phobia first encountered Reyes when she and several other members of the Brotherhood of Evil were seeking an ancient artifact called the Blue Beetle.

Said to have been originally discovered in a Mayan Pyramid, the Blue Beetle was prized by Phobia's employers, the Brain and Monsieur Mallah. During her efforts to obtain the item, Phobia was attacked by rival Super-Villains hired by the crime boss La Dama. In the ensuing chaos, the Blue Beetle fell into the hands of Jaime Reyes, who was transformed by the artifact into the Super Hero of the same name.

PHOBOS

DEBUT *Wonder Woman* (Vol. 1) #183 (Jul.–Aug. 1969)
BASE The Netherworld
HEIGHT 7ft 7in **WEIGHT** 459 lbs
EYES Red **HAIR** Flaming red
POWERS/ABILITIES Olympian god able to physically manifest an enemy's greatest fear; essentially invulnerable.
ALLIES Eris, Deimos, Circe
ENEMIES Wonder Woman, Batman, Ares
AFFILIATIONS Olympian Gods

Phobos is the God of Fear and twin brother of Deimos, God of Terror. The malevolent son of Ares, Phobos infamously attempted to help the God of War ignite World War III and destroy the Earth, before being stopped by Wonder Woman.

Phobos constantly orchestrates events to spread fear and he once merged with the villain Scarecrow before combining his body with the Dark Knight. Phobos' sister, Eris, inhabited Poison Ivy, and Deimos merged with The Joker, requiring the combined efforts of Wonder Woman and Batman to defend Gotham City from the siblings' threat.

The twins have also merged together to impersonate their father. Believing Amazons were specifically created to imprison their father, they sought the location of hidden Themyscira and planned to release him.

PIED PIPER

DEBUT *The Flash* (Vol. 1) #106 (Apr.–May 1959)
REAL NAME Hartley Rathaway
BASE Central City
HEIGHT 5ft 10in
WEIGHT 158 lbs
EYES Blue **HAIR** Red
POWERS/ABILITIES Brilliant engineer with augmented hearing; electronic flute induces mind-control, force-fields, and destructive vibrations.
ALLIES David Singh, The Flash, The Rogues
ENEMIES Gorilla Grodd

Hartley Rathaway was born deaf and his rich parents shunned him even after doctors fixed his hearing. However, Hartley had become obsessed with music and the wonders of acoustic science. He created incredible inventions and—afflicted by years of filial neglect and realizing he was gay—became flamboyant, attention-seeking Super-Villain Pied Piper. Hartley battled The Flash and joined The Rogues, before reforming and turning to writing music.

Hartley occasionally reanimated his Pied Piper identity, battling threats such as Grodd's super gorilla invasion and helping Lisa Snart (Golden Glider) out of a coma caused by an exploding Genome Recorder. However, Rathaway is generally content to enjoy semi-retirement building his relationship with police crime-lab director David Singh.

PLANETEERS, THE

DEBUT *Real Fact Comics* #16 (Sep.–Oct. 1948)
NOTABLE MEMBERS Col. Tommy Tomorrow; Gen. Vurian of Venus; SCO Hega; Capt. Brent Wood; Capt. Lenk; Cadet Hjaro; Cadet Lo-Duey of Mars.
ALLIES Interplanetary Zoo, Operation Noah's Ark
ENEMIES Chardu of Mercury, Dr. Suvu of Jupiter, Dr. Klik, Nkolo, Prime Minister Bsorbo of Roukar
AFFILIATIONS Super Sons, Takron-Galtos

Prior to *Flashpoint* the Planeteers was a multispecies organization created on Earth. Planeteers graduated from the Planeteer Academy before being trained in science, detective work, and military tactics. In essence a space navy, the Planeteers patroled space lanes, facilitated trade, explored uncharted regions, took rescue missions, and rooted out space pirates.

After *Rebirth*, the Planeteers became an intergalactic peacekeeping force. Based on the space station Tolerance, they administered their brand of justice in a heavy-handed way. After Doctor Manhattan's apparent time-tampering was unraveled in the *Doomsday Clock* affair, the original Planeteer set-up returned as a place for kind sentients to contribute to. This sadly did not include Rose Forrest, who applied, desperate to remove her alter ego, Thorn, from 25th-century Earth.

PLASMUS

DEBUT *New Teen Titans* (Vol. 1) #14 (Dec. 1981)
REAL NAME Otto von Furth
BASE Paris, France
HEIGHT 6ft 4in **WEIGHT** Variable
EYES Yellow **HAIR** None
POWERS/ABILITIES Malleable body; radioactive; acidic death-touch.
ALLIES Warp, Phobia, Secret Society of Super-Villains
ENEMIES Teen Titans, Blue Beetle

Trapped in a cave-in, German miner Otto von Furth spent several days exposed to unknown radiations before being rescued. As he lay dying, he was abducted from hospital by Nazi war criminal General Zahl. The General saved Otto by mutating his body further, until it stabilized as an amorphous mass of acidic, super-heated protoplasm. Now a living terror weapon, Otto called himself Plasmus and joined Zahl in the Brotherhood of Evil, even staying on with the group when his re-creator perished in battle.

Plasmus joined his occasional allies Warp and Phobia in the Secret Society of Super-Villains. He also robbed banks and corporations, claiming to be amassing loot from the kinds of institutions he held responsible for his monstrous state.

PHANTOM STRANGER

DATA

DEBUT *Phantom Stranger* (Vol. 1) #1 (Aug.-Sep. 1952)
REAL NAME Judas Iscariot
HEIGHT 6ft 2in **WEIGHT** 185 lbs **EYES** White **HAIR** Grey/White
POWERS/ABILITIES Immortality; skilled magic-user capable of flight, teleportation, energy-projection, invisibility, transformation, size-alteration, and the ability to stop time.
ALLIES Pandora, The Question, Chris Esperanza, John Constantine, Jim Corrigan, Doctor Terrence Thirteen
ENEMIES The Spectre, Haunted Highwayman, Sin Eater, Sons of Trigon
AFFILIATIONS Trinity of Sin, Council of Wizards, Justice League Dark

ROAD TO NOWHERE
Humanity's most reviled traitor learned over restless centuries that the only way to pay for his sin was saving the innocent and challenging the guilty.

AN UNWELCOME REUNION
As the centuries unfolded, it was inevitable that the restless Trinity of Sin would meet again: Sometimes as allies but more often in acrimony, as when the Phantom Stranger encountered Pandora.

The Phantom Stranger is eternally atoning for committing the greatest sin in human history: Betraying Jesus the Messiah to the religious authorities in exchange for 30 pieces of silver. In despair at his treachery, Jesus' former disciple, Judas Iscariot, tried to kill himself, but was brought before a Council of Wizards. He was deemed to be part of a Trinity of Sin—along with Pandora and The Question—and given a harsh punishment.

IN MYSTERIOUS WAYS
His noble intentions led to death and disaster, but Phantom's Stranger's failure was preordained to revive the Spirit of Vengeance when Earth needed him most.

Judas was compelled to walk among mankind on Earth forever and doomed to wear the blood-money for his betrayal around his neck. Returned to the scene of his crime, a Great Voice ordered him to don the transformative robe of the One he had betrayed and begin his penance.

As the Phantom Stranger, Judas wandered the Earth for centuries, seeking to atone for his crime. Unable to pause for long or enjoy human company, he roamed, waiting for the Voice to command him again.

The Voice later told the Phantom Stranger to help ex-Gotham City police detective Jim Corrigan save his kidnapped fiancée, Gwen. The Stranger found Gwen, but unknowingly led the detective into a trap, and both Corrigan and Gwen were killed. The Voice imbued Corrigan's soul with the Spirit of Vengeance and he became The Spectre. The Spectre accused the Phantom Stranger of betrayal and would have destroyed him, had the Voice not intervened. The curse of treachery still lay heavy upon the Phantom Stranger, but his necklace now held one less coin.

More recently, Phantom Stranger came into conflict with Wonder Woman when the Stranger turned her nemesis Paula Von Gunther into stone. Despite bringing Wonder Woman to the gates of Heaven itself, Wonder Woman fought for Von Gunther's life and won, using her Lasso of Truth to force the Stranger to admit he withheld Von Gunther's salvation in order to help balance the scales of his own legendary betrayal. After hearing the Stranger's confession, the Presence seemingly dissolved him into nothingness. While this appeared to be the end of the Phantom Stranger, his quest for redemption remained unfinished, and he will most likely return when truly needed.

ON THE RECORD

The Phantom Stranger of the 1950s was a complete mystery: a trenchcoated wanderer debunking charlatans, battling science-based threats, and defeating aliens from outer space.

As the 1960s closed, he returned as an enigmatic, mystic champion. In this incarnation, he confronted a legion of arcane enemies and eventually joined the Justice League of America. Such was his pervasive aura of mystery that, when his origins were finally revealed in *Secret Origins* #10 (Jan. 1987), readers were presented with four possible stories from which to choose.

MAN OF MYSTERY
The inscrutable Phantom Stranger instinctively seemed to know where and when someone needed his unique brand of problem-solving.

CLASSIC STORIES

Phantom Stranger (Vol. 2) #4 (Dec. 1969) Dr. Thirteen inadvertently liberates Tala, the demonic Queen of Evil; the Phantom Stranger defeats her, but gains an implacable enemy.

Phantom Stranger (Vol. 3) #1–4 (Oct. 1987–Jan. 1988) Reduced to a mere mortal, the Stranger battles Eclipso, Spirit of Wrath, before the villain transforms Earth into a realm of ultimate darkness.

Legends (Vol. 1) #1–6 (Nov. 1986–Apr. 1987) The Phantom Stranger foils Darkseid's attempts to destroy Earth's concept of heroism.

PLASTIC MAN

DEBUT *Police Comics* #1 (Aug. 1941)
REAL NAME Patrick Edward "Eel" O'Brian   **BASE** Cole City
HEIGHT 6ft 1in/variable   **WEIGHT** 178 lbs   **EYES** Blue   **HAIR** Black
POWERS/ABILITIES Completely malleable body; flexible skeleton; movable internal organs; extreme contortionism; shape-changing.
ALLIES Suave Pado Swakatoon, Obscura, Woozy Winks, Batman, Offspring (Luke O'Brian)
ENEMIES The Cabal, Granite Janet, Lex Luthor, Dr. Dratt, the Red Herring
AFFILIATIONS The Terrifics, Justice League, Spyral

FLEXIBLE RESPONSE
Plastic Man bends over backwards, sideways, and any old way to uphold the law.

Plastic Man has fought crime since the 1940s, using his astoundingly pliable form, deductive mind, and underworld knowledge to bring to justice some of the world's strangest villains. "Plas" worked as a private eye with dim but loyal assistant Woozy Winks, and was FBI liaison to the All-Star Squadron and Freedom Fighters during World War II. Decades later, he served with the Justice League.

Plastic Man knew how criminals thought because he was one. Patrick "Eel" O'Brian always outwitted the cops, but was betrayed by his own crew when a research lab heist for crime boss the Duchess went bad. Shot, doused in bizarre exotic chemicals, and left for dead, Eel did not die. While recuperating, he realized the ordeal had changed his body. He could now infinitely change his shape and appearance and resolved to follow the example of the good clerics who saved him to protect decent people. His character also changed and his memories seemed somehow altered.

Plastic Man never revealed he was still a wanted criminal. He maintained his original persona, cozying up to the mobsters he targeted while "Plas" fostered a reputation for silliness, and a habit of shapeshifting into common objects to surprise friends and foes alike.

Post-*Flashpoint*, O'Brian was an unrepentant thief, transformed when Earth-3's Crime Syndicate invaded and his weird chemical inundation came about when Owlman attacked him.

Following *Rebirth*, Plastic Man is seeking redemption and atonement. With new sidekick Suave Pado Swakatoon, and as a member of pandimensional Super Hero alliance the Terrifics, he faced threats including the Cabal and Secret Six.

PLASTIC FANTASTIC
Mobster Eel O'Brian never imagined that any of this metahuman nonsense could affect an ordinary guy like him.

THE TERRIFICS
When malign Barbatos broke through from the Dark Multiverse during the Metal Crisis, Plastic Man learned he has an unexplained affinity with extra-multiversal Nth Metal and immunity to the warping effects of Dark Matter: A possible explanation for his incredible abilities and unnatural, often surreal Super Hero experiences. This led to him being trapped in a trans-dimensional odyssey and an initially unwelcome alliance with Mister Terrific, Metamorpho, Phantom Girl, and a succession of alternate reality Super Heroes.

PLASTIQUE

DEBUT *The Fury of Firestorm* #7 (Dec. 1982)
REAL NAME Bette Sans Souci
POWERS/ABILITIES Explosives and munitions expert who can turn objects into bombs; able to project concussive blasts from her hands.
ENEMIES Firestorm, Checkmate, Wonder Woman, The Rogues, A.R.G.U.S., the Nuclear Men
AFFILIATIONS Suicide Squad, Secret Society

Canadian Bette Sans Souci was a terrorist armorer. She later went public as Plastique, a walking bomb in a costume covered with assorted incendiary charges. She acquired the ability to project concussive blasts and turn objects into bombs.

As she developed, her radical ideology waned. After serving with the Suicide Squad, Plastique became a thief and mercenary targeting targeting Firestorm before joining the Outsiders Secret Society.

In advance of the Crime Syndicate's invasion of Earth, she attempted to murder Madame Xanadu, infiltrated A.R.G.U.S., and tried to claim the bounty on the Rogues.

Following *Rebirth*, she battled the Justice League and bombed a wedding attended by Etta Candy and Wonder Woman. She was last seen holidaying on criminal paradise Zandia.

POWER COMPANY

DEBUT *JLA* (Vol. 1) #61 (Feb. 2002)
BASE San Francisco, California
MEMBERS/POWERS Josiah Power: Very powerful metahuman; **Manhunter**: Enhanced speed, rapid healing, martial arts; **Skyrocket**: Energy-manipulating harness; **Witchfire**: Magic-wielder; **Bork**: Super-strength, invulnerability; **Sapphire**: Telekinesis; **Striker Z**: Super-strength; capable of energy absorption and release; **Firestorm**: Flight, nuclear transmutation.
ALLIES Superman, Green Arrow, Wonder Woman, Nightwing
ENEMIES Black Dragon Society, Doctor Cyber, Cadre, Dragoneer, Strike Force, Jack Spheer, Crime Syndicate of America
AFFILIATIONS Conglomerate, Blood Pack, Hero Hotline, S.T.A.R. Corps, Captains of Industry, S.T.A.R. Labs

SUPER HEROES FOR HIRE
1 Striker Z   5 Sapphire
2 Bork   6 Witchfire
3 Josiah Power   7 Manhunter
4 Skyrocket

The Power Company was a Super Hero team created by attorney Josiah Power. When his metagene triggered in the middle of a trial, he was fired from his law firm. Power then devised a business model providing Super Hero services to paying clients. He recruited some minor champions and supplemented them with established characters, such as Firestorm.

Set up along the lines of a law firm, the front line Super Heroes were divided into "Partners" or "Associates," supported by specialists and administrative staff, who had extensive experience with the metahuman community and weird science. Power's personal assistant was former pop star Silver Shannon (of The Maniaks) and the Power Company boasted high profile contracts with the likes of S.T.A.R. Labs and St. Claire Industries. Despite initial success, the business is now "on hiatus."

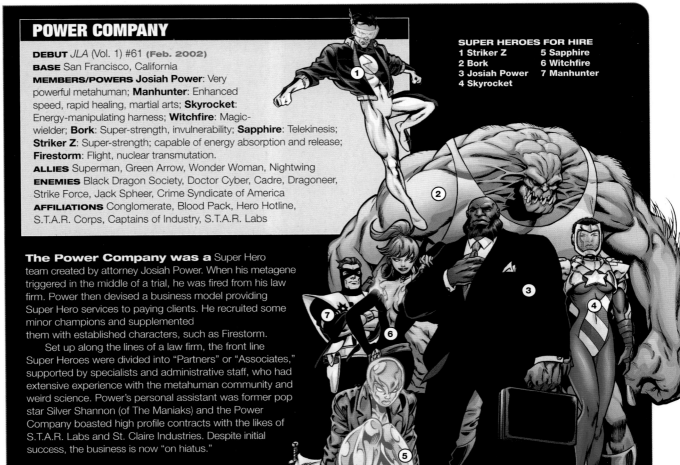

POISON IVY

DEBUT *Batman* (Vol. 1) # 181 (Jun. 1966)
REAL NAME Pamela Lillian Isley
BASE Gotham City
HEIGHT 5ft 8in **WEIGHT** 140 lbs
EYES Green **HAIR** Red
POWERS/ABILITIES Controls and manipulates all plant life; immune to poisons and toxins; can transmit toxins and poisons via a kiss; wields plant-based pheromones that can cause people to fall under her hypnotic spell; highly intelligent and adept at botany and chemistry.
ALLIES Harley Quinn, Clayface
ENEMIES Batman, the Batman Family, the Floronic Man
AFFILIATIONS Gotham City Sirens, the Green, Arkham Asylum inmates

A TOUCH OF POISON
All plant life is ripe for Poison Ivy's control. She can grow a vine with a thought, or turn a harmless Venus fly trap into a deadly attack dog.

BUDDING GENIUS
Although sunlight damaged her delicate pale skin, little Pamela's only escape from a life of domestic terror was beside her mother in their lush and well-tended garden.

Poison Ivy is more than a simple Super-Villain. She's a complex creature, often appearing more plant than human. Ivy is an eco-terrorist, and the lives of plants are her main concern. While her objective of saving the planet from mankind's pollutants and deforestation is a noble one, the means by which she works towards that goal are borderline insane, making her another formidable figure in Batman's Rogues Gallery.

Pamela Isley grew up in an abusive home. Her mother enjoyed growing plants, an activity Pamela became fond of. However, Pamela's father would routinely beat her mother, before buying her flowers as an apology, and she would take him back. Eventually, Pamela's father killed her mother, burying her in the garden. He was later taken into police custody, leaving Pamela alone.

In college, Pamela's interest in chemistry grew. She illegally developed pheromone pills, landing herself on academic probation. Using her pills and her natural charms, Isley seduced the dean into dropping all charges. Her next target was her father, whom Pamela visited in jail. Before leaving, she kissed him on the lips while wearing a toxic lipstick. He was found dead shortly after.

Pamela went on to intern for Wayne Industries, where she began to perfect her pheromone technology. During a struggle in the lab, she was splashed with chemicals, which granted her plant-controlling abilities. She soon embarked on a criminal career, believing it's her destiny to create a plant-based utopia, while also destroying the world of man.

While seeking help at the Sanctuary, Poison Ivy was killed when The Flash (Wally West) lost control of his powers. However, she was able to regrow herself, emerging more plantlike than ever and with green skin. Ivy was later completely restored, thanks to Lex Luthor. In the meantime, a part of her had gone on a road trip with Harley Quinn, who mistook this overgrowth clone for the real Poison Ivy. Feeling hurt and abandoned by her beloved Harley, Ivy severed ties with her, preferring to forsake Harley's new heroic direction for her more villainous roots.

ON THE RECORD

In her original incarnation, Poison Ivy hadn't evolved into the physical threat she'd represent in her later appearances. Before the *Crisis on Infinite Earths*, Ivy was merely an attractive criminal with a gimmick, and a crush on the Dark Knight Detective.

After *Crisis*, she fully displayed her plant powers, joining the Suicide Squad briefly before signing up with a more informal team, the Gotham City Sirens, in the 2000s. This post-*Crisis* version of Ivy also had a hand in the origin of another femme fatale, Harley Quinn, when she served her a concoction that gave Harley enhanced reflexes and strength.

KNIGHT MOVES
Poison Ivy proved her stature as one of Batman's main foes during "Knightfall," when she amassed a squad of enthralled warriors to take on the Dark Knight.

IN THE GARDEN OF EVIL
Poison Ivy was a dedicated and valiant member of the Birds of Prey, but only until she no longer had any use for them.

CLASSIC STORIES

***Batman* (Vol. 1) #181 (Jun. 1966)**
Poison Ivy debuts in Gotham City, proclaiming herself public enemy number one and catching the eye of the Dark Knight.

***Batman* (Vol. 1) #344 (Feb. 1982)**
Poison Ivy truly develops her plant-based powers as she attempts to destroy the Wayne Foundation.

***Batman: Poison Ivy* #1 (May 1997)**
In this one-shot, Poison Ivy's origin is retold for a modern audience, placing her first appearance much earlier in Batman's career.

***Batman: Shadow of the Bat* #88, *Batman* (Vol. 1) #568, *Detective Comics* (Vol. 1) #735 (Aug. 1999)**
Poison Ivy gains a green skin tone as she takes over Robinson Park during this chapter of the "No Man's Land" epic.

POWER GIRL (KARA ZOR-EL)

DEBUT *All-Star Comics* (Vol. 1) #58 (Jan.-Feb. 1976)
REAL NAME Kara Zor-El, Karen Starr
BASE Mobile
HEIGHT 5ft 11in **WEIGHT** 180 lbs **EYES** Blue **HAIR** Blonde
POWERS/ABILITIES Genius-level intellect; super-strength;
super-speed; flight; invulnerability; enhanced senses
all fueled by solar energy from a yellow sun.
ALLIES Huntress, Lois Lane, Tanya Spear,
Dr. Gerhard, Val-Zod, Harley Quinn
ENEMIES Desaad, Kaizen Gamorra, Brutaal, Darkseid
AFFILIATIONS Eight Wonders of the World, Michael Holt,
Vartox of Valeron

Kara Zor-El escaped Krypton and gained
astounding abilities under Earth-2's yellow sun. Adopted by Clark
Kent and Lois Lane, she was coached by Superman (her cousin,
Kal-El) and yearned to become a Super Hero.

When Superman, Batman, and Wonder Woman died after
Earth-2 was invaded by Apokolips, Kara and her friend Robin
were ejected from their universe. On Prime Earth, Kara rebranded
herself as technology entrepreneur Karen Starr, building a
company dedicated to bridging dimensions. As Power Girl, she
covertly secured funds and confiscated useful technologies in a
bid to return to Earth-2. Only Somya Spears, trusted assistant
of Robin—who had adopted the name Huntress—and chief
scientist Dr. Gerhard knew Karen's true nature and goals.
Power Girl and Huntress were eventually able to return home to
join Earth-2's surviving heroes in fighting Darkseid.

Following *Rebirth*, Huntress' origins changed and Power
Girl was lost in Limbo, probably due to time-tampering Doctor
Manhattan. When his meddling was undone, Karen Starr
returned to reality and action with the Justice Society.

ON THE RECORD

Power Girl evolved from a young
brat into the JSA's eventual leader.

Kara also served in the JLA and
Justice League International,
surviving numerous reality-altering
events virtually unchanged. After
an allergic reaction, she developed
aggressive mood-swings, leading
to her being possessed by Eclipso.

Power Girl repeatedly proved her
no-nonsense attitude was the way
to get the job done. This tactic only
failed when Harley Quinn took
advantage of Power Girl's
temporary amnesia to lead them on
a madcap tour of the Multiverse.

LOOKS LIKE TEEN SPIRIT
One of DC Comics' first legacy
heroes, Power Girl debuted in
1976 as a youthful rebel within
the company's oldest super team,
the Justice Society of America.

POWER RING

DEBUT *Justice League* Vol 2. #23 (Oct 2013)
REAL NAME Harold Jordan
BASE Coast City, Earth-3
HEIGHT Unkown
WEIGHT Unknown
EYES Brown
HAIR Brown
POWERS/ABILITIES While wearing the
Ring of Volthoom, Power Ring can create light
constructs, fire energy blasts, and fly.
ALLIES Deathstorm
ENEMIES Sinestro, Anti-Monitor
AFFILIATIONS Crime Syndicate

On Earth-3, Harold Jordan was a janitor
at Ferris Aircraft. In this reality, his abject
cowardice and lack of willpower caused him
to be chosen by the Ring of Volthoom as its
host. Unlike the rings of Earth-0's Green
Lanterns, the Ring of Volthoom gradually
destroys its wearer to keep itself powered up.

Now bearing the name Power Ring,
Harold was able to rise through the criminal
ranks and eventually join the Crime
Syndicate with other twisted versions of
the Justice League. However, he remained
a coward, a fact which his ring was never
slow to remind him of. Power Ring was part
of an invasion of Earth-0 by the Crime
Syndicate, but he was slain by Sinestro.

OVERPOWERED
The most cowardly man on Earth-3
seemed the perfect choice for the
Ring of Volthoom, which fed on fear.

POWER GIRL (TANYA SPEARS)

DEBUT *Worlds' Finest* #23 (Jul. 2014)
REAL NAME Tanya Spears
BASE New York City
HEIGHT 5ft 3in **WEIGHT** 120 lbs **EYES** Brown **HAIR** Black
POWERS/ABILITIES Genius intellect; superhuman strength; size-alteration,
virtual invulnerability
ALLIES Karen Starr, Huntress, Deathstroke, Wally West
ENEMIES Desaad, Adeline Kane
AFFILIATIONS Teen Titans, Defiance

Tanya Spears inherited the role of
Power Girl, after her predecessor, Karen Starr,
returned to Earth-2. She left her fortune, and Super
Hero name to the daughter of her friend, Somya
Spears, who had run Starr Industries, allowing the
Kryptonian to fight injustice and find a way home.

Tanya was a scientific prodigy. Aged 17, she
earned a postdoctoral fellowship at MIT. While
working at Starr Industries, Tanya was held by a terrorist stealing nuclear isotopes. She was saved
by Starr's Earth-2 partner Huntress, but not before being exposed to isotope radiation.

When Huntress and Karen prepared to return to Earth-2, Tanya was attacked by exiled
Apokolyptian Desaad, appropriating her new power to follow the pair and rejoin his master,
Darkseid. In the assault, Starr Industries' lab was destroyed, but when rescue workers started
digging her out of the rubble, Tanya discovered she had many of Power Girl's metahuman abilities.
She later learned that those powers were a parting gift from a grateful friend. Karen also legally
transferred her Power Girl codename and her money to Tanya. Seeking to understand her extraordinary
abilities and new, heroic direction in life, Tanya left Boston for New York, and joined the Teen Titans. At
a loss when the team broke up, she fell under the sway of Slade Wilson, Deathstroke, who was
seeking a fresh path for himself and leading a new team of young heroes: Defiance.

Learning Karen Starr was trapped in an interdimensional fold of Innerspace, Tanya sought to
extract her in astral form. When her vacant body was found, her teammates believed she had
taken her life. When burying her they were unaware that they had inadvertently marooned her
consciousness between dimensions.

THE DEVIL IN THE DETAIL
A valiant, superpowered young genius,
Tanya Spears is smart enough to realize
that any alliance with Deathstroke is
likely to come with some deadly terms
and conditions.

PRIMAL FORCE

DEBUT *Primal Force* (Vol. 1) #0 (Oct. 1994)
BASE Manhattan, New York City
MEMBERS/POWERS Doctor Mist:
Immortal magician and sage; **Claw:** Demonic right hand gives superpowers; **Nightmaster:** Magic sword; **Golem:** Super-strength; **Jack O'Lantern:** Magic lantern bestows superpowers; **Meridian Mychaels:** Teleportation martial artist; **Red Tornado:** Creates air vortexes; **Black Condor:** Flight, telekinesis; **Willpower:** Electromagnetism.
ALLIES Superman, the Water Woman, Zatanna
ENEMIES Cataclysm, Satanus, Cult of August, Master Chu, Prince Inferno

For 2,000 years mystic warriors the Leymen secretly protected humanity from magical threats. They were originally gathered by immortal mage Nommo—known today as Doctor Mist—and, armed with mystic Ley Pendulums, they patrolled the Earth via its network of Ley Lines.

When the modern cabal was eradicated during *Zero Hour*, Mist's sorcerous protocols came into play and a new squad was hastily gathered by Mist's agent, the Water Woman. This ill-prepared band was equipped with its own Ley Pendulums and began battling ancient and modern sorcerers and sects. Calling themselves Primal Force, they were drawn to many supernatural and magical crises, but eventually fell battling the monstrous Cataclysm. The survivors joined groups such as Shadowpact, and awaited the Water Woman's next call to arms.

THE LAST HURRAH
Despite their desperate determination and dedication, the last gathering of Leymen was a force destined to fail.
1 Golem
2 Black Condor
3 Will Power
4 Meridian Mychaels
5 Jack O'Lantern
6 Red Tornado
7 Claw

PREZ

DEBUT *Prez* (Vol. 1) #1 (Aug.-Sep. 1973)
REAL NAME Beth Ross
BASE Eugene, Oregon; Washington, DC, 2036
EYES Green **HAIR** Bleach blonde
POWERS/ABILITIES Honesty, common sense, compassion, straight talking, hatred of hypocrites.
ALLIES Vice President Preston Rickard, Amber Waves, Joni Andersen
ENEMIES Senator Jay Thorn, Senator Tom Downey, Boss Smiley, Grizzly Tobacco, Pharmaduke
AFFILIATIONS Li'l Doggies House of Corndogs, Anonymous

Working in a fast-food franchise, 19-year-old Beth Ross accidentally battered and deep-fried her own hair. When friends posted a video of the incident online, "Corndog Girl" went viral. In election year 2036, owing to public apathy and the venality of politicians, an amendment was passed allowing voting by email and social media. With Beth trending stratospherically, hacker collective Anonymous launched a campaign and, despite political chicanery, good-hearted Beth became President. Her first order of duty was to overturn centuries of institutional corruption. She filled her cabinet with "actual smart people" and made the most hated politician in America—Preston Rickard—her Vice President. As he himself pointed out, no one would try to assassinate her if he was next in line for the top job.

SOCIALLY AWARE
Beth had no interest in politics, but was determined that people like her dad shouldn't have to die because they were poor.

PROFESSOR IVO

DEBUT *Brave and the Bold* (Vol. 1) #30 (Jun.-Jul. 1960)
REAL NAME Anthony Ivo
EYES Black **HAIR** None
POWERS/ABILITIES Genius intellect; advanced knowledge of engineering, computer science, chemistry and biology; indefinitely extended lifespan; mutated form, which is bullet- and energy-blast-proof and toxin-resistant.
ALLIES Lionel Luthor, lex Luthor, T.O. Morrow, Amazo, The Outsider
ENEMIES Justice League, Justice League of America, Green Arrow
AFFILIATIONS Legion of Doom, Silas Stone, S.T.A.R. Labs, A.R.G.U.S., Secret Society of Super-Villains, Ivy University

Anthony Ivo is a true mad scientist, obsessed with results and caring nothing for the harm his work causes. He headed Ivy University's Cellular and Structural Biology Department before joining S.T.A.R. Labs to supervise their top-security Red Room in Detroit: A research repository for extraterrestrial, futuristic, and arcane technologies too dangerous for public knowledge. As a result of his discoveries, Ivo developed the A-Maze Operating System, which created machines able to mimic organic life at a cellular level. Ivo is terrified of dying and much of his research stems from a determination to live forever. He constructed the android Amazo to replicate the powers of the Justice League, and subsequently developed a serum that greatly enhanced his lifespan. So severe was his phobia that he cared little when it monstrously mutated his body. Fully embracing his evil side, he returned to constructing killer-androids and worked with the transdimensional Outsider in the Secret Society of Super-Villains.

With the return of Mother Perpetua, Ivo captured and tried to vivisect Martian Manhunter J'onn J'onnz, seeking to use his unique biology to create Apex Predators, composed of human and Martian DNA.

ON THE RECORD

Teenage US President Prez Rickard debuted in 1973, working tirelessly to make America a cooler, hipper, and more surreal place. His idealistic vision for the Land of the Free was bitterly contested by vested corporate interests—exemplified by Boss Smiley—and his tenure was plagued by various bizarre attacks. He was even saved from a marauding witch by Supergirl. His legacy in the modern, post-*Flashpoint* re-imagining can be seen in the person of Vice-President Preston Rickard.

DEMOCRACY IN ACTION
Prez was elected after the voting age was lowered to include teenagers, and he stormed in on a "Youth Protest" landslide.

ON THE RECORD

In his first incarnation, Professor Ivo was one of the Justice League of America's most pernicious foes. His quest for immortality and expertise in creating robots and androids tested the heroes many times, and he was the man responsible for the JLA's biggest body-count.

When a stripped-down JLA relocated to Detroit, they were targeted by an army of Ivo's killer-droids, which murdered Vibe and Steel, and caused the despondent team to disband.

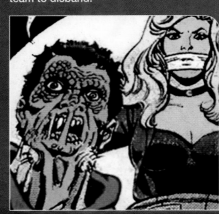

ETERNAL ENEMY
Ivo battled the JLA so often that he lost his mind and his humanity, until all that remained was hatred and madness.

PRINCESS PROJECTRA

DEBUT *Adventure Comics* #346 (Jul. 1966)
REAL NAME Dr. Wilimena Morgana Daergina
Annaxandra Projectra Velorya Vauxhall
BASE Legion HQ, 31st-century New Metropolis
HEIGHT 5ft 6in
WEIGHT 130 lbs
EYES Purple
HAIR Lavender
POWERS/ABILITIES hyper-real illusion
caster; strong sensory perceptions
ENEMIES Horraz, Crav the General Nah,
Mordru
AFFILIATIONS Legion of Super-Heroes,
royal family of Orando

ROYAL LEGIONNAIRE
Princess Projectra resigned following
the murder of her husband Karate Kid,
but she later returned to the Legion
in the guise of Sensor Girl.

Scion of the royal family on her homeworld
of Orando, Princess Projectra was devoted
to Earth's legendary Age of Heroes. Despite
being a child of unmatched privilege and
one of the wealthiest sentient beings in
the United Planets, Wilimena Morgana
Daergina voraciously studied history, and
earned doctorates in Ancient Studies for
Earth, Mars, and Thanagar. She was simply
in love with the concept of heroes and
jumped at the opportunity to become
one with the burgeoning Legion of
Super-Heroes.

Sleek, poised, and confident, she
offered to personally fund the Legion, but
is rather ill-at ease with her commoner
comrades. She even acknowledged to
Saturn Girl that joining the team would
benefit her own emotional growth.

PROFESSOR PYG

DEBUT *Batman* #666 (Jul. 2007)
REAL NAME Lazlo Valentin
BASE Gotham City
HEIGHT 5ft 11in **WEIGHT** 195 lbs
EYES Brown **HAIR** Brown
POWERS/ABILITIES Skilled surgeon
ALLIES Scarecrow, Bane
ENEMIES Batman
AFFILIATIONS Circus of Strange, Secret Society
of Super-Villains

Driven insane by exposure to Doctor
Dedalus' Spyral labyrinth, Lazlo Valentin
became pig-mask-wearing Professor Pyg.
Committed to Arkham Asylum, he was
prevented from escaping during a riot by
Batman and Nightwing. When the Crime
Syndicate of America's attack diverted
attention from Arkham, Pyg did escape.

Pyg's exploits consisted of kidnapping
unfortunate Gotham City citizens and
performing bizarre surgeries on them before
adding doll-face masks that turned them
into obedient minions called Dollotrons. In
the lawless Gotham City created as Batman
and other heroes were drawn into fighting
the Crime Syndicate and Secret Society of
Super-Villains, Scarecrow struck a deal with
Pyg to use his army of Dollotrons, but soon
after, Bane slaughtered the Dollotrons, and
forced Pyg to work for him instead.

A driven free spirit, Pyg frequently opens
new "clinics." His latest foes have included
the Teen Titans, Red Hood and the Outlaws,
Nightwing, and Batman.

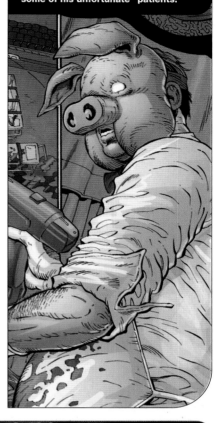

DRESSED TO KILL
In the pursuit of extreme medical
breakthroughs, Professor Pyg didn't
think twice about switching limbs on
some of his unfortunate "patients."

PROFESSOR ZOOM/REVERSE-FLASH

DEBUT *The Flash* (Vol. 1) #139 (Sep. 1963)
REAL NAME Eobard Thawne
BASE Central City; Keystone City in the year 2463
HEIGHT 6ft **WEIGHT** 195 lbs **EYES** Blue **HAIR** White
POWERS/ABILITIES Genius-level intellect; Future science Negative Speed
Force super-speed; manipulates time without affecting himself
ALLIES The Acolytes of Zoom
ENEMIES The Flash, Paradox
AFFILIATIONS Legion of Zoom

In the 25th century, orphan Eobard Thawne became obsessed
with ancient Super Hero The Flash. Finding a time capsule containing
his hero's uniform, Thawne engineered a Speed Force connection and
became a speedster hero, unaware that he had actually created a Negative
Speed Force that would impact all of reality. He also lacked enemies and
catastrophes to combat, and so began creating his own. When Barry Allen
visited his era, Thawne was initially ecstatic, but his admiration soured
when The Flash exposed Eobard's deception. After rehabilitation, Thawne
became a Professor and curator of The Flash Museum.

Refining his powers, "Professor Zoom," traveled back in time to win
The Flash's approval. Unfortunately, he discovered that the pair had no
special relationship. At heart a psychotic attention-seeker, Thawne felt
betrayed and determined to make Barry Allen's life a living hell.

Thawne's Negative Speed Force connection allowed him easy
access to all points in time, and he murdered Barry's mother and his
wife, Iris, altering time and reordering reality on a whim.

Thawne has been killed repeatedly too, but is virtually immune to
death, since he can simply attack his despised "betrayer" from different
moments in his own personal timeline. Thawne remains an unpredictable
and constant threat, a vicious Reverse-Flash bent on undoing all the good
Barry Allen has done, most recently corrupting his unborn future children
and assembling an army of Super-Villains into a Legion of Zoom.

ON THE RECORD

In his first appearance, Thawne
was called the Reverse-Flash, but for
much of his career was known as
Professor Zoom. Other pre-*Flashpoint*
villains had also called themselves
Zoom—each with a similar yellow
costume that was a reverse of The
Flash's; these included Citizen Abra, a
time-traveler from the 64th century,
and criminal profiler Hunter Zolomon.

NEED FOR SPEED
Thawne was obsessed with Barry Allen,
traversing timelines and dimensions to
carry on his maniacal battle against The
Flash and everything he loved.

PROMETHEUS

DEBUT *Prometheus* #1 (Dec. 1997)
BASE The Ghost Zone
HEIGHT 6ft 1in
WEIGHT 180 lbs
EYES Brown
HAIR White
POWERS/ABILITIES Genius intellect; technologically advanced armor and nightstick.
ENEMIES JLA, Batman, Midnighter, Vixen
AFFILIATIONS Injustice Gang

All that is known of Prometheus' history is that he witnessed his criminal parents gunned down in a fight with police, and devoted himself thereafter to destroying the forces of law and order.

He designed an armored suit with a cybernetic interface making him an expert martial artist, and established a base in the Ghost Zone. In the Zone, he built his Crooked House—a laboratory to develop technological resources. He also used his House as a base from which to strike out at the Justice League of America. He saw the JLA as the ultimate law-enforcement organization, and therefore most in need of destruction. A psychotic devotee of violence, Prometheus has bested the JLA singlehandedly at times, but has also been defeated by Catwoman and Green Arrow—proving advanced technology is not the only way to win a battle.

Unable to learn from his mistakes, his latest antihero schemes have been crushed by Midnighter and JLA member Vixen.

TECHNOLOGICAL PROWESS
Prometheus continually refined his armor. His computerized helmet was linked to his brain and he wielded an energized nightstick.

PSIONS

DEBUT *The Witching Hour* #13 (Feb.–Mar. 1971)
BASE Planet Maltus in the Vega Star System
HEIGHT Variable
WEIGHT Variable
EYES Yellow
HAIR None
POWERS/ABILITIES Genius-level scientific intelligence
ENEMIES Green Lantern Corps, Guardians
AFFILIATIONS Maltusian immortals

Created by Oans from bestial reptilians on planet Maltus, the Psions became ruthless experimenters just like their creators. Based on vast space science stations spread across the universe, Psions seek knowledge, stopping at nothing to further advance their technologies. They view their procedures on different species as a gift and strive to improve themselves through experimentation.

The Psions experimented on Tamaran Princess Koriand'r, unleashing her powers, and ran tests on the Guardian Quaros before Kyle Rayner and the New Guardians saved him. Quaros liberated other imprisoned Guardians before destroying the Psions, their long-suffering test subjects—and himself.

Psions monetize their obsessive research by hiring out to local powers, such as Harry Hokum. Whether testing Supergirl in deep space or weaponizing Earth citizens to test the progress of Starfire, their prime motivation seems to be expanding knowledge through terror and pain.

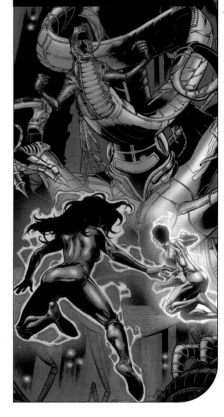

EXTRATERRESTRIAL TERROR
Psions never forget past research: Years after first torturing Starfire with their experiments, they returned to repeat and assess their procedures.

PRYSM

DEBUT *Teen Titans* (Vol. 2) #1 (Oct. 1996)
REAL NAME Audrey Spears
HEIGHT 6ft 4in
POWERS/ABILITIES Invisibility; energy absorption and projection of light.
ALLIES Argent II, Hot Spot, Risk
ENEMIES Warlord, H'San Natall
AFFILIATIONS Teen Titans

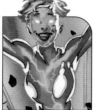

The alien H'San Natall created a human hybrid breeding program to install sleeper agents on Earth. One of these was Audrey Spears, who grew up inside a virtual fantasy world modeled on the popular shows of 1950s television. Escaping her artificial environment, she went to Earth with other hybrid teens Argent II, Hot Spot, and Risk, adopting the name Prysm for her ability to manipulate light. She later founded the post-*Zero Hour* Teen Titans.

Prysm hated the glassy appearance of her crystalline body structure, caused by the interaction of human and H'San Natall genomes. After meeting her true parents, she convinced the H'San Natall to stop their infiltration of Earth, and then remained with her parents in space, never feeling at home on Earth, nor with her hybrid teammates—particularly Risk, for whom she nursed unrequited romantic feelings.

PSIMON

DEBUT *New Teen Titans* (Vol. 1) #3 (Jan. 1981)
REAL NAME Simon Jones
HEIGHT 5ft 11in **WEIGHT** 145 lbs
EYES White **HAIR** None
POWERS/ABILITIES Immense telepathic and telekinetic powers; mind control
ALLIES Trigon, Doctor Siva, Troia
ENEMIES Teen Titans, Outsiders
AFFILIATIONS Fearsome Five, Injustice League, H.I.V.E.

During an experiment designed to breach dimensional barriers, physicist Simon Jones was struck by a beam of energy, which gave him psionic powers. As Psimon, he joined the Fearsome Five, often battling the New Teen Titans, where Raven discovered the source of Jones' power and that he was an agent of her demon-lord father, Trigon. For failing to kill the heroes, Psimon was exiled by Trigon, but he escaped. He continued to prey on humanity and was exiled to a prison planet alongside other Super-Villains. He proposed starting a civilization there instead of trying to escape. The Joker, unamused, crushed his head with a rock.

Post *Flashpoint*, Psimon was leading a scheme to steal and resell super-powers for H.I.V.E. and was eventually exposed as a pawn of future tyrannical conqueror Troia.

PSYCHO-PIRATE

DEBUT *All-Star Comics* #23 (Winter 1944–1945) (Charley Halstead); *Showcase* #56 (May–Jun. 1995) (Roger Hayden)
REAL NAME Roger Hayden
HEIGHT 6ft 1in **WEIGHT** 180 lbs
EYES Green **HAIR** Red
POWERS/ABILITIES Medusa Mask conveys ability to control others' emotions.
ALLIES Anti-Monitor, Bane
ENEMIES Power Girl, Black Adam, Amanda Waller, Hugo Strange

Roger Hayden was one of the Twenty—humans Brainiac bestowed psionic powers on. Hayden believed his Medusa Mask allowed him to control the virus. He escaped the H.I.V.E. Queen, who was draining the energies of the Twenty, and found Superman.

Hayden informed him Brainiac would use the Twenty as hosts for the minds of people from his destroyed home planet. Hayden tried to drain Superman's energy to free the Twenty, but Lois Lane defeated him.

Hayden was renditioned by Amanda Waller and conditioned by rogue psychiatrist Hugo Strange. Strange then used Hayden to attack Batman's Gotham Knights team before trading Psycho-Pirate to Bane for quantities of Venom. Hayden was extracted from Bane's base by a Batman black-ops team to cure a deranged Gotham Girl, but his powers were countered by Ventriloquist Arnold Wesker, whose multiple personalities were too much for the Medusa Mask.

EMOTIONAL CATHARSIS
After the death of original Psycho-Pirate, Charles Halstead, Roger Hayden used a single Medusa Mask to control the whole emotional spectrum.

PUNCHLINE

DEBUT *Batman* (Vol. 3) #89 **(Apr. 2020)**
REAL NAME Alexis Kaye   **BASE** Gotham City
HEIGHT Unknown   **WEIGHT** Unknown
EYES Green   **HAIR** Black
POWERS/ABILITIES Expert in making poisons
ALLIES The Joker
ENEMIES Batman
AFFILIATIONS None

Alexis Kaye was a disaffected college student, whose anger with the world she saw as falling apart around her made her the perfect acolyte for The Joker's nihilistic philosophy. She wanted to prove to her hero that she was not merely an obsessive fangirl, but a potential partner in crime. She created her own version of The Joker toxin and killed her college dean with it. The Joker, watching on from inside her wardrobe, was satisfied that Alexis—or Punchline, as she called herself—was up to the job of helping him in his next big plot against Batman.

It was not long before Punchline found herself face to face with her predecessor, Harley Quinn, and the two fought. Punchline cut Harley's throat, although Quinn was able to get herself patched up and back in the field to help Batman. As for the Dark Knight, Punchline had concocted a special toxin to take him out—a powerful combination of The Joker's recipe, Fear Toxin, and Venom. However, to Punchline's surprise, Harley managed to make an antidote using her knowledge of the plants in a secret garden Poison Ivy had built for her. Punchline escaped Batman's custody, but was later apprehended by Nightwing.

A POISONOUS PAIR
Punchline's obsession with The Joker led to her becoming his partner—in love and crime. This brought her into conflict with his ex, Harley Quinn.

QUEEN BEE

DEBUT *Justice League of America* (Vol. 1) #23 **(Nov. 1963)**
BASE Hiveworld Korll
HEIGHT 5ft 9in   **WEIGHT** 135 lbs
EYES Blue   **HAIR** Black
POWERS/ABILITIES Mind control; flight, superhuman speed and strength; hypno-pollen; alien technology; Magno-Nuclear rod; stinger gun
ALLIES The Cabal (Doctor Psycho, Hugo Strange, Amazo, Per Degaton)
ENEMIES Justice League, Plastic Man, Superman, Batgirl, Secret Six; Firestorm
AFFILIATIONS Anti-Justice League; Injustice Gang; Injustice League Unlimited; Secret Society of Super-Villains; H.I.V.E. (Holistic Integration for Viral Equality)

Intergalactic conqueror Zazzala of Korll has repeatedly attempted to enlarge her empire by enslaving humanity, but has always been thwarted, most frequently by the Justice League. In her earliest encounters she also sought ways to make herself and her drone armies immortal. However, repeated defeats at the hands of Super Heroes consumed her and she obsessively turned her insectoid traits—such as a hypnotic pollen created within her body and innate control over bees and other insects—to dominating the planet and species that has so frustrated her. She unsuccessfully allied with Lex Luthor and groups such as the Secret Society of Super-Villains before enacting her own criminal schemes as leader of covert multinational organisation the H.I.V.E.

After enduring further humiliating setbacks, she has retrenched—working to achieve her goals of global domination and human enslavement through a clandestine super-criminal Cabal that includes malignant telepath Doctor Psycho, warped psychologist Hugo Strange, terrorist Per Degaton and power-absorbing android Amazo. Even here, Zazzala's schemes have resulted in aggravation and setbacks, with as her latest machinations being foiled by pliable—and to her, ridiculous—opponent Plastic Man.

ON THE RECORD

Numerous female villains have used the title Queen Bee, beginning with 1940s gangster Lissa Raven Successors include thrill-seeking heiress Marcia Munroe—who battled Batman—and extradimensional tyrant Tazzala. Two anonymous* sisters usurped the Bialyan throne and shared the name when battling Justice League International. Following the *Flashpoint* event, a psionically-empowered Queen Bee ruled H.I.V.E.,one of 20 humans abducted and mutated by Brainiac, the Collector of Worlds. Her plans for enslaving humanity were eventually foiled by Superman.

HONEY TRAP
Queen Bee's purpose was liberating humanity from the pressures of free will, and she knew her biggest obstacle were its Super Heroes…

Q

QUEEN OF FABLES

DEBUT *Justice League of America* #47 (Nov. 2000)
REAL NAME Tsaritsa
HEIGHT 5ft 10in **WEIGHT** 130 lbs
EYES Green **HAIR** Red
POWERS/ABILITIES Vast magical abilities, including rearranging reality.
ENEMIES Justice League of America

Centuries ago, Tsaritsa, the Queen of Fables, arrived on Earth. She initiated a magical reign of terror until her enemy, Snow White, trapped her in the Book of Fables. At the dawn of the 21st century, Tsaritsa escaped to sow chaos in New York City by conjuring a horde of ogres, witches, and goblins. The Justice League of America clashed with Tsaritsa when she attacked Wonder Woman, believing the Amazon to be the daughter of her old nemesis because of Diana's physical resemblance to Snow White.

The Queen drew the JLA into the realm of fairy tales where they faced monsters on an enchanted Manhattan Island. Eventually, Wonder Woman used her lasso to defeat Tsaritsa, imprisoning her inside a new book—the United States Tax Code. However, she managed to free herself, and tried to seduce Superman and then turn a slanderous movie about Wonder Woman into the Amazon Queen's new reality.

QUICK, JOHNNY

DEBUT *More Fun Comics* #71 (Sep. 1941) (John Chambers); *Justice League of America* (Vol. 1) #29 (Aug. 1964) (Syndicate member); *Justice League* (Vol. 2) #23 (Oct. 2013) (Jonathan Allen)
REAL NAME Jonathan Allen
HEIGHT 5ft 11in **WEIGHT** 170 lbs
EYES Blue **HAIR** Blond
POWERS/ABILITIES Super-speed, concentrated and enhanced by a special helmet.

Jonathan Allen was trapped at a S.T.A.R. Labs facility when lightning struck. He gained superspeed and joined the Crime Syndicate of America. This was on Earth-3, a parallel world where evil was the dominant philosophy. When it was in danger, the Syndicate escaped to Prime Earth.

There, the Crime Syndicate tackled other foes. Johnny sent the Teen Titans into the future and killed Doom Patrol members but stumbled battling Super-Villains united to save the world. Captain Cold froze Quick's leg and Alexander Luthor—as Mazahs—broke his neck.

Following *Rebirth*, Earth-3 returned and Johnny Quick was resurrected in a reborn Syndicate. Apex Predator Lex Luthor invited them to join his Legion of Doom, but when Quick objected, Perpetua destroyed him.

QUESTION, THE

DEBUT *Blue Beetle* (Vol. 3) #1 (Jun. 1967)
BASE Mobile
REAL NAME Victor "Vic" Sage
HEIGHT 6ft 2in **WEIGHT** 185 lbs
EYES Blue **HAIR** Blonde
POWERS/ABILITIES Extensive martial arts training; incisive mind; detective skills; appearance and apparel altering gadgets.
ALLIES Lois Lane, Batman
ENEMIES Bible of Crime cult, Lady Shiva
AFFILIATIONS Justice League, Batman

ON THE RECORD

When *Crisis on Infinite Earths* first reshaped continuity, The Question migrated to Earth from another reality. His career ended when he died from cancer, but he ensured there would always be answers by training Gotham City detective Renee Montoya to become a new Question.

Following *Flashpoint*, The Question was reimagined as a mystic enigma. Eons ago—with Pandora and the Phantom Stranger—he faced the Council of Eternity to answer for his sins. Defiant and unrepentant, his punishment was having his identity and visage magically erased.

In modern times, he sought Pandora's Box, hoping to answer The Question of his identity. He united with the Phantom Stranger and Pandora as the Trinity of Sin, but eventually betrayed them. After this, he vanished, no one knows where.

NEXT QUESTION
Intrepid Gotham City detective Renee Montoya was unable to escape her strange destiny: to take on the role of the enigmatic Question.

Crusading reporter Vic Sage relentlessly confronted corruption and crime in Hub City, both in his public media persona and as The Question, a faceless vigilante who followed the dictates of his conscience but not necessarily the rule of law. He utilized his martial arts training and identity-masking gimmicks created by his old college professor Aristotle Rodor, but was helpless when targeted by the ultimate assassin Lady Shiva. She had been hired by the political elite Sage was constantly targeting.

Left to die, Sage was saved by Shiva, who saw his combat potential. She brought him to sensei Richard Dragon who trained him to master his body and mind. Sage returned to clean up Hub City before becoming a wanderer battling injustice by asking the right questions. Working with many Super Heroes, he is primarily a detective, consulting with Batman, the Justice League, and Superman who used his gifts to combat the invisible Mafia.

When Leviathan dramatically destroyed or subsumed most of the world's covert agencies, The Question joined a select team assembled by Batman and Lois Lane to unmask the mastermind behind the scheme.

TRINITY OF SIN
Phantom Stranger, Pandora, and The Question.

QUESTION, THE (RENEE MONTOYA)

DATA

DEBUT (as Montoya) Batman (Vol. 1) #475 (Mar. 1992)
(as The Question) 52 #48 (Apr. 2007)
BASE Gotham City
HEIGHT 5ft 8in   **WEIGHT** 144 lbs   **EYES** Brown   **HAIR** Black
POWERS/ABILITIES Very intelligent with strong set of ethics; natural team player; expertise in police procedure and knowledge of the law; skilled detective; excellent physical condition; expert martial artist; wears specialized mask that adheres to her face to hide her identity.
ALLIES Harvey Bullock, James Gordon, Batman, Batwoman, The Question, Lois Lane
ENEMIES Detective Nancy Yip, The Joker's Daughter
AFFILIATIONS Gotham City Police Department

ONE GOOD COP
Montoya was a no-nonsense cop and was one of the few people on the G.C.P.D. that could put the opinionated Harvey Bullock in his place.

A KEEN EYE
Montoya is a natural detective and not afraid of a fight. These traits made her very well suited to the rough-and-tumble policing of Gotham City.

Renee Montoya was a good and honorable cop, a rarity in Gotham City. Frequently partnered with the uncouth Harvey Bullock, Renee fought for her adopted city before feeling the call toward a different kind of heroics. Remembering a past version of herself from a time before a cosmic shift in reality, Renee became the faceless vigilante The Question again—for the first time.

A shining star during her Gotham City Police Department (G.C.P.D.) training, Renee Montoya was given Harvey Bullock as her superior and drill instructor. Renee's tenacity, quick wits, and drive soon earned her high marks, and her willingness to get involved in a brawl or two—as well as her extremely low tolerance for nonsense—put her in Bullock's good graces. After graduating, Renee opted not to stay in Gotham City. She moved to Blüdhaven, another city known for its high crime rate, and stayed there for a few years before returning to Gotham City and reuniting with her old mentor. She and Harvey picked up right where they left off, but this time as peers, and she once again became a valuable asset to the G.C.P.D. She helped fight against The Joker's Daughter as part of the Batman Task Force that supported Jim Gordon's tenure as Batman, and she also helped to root out Bullock's corrupt fellow officer and then girlfriend, Nancy Yip.

The DC Multiverse is often subject to reality-altering events, but few of its citizens realize that their own personal continuities have shifted around them. Renee, however, began to remember the pre-Flashpoint version of herself where she quit the police force and became the heroine called The Question. Recalling this past, Renee became The Question once more, and took a job gathering information for Lois Lane. She even began to work with Lois on the Unity Project, a service that offers to reconcile similar cases of broken identity due to timeline divergences for those who can also remember past realities.

ON THE RECORD

Before Flashpoint, Montoya began her career as an assistant to Commissioner James Gordon. The role came in advance of her part as a cop cast member in Batman: The Animated Series and Renee soon became a G.C.P.D. regular in the comics as Harvey Bullock's long-suffering partner. She became a Super Hero in her own right during the maxiseries 52, when her relationship with Batwoman Kate Kane was showcased, as was her protégé relationship with Vic Sage, the original Question. When The Question died, Montoya took his mantle, becoming the first female incarnation of that hero.

ANOTHER QUESTION
As the new Question, Renee Montoya adopted Vic Sage's signature blank face mask, which adhered to the skin when exposed to a chemical gas.

CLASSIC STORIES

***Gotham Central* #6–10 (Jun.–Oct. 2003)** Renee is revealed to be gay, while struggling to fight off the attentions of the obsessed Two-Face.

***Gotham Central* #38–40 (Feb.–Apr. 2006)** Montoya quits the Gotham City Police force after nearly killing a corrupt police officer, Jimmy Corrigan.

***52* #1–52 (May 2006–May 2007)** Montoya goes from life as an alcoholic to one as a Super Hero, stepping up to the plate as the new Question.

***Detective Comics* (Vol. 2) #41–44 (Aug.–Nov. 2015)** Montoya returns to the G.C.P.D. to join the Batman Task Force after years of serving on the Blüdhaven police force.

R.E.B.E.L.S.

DEBUT *R.E.B.E.L.S.* (Vol. 1) #0 (Oct. 1994)
REAL NAME Revolutionary Elite Brigade to Eradicate L.E.G.I.O.N. Supremacy
NOTABLE MEMBERS/POWERS Vril Dox II: Cloned son of Brainiac;
Phase: Can pass through solid matter; **Starfire:** Tamaranean
powers; **Lobo:** Czarnian powers, expert combatant;
Tribulus: Lightning generation and super-strength;
Adam Strange: Tactical expert, planetary adventurer;
Captain Comet: Pinnacle of human evolution with
multiple superpowers; **Wildstar:** Genetically-
altered human with superhuman abilities;
Strata and **Garv:** Dryadan durability.

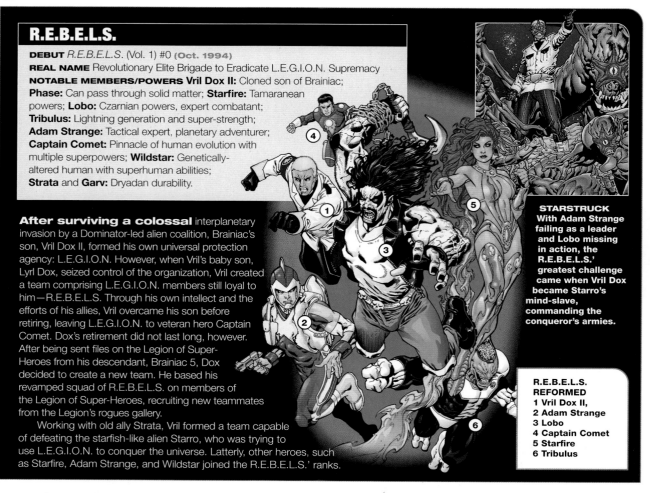

After surviving a colossal interplanetary
invasion by a Dominator-led alien coalition, Brainiac's
son, Vril Dox II, formed his own universal protection
agency: L.E.G.I.O.N. However, when Vril's baby son,
Lyrl Dox, seized control of the organization, Vril created
a team comprising L.E.G.I.O.N. members still loyal to
him—R.E.B.E.L.S. Through his own intellect and the
efforts of his allies, Vril overcame his son before
retiring, leaving L.E.G.I.O.N. to veteran hero Captain
Comet. Dox's retirement did not last long, however.
After being sent files on the Legion of Super-
Heroes from his descendant, Brainiac 5, Dox
decided to create a new team. He based his
revamped squad of R.E.B.E.L.S. on members of
the Legion of Super-Heroes, recruiting new teammates
from the Legion's rogues gallery.
    Working with old ally Strata, Vril formed a team capable
of defeating the starfish-like alien Starro, who was trying to
use L.E.G.I.O.N. to conquer the universe. Latterly, other heroes, such
as Starfire, Adam Strange, and Wildstar joined the R.E.B.E.L.S.' ranks.

STARSTRUCK
With Adam Strange
failing as a leader
and Lobo missing
in action, the
R.E.B.E.L.S.'
greatest challenge
came when Vril Dox
became Starro's
mind-slave,
commanding the
conqueror's armies.

**R.E.B.E.L.S.
REFORMED**
1 Vril Dox II,
2 Adam Strange
3 Lobo
4 Captain Comet
5 Starfire
6 Tribulus

RAVAGER

DEBUT *Deathstroke the Terminator* (Vol. 1) #15
(Oct. 1992)
REAL NAME Rose Wilson **BASE** Mobile
HEIGHT Unknown **WEIGHT** Unknown
EYES Blue **HAIR** White
POWERS/ABILITIES Martial-arts expert;
precognitive ability
ALLIES Jericho, Wintergreen,
Deathstroke, Hosun Park
ENEMIES Shado, Deathstroke
(Dark Multiverse)
AFFILIATIONS None

Rose Wilson was
Deathstroke's
daughter. Her father
kept Rose at arm's
length, fearing close
association with him
could be dangerous
for the girl, but Rose
grew to be more than capable of fighting
her own battles. Trained by Nightwing,
she had also inherited her father's
metagene, giving her a range of enhanced
abilities, but additionally had a skill all of
her own—being able to see images
from her future.
    Rose took the codename of Ravager,
which formerly belonged to her late
half-brother, before deciding to abandon it
and simply use her real name. Rose had the
makings of a great hero, but often found
it hard to shake off the violent influence of
her father, whom she still wanted to please.

RAGDOLL

DEBUT *Villains United* #1 (Jul. 2005)
REAL NAME Peter Merkel, Jr.
HEIGHT 5ft 11in **WEIGHT** 73 lbs
EYES Gray **HAIR** Red
POWERS/ABILITIES Superhumanly agile
ALLIES Black Alice, Catman, Jeannette
ENEMIES Batgirl, The Riddler
AFFILIATIONS Secret Six, Suicide Squad,
Legion of Zoom

When criminal Rag
Doll (Peter Merkel)
vanished, his
deranged son—also
Ragdoll—stepped into
his shoes. Merkel, Jr.
endured multiple
surgeries to achieve
his contortionist abilities and needs special
ointment to stop his skin splitting.
    Ragdoll participated in Bane's Blackgate
Penitentiary riot, before battling Batgirl after
her activist roommate was misled into
performing an act of terrorism. Shortly after,
The Riddler coerced him into fighting the
Secret Six by withholding his skin ointment.
Fortunately, the team outwitted The Riddler,
and Merkel, Jr. helped them and Scandal
Savage protect Black Alice from persecution
by the magical community. A mercenary with
the Secret Six, Ragdoll battled Plastic Man
before being killed on a Suicide Squad
mission. After being plucked from his own
past timeline, he joined the Legion of Zoom
to battle The Flash and remains at large.

RAGMAN

DEBUT *Ragman* (Vol. 1) #1 (Aug.–Sep. 1976)
REAL NAME Rory Regan
BASE Gotham City
POWERS/ABILITIES His sentient demonic
mantle suit of rags imparts superhuman speed,
strength, agility, and healing powers; demon sight
and perceptions; feeds on souls and emotions.
ALLIES Batman, Batwoman, Clayface
ENEMIES Morgaine le Fey, Nocturna
AFFILIATIONS Etrigan the Demon

War veteran Rory
Regan was the only
survivor of his unit.
His buddies died and
were sucked into the
Suit of Souls they
found in an ancient
desert vault. They
stayed inside Regan's head when he
returned to Gotham City, followed by an
army of demons seeking to reclaim the rags
that had bonded with him.
    Regan was now inextricably linked to a
Mantle of Hell: demonic armor that absorbed
souls to generate power. Able to steal the
life of living and never-born humans and
demons, Rory, his ex-wife, and child were
prey for various factions trying to retrieve it.
    Determined to atone for his sins, Regan
began fighting evil, encountering Batwoman
and other heroes. Briefly taking advice from
demon Etrigan, it became clear that all he
could depend on were his instincts and the
advice of the dead soldiers in his head.

RANKORR

DEBUT *Red Lanterns* #1 (Nov. 2011)
REAL NAME John (Jack) Moore
BASE Ysmault, Space Sector 666
HEIGHT 5ft 10in **WEIGHT** 166 lbs
EYES Green **HAIR** Red (formerly black)
POWERS/ABILITIES Possesses a
rage-fueled Red Lantern power ring.
ALLIES Atrocitus, Bleez, Guy Gardner
ENEMIES Lobo, Mr. Baxter
AFFILIATIONS Red Lantern Corps

John Moore and his
brother Ray were
raised in the United
Kingdom by their
grandfather. The
brothers reacted in
very different ways
when their grandfather
was murdered by a street thug named
Baxter. John tried to keep his grief to
himself, while the more volatile Ray furiously
claimed the police were covering up for the
killer. John then witnessed the police beat
his brother to death. This act released all the
pent-up rage in John, and at that moment,
a Red Lantern ring flew onto his finger and
John became the Red Lantern Rankorr.
    Rankorr tracked Baxter down, but before
he could kill him, John was whisked away
to Ysmault, the Red Lanterns' homeworld.
As an Earthling, Rankorr had to fight hard to
win the respect of Atrocitus and other Corps
members. After serving bravely, he met his
death at the hands of Lobo.

RAVAGERS, THE

DEBUT *The Ravagers* #1 (Jul. 2012)
BASE Los Angeles, California
NOTABLE MEMBERS/POWERS
Fairchild: Scientist, superhuman strength;
Terra: Geokinesis, flight; **Beast Boy:** Can
transform into any animal; **Thunder:** Creates
sound-wave blasts; **Lightning:** Electrokinesis;
Ridge: Super-strong and super-durable.
ALLIES Niles Caulder, Superboy, Teen Titans
ENEMIES Deathstroke, Harvest

While working for the
demented Super-
Villain Harvest,
scientist Caitlin
Fairchild's clone
helped a group of
Harvest's prisoners
escape. One of these
was Ridge, a member of Harvest's elite
personal army known as The Ravagers. In
defiance at their incarceration, the young
heroes adopted the name Ravagers and
briefly set up shop at Dr. Niles Caulder's
secret headquarters in Los Angeles.
    Soon after, their makeshift home was
invaded by Harvest's own Ravagers, Rose
Wilson and Warblade, and the assassin
Deathstroke. The heroes fought valiantly, but
were overcome by Deathstroke who took
them back to Harvest—except for Beast
Boy, whom Deathstroke believed to be
dead. The rest of the team, aside from Terra,
remained with Harvest until the villain's
defeat by the Teen Titans.

RĀ'S AL GHŪL

DATA

DEBUT *Batman* (Vol. 1) #232 **(Jun. 1971)**
BASE 'Eth Alth'eban
HEIGHT 6ft 5in **WEIGHT** 215 lbs
EYES Green **HAIR** Black with white streaks
POWERS/ABILITIES Expert swordsman and martial artist; extremely long lived thanks to his access to the age-retarding Lazarus Pits; genius-level intellect with a keen strategic skills; possesses an army of loyal assassins and many connections in nearly every nation on the globe.
ALLIES Talia al Ghūl
ENEMIES Batman, the Batman Family, Birds of Prey
AFFILIATIONS The League of Assassins

OUTLAW VS. OUTLAWS
Rā's al Ghūl clashed with Red Hood and The Outlaws after Jason Todd was briefly invited to join the League of Assassins.

LEGENDS CLASH
Batman and Rā's al Ghūl have battled each other many times. Their very first encounter led to a savage swordfight in the desert, with Talia al Ghūl looking on.

He is the legendary figure whose name roughly translates as "The Demon's Head." A villain who has earned that name a thousand times over, Rā's al Ghūl is one of the world's most infamous eco-terrorists and the leader of the League of Assassins, an ancient organization based in the mystical city of 'Eth Alth'eban. Rā's wants nothing more than to save the Earth by killing off the majority of the humans that "plague" it.

The stories of Rā's al Ghūl stretch back more than 700 years, making it nearly impossible to discern fact from fiction. Through the frequent use of the mystical Lazarus Pits and their life-renewing properties, Rā's has been able to survive for centuries. His reach is wide, with connections in most major governments, but he wasn't always so powerful. Having left his nomadic tribe to pursue a scientific career in the city, the man who would become Rā's al Ghūl found work as a humble physician to a great sultan. While attempting to save the life of the sultan's son, the doctor discovered the properties of the Lazarus Pits.

Resurrected from death, the sultan's son became deranged and ran amok, killing the physician's wife. The sultan refused to admit his son's guilt and imprisoned the doctor in a cage with her corpse, expecting him to die under the desert sun. However, he was rescued by local rebels, men he soon led back to the sultan's palace in an uprising that saw the doctor take the name Rā's al Ghūl. Rā's formed the League of Assassins, and embarked on an eco-terrorist mission to cull humanity and "save" the planet from over-population and pollution. He also fathered a daughter, Talia, with a woman named Melisande.

The villainous League of Assassins' Dr. Ebenezer Darrk had a falling out with Rā's and kidnapped Talia. Batman rescued her, and Rā's decided that the Dark Knight would be the ideal son-in-law to take over his operations. Batman saw things differently, and the two became archenemies, united only by their mutual love for Talia, the "Daughter of the Demon."

ON THE RECORD

Rā's al Ghūl's origin and history have been revised more than once since his debut in the 1970s. Likewise, the Lazarus Pits that restore his vitality have changed markedly over the years.

At first, there was a single pit. Later, multiple green, bathtub-sized pools were linked to major ley lines of mystic energy, and each pit could only be used once. They soon evolved into a handful of large pools found around the world, including at the Batcave. Their properties remained the same, and they were responsible for resurrecting many characters, such as the Red Hood, The Riddler, Wonder Woman, and even Batman.

THE DEMON LAUGHS
The Joker once cheated death after a dip in the Lazarus Pits' life-giving waters. Unlike most people, who emerge violently deranged, The Joker "enjoyed" a moment of calm.

RETURNED TO LIFE
After immersing himself in the Lazarus Pits, Rā's al Ghūl is returned to the age and health of a man in his prime. The Pits' side effect of brief madness may have altered his outlook over time, making him ever more extreme in his tactics.

CLASSIC STORIES

***Batman* (Vol. 1) #232 (Jun. 1971)**
Mentioned in an earlier story, Rā's al Ghūl finally makes his debut, fabricating a mystery just to test Batman's skills.
***Detective Comics* (Vol. 1) #444–448 (Jan.–Jun. 1975)** Rā's al Ghūl frames Batman for murder in a story told over five issues, a rarity for the time.
***Batman: Birth of the Demon* #1 (Dec. 1992)** Rā's is given an origin, exploring his tragic fall from an honorable physician to a corrupt terrorist leader.
***Detective Comics* (Vol. 1) #700–702, *Catwoman* (Vol. 2) #36, *Robin* (Vol. 4) #32–33, *Batman: Shadow of the Bat* #53–54, *Batman* (Vol. 1) #533–534 (Aug.–Oct. 1996)** In the Legacy storyline, Batman discovers that the evil mastermind behind the horrific "Clench" plague in Gotham City is none other than Rā's al Ghūl, aided and abetted by his new lackey, Bane.

RAVEN

DATA

DEBUT *DC Comics Presents* #26 (Oct. 1980)
REAL NAME Rachel Roth
BASE New York City
HEIGHT 5ft 6in **WEIGHT** 110 lbs
EYES Blue **HAIR** Black
POWERS/ABILITIES Empathic sensitivity and healing abilities; manipulation of darkness; time travel; teleportation; flight; projection of Soul-Self; other undefined magical powers.
ALLIES Beast Boy, Kid Flash (Wallace West), Starfire, Nightwing
ENEMIES Trigon, Mother Blood
AFFILIATIONS Teen Titans, Titans

EARTH FAMILY
Adopting the name Rachel Roth, Raven has rediscovered her human side, often staying with the family of her Aunt Alice.

FATHER AND DAUGHTER
Raven was haunted by her father and struggled with her demonic nature and immense powers.

Daughter of the cosmic demon Trigon, Raven struggles to master the baser impulses she has inherited from him. While her father sees her as the key to his plans to consolidate his power, Raven uses her vast mystical and psychic abilities to battle evil in all its forms alongside her adopted families, the Teen Titans and the Titans.

Raven grew up in the realm of Azarath, protected by a mystical order of monks and taught to control the demonic influence of her father, Trigon. Knowing Trigon would be hunting for her, she fled Azarath for her mother Arella's home planet, Earth, where she went into hiding. Raven eventually joined the Teen Titans alongside Wonder Girl (Cassie Sandsmark), Red Robin (Tim Drake), Best Boy, and Bunker. While the team's roster would change over the years, Raven learned to let her guard down and accept their friendship.

When the Titans parted ways, the newest Robin (Damian Wayne) saw an opportunity to form his own personal team. He captured Raven, Beast Boy, Starfire, and Kid Flash (Wallace West), and convinced them they were better working as a team than working individually. Raven stayed on with this version of the Teen Titans, and began to form a romantic relationship with Kid Flash.

When the mysterious Source Wall was damaged at the furthest reaches of known space, strange Source energy began transforming innocent civilians. To help those affected, Nightwing formed a Justice League-sanctioned branch of the Titans and quickly recruited Raven. During her tenure on the team, Raven was separated from her Soul-Self—the source of her powers—but overcame her attempted corruption at the hands of villain Mother Blood. She rejoined with her other half and her Titans family.

ON THE RECORD

A touchstone of Raven's story has always been her relationship with Beast Boy. They became close immediately after she gathered the New Teen Titans, and their attachment blossomed into romance after her death and rebirth in a new body.

When her relationship with Beast Boy fell apart, and following the death of Kid Flash (Bart Allen) and the battle with Titans East, Raven left the team. She later returned seeking help after being attacked by Wyld, a demonic being she had inadvertently created. She rekindled her relationship with Beast Boy after they had fought side by side to defeat Superboy-Prime.

HER BEST BOY
Following a close call with Brother Blood, who had attempted to marry her, Raven began a relationship with fellow Teen Titan, Beast Boy, which continued on-and-off for several years.

CLASSIC STORIES

New Teen Titans (Vol. 1) #4–6 (Feb.–Apr. 1981) Raven asks the Justice League to help her against her father, but they refuse because Zatanna doesn't trust Raven. She brings together the New Teen Titans, who imprison Trigon.
New Titans (Vol. 2) #121–130 (May 1995–Feb. 1996) Surrendering to Trigon's influence, Raven implants the seeds of his dead children into new bodies, spreading evil. One of the seeds turns out to be the soul of her own good self.
Teen Titans (Vol. 3) #30–31 (Jan.–Feb.) 2006 After narrowly escaping marriage to Brother Blood and triggering armageddon, Raven joins the Teen Titans to combat Blood and his demonic army.

RAVERS

DEBUT *Superboy and the Ravers* #1 (Sep. 1996)
BASE Event Horizon
MEMBERS/POWERS Superboy: flight, super-strength; **Kaliber**: Quardian with shrinking and growing powers; **Aura**: powerful magnetic abilities; **Hero Cruz**: force-field generated from Achilles Vest, H-Dial allows transformation into a Super Hero identity; **Rex, the Wonder Dog**: enhanced intelligence; **Sparx**: wields electricity.
ALLIES Highfather
ENEMIES InterC.E.P.T., Darkseid

The Event Horizon was a mobile, intergalactic party frequented by cliques of teens invited by club owner Kindred Marx—the catch was that only those with superpowers could get in. The Ravers, led by Superboy, were the most outrageous of the club's regulars.

By touching their hand-stamps, team members could teleport to the Event Horizon from anywhere in the universe. The Ravers came into conflict with rival clique Red Shift and the interdimensional police force known as InterC.E.P.T. They also helped Highfather of New Genesis foil Darkseid's attempts to tap into the power of the Source.

After the Raver Half-Life perished in a battle against the Qwardians of the Antimatter Universe, Kindred Marx closed down the Event Horizon, and most of the Ravers went their separate ways.

RAY, THE

DEBUT *Smash Comics* #14 (Sep. 1940)
REAL NAME Ray Terrill
BASE Vanity, Oregon
HEIGHT 5ft 9in **WEIGHT** 165 lbs **EYES** Brown **HAIR** Black
POWERS/ABILITIES Absorption and projection of light and electricity, flight, invisibility, other light and energy-derived powers.
ALLIES Caden Zapote, Batman, Aztek
ENEMIES Doctor Polaris, Sons of Liberty
AFFILIATIONS Justice League of America

New York Star **reporter** Lanford "Happy" Terrill, became the first Ray after being transformed by scientist Dr. Dayzl. Happy's son, Joshua, inherited his father's powers and became Ray's sidekick, Spitfire, before killing his mother in a tragic accident. Happy remarried and his second son Raymond also inherited light powers. The youthful hero later exposed the third Ray, Stan Silver, as a traitor within the ranks of the Freedom Fighters.

Some years ago, young Ray Terrill was told he was allergic to light and exposure would kill him, and grew up isolated and in darkness. When his only friend, Caden, used a camera flash while taking a picture, Ray crackled with energy and his mother told him he had hospitalized and probably killed Caden.

As a teen, "night boy" Ray ran away from home and discovered he had powers fueled by light absorption—including flight and invisibility—but would not explode and die. Constantly on the road, he eventually reached Vanity, Oregon, where Caden was running for Mayor. Watching invisibly, Ray saw Sons of Liberty terrorists try to murder Caden and exploded into bright, brilliant action to save him. Finding purpose at last, Ray remained as the local Super Hero. He was eventually recruited by Batman for his Justice League of America.

ON THE RECORD

Lucien Gates was transformed when hit by a particle beam. He learned he could fly, but only in a straight line—a reflective surface was needed to change his path.

Lucien's parents taught him to control his powers through meditation. He fought other creations of the misfired beam before it emerged these battles were staged by villain Thaddeus Filmore. Lucien defeated Filmore and remade his personality with light hypnotherapy. Lucien was then recruited into a new hero team under the auspices of S.H.A.D.E.

NIGHT BOY
Before realizing he had light-based superpowers, Raymond Terrill was known as Night Boy because he only came out when it was dark.

RED ARROW

DEBUT *Green Arrow* #18 (May 2013)
BASE Seattle/Star City
REAL NAME Emiko Queen
HEIGHT 5ft 2in **WEIGHT** 100 lbs
EYES Brown **HAIR** Black
POWERS/ABILITIES Skilled archer; acrobat; and hand-to-hand combatant.
ALLIES Green Arrow, Black Canary
ENEMIES Komodo, Shado, The Underground Men
AFFILIATIONS Teen Titan

KILLER QUEEN
After first joining forces with her brother Oliver, Emiko fought him to be the next Green Arrow—until, like most siblings, they made their peace.

The half-sister of Oliver Queen and daughter of archer-assassin Shado, Emiko Queen was kidnapped as an infant and reared by Komodo. Trained as an archer, Emiko wounded Green Arrow in her first battle, unaware of their family ties. Raised believing her parents were dead, she learned the truth when she saw them at The Outsiders' headquarters. Enraged, she turned on Komodo, but in the ensuing battle, her father, Robert Queen, was killed. Emiko then executed Komodo, and traveled to Seattle to aid Oliver against the Longbow Hunters.

Emiko wanted the title Green Arrow but Oliver resisted. He trained Emiko until she was ready to strike out on her own. As Red Arrow, Emiko fought alongside Green Arrow and Black Canary to defeat the Underground Men. Their partnership was short-lived, and Emiko reunited with her mother to attack Oliver. However, Emiko later rejected Shado to carve out her own path singly, with Oliver, and as part of the Teen Titans.

RED CLOUD

DEBUT *DC Nation* Vol 2 #0 (Jul. 2018)
REAL NAME Robinson Goode
BASE Metropolis
HEIGHT Unknown
WEIGHT Unknown
EYES Green **HAIR** Black
POWERS/ABILITIES Can transform into an intangible being, attacking even the strongest opponents by getting into their airways.
ALLIES Marisol Leone, Lex Luthor
ENEMIES Superman
AFFILIATIONS Invisible Mafia, Legion of Doom, Leviathan

Robinson Goode was a rookie reporter for the *Star Sentinel* newspaper when she stumbled into a top-secret experiment at S.T.A.R. Labs. She was tossed into a strange red gas and was transformed into the Red Cloud, an intangible being of immense power. She became an enforcer for the gangs of Metropolis, working for an organization called the Invisible Mafia.

However, in her Robinson Goode form, she also got a job at *The Daily Planet*, trying to ensure that the Invisible Mafia remained off the media radar. Red Cloud could hold her own against Superman, thanks to her intangibility, making her a valuable recruit for Lex Luthor's Legion of Doom.

RED DEVIL

DEBUT *The Fury of Firestorm* #24 (Jun. 1984) (as Eddie); *Blue Devil* #14 (Jul. 1985) (as Kid Devil)
REAL NAME Edward Alan Bloomberg
POWERS/ABILITIES Demonic power; flame breath; superhuman strength; burning skin
ALLIES Blue Devil, Rose Wilson, Zachary Zatara
ENEMIES Niles Caulder, Kid Crusader
AFFILIATIONS Teen Titans, Young Justice

Before meeting Daniel Cassidy, Eddie Bloomberg—a gopher in his aunt's film production company—dreamed of being an actor. Once he saw Cassidy's Blue Devil in action, however, Eddie would settle for nothing less than being a hero. At first, he used Cassidy's special effects as Kid Devil, acting as his idol's sidekick—but with little success or approval. Demon Neron offered Eddie true power in exchange for his soul—a trade he soon came to regret.

After losing his powers, Eddie returned to Hell and discovered Neron had only activated his metagene and never truly bestowed demonic abilities. Even without powers, Eddie continued to assist the Teen Titans, ultimately sacrificing his life to save theirs. He was resurrected following Rebirth, only to be killed by the original Wally West during a murder spree at the Super Hero Mental Health facility, the Sanctuary.

RED HOOD

DEBUT *Batman* (Vol. 1) #357 (Mar. 1983)
REAL NAME Jason Todd
BASE Mobile
HEIGHT 6ft **WEIGHT** 200 lbs **EYES** Blue **HAIR** Black
POWERS/ABILITIES Expert martial artist trained by Batman and secret order All-Caste; skilled detective and gymnast; street smart and a natural leader; expert marksman
ALLIES Bizarro, Artemis, Starfire, Arsenal, Batman
ENEMIES Untitled, Rā's al Ghūl, Black Mask
AFFILIATIONS The Outlaws

Jason Todd was the second Robin, and easily the most troubled. Angry and with a desperate need to prove himself, Jason's impulsive behavior led to his death at the hands of The Joker. Resurrected to become the heroic Red Hood, Jason now walks his own path, learning to handle the anger that forged him.

Batman knew Jason Todd was bold when Jason stole the tires off the Batmobile. With his dad in prison and his mother presumed dead, teenage Jason was trying to get by any way he could on the streets of Crime Alley. When Batman caught Jason red-handed, instead of punishing the boy, he bought him dinner. After enrolling Jason in Ma Gunn's School for Wayward Boys and then soon discovering Ma Gunn was running a secret crime ring from her orphanage, Batman took Jason in as the ward of his secret identity, Bruce Wayne. Batman trained Jason, and the sharp teen became the second Robin, replacing Dick Grayson, who had left to join the Teen Titans and would rename himself Nightwing.

Jason always had an edge to him, and that unchecked rage would soon lead to his death. When Jason discovered his mother was alive, he tracked her down, only to be brutally killed by The Joker. Through the help of Talia al Ghūl and the restorative properties of the Lazarus Pits, Jason was reborn. Angry at Batman for not punishing The Joker more severely for his death, Jason adopted the identity of the Red Hood, a name associated with The Joker's early years in Gotham City. He then set out to fight crime by breaking two of Batman's most important rules: no guns, and no killing.

The Red Hood would eventually form The Outlaws, a team of likeminded vigilantes. Jason has matured and mellowed a bit because of their companionship, although his methods are still much too severe for Batman's tastes.

ROBIN HOOD
Red Hood opted for a more literal interpretation of his name when he abandoned his red helmet for a lighter-weight hood.

ON THE RECORD

In his earliest appearances before *Crisis on Infinite Earths*, Jason Todd was a veritable clone of Dick Grayson. His parents were aerialists, and when they were murdered by Killer Croc, he joined Batman's war on crime. He adopted a costume exactly like that of Dick Grayson, and even dyed his hair black.

Jason was killed in the memorable "A Death in the Family" storyline, and remained that way for years, before being resurrected thanks not just to Talia al Ghūl's machinations, but also Superboy Prime shattering reality.

CALL-IN KILLER
Readers were urged to call in to a special DC 1-900 number to vote for whether Jason lived or died. A version of Jason surviving The Joker's handiwork was also drawn, owing to the uncertainty of the poll's outcome.

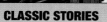

CLASSIC STORIES

Batman **(Vol. 1) #426-429 (Dec. 1988–Jan. 1989)** The Joker murders Jason Todd with a crowbar and an explosion in the momentous "A Death in the Family."

Batman **(Vol. 1) #635-638 (Feb.–May. 2005)** In the four-part "Under the Hood" story, Jason Todd makes his full return as the Red Hood, shocking his mentor in the process.

Red Hood: The Lost Days **#1-6 (Aug. 2010– Jan. 2011)** Jason's resurrection is expanded and further explained in his first solo miniseries.

RED LANTERN CORPS

DEBUT *Green Lantern* (Vol. 4) #25 (Jan. 2008)
BASE Styge Prime, Ysmault
MEMBERS All Corps members are able to vomit blazing bile; wearing Red Lantern rings affords flight, full environmental protection, intergalactic transportation, translation, violent energy projection, and hard-light constructs if the wielder can focus their thoughts. **Atrocitus**: Immortal magician; **Bleez**: Abused alien princess; **Rankorr**: Outraged Earthman; **Ratchett**: Tentacular Brain; **Vice**: Insectoid flesh-ripper; **Dex-Starr**: Incensed cat from Brooklyn; **Skallox**: Incinerated enhanced interrogator; **Zilius Zox**: Ball of fury; **Guy Gardner**: Undercover Emerald Warrior; **Kara Zor-El/Supergirl**: Constantly betrayed and marginalized Kryptonian.
ENEMIES Sinestro Corps, Green Lantern Corps, Blue Lantern Corps, Third Army, Volthoom, Relic, Guardians of the Universe, Black Lantern Corps, Krona, The Wheel
AFFILIATIONS Star Sapphire Corps

Atrocitus is one of "Five Inversions" who survived the Massacre of Sector 666. Manhunter robots carried out the slaughter, but Atrocitus held their creators, the Guardians of the Universe, responsible. Imprisoned for billions of years on Ysmault as part of the Oans' furtive cover-up, Atrocitus eventually broke free and, through magic and the blood of his fellow captives, harnessed his boiling fury.

Building a Central Power Battery to tap the Emotional Spectrum's light of Rage, he dispatched red power rings to find beings similarly wronged and driven by a hunger for retribution. All across the universe, Red Lanterns began exacting fearful vengeance on those deemed to have escaped justice. Their rings constantly stoked their blazing fury.

Possession by a red power ring lasts a lifetime. The bonding is permanent, and the bearer dies in agony if it is removed. Like all Spectrum Warriors, Red Lanterns have their own oath to recite when recharging their rings:

"With blood and rage of crimson red,
Ripped from a corpse so freshly
dead, Together with our hellish hate,
We'll burn you all, that is your fate."

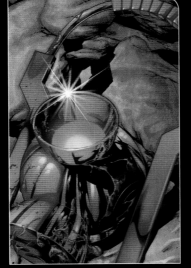

SEEING RED
Atrocitus assembled a fearsome force of ring bearers with a grudge.
1 Atrocitus
2 Bleez
3 Zilius Zox
4 Haggor
5 Ratchett
6 Skallox
7 Fury-6
8 Dex-Starr
9 Antipathy
10 Butcher (Rage entity)

ON THE RECORD

In pre-*Flashpoint* reality, Atrocitus became concerned that Red Lanterns were usually too consumed with rage to conceive or form light constructs with their rings to solve the situations they encountered. Instead, they would strike with a boiling napalm spew of crimson bile generated from within their bodies. Atrocitus eventually devised a way to restore a degree of rationality to his furious fellows by immersing them in the blood-pool on Ysmault.

THERE WILL BE BLOOD
Atrocitus murdered his fellow Five Inversions and used their blood to power the Red Lanterns' Central Battery. Before long, Hal Jordan and the Green Lantern Corps would feel the wrath of the Red Lantern Corps.

RED BADGE OF COURAGE
Red Lanterns are utterly fearless. Hunger for bloody justice fills them with a fiery fury, blinding them to everything except their targets.

ALL THE RAGE
Even a truly dedicated warrior like Guy Gardner lost all composure when filled with the scalding scarlet fire of Rage.

RED STAR

DEBUT *Teen Titans* (Vol. 1) #18 (Nov.–Dec. 1968) (as Starfire)
REAL NAME Leonid Konstantinovitch Kovar
BASE Moscow, Russia
HEIGHT 5ft 10in **WEIGHT** 180 lbs
EYES Green **HAIR** Blond
POWERS/ABILITIES Super-strength, speed, endurance, flight and pyrokinesis; trained scientist and researcher.
ENEMIES Le Blanc, Hammer and Sickle, Doctor Light, Superboy-Prime

With his Russian archaeologist father, Leonid Kovar was investigating a crashed alien vessel when it exploded. As a result, Leonid developed superhuman powers. He offered his services to the state and became Russia's first official Super Hero, Starfire.

While tracking international thief Le Blanc, he met the Teen Titans, subsequently changing his codename to Red Star. When Leonid left Russia to join the Titans, he formed a close relationship with were-woman Pantha and her foster-son, Baby Wildebeest.

Leonid returned to fight crime in his homeland, mostly over the objections of the Russian rulers. However, when the *Doomsday Clock* event triggered an international incident, Red Star grudgingly joined Russia's Peoples Heroes and battled Superman and Firestorm.

FULL CIRCLE
Russian Super Hero Starfire joined the Teen Titans as Red Star, before reluctantly resuming Russian government employ.

RED TORNADO

DEBUT *All American Comics* (Vol. 1) #3 **(Jun. 1939)** (Ma Hunkel); *Justice League of America* (Vol. 1) #64 **(Aug. 1968)** (Android John Smith); *World's Finest* (Vol. 1) #0 **(Nov. 2012)** (android Lois Lane)
POWERS/ABILITIES Generation of super-speed vortexes, flight, limited invisibility, enhanced strength and durability, air blasts and impact-deflection; computerized mind, enhanced senses.
ALLIES Red Volcano, Red Torpedo, Red Inferno, Cyborg, Will Magnus
ENEMIES T.O. Morrow, Amazo, Professor Ivo, Solomon Grundy, The Construct, Doctor Impossible

Red Tornado was constructed by Thomas Oscar Morrow to counteract the Super Heroes who interfered in his schemes. However, the android's frame was possessed by a wandering wind elemental, and achieved unanticipated power and sentience.

Joining the Justice League, "Reddy" enjoyed friendship and loyalty. He took on the human identity John Smith, married Kathy Sutton, and adopted a young orphan, Traya.

He has been destroyed and reconstructed repeatedly— with varying degrees of success—leading to serious impairment of function. He was operating on little more than instinct when coopted into the mystic rapid response squad Primal Force. However, after being appointed overseer and guardian of Young Justice, Red Tornado grew into a wise mentor.

Reddy longed to be human, but when an organic body was created for him, the mind-transfer process was subverted by Amazo and Professor Ivo.

After *Rebirth*, he became part of the Challengers of the Unknown, working with Carter Hall to solve the mystery of Nth Metal and holding back Dark Universe terror Barbatos. He also joined Earth's Super Heroes to help thwart Doctor Manhattan.

SPIN CYCLE
The man-made hero was a caring champion who treasured a humanity he could never share.

ON THE RECORD

After *Flashpoint*, Red Tornado was a robotic shell housing the personality of Earth-2's Lois Lane. When she was killed in the Apokolips invasion, her mind was uploaded to a machine that could generate cyclonic winds—a secret weapon assembled to fight Parademons.

Reunited with her foster-daughter Power Girl, Red Tornado led Earth-2's final fight against eradication, with the help of other doomed heroes such as substitute Batman Thomas Wayne, his granddaughter Huntress, and Kryptonian Val-Zod. Their brave efforts took the fight back to Darkseid, allowing humanity's last survivors to escape destruction in space arks.

STORMING IN
The newly created Red Tornado gatecrashed a Justice Society meeting and insisted he was once a member of the team.

REIGN

DEBUT *Supergirl* (Vol. 6) #5 (Mar. 2012)
EYES Black **HAIR** Red
POWERS/ABILITIES Superhuman strength, speed, and durability; highly advanced unarmed combat skills and swordsmanship, tactical and leadership training.
ALLIES Deimax, Perrilus, Flower of Heaven
ENEMIES Supergirl
AFFILIATIONS Worldkillers, Argo City

Reign was part of a clandestine Kryptonian experiment in which alien embryos were altered to create living weapons of vast power. They were designated Worldkillers after an ancient myth. Designed to fight and born to kill, five subjects were programmed with a hunger for destruction and gestated in a floating space laboratory. At some point, the scientists abandoned the project, leaving the subjects to grow to term in isolation. The newborns knew virtually nothing of their origins other than what could be gleaned from discarded datacores.

Reign, their leader, clashed with Supergirl in the ruins of Argo City when both went looking for answers. The Worldkiller quickly got the upper hand and Supergirl retreated to Earth. Reign followed, taking with her three companions, who wreaked havoc until Supergirl defeated them. Reign grudgingly withdrew, but swore to return.

RELIC

DEBUT *Green Lantern* (Vol. 5) #21 (Aug. 2013)
EYES White **HAIR** None
POWERS/ABILITIES Gigantic body, vast intellect, numerous technologies from another universe; manipulation and draining of all colors of Emotional Spectrum; powers of a New God.
ALLIES Highfather, Metron
ENEMIES Green Lantern Corps, White Lantern Kyle Rayner, Green Lantern Hal Jordan
AFFILIATIONS Lightsmiths, Black Lanterns

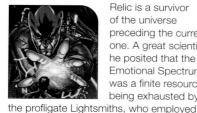

Relic is a survivor of the universe preceding the current one. A great scientist, he posited that the Emotional Spectrum was a finite resource being exhausted by the profligate Lightsmiths, who employed its colors as power sources. Ridiculed by his peers, he searched for the reservoir containing the emotional energies and found it in the Source Wall surrounding creation. The Lightsmiths went to war over the dwindling energies and his universe ended.

Relic was preserved in the Source and awoken by Kyle Rayner and the Templar Guardians. Seeing a new cosmos of beings making the same mistakes, Relic declared war on all Lantern Corps, resolved to save this universe. He destroyed Oa and then eradicated the Blue Lanterns before being trapped in the Source Wall, but was released by New Gods Highfather and Metron.

REPLICANT

DEBUT *The Flash Secret Files and Origins* (Vol. 1) #2 (Nov. 1999)
REAL NAME Anthony Gambi
BASE Keystone City
HEIGHT 7ft 5in **WEIGHT** 325 lbs
EYES Mirrored **HAIR** None
POWERS/ABILITIES Absorbs and replicates any technology or weaponry nearby.
ENEMIES The Flash, Dark Flash (Walter West), Uncle Sam and the Freedom Fighters
AFFILIATIONS The Rogues, S.H.A.D.E.

Anthony Gambi grew up around Super-Villains. With his mother dead and his father in jail, Tony lived with his uncle Paul, a tailor- turned-armorer who created and repaired the costumes of The Flash's arch foes the Rogues. They spoiled the boy, and Tony viewed them as modern-day Robin Hoods. When Captain Boomerang was crippled by a darker, more brutal Flash, Tony joined the Rogues. With powers provided by scientist T.O. Morrow, Tony could organically duplicate his idols' devices and weapons. As Replicant, Tony was soundly beaten by The Flash but escaped after discovering his newfound talent applied to any nearby technology. After allying with Abra Kadabra and inadvertently helping Wally West return, Replicant vanished. He was eventually captured by Father Time and S.H.A.D.E.

RESURRECTION MAN

DEBUT *Resurrection Man* (Vol. 1) #1 (May 1997)
REAL NAME Mitchell Shelley
HEIGHT 6ft 1in
WEIGHT 190 lbs
EYES Brown
HAIR White
POWERS/ABILITIES Immortality and resurrection, various metahuman powers; Tektite enhancement, accelerated healing.
ENEMIES Suriel, Body Doubles, Hooker, Vandal Savage

Mitchell Shelley was a biologist working for a clandestine organization to create cutting-edge weapons and tech. His big project was Tektite nanites, intended to allow wounded US soldiers in Iraq to regenerate or at least survive major trauma. After many failures, a breakthrough arrived. Unfortunately, Shelley was caught in a bomb blast and lost an arm. To save his life, his staff injected him with Tektites. The procedure worked and his arm was reattached. However, Shelley then began growing a whole new arm and the reattached arm was removed. Incredibly, this arm grew into a full clone of Shelley and set off on its own. Mitchell was now desperate to track down his clone for further research.

Meanwhile, the clone, which had few memories, searched for its past. Despite suffering from amnesia, it eventually realized it was being repeatedly killed and then resurrected by unknown enemies. Each time it was brought back to life, it possessed a different superpower.

DEATH BECOMES HIM
Mitch Shelley's clone died and was resurrected countless times, and on each occasion he found he had a new metahuman ability.

RIOT

DEBUT *Superman: Man of Steel* #61 (Oct. 1996)
REAL NAME Mr. Murphy
POWERS/ABILITIES Instant generation of psychically linked clones with enhanced strength and speed.
ALLIES Temple Bellachek
ENEMIES "Commodore" Murphy, Green Team, Mohammed Qahtanii, J.P. Houston, Cecilia Sunbeam

The disgraced and exiled heir to the Murphy fortune began attacking his own son, "Commodore" Murphy, as masked marauder Riot after being medically altered by wealthy maniac Temple Bellachek. Faking his death, Riot then staged a series of brutal assaults hoping to regain the fortune his son had inherited. Unfortunately for Riot, Commodore had also inherited his father's fascination with metahuman improvement.

Young Murphy had surreptitiously purchased nanite-based armor, which he shared with his associates in the trillionaires-only social club the Green Team. These rich kids perpetually frustrated Riot's murderous attacks, defeating his clone army with ease and even toppling Temple Bellachek's empire. Riot apparently died in a final battle with his son.

RISK

DEBUT *Teen Titans* (Vol. 2) #1 (Oct. 1996)
REAL NAME Cody Driscoll
HEIGHT 5ft 11in **WEIGHT** 175 lbs
EYES Blue-green **HAIR** Blond
POWERS/ABILITIES Superhuman strength, speed, and reflexes; invulnerability; psychic powers.
ALLIES Loren Jupiter, Ray Palmer, Prysm
ENEMIES H'San Natall, the Veil, Haze, Deathstroke the Terminator, Sinestro Corps, Superboy-Prime

Cody Driscoll was abducted by aliens, the H'San Natall. Aboard their ship, he learned that he and other kidnapped kids were part of a breeding program—human/alien hybrids, designed to counter Earth's Super Hero defenders. As Risk, he and hero Ray Palmer joined a new Teen Titans group. When the volatile team broke up, Cody returned to his Colorado trailer-park home. His adrenaline-triggered powers made him a thrill addict, and he turned to petty crime. He redeemed himself by fighting valiantly during the *Infinite Crisis*, losing his right arm battling Superboy-Prime. Seeking no favors from his former friends, Risk vanished. But when the Sinestro Corps attacked Earth, Risk again tackled Superboy-Prime and had his left arm torn off. His whereabouts are unknown.

RO, KANJAR

DEBUT *Justice League of America* (Vol. 1) #3 (Feb.–Mar. 1961)
BASE Dhor, Thanagar, mobile
HEIGHT 5ft 7in **WEIGHT** 147 lbs
EYES Yellow **HAIR** None
POWERS/ABILITIES Cunning; tactical analysis; strategic planning; wide array of advanced technology and weapons taken in conquest.
ALLIES Vril Dox
ENEMIES The Durlans, Khunds, Hyathis of Alstair, Kromm of Mosteel, Sayyar of Larr, Green Lantern Corps, Guardians of the Universe, Metamorpho, Starro the Conqueror, Justice League of America
AFFILIATIONS Thanagarian Ministry of Alien Affairs

CHAINS OF COMMAND
Despite his devious nature, Kanjar Ro's grand schemes frequently led to his being locked up beside his former possessions and chattels.

EYES ON THE PRIZE
Kanjar Ro is a consummate politician and pragmatist, eminently capable of turning any crisis to his personal advantage.

When a four-way war broke out in the Antares system, Dhorian dictator Kanjar Ro used cunning and duplicity to defeat his rivals. Imprisoning his foes, he luxuriated in the sybaritic joys of victory and was totally unprepared when the losers returned, united against him.

The unforgiving victors sold Kanjar into slavery, but he quickly turned the tables on his new owners and became a preeminent slave-trader and arms-dealer. A cosmic wanderer, he roamed space constantly seeking to re-establish a power-base, always looking for ways to exact revenge on those who had humiliated him. His brutal depredations brought him to the attention of the Guardians of the Universe and Kanjar Ro ended up in a Sciencell on Oa.

When the Guardians of the Universe died, an alliance of shape-shifting Durlans and barbaric Khunds attacked the Green Lantern Corps. These malignant invaders liberated Ro and several other galactic super-criminals, planning to press them into war service. Ro thus discovered that there was something he despised even more than groups of heroic do-gooders, and he led the Sciencell escapees in a coalition with the Green Lanterns against the invading alien alliance.

ON THE RECORD

The Silver Age Kanjar Ro was a quintessential alien evildoer. Ro was always hungry for conquest and used a variety of terrifying technologies. He was also small-minded and spiteful, obsessed with vengeance and with making the Justice League of America and Adam Strange his slaves.

Over time, however, Kanjar Ro evolved into an even more savage and bloodthirsty creature—a vile bureaucrat for the militaristic Thanagarians and later a petty dictator in conflict with Vril Dox II and his R.E.B.E.L.S.

ALIEN THREAT
The dictator of Dhor traveled the universe accumulating incredible weapons just to avenge the insults inflicted upon him by so-called primitive humans.

REVERSE-FLASH (DANIEL WEST)

DATA

DEBUT *The Flash* (Vol. 4) #0 (**Nov. 2012**)
REAL NAME Daniel West
BASE Belle Reve Penitentiary
HEIGHT 5ft 10 in **WEIGHT** 170 lbs
EYES Blue **HAIR** Brown
POWERS/ABILITIES Uses the extra-dimensional energy known as the Speed Force to travel back in time; costume acts like armor and includes part of the monorail he crashed into that was merged to his body by the Speed Force.
ALLIES Suicide Squad
ENEMIES The Flash, Rogues, League of Assassins
AFFILIATIONS Suicide Squad

SPEED STEALER
The Reverse-Flash killed those connected to the Speed Force, draining them of their energy to make himself more powerful. West even stole Speed Force energy from The Flash himself.

Like The Flash, Daniel West gained his amazing powers of speed following an accident. However, unlike his nemesis, West became the Reverse-Flash, using his powers for his own selfish needs. The speedster cared little for those who had to die to help him accomplish his ultimate goal—to use the Speed Force to alter his own past.

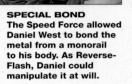

SPECIAL BOND
The Speed Force allowed Daniel West to bond the metal from a monorail to his body. As Reverse-Flash, Daniel could manipulate it at will.

Daniel West's life was marked by tragedy. Hidmother died in childbirth and his father was a violent drunk. When Daniel's father destroyed the boy's cricket collection, Daniel pushed him down a staircase, injuring him. Terrified of being punished, he ran away, and began a life of crime. While acting as a getaway driver, he was captured by The Flash and jailed. Shortly after Daniel's release, he was caught up in Gorilla Grodd's attack on Central City. He was saved by the Rogues, who trapped him in their Mirror World base. Daniel escaped by stealing a car but crashed into a new monorail fitted with a Speed Force battery. The accident threw Daniel back to Earth and imbued him with the Speed Force—fusing remnants of the monorail with his body and showing him others connected to the Speed Force. Daniel could now use the Speed Force to time travel, but needed more power. He started killing those connected to the Speed Force. He gained enough energy to travel back to his own past. When he tried to kill his father, the young Daniel and his sister Iris, who witnessed the attempt, were terrified. The Flash arrived and reabsorbed the stolen Speed Force, returning them both to the present. After a brief incarceration, he joined the Suicide Squad but died on a mission, heroically saving innocents from a bomb blast. It has since been discovered that Daniel West has a son, Wallace West. Wallace originally thought he was Daniel's nephew, but The Flash discovered the truth when Daniel was arrested.

SPEED DEMON
The accident that turned Daniel West into Reverse-Flash created a distinctive red and metallic-gray suit.

ON THE RECORD

Several villains have taken on the role of Reverse-Flash over the years. Eobard Thawne was from the 25th century and a fan of The Flash. He even built his own version of The Flash's Cosmic Treadmill and traveled back in time to meet his hero. However, when Eobard learned that he was destined to become a villain and would die at the hands of The Flash, he went insane and became the Reverse-Flash. In later appearances, he called himself Professor Zoom.

When Wally West became the third Flash, he fought a new Reverse-Flash named Hunter Zolomon, who had once been Wally's friend. Zolomon also went by the name of Zoom.

YOU'RE NO BARRY ALLEN
The original Reverse-Flash, Eobard Thawne, was quickly driven mad by his fixation with The Flash (Barry Allen), and was repeatedly defeated by his idol.

CLASSIC STORIES

Flash Comics #104 (Feb. 1949)
Named "the Rival" at the time, the original Reverse-Flash fights the first Flash, Jay Garrick.

The Flash (Vol. 4) #23.2 (Nov. 2013) Daniel West's origin is explored, and the cruelty of his father is exposed.

New Suicide Squad Annual #1 (Nov. 2015) Daniel dies heroically, saving innocent children from an exploding bomb.

RIDDLER, THE

DATA

DEBUT *Detective Comics* (Vol. 1) #140 (Oct. 1948)
REAL NAME Edward Nygma **BASE** Gotham City
HEIGHT 6ft 1in **WEIGHT** 183 lbs **EYES** Blue **HAIR** Brown
POWERS/ABILITIES Expert at creating riddles and death traps; genius-level intellect; computer and electronics whiz; morally corrupt with a penchant for cheating; carries cane in the shape of a question mark from which he can fire electrical blasts or create holograms; makes use of exploding jigsaw puzzle pieces and crossword puzzle nets.
ALLIES Dr. Death
ENEMIES Batman, the Batman Family, The Joker
AFFILIATIONS Arkham Asylum inmates, Secret Society of Super-Villains

THE WAR OF JOKES AND RIDDLES
A few years ago, The Joker found himself unable to laugh. The Riddler sought to team up with the Clown Prince of Crime, but instead, The Joker shot him in the chest. This sparked the "War of Jokes and Riddles," where the criminals of Gotham City chose sides and the casualties built up. Once The Riddler revealed that he had plotted the entire war to try to solve the riddle of how to make The Joker laugh, Batman was pushed beyond his limits. The Dark Knight had a moment of weakness and attempted to kill The Riddler in a fit of rage. The Joker saved The Riddler's life, and the irony of the situation finally caused The Joker to regain his mad laughter.

The Riddler is a conflicted criminal. His dreams of wealth and prosperity are often at odds with his love of finding a worthy competitor—namely the Batman—to challenge to a game of mental and physical gymnastics.

LASER FOCUS
The Riddler loves death traps, and Batman was forced to enter one in order to free Gotham City from the villain's hold.

Edward Nygma (going by Nigma a the time) found his ticket to the big time as an employee of Wayne Industries. Securing the role of advisor to Philip Kane—Bruce Wayne's uncle, who took over the Wayne corporation when Bruce left Gotham City to train to become the Batman—Nigma began plotting his takeover of the city.

An expert strategist, with a genius-level knowledge of history, it was not long before Nigma adopted the guise of a Super-Villain, calling himself The Riddler, and employing the help of fellow criminal Dr. Death after he shut down power to all of Gotham City.

In The Riddler's twisted mind, he wanted to help evolution by forcing the citizens of Gotham City to either "get smart or die." As a super-storm hit the city, The Riddler blew the retaining walls and grounded the city's blimps. With complete control of the electrical grid, The Riddler created a dystopia of sorts with the city's tunnels flooded and its bridges rigged to explode. Using research stolen from Dr. Pamela Isley (later Poison Ivy), The Riddler reduced the city to a plant-covered wasteland, holding the entire population hostage. With the help of Lucius Fox and James Gordon, Batman took up The Riddler's challenge of wits, and bested the Super-Villain before he could unleash total devastation. Gotham City was freed, and The Riddler was banished to Arkham Asylum for the first of many stays in the infamous penitentiary.

The Riddler would return to plague Batman many times, from fighting The Joker during the "War of Jokes and Riddles," working with the criminal genius called the Designer in order to discover the perfect plot to foil the Batman, to working as a brainwashed faux police detective when Bane briefly took over Gotham City. However, no matter how brilliant The Riddler's schemes, the Dark Knight was always several moves ahead.

WEAPON IN QUESTION
The Riddler is rarely without his signature question-mark cane and bowler hat.

ON THE RECORD
The Riddler debuted in the 1940s. His origin revealed that Edward Nigma (the "y" spelling was first used in 1992's *Batman: The Animated Series*) had always been amoral, acquiring an early love of games and puzzles after sneaking a peek at the solution to a classroom jigsaw puzzle assignment.

Later, while working as a carnival barker, The Riddler ultimately chose a life of crime, finding a worthy opponent in the form of Batman. This origin was left largely unchanged by the *Crisis on Infinite Earths* event, although it was later revealed that Edward's true birth name wasn't Nigma at all, but Nashton.

REINTRODUCING THE RIDDLER
In the mid-1960s, The Riddler became a mainstay of Batman's Rogues Gallery, finding all sorts of eccentric, entertaining ways to baffle the Dynamic Duo.

CLASSIC STORIES

Detective Comics (Vol. 1) #140 (Oct. 1948) The Riddler debuts, proving himself to be the "Prince of Puzzles" as his origin is revealed to the readers.
Batman (Vol. 1) #171 (May 1965) In an issue adapted for the pilot episode of the 1966 Batman TV show, The Riddler makes his Silver Age comic book debut.
Batman (Vol. 1) #452-454 (Aug.-Sep. 1990) The Riddler gets a supernatural upgrade in the haunting three-part story "Dark Knight, Dark City," which shows the villain being possessed by a demon named Barbatos.
Detective Comics (Vol. 1) Annual #8 (1995) The Riddler's origin is retold for the modern age, introducing his two female sidekicks, Query and Echo.

DATA

HA! HA! HA! HA!

R

ROBIN

DATA

DEBUT *Batman: Son of the Demon* (Sep. 1987) (unnamed baby); *Batman* (Vol.1) #655 (Sep. 2006) (Damian Wayne)
REAL NAME Damian Wayne **BASE** Gotham City and Brooklyn, New York **HEIGHT** 5ft 3in **WEIGHT** 114 lbs **EYES** Blue **HAIR** Black
POWERS/ABILITIES Expert martial artist and assassin trained by the League of Assassins, Batman, and Nightwing; skilled detective and extremely intelligent; very athletic with some gymnastic training; briefly possessed Superman-like powers; weapons include armored suit with Utility Belt and access to the equipment in the Batcave.
ALLIES Batman, The Batman Family, Nobody II, Goliath, Superboy (Jon Kent) **ENEMIES** Rā's al Ghūl, League of Assassins, Nobody, Deathstroke **AFFILIATIONS** Teen Titans

While Batman has been known to hide his feelings, Damian Wayne would be a hard son for even the most affectionate father to love. Headstrong, arrogant, and more than a little condescending to his fellow Super Heroes, Damian Wayne is the fifth and current Robin, and has managed to make enemies on both sides of the aisle despite his short tenure as a hero. The son of Bruce Wayne and the notorious League of Assassins leader, Talia al Ghūl, Damian was taught the ways of the League of Assassins by his mother. However, since joining his father, he has sided time and again with the Dark Knight's noble cause.

AT A GLANCE...

Assassin born
The son of Batman and criminal Talia al Ghūl, Damian Wayne was raised by his mother, and constantly surrounded by the members of the notorious League of Assassins. With no qualms about killing those who got in his way, Damian didn't quite fit the mantle of a Robin when he first traveled to Gotham City to live with his father.

Like father, like son
After spending some time with Batman, Damian realized the nobility of the Dark Knight's cause, and wished to become more like the father he began to idolize. To that end, he did his best to put his killer instincts to one side and abide by Batman's uncompromising rules.

Attitude adjustment
Working with Dick Grayson—who had stepped up to be Batman—taught Damian Wayne a thing or two about true heroism and respecting his elders. However, Robin still maintained a trademark arrogance that could alienate his fellow Super Heroes.

CLASSIC STORIES

***Batman: Son of the Demon* (Sep. 1987)** A romantic fling between Batman and Talia al Ghūl results in a child the Dark Knight knows nothing about: A boy who later becomes known as Damian.
***Batman* (Vol. 1) #655-658 (Sep.-Dec. 2006)** In "Batman and Son," Batman is introduced to his son, Damian, for the first time and attempts to curb the boy's ruthless form of vigilantism.
***Batman and Robin* (Vol. 1) #1 (Aug. 2009)** A new Batman and Robin are back in Gotham City: Dick Grayson as the Dark Knight and Damian Wayne as his youthful crime fighting partner.
***Batman, Inc.* (Vol. 2) #8 (Apr. 2013)** Damian Wayne meets his seemingly final fate as he valiantly fights his powerful "brother" clone, the Heretic.

Batman and the international terrorist named Rā's al Ghūl have battled for many years. While Rā's wants to "save the planet" by wiping out a huge percentage of the populace, Batman puts human life first and foremost, and has thwarted Rā's' plans on many occasions. However, despite the hostility between the Dark Knight Detective and the so-called Demon's Head, the two shared a common affection for Rā's daughter, Talia al Ghūl.

One of Batman's romantic flings with Talia resulted in the birth of a son, a boy named Damian Wayne. Accelerating the boy's growth through artificial means, Talia oversaw Damian's upbringing, training him in the many deadly arts known by Rā's al Ghūl's League of Assassins. Before he turned 10, Damian had mastered the violin, severed a tiger's head, harpooned a shark by hand, and killed humans and Man-Bats alike. He had become an assassin without remorse, one his mother was immensely proud of.

Knowing that her son could possibly be the heir to the al Ghūl empire, Talia presented the boy to Batman, hoping the Dark Knight could guide Damian to become more than the sum of what the masters of the League of Assassins could teach him. Rā's al Ghūl' had long wanted Batman himself to take over his empire, but knowing that was impossible, instilling Damian with some of Bruce Wayne's qualities seemed to be the next best thing.

While Batman has faced many challenges, taming Damian Wayne was among the most difficult. At first the boy seemed to be confused by Batman's ethics, but after seeing the Dark Knight in action, Damian realized that his father was a noble warrior.

Damian Wayne first officially adopted the mantle of Robin after Bruce Wayne was sent spiraling through time following a conflict with Darkseid. Realizing that Gotham City needed a Batman, Dick Grayson stepped into the role, with Damian Wayne as Robin by his side. The two fought new villains such as Mr. Toad and Professor Pyg, until Bruce Wayne returned and reclaimed the Batman mantle.

Despite gaining respect for Grayson during their crime fighting partnership, Damian was

DADDY ISSUES
Young Damian Wayne was initially unimpressed with his father—not understanding why he refused to kill his foes. In time, Damian realized how heroic his father truly was.

THE DEATH OF ROBIN
After Batman returned from traveling through time, he was given a quick glimpse of a future threat called Leviathan. To battle this oncoming foe, Batman formed a global team of heroes called Batman, Inc., and later learned that Leviathan was headed by none other than Damian Wayne's mother, Talia al Ghūl. During a confrontation with Leviathan's forces and the villain Heretic, Robin was mortally wounded. It was a loss that Batman was unable to accept, and the Dark Knight began searching for a way to bring his son back to life.

DEATH IN THE FAMILY
Young Damian Wayne was killed battling the Heretic, an adult clone of himself who had been raised by Talia. Following Robin's death, Batman swore revenge, redoubling his efforts to take down Leviathan once and for all.

> *"Show me respect, father, and fight me!"*
>
> **DAMIAN WAYNE**

very excited to join forces with his father. But he also found plenty of conflict within himself, especially when he felt forced to destroy the criminal called Nobody. Despite his son's huge misstep, Batman refused to give up on Damian, and worked hard on strengthening their bond. When Damian was murdered by the villain Heretic, Bruce Wayne found himself not just without a partner, but without a son, a truly devastating moment in the Dark Knight's already tragic life.

Determined to reunite with his son, Batman traveled to Apokolips, where he eventually succeeded in resurrecting Damian. Robin then decided to venture out into the world, seeking to correct past mistakes committed while trying to prove himself to the League of Assassins.

However, old habits die hard. Robin teamed with Superman's son Superboy (Jon Kent) on several adventures, but when Superboy took off to join the Legion of Super-Heroes, Robin found himself without a moral compass. Damian formed yet another Teen Titans, but instead of handing villains to the authorities, he began imprisoning them beneath the Titans' hideout. However, these powerful villains proved too strong, so Robin's approach became bolder. He murdered the cult leader Brother Blood, believing that death was the only true solution for career villains. Confronted by Batman, Robin quit as the Boy Wonder and ripped the R chest emblem from his uniform.

While this resignation didn't spell the end for Robin's adventures, it did change his family dynamic. It may now prove impossible for Batman to ever truly trust his son again.

ROBIN AND GOLIATH
While returning artifacts he had stolen from various cultures around the world, Robin employed the help of Goliath, a dragonlike bat creature he had adopted as a pet after slaying its family.

REBIRTH

LEADER OF THE GANG
After being resurrected, Damian Wayne became overbearingly ambitious. Assisting Nightwing in safeguarding Gotham City and teaming up with Superboy (Jon Kent), Robin also convinced Starfire, Raven, Beast Boy, and the new Kid Flash (Wallace West) to join him in a campaign to stop his immortal grandfather and would-be world conqueror Rā's al Ghūl.

Regrettably for Damian, although he arrogantly believed he had everything under control, he had no idea what his new allies thought of him.

FITTING FASHION
Damian's costume slightly differed from his predecessors', but kept the trademark yellow cape as a badge of honor.

ROBIN RISES
Batman was willing to go to hell and back to see his son returned to the land of the living, and had to nearly do just that after the tyrant of the planet Apokolips, Darkseid, stole Damian's casket. It seems that years ago, Talia al Ghūl had discovered a fraction of a crystal called the Chaos Shard. The crystal had helped accelerate Damian's growth and seemed to be a source of renewable energy. Darkseid wanted the shard, and his people took Damian's body and the crystal back to Apokolips with them. Batman was forced to follow in his special Hellbat armor, and finally returned to Earth with his resurrected son.

SECOND CHANCE
After returning to Earth, Batman resurrected his son by plunging the Chaos Shard into the boy's chest. It was a rebirth that briefly granted Damian powers akin to Superman's.

ON THE RECORD

After a brief appearance as a baby in 1987, Damian Wayne was reintroduced into the DC universe again in 2006. With a relatively short career in comics before the dramatic *Flashpoint* event of 2011, Damian's backstory has barely altered despite the shifting landscape of the world around him.

Conflicting backstories
Originally, Damian Wayne was simply the unnamed child of Talia and Batman who was left on an orphanage's doorstep after their romance soured. All but forgotten, when Damian returned in the later continuity of 2006, his backstory was tweaked to reveal he had been raised in a lab, and had never in fact been abandoned by his mother.

Tackling the Titans
Joining the Teen Titans has been a time-honored tradition for Robins, starting with one of the team's founding members, Dick Grayson. While the second Robin, Jason Todd, only briefly served with the team, the third Boy Wonder, Tim Drake, helped found a new incarnation of the team that nearly reached the greatness of Grayson's era. Before the *Flashpoint* series significantly altered the Teen Titans' continuity—erasing almost all the stories that had come before—Damian Wayne had decided the Titans needed his particular skill set. While Dick Grayson volunteered Damian's services to the Teen Titans as a member—thinking the team dynamic would be good for Robin's social skills—Damian was angered that he was not immediately welcomed as team leader, and his tenure with them was relatively short.

Titan trouble
After leaving the Teen Titans, Damian Wayne was soon back operating with the Batman Family. But even that working relationship was a constant struggle for the headstrong teen.

WHAT CHILD IS THIS?
Damian's name was initially only revealed when he came into Batman's life as a troubled adolescent boy, placing in some doubt that the baby depicted in *Batman: Son of the Demon* and Damian Wayne were one and the same.

RED ROBIN (TIM DRAKE)

DEBUT (as Tim Drake) *Batman* (Vol. 1) #436 **(August 1989)** (officially as Robin) *Batman* (Vol. 1) #457 **(December 1990)**
REAL NAME Timothy Jackson Drake
HEIGHT 5ft 6in **WEIGHT** 131 lbs **EYES** Blue **HAIR** Black
POWERS/ABILITIES Expert martial artist trained by Batman; skilled detective and gymnast; impressive intellect and a natural leader; computer expert; equipped with Utility Belt full of hi-tech gadgets; access to the Batcave and its technology.
ALLIES Batman, Nightwing, Spoiler, Superboy, Impulse, Wonder Girl
ENEMIES Arkham Asylum inmates, Blackgate criminals
AFFILIATIONS Young Justice, Teen Titans, Batman Incorporated, Gotham Knights

YOUNG JUSTICE
When Tim joined Young Justice, he briefly adopted the hero name Drake. Around this time, Tim unlocked memories of serving in an earlier incarnation of the team. While he seems to be remembering a past timeline that no longer exists, Tim's memories are as real as any in his newly altered reality.

He has gone by Robin, Red Robin, and simply Drake, but despite his costume and moniker changes, Tim Drake's mission has never changed. The third Robin to pick up the mantle, and the only one to do so by deducing Batman's secret identity, Tim earned his place at his mentor's side, applying his computer expertise, his natural leadership, and most of all, his tenacity, to help protect and defend the citizens of Gotham City.

Batman needs a Robin. Young Tim Drake was sure of it. He had studied Batman ever since he saw him for the first time at Haly's Circus. Tim was there the night Dick Grayson's parents died, and learned that Bruce Wayne later took Grayson in as his ward. When he saw Robin in action later by Batman's side, he put two and two together, and deduced the identities of Batman and Robin.

Tim's Batman obsession took up much of his life, despite being a great student who excelled at computer technology. As Dick Grayson grew up and became Nightwing, Tim learned Jason Todd became the second Robin. When Jason later died at the hands of the Joker, Tim watched Batman and studied him carefully, even taking pictures of the Dark Knight during a fight with a criminal. Batman was becoming unhinged, more violent. The solution was simple: he needed a Boy Wonder to help show him the brighter side of his mission.

To that end, Tim tried to convince Grayson to reclaim his role as Robin. But when Dick refused, Tim found himself rushing into action to help Batman fight the villain Two-Face. Hearing Tim's argument for the necessity of a Robin, Batman reluctantly agreed, and soon took Tim under his wing. After months of relentless training, coupled with Tim's natural abilities and determination, a new Robin was born.

Just like the Robins before him, Tim was destined to eventually chart his own path. He adopted the name of Red Robin and partnered with other young heroes like Spoiler and the Teen Titans. He eventually formed a team of heroes he dubbed the Gotham Knights, and they operated out of the Belfry, a hideout he designed in the Old Wayne Tower. While the Knights disbanded over the actions of rogue member Clayface, Tim soon joined some old friends in the heroic team Young Justice. Tim has evolved from rookie hero to seasoned professional over the years, one of Batman's most trusted allies.

ON THE RECORD

In the pre-*Flashpoint* timeline, Tim Drake fought for years beside Batman and evolved over time. He watched in horror as his father was killed by Captain Boomerang, and soon adopted the name Red Robin before striking out on his own. As Robin, he led Young Justice and then the Teen Titans, and formed an on again/off again relationship with Spoiler, who briefly took his place as the 4th Robin.

DARK DAYS
Tim's uniform changed many times during the pre-*Flashpoint* continuity. He originally dropped the green from his suit in favor of black and red, then later chose a black cowl that resembled that of his mentor.

CLASSIC STORIES

Batman (Vol. 1) #440-442, *The New Titans* #60-61 (Oct.-Dec. 1989) In the five-part "A Lonely Place of Dying," Tim makes his true debut and even briefly wears a Robin costume into battle.
Robin (Vol. 1) #1-5 (Jan.-May 1991) In his first solo miniseries, Tim studies under Lady Shiva and comes into conflict with the notorious King Snake.
Robin II: The Joker's Wild #1-4 (Oct.-Dec. 1991) Tim faces the Joker on his own, the very villain that killed his predecessor, Jason Todd.

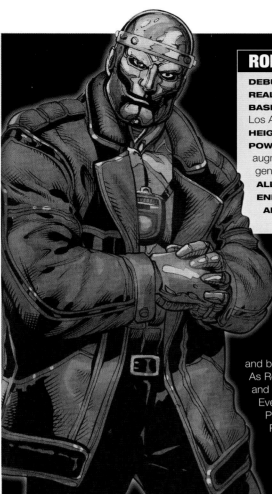

ROBOTMAN

DEBUT *My Greatest Adventure* (Vol. 1) #80 (Jun. 1963)
REAL NAME Clifford "Cliff" Steele
BASE Doom Patrol HQ, Midway City, Michigan; Las Vegas, Nevada; Los Angeles, California
HEIGHT 6ft 2in **WEIGHT** 295 lbs **EYES** Photocellular **HAIR** None
POWERS/ABILITIES Enhanced strength, speed, durability; electronically augmented senses; enhanced invulnerability; extendable limbs; heat generation
ALLIES Dr. Will Magnus, Elasti-Girl, Negative Man
ENEMIES Dr. Niles Caulder, Brotherhood of Evil, Brotherhood of Dada
AFFILIATIONS Doom Patrol, Justice League United

Life seemed over for rugged sportsman and compulsive daredevil Cliff Steele when he died in a car crash. However, Cliff's brain was secretly preserved by radical scientist Dr. Niles Caulder and transplanted into a succession of mechanical bodies. Although the savant's motives seemed benevolent, Caulder was in reality a master manipulator who engineered catastrophes so that he could conduct unregulated experiments on human beings. His successes were then press-ganged into his private superteam, the Doom Patrol.

Initially bitter and hostile, Cliff Steele gradually adjusted to his condition and became the backbone of the unit: a hero in every sense of the word. As Robotman, he faced each incomprehensible danger with a wry wisecrack and every nasty shock life threw at him with unshakable grit and determination. Eventually, Caulder's duplicity was exposed and Robotman became the Doom Patrol's moral compass. Seeing through the deranged genius' machinations, Robotman stayed with the team to limit the damage the fame-obsessed "Chief" might cause and to protect his more vulnerable friends on the squad.

Even this was not enough for the tireless, compassionate thrill-seeker. Robotman began operating as a substitute champion with Justice League United, and came to be regarded as a mentor and elder statesman for the next generation of Super Heroes.

ON THE RECORD

Cliff Steele was not DC Comics' first Robotman. In *Star-Spangled Comics* (Vol. 1) #7 (Apr. 1942), Robert Crane was killed by gangsters, and his best friend transplanted his brain into a marvel of mechanical engineering packed with crime-fighting gadgets. This prototype man of steel even had a faithful, talking-robot dog, named Robbie, to help battle the bad guys. Robert Crane was later reimagined as a scientist in a rebuilt robotic body on Earth-2.

WARTIME HEROICS
Robotman stopped Commander Steel—brainwashed by Nazi Baron Blitzkrieg—from assassinating President Roosevelt, as the rest of the All-Star Squadron rushed to intervene.

ROCKET RED BRIGADE

DEBUT *Green Lantern Corps* (Vol. 1) #208 (Jan. 1987)
BASE Russia
POWERS/ABILITIES Classified, but observed as enhanced strength, supersonic flight, limited invulnerability, electronic senses and a suite of ballistic and energy projection armaments.
ENEMIES Task Force X, Suicide Squad, Peacemaker
AFFILIATIONS Russian military command

The Rocket Red Brigade was commissioned by Russia's rulers as a military-controlled response to metahuman threats and proliferation. The technology is a combination of human ingenuity and alien bio-engineering, thanks to the contributions of Green Lantern Kilowog, who innocently offered his aid while on a fact-finding mission to Russia. Rocket Reds were part of the first Justice League International team. The first was exposed as an android Manhunter infiltrator, while the second—Dmitri Pushkin—died battling renegade O.M.A.C. units.

Currently composed of older units and more modern upgrades, Rocket Reds now solely protect Russian interests, with reports of potential international incidents involving Supergirl, Peacemaker, and China's New Super-Man.

RED ALERT
Rocket Reds were effective against conventional threats to the State, but seldom overcame Super Hero targets.

ROGOL ZAAR

DEBUT *Action Comics* (Vol. 1) #1000 (Jun. 2018)
REAL NAME Rogol Zaar
BASE Phantom Zone
HEIGHT Unknown
WEIGHT Unknown
EYES One white, one red
HAIR Black
POWERS/ABILITIES Super-strength and durability; wields an axe that responds to his call.
ALLIES Jax-Ur
ENEMIES All Kryptonians, Superman
AFFILIATIONS The Circle

The monstrous, super-strong Rogol Zaar had a burning hatred for Kryptonians. It was he who was responsible for the destruction of Krypton, enabled by a shadowy cabal called the Circle.

Decades later, Rogol Zaar came to Earth on a rage-fuelled quest to eliminate every remaining Kryptonian. He was so strong that even Superman could only fight him to a standstill. Zaar had also managed to destroy the Man of Steel's Fortress of Solitude, including the many inhabitants of confined within the bottled city of Kandor.

Supergirl eventually trapped Rogol Zaar in the Phantom Zone, although he later escaped. He was later apprehended by Superman, Supergirl, General Zod, and the Black Guard of Thanagar.

PHANTOM ZONE KILLER
Rogol Zaar was consumed with mindless hatred for Kryptonians and powerful enough to destroy them.

ROGUES, THE

DATA

DEBUT *The Flash* (Vol.1) #155 **(Sep. 1965)**
BASE Central City
MEMBERS/POWERS Captain Cold (Leonard Snart): Generates and controls ice; **Glider** (Lisa Snart): Astral projection, flight; **Mirror Master** (Sam Scudder): Access to the Mirror World; **Heat Wave** (Mick Rory): Fire projection; **Weather Wizard** (Marco Mardon): Weather manipulation; **Trickster** (Axel Walker): Gadgetry, cybernetic arm; **Pied Piper** (Hartley Rathaway): Sonic manipulation
ENEMIES The Flash, Gorilla Grodd, Crime Syndicate
AFFILIATIONS Injustice League

HARD TARGETS
Having rejected the Crime Syndicate's offer to join them, The Rogues returned to a Central City devastated by Gorilla Grodd. Before long they were targeted by the Syndicate's Power Ring and Deathstorm.

The Rogues were low-level criminals united in their hatred of The Flash. Employing exotic technologies to facilitate their crooked enterprises and in attempts to outfox the Scarlet Speedster, they abided by three rules they viewed as their code of honor: no unnecessary killing, not to use drugs, and not to fail in their crimes.

As The Flash, Barry Allen repeatedly battled The Rogues, each time doling out a bruising defeat. Eventually, Rogues' leader Leonard Snart—alias Captain Cold—tired of being bested and accepted an invitation from research scientist Dr. Darwin Elias. He approached Snart claiming his Genome Recoder could imbue The Rogues' bodies with the power of their weapons. However, the process malfunctioned; each Rogue gained superpowers, but at a cost. Heat Wave was badly burned; Weather Wizard became emotionally linked to the weather he generated, and Mirror Master was trapped in a Mirror World. In addition, Snart's sister, Lisa, who was dating Mirror Master and was also present, was separated from her body in astral form.

As Golden Glider, Lisa formed a new Rogues team, cutting Snart out of a heist before going to war with him. Captain Cold rejoined in time to face an invasion of Central City by Grodd's gorilla army, an episode that forced The Rogues to form an alliance with The Flash. The Rogues subsequently ran afoul of the Crime Syndicate, having rejected joining their ranks. After many skirmishes, The Rogues banished Syndicate allies the Secret Society to the Mirror World.

Despite constant membership revisions and frequent internal squabbles, The Rogues remained basically united until Captain's Cold's growing obsession with beating The Flash compelled him to ignore his own three rules. After Snart accepted power upgrades from Luthor's Legion of Doom to become King Cold, The Rogues mutinied. Led by Golden Glider they attacked their former leader in a concerted attack by The Flash and his speedster allies.

A NEW START
Having rejected the Crime Syndicate's offer to join them, The Rogues returned to Syndicate's Power Ring and Deathstorm.

AT THE ROGUES' MERCY
In one of their earliest capers, The Rogues teamed up to rob a department store. When The Flash arrived, the villains briefly thought they had disintegrated him with their weapons—only to find he had vibrated through the floor.

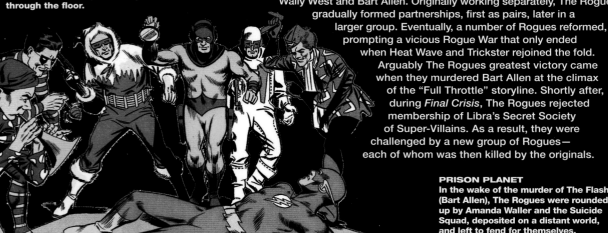

ON THE RECORD

Pre-*Flashpoint*, The Rogues were perennial thorns in the sides of not only Barry Allen but his speedster successors Wally West and Bart Allen. Originally working separately, The Rogues gradually formed partnerships, first as pairs, later in a larger group. Eventually, a number of Rogues reformed, prompting a vicious Rogue War that only ended when Heat Wave and Trickster rejoined the fold. Arguably The Rogues greatest victory came when they murdered Bart Allen at the climax of the "Full Throttle" storyline. Shortly after, during *Final Crisis*, The Rogues rejected membership of Libra's Secret Society of Super-Villains. As a result, they were challenged by a new group of Rogues— each of whom was then killed by the originals.

PRISON PLANET
In the wake of the murder of The Flash (Bart Allen), The Rogues were rounded up by Amanda Waller and the Suicide Squad, deposited on a distant world, and left to fend for themselves.

RORSCHACH (REGINALD LONG)

DEBUT *Doomsday Clock* (Vol. 1) #1 **(Jan 2018)**
REAL NAME Reginald Long
BASE New York City **HEIGHT** Unknown **WEIGHT** Unknown
EYES Brown **HAIR** Black
POWERS/ABILITIES Skilled in hand-to-hand combat
ALLIES Mothman, Saturn Girl, Johnny Thunder
ENEMIES Ozymandias
AFFILIATIONS None

Reggie Long's parents were killed in Ozymandias's attack on New York City, and the trauma of the event cut the young man so deeply that he ended up in a mental institution. Here he befriended inmate Byron Lewis, who had been one of the Minutemen as Mothman. Lewis managed to smuggle in Reggie's father's notes on Rorschach (Walter Kovacs), who had been a patient of his. Mothman also trained Reggie to fight using all the techniques of the Minutemen.

When Reggie discovered that Ozymandias (Adrian Veidt) was responsible for his parents' deaths, he escaped the institution and assumed the identity of Rorschach to take revenge. Reggie could not bring himself to kill his quarry, and was instead persuaded to help Veidt find Doctor Manhattan. The two traveled to an alternate Earth on their quest, but Reggie ended up locked in Arkham Asylum.

Helped to escape by Saturn Girl, Rorschach returned to Ozymandias and they found Doctor Manhattan. It was only then that Reggie discovered the terrible truth: he had been manipulated by Mothman and Ozymandias, and the original Rorschach, whom he had used as his inspiration, had ruined his father's life and career. Devastated, he cast aside his mask and fled, but Batman and Alfred later persuaded him to don it again to help save their world. Reggie returned to his own reality, his last act being to save Ozymandias's life so that he can face justice.

LEGACY HEROES
In his quest to discover which reality Doctor Manhattan had traveled to, the new Rorschach encountered members not only of the Justice League, but also the Legion of Super-Heroes and the Justice Society of America.

THE FIRST RORSCHACH

Walter Kovacs was a masked vigilante, his face obscured by an inkblot pattern of the kind used to assess psychiatric patients. It was this that gave him his name: Rorschach. He became known and feared for his remorseless, brutal brand of justice. Early in his career Rorschach teamed up with the second Nite Owl, but after the Keene Act outlawed costumed adventurers he defied the law and operated as a lone wolf. In the 1980s, Rorschach investigated the murder of the Comedian, recording his findings in his journal. Reuniting with Nite Owl and the new Silk Spectre, Rorschach discovered a plot by Ozymandias to devastate New York City. His comrades agreed to keep it a secret for the sake of world peace, but Rorschach could not. He told Doctor Manhattan to kill him instead, but Rorschach's journal would later reveal everything to a new generation.

ROSE AND THORN

DEBUT *Flash Comics* #89 (Nov. 1947)
REAL NAME Rose Canton
EYES Green
HAIR Brown
POWERS/ABILITIES Multiple personalities; relentless and remorseless drive to succeed
ALLIES Aunty Cate, Melinda, Mister Mittens
ENEMIES Thorn, Mr. Varker

Teenager Rose Canton's world changed when she woke up with a new rose tattoo and covered in someone else's blood. She couldn't remember anything and couldn't confide in her aunt Cate: It would only get Rose sent back to "the institution." More disturbingly, the popular girls who had tormented Rose at high school wanted to be friends now. Answers arrived as video messages on her phone from someone called Thorn, who looked like Rose.

Rose's father died when she was little. Now Thorn—a manic force of nature—was emerging from Rose's psyche to find out how and why, ripping her way through her dad's nasty old cronies before submerging back inside sweet, innocent Rose. Unless she wanted to return to the asylum, Rose had to let Thorn find out what they both needed to know.

ROSS, PETE

DEBUT *Superboy* (Vol. 1) #86 (Jan. 1961)
BASE Smallville, Kansas
HEIGHT 5ft 11in
WEIGHT 175 lbs
ABILITIES Steadfast loyalty, acute empathy
ALLIES Lana Lang, Clark Kent, Chief Parker, Kenny Braverman

Pete Ross may have been one of the select few who knew about Clark Kent's incredible abilities from early on. As Clark's powers grew by leaps and bounds, he felt increasingly scared and alone. Pete kept him grounded with tension-breaking banter about what he'd do if he had superpowers. Pete, Clark, and Lana Lang—the "Three Musketeers"—reunited one last time when Clark left Smallville. Pete wished his friend well in his journalism career, joking that, as he didn't have superpowers, he'd have to be a millionaire instead, or work in his dad's store.

Pre-*Flashpoint*, Pete, Clark, and Lana had also been the "Three Musketeers." When Pete became a Senator, he and Lana married and had a son, but after Pete accepted presidential candidate Lex Luthor's invitation to become his Vice President, the couple divorced. On Luthor's impeachment, Pete became President, returning to Smallville to open a general store when his term expired.

ROULETTE

DEBUT *JSA Secret Files and Origins* (Vol. 1) #2 (Sep. 2001)
REAL NAME Veronica Sinclair
HEIGHT 5ft 9in **WEIGHT** 140 lbs
EYES Green
HAIR Black
POWERS/ABILITIES Manipulator, martial artist; assessor of skills and abilities in others
ENEMIES Catwoman, Golden Glider, Vice

Mystery woman Veronica Sinclair loved games and made vast profits compelling others to play them. As well as running numerous casinos—and less respectable gambling ventures—as Roulette, she was a devious and accomplished criminal.

Declaring herself the "Greatest Thief in the World," she challenged other high-profile crooks to prove her wrong. Selina Kyle was one of the underworld figures Roulette most wanted to compete against. As Selina had retired, Veronica forced Catwoman to join her "Race of Thieves" by claiming to have kidnapped children as hostages.

Grotesquely presenting a bag of kids' teeth, Roulette had Selina battle other robbery superstars in a global test, but soon came to regret her rash actions. Selina not only triumphed in style, but also uncovered Veronica's real motives for the rigged competition. Capitalizing on Roulette's crippling obsessive-compulsive disorder, Selina retaliated, punishing her, but also making a deadly enemy of the gambler.

CATFIGHT!
Roulette's rigging of the "Race of Thieves"—a test of the participants' deception, dexterity, and disguise—led to conflict with Catwoman.

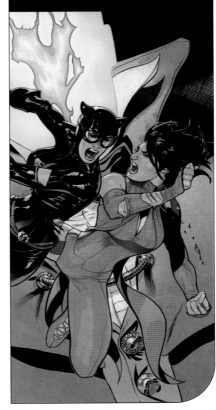

ROUNDHOUSE

DEBUT *Teen Titans* Special Vol 1 #1 (Aug 2018)
REAL NAME Billy Wu
BASE Mercy Hall, New York City
HEIGHT Variable **WEIGHT** Variable
EYES Blue **HAIR** Blond
POWERS/ABILITIES Can change his body into spherical forms of various sizes and substances using his suit; genius computer hacker
ALLIES: Kid Flash, Crush
ENEMIES The Other, Deathstroke, Brother Blood
AFFILIATIONS Teen Titans

Billy Wu was caught in a warehouse explosion with his twin sister Claire. She was tragically killed, but Billy survived, having acquired strange powers in the accident. He learned to control these weird shapeshifting abilities using a special suit that he built himself, revealing his new powers to the world via his popular ViewTube channel and calling himself Roundhouse.

This was how he came to the attention of Kid Flash, who brought him into the new Teen Titans lineup. However, Roundhouse was harbouring a grudge against team leader Robin, whom he believed to be responsible for his sister's death. He used teammate Djinn's powers to capture all his teammates, but soon regretted his actions and was later welcomed back into the team.

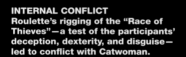

INTERNAL CONFLICT
Roulette's rigging of the "Race of Thieves"—a test of the participants' deception, dexterity, and disguise—led to conflict with Catwoman.

ROYAL FLUSH GANG

DEBUT *Justice League of America* (Vol. 1) #43 (Mar. 1966)
BASE Atlantic City, New Jersey; mobile
MEMBERS/POWERS Wild Card/Ace of Clubs (Amos Fortune): Probability manipulation; **King of Spades** (Joseph Carny): Immortality; **Queen of Spades** (Mona Taylor): Ability to impersonate any woman; **Jack of Spades**: Energy weapons; **Ten of Spades** (Wanda Wayland): Skilled fighter; **Ace Android**: Robotic super-strength; **King of Clubs** (Kerry): Energy-charged playing cards; **Queen of Clubs**: Playing cards that influence behavior; **Jack of Clubs/ Hi-Jack**: Specially adapted playing cards.
ALLIES Hector Hammond
ENEMIES The Rogues, Justice League, Superman, Batman, The Joker
AFFILIATIONS Secret Society of Super-Villains

When they first showed their hand,

the Royal Flush Gang were a quintet of outlandish thieves. They employed a variety of card-themed, reality-warping weapons and gadgets devised by crazy genius Amos Fortune. After the Justice League defeated them, the motif and concept were stolen by numerous crooks and masterminds. Eventually, the Gang became little more than a 52-man-strong mercenary unit riding flying card-sleds. The entire cadre was killed by The Joker in a feud with Alexander Luthor's Secret Society of Super-Villains, before Amos Fortune returned and franchised the Royal Flush concept throughout America's underworld.

The group's latest incarnation had no access to the advanced weaponry of the originals. No better than a pack of gun-toting thugs, this masked army of opportunistic killers traded off their predecessors' reputations. They rode flying cards while wearing card-suit masks.

After an invasion by Earth-3's Crime Syndicate, the extra-dimensional invaders placed a large bounty on the rebellious Central City Rogues for rejecting their rule. When the Royal Flush Gang attempted to collect the bounty, they proved no match for the Rogues, who wiped them out.

ON THE RECORD

Amos Fortune's Royal Flush Gang utilized arcane card lore and a selection of exotic weaponry. These devices were empowered by Fortune's discoveries in the manipulation of luck. The members were childhood friends from the same juvenile gang, and decked themselves out in costumes based on the suit of Clubs.

Much later, Hector Hammond revived the concept, gifting his squad with metahuman powers and weapons. For psychological impact and its connotations of death, he clad his team in spades.

LUCK OF THE DRAW
The criminal cardsharps always proved that fortune favored the bold, even if they usually folded in the final reckoning.

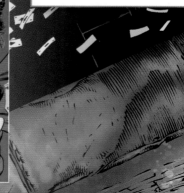

PURE BLUFF
The Royal Flush Gang rarely played with a full deck.
1 King of Spades
2 Jack of Spades
3 Ten of Spades
4 Ace of Spades
5 Queen of Spades

S.H.A.D.E.

DEBUT *Seven Soldiers: Frankenstein* (Vol. 1) #1 (Jan. 2006)
REAL NAME Super-Human Advanced Defense Executive
BASE S.H.A.D.E. City, The Ant Farm, Manhattan (exact location highly classified)
NOTABLE MEMBERS Father Time: Director; **Ray Palmer**: Chief Science-Liaison; **Agent Belroy**: Psychic intelligence gatherer
ALLIES Frankenstein, the Bride, G.I. Robot Squadron
ENEMIES Army of Monsters, Humanids, Brother Eye, the Rot
AFFILIATIONS Justice League Dark, Creature Commandos, S.H.A.D.E. Net, Checkmate

The Super-Human Advanced Defense Executive

(S.H.A.D.E.) was formed to counteract terrorism and contain all manner of supra-normal dangers to humanity. However, in recent years this ultra-secret government-sponsored group has concentrated exclusively on threats of a supernatural or paranormal nature and has been officially re-designated a "Counter-Disaster Organization." Their remit is to quietly head off metahuman crises before they can seriously impact upon the American public. S.H.A.D.E. is led by immortal superhuman Father Time and utilizes arcane lore and advanced technologies, much of it confiscated from the monsters, aliens, and super-maniacs they have defeated over the decades.

S.H.A.D.E.'s current HQ is a miniaturized city-sized citadel. The Ant Farm is a vast, futuristic fortress inside an indestructible metal globe reduced to three inches in diameter and floating 2,000 feet above New York City. Although S.H.A.D.E. possesses its own highly trained paramilitary force, the bulk of its operations is carried out by specialist operatives, like Frankenstein and the Bride, or the Creature Commandos. They are equipped with extraordinary ordnance from the Toybox—a repository of impounded superweapons, such as blockbusting Nazi War Wheels.

LEGION OF MONSTERS
Grim experience had proved that, for S.H.A.D.E., the best solution to fighting evil monsters was good ones, preferably carrying weapons.

The original S.H.A.D.E. was a counter-intelligence operation created by President Lyndon B. Johnson in the mid-1960s. As metahumans began to proliferate, the power and influence of the unit dwindled, until it was almost forgotten.

S.H.A.D.E. was saved by the *Infinite Crisis*. With all Earth's heroes fully occupied, Father Time became aware of an imminent invasion by the time-rending Sheeda and orchestrated the government's counterstrike through his own recruits, the Atomic Knights and Freedom Fighters.

THE EXPENDABLES
Father Time was content to let dispensable agents do the dirty work, and use the power of the US government to cover up his actions.

FUTURE PROOF
S.T.A.R. Labs is working on rational solutions to almost every physical problem facing mankind, but cannot ever escape its clandestine, conflict-tainted origins.

S.T.A.R. LABS

DEBUT *Superman* (Vol. 1) #246 (Dec. 1971)
REAL NAME Science and Technology Advanced Research Laboratories
BASE New York City, Metropolis
POWERS/MEMBERS Garrison Slate: founder; Jenette Klyburn; Kitty Faulkner; Kala Avasti; Murray Takamoto; Tina McGee; Valerie Perez. Dr. Glory:
FORMER MEMBERS Albert Michaels; Emil Hamilton; Silas Stone; Elinore Stone; Snapper Carr
ALLIES John Henry Irons, Superwoman
ENEMIES Lex Luthor, LexCorp, Algorithm
AFFILIATIONS The Teen Titans, Justice League, A.R.G.U.S.

Stemming from Operation Paperclip—a US Government project employing captured Nazi scientists on secret projects after World War II—S.T.A.R. Labs was founded by idealistic Garrison Slate. it proudly boasts independence from all governments: Earth's only cutting-edge, multi-disciplinary company specializing in "blue sky" science. It employs radical thinkers unwilling to work for soulless corporations or the military-industrial complex, probing all areas of scientific investigation, testing, exploration, and analysis.

A truly global enterprise, S.T.A.R. Labs has major facilities in many nations, including purpose-built skyscrapers in Manhattan and Metropolis. Non-political and offering immense resources, S.T.A.R. Labs is first port of call for Super Heroes requiring technical expertise, medical aid, or advice in coping with metahuman menaces. S.T.A.R. Labs has fought off takeover bids from Lex Luthor's LexCorp and infiltration from many covert groups, but has frequently been betrayed by its own employees such as Atomic Skull Albert Michaels and Parasite Rudy Jones. The biggest breach of ethics was uncovered recently by Young Justice, who found interdimensional researcher Dr. Glory had been corrupting her data for profit and had endangered Super Heroes Superboy (Conner Kent), and Impulse and Naomi McDuffie. With Glory arrested by the FBI, S.T.A.R. Labs now faces the task of cleaning house and regaining public trust as it continues to deal daily with constantly multiplying dangers of alien or post-metahuman technologies and unchecked, fringe-science innovation.

S.T.A.R. Labs quickly became a global mainstay of the pre-*Flashpoint* DC universe, acting as a prison for metahuman menaces and a medical resource for injured or mysteriously afflicted Super Heroes. The company even briefly operated its own team. S.T.A.R. Corps featured old company alumnus Rampage and a squad of neophyte metahuman anomalies—Brainstorm, Deadzone, Fusion, Ndoki, and Trauma—all created by out-of-control Project Mindstorm, as it probed the mysteries of the human metagene.

PROOF OF CONCEPT
S.T.A.R. Labs' employment package included fun, thrills, good pay, rewarding work, a dental plan—and possible metahuman transformation.

SABBAC

DEBUT *Captain Marvel, Jr.* (Vol. 1)
#4 (Feb. 1943) (Timothy Karnes);
The Outsiders. (Vol. 3) #8 (Mar. 2004)
(Ishmael Gregor)
REAL NAME Ishmael Gregor
BASE Hell
EYES Black **HAIR** Black
POWERS/ABILITIES Demonically-
fueled strength, speed, endurance, flight,
fire breath.
ALLIES Dr. Sivana, High Priest of Bagdan
ENEMIES Shazam, Shazam Family,
Superman, Nightwing, The Outsiders

Timothy Karnes was a huge disappointment
to the Lords of Hell. Thanks to their infernal
magic, he could transform into a monstrous
engine of destruction whenever he shouted
the acronym of their names; but as Sabbac,
he was an ineffectual agent, easily defeated
by Earth's Super Heroes. They were far
happier when New York City mob-boss
Ishmael Gregor murdered a bus full of
people as a blood-sacrifice and stole the
power from Timothy's expiring corpse.

Reveling in slaughter and chaos, the
new Sabbac undertook a vicious campaign
to amass wealth and bring about Hell on
Earth. When he opened a portal and started
recruiting demons from the Pit, he was
routed by the Outsiders. Sabbac has
returned many times, allying with coalitions
of Super-Villains and the demon Neron.

PURE EVIL
When it comes to sheer devilry, the
demonic Sabbac has few rivals. He is
prepared to go to any lengths to turn
Earth into a living hell.

SALAAK

DEBUT *Green Lantern* (Vol. 2) #149 (Feb. 1982)
BASE Mogo
HEIGHT 7ft 6in **WEIGHT** 207 lbs
EYES White **HAIR** None
POWERS/ABILITIES Skilled warrior and
strategist; genius intellect; indomitable will
enables command of a green power ring.
ENEMIES Sinestro, Guardians of the Universe,
Parallax

Salaak of Slyggia served the Corps for
years and single-handedly defended space
sectors from the Anti-Monitor during the
Infinite Crisis. When the Guardians
reconstructed the Green Lantern Corps,
he became protocol officer liaising between
the Guardians and their agents. However,
when the Guardians sought to replace their
servants with a mindless Third Army, Salaak
fought valiantly to thwart them. Painfully
aware that many of his comrades still
associated him with the treacherous
Guardians, Salaak gave up his post in Hal
Jordan's new administration and resolved to
earn the trust of his fellow Green Lanterns.

When the emerald Corps regrouped to
police the universe in a fragile coalition with
the Yellow Lantern Corps, Earthman John
Stewart was elected commander but
Salaak's clerical genius and multitasking was
what truly kept the 3600 Space Sectors
safe. As senior administrator and Keeper of
the Book of Oa, Salaak handled day-to-day
logistics, duty rosters and information flow,

INTERNAL CONFLICT
Salaak's bravery, brains, and loyalty
eventually convinced the Green
Lantern Corps
to trust him.

allowing the "beat cops" to safeguard
trillions of beings from threats such as
Brainiac 2.0, Larfleeze and Sinestro, and
every other intergalactic miscreant.
However, when the situation demanded, he
was ready to leave his command center on
Sentient world Mogo and hand out his
brand of emerald justice against problems
like the Controllers and Dark Stars.

SAINT WALKER

DEBUT *Final Crisis: Rage of the Red Lanterns* (Vol. 1) #1 (Dec. 2008)
REAL NAME Bro'Dee Walker
BASES Mogo, Odym, Astonia, Sector 1
EYES Black **HAIR** None
POWERS/ABILITIES Genius intellect, compassionate, and possesses
indomitable willpower; commands a blue power ring to materialize hard-light
constructs, translate languages, enable flight and protect against enemy
attack. His power ring also boosts and hyper-charges all green power rings
in immediate vicinity.
ALLIES Warth, Green Lantern Corps, Guy Gardner, Star Sapphires,
Indigo Tribe
ENEMIES Sinestro, Larfleeze, the Reach, Relic
AFFILIATIONS Ganthet and Sayd, Blue Lantern Corps,
New Guardians

Bro'Dee Walker was the first Blue Lantern, selected
by Oans Ganthet and Sayd after they quit the Guardians
of the Universe to create a corps empowered by hope.
A cleric on the doomed planet Astonia, Walker was chosen
for his ability to inspire his people in the face of extinction.
With his blue ring, he reinvigorated Astonia's sun, saving
his race. He then rescued Hal Jordan and his comrades
from Red Lanterns and later helped repel the rampaging
risen dead during the *Blackest Night*. His blue light
of Hope, combined with the green of Will, proved
devastatingly effective against the Black Lanterns.

Bro'Dee despaired when the Blue Lantern Corps
was wiped out by the fanatic Relic. His ring left him,
but when his hope for the future finally returned,
he regained the blue ring and set about spreading
harmony throughout the cosmos once more.

ON THE RECORD

For tyrants and villains,
Hope is the most dangerous
hue of the Emotional Spectrum.
A being possessing hope cannot
be cowed or controlled, only killed.
Despite the Guardian's misgivings
and plans to destroy free will, Saint
Walker became a trusted ally of the
Green Lanterns and served with
distinction in Kyle Rayner's
multi-spectrum task force, the
New Guardians. His assistance
was crucial in crushing the Oans'
oppressive Third Army.

AGAINST ALL HOPE
Although the Third Army was
designed to eliminate Free Will in
the universe, it would have just as
readily eradicated the light of Hope.

SAND

DEBUT *Adventure Comics* (Vol. 1) #69 **(Dec. 1941)**
REAL NAME Sanderson "Sandy" Hawkins
BASE Brooklyn, New York
HEIGHT 5ft 11in **WEIGHT** 162 lbs **EYES** Blue **HAIR** Blond
POWERS/ABILITIES Geokinesis, silicate transformation and phasing,
extended lifespan, psychic affinity with the planet, precognitive dreams; skilled
detective and criminologist, trained in combat.
ALLIES Wesley Dodds, Dian Belmont, John Law/Tarantula, Kendra Saunders
(Hawkgirl), Rex Tyler
ENEMIES Johnny Sorrow, Mordru, Ian Karkull, Geomancer,
Injustice Society, King of Tears
AFFILIATIONS Justice Society of America, All-Star Squadron,
Young All-Stars

Sandy Hawkins started his adventurous life during
World War II as sidekick to Sandman Wesley Dodds. Hawkins learned
crime-solving skills from his brilliant senior partner before succumbing to
a tragic accident. During a laboratory experiment to improve their crime-fighting
arsenal, Sandy was accidentally transformed into a huge, raging silicoid monster.
Fearing his experiment had created a pitiless menace, Dodds tranquilized the
inarticulate horror, keeping it imprisoned and unconscious for decades. Sandy
at last revived and escaped during an earthquake. His transformation had
attuned him to Earth's structure and he gradually learned to regain his human
shape. His new abilities included turning into sand and traveling through
geological strata at incredible speeds, hence his new moniker—Sand.

With Dodds disabled by age and infirmity, Sandy inherited his arsenal,
leading a multi-generational Justice Society of America. After adopting his
mentor's codename—and his awful power of prophetic dreaming—Sand
stood down to become the JSA's covert intelligence-gatherer. A tireless
avenger of injustice, Hawkins was excised from the timeline by Doctor
Manhattan but returned to continue his anti-crime crusade when the
Justice Society was restored to life and history.

NO SLEEP FOR THE WICKED
No matter what form he took,
Sand was a legacy hero who
took his glittering heritage and
evil-crushing duties seriously.

ON THE RECORD

Sandy the Golden Boy's Golden Age
debut coincided with Sandman's abrupt
transformation from an enigmatic, gas-
masked mystery man into a bombastic
masked acrobat, battling gangsters while
haunting their dreams with two-fisted
retribution. Years later, Sandy was
reintroduced in a 1974 Justice League/
Justice Society team up that revealed his
decades of petrification and
suspended animation.
His restoration to human
form in 1982 hinted that he
may have gained powers from
the experience, but it took the JSA's
21st-century revival to confirm it.

CRIME'S WORST NIGHTMARE
The Sandman and Sandy tirelessly pursued
evildoers in their dreams and then dealt swiftly
and forcefully with them in the real world.

SANDMAN (WESLEY DODDS)

DEBUT *Adventure Comics* (Vol. 1) #40 **(Jul. 1939)**
REAL NAME Wesley Dodds
HEIGHT 5ft 11in
WEIGHT 172 lbs
POWERS/ABILITIES Brilliant detective; gifted inventor specialising in
physics, chemistry and engineering; skilled acrobat and fighter; employs
gas gun and wirepoon grappling device; prescient dreams of evil deeds
ALLIES Sandy Hawkins, Dian Belmont, Speed Saunders
ENEMIES Scorpion, Dr. Death, Phantom of the World's Fair
AFFILIATIONS Justice Society of America

One of DC Comics' oldest heroes, Sandman was inspired
by 1930s pulp-fiction stars. Sporting a suit, hat, cape, and gas-mask,
he employed his detective skills, sleeping gas, and other gimmicks
against a legion of crooks.

Touched by the power of Morpheus, Lord of Dreams, World War I
veteran Wesley Dodds was plagued by nightmares of evil deeds.
Eventually he realized these were prescient visions, and used his vast
fortune, scientific genius and years of experience as a world traveler to
create the Sandman: eerie mystery man stalking America's vilest human
predators. He was a founder of the Justice Society of America, fighting
uncanny menaces and battling the military might of Nazi Germany and
Japan, but was always most comfortable hunting the darkest examples
of human evil.

During World War II, Sandman switched to gaudy tights and traded
his gutsy girlfriend Dian Belmont for a sidekick: Sandy the Golden Boy.
After years in retirement, Sandman returned in the
1960s, he reverted to his moody original gear and
methods. When Doctor Manhattan tampered with
the timeline, he was seemingly erased from
existence, but has since returned with his JSA
comrades to a restored reality.

IN THE SHADOWS
Even in a doomed
world, Sandman
found what was
necessary for
humanity to survive.

ON THE RECORD

After *Flashpoint*, **Sandman** was
reimagined on Apokolips-devastated
Earth-2. With Superman, Batman, and
Wonder Woman killed by Darkseid's
forces, a World Army arose to unite
and safeguard the remains of humanity.
Canadian super-spy Wesley Dodds was
the "Sandman": an infallible, teleporting
combat-master, expert with gas weapons,
leading a personally trained cadre of black
ops specialists. When Earth-2 was finally
consumed by Apokolips, Sandman was
instrumental in securing a fleet of colony
ships to ferry the last survivors of humanity
away from their doomed world.

THE SLEEP OF THE UNJUST
The Sandman punched heads and gassed
goons, scattering sand calling-cards as a
reminder to his targets to stay honest—or
face the consequences.

SARGON THE SORCERER

DEBUT *All-American Comics* (Vol. 1) #26 (May 1941)
REAL NAME Jaimini Sargent
BASE Temple of the Cold Flame
HEIGHT 5ft 10in **WEIGHT** 160 lbs
EYES Brown **HAIR** Black
POWERS/ABILITIES Highly skilled magician.
ENEMIES John Constantine, Justice League Dark, Frankenstein, S.H.A.D.E., Zatanna

Sargon the Sorcerer was formerly John Sargent: One of the most powerful magicians of the 20th century, who used his miraculous Ruby of Life to battle the forces of injustice and supernatural menaces, such as the Blue Lama. He eventually retired, studying lost lore and creating the Cult of the Cold Flame with mages Mister E. Tannarak, and Zatara.

His daughter Jaimini claims to have killed him, stealing his power and twisting the cult's aims. She and John Constantine searched for Croydon's Compass, a mystic artifact of great power. Unsure whether she was attracted to him for himself or his mystic resources, Jaimini variously tried to seduce, enslave, and eradicate the trickster-magician, but in vain. Her goals remain clear: To amass enough knowledge and power to do anything she wants.

SATANUS

DEBUT *Action Comics* (Vol. 1) #527 (Jan. 1982)
REAL NAME Lord Satanus
BASE Hell
HEIGHT/WEIGHT Variable **EYES** Red
POWERS/ABILITIES Supernal physical prowess derived from a demonic nature; dimensional travel, reality alteration, flight.
ENEMIES Kaiyo, Batman, Superman, Catwoman, Lois Lane

Lord Satanus is supreme overlord of demonic underworld the Dark Realm. A creature of almost limitless power and infinite life-span, Satanus lurks at the edges of reality looking for souls to torment and good lives to destroy. He has observed all aspects of human frailty, and occasional triumphs of virtue over adversity, which both amuse and repel him.

Though fiercely territorial over intrusions into his infernal realm, Satanus allowed Apokolips' trickster-demon Kaiyo to play her cruel games with Earth's greatest Super Heroes, Superman and Batman. She spitefully meddled with their lives and memories, drawing in Lois Lane, Catwoman and others, and providing Satanus with such great entertainment that the demon decided to imprison Kaiyo for the times that he craved further amusement.

SATURN QUEEN

DEBUT *Superman* (Vol. 1) #147 (Aug. 1961)
REAL NAME Eve Aries
BASE 31st century, mobile
HEIGHT 5ft 5in **WEIGHT** 110 lbs
EYES Green **HAIR** Red
POWERS/ABILITIES Telepathy, hypnotism, mind-control.
ALLIES Lightning Lord, Cosmic King
ENEMIES Saturn Girl, Legion of Super-Heroes, Superman, Batman

Eve Aries grew up in the telepathic community of Titan, but suffered a radical personality shift after leaving the influence of Saturn's moon. On her world, wicked thoughts and anti-social behavior were practically unknown and deviant attitudes were easily detected and rapidly addressed. Once beyond her people's influence, Eve was gripped by criminal tendencies and started using her psionic gifts to dominate lesser minds. The further Eve strayed from Titan, the more evil she became.

Saturn Queen went on a spree of robbery and worse, teaming with Lightning Lord and Cosmic King. They formed a Legion of Super-Villains, battling their own era's heroes and, after stealing time-travel technology, attacking Superman in his own time in an attempt to remake history.

SAWYER, MAGGIE

DEBUT *Superman* (Vol. 2) #4 (Apr. 1987)
REAL NAME Margaret Ellen "Maggie" Sawyer
BASE Metropolis
POWERS/ABILITIES Skilled detective, trained in special weapons protocols.
ALLIES Superman, Batman, James Gordon, Lois Lane, Batwoman (Kate Kane), Harvey Bullock
ENEMIES The Weeping Woman, Medusa, Ceto, Mother of All Monsters, Nocturna
AFFILIATIONS Metropolis Special Crimes Unit, G.C.P.D.

After her first marriage ended, Maggie quit the Metropolis Police Department to join the Gotham City force. While investigating the murderous Weeping Woman, Sawyer became romantically involved with Kate Kane aka Batwoman.

Sawyer was tipped to succeed James Gordon as Commissioner, but when he was framed for murder, the G.C.P.D. slipped back into old corrupt ways under interim Commissioner Jack Forbes. Sawyer worked with honest cops Jason Bard and Harvey Bullock to expose Forbes and restore Gordon. When her relationship with Kane foundered, Sawyer returned to Metropolis to head the city's Special Crimes Unit, facing threats such as Doomsday and the Legion of Doom, along with more insidious menaces like Intergang and the Invisible Mafia.

SATURN GIRL

DEBUT *Adventure Comics* (Vol. 1) #247 (Apr. 1958)
REAL NAME Imra Ardeen
BASE Legion of Super-Heroes HQ, 31st-century New Metropolis
POWERS/ABILITIES Wide array of psionic abilities including telepathy, mind-reading, thought-casting, mind-control, and illusion generation.
ALLIES Superboy, Garth Ranzz, Rokk Krinn, Superman, United Planets President R.J. Brande
ENEMIES Horraz Collective, Crav the General Nah, Mordru
AFFILIATIONS Legion of Super-Heroes, United Planets Youth Delegation for Peace

Imra Ardeen is a supremely powerful telepath, trained by elite mentalists on her birthplace, Saturn's moon, Titan. She was invited to join the United Planets Youth Delegation for Peace, with fellow exceptional teens Rokk Krinn and Garth Ranzz. While being interviewed by United Planets President R.J. Brande, their ship was attacked by terrorist species the Horraz Collective. The assault was repulsed by the teens and opportunistic Brande suggested a chance to make a real difference to civilization by reviving the mythic "Age of Heroes" as a Legion of Super-Heroes that could operate like Metropolis' legendary champion Superman. Imra realized that this was how she could best use her amazing psionic abilities.

When the Legion was established, Imra time-traveled to recruit Superboy Jon Kent, and became embroiled in the time-tampering of Doctor Manhattan and was largely responsible for undoing his machinations and restoring edited time, and Super Heroes like the Justice Society of America, to Earth's history. She helped the last survivors of Krypton punish the beings who actually destroyed the planet.

Her greatest achievement thus far is bringing United Planets founder Jon Kent into the Legion of Super-Heroes in preparation for an impending time of "Great Darkness" and multiversal doom.

ON THE RECORD

Saturn Girl was the first female comic book character to lead a team. When it was revealed that a Legionnaire would die on duty, she orchestrated events to be the only active Legionnaire. Lightning Lad uncovered the plot and died instead, but Imra brought him back, and won a second term as leader.

She later married Lightning Lad and had a son, Graym, unaware that their child had a twin whom Darkseid had stolen and turned into the monstrous Validus. When the secret was exposed, Imra convinced Darkseid to restore the child to human form. Now Legion Reservists, Imra and Garth aid the team when needed.

THE TEAM COMES FIRST
fiercely protective, Saturn Girl would go to any lengths and make any sacrifice to ensure the safety and wellbeing of her comrades.

SCALPHUNTER

DEBUT *Weird Western Tales* #39 (Mar.–Apr. 1977)
REAL NAME Brian Savage/Ke-Woh-No-Tay
BASE Opal City, 19th century
HEIGHT 6ft 1in **WEIGHT** 190 lbs
EYES Blue **HAIR** Black (later gray)
POWERS/ABILITIES Superb hand-to-hand fighter; excellent horseman; expert marksman and tracker.
ALLIES Bat Lash, Cinnamon, Jonah Hex, Shade
ENEMIES The Tuesday Club
AFFILIATIONS Rough Bunch, Black Lanterns

In the 1840s, the Kiowa tribe of Native Americans attacked the home of Matthew and Laurie Savage, kidnapping their young son Brian. Renamed Ke-Woh-No-Tay, meaning "He Who Is Less Than Human," Brian was raised by the Kiowa until he was captured during a raiding party and recognized. Sent to prison for a murder he did not commit, Brian escaped and caught the killers, procuring a pardon for himself in the process.

He became known as Scalphunter and befriended gambler Bat Lash, settling down in Opal City later in life. While only a ghost of Scalphunter has been glimpsed post-*Flashpoint*, he was resurrected during the *Blackest Night* event as a Black Lantern, joining forces with other Western icons.

SCANDAL

DEBUT *Villains United* #1 (Jul. 2005)
REAL NAME Scandal Savage
HEIGHT 5ft 10in **WEIGHT** 143 lbs
EYES Brown **HAIR** Brown (with blue streak)
POWERS/ABILITIES Expert fighter, natural leader, intelligent; gauntlets with retractable blades.
ALLIES Ragdoll, Jeannette, Secret Six
ENEMIES The Riddler

The daughter of infamous criminal Vandal Savage, Scandal hasn't quite followed in her dad's footsteps, but she hasn't led a civilian's life either. Blackmailed by the Riddler, who threatened to kill her two wives, Scandal was forced to do his bidding as the villain kidnapped Thomas Blake (the future Catman). Fearing for Blake's sanity, Scandal brought him a kitten to keep him company in his solitary jail cell.

Later—in company with two other mercenaries, Ragdoll and Jeannette—Scandal was forced to battle the Secret Six, Catman's allies. With neither team wanting to harm the other, they developed a mutual respect, especially when the Secret Six brought the Riddler to justice. Scandal subsequently offered to look after the young Secret Six member Black Alice, when it seemed as if she was being pursued by nearly every sorcerer in the world.

SCARAB

DEBUT *Robin* #124 (May 2004)
REAL NAME Maat Shadid
BASE Gotham City
HEIGHT 5ft 4in **WEIGHT** 125 lbs
EYES Brown **HAIR** Black
POWERS/ABILITIES Hi-tech, armored suit allows flight, enhanced communication and durability; helmet provides night-vision; forearm-mounted blasters fire energy bolts.
ALLIES Fellow Scarabs
ENEMIES Red Robin, Spoiler, Batman
AFFILIATIONS Covenant of Ka

The killer for hire known as Scarab first arrived in Gotham City when she was hired by another villain, Johnny Warlock, to assassinate Robin (Tim Drake). However, Scarab took the contract during a time of great turmoil between Batman and Robin; Tim Drake had temporarily quit his position as the Dark Knight's closest ally, which resulted in Batman enlisting Stephanie Brown as a replacement Robin.

Nevertheless, Scarab began targeting boys who met Robin's description until she was defeated by Stephanie and Batman. When Tim Drake graduated to the position of Red Robin, he would clash with Scarab several more times, discovering she was just one of many assassin Scarabs working for the Covenant of Ka syndicate.

SCARLET

DEBUT *Batman and Robin* (Vol. 1) #1 (Aug. 2009)
REAL NAME Sasha (last name unknown)
BASE Gotham City
HEIGHT 4ft 6in **WEIGHT** 78 lbs
EYES Blue **HAIR** Red
POWERS/ABILITIES Adept hand-to-hand combatant trained by the Red Hood.
ALLIES Red Hood
ENEMIES Professor Pyg, Flamingo

A young girl named Sasha traveled to the United States to start a new life with her father, Niko. When he was hired as a henchmen by the criminal Mr. Toad, Niko was lucky to escape his first encounter with Batman (Dick Grayson). Niko went to his apartment, but before he could get away with Sasha, the pair were ambushed by the murderous scientist Professor Pyg, who placed a Dollotron mask on them both to control their minds. Freed by Robin, Sasha fought back against Pyg, setting the villain on fire.

Sasha later smothered her father in his hospital bed as a mercy killing, and was discovered by the Red Hood (Jason Todd) and became his vigilante partner, using the codename Scarlet. They fought foes including the Flamingo and the Menagerie, often employing a deadlier brand of justice than Batman.

SCAVENGER

DEBUT *Aquaman* (Vol. 1) #37 (Jan.–Feb. 1968)
REAL NAME Peter Mortimer
HEIGHT 5ft 9in **WEIGHT** 176 lbs
EYES Brown **HAIR** Brown
POWERS/ABILITIES Underwater fighter; protective suit with air supply and advanced weapons; Scorpion Ship.
ALLIES Black Manta, Aquamarines
ENEMIES Aquaman, Tula, Mera, Dead Water
AFFILIATIONS Secret Society

Sub-sea thief Scavenger is one of Aquaman's greatest foes. Super-Villain Graves even grilled Scavenger to learn more about the Atlantean.

After Atlantis attacked Boston, Scavenger salvaged valuables from the ruins. Aquaman believed Scavenger was taking Atlantean weapons, but he was actually preparing an invasion of Atlantis—one the Sea-king barely managed to repel. Scavenger joined the Secret Society of Super-Villains, but was maimed in action. Hired by the US government to investigate mutations, Mortimer reluctantly worked with Aquaman and the Aquamarines.

Scavenger now understands the benefit of working with a powerful crowd and is constantly seeking allies. He has even been spotted in his armored suit at a Legion of Doom villains mixer.

SCORN

DEBUT *Superman* (Vol. 2) #122 (Apr. 1997) (Ceritak); *Detective Comics* (Vol. 2) #22 (Sep. 2013) (Clyde Anderson)
BASE Metropolis, mobile
HEIGHT 12ft **WEIGHT** 975 lbs
EYES White **HAIR** White
POWERS/ABILITIES Superhuman strength and senses; flight; tracking vision.

The hulking creature known as Scorn is actually named Ceritak, a citizen of a bottled city created by the sorcerer Tolos. His father, Cerimul, was a Council Elder of the city, but Ceritak was a rebel, and escaped the confines of his bottled prison when Superman weakened the dimensional barrier between the city and the rest of the world.

Ceritak was dubbed Scorn by the media, despite only wanting to explore the world, often by the side of his love, Ashbury, daughter of *Daily Planet* writer Dirk Armstrong. Making Metropolis his home, Scorn did his best to protect the city during his short time there, fighting the likes of the Cyborg Superman.

After *Flashpoint*, small-time criminal Clyde Anderson used the name Scorn. Bearing a grudge against the G.C.P.D., Anderson teamed up with the Super-Villain Wrath, but when Scorn didn't reach his target number of kills, he was murdered by his partner.

THE WRATH OF WRATH
The new Scorn was Wrath's partner, until the villain murdered him for not eliminating enough police officers.

SEA DEVILS

DEBUT *Showcase* (Vol. 1) #27 (Jul.–Aug. 1960)
NOTABLE MEMBERS Dane Dorrance; Judy Walton; Nick Walton
ALLIES Aquaman
ENEMIES Captain Moller
AFFILIATIONS Interpol

Seafaring vigilantes the Sea Devils are led by former Navy SEAL Dane Dorrance. The team also includes Judy and Nick Walton who were reputedly responsible for bringing down an oil rig mid-construction, among similar plots.

When the Sea Devils found Captain Moller using stolen Atlantean weaponry to kill whales, he turned his weapon on them. Aquaman came to their rescue, but Dane was angered, as Atlanteans had recently attacked surface people because of Aquaman's half-brother, Ocean Master.

The Devils and Aquaman joined forces to arrest Russian mobsters involved in toxic waste dumping, and destroyed a colossal mutated fish created by pollution. The Sea King made the Devils his Surface Liaisons and gifted them Diplomatic Immunity.

BIG BLUE
Belying his threatening appearance, Scorn had a kind heart and helped to defend Metropolis.

SCARECROW

DATA

DEBUT *World's Finest Comics* (Vol. 1) #3 **(Fall 1941)**
REAL NAME Dr. Jonathan Crane
BASE Gotham City
HEIGHT 6ft **WEIGHT** 140 lbs
EYES Green **HAIR** Brown
POWERS/ABILITIES Near genius intellect; brilliant chemist and
psychiatrist; weapons include fear gas that causes victims to experience
their worst nightmares.
ALLIES Professor Pyg, Merry-Maker, Harley Quinn, Mr. Freeze
ENEMIES Batman, the Batman Family
AFFILIATIONS The Secret Society of Super-Villains

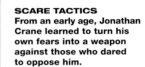

WHO SCARES THE SCARECROW?
The Scarecrow has spent his life becoming a bogeyman to scare innocents. Unluckily for Crane, he often clashes with a creature of the night that frightens even him: Batman.

Dr. Jonathan Crane has spent as much time lurking in the dark corners of the human psyche as he has hiding in the shadowy parts of Gotham City. Obsessed with the idea of fear in its many forms, Crane has adopted the role of the Scarecrow, a living embodiment of things that go bump in the night. A career Super-Villain, Scarecrow lives to clash with the Batman, intent on making the Dark Knight cower in fear.

SCARE TACTICS
From an early age, Jonathan Crane learned to turn his own fears into a weapon against those who dared to oppose him.

FEAR OF THE FATHER
Surrounded by skeletons and other horrors that would scare an adult, young Jonathan Crane grew up with fear, and would later embrace it.

Jonathan Crane was born into a life of fear due to the terrible upbringing inflicted on him by his heartless scientist father. Jonathan's mother died when he was young and he was brought up by his father, who was obsessed with all aspects of terror—a grim passion he would pass on to his son. When Jonathan was a young boy, his father would hook him up to heart rate monitors and shove him beneath a trap door. The small, dark chamber beneath was stuffed full of macabre items more suited to the set of a Gothic horror movie. As soon as Jonathan was set free by his father, the terrified boy would run as fast as he could into a nearby cornfield, screaming and scaring away the birds.

A shy boy, mocked by his peers, young Jonathan focused on his studies. He became a professor of psychology, but his peculiar teaching methods terrified his students and he was fired. He then became a psychologist, but after attacking a patient, decided to accept his "true self" and adopted the name and costume of the scarecrow on his family farm. He embarked upon a criminal career that used his specially designed fear toxins to terrify victims. Becoming a notorious figure in Gotham City, Scarecrow was recruited into the infamous "War of Jokes and Riddles" on the side of the Riddler, and became a brainwashed faux police detective during Bane's recent takeover of Gotham City. He's even branched out on occasion, taking his special brand of terror to Blüdhaven to terrorize Nightwing.

ON THE RECORD

While he is a key foe in Batman's modern-day Rogues Gallery, the Scarecrow's criminal career got off to a fairly slow start. Debuting in the 1940s, the villain only appeared once more before returning to commit new crimes in the 1960s.

The Scarecrow's ascendancy through Gotham City's criminal ranks continued in the following decades. His character grew darker and increasingly psychotic as he took on Batman and the Batman Family in such high-profile stories as *Batman: Dark Victory*, "Hush," "Knightfall," and even the cosmic saga *Blackest Night*.

NATURE OF THE BEAST
Before *Flashpoint* altered reality, Scarecrow was given a power upgrade courtesy of a scheming Penguin, who transformed Crane into the hulking, super-powered Scarebeast.

CLASSIC STORIES

World's Finest Comics (Vol. 1) #3 **(Fall 1941)** The Scarecrow debuts in Batman's chapter of this title, which stars both the Dark Knight and Superman in their own separate features.
Batman (Vol. 1) #189 (Feb. 1967) Not glimpsed since the Golden Age, the Scarecrow returns to frighten a new generation of readers, armed with his signature fear gas.
Batman (Vol. 1) #457 (Dec. 1990) Fledgling Robin Tim Drake proves his worth when he saves Batman from the Scarecrow and the villain's latest fear gas concoctions.

SCOTT, ALAN

DEBUT *All-American Comics* (Vol. 1) #16 **(Jul. 1940)**
HEIGHT 6 ft **WEIGHT** 175 lbs.
EYES Blue **HAIR** Blond
POWERS/ABILITIES Possesses a Green Lantern carved from the mysterious Starheart and corresponding ring capable of mystic force generation, flaming construct manipulation, force-field barriers, and flight, among other functions.
ALLIES The Flash (Jay Garrick), Wildcat (Ted Grant), "Doiby" Dickles
ENEMIES Solomon Grundy, Vandal Savage, Injustice Society of America
AFFILIATIONS Justice Society

FORCE OF WILL
While he's a bit older than when he first slipped on the Green Lantern Ring, Alan Scott is still vital and kicking after 80 years of crime fighting.

As the Green Lantern of the Golden Age, Alan Scott is a member of the Justice Society of America, the same team he helped found back in the 1940s. A survivor and a thinker, Alan has servd as an inspiration to not just Green Lanterns, but to everyone who knows a true hero when they see one.

Alan Scott was an engineer with an uncanny way of figuring out how things worked. He designed a bridge that could hold a great deal of weight, but before he could receive a healthy government contract for mass production, his bridge was sabotaged by a criminal and rival engineer named Dekker.

On July 16, 1940, Dekker's men blew up Scott's bridge, causing a train Alan was riding to crash. Everyone aboard the train was killed, including Alan's lover, a man named Jimmy Henton. Pinned under some wreckage, Alan would've died as well, if the dying Jimmy hadn't pointed out a mysterious glowing green light right within Alan's reach. It was a Green Lantern.

Enraged at the murderous Dekker, Alan sought him out. He used the power of the mysterious Green Lantern to pass right through the wall of Dekker's office. Dekker's men shot at him, but the bullets had no effect. The criminals couldn't believe what they were seeing, and assumed Alan must be a ghost. Alan brought them to justice, and soon became the Super Hero known as Green Lantern.

A founding member of the wartime Justice Society of America, Alan would be with the team in later incarnations as well, serving with the Justice Society into the present day. With his aging slowed by his Green Lantern, carved from the mystical Starheart, Alan shows no signs of retiring, and serves as a mentor to younger Society members, including Stargirl.

SHAPE OF THINGS
Alan Scott's Green Lantern Ring is more lantern-shaped than those worn by the Green Lantern Corps members.

ON THE RECORD

Alan Scott was the original Green Lantern, debuting in 1940 to battle all forms of evil with a magic ring. He shone for over a decade as one of the brightest lights of the Golden Age before changing tastes benched him and many other costumed champions.

Scott returned in the 1960s as a hero from alternate Earth-2; an affable elder statesman sharing experiences and adventures with his science-based counterpart Hal Jordan and other heroes of the Justice Society of America.

After *Crisis on Infinite Earths* rebooted continuity, Scott was given a new lease of life as the world's Sentinel. Still later, he would be reintroduced as a new Earth-2 hero following the *Flashpoint* miniseries event, until his post-*Crisis* characterization was restored during the *Doomsday Clock* miniseries.

CREATURE OF THE NIGHT
The earliest appearances of the Emerald Gladiator played up his mystical origins and uncanny power, as he terrorized crooks and killers.

THE OATH
When Alan met with the mother of Jimmy Henton, she spoke of her son's inner light, and inspired what would become Green Lantern's often repeated oath.

CLASSIC STORIES

***Green Lantern Comics* (Vol. 1) #30 (Feb.–Mar. 1948)** Green Lantern gets a pet. Streak the Wonder Dog will push Green Lantern out of his own title and into retirement within two years.

***Green Lantern* (Vol. 2) #61 (Jun. 1968)** Fed up with fighting a never-ending battle, Scott orders his ring to banish all evil from Earth and is instantly the only human left on an empty planet.

***Green Lantern Corps Quarterly* (Vol. 1) #5–6 (Jun.–Sep. 1993)** Suddenly rejuvenated as Sentinel, Alan discovers his green flame is the Starheart, repository of ancient magic, bound by the Guardians of the Universe when the cosmos was young.

SECRET SIX

DEBUT *Secret Six* (Vol. 1) #1 (Apr.–May 1968)
BASE Gotham City, suburbia
MEMBERS/POWERS Catman (Thomas Blake): Feline strength, power, speed, agility, and reflexes; **Ventriloquist** (Shauna Belzer): Telekinesis, voice manipulation, ventriloquism; **Black Alice** (Lori Zechlin): Absorption of magical powers; **Porcelain** (Kani): Able to turn objects brittle and fragile; **Big Shot** (Damon Wells/Ralph Dibny): Transformation, super-strength, pliable body; **Strix** (Mary Turner): Former Talon, trained human weapon with exceptional proficiency in unarmed combat and acrobatics.
ENEMIES The Riddler, Agent Robbins, Punster, Susan Dibny, Felix Faust, Aquaman, Shiva Woosan

The Secret Six is the designation given to a succession of clandestine, non-governmental special ops teams. All have been run by a leader dubbed Mockingbird who compels the services of the six through coercion and blackmail. The most recent incarnation was created by The Riddler, who tested a disparate group of metahumans he believed had stolen a gem he craved. After a fruitless year of isolation and torture, the Riddler (aka Mockingbird) allowed his suspects to escape after planting a mole within their ranks.

The fugitive Secret Six retreated to suburbia, laying low and slowly forging close bonds of fellowship. Following a series of attacks by Mockingbird's hirelings and a final confrontation with the Prince of Puzzlers, they solved the mystery and exposed the infiltrator. Despite this betrayal, the outcasts opted to stick together. Catman, Ventriloquist, Porcelain, and Big Shot grew increasingly protective of emotionally scarred Strix and especially Black Alice. The latter's predatory, magical nature began to manifest itself, drawing the group into a universe-threatening conflict with the planet's supernatural community and the ancient League of Assassins.

WALKING THE LINE
The Secret Six were wanted by criminals and cops, but only wanted to live together in peace and safety.

SECRET SIX—THE INFECTED
When Dark Multiverse bat-god Barbatos sought to absorb reality, his agent The Batman Who Laughs created a virus that empowered and twisted heroic personalities. The first to transform were Shazam (King Shazam), Donna Troy (Deathbringer), James Gordon (The Commissioner), Supergirl (Kara Zor-El)), Blue Beetle (Scarab) and Hawkman (Sky Tyrant): a new and lethally contagious Secret Six ready to lay low Earth's defenders with deadly violence and a horrific viral load.

SERGEANT ROCK

DEBUT *Our Army at War* (Vol. 1) #81 (Apr. 1959)
REAL NAME Franklin John Rock
BASE Various Operational Theaters of World War II
HEIGHT 6ft **WEIGHT** 183 lbs **EYES** Blue **HAIR** Auburn
POWERS/ABILITIES Excellent marksman and militarily trained combatant; peak human endurance, combat-honed instincts, overwhelming determination, leadership skills, and personal charisma.
ALLIES The Losers, Unknown Soldier, Jeb Stuart, Mlle. Marie
ENEMIES Nazi Germany, Iron Major, Japanese Empire, Vandal Savage
AFFILIATIONS United States Army, Easy Company, Suicide Squad, Justice League United

An indomitable fighting man, Sergeant Rock served in the US Army during World War II. Enlisting in 1941, he rose steadily in rank, soldiering from the burning sands of Africa to mainland Europe on D-Day. Leading from the front, he shepherded Easy Company from the beaches of Normandy into the heartland of Germany, always at the vanguard of the bloodiest battles.

Frank Rock was the quintessential soldier. He followed orders and got the job done swiftly and efficiently, witnessing extraordinary events during wartime, even the presence of super-powered beings on the battlefield. In later years, Frank most clearly recalls the horror of seeing men on both sides and an endless parade of greenhorns get maimed or killed. When hostilities ceased, Frank stayed a soldier, serving his country as both educator and clandestine agent.

His legacy lives on today through his grandson, Joseph. Becoming a career soldier after a family tragedy, Joe joined other combat veterans in a radical enterprise started up by a private military contractor. He took charge of a new Easy Company that uses cutting-edge ordnance to provide an effective human response to metahuman or supernatural threats.

SERAFINA

DEBUT *Forever People* #1 (Feb.–Mar. 1971)
REAL NAME Serafina Baldaur
BASE New Genesis
HEIGHT 5ft 7in **WEIGHT** 143 lbs
EYES Brown **HAIR** Brown
POWERS/ABILITIES Bio-bursts dazzle and
disorient targets; other powers of the New Gods.
ALLIES Infinity-Man, Vykin
ENEMIES Mantis, Darkseid

Serafina Baldaur is one of the Forever People, a group of New Gods who can collectively become the mind of the Infinity-Man by tapping the powers of the Mother Box. Infinity Man forces this merger against their will as a way to direct them against dangers from New Genesis and Apokolips. Infinity-Man meddled with the Forever People's first mission to Earth, which put them in conflict with the Lantern Corps. Despite Serafina's best efforts, this conflict broke out into a pitched battle between Infinity-Man and the Lanterns, who pooled their powers and faced him with Mecha-Darkseid. Serafina and the rest of the Forever People then learned that Infinity-Man was the agent of the New God Highfather, fighting on his behalf against the resurgent threat of Darkseid himself.

SEVEN DEADLY SINS

DEBUT *Whiz Comics* #2 (Feb. 1940)
BASE Rock of Eternity
MEMBERS Pride, Gluttony, Sloth, Anger, Envy, Greed, Lust
ALLIES Blight
ENEMIES The Wizard, Justice League Dark, Shazam, Shazam Family
AFFILIATION Rock of Eternity, Seven Magic Lands

Also known as the Seven Deadly Enemies of Mankind, these entities personify the mortal sins that have beset humanity since ancient times. Unleashed 10,000 years ago by Pandora, the Sins ravaged her village and began corrupting Earth. The wizards' council of the Rock of Eternity battled their dire influence for millennia, while Pandora—condemned by that same council—learned magic in her quest to recapture them.

After *Flashpoint*, Pandora's Box was revealed as the key to containing the Sins. When the Trinity of Sin battled over possession of the box and the Blight was unleashed on the world—along with the Crime Syndicate of America and a resurgent Secret Society of Super-Villains—Pandora learned her true power and was able to dispel the Sins herself.

SEVEN SOLDIERS OF VICTORY

DEBUT *Leading Comics* #1 (Winter 1941–42)
BASE Mobile
CURRENT MEMBERS/POWERS Bulleteer: Invulnerable metal skin and enhanced strength **Spawn of Frankenstein:** Enhanced strength, injury-resistant undead body **Klarion the Witch Boy:** Spellcasting and monstrous transformations **Manhattan Guardian:** Peak physical condition, skilled fighter **Mister Miracle II:** One of the world's greatest escape artists **Shining Knight II:** Skilled fighter and excellent swordswoman **Zatanna:** Vast magical powers triggered by saying spells backward
ALLIES Sideways, Superman (New Earth)
ENEMIES Iron Hand, Injustice League, Darkseid, Perrus the Benevolent
AFFILIATIONS Justice League of America, Justice Society of America, Super-Human Advanced Defense Executive.

LAWS' LEGIONNAIRES
Six of the original Seven Soldiers, before they had adopted their new team name. Only the Shining Knight remains a member of the team.

After independently stopping the villainous agents of the Iron Hand, seven heroes united to become the Laws' Legionnaires, more commonly referred to as the Seven Soldiers of Victory. The team comprised the Crimson Avenger, Billy Gunn; Shining Knight and his flying horse Winged Victory; Vigilante, the Spider; the Star-Spangled Kid; and Stripesy. The Crimson Avenger's aide, Wing, an unofficial eighth member, sacrificed his life in a battle against the Nebula Man in Tibet. The resulting temporal explosion scattered the group across the timestream. Before they reformed, Deadman organized a short-lived new incarnation of the team, including Adam Strange; Batgirl; Blackhawk; Mento; Metamorpho; and Shining Knight. They defended the planet Rann from the Injustice League.

Two later versions of the Seven fought the Sheeda, a powerful faerie race from the far future bent on harvesting humanity. The first Soldiers—Vigilante; I, Spyder; Gimmix; Boy Blue; Dyno-Mite Dan; and the Whip's granddaughter—numbered only six, after the Bulleteer's last-minute refusal to join. Destroyed by the Sheeda, a new team formed: Seven Soldiers who never actually met: Mister Miracle II ; the Spawn of Frankenstein; Zatanna; Clarion the Witch Boy; Shining Knight II; Manhattan Guardian; and the returning Bulleteer, who struck the fatal blow against the vile Sheeda Queen.

Following *Rebirth*, these Seven Soldiers came adrift in the Multiverse, falling victim to the returned Sheeda and the psychic parasite Perrus. At their lowest ebb, they were reinvigorated and returned to full strength when dimension-hopping teen Sideways substituted for the Manhattan Guardian and battled beside a time-lost alternate Superman to save them.

MAGNIFICENT SEVEN
The most recent incarnation of the Seven Soldiers assembled for action against the Sheeda:
1 Klarion the Witch Boy
2 Shining Knight II
3 Zatanna
4 Spawn of Frankenstein
5 Guardian
6 Bulleteer
7 Mister Miracle II

SECRET SOCIETY OF SUPER-VILLAINS

DEBUT *The Secret Society of Super-Villains* #1 (May–Jun. 1976)
NOTABLE CURRENT MEMBERS
BLACK MANTA Expert in hand-to-hand combat, weapons master.
ULTRA-HUMANITE Alien physiology, mind control, possession.
DEATHSTROKE Super-soldier, expert assassin.
KILLER FROST Heat absorption and cold generation.
HECTOR HAMMOND Powerful telepathic abilities.
RAPTOR Expert mercenary, pain immunity.
VANDAL SAVAGE Immortal, genius level intellect, acclaimed warrior.
REVERSE-FLASH (Eobard Thawne) Super-speed.
LEX LUTHOR Genius level intellect, billionaire.
ENEMIES Justice League, Teen Titans, Titans

Secret Society of Super-Villains is the villain team to end all villain teams, formed to balance the scales against Super Hero groups like the Justice League. The Secret Society has been a small gathering of villains as well as a massive organization, but it has always had one goal: The destruction of the forces of good.

AT A GLANCE...

The butler did it
The Outsider, leader of Earth-0's Secret Society, is Owlman's butler on Earth-3, Alfred Pennyworth. He raised an army of Super-Villains to help the Crime Syndicate take over Earth-0, but did not share their goal. When Black Manta found out, he defected from the group and put a permanent end to The Outsider and his machinations.

No honor among villains
Composed of power-hungry evildoers, The Secret Society has its share of competing agendas. Professor Ivo and The Outsider recruited the Society's members under false pretenses, telling them they would destroy the Justice League, without mentioning that they would then be subservient to the Crime Syndicate. Meanwhile Superwoman, Black Adam, and the Rogues all revealed themselves to be working at cross-purposes. Two of the defectors from the Society—Captain Cold and Black Manta—would play a decisive role in its defeat once they discovered The Outsider's true goal.

While there are rumors of several different Secret Society of Super-Villains forming in the past, the most infamous incarnation of this criminal-led organization was assembled by Professor Ivo and the mysterious Outsider—revealed to be none other than Earth-3's Alfred Pennyworth. This Secret Society of Super-Villains was to be The Outsider's army on Earth-0, ready and waiting for the arrival of the evil Crime Syndicate following the opening of Pandora's Box. Hunting the box, The Outsider took steps to isolate Pandora from those who would protect her, manipulating the Justice League, Justice League of America, and Justice League Dark into a three-way battle. In addition to these preparations, The Outsider placed a mole inside the Justice League, with Earth-3's Atomica masquerading as the Atom until the Crime Syndicate could finally make their appearance.

WHAT'S IN THE BOX?
The Outsider understood that Pandora's Box was in fact a technological device that could open portals between alternate Earths.

The Justice League understood that the Secret Society was forming and initiated a series of covert actions to discover the true nature of the threat. Catwoman was sent to infiltrate the Society, but was captured, interrogated, and shot—whereupon it was revealed that she was actually the Martian Manhunter in disguise. The Manhunter briefly touched minds with the shadowy villain known as The Outsider, but was unable to discern his identity. The Outsider then destroyed the Justice League's Watchtower, using the ruins as his new base and holding Nightwing in a machine with a bomb wired to the beating of his heart. He also held another prisoner, who turned out to be Alexander Luthor, the Shazam of Earth-3. The Justice League freed him and he went on a rampage, attacking hero and villain alike, but directing most of his rage at the members of the Crime Syndicate who had removed him from Earth-3.

Power Ring, Johnny Quick, Copperhead, and The Outsider all died in the climactic battle with the combined Justice League and Justice league of America. The heroes were helped by defecting members of the Society, notably Deathstroke and Black Manta, who killed The Outsider. The Secret Society of Super-Villains was disbanded again and its membership scattered or imprisoned. However, the Secret Society of Super-Villains still remains active, albeit a closely guarded secret. With an inner high council that meets to decide policy and settle disputes between Super-Villains, it seeks to unite the underworld from the shadows.

THE OUTSIDER
As the different Justice Leagues battled in Kahndaq, The Outsider finished gathering the new Secret Society of Super-Villains, capable of destroying the Justice League, in readiness for the arrival of the Crime Syndicate from Earth-3. He was a faithful servant of Earth-3's Owlman, completely dedicated—as any good butler should be.

STEADFAST LOYALTY
The Outsider humbles himself before Owlman, explaining how he brought the Secret Society together.

ALL HANDS ON DECK
The Secret Society of Super-Villains gathered to hear the Crime Syndicate's plans to finish off the Justice League. One notable absence—The Joker.

TRIBUNAL
A sampling of the Society's elite:
1. Killer Frost
2. Hector Hammond
3. Vandal Savage
4. Ultra-Humanite
5. Reverse-Flash
6. Black Manta

FROM THE SHADOWS

While the Society has been keeping a low profile as the Legion of Doom rose to power, they are still functioning behind the scenes. When Deathstroke formed a team of young heroes, Reverse-Flash (Eobard Thawne) kidnapped him and brought him before a council led by Vandal Savage. He was given the Riddler as his defense "attorney" and stood trial to see if he was still evil enough to be permitted to stay in the SSSV. When they used Hector Hammond's abilities to peer into Deathstroke's mind and see that he would murder everyone in the room if freed, the Society opted to keep him on as a member.

STRIKING OUT ON HIS OWN

Deathstroke, never a friend to the Justice League, liked the Crime Syndicate even less.

"All this time you were looking for who was behind this... as you say on your world... the butler did it."

The Outsider

ON THE RECORD

The first Secret Society of Super-Villains was created by Darkseid to coordinate his efforts to rid Earth of all Super Heroes who would oppose his rule. A new assembly of evil, overseen by the Ultra-Humanite, targeted the Justice League and Justice Society before being banished to limbo.

Leadership changes

Despero awakened the memories of several former Society members and set them against the Justice League just prior to *Infinite Crisis*. A fourth generation, the brainchild of Alexander Luthor, was known as Villains United. Control of the group's remaining members then passed first to the Wizard and then Calculator, bookending the *Infinite Crisis* event. Darkseid's prophet, Libra, then reformed the SSSV as *Final Crisis* loomed, before The Cheetah took over and masterminded the creation of the post-*Final Crisis* version of the Society.

In syndication

While leaders of the Secret Society come and go, its history with the Crime Syndicate of America stretches all the way back to the early 1960s, when a version of the Secret Society battled the original Crime Syndicate in one of the first cross-world "Crisis" stories. This story also established the conflict between the Crime Syndicate and the Justice League, a touchstone for the *Forever Evil* crossover event.

VILLAINS UNITED
Deathstroke is central to Alexander Luthor's Villains United, hand-picked from the Secret Society to battle the splinter group called the Secret Six.

SHADE, THE

DEBUT *The Flash Comics* #33 (Sep. 1942)
REAL NAME Richard Swift
BASE Opal City
HEIGHT 6ft 2in **WEIGHT** 170 lbs **EYES** Gray **HAIR** Black
POWERS/ABILITIES Immortality; summoning of "shadowmatter" from the Dark Zone; manipulation of shadows.
ALLIES Starman
ENEMIES Simon Culp, Dudley Caldecott

In 1838, Richard Swift was transformed into the Shade—a near-immortal capable of manipulating shadowmatter—in an occult ceremony conducted by his evil, shadow-wielding counterpart, Simon Culp. He left his family behind and became a vigilante, battling both mystical threats and ordinary criminals. He and Culp became mortal enemies because of Culp's original subterfuge that trapped Swift.

A ruthless self-proclaimed man of taste, he frequently purloined beautiful art, and clashed with Super Heroes such as The Flash, Starman, and Hawkman Carter Hall. A fellow immortal, Hall eventually befriended Swift and they became "off-duty" confidants.

When Jack Knight inherited Starman's mantle, he gradually convinced Swift to abandon criminality and retire to the Shadowlands with his true love, Hope O'Dare. But nearly 200 years after his creation, he was killed by Deathstroke. Ressurecting, Swift traced his would-be killer's employers: Descendants of his first wife bribing Egyptian luck deities with human sacrifices. The Shade learned the truth of their origin and dispelled them to their home dimension—after which he reluctantly killed the family who unleashed them.

Swift recently teamed up with The Flash to cleanse the Shadowlands of toxic influences, and advised a reborn Carter Hall: A task made harder since Hawkman was transformed by The Batman Who Laughs into the monstrous Sky Tyrant.

ON THE RECORD

Possibly due to the nature of shadowmatter, the Shade was one of the few people able to prevent a Black Lantern ring from attaching to him during *Blackest Night*. He also survived having his heart ripped out by Black Lantern David Knight. Sometimes a hero, sometimes a villain, the Shade was saved from a descent into villainy thanks to his long friendship with the hero Ted Knight, aka Starman.

DARK SHADOWS
Shadowmatter constructs take savage and lethal action without Richard Swift having to lift a finger.

SHADE, THE CHANGING MAN

DEBUT *Shade, The Changing Man* (Vol.1) #1 (Jun.–Jul. 1977)
REAL NAME Rac Shade
HEIGHT 5ft 6in **WEIGHT** 108 lbs **EYES** Blue **HAIR** Red
POWERS/ABILITIES M-vest emits energy that distorts perception, projects force-fields, and enables flight and dimensional travel.
ENEMIES Cain
AFFILIATIONS Justice League Dark

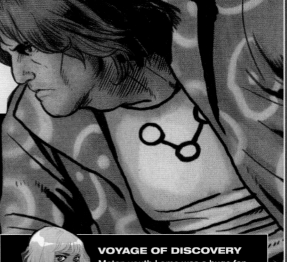

Tormented to near-madness by the death of his lover Kathy, Rac Shade created a simulacrum of her using the reality-warping power of the M-Vest, a relic of his origin in the mysterious world of Meta. He consented to join the Justice League Dark at the request of Madame Xanadu after Enchantress separated from June Moone, and played a critical role in the JLD's fight against resurgent occult powers. At the same time, he fought an internal struggle against a malfunctioning M-Vest, which plagued him with visions of a deformed Kathy. The combination of the M-Vest's overwhelming powers and his terrible grief resulted in a mental breakdown, and Shade quit the team just as the final battle with the vampire progenitor known as Cain loomed.

Drawn into the Area of Madness by the M-Vest, Shade reunited with the Kathy simulacrum and told her he would not be returning to the team because the coming changes would leave no place for him there—or, he feared, anywhere.

CONFLICT RESOLUTION
Shade's conflicted relationship with The Spectre of Kathy culminated in an explosive rejection of her.

VOYAGE OF DISCOVERY
Metan youth Loma was a huge fan of Rac Shade's poetry. She was determined to understand him, and so she stole a Madness Vest and voyaged to Earth. Inhabiting and reanimating the body of teen coma victim Megan Boyer, Loma explored many painful aspects of her new reality and learned a surprising amount about herself. Ultimately, she met her idol Rac Shade and a new adventure began...

ON THE RECORD

Rac Shade was a secret agent on the other-dimensional world of Meta. He came into possession of the M-Vest to keep it from being utilized in a conspiracy to take over Earth, which was being hatched in a neighboring dimension. It later transpired that he had to occupy a different body when the M-Vest brought him to Earth, which led to his relationship with a traumatized Kathy George.

BALANCE OF POWER
As soon as Shade unleashed the powers of the M-Vest, he realized that they would be difficult to control.

SHADOW CABINET

DEBUT *Shadow Cabinet* #0 (Jan. 1994)
BASE The Bleed
POWERS/ABILITIES Undisclosed
ENEMIES Daemonites, Hidden People, Kollective
AFFILIATIONS Stormwatch

Based in the interdimensional space The Bleed, which connects all realities of the multiverse, the mysterious Shadow Cabinet presides over the ancient alien defense organization Stormwatch. The four members, known as Shadow Lords, guided the group on its mission to defend Earth against both alien and paranormal threats, never revealing their identities or origins beyond the fact that they control technologies centuries in advance of anything available to humankind.

During the Martian Manhunter's membership in Stormwatch, the team clashed with the Shadow Lords over the Cabinet's manipulations. This led to a crisis that ended only when the time-controlling Kollective eradicated all traces of Stormwatch from the existing timeline. In the aftermath, the Shadow Lords formed a smaller, more clandestine team. They used a DNA sample from the Martian Manhunter to create Stormwatch's new leader, Forecaster. He mistrusted them, despite their promise to stop keeping secrets from the new team that might endanger their existence.

ON THE RECORD

The pre-*Flashpoint* version of the Shadow Cabinet was initially an ancient order of vigilante heroes based in the Shadowspire, and dedicated to protecting humanity from itself. Their leader, Dharma, maintained that they had to use controversial methods to achieve good ends. This brought them into conflict with other heroes.

ENDS JUSTIFY MEANS
The Shadow Cabinet stood as judge, jury, and executioner, believing hard choices were necessary to protect the common good.

SHARK

DEBUT *Green Lantern* (Vol. 2) #24 (Oct 1963)
REAL NAME Karashon
BASE Mobile
POWERS/ABILITIES Psionic manipulation of matter and energy; telepathy; flight.
ENEMIES Green Lantern, Aquaman, The Flash, Fuerza
AFFILIATIONS Weaponers of Qward, the Society, Terrible Trio

Radiation leaking from a nuclear power station transformed a tiger shark into a mutant humanoid monster. Developing vast intelligence and psionic powers, the Shark feasted on the psyches of his victims. He attacked Green Lantern Hal Jordan, hoping to consume his mind, but was defeated, and devolved to his original state.

The Shark regained humanoid form on several occasions, battling both Green Lantern and Aquaman, briefly seizing the Throne of Atlantis and installing himself as Karshon. Later, he was recruited by Green Lantern Guy Gardner to join a Super-Villain squad. During *Infinite Crisis*, the Shark participated in an attack on Atlantis, where he allied with King Shark, and apparently killed the undersea hero Neptune Perkins.

The Shark joined the Suicide Squad but was killed on a mission by a teammate in revenge for killing Fin's brother, Scale.

SHADO

DEBUT *Green Arrow: The Longbow Hunters* #1 (Aug. 1987)
HEIGHT 5ft 3in **WEIGHT** 121 lbs
EYES Brown **HAIR** Black
POWERS/ABILITIES Unsurpassed skill with a bow and arrow; superior acrobat and martial artist.
ALLIES Green Arrow
ENEMIES Komodo, Count Vertigo

Raised as an assassin, master archer Shado turned on her mentor Ito when paid to kill him by Robert Queen and Simon Lacroix. She and Robert fell in love and had a daughter, Emiko. Robert then enlisted Shado in his search for "the Green Arrow".

As Komodo, Lacroix kidnapped Emiko and turned her over to Count Vertigo, who imprisoned her for her refusal to reveal the Green Arrow's location—which she knew was, in fact, Oliver Queen, Robert's son. Oliver rescued Emiko and Shado spared the defeated Vertigo During the escape, Shado also revealed to Oliver that he had a half-sister: Emiko.

As Shado became a mercenary, Oliver invited Emiko into his home. Trained in archery and combat skills, she became his partner Red Arrow. The pair confronted Shado, who was working for the Ninth Circle to destabilize Seattle.

SHADOWPACT

DEBUT *Day of Vengeance* #1 (Jun. 2005)
BASE Oblivion Bar
MEMBERS/POWERS Nightmaster: Expert combatant with magical sword; **Blue Devil**: Enhanced strength, wields Trident of Lucifer; **Nightshade**: Teleportation, can form darkness into 3D shapes; **Ragman**: Absorbs sinners into his cloak and draws on their powers; **Detective Chimp**: Brilliant mind and can talk to animals; **Enchantress**: Vast magical abilities; **Zauriel**: Flight, enhanced strength, telepathy, sonic scream.
ENEMIES The Spectre, Eclipso, Pentacle

According to legend, teams of mystics have called themselves the Shadowpact during struggles against dark sorcery. The most recent group assembled in the Oblivion Bar after an insane Spectre had teamed with Eclipso on a destructive rampage. Shadowpact survived the battle with help from Shazam and Black Alice. The team later organized the cleanup after the destruction of the Rock of Eternity let loose the Seven Deadly Sins.

Following *Infinite Crisis*, Shadowpact spent a year battling and eventually defeating their evil opposites, the Pentacle, inside a sacrificial bubble of blood the villains had created around the town of Riverrock, Wyoming. The team returned to action against Doctor Gotham, and later welcomed Laurel, who took the Blue Devil's place.

AGAINST THE DARKNESS
The Shadowpact stands against occult and sorcerous threats, as it has for centuries and as it always will.
1 Blue Devil
2 Nightmaster
3 Nightshade
4 Ragman
5 Detective Chimp
6 Enchantress

SHAGGY MAN

DEBUT *Justice League of America* (Vol.1) #45 (Jun. 1966)
BASE Secret Society of Super-Villains mansion
HEIGHT 8ft 2in **WEIGHT** 550 lbs
EYES Red **HAIR** Brown
POWERS/ABILITIES Superhuman strength; near invulnerability; regeneration.
ALLIES Professor Ivo
ENEMIES Justice League of America

Shaggy Man was created by Professor Ivo as a genetic experiment that also involved the artificial synthesis of his tissue and fur. Recruited into the Secret Society of Super-Villains by his creator, Shaggy Man attacked the Justice League of America when they were infiltrating the Society's mansion headquarters to rescue Catwoman.

Proving himself invulnerable to the JLA's various powers, he singlehandedly subdued the entire team, except Hawkman. As he pursued Hawkman through the mansion, Stargirl freed the other members of the JLA, and they learned that the key to defeating Shaggy Man was cutting away his thick synthetic fur. Together Katana and Hawkman managed to do this, bringing the behemoth down and setting the stage for a mass breakout from the mansion.

SHAZAM!

DATA

DEBUT *Whiz Comics* (Vol. 1) #1 (labeled as issue #2 in indicia) (Feb. 1940)

REAL NAME William "Billy" Batson **BASE** Philadelphia, Pennsylvania

HEIGHT 6ft 1in **WEIGHT** 195 lbs

EYES Blue **HAIR** Black

POWERS/ABILITIES Power over the Living Lightning; immense magical powers, including flight, speed, strength; can share Living Lightning with others.

ALLIES The Wizard, Freddy Freeman, Mary Bromfield, Tawky Tawny

ENEMIES Black Adam, Seven Deadly Sins, Dr. Sivana, Mr. Mind, King Kid, Superboy-Prime, Monster Society

AFFILIATIONS Shazam Family, Justice League

Possessing the powers of the Living Lightning, Billy Batson is an unlikely hero—a cocky delinquent foster child constantly grappling with the responsibilities that come with his immense powers as the Keeper of Magic. Billy is still a teenager, and Shazam is the idealized grown-up version of him. At times, the responsibility of being the last standard-bearer of the Council of Eternity can seem impossible to live up to. However, Billy's foster siblings always have his back, and after a rocky start to their relationship, so does the Justice League. What he lacks in experience he makes up for in courage, and soon becomes known as Earth's Mightiest Mortal.

AT A GLANCE...

S stands for...
Shazam's powers were originally granted by Solomon, Hercules, Atlas, Zeus, Achilles, and Mercury, a deal brokered by The Wizard himself.

Family affair
Orphaned from an early age, troubled teenager Billy Batson found his family among his foster siblings. He can share his powers with them (and Tawky Tawny the tiger) in urgent situations, transforming them into the Shazam Family.

Say the magic word
By speaking the word "Shazam!" aloud, Billy Batson transforms himself and gains the use of the Living Lightning, the distilled essence of the powers bestowed by the six divine entities who empower him as the Keeper of Magic.

CLASSIC STORIES

Whiz Comics #2 (Feb. 1940)
Homeless newsboy Billy Batson is led into the tunnels beneath New York City, where The Wizard grants him the powers to become Shazam.

Shazam: Monster Society of Evil #1–4 (Apr.–Sep. 2007) In this origin story, Billy Batson becomes a host for Shazam, with whom he can merge by saying the word "Shazam!" They battle Doctor Sivana and an army of giant robots summoned by the Monster Society.

The Trials of Shazam! #1–12 (Oct. 2006–May 2008) The aging Billy takes on the role of The Wizard, as new Captain Marvel Freddy Freeman strives to prove himself worthy of Shazam's powers.

Billy Batson is the son of C.C. and Marilyn Batson from Zumbrota, Minnesota. They moved to Philadelphia when Billy was young, but he would never grow to know them. While Billy thought he had gotten lost from his family, the truth was that neither was a fit parent. Billy was sent into the foster system, but found a home with the kind Vasquez family and their five other foster children. Rebellious at first, Billy grew to be fiercely protective of his adoptive family. Meanwhile, an ancient Wizard, the last surviving member of a magical council based at the Rock of Eternity, saw the need for a new champion to meet the threat of a resurrected Black Adam, his former and now corrupted chosen representative. The Wizard summoned Billy to the mystical nexus called the Rock of Eternity and made him his new champion. With the word "Shazam!" Billy was transformed into an adult with superhuman powers beyond anything he could have imagined.

Black Adam attacked Shazam and nearly overwhelmed him before Billy brought in the rest of his foster family and shared the Living Lightning with them. Billy was unable to sustain the power sharing and only defeated Black Adam by challenging him to fight in mortal form. When Black Adam did this, he instantly suffered the effects of several centuries' aging… and collapsed into dust. Trying to do the right thing, Billy returned Black Adam's ashes to his home in Kahndaq, inadvertently causing a diplomatic incident. The Justice League, Justice League Dark, and Justice League of America all converged on Kahndaq to try and defuse the situation, but instead a

GATEWAY TO SHAZAM
Billy discovered the way to the Rock of Eternity, where The Wizard—and Billy's destiny—awaited him.

NEW ORIGIN
After Dr. Sivana freed ancient Black Adam from his tomb, The Wizard created a new champion to oppose him, and chose Billy Batson. Billy defeated Black Adam, first trying to reason with him, and then sharing his powers with his foster siblings—thereby passing the first test of The Wizard's faith in him.

CLASH OF CHAMPIONS
Billy came out on top in his first critical test as Shazam, but Black Adam was almost more than he could handle.

TRINITY WAR/FOREVER EVIL

Billy inadvertently set off a battle among the three Justice Leagues after he tried to return Black Adam's remains to their rightful resting place. Then he became the fulcrum of a battle over Pandora's Box, before the Outsider tapped his power to fulfill his goal of bringing the Crime Syndicate to Earth.

NO GOOD DEED GOES UNPUNISHED?

Even bad guys deserve to be buried. But when Shazam tried to do the right thing by Black Adam it sparked an almighty fight with Superman.

battle broke out with Shazam at its center. Despite all this, Shazam would join the Justice League for a time. But Billy's true team remained the Vasquez household. He and the rest of his Shazam family began to explore the Rock of Eternity, learning that Earth was only one of the seven magic realms, each formerly protected by a champion. The Shazam Family explored these worlds, just as Billy's father, C.C. returned to Billy's life. Wanting a relationship with his dad, Billy shared the Living Lightning with him, and he became the seemingly missing seventh champion.

However, C.C. was actually being mind-controlled by the evil worm known as Mr. Mind. Mind wanted control of the magic in all seven lands, and was using Billy's family to get it, partnering with Dr. Sivana. The two unleashed an entire Monster Society and even the Super-Villain Superboy-Prime, but the Shazam Family bested them. When the smoke cleared, Billy's father remembered nothing of recent events. He left Philadelphia after revealing to Shazam that he never wanted a relationship with his son. Billy fully embraced his new family, leading The Wizard to believe that the seventh champion had been the resurrected Black Adam all along, and someday, the goodness in Shazam would point Adam back to the light.

KING SHAZAM
When he was briefly infected by an evil Batman from the Dark Multiverse called The Batman Who Laughs, Billy became King Shazam, a cruel and twisted version of his superpowered self.

INTO THE MAGICLANDS
Accessible by the magic subway system at the Rock of Eternity, the Magiclands consisted of: the Earthlands (Earth); the carnival like Funlands; the videogame-centric Gameland; the haunting Darklands, the villainous Monsterlands; the talking animal home known as the Wildlands; and the mash-up of Oz and Wonderland called the Wozenderlands.

ON THE RECORD

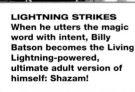

The Wizard originally known as Shazam was one of Earth's first heroes, making his mark in ancient Canaan millennia ago. He bestowed his powers on a successor, Teth-Adam, who became Black Adam. Thousands of years later, The Wizard gifted his powers to a boy named Billy Batson, beginning the career of this mighty DC hero.

LIGHTNING STRIKES
When he utters the magic word with intent, Billy Batson becomes the Living Lightning-powered, ultimate adult version of himself: Shazam!

A hero in crisis
Trapped in limbo for 20 years, Shazam and his family returned without aging in the 1970s. Following 1985's *Crisis on Infinite Earths*, Shazam's history was revised, with his most memorable run featured in *The Power of Shazam!* ongoing series. After The Wizard Shazam sacrificed his life to stop The Spectre's massacre of magicians, Shazam assumed his place at the Rock of Eternity. Freddy Freeman took the name Shazam and continued the legacy. In the post-*Flashpoint* timeline, Billy Batson was once again the primary hero, Shazam.

Other champions
Alexander Luthor was Mazahs, Earth-3's version of Shazam, who spoke his name to absorb the superpowers of other heroes and villains. Shazam also battled The Wizard's previous Champion, Black Adam, whose use of the word calls on the Egyptian gods Shu, Heru, Amon, Zehuti, Aton, and Mehen.

"I'm not supposed to be Shazam. The Wizard said so himself."
SHAZAM

DAY OF VENGEANCE
Billy Batson as Shazam took on The Spectre, who was out to destroy all magic and those who used it.

SHAZAM FAMILY

DATA

DEBUT *Captain Marvel Adventures* (Vol. 1) #18 (Dec. 1942)
BASE Philadelphia, Pennsylvania
MEMBERS/POWERS MARY BROMFIELD, EUGENE CHOI, DARLA
DUDLEY, FREDDY FREEMAN, PEDRO PEÑA Each member of the group
is able to share the magical powers of Shazam as long as Billy Batson
considers him or her family.
ALLIES The Wizard, Tawky Tawny, Rosa, Victor Vasquez
ENEMIES Black Adam, Seven Deadly Sins, Dr. Sivana, Mr. Mind, King Kid,
Superboy Prime, Monster Society

SIX OF THE BEST
It took the combined efforts
of the Shazam Family to take
down magic-wielding villain
Black Adam, but they pulled
together and got the job done.

**The Shazam Family is a group of foster siblings who
can each assume the powers of Shazam when Billy
Batson grants them. None of them has a biological
family link, but together they are as closely knit as
any group of brothers and sisters can be.**

Six foster siblings lived in the
Vasquez family household in Philadelphia.
One, Billy Batson, was granted the powers
of Shazam by a powerful ancient wizard.
He shared his secret with his foster brother,
Freddy Freeman, and it stayed between
them until the Super-Villain Black
Adam attacked, holding the rest of
the siblings hostage and
demanding Billy's powers. Billy
tried to meet this demand, but
accidentally bestowed the powers of
Shazam on his six siblings, instead.
They all battled Black Adam together,
but were then surprised and nearly
overwhelmed by the Seven Deadly Sins, who threatened
the city of Philadelphia after being unleashed by Dr. Sivana.

**STICKING
TOGETHER**
The kids who live
in the Vasquez
household have
been through a
lot, and they
always have each
other's backs.

During the battle, some of this superpowered foster
family discovered that they had variations on the powers
of Shazam: Eugene had technopathic powers; Pedro
showed even greater strength; and Darla possessed
incredible speed. Knowing he can share his Shazam
secret with his siblings makes it easier for Billy to handle his new responsibilities.
He and his sister Mary even eventually revealed themselves to their foster parents.
Headquartered at the Rock of Eternity, the Shazam Family discovered that Earth was
just one of the seven realms of the Magiclands. While exploring other dimensions, they
came under attack from Sivana and his new Monster Society. Working as a team, they
successfully bested the villains, prompting The Wizard who had granted Billy his powers to
realize that he needed to have faith in his chosen champion, and in the family he has built.

CLASSIC STORIES

Whiz Comics #21 (Sep. 1941)
Billy Batson meets three namesakes and
shares the secret of Shazam with each of
them—but they are reluctant to use it until
the evil Sivana captures them. The original
Billy sets out to rescue them, and all four
become Captain Marvels. To avoid
confusion, the three other Billies become
the Lieutenants Marvel.

**Marvel Family Comics #1 (Dec.
1945)** The family—now including Mary
Marvel, Captain Marvel, Jr., and Uncle
Marvel—bands together to take on Black
Adam for the first time as a group, setting
the stage for a decades-long rivalry
between Champions past and present.

ON THE RECORD

The Shazam Family was
originally known as the Marvel Family,
back when Shazam was going by the
name Captain Marvel. They later
appeared under their current name
after the death of The Wizard Shazam.

The Marvel Family was part of the
Fawcett stable and brought
into DC in the early 1970s. The pre-
Flashpoint Marvel Family made
an appearance in the prologue to the
"Darkseid War," during a flashback to
Crisis on Infinite Earths.

Dr. Sivana and Black Adam are the
Marvel/Shazam Family's oldest adversaries, both
making their villainous debuts in the 1940s and posing
a recurrent threat to Billy Batson and his loved ones
(and namesakes) ever since.

ALL IN THE FAMILY
The Marvel Family gathered
together to meet with The
Wizard Shazam, who
bestowed upon them their
tremendous powers.

MEET THE FAMILY
The Vasquez foster siblings
become the Shazam Family
for the first time.

1 Eugene Choi
2 Darla Dudley
3 Pedro Peña

4 Mary Bromfield
5 Freddy Freeman

SHAZAM JR.

DEBUT *Whiz Comics* (Vol. 1) #25 (Dec. 1941)
REAL NAME Freddy Freeman **BASE** Philadelphia
HEIGHT 5ft 10in **WEIGHT** 164 lbs **EYES** Blue **HAIR** Blond
POWERS/ABILITIES Possesses the powers and abilities of
Shazam when Billy Batson shares them with his foster family.
ALLIES Shazam **ENEMIES** Black Adam, Sivana, Superboy Prime
AFFILIATIONS Shazam Family

Teenager Freddy Freeman was
placed into foster care with the Vasquez family
after his parents went to prison. A gregarious,
likeable kid despite a permanent leg injury, Freddy
considered himself a fixer at high school, with a
tendency to bend rules—usually in harmless ways.
He swiftly befriended the new kid: selfish, surly Billy
Batson, and he was the first to learn about Billy's powers.
At first, Freddy encouraged Billy to treat his gifts as a
lark—and a way to make money. When Billy saved an old
woman, Freddy suggested Billy should ask for reward
money and he started taking the power of Shazam more
seriously—especially after Black Adam attacked, heralding
the Seven Deadly Sins. Billy shared his powers with Freddy
and the other children to overpower Black Adam, defeat the
demon Sabbac, and neutralize the Seven Deadly Sins.
Freddy's sense of fun was tested to the limit when
the kids accidentally unlocked the Seven Magic Lands,
unleashing a new Monster Society of evil upon Earth as well
as reviving psychotic alternate Earth terror
Superboy Prime. Thankfully, the power
of the united Shazam Family proved equal
to the task of pacifying the terrors.

JUST SAY THE WORD
Although Freddy regards
his superpowers as a source
of joy, he never refrains
from using them to protect
the helpless.

ON THE RECORD

Freddy Freeman joined the Marvel
Family just two years after the emergence
of Captain Marvel. Crippled and orphaned
by the sadistic Captain Nazi, young Freddy
was granted access to the power of
Shazam, which allowed him to walk again
and even fly as Captain Marvel, Jr. After a
series of trials that followed *Infinite Crisis*,
Freddy Freeman became the new Captain
Marvel (now calling himself Shazam), with
Billy Batson assuming The Wizard's place
and overseeing the Rock of Eternity.

THE NEW CAPTAIN
As Captain Marvel, Jr., Freddy Freeman
struggled with the temptation to exact revenge
on Captain Nazi, the man who crippled him.

SHAZAM'S SQUADRON OF JUSTICE

DEBUT *Justice League of America* #135
(Oct. 1976)
**MEMBERS/POWERS Bulletman and
Bulletgirl**: Married couple, each with a Gravity
Helmet that turns them into projectiles; **Ibis the
Invincible**: Magical powers granted by Thoth are
focused in the Ibistick; **Mister Scarlet**: Acrobatics,
various weapon proficiencies; **Pinky**: Acrobatics,
various weapon proficiencies; **Spy Smasher**:
Technical wizardry, unarmed combat expertise.
ENEMIES King Kull, Beastmen

Earth-S's Squadron of
Justice was deputized
by the god Mercury to
counter an assault by
King Kull, who plotted
to destroy humanity
and turn Earth-S over
to the Beastmen.
With the Shazam Family inactive because
of Shazam's paralysis, the Squadron allied
with the Justice League of America and the
Justice Society of America to combat villains
from three Earths: Earth-1 (JLA), Earth-2
(JSA), and Earth-S.

In a cataclysmic final battle with King Kull
at the Rock of Eternity, Superman was driven
into a murderous rage by red Kryptonite.
The Squadron restored Shazam's powers
and he broke the hold of the red Kryptonite,
with help from several Green Lanterns. The
Squadron then imprisoned Kull in magical
chains, preserving the Rock of Eternity and
thwarting the Beastmen's plot.

SHINING KNIGHT

DEBUT *Adventure Comics* #66 (Sep. 1941)
REAL NAME Ystin/Justin/Ystina
BASE Camelot
HEIGHT 6ft 2in
WEIGHT 185 lbs
EYES Green
HAIR Black
POWERS/ABILITIES Immortality; magical
armor and weapons; control over animals.
ENEMIES Sheeda, Morgaine le Fey

The gender-fluid,
immortal knight Ystin
has also been known
as Ystina, Sir Justin,
and the Shining
Knight, and was
present at Merlin's
rebirth in Avalon as
Adam One. As one of the Demon Knights—
ancestors of Stormwatch—Ystina battled
alien and demonic threats. Ystina was
granted immortality after a sip from the Holy
Grail during the fall of Camelot, but was
cursed with an unquenchable desire to drink
from the Grail again.

Ystin rode the winged horse Vanguard,
fighting alongside such Demon Knights as
Madame Xanadu and Jason Blood. He also
wielded the sword known as Caliburn or
Excalibur, marking him a champion of Camelot.
Ystina fought with the Demon Knights against
the vampire Cain and was bitten, fulfilling his
vision of one day becoming undead.

SHRIEK

DEBUT *Batman Beyond* (Vol. 2) #5 (Mar. 2000)
REAL NAME Walter Shreeve
BASE Neo-Gotham, Earth-12
HEIGHT 5ft 10in **WEIGHT** 170 lbs
EYES Brown **HAIR** Brown
POWERS/ABILITIES Armored suit that
generates destructive sound waves.
ENEMIES Batman

Walter Shreeve was
a gifted audio engineer
in Neo-Gotham.
Unable to find a more
legitimate way to profit
from his advanced
sound technologies,
Shreeve fashioned a
suit armed with sonic weaponry capable of
destroying buildings. Hired to assassinate
Batman, Shreeve almost succeeded, but
suffered hearing damage in the encounter
and was imprisoned in Blackgate. While
incarcerated, he gained the trust of a prison
doctor and began new research, developing
earphones to restore his hearing and
rebuilding his sonic technology.

Then he broke out of prison, attacking
Batman again and using low-frequency
sound weapons to destroy buildings, while
he tried to steal power crystals to amplify
his sound-projection weapons. He nearly
unmasked Batman, but was buried in a
collapsed building that he had weakened.
Presumed dead, he survived and later
plotted against Earth-12's Justice League.

SHRINKING VIOLET

DEBUT *Action Comics* (Vol. 1) #276 (May 1961)
REAL NAME Salu Digby
HEIGHT 5ft 2in **WEIGHT** 105 lbs
EYES Violet **HAIR** Black
POWERS/ABILITIES Ability to alter size
from subatomic to approx. 30ft tall, with
proportionate change in mass and strength.
ENEMIES Fatal Five, Dominators, Daxamites

Like other natives
from the planet Imsk,
Salu Digby can
change her size,
making her a key
member of the Legion
of Super-Heroes'
Espionage Squad.
Although a striking presence and a potent
warrior, she is as retiring as her codename.

In versions of the team prior to the
reality-alterations of Prime Earth, Shrinking
Violet endured a grim Possible Future with a
traumatic period of captivity, which had
consequences for her relationship with the
team, particularly her lover, Lightning Lass.

Alongside the Legion, Shrinking Violet
battled threats to 31st-century space by the
Dominators, Daxamites, and the Fatal Five.
She was one of the Legionnaires sent to
the 21st century when Ultra the Multi-Alien
destroyed their home timeline. Fighting
alongside the Justice League United, she
uncovered the truth of Ultra's origins and
saved the Legion's future by preventing Ultra
from becoming all-consuming Infinitus.

SIDEWAYS

DEBUT *Sideways* (Vol. 1) #1 (Apr. 2018)
REAL NAME Derek James
BASE Gotham City
HEIGHT 5ft 7in
WEIGHT 148 lbs
EYES Brown **HAIR** Brown
POWERS/ABILITIES Super-strength, can
open rifts to other places.
ALLIES Ernie, Tempus Fuginaut
ENEMIES Killspeed, Replicant, Showman
AFFILIATIONS Young Justice

When Challengers
Mountain, the
Challengers HQ,
dropped into Gotham
City during the invasion
of the Dark Multiverse,
schoolboy Derek
James fell into a fissure
in the unstable ground and became infused
with the strange energy coming off the
mountain. He reappeared on the other side of
town and was taken to hospital unconscious.

When he awoke he had new powers—
super-strength and the ability to open rifts in
space-time to travel between places almost
instantly. Derek immediately seized on the
idea of becoming a Super Hero, taking the
name Sideways and asking his friend Ernie
to design him a costume. At first he
struggled to adapt to his new life, but he
managed to control his powers. He
eventually joined the Young Justice team.

SIGNAL, THE (DUKE THOMAS)

DEBUT *Batman* (Vol. 2) #21 (Aug. 2013)
REAL NAME Duke Thomas
BASE Gotham City
EYES Yellow **HAIR** Black
POWERS/ABILITIES Genius; martial-arts; puzzle-solving skills; still-developing extrasensory powers; modified Eskrima sticks/grappling hooks; motorcycle with cloaking tech.
ALLIES Batman, Black Lightning, Dre-B-Robbin, Leslie Thompkins, Robin, DaxAtax, R-Iko, Robina
ENEMIES The Joker, Karma, The Riddler, Victor Zsasz, Johnny Bender Jr., the Preacher, the Nest
AFFILIATIONS Outsiders, We Are Robin, Lucius Fox Center for Gotham Youth

When Duke Thomas was young, the Joker drove his parents insane because they helped Bruce Wayne. Living in foster care, Duke joined the "We Are Robin" young anti-crime group. He became a lone street vigilante until Batman brought him into his inner circle and trained him.

Eventually, Duke learned that he was the son of immortal Super-Villain Gnomon and he had a vast range of metahuman powers linked to the mystic Eighth Metal, including "boosting" the abilities of others.

After working with assorted Bat-teams, Duke—now calling himself The Signal—is a key operative of The Outsiders team, led by Black Lightning.

SILENCER, THE

DEBUT *The Silencer* (Vol. 1) #1 (Mar. 2018)
REAL NAME Honor Guest
BASE Charleston, South Carolina
HEIGHT Unknown **WEIGHT** Unknown
EYES Brown **HAIR** Blonde
POWERS/ABILITIES Can create zones of silence; highly skilled in combat and with weapons; wears bodysuit with nanites that can perform individual tasks.
ALLIES Aftermarket, Detail, Quietus
ENEMIES Talia Al Ghūl, Wishbone, Smoke
AFFILIATIONS Leviathan

Honor Guest was very happy with her ordinary life in Charleston with her husband and son. But she was hiding a secret from them— a bloody past as the assassin Silencer. Honor possessed a metagene that enabled her to create "zones of silence"—the perfect way to carry out stealth missions. She had been given this ability at a young age by a project funded by Rā's al Ghūl, using his own genetic material. Honor was then sent to a school for assassins, where she was chosen as Talia al Ghūl's personal bodyguard, with the deal that one day she could leave and have a family.

It seemed Talia had kept her promise, but later her machinations ensured that Honor was pulled back into the Leviathan organization, putting her family at risk.

SILVER BANSHEE

DEBUT *Action Comics* (Vol. 1) #595 (Dec. 1987)
REAL NAME Siobhan McDougal
BASE Metropolis
HEIGHT 6ft 11in **WEIGHT** 180 lbs
EYES Blue **HAIR** White
POWERS/ABILITIES Death stare and lethal wail; superhuman strength, endurance, healing; sound manipulation, flight, teleportation.
ALLIES The Crone
ENEMIES Black Banshee, Superman, J'onn J'onzz, Batman, Supergirl
AFFILIATIONS Castle Broen, Clan McDougal, Satanus

First-born child Siobhan McDougal was denied leadership of ancient Clan McDougal due to her gender. When her father died, she illicitly performed the supernatural family succession ritual, and was cursed to Hell after her brother Bevan interrupted her.

Given magical powers by "The Crone," Siobhan was transformed into the Silver Banshee. In return she had to find a magical book, but this search brought her into conflict with Superman and others, and then she was dragged back to Hell by The Crone. She was freed by Supergirl and became a villain for profit.

After the *Flashpoint* event, she was replaced by Siobhan Smythe—seemingly a more beneficial Silver Banshee—who was fleeing her evil father, Black Banshee. Following *Rebirth*, Siobhan McDougal has been sighted in Metropolis, resuming her criminal career.

IF LOOKS COULD KILL
Silver Banshee can sentence her chosen victim to instantaneous death, but only if she knows their true name.

SILVER SWAN

DEBUTS *Wonder Woman* (Vol.1) #288 (Feb. 1982) (Helen Alexandros); *Wonder Woman* (Vol. 2) #15 (Apr. 1988) (Valerie Beaudry); *Wonder Woman* (Vol. 2) #171 (Aug. 2001) (Vanessa Kapetelis)
POWERS/ABILITIES Flight, vocal sonic attacks.
ALLIES Mars, Circe, Dr. Psycho
ENEMIES Wonder Woman

JEALOUSY TAKES FLIGHT
The Silver Swan was driven to villainous acts by her jealousy of Wonder Woman's beauty and renown.

Three women have been known as the Silver Swan. The first, Helen Alexandros, was granted the powers of flight and sonic voice attack by Mars, and she fought Wonder Woman at his behest before he withdrew her powers and she returned to normal life. The following two Silver Swans, Valerie Beaudry and Vanessa Kapatelis, achieved their powers by technological means, being altered by Henry Armbruster and Circe, respectively.

In each case, these women were manipulated using their jealousy of Wonder Woman's beauty and strength. Valerie had been deformed in the womb by nuclear testing. Wonder Woman had lived with Vanessa's family for a while. Vanessa blamed her for leaving, but she had actually been forced to because Dr. Psycho was manipulating Vanessa's mother.

However, as they battled Wonder Woman, the Amazon Queen's virtue and strength made both Valerie and Vanessa realize the error of their ways.

SILVERLOCK, OLIVE

DEBUT *Gotham Academy* #1 (Dec. 2014)
BASE Gotham City
HEIGHT 5ft 3in **WEIGHT** Not telling
EYES Violet **HAIR** Silver
POWERS/ABILITIES Keen investigative instincts, determination, pyrokinetic abilities.
ALLIES Maps Mizoguchi, Pomeline Fritch, Kyle Mizoguchi, Colton Rivera, Robin (Damian Wayne)
AFFILIATIONS Detective Club

ON THE CASE
Once Olive Silverlock uncovered mysterious goings-on in and around the halls of Gotham Academy, the Detective Club got serious.

Olive Silverlock was the daughter of Sybil Silverlock—the fire-starting Super-Villain Calamity. At Gotham Academy she and her friends stumbled across a secret society that was trying to contact a ghost—Millie Jane Cobblepot—whose journal Olive had in her possession. Her friends formalized their partnership as the Detective Club

The prestigious school was a haven for Super-Villains and mad scientists and a magnet for mystic events. Olive encountered Man-Bats, werewolves, witchcraft cults, and other weirdos all searching for another ancient volume—the Book of Old Gotham.

As Olive's own pyrokinetic powers intensified, her friends secured the tome and discovered that generations of Silverlock women had been possessed by a witch—Amity Arkham—who had been burned at the stake in the early years of Gotham City. Armed with this knowledge, Olive's friends freed her from Amity, just as the witch was using her to destroy the descendants of those who had condemned her: the Dents Cobblepots, Waynes, and others.

SINESTRO

DATA

DEBUT *Green Lantern* (Vol. 2) #7 **(Jul.–Aug. 1961)**
REAL NAME Thaal Sinestro
BASE Ranx, Warworld, Qward; mobile
HEIGHT 6ft 5in **WEIGHT** 205 lbs **EYES** Black **HAIR** Black
POWERS/ABILITIES Indomitable will; mastery of fear and intimidation; mastery of unarmed combat; Ultraviolet power ring capable of generating light-constructs, flight, protection, energy-projection.
ALLIES Parallax, Lyssa Drak, Lex Luthor
ENEMIES Hal Jordan, Guardians of the Universe, Red Lantern Corps
AFFILIATIONS Sinestro Corps, Green Lantern Corps, White Lantern Corps, Indigo Tribe, New Guardians, Ultraviolet Corps, Legion of Doom

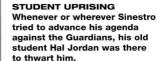

MIGHT IS RIGHT
On returning to the Green Lantern Corps, Sinestro realized the Guardians had adopted his ruthless methods for enforcing order.

Proud Thaal Sinestro of Korugar loved order. To preserve it, he pursued power in all its forms and became one of the most feared villains in the cosmos. He founded his own corps of cosmic terrorists and by dominating the cosmic entity Parallax, Sinestro became the lord of fear. He remains one of the most powerful beings in creation.

Anthropologist Sinestro was exploring an ancient city when a wounded Green Lantern crashed at his feet. Taking the Green Lantern ring rather than earning it, Sinestro became determined to make use of the powerful weapon. In fact, he proved to be one of the Corps' most effective agents. His sector was the most peaceful of all, but only because he ruled it as dictator.

Mentor to Green Lantern Hal Jordan, Sinestro was eventually banished to the Anti-Matter Universe of Qward for his crimes after Hal challenged his authoritarian rule. There the Qwardians tapped the power of the universal fear-entity to create their own power rings imbued with yellow energy, the only vulnerability of the Green Lanterns' rings. With his yellow ring, Sinestro struck remorselessly at the Guardians who had frustrated his dreams. A constant thorn in Green Lantern's side, Sinestro formed the Sinestro Corps and warred with the Green Lanterns. After a brief and unexpected return to the Green Lantern Corps, Sinestro was able to grow his Sinestro Corps forces substantially during a period where the Green Lanterns went missing.

Ruling from the artificial planet Warworld, Sinestro was challenged by the returning Hal Jordan. The two fought, and Hal unleashed his full energy, destroying Warworld in the process. Sinestro survived, but his quest for power did not end there. Joining Lex Luthor's Legion of Doom, Sinestro helped unlock one of the seven unseen forces of the universe, becoming the first Lantern to embrace the invisible spectrum. Unlike Lanterns on the emotional scale—like Green Lanterns and Red Lanterns where the user controls the light via emotions—the invisible spectrum controls the user. Sinestro used it to command a veritable army, but was blocked when John Stewart ultimately rejected his Ultraviolet Corps. Things got worse yet for Sinestro when he and the Legion of Doom succeeded in their goal of unleashing the mother of the Multiverse, Perpetua, only to have Perpetua imprison Sinestro in her throne to better harness his new Ultraviolet powers.

STUDENT UPRISING
Whenever or wherever Sinestro tried to advance his agenda against the Guardians, his old student Hal Jordan was there to thwart him.

FOND FATHER
The only softness in Sinestro's soul came from his sentimental but unshakable attachment to his estranged daughter, Green Lantern Soranik Natu.

CLASSIC STORIES

***Green Lantern* (Vol. 2) #9 (Nov.–Dec. 1961)** In his second appearance, Sinestro debuts his deadly yellow power ring, trapping and impersonating Hal Jordan in a devious plan to destroy the Guardians of the Universe.

***Green Lantern* (Vol. 2) #52 (Apr. 1967)** Reduced to energy and possessing an ancient automobile, Sinestro springs his strangest trap on Green Lanterns Hal Jordan and Alan Scott.

***Green Lantern* (Vol. 3) #50 (Mar. 1994)** Released by the Guardians to battle a Parallax-possessed Hal Jordan, Sinestro is seemingly killed by Jordan, who then destroys the Central Battery of Power and depowers the Green Lantern Corps.

SINESTRO CORPS

DEBUT *Green Lantern* (Vol. 4) #10 (May 2006)
BASE New Korugar
NOTABLE MEMBERS/POWERS SINESTRO Guiding light and master of Parallax; SORANIK SINESTRO, daughter of Sinestro; ARKILLO Deputy leader/drill sergeant; LYSSA DRAK Guardian of the Book of Parallax; KARU-SIL Reared by beasts; DEVILDOG Intergalactic assassin; MURR THE MELTING MAN Flesh-dissolving ravager; SLUSHH Sentient bag of acids; TRI-EYE Subterranean ambush-predator; SCIVOR Psionic persuader; SETAG RETSS Aquatic assassin; AMPA NNN Serial killer and organ collector; ROMAT-RU Mass-murderer of children; MAASH Three brains constantly at war with each other; SCHLAGG-MAN Killer bite; Low Blood-sucking parasite; TEKIK RENEGADE robot; Kryb, Infant thief. All members are capable of instilling great terror, operating yellow power rings that channel the part of the Emotional Spectrum that draws on universal fear.
ALLIES Weaponers of Qward, Manhunters
ENEMIES Green Lantern Corps, Guardians of the Universe, Red Lantern Corps, Justice League, Star Sapphire Corps, Blue Lantern Corps, Indigo Tribe
AFFILIATIONS Parallax

YELLOW POWER
1 Sinestro
2 Karu-Sil
3 Parallax
4 Slushh
5 Scivor
6 Kryb
7 Tri-Eye
8 Ampa Nnn
9 Romat-Ru
10 Maash
11 DevilDog
12 Arkillo
13 Murr the Melting Man
14 Schlagg-Man
15 Low
16 Tekik

SCIENCELL CORPS
When the Sinestro Corps and the Green Lanterns paired up to hunt down rogue Sinestro Corps agents, they caged their prisoners in the Sciencells inside the living planet Mogo.

Though no longer under his leadership, the Sinestro Corps was the perfect revenge scheme from Green Lantern Hal Jordan's longtime nemesis, Sinestro. Creating an army able to counter the Guardians of the Universe and kill their agents, the Sinestro Corps channeled the primal emotion of Fear.

The Sinestro Corps originally comprised the worst monsters in creation, filled with a hunger to hurt and the ability to "instill great fear"—possessing the power to realize their destructive desires. Their murderous drives were harnessed by charismatic Sinestro, who marshaled them into a disciplined force and had them launch a concerted attack on their green counterparts and Earth, while chanting their chilling oath: "In blackest day, in brightest night, beware your fears made into light. Let those who try to stop what's right, burn like my power... Sinestro's might!"

Ever since he formed his army, Sinestro waged a constant war with his old trainee Hal Jordan and the Green Lantern Corps. With only small truces made to battle threats bigger than his old grudge match, Sinestro spread fear throughout the galaxy through his many minions.

This effort culminated when Sinestro took control of the artificial planet Warworld and maneuvered it to the center of the universe where Oa used to be. After manipulating his daughter Soranik Natu to trick many worlds into thinking the Sinestro Corps was a force for good, he revitalized himself using the Parallax entity held at Warworld's core. Sinestro used a Fear Engine to terrorize a galaxy that was briefly without Green Lantern protectors. However, when John Stewart and the Green Lantern Corps united with the formerly missing in action Hal Jordan, Sinestro's ego got the better of him. He challenged Jordan to a one-on-one fight, and lost, and the empty Warworld was destroyed in the process.

ON THE RECORD

Sinestro's yellow power ring was created by the evil Weaponers of Qward during the Korugarian's exile to the Anti-Matter Universe. Its function and origins were never fully explained, but it remained a constant threat to Hal Jordan and other Green Lanterns for decades.

Before the terror weapons were mass-produced for the Sinestro Corps, Guy Gardner briefly used Sinestro's yellow power ring to facilitate his new career as an independent, maverick hero.

WAY OF THE WARRIOR
When Guy Gardner was kicked out of the Green Lanterns, his search for new powers made him a problem for his erstwhile allies.

CLASSIC STORIES

***Green Lantern: Sinestro Corps Special* #1 (Aug. 2007)** Sinestro declares all-out war on the Guardians, the Green Lantern Corps, the entire universe, and Earth's Super Heroes in particular. To conduct his campaign of terror, he recruits many of the worst menaces in the universe to his unholy cause.

***Green Lantern* (Vol. 4) #59–60 (Dec. 2010–Jan. 2011)** During the Brightest Day event, Parallax possesses Barry Allen, and Green Lantern Hal Jordan is forced to offer himself up as a host to save his best friend.

***Forever Evil* #4 (Feb. 2014)** Batman briefly becomes the Sinestro Corps operative for Space Sector 2814 after donning a yellow ring to battle Power Ring, the deranged Green Lantern antithesis from Earth-3.

FOLLOW THE LEADER
Soranik Sinestro now leads the Sinestro Corps, continuing her father's cruel legacy.

SIXPACK

DEBUT *Hitman* (Vol. 1) #9 (Dec. 1996)
REAL NAME Sidney Speck
BASE Gotham City
EYES Bloodshot **HAIR** Brown
POWERS/ABILITIES Expert in unarmed combat and weapons handling; incredibly high tolerance for alcohol.
ENEMIES Bane, Many Angled Ones

Sidney Speck remains one of the world's strangest and most unsavory costumed champions. As Sixpack, he led a team of dissolute heroes, Section 8.

With no abilities other than drunken bravado, he was always ready for a fight. His favorite weapon was a broken beer bottle.

A man of mystery, due to the damage booze had wrought on his memory, Sidney spent his days in Noonan's Bar regaling the clientele with tales of his Super Hero career. However, when Gotham City was invaded by demons, he led his men into battle and saw most of them die. After a prolonged period of sobriety, Sixpack began drinking again and revived Section 8, comprised of similarly delusional stalwarts Powertool, Bueno Excellente, Guts, the Grapplah, Dogwelder II, and Baytor.

SKEETS

DEBUT *Booster Gold* (Vol. 1) #1 (Feb. 1986)
BASE Vanishing Point
WEIGHT 5 lbs
POWERS/ABILITIES Flight; voice projection; historical records archive; numerous tools and weapons.
ALLIES Rip Hunter, Booster Gold, Will Magnus
ENEMIES Black Beetle, Per Degaton, Chronos, T.O. Morrow, Rex Hunter

When disgraced sports star Michael Carter fled the 25th century, he stole technological artifacts from the museum where he worked and headed back four centuries to become Super Hero Booster Gold. He also took Skeets, a robotic museum tour-droid he had packed with historical data. With his personality growing, Skeets became a companion and friend, helping to curb some of Carter's wilder get-rich-quick schemes.

Moreover, when the fugitive from the future became the unheralded guardian of the timestream, Skeets was reconstructed and remodeled by Time Master Rip Hunter. He now functions as a sentient monitor and beacon allowing Booster Gold to travel the ever-fluctuating corridors of time and return safely to his starting point without wrecking the course of history.

SLEEZ

DEBUT *Action Comics* (Vol. 1) #592 (Sep. 1987)
BASE Apokolips, Metropolis, mobile
HEIGHT 4ft 3in **WEIGHT** 181 lbs
EYES Black **HAIR** Bald
POWERS/ABILITIES Empathic nature; mind control; immortality; Apokoliptian strength and durability.
ALLIES Prince Uxas (Darkseid)
ENEMIES Mister Miracle, Superman, Big Barda, Newsboy Legion, Justice League of China, New Super-Man

Before Prince Uxas transformed into Darkseid and seized control of Apokolips, he was a typical spoiled aristocrat, frequenting unsavory places with deviant hedonist Sleez as guide and companion. Afterwards, Sleez was an embarrassment and Darkseid exiled him. The salacious New God gravitated to the seamiest backwaters of Metropolis, using his psychic abilities to push humans into slaking their darkest hungers for his profit and amusement, before his depredations were ended by Superman, Big Barda, and Mister Miracle. Sleez relocated to Project Cadmus and renewed his sordid antics, even creating second cloned iteration of the Newsboy Legion.

During a purge of Apokolips and New Genesis, Sleez fell to the deadly God Killer, but recently returned, feeding off the repressed populace of China and clashing with New Super-Man and the Justice League of China.

SLEEZY DOES IT...
Sleez feeds off the worst aspects of human nature to keep his energy levels high and an evil grin on his face.

SMOAK, FELICITY

DEBUT *The Fury of Firestorm* #23 (May 1984)
BASE Seattle, Washington
EYES Blue **HAIR** Blonde
POWERS/ABILITIES Brilliant computer technician, expert hacker, code-writer and breaker.
ALLIES Oliver Queen, John Diggle
ENEMIES The King, Zehra Darvish, The Cheetah
AFFILIATIONS Team Arrow, Mia Dearden, Steve Trevor, A.R.G.U.S.

Felicity Smoak is one of the world's greatest hackers: an infallible digital gun-for-hire. After successfully scrubbing her history from all records, she gained a peerless reputation among the wrong sort of people. For this reason she was hired by scheming billionaire John King to dismantle Queen Industries and assassinate Green Arrow.

King's problem with Green Arrow was that he considered him too weak and unfit to protect Seattle. However, though she was far from a saint, Felicity balked at murder and instead warned the Super Hero, catapulting her into conflict with her vindictive former employer. For betraying him, King used his connections to have Felicity arrested for hacking government servers. He expected she would be killed within hours of arriving at Federal Supermax prison, as he had arranged for her to share a cell with the vicious Super-Villain The Cheetah. This feral fury had harbored a grudge against Smoak ever since the hacker had exposed her family members to danger by publishing their addresses online.

Saved by Green Arrow, Felicity joined him, John Diggle, and a small army of heroes in stopping John King. Oliver Queen, knowing Felicity was considering an offer from Steve Trevor to work anonymously for top-secret government agency A.R.G.U.S., invited her to officially join Team Arrow. Although she initially stayed in contact with them, she has remained more than a little evasive over her final decision.

SMOAK AND MIRRORS
Felicity was clever, cunning, capricious, and capable of many things, but cold-blooded murder wasn't one of them.

ON THE RECORD

Entrepreneur Felicity Smoak was introduced in the mid-1980s, when computers were starting to be more commonplace. Her company was nearly ruined when Firestorm's negligence during a metahuman battle wiped out her proprietary software.

It was the first of many unhappy and unlucky encounters with the Nuclear Man. These only grew more complicated when she married Ed Raymond, father of one of the two people who made up the composite Super Hero.

FIRESTORM AND FIREBRAND
Tech-company pioneer Felicity backed down for no man, least of all a bumbling junior super-freak who was more hazard than hero.

SOLOMON GRUNDY

DEBUT *All-American Comics* #61 (Oct. 1944)
REAL NAME Cyrus Gold
BASE Slaughter Swamp, Gotham City
HEIGHT 7ft 5in **WEIGHT** 517 lbs **EYES** Black **HAIR** White
POWERS/ABILITIES Near-immortality due to undead nature; immense strength, stamina, and durability; elemental plant qualities, including regeneration.
ALLIES The Joker, Amygdala, Klarion the Witch Boy
ENEMIES Green Lantern, Batman, Justice Society of America, Justice League Dark
AFFILIATIONS Injustice Society, Suicide Squad, Injustice League Dark

SUICIDE SOLOMON
Grundy was briefly recruited into the Suicide Squad on a mission to stop another rampaging behemoth, Damage.

Solomon Grundy, Born on a Monday, Christened on Tuesday, Married on Wednesday, Took ill on Thursday, Grew Worse on Friday, Died on Saturday, Buried on Sunday. That was the end of Solomon Grundy. Or so they thought...

The hulking monster known as Solomon Grundy is believed to be the reincarnation of a man named Cyrus Gold. When he plunged into Gotham City's Slaughter Swamp and died, Gold was reborn, a creature of rotted wood and swamp muck, nearly brainless, yet able to recall the Solomon Grundy nursery rhyme from which his name was derived.

Originally a foe of Green Lantern (Alan Scott) and the Justice Society, Grundy's near-immortal form kept him in his "prime" for decades. When the crime fighter known as the Batman emerged in Gotham City, it wasn't long before he clashed with Grundy. Batman recognized the tragic creature's animal-like behavior, but has had repeated clashes with him over the years. Grundy fought on The Joker's side during the momentous "War of Jokes and Riddles," a battle that pitted him against Killer Croc. He would later fight fledgling heroes Gotham and Gotham Girl, nearly destroying Gotham City's Statue of Justice in the process. When incarcerated in Arkham Asylum, Grundy still found time for violence, battling not just Batman, but also Bane, Catwoman, and even Deathstroke.

Solomon Grundy's brain has rotted even further in recent months, and he was recruited as muscle for the Injustice League Dark, following the commands of Klarion the Witch Boy. However, their team fell to the Justice League Dark, leaving Grundy to wander the world aimlessly yet again.

APPROACHING SATURDAY
Grundy's appearance deteriorated along with his brain during his time serving with the Justice League Dark.

CLASSIC STORIES

***All-American Comics* #61 (Oct. 1944)** A shambling undead creature appears in a hobo encampment near Gotham City, unable to remember its origins. It is dubbed Solomon Grundy because one of its few memories is that it was "born on a Monday."

***All-Star Comics* #33 (Feb.–Mar. 1947)** Grundy's battles the Justice Society, and for his crimes is banished by Green Lantern to another planet.

***Justice League of America* (Vol. 2) #1–6 (Oct. 2006–Apr. 2007)** Solomon Grundy realizes he has a shot at true immortality if he can possess Professor Ivo's undying essence. However, he will only be able to survive the process if he has the upgraded Red Tornado android as armor.

UNDERGROUND MONSTER
Grundy has no problem lurking in the Gotham City sewers. A creature of the swamps, the quiet solitude of the filth and muck makes him feel right at home.

ON THE RECORD

Solomon Grundy's name comes from a old nursery rhyme. A foe of Golden Age Green Lantern (Alan Scott), the swamp creature proved a thorn in GL's side due to Lantern's ring having a vulnerability to wood. Grundy later became a recurring foe of Batman's when he wandered from Gotham City's Slaughter Swamp into its sewer system. He was reborn with a kind soul and became an ally of Starman (Jack Knight) before returning to his "roots." The *Seven Soldiers: Klarion* miniseries revealed an enslaved population of Grundys working underground in Limbo Town.

BORN ON A MONDAY
Solomon Grundy's powers made him a formidable foe, even for the Justice Society.

SORROW, JOHNNY

DEBUT *Secret Origins of Super-Villains* #1 (Dec. 1999)
HEIGHT 6ft 1in **WEIGHT** 192 lbs
POWERS/ABILITIES Uncovered face fatally shocks viewers; teleportation; intangibility.
ALLIES Despero, King of Tears
ENEMIES JSA, Justice League, Amanda Waller
AFFILIATION Injustice Society, Suicide Squad, Maxwell Lord

A silent-movie actor unable to make the transition to talkies, Johnny Sorrow stole a device called a Subspace Prototype. It malfunctioned, transporting him to another dimension—the Subtle Realms—where monstrous creatures made his visage so horrifying that anyone seeing it died from shock. Returned to Earth, Sorrow prepared for the invasion of his godlike master, the King of Tears, who was imprisoned by the Spectre and Justice Society of America. Decades later, Sorrow assembled a new Injustice Society to liberate his King, but lost to the Justice Society. He returned to the Subtle Realms and teamed with Despero to unleash the Seven Deadly Sins. Again beaten and banished by the Justice League and Justice Society, he returned, leading another Injustice Society, and as part of Amanda Waller's Suicide Squad program.

MAN BEHIND THE MASK
Remade in the hellish Subtle Realms, Johnny Sorrow acquired dangerous powers, a hunger for domination, and a face that nobody gets to see twice.

SPACE CABBIE

DEBUT *Mystery in Space* #21 (Aug.–Sep. 1954)
REAL NAME Unknown
HEIGHT 5ft 10in **WEIGHT** 175 lbs
ABILITIES Skilled pilot, navigator, engineer; robotic left leg.
ENEMIES New Gods, The Gang, Tommy Tomorrow, Planeteers

Orphaned as a child, the man known as Space Cabbie displayed a talent for interstellar navigation, and found his true calling as a cab driver behind the wheel of Old Gal—a small ship modified with unsanctioned Mother Box and Boom Tube technology. Over the years, Space Cabbie has seen more worlds than he can count and learned several alien languages, ferrying many prestigious personalities, such as Lobo, Starman, and Superman,

OUTTA SPACE
Rokko put Denise to the test and hyperjumped the Lanterns to safety.

Space Cabbie branched out as an intergalactic deliveryman—often of illegal goods—and fell foul of the Green Lanterns. However, when Earth was endangered, he pitched in to help and further risked his liberty and livelihood helping Super Sons Damian Wayne and Jon Kent in their battles against Rex Luthor and the militant Planeteers of Tommy Tomorrow.

TAXI TO THE STARS... AND BEYOND
Space Cabbie will get you where you need to go, whether it's around the block, through the galaxy... or even across time itself.

SPACE RANGER

DEBUT *Showcase* #15 (Jul.–Aug. 1958)
REAL NAME Rick Starr
BASE New York City; asteroid base near Mars
HEIGHT 6ft 2in **WEIGHT** 194 lbs
EYES Blue **HAIR** Black
ABILITIES Hand-to-hand combat; weapons expert.
ALLIES Myra Mason, Cryll, Hal Jordan
ENEMIES Gordanians, Jupiter's Jungle beasts

Rick Starr was the 22nd-century's Space Ranger, patrolling Earth's solar system from his asteroid base near Jupiter. Often joined on his starship, Solar King, by his girlfriend Myra Mason, on one solo mission, Starr nearly died after being stranded on Pluto. He was saved by an alien shape-changer, Cryll, and the two became good friends. Starr later foiled a Gordanian invasion of Earth with the help of Green Lantern Hal Jordan.

After *Flashpoint*, a new—21st century—Rikane "Ric" Starr appeared. Having left the Space Rangers, Ric traveled to planet Tolerance in the Tenebrian Dominion. Here he was branded a fugitive with a bounty on his head, and became an unwilling participant in popular glimmernet gameshow, *The Hunted*.

PATROLLING THE FINAL FRONTIER
Space Ranger and his shape-changing pal Cryll were armed and ever ready for all manner of alien threats.

PRIMETIME PREY
"Ric" Starr worked with Colonel T'omas T'morra to create blind spots during *The Hunted* games.

SPARX

DEBUT *Adventures of Superman Annual* #5 (1993)
REAL NAME Donna Carol Force
BASE New York City
HEIGHT 5ft 5in **WEIGHT** 130 lbs
EYES Blue/white **HAIR** Brown/white
POWERS/ABILITIES Faster-than-light travel; lightning emission; flight.
ALLIES Superboy
AFFILIATIONS Canadian Force, Ravers

Donna Carol "D.C." Force was the only member of the Force Family without metahuman powers. This changed when they discovered alien parasites in Metropolis whose bite triggered latent metahuman powers. The parasites nearly killed her—but also bestowed upon her a number of powers, essentially transforming her into a living thunderbolt. Staying to fight alongside Superboy, D.C.—now called Sparx—helped the New Bloods and veteran heroes combat the alien horde. Searching for her place in the world, Sparx discovered the Event Horizon, a neverending rave party that floated from reality to reality, world to world. Superboy was invited to the rave, and with Sparx, created a Super Hero team called the Ravers. Sparx was later considered for admission into the Teen Titans.

Post *Rebirth*, another alien parasite attack in rural Pine Ridge saw a young girl named Dana gain electrical powers in copycat incident. Her current location and status are unknown.

RAVE ON!
The alien parasites that initially threatened Sparx's life, not only gave her superpowers, they turned her into a fun-loving party animal!

SPECTRE, THE

DATA

DEBUT *More Fun Comics* #52 (Feb. 1940)
REAL NAME James Corrigan
BASE New York City
HEIGHT 6ft 1in **WEIGHT** 184 lbs **EYES** Blue **HAIR** Red
POWERS/ABILITIES Near omnipotent magical and physical abilities, limited only by the need to bond with a host.
ENEMIES Eclipso
AFFILIATIONS Justice Society of America, Gotham City Police Department, New York City Police Department

I AM VENGEANCE
When The Spectre and Jim Corrigan were recently separated, Batman reluctantly helped them reunite after learning The Spectre's origin.

Jim Corrigan is The Spectre, the mystical embodiment of divine wrath. Torn between his desire for revenge and his destined role as an instrument of justice, Corrigan fights both the evils of the world and his own baser human impulses.

When hard-boiled New York City cop Jim Corrigan was drowned by criminals while on the job, he was given a second chance at life as the physical personification of the Presence's wrath. He became The Spectre, a pale ghost clad in a green cloak, who often changed his form so as to appear massive to human beings. Able to perform nearly any magical feat on a whim, The Spectre sought out those he felt in need of vengeance, and punished them, not without a sense of irony in his fatal judgments.

UNDER THE CLOAK
Jim Corrigan still retains his humanity somewhere deep inside The Spectre. He can switch back and forth at will, although he often doesn't have a choice when it comes time to spring into action.

While Corrigan's appearance would have many believe that he is fairly young and new to his role as The Spectre, Corrigan is immortal so long as he remains The Spectre's host. When he was just getting his start, Corrigan served with the World War II era team of Super Heroes known as the Justice Society of America. Perhaps in an attempt to avoid explaining why his secret identity refused to age, Corrigan has moved around over the years, taking a job as a Gotham City detective most recently. However, after Batman helped save his life and rescue his Corrigan half, the Dark Knight informed The Spectre that he didn't want a murderer like him running free in his city. Corrigan agreed to move back to New York City, not comfortable being on the other end of a hero's judgment.

DIVINE RETRIBUTION
The Spectre's powers can run amok if not kept in check by being tethered to the conscience of a human host.

ON THE RECORD

Three men have hosted The Spectre. The first was Jim Corrigan, a classic 1940s noir cop who was killed by gangsters and rose from the dead to exact his revenge. Moderating his vengeful feelings, he became a charter member of the Golden Age Justice Society.

The Spectre's second host was Hal Jordan, the former Green Lantern who assumed the role after Corrigan refused. Jordan was chosen because The Spectre knew Hal was threatened with corruption by Parallax, and only The Spectre could purge Hal's soul.

After a period without a host, during which Eclipso turned The Spectre into a destructive force that wreaked havoc on Earth's magic users, the entity was forced into the recently deceased body of Gotham City cop Crispus Allen.

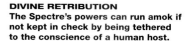

SPECTRES THREE
Left to right: the original James Corrigan Spectre took no prisoners; Hal Jordan became The Spectre's reluctant host; the angry, vengeful third Spectre, Crispus Allen.

CLASSIC STORIES

***More Fun Comics* #52–53 (Feb.–Mar. 1940)** The Spectre makes his first dramatic appearance after tough cop Jim Corrigan is drowned in a cement-filled barrel, and returns soon after to take supernatural revenge on his killers.

***Crisis on Infinite Earths* #10 (Jan. 1986)** The only being on Earth capable of holding his own against the Anti-Monitor, The Spectre buys Earth's other heroes precious time to execute their ultimate plan to save creation.

SPELLBINDER I, II, AND III

DEBUT *Detective Comics* (Vol. 1) #358 (Dec. 1966) (Spellbinder I); *Justice League International* (Vol. 2) #65 (Jun. 1994) (Spellbinder II); *Detective Comics* (Vol. 1) #691 (Nov. 1995) (Spellbinder III)
REAL NAME Delbert Billings (Spellbinder I); Fay Moffit (Spellbinder III)
BASE Gotham City
HEIGHT 5ft 11in (Billings); 5ft 6in (Moffit) **WEIGHT** 155 lbs (Billings); 137 lbs (Moffit) **EYES** Brown (Billings); Pink (Moffit)
HAIR Blue (Billings); Blue (Moffit)
POWERS/ABILITIES Can generate powerful illusions **ENEMIES** Batman

BEDAZZLED:
The first Spellbinder, Delbert Billings, tested his hypnotic powers on Batman, who soon saw through the illusions.

Art forger Delbert Billings decided to embellish his criminal career by developing optical devices that would enable him to hypnotize others. As Spellbinder, Billings committed a rash of robberies, but was ultimately routed by Batman and Robin.

A second Spellbinder—mystically powered and unrelated to Delbert Billings—was briefly active during Billings' incarceration and battled the Justice League as a member of the government-sanctioned "Leaguebusters," before vanishing to parts unknown.

Upon his release from prison, Delbert Billings attempted a criminal comeback, but made the mistake of his life when he turned down the demon Neron's offer for enhanced powers in exchange for his soul. However, while Billings would not agree to Neron's offer, his moll, Fay Moffit, jumped at the chance and promptly shot Delbert in the head. Neron gave Moffit the ability to cast psychedelic illusions, and she became the third and most sinister Spellbinder. However, her power to alter others' perceptions of reality is directly tied to her own vision. Cover her eyes and she is rendered powerless.

DEMONIC DEAL:
Fay Moffit knew a good deal when she saw it and accepted Neron's offer to succeed Delbert Billings as the new Spellbinder.

CASTING A WICKED SPELL
In the Possible Future of Neo-Gotham (Batman Beyond) elderly Bruce Wayne and new Batman Terry McGinnis frequently confront Dr. Ira Billings. This former school psychologist uses virtual technology and brainwashing techniques to play bizarre mind-games, punish the lackluster and get rich as the sinister Spellbinder.

JOKERS WILD
While incarcerated at the Slab prison, the third Spellbinder was among a throng of Super-Villains infected by the Clown Prince of Crime's toxin. During the jailbreak that followed, she almost killed Nightwing with an illusion of the inter-dimensional imp, Bat-Mite.

SPINNER, DOROTHY

DEBUT *Doom Patrol* (Vol. 2) #14 (Nov. 1988)
HEIGHT 5ft 3in **WEIGHT** 118 lbs
EYES Brown **HAIR** Brown
POWERS/ABILITIES Can bring imaginary friends and enemies to life for short periods.
ENEMIES Candlemaker
ALLIES Robotman, Beast Boy
AFFILIATIONS Doom Patrol

Dorothy's deformed, simian-like features made her hide from the world, so she used her psychic ability to bring imaginary friends to life. When she met the Doom Patrol, she found equally strange friends who accepted her as one of their own. However, her time with the team also unleashed her innermost fears, giving life to the Candlemaker. The savage entity decapitated the Doom Patrol's leader, the Chief, and terrorized the team, but was eventually snuffed out by Dorothy.

Dorothy was then imprisoned within the other-dimensional Dream Country with other powerful children who were brought there to expand the region's power. She escaped and later unwittingly destroyed Robotman when he tried to reunite Dorothy with her mother. She created a new Robotman from her mind, but Beast Boy and Fever rebuilt the original and got Dorothy the psychiatric care she needed.

CANDLE KILLER
Dorothy's deepest fears, frustrations, and fury found all-too-real and terrifying form in the Candlemaker.

SAVAGE PSYCHE
Years of retreating from the real world and keeping her emotions in check were unleashed when Dorothy joined the Doom Patrol.

SPIVOT, PATTY

DEBUT *DC Special Series* # 1 (Sep. 1977)
BASE Central City
HEIGHT 5ft 3in **WEIGHT** 133 lbs
EYES Blue **HAIR** Blonde
POWERS/ABILITIES Extremely intelligent forensic scientist with a real thirst for justice and seeing cases through to the end.
ALLIES Barry Allen, Solovar
ENEMIES Captain Cold, Gorilla Grodd
AFFILIATIONS Central City Police Department

Patty Spivot is the blood analysis specialist at the Central City Police Department crime land, where she works with forensic scientist Barry Allen. After years of working together, Barry finally worked up the nerve to ask Patty out on a date, and took her to a tech symposium. Unfortunately their brief romantic moment was interrupted by an armed robbery.

Despite this shaky start, they grew closer, but Patty soon realized she had a potential rival for Barry's affections. Reporter Iris West had a tendency to flirt with him while seeking leads for her articles.

After Barry was nearly killed in the line of duty, he and Patty took their blossoming relationship to the next level and officially became a couple. Patty then learned that Barry was also Central City Super Hero The Flash, but moved in with him anyway. However, she eventually left Barry after a terrifying encounter with his future self tainted him in her eyes.

GETTING SERIOUS
Despite a hesitant start, Patty Spivot knew that she and Barry Allen were destined to have a life together—even after he revealed he was The Flash.

SPOILER

DEBUT *Detective Comics* (Vol. 1) #647 **(Aug. 1992)**
REAL NAME Stephanie Brown
BASE Gotham City
HEIGHT 5ft 5in **WEIGHT** 110 lbs **EYES** Blue **HAIR** Blonde
POWERS/ABILITIES Adept gymnast and fighter; brilliant computer hacker; weapons include protective suit equipped with offensive and defensive devices; skilled motorcyclist.
ALLIES Tim Drake (Red Robin/Drake), Bluebird, Catwoman, Batman, Batman Family
ENEMIES Cluemaster, Hush, Lincoln March, Anarky, Ulysses Hadrian Armstrong (the General)
AFFILIATIONS Young Justice

Teenager Stephanie Brown knew had no idea that her father was costumed Super-Villain Cluemaster. After unintentionally walking in on his meeting with his cronies, including Signalman, Lock-Up, and Firefly, Stephanie began running for her life, as even her mother was in on the conspiracy.

Telling her story on her blog "Spoiler Alert," Stephanie soon adopted the vigilante name of Spoiler and a flamboyant purple costume. Acting alone, she used biking skills she had picked up during her childhood to lure Cluemaster into a trap, ultimately resulting in his arrest. Even after her father was seemingly killed by his former associate—Lincoln March of the Court of Owls—Spoiler opted to continue her Super Hero career. Catwoman trained her in fighting techniques, and Spoiler was constantly popping up in Batman's life.

Eventually she joined the Bat-family, becoming a Robin and Batgirl, before reverting to her original costumed persona. She developed a romantic relationship with Red Robin (Tim Drake) and was crushed when he died. However, when Drake reappeared, they reunited to investigate anomalies in the timestream.

TO THE VICTOR...
During a massive attack by the villain Mother, Spoiler helped protect Bluebird's brother Cullen and fought back against Mother with other heroes, including Red Robin and Midnighter.

ON THE RECORD

Before *Flashpoint*, Stephanie Brown was the only character to serve as both Robin and Batgirl. She debuted in the pages of *Detective Comics*, but soon became romantically involved with Tim Drake in his Robin role.

Having had a tumultuous life, including giving her baby up for adoption and troubles with her single mom, Spoiler eventually worked her way into Batman's good graces, briefly replacing Tim as Robin. Fired by the Dark Knight for not following his directions, she continued her crime-fighting career—with Barbara Gordon's blessing—adopting the name and costume of Batgirl.

HERO BY PROXY
As Batgirl, Stephanie fought crime on her college campus at Gotham University with the help of her own Oracle of sorts—computer expert Proxy. Thanks to a grant from Batman, Inc., Batgirl set up shop in her own Batcave-like hideout she called Firewall.

SPYRAL

DEBUT *Batman, Incorporated* (Vol. 1) #4 **(Apr. 2011)**
BASE St. Hadrian's Finishing School for Girls, England
NOTABLE MEMBERS Helena Bertinelli (Matron, Director of Spyral); **Doctor Dedalus** (Agent Zero, Otto Netz); **Tiger** (Agent 1); The Hood (Agent 24, George Cross); **El Gaucho** (Agent 33, Santiago Vargas); **Dick Grayson** (Agent 37); **Mr. Minos** (Former Head of Spyral); **Elisabeth Netz** (Frau Netz); **Dr. Poppy Ashemore**
ENEMIES Batman, Dick Grayson, Tiger

Led by the former "mafia princess" Helena Bertinelli, clandestine espionage agency Spyral was an organization with self-destructive underpinnings, creating violence to beget more violence. It was originally formed by Nazi scientist Otto Netz—Doctor Dedalus—when he turned to Super-Villainy. After Netz's death, the organization was briefly controlled by corrupt and devious Mr. Minos before passing to his daughter, Agent 0.

Minos had been gathering intel on Super Heroes, but his clumsy efforts attracted the attention of Batman. When Nightwing was publicly outed as Dick Grayson and seemingly executed by the Crime Syndicate, Batman exploited the situation to discover more about the mysterious organization. He persuaded Grayson to join Spyral as an undercover agent. All went smoothly for a while: Grayson worked with Spyral agent Bertinelli on several missions.

However, after she took over as the institution's new head, Spyral's computer consciousness—an artificial intelligence called Spyder—ordered her to kill Grayson. As a result, Grayson and Agent 1, Tiger, turned against Spyral and began taking out their agents one by one.

Barely surviving that debacle, Spyral was later eradicated when former Manhunter Mark Shaw launched his hostile takeover of all Earth's covert agencies, absorbing them into his Leviathan group.

SPY VS. SPY
Helena Bertinelli wanted to run Spyral along more principled lines, but found it near impossible thanks to Spyder, the organization's corrupt computer system.

ON THE RECORD

Spyral debuted shortly before the *Flashpoint* event. In the original version, Netz's daughter was not Agent 0, but the original Batwoman, Kathy Kane. She had a relationship with Batman, while also working for Spyral. This explained why the battle uniforms at St. Hadrian's Finishing School resembled the red and yellow of Batwoman's costume. After *Flashpoint*, Kathy Kane disappeared from the timeline, and Agent 0, Katarina "Luka" Netz, was introduced in her place.

SINS OF THE FATHER
The original Batwoman cut off her relationship with Batman after learning that Otto Netz was her father and that, years ago, she had been given up for adoption.

ST. CLOUD, SILVER

DEBUT Detective Comics (Vol. 1) #470 (Jun. 1977)
BASE Gotham City
HEIGHT 5ft 5in **WEIGHT** 131 lbs
EYES Blue **HAIR** Silver
POWERS/ABILITIES Highly intelligent and witty; excellent connections to Gotham City's elite social circles.
ALLIES Batman
ENEMIES Onomatopoeia, Rupert Thorne, The Joker, Deadshot

RELAXEZ-VOUS!
Silver was closer to Bruce Wayne than perhaps any of his previous girlfriends. She brought out his playful side, normally kept well under wraps.

Bruce Wayne first met Silver St. Cloud at a party on his yacht, and they were very taken with one another. After Bruce left briefly to battle Dr. Phosphorous, he returned to the yacht only for Silver to touch his hair and realize it was wet. Suspicious of Bruce from then on, Silver nevertheless began to date him. But when she saw Batman in action and recognized Bruce beneath the cowl, she broke off their relationship, unable to deal with Bruce's nighttime activities.

Fate brought the couple back together, and Silver and Bruce became engaged. As a result, Batman began to let his guard down, revealing his secret identity to a vigilante calling himself Baphomet, and even bringing the young man back to the Batcave and introducing him to Silver. Bruce was appalled to discover that Baphomet was none other than the murderous villain Onomatopoeia, who slashed Silver's throat in front of his horrified eyes.

STALKER

DEBUT Stalker #1 (Jun.–Jul. 1975)
HEIGHT 5ft 8in
WEIGHT 145 lbs
EYES Red
HAIR Black
POWERS/ABILITIES expert marksman, unparalleled hunting skills, magical knowledge; fires explosive blasts from hands; can create portals to other locations.
ALLIES Lyll'ana
ENEMIES Lucifer

A long time ago, young warrior king Stalker returned from battle to find his wife, Lyll'ana dying of fever. He prayed to his god to spare her life and that of his unborn child. He was visited by Lucifer, who made him a deal: a male soul of his bloodline for the health of his wife and child. His wife recovered, but died in childbirth. Stalker realized he was doomed to walk the Earth forever, presumably without a soul.

As a hitman in the modern world, Stalker was told by Lucifer to kill a woman, Clarissa Rowe. Stalker was shocked to find that she was pregnant and his descendant. He also realized that he had always had a soul, and that Lucifer was claiming this young boy as part of their deal. Realizing what a monster he had become Stalker drove Lucifer away from the infant.

STAR BOY

DEBUT Adventure Comics #282 (Mar. 1961)
REAL NAME Thom Kallor
BASE Legion HQ, 31st-century New Metropolis
HEIGHT 5ft 8in **WEIGHT** 160 lbs
EYES Brown **HAIR** Brown
POWERS/ABILITIES Can increase the weight of people or objects; Density manipulation, enhanced strength and durability, Legion of Super-Heroes combat training, flight ring.
ENEMIES Horraz, Crav the General Nah, Mordru

Thom Kallor was born in a floating observatory to astronomer parents from the planet Xanthu. As a result of his unique introduction to the universe, Thom developed the power to borrow mass from stars, to affect his own body and to alter the weight of any objects he concentrated on. He could also emit blasts of stellar energy.

Due to a possible connection with Earth's heroic Starman dynasty, Thom is an ardent fan of 21st-century culture and ephemera and frequently bores his teammates with some incomprehensible piece of arcane trivia from the legendary Age of Heroes. For all his bookish interests, Thom is a poweful and canny combat specialist, happy to go toe-to-toe with terrorists like the Horraz or galaxy-rending monsters like demon lord Mordru.

STAR SAPPHIRE CORPS

DEBUT Green Lantern (Vol. 4) #20 (Jun. 2007)
REAL NAME Violet Lantern Corps
BASE Zamaron
CURRENT MEMBERS/POWERS Carol Ferris, Fatality, Miri Riam, Queen Aga'po Each member uses all-consuming love to power a violet power ring that affords flight, protection, energy projection, and solid light-construct creation.
ALLIES Blue Lantern Corps, Indigo Tribe, Green Lantern Corps
ENEMIES Guardians of the Universe, Sinestro Corps

A multi-species group of females empowered by love, the Star Sapphires were created by the immortal women of Maltus. Having broken away from their emotion-suppressing males in the wake of Krona's wounding of the cosmic fabric, the Zamarons sought to ease universal conflict, using love to soothe aggression. Initially they employed violet crystals, but these ultimately proved wild and attuned to love's darker side. Eventually they were equipped with power rings using the refined Light of Love broadcast from a Central Power Battery. The Star Sapphire Corps also use conversion crystals to envelop resistant or hostile targets, gradually reprogramming potential recruits to pursue the interests of love at all costs. Until recently all members were female, except for Guy Gardner, who briefly found love on his odyssey through the Emotional Spectrum.

"The Star Sapphires have their own unique oath:
For hearts long lost and full of fright,
For those alone in blackest night,
Accept our ring and join our fight,
Love conquers all—with violet light!"

ON THE RECORD

The Zamarons have been altered radically and often since their introduction in 1962. Initially super-scientific Amazons roaming the cosmos in search of a new ruler, their selection of Carol Ferris met with stiff resistance from the Green Lantern.

They were later revealed as the long-missing females of the Oan Guardians, complete with their own agenda for how creation should be run. Their return signaled a reconciliation of immortals and a new Millennium for the Universe.

TOGETHERNESS
Pooling their resources, a male and female immortal came to Earth with the intent of creating a group of transformative New Guardians.

STAR SAPPHIRE

DEBUT *Green Lantern* (Vol. 2) #16 **(Oct. 1962)**
REAL NAME Carol Ferris
BASE Mobile
HEIGHT 5ft 9in **WEIGHT** 158 lbs **EYES** Blue **HAIR** Black
POWERS/ABILITIES Indomitable will and all-consuming love; capable of utilizing a violet gem or ring that affords flight, protection, energy projection and solid light-construct creation, astute businesswoman
ALLIES Green Lantern (Hal Jordan), Green Lantern (Kyle Rayner)
ENEMIES Sinestro, Larfleeze, Black Hand
AFFILIATIONS Star Sapphire Corps, Zamarons, Ferris Air/Ferris Aircraft, New Guardians

CLASSIC STORIES

***Green Lantern* (Vol. 2) #73-74 (Dec. 1969–Jan. 1970)** Carol's love for Hal together with Star Sapphire's increasing mental instability enable Sinestro to use her as a deadly weapon in an attack on their mutual foe—Green Lantern Hal Jordan.

***Superman* (Vol. 1) #261 (Feb. 1973)** Following a bizarre misunderstanding, the lethally protective but mentally muddled Star Sapphire launches an attack on Superman, believing that the Man of Steel has harmed her chosen consort, Green Lantern.

***Action Comics* (Vol. 1) #601 (Aug. 1988)** Under the influence of the ruthless Predator Entity, Star Sapphire kills Green Lantern Katma Tui to send a message to Hal, devastating John Stewart in the process.

EMOTIONAL ROLLERCOASTER Her time with the New Guardians showed Carol that love could not exist in an emotional vacuum.

Carol Ferris had no time for love, despite being torn between affection for test pilot Hal Jordan and being attracted to the hero Green Lantern. This emotional conflict led to mayhem after she was selected by warriors of an extraterrestrial matriarchy to wear the all-powerful Star Sapphire. With the gem, all Carol's subconscious desires could be realized and she repeatedly attacked the Green Lantern, determined to bend him to her will.

I SEE YOUR LOVE LIGHT SHINING Like everything in her life, Carol's relationships with teammates were always fraught with complications.

Hal Jordan's boss at Ferris Air, Carol Ferris had been chosen to become Star Sapphire, the Violet Light's equivalent to a Green Lantern. As Star Sapphire, she harnessed love's light—a light that affected Carol's mind after a time, even creating a subconscious third personality, named Predator. "He" drove her to brutality and murder, and was later revealed as a physical manifestation of the Entity embodying the accumulation of universal love. Eventually she was cured, but when the War of Light brought all shades of the Emotional Spectrum into conflict, the alien Zamarons sought a new path to universal love, asking Carol to lead their Star Sapphire Corps.

Now wearing a Star Sapphire power ring, Carol thrived as a hero, battling against the marauding Sinestro Corps and the ghastly risen dead of the Black Lanterns. She even reformed the uncontrolled passions of the Predator Entity, creating a more benign and positive aspect of love.

Following valiant participation in the coming of the White Entity of Life on the *Brightest Day* event and during the War of the Lanterns, Carol joined Kyle Rayner's multidenominational band of Spectrum Warriors as a New Guardian. Her long-held feelings for Hal Jordan began to waver, as she found herself increasingly drawn to Rayner. Carol eventually broke away from both Jordan and White Lantern Rayner to chart her own course. While Hal returned home to Earth recently to seemingly rekindle his relationship with Carol, it seemed just another fling that was destined not to last.

ON THE RECORD

Golden Age Star Sapphire was an alien invader who fought The Flash. She was reinvented as Carol Ferris, and since then a number of women have worn the transformative gem.

Dela Pharon became the Zamarons' second choice for queen, while Deborah Camille Darnell—aka Remoni-Notra—just wanted power. Hal Jordan's old flame Jillian Pearlman was simply overwhelmed by the gem itself as it sought to discover which woman Hal loved the most.

TAKING NO PRISONERS The very first Star Sapphire loved only the thrill of battle and the allure of conquest.

STARFIRE

DATA

DEBUT *DC Comics Presents* #26 (Oct. 1980)
REAL NAME Princess Koriand'r
BASE San Francisco; mobile
HEIGHT 5ft 9ins **WEIGHT** 158 lbs
EYES Green **HAIR** Red
POWERS/ABILITIES Converts ultraviolet radiation into energy, providing enhanced strength, speed, endurance, durability, gravity-repelling flight, and heat and energy projection; contact language assimilation; expertly trained warrior.
ALLIES Nightwing, Red Hood (Jason Todd), Arsenal, Cyborg, Raven
ENEMIES Blackfire, Helspont, Darkseid
AFFILIATIONS Teen Titans, The Outlaws, Justice League Odyssey

CLASSIC STORIES

New Teen Titans (Vol. 1) #23–25; *New Teen Titans Annual* #1 (Sep.– Nov. 1982) Starfire is recaptured by slavers and, with human allies, fights a climactic battle against her vicious usurping sister, Blackfire.

New Teen Titans (Vol. 2) #14–18 (Nov. 1985–Mar. 1986) Koriand'r and the Titans visit Tamaran, where the Princess is compelled by her parents to enter into a state marriage to prevent civil war. The decision does not go down well with her boyfriend, Dick Grayson.

New Titans (Vol. 1) #109 (Mar. 1994) After months of personal tragedy and escalating violence, Starfire undergoes a radical transformation and becomes a darker, meaner warrior woman.

SHINING STAR
Red Hood and Arsenal were fiercely protective of their alien ally Koriand'r, despite her staggering power and battle prowess.

An alien princess in exile, Koriand'r of Tamaran escaped a lifetime of brutality as a slave and lab rat for the Citadel and the Psions. Years after manifesting incredible energy powers, she led a revolt and escaped to Earth. An engine of righteous fury, she fights to ensure no other beings have to endure the pain and indignity that ruined her life.

As a child, Princess Koriand'r of Tamaran was trained in combat techniques alongside her sister Komand'r. Longtime rivals, Komand'r agreed for her sister to be sold into slavery. Kori spent her early life in drudgery and as a subject of scientific experimentation at the hands of the Psions.

After escaping to Earth, Kori adopted the name Starfire and spent time fighting evil alongside a number of young heroes—most notably Dick Grayson. Eventually, however, she suffered damage to her memories, and became insular. She was brought out of her shell by Red Hood, who looked after her when she became a member of his team, The Outlaws.

Following months of conflict on Earth, The Outlaws joined Starfire on a mission to occupied Tamaran. Her homeworld was now under attack from the parasitic Blight. Kori successfully liberated her people and reconciled with her sister, now known as Blackfire. Together they repelled another invasion from the Daemonite overlord Helspont.

Starfire returned to Earth and set up home in Florida. However, while investigating a slavery ring, she was taken hostage by Robin (Damian Wayne) in his attempt to recruit a new team of Teen Titans. She fought by the side of heroes including Raven and Beast Boy, before traveling to the mysterious Ghost Sector. There she became a member of Justice League Odyssey, helping to restore Tamaran's place in the universe, despite conflict with her sister when Starfire fell under the control of the evil Darkseid. Starfire was killed by her sister, before being brought back to life when she was plucked from an earlier point in the timestream.

YEARS A SLAVE
Imprisoned on the planet Takron, the young Koriand'r endured years of back-breaking hard labor and enforced drug-dependency.

GOLDEN GIRL
Though always confident and a little headstrong, Starfire was generally considered to be a team player, not a solo star.

ON THE RECORD

When Starfire was introduced in 1980, she was a naïve girl with staggering powers and a short temper. The alien princess trusted implicitly and always spoke her mind. Moreover, when she was in action with the New Teen Titans, she had to be constantly monitored because she had a tendency to go straight for the kill. After leaving the Titans, she served with distinction in the Justice League, the Outsiders, and interstellar peacekeeping force R.E.B.E.L.S.

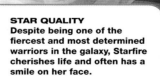

STAR QUALITY
Despite being one of the fiercest and most determined warriors in the galaxy, Starfire cherishes life and often has a smile on her face.

STARRO THE STAR CONQUEROR

DEBUT (Starro) *The Brave and the Bold* (Vol. 1) #28 **(Feb.–Mar. 1960)**; (Starro the Conqueror/Cobi) *R.E.B.E.L.S.* (Vol. 2) #5 **(Aug. 2009)**; (Jarro) *Justice League* (Vol. 4) #10 **(Dec. 2018)**

REAL NAME Cobi

EYES Black **HAIR** Bald

POWERS/ABILITIES Immense strength and durability; controls trillions of beings through Starro parasites; can spawn spores from body.

ALLIES The High Vanguard, Batman (Jarro)

ENEMIES R.E.B.E.L.S. Justice League, Legion of Doom

LEAGUE OF LEGENDS
A Starro alien discovered Earth and attempted to conquer it with its mind-control powers. Fortunately, it was defeated by the Justice League on the team's first official mission.

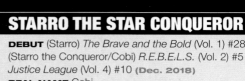

FACE-OFF
When a spore forced him to kill his own brother, Cobi escaped its control and ripped it from his head.

Starros are giant starfish-like aliens employing parasitic spores to enslave other species. Immense Starro Motherstars ventured across intergalactic space, brutally conquering and assimilating inhabited worlds with their spores as they went.

Starros attacked planet Hatorei and began incorporating the inhabitants, but the psychic link shared by the Hatorei enabled some of the populace to fight back. A youth named Cobi tore the Starro spore from his head, and when an immature Motherstar spore attacked, it became latched to his chest. They bonded, but Cobi was now in charge and exerted control over all the Starro species. He became Starro the Star Conqueror, controlling nine galaxies and exercising indomitable psychic control over trillions of beings. Starro the Star Conqueror's commanders were the High Vanguard, who were allowed to retain some of their free will.

Starro's forces made several attempts to conquer Earth. The first was met by a gathering of heroes who joined forces to defeat the invaders, thereby forming the Justice Society of America. Subsequent attacks launched by an undeterred Starro were thwarted by Vril Dox and L.E.G.I.O.N.

Recently, Starro joined Super Heroes in Team Mystery to turn back an invasion of Omega Titans and to—inspired by Martian Manhunter's heroism, sacrificed himself to save his new comrades. In the aftermath, Batman grew a tissue fragment into a new being. "Jarro" is a valiant, loving ally and considers himself the latest Robin, aiding the Justice League during the return of Perpetua. The heroes were unaware that Luthor's Legion of Doom also preserved a portion of Starro: regrowing it to aid their plans of conquest.

CONQUEROR OF WORLDS
When Cobi bonded with a Starro parasite, he became an almost unstoppable warrior who could take down armies by himself.

STARLING

DEBUT *Birds of Prey* (Vol. 3) #1 **(Nov. 2011)**

REAL NAME Evelyn Crawford

BASE Gotham City

EYES Brown **HAIR** Brown

POWERS/ABILITIES Highly skilled unarmed combatant; skilled and aggressive vehicle driver; extremely proficient with firearms.

ALLIES Black Canary, Batgirl, Katana

ENEMIES The Penguin, Choke

AFFILIATIONS Birds of Prey, Amanda Waller

Starling is a wanted mercenary and master strategist. The covert surveillance operative and combat specialist met Black Canary when both were infiltrating the Penguin's operation in Gotham City. They decided to stick together after they were exposed, forming the Birds of Prey.

Starling repeatedly proved her worth in battle against terrorists such as Basilisk and metahuman maniacs like Choke and Talon, but she was not a team player, fighting with new members and acting with increasing ruthlessness. All the while, she was secretly supplying reports to Amanda Waller on Black Canary's sonic powers.

When the Birds finally learned of her treachery, working for Mr. Freeze and manipulating her teammates into going against the Court of Owls, she vanished. She remains a fugitive at large.

STEEL (NATASHA IRONS)

DEBUT *Steel* (Vol. 2) #1 **(Feb. 1994)**

REAL NAME Natasha Irons

EYES Brown **HAIR** Black

HEIGHT 5ft 6in **WEIGHT** 106 lbs

POWERS/ABILITIES Supergenius intellect, semi-sentient Chrome Armor changes configuration and gives protection, rocket boots, magnetic hammer (as Steel); superhuman strength and endurance, flight (as Starlight); can turn into gas (as Vaporlock).

Natasha Irons shares a flair for technology with her uncle John Henry Irons. She soon involved herself in his career as the Super Hero Steel, and when he retired received a suit to become the new Steel. However, he was furious when she ditched city-cleanup duties to apply for the Teen Titans. Natasha then volunteered for Lex Luthor's Everyman Program, angering Henry further. Luthor's enhancement procedures gave her flight and other powers, and she joined Infinity, Inc. as Starlight. After developing the ability to turn to gas, she changed codenames to Vaporlock.

Natasha recently achieved her childhood dream to became part of a real team: the Justice League sponsored the Titans team tasked with helping victims of mutagenic changes caused by the Dark Multiverse invasion and the sundering of the Source Wall.

STEEL (JOHN HENRY IRONS)

DATA

DEBUT *The Adventures of Superman* #500 (June 1993)
REAL NAME John Henry Irons
BASE Metropolis
HEIGHT 6ft 7in **WEIGHT** 210 lbs **EYES** Brown **HAIR** Bald
POWERS/ABILITIES Genius inventor; armored suit boosts strength and allows flight via rocket boots; armor equipped with an array of hi-tech internal systems; utilizes weaponized self-propelled hammer.
ALLIES Steel (Natasha Irons), Superman, Lana Lang, Superboy (Kon-El)
ENEMIES Ultrawoman, Crash, Skyhook

PROTECTIVE SUIT
Irons' organic steel armor can prevent him from succumbing to otherworldly infections. He can extend the liquid metal to protect others.

WOMAN OF STEEL
Steel and Superwoman's relationship wasn't without its "minor" clashes.

John Henry Irons was named after a hammer-swinging American folk hero. He used his technical expertise to create a suit of power armor and became the heavy-hitting hero Steel. A close friend and ally of Superman, John Henry has stood by the Man of Steel's side during countless conflicts, and fought many of his own battles against the forces of evil. Irons is also the owner of Steelworks, a tech start-up dedicated to building a better world through technology.

Engineer John Henry Irons was on his way to becoming a giant in the field of technology, designing weapon systems for a military industrial firm. But when he saw his weapons fall into the wrong hands, he opted to leave his promising career, destroying his notes in the process. On the run from the deadly corporation, Henry disguised his identity and took a job working construction in Metropolis.

It was there that John Henry met Superman, when the Man of Steel saved his life on the construction site. John Henry was truly inspired by the chance encounter, so much so that when the alien beast known as Doomsday killed Superman in a violent brawl, John Henry decided to take up Superman's mantle and protect Metropolis. He adopted a suit of robotic armor with a red cape and S-Shield and became a true man of Steel.

Armed with his trusty hammer, Steel made a name for himself and kept up his Super Hero career even after Superman returned from the dead. In his private life, John Henry served as a mentor to his niece Natasha, who later followed in his footsteps as a new Steel and even joined the Titans. John Henry became romantically involved with Clark Kent's high school sweetheart, Lana Lang, and helped her in the crime-fighting field when Lana briefly became the hero Superwoman.

Steel continues his work on two fronts: aiding the world through technology with his company Steelworks and protecting the skies of Metropolis as Steel.

ON THE RECORD

In the pre-*Flashpoint* universe, engineer John Henry Irons created the Toastmaster advanced weapon for AmerTek Industries, but quit when his invention fell into the wrong hands. While Irons was working in construction, Superman saved his life after he fell from a skyscraper.

When the Man of Steel died in "The Death of Superman," Irons built an armored suit and became the hero Steel, one of four new champions who emerged to continue Superman's legacy. Irons was killed in battle during "Our Worlds at War," but returned to life after being placed in the Entropy Aegis armor. Unfortunately, the Aegis took control of him, and Superman had to save him again.

After *Flashpoint*, John Henry's origin was tied into the creation of Metallo, but his classic history was later restored during the "Superman Reborn" storyline.

TITLE FIGHT
After the death of Superman, Steel encountered the Last Son of Krypton's other successors, including Superboy (Kon-El).

CLASSIC STORIES

Superman: The Man of Steel **#22-26 (Jun.-Oct. 1993)** After the death of Superman, John Henry Irons builds the Steel armor and becomes a hero to continue the legacy of Metropolis' greatest champion.
Superman Versus Darkseid: Apokolips Now! **(Vol. 1) #1 (Mar. 2003)** When John Henry Irons is taken over by the Aegis armor, Superman leads an invasion of Apokolips to get his good friend back.
Infinity, Inc. **(Vol. 2) #1–12 (Nov. 2007–Oct. 2008)** Steel leads a new Infinity, Inc. team, which includes his niece Natasha—but they ultimately come into conflict with the team's backer, Lex Luthor.

STARGIRL

DATA

DEBUT *DCU Heroes:* Secret Files and Origins #1 **(Feb. 1999)**
REAL NAME Courtney Whitmore
BASE Mobile
HEIGHT 5ft 5in **WEIGHT** 127 lbs
EYES Blue **HAIR** Blonde
POWERS/ABILITIES Trained martial artist and gymnast; carries a Cosmic Staff that increases strength, speed, and agility, and affords flight, force-field generation, gravity and electromagnetic manipulation, heat emission, and energy projection and absorption
ALLIES S.T.R.I.P.E., Shazam
ENEMIES Secret Society of Super-Villains, Injustice Society
AFFILIATIONS Justice League of America, Justice League United, Justice Society of America

JUNIOR HERO
Stargirl has bonded with other young heroes, including the deceptively adult-looking Shazam.

Courtney Whitmore was a typical bratty kid until she found out about her stepfather's heritage as a costumed crime fighter/sidekick originally called Stripesy. Adopting gear from his former partner, the original Star-Spangled Kid, Courtney eventually became Stargirl. Although he was furious, there was nothing her stepfather Pat Dugan could do except train her to use the gear properly. He also recognized that she had found her true calling: helping people. In a year's time, she rose from fledgling hero to a media sensation.

Later, Stargirl was asked to join A.R.G.U.S.'s Justice League of America project but quickly realized it was for publicity purposes and that it wouldn't help her fight or save people. She was unaware that Director Amanda Waller also intended her to be a counter to Justice Leaguer Cyborg, should he ever go rogue.

Stargirl helped fight the Earth-3 Crime Syndicate's global invasion, and then joined another offshoot of the Justice League, the Justice League United. However, the final piece of the puzzle that was Courtney Whitmore's life fell into place when Superman encountered the powerful Dr. Manhattan, a near omnipotent being from another dimension. Dr. Manhattan went back in time and restored the Justice Society of America – the original team of mystery men heroes of the 1940s – to the timeline. During the butterfly effect that followed, the modern-day Justice Society returned, with Stargirl a proud member, once again carrying on the family tradition and legacy.

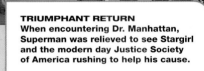

TRIUMPHANT RETURN
When encountering Dr. Manhattan, Superman was relieved to see Stargirl and the modern day Justice Society of America rushing to help his cause.

ON THE RECORD

On her debut, Courtney Whitmore was only allowed to be a Super Hero if her stepfather chaperoned her. Pat Dugan had been costumed crusader Stripesy in the 1940s and later turned his engineering genius to building the mechanical warsuit S.T.R.I.P.E. (Special Tactics Robotic Integrated Power Enhancer).

Unable to stop his wayward stepdaughter risking her life, he tagged along, but soon decided to let Stargirl go it alone as she graduated to a highly prized member of the Justice Society of America. Originally only armed with the first Star-Spangled Kid's Cosmic Converter Belt, she was later gifted the Cosmic Rod from Starman (Jack Knight).

READY FOR THE BIG TIME
After months battling beside his stepdaughter, Pat realized Courtney was capable of handling any trouble as a solo star.

CLASSIC STORIES

Stars and S.T.R.I.P.E. #0 **(Jul. 1999)** Courtney Whitmore and her stepdad Pat begin their adventures in Blue Valley, the home of the original Kid Flash.

JSA #1 **(Aug. 1999)** Courtney continues to follow in the footsteps of her Golden Age predecessor, fighting in the Justice Society of America alongside Starman (Jack Knight).

Justice Society of America (Vol. 3) #1 **(Feb. 2007)** Stargirl proves her staying power as a Justice Society member, now a veteran member compared to some of the new rookie recruits.

STARMAN I, II, III

DATA

DEBUT *Adventure Comics* (Vol. 1) #61 (Apr. 1941)
REAL NAME Ted Knight
BASE Opal City
HEIGHT 6ft 1in
WEIGHT 165 lbs
EYES Black
HAIR Black
POWERS/ABILITIES Cosmic Rod enables flight, object-levitation, energy-projection, extreme heat production, and force-field generation.
ALLIES Justice League, every Starman
ENEMIES The Mist, Solomon Grundy
AFFILIATIONS Justice Society of America

DEBUT *Starman* (Vol. 1) #1 (Oct. 1988)
REAL NAME William Payton
BASE Tucson, Arizona
HEIGHT 6ft 1in
WEIGHT 180 lbs
EYES Brown **HAIR** Variable (white, black, red)
POWERS/ABILITIES limitless stored solar energy for blast projection, radiation, enhanced durability, strength, flight, object-levitation, energy-projection, extreme heat production, force-field generation, teleport portals, clairvoyance.
ALLIES Superman, Martian Manhunter, Starman (Ted Knight)
ENEMIES Lex Luthor, Legion of Doom
AFFILIATIONS Justice League of America

DEBUT *Zero Hour* (Vol. 1) #1 (Sep. 1994)
REAL NAME Jack Knight
BASE Opal City
HEIGHT 6ft 1in **WEIGHT** 165 lbs
EYES Black **HAIR** Black
POWERS/ABILITIES Cosmic Staff enables flight, object-levitation, energy-projection, extreme heat production, and force-field generation.
ALLIES Ted Knight, Will Payton, Sadie Falk, O'Dare Family, the Shade, Jake "Bobo" Benetti, Phantom Lady, Mikaal Tomas, Solomon Grundy, Hamilton Drew, Black Condor, Charity
ENEMIES Kyle, Bliss, Nash, the Mist, Culp, Rag Doll Cult, the Infernal Dr. Pip, Spider
AFFILIATIONS Justice Society of America, Ralph and Sue Dibny, Stargirl

Ted Knight became Starman after inventing a Gravity Rod that gathered and focused ambient energy from the stars. Ted refined and improved his creation until he finally devised the awesome Cosmic Rod, used by generations of champions who followed him. His career was interrupted by a nervous breakdown, stemming from his contributions to the Manhattan Project, but upon recovery he resumed costumed crime-fighting until old age caught up with him. His eldest son, David, took over as Starman.

Other individuals to have held the mantle of Starman include Charles McNider—the hero Dr. Mid-Nite—who assumed the role during Ted Knight's breakdown. McNider was succeeded by David Knight, who was thrown back in time at the moment of his death, decades hence. Mikaal Tomas, an alien would-be conqueror, rejected his species' plans to invade Earth and became Starman, Earth's guardian. Another alien, Prince Gavyn of the Crown Imperial, protected his domain as Starman until he died fighting Eclipso; his essence struck Earthman Will Payton, transforming him into Starman and Farris Knight, a distant descendant of Jack Knight's, was the 853rd century's Starman.

When Doctor Manhattan used his powers to erase Starman and his JSA colleagues, they were spectacularly restored in time to battle the threat of Perpetua. Ted Knight was key to the Justice League's strategy, using his Cosmic Rod to connect every Starman in history into a strikeforce attacking her from multiple points in time.

STARSTRUCK
A fragment of Totality, the oldest source of energy in the universe, gave Will Payton incredible powers.

STARS IN THEIR EYES
The Astral Avenger crushed America's many enemies with his fists, backed up by the accumulated might and majesty of the heavens.

In 1988, Will Payton was struck by a beam of force from the Stellaron-5 satellite. The artificial moon had been intended to capture a fragment of reality-warping artifact the Totality, but had proven wholly inadequate, malfunctioning and spilling the exotic energies towards Earth.

Payton was utterly transformed and became a local Super Hero, battling bad guys and dodging the mysterious science cabal who had built the satellite and now craved the powers possessed by "the Starman". During this period, Payton met reincarnating hero Carter Hall. Lex Luthor traveled back in time and abducted Payton to increase his own knowledge of Totality energy. After being tortured and having his mind altered, Payton escaped and joined the modern-day Justice League's battle against Perpetua and Luthor's Legion of Doom.

Valiantly battling across time and space, Payton seemingly perished opening star-portals that enabled Super Heroes in many eras to attack Perpetua simultaneously. The ploy might have succeeded if the Mother of Multiverses had not personally intervened, crushing Starman in her colossal fist.

Jack Knight came from a dynasty of Super Heroes. His father was World War II Super Hero Starman, and he was also related to the first Phantom Lady. However, he was content to let older brother David wield the Cosmic Rod as champion of Opal City. Jack preferred to pursue his love of history and popular culture. That all changed after David was assassinated.

Jack Knight became Starman only after David's murder was followed by an attempt on his own life. Using a prototype staff his father had discarded, Jack vanquished the killers and became the city's protector. Despite reservations, he was drawn to the life of adventure and exploration, although he refused to wear a costume.

Jack saved Opal City from numerous menaces, and even helped to revive the Justice Society of America for the modern age.

He was truly unconventional. He turned Super-Villains such as Bobo Bennetti, Solomon Grundy, and the Shade from the path of evil, and preferred to debate rather than fight. However, when necessity demanded, he pulled no punches. During an all-out battle for Opal, he led a coalition of unlikely champions against the savage forces of magical terrorist Culp.

Jack's greatest joy came from using his power to learn forgotten secrets. He once traveled through time and space to map the connection between all heroes who had ever called themselves Starman. Upon the birth of his daughter, Jack retired, passing the Cosmic Staff to teenage hero Courtney Whitmore, who carried on the legacy as Stargirl.

When Doctor Manhattan seemingly reordered history and erased the 1940s Super Hero generation, Jack vanished too, and, despite the restoration of many other heroes, he has not yet been sighted.

STARLIT KNIGHT
Jack Knight never let the astounding power in his hands overwhelm the wonder in his eyes or joy in his heart.

COSMIC HEROES
Other individuals to have held the illustrious mantle of Starman include Doctor Mid-Nite (Charles McNider); David Knight; Mikaal Tomas; Prince Gavyn of the Crown Imperial; and Farris Knight, the 853rd-century's Starman.

Doctor Mid-Nite **David Knight** **Mikaal Tomas** **Prince Gavyn** **Farris Knight**

STEWART, JOHN

DEBUT *Green Lantern* (Vol. 2) #87 (Dec. 1971–Jan. 1972)
REAL NAME John Stewart
BASE Mobile
HEIGHT 6ft 1in **WEIGHT** 210 lbs **EYES** Black **HAIR** Brown
POWERS/ABILITIES Indomitable willpower commanding a power ring that
is able to materialize hard-light constructs, translate languages, facilitate
in-planet and intergalactic flight, and protect against hostile environments
and enemy attack; vast knowledge of architecture and construction; military
training; natural leader.
ALLIES Green Lantern (Hal Jordan), Green Lantern (Guy Gardner), Fatality
ENEMIES Darkstars, Sinestro, Legion of Doom
AFFILIATIONS Green Lantern Corps, Justice League

**John Stewart is the go-to leader of the Green Lantern Corps.
A natural leader with a tactical, military-trained mind, John has also
been a frequent member of the Justice League, and can step up to
command the League when needed or take orders when a mission
doesn't fall under his realm of expertise. A longtime Green Lantern,
John has felt the weight of making mistakes in this dangerous field,
and he's sworn not to repeat them at any cost.**

John Stewart was a sniper for the US Marines, knowing the darkness
that came with following orders. He decided to leave that life behind him and become
an architect. He would soon discover a career that combined both his passion for
design and efficiency, and his need to protect and serve when he was brought into the
Green Lantern Corps as Hal Jordan's backup after successfully passing the Guardians
of the Universe's test. While he would form bonds with many of his fellow Lanterns,
John would also make the greatest mistake of his career when his arrogance
contributed to the destruction of the planet Xanshi. He also faced personal tragedy
when his wife Katma Tui was murdered. John spent his career working through
his guilt over Xanshi and dealing with his grief over Katma, becoming one of
the best Green Lanterns in the process.

Later the leader of the Green Lantern Corps, Stewart helped battle
Sinestro, Larfleeze, and dozens of other threats. He was instrumental
in brokering and alliance between the Sinestro Corps and the Green
Lanterns, and when the peace didn't last, he shut the Sinestro
Corps down by planting an imperfection in their power battery.
John then joined the Justice League and concentrated most
of his efforts with that team.

When damage to the Source Wall—the protective
barrier at the edge of the known universe—altered the
very energies of the cosmos, John became the bearer
of an Ultraviolet power ring for a brief time, infected by
Sinestro's influence. However, by embracing his
emotions rather than fighting them, John helped hold
off Sinestro's forces, and restored his Green Lantern
status through sheer willpower.

ULTRAVIOLENT
**John initially let his emotions get
the better of him when he briefly
became an Ultraviolet Lantern.**

ON THE RECORD

A signature feature of John
Stewart's career as a Green Lantern
has always been the conflict
between peaceful goals and violent
means. He has suffered a great deal
personally since first accepting a
power ring, losing his wife Katma
Tui and suffering the guilt of
accidentally destroying the planet
Xanshi. A somewhat brighter point
in his life came when he had the
chance to put his architectural
training to work designing the
new Justice League of America
headquarters in Washington DC.

POWER RING
John Stewart feels the power of the Green
Lantern power ring after being deemed
fit by the Guardians of the Universe.

CLASSIC STORIES

Justice League of America
(Vol. 1) #110 (Mar. –Apr. 1974)
When Hal Jordan slips in the shower,
Stewart is summoned to wear the
ring and fight alongside the Justice
League against the Key.

Action Comics **(Vol. 1) #601 (Aug.
1988)** John is stricken with grief
when he discovers his wife, Katma
Tui, dead at the hands of Star
Sapphire.

***Green Lantern: Mosaic* #1 ((Jun.
1992)** John Stewart stars in his own
title, charged with protecting a brave
new Oa and helping build a society of
disparate cultures.

STEPPENWOLF

DEBUT *New Gods* (Vol. 1) #7 (Feb.–Mar. 1972)
BASE Apokolips
HEIGHT 6ft **WEIGHT** 203 lbs **EYES** Black **HAIR** Red
POWERS/ABILITIES Enhanced strength, durability and brutality; cable snare weapon fires energy beams to entrap opponents; electro-ax; expert swordsman.
ALLIES Darkseid
ENEMIES Superman, Kalibak, Desaad, Granny Goodness
AFFILIATIONS Dog Cavalry, Darkseid's inner circle

Steppenwolf is Darkseid's uncle and was a contender to rule Apokolips. Darkseid used his uncle to start a war between Apokolips and New Genesis—one which ended when Steppenwolf was killed by Izaya the Inheritor.

Revived thanks to advanced Apokoliptian technology, Steppenwolf returned to court just in time to see his sister—and Darkseid's mother—Queen Heggra assassinated by his nephew's cronies Goodness and Desaad. The war continued to rage on, decimating systems, but Steppenwolf reveled in the carnage as the head of Darkseid's terrifying Dog Cavalry. A competent warrior thirsty for battle, Steppenwolf is happy to follow Darkseid. He died once more during the Death of the New Gods event, slaughtered by an out-of-control Infinity-Man. He resurrected, continuing to serve Darkseid and seek fresh combat.

FEAR AND FURY
Steppenwolf sought to carve out his own Earthly empire beside his savage Amazon daughter, Fury.

ON THE RECORD

After *Flashpoint*, general Steppenwolf led the invasion of Earth until Cyborg hacked Apokoliptian Boom Tubes, trapping them on Earth-2. Undaunted, he attempted to conquer that world in Darkseid's name, killing their Wonder Woman and Kal-L. Batman sacrificed himself by spreading a virus among the Parademons, leaving Steppenwolf at the mercy of the World Army and the Wonders. Steppenwolf died at the hands of Superman clone Brutaal, but was revived again.

OLD SOLDIERS NEVER DIE
Darkseid's uncle despised petty politics and double-dealing, living only for the addictive thrill of combat and butchery.

STOMPA

DEBUT *Mister Miracle* (Vol. 1) #6 (Jan.–Feb. 1972)
BASE Apokolips
HEIGHT 5ft 8in **WEIGHT** 330 lbs
POWERS/ABILITIES Heavy-matter boots can pulverize even the densest material.
ENEMIES Supergirl, Superman, Wonder Woman, Lois Lane, Kalibak, Oddfellows
ALLIES Female Furies,

Reared on Apokolips and personally trained by Granny Goodness, Stompa is the backbone of the Female Furies in Darkseid's Special Powers Force. As her name implies, Stompa crushes enemies of Darkseid beneath her boots. She is stronger than a Parademon and just as mean.

She was among the Furies dispatched to Earth to capture Kara Zor-El, so Darkseid could shape the young Supergirl to his will. This brought Stompa and her team into conflict with Earth's finest heroes, as two worlds struggled for the young Kryptonian's soul. When Darkseid fell, Stompa was loyal to his memory, battling the forces of his son Kalibak and resisting when both Lex Luthor and Superman briefly ruled Apokolips. When a weakened Darkseid returned, Stompa and the Furies sought empowering artifacts for him but were defeated by Wonder Woman and Steve Trevor.

STORMWATCH

DEBUT *Stormwatch* #1 (Mar. 1993)
BASE Eye of the Storm, Skywatch
CURRENT MEMBERS/POWERS Apollo: Photon-powered energy projection, flight, superhuman strength; **Jack Hawksmoor**: Alien technology grants superpowers in urban environments; **Jenny Quantum**: Teleportation, force-field projection; **Midnighter**: Cybernetically enhanced strength, speed, and senses, as well as advanced hand-to-hand combat skills; **Projectionist**: Perception of and control over electronic communications.
ALLIES Shadow Cabinet
ENEMIES Daemonites, Hidden People

The origins of Stormwatch reach back into the Middle Ages, when its members were known as Demon Knights. Among their first members were Artisan, Madame Xanadu, and Vandal Savage. They first became known as Stormwatch during the 14th century, when they battled the extraterrestrial Daemonites. The group was typically formed around a Century Baby—a person given powers by virtue of being born at the stroke of midnight as a new century dawned. Stormwatch revealed itself to the world's governments in the 18th century, which its ruling Shadow Council soon decided was a mistake. They worked to erase the group's existence from known history, and were successful by the beginning of the next century.

As the 21st century dawned, the group was in danger of losing its way, as its historical mission of combating alien threats now faced competition from the Justice League. Adam One (the avatar of Merlin, one of Stormwatch's original members) recruited a new Century Baby, Jenny Quantum, to maintain the group in the new era. Other core members included Jack Hawksmoor, Apollo, and the Midnighter, and briefly the Martian Manhunter. They battled the Daemonites, the Hidden People, and the Red Lanterns, among other threats, while keeping their existence and membership secret.

KEEPING WATCH
The core members of Stormwatch, maintain their vigil against threats from the vastness of space.
1 Midnighter
2 Jack Hawksmoor
3 Jenny Quantum
4 Projectionist
5 Apollo

ON THE RECORD

The original Stormwatch was formed in the wake of a disaster on board Monitor One, a UN space station. The event transformed the station's Team One into the dangerous Warguard, who were defeated and a new team—Stormwatch—recruited in its place. Its members were "Seedlings," humans who had been granted super-powers. Now based on an orbital platform called Skywatch, they monitored both terrestrial and alien threats.

THE PRICE OF VIGILANCE
Though no hostile force could long deter Earth's metahuman watchmen, internal dissent and hidden agendas would eventually tear the team apart.

STRANGE, ADAM

DEBUT *Showcase* #17 (Nov.-Dec. 1958)
BASE Rann **HEIGHT** 6ft **WEIGHT** 175 lbs **EYES** Blue **HAIR** Blond
POWERS/ABILITIES Expert pilot; brilliant tactician; uses Rannian technology, including guns and space suit **ALLIES** Alanna, Sardath, Hawkman, Superman **ENEMIES** Byth Rok, Ultra the Multi-Alien **AFFILIATIONS** Justice League United, planet Rann

Before *Crisis on Infinite Earths* anthropologist Adam Strange was struck by a random Zeta beam fired from Alpha Centauri and teleported to atomic-war-ravaged Rann, where he became a hero, fighting invasions and defeating uncanny threats. He also fell in love with Alanna, a hero in her own right.

Post-*Flashpoint* he was working a dig in northern Ontario with his student Alanna Lewis when an uncanny beam of light made her disappear. He discovered a strange skeleton, which he showed to the heroes Animal Man and Star Girl. They found what appeared to be an alien grave and an underground base. Fighting off an attack by aliens, Strange was knocked into the base. Arming himself with a jet-pack-powered space suit and ray gun, he rejoined the fight. He and the rest of Justice League United were then transported to Rann, where they learned Byth Rok was responsible for Alanna's abduction.

The Zeta Beam, which had transported them to Rann, abruptly returned them to Earth. Strange was reunited with Alanna as he and the JLU battled Ultra the Multi-Alien. Moving back and forth between Earth and Rann, Strange (by now married to Alanna) fought Byth Rok with help from the time-displaced Legion of Super-Heroes. Strange and the JLU later joined the Justice League of America's counterattack against Vandal Savage when he besieged the JLA's Watchtower.

Following *Rebirth*, Strange is Earth's unofficial ambassador to the stars. He has often fought with or against Hawkman and the Thanagarians. He also worked with Superman as he strove to create the United Planets organization, and with the Justice League against Leviathan, the Legion of Doom, and others.

HAVE JET-PACK, WILL TRAVEL
Adam Strange experiments with the new technological wonders he found in the alien scientists' underground base.

Adam Strange was introduced in 1958 in DC's *Showcase* title, which also launched the career of the Silver Age Flash (Barry Allen). In his debut story, Adam was an anthropologist and adventurer, who was transported to Rann by a Zeta Beam experiment conducted on the scientifically advanced planet Rann. On his arrival, he fell for Alanna, daughter of the scientist Sardath, who had created the Zeta Beam.

More adventures followed, each limited to the fluctuating duration of the Zeta Beam's powers—which prolonged the blooming romance between Strange and Alanna. They were married on Rann, with the Justice League of America present.

BRAIN OVER BRAVADO
With every new threat he faced, Adam Strange became more famous for relying on his wits as much as his weaponry... and iconic wardrobe.

STRANGE, HUGO

DEBUT *Detective Comics* #36 (Feb. 1940)
BASE Gotham City
HEIGHT 5ft 10in **WEIGHT** 170 lbs **EYES** Gray **HAIR** None
POWERS/ABILITIES Trained in psychology; brilliant deductive mind.
ALLIES Bane **ENEMIES** Batman, Deathstroke,
AFFILIATIONS The Cabal, Task Force X, Secret Society of Super-Villains

Psychologist Hugo Strange was one of Batman's earliest villains and has plagued him in every incarnation. He is obsessed with why heroes exist and what motivates them: frequently impersonating Batman and becoming lost in the masquerade.

Following *Flashpoint*, he was recruited to Wayne Industries by acting CEO Philip Kane while Bruce Wayne was on extended leave following his parents' murder. Strange was tasked with researching the mysteries of the mind by exploring the overlap between the physiology and the psychology of the brain. After Wayne's return, Strange left to establish a research lab at Arkham Asylum, studying the aberrant brains of its inmates and forming a working relationship with Harleen Quinzel. He also reconnected with his estranged son, when Eli Strange was caught cheating at cards by Russian gangsters and narrowly avoided being killed. Strange brought Eli in on a plot to release the Scarecrow's Fear Gas over Gotham City.

While at Arkham, Strange was recruited into the Secret Society of Super-Villains by the Outsider, where his role was largely advisory. He also continued his medical practice, working with Roy Harper, among others. This allowed him to involve the Outlaws in yet another scheme.

As mercenary as he is inquisitive, Strange has worked with the Psycho-Pirate and sought to cure Bane's dependence on Venom. While secretly a member of the criminal Cabal vexing Plastic Man he has also recently treated Deathstroke in Arkham, a course of therapy that resulted in an explosive mass breakout.

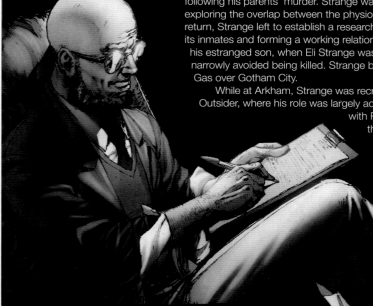

ALL IN THE MIND
As a professional psychologist, Hugo Strange was in a powerful position of authority to advance his own evil schemes.

Hugo Strange was one of very few people who had deduced Batman's secret identity. He rose to fame as a psychological consultant on Gotham City talk shows, speculating on Batman's psyche and motivations.

Fortunately for Batman, Strange's own psychological instability always made it difficult for him to remember what he knew for very long, so the Dark Knight avoided the danger of having his identity widely known.

MASKED MANIA
The master schemer was driven by a singular obsession with Batman.

STRIFE

DEBUT *Wonder Woman* (Vol. 1) #183
(Jul.–Aug. 1969)
REAL NAME Eris
BASE Olympus
EYES Gold
HAIR White
POWERS/ABILITIES Vast supernatural
powers granted to Olympian Gods.
ENEMIES First Born
AFFILIATIONS Olympus

NOTHING BUT TROUBLE
Strife certainly lived up to her name,
stirring up dissension wherever and
whenever she could.

Sister to Ares, Strife was spiteful in an almost childlike way. It was her nature to disrupt any peace or alliance and she delighted in creating confusion among enemies and allies alike. This made her true allegiances extremely difficult to discern.

Strife saw the disappearance of Zeus from Olympus as a perfect chance to cause chaos among the Amazons, as well as on Mount Olympus. She appeared on Themyscira and carefully let slip the secret of her half-sister Wonder Woman's origin, causing Diana to leave Themyscira for a time, and revealing the Amazon Queen Hippolyta's dalliance with Zeus. At the same time, Strife fomented division among the Amazons, leading to the creation of Donna Troy and a civil war on Themyscira. This, in turn, resulted in the unprovoked massacre of the Sons of Hephaestus.

STRIPESY

DEBUT *Star-Spangled Comics* #1 (Oct. 1941)
REAL NAME Patrick Dugan
BASE Blue Valley, Nebraska
HEIGHT 6ft 1in
WEIGHT 210 lbs
EYES Blue
HAIR Red
POWERS/ABILITIES Great intellect and
skill as a mechanic.

SUPER SIDEKICK
Patrick Dugan earned his Super Hero
stripes as Star-Spangled Kid's
steadfast partner.

Pat Dugan was Sylvester Pemberton III's chauffeur when they respectively became Stripesy and the Star-Spangled Kid. After many World War II exploits, the duo joined the Seven Soldiers of Victory, and after one mission were briefly stranded in time. On Pat's return to the present he married and had a son, Michael. Sadly, Pat's exposure to the timestream caused Michael to rapidly age, a process that was only halted by the magical heroes of the JSA.

Pat later divorced and married Barbara Whitmore. When Pat's stepdaughter, Courtney Whitmore, laid claim to the Star-Spangled Kid's cosmic belt, Pat returned to Super Hero action in a robot battlesuit and the duo became Stargirl and S.T.R.I.P.E. The family moved to Metropolis to work with John Henry Irons' Steelworks, and later returned to Blue Valley.

STRIX

DEBUT *Batgirl* (Vol. 4) #9 (Jul. 2012)
REAL NAME Mary Turner
BASE Gotham City
HEIGHT 5ft 6in
WEIGHT 125 lbs
EYES Brown
HAIR Black
POWERS/ABILITIES Immortality; healing;
acrobatics; martial arts; swordsmanship
ALLIES Catwoman, Batgirl
ENEMIES Court of Owls, Starling, Mr. Freeze
AFFILIATIONS Birds of Prey, Secret Six

LOOKING FOR A HOME
Strix had to endure more than her fair
share of trouble before she found a
welcome in the Secret Six.

Young Mary Turner lost her family and suffered disfiguring burns when a Japanese fire balloon exploded in her Oregon hometown during World War II. A circus acrobat, she was recruited into the Court of Owls, which gave her a Talon's powers of immortality and healing.

During the Court of Owls' war with the Batman Family, she switched sides out of sympathy for Batgirl. Joining the Birds of Prey, she fought agents of Basilisk and her former masters.

After being betrayed to Mr. Freeze by Birds of Prey agent Starling, Strix fled. She eventually found a home and family with Catman, Black Alice, Ventriloquist, Porcelain and Big Shot Ralph Dibny in the Secret Six.

STRONG, TOM

DEBUT *Tom Strong* (Vol. 1) #1 (Jun. 1999)
REAL NAME Tomas Strong
BASE Millennium City
HEIGHT Unknown
WEIGHT Unkown
EYES Blue
HAIR Brown/white
POWERS/ABILITIES Super-strength, speed
and durability, genius intellect
ALLIES Dhalua Strong, Tesla Strong, King
Solomon, Pneuman, The Terrifics
ENEMIES Paul Saveen, Doc Dread
AFFILIATIONS America's Best

A DARK LESSON
Tom Strong learned the hard way that
venturing into the Dark Multiverse
brought only deadly peril.

Tom Strong had grown up mostly within a high-gravity chamber on the island of Attabar Teru, giving him super strength in body and mind. Grown into a "science hero," his adventures usually featured his family: wife Dhalua and daughter Tesla, the robot Pneuman, and the hyperintelligent ape King Solomon, who was Tom's assistant.

However, when Tom decided to explore the Dark Multiverse, he chose to do it alone. Discovering that it was packed with horrors and terrible dangers, Tom made his escape, leaving a warning message to anyone who might stray into the Dark Multiverse. Later that message was found by the Terrifics, and they teamed up to help Tom when his family were abducted by Doc Dread.

SUICIDE SQUAD

DATA

DEBUT *The Brave and the Bold* #25 (Aug.-Sep. 1959)
REAL NAME Task Force X
BASE Belle Reve Penitentiary
NOTABLE RECENT MEMBERS/POWERS
DEADSHOT Expert marksman; **HARLEY QUINN** Troubled former psychiatrist, unpredictable fighter; **OSITA** Enhanced strength and endurance, metal arm, natural leadership qualities; **THYLACINE** Heightened senses, expert trakcer and hunter; **DEADLY SIX** Able to choose from six deadly sins in order to influence others to do his bidding; **ZEBRA-MAN** Telekinesis, force field projection, magnetism control; **CHAOS KITTEN** Scrappy fighter; **WINK** Teleporter; **THE AERIE** Flight, able to communicate with birds; **FIN** Underwater breathing and enhanced swimming speed, telepathic, can communicate with sea life; **CAPTAIN BOOMERANG** Boomerang expert and former spy; **KATANA** Martial arts expert wielding magic Soultaker sword; **ENCHANTRESS** Powerful sorceress; **KILLER CROC** Crocodile-like skin and superhuman strength; **RICK FLAG JR.** Expert soldier, trained leader; **AMANDA WALLER** Highly trained soldier, expert covert operative; brilliant leadership abilities.
ENEMIES League of Assassins, Basilisk, Maxwell Lord, Eclipso, Black Mask, Maxwell Lord, Justice League

The Suicide Squad is the nickname for Task Force X, a team of Super-Villains originally brought together by Amanda Waller to perform highly dangerous black ops missions. The members are among the most ruthless, craziest, and cold-blooded killers in the world—the majority have been sentenced to life-imprisonment in Belle Reve Penitentiary. The Squad has an ever-changing membership, but some villains—like Deadshot and Harley Quinn—have survived several missions. If they live, members are rewarded with reduced jail terms. They might even one day walk free... if they can last long enough.

After World War II, the US government began to investigate extraterrestrial and paranormal threats. To that end, they created Task Force X, a group of specialized soldiers, scientists, and intelligence officers unofficially dubbed the Suicide Squad. Led by Captain Rick Flag, Sr., astronomer Dr. Hugh Evans, space medicine expert Karin Grace, and physicist Jess Bright, this Suicide Squad worked with Argent head King Faraday to protect the world.

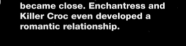

Decades later, a brilliant, but often heartless tactician named Amanda Waller decided to bring the concept back. However, she wanted a fighting force of completely expendable and easily deniable soldiers; Waller wanted Super-Villains. Working with the government, Waller formed her first Task Force X, her Suicide Squad. She teamed powerhouse criminals Emerald Empress, Johnny Sorrow, Lobo, Dr. Polaris, and Rustam together with less than ideal results.

STRANGE BEDFELLOWS
Some Suicide Squad members became close. Enchantress and Killer Croc even developed a romantic relationship.

Amanda's later teams were more manageable. She found success with slightly more controllable criminals like Harley Quinn, Deadshot, and Captain Boomerang. Bombs embedded in their heads allowed Waller to kill anyone who disobeyed her. The Squad fought threats from terrorist organizations and Super-Villains on foreign soil, staging missions that official troops could not. Waller soon appointed heroic additions to her team in the form of Rick Flag, Jr. and Katana, and found other longtime Squad members, including Killer Croc and the Enchantress.

The Squad suffered from external threats, ranging from the Justice League to Maxwell Lord re-uniting Waller's original Suicide Squad in a mad attempt to obtain the powers of the supernatural villain Eclipso. The Squad always triumphed, with some members living to see another day. Eventually, Killer Croc, Harley Quinn,

AT A GLANCE...

Loyalty insurance
Criminals chosen by Amanda Waller for missions had a nano-bomb injected inside their necks. If they went rogue, the bomb would explode—a sure way to guarantee their loyalty to Amanda's cause.

Belle Reve
Amanda took her potential candidates from the notorious Belle Reve Penitentiary, which houses metahuman criminals and Super-Villains. Close to the Gulf of Mexico, the prison is surrounded by swampland.

TERROR ATTACK
An early Suicide Squad mission took the fight to the Basilisk terrorist network.

CLASSIC STORIES

***TThe Brave and the Bold* #25 (Aug.-Sep. 1959)** The original Suicide Squad makes its first appearance as Colonel Rick Flag leads a team of scientists against a monster that terrorizes a seaside resort.

***Legends* #1 (Nov. 1986)** Amanda Waller and Rick Flag Jr. start Task Force X as an ancient evil threatens the world.

***Suicide Squad* (Vol. 1) #26 (Apr. 1989)** Rick Flag Jr. is seemingly killed by a nuclear bomb.

***Suicide Squad* (Vol. 4) #1 (Nov. 2011)** Amanda Waller puts Deadshot and his fellow Super-Villains through a deadly fake mission to see if they are suitable for Task Force X.

JUSTICE LEAGUE VS. SUICIDE SQUAD
After looking into Task Force X, Batman brought the team to the Justice League's attention. The heroes decided to shut Amanda Waller's pet project down. They confronted the Squad during a mission, and a ferocious battle ensued.

However, when Maxwell Lord broke some of the most powerful criminals on the planet out of the top-secret prison called the Catacombs, the Justice League and the Suicide Squad joined forces. It took the combined might of both teams to end this high priority threat.

TEST OF STRENGTH
When the Justice League confronted the Suicide Squad, Amanda Waller gave her team an order in no uncertain terms: "Do not let the Justice League take you alive. Or you're dead."

KILLED IN ACTION

Some Suicide Squads are luckier than others. When the main Squad was busy running a mission on Atlantis, Amanda Waller recruited a team consisting of the archer Merlyn, vampire Scream Queen, Titan villain Shimmer, martial artist Tao Jones, blade expert Skorpio, contortionist Rag Doll, and explosive generator Baby Boom. This ragtag bunch were charged with capturing Belle Reve escapee Cadence Laramie, who seemed able to summon and control ghost creatures. Laramie and all the members but Merlyn were killed in action, although it was later revealed that Shimmer faked her own death, and Rag Doll might have survived, too.

IN TOO DEEP
Some Suicide Squad recruits just didn't have what it takes to face down hordes of supernatural spirits and a very angry Swamp Thing.

"I want to use prisoners with nothing to lose and everything to gain. I want to create a Suicide Squad."

Amanda Waller

DEADLY FORCE
Deadshot and his team of Revolutionary Suicide Squad members decided to end Task Force X or die trying.
1 Osita
2 Chaos Kitten
3 Harley Quinn
4 Wink
5 The Aerie
6 Deadshot
7 Zebra-Man
8 Fin

REBIRTH

BUSINESS AS USUAL

With the world spiraling into even greater chaos than usual, Amanda Waller resurrects and redeems disgraced military legend Rick Flag, entrusting him with restoring Task Force X to full combat effectiveness.

Can the traumatized and disaffected veteran possibly be a match for Waller's rebellious and unwilling recruits, and the deadly modern menaces that she happily pits the Suicide Squad against?

and Deadshot all earned their freedom, but the government "forgot" to inform Harley and Deadshot of this fact, continuing to use them on Suicide Squad missions.

A soldier called Osita learned of Task Force X after witnessing her wife's death at the hands of Captain Boomerang during a Squad mission. She formed the Revolutionaries, and they successfully infiltrated the Suicide Squad in order to seek out the mysterious new head calling the shots. Meanwhile, Amanda Waller found herself answering to a superior named Lok. When Lok decided to use the Revolutionaries as Squad members, Waller quit Task Force X. That made it much easier for Deadshot when Lok instructed him to assassinate his longtime ally, Captain Boomerang. Deadshot shot and killed Lok instead, and he and this new Squad of Revolutionaries became outlaws alongside Harley Quinn and Zebra-Man.

This Squad began hunting for the man responsible for their situation: Ted Kord. However, Kord had been replaced by Black Mask, who was impersonating the billionaire. The Squad succesfully discovered Black Mask's plot, but not before Deadshot was seemingly killed.

ON THE RECORD

The Suicide Squad has changed a great deal since its first appearance in the *The Brave and the Bold*. The original Suicide Squad was a group of heroes led by Colonel Rick Flag— the pilot of their base, the Flying Laboratory. The team also included chief medic Karin Grace, a physicist called Jess Bright, and astronomer Dr. Hugh Evans. They investigated Fortean subject matter and often fought strange monsters and aliens.

Villainous legends
During the "Legends" miniseries, the modern Suicide Squad made their first dramatic appearance. This team was made up of imprisoned Super-Villains drafted into the Suicide Squad by Amanda Waller. The team would include villains such as Captain Boomerang, Deadshot, and mainstay heroes like Rick Flag Jr., Bronze Tiger, and even Oracle (Barbara Gordon).

Task Force Omega
A later Suicide Squad—named Task Force Omega— was led by Sgt. Rock. Everyone except Major Disaster seemingly died on the team's first mission. Sgt. Rock recruited more villains for the team, bringing in the likes of Deadshot and Killer Frost. The team was eventually captured by a group called Onslaught. Some members were rescued by the Justice Society, who could only find a mask of Sgt. Rock in the cell where he was been held, implying their leader had been an impostor.

SUPERBOY (JON KENT)

DATA

DEBUT *Convergence: Superman* #2 **(Jul. 2015)**
REAL NAME Jonathan Samuel Kent
BASE New Metropolis, 31st century New Earth
HEIGHT 5ft 11in **WEIGHT** 155 lbs **EYES** Blue **HAIR** Black
POWERS/ABILITIES Super-strength; super-speed; flight; invulnerability; numerous sense-based abilities; accelerated healing; all fueled by exposure to solar energy from a yellow sun.
ALLIES Superman, Lois Lane, Robin (Damian Wayne), Saturn Girl
ENEMIES Crav, the General Nah, Eradicator, the Gang, Kid Amazo
AFFILIATIONS Legion of Super-Heroes

BOY OF STEEL
Superboy aged rapidly, but retains his boyish enthusiasm and a faith in humanity only rivaled by that of his father, Superman.

LEGION FOUND
Superboy was a perfect fit for the new Legion of Super-Heroes. In the 31st century he was able to see his hopes for a better world actually come to fruition.

The son of Superman and Lois Lane, Jon Kent is heir to the greatest legacy in the universe. As Superboy, he originally teamed with his best friend Robin (Damian Wayne), before traveling to the future of the 31st century to teach an entire generation the ways of truth and justice.

Superman and Lois Lane had lived through countless Super-Villain battles, invading aliens, and reality-warping events. During those years of heartache and chaos, they still managed to find time for each other and get married. But when they were ready to settled down and start a family, they both decided a change was in order.

Leaving their jobs as reporters at Metropolis' *Daily Planet*, the couple raised their son, Jon Kent, on a farm in Hamilton County, some 300 miles north of the city, although Superman kept up his heroic actions from the shadows from time to time. But before long, big-city life beckoned, and the family moved back to Metropolis.

As Jon grew and matured along the way, he followed in his father's footsteps as Superboy, putting his own Kryptonian powers to good use. With his dad's blessing, he partnered with Robin (Damian Wayne) and even set up a hideout in the form of the Fortress of Attitude, an underwater headquarters well-equipped and monitored by both Batman and Superman.

However, when Robin refused Jon's request to join the Teen Titans, Jon felt aimless. He took a trip across the galaxy with his grandfather, Jor-El, where he accidentally traveled through a black hole and ended up a prisoner of Ultraman of the evil Crime Syndicate. By the time Jor-El helped rescue Jon and return him home to Earth, Jon had gone from an 11-year-old to a 17-year-old. Due to the black hole travel, however, Jon had only been gone three weeks Earth time. Upon his return, Jon helped stop an intergalactic battle with an idea to form a United Planets, based on Earth's own United Nations. On the first assembly of this body, dubbed Unity Day, Jon was invited to join the future team called the Legion of Super-Heroes and travel to the 31st century. Feeling this was his destiny all along, Jon did just that, teaching 21st century heroics to an entire generations of new allies.

ON THE RECORD

The fact that Jonathan Kent was born into a continuity event and survived several more reboots is a testament to the popularity of the character. Born in a pocket universe of sorts when the pre-*Flashpoint* Superman and Lois Lane had a child during the *Convergence* event, the classic Kent-Lane family survived and made it into the main DC universe, later merging with their New 52 counterparts. Jon's history was tweaked so that he was born on Earth-0, effectively melding Superman's post-*Crisis* reality with the current continuity.

PAGING DOCTOR WAYNE
Before the *Rebirth* event, the Batman from the *Flashpoint* universe, Dr. Thomas Wayne, was present for the birth of baby Jonathan.

CLASSIC STORIES

Action Comics **(Vol. 1) #976 (May 2017)** During a battle with Mr. Mxyzptlk, Jon helps restore Superman's history by reminding his parents of their family's love.

Super Sons **#10 (Jan. 2018)** Superboy and Robin are rewarded for their heroics with their own headquarters, one Jon names the Fortress of Attitude.

Legion of Super-Heroes **(Vol. 8) #1 (Jan. 2020)** Superboy is amazed at the future of the 31st century as he visits New Metropolis for the first time.

SUPERBOY (KON-EL)

DEBUT *The Adventures of Superman* (Vol. 1) #500 (June 1993)
REAL NAME Kon-El; Conner Kent (adoptive name)
BASE Mobile
HEIGHT 5ft 7in **WEIGHT** 145 lbs **EYES** Blue **HAIR** Black
POWERS/ABILITIES Limited tactile telekinesis that imitates super
strength, durability, speed, stamina, and flight; augmented senses and
enhanced vision abilities deriving from partial Kryptonian genetic structure
under a yellow sun.
ALLIES Superman, Red Robin, Wonder Girl, Impulse
ENEMIES S.T.A.R. Labs
AFFILIATIONS Young Justice

WORLD'S FINEST
Superboy's eternal optimism seemed to constantly clash with Robin's pessimism. That sort of thing is bound to happen when one was raised by the world's greatest hero and the other was raised by Talia al Ghūl and her League of Assassins. Despite their differences, the two became close friends.

Some heroes are made, not born. A combination of Superman and Lex Luthor's DNA, Superboy was an outsider from his inception. Raised in a lab, and aged to maturity in the public spotlight, Superboy went from a young teenager with an attitude to a more mature veteran of the Super Hero team Young Justice.

LEGION FOUND
Superboy was a perfect fit for the new Legion of Super-Heroes. In the 31st century he was able to see his hopes for a better world actually come to fruition.

When Superman died saving Metropolis from the menace of the alien beast known as Doomsday, four faux Supermen emerged, each claiming to be the original. One of those four was Superboy, a teenage clone of Superman created in a lab by the secretive organization known as Cadmus. Kon-El, as Superboy would later be called, was in reality half human and half Kryptonian, made from both Superman's DNA and that of the Man of Steel's arch enemy, Lex Luthor. Rebellious and a true teenager at heart, Superboy soon developed his own identity and forged his way in the world.

Kon-El's adventures soon brought him in contact with the then Robin (Tim Drake) and the super-speedster Impulse. Together they formed the hero team Young Justice, and then years later, graduated to become Teen Titans. Superboy developed a romance with Wonder Girl (Cassandra Sandsmark), and even adopted the name Conner Kent, living for a time with Superman's Earth parents in Smallville, Kansas.

When investigating shady dealing at the hi-tech facility S.T.A.R. Labs, Superboy was transported to the dimension known as Gemworld. There he built a life for himself, albeit reluctantly. Finally, when his old teammates rescued him and brought him to Earth-0, Superboy was surprised to see that so much had changed. Being on Gemworld, he'd missed several continuity-altering events, including *Flashpoint* and *Rebirth*. The world had changed, but Superboy still remained the same. And somehow, when he made contact with his loved ones, they remembered not just him, but the world he was from.

Truly alien in a brave new world, Superboy nonetheless continues his battle against the forces of evil, his load lightened by his old teammates and friends in the newest incarnation of the Young Justice team.

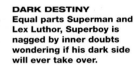

DARK DESTINY
Equal parts Superman and Lex Luthor, Superboy is nagged by inner doubts wondering if his dark side will ever take over.

ON THE RECORD

As first conceived, Superboy was a light-hearted look at "the adventures of Superman when he was a boy." Wearing his Superman costume and fighting crime as a teenager in Smallville, young Clark Kent was drafted into the Legion of Super-Heroes, a team of crime fighters one thousand years into the future. While the Kon-El version of Superboy was created following the "Death of Superman" saga, the character was altered when introduced into the post-*Flashpoint* era. A reality has been since altered due to the *Rebirth* event, this Kon-El was a founding member of the Teen Titans.

TITANS TOGETHER
The Superboy who helped found the Titans in the *New 52* was more stoic than the original incarnation of Kon-El.

CLASSIC STORIES

The Adventures of Superman (Vol. 1) #501 (Jun. 1993) Superboy bursts into Metropolis in Superman's absence, claiming to be the real Man of Steel and not taking kindly to anyone who calls him a "boy."
Superboy (Vol. 3) #1 (Feb. 1994) Superboy sets up shop in Hawaii, pursing the ideal life of a superpowered teenager.
Final Crisis: Legion of Three Worlds #1-5 (Oct. 2008-Sep. 2009) Kon-El returns from the dead for a rematch with his killer, Superboy-Prime.

SUPERGIRL

DATA

DEBUT *Action Comics* (Vol. 1) #252 **(May 1959)**
REAL NAME Kara Zor-El
BASE National City
HEIGHT 5ft 5in
WEIGHT 120 lbs
EYES Blue
HAIR Blonde
POWERS/ABILITIES Super-strength, speed, flight, invulnerability, enhanced senses, and rapid-healing fueled by direct and close exposure to solar energy from a yellow sun; expert on Kryptonian technology and culture.
ALLIES Superman, Jeremiah Danvers, Batgirl, Dr. Shay Veritas, Ben Rubel, Superboy (Jon Kent), Superboy (Kon-El), Lois Lane, Krypto
ENEMIES Cyborg Superman (Zor-El), Fatal Five, Rogol Zaar
AFFILIATIONS Department of Extranormal Operations, The Infected

While older than her cousin, Supergirl crash-landed on Earth years after baby Kal-El. Unlike the man who would grow to become Superman, Kara Zor-El spent her childhood on Krypton, Earth culture remaining alien to her. Now attempting to defend a world she doesn't fully understand, Kara has followed in her cousin's footsteps to become Supergirl.

Kryptonian scientist Zor-El had a rivalry with his brother Jor-El. With Krypton on the brink of destruction, Jor-El rocketed his son Kal-El toward the far away planet Earth in order to save the child's life. Zor-El did the same with his daughter Kara, but then took things a step further. Zor-El struck a deal with the Super-Villain Brainiac to save and preserve his metropolis of Argo City. However, Argo was destroyed anyway, and Zor-El became a ghost trapped in the hi-tech machine that is Brainiac.

Meanwhile, Kara's rocket crash-landed in Siberia. She was overwhelmed; unable to control the powers she had suddenly acquired from exposure to Earth's yellow sun. Finally regaining her senses a bit, she met her baby cousin Kal-El, discovering that he had somehow arrived years earlier than her and aged into the hero known as Superman. She soon followed suit as the heroic Supergirl.

On Earth for only a few months before she lost her powers, Kara made a deal with the Director of the Department of Extranormal Operations, Cameron Chase. Chase agreed to rocket Kara toward the sun to restore her abilities, but it would come at a cost. Worried Kara was a potential danger to the people of Earth, she assigned a married pair of agents, Jeremiah and Eliza Danvers to Kara's case. Kara would live with the Danvers and adopt the secret identity of sixteen-year-old Kara Danvers.

PREEMPTIVE PROTECTION
Kara had no idea that Zor-El had altered her physiology when she obeyed his wishes to escape Krypton's doom in his space pod.

AT A GLANCE...

Secret Identity
While only a high schooler, Kara Zor-El has more life experience under her golden belt than most adults three times her age. While attending National City Technical High School or working at Catco, Kara hides her famous appearance behind a pair of glasses that automatically darken her hair color.

Cuts like a Blade
Living in a world where her very existence caused distrust due to her tremendous powers, Supergirl began working with the Department of Extranormal Affairs out of their National City headquarters called the Blade. D.E.O. Director Cameron Chase couldn't afford not to be suspicious of Supergirl if she was to keep the country safe.

Enrolled in National City Technical High School, Kara thought it would be easy to adjust to life in a culture so primitive compared to the advanced society to which she was accustomed. Gifted in science on Krypton, Kara discovered she would have quite the learning curve on Earth, adjusting to this world's rudimentary tools. English was not spoken on Krypton, so just trying to wrap her mind around

MEET THE DANVERS
The Danvers attempted to give Kara a normal life and even subjected her to many different Earth cuisines, including the food court at the National City Mall.

CLASSIC STORIES

Action Comics (Vol. 1) #252 (May 1959) Superman's cousin arrives on Earth and, hidden in an orphanage under the name Linda Lee, immediately begins training as his secret weapon.

Action Comics (Vol. 1) #285 (Feb. 1962) After years of operating in total secrecy, Supergirl publicly premieres to an adoring and astonished world and quickly becomes the world's favorite female hero.

Crisis on Infinite Earths (Vol. 1) #7 (Oct. 1985) Supergirl's greatest triumph comes as, to save all reality, she sacrifices herself battling the Anti-Monitor.

Supergirl (Vol. 1) #10 (Sep–Oct. 1974) A most unlikely team up occurs when the Girl of Steel saves teenage American President Prez Rickard from two assassination attempts by a witch.

House of El
Supergirl has found family in not just Superman, but also Superboy (Kon-El), Superboy (Jon Kent), and even Lois Lane.

ZOR-EL RETURNS
One of Supergirl's first battles was with Cyborg Superman, but this half-robotic foe wasn't the Cyborg Superman from Clark Kent's past. Instead, this version was loaded with the consciousness of her father, Zor-El. Mad with grief, Zor-El soon rebuilt Argo City and populated it with the cybernetic reanimated corpses of its dead civilization.

RAGE AGAINST ROGOL

After the alien called Rogol Zaar came to Earth and attempted to destroy it, Supergirl discovered that Rogol claimed to have destroyed Krypton in much the same fashion. More personally affected by Rogol's crimes than even Superman—who had no personal memories of Krypton—Supergirl hunted Rogol down and helped imprison him in the Phantom Zone for his crimes.

DRESSED TO KILL

Supergirl armed herself with Rogol's axe as she set out into outer space to learn everything she could about the killer, accompanied by none other than her Super Dog, Krypto.

> "All these sudden powers... and I can barely control them."
>
> SUPERGIRL

simple communication became a Herculean task for the Girl of Steel, and her classmates often gawked at her bizarre accent.

When her physics work was noticed by Catco Worldwide Media head Cat Grant, Kara was given a job alongside her classmate Ben Rubel, whom she later began to date. However, her day job always played second fiddle to protecting National City. To that end, she faced her father in the form of a corrupted Cyborg Superman, and fought the likes of Emerald Empress and Magog. She soon came into conflict with the D.E.O. itself and parted ways with them.

Involving a journey through space, infection from the Dark Multiverse, and learning Eliza Danvers was killed, Supergirl's life kept up a hectic pace that proved difficult for even her super-speed. As a new chapter in her life unfolds, the Girl of Steel has truly rededicated herself to defending her adopted planet.

THE INFECTED
When a Jokerized Batman from the Dark Multiverse called the Batman Who Laughs came to Earth-0, he created his own Secret Six and infected Supergirl briefly with a tainted Batarang.

LOOKING FOR A CAUSE
Supergirl Kara Zor-El is one of the mightiest beings in the universe, but struggles to find a heroic purpose to match her superpowers.

ON THE RECORD

There were numerous early attempts to create a female equivalent of the Man of Tomorrow. The particular prototype which clicked best with fans and prompted Kara Zor-El's official entry into the DC pantheon appeared in 1958 in *Superman* (Vol. 1) #123, when Jimmy Olsen's wish for a female companion for his pal Superman came true.

Putty in his hands

After DC continuity was rebooted in the 1980s, Supergirl was re-imagined as an artificial, protoplasmic life-form. Grown by a benevolent, alternate-world Lex Luthor, her psionic abilities mimicked Superman's powers. The shape-shifter Matrix migrated to Earth and chose Supergirl as her preferred form. She alienated everyone by becoming the girlfriend of Lex Luthor when the villain transplanted his brain into a younger cloned body.

Eventually, Supergirl merged her body and personality with troubled student Linda Danvers to save her from demonic possession. They ultimately evolved into a powerful supernatural entity known as the Earth Born Angel of Fire.

Supergirl's dark side

A tougher, rebellious Girl of Steel crashed to Earth in a reprise of her origin for the 2000s. More powerful than her cousin Kal-El, Kara caused a rift between Superman, Batman, and Wonder Woman. She also became a disciple of evil New God Darkseid before joining the right side.

OVERPOWERED
Darkseid looked on approvingly as Supergirl showed Superman who was boss.

Tomorrow's world

Believing that she was experiencing a prolonged dream, Supergirl joined the Legion of Super-Heroes. In a dystopian future, where teenagers were oppressed by adults throughout a vast federation of United Planets, Kara Zor-El led this rebellious group to triumph and glory.

SUPERMAN

DATA

DEBUT *Action Comics* (Vol. 1) #1 (Jun. 1938)
REAL NAME Kal-El; Clark Kent (adoptive name)
BASE Metropolis
HEIGHT 6ft 3in **WEIGHT** 235 lbs
EYES Blue **HAIR** Black
POWERS/ABILITIES Super-strength; super-speed; flight; invulnerability; numerous sense-based abilities; accelerated healing; all fueled by exposure to solar energy from a yellow sun.
ALLIES Lois Lane, Superboy (Jon Kent), Batman, Wonder Woman, Supergirl, Steel, Superboy (Kon-El), Jimmy Olsen
ENEMIES Lex Luthor, Brainiac, General Zod, Doomsday, Parasite, Metallo, Mr. Mxyzptlk
AFFILIATIONS Justice League

Superman is the world's greatest hero. He is a tireless champion dedicated to protecting life and battling injustice not only in his city of Metropolis, but also all over his adopted world and across the universe. With his fantastic powers and abilities, fueled by his alien cells—which hyper-efficiently process the solar energy of Earth's yellow sun—Superman is an unstoppable force for good and a steadfast punisher of evil. Superman is a founding member of the Justice League, and an inspiration to countless other heroes, continuing into the 31st century and beyond.

AT A GLANCE...

Real and Present Dangers
The Man of Steel is not impervious to harm. He is weakened and will eventually die if exposed to Kryptonite—radioactive remnants of his old homeworld. He has no defense against magic and his mind will succumb to sufficient psionic assault, but his real vulnerability is his dependence on yellow solar radiation. Deprived of it, he becomes a mere mortal.

Fortress of Solitude
Even a Superman needs a place to hang his cape. The Man of Steel keeps his menagerie of alien creatures, advanced medical facilities, confiscated weapons, and other dangerous devices in a vast crystalline stronghold derived from recovered Kryptonian technologies. His famous Fortress of Solitude is currently located in the Bermuda Triangle.

CLASSIC STORIES

Action Comics (Vol. 1) #1 (Jun. 1938) A different kind of hero debuts with Superman creating a new literary genre and sparking a revolution in popular fiction.
Superman (Vol. 1) #423 & Action Comics (Vol. 1) #583 (Sep. 1986) An era ends in tribute to 50 years of continuity as the Superman family retires to make way for a potent re-imagining of the characters.
Superman (Vol. 2) #75 (Jan. 1993) After an epic storyline across multiple titles, a horrific pitched battle with Doomsday results in the "Death of Superman."
Superman (Vol. 1) #701-714 (Sep. 2010-Oct. 2011) Following a mighty war against the people of New Krypton, which found him exiled from Earth, Superman reconnects with ordinary Americans by walking across the country.

Suit of Steel
Superman has worn a few other costumes during his career, but returns time and time again to his classic, iconic uniform. For a while, he wore a version with a red belt that didn't feature his signature red tights. However, he gifted this *Rebirth* costume to Lois when she and their son Jon traveled the galaxy with Superman's father, Jor-El.

Years ago, the planet Krypton was on the verge of destruction, plagued by devastating earthquakes and other disasters. Krypton was a highly advanced civilization, one revolving around a red sun, yet it had fallen into a state of crisis. Although scientist Jor-El petitioned the Kryptonian Council to evacuate the planet, he was called an alarmist and ignored. After one final plea, Jor-El and his wife Lara were left with no other choice. With destruction all around them, they placed their only son, baby Kal-El, in a small rocket ship programmed to carry him away to the safety of the planet Earth. Jor-El had done the calculations and realized that Earth's yellow sun would supercharge Kal-El's cells, allowing him to thrive in a way he never could on Krypton.

When Kal-El's ship crashed on Earth it was spotted by Kansas farmers Jonathan and Martha Kent. A childless couple eager for a baby, they rescued the little star-child and raised him as a perfectly normal little boy in their hometown of Smallville, naming him Clark Kent. However, as Clark grew older, foreboding hints of his true nature manifested themselves. His physical strength and speed grew exponentially. He was never sick, and as his teen years progressed, his senses became acutely sharper than those of his peers. Clark learned early on that anyone in need had to be helped, and it was his duty to do the right thing. It was thanks to his parents' love, warmth, and social conscience that he grew up with the upright moral principles that shaped his later life.

Attending high school with his best friends Pete Ross and Lana Lang, Clark did his best to keep his continually evolving powers to himself, even from a rather nosy older fellow student named Lex Luthor. However, when a tornado hit town during a county fair, Clark used his powers to save Lana's life, and discovered that he could fly. While he and Lana began a childhood romance, Clark realized that his powers were too big for Smallville, and soon left to explore the world.

During his travels, Clark realized that truth and justice were exponentially important to him. Inspired to report that truth on a daily basis, he moved to Metropolis and pursued a career as a journalist. He got a job at *The Daily Planet*, working under Perry White, where he met his fellow reporter, Lois Lane, and photographer and general office gopher, Jimmy Olsen. Clark had perfected a mild-mannered routine by this point in his life, not afraid to let his Midwest honesty be mistaken for naiveté from many a jaded Metropolis citizen. He had learned to hide behind eyeglasses and relaxed posture

LAST SON OF KRYPTON
Baby Kal-El was sent to Earth to escape the destruction of Krypton. As an adult, he would discover that his father, Jor-El, escaped death that day as well... for a time.

THICK AS THIEVES
Growing up in Smallville, Clark was best friends with Pete Ross and Lana Lang. He also knew Lex Luthor, but Lex was a little older, and according to Clark, just as difficult then as he is now.

KRYPTON'S DESTROYER?

When Jor-El and Lara sent Kal-El away from Krypton, neither was aware that there may have been something far more sinister in play when it came to their planet's destruction. A warrior named Rogol Zaar feared Krypton's advanced science and predicted they would ruin other civilizations in their continued development. Rogol claimed that he was truly responsible for the destruction of Krypton, and in fact, later tried to destroy Earth when he found that it, too, had been "infected" by Kryptonians.

Although he was brought to justice by Superman, Supergirl, Superboy (Jon Kent), and others, the mystery of his claims still eats away at the heroes.

ROGOL RAGE
Supergirl felt more anger toward Rogol's crimes than Superman. As Kal-El's older cousin, she grew up on Krypton, where Clark has no memories of the planet.

years ago, in order to disguise his natural strength and power.

This quiet and reserved Clark Kent was a drastic contrast to the man in a red cape who would appear later that day. When Clark tagged along with Lois to investigate Lex Luthor's latest enterprise, he was forced to leap into action when Lois was accidentally knocked off a rooftop's ledge. Changing in secret into a blue and red costume, adorned with the "S"-shaped house of El crest on its chest, Clark flew up and rescued not just Lois, but also a falling helicopter. Lois was awestruck, and soon coined the name "Superman" when she stole the headlines of the next edition of *The Daily Planet*.

Superman's exploits made him a sensation, inspiring other metahumans and masked heroes to emerge from the shadows and work under the avid gaze of an adoring public—and that of the increasingly

WHO'S GOT YOU?
While she had already met him as Clark, Lois was much more impressed when she met Superman for the first time.

MAN OF TOMORROW
For all his incredible abilities, Superman's greatest strength is his unflagging determination to protect his adopted world.

"This is my fight to finish! This is a job for Superman!"

KAL-EL

JOR-EL RETURNS

The Superman family has grown throughout the years. Not only did Superman's cousin Supergirl survive their planet's destruction, but so did the nefarious General Zod and his wife Ursa, who escaped thanks to the other dimensional Phantom Zone. Superman would even discover that his father Jor-El was transported away from Krypton at the last moment. However, Jor-El would prove not quite the father figure Kal-El had dreamed of. Jor-El was coldly scientific, and was proven to have created the genetically altered planet-destroying monster Rogol Zaar. For his crimes, he was sent back to Krypton at the moment of its destruction, despite Superman's protests.

EVOLUTIONARY GAP
Captain Comet's mind control turned the people of Metropolis into a howling mob determined to stop Superman.

SUPERMAN

COVER STORY
The Daily Planet offered Clark the opportunity to meet like-minded people and provided a platform for him to do some good as Superman.

nervous military and federal authorities. Nevertheless, when the evil despot Darkseid invaded Earth, Superman joined forces with Batman, Wonder Woman, and others, forming the first incarnation of the Justice League.

Over the years, Superman has fought countless threats, from the villainous schemes perpetrated by the seemingly altruistic billionaire Lex Luthor, to the hijinks of the 5th dimensional imp Mr. Mxyzptlk, to the direct, organized attacks of rogue surviving Kryptonian General Zod. Superman's relationship with Lois continued to blossom despite the chaos, and he eventually revealed his secret identity to her.

When Superman encountered the beast known as Doomsday, he met his greatest challenge to date. He was killed by the beast, but with the help of Kryptonian technology and a link to his father, Jonathan Kent, Clark returned to the land of the living. He later married Lois, but soon suffered a power change, and became a being of pure energy, requiring a specialized blue suit just to contain his being. As always, the Man of Steel adapted, and eventually returned to his true form.

REBIRTH

SUPERMEN?

After the continuity-altering event known as *Flashpoint*, the Superman that was reborn into the main universe, Earth-0, was younger than the previous incarnation and had a different personal history, as well as only a casual friendship with Lois Lane.

Interference from the near-omnipotent being Doctor Manhattan had split Superman's continuity in two, with the other half living in the shadows with his wife Lois and their son Jon Kent. During a battle with the 5th-dimensional imp called Mr. Mxyzptlk, Superman managed to merge his personal histories into one streamlined timeline, his past and life becoming one with that of the so-called "New 52" Superman.

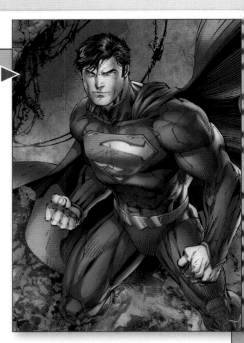

HOSTAGE CRISIS
When scientist Lex Luthor and the army captured the Metropolis vigilante, they learned the limitations of their power—and the risks of antagonizing Superman.

Some time later, Clark and Lois had a son and named him Jonathan Samuel Kent. In order to give Jon the life he needed, Clark and Lois took sabbaticals from the Daily Planet and moved to California for a time, where Clark worked as Superman in the shadows, stepping away from his duties in the Justice League. He eventually returned, realizing that his family belonged in Metropolis.

In his continued pursuit of the truth, Superman has recently revealed his double identity to the world. A public figure now as both Clark Kent and Superman, he continues to report for *The Daily Planet* and wages his never-ending pursuit of justice, no matter what the universe throws his way.

REBIRTH

SINO SUPER-MAN

During his final days, Superman's power waned. He was even attacked by Chinese superhumans seeking to steal his genetic material for their enigmatic leader, Dr. Omen. Soon after Kal-El's final battle, a new Chinese Super Hero debuted and it appeared that the Middle Kingdom had finally achieved the impossible dream of putting their own patriotic Super-Man onto the world stage. Kenji Kong, a brash young man, takes to this new role with great relish, determined to be China's Number One hero.

SUPER THREATS
Superman has faced death on multiple occasions, yet lived to tell the tale. His rogues gallery consists of some of the most powerful villains in the universe.

When Superman first appeared on the scene, he was as likely to go after greedy mine-owners and armaments manufacturers as mobsters and mad scientists. However, as he developed, the Man of Tomorrow specialized in battling monsters, crushing invasions, and tackling criminals no ordinary emergency services could handle. He became an accredited representative of the legal authorities.

Following a reordering of reality in *Crisis on Infinite Earths*, Superman was dramatically reimagined for a new generation. Much of his history was dialed back to parallel his earliest adventures, and his foster parents Jonathan and Martha Kent were resurrected to add a family element to the life of the interstellar orphan.

The Ultimate Sacrifice

When the alien beast Doomsday burst from the Earth on a destructive path to Metropolis, no force could stop it. After the creature smashed the Justice League and brutalized Superman, the city looked finished. However, its unyielding champion was determined to stop Doomsday at all costs. Despite his terrible injuries, Superman returned to the fray. He finally triumphed over the creature, but paid the ultimate price for victory with his life.

Superman's body was interred in Metropolis' Centennial Park. It was stolen by the military research group Cadmus for experimentation purposes, before being recovered by the fallen hero's friends and revived using Kryptonian technology. However, it was just an animated cadaver, as Superman's spirit was long gone.

It took the unfailing devotion of his Earth-born father to retrieve Clark from the afterlife. Grieving for his son, Jonathan Kent suffered a heart attack, and ascended to an eerie netherworld, from where he brought Clark back to stand at the forefront of Earth's champions.

DOOMSDAY SCENARIO
Despite being bloodied by attacks from the alien invader, Doomsday Superman fought to defend Metropolis.

The Rise and Fall of New Krypton

The Man of Steel's uniqueness ended when citizens of the Bottled City of Kandor were restored to normal size. Under the leadership of Alura Zor-El and General Zod, legions of new supermen built a New Krypton. Before long, growing tensions and suspicions culminated in a "100-Minute War" against mankind, with Superman and Supergirl caught in the middle. With the help of Superboy and Lor-Zod, Zod was ultimately trapped in the Phantom Zone and Earth was safe once again.

Superman Reborn

After the events of the miniseries *Flashpoint*, Superman's life would receive a drastic overhaul not seen since his reboot following the events of *Crisis on Infinite Earths*. While the post-*Crisis* Superman had married Lois Lane, their marriage had never happened in the new reality of this *New 52* era. Superman's costume appeared more like a suit of armor, and his early history was rewritten to include a period of time where he simply wore a T-shirt to fight crime. This Superman was eventually killed off, as another Superman, the version from the pre-*Flashpoint* universe, emerged from the shadows. During the four-part "Superman Reborn" storyline that crossed from *Superman* to *Action Comics*, the history of these two Supermen was merged. The result was a Superman who contained the best of all continuities. He had indeed battled Doomsday and died, married Lois Lane, and had a son, and even formed the Justice League by battling Darkseid.

THOROUGHLY GROUNDED
The Last Son of Krypton's resolute sense of justice is molded by the love, support, and good advice of his adoptive parents, Jonathan and Martha.

WAR OF THE SUPERMEN
Superman and Zod clashed over the Kryptonian zealot's desire to turn Earth into a new Krypton.

SUPERMAN REVENGE SQUAD

DEBUT *Superboy* (Vol. 1) #94 (Jan. 1962)
BASE The Moon
MEMBERS/POWERS Cyborg Superman:
Manipulation of electronic devices, Kryptonian powers; **Eradicator:** Android with Kryptonian powers; **Metallo:** Superhuman strength and durability, powered by Kryptonite heart; **Blanque:** Telepathy, telekinesis, pyrokinesis **Mongul:** Superhuman strength, stamina, and speed, invulnerability, flight
ALLIES General Zod
ENEMIES Superman

Hank Henshaw (Cyborg Superman) assembled a team of some of Superman's most dangerous enemies, making their mission statement their name: Superman Revenge Squad. Consisting of Henshaw, Eradicator, Metallo, Blanque, and Mongol, Cyborg Superman had one more recruit to make if the team were to successfully break into the Fortress of Solitude: General Zod. At first Zod resisted the idea of a team-up, refusing to follow orders, but he realized that he could use the Squad to achieve his dearest wish: To use the Phantom Zone Projector at the Fortress of Solitude to release his wife and son from their other-dimensional prison. After they had served his purpose, Zod disbanded the team, but kept the Eradicator as an ally for his family.

SUPERMEN OF AMERICA

DEBUT *Supermen of America* #1 (Mar. 1999)
BASE Metropolis
MEMBERS/POWERS
Brahma (Cal Usjak): Super-strength and invulnerability; **Loser** (Theo Storm): Possesses powerful dermal force field; **Maximum** (Max Williams): Channels bursts of superhuman energy; **Outburst** (Mitch Anderson): Manipulates magnetic fields; **Pyrogen** (Claudio Tielli): Flame-controlling pyrokinetic; **White Lotus** (Nona Lin): Martial artist; mystic aura generates a force field she can manipulate.
ALLIES Lex Luthor
ENEMIES O.M.A.C.

A heroic power vacuum left by Superman's brief departure from Metropolis to defend Earth gave rise to the Supermen of America. This team of teen heroes was unexpectedly sponsored by Superman's perennial opponent, Metropolis mogul Lex Luthor.

When Junior K-D, the lead singer of the band Crossfire, was gunned down during a benefit concert in Metropolis, the ensuing chaos forced teen hero Outburst into action. Inspired by Superman, Outburst eagerly accepted Lex Luthor's offer to recruit a force of young metahumans. He had soon gathered Brahma, Loser, Psilencer, Pyrogen, and White Lotus to serve as Supermen of America. The group helped to quell gang violence on Metropolis' streets and even tackled Super-Villains emboldened by Superman's temporary

HERE COME THE SUPERMEN!
1 Outburst   4 Loser
2 Brahma   5 Pyrogen
3 White Lotus 6 Maximum

absence.

When Psilencer was struck down by a gang member's bullet, he was replaced by the super-athletic Maximum. The Supermen of America eventually left Lex Luthor's employ, later participating in the global fight against O.M.A.C.'s units prior to the *Infinite Crisis*, an event that left many of their members grievously injured.

SUPERWOMAN

DEBUT *Justice League* (Vol. 2) #23 (Oct. 2013)
REAL NAME Lois Lane
BASE Themyscira, Earth-3
HEIGHT 6ft **WEIGHT** 165 lbs
EYES Blue **HAIR** Black
POWERS/ABILITIES Super-strength, stamina and durability, flight, and heat vision.
ALLIES Ultraman, Owlman, Alexander Luthor [NB As with other Crime Syndicate members, there's an argument for saying they have no allies as they all betray each other in the end]
ENEMIES Grail, Anti-Monitor
AFFILIATIONS Crime Syndicate

On Earth-3, Lois Lane is a powerful Amazon known as Superwoman. Ruthless and manipulative, she joins the Crime Syndicate. The team invade Earth-0 with Superwoman wielding the barbed Lasso of Submission, exerting control over almost any being.

Pregnant by Alexander Luthor, she plays teammates Owlman and Ultraman off against each other by claiming that each of them is the father of her baby. Superwoman gives birth during a battle against the Anti-Monitor and the heirs of Darkseid, but is killed by Darkseid's daughter Grail, who wants to use the child for her own ends.

T.O. MORROW

DEBUT *The Flash* (Vol. 1) #143 (Mar. 1964)
REAL NAME Dr. Thomas Oscar Morrow
BASE Detroit, Michigan
HEIGHT 5ft 11in **WEIGHT** 187 lbs
EYES Blue **HAIR** Black
POWERS/ABILITIES Scientist with advanced knowledge of robotics and future studies; access to the highly classified Red Room at S.T.A.R. Labs.
ALLIES Dr. Silas Stone, Dr. Will Magnus, Sarah Charles
ENEMIES FBI
AFFILIATIONS Red Room, S.T.A.R. Labs

Brilliant scientist Dr. Thomas Morrow was fascinated by future technologies from an early age, having been influenced by science fiction, especially the works of H.G. Wells. He earned Masters' degrees from Harvard University in Emerging Technologies, Strategic Foresight, and Future Studies, before focusing on time travel. He was forced to forsake his scientific endeavors after an accident nearly killed him.

Recruited by S.T.A.R. Labs Detroit, Morrow helped Dr. Silas Stone establish the clandestine Red Room facility. He was working in the lab when a Parademon attack caused extensive injuries to Silas' son, Victor. This caused Dr. Stone to graft the experimental metal Promethium to Victor, using an equally experimental nanite technique for neural integration. The result was the hero Cyborg, who went on to become a founding member of the Justice League. T.O. Morrow continues his work at S.T.A.R. Labs to this day, working closely with Dr. Silas Stone and Cyborg. For unknown reasons, he is currently under investigation by the FBI. He was instrumental in maintaining Cyborg's sanity and systems when Victor was trapped in the Digiverse.

ON THE RECORD

The quintessential mad scientist, T.O. Morrow was created in the 1960s and was a staunch enemy of the JLA. He created the android Red Tornado to use as a weapon against the League, until it rejected its programming and became a hero itself. After repeated clashes with the League, Morrow worked closely with fellow nutty Professor Ivo. Later, he set up shop on the scientific sanctuary of Oolong Island with a who's who of the most villainous scientists.

TOMORROW AND TOMORROW: T.O. Morrow worked with Professor Ivo, to create the android Tomorrow Woman (inset) to infiltrate and destroy the Justice League. However, Tomorrow Woman was too smart to play ball.

SWAMP THING

DATA

DEBUT *House of Secrets* #92 (Jun.–Jul. 1971)
REAL NAME Alec Holland
BASE Mobile
HEIGHT Variable   **WEIGHT** Variable
EYES Red   **HAIR** None
POWERS/ABILITIES Former avatar of the Green, the cosmic energy that animates all plant life; can appear wherever there is life; can manipulate plant matter; travel in time; shape size and shape; possesses prodigious strength and regenerative powers.
ALLIES John Constantine, Abby Arcane
ENEMIES Anton Arcane, Floronic Man
AFFILIATIONS The Green, Justice League Dark

GREEN CHAMPION
Holland's bio-restorative formula was seen as a boon by the Green, but a threat by the Rot.

Swamp Thing was the avatar of the Green: The mysterious force inherent in all plant life. Given physical form by botanist Alec Holland, he fought valiantly for the Parliament of Trees before their destruction by dark forces. Still nature's protector, Swamp Thing has joined up with other magical heroes to battle things that go bump in the night.

Botanist Alec Holland died in an explosion at his laboratory in the swamp when it was sabotaged by criminals. Soaking in Alec's experimental bio-restorative plant formula, vegetation in the Louisiana swamp formed a humanoid Swamp Thing body, and believed itself to be Alec Holland reborn in monstrous form. In reality, this body was an avatar of the Green, a servant of the Earth's Parliament of Trees, primordial planet elementals.

After this Swamp Thing died, Alec was reborn in human form. Suffering from memories belonging to the Swamp Thing, it wasn't long before he met Abigail Arcane, whom he recognized from those same fleeting thoughts. Alec was drawn into an elemental war between the Green and the force of death and decay called the Rot. He was transformed into Swamp Thing by the Parliament of Trees and fought the Rot, finally overcoming its new avatar, Anton Arcane.

Adjusted to life as Swamp Thing, Alec's world was once again uprooted when the machinations of the witch Hecate burned down the Parliament of Trees. Swamp Thing was soon reduced to little more than a handful of green mush. The Parliament of Flowers sought to fill the gap with a new protector, but their choice for avatar was usurped by the villainous Floronic Man. However, thanks to the crafty nature of John Constantine, a new Swamp Thing was born, one that remembered Holland's memories and much more.

Swamp Thing continues to lend his considerable might and control over plant life to help his friends in the Justice League Dark, discovering the world again in the process.

AVATAR OF THE GREEN
The Swamp Thing was the living embodiment of the elemental force that animates all plant life in the known universe.

CLASSIC STORIES

House of Secrets #92 (Jun.–Jul. 1971) In this prototype for Swamp Thing's origin story, readers meet scientist Alex Olsen and learn of his transformation into a Swamp Thing.

Saga of Swamp Thing #34 (Mar. 1985) The mutual attraction between Swamp Thing and Abigail Cable, daughter of his nemesis Anton Arcane, blossoms into love.

Swamp Thing (Vol. 2) #37-50 (Jun. 1985–Jul. 1986) John Constantine guides the Swamp Thing towards an understanding of his true powers as a member of the Parliament of Trees.

Swamp Thing (Vol. 2) #166–171 (May–Oct. 1996) Having subsumed each of Earth's elemental Parliaments, The Swamp Thing takes his place in the Parliament of Worlds as its representative of the entire planet.

ON THE RECORD

From his origins in the pulp horror tradition, the character of the Swamp Thing has evolved over the years to become a way to explore environmental issues.

The 1972 Alec Holland origin story transformed him into the Swamp Thing after chemical exposure, engaging the emerging environmental consciousness of the time. Later, the character came to represent the entire natural world, at war not just with individual villains, but with the human impulse to dominate and destroy nature.

NATURE'S REVENGE
The Swamp Thing has always been a warning of the dire consequences of polluting the natural world.

IN THE NAME OF THE FATHER
While he was raised by his stepfather and took the Holland name as his own, Alec Holland's real father was Lloyd Bernard McGinn. When he was killed by the Headhunter, Swamp Thing teamed with Batman to track down the killer, and Alec promptly killed him, despite Batman's "no killing" stance.

TALIA AL GHŪL

DATA

DEBUT *Detective Comics* (Vol. 1) #411 **(May 1971)**
HEIGHT 5ft 8in **WEIGHT** 120 lbs
BASE Mobile
EYES Brown **HAIR** Brown
POWERS/ABILITIES Accomplished fighter and assassin; adept in ballet and horseback riding; talented chemist; highly intelligent and a cunning strategist; access to huge terrorist networks; charismatic leader.
ALLIES Rā's al Ghūl, Heretic, Red Hood, the Silencer
ENEMIES Batman, Batman Family, Batman, Inc., Leviathan (Mark Shaw)
AFFILIATIONS League of Assassins, Leviathan

DAMSEL CAUSING DISTRESS
She first met Batman when held captive by an enemy of Rā's al Ghūl. However, Talia has since become a threat in her own right, leading her own terrorist group for a time, a clandestine organization called Leviathan.

She is the daughter of the demon, the child of eco-terrorist Rā's al Ghūl, born into the world surrounded by the worst assassins known to man. She is the mother of Robin (Damian Wayne), and the estranged love of Batman. She is Talia al Ghūl, a conflicting mix of passion and apathy, compassion and ruthlessness. While the Dark Knight would wish to believe otherwise, at her core, Talia is truly her father's daughter.

PARENTAL CONTROL
Rā's al Ghūl and Talia's relationship is complex. While he wants nothing more than total control over her, he was proud when she broke away and started Leviathan.

When international terrorist Rā's al Ghūl met a young hippie named Melisande, the two formed a close bond that Rā's hadn't shared with a woman in quite some time. As the founder of the League of Assassins, and despite having lived for centuries thanks to the life-extending properties of the fabled Lazarus Pits, Rā's had little time for love. Nevertheless, he and Melisande had a child, and named her Talia al Ghūl.

Talia was raised among assassins and killers, but she doted on her father. She soon followed in his footsteps, training in numerous fighting styles, and also mastering skills such as chemistry, ballet, and horse riding. Thanks to her father's vast wealth, she had everything she wanted, but it wasn't until she was kidnapped by Dr. Darrk that she met someone who interested her: Batman.

Despite her father's ongoing conflict with the Dark Knight, Talia and Batman shared a passionate romance and had a child named Damian. While Damian would later take his place by Batman's side as the new Robin, Talia felt shunned by the Dark Knight, and declared war against him, starting her own secret society called Leviathan. With a vast array of assassins at her control, Talia worked closest with the Silencer, but even when he couldn't protect Leviathan when former Manhunter Mark Shaw decided to claim the group as his own. After ousting Talia, Shaw made Leviathan a greater threat, taking out nearly every other spy organization. Talia has sworn revenge, even willing to team up with Batman and Robin to get it.

LOVE LOST
Like her son, Damian, before her, Talia has been resurrected in the Lazarus Pits. However, Damian refused to return his mother's love when she tried to revive their relationship.

ON THE RECORD

First appearing in the 1970s, Talia al Ghūl matured into a formidable presence before the continuity-altering events of the *Flashpoint* miniseries. Breaking away from her father's influence in the 2000s, Talia took over LexCorp for Lex Luthor when he was elected to the position of President of the United States.

Going under the name Talia Head, she ran Luthor's company as its CEO. Having proved herself to be a shrewd businesswoman, she later purposely bankrupted LexCorp. Talia also served in the inner circle of two incarnations of the elite Secret Society of Super-Villains, working alongside Luthor and the likes of Black Adam, Deathstroke, Vandal Savage, and Gorilla Grodd.

SISTER, SISTER
In 2003, it was revealed that Talia had an older stepsister, Nyssa Raatko. Introduced in *Batman: Death and the Maidens*, Nyssa manipulated Talia into helping her murder their father.

TAKION

DEBUT *Takion* #1 (Jun. 1996)
REAL NAME Joshua Sanders
BASE New Genesis
HEIGHT 6ft 2in
WEIGHT Variable
EYES Red
HAIR Flaming yellow
POWERS/ABILITIES Flight; energy blasts; matter manipulation; super-speed; super-strength; powered by the all-powerful Source
ENEMIES Stayne, Darkseid, Infinity-Man

Blind from birth, psychologist Joshua Sanders was overcome with a tremendous surge of energy and suddenly knew everything there was to know. In that instant, he was whisked away to New Genesis, where his developing sight gazed upon Izaya, the New God's Highfather, who had chosen Joshua as his champion. Now known as Takion of the Source, he would take Izaya's place in the event of the latter's death.

Takion soon faced the threat of Stayne, created by Darkseid to counter the New Gods' existence. Despite frequent conflict, Takion's power grew, and he became the new Highfather for a time. Eventually, Takion was seemingly killed by the Infinity-Man, under direction from the Source. However, he has been glimpsed recently among the New Gods watching over Earth-51.

TALON

DEBUT *Talon* #0 (Nov. 2012)
REAL NAME Calvin Rose
BASE Gotham City
HEIGHT 5ft 10in **WEIGHT** 174 lbs
EYES Brown **HAIR** Brown
POWERS/ABILITIES Expert escape artist; adept in several fighting styles; knowledge of electronics and security systems; expert assassin but now practices non-lethal crime fighting; access to funding and weaponry from Batman, Inc.; armored suit fires grappling line and darts; customized Utility Belt.
ALLIES Batman, the Batman Family, Strix, Casey Washington
ENEMIES Court of Owls, Bane, Lord Death Man, Sebastian Clark
AFFILIATIONS Batman Incorporated

Like all the Talons who were forged by the nefarious secret society called the Court of Owls, Calvin Rose lived a hard life. Calvin's father was abusive and, at only eight years of age, Calvin was locked and abandoned in an outdoor dog kennel. He waited for three days for his father to return and free him, but after the third night, he realized he was alone in the world. Calvin broke out of his cage, took to the road, and was discovered by an escape artist who worked at the traveling Haly's Circus. In time, Calvin became the escape artist's successor—which was when he learned Haly's Circus' dark secret.

Every generation the Court of Owls trawled the circus looking for prospective new assassins, called Talons, who would be schooled and conditioned to do their bidding. Calvin was recruited, but after killing another Talon to complete the Court's rigorous and ruthless training, he realized he could not be one of their operatives and defected. He also saved the life of Casey Washington, a target he was supposed to eliminate. Armed with a modified Talon suit, Calvin set out to destroy the Court of Owls, later working alongside Batman.

TALON, INCORPORATED
Calvin Rose was later recruited into another society, this one on the side of the angels. He gladly accepted membership of Batman Incorporated.

TALONS

DEBUT *Batman* (Vol. 2) #2 (Dec. 2011)
BASE Gotham City
NOTABLE MEMBERS William Cobb; Alexander Staunton; Ephraim Newhouse; Henry Ballard; Uriah Boone; Mary Turner; Alton Carver
POWERS/ABILITIES Brainwashed to be blindly loyal; highly trained in the use of various weapons as well as combat, assassination, and infiltration techniques; exceptionally fit and agile; ability to cheat death thanks to formula injected into their bloodstream by the Court of Owls.
ENEMIES Batman, Birds of Prey, the Batman Family, Talon (Calvin Rose), Mr. Freeze, Jonah Hex
AFFILIATIONS Court of Owls

A clandestine organization active since the birth of Gotham City, the Court of Owls is a powerful, well-connected cabal of Gotham society's elite. However, to bend an entire city to its will, the Court deployed a succession of lethal enforcers: A near-invisible assassin haunting the night, killing, before vanishing without a trace. The "Talon" served the Court after undergoing a series of demanding challenges, including physical and mental conditioning ensuring loyalty to their cause above all else.

To recruit Talons, the Court looked to Haly's Circus to find suitable candidates whose talents and skills they could refine. For generations, the best and brightest acts were abducted and forged into obedient, unstoppable killing machines. Recently, the Court developed a chemical formula granting superhuman endurance and the ability to be reanimated from death. This allowed the Court to unleash numerous Talons simultaneously, attacking the Dark Knight and thwarting his efforts to destroy the Court.

THE SECRET IS OUT
The upper echelons of the Court of Owls as well as many of their Talon enforcers know that Bruce is Batman.

With the Court and its international parent organization, The Parliament of Owls, now shattered by the Dark Robins attending the Batman Who Laughs, the Talons are largely leaderless, although individuals have been encountered by Batman and Green Arrow, who ended a human trafficking scheme providing quarry for Talons to hunt.

TAMARANEANS, THE

DEBUT *The New Teen Titans* (Vol. 1) #3 (Jan. 1981)
BASE Tamaran, Ghost Sector
NOTABLE MEMBERS/POWERS Starfire (Koriand'r): Energy projection, flight, language assimilation through touch; **Blackfire** (Komand'r): Firearms expertise, flight; **Sister Kala** (Kaland'r): Pyrokinesis, leadership, flight.

Long ago, Tamaran was freed from its enemies by X'Hal. When she left, many disciples followed her, settling on a barren planet where Sister Kala (Kaland'r)—a future ally of White Lantern Kyle Rayner—was born. Remaining Tamaraneans flourished on their birthworld where, years later, princesses Koriand'r and Komand'r were born.

When they were young, Tamaran was invaded by the Citadel. In exchange for Koriand'r, the Citadel made Komand'r ruler of Tamaran. Koriand'r escaped, becoming the hero Starfire on Earth. She later returned to Tamaran to help her people battle Blight. Komand'r took a different path, and united her people with Super-Villain Helspont.

Brainiac stole Tamaran, but his collection of planets was released after he was destroyed during the Omega Titans invasion. Tameran now rests in the Ghost Sector, where Komand'r and the heroes of Justice League Odyssey defend it.

TARANTULA II

DEBUT *Nightwing* (Vol. 1) #71 (Sep. 2002)
REAL NAME Catalina Flores
HEIGHT 5ft 7in **WEIGHT** 135 lbs
EYES Brown **HAIR** Black
POWERS/ABILITIES Adept hand-to-hand combatant; intelligent and well-traveled; weapons include gun that fires webbing-like netting and grappling lines.
ENEMIES Jefe, the Skeletons

Inspired by 1940s Super Hero John Law, former FBI agent Catalina Flores took on his codename and became a second Tarantula. Preying on gangsters and bad cops, her extreme methods brought her into conflict with Nightwing. After murdering Blüdhaven's corrupt Chief of Police, she appeared to join the city's top criminal Blockbuster, but killed him, too. Nightwing blamed himself and had a nervous breakdown, which Tarantula exploited.

Despite Batman banning her from Gotham City, she took control of one gang, renaming them Las Arañas, protecting them during the mob clash dubbed War Games, destroying The Penguin's powerbase, and then leaving town. She became a wandering vigilante and mercenary. She died saving the Secret Six, but returned after *Rebirth*, battling beside Green Arrow against the bone-obsessed killers, Skeletons.

TATTOOED MAN

DEBUT *Green Lantern* (Vol. 2) #23 (Sep. 1963)
REAL NAME Abel Tarrant
HEIGHT 6ft **WEIGHT** 195 lbs
EYES Blue **HAIR** Brown
POWERS/ABILITIES Can bring to life any tattoo on his body and control it with his mind.
ALLIES Scavenger, Clayface, Dr. Alchemy
ENEMIES Green Lantern Hal Jordan, Justice League
AFFILIATIONS Secret Society of Super-Villains

The Tattooed Man was a member of a Secret Society of Super-Villains group. He was present when the Justice League raided their hideout and arrested members, thanks to the leadership of then League member, Lex Luthor.

Before *Flashpoint*, the Tattooed Man was primarily an enemy of Green Lantern Hal Jordan. Able to bring his tattoos to life and control them, he proved a powerful foe. After attempting to reform, Tarrant was killed by Mirror Master when he doublecrossed the villain. Two other Tattooed Men emerged pre-*Flashpoint*: Titans member Mark Richards, and John Oakes.

Oakes' whereabouts are unknown, but Richards died in the mass-murder event at Sanctuary.

TATTOOED TOO
Mark Richards seemed more heroic than previous Tattooed Men. However, he was soon recruited by Deathstroke into an unscrupulous incarnation of the Titans.

TAWKY TAWNY

DEBUT *Captain Marvel Adventures* #79 (Dec. 1947)
BASE Philadelphia
HEIGHT 6ft 2in **WEIGHT** 480 lbs
EYES Yellow **HAIR** Orange, black, and white
POWERS/ABILITIES Charming, urbane, witty and sensitive, strength and power of a 480lb tiger.
ENEMIES Black Adam
AFFILIATIONS Vasquez family

Before *Flashpoint*, Tawky Tawny was a humanoid tiger, often helping Shazam. Post-*Flashpoint*, Tawny was a tiger at a zoo. Visiting Tawny was the oldest memory that orphan Billy Batson had. He would talk to the big cat and feed him hamburgers. After Billy was given the powers of Shazam, Black Adam began hunting him. Their fight led to the zoo, where Adam threw Shazam against Tawny's cage, freeing him. He was then imbued with some of Shazam's powers and the big cat injured Black Adam.

After *Rebirth*, Tawny was an unhappy citizen of the Wildlands, where talking animals had killed all humans. When the Shazam Family accidentally opened the Magic Lands, he migrated to Earth and now lives with the Vasquez household.

TEAM 7

DEBUT *The Kindred* #3 (May 1994)
NOTABLE MEMBERS
John Lynch (team leader); **Canary** (Dinah Drake, later Black Canary); **Kurt Lance**; **Slade Wilson** (later Deathstroke); **Cole Cash** (later Grifter); **Captain Summer Ramos**; **James Bronson** (later Majestic); **Alex Fairchild**; **Amanda Waller**; **Dean Higgins** (later Regulus); **Steve Trevor**.
ENEMIES Eclipso, Basilisk, Pandora, Spartan
ALLIES Essence

Over five years ago, an elite black-ops team was formed under the name Team 7 by John Lynch. He originally recruited Dinah Drake and Kurt Lance to choose only the very brightest and bravest (Kurt and Dinah would later be married, and Dinah would adopt the name Black Canary when Lynch augmented her abilities, sparking her famed Canary Cry).

The pair recruited mercenaries Slade Wilson and Alex Fairchild, as well as operatives James Bronson, pilot Captain Summer Ramos, ex-special forces soldier Cole Cash, NSA analyst Amanda Waller, and military intelligence agent Dean Higgins. Team 7 overcame the threat of Eclipso, yet Fairchild and Ramos were murdered battling the rogue Spartan programming. The team disbanded after Bronson transformed into the powerhouse Majestic.

TEEN LANTERN

DEBUT *Young Justice* Vol 3 #1 (Mar 2019)
REAL NAME Keli Quintela
BASE La Paz, Bolivia
HEIGHT Unknown **WEIGHT** Unknown
EYES Brown **HAIR** Black
POWERS/ABILITIES Using battery pack and gauntlet, can fly and create light constructs with Green Lantern energy.
ALLIES Jinny Hex, Naomi, Wonder Twins, Batwoman (Earth-3)
ENEMIES Lex Luthor, Hack (Earth-3)
AFFILIATIONS Young Justice

When Keli Quintela came across what appeared to be a dying Green Lantern in a junkyard in her home city of La Paz, he gave her a gauntlet attached to a battery pack. Although Keli's friend Marcos told her that Green Lanterns got their power from rings, her mysterious inheritance seemed to give her the same capability, and was possibly a "hack" of Green Lantern energy. Keli went to Metropolis to find out more, where she ended up joining a new Young Justice lineup. She introduced herself as Teen Lantern, despite actually being only 11 years old. Teen Lantern can use Green Lantern energy, apparently without attracting the attention of the Green Lantern Corps.

TEMPEST

DEBUT *Adventure Comics* (Vol. 1) #269 (Feb. 1960)
REAL NAME Garth
BASE Atlantis
HEIGHT 5ft 10in **WEIGHT** 235 lbs **EYES** Purple **HAIR** Black
POWERS/ABILITIES Atlantean warrior adept with many weapons; able to breathe underwater, swim at extreme speeds and resistant to tremendous pressure; super-strong, fast, durable, enhanced senses and reflexes, laser vision; intelligent and an adept hand-to-hand combatant; weapons include hi-tech trident; skilled magic user.
ALLIES Aquaman, Mera, Omen
ENEMIES Mr. Whisper, Mammoth
AFFILIATIONS Atlantis, School of Silence, Teen Titans

The Atlantean Garth was called Aqualad when he first worked on land with the Teen Titans, but many of those memories were erased by timestream manipulation and plots by old enemies. Not only did Garth forget that part of his past, but so did the rest of the world. He reemerged in Atlantis; part of a strike force assembled by Mera to hunt Aquaman. Ultimately, Garth discovered his orders weren't from her, but an impostor paving the way for the invading Thule. Garth and Aquaman succesfully turned the tide against the invaders.

A soldier and sorcerer (having spent years in Atlantis' mystical School of Silence), Garth used deadly force to stop organ smugglers dealing in Atlantean lungs, and found himself fighting Dick Grayson and Donna Troy. Realizing they knew each other from some forgotten past, the trio became uneasy allies, rediscovering their shared history as founding members of the first Teen Titans. Now restored to full capacity, Garth reunited with his old allies in the Titans as Tempest, battling the Fearsome Five and H.I.V.E., beginning a doomed relationship with telepath Omen, and helping his old friends defeat Troia: A crazed and murderous future version of Donna Troy.

He is currently active in Atlantis, battling the Trench subversion in Xebel, as well as surface criminal depredations.

TERRA

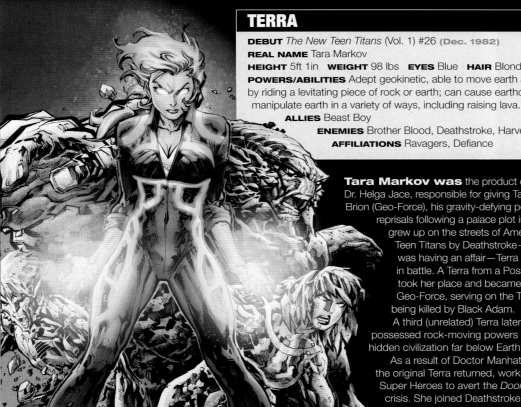

DEBUT *The New Teen Titans* (Vol. 1) #26 (Dec. 1982)
REAL NAME Tara Markov
HEIGHT 5ft 1in **WEIGHT** 98 lbs **EYES** Blue **HAIR** Blonde
POWERS/ABILITIES Adept geokinetic, able to move earth and rocks; can fly by riding a levitating piece of rock or earth; can cause earthquakes and manipulate earth in a variety of ways, including raising lava.
ALLIES Beast Boy
ENEMIES Brother Blood, Deathstroke, Harvest
AFFILIATIONS Ravagers, Defiance

Tara Markov was the product of experiments by Dr. Helga Jace, responsible for giving Tara's brother, Prince Brion (Geo-Force), his gravity-defying powers. After escaping reprisals following a palace plot in Markovia, Tara grew up on the streets of America. Planted in the Teen Titans by Deathstroke—with whom she was having an affair—Terra went insane and died in battle. A Terra from a Possible Future reality took her place and became like a sister to Geo-Force, serving on the Team Titans before being killed by Black Adam.

A third (unrelated) Terra later emerged. Atlee also possessed rock-moving powers but originated from a hidden civilization far below Earth's surface.

As a result of Doctor Manhattan's time-tampering, the original Terra returned, working with other Super Heroes to avert the *Doomsday Clock* crisis. She joined Deathstroke in his super-team Defiance, alternately attempting to seduce him and biding her time until she could destroy him. Ultimately, she helped put him behind bars in Arkham Asylum.

TEEN TITANS

DATA

DEBUT *The Brave and the Bold* #54 (Jun.–Jul. 1964)
BASE Brooklyn, New York
RECENT MEMBERS/POWERS
Robin (Damian Wayne) Formidable intellect, expert martial artist;
Kid Flash (Wallace West) Super-speed, accelerated healing;
Red Arrow (Emiko Queen) Expert archer and martial artist;
Crush (Xiomara Rojas) Enhanced strength, stamina, and
endurance; Roundhouse (Billy Wu) Genius-level intellect, able to
transform into a ball, propulsion; DJINN Other-dimensional genie
powers; Starfire (Princess Koriand'r) Expert warrior, Tamaranean
physiology provides enhanced strength, speed, endurance, and flight;
Raven (Rachel Roth) Magical powers from demonic ancestry;
Beast Boy (Garfield Logan) Assumes the form of any animal.
ALLIES Justice League, Titans
ENEMIES Manchester Black, Ra's al Ghul, Deathstroke,
Brother Blood

Some were the sidekicks of the Justice League looking to leave their own mark on the world. Others were aimless teen heroes seeking friendship and a way to help their communities. But all of them were heroes. And when they banded together they became even more. They became Teen Titans.

The original Teen Titans were Robin (Dick Grayson), Aqualad (Garth), Wonder Girl (Donna Troy), Hawk and Dove (Hank and Don Hall), Speedy (Roy Harper), Caveboy (Gnarrk), Herald (Mal Duncan), Lilith Clay, and Kid Flash (Wally West). From their Teen Titans Club House in Hatton Corners, the teenagers fought crime, commiserated with one another about issues with their mentors in the Justice League, and became close friends. When faced with the threat of Mister Twister, the group was forced to forget their time together as Titans, sacrificing their memories to save the world.

Years passed, and those original Teen Titans grew up. A new generation of heroes began to emerge, many inspired by those same Justice League mentors. One of those teenage heroes, Red Robin (Tim Drake), uncovered a plot by the organization N.O.W.H.E.R.E. to capture adolescent metahumans and turn them to its own mysterious ends. Recruited by Red Robin against N.O.W.H.E.R.E. and its leader Harvest, the Teen Titans were born anew, unaware of their predecessors who originally coined the team's name.

While this new incarnation included core members Red Robin, Superboy (Kon-El), Kid Flash (Bart Allen), Wonder Girl (Cassie Sandsmark), and Bunker, the team would go through several incarnations, gaining members like Raven, Beast Boy, and Power Girl (Tanya Spears) along the way. However, Red Robin eventually disbanded the team, unsure of the direction he wanted his life to head.

N.O.W.H.E.R.E. MAN Harvest had big plans for the Teen Titans—if they survived the Culling.

AT A GLANCE...

Teen spirit
The Teen Titans take both parts of their group's name seriously. They're a formidable fighting force, but they don't handle things the same way as other groups, because they're the next generation— headstrong, idealistic, and prone to lots of arguing.

The Robin Touch
The original Teen Titans were led by the first Robin (Dick Grayson). Every successful incarnation of the Titans seems to have a Robin at its center, which is not surprising as all Robins are trained in strategy and leadership techniques by Batman himself.

Surrogate family
The Teen Titans tend to come from difficult backgrounds, and the team represents a surrogate family, with all that entails. They argue, they bicker, they occasionally make each other miserable… but when the chips are down, they're always there for each other.

CLASSIC STORIES

***New Teen Titans* (Vol. 2) #1–5 (Aug. 1984–Feb. 1985)** In "The Terror of Trigon," the group are forced to confront their darkest alternate selves as Raven's demonic father attempts to enslave and destroy the Earth.

***Teen Titans* (Vol. 3) #1–7 (Sep. 2003–Mar. 2004)** Reeling from the deaths of Donna Troy and Omen, the group try to figure out where it fits in, juggling adolescent problems and being the Teen Titans—as wel as brawling with the Justice League along the way.

***Tales of the Teen Titans* #42–44, *Tales of the Teen Titans* Annual #3 (May 1984–Jul. 1984)** The Titans face down H.I.V.E. and Deathstroke in "The Judas Contract," which features the first appearance of Dick Grayson as Nightwing.

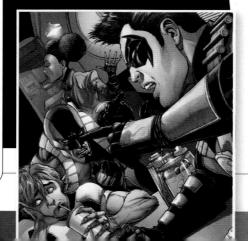

REBIRTH

KIDS' STUFF
Every incarnation of the Teen Titans has been beset by headstrong natures and internal strife. That's bad enough against ordinary Super-Villains, but when Damian Wayne gathers Starfire, Raven, Beast Boy, and the newest Kid Flash to battle his grandfather Rā's al Ghūl, is the arrogant little bully leading the kids to their inevitable doom?

TITANS, GO!
Robin (Damian Wayne) takes charge of the new Teen Titans.
1 Robin
2 Kid Flash
3 Starfire
4 Beast Boy
5 Raven

REMEMBER THE TITANS
Now adults, the original Teen Titans regained their memories when they were forced to once again battle Mister Twister. Most of the team decided to stick together as the Titans, joined by another original member, The Flash (Wally West), who had been lost in the mysterious Speed Force. The team later fell under Justice League control and shifted its roster, allowing new blood to team with classic Titan members.

TROUBLED TEENS
Robin's Teen Titans team was well-intentioned, but crossed moral boundaries in its pursuit of justice.

ON THE RECORD

In their initial incarnation, the Teen Titans were assembled from existing sidekicks and new junior versions of established heroes. Aqualad, Kid Flash, and Robin teamed up to defeat Mister Twister, and later recruited Donna Troy—then Wonder Woman's younger sister—into the team, completing their original lineup. From the Titans Lair they embarked on a series of teen-themed adventures against villains such as Ding Dong Daddy and the Mad Mod, giving the series a defining youth-culture flavor that continued in later iterations.

"...We might be good or evil, black or white, man or woman, straight or gay. But one thing you can count on... we are very, very dangerous."

BUNKER

Fortunately for the Titans' legacy, there were other Robins who felt differently. Damian Wayne jumped at the chance to command his own team. His recruitment methods could've used a bit of work, however. Instead of meeting with his prospective teammates one by one, Damian attacked and abducted Beast Boy, Raven, Starfire, and Kid Flash (Wallace West). It was Robin's way of showing these heroes that individually they're weak, but together they're strong. And surprisingly, it worked. A new era of Teen Titans was underway.

Operating out of their T-shaped Titans Tower in San Francisco, Robin's Teen Titans first fought Damian's grandfather, the notorious eco-terrorist Rā's al Ghūl, and quickly added the new Aqualad (Jackson Hyde) to their ranks. Despite surviving threats like Deathstroke and Black Manta, the team eventually lost their tower home and disbanded. But Robins are a persistent bunch. Damian was positive that the Teen Titans were a good idea, but they need to adapt for the times. So he recruited Kid Flash back onto his team, who insisted on giving new hero and human wrecking ball Roundhouse a chance as well. The trio added archer Red Arrow, genie Djinn, and the daughter of Lobo, Crush, to their roster, and fought crime out of a converted warehouse in Brooklyn. However, only Red Arrow knew that Robin was secretly imprisoning the villains they defeated in cells of the basement of their Mercy Hall hideout.

Damian's prison was revealed when Robin took Deathstroke captive. Deathstroke broke free and was only stopped when Red Arrow seemingly killed him. It took time, but the team began to repair from Robin's betrayal, and took their villain-rehabilitation program to the next level, brainwashing them to erase their criminal tendencies.

As the team slipped more and more into a morally gray area, they were captured by Lobo and delivered to a villain called The Other, an adult clone of Damian formerly called Heretic. The Teen Titans bested The Other, and soon clashed with the evil genie Elias in an adventure that saw Djinn leave the team with Jakeem Thunder to embark on a spiritual quest. The team disbanded, unable to follow Robin's leadership as he became more and more extreme.

To make matters worse, Djinn's brainwashing magic had faded, and the villains the Teen Titans had "reformed" all reverted to normal. Reeling from the death of the Wayne Family's beloved butler Alfred Pennyworth, Robin decided that he had to take the next step to remove these villains from society. He killed the evil cult leader Brother Blood and then set out to murder the assassin known as the KGBeast. The Teen Titans reunited to stop him, but Robin simply ripped the "R" off his costume and quit the team, leaving the fate of the once lighthearted and honorable Teen Titans in question.

Infiltrations and manipulations
With the introduction of the telepath Raven in 1980, a new Teen Titans team was formed, featuring three existing members—Kid Flash, Wonder Girl, and Robin—and new additions Cyborg, Starfire, and Changeling (formerly Beast Boy). Raven manipulated the team into joining forces against her demonic father Trigon, after which they stayed together to face Deathstroke the Terminator and his protégé Terra, who had infiltrated the Titans.

Graduation day
The next epochal shake-up in the Teen Titans' lineup came after the (no longer Teen) Titans and Young Justice resisted interference from the secretive Optitron Corporation. They then tangled with a Superman robot that killed both Omen and Donna Troy. In the aftermath, both teams disbanded, with some members forming a new Teen Titans and others joining the Outsiders. Donna Troy, who had been resurrected after *Infinite Crisis*, would rejoin briefly but then leave to pursue membership in the Justice League of America.

Growing pains
The following years saw further upheaval—leadership shake-ups and a changing roster. Cyborg and Starfire left for the JLA, and Damian Wayne took on a leadership role, teaming up with Red Robin before a clash between them led to Damian's exit. With Red Robin in charge, the Teen Titans battled Superboy-Prime in a story that prefigured their post-*Flashpoint* debut.

FINAL MOMENT
Donna Troy thought she had the Cyborg Superman down, but that proved to be a fatal mistake.

TERRIFICS, THE

DEBUT *The Terrifics* (Vol. 1) #1 *(Apr 2018)*
BASE Terrifics Island
MEMBERS/POWERS Mister Terrific: Genius intellect; **Metamorpho**: Can turn body into any element; **Phantom Girl**: Intangibility, fires dark energy blasts; **Plastic Man**: Can stretch into any shape.
ALLIES Justice League, Tom Strong, Element Dog, T-Council
ENEMIES Doc Dread, The Dreadfuls, The Dark Elder, The Terribles

When Mr. Terrific visited unscrupulous businessman Simon Stagg, he discovered that Stagg was trying to open a doorway to the Dark Multiverse, having transformed Metamorpho into Nth Metal. Mr. Terrific had brought Plastic Man in his comatose "egg" form, knowing he was one of the few beings unaffected by Nth Metal; but before he could bring Plastic Man into play, both of them were sucked into the Dark Multiverse with Metamorpho. Here they met Phantom Girl, who had been lost in the Dark Multiverse for years.

Although the four of them made it safely back, the interdimensional journey had created a bond of dark energy between them that meant that they would explode if they were further than one mile apart. And so The Terrifics were born—a team created from necessity. After another trip between dimensions, The Terrifics' bond was broken and they separated, much to the distress of Phantom Girl. But when Mr. Terrific was in danger in the Multiverse, the team reformed to save him. Now they would stay together not because they had to, but because they wanted to.

Along the way, The Terrifics acquired additional members: Element Dog, Plastic Man's son Offspring, and Ms. Terrific, a version of Mr. Terrific's late wife from another reality.

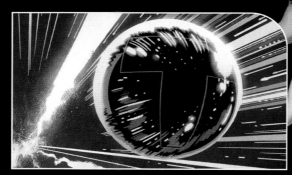

OPPOSITES ATTRACT
The Terrifics comprised very different personalities and abilities, but, despite this, the team possessed an alchemy that worked; a bond that was like that of a family.

THANAGARIANS, THE

DEBUT *The Brave and the Bold* (Vol. 1) #34 (Mar. 1961)
BASE Thanagar Prime
POWERS/ABILITIES Great strength and speed; long-lived and fast-healing with resistance to temperature extremes and acute senses.
ALLIES Justice League United, Legion of Super-Heroes, Rann **ENEMIES** Onymar Synn, Hyanthis, Byth Rokk, Rann
AFFILIATIONS United Planets

Thanagar's is a militaristic culture; soldiers and law keepers are patterned on feathered raptors. Often referred to as "Hawkworld" it has suffered wars and rebellions. Thanagar's unique abundance of Nth metal—a mineral with supernatural properties—allowed Thanagarians to perfect anti-gravity technologies: flying at incredible speeds. The ore also empowered ancient demon Onimar Synn, who has dominated Thanagarians repeatedly over millennia.

After being liberated from renewed enslavement to the "Sin Eater," their capital became Thanagar Prime, with warrior Shayera Hol as Empress. The vaults on that notorious intergalactic banking world having been compromised by cosmic events such as the return of Perpetua, Thanagar's leaders agitated for a federation of worlds and the establishment of the United Planets.

THINKER

DEBUT *All Flash* #12 (Fall 1943)
BASE Belle Reve Penitentiary, Louisiana
POWERS/ABILITIES Hyperintelligence
ALLIES James Gordon Jr., Harley Quinn
ENEMIES All Flashes, Cyborg, Amanda Waller, O.M.A.C., Suicide Squad, Unknown Soldier

The codename Thinker has been used by many criminals since 1940s District Attorney Clifford DeVoe first realized he was far smarter than the gangsters he prosecuted. Initially just with brilliant cunning, and later with a brainpower-augmenting "Thinking Cap," DeVoe plagued original Flash Jay Garrick and the Justice Society of America for decades, singly and as a founding member of the Injustice Gang of the World.

Decades later, his title fell to teen bully Cliff Carmichael, whose mental issues were treated with circuits from DeVoe's Thinking Cap. Carmichael incorporated the tech into his own body, linking with computer systems to terrorize the world, but was defeated by a succession of Firestorms. Remanded into Amanda Waller's custody, Carmichael served in the Suicide Squad before his talent for betrayal led to his death. The third Thinker was minor criminal Des O'Connor. His innate telepathic powers were no match for the resolve of Batman.

THIRD ARMY

DEBUT *Green Lantern Annual* (Vol. 5) #1 (Oct. 2012)
POWERS/ABILITIES Superhuman strength; can survive vacuum, extreme cold, and radiation of space; communal mind link—they multiply by converting victims into versions of themselves.
ENEMIES White Lantern Kyle Rayner, Guy Gardner, Green Lantern Corps, Red Lantern Corps, Zamarons, Star Sapphire Corps
AFFILIATIONS Guardians of the Universe

The Third Army were a mind-linked bio-weapon designed by the Guardians of the Universe, and activated using the power of Volthoom, the First Lantern. The Army was released after the immortals decided that true order was only possible if free will was eradicated from the cosmos.

The Third Army were programmed to assimilate all life into their ranks. Though possession of a power ring from any Spectrum Corps offered protection from conversion, the drones were strong enough to dismember Lanterns and remove the rings.

Despite intense resistance from assorted color Corps, the creatures were on the verge of total triumph. However, protracted battles forced the Guardians to tap more of Volthoom's power, awakening their captive. He reclaimed his power and the Third Army disintegrated.

THIRST

DEBUT *Aquaman* (Vol. 6) #5 (Jun. 2003)
BASE Secret Sea
HEIGHT 6ft 8in **WEIGHT** Variable
EYES Black **HAIR** None
POWERS/ABILITIES Life energy absorption, water and moisture absorption, creation of zombie slaves.
ALLIES Hagen, Black Manta
ENEMIES Aquaman, the Waterbearer, Lady of the Lake, Sentinels of Magic

The Thirst is a mystical construct derived from river mud; an antithetical being who hunted the sorcerous deities who guarded the Secret Sea. This vast metaphysical ocean was comprised of the communal imagination of humanity and underpinned the health of the planet's watery arteries and ultimately the life of mankind.

The Thirst was reawakened when Aquaman used his mystic water-hand to perform evil acts. It stalked the sea king while scheming to drain all life on Earth. Anything the Thirst drained would be reborn as a withered husk subservient to its will.

After numerous battles with Aquaman, the arid atrocity was tricked into merging with its Atlantean adversary. Knowing that he could defeat the Thirst from within, Aquaman surrendered their combined totality to the spiritual perfection of the Secret Sea.

THOMPKINS, DR. LESLIE

DEBUT *Detective Comics* (Vol. 1) #457 (Mar. 1976)
BASE The East End, Gotham City
HEIGHT 5ft 7in   **WEIGHT** 130 lbs   **EYES** Blue   **HAIR** Gray
POWERS/ABILITIES Trained doctor and psychologist, with extensive experience in trauma injuries and drug dependency.
ALLIES Alfred Pennyworth, Bruce Wayne, Stephanie Brown, James Gordon, Jason Todd
ENEMIES Black Mask Society, Killer Croc
AFFILIATIONS Duke Thomas, Gotham City Child Services

Physician Leslie Thompkins comforted young Bruce Wayne on the night his parents were gunned down and, with family retainer Alfred Pennyworth, tried to provide the boy with a semblance of normality in his life. Despite her best efforts, Bruce became increasingly obsessive in the years following the murder. As he pursued the training that would carry him on his chosen path, Thompkins lost touch with him. When a bat-clad vigilante began punishing Gotham City gangsters, crooked cops and Super-Villains, Thompkins deduced that behind the mask and gadgets was the shattered child she had known. A skilled clinician and deeply compassionate, she forsook private practice to work in medical centers for Gotham City's deprived citizens. Her work brought her into contact with many of Batman's allies and associates, such as juvenile delinquent Jason Todd and Stephanie Brown, estranged daughter of costumed criminal Cluemaster. Thompkins is strictly neutral, treating heroes, villains and innocent bystanders equally. During the No-Man's Land crisis following an earthquake that crushed the city, her clinic was a beacon of hope.

Dr. Thompkins spends time re-homing orphans and runaways in Gotham City's Child Protection system. This brought her into contact with some of the City's most conflicted characters, such as Duke Thomas and Catwoman. She actively contested Batman and Batwoman's continued use of teenagers in their war, and became personally involved in it—another potential victim in the Joker's crusade against Batman.

HEART AND SOUL
Leslie Thompkins' greatest regret was that she was unable to persuade Batman's "family" to adopt less violent methods to keep Gotham City's monsters at bay.

ON THE RECORD

Leslie Thompkins was introduced in the classic Batman story "There is No Hope in Crime Alley." Here Batman was shown to visit a sordid backstreet of Gotham City on a particular night every year. This time, however, he saves a gentle old lady from muggers and a flashback reveals how that gentle stranger once reached out to the terrified young Bruce Wayne after the murder of his parents. Leslie offered love and comfort during the most horrific moment of his life.

ANGEL OF HOPE
Leslie Thompkins always knew that orphaned little Bruce would grow up to be a most remarkable man.

THUNDER AND LIGHTNING

DEBUT *New Teen Titans* (Vol. 1) #32 (Jun. 1983)
REAL NAMES Alexei and Ayla
EYES Black (Alexei); Brown (Ayla)
HAIR Brown (Alexei); Blonde (Ayla)
POWERS/ABILITIES Alexei: Able to generate destructive sonic wave-fronts by clapping his hands together; Alya: Can absorb energy and generate electrical blasts.
ENEMIES Harvest, N.O.W.H.E.R.E., Brother Blood, Niles Caulder
ALLIES The Ravagers

Metahuman siblings Alexei and Ayla don't know who they are or where they come from. Their earliest memories are of being experimented upon by N.O.W.H.E.R.E. technicians, who sought to boost their powers and make them the most potent living weapons possible.

As victors of the brutal gladiatorial contests known as the Culling, Thunder and Lightning were expected to join Harvest's murderous elite kill-squads. However, they were rescued by undercover operative Caitlin Fairchild, the Teen Titans, and a few time-displaced Legionnaires. Alexei and Ayla joined Fairchild's fugitive band of Ravagers but could find no peace. On the run from time-traveling tyrant Harvest, the twins stumbled from one battle to another and have since gone into hiding.

THUNDER III

DEBUT *Outsiders* (Vol. 3) #1 (Aug. 2003)
REAL NAME Anissa Pierce
BASE Brooklyn, New York; New Orleans, Louisiana
HEIGHT 5ft 7in   **WEIGHT** 119 lbs
EYES Brown   **HAIR** Black
POWERS/ABILITIES Can increase mass and density; super-strength and invulnerability; creates shockwaves by striking the ground.

The daughter of Super Hero Black Lightning, Anissa Pierce followed her father's wishes and went to college before starting her own crime-busting career. However, on the day she qualified as a doctor, she donned a costume for the first time and began helping people in a more unique way as the Super Hero Thunder. Her sister Jennifer later took up costumed crime-fighting as Lightning. Just after her solo debut, Anissa accepted a place with The Outsiders, reasoning that the best place to learn was with seasoned professionals. Soon she was tackling some of the most terrifying villains around, like Simon Hurt and Brother Blood, and also started a relationship with her teammate Grace.

Anissa was seriously wounded many times. Once, after triggering a booby-trap, she was in a coma for months, and later went into semi-retirement.

THUNDER, JAKEEM

DEBUT *The Flash* (Vol. 2) #134 (Feb. 1998)
REAL NAME Jakeem Johnny Williams
BASE Keystone City; New York City
HEIGHT 5ft 7in   **WEIGHT** 130 lbs   **EYES** Brown   **HAIR** Black
POWERS/ABILITIES Inherited control of "Thunderbolt" Genie from the original Yz/Johnny Thunder to deploy Fifth Dimensional science.
ALLIES Yz/Johnny Thunder, Djinn, Stargirl
ENEMIES Triumph, Solomon Grundy, Mordru

After meeting the first Flash, orphan Jakeem Williams kept the pen Jay Garrick had used to sign autographs. Nobody realized that it housed elderly Johnny Thunder's Fifth Dimensional companion, Yz. The Thunderbolt bonded with Jakeem, and when a malign sprite from Yz's dimension invaded Earth, Yz and Jakeem were instrumental in helping the JSA defeat it. To accomplish the feat, Yz had to merge with fellow thunderbolt Lkz into a whole new entity—Yzlkz—activated whenever Jakeem clicked the pen and uttered the phrase, "So Cûl" (so cool).

An orphaned street kid, Jakeem was initially reluctant to join the JSA, but soon made friends with younger members such as Stargirl. As one of the team's "legacy heroes," he became an invaluable member of both the JSA and its First Strike component the All-Star Squadron.

THUNDER, JOHNNY

DEBUT *Flash Comics* (Vol. 1) #1 (Jan. 1940)
REAL NAME Jonathan L. Thunder
BASE New York City; Gotham City; the Fifth Dimension
HEIGHT 5ft 8in   **WEIGHT** 125 lbs
EYES Blue   **HAIR** Blond
POWERS/ABILITIES Absolute control over a wish-granting "Thunderbolt" Genie—in reality an energy being able to employ science from the Fifth Dimension.

Johnny Thunder was the seventh son of a seventh son born under mystical circumstances. As an infant, he was taken by cultists from Bahdnisia, and through arcane rites was bonded to a powerful wishing genie. Under fortuitous circumstances—luck always favored Johnny—he was rescued before his seventh birthday and returned to his family in Brooklyn. For years, he never realized the phrase "Cei U" (say you) activated Yz, his invisible wish-granting Thunderbolt, for an "hour of power." An honest, decent soul, Johnny became an unlikely hero helping those in need through his "luck."

Johnny served the JSA with implausible distinction for many decades. He was murdered by the Ultra-Humanite, but his personality was absorbed by Yz. They now abide in the Fifth Dimension.

THUNDER, JONNI

DEBUT *Jonni Thunder* (Vol. 1) #1 (Feb. 1985)
BASE Los Angeles, California
HEIGHT 5ft 6in **WEIGHT** 130 lbs
EYES Green **HAIR** Blond
POWERS/ABILITIES Partially controlled ability to possess a high-voltage electrical entity.
ALLIES Harry Trump, Shamus, Skyman
ENEMIES Clarence "Slim" Chance, Red Nails
AFFILLIATIONS J. Thunder Detective Agency, Infinity Incorporated

Jonni Thunder was a tough-as-nails Los Angeles private eye. She gained accidental control of a magical thunderbolt, which lived in an old lamp belonging to her father, a former cop. His former partner Slim Chance desperately sought the artifact, eventually attempting to kill Jonni for it.

After Jonni brought Chance to justice, she remained on the fringe of the LA metahuman community. She was always reluctant to acknowledge her powers, but she did work closely with millionaire hero Sylvester Pemberton in his roles as Skyman and founder of Infinity Incorporated.

An alternate Jonni Thunder recently appeared on Earth-2, liberated from World Army incarceration by John Constantine. She joined Brainwave in trying to enslave the last survivors of humanity, and it is unknown if she survived the planet's annihilation.

TIMBER WOLF

DEBUT *Adventure Comics* (Vol. 1) #327 (Dec. 1964)
REAL NAME Brin Londo
BASE Legion HQ, 31st-century New Metropolis
EYES Brown/Golden **HAIR** Brown
POWERS/ABILITIES Human/wolf hybrid; enhanced senses, strength, speed, and agility, sharp claws.
ENEMIES Horraz, Crav the General Nah, Mordru

Zuunian Brin Londo gained super-strength, speed, agility plus enhanced senses and durability after being the subject of illegal experiments by his own father.

Zuun is a desolate, depleted world, and the experiments were intended to create a super-powered warrior to defend what little resources the planet still possessed. The harsh early life of pain and duty made Brin a ferocious defender of the weak: an animalistic alpha dog always ready to spring into action or die to preserve his "pack."

The tough attitude and willingness to fight make him one of the teams' greatest assets in action, but his gruff exterior masks a sensitive philosophical side. He is a confirmed advocate of the United Planets for the simple reason that his childhood proves how bad life might be without peace and civilization.

TIME MASTERS

DEBUT *Showcase* #20 (May–Jun. 1959) (as Rip Hunter and crew); *Time Masters* #1 (Feb. 1990) (as Time Masters team)
BASE Vanishing Point, Rip Hunter Time Lab, Arizona Lab, Arizona
MEMBERS Rip Hunter, Dan Hunter, Tony, Bonnie Baxter, Corky Baxter, Jeff Smith, Booster Gold, Superman, Green Lantern Hal Jordan
ALLIES Starfire II, Claw the Unconquered, Skeets
ENEMIES Illuminati, Vandal Savage, Gog, Black Beetle, Per Degaton, Despero

The Time Masters are a loose affiliation of explorers and heroes assembled by scientist, and time-traveler, Rip Hunter to unearth the secret history of Earth and preserve the sanctity of the timeline.

Hunter convened a second team to rescue Batman after he was cast adrift in the timestream by Darkseid. Superman, Green Lantern, and Booster Gold tracked the Dark Knight from era to era, but Batman returned to his original time through his own efforts.

A later team, consisting of Hunter, Booster Gold, and his sister Michelle Carter currently act as clandestine custodians of the timestream; protecting reality from villains seeking to bend history to their desires. Other than a recent alliance of Rip Hunter and the Green Lantern Corps to stop future-born time-meddler Sarko, the Time Masters have been missing in action since Doctor Manhattan used his powers to erase them from history.

TIME TRAPPER

DEBUT *Adventure Comics* (Vol. 1) #318 (Mar. 1964)
BASE The End of Time
POWERS/ABILITIES Immortality, transformation, manipulation of the timestream.
ALLIES Glorith
ENEMIES Mordru, Legion of Super-Heroes, Superman, Parallax

The Time Trapper is a sentient force resident at the end of space/time. An aspect of cosmic entropy, it easily weathers the dramatic changes wrought by reality-revisions such as the *Infinite Crisis* and *Zero Hour*. Each time the Multiverse has changed or shifted, the Trapper has been personified by a new being. Previous examples have included: Cosmic Man, Rokk Krinn; Time Witch, Glorith; a Malthusian Controller, Lori Morning; and even the psychotic Superboy-Prime.

The Trapper has spent much of his attention challenging the 31st-century Legion of Super-Heroes and claims to have been instrumental in their creation as a weapon against his true enemy, Mordru. However, having complete control over the future, his ultimate goal remains constant: To bring about the dissolution of Creation in preparation for a new Big Bang.

TITANS, THE

DEBUT *Titans Hunt* Vol. 1 #1 (Dec 2015)
BASE Hall of Justice, Washington D.C.
MEMBERS/POWERS Miss Martian: Telepathy; **Donna Troy**: Amazonian warrior; **Beast Boy**: Shapeshifter; **Green Lantern** (Kyle Rayner): Ability to form light constructs and fly; **Raven**: Extensive magical powers, including the ability to separate her soul-self from her physical body; **Steel**: Genius engineer, armor made from semi-sentient metal, kinetic hammer.
ALLIES Justice League, Teen Titans, Ben Rubel
ENEMIES Deathstroke, H.I.V.E., Troia, Blood Cult

The original Titans team grew out of the Teen Titans, as former Super Hero sidekicks sought to forge a path separate from their mentors. The Titans were characterized not only by heroics and a desire to help people, but by a close bond of friendship. After the disbanding of that team, former member Nightwing decided to assemble a new lineup in response to the breaking of the Source Wall. Energy from this cosmic cataclysm was causing problems on Earth, with ordinary people suddenly gaining metahuman powers. The Justice League was fully occupied with facing the main threat, and so a new team was needed to deal with earthbound problems.

Nightwing chose his members carefully, getting a range of skill sets to cope with any scenario. However, when he was shot and badly wounded on a mission, the team were forced to try and carry on without him. Donna Troy, another member of the original Titans, assumed leadership, determined to inject some of that spirit into the new iteration. Nightwing had wanted the Titans to be as fearless as they had been as kids but as strong as the Justice League, and Donna inspired her teammates to be just that. Gaining Green Lantern Kyle Rayner as a member, the team was ready to go from strength to strength.

NEW TITANS Nightwing's new Titans lineup, assembled in the wake of the death of a girl struggling with new powers, had the patron saint of lost causes as its totem.

TOMAHAWK

DEBUT *Star-Spangled Comics* (Vol. 1) #69 (Jun. 1947)
POWERS/ABILITIES Advanced unarmed combat skills; proficiency with knife, spear, bow and arrows, and throwing hatchet.
ALLIES Blue Jacket, Tecumseh, the Prophet
ENEMIES General Anthony Wayne, General George Washington, General Arthur St. Clair
AFFILIATIONS Iroquois Tribe, Shawnee Tribe

Born of Iroquois and Shawnee blood, Tomahawk was a mighty warrior among the Indian nations. He battled long and hard against the white invaders who were inexorably swallowing up their land.

When George Washington ordered ruthless General Anthony Wayne to wipe out every Indian settlement in the territory, Tomahawk's family were killed and he swore vengeance on all Americans. He had allies among the British forces occupying the colonies, but when he sought their help, he was betrayed as the white men worked together to force the Indians out.

Tomahawk's braves won another battle against the united invaders, and he took revenge on the man who killed his kin, but he realized his people would never know peace and security again.

TOMAR-TU

DEBUT *Green Lantern* (Vol. 2) #6 (May–Jun. 1961)
BASE Xudar, Space Sector 2813
HEIGHT 6ft 2in **WEIGHT** 210 lbs **EYES** Red **HAIR** No hair, orange fins
POWERS/ABILITIES Commands a Green power ring able to materialize hard-light constructs, translate languages, generate in-planet and intergalactic flight, and protect against hostile environments and enemy attack; latterly Darkstar Mantle providing flight, force fields, energy blasts, sensor array, teleportation
ALLIES Kilowog, John Stewart,
ENEMIES Hal Jordan, Romat-Ru
AFFILIATIONS Darkstars, Green Lantern Corps, Controllers

Tomar-Tu inherited the space sector of his illustrious father Tomar-Re, following his civilian endeavors against mad Guardian Appa Ali Apsa. When the renegade Oan assembled his mosaic world from abducted cities of many civilizations, Tu was leader of the resistance. When the crisis was averted, Hal Jordan recommended him for the vacant beat of Space Sector 2813.

Following Sinestro's war on the Green Lanterns, Tu felt compelled to testify against a colleague after GL Laira executed Sinestro Corpsman Amon Sur in cold blood. Years later, he followed in her footsteps. When child killer Romat-Ru taunted Tu and threated more children, the weary Green Lantern killed him. Arrested and resigned to pay for his crime, Tu was then co-opted by a Darkstar mantle. Seduced by the offer of immense power and leadership of a hardline army, Tu helmed the Darkstar campaign to execute all murders in the universe. His battle with the Green Lanterns resulted in his death and the succession of youthful Somar-Le to the role of Green Lantern of Xudar and Sector 2813.

ON THE RECORD

Tomar-Re patrolled the Space Sector adjacent to Hal Jordan's and became his friend and mentor. A scientist and warrior, he was elevated to the elite Green Lantern Honor Guard. He safeguarded Jordan and Sinestro when Black Hand trapped them in Nekron's Dead Zone. Dispatched by the Guardians to stop planet Krypton exploding, he was blinded. Tomar had no idea that his temporary affliction was instrumental in the creation of the universe's greatest hero: Superman.

LANTERN CALLING
Tomar-Re used his power ring to contact Hal Jordan and request his help in saving the planet Aku.

TOMORROW, TOMMY

DEBUT *Real Fact Comics* #6 (Jan. 1947)
REAL NAME T'omas T'Marra
BASE Tolerance, Tenebrian Dominion
EYES Blue **HAIR** Blond
POWERS/ABILITIES Cunning planner and problem-solver with advanced combat skills.
ALLIES Brent Wood, Tuftan the Tiger Prince
ENEMIES Jediah Caul, Star Sapphire, Stealth, Rikane Starr, Knights of the Galaxy

Tommy Tomorrow's most consistent history is as a valiant explorer, peacekeeper, and an agent of the Planeteers. In another time and dimension he was Kamandi, the Last Boy on Earth, struggling to re-establish humanity on a planet teeming with intelligent and aggressive animals. In yet another reality, Major Thomas Tomorrow is a military martinet with a secret agenda.

His most recent transformation took him to the Tenebrian Dominion as Colonel T'omas T'Marra: a double-dealing opportunist secretly running the galaxy's most popular entertainment. Glimmernet sensation *The Hunted* is a gameshow where viewers can win big prizes simply by catching and killing the featured stars. Naturally, T'Marra has more than one reason to keep the runners running and the pursuers confused.

TOYMAN (WINSLOW SCHOTT)

DEBUT *Action Comics* (Vol. 1) #64 (Sep. 1943)
REAL NAME Winslow Schott
BASE Metropolis
EYES Blue **HAIR** Brown
POWERS/ABILITIES Inspired engineer, brilliant in mechanical, robotics and circuit-design.
ENEMIES Lex Luthor, Superman

Many men have claimed the title of Toyman, transforming toys into weapons of profit and vengeance. The first was Winslow Schott, a failed toymaker who has plagued every incarnation of Superman over many reality-alterations, warping wholesome childhood fantasies into a deadly criminal arsenal. Others have included super-thief Jack Nimball, and Schott's son Anton, whose twisted mind turned children into living dolls—until he killed them. Following *Rebirth*, Schott attacked Metropolis to gain revenge on Lex Luthor, who had crushed his toy company in a hostile takeover. Schott responded by weaponizing his designs and unleashing explosive destruction all over the city to ruin the now Lexcorp-owned business. As Superman crushed his giant robots and deadly drones, Schott never realized Luthor's true game-plan: forcing the inventive Toyman to create new technology Lexcorp could steal and sell to the military.

TOYMASTER

DEBUT *Batman/Superman* (Vol. 1) #5 (Jan. 2014)
REAL NAME Hiro Okamura
BASE Gotham City
HEIGHT Unknown **WEIGHT** Unknown
EYES Brown **HAIR** Black
POWERS/ABILITIES Genius intellect.
ALLIES Superman, Batman
ENEMIES Mongul, Ultra-Humanite
AFFILIATIONS None

Hiro Okamura was a very rich, very intelligent teenager who used his genius to create cutting-edge games and other tech. After inadvertently aiding Mongul in an attempt to use Earth's population to kill Superman, Hiro became an ally of the Man of Steel. Later, when Toymaster was forced by Mongul to build a set of robots to defeat the Justice League in an arena battle, he secretly enabled the robots to be taken over and combined by the League into one giant mechanoid to defeat Mongul.

He also built many other devices designed to repel another incursion by the Dark Multiverse, including a giant robot that combined visual aspects of the Trinity: Wonder Woman, Superman and Batman.

TRACI 13

DEBUT *Superman* (Vol. 2) #189 (Feb. 2003)
BASE Metropolis **HEIGHT** 5ft 5in
WEIGHT 127 lbs **EYES** Brown **HAIR** Black **POWERS/ABILITIES** Urban magic; cast spells. **ALLIES** Leroy, Blue Beetle, Kid Eternity, Zatanna, Baron Winters, Detective Chimp
ENEMIES Otherkind, Shadowriders, Heartbreakers, Eclipso, Brother Blood, the Futuresmith **AFFILIATIONS** Night Force

Traci Thirteen inherited her witchly powers from her mother—a member of human sub-species Homo Magi—and when Mrs. Thirteen died, Traci's dad blamed her, forbidding Traci from ever using her gifts. When he suddenly vanished, Traci began accruing mystical knowledge and established herself in Metropolis as freelance supernatural problem-solver Girl 13, AKA Traci 13. Traci was later reunited with her father, who had been possessed by Heartbreaker demons after her mother died.

Traci then formed a witches' society: the Sisterhood of the Sleight Hand offering mystical aid to mortal heroes. She briefly worked with Baron Winters' Night Force to stop a supernatural murder spree, and when not working at the Oblivion Bar, now battles beside Justice League Dark to stop the predations of the Otherkind.

TRENCH, THE

DEBUT *Aquaman* (Vol. 7) #1 (Nov. 2011)
BASE Marianas Trench, Pacific Ocean
EYES Black **HAIR** None
POWERS/ABILITIES Water-breathing; immense strength; neuro-toxic secretions; mimicry; bioluminescence; steel-rending teeth and claws; weave cocoons to transport prey.
ENEMIES Aquaman, Mera
AFFILIATIONS King Atlan, Dead King's Scepter, Atlantis, Xebel

The cannibalistic Trench subsisted in utter darkness at the bottom of Earth's Marianas Trench for eons, unsuspected and forgotten by the sub-sea empire of Atlantis, which had developed in shallower regions. In recent times, shifts in sea-floor geology allowed the Trench to rise from the depths, to discover waters and land teeming with potential sustenance.

They were eventually turned back by Aquaman and Mera, who found the beasts were actually gathering food to feed their next generation. When Queen Mera held her royal wedding ceremony in Xebel, the proceedings were disrupted by the return of an army of Trench, demanding the return of an unknown object. When they were eventually driven off by Aqualad Jackson Hyde, the previously non-communicative monsters swore to take their revenge.

TREVOR, STEVE

DEBUT *All-Star Comics* (Vol. 1) #8 (Dec. 1941–Jan. 1942)
REAL NAME Steven Rockwell Trevor
HEIGHT 6ft 1in **WEIGHT** 195 lbs **EYES** Blue **HAIR** Blond
POWERS/ABILITIES Expert pilot and military tactician.
ALLIES Wonder Woman, Etta Candy, Barbara Minerva
ENEMIES Colonel Andres Cadulo, Phobos, Deimos, Veronica Cale/
Godwatch **AFFILIATIONS** A.R.G.U.S., Justice League of America,
Oddfellows, US Air Force, US Navy Seals, Team 7

A.R.G.U.S. ORIGINS
The President personally asked Trevor to become the founder and acting director of A.R.G.U.S.

A true warrior, decorated pilot and respected command officer, Steve Trevor met the Amazon Diana when his plane crashed on hidden island Themyscira. She nursed him back to health and —after winning a fierce worthiness contest—escorted him and the bodies of his fallen comrades back to the outside world. A veteran soldier, well-respected in the intelligence community, Trevor became her advocate— guiding her through the labyrinth of security organizations such as the DEO and A.R.G.U.S.—and inevitably, her lover. As Wonder Woman, Diana saved him when Trevor was kidnapped by Colonel Andres Cadulo as a vessel of transformation for plant god Urzkartarga, but their relationship stalled when Phobos and Deimos—the spiteful sons of war god Ares—altered their minds and memories.

Eventually, the lovers were reunited. Trevor retired from the military and took command of the Oddfellows—the Black Room field regiment of A.R.G.U.S.: investigating metahuman and unnatural activities. With Diana, Trevor has faced terrorists, gods such as Ares and Darkseid, a global virus, paramilitary force Poison and Veronica Cale's Super-Villain agency Godwatch. With the Multiverse unraveling thanks to threats like Perpetua and the Dark Multiverse invasion, Trevor remains steadfast, valiant and ready for action.

DARKSEID INVASION
Steve Trevor was at Wonder Woman's side when Darkseid unleashed his terrifying Parademons on Earth.

TRICKSTER

DEBUT *The Flash* (Vol. 2) #183 (Apr. 2002)
REAL NAME James Jesse Axel Walker
BASE Central City
HEIGHT 5ft 7in **WEIGHT** 150 lbs **EYES** Blue **HAIR** Blond
POWERS/ABILITIES High intelligence, brilliant conman; skilled acrobat and escapologist; anti-gravity boots, numerous modified gadgets based on practical jokes and clowning.
ALLIES Captain Cold, Mirror Master, Weather Wizard, Heat Wave
ENEMIES The Flash, Johnny Quick, Captain Cold
AFFILIATIONS Legion of Zoom, Secret Society of Super-Villains, Rogues, FBI

The first Trickster was James Jesse—stage name of Giovanni Giuseppe—a trapeze artist scared of heights and his abusive conmen parents. Turning to crime, he pitted his wits against The Flash, Blue Devil and others, before turning FBI informant and retiring. Returning to crime, he was again defeated by The Flash and imprisoned in Super-penitentiary Iron Heights.

Sometime later, Super-Villain Blacksmith needed someone with similar skills in her gang and selected wayward teenager Axel Walker, giving him upgraded Trickster gimmicks. After suffering appalling treatment in prison, Jesse broke out—the first ever to do so—and restarted his own crime career. He began spectacularly but secretly: saving Walker from certain death.

The self-proclaimed "greatest conman to ever live" swore to restore his tattered reputation. His scheme was stunning: making all Central City dangerously happy, by employing the mind-bending Sage Force to control the population. When The Flash and Commander Cold stopped the enforced jolly torment, Jesse was content that he had at least heaped revenge on Iron Heights' brutal warden, Gregory Wolfe. The Trickster is now a member of the Reverse-Flash's Legion of Zoom.

EASY MONEY
The Trickster puts his anti-gravity footwear to good use, escaping from the scenes of his crimes.

TRIGON

DEBUT *New Teen Titans* (Vol. 1) #2 (Dec. 1980)
BASE Azarath
HEIGHT Variable **WEIGHT** Variable **EYES** Yellow **HAIR** Black
POWERS/ABILITIES Demonic powers including draining souls, unleashing energies, transmutation of elements, destroying planets.
ENEMIES Teen Titans, The Divine

An ancient trinity of cosmic entities known as the Divine attempted to eradicate evil from the universe. Punishing the brutal conqueror of a world, they sentenced him to be consumed by the Heart of Darkness, but he fought back, feeding on the Heart, assimilating the evils of a billion worlds and transforming into all-powerful demon, Trigon.

He ruled the Under-Realms, but could not pass a mystic barrier built by the Divine and to spread his evil, fathered children on denizens of target worlds. One of these was human girl Raven, whom Trigon believed would unify all dimensions under his rule. When she fled to sanctuary dimension Azarath, Trigon began a campaign to call forth her dark side.

After many humiliating defeats by the Teen Titans, Trigon's ambitions came closer to fruition when he allied with 2morrowTek, who genetically engineered hosts for his progeny. The scheme was thwarted by Raven in alliance with amoral mystic enigma Baron Winters. Recently, his dreams came true after the Untitled brought Trigon to Earth. He was intercepted by Essence, Red Hood and Artemis, and the demon lord seemingly perished battling Bizarro.

ON THE RECORD

Trigon's home dimension of Azarath was once said to be a place of peace, overseen by powerful sorcerers who raised Raven under their protection when she rejected her father's evil, and fought to prevent Trigon from breaching the barriers between their dimension and Earth's.

Trigon finally succeeded and Raven, seeing no other choice, agreed to rule with him if he spared Earth. Knowing he wouldn't keep his side of the bargain, she gathered the New Teen Titans to fight against his coming invasion. Their defeat of Trigon was their signature achievement.

RAVEN'S SACRIFICE
Facing Trigon in the Temple of Azarath, the Titans were easily defeated. Raven realized that the only way to save Earth was to join her father. Together they vanished in a cloud of smoke.

TRIAD

DEBUT *Action Comics* (Vol. 1) #276 (May 1961)
REAL NAME Luornu Durgo
BASE Legion HQ, 31st-century New Metropolis
HEIGHT 5ft 6in **WEIGHT** 125 lbs
EYES Amber, purple **HAIR** Brown
POWERS/ABILITIES Can divide into three or more different bodies; martial-arts training takes advantage of fighting with multiple bodies as a unit.
ENEMIES Horraz, Crav the General Nah, Mordru

Although Luornu Durgo only has one name, she considers herself a plurality of three. Known at various times as Triplicate Girl and Duplicate Girl, she was born on Cargg, where the triple suns give native Carggites the ability to split into identical duplicates. Unlike most Carggites, however, Luornu's duplicates manifest individual personalities. They all experience the world individually but when they remerge, the accumulated memories are processed by one single gestalt personality.

Luornu joined the Legion of Super-Heroes to do as much good as possible, but after enduring the red-tape of the United Planets, constantly debates with herselves if they wouldn't be more useful fighting crime back on Cargg.

TROY, DONNA

DEBUT *The Brave and the Bold* (Vol. 1) #60 (Jun.–Jul. 1965)
BASE New York City
HEIGHT 5ft 9in **WEIGHT** 135 lbs **EYES** Brown **HAIR** Black
POWERS/ABILITIES Amazonian physiology bestows enhanced intellect and superhuman strength, endurance, agility, and durability; advanced healing factor; expert fighter; weapons include Amazon armor and swords.
ALLIES Dick Grayson, Arsenal, Wonder Woman, Wally West (first Kid Flash)
ENEMIES Mr. Twister, Aegeus, Troia
AFFILIATIONS The Titans, Amazons

Donna Troy was a valiant hero in every iteration of Earth's reality. She has fought injustice in the Teen Titans and their adult incarnation, but her origins have radically shifted in every instance. After *Rebirth*, she discovered the horrific answer: She was not an Amazon, a human mystically empowered or even a small girl raised and modified by the Titans of Myth. After the return of original Kid Flash Wally West began unraveling malicious alterations to the timestream, Donna learned that she was not even alive, but a construct of clay animated by magic: An Amazon golem created to destroy Princess Diana if she ever went rogue.

With false memories crafted by the Amazons, Donna had carved out a life as a Super Hero, but even that comfort was taken from her after the Titans were attacked by a horror from the future. Troia was Donna Troy after all her friends had died: a psychotic killer who had traveled back to eradicate them before they could ever leave her. Donna defeated Troia, swearing that she would never let this possible future come to pass. She and her Titan allies now continue their crusade for justice across the Multiverse.

FORGOTTEN TITANS
When Donna Troy discovered she had mysterious shared memories with other heroes, including Dick Grayson and Arsenal, she teamed up with these so-called Titans and came into conflict with the dastardly Mister Twister.

ON THE RECORD

Donna Troy's backstory has been an ever-evolving one, nearly from the time of her creation. Originally conceived as Wonder Girl, Donna was meant to be a teenage version of Wonder Woman as a founding member of the newly formed Teen Titans. She became one of the team's mainstays, taking the independent name Donna Troy, and appearing only once in a Wonder Woman story during the Bronze Age.

Continuity was altered in the 1980s to recreate Donna as a girl chosen for training by the Titans of Myth, during which she adopted the name Troia. In the 1990s, Donna was reestablished once more, but this time as a magical doppelgänger of Wonder Woman brought to life, while Diana was out of action for a while.

THE RETURN
Donna Troy's history was somewhat streamlined after she was killed by a rogue Superman robot. She came back as a combination of all her past selves, but relied primarily on her Titans of Myth origin.

TUI, KATMA

DEBUT *Green Lantern* (Vol. 2) #30 (Jul. 1964)
BASE Coast City
HEIGHT 5ft 11in **WEIGHT** 131 lbs
EYES Blue **HAIR** Black
POWERS/ABILITIES Green Lantern ring allows flight, force-fields, and space travel.
ALLIES Green Lanterns: John Stewart, Hal Jordan, and Kilowog
ENEMIES Sinestro, Star Sapphire

NOTHING SINISTER
Though from the same planet as Sinestro, the only other trait Katma Tui shared with the corrupt Green Lantern was her skill with a power ring.

Born on the planet Korugar, Katma Tui became the Green Lantern for Space Sector 1417, replacing the corrupt Lantern-turned-Super-Villain, Sinestro. Despite a difficult start, with the Korugarians distrusting the Green Lanterns and regarding their new protector as "Katma Tui the Lost," Katma went on to prove herself many times over.

After several successful missions, she was assigned to train another Green Lantern, John Stewart, and, after a rocky start to their relationship, they fell in love. She eventually journeyed to Earth with John to help form Earth's own Green Lantern Corps, and the two married. Some time later, during a home invasion by Star Sapphire, Katma was viciously killed. John never fully recovered from the loss, haunted by her death for years after.

Katma would see life in a fashion one last time when resurrected as part of the Black Lantern Corps. However, this evil, undead version of the once well-respected hero was ultimately destroyed.

TULA

DEBUT *Aquaman* (Vol. 1) #33 (May–Jun. 1967)
REAL NAME Tula Marius
BASE Atlantis
HEIGHT 5ft 5in **WEIGHT** 119 lbs
EYES Blue **HAIR** Brown
POWERS/ABILITIES Atlantean warrior adept with many weapons; able to breathe underwater, swim at extreme speeds; super-strong, durable, enhanced senses and reflexes
ALLIES Mera, Aquaman, Sea Devils, Murk, Tempest, Ocean Master **ENEMIES** Scavenger, Black Manta, The Trench, Coram Rath

EASILY MISGUIDED
In her relatively short career as commander of the Drift, Tula has mistakenly followed a corrupt Mera impostor and the villain Ocean Master.

Atlantean Tula first became known to the surface world when Ocean Master—Aquaman's half-brother Orm—led an invasion against the US and surface world. When Aquaman defeated Orm, reclaiming the throne of Atlantis, he met with Tula who commanded the Drift, an elite faction of the Atlantean army. Tula had her own allegiances. As Orm's sister, she was determined to liberate him from Belle Reve prison with the help of loyalists such as Murk and Swatt. The plan failed because Atlantis was attacked by the Scavenger, and dutiful Tula and her allies went home to help.

Tula later proved her loyalty toward Mera, accepting her as queen for the sake of peace. Tula also accepted Aquaman and he made her regent of Atlantis. She was arrested when Coram Rath usurped the throne, but fled to Amnesty Bay with Mera. When Mera became queen again, Tula acted as a bodyguard to the royal family.

TURTLE, THE

DEBUT *All-Flash* (Vol. 1) #21 (Dec. 1945)
REAL NAME Unknown
BASE Hall of Doom
HEIGHT Unknown
WEIGHT Unknown
EYES Green
HAIR Gray/Blond
POWERS/ABILITIES Connection to the Still Force
ALLIES Gorilla Grodd
ENEMIES The Flash, Justice League
AFFILIATIONS Legion of Doom

HOLDING THE BABY
Super-intelligent Gorilla Grodd of The Flash's rogues gallery made a most improbable carer for the childlike villain The Turtle.

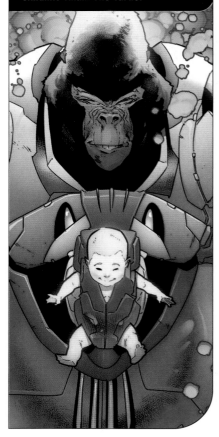

The Turtle was a scientist who had experimented with the Still Force, a powerful energy that represented inertia and was the opposite of the Speed Force. When an accident infused him with the power of the Still Force, he became obsessed with discovering the truth behind it and was drawn to The Flash, with whom he now felt an elemental connection. He was the first villain The Flash fought, and nearly turned out to be the last when a future version of The Turtle, then ruler of Central City, traveled in time to try and steal The Flash's Speed Force.

Following this defeat, The Turtle was reborn in the body of a baby. Recognizing the potential of the child to help him access all the hidden powers of the Multiverse, Lex Luthor took him to be part of his new Legion of Doom, securely strapped to the chest of Gorilla Grodd so that the ape could use his mental abilities to amplify and project the child's power.

TWEEDLEDEE AND TWEEDLEDUM

DEBUT *Detective Comics* #74 (Apr. 1943)
REAL NAMES Deever and Dumpson Tweed: formerly Dumfree Tweed
BASE Gotham City
ALLIES Mad Hatter, Scarecrow, Kite Man, Hugo Strange
ENEMIES Batman, Bane
AFFILIATIONS Secret Society of Super-Villains, Wonderland Gang

DOUBLE TROUBLE
Tweedledee and Tweedledum seemed little more than a couple of musclebound thugs, but they aspired to be gang leaders in their own right.

Deever and Dumfree Tweed were cousins united in their love of Alice in Wonderland. Rotund, and immensely strong they decided to get rich as themed villains. After many battles against Batman, Dumphree was eventually replaced by cousin Dumpson but the diabolical duo remained little more than henchmen. After a stint with the Secret Society of Super-Villains, they united with the Mad Hatter in his Wonderland Gang for a series of robberies. Most believed the Hatter was in charge, but frequently the devious Tweeds controlled him, using one of his own mind-slave devices.

Cunning and ambitious, the Tweeds grew ever bolder, but never managed to defeat the Dark Knight. While incarcerated in Arkham Asylum, they fell under the sway of warped psychologist Hugo Strange and escaped imprisonment when Deathstroke wrecked his latest plot. When Bane seized control of Gotham, Tweedledum and Tweedledee declined to join his army, forming their own gang with Kite Man and Scarecrow. Both were reported killed fleeing from Batman.

TWO-FACE

DATA

DEBUT *Detective Comics* (Vol. 1) #66 (Aug. 1942)
REAL NAME Harvey Dent
BASE Gotham City
HEIGHT 6ft **WEIGHT** 182 lbs **EYES** Blue **HAIR** Brown
POWERS/ABILITIES Dangerous split personality makes him unpredictable; expert knowledge of law and police procedure; extremely intelligent and a brilliant strategist; relies on lucky coin to make decisions.
ALLIES Gilda Dent (deceased), Bruce Wayne (formerly), Amygdala, Solomon Grundy **ENEMIES** Batman, Batman Family, Erin McKillen
AFFILIATIONS The Secret Society of Super-Villains, Arkham Asylum inmates

Harvey Dent has led a deeply conflicted life. Possessing a split personality that veers between two extremes—good and evil— Dent goes by the name of Two-Face. It is an apt description of his physical appearance. Scarred by acid into outwardly becoming the monster he once hid away from the world, Two-Face has become a tragic figure and one of Batman's most unpredictable and dangerous opponents.

BIRTH OF TWO-FACE
In a violent, life-changing act of revenge, criminal Erin McKillen tied DA Harvey Dent to his desk and poured acid on his face, claiming that the world could now see how two-faced he truly was.

Harvey Dent lived an enviable life

in Gotham City. As a premier defense attorney with handsome features and a beautiful wife named Gilda, he had it all. Dent had gotten some of the city's worst criminals back on the street by using his knowledge of the law's technicalities. However, after working for the notorious McKillen Clan he was starting to rethink his priorities. Twin sisters Shannon and Erin McKillen had been old friends of Bruce Wayne since childhood, but both turned to crime in later years, even going as far as hiring a hit on Commissioner James Gordon. It was after this failed assassination attempt that Dent was approached by his old friend Bruce Wayne. Wayne admired Dent's legal skill and wanted him to run for District Attorney, turning his expertise towards putting criminals away rather than setting them free. Dent agreed to run for office, and soon he found himself partnering with both Jim Gordon and the Batman, setting his sights on the McKillen sisters.

After the McKillen twins were jailed, thanks in part to Harvey Dent's exemplary work as District Attorney, Shannon McKillen killed herself to give Erin a chance to break out. One of Erin's first stops was to Dent's office where she set about enacting savage revenge on the double-crossing lawyer she held responsible for her sister's death. She stabbed and killed Gilda, then knocked Harvey unconscious. When Harvey awoke, he was tied to his office desk, and Erin was pouring acid on his face, scarring him for life. It was on that day that Harvey Dent adopted the name Two-Face. He soon showed his talent as a cunning, if psychotic, master criminal who relies on a scarred coin to make his decisions for him, forever torn between his old, noble self and his dark side.

Two-Face's descent into madness worsened over the years. After failing at an attempt to take his own life, Two-Face scarred the entire left side of his body, in some mad attempt to experience complete good and complete evil. For a time, he even ran his own church of fanatical followers, until Batman saw him incarcerated once again.

CLASSIC STORIES

***Batman* (Vol. 1) #234 (Aug. 1971)**
Two-Face is reintroduced to Bronze Age comic readers in a classic tale that saw the villain seek gold hidden aboard an old ship.

***Batman* (Vol. 1) Annual #14 (Dec. 1990)** Two-Face is given an updated origin that ties neatly into "Batman: Year One" and deals with his fractured psyche.

***Batman: The Long Halloween* #1-13 (Dec. 1996-Jan. 1998)**
Harvey Dent's wholesale descent into madness is chronicled month-by-month as the mysterious Holiday serial killer strikes in Gotham City.

***Detective Comics* (Vol. 1) #817-820 and *Batman* (Vol. 1) #651-654 (May-Aug. 2006)** In the "Face-to-Face" storyline, a healed Harvey Dent attempts to follow in Batman's footsteps as a hero in Gotham City, only to be reborn as Two-Face.

ON THE RECORD

One of Batman's oldest enemies, Two-Face first debuted in the 1940s, his original alias being Harvey Kent. With his last name being perhaps a little too close to the alter ego of a certain Kryptonian Super Hero, Harvey's surname was changed to "Dent" as he continued to be a thorn in Batman's side over the decades.

After the *Crisis on Infinite Earths* event, Harvey Dent was reintroduced during "Batman: Year One" as Gotham City's golden boy, a white knight in the city's crusade against crime. Through several different origin stories that followed, it was disclosed that Harvey had always struggled with a dark dual personality. His true split self only emerged fully when the over-zealous District Attorney's face was irreparably scarred by gangster Sal Maroni.

A MAN DIVIDED
Harvey Dent's modern origin revealed that he had been abused by his father, a traumatic event that split his personality years before Two-Face was born. Later, even after plastic surgery to fix his face, Harvey couldn't let go of his dark past.

TWO OF A KIND
Batman and Two-Face share a long history. It was Bruce Wayne who introduced Harvey Dent to his future wife, Gilda. Despite Harvey's past crimes, Batman wants nothing more than to restore the sanity of his old friend.

ULTRA-HUMANITE

DEBUT *Action Comics* (Vol. 1) #13 (Jun. 1939)
BASE Mobile   **REAL NAME** Unknown
HEIGHT 7ft 9in   **WEIGHT** 666 lbs   **HAIR** white   **EYES** Red
POWERS/ABILITIES Super-genius IQ; master of science, psionic abilities—telepathy, telekinesis, hypnosis, brain blasts; modified ape body affords enhanced strength, speed, agility, and durability.
ENEMIES Justice League, Deathstroke the Terminator, Superman, Batman
AFFILIATIONS Secret Society of Super-Villains

A mad scientist menacing humanity since the end of World War I, the Ultra-Humanite has committed atrocities and battled generations of Super Heroes including the All-Star Squadron, Justice League, and the Terminator's Defiance team.

Initially a frail human, he modified his own form while spreading chaos and destruction, continually evading justice by transplanting his brain into new bodies, ranging from a movie actress to a giant insect. His current form is a mutated albino ape that he bred over many years, enhancing his intellect even further and granting him sufficient super-powers to lead the treacherous malcontents of the Secret Society of Super-Villains against Infinity Inc. and the Justice Society of America. In one clash, he killed the Crimson Avenger and Johnny Thunder. However, after usurping the magic of Thunder's Thunderbolt, he was shot dead by a new Crimson Avenger, but is notorious for having ways to escape the grave.

His recent return in a subservient role in Vandal Savage's Super-Villain Society team and subsequent easy defeat at the hands of Deathstroke revealed that Ultra-Humanite's keen intellect may be starting to give way to the savage primordial instincts of the bestial body he's inhabiting.

ON THE RECORD

After *Flashpoint*, Ultra-Humanite was trapped in the Phantom Zone for eons. He briefly escaped to Earth when schoolboy Clark Kent was scared during a crop fire in Smallville. However, Clark was too emotional and the villain retreated. Twenty years later he reappeared when the Phantom Zone was ruptured by Superman's battle against Doomsday and Brainiac.

Possessing many Smallville residents, Superman's emotions again repulsed Ultra-Humanite. He explosively released his victims and retreated to the Phantom Zone.

ULTRA-ABSORBENT
The predatory Ultra-Humanite was only as strong as its last psychic feast.

ULTRA BOY

DEBUT *Superboy* #98 (Jul. 1962)
REAL NAME Jo Nah
BASE Legion Headquarters, New Earth
HEIGHT 6ft   **WEIGHT** 190 lbs
EYES Brown   **HAIR** Brown
POWERS/ABILITIES Vast strength, speed, invulnerability, flight, vision like Superman—but canonly use one power at a time.
ENEMIES Daxamites, Dominators, Fatal Five, Krav the General Nah

Rimbor is a United Planets world wracked by civil war, but Ultra Boy Jo Nah strives to use his powers to proudly represent both sides. A member of the Legion of Super-Heroes. Impetuous and impatient, Jo always seeks the most direct solution to any problem, a useful quality as one of the team's heavy hitters, with powers matching Superboy's, even if only accessible one at a time.

However, his capacities are stretched to the limit after he is elected the second Legion leader. Not only has he the devious political machinations of UP President R. J. Brande to navigate, but his own father—Crav the General Nah—is a powerful and sworn foe of the Legion, determined to destroy all Ultra Boy cherishes and stands for.

UNCLE SAM

DEBUT *National Comics* (Vol. 1) #1 (Jul. 1940)
HEIGHT 6ft 5in; variable   **WEIGHT** 140 lbs   **EYES** Blue   **HAIR** White
POWERS/ABILITIES Super-strength, speed, invulnerability, immortality; enhanced senses, charisma, and reflexes; clairvoyance; ability to alter size; interdimensional teleportation; all fuelled and sustained by the American people's belief in the ideals of Liberty and Democracy.
ALLIES The Ray, Phantom Lady, Doll Man, Human Bomb, Firebrand, the Spectre, Superman, Justice League of America
ENEMIES Fascism, Nazis, All Tyrants, Secret Society of Super-Villains, Imperiex, Black Adam, Sinestro
AFFILIATIONS Freedom Fighters, the Multiversity, S.H.A.D.E.

Uncle Sam is among the youngest of the quasi-mystical National Avatars on the many Earths of the Multiverse. Created by the Founding Fathers as the colonies fought the War of Independence, he is the embodiment of America's communal spirit. Reanimating and empowering a fallen patriot, he fought the British as Minute Man.

Uncle Sam returned during every war and crisis threatening the USA, tailoring his manifestations to suit the tone of the times. When the Civil War broke out, his essence divided too, inhabiting a soldier on each side, battling as both Johnny Reb and Billy Yank.

His current look evolved in 1870 after manifesting to crush political corruption. He maintained it for both World War I and II. During this time he also first encountered multiple metahumans and Super Heroes. On Prime Earth, people are increasingly polarized, causing his power levels to fluctuate wildly.

Uncle Sam frequently works with iterations of the Freedom Fighters. His greatest triumph occurred on Earth-X, where Nazis won World War II. After fading away, Sam was revived to overturn the conquest and liberate America after his costumed allies stirred the crushed populace to again believe in the power of liberty, equality, and democracy.

I WANT YOU
After *Flashpoint*, Samuel Wilson led the Super Human Advanced Defense Executive (S.H.A.D.E.), a branch of Homeland Security employing metahumans the Ray, Phantom Lady, Human Bomb, and Doll Man, as undercover Freedom Fighters. As Uncle Sam, Wilson commands trained agents and vast intelligence and surveillance resources, recruiting heroes who can tackle America's enemies without drawing too much public scrutiny.

He may possess metahuman abilities but carefully conceals them, preferring to operate behind the scenes, strategically evaluating threats and decisively expending S.H.A.D.E. assets to "defend the 21st century."

ULTRAMAN

DEBUT *Justice League of America* (Vol. 1) #29 (Aug. 1964)   **REAL NAME** Kal-Il
POWERS/ABILITIES From Kryptonite gains super-strength, speed, and stamina, fligh, heat vision, enhanced senses and the ability to breathe out with the force of a hurricane
ALLIES Superwoman (as with others in Crime Syndicate, he is not really allied to anyone but only fights for himself)
ENEMIES Anti-Monitor, Alexander Luthor
AFFILIATIONS Crime Syndicate

In the universe of Earth-3, Krypton was populated by ruthless beings who cared only for strength. Young Kal-Il was the sole survivor of the planet's destruction. Sent to Earth-3 on an escape rocket by his parents, they despised his vulnerable infant form.

On Earth-3, Kal intimidated Jonny and Martha Kent into taking care of him, killing the dysfunctional couple when he had no further need for them. He became Ultraman, eating Kryptonite to maintain his superpowers. Ultraman led the Crime Syndicate to Earth-0 after Earth-3 was destroyed, but he was defeated after being exposed to sunlight. Ultraman was imprisoned but later released to battle Anti-Monitor. He was killed in this conflict.

UNTITLED, THE

DEBUT *Red Hood and the Outlaws #4*
(Feb. 2012)
POWERS/ABILITIES Virtually immortal
beings of pure evil; intangibility; darkness
manipulation; shapeshifting.
ENEMIES All-Caste, Jason Todd (Red Hood),
Outlaws (Starfire, Arsenal, Bizarro, Artemis),
Essence

Eons ago, before "the sun began to cast
shadows over the Earth," a clan of nine
brothers and sisters—The Untitled—
discovered the waters of Absolute Evil.
One by one, they drank deep of the flowing
waters, gaining dark, unspeakable powers
and immortality. However one sister, Ducra,
resisted the evil. She formed the All-Caste,
a mystical martial arts clan. The bitter
antagonism between The Untitled and the
All-Caste lasted for thousands of years, but
eventually The Untitled tracked the All-Caste
to their secret Himalayan base and
practically eradicated them. The Untitled's
brutal actions enraged former Robin Jason
Todd, who had recuperated there, trained
by the All-Caste after being killed by The
Joker and resurrected by immersion in a
Lazarus Pit. Todd fell in love with Ducra's
daughter, Essence, so had many reasons
for hating The Untitled. As Red Hood, he
hunted The Untitled with the help of his
Outlaws team, and believed them destroyed,
but the devil clan re-emerged to battle his
latest squad of unlikely heroes.

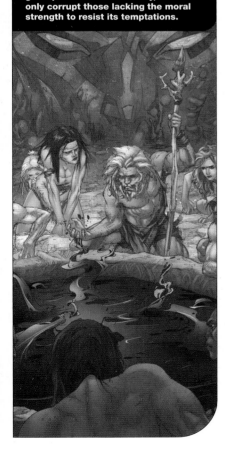

DARK EVOLUTION
The tainted black waters imparted
great power and immortality, but could
only corrupt those lacking the moral
strength to resist its temptations.

UNKNOWN SOLDIER

DEBUT *Our Army at War* (Vol. 1) #168 (Jun 1966)
REAL NAME Classified Top-Secret
HEIGHT 5ft 9in **WEIGHT** 155 lbs **HAIR** None **EYES** Black
POWERS/ABILITIES Expertise with all forms of military ordnance and most
unarmed combat disciplines; master of disguise with excellent strategic and
tactical skills and an uncontrollable ability to tap into the memories of soldiers
throughout history.
ALLIES Amanda Waller, Komal Akbari, Damage
ENEMIES Al-Isri, Ali "Ollie" Hassan, Roman, Crime Syndicate, Col. Marie Jonas

CAREER SUICIDE
Running roughshod over a squad
of government-sanctioned
criminal maniacs was a new
challenge for the "Immortal G.I."

The Unknown Soldier joined
the Army after his family was killed
in London during a terrorist attack.
Disfigured in combat in Afghanistan, he
was retrained as a clandestine operative,
carrying out black-ops missions all over
the world for the covert organization
Advanced Medical Military Operations.
    Wounded again in Dubai, during
his recuperation he learned he
was the latest in a line of
Unknown Soldiers stretching
back to the Middle Ages—and
perhaps beyond. He also
began suffering flashbacks and
hallucinations, possibly
caused by nanites
A.M.M.O. had implanted to
track him while he was in
the field.
    Rebelling against his increasingly untrustworthy A.M.M.O.
bosses, he tried disappearing and taking up civilian life, but war
and conflict seemed to seek him out. After his return from
Afghanistan, A.R.G.U.S. chief Amanda Waller brought him into
her Suicide Squad, placing him in charge of a detachment
dubbed the Reverse Squad. Their first mission was to capture
O.M.A.C. and Crime Syndicate members who had survived the
final battle with the Justice League. The immortal G.I. has been
reported saving mutated US soldier Ethan Avery from the
criminal experiments of Colonel Marie Jonas and infiltrating
US Black Ops missions in a crusade to save honest
soldiers from the illegal orders of their rogue commanders.

ON THE RECORD

The original Unknown Soldier was radically re-imagined
in 2008 as a Ugandan doctor, Moses Lwanga. Caught
up in an insurgency, the good doctor learned that his
personality and memories were fabricated by the previous
Unknown Soldier.
    His predecessor had attempted to transfer his
persona and skills to Lwanga to create peace instead
of perpetuating war.

THE KNOWN UNKNOWN
The Unknown Soldier strides into battle, his face bandaged
to both hide his disfigurement and protect his identity.

THE FACE OF WAR
All Unknown Soldiers
surrender personal
identity to become a
symbol of unflinching
resistance and
military superiority.

UPSIDE-DOWN MAN

DEBUT *Justice League* Dark (Vol. 2) #1 (Sep. 2018)
REAL NAME None
BASE The Other Place
HEIGHT Unknown **WEIGHT** Unknown
EYES None **HAIR** None
POWERS/ABILITIES Extensive magical powers including telekinesis, regeneration and energy projection.
ALLIES Nabu, Circe
ENEMIES Justice League Dark, Hecate
AFFILIATIONS Otherkind, The Rip

The Upside-Down Man was a being made of pure magic, whose realm was simply called the Other Place, found around the Dark Multiverse. He was originally supposed to be the balancing force for the magic of Hecate, but she trapped him in the Dark Multiverse, not wanting the horrors he brought with him to be part of her world. For millennia he waited and watched for an opportunity to come to Earth-0 and destroy all the magical beings. When it came, he revealed himself to the Justice League Dark at the Tower of Fate. He had no true form, but assembled a body for himself in a gruesome parody of a human form, upside-down, with no features except ear holes and a leering, fanged mouth.

URSA

DEBUT *Action Comics* (Vol. 1) #845 (Jan. 2007)
REAL NAME Ursa **BASE** Jekuul
HEIGHT Unknown **WEIGHT** Unknown
EYES Brown **HAIR** Black
POWERS/ABILITIES The usual powers of a Kryptonian under a yellow sun, including flight, super-strength, speed, and durability, X-ray vision, heat vision and freeze breath.
ALLIES General Zod, Lor-Zod **ENEMIES** Superman **AFFILIATIONS** House of Zod

Ursa was a Kryptonian, married to General Zod, who had survived the destruction of their planet due to being imprisoned in the Phantom Zone. Ursa had a son with Zod, named Lor, and the three of them referred to themselves as the Last Family of Krypton. Zod broke into the Fortress of Solitude and used the Phantom Zone Projector to release Ursa and Lor. They planned to start a new Krypton on a planet called Jekuul. When Kyle Rayner arrived on Jekuul Ursa nearly killed him, having a hatred of Green Lanterns for allowing the destruction of Krypton. She was quick to anger and warlike, teaching her son that battle was an art form. However, Ursa supported Zod's alliance with Superman to defeat Rogol Zaar and avenge Krypton. Afterwards, Ursa took charge of infrastructure in the project to rebuild Krypton.

VANDAL SAVAGE

DEBUT *Green Lantern* (Vol. 1) #10 (Winter 1943)
REAL NAME Vandar Adg
BASE Mobile
HEIGHT 5ft 10in **WEIGHT** 176 lbs **EYES** Brown **HAIR** Black
POWERS/ABILITIES Immortal; cannot be killed through traditional means; wounds heal regardless of severity; incredibly intelligent with ancient connections throughout the world; briefly possessed superhuman strength, endurance, durability, and flight when supercharged by the returning comet that gave him his powers.
ALLIES Signalman, Giganta, Madame Xanadu, Jason Blood, Shining Knight
ENEMIES Lex Luthor, Legion of Doom, Agent Kassidy Sage, Hawkman, Superman, The Flash, Batman, Wonder Woman, Scandal Savage, Green Lanterns, Mordru
AFFILIATIONS Legionnaires Club, Demon Knights, Justice League United, the House of Savage

Vandal Savage has stalked Earth for millennia. He attributes this to various causes including a mystic meteor, blood sacrifice rituals to forgotten gods and even harvesting the organs of his countless descendants. Decades ago, he was Cherry Blossom Killer Jonathan Savage: abandoning a wife and daughter to fulfil these rituals. Over 1,000 years ago, he founded the Demon Knights, a fractious team of early superhumans and immortals to fight the sorcerer Mordru. Over 40,000 years ago, he was Neanderthal caveman Vandar Adg who stumbled upon a fragment of a comet during a battle with Cro-Magnon rivals. That is the true source of his power and immortality: an aspect of primordial creation heralding the return of Creations dark mother Perpetua.

Having haunted all of history, covertly stoking wars and schooling tyrants, in the 20th century Savage began clashing with numerous Super Heroes, He joined many iterations of Super-Villain teams, battled legendary mystic warrior Pandora, and even (reluctantly) joined Justice League United. All the while, he had been biding his time for the return of his precious comet to Earth. He duelled Batman and host of heroes across time and space to recover a mysterious Faberge Egg containing a White Lantern power ring before his latest Injustice Gang lost a war against Lex Luthor's Legion of Doom for possession of the comet—actually reality-bending artefact the Totality. Although reported beaten to death, the immortal villain has a knack of returning…

NEVER-ENDING SAVAGERY: Despite several "deaths," Vandal Savage always returned to reclaim his hold on mankind, thanks to the life-sustaining powers of the comet fragment he first retrieved.

STAYING ALIVE
Vandal Savage blieved that slaughtering Superman—even a powerless one—would extend his life for centuries to come.

ON THE RECORD

Vandal Savage originally debuted in the Golden Age of Comics in the pages of *Green Lantern*. He fought the first Green Lantern Alan Scott, and over the years would come to face nearly every major character in the DC Comics stable.

Before *Crisis on Infinite Earths* altered continuity, Vandal was an Earth-2 resident and battled the Justice Society of America. After the Crisis, he became the prime adversary of The Flash (Wally West), before emerging as the arch-nemesis of the youthful hero Damage, the long-lived Resurrection Man, and even the time-traveling hero Rip Hunter.

THE MAN WHO WANTED THE WORLD!
In his 1943 debut, Vandal Savage fought Earth-2 Green Lantern Alan Scott and his doughty sidekick "Doiby" Dickles. Savage would go onto become a recurring JSA foe in his early comic book exploits.

VALE, VICKI

DEBUT *Batman* (Vol. 1) #49 (Oct.–Nov. 1948)
BASE Gotham City
HEIGHT 5ft 8in
WEIGHT 115 lbs
EYES Red
HAIR Green
POWERS/ABILITIES Ace reporter; extremely intelligent; adept at self-defense.
ALLIES Bruce Wayne, Jason Bard
ENEMIES The Penguin, Carmine Falcone

HOLD THE FRONT PAGE
Gotham City Gazette star reporter Vicki Vale eventually saw through Police Commissioner Jason Bard's duplicity, achieving yet another scoop.

Star reporter Vicki Vale of *The Gotham City Gazette*, was a member of the city's elite. Thanks to her busy social life, she knew Bruce Wayne, and grew even closer to the notorious bachelor when he helped take the *Gazette* online.

Despite always vetting her sources, Vale was duped when she began a romance with Jason Bard. As he quickly ascended the ranks of the city Police Department—eventually becoming commissioner—Vicki helped his rise by publicizing his heroic deeds. She didn't realize that he was pursuing a vendetta against Batman, using his growing power to stop the Dark Knight for good. Vale finally discovered the truth, and Bard eventually turned over a new leaf, offering her an exclusive confession for the *Gazette* to get back in Vicki's good graces. In the aftermath, Vale took a job in television, as the anchor on Gotham 4 News.

VERITAS, SHAY

DEBUT *Superman* (Vol. 3) #13 (Dec. 2012)
REAL NAME Dr. Shay Veritas
BASE Mobile, formerly DEO Ghost Site #252 "The Scabbard," formerly The Block (near the Earth's core)
HEIGHT 5ft 5in **WEIGHT** 109 lbs
EYES Brown **HAIR** Purple
POWERS/ABILITIES Genius-level intelligence; access to advanced scientific equipment, trained Super Hero.
ALLIES Superman, Supergirl, Cameron Chase, Michael Holt
ENEMIES Doomsday, Lobo
AFFILIATIONS The T-Council, The Terrifics, DEO, Crucible Academy

TRUTH OR DARE
Injury may have prevented science genius Shay Veritas completing her Super Hero training, but that doesn't stop her jumping into action.

Dr. Shay Veritas is an eminent omniologist, expert in virtually every discipline of knowledge. She was originally based at the Block—an advanced research facility near the Earth's core. Equipped with incredible technologies, Dr. Veritas was Superman's medical specialist, and she took every opportunity to assess the range and magnitude of his powers. She also became his technical advisor for difficult or perplexing cases.

Veritas was trained as a Super Hero at the intergalactic Crucible Academy, but had to leave following injury. Home on Earth, she became a scientific and medical consultant, entrusted with Superman and Supergirl's most personal secrets. She later worked in a similar capacity for Cameron Chase at the Department of Extranormal Operations. Unable to shake the taste for superheroic action, Veritas has worked with Red Hood and the Outlaws and is a member of Mister Terrific's super-science thinktank the T-Council.

VENTRILOQUIST AND SCARFACE

DEBUT *Detective Comics* (Vol. 1) #583 (Feb. 1988)
REAL NAME Arnold Wesker (Ventriloquist)
BASE Gotham City
HEIGHT 5ft 7in **WEIGHT** 142 lbs **EYES** Blue **HAIR** Bald
POWERS/ABILITIES brilliant planner and tactical analyst; utterly ruthless when acting through his Scarface dummy.
ALLIES "Scarface," The Joker
ENEMIES Batman, Batgirl, The Riddler, Bane

In the early years of Batman's career, crime boss Arnold Wesker succumbed to insanity, refusing to speak and only giving orders through a wooden puppet based on a 1920's Chicago gangster. As the Ventriloquist and Scarface they terrorized Gotham City, leading many to believe the dummy was actually possessed by an evil spirit. When The Joker and The Riddler went to war over ownership of the city, Ventriloquist and Scarface joined The Joker's army of recruits and was locked in Arkham Asylum by Batman.

After facing the Dark Knight several times—including a perilous period working for Venom-fuelled megalomaniac Bane—Wesker was reported killed and Scarface adopted by the equally unbalanced Peyton Riley. She acted out the role of Scarface's moll, using the dummy's reputation to earn a place for herself in the underworld. Another pair, Shauna Belzer and Ferdie, temporarily traded on the pair's killer reputation, before joining antihero superteam the Secret Six.

Wesker ultimately returned to reclaim Scarface, but his criminal alliance with The Penguin, Black Mask and Great White Shark again landed him in Arkham. In recent times, he was pressganged by Batman into a team to tackle Bane. The Dark Knight gambled that Wesker's multiple personality disorder would counteract the mind-bending, mood-altering powers of Bane's partner, Psycho-Pirate.

PUPPET DICTATOR
Ventriloquist Arnold Wesker's personality was totally subsumed in the vicious character of his Scarface dummy.

ON THE RECORD

After *Flashpoint*, altered reality, Arnold Wesker was superseded by Shauna Belzer, a demented telekinetic who mercilessly bullied and eclipsed her child star twin brother, Ferdie. "Shabby Shauna" grew to resent Ferdie and when her powers peaked, she murderously used them on all her tormentors. When, at a friend's birthday party, Shauna encountered a ventriloquist, she fixated on his dummy. Naming it Ferdie, she formed a twisted relationship with the puppet. using Ferdie to give vent to her dark side, and murder anyone who crosses her.

DEADLY DOUBLE ACT
Shauna and Ferdie constantly bickered, but it was always other people who paid the ultimate price.

VIXEN

DEBUT *Action Comics* (Vol. 1) #521 (Jul. 1981)
REAL NAME Mari Jiwe McCabe
BASE Mount Justice, Happy Harbor, Rhode Island
HEIGHT 5ft 9in **WEIGHT** 140 lbs **EYES** Amber **HAIR** Black
POWERS/ABILITIES Uses the mystical Tantu Totem to channel abilities of any animal, allowing her enhanced strength, speed, flight, and mimic any animal feat or characteristic.
ALLIES Justice League of America
ENEMIES Queen of Fables, Ocean Master, Prometheus
AFFILIATIONS Mndawe Foundation, Justice League International, Justice League of America, Justice Foundation

Super Hero Mari McCabe is a fashion model from African nation Zambesi. Inheritor of the Tantu Totem, she can channel the abilities of any animal by tapping into the Red, the morphogenetic field of all life on Earth. As Vixen, Mari served with many incarnations of the Justice League—including the United Nations' Justice League International team, led by Booster Gold. She participated in their first mission, defeating planet-plundering alien Peraxxus and his Signal Masters. Seriously injured in a bomb attack at the UN, McCabe then quit the team to recuperate. When Ocean Master's Atlanteans attacked Boston—taking many Justice Leaguers captive—Vixen was ready for action. Drafted in as a temporary member, she helped drive back the Atlantean tide. In the aftermath she was considered for full membership, but failed to make the final cut. When Batman formed his own Justice League of America team, Vixen became his trusted lieutenant, and through increasingly significant missions grew into a position of leadership. Facing the Extremists, wild man Makson, and the godlike Kingbutcher she proved her mettle before personally defeating Prometheus and uniting Earth's wishers against the reality-shifts of the Queen of Fables. As their spokesperson, Vixen transformed the team into the multi-national Justice Foundation.

PRIMAL FURY
The Tantu Totem allows Vixen to channel the abilities of any animal, making her a formidable opponent.

LEAGUE CASUALTIES
The bombing of the Justice League's ceremony at the UN killed League member Gavril Ivanovich and severely injured Vixen.

ON THE RECORD

The pre-*Flashpoint* Vixen served as a member of many teams, including the Suicide Squad, Justice League of America, Birds of Prey, and Justice League Task Force. On one adventure she faced the African trickster-god Anansi within the Tantu Totem itself. She also returned to Africa and came to terms with her past by facing her mother's murderer—Aku Kwesi, a warlord who was taking control of local villages with help from Intergang.

WRATH OF THE VIXEN
Mari returned to Zambesi to avenge her mother and put an end to Intergang's schemes. But her enemy was far stronger than she realized, and the battle was not an easy one.

VIGILANTE II

DEBUT *New Teen Titans Annual* (Vol. 1) #2 (Aug. 1983)
REAL NAME Adrian Chase
BASE New York City
HEIGHT 6ft 2in **WEIGHT** 197 lbs
EYES Blue **HAIR** Blond
POWERS/ABILITIES Superb athlete; expert with knives and firearms; master of multiple martial arts; meditates to heal injuries.
ALLIES Teen Titans, Nightwing
ENEMIES New York Mafia, Electrocutioner, Saber, Cannon, Peacemaker

Adrian Chase was once a crusading District Attorney in New York City, using the legal system to take on the Mob. However, after a vengeful gang boss killed his wife and children in a bombing, the lawyer was contacted by a mysterious group dedicated to fighting evil from outside the law. They trained him in martial arts and meditation, and on returning to New York, he embarked on a crime-fighting career as Vigilante.

Despite his noble intentions, Adrian found himself sliding toward darkness as his war against crime progressed. When he tried to retire, his friend Alan Welles and then his court bailiff Dave Winston took up the mantle—but both were killed in action. Adrian finally decided to become Vigilante once again, but could not deal with the stress and took his own life. The identity was later taken up by rogue police officer Pat Trayce; the mysterious Justin Powell; and then Adrian's own brother, Dorian Chase.

VIOLENT METHODS
Despite initially trying to use non-lethal techniques, Adrian's descent into darkness resulted in him killing without hesitation.

VIBE

DEBUT *Justice League of America Annual* (Vol. 1) #2 (1984)
REAL NAME Francisco "Cisco" Ramon
BASE Detroit, Michigan
HEIGHT 5ft 7in **WEIGHT** 145 lbs
EYES Brown **HAIR** Black
POWERS/ABILITIES Taps into the vibrational strands that hold reality together, allowing him to project vibrations at others; can see objects vibrating at unique frequencies.
ALLIES Dale Gunn, Breacher, Gypsy
ENEMIES Suicide Squad, Rupture, Parademons
AFFILIATIONS Justice League of America

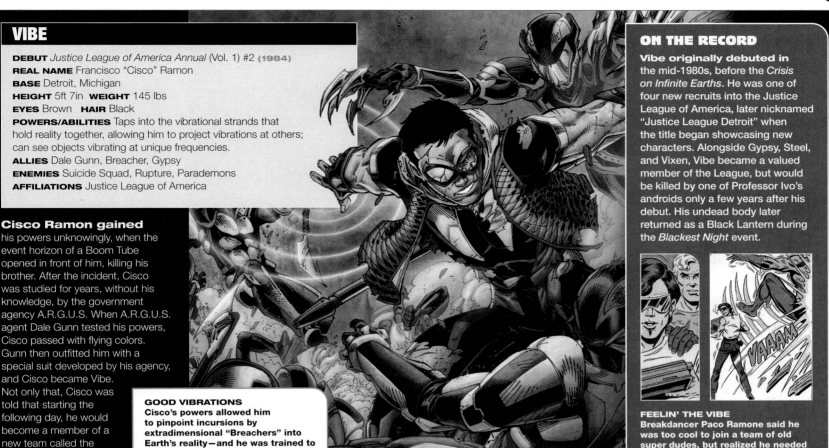

Cisco Ramon gained his powers unknowingly, when the event horizon of a Boom Tube opened in front of him, killing his brother. After the incident, Cisco was studied for years, without his knowledge, by the government agency A.R.G.U.S. When A.R.G.U.S. agent Dale Gunn tested his powers, Cisco passed with flying colors. Gunn then outfitted him with a special suit developed by his agency, and Cisco became Vibe. Not only that, Cisco was told that starting the following day, he would become a member of a new team called the Justice League of America.

GOOD VIBRATIONS
Cisco's powers allowed him to pinpoint incursions by extradimensional "Breachers" into Earth's reality—and he was trained to deal with them if they proved hostile.

ON THE RECORD

Vibe originally debuted in the mid-1980s, before the *Crisis on Infinite Earths*. He was one of four new recruits into the Justice League of America, later nicknamed "Justice League Detroit" when the title began showcasing new characters. Alongside Gypsy, Steel, and Vixen, Vibe became a valued member of the League, but would be killed by one of Professor Ivo's androids only a few years after his debut. His undead body later returned as a Black Lantern during the *Blackest Night* event.

FEELIN' THE VIBE
Breakdancer Paco Ramone said he was too cool to join a team of old super dudes, but realized he needed them as much as they needed Vibe.

VIKING PRINCE

DEBUT *The Brave and the Bold* (Vol. 1) #1 (Aug.–Sep. 1955)
REAL NAME Jon Haraldson
HEIGHT 5ft 11in **WEIGHT** 171 lbs
EYES Blue **HAIR** Blond
POWERS/ABILITIES Skilled warrior and great narrator; cannot be harmed by fire, water, wood, or metal.
ALLIES Sgt. Rock, Black Canary
ENEMIES Krogg the Red

Many legends are told of the mysterious time-lost warrior called the Viking Prince. According to some tales, he crossed the Atlantic to find Vinland; in others, he fell in love with a Valkyrie and wished to die to be with her, but was cursed by Odin so that fire, water, wood, and metal could not slay him.

As well as sailing across the seas and battling monsters and other mighty foes, he was transported through time on several occasions. The Lord of Time forced the Viking Prince to join the Five Warriors From Forever to face the Justice League of America. He was stranded with other temporal exiles on Dinosaur Island, and later, in World War II, fought beside Sgt. Rock of Easy Company. Killed by explosives while battling the Nazis, perhaps the Viking Prince finally beat Odin's curse and achieved the death he long desired.

VOODOO

DEBUT *W.I.L.D. Cats* (Vol. 1) #1 (Aug. 1992)
BASE Dead City of the Daemonites, Europa
EYES Brown **HAIR** Brown
POWERS/ABILITIES Shapeshifting; mimicry; telepathy; poison quills; life support; can extrude wings or claws from body.
ENEMIES Black Razors, Black Jack, Green Lantern (Kyle Rayner)

HYBRID ABILITIES
Voodoo's wings and razor-sharp claws made her formidable in close combat, while her shapeshifting made her highly suited for espionage.

Priscilla Kitaen was an exotic dancer with the stage name "Voodoo," who was captured by the alien Daemonites. They subjected her to procedures that transformed her into a shape-changing human/alien hybrid, but when she escaped, the Daemonites used her DNA to create another hybrid: Voodoo.

Voodoo took over Priscilla's old identity (and even her job) to blend in and gather data on Earth's superhuman population, but she was found by the alien-hunting Black Razors. She took refuge in a safe house, but Green Lantern (Kyle Rayner) tracked her down, forcing her to return to the Daemonite mothership. Voodoo was furious when a Daemonite commander explained that she was just a genetic experiment, but agreed to work with them after being offered command of all hybrids on Earth. Voodoo set out to kill Priscilla and faced her on Jupiter's moon, Europa. However, Priscilla convinced her that she didn't have to follow the Daemonites, and could choose her own destiny.

VUNDABAR, VIRMAN

DEBUT *Mister Miracle* (Vol. 1) #5 (Nov.–Dec. 1971)
BASE Apokolips
HEIGHT 5ft 2in **WEIGHT** 103 lbs
EYES Blue **HAIR** Black
POWERS/ABILITIES As a New God, Virman is immortal and has superhuman physical attributes; a relatively skilled strategist.
ENEMIES Mister Miracle, Big Barda, Justice League International

A product of one of Granny Goodness' infamous orphanages, Virman Vundabar was a member of Darkseid's inner circle. He was obsessed with military discipline and devoted to Granny, but despite his best efforts he repeatedly failed to capture Mister Miracle himself.

When Darkseid was lost in the Source Wall, Virman sided with Granny as the dark lord's henchmen jockeyed for influence. When Darkseid returned, Vundabar made a foolhardy grab for power by trying to assassinate his lord, and was destroyed by Darkseid's Omega-Beams. He was later resurrected by Darkseid, only to be killed again by the Infinity-Man. Reborn on Earth, Vundabar ran the Dark Side Club's gladiatorial competitions. He finally suffered the ignominy of being beheaded by the Clock King, one of the club's fighters.

WALLER, AMANDA

DEBUT *Legends* #1 (Nov. 1986)
BASE Belle Reve Penitentiary
EYES Brown **HAIR** Black
POWERS/ABILITIES A wealth of field experience with superpowered beings; superb leader and analyst with military expertise.
ALLIES James Gordon, Jr.
ENEMIES Black Spider, Basilisk, Regulus, Crime Syndicate, O.M.A.C.
AFFILIATIONS Suicide Squad, Team 7, NSA, A.R.G.U.S., Lexcorp, Justice League of America

Brilliant NSA analyst Amanda Waller served in elite special ops unit Team 7. Her intelligence, management skills, and ability to make hard decisions landed her the job as head of A.R.G.U.S. and Commander of Task Force X/Suicide Squad, a covert team staffed by convicted Super-Villains. Controlling superpowered criminals required someone equally ruthless. Waller demonstrated a willingness to lie, cheat, and allow candidates to be tortured and killed.

Although reviving the Squad was her pet project, running it has caused endless heartbreak. Family and friends have died because of Waller's relentlessness. She has been removed and returned to control of Task Force X many times. She was caught off-guard when Squad member Black Spider proved to be a planted infiltrator, and took her beloved Nana hostage. Although Waller fought back with skill, she was unable to prevent Nana's murder.

When she was replaced by political appointee Emilia Harcourt, Waller ordered herself assassinated by marksman Deadshot, simply so that she could operate in complete anonymity to expose a traitor and foil a plot for world domination. Whatever the obstacle, Waller perseveres and overcomes.

MEAN TEAM
Amanda Waller came to prominence as part of Team 7, countering the emerging metahuman threat alongside Steve Trevor, Deathstroke, Grifter, and others.

SUICIDAL TENDENCIES
Amanda Waller handpicked the members of Task Force X—the Suicide Squad—including King Shark, El Diablo, Black Spider, Deadshot, and Harley Quinn.

ON THE RECORD

Pre-*Flashpoint*, Amanda Waller was an abrasive and controversial figure who frequently ignored the rules—and paid the price. She was found guilty of unauthorized deployment of the Suicide Squad against the occult Loa cartel, and later jailed for other offenses by President Lex Luthor.

She was subsequently freed and assigned a position in UN agency Checkmate, but was forced to resign after it was discovered that she had illegally deported Super-Villains to the hostile planet of Salvation.

PUSHY ATTITUDE
Amanda "the Wall" Waller's arrogance earned her few friends in the Super Hero community. Waller's relationship with Batman was especially fraught.

WARLORD

DEBUT *First Issue Special* #8 (Nov. 1975)
REAL NAME Travis Morgan
BASE Skartaris
HEIGHT 6ft **WEIGHT** 188 lbs
EYES Blue **HAIR** White
POWERS/ABILITIES Brilliant strategist; natural leader; expert hand-to-hand combatant; extraordinary swordsman; extremely athletic.
ALLIES Shakira, Jennifer Morgan, Machiste
ENEMIES Deimos

On June 16, 1969, Air Force pilot Lieutenant Colonel Travis Morgan was flying an SR-71 Blackbird at 80,000 ft on a spy mission over Russia when he was shot down and sent spiraling to Earth. Bailing out and expecting to freeze to death in chilling water, Morgan instead parachuted into Skartaris, a land of eternal sunlight where mythical creatures and prehistoric beasts roamed. There he became known as Warlord, a warrior who battled and eventually killed Skartaris' corrupt mage, Deimos.

While he ventured from Skartaris a few times, including a memorable visit to Seattle to partner with Green Arrow, Warlord found a home in this land hidden inside the Earth. He died in a duel with his own son, Joshua Morgan. Joshua later honored his father's legacy by taking up the Warlord mantle.

WARP

DEBUT *The New Teen Titans* #14 (Dec. 1981)
REAL NAME Emil LaSalle
HEIGHT 5ft 8in **WEIGHT** 134 lbs
EYES Brown **HAIR** Brown
POWERS/ABILITIES Flight; able to open a hole in space to teleport.
ALLIES Phobia, Plasmus, Brain, Monsieur Mallah
ENEMIES Blue Beetle, Brutale, La Dama, Rompe-Huesos, Coyote, The Joker
AFFILIATIONS Secret Society of Super-Villains, Brotherhood of Evil

Before *Flashpoint*, Frenchman Warp was a major foe of the Teen Titans. After serving with the Brotherhood of Evil and Secret Society, Warp became a mercenary with old comrades Phobia and Plasmus, sent to retrieve an artifact called the Blue Beetle. But crime boss La Dama also wanted it, and sent her own lackeys Brutale, Rompe-Huesos, and Coyote after it.

The Blue Beetle had already possessed teenager Jaime Reyes, transforming him into an alien armored warrior. Reyes repurposed the sentient weapon into a Super Hero, routing Warp and his cronies. Warp then joined the Outsider's Secret Society, but was defeated. Warp also got between Lex Luthor and The Joker as they fought for control of the Legion of Doom, and the Harlequin of Hate destroyed his mind.

WAVERIDER

DEBUT *Armageddon 2001* #1 (May 1991)
REAL NAME Michael Jon Carter
BASE The Vanishing Point
HEIGHT 6ft 5in **WEIGHT** 215 lbs
EYES Blue **HAIR** Blond
POWERS/ABILITIES Can see the future of any individual; one with the timestream, allowing time-travel; superhuman strength, durability.
ENEMIES Monarch

TIME TRAVELER
Waverider's ability to surf the timestream enables him to discover secrets hidden in the past and also gain knowledge of future events.

The original Waverider was Matthew Ryder, a scientist from a future reality in the year 2030 ruled by the tyrant Monarch. Resolved to stop Monarch's iron rule before it began, he became Waverider. Knowing only that Monarch was a former Super Hero, Waverider went back in time to investigate possible futures for many heroes and discovered that Hawk was destined to become the Super-Villain in question.

The first Waverider was killed in the line of duty. However, during the Convergence event, an aged Booster Gold (Michael Jon Carter) from an alternate Earth became the new Waverider when he was fed into the timestream by Earth-0's Booster Gold. This Waverider took on a career in the Multiverse, initially helping Telos and various Super Heroes convince Brainiac to realign the Multiverse.

WATCHMEN, THE

DEBUT *Watchmen* #1 (Sep. 1986)
MEMBERS/POWERS OZYMANDIAS (Adrian Veidt) Genius, polymath, tycoon, and master martial artist; **SILK SPECTRE** (Laurie Juspeczyk) Skilled hand-to-hand fighter; **NITE OWL** (Daniel Dreiberg) Gadgeteer and inventor, owner of flying Owlship; **COMEDIAN** (Edward Blake) Combat veteran and firearms expert; **RORSCHACH** (Walter Kovacs) Investigator and brawler; **DOCTOR MANHATTAN** (Dr. Jon Osterman) Near-omnipotent; able to control and manipulate matter at a quantum level.
ALLIES The Minutemen
ENEMIES Moloch the Mystic, Big Figure, Lady Sin
AFFILIATIONS The Crimebusters

BEFORE WATCHMEN
The Minutemen were America's original costumed crime-fighters. Operating throughout the 1940s, it was Captain Metropolis who instigated the team when he approached Silk Spectre and her manager, Laurence Schexnayder, to suggest joining forces. The team comprised:
1 Silk Spectre (Sally Juspeczyk)
2 Nite Owl (Hollis Mason)
3 The Comedian (Edward Blake)
4 Mothman (Byron Lewis)
5 Cpt. Metropolis (Nelson Gardner)
6 Hooded Justice (Unknown)
7 Dollar Bill (William Brady)
8 Silhouette (Ursula Zandt)

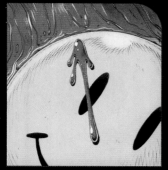

NO LAUGHING MATTER
Investigating a routine homicide, Rorschach found a bloodstained badge—his first clue that the victim, Edward Blake, was none other than the Comedian.

Though never referred to as The Watchmen at the time, these costumed adventurers were once the US's most celebrated heroes. However, a public backlash against vigilante violence forced them to go their separate ways in the 1970s. In 1985, as Cold War tensions between the US and the USSR escalated, one of these feted heroes was found murdered. Investigating the crime, his old teammates were forced to deal with issues from their past, and uncovered evidence of a conspiracy with far-reaching ramifications.

In a universe separate from Earth-0, costumed heroes emerged in the late 1930s, and by the 1940s had teamed up as the crime-fighting Minutemen. They were succeeded by a new generation of heroes called the Crimebusters. Among this second generation was Doctor Manhattan. As a result of a lab accident, Doctor Manhattan was the only hero on Earth with superhuman powers. Able to control quantum forces, he was a living nuclear deterrent, altering the power balance between the US and the USSR.

In the 1960s and 1970s, the public turned against costumed vigilantes, and the Keene Act was passed in 1977, banning vigilante activity. The Watchmen retired, except for Doctor Manhattan and the Comedian, who worked for the government, and Rorschach, who refused to concede. When the Comedian was murdered in 1985, Rorschach suspected that former heroes were being targeted. To compound matters, Doctor Manhattan was then accused of being the cause of cancer in some of his former associates. He exiled himself on Mars, which increased tensions with the USSR. Rorschach and Nite Owl uncovered evidence of a bizarre plot that would kill millions, yet result in world peace—and the mastermind appeared to be their fellow adventurer, Ozymandias.

Ozymandias' plan briefly worked, but by 1992 he had been discovered. Doctor Manhattan ripped through the barriers of the DC Multiverse and studied Superman. Manhattan altered reality repeatedly as the DC heroes and villains reached breaking point in a massive international feud. Inspired, he returned to his own world where he helped heal the planet's vegetation, removed its nuclear capability, and raised a son to be as honorable as Clark Kent. He gifted his son with his remaining powers before fading away into nonexistence.

WHO WATCHES THE WATCHMEN?
1 Ozymandias, 2 Silk Spectre, 3 Doctor Manhattan, 4 Comedian, 5 Nite Owl, 6 Rorschach

CLASSIC STORIES

***Watchmen* #1–12 (Sep. 1986–Oct. 1987)** Arguably the defining comic of its decade, *Watchmen* recounts a dark and disturbing tale of murder and conspiracy in a world on the brink of nuclear annihilation.

***Before Watchmen: Minutemen* #1–6 (Aug. 2012–Mar. 2013)** A prequel that explores the history of The Watchmen's predecessors from the perspective of the original Nite Owl, as chronicled in his book *Under the Hood*.

***Before Watchmen: Ozymandias* #1–6 (Sep. 2012–May 2013)** Ozymandias is perhaps the most distant and mysterious character in *Watchmen*. This miniseries looks at his early adventures and first encounters with the other *Watchmen* characters.

LIFE ON MARS
Accused of being a cause of cancer, Doctor Manhattan retreated to Mars—to think, to remember, and to build.

WAYNE, THOMAS AND MARTHA

DEBUT *Detective Comics* (Vol. 1) #33 **(Nov. 1939)**
BASE Gotham City
HEIGHT 6ft 2in (Thomas); 5ft 4in (Martha)
WEIGHT 210 lbs (Thomas); 108 lbs (Martha)
EYES Blue (Thomas and Martha); **HAIR** Black (Thomas); Brown (Martha)
POWERS/ABILITIES Gotham City power couple with connections in the city's elite social circles and business world; charitable and intelligent with an eye for philanthropy; loving parents; Thomas Wayne was also a skilled surgeon.
ALLIES Bruce Wayne, Lucius Fox, Alfred and Jarvis Pennyworth
ENEMIES Joe Chill, Court of Owls

Thomas Wayne was heir to the Wayne family fortune. He was the latest member of a proud dynasty, including one of the city's most influential figures, Alan Wayne—that dated back to the founding of Gotham City itself. Although he did not need to work, Thomas was extremely intelligent and, in addition to working closely with the family business, Wayne Industries, he became a surgeon. He also found another stimulating challenge in his courtship with the equally brilliant Martha Kane. Hailing from another of Gotham City's first families, Martha was renowned for her kind heart and philanthropy. She and Thomas were married, and had a son named Bruce. After a young Bruce got in trouble for sneaking into Gotham City to see the film *The Mark of Zorro*, Thomas Wayne decided a family outing was in order, and the three went to see the movie later that night. In a random act of violence, perpetrated by a small-time crook named Joe Chill, Thomas and Martha were shot and killed in an alley near the Monarch Theater. Bruce was left an orphan, and the murder of his parents would later inspire him to create his alter ego, Batman, sworn to protect the innocent in crime-infested Gotham City.

A Thomas Wayne from an alternate reality—where he was Batman—initially helped Bane take over Gotham City, before betraying and seriously wounding the Super-Villain with a gunshot to the head.

ON THE RECORD

While their famous son, Batman, debuted in *Detective Comics* #27 (May 1939), his origin was not related until November of that year. In a famous two-page introduction, Thomas and Martha Wayne first appeared, with only Thomas given a first name.

In later years, Batman's origin was fleshed out, particularly in *Batman* #47 (Jun.–Jul. 1948); Martha was given her first name, as was the Wayne's killer, Joe Chill.

In 1956, it was revealed that Thomas Wayne had actually worn a Batsuit to a costume party that served as inspiration to a young Bruce, in a story that provided an employer for Joe Chill—organized criminal Lew Moxon—on that fateful night.

BATMAN SR.
Long before the *Flashpoint* event, Thomas Wayne tried on the original Batsuit. During *Flashpoint*, in an alternate universe, Thomas served as that world's Batman.

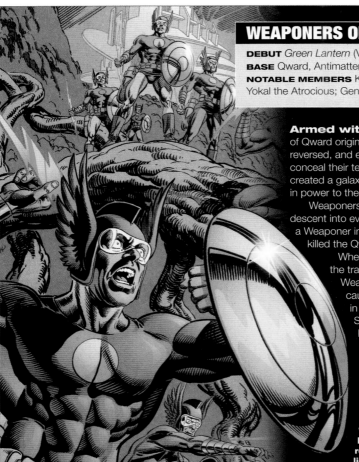

WEAPONERS OF QWARD

DEBUT *Green Lantern* (Vol. 2) #2 **(Sep.–Oct. 1960)**
BASE Qward, Antimatter Universe
NOTABLE MEMBERS Kramen; Drik; Chomin; Kiman; Yokal the Atrocious; General Fabrikant.

Armed with devastating Qwa-bolts, the Weaponers of Qward originated in the Antimatter Universe, where morality is reversed, and evil dominates. On Qward, honest decent citizens conceal their tendencies fearing pain of death. The Qwardians created a galaxy-spanning military empire, equal and opposite in power to the Guardians of the Universe and Green Lantern Corps.

Weaponers originally found an enemy in Sinestro. Before his own descent into evil, the Korugarian found a Green Lantern ring and battled a Weaponer in the positive matter universe. Hungry for power, Sinestro killed the Qwardian, kickstarting his own Green Lantern career.

When Green Lantern Hal Jordan exposed Sinestro's villainy, the traitor was banished to Qward, where opportunistic Weaponers equipped him with a yellow power ring to cause chaos and promote their doctrine of corruption in the positive matter universe. After years of marauding, Sinestro recruited his own Sinestro Corps to challenge his former masters and Qwardian allies.

A broken empire, Weaponers ranks were devastated when Sinestro and Superman clashed for control of yellow Fear Entity Parallax. They were all but eradicated when Multiversal creator Perpetua unleashed her restored Anti-Monitor on Qward.

WEAPON MASTERS
Before the *Flashpoint* event, the Weaponers relied heavily on their yellow shields and lightning-bolt weapons.

ON THE RECORD

In *Green Lantern* (Vol. 2) #2, Hal Jordan met Telle-Teg, a refugee from Qward who was one of the few people on his planet rebelling against the evil Weaponers. When a Destroyer from Qward followed Telle-Teg, Green Lantern fought the villain, and eventually made his way to Qward as well.

There he learned the Weaponers had designs on taking all the power batteries in the universe. They soon managed to steal Hal's power battery and bring it to their capital city, Qwar-Deen. In the second part of this first adventure, Green Lantern was able to steal back his battery and stop the two Qwardians on Earth, who were posing as door-to-door salespeople.

BOLT OF DESTRUCTION
Telle-Teg tried to protect Green Lantern as his ring was powerless against the golden Qwa-bolts. Telle-Teg died, but Hal found a way to defeat the Weaponers of Qward.

WEATHER WIZARD

DEBUT *The Flash* (Vol. 1) #110 (Dec. 1959–Jan. 1960)
REAL NAME Marco Mardon
BASE Central City
HEIGHT 6ft 1in **WEIGHT** 184 lbs **EYES** Blue **HAIR** Black
POWERS/ABILITIES Able to manipulate the weather, manifesting storms, lightning, tornadoes, and other weather phenomena; manipulates wind in order to fly; using powers affects his mood
ALLIES Captain Cold, Mirror Master, Heatwave, Glider, Trickster
ENEMIES The Flash, Elsa Mardon
AFFILIATIONS The Mardon Family, the Rogues

At 22 years old Claudio Mardon became leader of a major crime family when his father died. Claudio wanted to prove himself worthy of the Mardon name but soon realized he was out of his depth. His brother Marco wanted nothing to do with organized crime, and shunned the tainted legacy until Claudio was shot dead. This was no rival mob hit, but a murder scheme orchestrated by the victim's ambitious wife Elsa. She was concerned Claudio was surrendering too much family territory in the name of peace.

Enraged, Marco returned, just as Elsa had anticipated he would. As The Flash debuted, Marco assumed the name and mantle of Weather Wizard and electrocuted his sister-in-law with lightning.

The Flash became a sworn enemy, and it became clear that the technology Mardon used was driving him crazy. Weather Wizard joined infamous Super-Villain team the Rogues, content to follow orders and get rich. This changed after leader Captain Cold accepted an offer of greater power from Lex Luthor's omnipotent sponsor Perpetua. As "King Cold" reshaped Central City into his personal playground, Mardon joined rebel Rogues Golden Glider, Heat Wave, and Mirror Master in The Flash's resistance squad.

STORMY WEATHER
Tired of facing The Flash (and certain defeat) at one point, Weather Wizard tried his luck in Gotham City where he met and was bested by the team of Batman and Robin.

WEST, IRIS

DEBUT *Showcase* #4 (Sep.–Oct. 1956)
BASE Central City
HEIGHT 5ft 6in **WEIGHT** 130 lbs **EYES** Blue **HAIR** Brown
POWERS/ABILITIES Trained journalist with a suspicious nature, dogged determination and the instincts of a detective.
ALLIES Barry Allen, Daniel West (formerly), Hartley Rathaway, Wally West (The Flash III), Wallace West (Kid Flash)
ENEMIES Reverse-Flash/Daniel West
AFFILIATIONS Gotham Gazette, Speed Force

Iris West grew up handling trouble. After crippling their abusive father, her brother Daniel left her to care for him. Daniel turned to a life of crime and was caught by new Super Hero, The Flash. Despite her burdens, Iris got a journalism degree and interned at the Gotham Gazette where she met easy-going Barry Allen.

They met again years later when he was a forensic scientist for Central City Police Department. Barry quickly realized Iris was either using him to get information on The Flash or about her brother's case. Their relationship stalled, but they remained friends.

When Iris gained powers from the Speed Force, The Flash gave her a special outfit: Protecting her from a Reverse-Flash targeting The Flash's associates. When the psychopath was revealed as Daniel, she sacrificed her powers and regretfully helped put him back behind bars. As Iris and Barry's relationship matured, Daniel's son Wallace moved in, and thanks to a bizarre event, became a speedster too: Kid Flash.

Life became truly complicated after the apparent time manipulations of Doctor Manhattan began unraveling. Soon, a grown Wally West materialized: another nephew from another life and the original Kid Flash. Now privy to the secrets of prior existence, Iris learned Barry was The Flash and was targeted by a different Reverse-Flash. Eobard Thawne revealed how he murdered her once before and was about to repeat the act when she killed him. After an abortive murder trial in the 25th century, Iris returned to her own time, joining The Flash in a Speed Force Quest.

Despite all the terrors and hardships Iris has endured, her greatest trial was learning that she and Barry were once married, and agonizing over how to break the news to him.

FLEET OF FOOT
No matter how fast The Flash was or carefully Barry worked, his wife Iris was always two steps ahead of her.

WEST, WALLY

DATA

DEBUT *The Flash* #110 (Dec. 1959/Jan. 1960)
REAL NAME Wallace (Wally) Rudolph West
BASE Keystone City
HEIGHT 6ft **WEIGHT** 175 lbs
EYES Green **HAIR** Red
POWERS/ABILITIES Super-speed; accelerated healing; he can think quickly, mapping out the potential outcomes of a situation, and read books in an instant; can vibrate his molecular structure fast enough to pass directly through objects.
ALLIES Linda Park, The Flash (Barry Allen), Kid Flash (Wallace West), Impulse, Dick Grayson, Jai West, Iris West
ENEMIES The Rogues, Gorilla Grodd, Professor Zoom/Reverse-Flash
AFFILIATIONS Justice League, Teen Titans, Titans

His Name is Wally West. He was the Fastest Man Alive. From Kid Flash to The Flash, from accidental killer to pilot of Metron's Mobius Chair, Wally West has lived one of the strangest lives of any speedster, traversing multiple plains of existence just to find his way back home.

The nephew of Barry Allen's longtime love, Iris West, Wally West grew up idolizing The Flash while living in the small town of Blue Valley. When his aunt arranged for Wally to meet The Flash in Central City, he was thrilled. However, he had no idea that his life would be completely changed that day when lightning literally struck twice.

SEAT OF POWER
In his new role as a guardian of the Multiverse, Wally set out to help mend space, time, and reality, all of which were damaged and fractured.

WALLY'S RETURN
Wally adopted a new costume that paid homage to his classic yellow and red Kid Flash suit when he found his way out of the Speed Force and into the *Rebirth*-era.

As The Flash told Wally of his origin, lightning shot through a window, splashing altered chemicals onto Wally, and granting him access to the Speed Force that grants Barry Allen his own Flash powers.

First becoming Kid Flash, a founding member of the Teen Titans, Wally eventually accepted the role of The Flash after Barry sacrificed his life to save the universe during the events of *Crisis on Infinite Earths*. Just as heroic as his mentor, The Flash defended Keystone City from all manner of threats and rogues, and helped protect the world as a longtime member of the Justice League. In his private life, Wally married reporter Linda Park and had two children, Jai and Iris.

But after Barry returned and reality was altered during the *Flashpoint* event, Wally did not emerge in the so-called "New 52" universe that resulted. Lost in the Speed Force, Wally eventually made his way back to the real world. He appeared to Barry, who helped pull his former sidekick out of the Speed Force. And just like that, Barry's memories of his original sidekick came flooding back to him. The same thing happened to the memories of Wally's fellow Titans when he met with them. However, Linda remained lost to him, and his children simply didn't exist in this reality.

While he rejoined the Titans for a time, Wally's mind couldn't handle his reality shattering as it had. He sought out help at Sanctuary, a peaceful rehabilitation center where heroes could receive therapy. However, Wally's mind was unstable, and in one terrible instant, he lost control of his powers, killing several innocent heroes. Wally panicked and tried to cover up his terrible mistake by framing others, but was eventually incarcerated at Blackgate Prison. There he was visited by the Multiverse traveler Tempus Fuginaut, who eventually seated Wally in the New God Metron's Mobius Chair, in order to help correct mistakes in the timeline. In the process, Wally and Fuginaut were able to help Wally's children find their way back to reality and their mother.

ON THE RECORD

Pre-*Flashpoint*, Wally West first joined Justice League Europe before graduating to Justice League America. Often the lighthearted jokester on a team of older, more serious mentors, Wally nevertheless earned his stripes, even surpassing Barry Allen in terms of sheer speed.

FRENCH EVOLUTION
Justice League offshoot Justice League Europe were based in Paris. Here they strike a pose similar to that on the cover of *Justice League* #1 (May 1987), a copy of which is held by Metamorpho.

WHITE LANTERN CORPS

DEBUT *Blackest Night* (Vol. 1) #7 (Apr. 2010)
CURRENT MEMBERS/POWERS Kyle Rayner, Swamp Thing. All resurrected ring-wearers are able to fly, generate white energy blasts, force fields and light-constructs.
NOTABLE PREVIOUS MEMBERS Hal Jordan, Thaal Sinestro, Simon Baz, Maxwell Lord, Deadman, Hank Hall, Superman, Kid Flash, Firestorm, Aquaman, Martian Manhunter, Captain Boomerang, Jade, Professor Zoom, Green Arrow, Donna Troy, Hawkman, Hawkgirl, Ice, Osiris, Animal Man.
ALLIES Green Lantern Corps, Blue Lantern Corps, Indigo Tribe
ENEMIES Nekron, Black Lantern Corps, Black Hand
AFFILIATIONS Star Sapphire Corps, Red Lantern Corps, Sinestro Corps

The White Entity is the most enigmatic of all beings embodying aspects of the Emotional Spectrum. Only manifesting in times of ultimate cosmic peril and seemingly choosing its agents for specific purposes and missions, the White Entity can wholly resurrect the dead, rather than merely reanimate corpses, like Nekron.

The White Lantern Corps came into being when Hal Jordan merged with an entity that had lain dormant and hidden for millennia on Earth. As the Blackest Night ended, Hal brought Nekron's avatar—Black Hand—back to life, forcing the Death Lord to retreat to his Dead Zone and reducing his Black Lantern Corps to dust.

When Kyle Rayner mastered all seven colors of the Emotional Spectrum, he became the White Lantern, roaming the universe and preserving life from forces beyond the power of reality's regular champions. Following *Rebirth*, when Rayner and the Guardians sought to restore the defunct Blue Lantern Corps, his white ring shed six of its color components, reducing him to Green Lantern Status.

White energy is seemingly all-powerful, but operates in unpredictable ways: Batman was once catapulted across time and space at a White ring's mercy as it sought to stop Vandal Savage possessing it. Later, while battling the Legion of Doom and Sinestro's Ultraviolet Lantern Corps, the Justice League linked all Earthly life, briefly transforming the world into an untouchable and unconquerable White Lantern Planet.

DEATH IS NOT THE END
Alive or dead, Life's greatest defenders could not resist the urgent siren call of the mysterious White Entity.

ON THE RECORD

As epilogue to the *Blackest Night*, the unholy cosmic terror was followed by a *Brightest Day*.

A dozen deceased heroes and villains returned, each with a mysterious mission to fulfill. Closely observed by revived revenant Boston Brand, the White Lanterns pursued their ascribed goals, searching for fulfillment.

Their efforts eventually led to the return of Earth's elemental protector, as Alec Holland once again took up the mantle of Swamp Thing—avatar of The Green.

RENEWAL AND REBIRTH
The White energies of the *Brightest Day* were used to purge Swamp Thing of Nekron's pestilent influence and revive the guardian of Earth's ecology.

WHITE MARTIANS

DEBUT *Justice League* (Vol. 1) #71 (May 1969)
EYES Red **HAIR** None
POWERS/ABILITIES Telepathy, telekinesis, flight, enhanced senses, and shapeshifting.
ALLIES Ma'alefa'ak, Phobos
ENMIES J'onn J'onzz, Earth's Super Heroes
AFFILIATIONS Perpetua, The Epiphany, Martian Manhunter, Martian Man-Eater, Red Rising

TEETH BARED
The White Martians overtly hostile and aggressive intentions even extended to having an extra mouth filled with pointed teeth in their stomachs.

Martians are an ancient race of telepathic shape-shifters who had mastered all arts and sciences. White Martians are aggressive, and resented sharing the Red Planet with intellectual, philosophical Green Martians. Both are the product of genetic tampering by the Guardians of the Universe, who sought to pacify and tame an earlier species known as "The Burning," whose expansion potential threatened all life. Reality shifts in the fluctuating Multiverse have altered their history many times.

After *Flashpoint*, White Martians were the Red Planet's sole inhabitants. However, when their world began to die, they abandoned philosophy for dark blood-magic in their quest for survival.

A recent re-examination of Green Martian J'onn J'onzz's origins revealed that by the time of Mars' extinction event plague, Whites had been subsumed into a greater multi-culture of shapeshifters, but were regarded as a criminal sub-class because they preferred to retain their aggressive battle forms.

WHITE WITCH

DEBUT *Adventure Comics* (Vol. 1) #350 (Nov. 1966)
REAL NAME Xola Aq
BASE 31st-century Legion HQ, New Metropolis, New Earth
HEIGHT 5ft 8in **WEIGHT** 118 lbs
EYES Red **HAIR** Pale Blonde
POWERS/ABILITIES Skilled magic-user; reads auras; connection to magical forces throughout the universe
ALLIES Doctor Fate, Saturn Girl
ENEMIES Mordru
AFFILIATIONS Legion of Super-Heroes, Sorcerer's World Zerox

SINS OF THE FATHER
Xola Aq is a white witch with the blackest of secrets—her father is an evil entity, a Lord of Chaos, by the name of Mordru...

After studying the cosmomystic arts on Sorcerer's World Zerox for more than a century, Xola Aq became known as the White Witch—one of the most proficient magic wielders in the universe. Arrogant, impatient, and constantly holding back bubbling rage, she joined the Legion of Super-Heroes in anticipation of a forthcoming universal crisis. Her haughty pride in her achievements suffered a great blow when she learned that her father is Mordru the merciless, a supernatural threat to life and liberty across all reality, and the greatest mage of the age.

One of the few Legionnaires able to screen her thoughts from Saturn Girl, Xola Aq secretly burns with the fear that all her triumphs are owing to the blood of a mystic monster, rather than own hard work and sheer ability.

WHITE, PERRY

- **DEBUT** *Superman* (Vol. 1) #7 (Nov.–Dec. 1940)
- **BASE** Daily Planet, Metropolis
- **HEIGHT** 5ft 10in **WEIGHT** 200 lbs
- **EYES** Blue **HAIR** Brown
- **POWERS/ABILITIES** Incisive mind, keen journalistic instincts, deductive reasoning, organizational and logistics expertise, inspirational leader and mentor with great personal charisma.
- **ALLIES** Lois Lane, Jimmy Olsen, Clark Kent, Ron Troupe, Miko Ogawa, Heather Kelly
- **ENEMIES** Morgan Edge, Izzy Izquierdo, Glen Glenmorgan, Lex Luthor
- **AFFILIATIONS** *The Daily Planet*, Cat Grant, George Taylor

WORDS OF WISDOM
Perry White could juggle 10 stories at once and still be ready with a dozen fresh angles and an idea for the next big thing.

Perry White was a crusading, prize-winning journalist with the Metropolis-based *Daily Planet* for decades before taking a desk job. Once installed in an office, however, Perry surprised himself, and others, by proving to be an even greater editor than he was a roving news hound. An old-fashioned two-fisted reporter, Perry covered wars and political scandals, gang wars and murders, always aware that the public has a right to know and journalists have a sworn duty to root out the truth and tell their loyal readership.

As Editor and Editor-in-Chief, he made his own ironclad ethics and standards the yardstick by which all staff had to measure themselves. His is an increasingly difficult job in a multimedia world where integrity loses out to sensationalism every day. Perry's greatest role is as a mentor; teaching the next generation how to balance story against personal interest and how, in the end, journalism is a business not entertainment or a soapbox.

Recently, working for *The Daily Planet* has become one of the most dangerous jobs in the news business, drawing Perry and his team into regular contact with aliens, monsters, and superpowered madmen. However, his uncanny ability to discover and train great reporters like Lois Lane, Clark Kent, and Ron Troupe—and get the best out of them—is legendary throughout the industry. He has also steadfastly resisted every effort to lure him away from his beloved *Daily Planet*.

ON THE RECORD

An irreplaceable part of the "Superman Family," Perry White is one of the most iconic supporting characters in the history of comics. However, he was actually created for the *Superman Radio Show* in February 1940 and only introduced on the printed page at the year's end.

Before White's appearance, Clark Kent had jumped to the barked orders of Editor George Taylor and the great Metropolitan newspaper they worked for was the called the *Daily Star*.

HOLD THE PRESSES!
Hard-bitten, hard-boiled, and beefy, Perry knew that to get good stories you had to make your reporters hustle, but when things got tough you could trust them with your life.

WILDCAT

- **DEBUT** *Sensation Comics* (Vol. 1) #1 (Jan. 1942)
- **REAL NAME** Theodore "Ted" Grant
- **HEIGHT** 6ft 5in **WEIGHT** 250 lbs **EYES** Blue **HAIR** Grey
- **POWERS/ABILITIES** Boxer and mixed martial arts fighter in peak physical condition; Nine Lives curse bestowing virtual immortality
- **ALLIES** Stretch Skinner, Batman, Catwoman, Black Canary
- **ENEMIES** Brainwave, Yellow Wasp, Johnny Sorrow
- **AFFILIATIONS** JSA, Catwoman, Birds of Prey

In 1941, boxer Ted Grant was framed for murder and on the run when a comic book inspired him to don a costume and track down the real killer. As Wildcat, Ted cleared his name and, loving the double life, kept going. Specializing in sports-related crimes, he often helped his manager, Stretch Skinner, with the detective agency he ran as a sideline.

During World War II, Wildcat joined the Justice Society of America and All-Star Squadron. Cursed by the Spirit King, Ted was saved by magical ally Zatara who altered the spell, granting him nine lives. No matter how many times he died, he always had nine left. Ted scarcely aged, but saw almost everyone he loved pass away. He found renewed purpose teaching boxing to deprived kids and training future heroes. His students included Bruce Wayne, Selina Kyle and Dinah Drake (latterly Batman, Catwoman and Black Canary), and he now trains all new JSA recruits in hand-to-hand combat. Grant bears a troubled legacy. His goddaughter Yolanda Montez took on the mantle of Wildcat when Ted was crippled during *Crisis on Infinite Earths*, while his boxing protégé Hector Ramirez stole an old costume to become a Super Hero and was murdered by Killer Croc. Ted's own son Tom Bronson is a metahuman, and although initially resistant to fighting now serves with the Justice Society All-Stars as were-panther Tomcat.

GENTLE GIANT: Gruff and forthright, Wildcat believed every person was equal and that bad people should be decked whatever their gender or situation.

WILDCAT (YOLANDA MONTEZ)

- **DEBUT** *Infinity, Inc.* (Vol. 1) #12 (Mar. 1985)
- **REAL NAME** Yolanda Maria Dorothea Lucia Montez **BASE** Central City
- **HEIGHT** 5ft 8in **WEIGHT** 123 lbs
- **EYES** Blue **HAIR** Brown
- **POWERS/ABILITIES** Superhuman strength and speed, cat-like reflexes and agility; claws.
- **ALLIES** Ted Grant, Nuklon, Alexander Montez
- **ENEMIES** Dr. Benjamin Love, Psycho Pirate
- **AFFILIATIONS** JSA, Infinity Inc.

Before Yolanda Montez's birth, her mother was given experimental drugs by deranged doctor Benjamin Love: experiments that resulted in children born with mutant abilities. Yolanda concealed catlike powers hidden until her godfather—Wildcat Ted Grant—was crippled during the *Crisis on Infinite Earths*. She then assumed his Super Hero identity as Wildcat II. She served with Infinity, Inc. before joining a covert ops team hunting Eclipso in the nation of Parador. Yolanda died at vengeful monster's hands.

A new Yolanda Montez appeared on Earth-2 in the aftermath of *Flashpoint*. As Avatar of the Red, she channeled the lifeforce of fauna. Following Doctor Manhattan's apparent tampering with time in *Doomsday Clock*, the original Yolanda was back in action beside the original Wildcat.

WONDER GIRL

DATA

DEBUT (as Cassie) *Wonder Woman* (Vol. 2) #105 **(Jan. 1996)** (as Wonder Girl) *Wonder Woman* (Vol. 2) #111 **(July 1996)**
REAL NAME Cassandra "Cassie" Sandsmark **BASE** Metropolis
HEIGHT 5ft 3in **WEIGHT** 115 lbs **EYES** Blue **HAIR** Blonde
POWERS/ABILITIES Super-strength, agility, and speed; flight; armed with War Bracelets and a magical lasso.
ALLIES Superboy, Robin (Tim Drake), Impulse, Wonder Woman, Zeus
ENEMIES Trigon, Cassandra
AFFILIATIONS Young Justice, Teen Titans

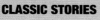

FIGHTING DESTINY
Confronting Superboy who, on orders from N.O.W.H.E.R.E., was trying to kidnap her, Cassie never suspected that, she and Kon-El would one day fall in love.

The daughter of archaeologist Helena Sandsmark and the demigod Lennox, Cassie Sandsmark was destined for great adventure. She began to find it as Wonder Girl, fighting alongside the youthful superhero teams the Teen Titans and Young Justice. Niece to Wonder Woman and the granddaughter of Zeus himself, Cassie strives to find herself in a world that is constantly changing all around her.

AMAZON AT HEART
Cassie Sandsmark has regained her memories of serving on the first incarnation of Young Justice. Whether or not she remembers her pre-*Flashpoint* origin remains to be seen.

Growing up with her single mother after her father left them, Cassie Sandsmark traveled the world to different archaeological digs. Frustrated and lonely, she began stealing art and artifacts, coming under the sway of an older thief, the charismatic Diesel. He and the teenage Cassie were exploring a temple near a Cambodian dig site when Diesel was attacked by a seemingly sentient being of liquid metal. A stunned Cassie was able to control it using a pair of bracelets that she found nearby. The bracelets were part of the Silent Armor, an alien parasite that enabled superpowers, but also constantly tried to subvert Cassie's will.

SILENT ARMOR
For a time, Cassie possessed the ability to unlock special silent armor. This power seems to have dissipated thanks to shifts in reality.

Cassie continued her life of crime until recruited by Red Robin (Tim Drake) to join the Teen Titans. Her battle to control the Silent Armor culminated when Diesel took it from her and she was forced to use the Armor's magical lasso to get it back. He died, and the Armor attracted the attention of the demon Trigon, who taunted Cassie by telling her he knew the identity of her father. Adrift in the world, Cassie went to Wonder Woman's then home in London, where she discovered that her father was the deceased demigod Lennox. Cassie also learned that Wonder Woman was her aunt. After a conflict with another of her aunts—the demigod, and her namesake Cassandra—realized that her true family was the Teen Titans, whom she joined as Wonder Girl.

That family would evolve as reality continued to shift. After defeating Despero while in Jacksonville, Florida, Wonder Girl was visited by her grandfather Zeus, who offered her a powerful necklace, one that corresponded with her bracelets and lasso. Cassie declined them, choosing to improve herself first in order to deserve the power he offered.

That quest brought her to Metropolis for college, where she chanced into a fight alongside Tim Drake. She soon rediscovered her long-lost friends from the pre-*Flashpoint* reality: Impulse and Superboy (Kon-El). Wonder Girl's memories were unlocked as she joined the team Young Justice, and she began to remember serving on the previous incarnation of this team. What she will do with these memories or her Olympian powers remains to be seen.

ON THE RECORD

The previous version of Cassie Sandsmark was not at all reluctant to be associated with Wonder Woman, having seized the mantle of a hero when Wonder Woman came to Cassie's hometown of Gateway City. Temporarily "borrowing" the Amazing Amazon's Sandals of Hermes and Gauntlet of Atlas, Cassie gained prodigious strength and the ability to fly—superpowers she used to help smash a clone of Doomsday.

Later, taking on the name Wonder Girl—an identity used before her by Donna Troy—she helped Wonder Woman defeat a manifestation of entropy called Decay.

AMAZONIAN ALLIANCE
As the symbol on her costume suggested, Wonder Girl was closely allied to Wonder Woman and the Amazons.

CLASSIC STORIES

***Young Justice* (Vol. 1) #4 (Jan. 1999)**
Cassie Sandsmark, wearing a black wig and goggles to mimic the appearance of her idol Donna Troy, joins up with Young Justice as Wonder Girl.

***Teen Titans* (Vol. 3) #1 (Sep. 2003)**
The new Teen Titans are formed, with Wonder Girl as one of the founding members, just as the previous Wonder Girl, Donna Troy, helped found the first Teen Titans. Romance with Superboy looms, and she discovers the truth about her father's identity.

WILDFIRE

DEBUT *Superboy* (Vol. 1) #195 (Jun. 1973)
REAL NAME Drake Burroughs
BASE Legion HQ, 31st century New Earth
HEIGHT 6ft 2in **WEIGHT** Variable
POWERS/ABILITIES Composed of anti-energy; can project and absorb energy across the electromagnetic spectrum; flight; solid form only when inside containment suit.
AFFILIATIONS Legion of Super-Heroes

Drake Burroughs was testing a radical new propulsion system when he was engulfed by an energy release that should have killed him. Instead, he became an ephemeral cloud of undetectable sentient energy, requiring a containment suit to keep himself from dispersing. Wanting to put his misfortune and new powers to good use, he applied to the Legion of Super-Heroes. He was initially rejected, as his powers seemed to mechanically duplicate other members natural gifts. It was only when he apparently sacrificed himself in action—revealing that his suit was an Energy Release Generator and he was his own unique super-power—that he was accepted.

Wildfire is impetuous and extremely self-confidant, considering himself one of the team's combat big guns and is always in the forefront of any battle.

WIZARD

DEBUT *All-Star Comics* #34 (Apr.–May 1947)
REAL NAME William Asmodeus Zard
HEIGHT 6ft **WEIGHT** 182 lbs
EYES Blue **HAIR** Black
POWERS/ABILITIES Magical powers include casting of illusions, hypnotism, and projection into the astral plane.
ENEMIES Justice Society of America, Justice League of America
AFFILIATIONS Injustice Society

A career criminal from a young age, William Zard was in and out of prison all through the 1930s. Deciding to refashion his criminal life, he left the US and traveled to a Tibetan monastery. Here he studied with a master lama and learned hypnotism and astral projection, before using those newfound skills to murder his teacher.

Zard then became the Wizard, returning to post-war USA and offering his services to the Justice Society of America in the mistaken belief that they were a criminal organization just pretending to be heroes. They, of course, refused, provoking Zard's lasting enmity and causing him to form the Injustice Society as a villainous counterpart to the JSA. They clashed numerous times as Zard increased his magical knowledge and expanded his list of enemies to include the Justice League of America.

WIZARD, THE (SHAZAM'S WIZARD)

DEBUT *Whiz Comics* #2 (Feb. 1940)
REAL NAME Mamaragan
BASE Rock of Eternity
HEIGHT 6ft **WEIGHT** 175 lbs
EYES Blue **HAIR** White
POWERS/ABILITIES Vast magical powers; immortality
ALLIES Shazam
ENEMIES Black Adam, the Seven Deadly Sins, Mister Mind, Sivana

The last survivor of the Council of Wizards bestowed the powers of Shazam on Billy Batson after initially rejecting him. The Wizard felt that Batson was not perfectly good and thus unsuitable for the role of his champion. The Wizard had long ago created Black Adam, as his champion: a frightened orphan just like Billy, but who later killed the other Council members and would eventually become Billy's nemesis. The Wizard confided in Pandora that he finally accepted Billy because he anticipated his own end and needed a successor. He also apologized for her wrongful conviction by the assembled Wizards in millennia past, when they made her part of the Trinity of Sin along with Phantom Stranger and The Question. The Wizard was later revealed to be the physical form of the god Mamaragan, lending his name to the new SHAZAM acronym, granting Billy Batson his powers and new heroic name.

With reality altered after *Rebirth*, The Wizard returned to life as the last of the Council, interfering with Billy and the family he shared his powers with, and even traveling to Earth to berate and challenge him. In a tense duel, Shazam took control of the magic, leaving The Wizard to ruefully assess his choices and future.

WRATH

DEBUT *Batman Special* #1 (Jun. 1984)
REAL NAME Elliot Caldwell
BASE Gotham City
HEIGHT 6ft 2in **WEIGHT** 205 lbs
EYES Blue **HAIR** Black
POWERS/ABILITIES Suit and device technology mirroring Batman's; trained combatant, both unarmed and with a variety of firearms; brilliant mind.
ALLIES Emperor Blackgate
ENEMIES Batman, Spoiler
AFFILIATIONS Scorn

CEO E.D. Caldwell was a business magnate who attempted to buy Wayne Industries. Bruce Wayne refused, knowing Caldwell Tech was a weapons company that would turn Wayne Industries' research to violent ends. At the same time, a series of murders targeting policemen attracted Batman's attention and he learned the truth about Caldwell: he was a killer calling himself Wrath. Modeling his appearance on Batman, he was using Caldwell Tech as a front to destroy Gotham City Police Department and create an army of his own, using both his and Wayne technologies.

The Dark Knight later discovered Caldwell's hatred of police began when his father was murdered during a diamond heist by corrupt cops. With this knowledge, Batman confronted and defeated Wrath, imprisoning him in Blackgate—where he began a villainous partnership with the criminal Emperor Blackgate. Caldwell eventually escaped, taking over a TV studio and demanding Batman fight him live on air to confirm Wrath's A-list villain status. Instead, he and his army of terrorists were soundly crushed by apprentice Super Hero Spoiler.

ON THE RECORD

The original Wrath also modeled himself after Batman, and focused his obsession on destroying those he blamed for the deaths of his parents—law enforcement officers.

After years as an assassin for hire, he returned to Gotham City and plotted to assassinate Commissioner James Gordon. However, he died in a fall from the roof of a building where he was fighting Batman. His adopted son, trained to be the Robin to Wrath's Batman, later adopted the Wrath's name and mission as well, before being caught by Batman and Nightwing.

WRATHFUL OBSESSION
The first Wrath was haunted and inspired by Batman—and determined to destroy him.

WONDER TWINS

DEBUT *Super Friends* (Vol. 1) #7 (Oct. 1977)
REAL NAME Jayna and Zan
BASE Hall of Justice
HEIGHT Unknown
WEIGHT Unknown
EYES Violet **HAIR** Black
POWERS/ABILITIES Shapeshifting: Jayna into any animal form, Zan into water
ALLIES Young Justice, Superman, Gleek, Polly Math
ENEMIES Mr Mxyzptlk, Lex Luthor, League of Annoyance
AFFILIATIONS Astrisk

ALIEN FRIENDS
The shapeshifting Wonder Twins proved too much for Mr. Mxyzptlk and impressed the Justice league with their crime-fighting skills.

Twins Jayna and Zan were born on the planet Exxor, a utopian place with virtually no crime or social problems. However, their grandfather had been responsible for terrible purges of those deemed unworthy of the planet, and the twins' father asked Superman to take the teenagers to Earth to escape their family's shame.

As well as being enrolled in high school, Jayna and Zan were given internships at the Hall of Justice, where they defeated Mr. Mxyzptlk in their first week on the job. Both twins were shapeshifters, with Jayna able to transform into any animal and Zan to become water in any of its forms. After impressing the Justice League with their fresh approach to crime fighting, the twins were given a new department, Astrisk (Assessing Strategic Threats Requiring Innovative Skills and Knowledge).

WORLD FORGER

DEBUT *Dark Nights: Metal* (Vol. 1) #4 (Feb. 2018)
REAL NAME Alpheus
BASE Sixth Dimension
HEIGHT Variable
WEIGHT Variable
EYES Yellow
HAIR None
POWERS/ABILITIES Godlike powers of creation using the energy of the World Forge
ALLIES Monitor, Justice League
ENEMIES Perpetua
AFFILIATIONS None

MULTIVERSAL MAKER
Even when seemingly destroyed, the godlike powers of the World Forger ensured his survival as he attempted to build a perfect world.

The World Forger, also known as Alpheus, is the son of Perpetua and the brother of the Monito and Anti-Monitor. He was tasked by his mother to create worlds to populate her Multiverse, using his hammer and the energy of the World Forge. When he learned that Perpetua was not obeying the natural order of the Omniverse, the World Forger joined his brothers in trying to resist her, but the Anti-Monitor betrayed them.

Later, Alpheus was able to assist the Justice League by sacrificing himself to open a portal to unite their members scattered through time and space. Although he was destroyed, such is his power that he can revive himself in the Sixth Dimension.

XA-DU

DEBUT *Adventure Comics* (Vol. 2) #283 (Apr. 1961)
BASE Phantom Zone
EYES Black **HAIR** Black
POWERS/ABILITIES Kryptonian superpowers, including flight, heat vision, super-strength; ecto-suit
ALLIES Mr. Mxyzptlk, Brainiac, Little Man
ENEMIES Superman, Supergirl, Batman, Wonder Woman
AFFILIATIONS Anti-Superman Army

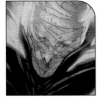

Kryptonian Xa-Du conducted forbidden experiments in suspended animation, leaving many patients virtual zombies. For these crimes, Xa-Du was the first prisoner condemned to the interdimensional Phantom Zone. Xa-Du swore revenge on the man who had discovered the Zone—fellow scientist Jor-El—and all his kin. After Krypton exploded, Xa-Du built an ecto-suit inside the Zone, allowing him to escape and travel to Superman's Fortress of Solitude. He despatched despised Kal-El into the dreaded Zone, but Superman disabled the ecto-suit, sending Xa-Du's back to the Phantom Zone. As the Phantom King, Xa-Du returned to Earth as the Phantom King several times, allying with Mr. Mxyzptlk, Brainiac, and Little Man to combat their mutual enemy.

XERO

DEBUT *Xer0* #1 (May 1997)
REAL NAME Coltrane Walker
BASE National City
POWERS/ABILITIES Can fire laser blasts; able to phase; master of unarmed combat.
ALLIES Frank Decker
ENEMIES Doctor Polaris, targets of Xer0's agency

Coltrane "Trane" Walker was an African-American athlete who played for the National City Vipers basketball team. He was also a technologically enhanced secret agent for a covert government agency, who disguised himself as a blond and blue-eyed Caucasian. He became renowned for his efficiency in cleaning up after espionage operations, including eliminating any witnesses. Walker was killed on his first mission, but was resurrected by an experimental enzyme that restored his physical health but drained him of all emotion. This not only made him a star basketball player, but also a remorseless killer, and he became known in the business as Xer0, aka the "Closer." Walker died again in a test of his capabilities set up by his superior, Frank Decker, and was once again brought back to life. This time, Walker's rebirth left him brain-damaged. It remains to be seen whether his agency will attempt to return Walker to his role as Xer0.

XS

DEBUT *Legionnaires* #0 (Oct.1994)
REAL NAME Jenni Ognats
BASE 31st century Earth **EYES** Brown
HAIR Black **POWERS/ABILITIES** Super-speed; tapping the Speed Force
ALLIES Legion of Super-Heroes, Bart Allen
ENEMIES Tangleweb, Savitar

TESTING THE LIMITS:
In addition to superspeed, XS could fly thanks to her Legion flight ring, but she was not prepared for the time-travel she would do on the Legion's behalf.

Granddaughter of Barry Allen—the second Flash—Jenni Ognats was born a millennium from now on planet Aarok, As a teenager, Jenni inherited the family's power of super-speed. She could also agitate her molecules to vibrate through solid matter. Although initially difficult to coordinate while traveling at maximum velocity, she eventually established fine control and became the hero XS. Jenni joined the Legion of Super-Heroes and, on an early mission, traveled to the 20th century, teaming up with her cousin Bart Allen, hero-in-training Impulse. Together, they united with Superboy to fight villainous speedster Savitar, who was intent on eradicating all super-fast rivals. Jenni later journeyed to the 100th century and became trapped at the end of time. After the Time Trapper intervened, Jenni was able to return to her own century.

All Speed Force users are highly attuned to reality shifts, and XS dropped out of existence during the many crises besetting the Multiverse. Following *Rebirth*, Jenni returned to the memory of her cousin Bart, so her physical comeback seems likely.

343

WONDER WOMAN

DATA

DEBUT *All Star Comics* #8 (Dec. 1941–Jan. 1942)
REAL NAME Diana
BASE Washington, D.C.
HEIGHT 6ft **WEIGHT** 165lbs **EYES** Blue **HAIR** Black
POWERS/ABILITIES Divinely bestowed strength, speed, and durability matching the Olympian gods; expertise in many forms of armed and unarmed combat; flight; Lasso of Truth compels those in its coils to tell the truth; can speak with animals.
ALLIES Batman, Superman, Aquaman, Steve Trevor, Donna Troy, Hippolyta
ENEMIES Circe, The Cheetah, Giganta, Dr. Psycho, Silver Swan
AFFILIATIONS Justice League of America, Amazons, Justice League Dark

Wise as Athena, stronger than Hercules, swift as Hermes, and beautiful as Aphrodite, Wonder Woman is Diana, daughter of Zeus. She is the princess of an ancient tribe of warrior woman known as the Amazons, and a founding member of the Justice League. After a childhood spent learning the arts of war on the island of Themyscira, she ventured into the world of mortals as the Amazons' ambassador of peace. Diana abides by a strict ethical code; her goal is peace and harmony between women and men. But she knows there's a very long way to go before this can be achieved.

AT A GLANCE...

Amazon Princess
Diana spent her childhood trained by the the Amazons of Themyscira. Their world exists outside our own, and they live their lives with great dedication to their Patrons, the Olympian Gods.

Bracelets
Once destroyed in the uprising that originally freed the Amazons, Wonder Woman's bracelets used to belong to her mother, Hippolyta. They were re-forged using Amazonium, a rare metal found deep inside Themyscira. To date, they are the strongest bracelets worn by any Amazon.

If nothing else, Diana of Themyscira stands for truth. However, it wasn't until recently that she realized she had been living a lie. Diana was born on the island of Themyscira, the daughter of Zeus and the Amazon Queen Hippolyta. However, her origins were hidden for decades to protect her from the wrath of Zeus's wife Hera, who was known to hunt down and kill her husband's illegitimate children. This gave rise to the legend that Queen Hippolyta had sculpted Diana from clay.

Growing up on Themyscira as the only child of her people, Diana was loved by the Amazons and doted on by Hippolyta. While she excelled in the ways of war, her thoughts were always of peace. It was this kind heart that took pity on American Steve Trevor, when he and five other Navy Seals crashed their plane on the shores of the island paradise. While his friends died in the wreck, Steve was healed in part due to the Amazons' purple ray and the medical expertise of the Amazon named Epione.

As Diana bonded with Steve, the Council of Themyscira met to discuss these soldiers that had landed on their sacred soil. There were no men on Themyscira, and Queen Hippolyta was tasked with deciding if this was an invasion, or perhaps the work of her old enemy, Ares, the God of War. To that end, the Council decided to choose a champion to send back to "Man's World." The chosen ambassador would accompany Steve Trevor and assess this new threat to the Amazons' way of life. To fairly choose this warrior, Hippolyta advanced the schedule of the Amazon's traditional games, feats of skill that would prove which Amazon was the most worthy. However, the winner of the games would forsake her natural immortality and never be allowed to return to Themyscira.

Hippolyta knew the outcome before the games even began. And as predicted, Diana was one of the last three women standing after the initial trials of battle. To choose the victor, Hippolyta asked each woman to deflect a bullet from a gun found in the wreckage of Steve Trevor's plane. Only Diana successfully deflected the shot with her bracelets, and soon she and Trevor were leaving the island for the United States aboard his reconstructed plane, albeit with an extra added feature thanks to the Amazons' technology: the aircraft was now invisible.

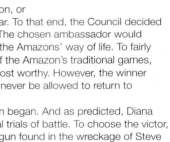

COMMUNING WITH THE GODS
While in a Navy holding cell, Wonder Woman was visited by the Olympian Gods in animal form.

CLASSIC STORIES

***Wonder Woman* (Vol. 1) #212–222 (Jun.–Jul. 1974 to Feb.–Mar. 1976)** After losing her powers, Diana has to perform 12 labors to earn her way back into the Justice League—and Hercules can't help her.

***Wonder Woman* (Vol. 2) #1–6 (Feb.–Jul 1987)** Introduces Wonder Woman's modern history and her mission as an ambassador of peace, along with the now-classic origin of her powers as gifts from various Greek gods.

***Wonder Woman* (Vol. 2) #90–93, #0 (Sep. 1994–Jan. 1995)** Angry at Diana for the perceived failures of her mission in the outside world, Hippolyta declares a contest to determine a new Wonder Woman. This is won by the Amazon Artemis, who briefly claims Diana's title.

***Wonder Woman* (Vol. 2) #219 (Sep. 2005)** Faced with an impossible choice, Wonder Woman kills Maxwell Lord, freeing Superman of his mind control, but leaving her future with the Justice League in doubt.

Roping Them In
Wonder Woman's Lasso of Truth is called the Golden Perfect by the Amazons. It is able to compel those it comes in contact with to tell the truth. It is also virtually unbreakable.

AMAZON TECH
Wonder Woman sometimes employs an Invisible Jet, one that is undetectable by the naked eye and by most radar systems. This remarkable camouflage effect is achieved by the use of individual tiles that appear purple from the inside. Surprisingly, the Amazons can convert any aircraft to make it invisible using this technology.

NOW YOU SEE HER, NOW YOU DON'T
Wonder Woman's Invisible Jet is ideal for secret missions in faraway places. In addition to transporting useful equipment, it enables her to come and go undetected by enemies, and can provide a handy refuge when evading pursuit.

> *"You know who I am. Who the world needs me to be. I'm Wonder Woman."*
>
> **WONDER WOMAN**

WARRIOR FOR THEMYSCIRA
Wonder Woman is not against taking up arms in the cause of peace. More often than not, however, she wins her battles by showing love and mercy toward her opponents.

TWINNING
Jason and Wonder Woman didn't always see eye to eye, but they certainly looked like twin siblings, especially when Jason was clad in his god-made armor.

Clad in red, white, blue, and gold, with an eagle adorned on her chest, Diana was given the Golden Perfect – better known as the Lasso of Truth – an unbreakable rope enchanted by the Greek Gods. She and Steve returned to the U.S., where Diana met Lieutenant Etta Candy and an expert called in to help translate Diana's strange ancient language, Dr. Barbara Ann Minerva. Diana revealed to Dr. Minerva that she had been visited by the Greek Gods and had been given "gifts," including incredible strength.

When Diana stopped a shooting at a shopping mall orchestrated by the villainous Sear Group, she discovered her ability to fly and move at super-speed. She also soon realized that her lasso helped her talk to her new American friends, as well as to animals. Minerva and Diana then learned that the Sear Group was run by a villain who appeared to be Ares, God of War. Diana defeated Ares and his planned chemical attack, much later discovering that this Ares was a ruse created by Ares's children Phobos and Deimos. After saving the United Nations from this attack, Diana earned a Super Hero name of her very own: Wonder Woman.

Diana soon helped found the Justice League in order to repel an invasion by the evil New God Darkseid of Apokolips. She became a legend in her own right, fighting the likes of The Cheetah, Circe, Dr. Poison, Giganta, and dozens of other threats. While she and Steve Trevor originally shared a relationship, she soon fell in love with Superman, although that relationship ended when this version of Superman died, later to merge energy with the Superman of the pre-*Flashpoint* reality. She and Steve later rekindled their relationship after he set up a home for her on the Virginian Coast.

DARK MAGIC
Wonder Woman was briefly possessed by the goddess Hecate while fighting alongside her magical allies in the Justice League Dark.

THE AMAZO VIRUS

Lex Luthor's organic virus version of the Amazo android operating system transformed Dr. Armen Ikarus into Patient Zero. The virus gave him the uncanny ability to mimic any superpower he encountered. In the event, Wonder Woman subdued him long enough for Batman to get a sample of the virus to begin ascertaining its origin.

One of the few heroes who was immune to the virus, Wonder Woman then convinced Superman to work with Lex Luthor to discover a cure. Diana was also the one who figured out that Patient Zero could not mimic cold powers, laying the groundwork for Superman to neutralize the threat with his freeze breath, while Lex Luthor began distributing the vaccine.

PATIENT ZERO
He could mimic almost any superpower after being infected with the Amazo virus, but even Patient Zero was not able to simply shrug off the Lasso of Truth.

WONDER WOMAN

The life of the daughter of Zeus is complicated. For years, Wonder Woman was duped into believing that she could come and go from Themyscira as she pleased. She soon learned that her mind had been manipulated, and she was destined to never see her mother again, as past memories raced back to her. She had also believed that she had trained with Ares, the God of War and accepted his mantle when he died. That proved to be another manipulation of her reality, one that even Diana doesn't fully understand.

When Diana's half-brother Hercules was killed by Super-Villain Darkseid's daughter, the half-Amazon Grail, Wonder Woman learned she had a twin brother named Jason.

She sought Jason out, learning he had been taken from Themyscira as a baby by General Philippus and was given to an immortal in the outside world named Glaucus to raise as his own. When Diana finally met Jason, however, he betrayed her, siding at first with Grail. While Jason later realized the error of his ways, Grail was able to complete her mission. She brought Darkseid back to his prime using Zeus's energy. Darkseid and Zeus then clashed, with Zeus perishing in the conflict. Wonder Woman had gained a brother, but lost a father all in a single moment.

Jason adopted a suit of armor from the gods and fought valiantly by Wonder Woman's side, despite his rather unrefined behavior. When mysterious Dark Gods attacked Earth, Jason allowed himself to be taken by these powerful entities in order for Diana and the Justice League to live free. Despite being rocked by yet another

WONDER WOMAN IN WWII
A story has surfaced of Wonder Woman saving the life of the President of the United States in 1939, and inspiring the first generation of heroes. How this event was possible remains a mystery.

DIVIDED LOYALTIES
Wonder Woman partnered with the *New 52* version of Superman, with whom she had just begun a romantic relationship, to thwart General Zod's plot to extract Doomsday from the Phantom Zone. In a last-ditch move, she split an atom with her sword to destroy the Phantom Zone Gate. While her relationship with Superman seemed easy and natural, it was fated not to last.

STAR-CROSSED LOVERS?
Wonder Woman's relationship with Superman caused some tension in the Justice League—and indirectly led to the creation of Amanda Waller's competing Justice League of America.

tragedy, Wonder Woman continued to fight on, facing threats old and new, and even leading a team of magical heroes, the Justice League Dark.

With the help of the enchanted sword of Antiope, Diana was astonished she was able to find her way back to the real Themyscira. She reunited with her mother, and now has the ability to travel back and forth from the outside world at will. In fact, when Wonder Woman's bracelets were shattered by The Cheetah, who was wielding the fabled God Killer sword, Hippolyta was able to gift Diana with even stronger replacements during one of her many visits to Paradise Island.

With her past restored and her future bright, Wonder Woman is steadfast in her unending battle for justice and equality.

AMAZING AMAZONS
Wonder Woman entrusted the Bana-Mighdall champion Artemis with a barbed lasso renamed the Golden Promise—originally the evil Superwoman's Lasso of Submission. While both have Amazonian roots, Artemis's people were a nomadic tribe who worshipped the Egyptian Pantheon.

REBIRTH

TRUTH SEEKER
Before the event known as *Rebirth*, another in a series of manipulations of the DC universe by the powerful Doctor Manhattan, Diana believed herself a student of Ares and his heir as the God of War. However, when she found she could crush Ares's supposedly indestructible helmet in her hands as if it were paper, she realized that this was not the truth of her situation. She set out to discover her new status quo, realizing that every interaction she had had with the Amazons after her original departure into "Man's World" had been a lie.

ON THE RECORD

From the outset, Wonder Woman has been portrayed as a complex amalgamation of feminist icon and glamorous Super Hero. Over the years, the character has been a vital touchstone for comics' portrayal of women. She has also generally been known for her ability to find nonlethal solutions, even in the midst of bloody battles.

Changing with the times

With her character established in comics' Golden Age, Wonder Woman transformed during the Silver Age, becoming reborn for the feminist era. A 1959 origin story was the first to trace her powers to the blessings of the Olympian gods. Demeter granted her strength, Athena wisdom, Artemis the Eyes of the Hunter, Hestia control over the Fires of Truth, Aphrodite beauty, and Hermes the power of flight. Surrendering her powers from 1968 to 1972, the now-mortal Diana Prince trained in martial arts with the blind master I Ching and wore mod fashions in a series of adventures taking her around the globe.

Keeping the peace

Following *Crisis on Infinite Earths*, Wonder Woman was recreated as an emissary bringing a message of peace to "Patriarch's World" from Themyscira—the new name for Paradise Island, with a new history to go with it. The romance aspects of her character, diminishing since the 1960s, almost completely disappeared, and new layers were added to the original story of Hippolyta forming her from clay.

THEMYSCIRA'S CHAMPION
A strong believer in Amazonian ideals, Wonder Woman tried to spread a message of peace and mercy in the wider world.

AMAZON ARSENAL
Wonder Woman is rarely without her bracelets and lasso, which alone are enough to handle most enemies. But if the occasion demands it, she has additional armor and weaponry at her disposal— some of it claimed as trophies on the battlefield.

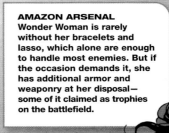

Battle royale

Diana's role and obligations in the outside world caused tensions back at home on Themyscira, eventually leading to all-out war between the different factions of Amazons on Themyscira and in the desert kingdom of Bana-Mighdall. This epic conflict destroyed Themyscira and led to the abolition of the Amazon royal family, however, Themyscira was later rebuilt as an archipelago of floating islands.

PARADISE LOST
When war came to Themyscira, Wonder Woman put her life on the line without compromising her ideals.

Fatal consequences

The most notable exception to Wonder Woman's commitment to nonlethal combat was her necessary killing of Maxwell Lord, who had seized control of Superman's mind. This choice had devastating consequences, alienating her from Batman and Superman—both of whom condemned her actions, but without suggesting what else she might have done—and laying the groundwork for the multiverse-shattering event known as *Infinite Crisis*.

THE HARDEST CHOICE
Seeing no other way to protect the world from Superman, Wonder Woman broke her own cardinal rule and killed Maxwell Lord.

XYLON

DEBUT *R.E.B.E.L.S.* (Vol. 2) #4 (Jul. 2009)
POWERS/ABILITIES Telepathy, exemplary marksmanship.
ALLIES R.E.B.E.L.S., L.E.G.I.O.N.
ENEMIES Starro the Conqueror, Kanjar Ro

Xylon was a member of the alien race known as the Dominators, a highly advanced and violent civilization that lived at the edge of the universe in a strict caste society. Each Dominator's position in society was determined by the size of a red dot that appeared on their forehead.

After serving as the Fleet Admiral of the Xylon Expanse, and later as Warrior Caste Commander, he became the first Dominator to take an individual name. Now calling himself Xylon, he joined Vril Dox's R.E.B.E.L.S. (Revolutionary Elite Brigade to Eradicate L.E.G.I.O.N. Supremacy), the splinter group of the intergalactic peacekeeping force L.E.G.I.O.N. (Licensed Extra-Governmental Interstellar Operatives Network). Working alongside his newfound allies they were able to defeat Starro the Conqueror.

Soon after this first battle, and in defiance of the Dominator caste system, the rebellious Xylon replaced the telltale red dot on his forehead with the L.E.G.I.O.N. symbol.

CASTE AWAY
When the R.E.B.E.L.S. transitioned into a reformed L.E.G.I.O.N., Xylon took its symbol as his own.

STATUS SYMBOL
The large red dot on the forehead of the Fleet Admiral of the Xylon Expanse denotes his high social ranking within the Dominators.

YAT, SODAM

DEBUT *Tales of the Green Lantern Corps Annual* (Vol. 1) #2 (Sep. 1986)
BASE Sector 1760
EYES Green **HAIR** Greyish black
POWERS/ABILITIES Daxamite superpowers and a Green Lantern power ring generating hard-light constructs, flight and travel through space.
ALLIES Justice League
ENEMIES Mongul, Sinestro, Durlans
AFFILIATIONS Green Lantern Corps

On his homeworld Daxam, young Sodam Yat dreamed of traveling to other planets. When alien Tessog crashed near him, Yat secretly nursed him. However, his outraged parents killed the extraterrestrial, making Yat believe the alien heralded an invasion force. When Yat later saw Tessog's stuffed body in a museum, the shock restored his memories. Horrified, he rebuilt Tessog's spaceship to escape Daxam, but was chosen as a Green Lantern and acquired a power ring. The Guardians opted to conceal two prophecies from Yat: That he would become the ultimate Green Lantern and he would be the last survivor of the Lantern Corps.

Yat defended sentient planet Mogo during the Sinestro Corps War. The Guardians empowered Yat with the Ion Force—living embodiment of willpower—and he brought glory to the Corps.

Yat suffered a rare defeat when captured by Durlans, who removed his ring and experimented on him. He escaped with the aid of the Green Lantern Corps and liberated Daxam from the shapeshifters. He battled beside the Justice League to defeat Cyborg Superman Hank Henshaw, and later risked death from toxic elements in Earth's atmosphere to aid the Justice League against The Eradicator and an army of all-conquering Daxamites in the War of the Supermen.

SODAM'S RETURN
After he was captured by the Durlans, Sodam Yat was held on the planet Corona Seven. He was harshly interrogated but later freed by the Green Lantern Corps.

ON THE RECORD

Sodam Yat has repeatedly lived up to the prophecy declaring him the ultimate Green Lantern. He has challenged some of the most fearsome villains in the universe, including Mongul, Darkseid, and even the Anti-Monitor. In *Green Lantern Corps* (Vol. 2) #17 (2007), Yat came close to death from lead poisoning, after being exposed to the metal during a fight with Superboy-Prime. He battled courageously, but as a result of that incident Yat will die within minutes if he ever removes his ring.

ION FORCE
Sodam Yat is able to access and generate the green willpower energy of the symbiotic Ion Force, which bestows him with immense power.

YA'WARA

DEBUT *Aquaman* (Vol. 7) #7 (May 2012)
BASE Brazil
EYES Blue **HAIR** Black
POWERS/ABILITIES Telepathic communication with animals; uses magic pendant to teleport.
ALLIES Aquaman, the Others
ENEMIES Black Manta, Madame Xan, Mayhem

Ya'Wara is a powerful warrior of the Tapirape, an indigenous Brazilian tribe that lives deep in the Amazon rainforest. An Amazon deity granted her the power to communicate telepathically with animals, which she uses as a fierce protector of wildlife and the Earth's fragile environments. She is a skilled fighter, equally good at hand-to-hand combat and wielding her twin daggers. If that fails, her loyal pet jaguars are never far from her side.

Ya'Wara also possesses a pendant that allows her to teleport almost anywhere, including to the moon. This pendant was one of seven ancient magical relics that were created by Atlan, the first king of Atlantis. The relic also brought her in touch with Aquaman, with whom she also shared a telepathic connection. Together, they briefly joined forces with the team known as the Others, to search for the other relics.

During a fight with Black Manta and his cohorts, who were also looking for Atlan's mystical artifacts, one of Ya'Wara's jaguars was killed. She responded by slaughtering the hunters, much to Aquaman's horror. In a final confrontation, Manta stole Ya'Wara's pendant and used it to escape.

ANIMAL INSTINCTS
Believing Stephen Shin had betrayed The Others to Black Manta, Ya'Wara was set to kill him, when Aquaman and Mera intervened.

YEUNG, EDGAR FULLERTON

DEBUT *Harley Quinn Annual* (Vol. 2) #1 (Dec. 2014)
POWERS/ABILITIES Self-designed robotic bodies provide mobility, articulated limbs, and weapons systems to his limbless, egg-like form.
ENEMIES Cap'n Horatio Strong

The brilliant, egg-bodied being Edgar Yeung, also known as Egg Fu, has a weird origin that involves the Great Ten, Chinese sleeper agents, extra-strong glue, and a giant bird's nest. When he was evicted from his SoHo apartment and could not find a new place because of his odd appearance, he hatched a desperate plan: kidnap Poison Ivy so that she could brew a potion to make people like him. Ivy's friend Harley Quinn went one better, and offered him a room in her apartment. "Eggy" moved in, got a job at the sideshow downstairs, and joined in Harley's wacky adventures. He also did the housework, renovations, and the training of Quinn's "Gang of Harleys" team.

Pre-*Flashpoint*, the egg-shaped role was taken by evil genius Chang Tzu who, with his Science Squad, created the dread Four Horsemen of Apokolips. He was killed in succession by Will Magnus and his mini-Metal Men, Wonder Woman, and Power Girl, only to rise again in a new cyborg body.

YOUNG ALL-STARS

DEBUT *Young All-Stars* (Vol. 1) #1 (Jun. 1987)
MEMBERS/POWERS Iron Munro (Arnold Munro): Chemically created Superman; **Dan the Dyna-Mite** (Danny Dunbar): Atomic-charged tiny titan; **Flying Fox**: Canadian First Nations mystic; **Fury** (Helena Kosmatos): Amazon warrior, fueled by the anger of the mythic Furies; **Neptune Perkins**: Aquatic adventurer; **Sandy the Golden Boy** (Sanderson Hawkins): Acrobatic detective; **Tigress** (Paula Brooks): Martial artist, weapons master, tracker and manhunter; **Tsunami** (Miya Shimada): Controller of tidal forces; **Nisei** (Japanese-American): Sub-sea storm bringer.
ALLIES Justice Society of America, All-Star Squadron
ENEMIES Ultra-Humanite, Axis Amerika, Baron Blitzkrieg, Mekanique, Black Circle, Per Degaton, Hugo Danner, Bedlam, Darkseid
AFFILIATIONS Justice Society of America

During World War II, a wave of metahumans and mystery men arose to battle the forces of fascism. Many of these costumed heroes had juvenile sidekicks and, as the conflict intensified, felt increasingly unhappy about subjecting them to the horrors that were unfolding on a daily basis.

In 1942, the Young All-Stars was created as a youth auxiliary to the All-Star Squadron. Here the frustrated kids and a number of new champions were usefully kept away from the action to appear at Bond Drives and publicity appearances, raising funds for the war effort. However, they were targeted by Nazi super-squad Axis Amerika and soon found themselves undertaking a non-stop crusade against evil every bit as deadly as anything the adult heroes faced on the battlefront.

The Young All-Stars broke up due to personality conflicts before the war ended, although many of the team continued as individual heroes—and villains—in the postwar years.

KID COMMANDOS
The world's first superpowered teen team eventually joined the ranks of the adult All-Star Squadron.
1 Neptune Perkins
2 Flying Fox
3 Iron Munro
4 Fury I
5 Dan the Dyna-Mite
6 Tsunami

YOUNG JUSTICE

DEBUT *Young Justice: The Secret* (Vol. 1) #1 (Jun. 1998)
BASE Secret Sanctuary, Happy Harbor, Rhode Island
FORMER MEMBERS Robin/Drake; **Superboy** (Kon-El/Connor Kent); **Impulse** (Bart Allen); **Wonder Girl** (Cassie Sandsmark); **Arrowette** (Bonnie King); **Red Tornado**; **Secret** (Greta "Suzie" Hayes); **Empress** (Anita Fite); **Batgirl** (Cassandra Cain); **Slobo**; **Ray Terrill**
CURRENT MEMBERS/POWERS Robin (Tim Drake): Genius, computer expert, martial artist, acrobat; **Superboy** (Kon-El/Connor Kent): Limited Kryptonian powers; **Impulse** (Bart Allen): Super-speed; **Wonder Girl** (Cassie Sandsmark): Super-strength, speed, invulnerability, flight; **Arrowette** (Bonnie King): Archer; **Jinny Hex** (descendent of the West's greatest gunfighter with crate full of magic weapons); **Amethyst** (mystic princess of Gemworld); **Teen Lantern** (hacker of Oan Green Energy); **Naomi** (Naomi McDuffie): enhanced speed, strength, durability, energy projection, golden armor
ALLIES Snapper Carr, Donald Fite, Forever People, Warlord
ENEMIES Agenda, Klarion, Harm, Buzz, Mr. Mxyzptlk, D.E.O., Dark Opal, Bedlam, Darkseid, Dr. Glory/S.T.A.R. Labs
AFFILIATIONS Wonder Twins, Hall of Justice

Young Justice began after magic exiled all Earth's adults to another world, leaving only sidekicks and junior heroes to conquer genie-possessed child Bedlam and restore the status quo. Crisis averted, Robin (Tim Drake), Impulse (Bart Allen), and Superboy (Conner Kent) hung out to have fun without adult supervision. A loose affiliation was born.

After rescuing immaterial girl Secret from a Department of Extranormal Operations holding center, the teens resolved to stay together as a team and keep doing good. As membership grew, adults started interfering. When Young Justice took over the JLA's old mountain headquarters, they had to accept android Red Tornado as a live-in guardian. Eventually Young Justice became a beacon for every young hero in the business.

After many frantic adventures and nonstop mayhem, Nightwing forcibly disbanded the team after Troia and Omen were killed by Brainiac-controlled super-robots. The bitter survivors renamed themselves Teen Titans and continued under the supervision of wiser heads—Cyborg, Starfire, Beast Boy, and Raven. Following a number of reality shifts including *Flashpoint* and *Rebirth*, Bart Allen returned to Earth-0 and discovered none of his old friends remembered him. Determined to find out why, he started searching and triggered a series of events pulling the old team back together while recruiting new teammates, Amethyst, Jinny Hex, Teen Lantern, Naomi and others. Their adventures crossed many universes, and included defeating tyrants such as Dark Opal, and exposing S.T.A.R. Labs' boss as criminal scientist Dr. Glory. The team became a beacon for all Earth's underage Super Heroes.

JUST KIDDING
The junior sidekicks all had a lot to prove and didn't need adults holding their hands or holding them back.

JUNIOR JUSTICE LEAGUE
1 Superboy
2 Jinny Hex
3 Robin/Drake
4 Wonder Girl
5 Amethyst
6 Impulse
7 Naomi
8 Teen Lantern

ALL TOGETHER NOW
From an accidental start, Young Justice attracted many young heroes into its ranks and, for a time, became a formidable fighting force.

ZATANNA

DEBUT *Hawkman* (Vol. 1) #4 (Oct.–Nov. 1964)
REAL NAME Zatanna Zatara **BASE** Mobile
HEIGHT 5ft 9in **WEIGHT** 125 lbs **EYES** Blue **HAIR** Black
POWERS/ABILITIES Expert magician with knowledge of innumerable spells, which she can use to teleport, create mystic barriers, fire energy bolts, control the elements, heal bodies, and manipulate minds; generally casts an enchantment by reciting a word backward, but can also cast a spell by other means.
ALLIES John Constantine, Giovanni Zatara, Batman
ENEMIES Nick Necro, Enchantress, Felix Faust, Blackbriar Thorn, Upside-Down Man
AFFILIATIONS Justice League Dark

ZATARA BURNS
Zatanna was plagued by the memory of her father being burned alive in a magic ritual that went terribly wrong, and blamed Constantine for his death.

Zatanna Zatara is one of the most powerful magicians in the world, able to alter reality with a single word. As a member of Justice League Dark she helps defend the Earth from supernatural threats. However, this mighty sorceress has learned to her cost that magical power can be a curse as well as a blessing.

HAT TRICKS
Zatanna enchanted audiences with her stage magic routine—but they were unaware she was capable of real sorcery.

Zatanna Zatara is the daughter of famed magician Giovanni Zatara. While she would eventually become a stage magician like her father, Zatanna learned she could access real magic at an early age. As a girl, when she brought a rabbit back to life, her father nearly died from the resulting magical backlash. Magic has its benefits, but Zee learned that day that it also has its price.

As she traveled with her father, mastering real magic and stage magic, she met and helped train a young Bruce Wayne (the future Batman), who wanted to know the ins and outs of the misdirection world. Soon Zatanna studied with the corrupt Nick Necro and the less-corrupt and usually well-intentioned John Constantine. Zatanna and Constantine eventually vanquished Necro, but tragedy later struck when a ritual led by Constantine went awry and burned Zatanna's father alive.

Several years later, the world was threatened by the malevolent Enchantress and the Super Heroes of the Justice League proved helpless against her witchcraft. Realizing that the world needed a new, specialized Justice League to fight supernatural threats, Madame Xanadu recruited Zatanna, John Constantine, Deadman, and Shade the Changing Man into a new team: Justice League Dark. After vanquishing the Enchantress, the team regrouped to take on the newly awakened vampire lord Cain.

After the Source Wall at the far reaches of the universe was pierced, unleashing strange new energies into the world, Zatanna found herself in a new incarnation of the Justice League Dark, this time aside Wonder Woman, Detective Chimp, Swamp Thing, and Man-Bat. Fending off powerful forces, like the goddess Hecate and the villainous Upside-Down Man, Zatanna soon learned that the Upside-Down Man was holding the spirit of her father Zatara. She embarked on a mission to return him to the mortal plane, not realizing that every step of the way was all part of her father's meticulous master plan to vanquish the Upside-Down Man's evil once and for all.

MISTRESS OF MAGIC
Zatanna possesses mastery over mystical and cosmic forces, powers as ancient as the universe itself.

ON THE RECORD

The pre-*Flashpoint* version of Zatanna is also haunted by the death of her father, and obsessed with bringing him back from Hell. She joined the Justice League, playing a key role in the *Identity Crisis* event. After Doctor Light molested Sue Dibny and threatened the League's loved ones, Zatanna used magic to alter his mind. The ethics of this caused a schism in the League—especially when it was revealed that Zatanna had also altered the memories of her teammates.

MIND BENDING
Zatanna employs controversial, mind-altering magic to neutralize the threat of Super-Villain Doctor Light.

CLASSIC STORIES

***Seven Soldiers: Zatanna* #1-4 (Jun.–Dec. 2005)**
After Zatanna loses her magical powers in a clash with the magical entity Gwydion, the intrepid enchantress and her apprentice Misty Kilgore embark on a quest to recover them.

***Justice League of America* (Vol. 2) #39-40 (Jan.–Feb. 2010)** During *Blackest Night*, Zatanna battles her undead father in a dramatic sorcerous duel. In the aftermath, she quits the Justice League.

***Black Canary and Zatanna: Bloodspell* (2014)**
When Black Canary tangles with a magic-wielding gang, she goes looking for magical help—which leads her to her first encounter with her future friend Zatanna.

ZATARA

DEBUT *Action Comics* (Vol. 1) #1 **(Jun. 1938)**
REAL NAME Giovanni "John" Zatara
BASE Shadowcrest Mansion, Gotham County
HEIGHT 5ft 11in **WEIGHT** 170 lbs **HAIR** Black **EYES** Blue
POWERS/ABILITIES profound mystical knowledge; can cast a wide variety of magic spells by speaking a word or phrase backward; excellent stage showman and a master of prestidigitation.
ALLIES Batman, Superman, John Constantine, Sargon, Nick Necro
ENEMIES Wotan, King Inferno, Allura, Lobo
AFFILIATIONS Cult of the Cold Flame, All-Star Squadron, Justice League Dark

Giovanni "John" Zatara learned conjuring as a child, after his uncle gave him a magic kit. He discovered he was a true sorcerer while performing: instinctively casting a spell to extinguish a fire. He learned he was descended from *Homo magi*—a human subspecies naturally manipulating magical forces—and fell in love with a woman named Sindella. Their daughter, Zatanna, inherited the gift of magic. Zatara arduously schooled her in all arcane arts, only revealing after his death that he had foreseen the coming of the Otherkind. Zatanna would be ready when the original multiversal creators of Magic returned to reclaim it. At 18, Zatanna defeated evil elemental Allura to rescue Zatara from banishment. For a few years they were together, although Zatanna's relationships with Nick Necro and John Constantine—and Zatara's secret deals with the latter—foretold more trouble to come. Zatara died protecting Zatana during a ritual that misfired. Damned, he was rescued during the Reign in Hell conflict and believed he had found oblivion, but returned as a Black Lantern during the Blackest Night. Banished to The Other Place with Sargon the Sorcerer, he holds back Otherkind horrors.

LOVE WILL TEAR US APART
Zatara loved his daughter Zatanna so much that he sacrificed himself to save her—and was damned in the process.

SPELLBOUND
Zatara would do anything to protect his young daughter Zatanna—as puppeteer and criminal Oscar Hempel discovered. Zatara turned Oscar into a living puppet! Something that would come back to haunt Zatanna in later life.

ZAURIEL

DEBUT *JLA* (Vol. 1) #6 (Jun. 1997)
BASE The Silver City, Heaven
EYES Glowing white **HAIR** Variable
POWERS/ABILITIES Angel physiology; Divinely enhanced senses; bodily transformation; casts spell-casting; winged flight; sonic scream.
ENEMIES Sin Eater, Felix Faust, the Blight, Nick Necro
AFFILIATIONS Eagle Host of Heaven, Justice League Dark

GUARDIAN ANGEL
As a member of the angelic host, Zauriel has watched over the Phantom Stranger for thousands of years, appearing in many guises.

A Guardian Angel of the Eagle Host, Zauriel has a deep affinity for humanity. He joined the Justice League in many battles to preserve life, even against rival Angels of the Bull Host. Following *Flashpoint*, Zauriel safeguarded tormented hero Phantom Stranger for millennia, helping against The Question after the accursed wanderer betrayed him and fellow "sinner" Pandora. Zauriel was forced to frequently intervene whenever the Stranger attempted to re-enter heaven in violation of divine edicts.

Zauriel was lured into the House of Mystery and constrained by John Constantine. The Stranger's Justice League Dark teammates needed angelic might. Motivated by love for the Stranger, Zauriel agreed, joining their fight against the Blight, Nick Necro, and Felix Faust. Ultimately, the heroes triumphed, but Zauriel died. Phantom Stranger confronted his own demons and God himself to achieve Zauriel's resurrection, and the angel returned in female form.

ZEUS, MAXIE

DEBUT *Detective Comics* (Vol. 1) #483 (Apr.–May 1979)
REAL NAME Maximillian Zeus
BASE Arkham Asylum
HAIR Brown **EYES** Brown
POWERS/ABILITIES Despite delusions of divinity, Maxie Zeus has no powers, though he is a cunning gang leader, employing technology to "prove" his divinity.
ENEMIES Batman

DIVINE DELUSION
Maxie Zeus believed he was a Greek god and dressed and bulked up accordingly. Little did he know he was just Deacon Blackfire's puppet.

History professor Maximilian Zeus was driven insane by the death of his wife. His obsession with Classical mythology led him to conclude that he was an incarnation of Greek god Zeus, and he became a crime lord in Gotham City. Unconcerned by loss of human life, Zeus and his gang committed mythologically inspired crimes, before he was arrested by Batman and incarcerated in Arkham Asylum. Crazed acolytes of deceased villain Deacon Blackfire chose Maxie's muscled body to house the spirit of their leader. Blackfire performed a ritual to merge Gotham City with Hell, but The Spectre intervened and exorcized Blackfire. Maxie's body was recovered by Detective Jim Corrigan. Zeus recovered, but still believed he was an Olympian god.

Zeus frequently slips out of Arkham. acting as a self-appointed oracle to Batman, obscurely warning him of the threat of Bane and others. On one occasion, Zeus was badly beaten by an increasingly out-of-control Dark Knight.

The DC universe is populated with a myriad of memorable characters. The *DC Comics Encyclopedia* presents as many of these as possible, and Roll Call spotlights some of the more notable players who round out that rich and diverse DC universe.

ACRATA
DEBUT *Superman Annual* (Vol. 2) #12 (Aug. 2000)
REAL NAME Andrea Rojas **BASE** Mexico City
ALLIES Iman, El Muerto, Superman **ENEMIES** Duran, Eclipso
BACKGROUND Deriving teleportation powers from an ancient Mayan symbol, Acrata and her occasional allies Iman and El Muerto defended Mexico City from sorcerer and eco-terrorist Duran, aided by Superman. Besides her superhuman abilities, Acrata had a penchant for dispensing literary quotations at moments of high tension, perhaps inspired by her learned father, Professor Bernardo Rojas.

AGENT LIBERTY II
DEBUT *Superman* #691 (Oct. 2009)
BASE Washington, D.C.
ENEMIES Ursa
BACKGROUND It was never revealed whether the second Agent Liberty was related to the murdered Benjamin Lockwood, the first Agent Liberty, or the paramilitary group the Sons of Liberty. Agent Liberty II served as a bodyguard to the then President of the United States, Martin Suarez, and lost her life when the Kryptonian villain Ursa attacked the White House.

AIR WAVE II
DEBUT *Green Lantern* #100 (Jan. 1978)
REAL NAME Harold "Hal" Lawrence Jordan
BASE Dallas
ALLIES Justice Society of America **ENEMIES** Kobra, Lex Luthor
BACKGROUND Harold Jordan, named after Hal Jordan of the Green Lantern Corps, is the son of Air Wave I. He inherited his father's helmet, which allowed him to change his molecular structure and fly at super-speed. He perished during the *Infinite Crisis* but was reanimated as a member of the Black Lantern Corps.

AMAZING GRACE
DEBUT *Superman* #3 (Mar. 1987)
BASE Apokolips
ALLIES Darkseid **ENEMIES** Superman
BACKGROUND The sister of Darkseid's star propagandist, Glorious Godfrey, Amazing Grace was able to manipulate the will of others with her beauty and persuasive powers. She was a master of mind control who lived in the slums of Apokolips. She located resistance groups and beguiled their leaders, drawing them out long enough for Darkseid to annihilate them.

AMYGDALA
DEBUT *Batman: Shadow of the Bat* #3 (Aug. 1992)
REAL NAME Aaron Helzinger **BASE** Gotham City, Blüdhaven
ALLIES Nightwing **ENEMIES** Batman
BACKGROUND In an effort to cure his homicidal rages, Aaron Helzinger underwent an operation in Arkham Asylum to have his amygdala cluster removed. However, the procedure had the opposite effect, leaving him permanently furious and bringing him into conflict with Batman. Helzinger received an implant that controlled his anger, allowing him to become a friend and ally of Dick Grayson, alias Nightwing.

ANANSA THE SPIDER QUEEN
DEBUT *Animal Man* #81 (Mar. 1995)
BASE Montana
ALLIES Her children **ENEMIES** Animal Man
BACKGROUND Anansa was a giant humanoid spider with the power to read minds. Prepared to do whatever it took to protect her offspring, she harvested human bodies to feed them. Her spider-children soon learned how to abduct and cocoon humans so that Anansa could feed off their dreams. The Spider Queen eventually abducted Animal Man and his son.

ANDROMEDA
DEBUT *Legion of Super-Heroes* #6 (Apr. 1990)
REAL NAME Laurel Gand
ALLIES Legion of Super-Heroes
ENEMIES Composite Man, Superboy-Prime
BACKGROUND Gand came from the planet Daxam in the 30th century. She was a member of the Legion of Super-Heroes where she represented her home planet. Gand possessed similar powers to Superman, including super-strength, heat-vision, and the ability to fly. However, she was hypersensitive to the element lead.

ANGLE MAN
DEBUT *Wonder Woman* #70 (Nov. 1954)
REAL NAME Angelo Bend
BASE Milan
ALLIES Devastation, Circe
ENEMIES The Cheetah, Catwoman
BACKGROUND Angle Man was a master thief who used a magical weapon called an Angler. It allowed him to teleport, bend space, alter gravity, and warp perception. He worked alone and also with the Secret Society of Super-Villains.

ANIMA
DEBUT *New Titans Annual* #9 (Jul. 1993)
REAL NAME Courtney Mason
ALLIES Cyborg, Superboy, Hawkman
ENEMIES The Nameless One
BACKGROUND Courtney Mason's body contained the Animus, a shadow being that possessed powerful abilities such as super-strength, flight, and shape-changing powers. It gave Courtney the power to leech bio-energy from both living and non-living things. She died in a battle with the villain Prometheus.

ANTITHESIS
DEBUT *Teen Titans* #53 (Feb. 1978)
BASE Limbo **ALLIES** Bromwell Stikk **ENEMIES** Teen Titans
BACKGROUND The vile creature known as the Antithesis used its powers of telepathy and mental manipulation against the Justice League of America. It hypnotized them by absorbing their negative emotions, and forced them to commit crimes, until they were stopped by the Teen Titans. The heroes Nightwing and the Herald defeated the Antithesis and exiled the creature to Limbo.

APPARITION
DEBUT *Action Comics* #276 (May 1961)
REAL NAME Tinya Wazzo
BASE Legion World, U.P. Space
ALLIES Saturn Girl, Timber Wolf **ENEMIES** Princess Projectra
BACKGROUND Apparition was a native of the planet Bgztl. Also known as Phantom Girl, Apparition had the ability to phase all or any part of her body into an intangible or phantom state she and, hence could not be harmed by conventional methods of attack. She fought alongside the Legion of Super-Heroes.

AQUAWOMAN
DEBUT *Earth 2* #18 (Feb. 2014)
REAL NAME Marella
UNIVERSE Earth-2 **BASE** Atlantis
ALLIES Batman **ENEMIES** Darkseid
BACKGROUND Aquawoman was the female ruler of Atlantis on Earth-2 and was skilled at hydrokinesis. After being imprisoned by the World Army in the Black Basement beneath Arkham Asylum, she was freed by Batman and joined him in a battle against Darkseid. Marella disliked being called "Aquawoman."

ARGENT II
DEBUT *Teen Titans* #1 (Oct. 1996)
REAL NAME Antonia Louise "Toni" Monetti
BASE New Jersey
ALLIES Teen Titans **ENEMIES** H'San Natall
BACKGROUND Teenager Toni Monetti was abducted by aliens and given the superpower to generate silver plasma and shape it to whatever form she desires. Her ability to control bursts of silver plasma energy earned her the codename "Argent." Toni was an on-and-off member of the Teen Titans.

ARGUS
DEBUT *The Flash Annual* #6 (1993)
REAL NAME Nicholas Kovak (aka Nick Kelly)
BASE Keystone City
ALLIES The Flash III **ENEMIES** Keystone's mobsters
BACKGROUND Kovak was working as an FBI agent when he was attacked by a space alien. The attack altered Kovak's body chemistry, allowing him to become virtually invisible in shadows and see beyond the normal spectrum. As the Super Hero Argus, he often teamed up with The Flash—although he preferred to operate alone.

ARKHAM KNIGHT
DEBUT *Detective Comics* #1000 (May 2019)
REAL NAME Astrid Arkham **BASE** Gotham City
ALLIES Knights of the Sun **ENEMIES** Batman
BACKGROUND The daughter of Arkham Asylum warden Jeremiah Arkham, Astrid Arkham was raised in the institution, befriending many of its criminally insane inmates. Blaming Batman for the death of her mother, Astrid adopted the guise of Arkham Knight, deploying an arsenal of weaponry and a group of fanatical followers, the Knights of the Sun, in her war on the Dark Knight.

ARRAKHAT
DEBUT *Robin* #78 (Jul. 2000)
BASE O'salla Ben Duuram **ALLIES** Arghulian, Tapeworm **ENEMIES** Robin, Connor Hawke **BACKGROUND** The demon Arrakhat was an evil djinn from the O'salla Ben Duuram, which translates as "Oasis of the Damned," one of the descending circles of Hell. He manifested as an armored demon wielding a flaming scimitar. Arrakhat's formidable powers were mystical in nature. When summoned, Arrakhat had the ability to grant three deaths instead of three wishes.

ARTEMIZ
DEBUT *Suicide Squad* #35 (Nov. 1989)
BASE Apokolips
ALLIES Darkseid's Female Furies **ENEMIES** Superboy, Supergirl
BACKGROUND This skilled archer was recruited by Granny Goodness to become one of Darkseid's Female Furies. She commanded a pack of cybernetic warhounds who helped her to hunt down enemies. Although highly skilled in hand-to-hand combat, her main role in the Female Furies was that of a huntress. Artemiz battled the Suicide Squad, Supergirl, and Superboy.

ARYAN BRIGADE
DEBUT *Justice League Task Force* #10 (Mar. 1994)
BASE Pine Heights, Nebraska
ALLIES Aryan Nation, the Cadre **ENEMIES** Justice League Task Force
BACKGROUND The Aryan Brigade was a team of white supremacist terrorists that created a virus to destroy non-white human DNA. This fanatical team would have exterminated most of the globe's population if it had not been stopped by the Justice League. The five metahumans who made up the group were Backlash, Blind Faith, Golden Eagle II, Heatmonger, and Iron Cross.

ASCENDANT
DEBUT *Dark Nights Metal* #6 (May 2018)
REAL NAME Prince Elligh **BASE** mobile
ALLIES Neon; Viking Judge; The Unexpected **ENEMIES** Bad Samaritan
BACKGROUND Elligh, Prince of Orcks survived an accident that erased his entire culture from the timeline. For 100,000 years the Ascendant secretly watched over humanity as it developed, confiscating dangerous Orck technology. He eventually joined Neon the Unknown's nomadic super-team The Unexpected. After years of clandestine heroics, he was killed by mystic predator the Bad Samaritan.

ASMODEL
DEBUT *JLA* #7 (Jul. 1997)
BASE Heaven
ALLIES Neron **ENEMIES** Zauriel, Justice League of America
BACKGROUND Asmodel was once the commander of the Angel Army of Heaven, but he rebelled and was consigned to Hell. There he obtained the rank of Archfiend and became a servant of the demon Neron. Asmodel wielded a flaming staff and had few rivals as a military commander. He was immortal and invulnerable, with vast super-strength, super-speed, acidic blood, and the power of flight.

ATMOS
DEBUT *Legion of Super-Heroes* #32 (Mar. 1987)
REAL NAME Marak Russen
BASE Planet Xanthu in the 31st century
ALLIES Uncanny Amazers **ENEMIES** The Blight
BACKGROUND Atmos was a member of the Uncanny Amazers, the planet Xanthu's counterpart to the Earth-based Legion of Super-Heroes. A living nuclear reactor, Russen's powers included super-strength, speed, and flight. He could generate a protective force field and survive unaided in the vacuum of space.

AUCTIONEER
DEBUT *Action Comics* #841 (Sep. 2006)
BACKGROUND The Auctioneer was a powerful, giant alien passionate about collecting and reselling items from across the cosmos. His starship was large enough to house entire buildings. He took an interest in Earth and pocketed monuments like the Eiffel Tower and the Golden Gate Bridge. He even captured Superman and other metahumans to sell at auction, but the Man of Steel, allied with Nightwing, Aquaman, and others, escaped. When Superman vowed to release the Auctioneer's private database, the alien withdrew.

AZAZEL
DEBUT *Sandman* #4 (Apr. 1989)
BASE Hell
ALLIES Lucifer **ENEMIES** John Constantine, Morpheus
BACKGROUND Azazel is one of the most powerful demons in Hell, ruling alongside Lucifer and Beelzebub. When Lucifer closed Hell for a time, Azazel tried to claim it for his own and failed. He was then trapped by Morpheus, the Dream King, and locked away in a jar. However, he is not to be underestimated. Azazel commands mystic and eldritch forces that allow him to eradicate a demon from existence.

BAD SAMARITAN
DEBUT *The Outsiders* #3 (Jan. 1986) *second - The Unexpected* Vol 3 #1 (Aug. 2018) **REAL NAME** Zviad Baazovi **ENEMIES** The Outsiders
BACKGROUND Baazovi is loyal to no organization, or country. He is a ruthless assassin and a master of disguise. His eyes are sensitive to bright light, or so he claims. In all his encounters with the Outsiders, he has escaped and remains at large. A second Bad Samaritan—a man named Alden Quench—was exposed to the World Forge and endowed with the Fires of Destruction, a force that put Alden in unwilling communication with the Dark Monitor.

BALLOON BUSTER
DEBUT *All-American Men of War* #112 (Nov.–Dec. 1965)
REAL NAME Steven Henry Savage, Jr.
BASE France
BACKGROUND The son of legendary cowboy Brian "Scalphunter" Savage, Steve Savage, Jr. was a matchless marksman and a skilled biplane pilot. He fought fearlessly in World War I and earned the nickname "Balloon Buster," after using his exceptional flying skills to down several German attack balloons. He disappeared in South East Asia in 1924.

BARON BEDLAM
DEBUT *Batman and the Outsiders* #1 (Aug. 1983)
REAL NAME Frederick DeLamb **BASE** Markovia
ALLIES Masters of Disaster **ENEMIES** Batman, The Outsiders
BACKGROUND Following in the footsteps of his Nazi-collaborating father, Frederick DeLamb attempted to seize the throne of the small European country of Markovia. He was stopped by the nation's crown prince, Brion Markov—alias Geo-Force—and his new allies Batman and The Outsiders. Though DeLamb lost his life, he was later resurrected as a clone and launched a second coup.

BAT-MAN OF CHINA
DEBUT *New Super-Man* #1 (Sep. 2016)
REAL NAME Wang Baixi **BASE** Shanghai
ALLIES Super-Man, Wonder-Woman **ENEMIES** Freedom Fighters of China
BACKGROUND Tech genius Wang Baixi was recruited by China's Ministry of Self-Reliance to become the country's Batman. He was trained at the Academy of the Bat, earning the right to wear the cowl against stiff competition. After encountering Kong Kenan—China's self-styled Super-Man—Baixi formed a team with Kenan and Peng Deilan, alias Wonder-Woman: the Justice League of China.

BAT-QUEEN
DEBUT *Detective Comics* #402 (Aug. 1970)
REAL NAME Francine Lee **BASE** Gotham City
ALLIES Wrath
ENEMIES Man-Bat, Batman, G.C.P.D.
BACKGROUND Lee was a scientist who married Dr. Kirk Langstrom, the monstrous Man-Bat. Forced to ingest the Man-Bat serum made by her husband she became a feral She-Bat, calling herself Bat-Queen. A deranged Lee terrorized Gotham City with a string of killings and was eventually defeated by Langstrom.

BATWOMAN BEYOND
DEBUT *Batman Beyond* (Vol. 6) #25 (Dec. 2018)
REAL NAME Elainna Grayson **BASE** Gotham City
ALLIES Batman Beyond **ENEMIES** Blight
BACKGROUND The daughter of mayor of Blüdhaven Dick Grayson—the original Robin, later Nightwing—former soldier Elainna Grayson did her best to abide by her father's wish that she not become a crime fighter. She took on the mantle of Batwoman when Terry McGinnis—the Batman of the future—lost his memory, utilizing Terry's Batsuit before gaining a suit of her own.

BAYTOR
DEBUT *The Demon* #43 (Jan. 1994)
BASE Gotham City
ALLIES Tommy Monaghan **ENEMIES** Etrigan
BACKGROUND Baytor was a minor demon who briefly proclaimed himself the ruler of Hell. After his attempted coup failed, he fled to Earth and settled in crime-torn Gotham City. He worked as a bartender in Noonan's Bar where he met Tommy Monaghan and joined his gang of criminals and mercenaries. Baytor could project a liquid onto his enemies; when it dried, it caused them to shatter.

BEEFEATER
DEBUT *Justice League Europe* #20 (Nov. 1990)
REAL NAME Michael Morice
BASE Ipswich, England
ALLIES Justice League International **ENEMIES** The Auctioneer
BACKGROUND Morice first became a liaison to Justice League International and later a costumed hero in charge of Basement 101, Britain's prison facility for meta-villains. Morice inherited his father's collapsible battle rod, which projected force blasts. However, his inept use of it left a lot to be desired.

BEELZEBUB
DEBUT *Sandman* #4 (Apr. 1989)
BASE Hell
ALLIES Azazel, Lucifer **ENEMIES** Supergirl
BACKGROUND Beelzebub is one of the three rulers of Hell. Also called the Lord of the Flies, he has vast demonic powers and can take the form of a giant fly. Beelzebub has dominion over decay and decomposition and has existed since the creation of death. He has crossed paths with the Earth-based heroes Kid Eternity and Supergirl, and continues to spread his evil throughout the universe.

BEK, GARRYN
DEBUT *Invasion* #1 (Jan. 1989)
BASE Cairn
ALLIES Vril Dox II **ENEMIES** Kanis-Biz
BACKGROUND Bek was a police administrator on the drug-trafficking planet of Cairn and an exceptional coordinator and a starship pilot. Imprisoned by the alien team Alliance, which was bent on destroying Earth, Bek escaped along with his cell mate, Vril Dox II. He then transformed Cairn's entire police force into a peacekeeping agency known as L.E.G.I.O.N.

BELIAL
DEBUT *Captain Marvel, Jr.* #4 (Feb. 13, 1943)
BASE Hell
ALLIES Sabbac
ENEMIES Captain Marvel, Jr.
BACKGROUND The eldest son of Trigon, Belial was one of the most ambitious demons in Hell. He used arcane dark arts and his intellect to make up for his relative lack of demonic strength. He also ran the Lucky Devil casino in Las Vegas. Belial's schemes on Earth were usually thwarted by Captain Shazam, Jr.

BLACK BANSHEE
DEBUT *Supergirl* #8 (Jun. 2012)
REAL NAME Garrett Smythe
BASE Dublin
ENEMIES Supergirl, Silver Banshee
BACKGROUND As the Black Banshee, Smythe was a skilled master of the magical arts. He possessed superhuman strength and was able to emit an incredibly destructive hypersonic scream. He traveled to Earth to battle his daughter Siobhan, the Silver Banshee, and also Supergirl.

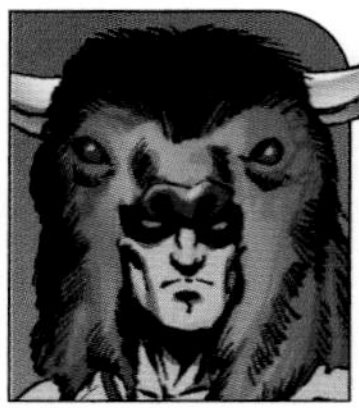

BLACK BISON
DEBUT *The Fury of Firestorm* #1 (Jun. 1982)
REAL NAME John Ravenhair, Black-Cloud-In-Morning
BASE New York City
BACKGROUND Seeking to right the wrongs that had been done to his Native American ancestors, Ravenhair donned a traditional tribal costume and launched a crime spree that included a battle with Firestorm. Black Bison became a member of the Secret Society of Super-Villains, and used a tribal coup stick to control the weather and to animate objects.

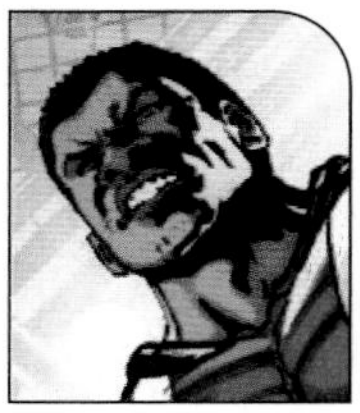

BLACK CONDOR
DEBUT *The Multiversity: Mastermen* #1 (Apr. 2015)
REAL NAME Marcus Robbins
ALLIES Uncle Sam, The Human Bomb
ENEMIES Cyborg Overman, The Plastic Men
BACKGROUND Marcus Robbins was a freedom fighter native to Earth 10, a world where the Nazi's conquered America. Using both a wingsuit and an experimental formula, Marcus was able to free the Human Bomb and start a revolution.

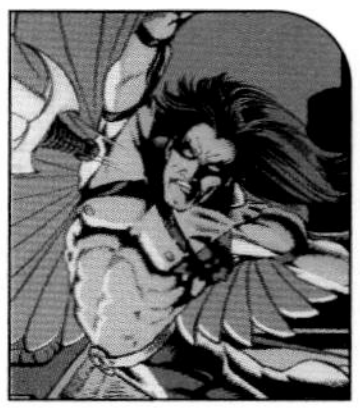

BLACK CONDOR II
DEBUT *Black Condor* #1 (Jun. 1992)
REAL NAME Ryan Kendall **BASE** Opal City
ALLIES Primal Force **ENEMIES** The Shark, Sky Pirate
BACKGROUND As the second Black Condor, Kendall used telekinesis and was an expert knife-thrower. Acquiring his powers from a monstrous radiation experiment conducted by his grandfather, Kendall was recruited to his new role by the first Black Condor, Richard Grey—the high-flying 1940s Freedom Fighter. Kendall served in the JLA, but later died during the *Infinite Crisis*.

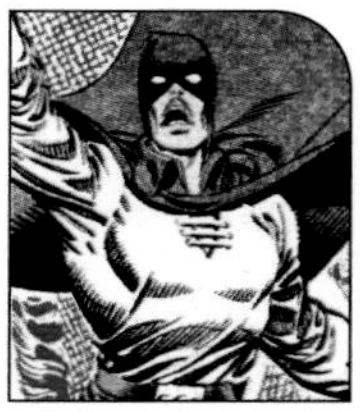

BLACK PIRATE
DEBUT *Action Comics* #23 (Apr. 1940)
REAL NAME Jon Valor
ALLIES Bruce Wayne **ENEMIES** Blackbeard
BACKGROUND The legend of the Black Pirate began in 1588 when British nobleman Jon Valor donned a pirate's costume and sailed the high seas in the cause of justice. Centuries later, his grandson Jack was inspired by Batman to fight crime as the new Black Pirate. Yet Jack Valor's spirit couldn't rest until his name was cleared, which it was with the help of Jack Knight, Ralph and Sue Dibny, and Hamilton Drew.

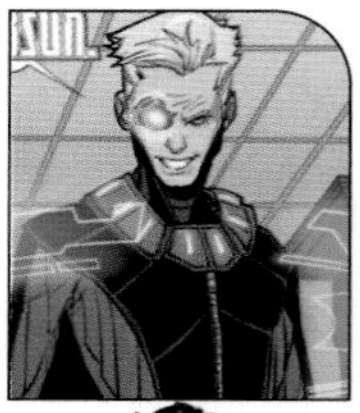

BLACKSUN
DEBUT *Batgirl* (Vol. 5) #6 (Feb. 2017)
REAL NAME Ethan Cobblepot **BASE** Burnside
AFFILIATION VicForm **ENEMIES** Batgirl, The Penguin
BACKGROUND The estranged son of Oswald Cobblepot, The Penguin, Ethan Cobblepot ran tech outfit VicForm from the Gotham City district of Burnside. His data-mining and mind-manipulation methods attracted the attention of both Barbara Gordon, aka Batgirl, and The Penguin. Adopting the identity Blacksun, Ethan tried to kill The Penguin and take control of Burnside, but was thwarted by Batgirl.

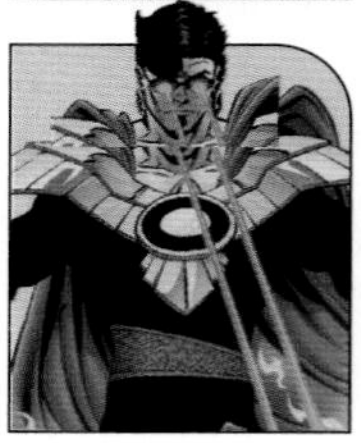

BLACK ZERO
DEBUT *Superboy* #61 (Apr. 1999)
REAL NAME Kon-El
BASE Metropolis
ALLIES Doomsday **ENEMIES** Earth's Superboy
BACKGROUND An evil clone of Superman from an alternate Earth, Black Zero possessed nearly all of the Man of Steel's powers. He had superhuman strength and speed, was invulnerable, and possessed psionic vision, similar to heat-vision. Black Zero invaded our planet, only to be destroyed by Earth's Superboy.

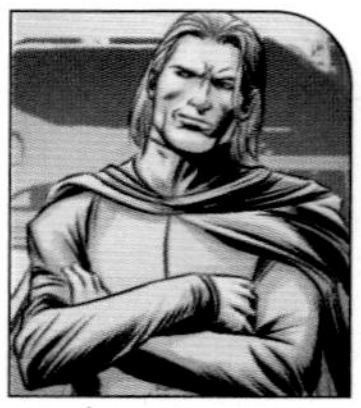

BLANQUE
DEBUT *Superman: Lois and Clark* #3 (Feb. 2016)
REAL NAME unknown **BASE** various
ENEMIES Superman
BACKGROUND His origins a mystery, the being known as Blanque was a formidable foe for Superman, his psychic abilities proving hard to counter. Superman managed to imprison Blanque in his Fortress of Solitude, until Hank Henshaw (once known as the Cyborg Superman) unwittingly allowed him to break free. Superman recaptured him, but Blanque escaped and joined the Superman Revenge Squad.

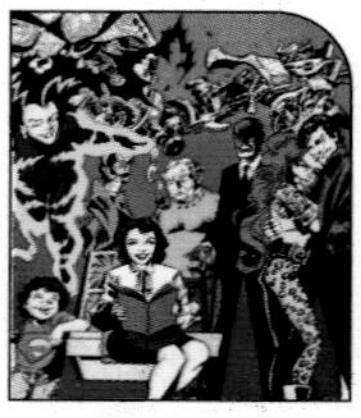

BLASTERS, THE
DEBUT *Invasion!* #1 (Jan. 1989) **MEMBERS** "Snapper" Carr: Teleportation; Churljenkins: Piloting; Dust Devil: Tornado control; Crackpot: Telepathy; Frag: Energy projection; Gunther: Enhanced intellect; Looking Glass: Deflection; Jolt: Force-field creation. **ALLIES** L.E.G.I.O.N., Valor, Omega Men
ENEMIES The Dominators, Spider Guild, Doctor Bendorion
During an invasion of Earth, 50 humans were captured and experimented on by the Dominators race. The survivors discovered they had superpowers after their dormant "metagenes" kicked in. After escaping, this international group became The Blasters.

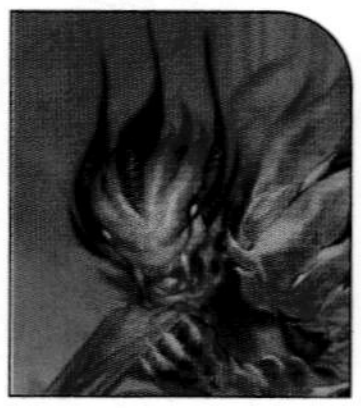

BLIGHT
DEBUT *Justice League Dark* (Vol. 1) #24 (Dec. 2013)
ALLIES Seven Deadly Sins
ENEMIES John Constantine, Phantom Stranger, Pandora, Justice League Dark
Born of mankind's collective unconscious, Blight is a personification of sin given physical form. Once this abomination gained sentience, it occupied a mortal named Chris Esperanza and began attacking Earth. The Phantom Stranger intervened and eventually—with the aid of John Constantine and the Justice League Dark—freed the young host from the influence of the collective unconscious of humanity.

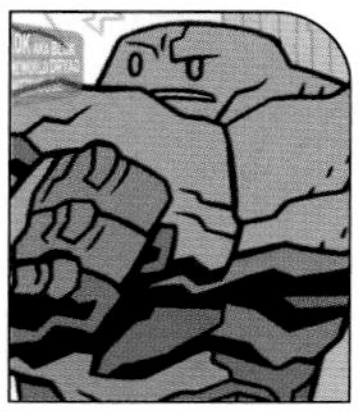

BLOK
DEBUT *Superboy and the Legion of Super-Heroes* #253 (Jul. 1979)
REAL NAME Blok **BASE** Legion HQ
AFFILIATION Legion of Super-Heroes **ENEMIES** League of Super-Assassins, Dark Man **BACKGROUND** A silicon-based native of the planet Dryad, Blok was a member of the League of Super-Assassins, who were manipulated by the Dark Man into attacking the Legion of Super-Heroes. After a period in Everest Planetary Prison, Blok agreed to help the Legion of Super-Heroes find the Dark Man, and subsequently became a longstanding member of the team.

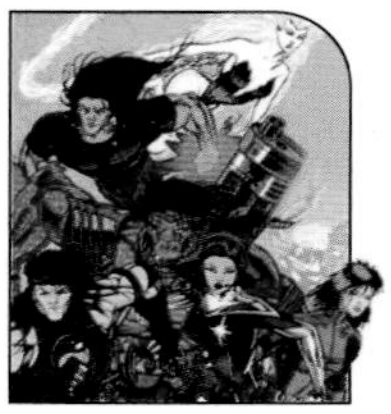

BLOOD PACK
DEBUT *Showcase '94* #12 (Dec. 1994)
ALLIES New Bloods **ENEMIES** Quorum
BACKGROUND When parasites invaded Earth during the Bloodlines crisis, several teenagers acquired superpowers, including Ballistic, a super-strong weapons expert; Geist, who could turn invisible; Sparx, who controlled electrical energy; Nightblade, with enhanced regenerative powers; and Loria, a steel-skinned warrior. Led by established heroine Jade, the team got corporate support and formed the Blood Pack team. Several members were killed by Superboy-Prime during the *Infinite Crisis*.

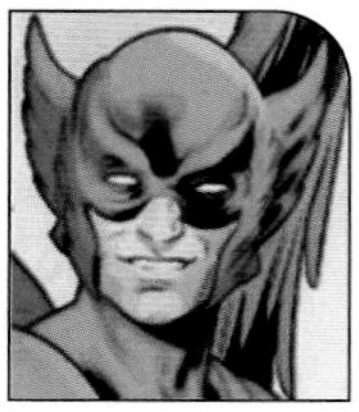

BLUE JAY
DEBUT *Justice League of America* #87 (Feb. 1971)
REAL NAME Jay Abrams **BASE** Angor, Paris
ENEMIES Extremists **BACKGROUND** Hailing from the planet Angor, Jay Abrams had the power to shrink and sprout wings. After encountering the Justice League, he and fellow Champion of Angor Silver Sorceress escaped Angor's destruction and made a new home on Earth. For a time, Abrams led Justice League Europe, but ultimately met his end at the Sanctuary facility, accidentally killed by Wally West, The Flash.

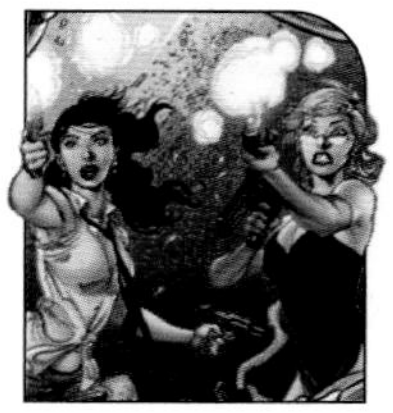

BODY DOUBLES
DEBUT *Resurrection Man* #1 (Mar. 1996)
REAL NAMES Bonny Hoffman and Carmen Leno
ALLIES Secret Society of Super-Villains **ENEMIES** Resurrection Man
BACKGROUND The Body Doubles were hired killers who worked for the Requiem, Inc. Assassination Agency. They were martial arts experts and employed the latest hi-tech weaponry, including deadly gadgets hidden in their makeup cases. They often came into conflict with the hero Resurrection Man and even tried to take on Catwoman, but the Princess of Plunder soon put them in their place.

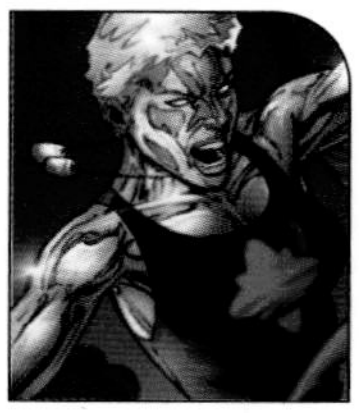

BOMBSHELL
DEBUT *Teen Titans* (Vol. 3) #39 (Nov. 2006)
REAL NAME Amy Allen **BASE** San Francisco
ENEMIES Project Quantum
BACKGROUND Undergoing the same experimental alloy process as Captain Atom, soldier Amy Allen was granted near-invulnerability, enhanced stamina and strength, flight, and atomic blasts. She was recruited into the Teen Titans, but betrayed the team in an effort to kidnap the resurrected Jericho on behalf of the villainous Titans East. She later redeemed her actions by rejoining the Teen Titans.

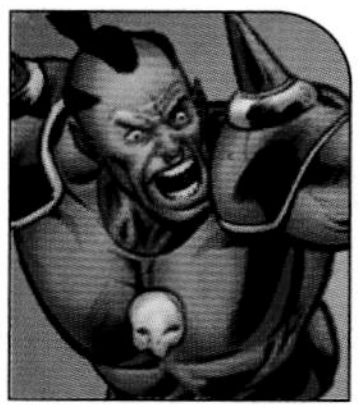

BOLPHUNGA
DEBUT *Green Lantern* (Vol. 2) #188 (May 1985)
ALLIES Burlls, Fatality, Quade
ENEMIES Green Lanterns
BACKGROUND Known as "Bolphunga the Unrelenting" for his tenacious pursuit of enemies and fugitives, this intergalactic warrior earned a fierce reputation as a bounty hunter who was obsessed with violence. Although of low intelligence, Bolphunga possessed superhuman strength and stamina. Green Lantern Guy Gardner was a frequent target.

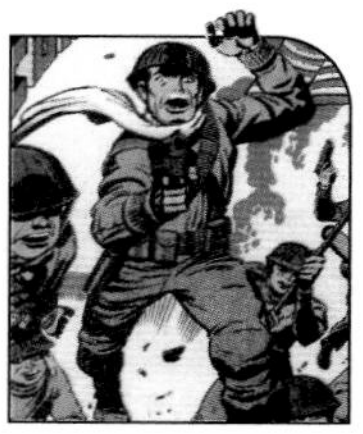

BOY COMMANDOS
DEBUT *Detective Comics* #64 (Jun. 1942)
BASE Metropolis, mobile
ALLIES The Guardian, Newsboy Legion **ENEMIES** Agent Axis
BACKGROUND In 1942, Captain Eric "Rip" Carter led four brave orphaned boys—Alfy Twidgett, Andre Chavard, Daniel "Brooklyn" Turpin, Jan Haasan—on missions throughout war-torn Europe, as the Boy Commandos. Percy Clearweather and Tex joined after the war ended. As adults, the individual team members still fought injustice, with Turpin joining Metropolis' Special Crimes Unit.

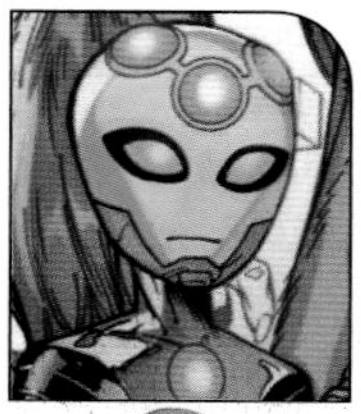

BRAINIAC 6
DEBUT *Adventures of the Super Sons* #1 (Oct. 2018)
REAL NAME unknown **BASE** Metropolis
ENEMIES Superboy, Robin
BACKGROUND A member of an alien race that idolized Earth's costumed adventurers, the youngster who would become Brainiac 6 was recruited by Rex Luthor, a fellow alien juvenile who modeled himself on Lex Luthor. Transformed by Rex into a junior version of Brainiac, Brainiac 6 joined Rex's Gang in their attack on Earth, using his criminal intellect to battle the Super-Sons.

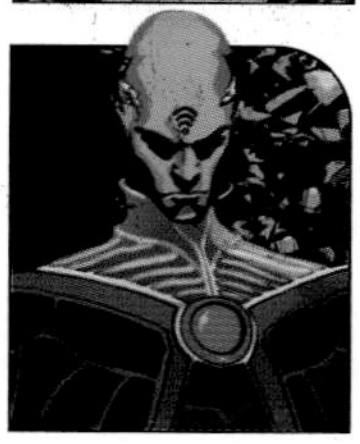

BRAINSTORM II
DEBUT *Mister Terrific* #2 (Dec. 2011)
REAL NAME Dominic Lanse **BASE** California
BACKGROUND The original Brainstorm, Axel Storm, built a mind-control helmet to control stellar radiation. But while using it, he was driven mad and went on a crime spree, battling the JLA multiple times. Later, Dominic Lanse acquired the ability to influence the minds of others. His mind-manipulating powers also indirectly caused the death of Paula Holt, Mr. Terrific's wife. There is no known connection between the two men.

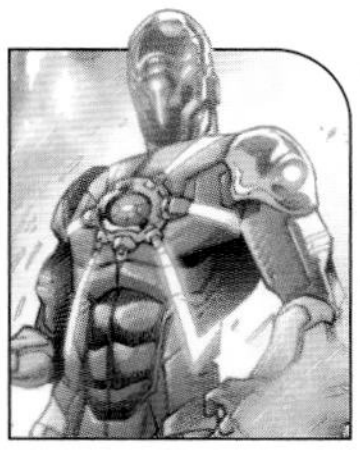

BREACHER
DEBUT *Justice League of America's Vibe* #3 (Jun. 2013)
REAL NAME Quell Mordeth
BASE Piradell
ALLIES Gypsy, Vibe **ENEMIES** Rupture
BACKGROUND After being exposed to massive amounts of energy, Mordeth acquired the power to expel energy from his body and teleport between dimensions. He traveled from another reality to warn Earth about Darkseid's invasion. Mordeth became a freedom fighter who fought for his people against the villainous Rupture.

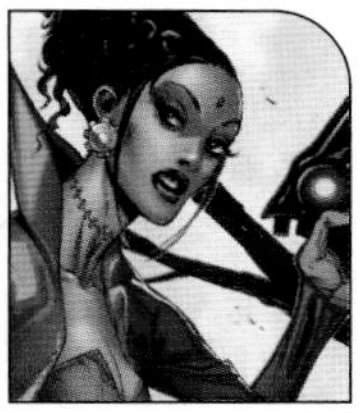

BRIDE, THE
DEBUT *Seven Soldiers: Frankenstein* #3 (Apr. 2006)
REAL NAME Bride of Frankenstein **BASE** S.H.A.D.E. HQ
AFFILIATION S.H.A.D.E. **ENEMIES** Zbigniew X
BACKGROUND Created by Dr. Victor Frankenstein as a mate for his Monster, The Bride rejected her intended companion. After the villainous Red Swami grafted an extra pair of arms onto her and turned her into an assassin, The Bride was recruited by the Super-Human Advanced Defence Executive. She was reunited with Frankenstein's Monster when he also joined S.H.A.D.E.

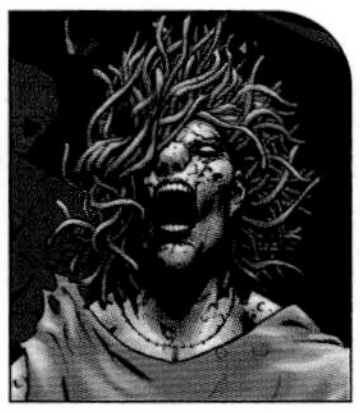

BROTHER POWER
DEBUT *Brother Power the Geek* #1 (Sep.–Oct. 1968)
ENEMIES Lord Sliderule
BACKGROUND Strauck by a lightning bolt a store mannequin was brought to life as Brother Power, the Geek. The Earth's only "puppet elemental," the pacifist Brother Power will do anything to avoid hand-to-hand combat. He has superhuman durability and strength, and is highly pliable and resistant to injury. Brother Power ran for Congress, was imprisoned as a circus freak, and enslaved on an assembly line by the villain Lord Sliderule. He has also crossed paths with Batman and the Phantom Stranger.

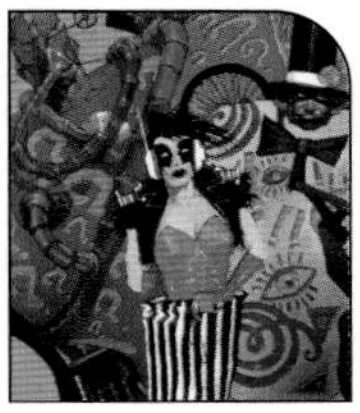

BROTHERHOOD OF DADA, THE
DEBUT *Doom Patrol* (Vol. 2) #25 (Aug. 1989)
NOTABLE MEMBERS Mr. Nobody, Sleepwalk, Frenzy, the Fog, the Quiz, Number None, Love Glove, Alias the Blur, the Toy **ENEMIES** The Doom Patrol
BACKGROUND Rejected by The Brotherhood of Evil, Mr. Nobody assembled a group of outcasts dedicated to the absurdity of life: The Brotherhood of Dada. The team included Sleepwalk, whose super-strength only manifested while asleep; the Fog, a psychedelic cloud; and the Quiz, who had "every superpower you haven't thought of yet." However, they were no match for the bizarre heroes of the Doom Patrol.

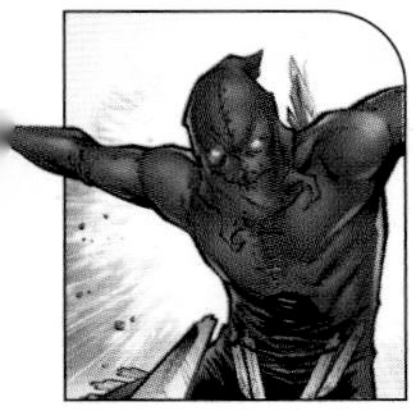

BRUTALE
DEBUT *Nightwing* #22 (Jul. 1998)
REAL NAME Guillermo Barrera **BASE** Hascaragua
ALLIES La Dama, Coyote, Rompe-Huesos **ENEMIES** Blue Beetle, Nightwing
BACKGROUND A master of knives, Barrera is quite formidable with this weapon of choice. He was an assassin from South America who moved to the US and donned a gargoyle costume to became the deadly Brutale. Under the direction of various employers, he repeatedly battled heroes like Nightwing and the Blue Beetle. He later became a member of the Secret Society of Super-Villains.

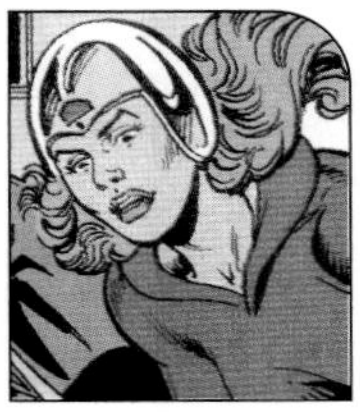

BULLETGIRL II (WINDSHEAR)
DEBUT *The Power of Shazam!* #32 (Nov. 1997)
REAL NAME Deanna Barr **BASE** Fawcett City
ALLIES Captain Marvel **ENEMIES** Chain Lightning
BACKGROUND During the 1940's, Susan Kent fought alongside her husband Jim Barr as the heroine Bulletgirl. Decades later, their daughter Deanna Barr inherited he mother's crime-fighting codename. Her anti-gravity helmet enables her to fly and create an invisible electromagnetic field. With the help of her father she used her abilities to rescue the depowered Shazam Family from Chain Lightning.

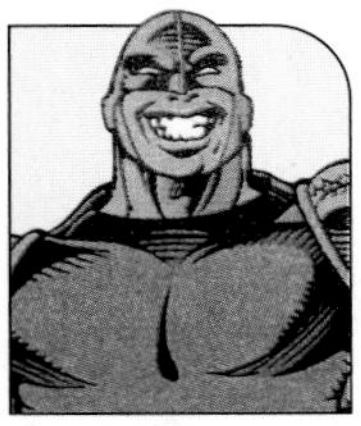

BUSHMASTER
DEBUT *Super Friends* #8 (Nov. 1977)
REAL NAME Bernal Rojas
BASE The Dome
ALLIES Justice League International **ENEMIES** Queen Bee of Bialya
BACKGROUND Rojas was a herpetologist who created a cybernetic costume that allowed him to duplicate certain reptile abilities. He donned this garish suit that was equipped with a venom gun and heat sensors to become a Super Hero. He became a member of the Global Guardians, but was shot and killed by bank robbers.

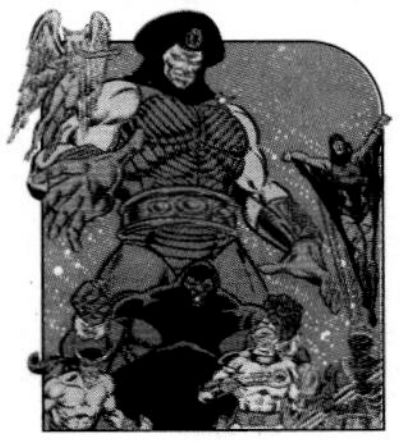

CADRE
DEBUT *Justice League of America* #235 (Feb. 1985)
ALLIES Aryan Brigade, New Extremists
ENEMIES Justice League Detroit
BACKGROUND The Cadre was a group of superpowered villains that received their powers from an alien known as the Overmaster. The team existed in many forms. The original members included Black Mass, Crowbar, Fastball, Nightfall, Shatterfist, and Shrike. Over time, the group lost several members, which were replaced by newly empowered recruits.

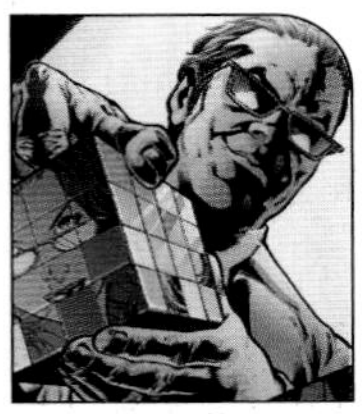

CALCULATOR
DEBUT *Detective Comics* #463 (Sep. 1976)
REAL NAME Noah Kuttler **ALLIES** Doctor Psycho, Doctor Light, Deathstroke
ENEMIES Batgirl, Birds of Prey
BACKGROUND After a failed career as a costumed villain, Kuttler, with his genius level intellect, reinvented himself as a computer expert and became a member of the Secret Society of Super-Villains. He eventually converted from a costumed crook to an information-broker for villains.

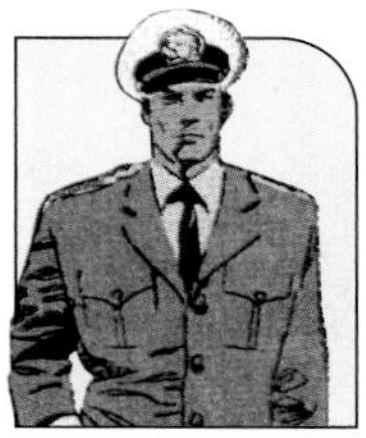

CAPTAIN COMPASS
DEBUT *Star-Spangled Comics* #83 (Aug. 1948)
REAL NAME Mark Compass
BASE The High Seas
ALLIES Penny Steamship Lines
BACKGROUND A skilled fighter with a keen deductive mind, Mark Compass served as a frogman in the US Navy, and later commanded his own vessels. After leaving the Navy, he joined Penny Steamship Lines as a roving nautical detective, solving mysteries and preventing crimes aboard the *S.S. Nautilus*.

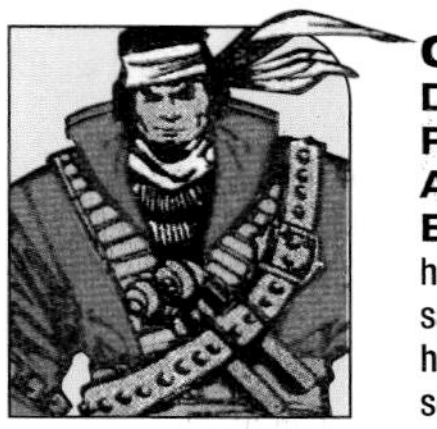

CAPTAIN FEAR
DEBUT *Adventure Comics* #425 (Dec. 1972–Jan. 1973)
REAL NAME Fero **BASE** The Caribbean
ALLIES His crew of pirates **ENEMIES** Baron Hemlocke
BACKGROUND When a young Fero was taken captive in a Spanish raid, he vowed to extract vengeance from all Spaniards. He became Captain Fear and sailed across the Caribbean in the 16th century, protecting his countrymen. He and his crew were later killed by demonic forces, who doomed them to wander the seas as spirits.

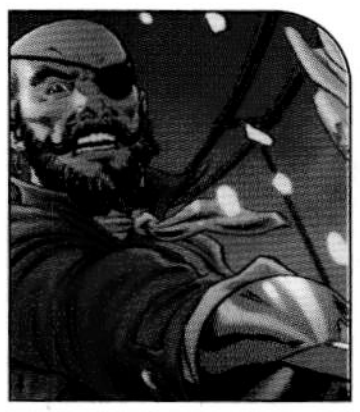

CAPTAIN STINGAREE
DEBUT *Detective Comics* #460 (Jun. 1976)
REAL NAME Karl Courtney
BASE Gotham City
ALLIES Cavalier, Captain Cold **ENEMIES** Batman, Secret Six
BACKGROUND Courtney was obsessed with pirates and donned pirate garb to launch his criminal career. He was an expert swordsman, but not a successful villain. He joined the Secret Society of Super-Villains and died fighting the Secret Six alongside his secret lover, Cavalier, and other Super-Villains.

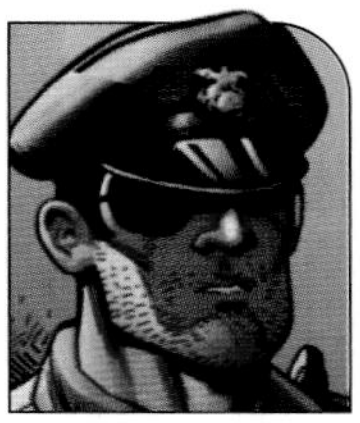

CAPTAIN STORM
DEBUT *Capt. Storm* #1 (May–Jun. 1964)
REAL NAME William Storm **BASE** Europe and the South Pacific
BACKGROUND Storm was a skipper on a patrol boat during World War II. He lost his ship, crew, and one of his legs during the war. Courageous and patriotic, Storm was determined to stay in the US Navy. He was eventually recommissioned, after which he joined a band of military misfits known as the Losers. After several adventures, Storm was trapped on Dinosaur Island. He was later rescued by Superman and taken to Star Labs, where he was outfitted with a robot leg.

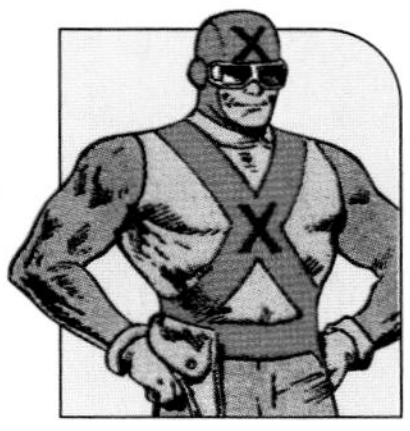

CAPTAIN X
DEBUT *Star Spangled Comics* #1 (Oct. 1941)
REAL NAME Richard "Buck" Dare
ALLIES The Group **ENEMIES** KGB, Stalnoivolk
BACKGROUND Richard Dare was a pilot during World War II and flew top-secret missions in a special aircraft called *Jenny*. It was an experimental plastic plane that was virtually invisible and used Uranium-235 as its atomic fuel source. Captain X remained active during the Cold War until he was killed by KGB agent Stalnoivolk. Dare is the grandfather of Ronnie Raymond (Firestorm the Nuclear Man).

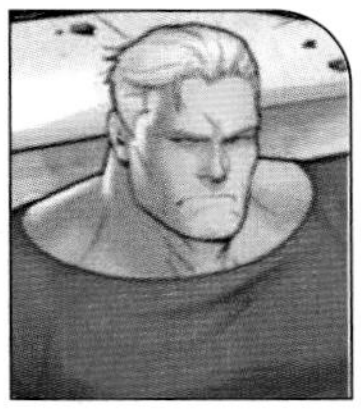

CAPTAIN TRIUMPH
DEBUT *Crack Comics* #27 (Jan. 1943)
ALLIES Liberty Belle
ENEMIES Baron Bragg, Dr. Manfree
BACKGROUND After his twin brother's plane is sabotaged, Lance G allant is empowered by the Fates to stand as a champion. Able to fuse with his twin's ghost, Lance becomes Captain Triumph. After many adventures during the second World War, Triumph is temporarily transported to the 21st century by Harley Quinn.

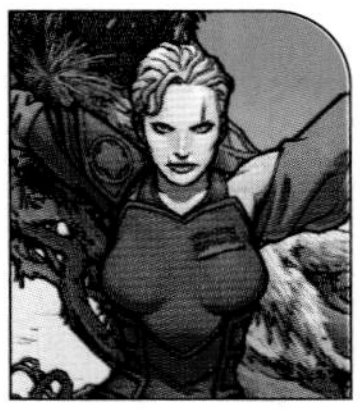

CAPUCINE
DEBUT *Swamp Thing* #20 (Jul. 2013)
ALLIES Swamp Thing **ENEMIES** Etrigan
BACKGROUND Capucine was a French warrior from the 12th century who was granted 1,000 years of immortality. She was a lethal fighter who honed her skills over centuries of combat. She had superhuman abilities and was skilled at hand-to-hand combat. She enlisted Swamp Thing to help her fight the demon Etrigan, who had come for her soul. After defeating Etrigan and at the end of her long life, Swamp Thing placed her in the Green, where she could exist for eternity.

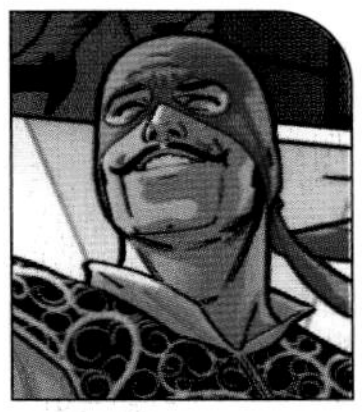

CAVALIER
DEBUT *Detective Comics* #81 (Nov. 1943)
REAL NAME Mortimer Drake **BASE** Gotham City
ALLIES Captain Stingaree, Black Lightning **ENEMIES** Batman, Secret Six
BACKGROUND Drake was a Batman villain obsessed with antiquated costumes and weaponry. A skilled swordsman, he was one of the Secret Society of Super-Villains who battled the Secret Six. During the brawl, Bane performed a "Backbreaker" on Drake and broke his back. The Cavalier recovered and joined the Suicide Squad, but was killed by Chaos Kitten on his first mission.

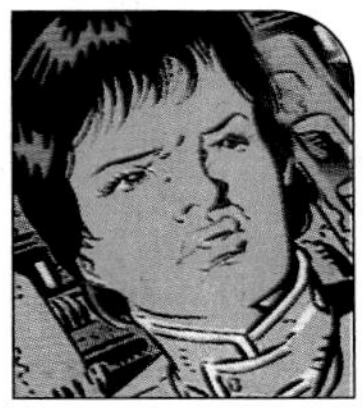

CELESTE
DEBUT *Legion of Super-Heroes* #6 (Apr. 1990)
REAL NAME Celeste McCauley
ALLIES Legion of Super-Heroes **ENEMIES** The Dominators
BACKGROUND Celeste was a member of the 30th-century Legion of Super-Heroes. During a fight with Glorith the Sorceress, Celeste became a being of pure energy. Later, she was caught in the blast of a dead Green Lantern's exploding power ring and became the living embodiment of Green Lantern energy. Celeste had an indomitable will, could fly, and become invisible.

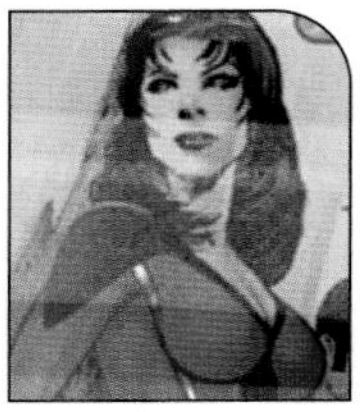

CELSIUS
DEBUT *Showcase* #94 (Aug.–Sep. 1977)
REAL NAME Arani Desai Caulder **BASE** Kansas City
ALLIES The Chief
ENEMIES General Immortus
BACKGROUND Possessing a formidable intellect, Arani was an Indian woman given the gift of immortality by her husband, Niles Caulder. She found she could now also project rays of intense heat or cold. She joined the Doom Patrol, but died during an alien invasion of Earth and was later reanimated as a Black Lantern.

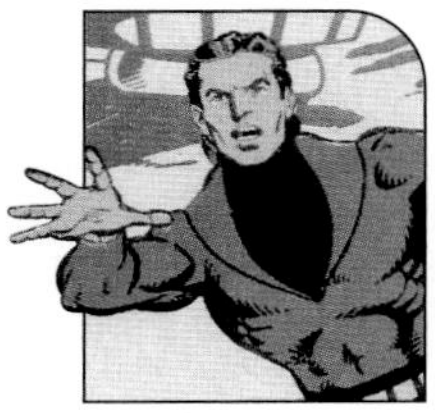

CHEMICAL KING
DEBUT *Adventure Comics* #371 (Aug. 1968)
REAL NAME Condo Arlik
ALLIES Legion of Super-Heroes **ENEMIES** Dark Circle
BACKGROUND Arlik left his planet Phlon to join the 30th century Legion of Super-Heroes and became one of the Legion Academy's first members. His mutant abilities enabled him to act as a "human catalyst" to slow down or speed up chemical reactions. On an undercover mission to Australia with Timber Wolf, he sacrificed his life to prevent Deregon, a Dark Circle agent from starting World War VII.

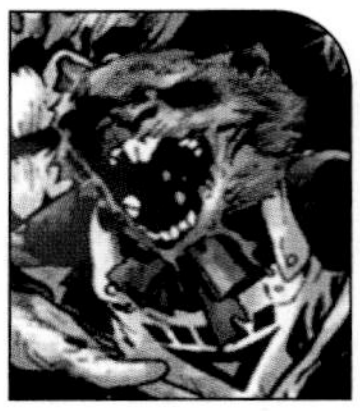

CH'P
DEBUT *Green Lantern* #148 (Jan. 1982)
BASE H'lven
ALLIES Lantern Salaak **ENEMIES** Doctor Ub'x and his Crabster Army
BACKGROUND As the Green Lantern of Sector 2014, Ch'p defeated an invasion of his homeworld by Ub'x and his army. He was run over by a truck and died on Oa. Like many other deceased Green Lanterns, he was later resurrected as a Black Lantern, who then began attacking the still-living Green Lanterns. The Black Lantern Central Power Battery was eventually destroyed and Ch'p died once again.

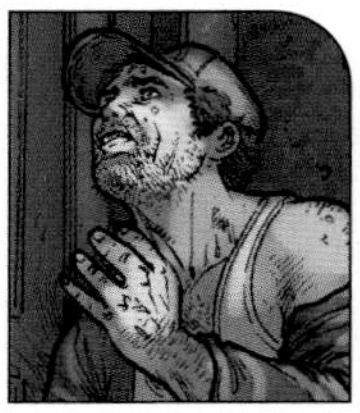

CHILL, JOE
DEBUT *Detective Comics* #33 (Nov. 1939)
REAL NAME Joseph Chilton
BASE Gotham City
BACKGROUND Chill was a low-level criminal whose actions created one of the greatest Super Heroes of all. On one fateful night, Chill robbed Bruce Wayne's parents and then killed them. Before he became Batman, Bruce tracked him down, demanding to know why. Bruce was prepared to murder Chill in revenge, but when the thug begged for his life, Bruce relented and spared him.

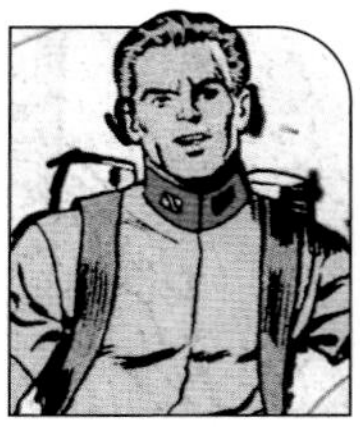

CHRIS KL-99
DEBUT *Strange Adventures* #1 (Aug.–Sep. 1950)
REAL NAME Christopher Ambler
BACKGROUND Born in the 21st century, Chris KL-99 was a brilliant scientist, astronaut, and astronomer. He piloted an interplanetary vessel named *The Pioneer* and explored new worlds in search of his parents' graves. Occasionally traveling with the Martian adventurer Halk and the Venusian scientist Jero, Chris discovered more inhabited planets than anyone in history. During the *Crisis on Infinite Earths*, Chris helped build a time-travel conduit to send heroes back to the dawn of mankind.

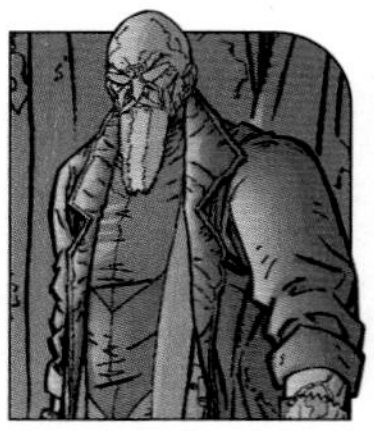

CICADA
DEBUT *The Flash* #170 (Mar. 2001)
REAL NAME David Hersch **BASE** Keystone City
ALLIES Magenta **ENEMIES** The Flash
BACKGROUND Cicada was an insane megalomaniac who, after being struck by lightning, could achieve immortality by consuming the life forces of others. He was a villain who believed that The Flash (Wally West) was a fellow "brother of the lightning." He kidnapped him, but The Flash emerged triumphant. After a stint in prison, Cicada joined the Secret Society of Super-Villains during the *Infinite Crisis*.

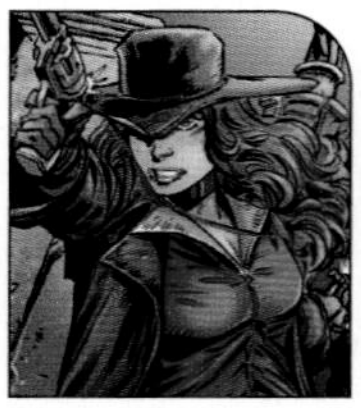

CINNAMON
DEBUT *Weird Western Tales* #48 (Sep.–Oct. 1978)
REAL NAME Katherine Manser **ENEMIES** August 7
BACKGROUND When her father was gunned down, young Katherine Manser was sent to a cruel orphanage where she was nicknamed Cinnamon. She escaped and became a savage fighter for justice. Teaming up with the gunslinger Nighthawk, the two became outlaw hunters during the late 1800s. Unbeknownst to Cinnamon, she is a reincarnation of an Egyptian Princess called Chay-Ra, and is in turn a predecessor to Hawkwoman.

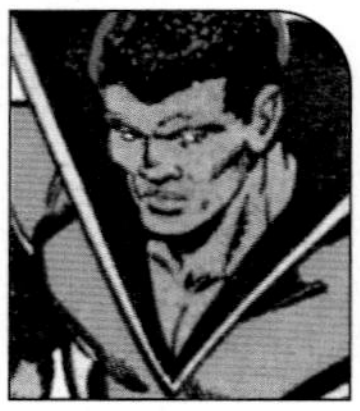

CLAY, JOSHUA
DEBUT *Showcase* #94 (Aug.–Sep. 1977)
BASE Happy Harbor, Rhode Island **ALLIES** Negative Woman, Robotman
ENEMIES Niles Caulder
BACKGROUND Clay was a Vietnam Vet who was able to project powerful bolts of energy from his hands. He deserted his military unit, took the name Tempest, and joined the Doom Patrol. Clay was subsequently murdered by the Chief, but reanimated as one of the Black Lantern Corps, with the power to control weather. Like many other Corps heroes, he was later resurrected.

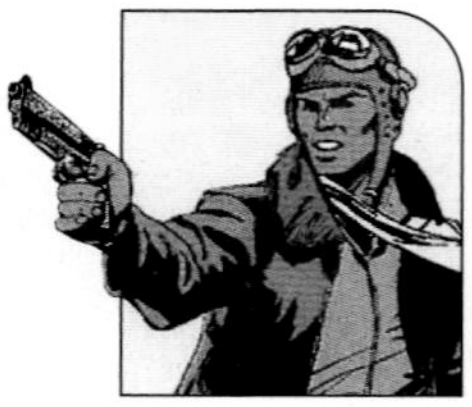

CLOUD, JOHNNY
DEBUT *All-American Men of War* #82 (Nov.–Dec. 1960)
REAL NAME Flying Cloud
BASE Europe **ALLIES** The Losers **ENEMIES** Nazis
BACKGROUND Flying "Johnny" Cloud was a Navajo US Air Force pilot who fought bravely during World War II, leading the "Happy Braves" air patrol. He was later recruited by PT-boat commander Captain Storm to join the military misfits known as the Losers. He saved Sergeant Rock's Easy Company from a battery of Nazi artillery, but was killed by an enemy fighter plane.

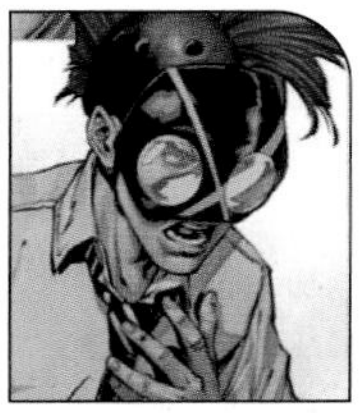

CLOWNHUNTER
DEBUT *Batman* (Vol. 3) #96 (Oct. 2020)
REAL NAME unknown **BASE** Gotham City
ALLIES Denizens of the Narrows **ENEMIES** The Joker
BACKGROUND The boy who became Clownhunter was set on the path to vigilantism when he saw his parents murdered by The Joker. Saved by Batman, he grew into a quiet, weird kid who idolized the Dark Knight. When The Joker War erupted, he became Clownhunter, defending his neighborhood, the Narrows, from The Joker's henchmen, armed with a baseball bat with a Batarang strapped to it.

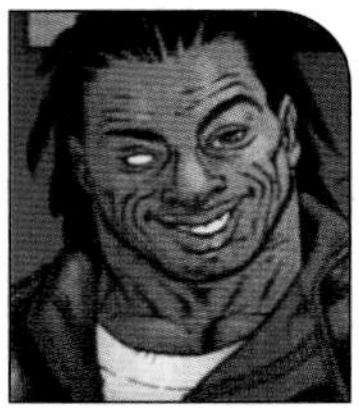

COLDCAST
DEBUT *Action Comics* #775 (Mar. 2001)
REAL NAME Nathan Jones **BASE** Chicago
AFFILIATION Elite, Justice League Elite **ENEMIES** Manchester Black
BACKGROUND Gaining energy powers as a teenager on the mean streets of Chicago, Nathan Jones was later recruited by Manchester Black into renegade team The Elite. After initially opposing Superman, Jones later worked with him, becoming a member of undercover ops outfit the Justice League Elite. A promising relationship with fellow teammate Menagerie ended when she framed him for murder.

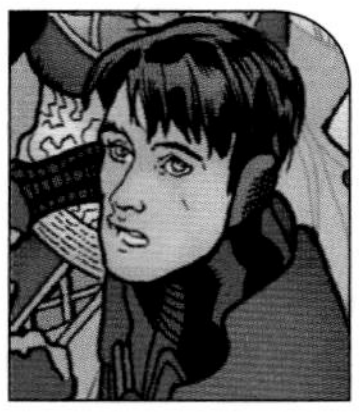

COLOSSAL BOY
DEBUT *Action Comics* #267 (Aug. 1960)
REAL NAME Gim Allon **BASE** Legion HQ
AFFILIATION Legion of Super-Heroes **ENEMIES** Fatal Five
BACKGROUND Hailing from Earth, Gim Allon gained his ability to grow to giant size on Mars when a meteor crashed near him and bathed him in radiation. Having trained to join the Science Police, Allon instead took the name Colossal Boy and joined the Legion of Super-Heroes. He became involved with teammate Shrinking Violent, who turned out to be a Durlan spy.

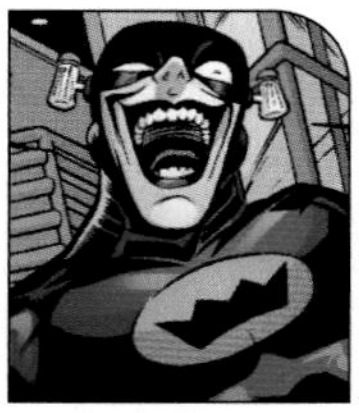

CONDIMENT KING
DEBUT *Birds of Prey* #37 (Jan. 2002)
REAL NAME Mitchell Mayo **BASE** Gotham City, Coney Island
ALLIES The Penguin **ENEMIES** Batgirl, Batman
BACKGROUND Mentally unbalanced former fast-food restaurant employee Mitchell Mayo adopted the guise of the Condiment King during Barbara Gordon's first year as Batgirl. Armed only with condiment bottles, he was easily apprehended by Batgirl and Robin (Dick Grayson), but later upgraded to condiment guns. After repeated stints in Arkham Asylum, Mayo turned legit and opened up a hot-dog joint.

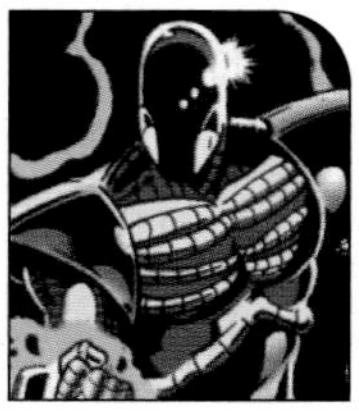

CONDUIT
DEBUT *Superman: The Man of Steel* #0 (Oct. 1994)
REAL NAME Kenneth Braverman **BASE** Metropolis
ALLIES Pipeline **ENEMIES** Superman
BACKGROUND Born in Kansas as the baby Kal-El's rocket landed, Kenny Braverman's exposure to kryptonite resulted in bouts of childhood illness. Attending Smallville High School, Braverman hated playing second fiddle to Clark Kent. After developing powers and undergoing CIA experiments, he became Conduit, using his Pipeline organization to wage war on Clark/Superman, leading to his own death.

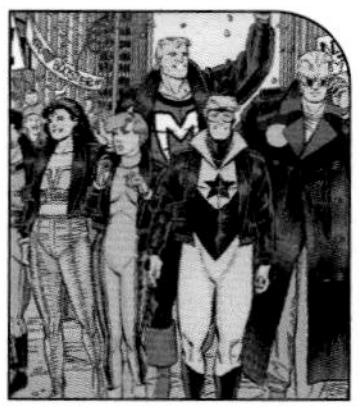

THE CONGLOMERATE
DEBUT *Justice League Quarterly* #1 (Dec. 1990) **MEMBERS** Booster Gold (Michael Carter); Echo (Terri Eckhart); Gypsy (Cindy Reynolds); Jesse Quick (Jesse Chambers); Hardline (Armando Ramone, formerly Reverb); Maxi-Man (Henry Hayes); Nuklon (Albert Rothstein); Praxis (Jason Praxis); Vapor (Carrie Donahue); Templar (Colin Brandywine). **ENEMIES** Despero **AFFILIATIONS** S.T.A.R. Labs
The Conglomerate was a short-lived attempt by Booster Gold to compete with the JLI. A second team of Qwardian villains was matched against the JLI for a pay-per-view battle. Templar lead a third version of new and original employees.

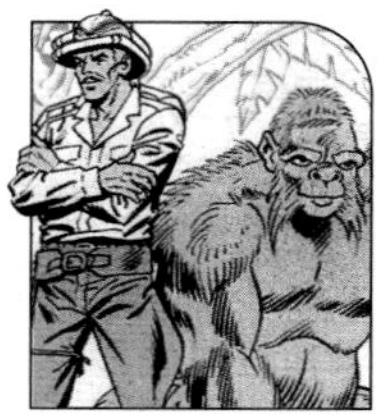

CONGORILLA
DEBUT *Action Comics* #248 (Jan. 1959)
REAL NAME Congo Bill **BASE** Africa
ALLIES Mikaal Thomas **ENEMIES** Prometheus
BACKGROUND Congo Bill was an explorer and naturalist in Africa who obtained a magical Golden Gorilla ring that allowed him to transform into a giant ape known as Congorilla. He used his powers as a crime fighter, teaming up with members of the Justice League. He later took on the role of Warden of Monster Rock. While there, he trained the young hero damage to control his powers.

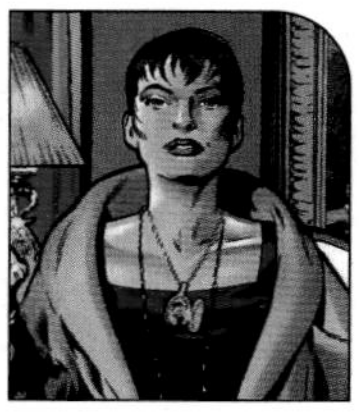

CONTESSA
DEBUT *Superman: The Man of Tomorrow* #1 (Jun. 1995)
REAL NAME Erica Alexandra del Portenza
ALLIES Klarion the Witch Boy
ENEMIES Lex Luthor
BACKGROUND The mysterious Contessa del Portenza was the former wife of Lex Luthor and the mother of his daughter, Lena. She was the head of the criminal genetics group known as the Agenda, and rumored to be immortal. It was unknown whether she survived an assassination attempt authorized by Lex Luthor.

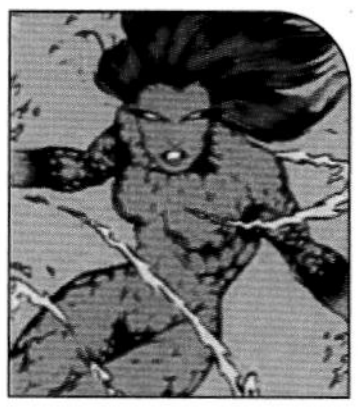

CORONA
DEBUT *Aquaman: Time and Tide* #3 (Feb. 1994)
REAL NAME Kako
BASE Alaska
ALLIES Aquaman **ENEMIES** Ocean Master
BACKGROUND Aquaman met a young Inuit girl named Kako in Alaska, and returned to Atlantis, unaware that Kako was pregnant with his son. Years later, she was murdered by the Deep Six and then resurrected as a fire elemental called Corona. In her new guise, she acquired the powers of pyrokinesis and flight.

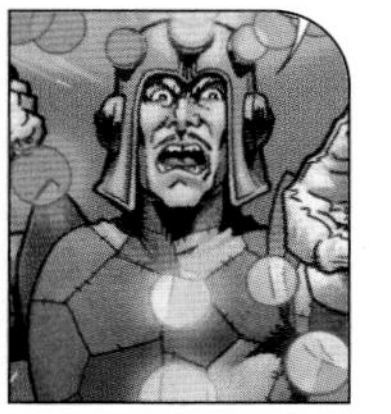

CRAZY QUILT
DEBUT *Boy Commandos* #15 (Jun. 1946)
REAL NAME Paul Dekker **BASE** Gotham City
ALLIES Secret Society of Super-Villains **ENEMIES** Robin, Batman
BACKGROUND Artist-turned-gangster Paul Dekker became Crazy Quilt when his eyesight was damaged by a gunshot, resulting in him only being able to see bright colors. Utilizing a color-helmet in his crimes, Dekker was repeatedly foiled by the first Robin, Dick Grayson. Dekker developed an antipathy toward the young crimefighter, culminating in him savagely beating the second Robin, Jason Todd.

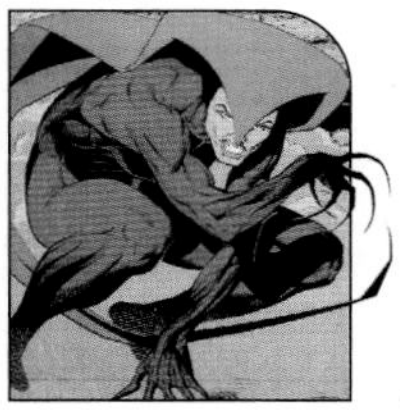

CRIMSON FOX
DEBUT *Justice League Europe* #6 (Sep. 1989)
REAL NAMES Vivian and Constance D'Aramis **BASE** Paris
ALLIES Justice League Europe **ENEMIES** Maurice Puanteur, Mist
BACKGROUND Vivian and Constance D'Aramis were twin sisters whose mother died at the hands of a corporation owned by their father. Vowing to avenge her, they ruined his business by setting up the rival Revson Corporation. They then created shared identities that would allow one to run the business and the other to fight crime as Le Renarde Rousse, the Crimson Fox.

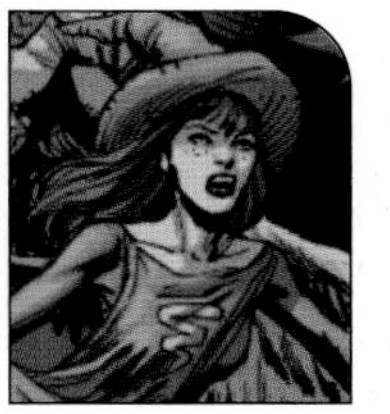

CYCLONE
DEBUT *Justice Society of America* (Vol. 3) #1 (Feb. 2007)
REAL NAME Maxine Hunkel **BASE** New York City
AFFILIATION Justice Society of America **ENEMIES** Fourth Reich
BACKGROUND The granddaughter of Ma Hunkel—the original Red Tornado—as a child Maxine Hunkel was injected with nanobytes by mad scientist T.O. Morrow. She began to manifest wind-manipulation powers while at Harvard University, and was recruited into the Justice Society of America by Power Girl and Mr. Terrific. Prone to depression, Cyclone found family and guidance in the JSA.

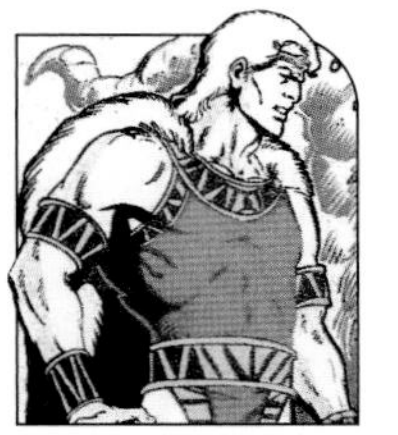

DAANUTH, GARN
DEBUT *Warlord* #59 (Jul. 1982)
ALLIES Majistra
ENEMIES Justice League of America, Warlord
BACKGROUND Daanuth was a powerful sorcerer and master of dark magic who tried to destroy his home, Atlantis. He possessed powers of flight and astral projection and was able to control the minds of others. Although he died in a fight with the Justice League, his evil legacy lived on in the form of Bedlam, a being created by an artifact suffused with Daanuth's magical power.

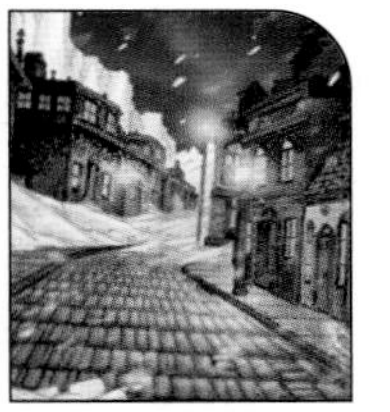

DANNY THE STREET
DEBUT *Doom Patrol* #35 (Aug. 1990)
ALLIES Doom Patrol, Titans, **ENEMIES** N.O.W.H.E.R.E.
BACKGROUND An ally of the Doom Patrol and Teen Titans, Danny the Street was a living, sentient, transvestite street. He communicated through signs and billboards, but could not speak. After an attack, Danny the Street was reduced to a single, sentient brick. Crazy Jane carried this brick with her, and eventually a man named D used Danny the Brick to kill a god. After this, Danny the Brick evolved into Danny the World.

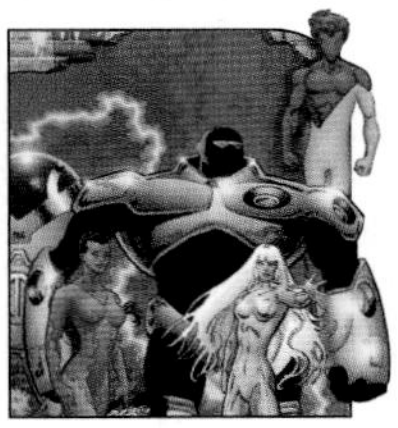

DARK NEMESIS
DEBUT *Teen Titans* #7 (Apr. 1997)
BASE Metropolis **ALLIES** Pylon, the Veil **ENEMIES** Teen Titans
BACKGROUND Dark Nemesis was a team of mercenary superpowered villains—Axis, Blizzard, Carom, and Scorcher—hired to battle human/alien hybrids. When Scorcher was revealed to be one of these hybrids, she was killed by Axis. A new Scorcher was recruited, before Dark Nemesis took on a mission for the Veil to capture the Teen Titans. They almost succeeded, but the Atom's last-minute intervention turned the tide, and Dark Nemesis was defeated and incarcerated in Slabside Penitentiary.

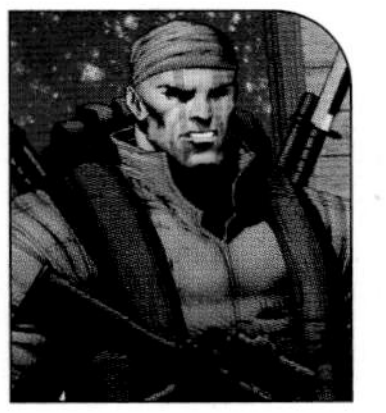

DEATHBLOW
DEBUT *Grifter* (Vol. 3) #9 (Jul. 2012)
REAL NAME Michael Cray
ALLIES Sister Mary, Sigma
ENEMIES Black Angel, Damocles
BACKGROUND Cray was a Navy SEAL who was recruited to join the newly formed Team 7. The team was exposed to the Gen-Factor, which gave them superpowers, but it took years until Cray discovered that he had the power to regenerate his body parts. After he was killed, he even managed to return to life.

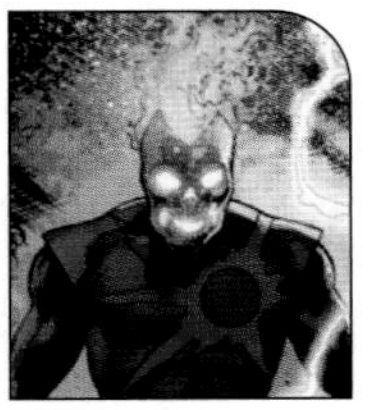

DEATHSTORM
DEBUT *Brightest Day* #10 (Nov. 2010)
REAL NAME Martin Stein
ALLIES Power Ring
ENEMIES Justice League
BACKGROUND When Pandora's Box was opened during the Trinity War, the Earth-3 creature Deathstorm emerged along with his fellow Crime Syndicate team members and attacked the Justice League. Deathstorm was originally Martin Stein, who harnessed the powers of the Firestorm Matrix for his evil plans.

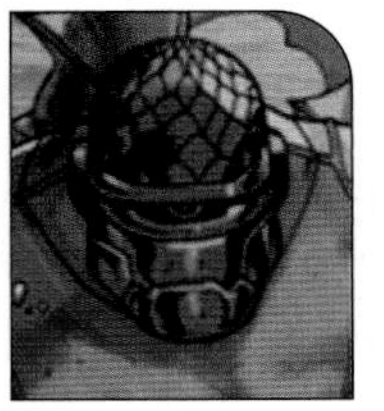

DEEP SIX
DEBUT *New Gods* #2 (May 1971)
BASE Apokolips **ALLIES** Darkseid
ENEMIES Aquaman, Orion **BACKGROUND** Amphibious warriors who existed only to do the bidding of Darkseid, the Deep Six—Gole, Jaffar, Kurin, Shaligo the Flying Finback, Slig, and Trok—were dispatched to Earth to assist in the planet's enslavement. Despite their deployment of monstrous mutated sea beasts, they were destroyed by Orion, but were later resurrected by Darkseid to battle first the New God Lightray, then Aquaman.

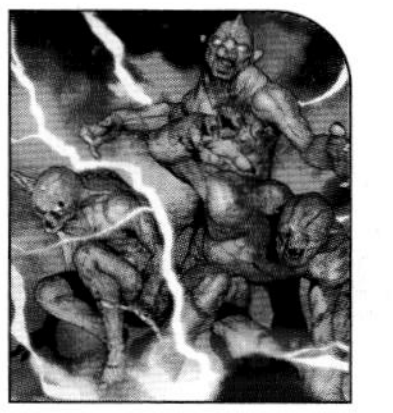

DEMONS THREE
DEBUT *Justice League of America* #10 (Mar. 1962)
BASE The Inferno **ALLIES** Felix Faust
ENEMIES Timeless Ones, JLA
BACKGROUND The deadly trio of Abnegazar, Rath, and Ghast, also known as Demons Three, ruled the galaxy a billion years ago, but they were banished to Hell. They have returned to Earth several times, often summoned by the sorcerer Felix Faust to battle the Justice League of America. Their powers include the ability to travel through time and space, give life to inanimate objects, and fire bolts of energy.

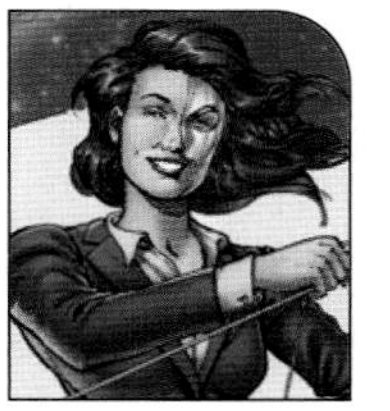

DIRECTOR ZITHER
DEBUT *The Fury of Firestorm: The Nuclear Men* (Vol. 1) #1 (Nov. 2011)
REAL NAME Candace Zither **BASE** Zithertech Compound, Nevada
ENEMIES Firestorm, Pozhar **BACKGROUND** Attempting to replicate the experiment that created nuclear-powered hero Firestorm, Candace Zither inadvertently transformed her husband Roger into the monster Helix. After this failure, Zither sent a team out to seize a sample from the Firestorm experiment. This led student Jason Rusch to trigger the Firestorm Protocol and merge with jock Ronnie Raymond. Candace Zither was later seemingly vaporized by Firehawk.

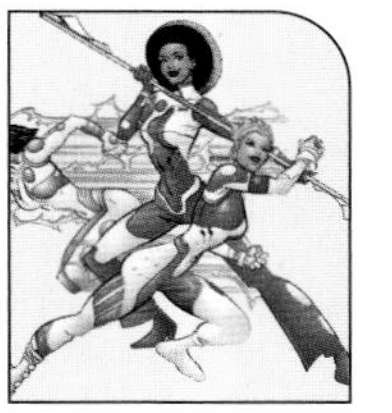

DNANGELS
DEBUT *Superboy* (Vol. 4) #87 (Jul. 2001) **BASE** Metropolis
MEMBERS Cherub, Seraph, Epiphany **ALLIES** Superboy **ENEMIES** Supergirl The DNAngels were created by a $2 billion cloning program. Speedster Cherub was made by mixing the DNA of Impulse with that of Superboy's dead girlfriend Tana Moon; Epiphany was based on Wonder Girl Cassie Sandsmark's DNA; Seraph gained telekinesis powers from the genetic code of Superboy. Their first mission was to recover an infant clone of Jim Harper (Guardian), believed stolen by Superboy. Later, the group worked for the League of Assassins.

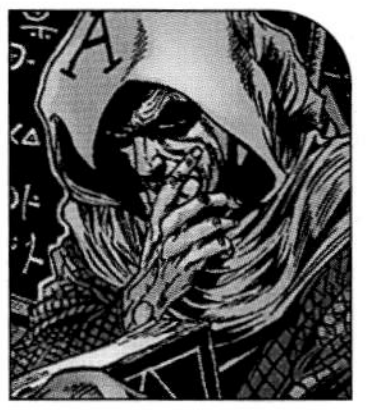

DOCTOR ALCHEMY
DEBUT *Showcase* #13 (Mar.–Apr. 1958)
REAL NAME Albert Desmond **BASE** Central City
ALLIES Captain Cold, Mirror Master, Trickster **ENEMIES** The Flash
BACKGROUND Albert Desmond suffered from dissociative identity disorder; his evil side used his chemistry knowledge to become Dr. Alchemy and battle The Flash. He came into possession of the magical Philosopher's Stone, which created a twin construct named Alvin who briefly became Doctor Alchemy. When the construct was eventually destroyed, Albert resumed his criminal identity.

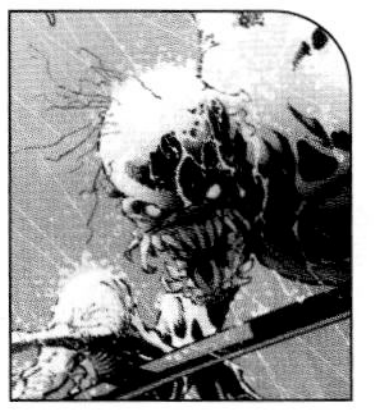

DOCTOR DEATH
DEBUT *Detective Comics* #29 (Jul. 1939)
REAL NAME Karl Helfern **BASE** Gotham City
ALLIES The Riddler
ENEMIES Batman
BACKGROUND Karl Helfern was a brilliant scientist who worked at Wayne Industries, trying to create a serum to strengthen human bones. After he lost his job and suffered a mental breakdown, he took the name Doctor Death and started working for the Riddler. Their plan failed when Doctor Death lost his life in a battle with Batman.

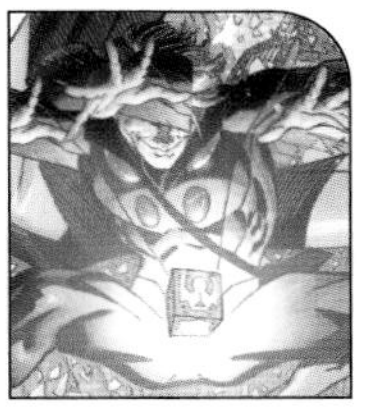

DOCTOR IMPOSSIBLE
DEBUT *Earth 2* #18 (Feb. 2014)
REAL NAME Jimmy Olsen
UNIVERSE Earth-2
ALLIES Thomas Wayne, Red Tornado **ENEMIES** Terry Sloane
BACKGROUND On Earth-2, Jimmy Olsen was a computer hacker known as Accountable. He was captured by the World Army and imprisoned at Arkham Asylum. After he was freed by Batman, Olsen acquired the powers of a New God and took the name Doctor Impossible. He was now able to fly and project energy.

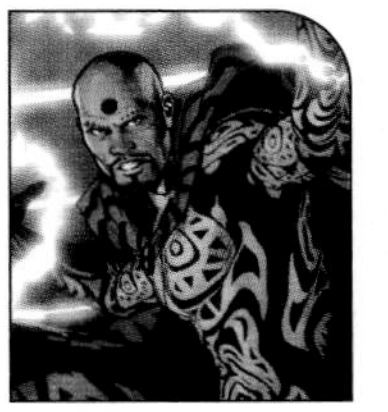

DOCTOR MIST
DEBUT *Super Friends* #12 (Jun.–Jul. 1978)
REAL NAME Nommo Balewa **BASE** South Africa
ALLIES Felix Faust, Nick Necro
ENEMIES Amethyst, Frankenstein
BACKGROUND African wizard Nommo Balewa gained immortality and magical powers thousands of years ago to become Doctor Mist. He was a member of the magical division of A.R.G.U.S., the military team that supported the Justice League, but betrayed them in order to obtain the Books of Magic.

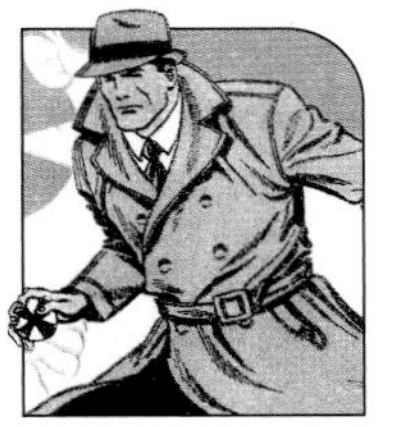

DOCTOR OCCULT
DEBUT *New Fun* #6 (Oct. 1935)
REAL NAME Richard Occult **BASE** New York City
ALLIES Rose Psychic, Justice Society of America
ENEMIES Nick Necro
BACKGROUND Doctor Occult and his partner/lover Rose Psychic ran a detective agency that specialized in supernatural crimes. During World War II, he joined the All-Star Squadron. Occult and Rose Psychic later merged into a single being, and helped the JSA with mystic crises. He was murdered by the sorcerer Nick Necro.

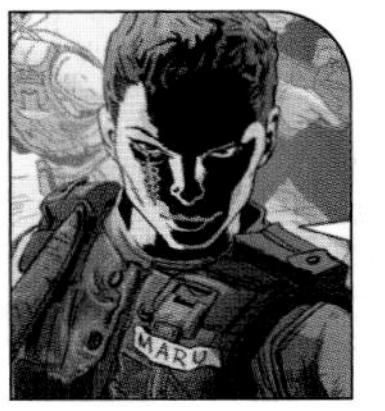

DOCTOR POISON
DEBUT *Sensation Comics* #2 (Feb. 1942)
REAL NAME Marina Maru **BASE** Washington, DC
ALLIES Godwatch **ENEMIES** Wonder Woman
BACKGROUND Leader of paramilitary outfit Poison, Marina Maru was enlisted by Veronica Cale and her Godwatch organization against Wonder Woman. But Maru's history with Diana of Themyscira stretched back further: Shortly after Wonder Woman left Themyscira for the first time, she fought soldiers infected with the Maru Virus, a psychoactive agent created by Poison.

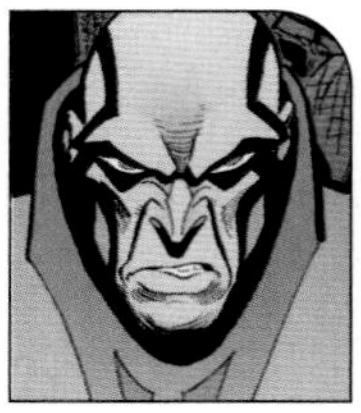

DOMINUS
DEBUT *Action Comics* #747 (Aug. 1998)
REAL NAME Tuoni
ALLIES Kem-L
ENEMIES Kismet, Superman
BACKGROUND Tuoni was once a priest who was incinerated and exiled to the Phantom Zone after he attacked his former lover, Kismet. Kryptonian technology resurrected him, and he became the powerful Super-Villain Dominus, able to create multiple realities based on his opponents' worst fears.

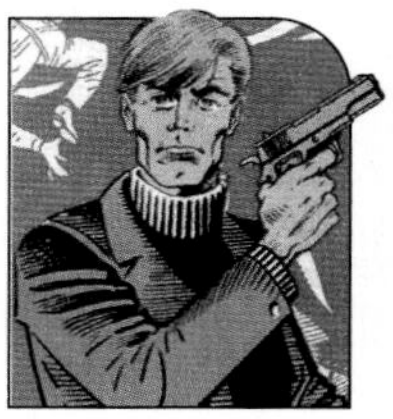

DOUBLE, JONNY
DEBUT *Showcase* #78 (Nov. 1968)
REAL NAME Jonathan Sebastian Double
BASE San Francisco **ALLIES** Wonder Woman
ENEMIES Kobra, Doctor Tzin-Tzin
BACKGROUND Jonny Double was a former police detective who formed his own detective agency, working alongside a waitress, Crystal Cross, and a pool shark known as Fish-Eye. Although Double mostly worked on local crimes, he counted Supergirl and Wonder Woman as allies and fought the super-terrorist Kobra.

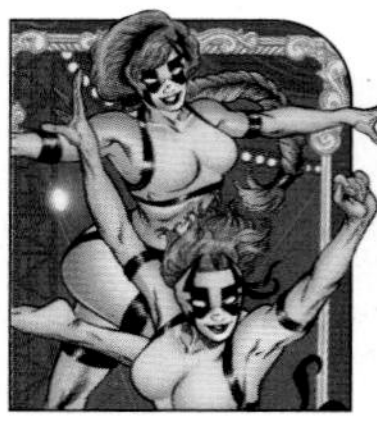

DOUBLE DARE
DEBUT *Nightwing* #32 (Jun. 1999)
REAL NAME Margo and Aliki Marceau
ALLIES Cheshire, Calculator, Deathstroke
ENEMIES Blockbuster, Secret Six
BACKGROUND The Marceau sisters were acclaimed circus acrobats who led secret lives as the costumed thieves Double Dare. While in Blüdhaven, the sisters made an enemy of crime boss Blockbuster and also competed for the affections of Nightwing. Double Dare later joined the Secret Society of Super-Villains.

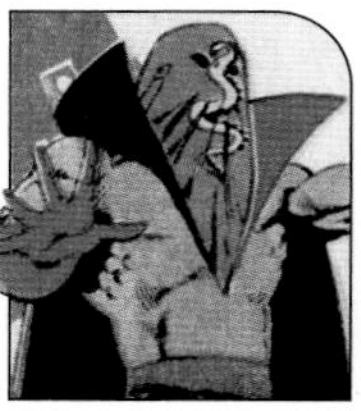

DRAGON KING
DEBUT *All-Star Squadron* #4 (Dec. 1981)
ALLIES His daughter Shiv **ENEMIES** All-Star Squadron, Shining Knight
BACKGROUND The Dragon King was a brilliant Japanese scientist who created a nerve gas during World War II. However, his biggest achievement was devising a mystical energy field around Axis countries that stymied any magically powered beings that came within its zone of influence. After the war, he experimented on himself, transforming into a deadly human/reptile hybrid. He seemingly perished during a fight with Star-Spangled Kid, S.T.R.I.P.E., and the Shining Knight.

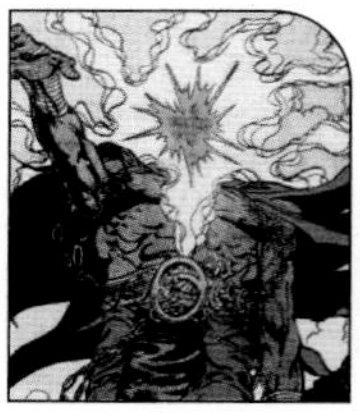

DREAMSLAYER
DEBUT *Justice League Europe* #15 (Jun. 1990)
ALLIES The Extremists **ENEMIES** Justice League Europe
BACKGROUND Dreamslayer was a powerful sorcerer that led the terrorist group known as the Extremists and was responsible for annihilating the planet Angor. Finding his way to Earth, he came up against Justice League Europe, killing the Silver Sorceress, but not before she dispatched him to the astral plane. He escaped but was soon banished to the dimension of terrors. He later returned, sacrificing himself alongside former team member Havok to resurrect Angor.

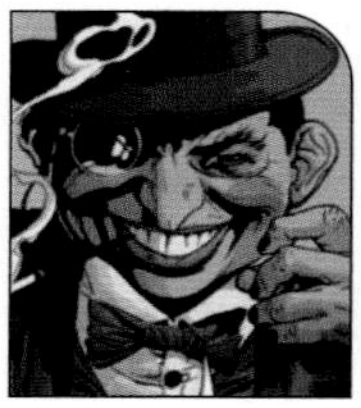

DUMMY
DEBUT *Leading Comics* #1 (Dec. 1941)
REAL NAME unknown **BASE** New York City
ALLIES Injustice Unlimited **ENEMIES** Vigilante, Infinity, Inc.
BACKGROUND When dying criminal mastermind The Hand decided to set the Seven Soldiers of Victory their greatest challenge ever, Dummy was among the villains he selected for the task. The diminutive puppet-like malefactor went up against Vigilante on that occasion, and subsequently fought the masked crimefighter multiple times, before taking on Infinity, Inc. as the new leader of Injustice Unlimited.

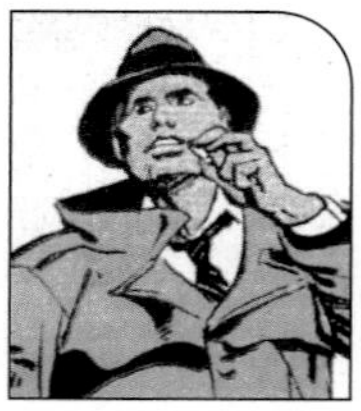

DUSK, NATHANIEL
DEBUT *Nathaniel Dusk* #1 (Feb. 1984)
BASE New York City
BACKGROUND Dusk was a private investigator active in the 1930s. In the events of the *Doomsday Clock* series, Dusk was a private-eye character made famous by actor Carver Colman who became an associate of Doctor Manhattan. Colman was eventually murdered by his mother. However, Doctor Manhattan then rewrote reality, by pushing Carver to admit to the world that he was a homosexual—an act that changed Carver's fate for the better.

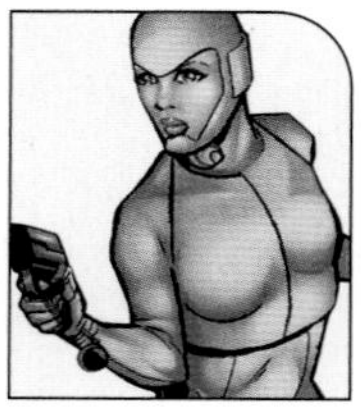

ECHO
DEBUT *Batman: Legends of the Dark Knight* #119 (Jul. 1999)
REAL NAME Isabella Cheranova
POWERS/ABILITIES **ENEMIES** Batman **BACKGROUND**
Echo was a Soviet agent assassin. She was selected to be implanted with organic "wetware" as part of the Turing Project—and was the only test subject to survive. The implant allowed her to pick up electromagnetic signals (incl. radio waves) and read minds; a holographic camouflage suit made her invisible for short periods. After a brief battle with Batman in Gotham City, she disappeared.

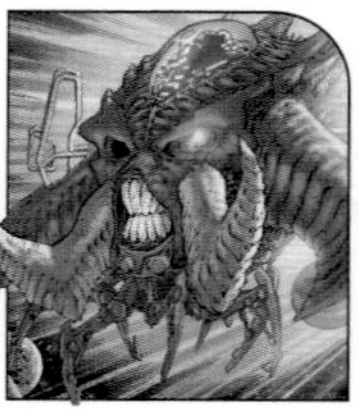

EKRON
DEBUT *Adventure Comics* #352 (Jan. 1967)
ENEMIES Lobo, Lady Styx
BACKGROUND Ekron is a mysterious ancient construct believed to have been built by the Guardians. Its eyes can fire energy beams and manipulate the minds of others. Following *Infinite Crisis*, the bounty hunter Lobo obtained one of its eyes, leaving Ekron (and its operator, the Green Lantern of Vengar) defenseless against Lady Styx's invading army. Ekron's pursuit of its eye brought it into conflict with Lobo and the outer-space exiles Animal Man, Adam Strange, and Starfire.

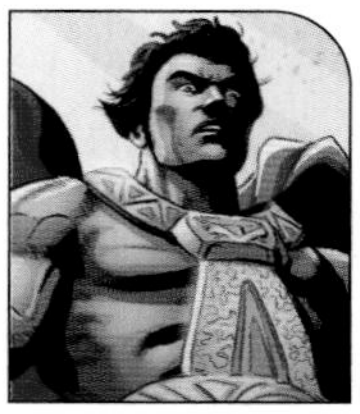

EL DORADO
DEBUT *Suicide Squad Most Wanted: El Diablo and Amanda Waller* #5 (Feb. 2017)
REAL NAME Unknown **BASE** Mexico **ENEMIES** Jake Dalesko
BACKGROUND When Amanda Waller sent a Task Force Y team to retrieve Suicide Squad member El Diablo and his allies near the Mexican border, El Dorado and his Justicia team interceded. With teammates Acrata, El Muerto, and Iman, he enlisted the aid of the Suicide Squad in taking down Checkmate's White King, Jake Dalesko, but not even El Dorado's great strength could prevail.

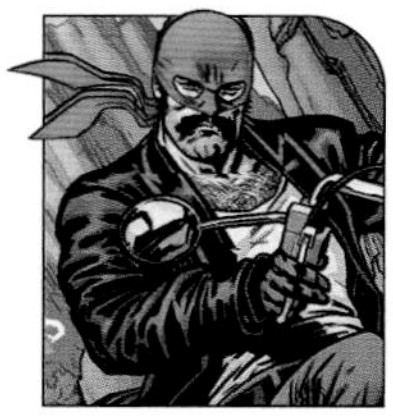

EL GAUCHO
DEBUT *Detective Comics* #215 (Jan. 1955)
REAL NAME Santiago Vargas **BASE** Buenos Aires
ALLIES Batman, Club of Heroes
ENEMIES Club of Villains
BACKGROUND Inspired by Batman's heroic exploits, Vargas became a costumed crime fighter in Argentina, notably opposing powerful drug cartels. He joined Wingman, Freight Train, Looker, Batwing, Halo, and the Hood to form the Dead Heroes Club, a division of Batman Incorporated.

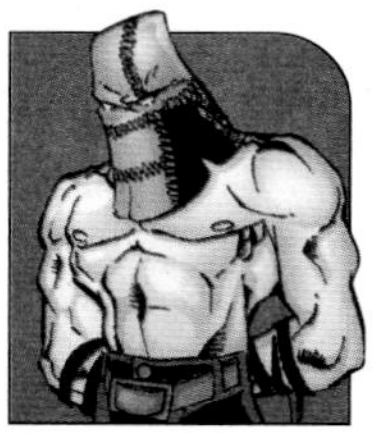

EL MUERTO
DEBUT *Superman Annual* #12 (Aug. 2000)
REAL NAME Pablo Valdez **BASE** Mexico City **ENEMIES** Duran
BACKGROUND Valdez idolized Superman but lacked superpowers. After Valdez died fighting crime, he was resurrected through mysticism and became the undead Super Hero El Muerto. This time, however, he hated Superman for not being there to prevent his death. El Muerto teamed up with fellow heroes Acrata and Iman to defend Mexico City from the sorcerer Duran and eventually reconciled with the Man of Steel. He later joined Justicia—the heroes of Mexico.

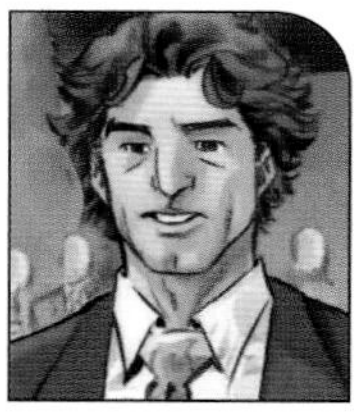

ELIAS, DARWIN
DEBUT *The Flash* #1 (Nov. 2011)
REAL NAME Dr. Darwin Elias
BASE Central City
ALLIES The Flash **ENEMIES** The Rogues
BACKGROUND Dr. Darwin Elias was a wealthy, intelligent, and dedicated scientist who helped The Flash utilize all aspects of the energy source known as the Speed Force. When The Flash temporarily disappeared from Central City, Elias tried to take control of the Speed Force himself, but was defeated by The Flash.

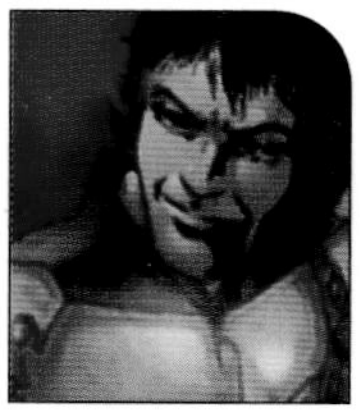

EMINENCE OF BLADES
DEBUT *Stormwatch* #1 (Nov. 2011)
REAL NAME Harry Tanner
ALLIES The Engineer **ENEMIES** Scourge of Worlds
BACKGROUND Tanner was a member of Stormwatch; he was also thought to be centuries old. One of the best swordsmen on Earth, he could imbue his blades with energy. He also possessed a unique form of telepathy that masked a deceptive and persuasive nature and rightfully earned him the title "The Prince of Lies." He would betray his teammates if he felt it was in his best interests to do so.

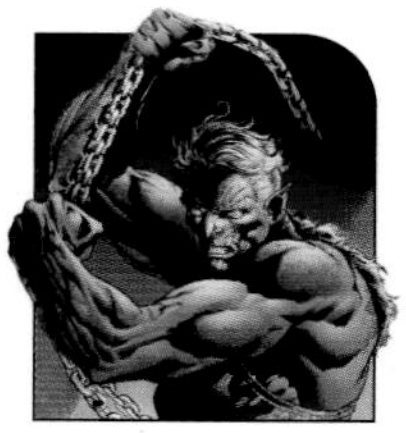

EMPEROR PENGUIN
DEBUT *Detective Comics* #13 (Dec. 2012)
REAL NAME Ignatius Ogilvy **BASE** Gotham City
ALLIES Poison Ivy, Bane **ENEMIES** Batman, The Penguin
BACKGROUND Ignatius Ogilvy was a common street thug when he joined The Penguin's gang, but he was smart and eventually became the group's second-in-command. He then betrayed The Penguin and took over the gang as Emperor Penguin. Later, he ingested a concoction of several drugs, including Man-Bat serum and Venom, that gave him superpowers and a monstrous appearance.

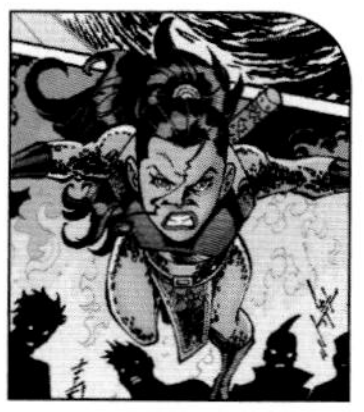

EMPRESS
DEBUT *Young Justice* #16 (Jan. 2000)
REAL NAME Anita Fite
ALLIES Arrowette
ENEMIES Agua Sin Gaaz
BACKGROUND Anita Fite inherited mystical powers from her grandmother, who was a powerful voodoo priestess. Fite was inspired by Arrowette and battled crime as Empress, often fighting alongside Young Justice. She possessed mind-control powers and the ability to teleport, as well as being skilled at hand-to-hand combat.

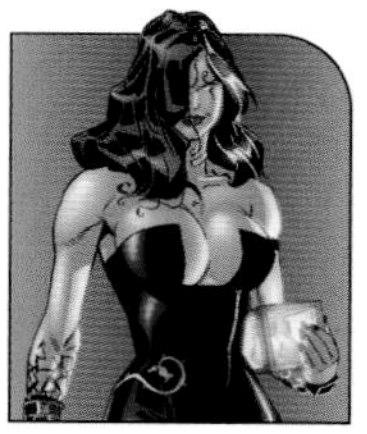

ENCANTADORA
DEBUT *Action Comics* #760 (Dec. 1999)
REAL NAME Lourdes Lucero **BASE** Metropolis
ALLIES General Zod **ENEMIES** Etrigan, Rā's al Ghūl, Superman
BACKGROUND Lucero was the daughter of an archaeologist who discovered the magical Mists of Ibella. She used the Mists to become La Encantadora and spent her life trying to defeat Superman, despite the Man of Steel invariably coming to her rescue when her plans went awry. She once almost killed him by releasing a cell-destroying nanobot into his body with a kiss, but immediately regretted the act.

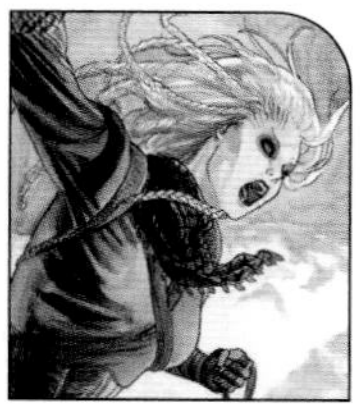

ESSENCE
DEBUT *Red Hood and the Outlaws* #1 (Nov. 2011)
BASE Himalayas
BACKGROUND Essence was the daughter of Ducra, the leader of an ancient group of warrior monks known as the All-Caste. After the All-Caste was slaughtered by their enemy, the Untitled, Ducra's mystical powers were transferred to Essence. Now, she was seemingly immortal and could manipulate darkness, enabling her to disappear into shadows. Essence had trained with Jason Todd while he was with the All-Caste and Todd mistakenly believed that she had betrayed them to the Untitled.

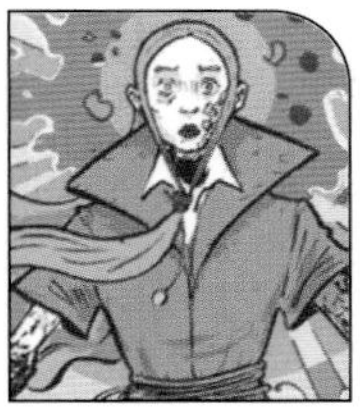

ETERNITY GIRL
DEBUT *JLA/Doom Patrol Special* #1 (Mar. 2018)
REAL NAME Caroline Sharp **BASE** Alpha 13 HQ
ALLIES Alpha 13, Lord Crash **ENEMIES** Madame Atom
BACKGROUND Sharp pushed herself both academically and physically, gaining two master's degrees, Olympic-level gymnastic prowess, and a career at government agency Alpha 13. Exposure to Madame Atom's atomic drill granted her matter-reconfiguration powers and immortality. For a time she operated as Chrysalis, before overcoming depression to become the multiversally aware Eternity Girl.

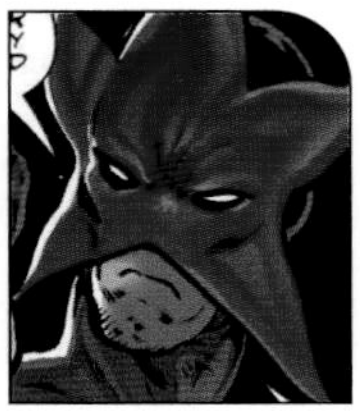

EVIL STAR
DEBUT *Green Lantern* #37 (Jun. 1965)
BASE Planet Aoran **ALLIES** Legion of Doom **ENEMIES** Green Lantern
BACKGROUND Evil Star was a scientist who attempted to achieve immortality by inventing the Starband, which harnessed the energy of stars. It also gave him the power to fly, create force blasts, and control the Starlings—miniature versions of himself. Having destroyed his own world when it dared to turn against him, Evil Star tried to overthrow the Guardians of the Universe, but was defeated. The villain was later drained of his power by Countess Belzebeth.

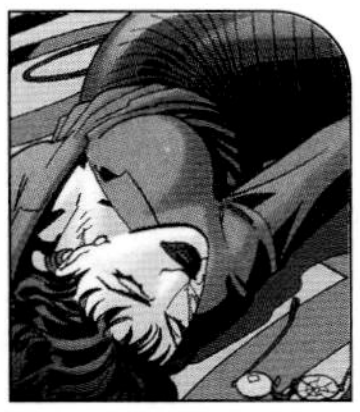

FAIRCHILD, VESPER
DEBUT *Batman* #540 (Mar. 1997)
BASE Gotham City
ALLIES Bruce Wayne **ENEMIES** Lex Luthor
BACKGROUND Nighttime radio talk-show host and investigative journalist Vesper Fairchild was romantically involved with Bruce Wayne for a short period. She was murdered at Wayne Manor and Bruce was charged with her death and forced to become a fugitive in order to find the real killer. He finally managed to clear his name and prove that Lex Luthor had hired the assassin David Cain to eliminate her.

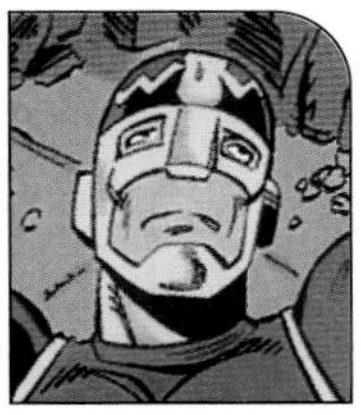

FASTBAK
DEBUT *The New Gods* #5 (Oct.–Nov. 1971)
BASE New Genesis **ALLIES** Highfather **ENEMIES** Darkseid
BACKGROUND Fastbak was one of the youngest of the New Gods on the planet New Genesis and was renowned for his ability to fly at high speeds, thanks to the aeropads in his boots. His body was resistant to friction heat, even through the upper atmosphere. Fastbak was believed to have died during the Death of the New Gods event, though he was briefly seen alive during the temporally unstable Flash War.

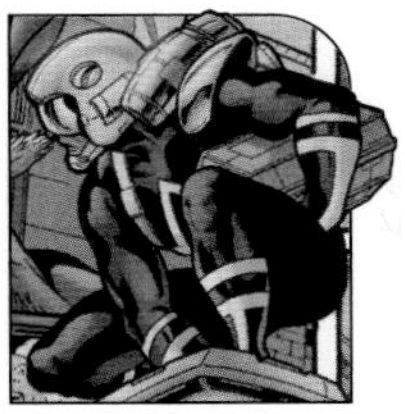

FASTBALL
DEBUT *Justice League of America* #234 (Jan. 1985)
REAL NAME John Malone
BASE Detroit
ALLIES The Cadre **ENEMIES** Justice League, the Power Company
BACKGROUND Malone was recruited by the Overmaster to join the Cadre. As Fastball, he had super-fast reflexes and specialized in throwing explosive spheres. After the Justice League defeated him, he joined Doctor Polaris but was defeated again by the Power Company. Fastball died at the hands of an O.M.A.C. unit.

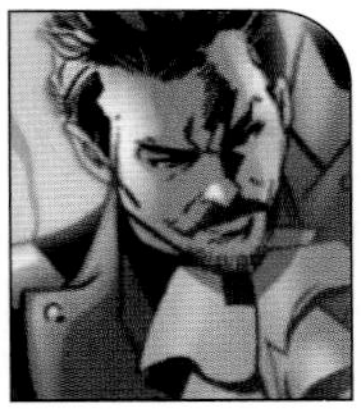

FAUST, SEBASTIAN
DEBUT *Outsiders: Alpha* #1
REAL NAME Sebastian Faust **BASE** Kahndaq
AFFILIATION The Outsiders, A.R.G.U.S. **ENEMIES** Asmodel, Diablos
BACKGROUND As a baby, Sebastian Faust had his soul traded to a demon by his father, the evil magician Felix Faust, in return for immortality for the elder Faust. Instead, Sebastian became the world's first infant soul-mage. Unlike his father, the younger Faust generally used his abilities for good, whether with The Outsiders or as a director of A.R.G.U.S.

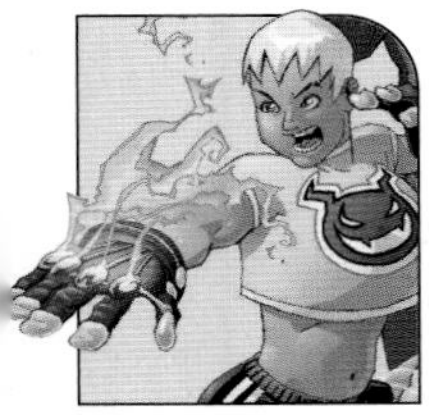

FEVER
DEBUT *Doom Patrol* #1 (Dec. 2001)
REAL NAME Shyleen Lao
BASE New York City
ALLIES Thayer Jost **ENEMIES** Virman Vundabar
BACKGROUND Lao could generate intense heat over short distances, allowing her to soften metal and other substances. As Fever, she became the youngest member of the newly reformed Doom Patrol, even though she had not completely mastered her powers. Fever was murdered by a member of the Dark Side Club.

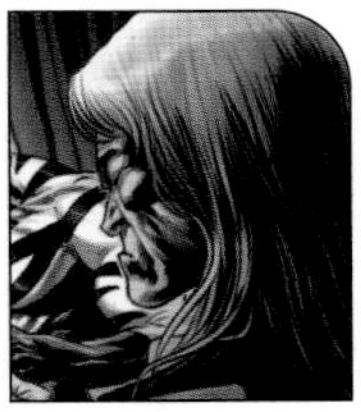

FIDDLER
DEBUT *All-Flash* #32 (Jan. 1948)
REAL NAME Isaac Bowin **BASE** Keystone City
AFFILIATION Injustice Society, Injustice Unlimited
ENEMIES The Flash **BACKGROUND** A petty thief who plied his trade in India, Isaac Bowin learned a fakir he was imprisoned with how to use music to hypnotize. Utilizing a fiddle, Bowin embarked on a new criminal career in Keystone City, a move which brought him into conflict with the original Flash, Jay Garrick. A member of the Injustice Society, latterly he joined the Legion of Doom.

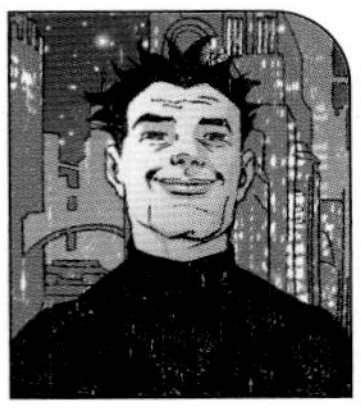

FILM FREAK
DEBUT *Batman* #395 (May 1986)
REAL NAME Burt Weston, aka "Edison"
BASE Gotham City
ALLIES Angle Man **ENEMIES** Catwoman
BACKGROUND A failed movie actor, Weston became a criminal and committed many thefts that were inspired by scenes from classic movies. He stole a nuclear bomb, placed it in a movie theater, and took over a TV studio so that he could broadcast his nuclear threat. Catwoman defeated him and defused the bomb.

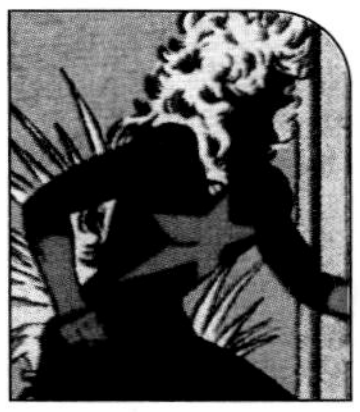

FIREBIRD
DEBUT *Firestorm, The Nuclear Man* #69 (Mar. 1988)
REAL NAME Serafina Arkadina **BASE** Russian Federation
ALLIES Ronnie Raymond, The People's Heroes **ENEMIES** Aliens
BACKGROUND Arkadina had psychic abilities, including telekinesis, telepathy, and hypnotic powers. As Firebird, she joined other superpowered Russian teenagers to form Soyuz. The government initially opposed the team, but eventually sanctioned Soyuz after they bravely fought off an alien invasion. More recently, Firebird has been a part of a Russian superteam called The People's Heroes.

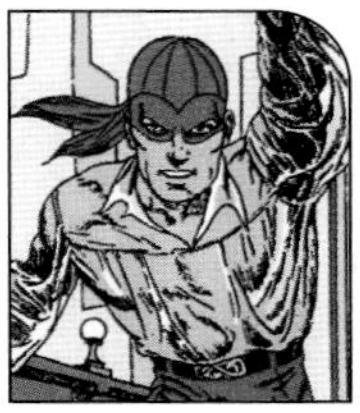

FIREBRAND I
DEBUT *Police Comics* #1 (Aug. 1941)
REAL NAME Rod Reilly **BASE** New York City
ALLIES Slugger Dunn **ENEMIES** Secret Society of Super-Villains
BACKGROUND Bored millionaire Rod Reilly decided to improve his athletic skills. He trained with an ex-heavyweight boxer, and then donned a red and pink costume to fight crime as Firebrand in New York City. Reilly served as a sailor during World War II and joined Uncle Sam's Freedom Fighters to battle the Nazis. His sister, Danette, later gained fiery superpowers and became the second Firebrand.

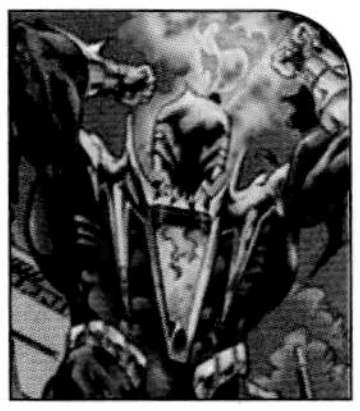

FIREBRAND III
DEBUT *Firebrand* #1 (Feb. 1996)
REAL NAME Alexander "Alex" Sanchez **BASE** New York City
ALLIES Noah Hightower **ENEMIES** Checkmate
BACKGROUND Sanchez was a policeman who lost the use of his legs after a criminal bombed his apartment. His life was turned around when philanthropist Noah Hightower provided him with robotic legs and hi-tech armor that could shoot energy bolts, thus creating Firebrand III. He was later killed by the villain Checkmate-Knight in a gladiatorial contest rigged by Roulette.

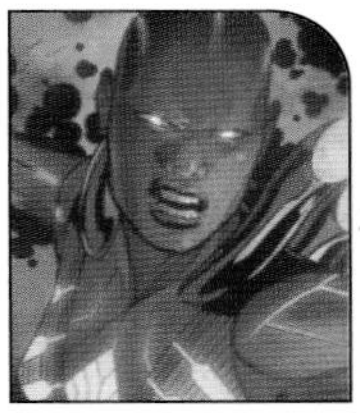

FIREBRAND V
DEBUT *Justice League of America* (Vol. 5) #29 (Jun. 2018)
REAL NAME Janet Fals **BASE** Mammoth City
AFFILIATION Unexpected **ENEMIES** Bad Samaritan
BACKGROUND Defying her CIA operative father's wish that she enlist, Janet Fals instead became a paramedic, dedicating herself to saving rather than taking lives. When she was killed in the line of duty, Fals' father had her resurrected. Her heart was replaced with a Conflict Engine which required her to fight or die, leading to her becoming involved with underground team the Unexpected.

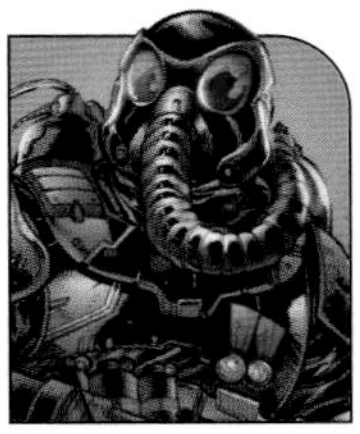

FIREBUG III
DEBUT *Deadshot* #1 (Feb. 2005)
BASE Gotham City **ENEMIES** Deadshot, Batman
BACKGROUND Little is known about the third villain to use the name Firebug, who, like his predecessors, specialized in arson-based crimes. Firebug wore an outfit containing a dangerous napalm derivative, and he projected the intensely flammable liquid from flamethrowers in the fingertips of his gloves. Deadshot defeated the villain when he shot Firebug and ignited the deadly liquid in his costume, encasing the arsonist in flames.

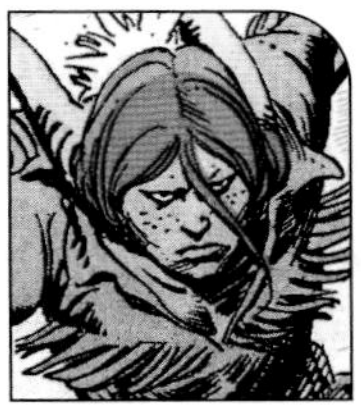

FIREHAIR
DEBUT *Showcase* #85 (Sep. 1969)
BASE Great Western Plains
ALLIES Hawk **ENEMIES** Wise Owl
BACKGROUND Firehair was an infant when he became the sole survivor of a wagon train massacre by a tribe of Blackfoot Indians in the early 1800s. His life was spared by the chief, Grey Cloud, and he grew up to be a great warrior and expert horseman. Firehair left the tribe to discover his true heritage and joined forces with the young gunslinger Hawk, son of Tomahawk.

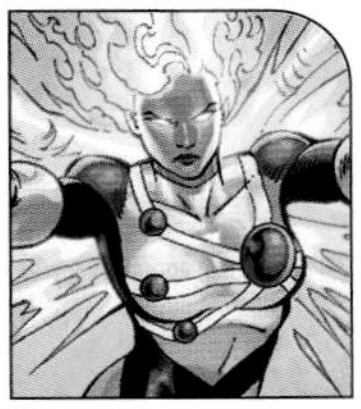

FIREHAWK
DEBUT *The Fury of Firestorm* #1 (June 1982)
REAL NAME Lorraine Reilly **ALLIES** Firestorm, Justice League
ENEMIES Multiplex, Tokamak, The Enforcer
BACKGROUND The daughter of a United States senator, Lorraine found herself the target of enemies of the USA. Consequently, she was kidnapped, experimented on, and transformed into Firehawk, a nuclear-powered superhuman. Firehawk was briefly mind-controlled and forced to battle Firestorm. However, the pair eventually became allies.

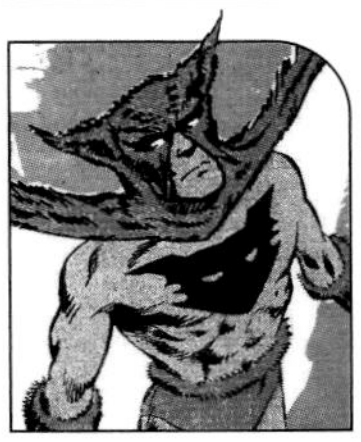

FLYING FOX
DEBUT *Young All-Stars* #1 (Jun. 1987)
ALLIES Iron Munro, Fury
ENEMIES Axis Amerika, the Nazis
BACKGROUND Flying Fox was a member of the First Nations tribe in Canada. After he was murdered by the Nazis, he was magically brought back to life and given a special mask and cape that gave him the powers of flight and invisibility. He also possessed the ability to cast fire from his hands. Flying Fox traveled to America, where he joined the All-Star Squadron and fought the Nazis.

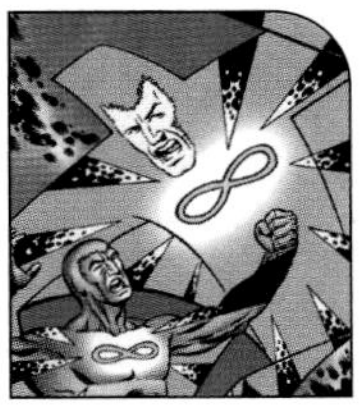

FOLDED MAN
DEBUT *The Flash* #153 (Oct. 1999)
REAL NAME Edwin Gauss **BASE** Central City
ALLIES Secret Society of Super-Villains **ENEMIES** The Flash
BACKGROUND Gauss was a physicist who created a special suit that allowed him to transform his body and teleport between dimensions. He became the Folded Man, capable of flattening into a 2D form or expanding to a 4D state. A recurring Flash (Wally West) foe, he was often able to escape Scarlet Speedster with his multi-dimensional powers.

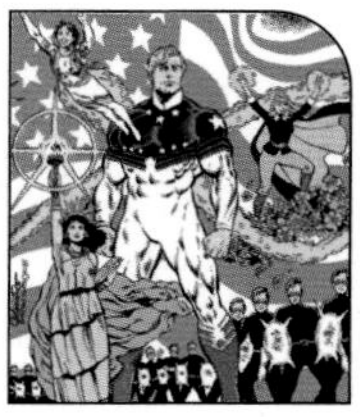

FORCE OF JULY
DEBUT *Batman and the Outsiders Annual* #1 (Sept. 1984)
BASE American Security Agency HQ **ALLIES** American Security Agency
ENEMIES Outsiders
BACKGROUND Created by American Security Agency head B. Eric Blairman as an ultra-patriotic super-team, Force of July numbered Major Victory, Lady Liberty, Mayflower, Silent Majority, and Sparkler. After failing to frame the Outsiders for a presidential assassination attempt, Force of July returned to battle the Outsiders and Green Arrow. An encounter with Suicide Squad saw most of the team killed.

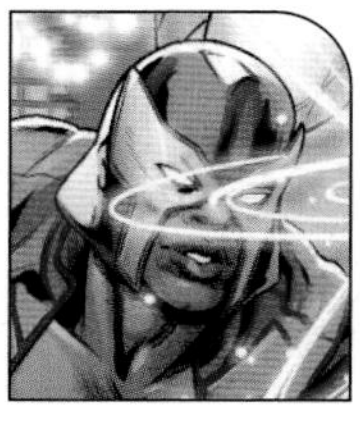

FREEDOM BEAST
DEBUT *Animal Man* #13 (Jul. 1989)
REAL NAME Dominic Mndawe **BASE** Capetown
ALLIES Animal Man, Global Guardians **ENEMIES** Prometheus
BACKGROUND After Mndawe was chosen to inherit the duties of B'Wana Beast, he acquired a magic elixir and helmet that enabled him to control minds and merge animals into hybrid creatures. Renaming himself Freedom Beast, he fought crime in Africa, often with his friend and ally, Animal Man. Mndawe has been a member of the Global Guardians and operates the Mndawe Foundation in Africa.

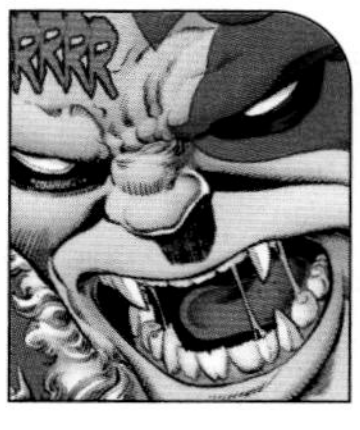

FRINGE
DEBUT *Teen Titans* #4 (Jan. 1997)
BASE H'San Natall empire, deep space
ALLIES Teen Titans **ENEMIES** Pylon, the Veil
BACKGROUND A half-human, half-alien hybrid, Fringe was abandoned by his parents because of his appearance and superhuman strength. He was found by a mysterious magical being known as the Entity, who granted him psychic powers. Hunted and captured by the villains Pylon and the Veil because of his alien genetics, he was rescued by the Teen Titans and later joined the team.

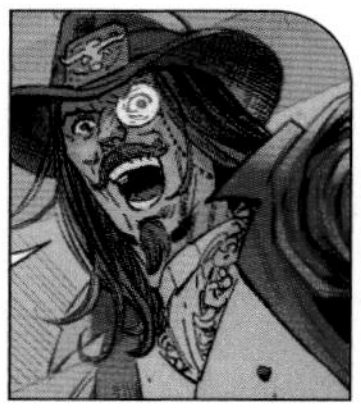

GAMBLER
DEBUT *New Titans* #68 (Jul. 1990)
REAL NAME Steven Montgomery Sharpe V **BASE** Gotham City
ENEMIES Justice Society of America, Teen Titans, Justice League
BACKGROUND The first Gambler, Steven Sharpe III, was a master of disguise, a skilled thief, and handy with a Derringer; he frequently battled the first Green Lantern, Alan Scott. After the Gambler lost his fortune, he committed suicide. His grandson, Steven Sharpe V, took his ID and plotted to defeat the JSA. He went on to battle the Teen Titans and the Justice League, never with much success.

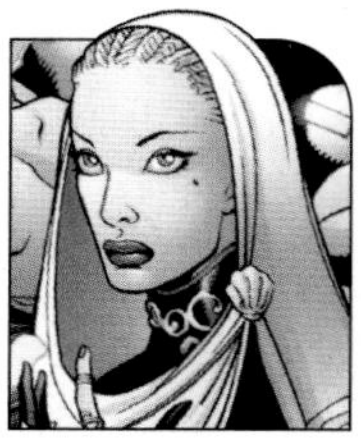

GAMEMNAE
DEBUT *JLA* #70 (Oct. 2002)
BASE Poseidonis, Atlantis
ALLIES League of Ancients **ENEMIES** Justice League
BACKGROUND A powerful sorceress, Gamemnae was cast out of Atlantis 3,000 years ago. She enslaved Aquaman and transported Atlantis to 1,004 BCE. Her ultimate plan to conquer the universe was thwarted by the Justice League, which rescued Aquaman and restored Atlantis to its proper place. Gamemnae died in a battle with Manitou Raven, one of the Ancients who had originally helped her.

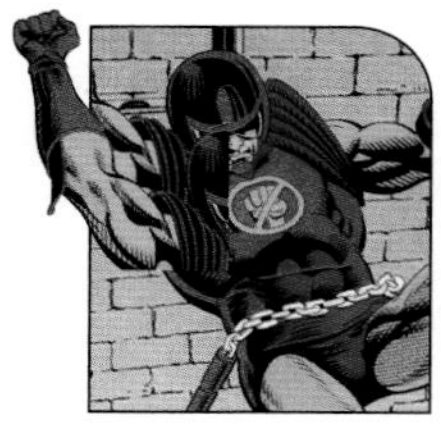

GANGBUSTER
DEBUT *Adventures of Superman* #428 (May 1987)
REAL NAME José Delgado
BASE Suicide Slum, Metropolis
ALLIES Hawkman, Dr. Light **ENEMIES** Street gangs, Bizarro Supergirl
BACKGROUND Delgado grew up fighting in the streets of Suicide Slum and later became a Golden Gloves boxing champion. He returned to his neighborhood to fight crime as Gangbuster, but suffered a spinal injury while fighting Combattor. An implant allowed him to patrol the streets of Metropolis once again.

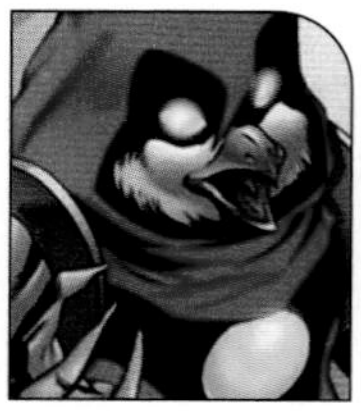

GATES
DEBUT *Legion of Super-Heroes* #66 (Mar. 1995)
REAL NAME Ti'julk Mr'asz **BASE** Vyrga
ALLIES Legion of Super-Heroes **ENEMIES** Superboy-Prime, Alastor
BACKGROUND Mr'asz was an outspoken radical on the planet Vyrga, and was one of the few members of his race with the power to create portals and travel through outer space. Much to his dismay, he was drafted as a member of the Legion of Super-Heroes in the 30th century, a group he had labeled "fascists." Even so, he acquitted himself well against the villainous likes of Mantis, Validus, and Rās al Ghūl.

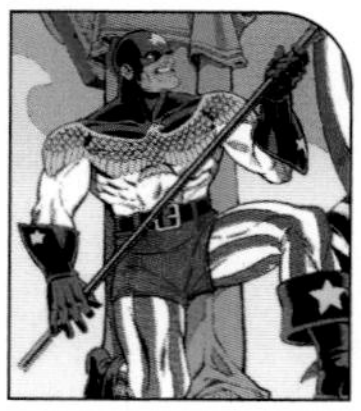

GENERAL GLORY
DEBUT *Justice League of America* #46 (Jan. 1991)
REAL NAME Joseph Jones **ALLIES** Justice League of America
ENEMIES Captain Schmidt **BACKGROUND** US soldier Jones was mystically bestowed with superpowers by Lady Liberty during World War II. As General Glory he was joined by a young partner, Ernest E. Earnest, alias Ernie. He also worked alongside his UK counterpart Beefeater and a time-traveling Booster Gold to stop a Nazi scientist from creating a time machine. The General later assumed a role in the Outsiders, helping to defeat the parasitic Untitled.

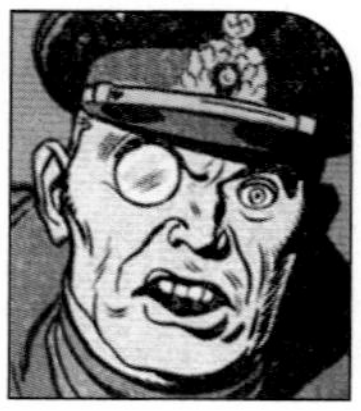

GENERAL ZAHL
DEBUT *Doom Patrol* #121 (Sep.–Oct. 1968)
ALLIES Brotherhood of Evil **ENEMIES** Doom Patrol, Robotman
BACKGROUND During World War II, Zahl was the ruthless commander of a Nazi U-boat, achieving one of the highest kill rates in the German fleet. After the war, he fled to Argentina to work as a mercenary, where he came into conflict with Niles Caulder, head of the Doom Patrol. Zahl later joined forces with Madame Rouge from the Brotherhood of Evil to ambush the Doom Patrol and destroy their island base. He died in a gun battle with Robotman.

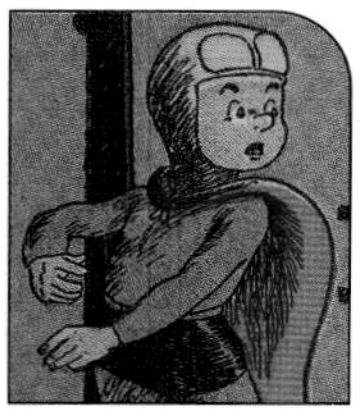

GENIUS JONES
DEBUT *Adventure Comics* #77 (Aug. 1942)
REAL NAME Johnny Jones
UNIVERSE Earth-2 **BASE** New York City
ALLIES I, Vampire, Doctor Thirteen, Anthro **ENEMIES** Black Manta
BACKGROUND Stranded on a desert island, Johnny Jones burned 734 books to attract the attention of a passing ship, but not before he absorbed every bit of knowledge from the books. After he returned home, he took the name Genius Jones and offered to answer any question for a fee.

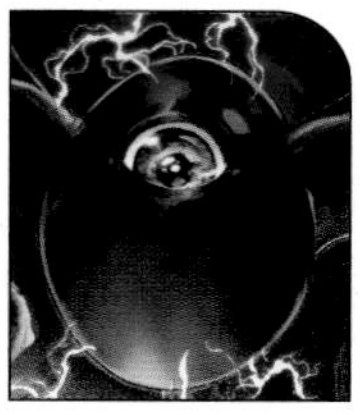

GENTRY, THE
DEBUT *The Multiversity* #1 (Oct. 2014)
ALLIES Mr. Stubbs, the Dark Monitor **ENEMIES** Society of Super-Heroes
BACKGROUND Intellectron, Dame Merciless, Demogorgunn, Hellmachine, and Lord Broken were five enormously powerful alien forces known as the Gentry. Capable of warping the laws of physics, they came to destroy Earth-7 and then moved on to corrupting other worlds with the aid of the Dark Monitor. Each member of the Gentry was the personification of a cultural fear or bad thought, and their goal was to take control of every mind in existence.

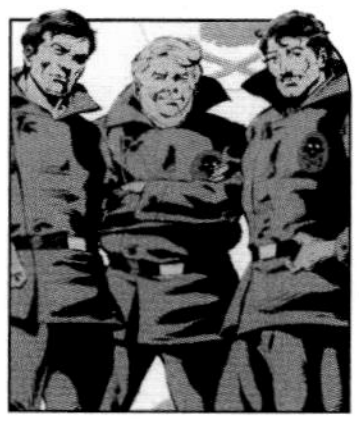

GHOST PATROL
DEBUT *Flash Comics* #29 (May 1942)
BASE France
ALLIES Shadowpact **ENEMIES** The Nazis
BACKGROUND Among the unsung heroes of World War II, the Ghost Patrol was three deceased members of the French Foreign Legion. Slim, Fred, and Pedro returned from beyond the grave to join the fight against Nazi Germany. With the ability to control their ectoplasm, changing from solid to insubstantial, the spectral trio proved effective soldiers, especially on clandestine sabotage missions.

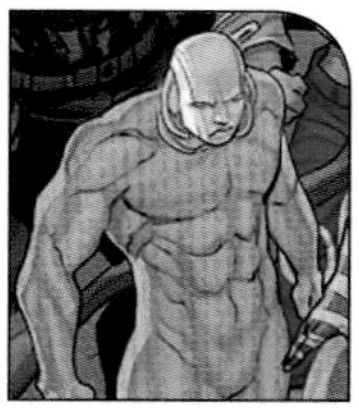

GIRDER
DEBUT *The Flash: Iron Heights* (Aug. 2001)
REAL NAME Tony Woodward **BASE** Central City
ALLIES Chroma, Tar Pit **ENEMIES** The Flash
BACKGROUND Steelworker Tony Woodward tumbled into a vat of molten steel that also contained debris from a S.T.A.R. Labs experimental project. Amazingly, he survived, and emerged with a body of living steel. Taking the codename Girder, he started a life of crime. Girder possessed a virtually indestructible metal body and superhuman strength.

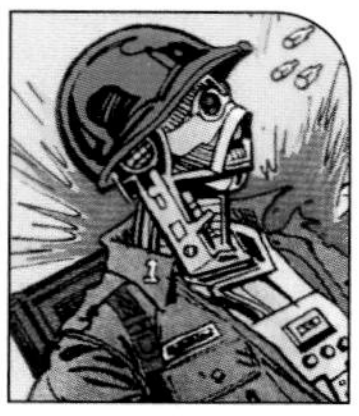

G.I. ROBOT
DEBUT *Weird War Tales* #101 (Jul. 1981)
REAL NAME J.A.K.E. 2 **BASE** Pacific Islands
BACKGROUND US scientists developed the super-strong G.I. Robot during World War II. The first model, J.A.K.E., developed artificial intelligence and sacrificed itself to save an American fleet. The next model, J.A.K.E. 2, was more powerful, being able to spray bullets from its fingers and shoot flames from its mouth. It fought with the Creature Commandos during the war and the military created an army of J.A.K.E. 2s. During *Final Crisis*, G.I. Robot was enlisted to fight Justifiers and other anti-life drones.

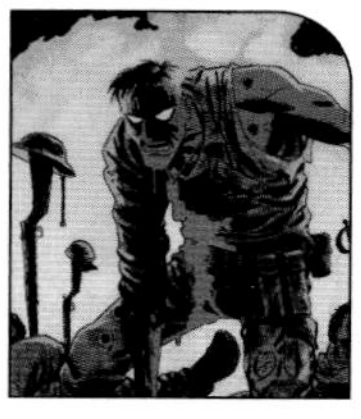

G.I. ZOMBIE
DEBUT *Star-Spangled War Stories Featuring G.I. Zombie* (Vol. 1) #1 (Sep. 2014)
REAL NAME Jared Kabe **ALLIES** Carmen King, Gravedigger
ENEMIES Jeff Kennedy, Leo Conroy **BACKGROUND** Jared Kabe has been dead for as long as he can remember. He is a soldier deployed by his commander, codename Gravedigger, to handle problems ranging from enemy armies to domestic terrorists with bio-weapons. Kabe combines martial skills with a shrewd mind and unnatural powers such as regeneration from injury, and freedom from fatigue. He tends to lose his abilities if he does not periodically eat human flesh.

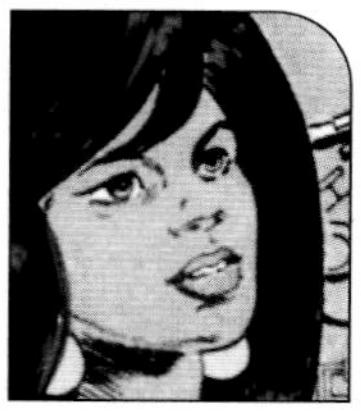

GLOSS
DEBUT *Millennium* #2 (Jan. 1988)
REAL NAME Xiang Po **ALLIES** Tasmanian-Devil, Crimson Fox III, Jet
ENEMIES Prometheus **BACKGROUND** Chinese-born Xiang Po was one of 10 humans chosen to become one of the immortal Guardians of the Universe. She acquired the ability to control the Dragon Lines of Power, energy fields that coursed through the Earth. With this power, Gloss could create force fields, duplicate herself, and teleport. She joined the Global Guardians, and then later became a member of China's government-sponsored team, The Great Twenty.

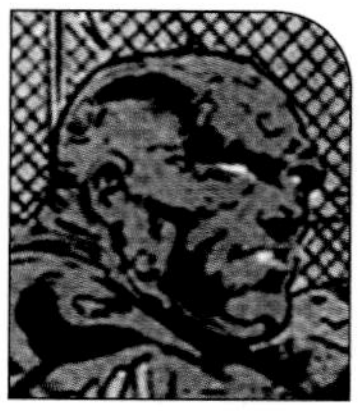

GOLEM
DEBUT *Suicide Squad* #45 (Sep. 1990)
REAL NAME Moyshe Nakhman
BASE Jerusalem
ALLIES Hayoth group **ENEMIES** Kobra
BACKGROUND Golem is a 300-lb monster that can alter the chemical composition of his body and take on the nature of any substance near him, including metal, water, and sand. He fought as a member of the Hayoth group and captured the terrorist Kobra in Israel. He later battled Superman and the Suicide Squad.

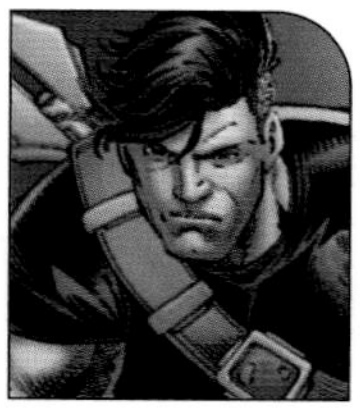

GNARRK
DEBUT *Teen Titans* #32 (Apr. 1971)
REAL NAME Gnarrk **BASE** Los Angeles
AFFILIATION Teen Titans **ENEMIES** Mr. Twister
BACKGROUND During a trip to the Stone Age, Teen Titans Kid Flash and Mal Duncan encountered a caveman who inadvertently returned with them to the present. Naming him after his guttural grunts, the Titans civilized Gnarrk and integrated him into the team, resulting in a relationship with teammate Lilith. Later, Gnarrk was among those accidentally killed by Wally West at the Sanctuary facility.

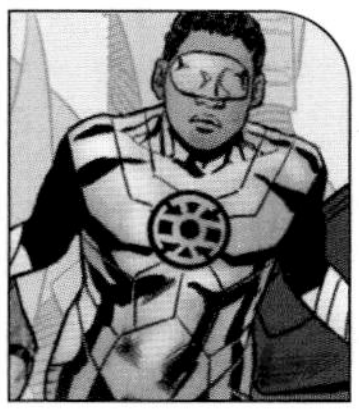

GOLD LANTERN
DEBUT *Superman* (Vol. 5) #14 (Oct. 2019)
REAL NAME unknown **BASE** Legion HQ
AFFILIATION Legion of Super-Heroes **ENEMIES** Tortor, Horraz
BACKGROUND A thousand years on from the heyday of the Green Lantern Corps, the Legion of Super-Heroes welcomed Gold Lantern into their ranks. Armed with a gold power ring, Gold Lantern was able to project and manipulate energy on an awesome scale, as demonstrated when he transmuted almost the entirety of New Earth's ocean system whilst battling Tortor of the Horraz Collective.

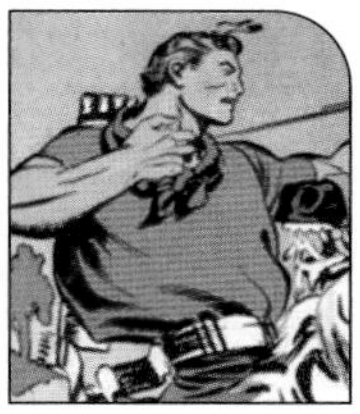

GOLDEN ARROW
DEBUT *Whiz Comics* #2 (Feb. 1940)
REAL NAME Roger Parsons
ALLIES Nugget Ned **ENEMIES** Brand Braddock
BACKGROUND Roger was the son of Paul Parsons, inventor of a new gas for balloon transportation. When his father was killed by rival Brand Braddock, Roger was raised by a prospector, Nugget Ned. He grew up to become a fearless fighter and a skilled archer. Dipping his homemade arrows in gold, he took the name Golden Arrow and set out to avenge his father's death and fight for justice on the western frontier.

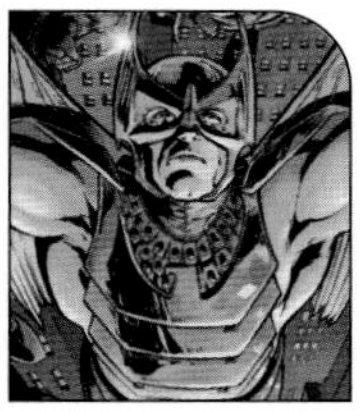

GOLDEN EAGLE
DEBUT *Justice League of America* #116 (Mar. 1975)
REAL NAME Cha'al Andar/Charley Parker **BASE** Midway City
AFFILIATION Teen Titans **ENEMIES** Hawkman, Hawkgirl
BACKGROUND Born on Earth to a Thanagarian father and human mother, Cha'al Andar—human name Charley Parker—grew up unaware of his heritage. Propelled into crime by his corrupt foster family, he turned his life around with the help of Hawkman. Donning Thanagarian battle armor to become Golden Eagle, Parker joined the Teen Titans, but later developed a hatred of Hawkman.

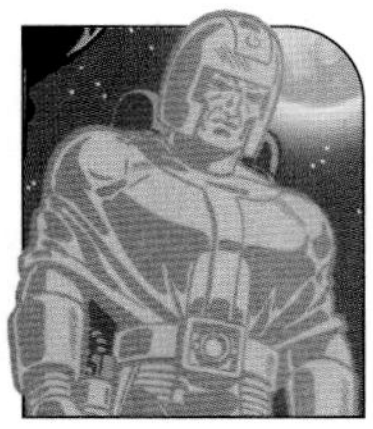

GOLDFACE
DEBUT *Green Lantern* #38 (Jul. 1965)
REAL NAME Keith Kenyon **BASE** Keystone City
ALLIES The Flash (Wally West) **ENEMIES** Green Lantern, Blacksmith
BACKGROUND Kenyon discovered a chest of gold, the molecular structure of which had been altered by chemical waste. It gave his body a gold-plated tone. He took the name Goldface and embarked on a life of crime, often clashing with the Green Lantern Corp, and murdering Green Lantern Tomar-Te. Goldface later died in prison, executed by the Darkstar Tomar-Tu.

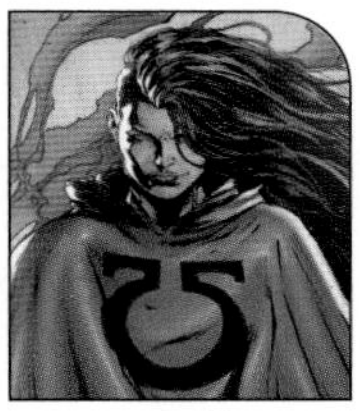

GRAIL
DEBUT *Justice League* #40 (Jun. 2015)
ALLIES Anti-Monitor **ENEMIES** Justice League, Green Lantern
BACKGROUND Grail was the daughter of Darkseid and the Amazonian assassin Myrina. It was prophesied at her birth that Grail would cause great destruction in the universe. As a hybrid Amazon/New God, Grail possessed almost limitless powers, including great strength, will corruption, and immortality. She allied herself with the Anti-Monitor and declared war on her father. During the cataclysmic conflict that ensued, she came very close to destroying the Justice League.

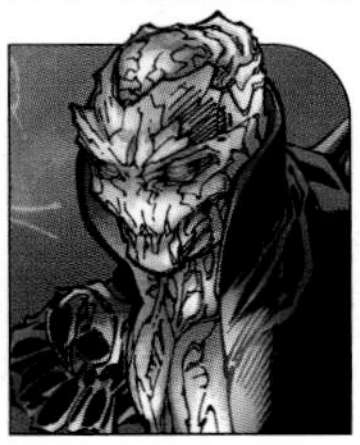

GRAVES, DAVID
DEBUT *Justice League* #6 (Apr. 2012)
ALLIES Several demonic entities **ENEMIES** Justice League
BACKGROUND David Graves was an author and historian who blamed the Justice League for the death of his family after they were exposed to a virus from Apokolips. He traveled to Asia and sought help from demons; he then stole the mystical Orb of Ra from A.R.G.U.S. Horribly disfigured, Graves tried to destroy the Justice League but was defeated. While incarcerated in Belle Reve prison, warden Amanda Waller suggested Graves write a book entitled *How to Defeat the Justice League*.

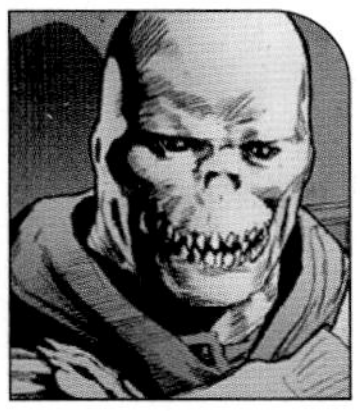

GREAT WHITE SHARK
DEBUT *Arkham Asylum: Living Hell* #1 (Jul. 2003)
REAL NAME Warren White **BASE** Gotham City
ALLIES The Penguin, Black Mask **ENEMIES** Batman
BACKGROUND Acquiring the nickname Great White Shark due to his ruthless fraud activities, financier Warren White escaped prison by pleading insanity. Unfortunately he was sent instead to Arkham Asylum. A series of encounters with the institute's psychopathic inmates left him with gill-like scars and a pallid, shark-like appearance, setting him up for a promising new career as a Gotham City crime lord.

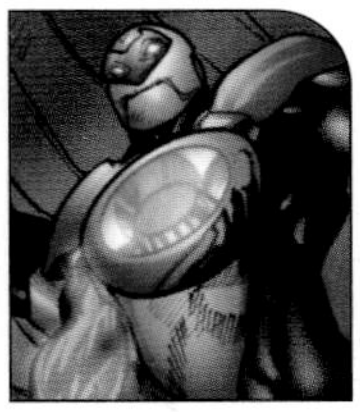

GREEN MAN
DEBUT *Green Lantern* #164 (May 1983)
BASE Space Sector 2828
ALLIES Alpha Lantern Corps, Omega Men **ENEMIES** Superboy-Prime
BACKGROUND Green Man came from the watery planet Uxor and was a Green Lantern for many years. He disobeyed the Guardians of the Universe to destroy the Spider Guild, left the Green Lantern Corps, and joined the Omega Men. After he was killed by the Durlans, a second Green Man was chosen from Uxor, and he became a member of the elite Alpha Lantern Corps.

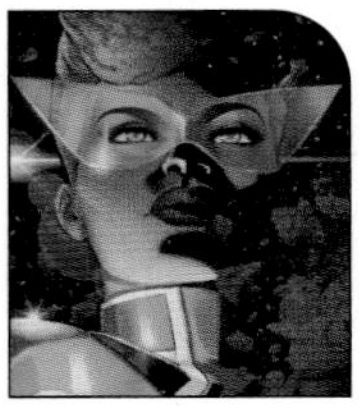

GREEN LANTERN
DEBUT *Far Sector* #1 (Jan. 2020)
REAL NAME Sojourner "Jo" Mullein **BASE** City Enduring
AFFILIATION Green Lantern Corps **ENEMIES** Cloud Kratocracy
BACKGROUND After being fired from the police force for reporting her partner for beating up a suspect, former soldier—and now ex-cop—Sojourner Mullein received an intriguing job offer. Enlisted in the Green Lantern Corps, Mullein was assigned to the most distant sector of the universe—far beyond the Corps' usual purview—to investigate the first murder in the City Enduring for five centuries.

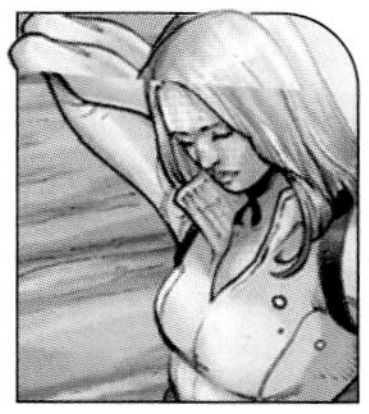

GRETEL
DEBUT *Batgirl* #5 (Mar. 2012)
REAL NAME Lisly Bonner **BASE** Gotham City
ENEMIES Boss Whittaker, Batman, Batgirl
BACKGROUND Bonner was an investigative reporter for the *Gotham Flame* who was shot in the head by gangster Boss Whittaker. She survived and discovered that she had acquired hypnotic powers. Taking the name Gretel, she murdered Whittaker and his family, and began a life of crime in Gotham City. When she tried to kill Bruce Wayne, she came up against Batman and Batgirl and was soundly defeated.

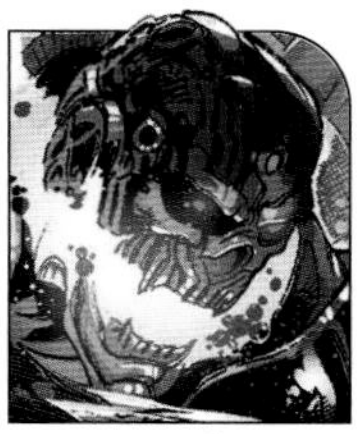

GRID
DEBUT *Justice League* #23 (Oct. 2013)
ALLIES Crime Syndicate **ENEMIES** Justice League
BACKGROUND Grid was a software program that gathered information for Cyborg. The program grew and evolved into a living computer virus. In its new, malevolent form, this sentient form of artificial intelligence attacked the Justice League, forming an alliance with Earth-3's Crime Syndicate. For its invaluable services, Grid demanded two things: a body, culled from the robotic prostheses of Cyborg, and emotions, which was its ultimate goal.

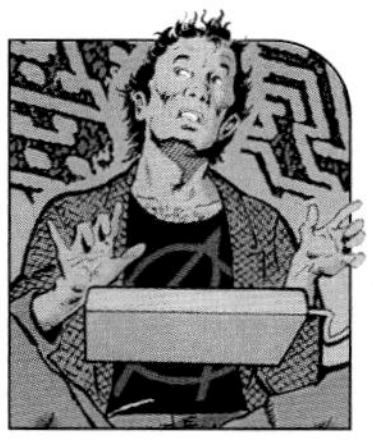

HACKER
DEBUT *The Hacker Files* #1 (Aug. 1992)
REAL NAME Jack Marshall
BASE Raleigh
ALLIES Sarge Steel, Speed Metal Kids **ENEMIES** Walter Sutcliffe
BACKGROUND Marshall worked for Digitronix, where he created a top-selling computer. After he was fired for requesting a share of the company's profits, he took the user name Hacker and stole back his data. He allied with the Speed Metal Kids, a group that solved computer-related problems around the world.

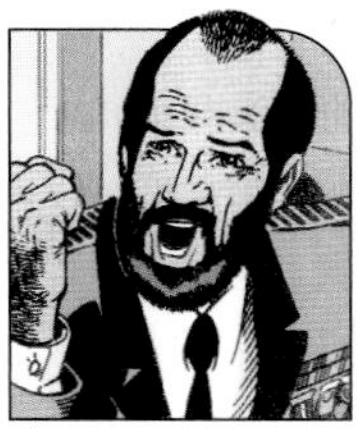

HARJAVTI, RUMAAN, AND SUMAAN
DEBUT *Justice League* #2 (Jun. 1987)
BASE Bialya
ALLIES The Joker **ENEMIES** Queen of H.I.V.E., Justice League International
BACKGROUND Rumaan Harjavti was a dictator in the African nation of Bialya. He joined forces with The Joker in an attempt to defeat the Justice League, and later teamed with the villain Queen Bee (Queen of H.I.V.E.) to fight the Global Guardians. After Harjavti was murdered by Queen Bee, his identical twin brother Sumaan assumed his identity and became ruler of Bialya.

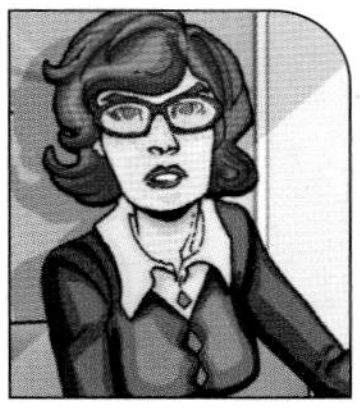

HARLEQUIN
DEBUT *All-American Comics* #89 (Sep. 1947)
REAL NAME Molly Mayne **BASE** Gotham City
ALLIES Justice Society, Infinity, Inc. **ENEMIES** Injustice Society
BACKGROUND An assistant to radio station boss Alan Scott, Molly Mayne became infatuated with his alter ego, Green Lantern. Donning an elaborate disguise, and armed with hypnotic spectacles, Mayne became criminal Harlequin to catch Green Lantern's attention and joined the Injustice Society for a time. Mayne became an ally of the Justice Society and a government agent, eventually marrying Scott.

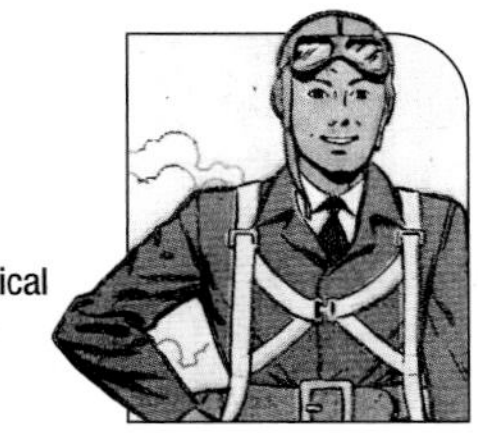

HARRIGAN, HOP
DEBUT *All-American Comics* #1 (Apr. 1939)
ALLIES All-Star Squadron, Prop Wash **ENEMIES** Silas Crane, the Nazis
BACKGROUND Hop Harrigan had no formal training as a fighter pilot. Even so, he was one of the top flying heroes of World War II. He flew secret missions for the US Army Corps, fighting Nazis in South America, and Japanese forces throughout the Pacific. He occasionally used the alias Guardian Angel and sometimes joined forces with the All-Star Squadron. After the war, Harrigan fought crime for a brief period under the name Black Lamp.

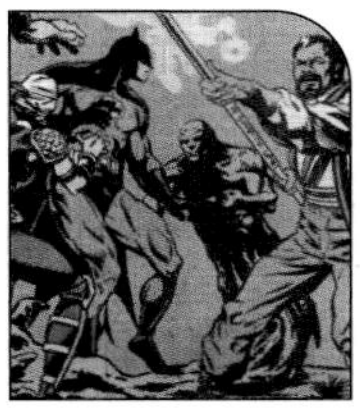

HAYOTH
DEBUT *Suicide Squad* #45 (Sep. 1990)
BASE Israel **ALLIES** Doctor Simon LaGrieve
ENEMIES Kobra **BACKGROUND** The Hayoth was a group of superpowered soldiers who acted as a strike force for the Israeli military. Dybbuk was a sentient form of artificial intelligence; Golem was a shapeshifter; Judith was a skilled martial arts warrior; and Ramban was a magician. The team came into conflict with the Suicide Squad, Superman, and Atom. Later, a former member of Hybrid called Pteradon joined.

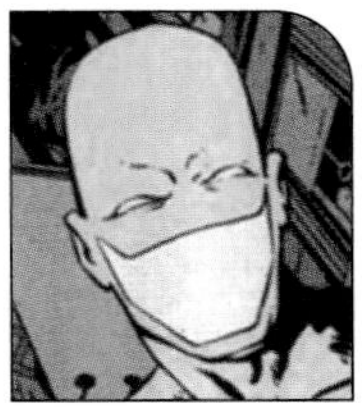

HECKLER
DEBUT *The Heckler* #1 (Sep. 1992)
REAL NAME Stuart Moseley **BASE** Delta City
ALLIES Ledge, Mr. Dude **ENEMIES** Boss Glitter, John Doe, Cosmic Clown
BACKGROUND Stuart Moseley was leading a quiet life running a Skid Row diner in Delta City when he heard a voice telling him to don the yellow and orange tights of the Heckler and fight crime. Armed with sarcastic wit but no superpowers, the Heckler was remarkably resilient and recovered quickly from physical damage. He was known to hang out with fellow zany heroes Plastic Man and Ambush Bug.

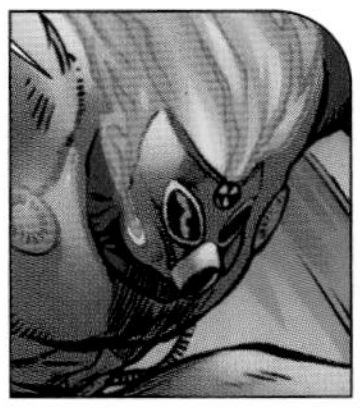

HELIX
DEBUT *The Fury of Firestorm* #3 (Jan. 2012)Base Zither-Tec
REAL NAME Roger Zither **ALLIES** Candace Zither **ENEMIES** Firestorm **BACKGROUND** Zithertech-Tech director Candace Zither transformed her husband Roger into the nuclear-powered Helix during experiments that also led to the creation of Firestorm. Helix was unleashed to battle the two men who together created Firestorm—Jason Rusch and Ronnie Raymond. An organization named Helix was a team of genetically engineered humans who fought Infinity, Inc. and other heroes, before joining the Dept. of Extranormal Operations.

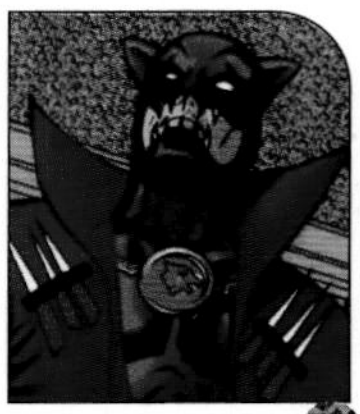

HELLHOUND
DEBUT *Catwoman Annual* #2 (July 1995)
REAL NAME Kai **BASE** Gotham City
ENEMIES Black Canary, Catwoman
BACKGROUND Kai was the top martial arts student at a secret dojo in Gotham City until Catwoman joined the facility and bested him. Filled with jealous rage, he vowed to top Catwoman in her crime sprees. He became Hellhound, a mercenary with a penchant for knives and daggers. When he died, his identity and legacy were bought by Jack Chifford, who joined the Secret Society of Super-Villains.

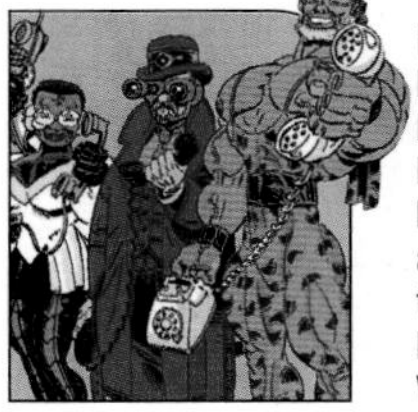

HERO HOTLINE
DEBUT *Action Comics Weekly* #637 (Jan. 1989)
BASE New York City
BACKGROUND Not every problem requires the help of a superpowered hero. Tex Thomson set up a hotline phone number (1-800-555-HERO), known as the Hero Hotline, so that the public could summon lesser-powered heroes to handle routine emergencies. Members included Stretch, Hotshot, Diamondette, Microwavabelle, Private Eyes, Marie the Psychic Turtle, Rainbow Man, Mr. Muscle, Voice Over, and Zeep the Living Sponge.

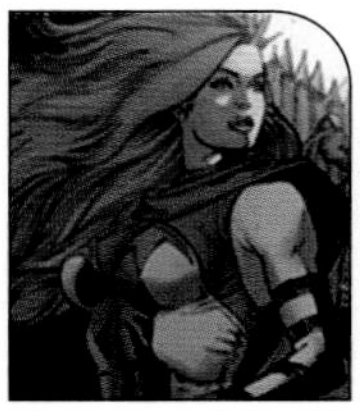

HORSEWOMAN
DEBUT *Demon Knights* #1 (Nov. 2011)
REAL NAME Clytemnestra **BASE** Avalon
ALLIES Demon Knights **ENEMIES** Questing Queen
BACKGROUND Horsewoman was a mysterious figure who occasionally joined the Demon Knights during medieval times and was always seen riding a horse. A skilled archer, she could also communicate telepathically with horses, thought to be her way of tapping into the animal lifeforce the Red. Although a paraplegic, she used a magical saddle and rope to mount her horses.

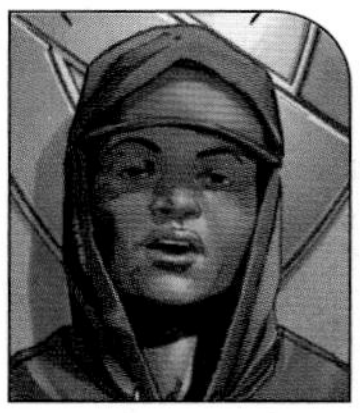

HOT SPOT
DEBUT *Teen Titans* (Vol. 2) #1 (Oct. 1996)
REAL NAME Isaiah Crockett **BASE** Ivy University, Rhode Island
BACKGROUND Aged 16, Crockett was abducted by an alien race, the H'San Nattal. He learned that he was an alien-human hybrid with thermokinetic powers created by the H'San Natall to assist their conquest of Earth. Isaiah escaped with fellow hybrid abductees Toni and Cody Moretti (Argent and Risk) and Audrey Spears (Prysm). They teamed up as a new incarnation of the Teen Titans. Hot Spot was accidently killed by Wally West in an accident in the Sanctuary facility.

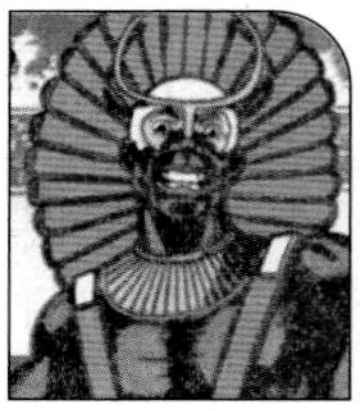

HOUNGAN
DEBUT *The New Teen Titans* #14 (Dec. 1981)
REAL NAME Jean-Louis Droo **BASE** Paris
ALLIES Brotherhood of Evil **ENEMIES** New Teen Titans
BACKGROUND Houngan, a voodoo priest, convinced Droo, a computer scientist, to merge his computer skills with dark voodoo arts. Droo created a computerized voodoo doll and electronic needle stylus that could inflict terrible pain and bring death to his victims. Taking on the name Houngan, he joined the New Brotherhood of Evil and became a loyal follower of the Brain.

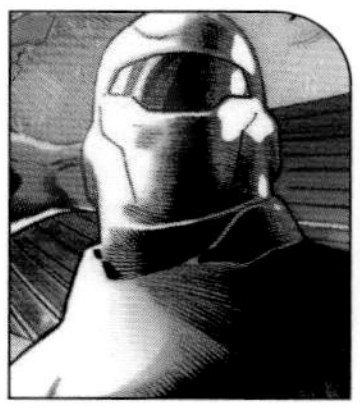

HUMAN BOMB
DEBUT *Freedom Fighters* #1 (Jun. 2019)
REAL NAME David Mathis
BASE Blue Tracer
ALLIES Uncle Sam, Phantom Lady, Freedom Fighters
BACKGROUND The original Human Bomb, Roy Lincoln, was captured and killed by the Plastic Men in the 1960s. His grandson pysicist Dave Mathis later took on the mantle, using his capacity to generate massive explosions to battle against the Nazi party of Earth 10 alongside the Freedom Fighters..

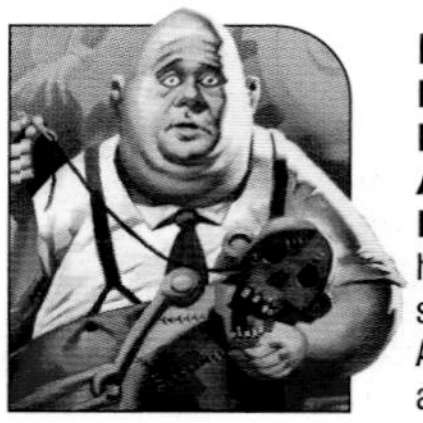

HUMPTY DUMPTY
DEBUT *Arkham Asylum: Living Hell* #2 (Aug. 2003)
REAL NAME Humphry Dumpler **BASE** Gotham City
ALLIES Warren White, Black Mask **ENEMIES** Death Rattle, Two-Face
BACKGROUND Dumpler suffered from an unfortunate name, an egg-shaped head, and a compulsive desire to repair broken items. This led him to derail a subway train and damage a clocktower, killing a dozen people. Committed to Arkham Asylum, he joined Black Mask's new group when the villain destroyed the asylum, and later became a member of the Secret Society of Super-Villains.

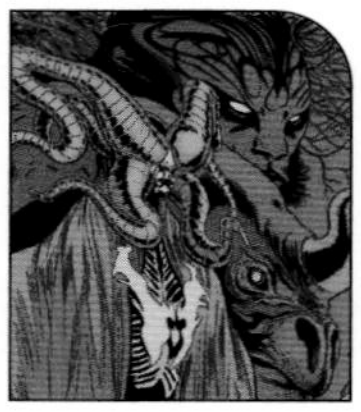

HUNTERS THREE
DEBUT *Animal Man* #1 (Nov. 2011)
ALLIES The Rot **ENEMIES** Animal Man
BACKGROUND The Hunters Three were once men and women who were members of the Red, the lifeforce that connects all animal life in the universe. The Red also gave Animal Man his superpowers. After they died, the Hunters Three became agents of the Rot, the force associated with death and decay. The group then took the form of hideous monsters and became relentless in their deadly pursuit of Animal Man and his family.

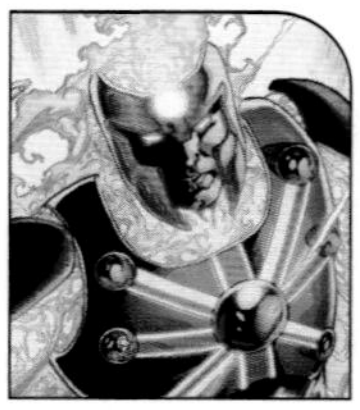

HURRICANE
DEBUT *Fury of Firestorm: The Nuclear Men* #8 (Jun. 2012)
BASE London, England
ALLIES Firehawk **ENEMIES** The Rogues, Pozhar
BACKGROUND Hurricane was created by Zithertech, and became Britain's officially sanctioned Firestorm. He could generate energy blasts and create constructs. Hurricane fought bravely alongside the French Firestorm, Firehawk, against rogue Firestorms; he died battling the energy-transforming monster Pozhar, when his Zithertech creators activated a kill switch in his suit.

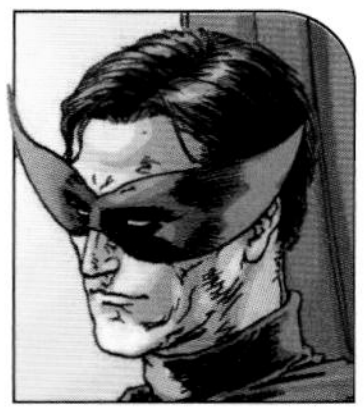

HURT, SIMON
DEBUT *Batman* #673 (Jun. 2008)
REAL NAME Thomas Wayne **BASE** Gotham City **ALLIES** Black Glove
ENEMIES The Joker **BACKGROUND** Hurt had many aliases, including Doctor Death, El Penitente, and Jack the Ripper. He was one of Bruce Wayne's distant ancestors, and a devil- worshipper. After gaining immortality, Hunt cofounded the Black Glove organization that menaced Bruce and his family. After an attempt to kill Batman failed, he was drugged and buried alive by The Joker. He later returned, brainwashing the dollotron called Deathwing as part of a plot against Nightwing.

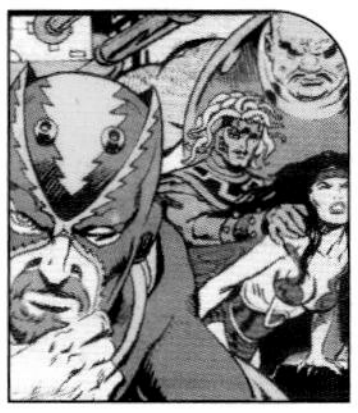

HYBRID
DEBUT *The New Teen Titans* #24 (Oct. 1986)
ALLIES Dayton **ENEMIES** Teen Titans, Blue Beetle
BACKGROUND Following the *Crisis on Infinite Earths*, a deranged Mento formed the Hybrid, a new version of the Doom Patrol. He gathered together injured people from around the world and infused their bodies with the alloy Prometheum to give them superpowers. The result was a team of hapless villains that included Pteradon, Gorgon, Harpi, Behemoth, Sirocco, Prometheus, and Touch-N-Go. The team fell into disarray when Mento was cured of his madness by the Teen Titans' Raven.

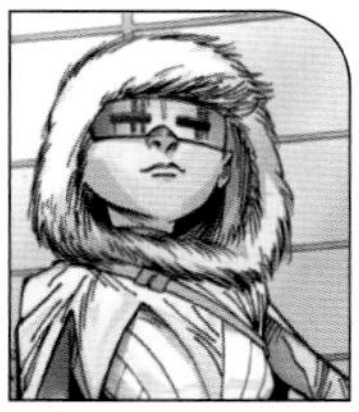

ICE PRINCESS
DEBUT *Adventures of the Super Sons* #1 (Oct. 2018)
REAL NAME unknown **BASE** Metropolis
AFFILIATION The Gang **ENEMIES** Robin, Superboy
BACKGROUND Like all the denizens of the planet Cygnus, the girl who would become Ice Princess grew up watching the exploits of Earth's heroes. But guided by Rex Luthor—who modeled himself on Lex Luthor—Ice Princess was instead inspired by Earth's villains. She was transformed by Rex into a junior version of Captain Cold, complete with her own version of a Cold Gun.

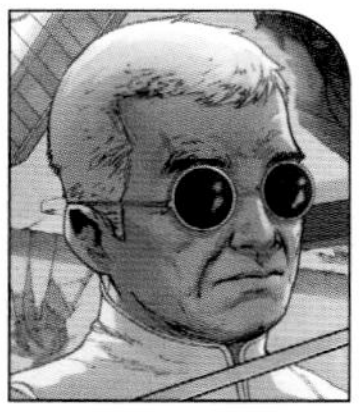

I-CHING
DEBUT *Wonder Woman* #179 (Nov.–Dec. 1968)
ALLIES Batman, Robin, Nightwing
ENEMIES Rā's al Ghūl, All-Yang
BACKGROUND I-Ching is an expression of Yin in human form, while his twin brother All-Yang is an expression of Yang. When All-Yang disappeared, I-Ching was forced to embody both forces. I-Ching helped Wonder Woman hone her fighting skills after she temporarily lost her powers, and teamed with Batman to bring down Rā's al Ghūl. He later helped train the hero Super-Man of China.

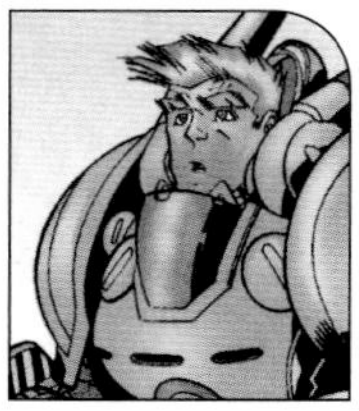

IMAN
DEBUT *Superman Annual* #12 (Aug. 2000)
REAL NAME Diego Irigoyen **BASE** Mexico City
ALLIES El Muerto, Acrata, Superman **ENEMIES** Duran, Darkseid
BACKGROUND Astronaut Irigoyen was on a mission in outer space when his mother was kidnapped and murdered. Upon his return, a grieving Irigoyen designed a superpowered, metallic battle suit that allowed him to fight crime in Mexico as the hero Iman. Diego also teamed up with his hero Superman and fellow local heroes El Muerto and Acrata. He later joined Mexico's Super Hero team Justicia.

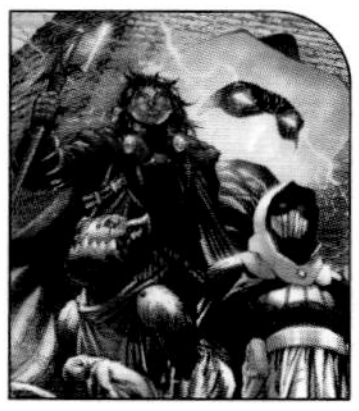

IMMORTAL MEN
DEBUT *Dark Days: The Forge* #1 (Aug. 2017)
BASE Campus **ALLIES** Council of Immortals **ENEMIES** Conquest
BACKGROUND A secretive team formed by Klam Arg—the ancient Immortal Man—to preserve mankind's future in the face existential threats, the Immortal Men operated from the shadows across human history. Latterly, their number reduced by their war against clandestine organization Conquest, the team—Immortal Man, Ghost Fist, Reload, Stray, and Timber—recruited the young superhuman Caden Park to their cause.

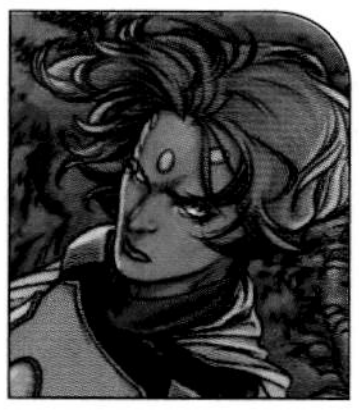

INDIGO
DEBUT *Titans/Young Justice: Graduation Day* #1 (Jul. 2003)
ENEMIES The Outsiders, Teen Titans
BACKGROUND A robotic being from the future, Brainiac 8 (a descendant of the original Brainiac) traveled back in time to pose as the naïve hero Indigo. By "accidentally" unleashing a defective Superman robot, Indigo triggered the death of Donna Troy. Indigo joined the Outsiders, but it transpired that Indigo had killed Donna to ensure the future of the Computer Tyrants of Colu. Indigo menaced Supergirl as a member of the Fatal Five, but was torn in half by Supergirl's father, Zor-El.

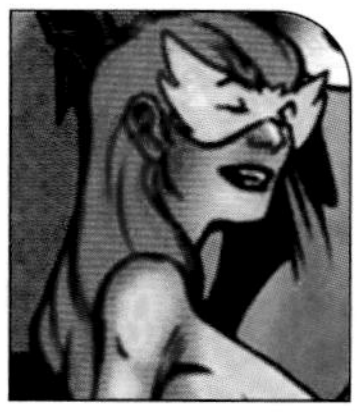

INSECT QUEEN
DEBUT *Legion of Super-Heroes* #82 (Jul. 1996)
REAL NAME Lonna Leing **BASE** Xanthu
ALLIES Legion of Super-Heroes **ENEMIES** Khunds, Robotica
BACKGROUND Leing came from the planet Xanthu in the 31st century. She possessed the ability to transform into an insect and use its powers. As a member of the Uncanny Amazers, a group of super beings created to counter Khunds incursions, she came into conflict with the Legion of Super-Heroes. However, she formed an alliance with them when the cyborg world Robotica invaded Xanthu.

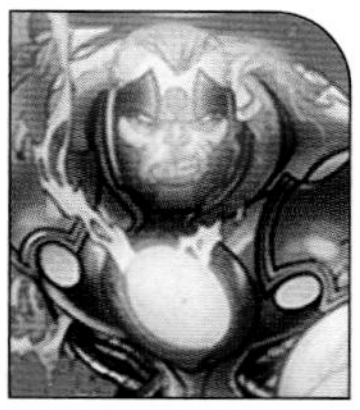

INVICTUS
DEBUT *Green Lantern: New Guardians* #5 (Mar. 2012)
BASE Orrery
ALLIES Angels of Vega **ENEMIES** Larfleeze
BACKGROUND Invictus was the leader of the Angels of Vega, a peaceful race that existed millions of years ago and was destroyed by Larfleeze. He emerged from the destruction with mighty powers, such as the ability to project blasts of energy from his body. He broke the barrier between dimensions and constructed the Orrery, his own recreation of the Vega system.

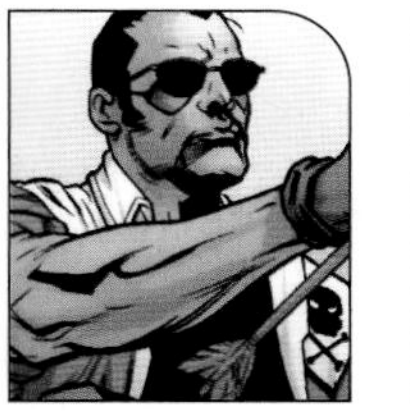

I, SPYDER
DEBUT *Seven Soldiers* #0 (Apr. 2005)
REAL NAME Thomas Ludlow Dalt **BASE** Keystone City
ALLIES Seven Soldiers of Victory **ENEMIES** Sheeda
BACKGROUND Dalt was the son of the first villainous Spider, Tom Ludlow Hallaway. He was a skilled fighter and archer, who killed his brother Lucas, the second Spider, to become the one and only "I, Spyder." After the Seven Unknown Men granted him immortality and heightened his abilities, Dalt joined the Seven Soldiers of Victory to fight against the Sheeda, a malevolent race of faeries and deadly foes of humanity.

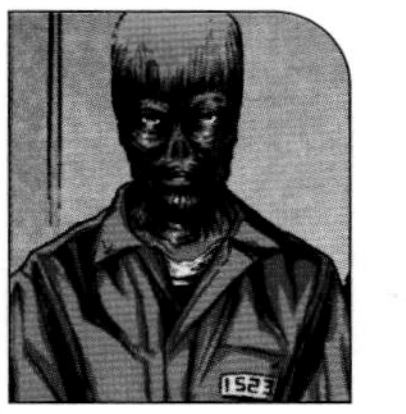

JANE DOE
DEBUT *Arkham Asylum: Living Hell* #1 (Jul. 2003)
BASE Gotham City
ALLIES Black Mask, Mr. Zsasz, Firefly **ENEMIES** Great White Shark, Batman
BACKGROUND Jane Doe was the alias used by a serial killer who studied the personalities of her victims, killed them, and then perfectly assumed their identities, male or female. She had an uncanny ability to mimic body language and speech patterns, and in one incident, even donned the skin of a police officer to break into the G.C.P.D. to murder Gotham City's DA and shoot James Gordon.

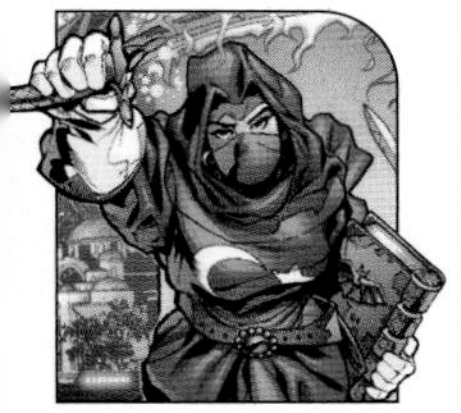

JANISSARY
DEBUT *JLA Annual* #4 (Aug. 2000)
REAL NAME Selma Tolon **BASE** Bursa
ALLIES JLA, Wonder Woman **ENEMIES** Circe
BACKGROUND Tolon was a medical student who returned home to Turkey and discovered the scimitar of Sultan Suleiman the Great, and the spell-casting Eternity Book of Merlin the Magician. These mystical items empowered her with flight and super-strength, and she became the Super Hero Janissary. She used her powers to defend her homeland but also to aid Wonder Woman when Circe attacked New York.

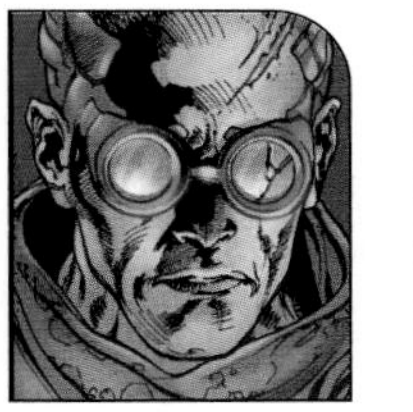

JAX-UR
DEBUT *Adventure Comics* #289 (Oct.1961)
CURRENT VERSION *Action Comics* #13 (Dec. 2012)
ALLIES General Zod
ENEMIES Nightwing, Flamebird
BACKGROUND Jax-Ur was a brilliant, but deranged scientist on Krypton who conducted an infamous experiment that destroyed Wegthor, one of the planet's inhabited moons. He was banished to the Phantom Zone for this crime, and later allied himself with the monstrous world killing creation of Jor El, Rogol Zaar.

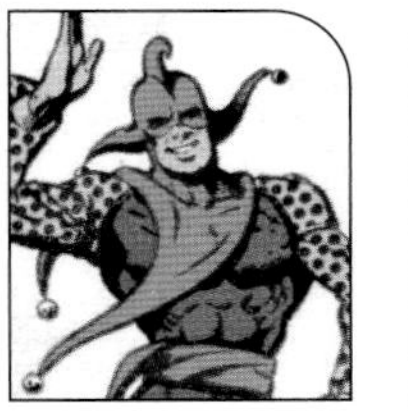

JESTER
DEBUT *Smash Comics* #22 (May 1941)
REAL NAME Charles Lane
ENEMIES Stoneface, Lady Satan
BACKGROUND Chuck Lane was a police officer who discovered that he was descended from King Arthur's court jester, Walter Delane. The Jester decided to honour this heritage as a vigilante, and eventually joined both the All-Star Squadron and the Freedom Fighters. Kane later discovered that a secret society group known as the Arcadians were manipulating him.

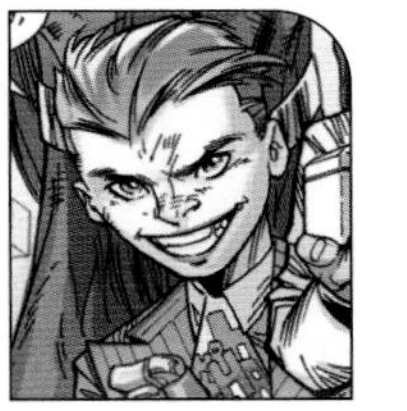

JOKER JR.
DEBUT *Adventures of the Super Sons* #1 (Oct. 2018)
REAL NAME unknown **BASE** Metropolis
ALLIES Robin, Superboy **ENEMIES** The Gang
BACKGROUND A native of the planet Cygnus, Joker Jr. was transformed into a pint-sized version of Gotham's Clown Prince of Crime by Rex Luthor, who was inspired by Earth's villains, especially Lex Luthor. Rex murdered Joker Jr.'s parents and doused him in chemicals to give him the correct pallor. But Joker Jr. rebelled, and teamed up with the Super-Sons to oppose Rex.

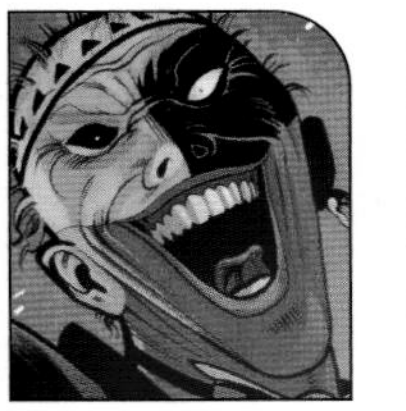

JOKER KING
DEBUT *Batman Beyond* (Vol. 4) #5 (Jul. 2011)
REAL NAME Doug Tan **BASE** Gotham City **ALLIES** Pally Otchee
ENEMIES Batman (Terry McGinnis), Bruce Wayne **BACKGROUND** Growing up in the near future, Doug Tan was a troubled young man obsessed with The Joker and the "Jokerz" youth subculture. Tan wanted to reveal The Joker's real message to the world: Life is meaningless, and the joke is on you. He clashed with an elderly Bruce Wayne and his young protégé—that era's Batman. Following a battle with Batman and Wayne, The Joker King fell from a ledge to his death.

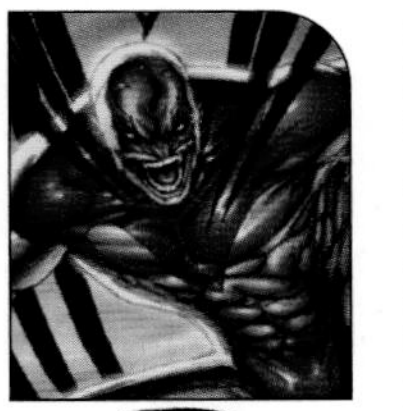

KESTREL
DEBUT *Hawk and Dove* (Vol. 2) #1 (Oct. 1988)
REAL NAME none **BASE** Washington, DC
ALLIES Lords of Chaos **ENEMIES** Hawk and Dove
BACKGROUND The embodiment of murder, Kestrel was created by two Lords of Chaos, M'Shulla and Gorrum. Requiring a human host, Kestrel possessed the body of an unnamed man and was dispatched to prevent the formation of a new Hawk and Dove team. When that failed, the vessel was destroyed, and Kestrel returned in multiple hosts, including Hank "Hawk" Hall's girlfriend, Renata Takamori.

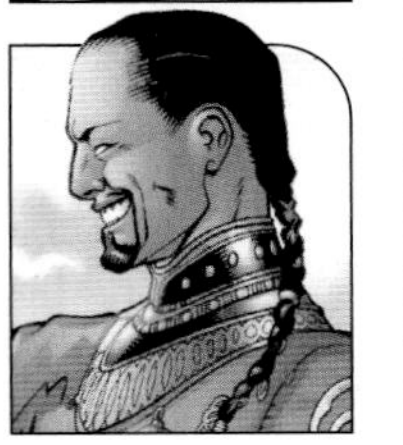

KHAN, RAMA
DEBUT *JLA* #62 (Mar. 2002)
BASE Jarhanpur **ALLIES** Gamemnae **ENEMIES** Justice League of America **BACKGROUND** Rama Khan, a great magician, possessed the powers of immortality and super-strength. In a battle with Wonder Woman, he shattered her hitherto unbreakable Lasso of Truth. This act unraveled reality, as existence became defined by belief rather than truth. The elemental defender of Jarhanpur, Khan fought the Justice League several times, including the mighty clash that took place in 1,004 BCE.

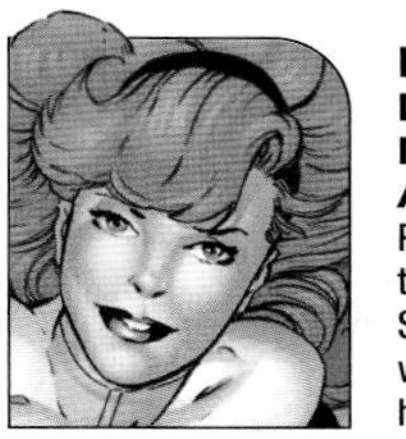

KINETIX
DEBUT *Legion of Super-Heroes* (Vol. 4) #66 (Mar. 1995)
REAL NAME Zoe Saugin **BASE** Metropolis, 31st Century, Earth-247
ALLIES Shrinking Violet, XS, Leviathan **ENEMIES** Emerald Eye, Superboy-Prime **BACKGROUND** Zoe Saugin gained her ability to animate and transform objects after exposure to several mystical artifacts. Joining the Legion of Superheroes, she took the name Kinetix and was instrumental in the teams' battles with Emerald Empress and Mordru. After years of service, she fell in battle alongside her fellow Legionnaires against Superboy-Prime during the *Final Crisis* event.

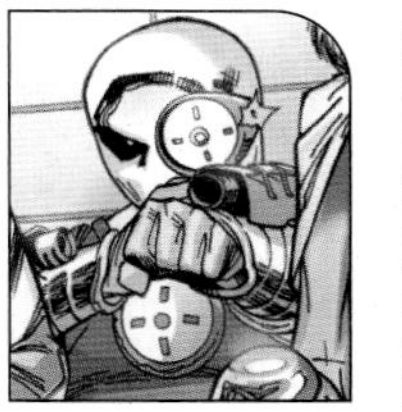

KID DEADSHOT
DEBUT *Adventures of the Super Sons* #1 (Oct. 2018)
REAL NAME Unknown **BASE** Metropolis
AFFILIATION The Gang **ENEMIES** Robin, Superboy
BACKGROUND His appearance modeled on the sharpshooting villain, Kid Deadshot was among those aliens recruited and transformed by Rex Luthor, who was inspired by Lex Luthor and Earth's villains. Like his senior namesake, Kid Deadshot was armed with wrist-mounted guns, and exhibited a similar gruff demeanor, though he professed himself to be an even more accurate shot.

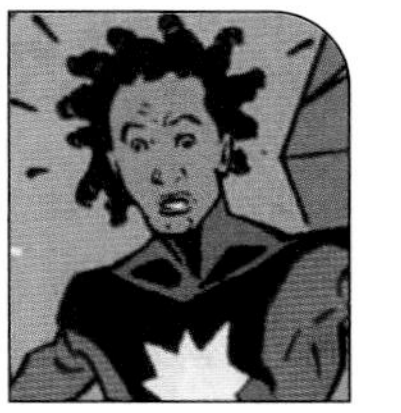

KID QUANTUM
DEBUT *Legion of Super-Heroes* (Vol. 4) #33 (Sept. 1992)
REAL NAME James Cullen **BASE** Legion HQ
AFFILIATION Legion of Super-Heroes **ENEMIES** Tanglefoot
BACKGROUND Hailing from the planet Xanthu, James Cullen was down to the final three contestants in the annual planetary champion competition when he was selected to become Xanthu's Legion representative. Overconfident, and reliant on a stasis field-generating belt, he was killed on his debut mission when the belt shorted out. After his death, his sister, Jazmin, inherited the mantle of Kid Quantum.

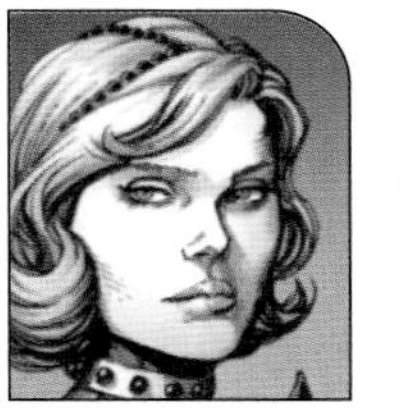

KILLER FROST
DEBUT *Firestorm* (Vol. 2) #21 (Mar. 1984)
REAL NAME Louise Lincoln **BASE** New Jersey
AFFILIATION Injustice League **ENEMIES** Firestorm
BACKGROUND A colleague of Crystal Frost—the original Killer Frost—Dr. Louise Lincoln was traumatized when Frost died battling Firestorm. Carrying on Frost's experiments with sub-zero temperatures, Lincoln was caught in the blast when laboratory apparatus exploded. Now possessed of icy powers, she assumed the mantle of Killer Frost and continued her forebear's vendetta against Firestorm.

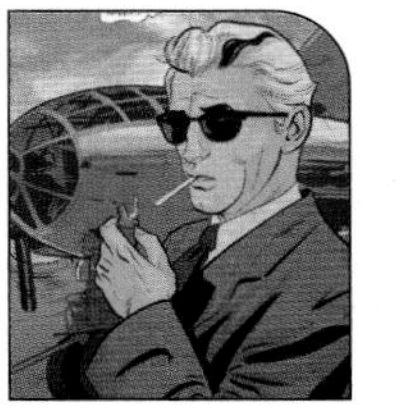

KING FARADAY
DEBUT *Danger Trail* #1 (Jul.–Aug. 1950)
CURRENT VERSION *Suicide Squad* #27 (Dec. 2017)
ALLIES Rick Flagg, Suicide Squad, **ENEMIES** Red Wave Monster
BACKGROUND King Faraday was an early recruit of the original Suicide Squad —a shortlived incarnation of the team that was infected with an alien parasite known as the Red Wave Monster. In the aftermath of this encounter, Faraday, having been kept alive by the power of the Red Wave far past his years, became an advisor to the Squad's chief, Amanda Waller.

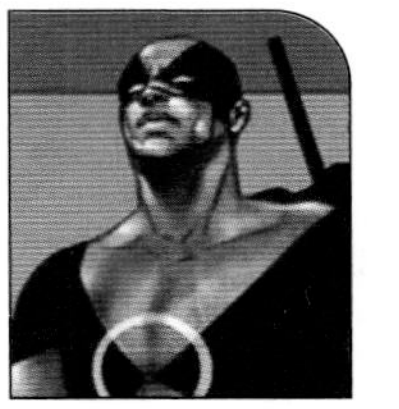

KINGDOM, THE
DEBUT *Batwing* #1 (Nov. 2011)
BASE Democratic Republic of the Congo
ALLIES Batwing **ENEMIES** Massacre
BACKGROUND The Kingdom were comprised of Dawnfire, Deity, Earth Strike, Josiah Kone, Razorwire, Staff, Steelback, and Thunder Fall. They fought to bring freedom to the Democratic Republic of the Congo and then disappeared. Batwing later discovered that Massacre had murdered three of the group's members. The others were scattered across the globe, leaving the team in limbo.

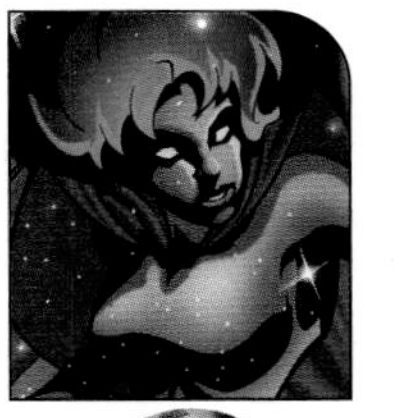

KISMET
DEBUT *Adventures of Superman* #494 (Sep. 1992)
REAL NAME Ahti
ALLIES Eternity, Superman **ENEMIES** Dominus, Krona
BACKGROUND Kismet was a cosmic entity and a Lord of Order. Wielding powers such as astral projection, time travel, and reality manipulation, she was charged with protecting the universe from evil. Ahti's rise to the role of Kismet created an eternal enemy of Dominus, who craved the position for himself. She frequently helped Superman and played a crucial role in ending the Imperiex War.

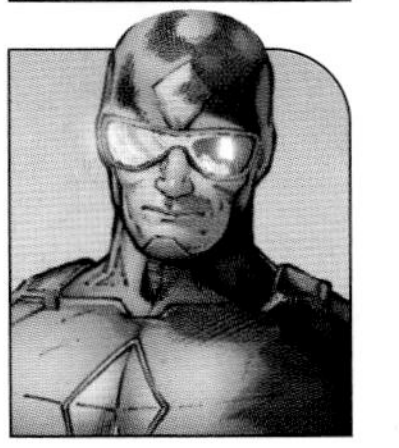

KITE-MAN
DEBUT *Batman* #133 (Aug. 1960)
REAL NAME Charles Brown **BASE** Gotham City
ALLIES Tweedledum, Tweedledee **ENEMIES** Batman
BACKGROUND After studying wind in school, Charles Brown fell into a life of crime, designing the aerodynamics of The Joker's Jokermobile, but otherwise regarded as a loser—even by his wife. He became Kite-Man when the Riddler murdered his son during the War of Jokes and Riddles, adopting the identity in honor of his boy, with whom he used to fly kites.

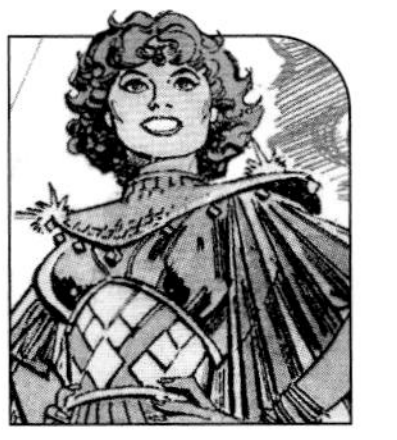

KOLE
DEBUT *Crisis on Infinite Earths* #3 (Jun. 1985)
REAL NAME Kole Weathers **BASE** New York City
ALLIES Team Titans **ENEMIES** Thia
BACKGROUND As a teenager, Kole became a victim of her father's flawed scientific experiments. A nuclear explosion triggered her meta-gene, enabling her to project crystal forms. She joined the Teen Titans and fought bravely until she seemingly lost her life during the *Crisis on Infinite Earths*. She returned later after an accidental massacre at the rehabilitation center known as the Sanctuary.

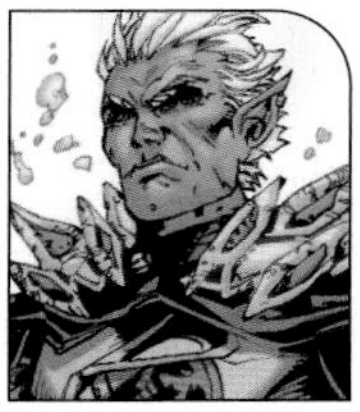

KORDAX
DEBUT *Atlantis Chronicles* #4 (Jun. 1990)
BASE Atlantis
ALLIES Koryak **ENEMIES** Poseidonians, Aquaman
BACKGROUND Born of Atlantean royalty, Kordax was sent away because of his ugly appearance. Kept alive by dark magic, Kordax returned thousands of years later and battled Aquaman, eventually assuming control of the terrorist group Scorpio. Eventually, Aquaman defeated Kordax, trapping his ancestor in a prison of his own mind.

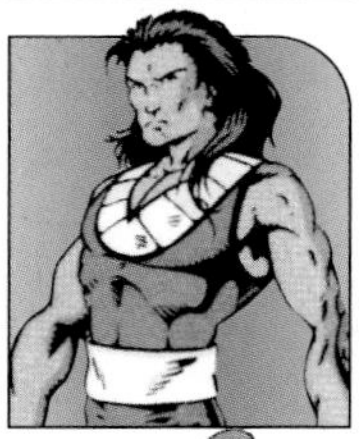

KORYAK
DEBUT *Aquaman* #5 (Jan. 1995)
BASE Atlantis
ALLIES Aquagirl **ENEMIES** Anton Geist, Spectre
BACKGROUND Koryak was the son of Aquaman and Kako. He grew up unaware of his father's identity or the truth of his royal heritage. Later, Koryak moved to Atlantis and rebelled against his father's wishes. He journeyed to the tunnels below the city of Poseidonis and accidentally freed the evil Kordax, which led to a devastating war. Koryak was later killed when The Spectre attacked Atlantis.

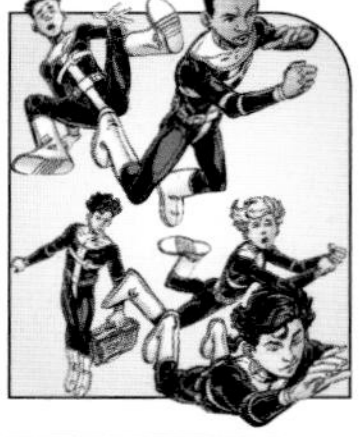

LAB RATS
DEBUT *Lab Rats* #1 (Apr. 2002)
BASE The Campus **ALLIES** Abigail Gooss
ENEMIES Robert Quinlan
BACKGROUND The Lab Rats was a group of teenagers who became test subjects for a mysterious experiment in virtual-reality combat. Alex, Dana, Gia, Isaac, Trilby, Wu, and Poe went to a secret training ground, the Campus, where they were subjected to virtual dangers. Gia was the first to die. Her six remaining teammates escaped, but later lost their lives in the real world.

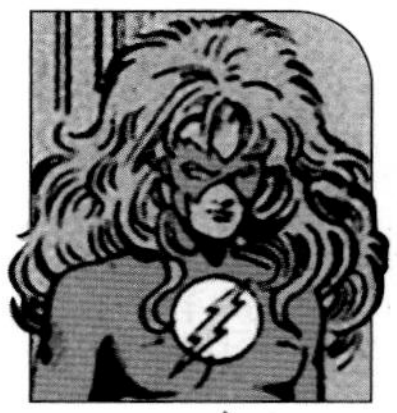

LADY FLASH
DEBUT *The Flash* #7 (Dec. 1987)
REAL NAME Ivana Christina Borodin Molotova **ALLIES** Blue Trinity
ENEMIES The Flash **BACKGROUND** Two boys and a young girl named Christina were entrusted to a Soviet scientist, who created a serum, Velocity 9, that could grant super-speed. Under the team name Blue Trinity, the three of them often battled The Flash. After allying herself with Vandal Savage, Christina became Lady Flash. Since this she has bounced back and forth between being a hero or villain. Most recently she joined the Russian team, The People's Heroes.

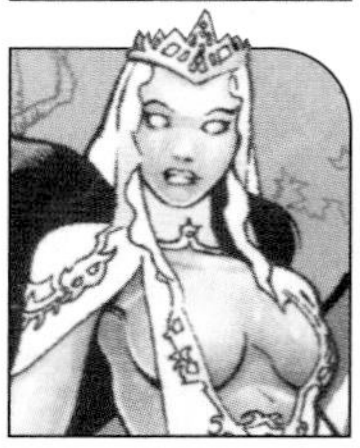

LADY OF THE LAKE
DEBUT *Aquaman* #1 (Feb. 2003)
REAL NAME Vivienne
BASE The Secret Sea
BACKGROUND The Lady of the Lake was a water spirit of seemingly limitless powers who aided both Aquaman and Britain's King Arthur. She was immortal and oversaw the Secret Sea, an enchanted realm that was also known as the Waters of Truth. When Aquaman lost his hand, she replaced it with a hand composed of magical water that received its powers from the Lady.

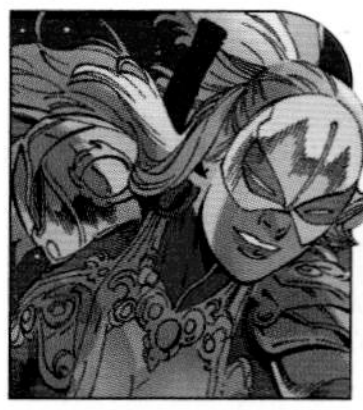

LADY VIC
DEBUT *Nightwing* #4 (Jan. 1997)
REAL NAME Lady Elaine Marsh-Morton **BASE** England
ALLIES Double Dare, Bane **ENEMIES** Deadshot, Nightwing
BACKGROUND Lady Vic was a true-blue aristocrat, a skilled martial artist, a superb athlete, and a ruthless killer-for-hire, fond of wielding her family's heirloom weapons. While under contract with Blockbuster, Lady Vic clashed repeatedly with Nightwing. She was later discovered dead by the Teen Titans, having been killed by the Super-Villain Heretic.

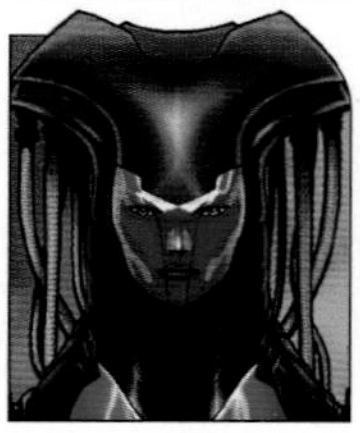

LADY WEEDS
DEBUT *Swamp Thing Annual* #2 (Dec. 2013)
BASE Servus, Arctic Circle
ENEMIES Swamp Thing
BACKGROUND "Born" in the 19th century, Lady Weeds was a powerful avatar of the Green, the elemental force that connects all forms of plant life on Earth. Her cruel nature led her to break away from the Green and betray Swamp Thing. As a result, she was paralyzed and lost her powers. She later became an avatar of the Machine Kingdom with a new body composed entirely of metal.

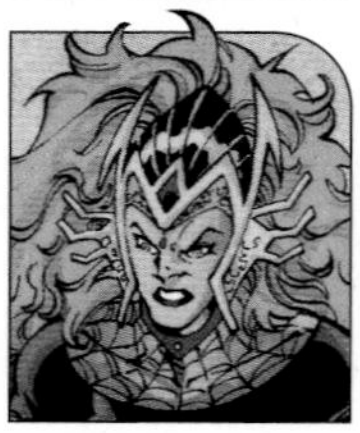

LADY ZAND
DEBUT *Young Justice* #50 (Dec. 2002)
BASE Zandia
ENEMIES Young Justice, Solstice, Wonder Girl
BACKGROUND Lady Zand possessed many elemental powers, including the ability to command the soil of her homeland and transform into a towering giant composed of rock and earth. She was the cruel and quick-tempered ruler of Zandia, a Baltic island and secret haven for fugitive Super-Villains. It was also the headquarters for the worldwide Church of Blood.

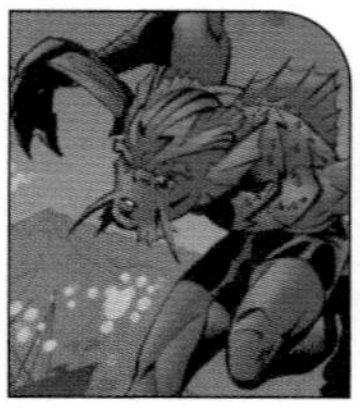

LAGOON BOY
DEBUT *Aquaman* (Vol. 5) #50 (Dec. 1998)
REAL NAME unknown **BASE** Atlantis
AFFILIATION Titans East **ENEMIES** Kobra, Black Manta
BACKGROUND When Aquaman decreed that his underwater kingdom would represent not just Atlanteans, but every undersea creature, Lagoon Boy was among those who became citizens. He and his friends, the humanoid whale Blubber and mermaid Sheeva, became fascinated by the surface world, and Lagoon Boy joined Young Justice and Titans East. He was among those slain at the Sanctuary.

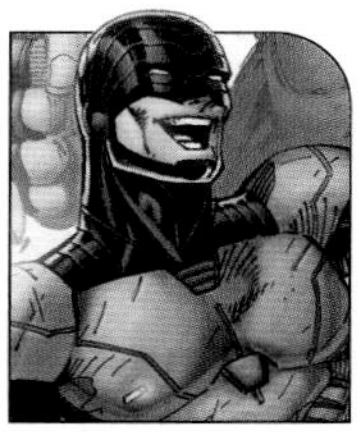

LANCE, KURT
DEBUT *Teen Titans* #8 (Jun. 2012)
BASE Gotham City
ALLIES Amanda Waller **ENEMIES** Black Canary
BACKGROUND Little is known about the early years of Lance before he became a member of a group of heroes known as Team 7. Equally mysterious were the events surrounding his alleged death after he married Dinah Drake, the Black Canary. Drake believed that she had killed him with her Canary Cry, but Lance was in fact alive and working with Amanda Waller to track down the Teen Titans.

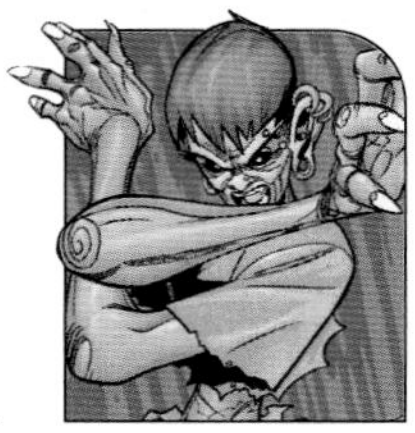

LEATHER
DEBUT *Nightwing* #62 (Dec. 2001)
REAL NAME Mary Kay Tanner **BASE** Peckinpah, Texas
ALLIES The Joker **ENEMIES** Nightwing
BACKGROUND Mary was born with metahuman powers as a result of her mother's use of illegal, experimental narcotics, which gave her leathery skin and razor-sharp claws. In her teens, she joined a gang that smuggled illegal immigrants between Mexico and the US. Her psychotic temper and deadly barbed whips made her a formidable opponent. She was imprisoned, but later freed by The Joker.

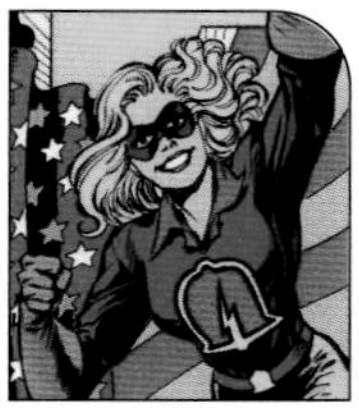

LIBERTY BELLE
DEBUT *Boy Commandos* #1 (Dec. 1942)
REAL NAME Elizabeth "Libby" Lawrence-Chambers **BASE** New York City
ALLIES All-Star Squadron **ENEMIES** Baron Blitzkrieg, Captain Nazi
BACKGROUND A descendant of the Revolutionary War heroine Miss Liberty, Libby gained superpowers through a mystic link to the Liberty Bell and became Liberty Belle, a founder member of the All-Star Squadron. After being irradiated by Baron Blitzkrieg, Libby gained the ability to manipulate sound. Decades after the war, Libby donned her costume once more to fight with the JSA during *Infinite Crisis*.

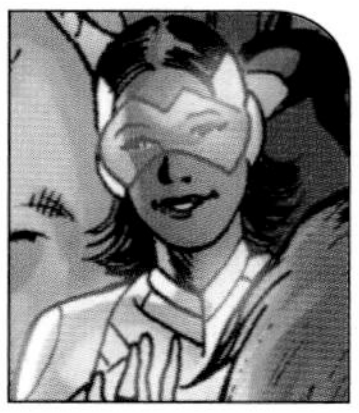

LIGHT LASS
DEBUT *Adventure Comics* #308 (May 1963)
REAL NAME Ayla Ranzz **BASE** Legion HQ
AFFILIATION Legion of Super-Heroes **ENEMIES** Darkseid, Lighting Lord
BACKGROUND Along with her twin Garth and older brother Mekt, Ayla Ranzz of Winath gained electricity powers from the Lightning Monsters of Korbal. She joined the Legion of Super-Heroes disguised as her brother, before being admitted as Lightning Lass. Subsequently, her abilities were altered by Legionnaire Dream Girl to gravity powers, prompting a change of identity to Light Lass.

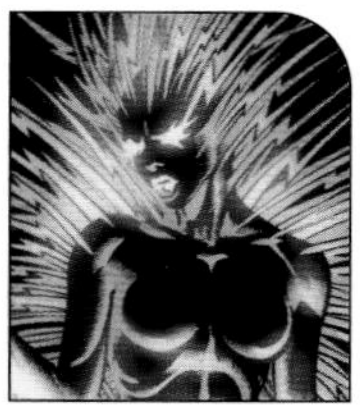

LIGHTNING
DEBUT *Justice Society of America* (Vol. 3) #12 (Mar. 2008)
REAL NAME Jennifer Pierce **BASE** New York City
AFFILIATION Justice Society of America **ENEMIES** Black Lanterns, Scythe **BACKGROUND** The youngest daughter of Jefferson Pierce, alias Black Lightning, Jennifer Pierce inherited the ability to generate an electric field. She joined the Justice Society at age 16 on the recommendation of her father, who figured the team would help her control her powers. Jennifer became a key member of the team, forming close friendships with fellow teens Stargirl and Cyclone.

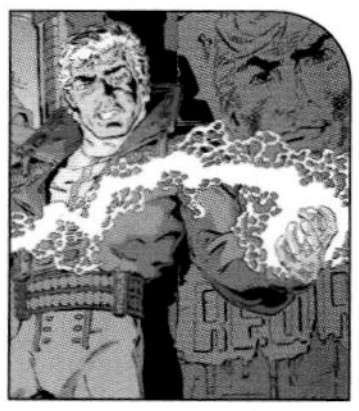

LIGHTNING LORD
DEBUT *Superman* #147 (Aug. 1961)
REAL NAME Mekt Ranzz **BASE** Winath
ALLIES Legion of Super-Villains
ENEMIES Legion of Super-Heroes
BACKGROUND When Mekt Ranzz and his siblings were attacked by lightning beasts on Korbal, they gained the power to absorb electricity and project powerful energy bolts. Mekt's siblings joined the Legion of Super-Heroes, but he decided to use his powers for evil under the name Lightning Lord.

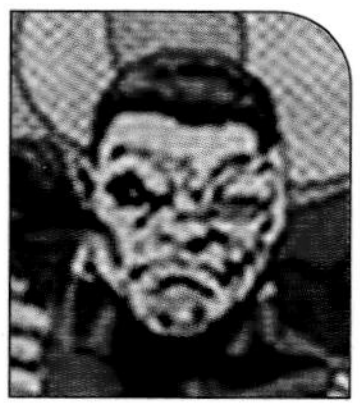

LINEAR MAN
DEBUT *Adventures of Superman* (Vol. 1) #476 (Mar. 1991)
REAL NAME Travis O'Connell **BASE** Vanishing Point
ALLIES Superman **ENEMIES** Booster Gold **BACKGROUND** Travis O'Connell is a member of time-travel regulation team the Linear Men. He went rogue to hunt down Booster Gold for unauthorized use of time-travel technology and transport him back to the 25th century. When O'Connell tried to apprehend Booster, Superman intervened, and was sucked into a time vortex. In a valiant attempt to correct his error, O'Connell sacrificed himself, saving the timeline in the process.

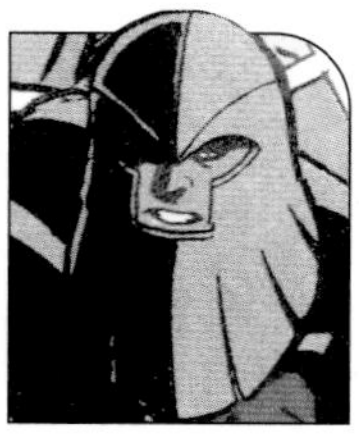

LIONHEART
DEBUT *Justice League International Annual* #4 (Summer 1993)
REAL NAME Richard Plante **BASE** London, England
ALLIES Justice League International **ENEMIES** Alien Parasites
BACKGROUND Plante, a direct descendant of King Richard I, was a former dockworker who donned a hi-tech battle suit that gave him enhanced strength and the ability to fly. As the hero Lionheart, he wielded an energy-sword and fought crime, occasionally working with the Justice League International. His first mission was to prevent an invasion of alien parasites from wreaking hell on his home turf.

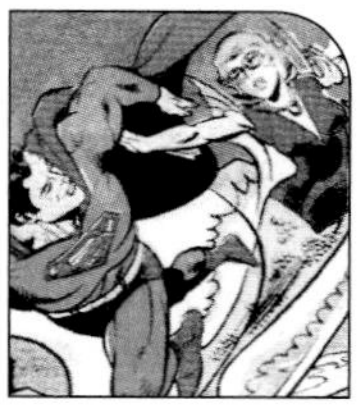

LITTLE MERMAID
DEBUT *Super Friends* #9 (Dec. 1977)
REAL NAME Ulla Paske **BASE** Denmark
ALLIES Global Guardians, JLE **ENEMIES** Jack O'Lantern, Queen Bee, Bialya
BACKGROUND An Atlantean hybrid, Ulla Paske possessed mutant powers that allowed her to fly, breathe underwater, and transform her legs into fins. As the Little Mermaid, she became a founding member of the Global Guardians and also worked alongside the Justice League. In the battle for Bialya, Paske was apparently killed by the villain Jack O'Lantern, but she was later seen in action with the Guardians.

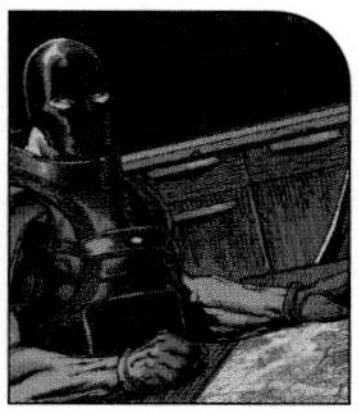

LOCK-UP
DEBUT *Robin* (Vol. 4) #24 (Jan. 1996)
REAL NAME Lyle Bolton **ENEMIES** Batman, Robin, Nightwing
AFFILIATIONS Secret Society of Super-Villains, Cluemaster's gang
BACKGROUND Lyle Bolton was expelled from the Police Academy and kicked out of various security jobs for brutality. Adopting the codename "Lock-Up," Bolton began capturing felons as a vigilante and taking out any police who got in his way. When his facility was discovered, Lock-Up tried to drown his prisoners, but was stopped by Batman, Robin, and Nightwing.

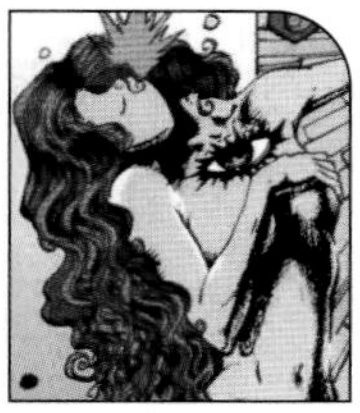

LODESTONE
DEBUT *Doom Patrol* #3 (Dec. 1987)
REAL NAME Rhea Jones **BASE** Kansas City
ALLIES Arani Desai **ENEMIES** Geomancers
BACKGROUND Rhea Jones was exposed to an overdose of electromagnetic radiation as a teenager. Due to this, she acquired super-strength, the power of flight, and the ability to attract or repel metallic objects. She was recruited to become a member of the Doom Patrol. She underwent a metamorphosis that heightened her powers and altered her looks, before teaming up with a Superboy clone.

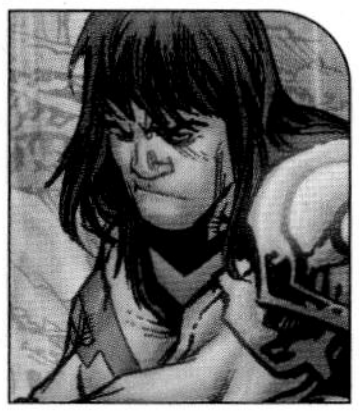

LONAR
DEBUT *Forever People* #5 (Oct.–Nov. 1971)
BASE New Genesis **ALLIES** Blue Beetle
ENEMIES Darkseid
BACKGROUND Lonar was one of the New Gods, renowned for his bravery and fighting skills as he rode into battle astride his flying steed Thunderer. He defended New Genesis from invasions by Darkseid, and never hesitated to protect other lands from the Dark Lord. He formed an unlikely alliance with Blue Beetle on the planet Tolerance during a bounty-hunting game show known as *The Hunted.*

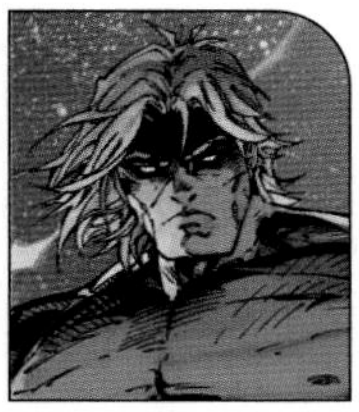

LOOSE CANNON
DEBUT *Action Comics Annual* #5 (1993)
REAL NAME Eddie Walker **BASE** Metropolis
ALLIES Maggie Sawyer, Eradicator
ENEMIES Lissik, Glonth, Pritor
BACKGROUND Eddie was a teenager with mobility issues that forced him to rely on crutches to walk. When his closest friend was attacked by mutated deer, he transformed into a massive, blue-skinned behemoth. Over time, he discovered that this transformation was due to an infection with an alien parasite.

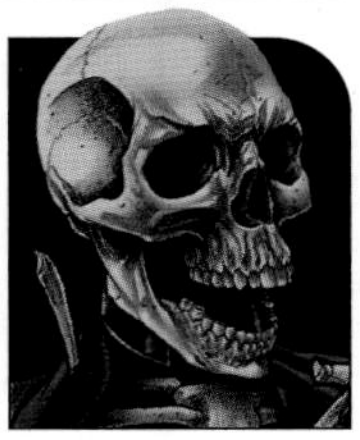

LORD DEATH MAN
DEBUT *Batman* #180 (May 1966)
BASE Japan **ENEMIES** Batman, The Outsiders, Mr. Unknown
BACKGROUND Lord Death Man was a mysterious crime boss who could return from the dead. In one gruesome incident, he came back to life mid-autopsy and slaughtered several people in a hospital. Lord Death Man also had superhuman strength and stamina, which he used to battle Batman, The Outsiders, and Talon. Rās al Ghūl even sought to siphon the regenerative fluids from Lord Death Man's body.

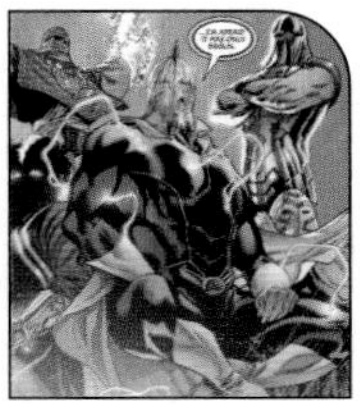

LORDS OF ORDER
DEBUT *1st Issue Special* #9 (Dec. 1975)
BASE mobile **ALLIES** Ken Nelson
ENEMIES Lords of Chaos
BACKGROUND From the dawn of time, the Lords of Order defended reality against the Lords of Chaos. Mystical beings composed of energy, the Lords often manifested in physical form, including in the shape of Amethyst, Princess of Gemworld, and Arion, the ancient Atlantean demigod. Chief among the Lords was Nabu, whose spirit resided in the Helmet of Fate, source of Doctor Fate's power.

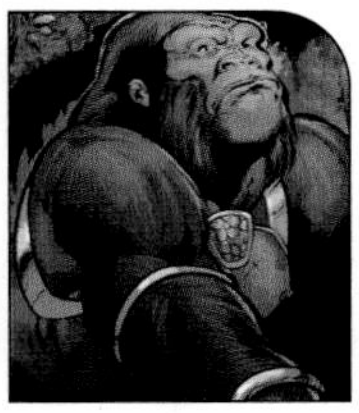

LORD SOLOVAR
DEBUT *The Flash* #106 (Apr.–May 1959)
BASE Gorilla City
ALLIES The Flash
ENEMIES Gorilla Grodd
BACKGROUND Solovar was the king of the superpowered apes in Gorilla City. One of his duties was to absorb the calm, positive thoughts of his subjects. Solovar was a gifted telepath and a benevolent ruler. When Gorilla Grodd threatened to usurp his throne, Solovar sought the help of the second Flash, Barry Allen.

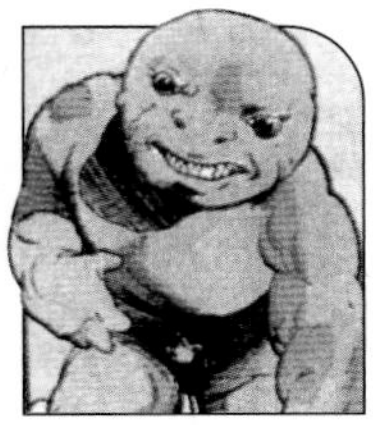

LUMP
DEBUT *Mister Miracle* #7 (Mar.–Apr. 1972)
BASE Apokolips **ALLIES** Granny Goodness **ENEMIES** Mister Miracle, Batman
BACKGROUND The Lump was a monster on Apokolips that could mold his body into any form. He used this ability to lure enemies into the Arena of the Gods, a realm that existed inside the Lump's own mind. The New God Mister Miracle fought a battle within the creature's mind-world and triumphed by driving the Lump insane. The Lump seemingly lost his life battling Batman, but later reappeared on Apokolips.

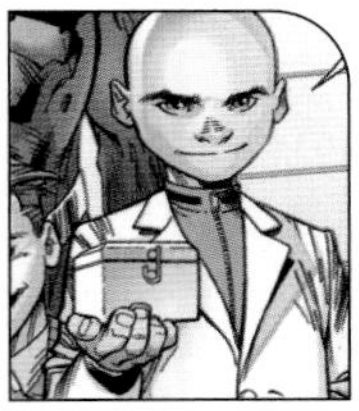

LUTHOR, REX
DEBUT *Adventures of the Super Sons* #1 (Oct. 2018)
REAL NAME Unknown **BASE** Metropolis
AFFILIATION The Gang **ENEMIES** Robin, Superboy
BACKGROUND Hailing from the planet Cygnus, Rex Luthor was inspired by the evil machinations of Earth's Lex Luthor to form his own Gang, recruiting and transforming fellow aliens into juvenile versions of Earth's villains. His ultimate aim was to obtain a powerful Hypercube. He led his Gang to Earth in search of it, but met defeat at the hands of the Super-Sons.

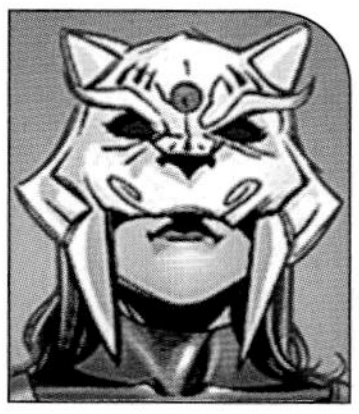

LYNX
DEBUT *Robin* #1 (Jan. 1991) **REAL NAME** Ling **BASE** Gotham City
ALLIES Ghost Dragons, King Snake, the Penguin **ENEMIES** Robin, Batgirl
BACKGROUND Ling started out as a thief on the streets of China, working for King Snake and his Ghost Dragons gang. She took the name Lynx and became a hired assassin for the Penguin in Gotham City, eventually returning to Hong Kong, deposing King Snake, and taking over the Ghost Dragons. Ling died trying to extend her operations into Gotham City. A second individual calling herself Lynx repeatedly clashed with Red Robin while claiming to be an undercover cop.

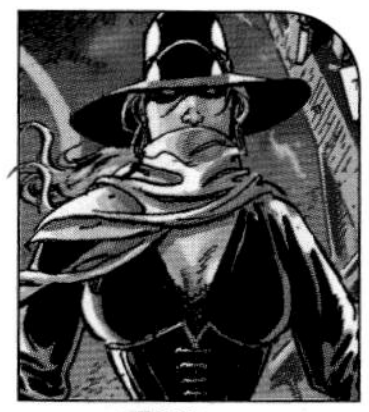

MADAME .44
DEBUT *All Star Western* #117 (Feb.–Mar. 1961)
REAL NAME Jeanne Walker
BASE Mesa City
BACKGROUND Walker's father was killed when thieves bombed his gold mine. She was trapped inside and, as she dug her way out, she wandered into a mysterious land with two moons. Walker defeated Kerberos, the demonic ruler of this strange world and, newly emboldened, emerged from the mine as the pistol-toting hero Madame .44, determined to seek justice for her father's murder.

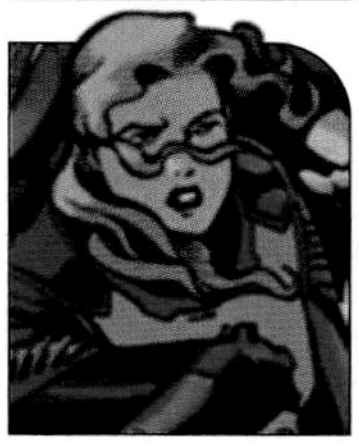

MADEMOISELLE MARIE
DEBUT *Star-Spangled War Stories* #84 (Aug. 1959)
REAL NAME Josephine Tautin
BASE The Castle, Switzerland
BACKGROUND Many brave French women have fought for justice using the name Mademoiselle Marie. One of the most famous operated behind enemy lines in occupied France during World War II, working as a saboteur, spy, and soldier for the French underground. Fearless and deadly, she frequently fought alongside Sgt. Rock. Josephine Tautin was the latest hero to take the name Mademoiselle Marie.

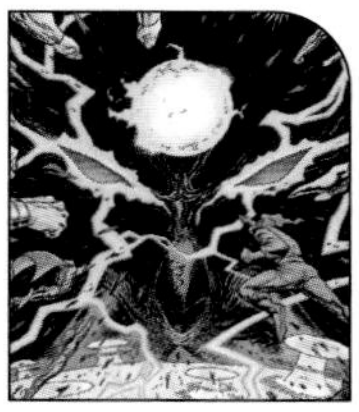

MAGEDDON
DEBUT *JLA #37* (Jan. 2000)
ENEMIES Orion, Justice League
BACKGROUND Mageddon was created by the Old Gods as a sentient war machine. A living doomsday device, it could project lethal energy blasts and take control of anyone's mind, changing any species into warlike savages. It traveled the universe and eventually targeted Earth, where it battled Orion and the Justice League. After the Mexican-American Super Hero Aztek sacrificed himself to weaken Mageddon, Superman was able to absorb its energy and disable the machine.

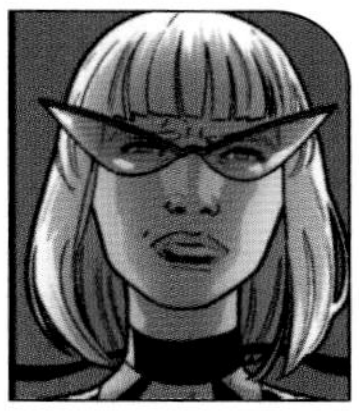

MAGPIE
DEBUT *Man of Steel* #3 (Nov. 1986)
REAL NAME Margaret Pye **BASE** Gotham City
AFFILIATION Suicide Squad **ENEMIES** Batman, Superman
BACKGROUND Acquiring the nickname Magpie as a kid due to her love of pretty things, as an adult Margaret Pye became curator of the Gotham Museum of Antiquities, where the lure of so many priceless artifacts became too much to bear. She began stealing valuables, boobytrapping the crime scenes, resulting in multiple deaths. She was later killed on a Suicide Squad mission.

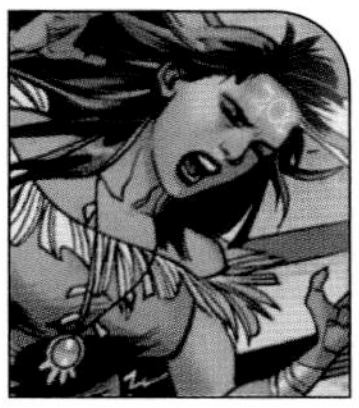

MANITOU DAWN
DEBUT *JLA* #75 (Jan. 2003)
REAL NAME Dawn **BASE** The Factory
AFFILIATION Justice League Elite **ENEMIES** Menagerie
BACKGROUND Originating in the Obsidian Age of Atlantis, around 1,000 BCE, Manitou Dawn and her husband, Manitou Raven, were recruited by the League of Ancients. After battling a time-traveling JLA, the pair accompanied the League to the future, joining Justice League Elite, where Dawn became involved with Green Arrow. When her husband was killed, Dawn assumed her husband's shamanic abilities.

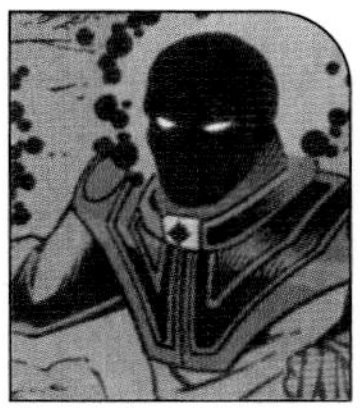

MANO
DEBUT *Adventure Comics* #352 (Jan. 1967)
REAL NAME Unknown **BASE** Angtu
AFFILIATION Fatal Five **ENEMIES** Legion of Super-Heroes
BACKGROUND Raised on the polluted planet of Angtu, Mano was a mutant born with the ability to disintegrate anything he touched with the glowing disc on his right hand. Shunned by his fellow citizens, and alone and embittered, he destroyed his own planet with one touch, wiping out the rest of his race. He operated as a hired assassin before joining the Fatal Five.

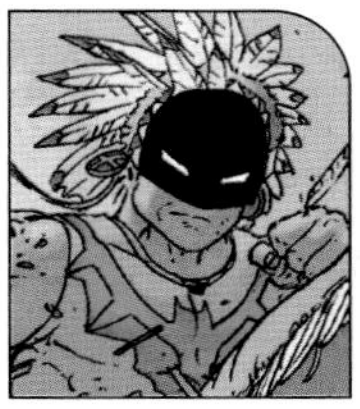

MAN-OF-BATS
DEBUT *Batman* #86 (Sep. 1954)
REAL NAME William "Bill" Great Eagle **BASE** South Dakota
ALLIES Raven Red, Batman Inc. **ENEMIES** Leviathan, Dr. Hurt
BACKGROUND Native American Eagle was so inspired by Batman that he gave up his career as a doctor and became Man-of-Bats, a vigilante crime fighter. His son became Red Raven and they joined the Club of Heroes and later Batman Inc. together. They both became valuable allies to Batman and helped to defeat the Black Glove and Leviathan organizations.

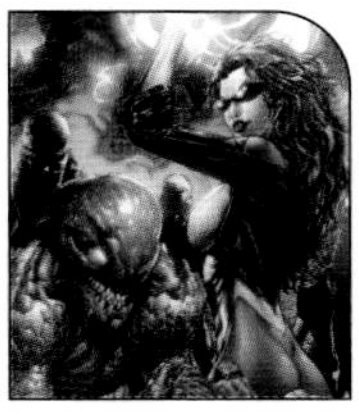

MASTERS OF DISASTER
DEBUT *Batman and the Outsiders* #9 (Apr. 1984)
BASE Gotham City **ALLIES** Baron Bedlam **ENEMIES** The Outsiders
BACKGROUND A group of mercenaries whose powers were all related to the elements, the Masters of Disaster originally comprised Coldsnap, Heatstroke, Shakedown, Windfall, and their leader, New-Wave. The group was hired to torture and kill Black Lightning, bringing them into conflict with Batman and The Outsiders. The two teams tangled multiple times; eventually, Windfall (New-Wave's sister) defected to The Outsiders.

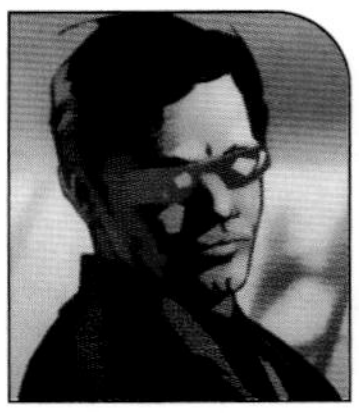

MATTER-EATER LAD
DEBUT *Adventure Comics* #303 (Dec. 1962)
REAL NAME Tenzil Kem **BASE** Legion HQ
AFFILIATION Legion of Super-Heroes **ENEMIES** Omega
BACKGROUND Like all natives of the planet Bismoll—where microbes made all food poisonous—Tenzil Kem was born with the ability to eat anything without being harmed. Joining the Legion of Super-Heroes, he used his super-strong jaws, teeth, and constitution to save the universe when he ingested the Miracle Machine. The episode drove him insane, but he later recovered and became a senator.

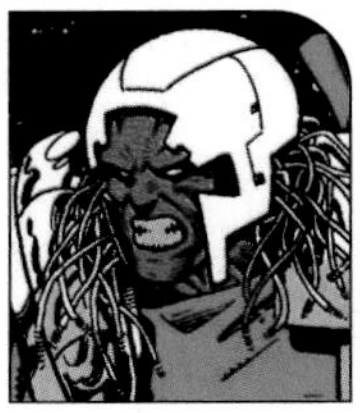

MASSACRE
DEBUT *Adventures of Superman* #509 (Feb. 1994)
REAL NAME Unknown
ALLIES Maxima **ENEMIES** Superman, Green Lantern
BACKGROUND A murderous alien that travels the galaxy, taking lives for sport. Massacre has clashed with Superman on multiple occasions, going so far as to attack the Man of Steel on Earth. Though Massacre was found guilty of genocide by an alien Tribunal, the creature escaped death and resurfaced in service of Maxima. Eventually he was sent to planet sized prison and has not been seen since.

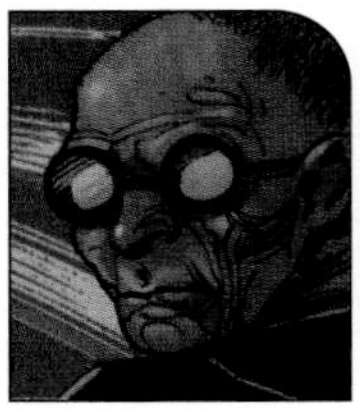

MATSUDA, SHIHAN
DEBUT *Detective Comics* #0 (Nov. 2012)
BASE The Himalayas
ALLIES Bruce Wayne **ENEMIES** Mio
BACKGROUND After the death of his parents, Bruce Wayne traveled to a remote monastery in the Himalayas, where he trained with the legendary monk warrior Shihan Matsuda. A master of mind-control, Matsuda told Wayne that he was destined to soar like a god, and he trained the young man in combat and the use of weapons. Matsuda was murdered by his daughter, Mio.

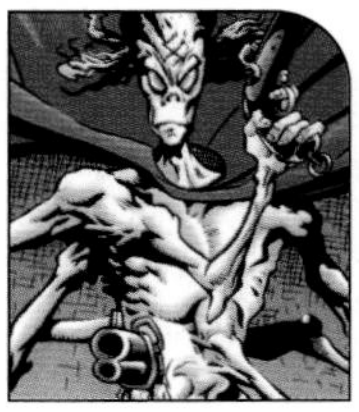

MAWZIR
DEBUT *Hitman* #1 (Apr. 1996)
BASE Hell **ALLIES** Arkannone **ENEMIES** Tommy Monaghan, Catwoman
BACKGROUND In the last days of World War II, the evil souls of five Nazi soldiers were transformed into a ten-armed demon called Mawzir by Arkannone, the Lords of the Gun. Mawzir frequently clashed with Catwoman and Tommy Monaghan. After Monaghan destroyed the Mawzir, the Arkannone brought the monstrous creature back to life. Mawzir later died again when Midnighter headbutted a bullet through the demon's brain.

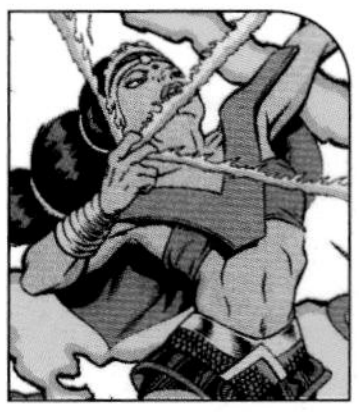

MAYA
DEBUT *Justice League Europe* #47 (Feb. 1993)
REAL NAME Chandi Gupta **BASE** India
ALLIES Justice League Europe **ENEMIES** Overmaster, Sonar
BACKGROUND As a teenager, Gupta acquired an array of elemental powers from the deity Maya. She was able to control and emit fire and water, and used her powers to fight crime, firing mystic arrows composed of those two elements. She allied with the Justice League to stop the villain Sonar from conquering Europe, and later, with the JLE's help, thwarted the alien Overmaster's plan to annihilate Earth.

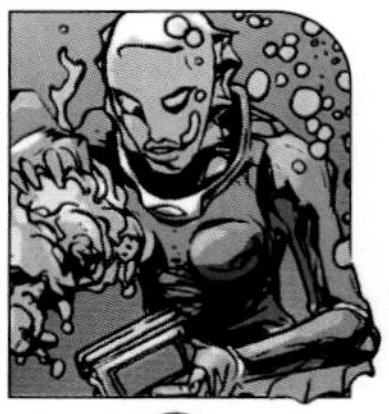

MAZURSKY, NINA
DEBUT *Flashpoint: Frankenstein and the Creatures of the Unknown* #1 (Aug. 2011)
ALLIES Creature Commandos **ENEMIES** Humanids
BACKGROUND Mazursky was a scientist who worked for the counter-terrorism agency S.H.A.D.E., creating stronger strains of human genetics. Her first subjects were the dangerous monsters who became known as the Creature Commandos. Mazursky developed a second, more successful generation of Creature Commandos, but thanks to her experiments, she was transformed into a human/amphibian hybrid herself.

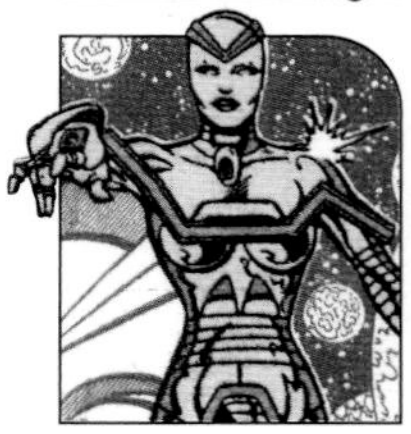

MEKANIQUE
DEBUT *Infinity Inc.* #19 (Oct. 1985)
ALLIES Per Degaton, Professor Malachi Zee **ENEMIES** All-Star Squadron
BACKGROUND Mekanique was a robot from the 23rd century that was sent back in time to alter history and prevent a slave rebellion from occurring. The robot arrived in 1942 and used its powerful energy blasts to battle the All-Star Squadron. It later joined forces with Commander Steel to fight his grandson, Steel, Infinity Inc., and the Justice League. After it lost that battle, Mekanique vanished, but a lookalike, golden-plated robot called Matrix was later spotted on Earth-2.

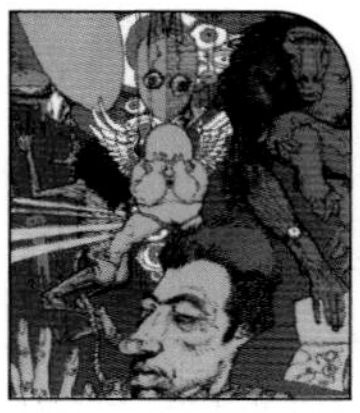

MEN FROM N.O.W.H.E.R.E.
DEBUT *Doom Patrol* (Vol. 2) #35 (Aug. 1990)
ALLIES Darren Jones **ENEMIES** Doom Patrol **BACKGROUND** The Men from N.O.W.H.E.R.E. used invisible guns, transformed children's toys into weapons and teleported via tears in their coats. They were created during World War II by the Agency, whose mission was to eliminate anything different or eccentric. After their deaths, a false version of the Men from N.O.W.H.E.R.E. was created by a device known as the Delirium Box. Their leader, insane Pentagon operative Darren Jones, sent them to kill Danny the Street, but the Doom Patrol defeated them.

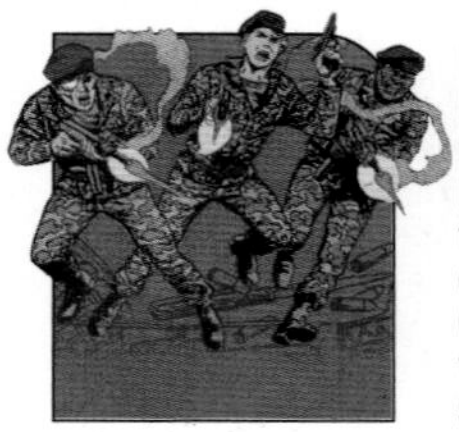

MERCENARIES, THE
DEBUT *G.I. Combat* #242 (Jun. 1982)
ENEMIES Colonel Q
BACKGROUND The Mercenaries were three men who had deserted the French Foreign Legion to become successful soldiers of fortune. The group consisted of the American Gordon, the British Philip "Prince" Edwards, and the German Horst Brenner. Together, they traveled the world fighting for any army that would pay them. The three were masters of armed and unarmed combat and showed great loyalty to their paying employers.

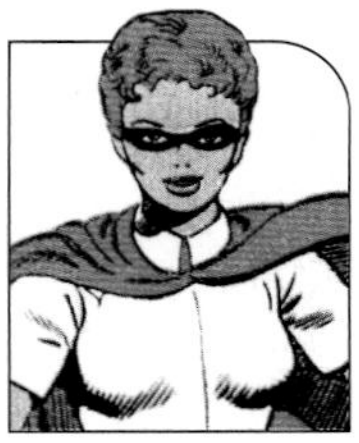

MERRY, GIRL OF 1,000 GIMMICKS
DEBUT *Star Spangled Comics* #81 (Jun. 1948)
REAL NAME Merry Pemberton King **BASE** Civic City
ALLIES Star-Spangled Kid, Stripesy **ENEMIES** Brainwave
BACKGROUND Pemberton was quick-witted and a superb athlete. The adoptive sister of the Star-Spangled Kid, she became Gimmick Girl, using a variety of crime-fighting gadgets. She stood in for Stripesy when he was injured and in her later years helped form a team of senior heroes known as Old Justice. She was the mother of the Super-Villain Brainwave and the ill-fated hero Gimmix.

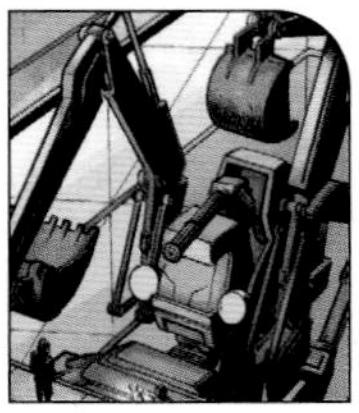

METALEK
DEBUT *Action Comics* #11 (Sep. 2012)
ENEMIES The Multitude, Superman
BACKGROUND The Metaleks were aliens who traveled to Earth after their own planet was destroyed by the Multitude. Taking the form of sentient heavy-duty construction equipment, such as giant ditch diggers and plows, the Metaleks tried to alter their new world to suit their needs. However, they soon came into conflict with the people of Earth. Some Metaleks were captured by the British government, and others were defeated by Superman.

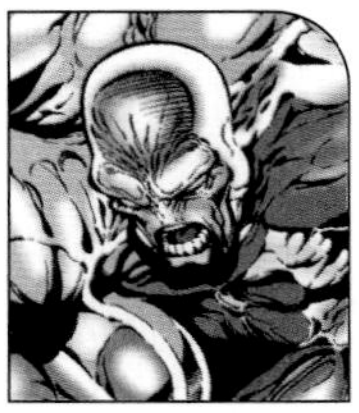

MINION
DEBUT *New Titans* #114 (Sep. 1994)
REAL NAME Jarras Minion
ALLIES Teen Titans, Cyborg **ENEMIES** Raven
BACKGROUND Minion escaped the destruction of his home planet Talyn by donning a powerful, cybernetically bonded suit of armor, the Omegadrome. He traveled to Earth, where he teamed with the Teen Titans to defeat Psimon, the villain he learned was responsible for Talyn's destruction. Minion joined the New Teen Titans, helping them defeat the evil Raven, and eventually gave his armor to Cyborg.

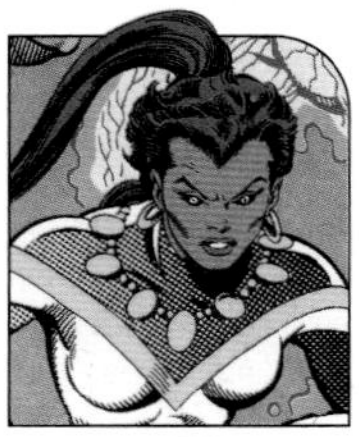

MIRAGE
DEBUT *The New Titans Annual* #7 (1991)
REAL NAME Miriam Delgado **BASE** New York City
ALLIES New Titans **ENEMIES** Lord Chaos
BACKGROUND Delgado could disguise herself as another person by creating psychic illusions around her body. She became Mirage and joined the Team Titans, who traveled back in time to prevent the birth of the godlike villain Lord Chaos, the son of Donna Troy. Their mission only succeeded with the aid of the Teen Titans, and Mirage later fell in love with Nightwing, disguising herself as his girlfriend, Starfire.

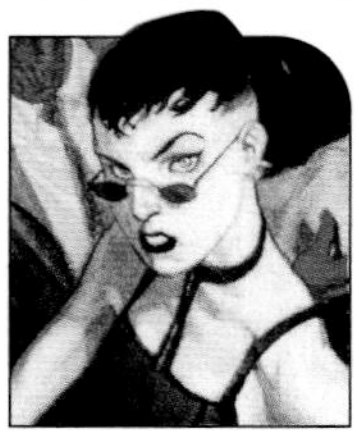

MIST I AND II
DEBUT *Adventure Comics* #67 (Oct. 1941) (Mist I);
Starman #0 (Oct. 1994) (Mist II)
REAL NAME Nash (last name unknown) **BASE** Opal City
ALLIES Kyle, Mary Shazam **ENEMIES** Jack Knight (second Starman)
BACKGROUND The first Mist was a scientist who created a device to transform objects and living things into a thin mist, making them invisible. Mist passed his hatred of the Knight family on to his son Kyle—killed by Starman Jack Knight—and to his granddaughter, Nash, who became the second, far deadlier Mist.

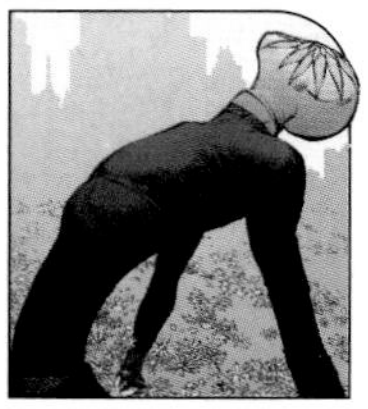

MISTER BLOOM
DEBUT *Batman* #43 (Oct. 2015)
BASE Gotham City
BACKGROUND Likened to a noxious weed, spreading his evil seeds across Gotham City, Mister Bloom was both a Super-Villain and a power broker. His seeds were deadly Man-Bat-based implants that granted superpowers to a new wave of criminals, such as Precious Precious, Gee Gee Heung, and Qi Tsu. Mister Bloom used those same implants to transform himself into a super-strong killer with sharp claws and the ability to stretch his body to an extraordinary lengths.

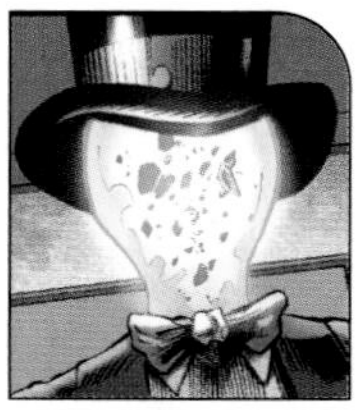

MISTER COMBUSTIBLE
DEBUT *Detective Comics* #6 (Apr. 2012)
BASE Gotham City
ALLIES The Penguin **ENEMIES** Batman
BACKGROUND Mister Combustible was a small-time criminal with a knack for explosives. As a trainee mobster, he joined the Penguin's gang, and for a while became one of Bane's foot soldiers after the Crime Syndicate let the inmates of Arkham Asylum loose on Gotham City. During the ensuing Arkham War, his unique, glass-shaped head was shattered by the Ventriloquist's living puppet, Ferdie.

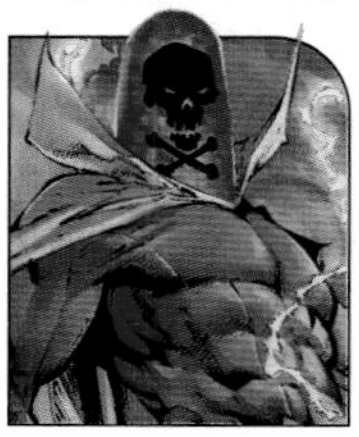

MISTER TOXIC
DEBUT *Detective Comics* #6 (Apr. 2012)
REAL NAME Hugh Marder **BASE** Gotham City
ALLIES The Penguin **ENEMIES** Batman
BACKGROUND Marder was the CEO of the Wayne Industries affiliate Mecha-North Corporation by day, and the Gas Man by night. He later appeared as Mister Toxic, with the power to emit a deadly gas and energy bolts at will. In a battle with Batman at the Mecha-North laboratory, it was revealed that Marder had died in a radiation accident, and Mister Toxic was his clone.

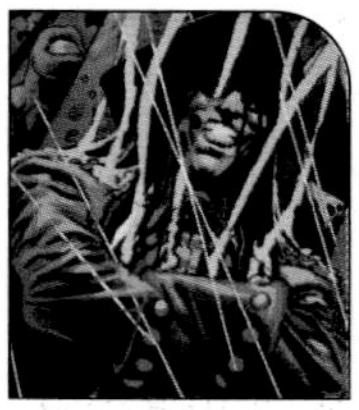

MISTER TWISTER
DEBUT *Brave and the Bold* #54 (Jul. 1964)
REAL NAME Bromwell Stikk **BASE** Hatton Corners
ALLIES Mammoth **ENEMIES** Teen Titans
BACKGROUND When Bromwell Stikk tried to call in a debt of carrier pigeon feathers accrued since his colonial ancestor struck a bizarre bargain with the denizens of Hatton Corners, he was laughed out of town. Arming himself with a staff that gave him elemental powers, he became Mister Twister, battling the Teen Titans. He later assumed a more demonic countenance with enhanced abilities.

MOGO
DEBUT *Green Lantern* #188 (May 1985)
BASE Sector 2261
ALLIES Kyle Rayner, Green Lantern Corps
ENEMIES Despotellis
BACKGROUND Mogo was a living, sentient planet that became the Green Lantern of Sector 2261. It was responsible for the crucial tracking system of the power rings, guiding the rings to new Green Lanterns. The planet played an important role in the battle against Superboy-Prime.

MONGREL
DEBUT *Hawkman Annual* #1 (Sep. 1993)
REAL NAME Josh Xan
ALLIES Hawkman, Quorum   **ENEMIES** Solomon Grundy, Superboy-Prime
BACKGROUND Alien parasites gave Vietnamese African-American Xan the power to fire deadly bolts of "darkforce" energy from his hands. He took the name Mongrel and used his superpower to assist Hawkman during the Bloodlines crisis. He then joined other teenagers who had acquired powers from the aliens to fight crime as the Blood Pack. He was killed with his teammates by Superboy-Prime.

MONOCLE
DEBUT *Flash Comics* #64 (May 1945)
REAL NAME Jonathan Cheval   **BASE** New York City
ALLIES Merlyn, Deadshot   **ENEMIES** Hawkman, JSA
BACKGROUND Cheval was an optician who turned to crime after he lost all his money. He used his optic skills to become the Monocle and fashion lens-based weapons that could project light, heat, lasers, and cosmic rays. He became a member of the Secret Society of Super-Villains, battled Manhunter, and later died at the hands of Ultraman.

MONSTER BOY
DEBUT *Superman* (Vol. 5) #14 (Oct. 2019)
REAL NAME Arune Singh   **BASE** Legion HQ
AFFILIATION Legion of Super-Heroes   **ENEMIES** Horraz
BACKGROUND Hailing from the planet Tor-Etto, Arune Singh was dubbed Monster Boy when he joined the Legion of Super-Heroes—"monster" being an earned title of respect in his culture. Able to change into monstrous shapes, he met some resistance at his Legion interview, as the team already had a changemorph—until he transformed into a giant flying beast, to the Legionnaires' delight.

MONSTRESS
DEBUT *Legion of Super-Heroes* (Vol. 4) #82 (Jul. 1996)
REAL NAME Candi Pyponte-LeParc III   **BASE** U.P. Space, 31st century
ALLIES Star Boy, Atom'X, Insect Queen   **ENEMIES** Element Lad, the Blight
BACKGROUND Candi Pyponte-Le Parc III was transformed after being caught in a gene bomb explosion. Gifted with superpowers and an impossibly sunny disposition, Monstress applied for membership with the Legion of Super-Heroes during a recruitment drive. She died in battle against her former friend Element Lad. A statue was erected in her memory on Legion World.

MORTALLA
DEBUT *Orion* #6 (Nov. 2000)
BASE Apokolips
ALLIES Darkseid   **ENEMIES** Orion
BACKGROUND It was unclear whether Mortalla was the wife or mistress of Darkseid, but no one doubted her deadly powers—she could kill opponents with a single touch. Her preference, however, was to use fear as a weapon to defeat her enemies. After Darkseid's apparent death and Orion's assumption of the Dark Lord's throne, Mortalla seduced Orion. She was later killed by an unknown assassin.

MOVEMENT, THE
DEBUT *The Movement* #1 (Jul. 2013) **BASE** Coral City
MEMBERS Virtue, Katharsis, Mouse, Tremor, Vengeance Moth, Burden
ENEMIES James Cannon, Coral City Police Department, the Graveyard Faction
BACKGROUND In crime-ridden Coral City, a group of renegade superpowered teenagers decided to make a difference and started the Movement. The group's mission included rescuing misunderstood youth—such as troubled teenager Burden—from the police, as well as exposing corrupt police officers. The Movement subsequently gained influence in other cities, including Metropolis.

MRS NYXLY
DEBUT *Action Comics* #1 (Nov. 2011)
REAL NAME Nyxlygsptlnz   **BASE** Metropolis
ALLIES Mr. Mxyzptlk, Superman   **ENEMIES** Vyndktvx
BACKGROUND Mrs. Nyxly's real name was Nyxlygsptlnz. A powerful imp from the fifth dimension, she was the daughter of King Brpxz and the wife of Superman's foe, Mr. Mxyzptlk. Nyxlygsptlnz was hiding in Metropolis from her husband's jealous rival, Vyndktvx, who had killed her father and seriously hurt her husband. She came to the Man of Steel's aid when he confronted Vyndktvx and the Anti-Superman Army.

MURK
DEBUT *Aquaman* #17 (Apr. 2013)
BASE Atlantis   **ALLIES** Orm   **ENEMIES** Scavenger
BACKGROUND Murk was a fierce soldier, dedicated to protecting Atlantis from the "evils of man." Incredibly strong and ruthless, Murk was trained in the fire pits, and led the elite army known as the Men-of-War. He fought for King Orm, battling the Fire-Trolls and the Deep Six, but after Aquaman returned to the throne, Murk rebelled against his new king's tolerant attitude toward humans. Eventually, Murk came to respect his new king, and served as a bodyguard to the royal family.

MUSKETEER
DEBUT *Detective Comics* #215 (Jan. 1955)
REAL NAME Jean-Marie (last name unknown)
ALLIES Batman, Club of Heroes
ENEMIES Black Glove
BACKGROUND Mysterious Frenchman the Musketeer was inspired by the exploits of Batman to commence a career as a costumed crime fighter. He was one of the founding members of the Global Guardians and later answered the call of his idol to join Batman Inc. in the fight against the Black Glove.

NAIAD
DEBUT *Firestorm the Nuclear Man* #90 (Oct. 1989)
REAL NAME Mai Miyazaki
ENEMIES Shogun Oil Company
BACKGROUND Japanese-born Mai Miyazaki was a passionate environmental activist who piloted her boat Naiad near a leaking oil rig in the Pacific Ocean. The rig's captain set fire to the oily waters, engulfing Miyazaki in flames. She was rescued by the Earth spirit Maya and granted powers to become the planet's Water Elemental. In her new role as Naiad, she could control water in all its forms.

NAIF AL-SHEIKH
DEBUT *Justice League Elite* #1 (Sept. 2004)
REAL NAME Naif al-Sheikh   **BASE** The Factory   **AFFILIATION** Justice League Elite   **ENEMIES** Wolfwood   **BACKGROUND** Saudi Arabian intelligence operative Naif al-Sheikh harboured a hatred of superhumans, the result of his wife and children being murdered by an assassin named Wolfwood. Al-Sheikh was recruited into the black ops Justice League Elite by leader Vera Black, acting as the team's liaison to the world's governments. When the team disbanded, he and Vera formed a new version of the group.

NECRO, NICK
DEBUT *Justice League Dark* #12 (Oct. 2012)
REAL NAME Nicholas Edgar Nolan   **BASE** Hell   **ENEMIES** Cult of the Cold Flame, Justice League Dark   **BACKGROUND** Master sorcerer Nick Necro was dating Zatanna Zatara when he was approached by John Constantine, who begged him for instruction. Together they formed a formidable coven to battle the Cult. Eventually Zatanna cheated on him with Constantine, and Nick attempted to lure the pair into a mystical trap. The ritual misfired and Necro was dragged to Hell. He was released by Felix Faust, only to be killed by Constantine.

NEON THE UNKNOWN
DEBUT *Hit Comics* #1 (Jul. 1940)
REAL NAME Tom Corbett, Langford Terrill   **ALLIES** Uncle Sam and the Freedom Fighters   **ENEMIES** The Axis forces
BACKGROUND Tom Corbett became the first Neon the Unknown after he drank from a lake of magic waters and gained the powers to fly and project powerful energy bolts from his hands. He joined the Freedom Fighters and fought during World War II. He disappeared after the war and was later found by Langford Terrill, the original Ray. Terrill drank from the same lake waters and became the second Neon.

NERGAL
DEBUT *Green Lantern Annual* #9 (Sep. 2000)
BASE Kurnugi
ENEMIES Ninurta, Justice League of America
BACKGROUND Nergal was an immortal alien with almost unlimited powers who left the planet Oa and traveled the universe for millennia before settling on Earth. Nergal became a tyrannical god to the Mesopotamians, but was defeated by one of Earth's first Green Lanterns and sent to the portion of Hell known as Kurnugi. Nergal escaped and was defeated again, this time by the Justice League of America.

NIGHTBLADE
DEBUT *Green Lantern Annual* #2 (1993)
REAL NAME Nik Mayak
ALLIES Blood Pack   **ENEMIES** Solomon Grundy, Superboy-Prime
BACKGROUND An automobile accident cost Nik Mayak the use of his legs, but he worked hard in the hospital to train his upper body and practiced knife-throwing. After alien parasites attacked the hospital and drank Mayak's spinal fluid, he gained the power to regenerate his damaged legs. Newly healed, he fought crime as Nightblade and became a member of the Super Hero team Blood Pack.

NIGHTHAWK
DEBUT *Western Comics* #5 (Sep.–Oct. 1948)
REAL NAME Hannibal Hawkes   **BASE** The Old West
BACKGROUND A reincarnation of Prince Khufu, Hawkes was a boy when he set sail on a whaling ship in 1861. After the ship's captain was murdered, Hawkes vowed to fight injustice in the West. Years later, he teamed up with another gunslinger, Cinnamon, and the pair became the most feared outlaw hunters in the West. Both heroes used a special medallion, found at an Indian burial site, which gave them enhanced strength and healing abilities.

NIGHTRUNNER
DEBUT *Detective Comics Annual* #12 (Feb. 2011)
REAL NAME Bilal Asselah
BASE Clichy-Sous-Bois, France   **ALLIES** Batman, Robin
BACKGROUND Bilal Asselah was a superb athlete and a college student in Paris, France. Spurred on by the death of his best friend in a race riot, Bilal became Nightrunner and fought to prevent civil war erupting in his city. Batman and Robin recruited him as the French member of Batman Incorporated, and they defeated a child slavery ring. Despite initial misgivings, Bilal became the protector of Paris.

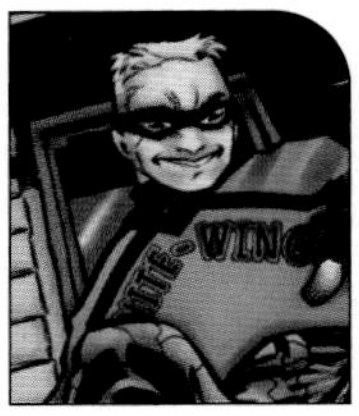

NITE-WING
DEBUT *Nightwing* (Vol. 2) #8 (May 1997)
REAL NAME Thaddeus "Tad" Ryerstad **BASE** Blüdhaven
ALLIES Nightwing **ENEMIES** Blockbuster **BACKGROUND** Growing up in a broken home in Blüdhaven, Thaddeus "Tad" Ryerstad sought solace in comic books. After causing his criminal father's death by outing him as a police informer, Tad went through a succession of foster homes before winding up on the street. Inspired by comics and by local hero Nightwing, he became violent vigilante Nite-Wing, eventually being imprisoned for multiple murders.

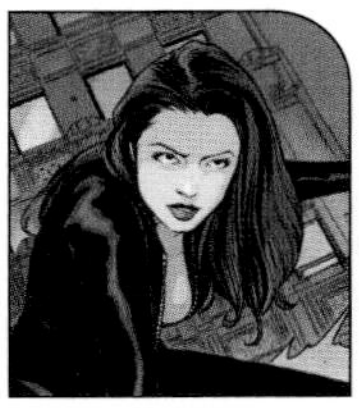

NOCTURNA
DEBUT *Detective Comics* #529 (Aug. 1983)
REAL NAME Natalia Mitternacht **BASE** Gotham City
ALLIES Secret Society of Super-Villains **ENEMIES** Batman, Batwoman
BACKGROUND Natalia Mitternacht (AKA Natalia Knight) was sentenced to Arkham Asylum for killing her husband. She escaped and stalked the streets of Gotham City as Nocturna, exhibiting many of the traits of vampirism, including hypnosis. She had many clashes with Batman, Batwoman, and spent some time as a member of the Secret Society of Super-Villains.

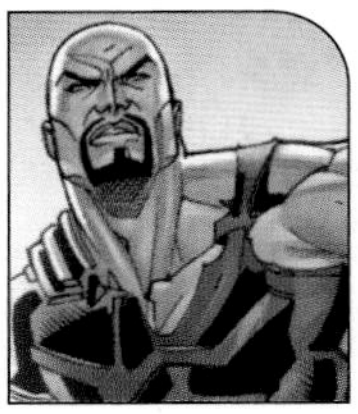

NON
DEBUT *Action Comics* #845 (Jan. 2007)
REAL NAME Non **BASE** New Krypton
ENEMIES Superman **ALLIES** Zod, Ursa
BACKGROUND One of the most brilliant minds on Krypton, scientist Non concurred with his protegé Jor-El that the planet would soon be destroyed. When Non refused the orders of the Ruling Council of Krypton to stay silent on the matter, he was lobotomized. Nursed back to health by Zod and Ursa, he was consigned to the Phantom Zone with them, until all three escaped.

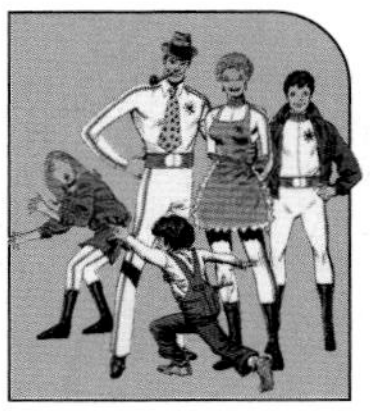

NUCLEAR FAMILY
DEBUT *The Outsiders* #1 (Nov. 1985)
BASE California **ALLIES** Secret Society of Super-Villains
ENEMIES The Outsiders
BACKGROUND The Nuclear Family was a family of androids named Dad, Mom, Bigg, Sis, Brat, and Dog. A deranged scientist named Eric Shanner created the group, and gave each member lethal superpowers, including the ability to emit nuclear radiation and intense heat. The Nuclear Family appeared to have been destroyed during a battle with the Outsiders, but later returned to battle Firestorm.

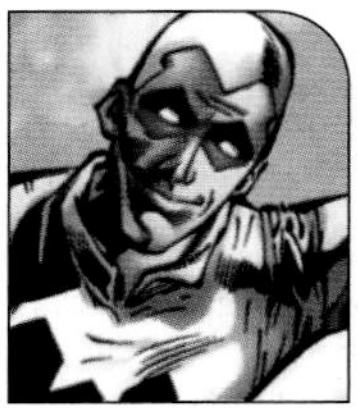

OFFSPRING
DEBUT *The Kingdom: Offspring* #1 (Feb. 1999)
REAL NAME Luke O'Brian **BASE** San Francisco
AFFILIATION Teen Titans **ENEMIES** Terror Titans
BACKGROUND The son of Eel O'Brian, alias Plastic Man, Luke O'Brian was mostly raised by his mother. By the age of ten, Luke was using his inherited elasticity powers in service of a street gang, prompting an intervention by Plastic Man's JLA teammate Batman. Thereafter, he and his dad developed a sometimes fraught relationship, and for a time Luke joined the Teen Titans.

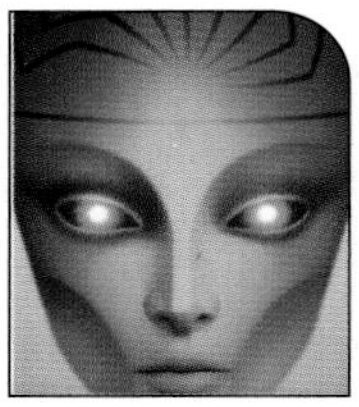

ORACLE
DEBUT *Batgirl* (Vol. 5) #37 (Sep. 2019)
REAL NAME Oracle **BASE** Burnside
ALLIES Terrible Trio **ENEMIES** Batgirl
BACKGROUND After Barbara Gordon abandoned her identity as tech specialist Oracle and returned to being Batgirl, the AI she had created was evolved into its own body by Lex Luthor. Found in a Blue Ridge Mountains base by the Terrible Trio, this robotic Oracle launched an assault on Batgirl's Gotham City territory of Burnside, intending to kill her creator and control the neighborhood.

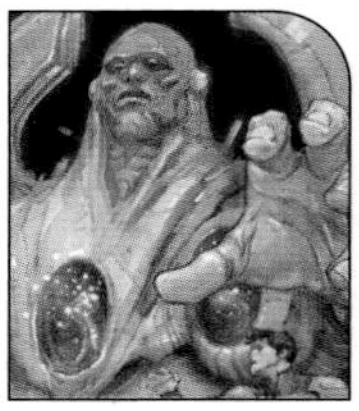

ORACLE, THE
DEBUT *Supergirl* (Vol. 6) #16 (Mar. 2013)
BACKGROUND The enigmatic, all-powerful cosmic being known as The Oracle awoke when the Kryptonian clone H'El journeyed to Earth, determined to destroy it in a mad quest to save Krypton, his long-dead planet. Since the dawn of time, The Oracle has had the same role: To both serve as a witness to every dying world and also to warn of a planet's imminent destruction. After Supergirl saved Earth from H'El's machinations, The Oracle faded away. He later reappeared for the destruction of Earth-2, as well as during the *Convergence* event.

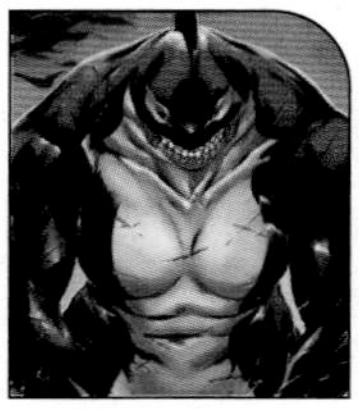

ORCA
DEBUT *Batman* #579 (Jul. 2000)
REAL NAME Grace Balin **BASE** Blüdhaven
AFFILIATION Whale's Enders **ENEMIES** Batman, Nightwing
BACKGROUND Paralyzed in an accident, marine biologist Grace Belin used a gene serum derived from killer whales to regenerate her spine, in the process transforming her into Orca. The product of a lower-working class background, Balin used her new abilities to steal from the rich in order to help Gotham City's poor. She later became a member of Blüdaven crime outfit the Whale's Enders.

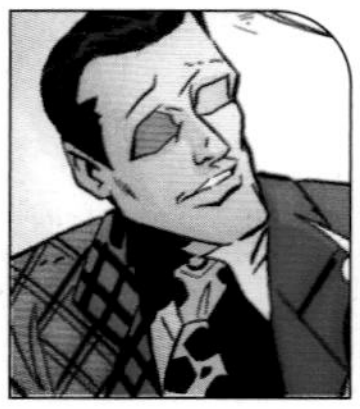

ODD MAN
DEBUT *Detective Comics* #487 (Dec. 1979–Jan. 1980)
REAL NAME Clayton "Clay" Stoner **BASE** River City
ENEMIES Pharaoh, Queen of the Nile **AFFILIATION** Hero Hotline
BACKGROUND River City's sole champion, the Odd Man lived up to his name. His clownish garb, concealed gimmicks and wacky weapons, proved surprisingly effective in disorienting and defeating opponents. He retired after accidently transforming the Nile Queen and Pharaoh—two jewel thieves posing as reincarnated Egyptians—into stone.

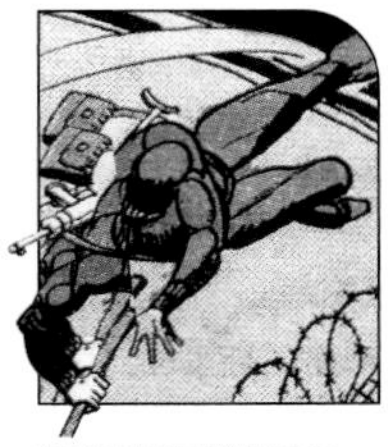

O.S.S. SPIES AT WAR
DEBUT *G.I. Combat* #192 (Jul. 1976)
BASE Washington, DC
ALLIES Blackhawk squadron
BACKGROUND When World War II began, the US Government assembled a group of men and women to form the Office of Strategic Services. The O.S.S. operated as spies, working as liaisons to the Blackhawk squadron and undertaking dangerous covert missions. The team members used codenames, including Falcon, Shadow, Sprinter, and Mongoose. After the war, the group was absorbed into the CIA.

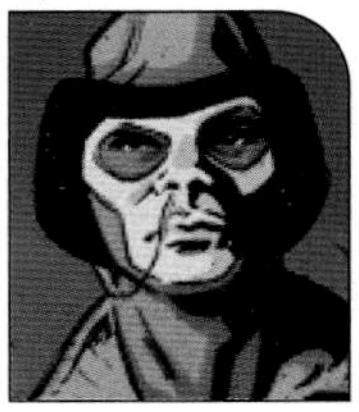

PAPA MIDNITE
DEBUT *Hellblazer* #1 (Jan. 1988)
REAL NAME Linton Midnite **BASE** Club Midnite, NYC
ENEMIES John Constantine, Neron
BACKGROUND Linton Midnite was a voodoo priest from Haiti and a nightclub owner. The demon Neron took over his club and Papa Midnite tricked his old foe, occult sleuth John Constantine, into helping him get it back. Neron sent them both to Hell, but Constantine escaped, leaving Papa Midnite to his fate. Under the leadership of Circe, Midnite joined the Injustice League Dark.

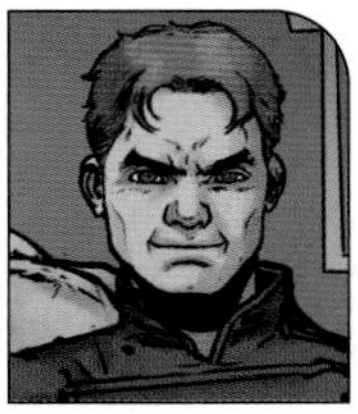

PER DEGATON
DEBUT *All-Star Comics* #35 (Jun. 1947)
REAL NAME Per Degaton **BASE** mobile **ALLIES** Mekanique
ENEMIES, Justice Society, All-Star Squadron, Infinity, Inc.
BACKGROUND When the Time Trust sent the Justice Society of America to the future to retrieve a bomb-defense beam, lab assistant Per Degaton sabotaged the beam out of petty jealousy. Later, now working for Professor Zee, he killed Zee and appropriated his time machine in order to conquer the world. Degaton's repeated time meddling brought him into conflict with both the JSA and Infinity, Inc.

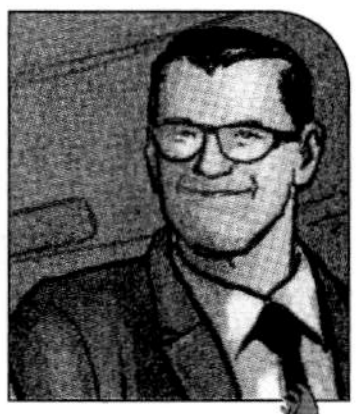

PERIL, JOHNNY
DEBUT *Comic Cavalcade* #19 (Feb.–Mar. 1947)
BACKGROUND Johnny Peril's past was shrouded in mystery, and his name was almost certainly an alias. His occupations included reporter, soldier-of-fortune, and private detective specializing in the occult. It was in this last capacity that he became involved in supernatural incidents, working alongside psychic Heather Storm. As Dr. John Peril, he worked as a scientist at US agency A.R.G.U.S., using his knowledge of biology and technology to combat malign magical forces.

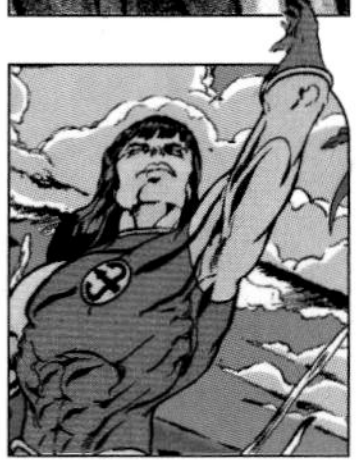

PERKINS, NEPTUNE
DEBUT *Flash Comics* #66 (Aug.–Sep. 1945)
BASE Hawaii
ALLIES Young All-Stars **ENEMIES** Secret Society of Super-Villains
BACKGROUND Neptune Perkins was a human/dolphin hybrid who could hold his breath underwater for seven minutes. His webbed hands and feet made him an exceptionally powerful swimmer, and he could also communicate with sea creatures. He became a member of the Young All-Stars and fought with them during World War II. Years later, Perkins died defending Atlantis during *Infinite Crisis*.

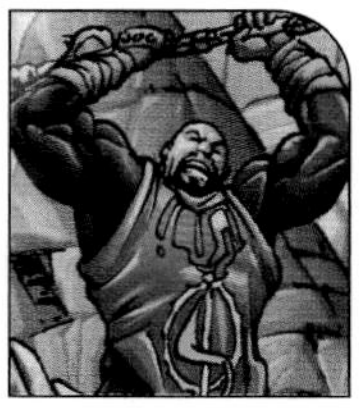

PERSUADER
DEBUT *Adventure Comics* #352 (Jan. 1967)
ALLIES Fatal Five
ENEMIES Legion of Super-Heroes, Batman, Blue Beetle
BACKGROUND Several villains were known as the Persuader, but all of them used an "atomic axe" that could cut through anything. The alien Nyeun Chun Ti was the first Persuader and joined the Fatal Five. A second Persuader, Cole Parker, was a member of the Suicide Squad. Elise Kimble, allegedly an ancestor of Nyeun Chun Ti, later became the Persuader as an assassin-for-hire and member of the Terror Titans.

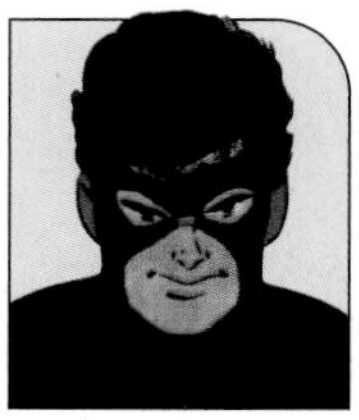

PERUN
DEBUT *Firestorm* #70 (Apr. 1988)
REAL NAME Ilya Trepliov **BASE** Russian Federation
ALLIES Firestorm **ENEMIES** Imperiex
BACKGROUND Ilya Trepliov became the Super Hero Perun when he was only 17. Named after a Russian God of Thunder, Perun could mentally control electricity and channel it in any way he desired. He joined the Russian team of superpowered heroes known as Soyuz, and together they protected Earth from the alien invader Imperiex. Later he became a member of The People's Heroes.

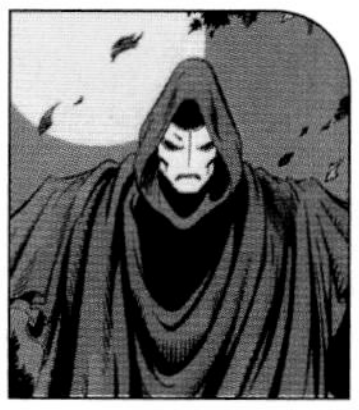

PHANTASM
DEBUT *The New Titans Annual* (Vol.2) #3 (1987)
REAL NAME Danny Chase **ENEMIES** Wildebeest Society
BACKGROUND Danny Chase possessed the power of telekinesis and was a member of the Teen Titans. After several Titans were murdered by the Wildebeest Society, Chase faked his death. He then donned a mask and costume to become Phantasm. In a battle with the Wildebeest Society, his powers became linked with the hero Raven and her mother, Arella. Chase and Arella died, but their essences united to form an even more powerful Phantasm.

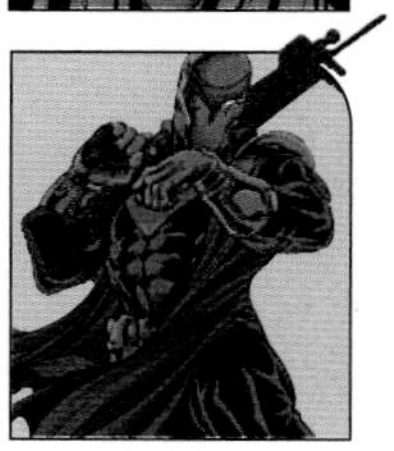

PLUNDER
DEBUT *The Flash* #165 (Oct. 2000)
BASE Mirror image dimension
ALLIES Mirror Master, Captain Cold **ENEMIES** The Flash, Professor Zoom
BACKGROUND Plunder was a bounty hunter and deadly marksman from another dimension who worked for the Thinker and teamed up with Mirror Master and Captain Cold to invade Keystone City. He later murdered police detective Jared Morillo and assumed his identity, before being exposed. He was defeated by Professor Zoom and sent back to his dimension.

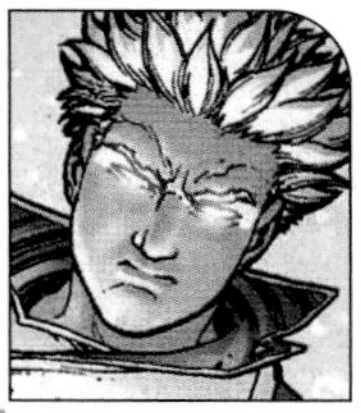

POLAR BOY

DEBUT *Adventure Comics* (Vol. 1) #306 (Mar. 1963)
REAL NAME Brek Bannin **BASE** Legion HQ, 31st-century Metropolis
ENEMIES Ambush Bug, Plant Men, Captain Freeze **BACKGROUND** Brek Bannin was the youngest candidate to audition for the Legion of Super-Heroes. Unfortunately, he lost control of his ability to project waves of intense cold and was rejected. Brek formed a replacement team: the Legion of Substitute Heroes. Over time, Polar Boy proved his worth and was rewarded by being inducted into the Legion of Super-Heroes—eventually rising to the rank of team leader.

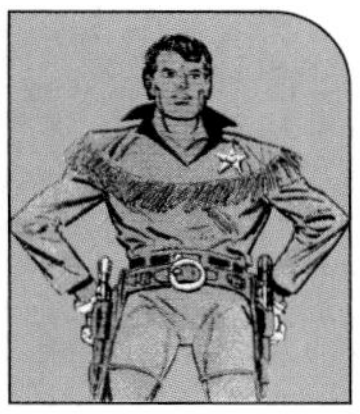

POW-WOW SMITH

DEBUT *Detective Comics* #151 (Sep. 1949)
REAL NAME Ohiyesa **BASE** Elkhorn **ALLIES** Hank Brown (deputy)
BACKGROUND The frontier town of Elkhorn was plagued by armed gangs until Ohiyesa (sarcastically nicknamed Pow-Wow Smith), the only Indian lawman in the west, rescued them. An expert marksman and horseman, Smith was also a great detective. In the 1940s, a descendant of Ohiyesa's adopted the name Pow-Wow Smith and became a detective; his son later took up the mantle, fighting alongside Robin, Huntress, and Nighthawk to bring the latest version of the Trigger Twins to justice.

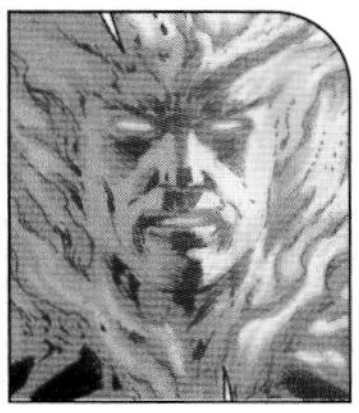

POZHAR

DEBUT *The Fury of Firestorm* #62 (Aug. 1987)
REAL NAME Mikhail Arkadin **BASE** Moscow, Russia
BACKGROUND Professor Mikhail Arkadin was the Russian Firestorm Pozhar. He claimed to have worked with Martin Stein to invent the protocols that created the original Firestorm program. After manipulating Firestorm Ronnie Raymond, he combined with him to become the energy being Scorn. Though believed dead after a battle with Firestorms Jason Rusch, Firehawk, Hurricane, and Rakshasi, Pozhar later reappeared as a member of Russian super-team the People's Heroes.

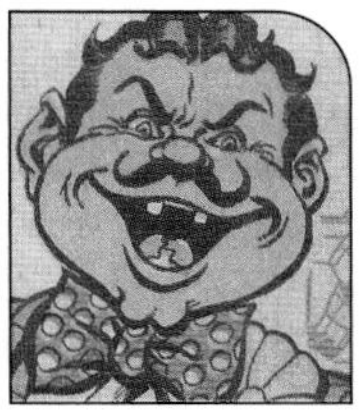

PRANKSTER

DEBUT *Action Comics* #51 (Aug. 1942)
REAL NAME Oswald Loomis **BASE** Metropolis
BACKGROUND A fading children's TV star, Loomis turned to crime after his TV show ratings began to lag. His motivation often fuelled more from a need for attention than a desire for wealth. The Prankster continually harass Superman and the citizens of Metropolis, typically by employing extremely dangerous gimmicks and pranks. A second version of the Prankster (also named Oswald Loomis) surfaced to trouble Nightwing. What his relation to the original is remains unknown.

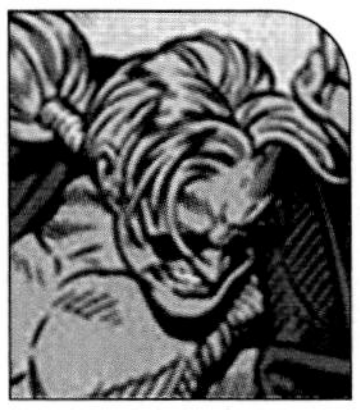

PRAXIS

DEBUT *The Spectre* (Vol. 2) #24 (Feb. 1989)
REAL NAME Jason Praxis **BASE** Portland, Oregon
ENEMIES Richard Redditch, Ghast, Dexter Defarge **BACKGROUND** Police detective Jason Praxis gained psionic powers after a manhunt for a super-powered serial killer went awry. Though he briefly joined a Super Hero team founded by Booster gold, his reluctance to use his powers led him back to detective work. Praxis joined FBI agent Deanna Walker to stop magician Dexter Defarge resurrecting the demon Ghast. Soon after he went into semi-retirement.

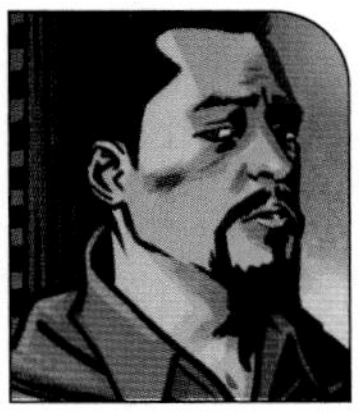

PRINCE RA-MAN

DEBUT *House of Secrets* #73 (Jul. 1965)
REAL NAME Mark Merlin **BASE** Mystery Hill Mansion
ALLIES Kranak **ENEMIES** Eclipso
BACKGROUND Transported to the other-dimensional world of Ra, occult detective Mark Merlin gained mind-over-matter powers. However, the only way he could return to his own world was via the body and mind of ancient Egyptian Prince Ra-Man. Taking Merlin's place at Mystery Hill Mansion, Prince Ra-Man embarked on a career as a sorcerer, battling Eclipso and other mystical threats.

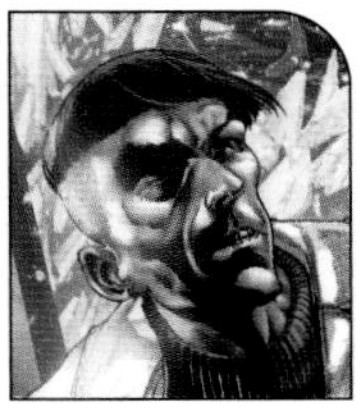

PROFESSOR MILO

DEBUT *Detective Comics* #247 (Sep. 1957)
REAL NAME Achilles Milo **BASE** Gotham City
ALLIES General Immortus **ENEMIES** Batman
BACKGROUND Renegade scientist Professor Achilles Milo repeatedly used his expertise with chemistry to bedevil Batman. Concocting a range of drugs and gasses, Milo variously induced a fear of bats in the Dark Knight; sapped his will to live; and transformed Anthony Lupus into a werewolf to kill Batman. After assuming control of Arkham Asylum, he was subsequently committed to the institution.

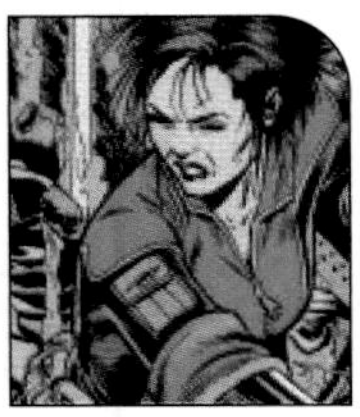

PSYBA-RATS

DEBUT *Robin Annual* #2 (Sep. 1993)
BASE Gotham City **ALLIES** Robin **ENEMIES** The Collector
BACKGROUND Hired by the Collector to break into Wayne Industries, the Psyba-Rats was a team of five teenagers who operated as techno-thieves. After the Collector killed two members of the group, the three remaining—Sharp, Hackman, and Channel—were attacked by an alien and gained superpowers. Taking the names Razorsharp, Channelman, and Hackrat, they sought revenge on the Collector. The hero Robin joined them, and the team made him an honorary Psyba-Rat.

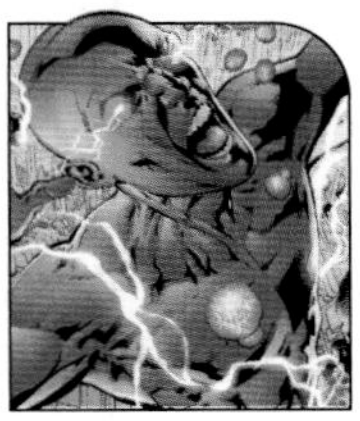

QUANTUM MECHANICS

DEBUT *JLA: Heaven's Ladder* (Nov. 2000)
BACKGROUND Born in the wake of the Big Bang, the Quantum Mechanics were ancient, almost godlike beings, who roamed the universe in search of divine enlightenment. Aware that their race was finally dying out, they decided to create a perfect afterlife and started collecting planets in order to build a ladder to their version of Heaven. One of the planets was Earth, which brought them into conflict with the Justice League of America. Eventually, the JLA was able to save Earth and also help the Quantum Mechanics to ascend to their afterlife.

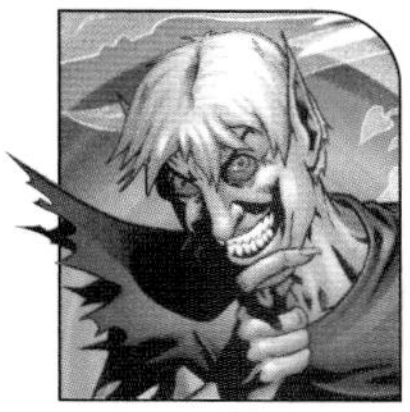

QWSP

DEBUT *Aquaman* #1 (Jan.–Feb. 1962)
BASE The Fifth Dimension
ALLIES Aquaman, Aqualad (when good) **ENEMIES** JLA (when bad)
BACKGROUND Qwsp was an imp from the Fifth Dimension who traveled to Earth, where he could reshape reality, and manipulate time and matter. Formerly a friend to Aquaman, Qwsp turned evil when the sea king became a grim warrior and teamed up with the evil genie Lkz to battle the JLA. For his crimes, the rulers of his dimension sentenced Qwsp to one million infinities in an eight-dimensional maze.

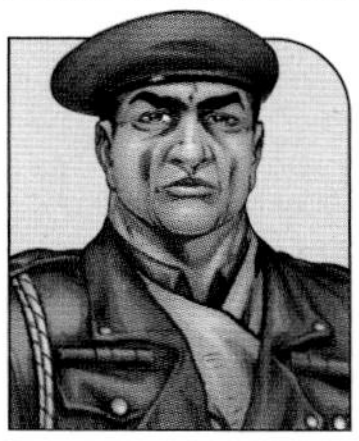

RAJAK, COLONEL

DEBUT *Adventures of Superman* #590 (May 2001)
REAL NAME Ehad Rajak **BASE** Bialya
BACKGROUND The African country of Bialya has seen its share of iron-fisted leaders come and go. After Colonel Rajak took control he perpetuated the anti-American stance for which the nation had become well known. President Luthor asked Superman to help rescue the *Newstime* journalist Andrew Finch from the country, hoping to avoid direct military intervention. Finch, however, was actually a CIA assassin working under Luthor's orders. Superman rescued Finch but prevented him eliminating Rajak.

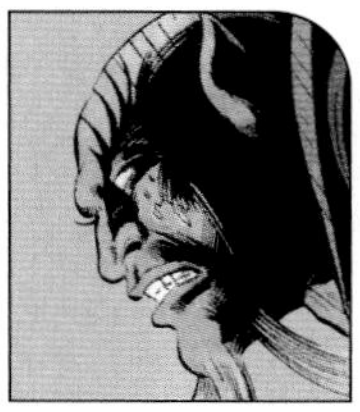

RAMULUS

DEBUT *World's Finest* #21 (Summer 1942)
ENEMIES The Sandman, Sandy the Golden Boy
BACKGROUND Originally known as the villain Nightshade, Ramulus created mechanized plants to terrorize his victims. When the Sandman (Wesley Dodds) and his protégé, Sandy, fought him, Nightshade lost control over his plants and was seemingly killed by them. Somehow surviving, Nightshade was found by the Aztec priestess Nyola. Given greater control over his techno-flora, and the ability to manipulate living vegetation, Nightshade became Ramulus and joined Nyola's Monster Society of Evil.

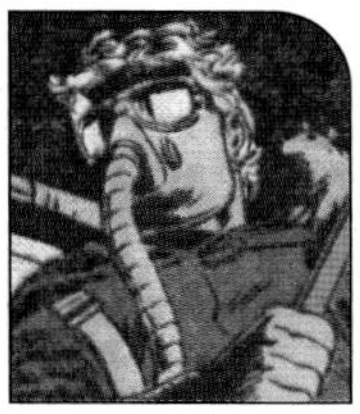

RATCATCHER

DEBUT *Detective Comics* #585 (Apr. 1988)
REAL NAME Otis Flannegan **BASE** Gotham City allies Menace
ENEMIES Batwing **BACKGROUND** A spell in Blackgate prison turned rat exterminator Otis into a hardened criminal. Taking the name "Ratcatcher," Otis used poisonous gases and sewer rats to murder. Batman discovered the Ratcatcher's activities, and the two clashed multiple times. After facing Batwing, the Ratcatcher supposedly reformed, and moved into the basement of the building that vigilante Mother Panic inhabited.

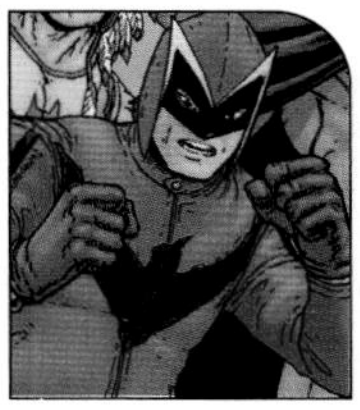

RAVEN RED

DEBUT *Batman* #86 (Sep. 1954)
REAL NAME Charles Great Eagle **BASE** South Dakota
ALLIES Man-of-Bats, Batman **ENEMIES** Leviathan, Black Glove
BACKGROUND Charles Eagle was the son of William Eagle, aka Man-of-Bats, who fought for his fellow Native Americans' rights. Charles became Raven Red and also fought crime, but unlike his father, he longed to take on international villains. Both father and son joined Batman Inc. to battle the crime organizations Leviathan and Black Glove.

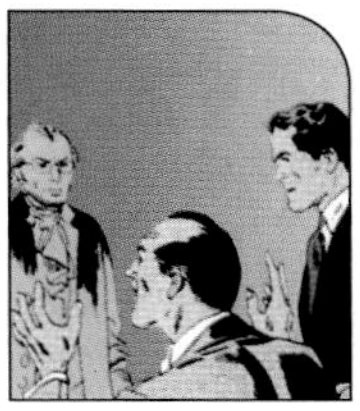

RAYMOND, ROY—TV DETECTIVE

DEBUT *Detective Comics* #153 (Nov. 1949)
BASE Metropolis
BACKGROUND Roy Raymond found fame as the host of the TV show *Impossible—But True!*, in which he showcased strange and exotic items. Describing himself as a "TV Detective," Raymond traveled around the world with his assistant Karen Colby debunking hoaxes and exposing fraudulent claims; Raymond even created hoaxes himself to help the police trap criminals. His son, Roy Raymond, Jr., continued his father's work and later fought crime as the costumed hero Owlman.

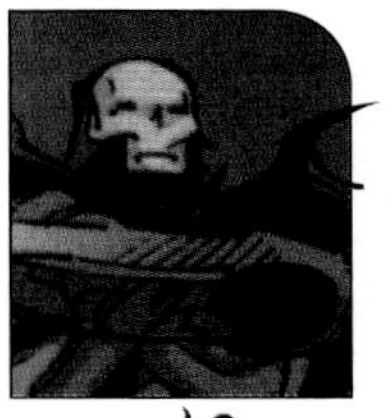

REAPER

DEBUT *Batman* #237 (Dec. 1971)
BASE Gotham City
ENEMIES Batman
BACKGROUND The first Reaper was a World War II concentration camp survivor named Benjamin Gruener, while a later incarnation was the vigilante Judson Caspian. Joe Chill, Jr. saw his father murdered by the Reaper and later took the identity of the villain himself. Recently, Gruener was revived from cryogenic suspension and returned to the role of the Reaper.

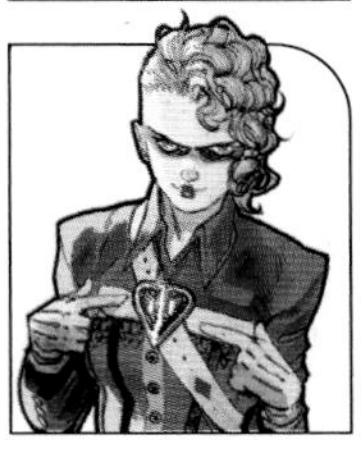

RED ALICE

DEBUT *Detective Comics* #854 (Aug. 2009)
REAL NAME Beth Kane **BASE** Gotham City
AFFILIATION Religion of Crime **ENEMIES** Batwoman
BACKGROUND As children, twin sisters Kate and Beth Kane were inseparable—until Beth was kidnapped by terrorists at age 12. Believed dead by her sister, Beth grew up to become the High Madame of the Religion of Crime. Calling herself Alice after Lewis Carroll's novels, she led an attack on Gotham City that was halted by Kate, now Batwoman. Later, she adopted a new guise: Red Alice.

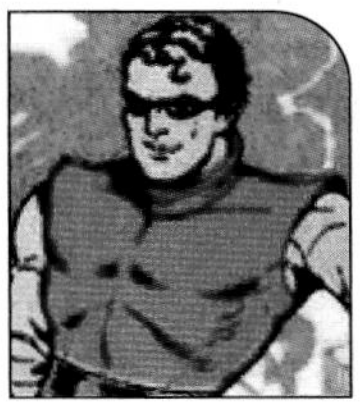

RED BEE

DEBUT *Hit Comics 1* (July 1940)
REAL NAME Richard Raleigh, Jenna Raleigh
ALLIES All-Star Squadron /Freedom Fighters, S.H.A.D.E.
BACKGROUND Assistant District Attorney Richard Raleigh was the first Red Bee, a World War II hero brandishing a special stinger gun. He was aided in his fight against crime by trained bees. He joined the All-Star Squadron and was believed to have died fighting Baron Blitzkrieg. After his death, his super-powered grandniece Jenna became Red Bee, wearing a battle suit that simulated a bee's sting.

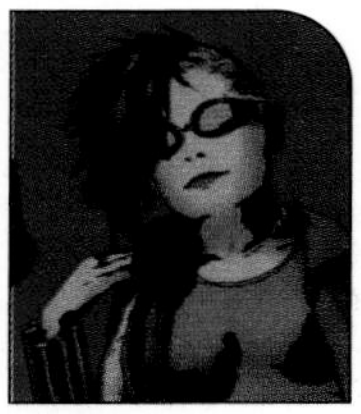

RED DART

DEBUT *World's Finest* #95 (Aug. 1958)
ALLIES Longbow Hunters **ENEMIES** Green Arrow, Green Lantern
BACKGROUND At least three villains have been Red Dart. The first was Green Arrow foe John "Midas" Mallory; followed by an unknown thief who stole Kyle Rayner's Green Lantern Power Ring. The current Red Dart is a member of Richard Dragon's Longbow Hunters. With a penchant for trick darts, she teamed up with Brick and Killer Moth to collect a bounty on Green Arrow's life. The Emerald Archer defeated all three.

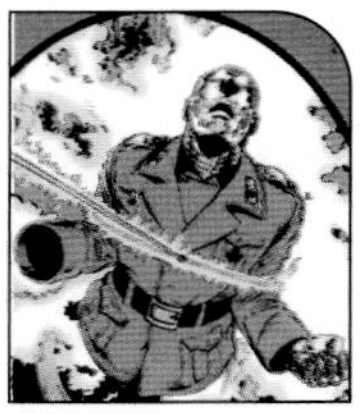

RED PANZER

DEBUT *Wonder Woman* #228 (Feb. 1977)
ENEMIES Wonder Woman, Titans
BACKGROUND The first villain known as Red Panzer was the former Nazi general Helmut Streicher, who donned a crimson battle suit that fired energy blasts. After his death, three criminals were inspired to continue as Red Panzer—a neo-Nazi and a teenager who became a member of Vandal Savage's villainous team, Tartarus. The most recent Red Panzer was recruited from Tartarus by Savage and lived on the island nation of Zandia, when he was not striking at his constant foe, Troia.

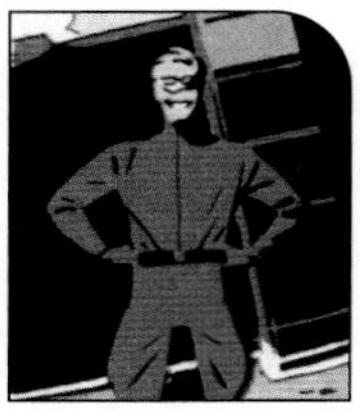

RED TORPEDO

DEBUT *Crack Comics* #1 (May 1940)
REAL NAME James Lockhart **ALLIES** the Freedom Fighters
BACKGROUND The first, most famous Red Torpedo was former US Navy Captain Jim Lockhart, whose submarine, the Torpedo, could travel to the bottom of the ocean and also fly. Lockhart donned a costume and fought as Red Torpedo alongside the Freedom Fighters. A later Red Torpedo—a female android possessing hydrokinesis, flight, and super-strength—was created and later abandoned in the ocean by Super-Villain scientist T.O. Morrow; she was later rescued by Red Tornado.

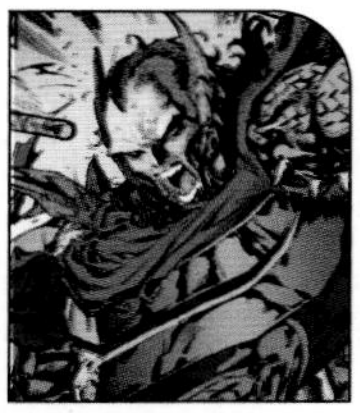

REGULUS

DEBUT *Team 7* #0 (Nov. 2012)
REAL NAME Dean Higgins **ENEMIES** Team 7, Birds of Prey, Suicide Squad
BACKGROUND Dean Higgins was working for US Military Intelligence when he was recruited by John Lynch to join the metahuman specialists known as Team 7. His final mission with the group was to secure Pandora's Box, but a freak accident caused his brain to meld with the brain of world terrorist Kaizen Gamorra. Higgins called himself Regulus and assumed control of the Basilisk terrorist network. His stated goal was to control or destroy every metahuman on Earth.

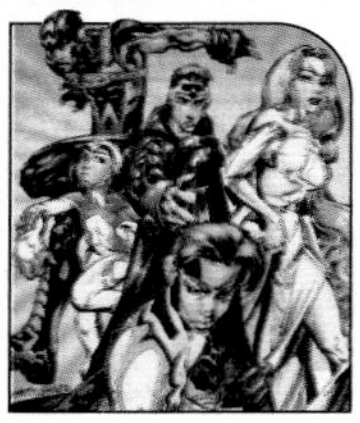

RELATIVE HEROES

DEBUT *Relative Heroes* #1 (Mar. 2000)
ALLIES Impulse, Young Justice **ENEMIES** D.E.O., Girth, Napalm, Kittyhawk
BACKGROUND After their parents died in a car crash, the Weinberg children united to form Relative Heroes. While team leader Houston had no superpowers, his siblings did: Temper could control electricity; Allure possessed magical persuasive abilities; Blindside had the power of invisibility; and Omni could imitate the powers of those around him. Pursued and captured by the D.E.O., the group learned that Omni was an alien, but they convinced the residents of his world to let Omni remain on Earth.

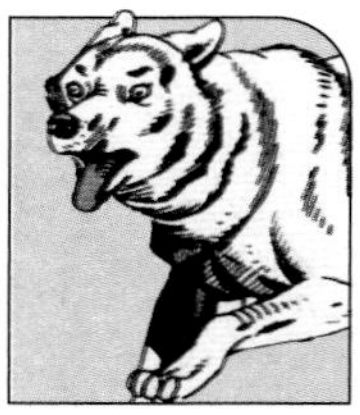

REX, THE WONDER DOG

DEBUT *The Adventures of Rex, The Wonder Dog* #1 (Jan.–Feb. 1952)
ALLIES Danny Daniels
BACKGROUND Rex, the Wonder Dog was an ordinary puppy that was transformed into a super-strong dog by a scientific experiment. Rex fought bravely during World War II and the Korean War as part of the elite K-9 Corps, taking part in many combat parachute jumps. He was later adopted by a young man named Danny Daniels and the pair's adventures took them around the world. The resourceful Rex eventually joined the US government's Bureau of Amplified Animals.

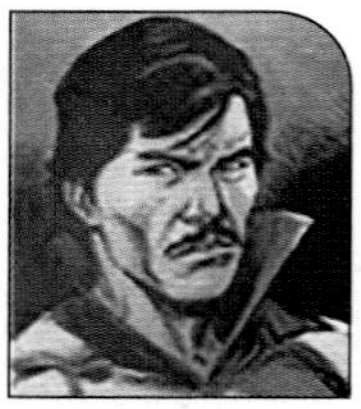

RISING SUN

DEBUT *Super Friends* #8 (Nov. 1977)
REAL NAME Isumi Yasunari **BASE** Tokyo, Japan
BACKGROUND Several members of the Yasunari family developed cancer as a result of the atom bomb that destroyed Nagasaki, Japan, during World War II. As a young man, Isumi Yasunari discovered he could absorb solar radiation. He became the hero Rising Sun and used his newfound power to project intense heat and flames from his body as he defended Japan from evildoers. Rising Sun became a member of the Global Guardians and fought alongside them for many years.

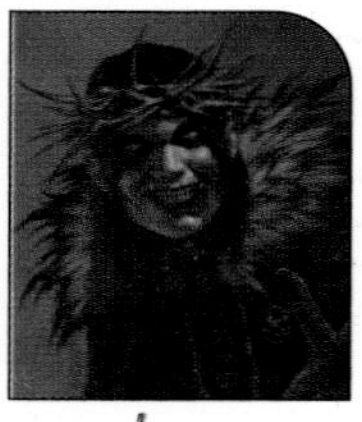

ROBIN KING

DEBUT *Dark Nights: Death Metal* #2 (Sep. 2020)
REAL NAME Bruce Wayne **BASE** Gotham City
ALLIES Batman Who Laughs **ENEMIES** Batman
BACKGROUND As a child, Bruce Wayne was prone to violent impulses—attacking Alfred, the family butler; microwaving the family cat; hurting his friends. One night, after his parents took him to see a movie, Bruce murdered them. Transforming himself into the Robin King, Bruce escaped the Dark Multiverse with the Batman Who Laughs and joined the invasion of the Prime Multiverse.

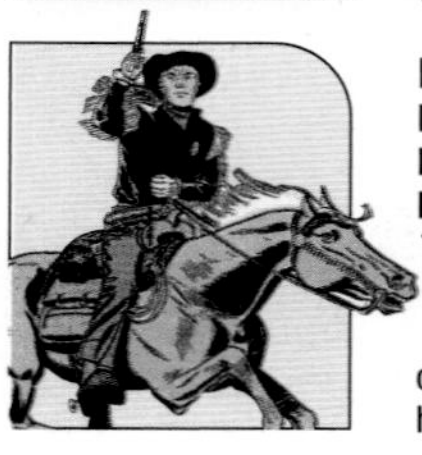

ROVING RANGER

DEBUT *All Star Western* #58 (Apr.–May 1951)
REAL NAME Jeff Graham **BASE** Mid-19th century Texas
BACKGROUND A captain in the Confederate army, Jeff Graham joined the Texas Rangers after the Civil War ended. As a Ranger, he brought lawbreakers to justice, including the infamous bandit El Dorado, in reality Bud Huston, a former fellow Confederate officer whom Graham convinced to give up his criminal ways. Along with other "History's Heroes," the Roving Ranger was transported to the present and helped prevent the Ultra-Humanite from stealing a space shuttle from Cape Canaveral.

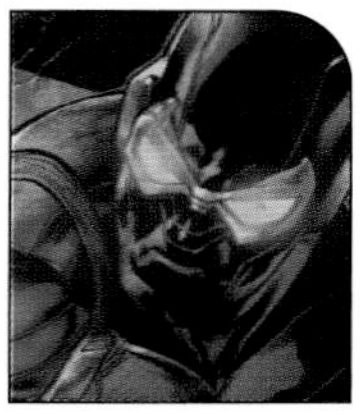

SAIKO

DEBUT *Nightwing* (Vol. 3) #1 (Nov. 2011)
REAL NAME Raymond McCreary **ALLIES** Raya Vestri, Zane, Bryan Haly
ENEMIES Court of Owls **BACKGROUND** Growing up as an acrobat at Haly's Circus, McCreary was jealous of Dick Grayson. Raymond endured cruel training as an assassin by the Court of Owls, which then left him to die. Years later, as contract killer Saiko, McCreary turned his rage towards Grayson, aka Nightwing, convinced that his former rival was responsible for the cruelties he had endured. Saiko perished in a fire he set off trying to destroy both Haly's Circus and Nightwing.

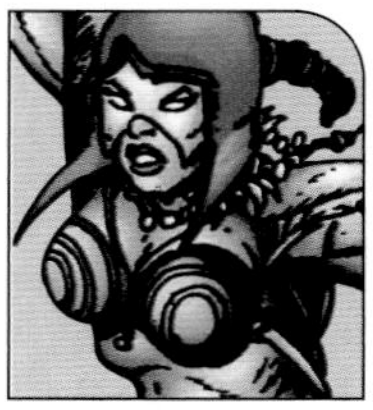

SALA

DEBUT *Green Lantern Annual* (Vol. 3) #9 (2000)
BASE Nabeul, Tunisia **ALLIES** Green Lantern Kyle Rayner, JLA
ENEMIES Ereskigal, Humbaba, Nergal, Pazuzu, Tiamat
Though she is a descendent of a refugee Malthusian named Istar. Lady of Battle, archaeologist Sala Nisaba only discovered the first clues to her heritage after she grasped the lost Goddess's ringstaff. Using the ringstaff, she joined Green Lantern Kyle Raynor in battle against a demonic entity that now threatened Earth. She later joined with earth's mystics to reconstruct the shattered Rock of Eternity.

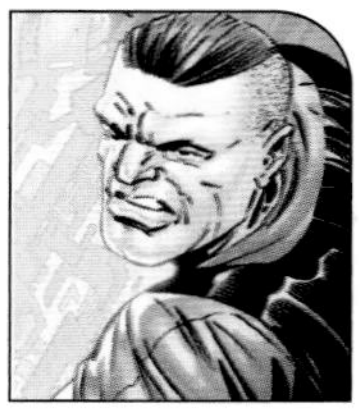

SARGE STEEL

DEBUT *Sarge Steel* #1 (Dec. 1964)
ALLIES Maribel, Little Kipper
BACKGROUND The mysterious espionage agent known only as Sarge Steel held many jobs, including a stint leading the Central Bureau of Intelligence and working with the government combat team Checkmate. Project Cadmus hired Steel to investigate O.M.A.C. attacks, and he led a team of agents, including Maribel and Little Knipper. Steel lost a hand during a battle with O.M.A.C., but grew even more formidable with a replacement hand made of solid steel.

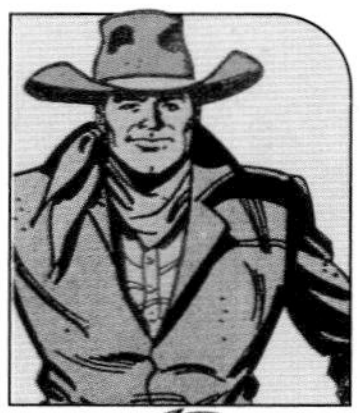

SAVAGE, MATT: TRAIL BOSS

DEBUT *Western Comics* #77 (Sep.–Oct. 1959)
BASE The Texas Trail
BACKGROUND Matt Savage was a legendary trail boss on the Dogiron trail in Texas during the 1860s. He led 2,000 steers and his seven-man Dogiron Crew through flood and drought, Indian attacks, and thundering stampedes. Savage possessed a keen sense of fair play, but he never hesitated to use his fast guns or quick fists to battle cattle rustlers and outlaws. Jebediah Kent, an ancestor of Clark Kent's adoptive father, Jonathan, briefly worked for Savage's team.

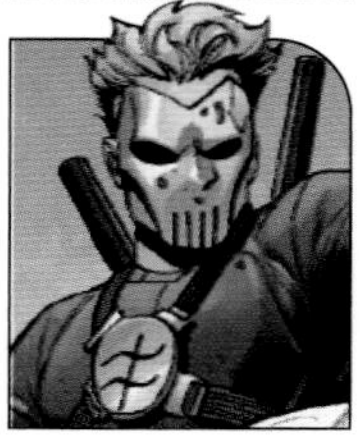

SAVANT

DEBUT *Birds of Prey* #56 (Aug. 2003)
REAL NAME Brian Durlin **BASE** Gotham City
ENEMIES Batman, Black Canary
BACKGROUND Durlin suffered from a chemical imbalance that gave him sporadic amnesia. After his father disinherited him, he took the name Savant and turned to a life of crime, often blackmailing his victims. After he kidnapped Black Canary, Savant was arrested; he then joined the Suicide Squad. As a test, he was secretly tortured to reveal details of the Squad. When he cracked, he was killed.

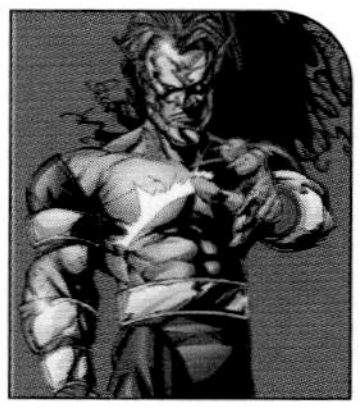

SAVITAR

DEBUT *The Flash* #108 (Dec. 1995)
BASE Tibet **ENEMIES** The Flash (Wally West), The Flash (Barry Allen)
BACKGROUND Savitar was a former Eastern bloc military pilot who was able to tap into the Speed Force. This allowed him to move his body at near light speed and absorb motion from other objects and people. He believed that his super-speed was a divine gift and named himself after Savitar, the Hindu god of motion. Over time, he became obsessed with stripping the Speed Force from other heroes, but was ultimately absorbed into the energy field, where he was trapped.

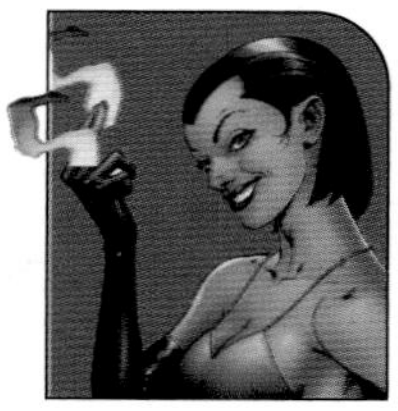

SCORCH

DEBUT *Adventures of Superman* #582 (Sep. 2000)
REAL NAME Aubrey Sparks **BASE** Pisboe, Virginia
ALLIES The Joker **ENEMIES** Superman
BACKGROUND Aubrey Sparks was transformed into the Super-Villain Scorch when The Joker briefly gained Mr. Mxyzptlk's cosmic powers. The Joker recruited her for his Joker League of Anarchy team. Scorch went on to battle Superman and later fell in love with the Martian Manhunter. Tormented with memories of her human self, she came under the supervision of the Department of Extranormal Operations.

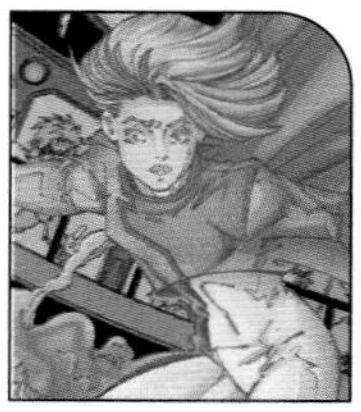

SECRET

DEBUT *Young Justice: The Secret* #1 (Jun. 1998)
REAL NAME Greta Hayes **ALLIES** Young Justice
BACKGROUND Greta Hayes was an ordinary teenager who became Secret, a mysterious phantom girl able to take a ghost-like form. This allowed her to pass through solid objects and create psychic manifestations. She joined Robin, Superboy, and Impulse to form the team Young Justice. Secret was later corrupted by Darkseid, which caused her to turn on her teammates. After Robin saved her, Darkseid punished Secret by restoring her humanity—which suited her perfectly.

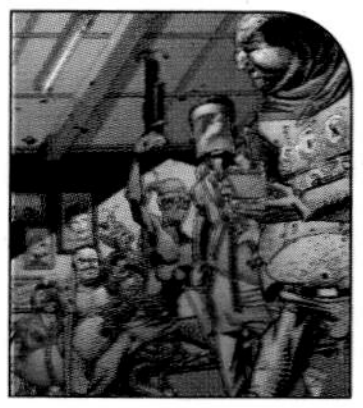

SECTION EIGHT

DEBUT *Hitman* #18 (Sep. 1997)
BASE Gotham City **ALLIES** Hitman, Batman
BACKGROUND Section Eight was a mostly befuddled team of semi-heroes with a headquarters in the sewers beneath Gotham City. The team's name was taken from the US military designation "section eight," meaning "mentally unfit for duty." The tubby leader of the team was Sixpack, who gathered various misfits together to stumble into crime scenes alongside Hitman and Batman. Three of the longest-serving members were Bueno Excellente, Baytor, and Dogwelder.

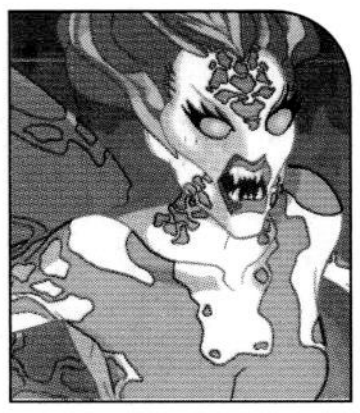

SENSOR
DEBUT *Legionnaires* #43 (Dec. 1996)
REAL NAME Jeka Wynzorr
ALLIES Legion of Super-Heroes **ENEMIES** Universo
BACKGROUND Sensor was a snake-shaped member of the Legion of Super-Heroes who used her illusion-casting power to disguise herself as a human being. Originally a princess from the planet Orando, a world ruled by large snakes, she renounced her heritage to travel the universe. After joining the Legion, Sensor helped to build the artificial planetoid Legion World and later defeated the Super-Villain Universo.

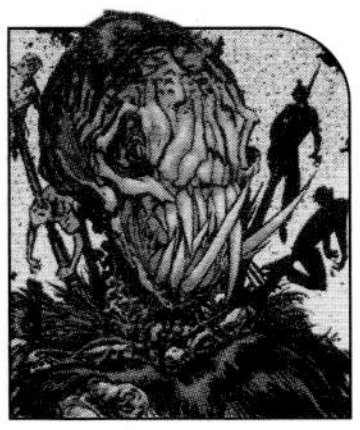

SETHE
DEBUT *Swamp Thing* #1 (Nov. 2011)
ENEMIES Swamp Thing, Abigail Arcane
BACKGROUND Sethe was the overwhelming presence of death and decay on Earth. As the Avatar of the Rot, he stood in terrifying opposition to the forces of life known as the Red and the Green. Responsible for all the plagues that have ravaged humankind, he could control the elements and bring death to anything he touched. Sethe battled Swamp Thing, the champion of the Green, but it was Abigail Arcane who ultimately defeated the vile villain.

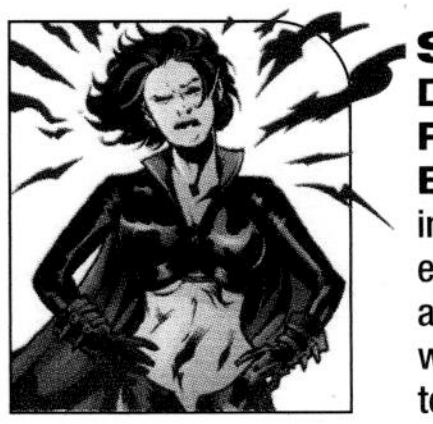

SHADOW LASS
DEBUT *Adventure Comics* #365 (Feb. 1968)
REAL NAME Tasmia Mallor **BASE** Talok VIII
BACKGROUND Tasmia Mallor could connect with the source of all darkness in the universe. She could project darkness over large areas of space, trapping enemies who would become disoriented and fearful. Tasmia was also a superb athlete and her homeworld's hand-to-hand combat champion. When her planet was invaded by the Fatal Five, she joined the Legion of Super-Heroes and helped to defeat the invaders.

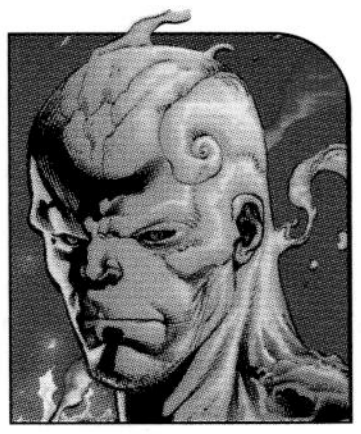

SHIFT
DEBUT *Titans/Young Justice: Graduation Day* (Vol. 1) #3 (Aug. 2003)
BACKGROUND When Metamorpho fell to Earth following the destruction of the JLA's satellite, a fragment of him broke loose and formed its own consciousness. Unaware of his origin, this clone became Shift and later joined the Outsiders. Shift's unstable molecular structure allowed him to transform himself and other objects into chemical compounds. After he accidentally killed a number of people during Black Lightning's escape from Iron Heights Penitentiary, the grief-stricken Shift chose to reintegrate his body with Metamorpho.

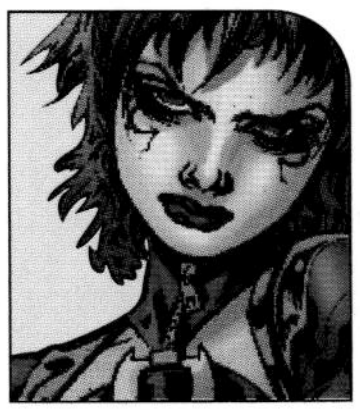

SHIMMER
DEBUT *The New Teen Titans* (Vol. 1) #3 (Jan. 1981)
REAL NAME Selinda Flinders **ENEMIES** Teen Titans, Psimon
BACKGROUND Selinda Flinders and her brother Baran were born with superpowers, with Selinda able to transform one element or compound into another. Both siblings were recruited by Doctor Light for his Fearsome Five team: Selinda took the name Shimmer and her brother became Mammoth. They battled the Teen Titans several times, but Shimmer was ultimately betrayed and killed by her own teammate, Psimon. Later, Doctor Sivana resurrected her for his new Fearsome Five.

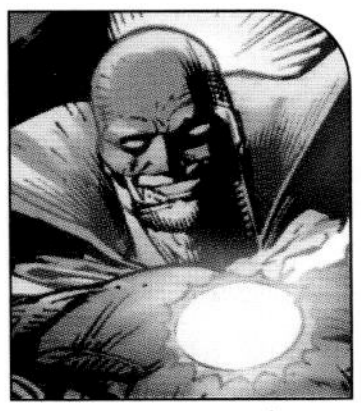

SIGNALMAN
DEBUT *Batman* #112 (Dec. 1957)
REAL NAME Phillip Cobb **BASE** Gotham City
AFFILIATION Secret Society **ENEMIES** Batman
BACKGROUND Small-time crook Phillip Cobb's efforts to form a gang in Gotham City were going nowhere. Then the Bat-Signal blazing in the night sky inspired him to become the Signalman and use signs and signals in his crimes. For a short while he changed his masked identity to the Blue Bowman, but reassumed his Signalman guise, arming himself with a Signal-Laser.

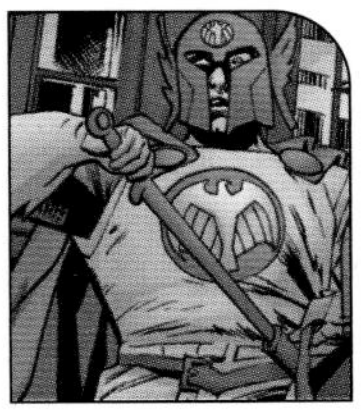

SILENT KNIGHT
DEBUT *Brave and the Bold* #1 (Aug. 1955)
REAL NAME Brian Kent **BASE** England
ALLIES Lady Celia **ENEMIES** Sir Oswald Bane
BACKGROUND In 6th-century England, Sir Edwin Kent and Sir Oswald Bane ruled their small kingdom jointly—until Sir Edwin murdered Sir Oswald. Sir Edwin's son, Brian, trained to be a knight to prove his worthiness to rule. After finding a mysterious suit of armor, sword, shield, and helmet in the Forest Perilous, Brian became the Silent Knight—a symbol of freedom to the oppressed.

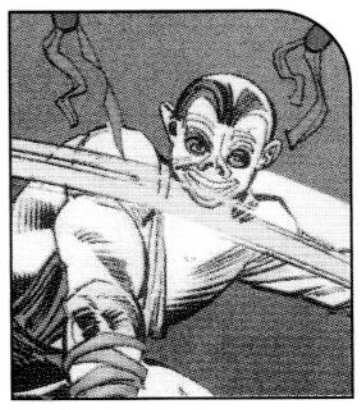

SILVER MONKEY
DEBUT *Detective Comics* #685 (Mar. 1995)
BASE Asia **ENEMIES** Batman, Robin, Nightwing
BACKGROUND Silver Monkey was the codename of the mysterious mercenary and deadly martial artist who was hired by crime lord General Tsu to murder King Snake during a gang war in Asia's Golden Triangle. Batman, Robin, and Nightwing joined the battle when it moved to Gotham City, barely preventing Silver Monkey from killing King Snake. Silver Monkey surfaced years later on the eve of another Gotham City gang war; he was believed to have been killed by Scarface.

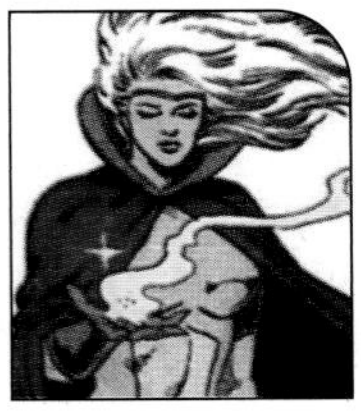

SILVER SORCERESS
DEBUT *Justice League of America* #87 (Feb. 1971)
REAL NAME Laura Neilsen **BASE** Angor, Paris
AFFILIATION Champions of Angor, Justice League **ENEMIES** Extremists
BACKGROUND Escaping the destruction of her homeworld Angor, Laura Neilsen and her fellow Champions of Angor traveled to Earth to prevent a similar nuclear holocaust occurring there. With teammate Blue Jay, she joined Justice League Europe, using her magical abilities to battle robot duplicates of Angorian villains the Extremists. She lost her life at the hands of the Extremists' Dreamslayer.

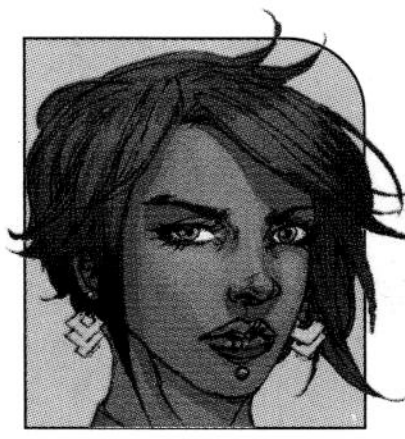

SINGH, NAOMI
DEBUT *Green Arrow* Vol 5 #1 (Nov. 2011)
BASE Seattle, Washington State **ALLIES** Jax, Oliver Queen, John Diggle, Henry Fyff, Emiko **ENEMIES** Richard Dragon, Killer Moth, Billy Tockman, Count Vertigo **BACKGROUND** Naomi Singh was Green Arrow's most trusted assistant, running his innovations division Q-Core and, with assistants Henry Fyff and Jax, providing him with intel weapons. Though she occasionally lends Team Arrow a hand, she prefers to stay hidden; her current whereabouts are unknown.

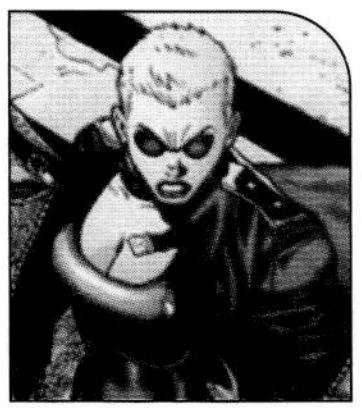

SISTER SUPERIOR
DEBUT *JLA* #100 (Aug. 2004)
REAL NAME Vera Lynn Black **BASE** The Factory
AFFILIATION Justice League Elite **ENEMIES** Manchester Black
BACKGROUND To atone for the sins of her brother, Manchester Black, Vera Black outfitted herself with cybernetic arms and took control of Manchester's former team, the Elite, calling herself Sister Superior. After working with the JLA to save the Earth from destroying itself, Vera headed up a new covert ops team, Justice League Elite, in the process overcoming a psychic assault by her dead brother.

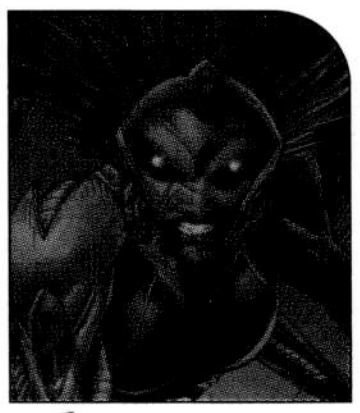

SKITTER
DEBUT *Teen Titans* #2 (Dec. 2011)
REAL NAME Celine Patterson **ENEMIES** Grymm
BACKGROUND Celine Patterson was a young girl when she underwent a metamorphosis and emerged from a cocoon as a metahuman with the powers and appearance of a spider. She possessed superhuman strength and could project webs and a corrosive substance from her body. When N.Y.P.D. officers ambushed the Teen Titans, Skitter rescued them by spinning webs around the cops. In honor of her bravery, she became a member of the Teen Titans.

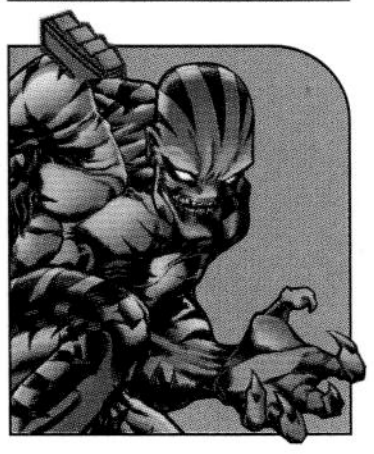

SKORPIO
DEBUT *Steel* (Vol. 2) #37 (Apr. 1997)
REAL NAME Dennis "Sam" Ellis **BASE** New Jersey
BACKGROUND A resident at the Garden State Medical Center, Ellis became Dr. Arthur Villain's bodyguard. He wore a reptilelike suit and became Skorpio. After his activities brought him into conflict with Steel, Ellis lost his medical license and was arrested. He joined Alexander Luthor's Secret Society of Super-Villains and was one of the first criminals sent to the prison-planet Salvation. While a Suicide Squad member, he was killed by angry spirits during a battle with Swamp Thing.

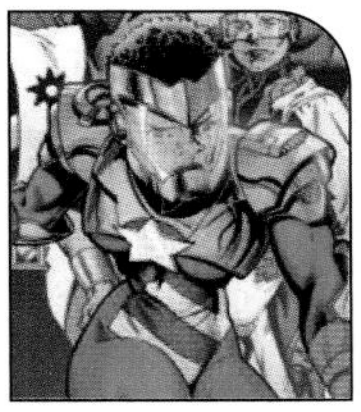

SKYROCKET
DEBUT *JLA* #61 (Feb. 2002)
REAL NAME Celia Forrestal **BASE** San Francisco, California
BACKGROUND US Navy aviation instructor Celia Forrestal was the daughter of two Argo Industries scientists. Her parents invented the Argo Harness, which could absorb, convert, and redirect energy. The terrorist group Scorpio, attempting to steal the device, killed her parents. Celia donned the Argo Harness, became the hero Skyrocket, and joined the Power Company. She also aided rescue efforts during the *Infinite Crisis* and was part of an all-female team created by Wonder Woman.

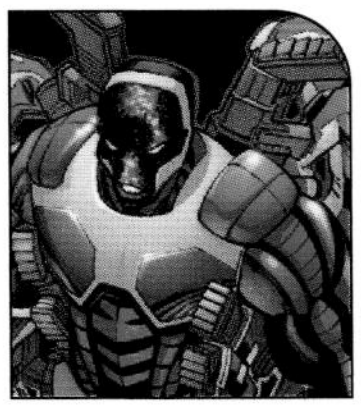

SLATE GANG
DEBUT *Static Shock* #1 (Nov. 2011)
BASE New York City **ENEMIES** Static
BACKGROUND The Slate Gang consisted of Cole Brick, Jann Jon, Kaitlin Stone, Kim Dagar, Nico Patrollus, and Trey Uhuru. This powerful syndicate specialized in technology theft and illegal surveillance, but their unlawful businesses were disrupted by the arrival of the hero Static. The team ordered the monster Virule—a killing machine composed of a living virus—to assassinate Static. After Virule failed in its mission, the team lost much of its prestige and influence.

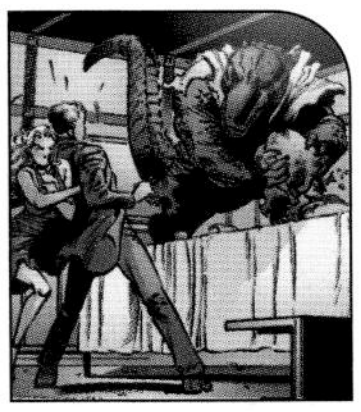

SOBEK
DEBUT *52* #26 (Nov. 2006)
REAL NAME Yurrd **ENEMIES** Black Adam, Batman, Superman
BACKGROUND The giant crocodile Sobek has been known as Famine, one of the Four Horsemen of the Apokolips. He was bioengineered by the villain Doctor Sivana to become a ravenous murderer, and one of his first crimes was to devour the unsuspecting Osiris. Black Adam slaughtered Sobek in revenge, but the crocodile's spirit returned, along with the other Horsemen, to the wastelands of Bialya to feed on the misery of the nation's refugees and later battle Batman and Superman.

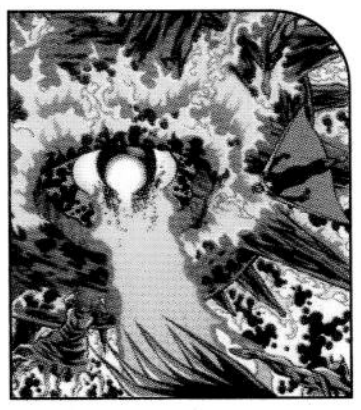

SOLARIS II
DEBUT *DC One Million* #1 (Nov. 1998)
ENEMIES Superman dynasty
BACKGROUND The first Solaris was a NASA engineer named Clifton Lacey, who created the deadly Heliotron and died in a battle with Kobra. The second Solaris was a man-made tyrant sun from the 853rd century that tried to destroy several planets with a techno-virus. Solaris first battled Superman-Prime in the 853rd century, and then traveled through time to combat members of the Superman dynasty. Solaris exerted its gravitational pull to wrench planets into its own orbit.

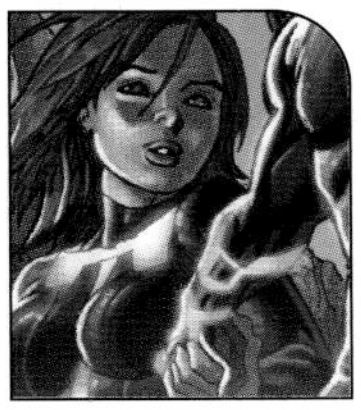

SOLSTICE
DEBUT *Teen Titans* (Vol. 3) #89 (Jan. 2011)
REAL NAME Kiran Singh **BASE** Delhi, India
AFFILIATION Teen Titans **ENEMIES** Legion of Doom
BACKGROUND Hailing from Delhi, India, Kiran "Solstice" Singh had the power to generate light energy. After meeting Wonder Girl in a London museum, Kiran joined the Teen Titans when her parents went missing on an archaeological dig in Pakistan. Taking on a new appearance after being experimented on by N.O.W.H.E.R.E., Kiran was among those killed at the Sanctuary facility.

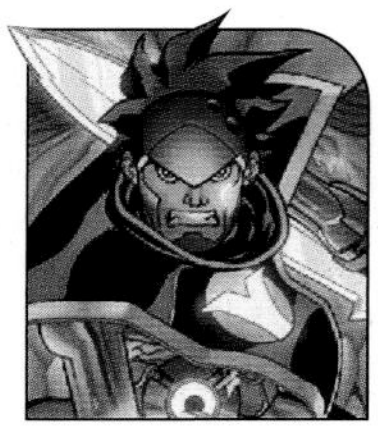

SON OF VULCAN
DEBUT *Son of Vulcan* (Vol. 2) #1 (Aug. 2005)
REAL NAME Miguel Devante **BASE** Derby Youth Home, Charlton's Point
BACKGROUND Miguel "Mikey" Devante was a 14-year-old metahuman orphan. When the Floronic Man took Mikey and others hostage, the hero Vulcan came to their rescue. However, it was Mikey who saved the day by chopping off Floronic Man's arm. Vulcan chose the boy as his successor, Son of Vulcan. After his mentor's death, Miguel took the name Vulcan and fought alongside the Teen Titans, battling the likes of Bork of the Power Company and Trigon, the latter seriously injuring him.

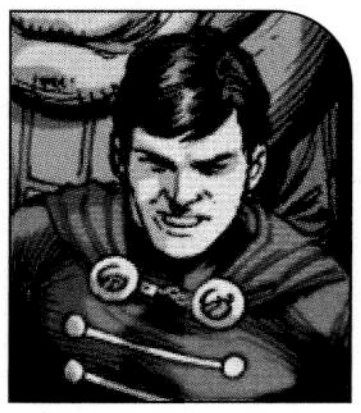

SONAR
DEBUT *Green Lantern* (Vol. 2) #14 (Jul. 1962)
REAL NAME Bito Wladon **BASE** Balkan country of Modora
ENEMIES Green Lantern
BACKGROUND The first Sonar was a sonic-altering alien monarch who battled Green Lantern. The newest Sonar was Bito Wladon, a terrorist from war-torn Modora. He exploded bombs in Coast City to draw attention to his country's plight. Green Lantern stopped him destroying the United Nations building, but Sonar escaped.

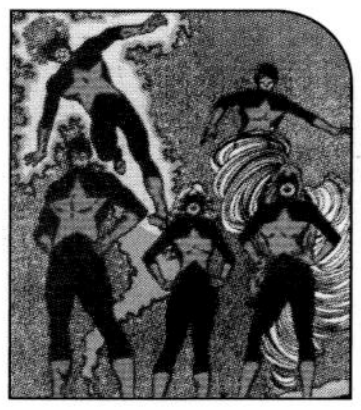

SOYUZ
DEBUT *Firestorm, the Nuclear Man* (Vol. 2) #70 (Apr. 1988)
BASE Russia **ALLIES** Firestorm **ENEMIES** Zuggernaut
BACKGROUND This team of superpowered Russian teens came together to rescue the family of Mikhail Arkadin, the Russian Firestorm. Calling themselves Soyuz, Arkadin's niece, Serafina, a telepath, became Firebird and based her teammates' names on Russian mythology. They included Morozko, Perun, Rusalka, and Vikhor, and among their powers were the abilities to control electricity, water, and cold weather. They have remained active fighting crime in Eastern Europe.

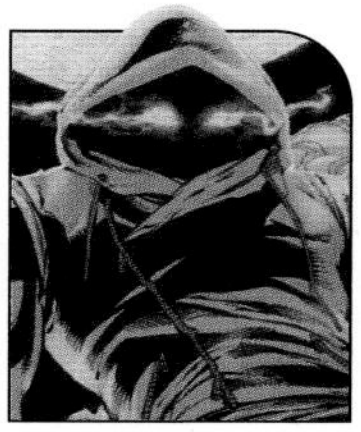

SPARK
DEBUT *Catwoman* (Vol. 4) #7 (May 2012)
BASE Gotham City **HEIGHT** 6ft **WEIGHT** 190 lbs **POWERS/ABILITIES** Control over various forms of electromagnetism. **ALLIES** Catwoman Spark made himself known to Catwoman when he saved her from being arrested by creating a diversion. He then proposed that they should pool resources and talents, and start pulling heists together. Spark is killed by Catwoman's long-time friend, Gwen Altamont, after the Penguin leaked information that the thief had ties to corrupt cops that had been trying to kill Catwoman.

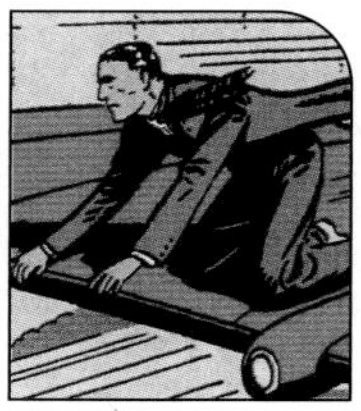

SPEED SAUNDERS
DEBUT *Detective Comics* #1 (Mar. 1937)
REAL NAME Cyril Saunders **ALLIES** Justice Society of America
BACKGROUND As a young man, Cyril Saunders traveled the world in search of adventure, becoming an expert explorer, tracker, climber, and survivalist. It was strongly rumored that he founded the World War II spy agency known as the Office of Strategic Services, and he also teamed up with the Justice Society of America during the 1940s. He became the guardian of his granddaughter, Shiera Saunders, and trained her to become the new Hawkgirl.

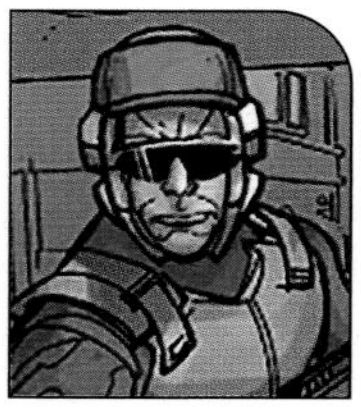

SPORTSMASTER
DEBUT *All-American Comics* #85 (May 1947)
REAL NAME Lawrence Crock **BASE** Gotham City
ALLIES Huntress **ENEMIES** Green Lantern
BACKGROUND Lawrence Crock could turn his hand to any sport, but his obsession with winning saw him cripple a football player, ending his professional career. Instead, he turned to crime, attempting to rob a polo match, before adopting a costumed identity: Sportsmaster. Crock joined the Injustice Society and struck up a fruitful partnership—criminal and romantic—with Huntress (originally Tigress).

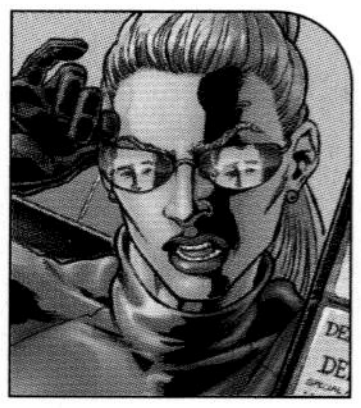

SPY SMASHER
DEBUT *Birds of Prey* (Vol. 1) #100 (Jan. 2007)
REAL NAME Katarina Armstrong **ALLIES** Various US government agents
ENEMIES Oracle (Barbara Gordon), Black Canary, Birds of Prey
BACKGROUND Katarina Armstrong was a soldier who became the modern-day successor to World War II hero Spy Smasher. Armstrong deduced Gordon's ID as Oracle and attempted to shut her down. Barbara won the fight, but Spy Smasher refused to back down. Surrounded by the Birds of Prey and many of Oracle's other friends, she realized this was one war she couldn't win.

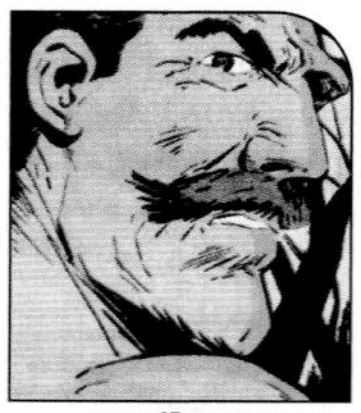

STALNOIVOLK
DEBUT *Firestorm the Nuclear Man* #67 (Jan. 1988)
REAL NAME Ivan Illyich Gort **BASE** Moscow, Russia
BACKGROUND Ivan Illyich Gort was given the name Stalnoivolk and transformed by the Soviet government into a superpowered agent to fight the Nazis during World War II. His aging was also slowed, and he became immune to pain and injury. He remained loyal to dictator Josef Stalin after the war and was an active participant in the government's bloody purges. Decades later, he traveled to the US to work as a KGB agent against Firestorm and eventually joined the Suicide Squad.

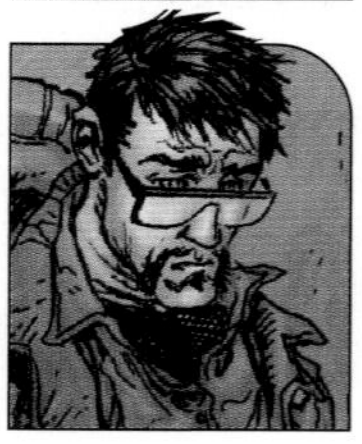

STAR HAWKINS
DEBUT *Strange Adventures* #114 (Mar. 1960)
BASE Tolerance, Tenebrian Dominion
BACKGROUND Down-at-heel private eye Star Hawkins was hired to investigate the identity of the Legend, the longest-surviving member of the bounty-hunting game show *The Hunted.* After Hawkins discovered that said Legend was none other than Lady Styx, the ruthless ruler of the Tenebrian Dominion, his faithful robot assistant Ilda activated an internal bomb that allowed him to escape.

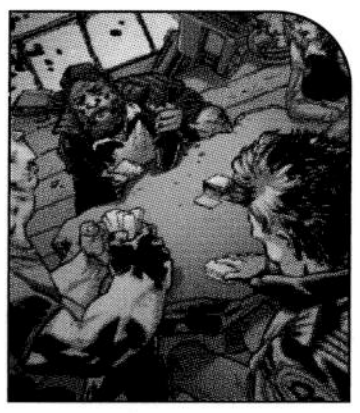

STAR ROVERS
DEBUT *Mystery in Space* (Vol. 1) #66 (Mar. 1961)
BACKGROUND The Star Rovers were a group of mercenary smugglers led by Homer Gint, comprising Chuddu, Karel Sorensen, and Rick Purvis. One of their earliest jobs was smuggling Carol Ferris, Arkillo, and Saint Walker into the Tenebrian Dominion. Instead, the Star Rovers sold them to agents searching for contestants in *The Hunted* game show. Later, the group was hired by Larfleeze, wielder of the Emotional Spectrum's orange light of Avarice, to recover valuable stolen items, including his Orange Lantern Power Battery.

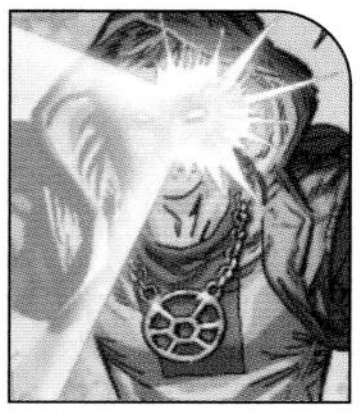

STEADFAST
DEBUT *The Flash* (Vol. 5) #69 (Jun. 2019)
REAL NAME unknown **BASE** Central City
ALLIES The Flash **ENEMIES** Black Flash
BACKGROUND The individual named Steadfast had chosen a life of quiet solitude in the mountains—until the Force Barrier broke, and he was gifted the Still Force, and the knowledge of time that accompanied it. Appearing to Barry Allen, alias The Flash, Steadfast showed him his true past, before enlisting his aid in finding out what was wrong with the Speed Force.

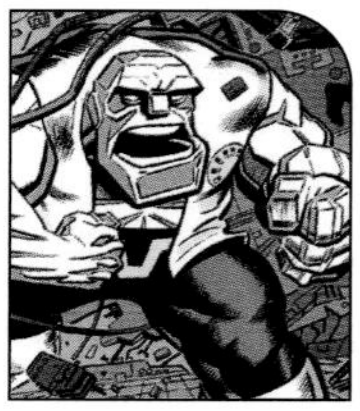

STRATA
DEBUT *Invasion!* #2 (Feb. 1989)
BASE The planet Cairn **ALLIES** L.E.G.I.O.N., R.E.B.E.L.S., InterC.E.P.T.
BACKGROUND Strata came from the planet Dryad, where the inhabitants were virtually invulnerable, rock-like humanoids. Strata teamed with Vril Dox to become a founding member of interstellar law-enforcement agency L.E.G.I.O.N. In an altercation with the bounty hunter Lobo, Strata's skin shattered, revealing that Strata was female. She served as chief training officer of L.E.G.I.O.N. and married team member and fellow Drayd, Garv. She later worked for the R.E.B.E.L.S. and InterC.E.P.T.

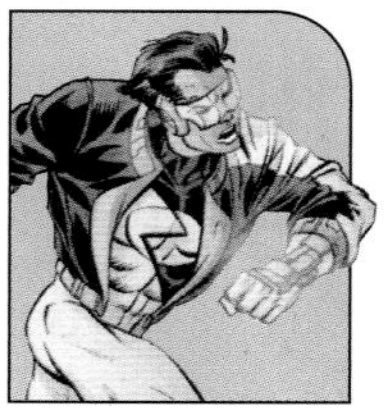

STRIKER Z
DEBUT *JLA* #61 (Feb. 2002)
REAL NAME Danny Tsang **BASE** San Francisco
BACKGROUND Stuntman Danny Tsang fell into a vat of experimental fuel-cell plasma. The liquid transformed him into a human battery, capable of fueling the hi-tech devices and flight jacket designed by his friend, a former S.T.A.R. Labs engineer named Charlie Lau. While wearing the jacket, Danny could generate sonic energy and shoot cannon blasts. As Striker Z, he worked for superpowered legal firm Power Company, and was badly hurt in a fight with Doctor Impossible.

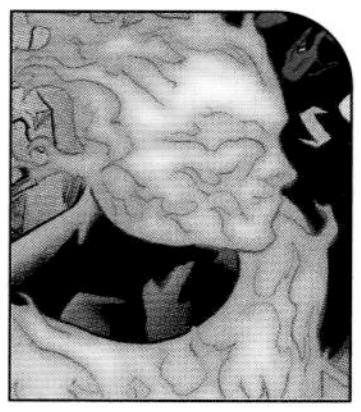

SUN BOY
DEBUT *Action Comics* #276 (May 1961)
REAL NAME Dirk Morgna **ALLIES** Legion of Super-Heroes
ENEMIES Superboy-Prime
BACKGROUND Dirk Morgna could generate and manipulate solar energy and was invited to join the Legion of Super-Heroes as Sun Boy. As Sun Boy, his entire body appeared to be aflame. Sun Boy can control and direct this energy as he chooses; however, he is afraid of the dark. He was killed by Superboy-Prime, but returned as a Black Lantern during the *Blackest Night* event.

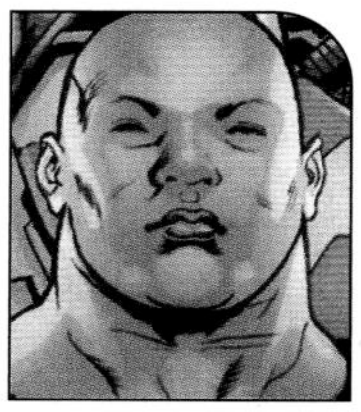

SUMO, SONNY
DEBUT *Forever People* (Vol. 1) #4 (Aug.–Sep. 1971)
ALLIES New Gods, Super Young Team **ENEMIES** Darkseid, Megayakuza
BACKGROUND Noble, super-strong prize fighter Sonny Sumo was unaware his brain held a portion of the Anti-Life Equation, which gave him power to defeat even almighty Darkseid. After freeing the Forever People, Darkseid blasted Sonny back to Feudal Japan. During *Final Crisis*, Sonny reappeared at a metahuman nightclub, where he swiftly dispatched a drunken cyborg called Megayakuza before joining Mister Miracle and the Super Young Team to oppose an Apokoliptian invasion of Earth.

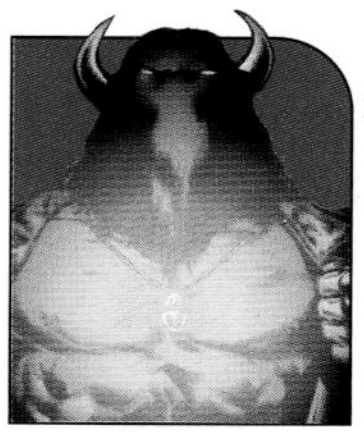

SUPER-CHIEF II
DEBUT *All-Star Western* #117 (Feb.–Mar. 1961)
REAL NAME Jon Standing Bear **BASE** North America
BACKGROUND Jon Standing Bear descended from Flying Stag, the greatest warrior of the Wolf Clan in the 1400s, who became the Supreme Chief of the Iroquois Nations. But none of that mattered to the jaded ex-con and war veteran until, at his father's funeral, he was given the Moon Stone, a family heirloom that bestowed longevity, super-strength, super-speed, and flight. Like his ancestor, Jon became Super Chief; he also helped found a new JLA with Firestorm, Firehawk, and Ambush Bug.

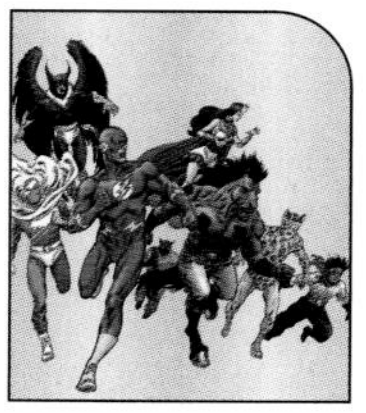

SUPER-MALON
DEBUT *The Flash Annual* #13 (Sep. 2000)
BASE Buenos Aires, Argentina **ALLIES** The Flash **ENEMIES** Gualicho
BACKGROUND Following in the footsteps of the Gaucho, a 1950s Argentinean hero, a team of metahumans came together to fight crime as Super Malon. Led by the sorceress Salamanca, the team included superspeedster El Yaguarette, swashbuckling Cimarron, wolf-like El Lobizon, wind-surfing Pampero, horse-like El Bagual, bird-like Cachiru, and master-thief Vizacacha. They joined The Flash to fight the wizard Gualicho, and helped Wonder Woman defeat The Cheetah.

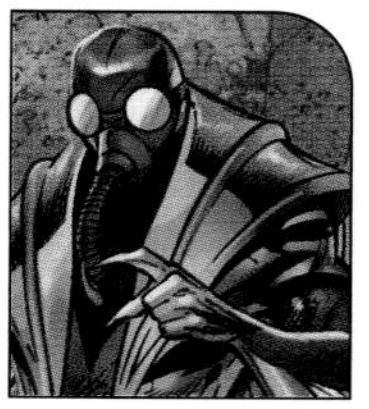

SWATT
DEBUT *Aquaman* (Vol. 7) #19 (Jun. 2013)
BASE Atlantis
BACKGROUND Swatt was perhaps the only resident of Atlantis unable to breathe underwater. When in Atlantis, he wore a pressure suit that allowed him to do this, even in the deepest parts of the ocean. His physiology led Swatt to spend a lot of time on the surface world, an activity that King Orm had forbidden. Like all Atlanteans, Swatt was super-strong; he also possessed the unique ability to control and discharge electricity, allowing him to harm enemies—or start a vehicle.

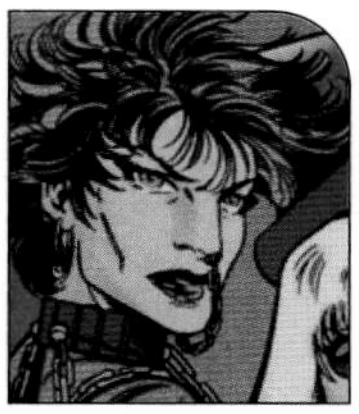

SYONIDE
DEBUT *Batman and the Outsiders* #19 (Mar. 1985)
ALLIES Tobias Whale, Fauna **ENEMIES** The Outsiders
BACKGROUND The first Syonide was a bounty hunter who worked for mob kingpin Tobias Whale. Wracked with guilt, he committed suicide. Whale recruited a mysterious, cold-hearted hitwoman to become the new Synonide and his personal bodyguard, but she died in a battle with the original Outsiders. A third Syonide joined Lady Eve's Strike Force Kobra, working with the villainess Fauna. She seemingly died fighting a reformed Outsiders, but was later seen as part of Queen Bee's team.

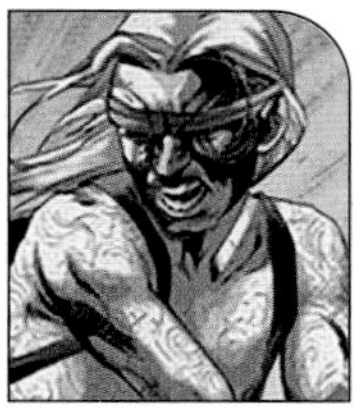

TANNARAK
DEBUT *Phantom Stranger* (Vol. 2) #10 (Nov.–Dec. 1970)
BASE New York City **ENEMIES** John Constantine
BACKGROUND Born over a century ago, Tannarak was an immortal and powerful sorcerer, able to project magical energy blasts from his hands. He was also a master of alchemy. He owned the interdimensional Bewitched nightclub in San Francisco, but he lost it to Brother Night. He was one of the founding members of the occult group, the Cold Flame, which often clashed with John Constantine.

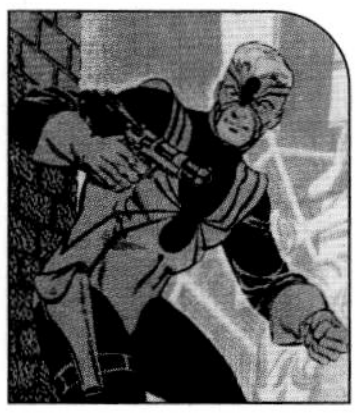

TARANTULA
DEBUT *Star-Spangled Comics* #1 (Oct. 1941)
REAL NAME Jonathan Law **BASE** Blüdhaven
BACKGROUND Jon Law was a crime novelist in the 1930s who wrote about Super Heroes and longed to become one himself. He began fighting crime as Tarantula, his name and weapons being inspired by his pet spider. His equipment included a web-gun that shot sticky webbing. A skilled acrobat, he joined the wartime heroes known as the All-Star Squadron. Decades later, he moved to Blüdhaven, where he was murdered by Blockbuster (Roland Desmond).

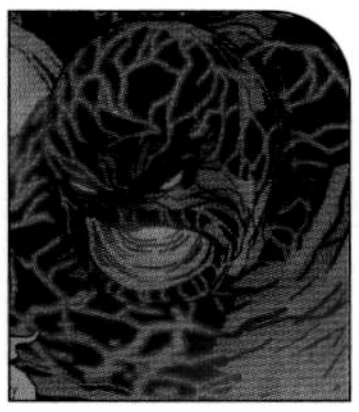

TAR PIT
DEBUT *The Flash* #174 (Jul. 2001)
REAL NAME Joseph "Joey" Monteleone **BASE** Keystone City
ENEMIES The Flash
BACKGROUND Armed robber Joey was in Iron Heights Penitentiary when he found he could transfer his consciousness outside the prison. His astral form became stuck in a vat of hot tar, turning him into Tar Pit, a large, sticky monster. As his human body sank into a coma, Tar Pit roamed Keystone City, causing trouble for The Flash.

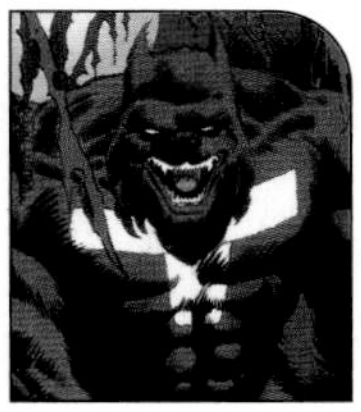

TASMANIAN DEVIL
DEBUT *Super Friends* #9 (Dec. 1977)
REAL NAME Hugh Dawkins **BASE** Sydney, Australia
ALLIES Global Guardians, Infinity Inc., JLA **ENEMIES** Prometheus
BACKGROUND Hugh Dawkins claimed his mother was a werewoman who was worshipped by his father in a Tasmanian devil cult. Hugh discovered that he had inherited his mother's powers and could transform into the hulking, super-strong Tasmanian Devil. He became a crime fighter in Australia, helping to form the Global Guardians, and later joined an Australian team called The Sleeping Soldiers.

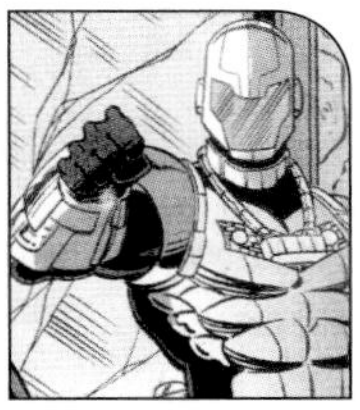

TECHNOCRAT
DEBUT *Outsiders* #1 (Nov. 1993)
REAL NAME Geoffrey Barron
ALLIES The Outsiders, Geo-Force **ENEMIES** Faust, Sanction
BACKGROUND Barron invented the Technocrat 2000 battle armor, which enabled flight and housed hi-tech weaponry. While demonstrating the suit in Markovia, Barron was attacked by the sorcerer Faust, who changed Barron's assistant, Charlie Wylde, into a bear-like beast. Barron became the hero Technocrat and, with Wylde, formed a new Outsiders team. After they disbanded, Technocrat joined Geo-Force.

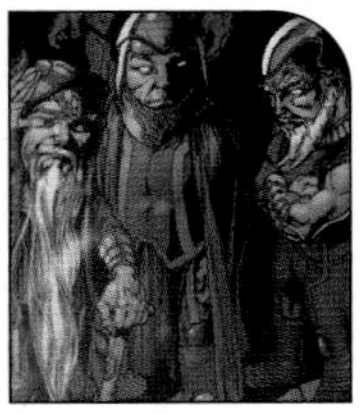

TEMPLAR GUARDIANS
DEBUT *Green Lantern Annual* #1 (Oct. 2012)
ALLIES Green Lantern Corps **ENEMIES** Guardians of the Universe
BACKGROUND The Templar Guardians were Reegal, Gurion, Paalko, Quaros, Yekop, and Zalla, a group of Oans who were members of the Guardians of the Universe. Their duty was to guard the crazed First Lantern, who had been sealed within the Chamber of Secrets to keep the universe safe. Reegal died in a battle with the Guardians of the Universe when they tried to free the First Lantern. The Templar Guardians were later elevated to the role of Guardians of the Green Lantern Corps.

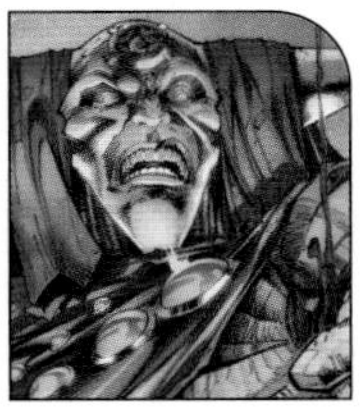

TEMPUS FUGINAUT
DEBUT *Sideways* #1 (Apr. 2018)
REAL NAME Unknown **BASE** Branefold Interior
ALLIES Sideways **ENEMIES** Dark Multiverse **BACKGROUND** Tempus was tasked by his fellow cosmic Fuginauts with terminating dimension-hopping hero Sideways, who had been judged a threat to space-time. However, when the dimensional lines began breaking down, Tempus enlisted Sideways' aid in sealing the disruptions. With the threat of the Dark Multiverse rising, Tempus guided former Flash Wally West to assume control of the Mobius Chair.

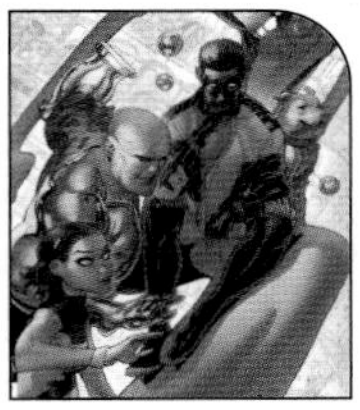

TERRIBLES, THE
DEBUT *The Terrifics* #19 (Oct. 2019)
BASE Htrae **ALLIES** Bizarro
ENEMIES The Terrifics
BACKGROUND On the backwards world of Htrae, Bizarro and inventor Mr. Terrible, frustrated at their inability to halt the tide of progress on their planet, set their sights instead on Earth. Forming a team composed of Bizarro analogues of Earth's Terrifics—Change-O-Shape-O, Disposable Man, and Figment Girl—these Terribles sought of a power source to transport their homeworld to the past.

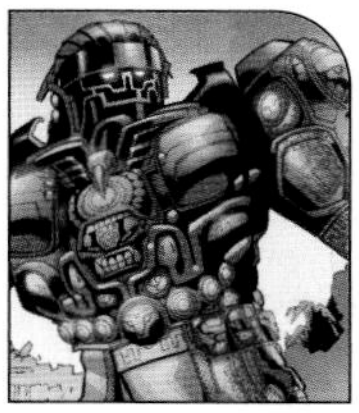

TEZUMAK
DEBUT *JLA* #66 (Jul. 2002)
BASE South America
ALLIES Justice League of America **ENEMIES** Gamemnae
BACKGROUND Tezumak was a pre-Aztec Mexican monk, whose suit of armor—oiled with sacrificial blood—enhanced his strength and endurance. He joined the sorceress Gamemnae to fight the Justice League of America, who had traveled back in time to search for Aquaman. When Tezumak learned that Gamemnae's real aim was to achieve power and exterminate the JLA, he sacrificed his life to defeat her.

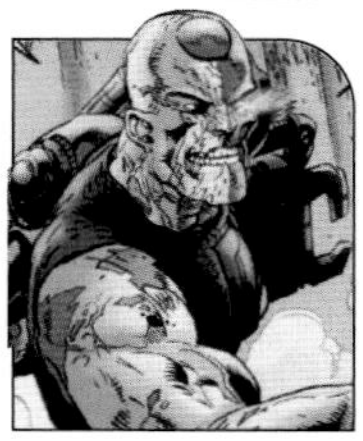

THAROK
DEBUT *Adventure Comics* (Vol. 1) #352 (Jan. 1967)
BASE 31st-century Zadron, mobile **ENEMIES** Legion of Super-Heroes, Polar Boy **BACKGROUND** Tharok was a thief until a caper went wrong and half his body disintegrated. A robotic frame was constructed to replace the missing parts of his skeleton that also amplified Tharok's intelligence. Tharok convinced four of his criminal confederates to team up with him as a Fatal Five, whose combined power could control the universe. After tapping the power of the Promethean Giants and ascending to a higher form, Tharok was finally contained—frozen by Polar Boy.

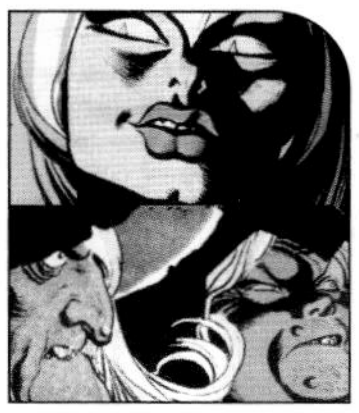

THREE WITCHES, THE
DEBUT *The Witching Hour* #1 (Feb.–Mar. 1969)
BACKGROUND The Three Witches were immortal goddesses who appeared in various guises. Possessing unlimited supernatural powers, they were aware of every event on the physical and metaphysical planes. They represented three aspects of one being: the mother (Mildred), the crone (Mordred), and the maiden (Cynthia). Their magical powers were strongest at midnight, and they would answer any three questions if asked as part of a ritual. During the Imperiex War, the Three Witches assumed the roles of the Greek Fates to destroy Themyscira.

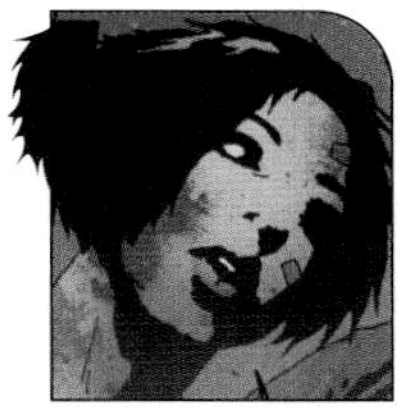

TIG
DEBUT *I, Vampire* #3 (Jan. 2012)
REAL NAME Tig Rafelson
ALLIES Andrew Bennett **ENEMIES** Mary, Queen of Blood
BACKGROUND Tig was a 16-year-old vampire hunter when she met vampire Andrew Bennett, who, with his friend John Troughton, was searching for Mary, Queen of Blood and her gang. Tig attacked Bennett and, although she learned he was not dangerous, remained distrustful. Despite her skepticism, Tig joined the hunt for Mary. She later revealed that her father, who had become a vampire, had tried to kill her.

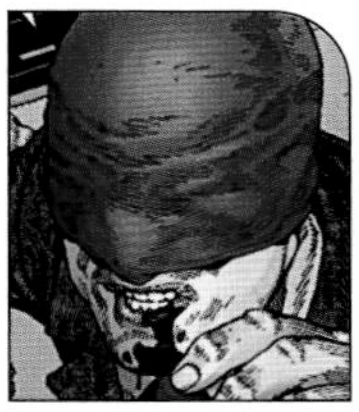

TIGER SHARK
DEBUT *Detective Comics* #878 (Aug. 2011)
REAL NAME Unknown **BASE** Gotham City
ALLIES The Penguin, Killer Croc **ENEMIES** Batman, Nightwing
BACKGROUND Gotham pirate Tiger Shark came to prominence when he murdered the assistant of Sonia Zucco—daughter of Tony Zucco, the mobster who killed Dick "Nightwing" Grayson's parents—and stuffed her corpse inside a killer whale. Tiger Shark became a fixture of the Gotham City crime scene. Later, dosed with the Blockbuster serum, a monstrous Tiger Shark fought Nightwing.

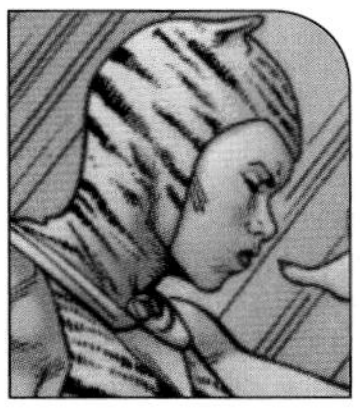

TIGRESS
DEBUT *Sensation Comics* #68 (Aug. 1947)
REAL NAME Paula Brooks **BASE** New York City
ENEMIES Axis Amerika, Justice Society **BACKGROUND** Adopting the crossbow-wielding costumed identity Tigress to get close to her idol, the All-Star Squadron's Manhunter (Paul Kirk), Paula Brooks joined World War II heroes the Young All-Stars. Struck down in battle with Axis Amerika, she revived a changed woman, becoming the villain Huntress. She partnered with Sportsmaster, the pair producing a daughter, Artemis Crock, who inherited the Tigress mantle.

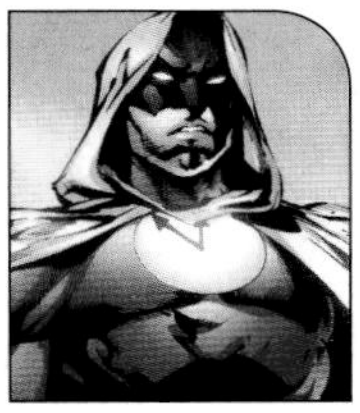

TIME COMMANDER
DEBUT *The Brave and the Bold* #59 (Apr.–May 1965)
REAL NAME John Starr **BASE** Gotham City
ALLIES Time Foes **ENEMIES** Batman, Green Lantern, Team Titans
BACKGROUND Starr developed a time-shifting hourglass, which he used, unsuccessfully, to battle Batman and Green Lantern. He later joined other time-themed villains—Chronos, Clock King, and Calendar Man—to form the Time Foes. He died fighting a teen team from the future. Starr's protégé, Sterling Fry, became the new Time Commander and fought Hourman to obtain the tachyon particles in the hero's hourglass.

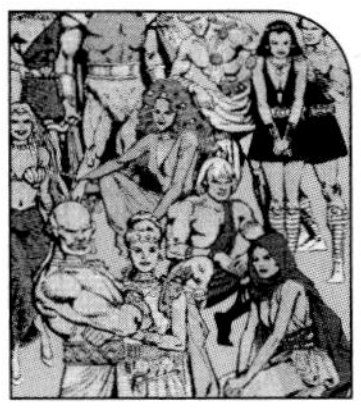

TITANS OF MYTH
DEBUT *New Teen Titans* (Vol. 1) #11 (Sep. 1981) **BASE** Tartarus
ENEMIES Gods of Olympus, Teen Titans, Wonder Woman, Hindu Gods
BACKGROUND The Titans are a primordial group of extradimensional entities who dominated parts of Earth in pre-history. Attaching themselves to the tribes of ancient Greece, they fed off the enforced adoration of mortals. Zeus exiled the Titans and created his own pantheon: the Greek Gods. Centuries later, the Titan Cronus spawned a newer, deadlier family, employing them to attack Olympus. They were defeated by Gaea, Wonder Woman, and the Greek and Hindu pantheons.

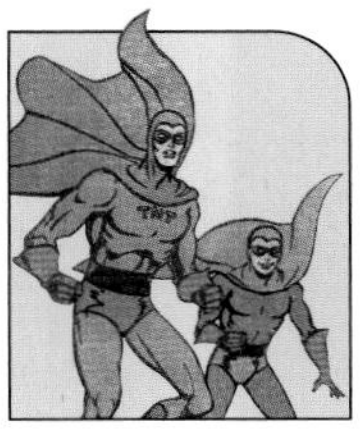

TNT AND DAN THE DYNA-MITE
DEBUT *Star-Spangled Comics* #7 (Apr. 1942)
REAL NAMES Thomas "Tex" N. Thomas (TNT); Daniel Dunbar (Dyna-Mite)
ALLIES All-Star Squadron, Old Justice **ENEMIES** Nazi forces
BACKGROUND After an experiment went awry, science teacher Thomas and his star pupil Dan became TNT and Dan the Dyna-Mite, atomic-powered heroes able to hurl energy bolts from their hands. They joined the All-Star Squadron during World War II and fought together until TNT was killed by Nazi saboteurs. Dan later joined the Young All-Stars and, decades after the war, resurfaced as a member of Old Justice.

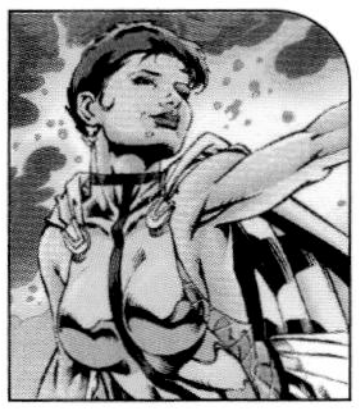

TOMORROW WOMAN
DEBUT *JLA* #5 (May 1997)
REAL NAME Clara Kendall **BASE** JLA Watchtower
ALLIES JLA, Hourman **ENEMIES** Professor Ivo, T.O. Morrow, Taint
BACKGROUND Tomorrow Woman was an android created by Professor Ivo and T.O. Morrow to infiltrate the Justice League of America. With superpowers including telekinesis and telepathy, she soon became invaluable to the team. Instead of destroying the JLA, she developed a conscience, disobeyed her villainous creators, and sacrificed herself to save the team.

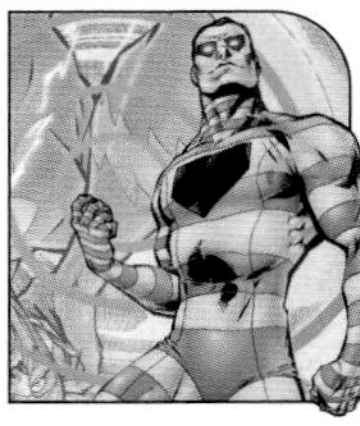

TOP, THE
DEBUT *The Flash* #122 (Aug. 1961)
REAL NAME Roscoe Dillon **BASE** Central City/Keystone City
ALLIES Mirror Master **ENEMIES** The Flash
BACKGROUND Claiming that his superpowers came from the Speed Force, the criminal The Top could generate and control centrifugal force, spinning at incredible speeds. He could also lift or smash objects with his spinning powers. He became an enemy of The Flash and joined other Super-Villains to form The Rogues criminal gang.

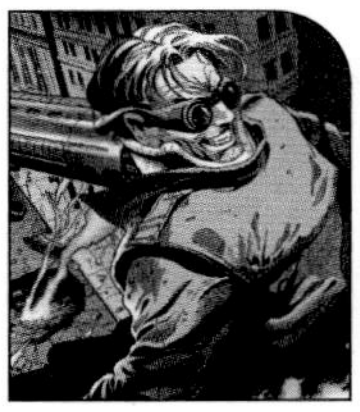

TORQUE
DEBUT *Nightwing* #1 (Oct. 1996)
REAL NAME Dudley Soames **BASE** Blüdhaven
ALLIES Blockbuster **ENEMIES** Nightwing
BACKGROUND Soames was one of Blüdhaven's most corrupt cops, working secretly for the mobster Blockbuster. After Blockbuster broke Soames' neck, twisting it right around, Soames vowed revenge and became the villain Torque. Defeated by Nightwing, he was sent to prison, where he enlisted the aid of the vigilante Nite-Wing to escape. Soames planned to kill his new partner, but instead Nite-Wing murdered Torque.

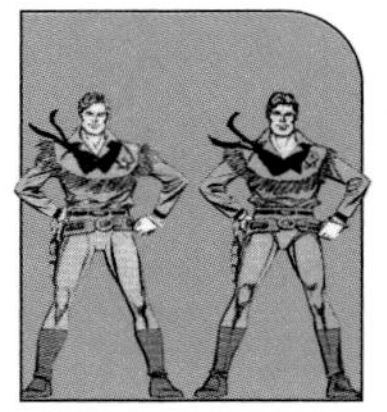

TRIGGER TWINS
DEBUT *All-Star Western* #58 (Apr.–May 1951)
REAL NAME Walter and Wayne Trigger
BASE Rocky City
BACKGROUND Walt and Wayne Trigger were identical twin brothers who fought for law and order in the Old West. Walt was Rocky City's sheriff, and Wayne ran the general store. When needed, Wayne secretly took Walt's identity and even rode a twin of his horse. Two modern-day Trigger Twins, Tom and Tad Trigger, were Gotham City criminals who fought Batman, Robin, Nighthawk, and The Flash.

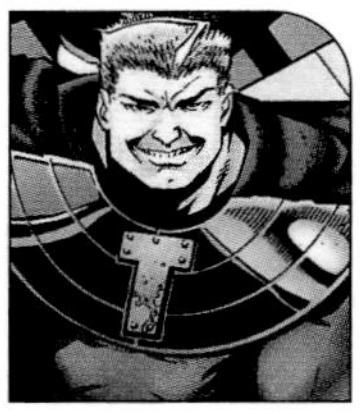

TRIUMPH
DEBUT *Justice League America* #91 (Aug. 1994)
REAL NAME William MacIntyre **BASE** JLA Watchtower
BACKGROUND Triumph was a Super Hero who controlled the electromagnetic spectrum. He joined the JLA to battle the alien Plasma-Man, directing all his energy at Plasma's spacecraft. The resulting power surge damaged the space/time continuum, and Triumph disappeared, irrevocably altering history. He reemerged a decade later and sold his soul to the demon Neron to regain his lost time. He then came under the influence of an evil Thunderbolt named Lkz and died in a battle with the Justice League.

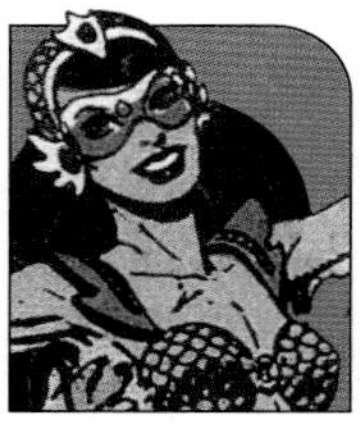

TSUNAMI
DEBUT *All-Star Squadron* #33 (May 1984)
REAL NAME Miya Shimada **BASE** San Francisco, California
ALLIES Young All-Stars, Aquaman **ENEMIES** Axis forces, Rhombus
BACKGROUND Shimada was a Japanese American who could control water. Disgusted by the prejudice she faced in the US during World War II, she became Tsunami and helped the Japanese Navy. After several battles against the All-Star Squadron, she switched sides and joined the Young All-Stars to fight the Japanese military. After the war, she and the sorcerer Atlan had a daughter who became the aquatic hero Deep Blue.

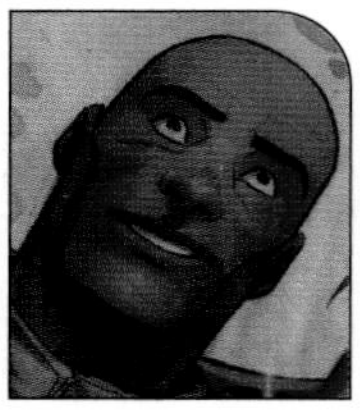

TURBINE
DEBUT *The Flash* #7 (May 2012)
REAL NAME Roscoe Hynes **BASE** Keystone City **ALLIES** The Rogues
ENEMIES Gorilla Grodd
BACKGROUND Hynes was a World War II Tuskegee Airman who became trapped in the Speed Force for seven decades and gained speed powers. The Flash's arrival in the Speed Force pulled Hynes to present-day Keystone City. Taking the name Turbine, he fought alongside the Rogues during the gorilla invasion of the city. After landing in prison, Turbine was murdered by Captain Cold.

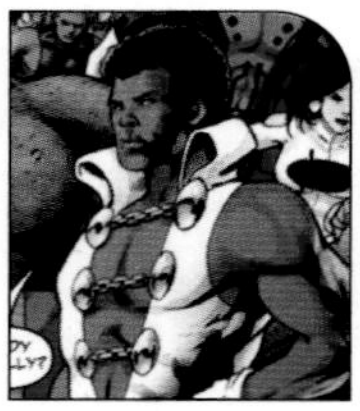

TYROC
DEBUT *Superboy* #216 (Apr. 1976)
REAL NAME Troy Stewart **BASE** Marzal
AFFILIATION Legion of Super-Heroes **ENEMIES** Betas
BACKGROUND The champion of dimension-shifting island Marzal, Troy Stewart generated sonic screams that could variously create anti-gravity fields, explosions, teleportation, and other effects. He encountered the Legion of Super-Heroes when his island appeared in their future. Initially suspicious, Stewart joined for a time before returning to his responsibilities on Marzal.

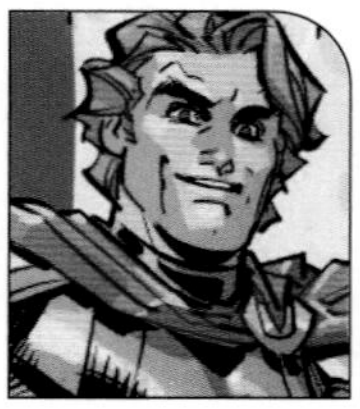

ULTRAA
DEBUT *Justice League of America* #153 (Apr. 1978)
CURRENT VERSION *The Multiversity: Ultra Comics* #1 (Mar. 2015)
ALLIES Queen Maxima **ENEMIES** Captain Atom, Ultra
BACKGROUND A warlord from the planet Almerac, Ultraa arrived on Earth in search of his consort Lady Maxima. When she bestowed her favors on Captain Atom instead, a brutal battle ensued that Ultraa appeared to win. Despite this, he was rejected by Maxima and sent home. Ultraa later attempted to seize the crown of Almerac. With Wonder Woman's aid, Maxima was able to thwart this endeavor.

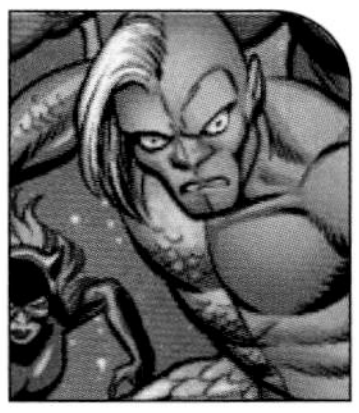

ULTRA THE MULTI-ALIEN
DEBUT *Mystery in Space* #103 (Nov. 1965)
REAL NAME Arn Ace **BASE** The Moon of Thalsalla
BACKGROUND Arn Ace was piloting a tourist space cruiser when he was caught in the magnetic field of a comet. The radiation forced him into suspended animation, and he was whisked away to another solar system. After crash-landing, Arn was attacked by four aliens, each wielding a different experimental weapon. These weapons caused Arn to mutate, taking on the properties of each alien that fired upon him. Unable to transform back, he became Ultra, the Multi-Alien.

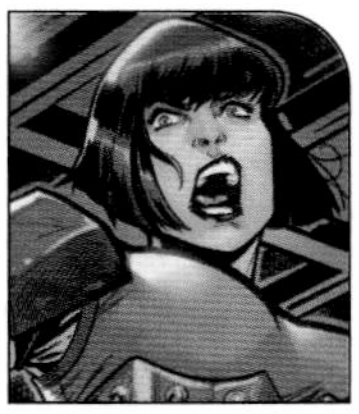

VALDA
DEBUT *Arak, Son of Thunder* #3 (Nov. 1981)
BASE Aix-le-Chapelle, Frankland, 8th century
ALLIES Arak **ENEMIES** Baledor, Angelica
BACKGROUND Valda, aka Iron Maiden, was one of the bravest knights in 8th-century Europe. After her mother's death, she was tutored by the sorcerer Malagigi and trained in swordfighting by the ghost of Amadis of Gaul. Knighted after defeating her uncle, Rinaldo, Valda teamed up with Arak, Son of Thunder, with whom she fell in love. Valda later traveled to the present and joined Shadowpact to fight The Spectre.

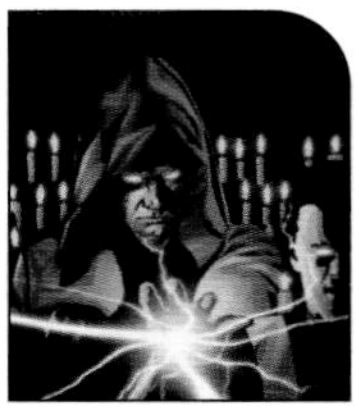

VALIDUS
DEBUT *Adventure Comics* #352 (Jan. 1967)
REAL NAME Garridan Ranzz **BASE** mobile
AFFILIATION Fatal Five **ENEMIES** Legion of Super-Heroes
BACKGROUND One of the galaxy's most dangerous beings, Validus the child of Legionnaires Lightning Lad and Saturn Girl. Abducted by Darkseid, baby Garridan Ranzz was propelled back in time and mutated into the monstrous Validus. With his allies in the Fatal Five, Validus, aka the Lord of Lightning, frequently fought the Legion. Eventually, Darkseid's curse was broken, restoring Garridan Ranzz.

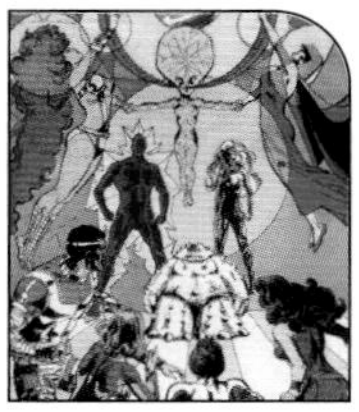

VANGUARD
DEBUT *The New Teen Titans* (Vol. 2) Annual #1 (1985)
BASE Mobile **NOTABLE MEMBERS** Anti-Matterman, Black Nebula, Drone, Scanner, Solaar, White Dwarf **ENEMIES** Brainiac
BACKGROUND The Vanguard is a team of superpowered beings, helping worlds with their cosmic powers. Mistaking Superman for a threat, the Vanguard tried to capture him. The Teen Titans came to Superman's aid, but quickly realized that this Man of Steel was a robot duplicate. The real Superman had been captured by Brainiac. With help from the Teen Titans, the Vanguard defeated Brainiac.

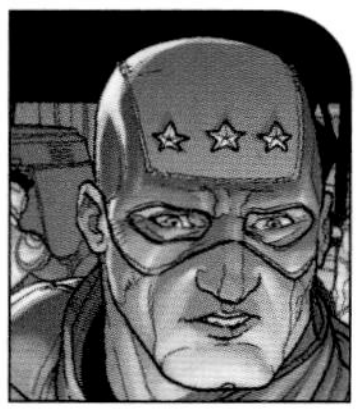

VETERAN
DEBUT *Robin* #138 (Jul. 2005)
REAL NAME Nathan Howe
ALLIES US Military, Superman, Robin **ENEMIES** The Auctioneer
BACKGROUND The Veteran was a legendary (and seemingly indestructible) Super Hero, rumored to have fought in all of America's wars, and earning the rank of General in Operation Desert Storm. A superb combatant, marksman, and strategist, the Veteran commanded his own elite squad of solders to handle everything from street crime to metahuman threats. He also fought alongside Robin and Superman.

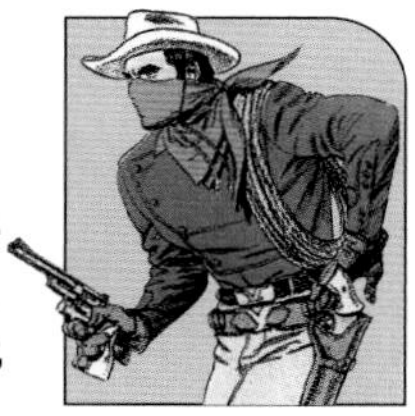

VIGILANTE I
DEBUT *Action Comics* #42 (Nov. 1941)
REAL NAME Greg Sanders **BASE** New York City
ALLIES Stuff, the Chinatown Kid, El Diablo **ENEMIES** The Dummy, Sheeda
BACKGROUND When Greg Sanders' father was killed by bandits, he left a career as "the Prairie Troubadour" to become the crime fighter Vigilante. Moving to New York, he partnered with young marital artist Stuff, the Chinatown Kid, and even teamed with Superman to track down a werewolf. He later formed a new Seven Soldiers of Victory team to fight the far-future Sheeda, but they were massacred in the battle.

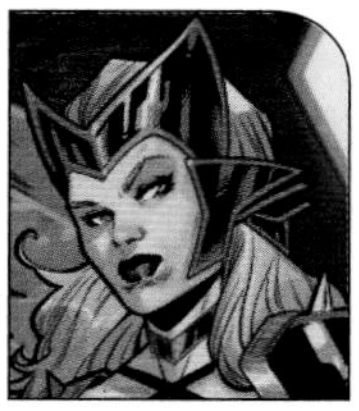

VON GUNTHER, PAULA
DEBUT *Wonder Woman Annual* #3 (Apr. 2019)
ALLIES Sons of Liberty, Valkyries
ENEMIES Amazons, Wonder Woman
BACKGROUND As a child, Paula von Gunther was rescued by Wonder Woman from a violent group known as the Sons of Liberty. Growing up to become a member of A.R.G.U.S., Paula discovered that she was a descendant of a faction of Valkyries that warred with the Amazons. She soon became the villain known as Warmaster, so that she might battle her former friend and savior.

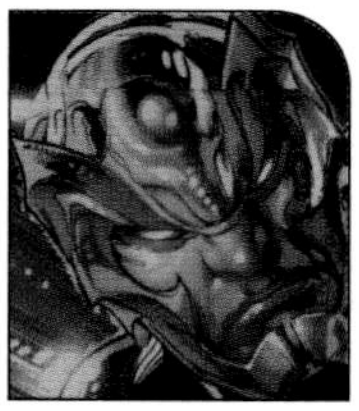

VOSTOK-X
DEBUT *Aquaman* #7 (May 2012)
ALLIES The Others, Aquaman **ENEMIES** KGBeast, Black Manta
BACKGROUND Vostok was a Russian cosmonaut-trainee who spent years in an isolation chamber preparing for space travel. When Russia's space program was shelved, Vostok fled to Siberia and aided Aquaman against Black Manta. Vostok later donned an Atlantean helmet that granted him the ability to survive without food, sleep, oxygen, or water. He joined Aquaman and the Others to fight the KGBeast, and later other Russian metahumans in the The People's Heroes.

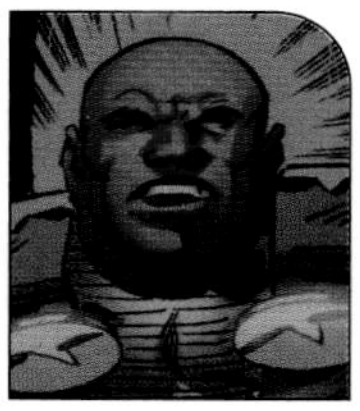

VYKIN BALDAUR
DEBUT *Forever People* #1 (Feb.–Mar. 1971)
ALLIES Forever People, Highfather
ENEMIES Darkseid, Mantis, Guy Gardner
BACKGROUND Vykin was a Warrior Class 7 New God, raised on New Genesis with his twin sister Serafina. A highly skilled combatant, he also possessed super-strength and could control his density. Vykin traveled to Earth to fight alongside the heroic Forever People. Though Vykin had a somewhat testy relationship with some members of the team, he eagerly joined the battle against the Red Lantern Guy Gardner.

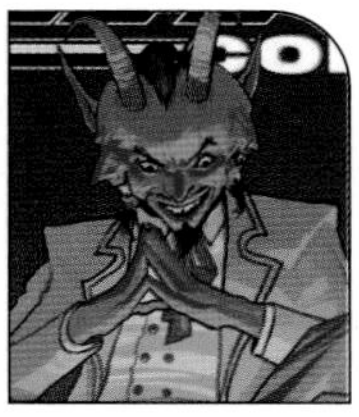

VYNDKTVX
DEBUT *Action Comics* #1 (Nov. 2011)
ALLIES Anti-Superman Army **ENEMIES** Superman, Mr. Mxyzptlk
BACKGROUND Vyndktvx was an imp in the 5th dimension and the court magician of King Brpxz. When the king chose Mr. Mxyzptlk as his favorite and permitted him to marry his daughter, Vyndktvx flew into a rage and vowed to kill his rival. He killed the king by mistake and trapped Mr. Mxyzptlk in a glass coffin. Vyndktvx then attacked Superman several times, gathering Super-Villains to form an Anti-Superman Army. He failed and was banished to a 5th-dimension prison for eternity.

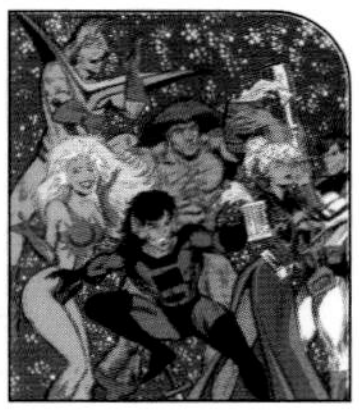

WANDERERS, THE
DEBUT *Adventure Comics* (Vol. 1) #375 (Dec. 1968)
MEMBERS Aviax (formerly Ornitho); Dartalon (formerly Dartag); Re-Animage (formerly Immorto); Psyche; Quantum Queen; Celebrand (original team leader)
A Super Hero team from the 30th century transformed into villains after exposure to the Nefar Nebula, the Wanderers stole the Seven Stones of Alactos and battled former friends the Legion of Super-Heroes. The team were later mysteriously found. The Controller Clonus cloned new bodies for most of them. They worked for the United Planets, but disappeared while exploring a strange anomaly in space.

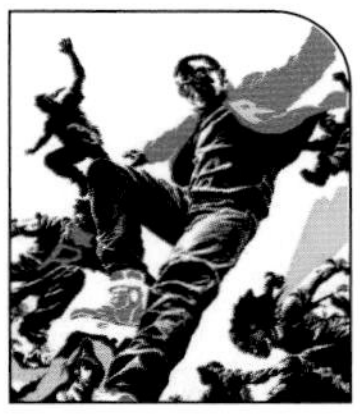

WE ARE ROBIN
DEBUT Convergence: World's Finest #2 (Jul. 2015)
BASE Gotham City **MEMBERS** Duke Thomas; Daxton Chill (DaxAtax); Andre "Dre" Cipriani (Dre-b-Robbin); Isabella Ortiz (Robina); Troy Walker (The Troy Wonder); Riko Sheridan (R-iko) **BACKGROUND** The Robin movement began when Batman was thought dead after a battle with The Joker. James Gordon took over the role of Batman; Alfred Pennyworth recruited heroic teens as Robins. The Court of Owls caged the teens, but the real Robins (Damian Wayne, Dick Grayson, Red Hood, and Red Robin) saved the kids and helped them fight back.

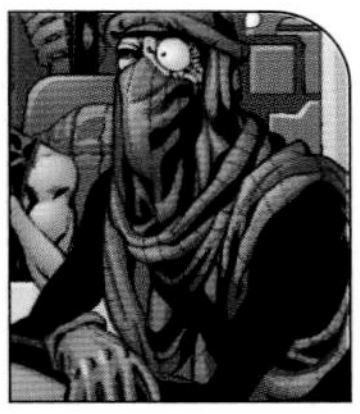

WEIRD, THE
DEBUT *The Weird* #1 (Apr. 1988)
ALLIES Stormwatch, Justice League
ENEMIES Macrolatts
BACKGROUND The Weird came from an alternate dimension inhabited by Zarolatts, a race of largely passive energy beings. When their tyrannical overlords, the Macrolatts, decided to attack Earth, the Weird intervened and animated a human corpse, enabling the Weird to alter his own molecular density and that of anything he touched. He later joined heroes like the Engineer and Hellstrike to form the team Stormwatch.

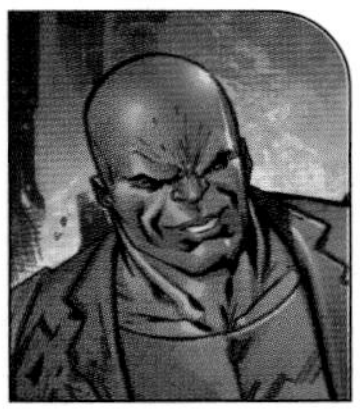

WHALE, TOBIAS
DEBUT *Black Lightning* #1 (Apr. 1977)
REAL NAME Tobias Whale **BASE** Cleveland
AFFILIATION The 100 **ENEMIES** Black Lighting
BACKGROUND The boss of the Metropolis branch of organized crime group the 100, Tobias Whale found himself on the wrong end of justice courtesy of new hero Black Lightning—alias schoolteacher Jefferson Pierce—when Whale killed one of Pierce's students. Becoming a perennial nemesis of Black Lightning, Whale was later revealed as the nephew of the genuine Whale, who operated in Cleveland.

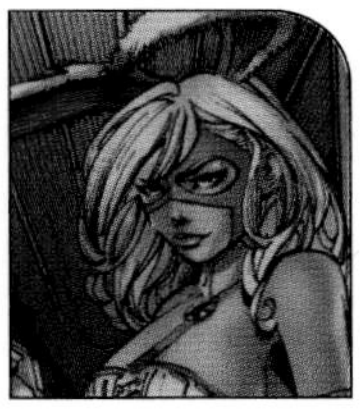

WHITE RABBIT
DEBUT *Batman: The Dark Knight* #1 (Nov. 2011)
REAL NAME Jaina Hudson **BASE** Gotham City
ALLIES Clayface, Bane **ENEMIES** Batman
BACKGROUND Jaina Hudson was a prominent Gotham City socialite who dated Bruce Wayne. She was also the mysterious White Rabbit, and seemed to be able to physically separate her two personas. Batman first encountered White Rabbit when she freed inmates from Arkham Asylum. He discovered she was working with the villain Clayface, and she almost managed to inject the Dark Knight with a dangerous toxin.

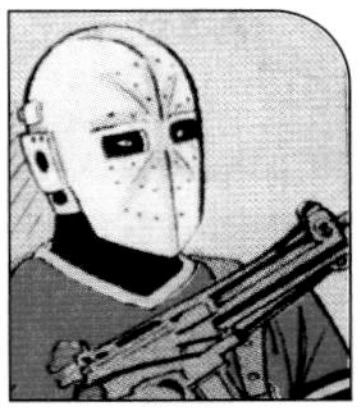

WILD DOG
DEBUT *Wild Dog* #1 (Sep. 1987)
REAL NAME Jack Wheeler **BASE** Quad Cities, Iowa
BACKGROUND Jack Wheeler faced several tragedies, first when his fellow US Marine troops were killed by a terrorist bomb in Beirut and, later, when a mobster murdered his girlfriend. Returning to his hometown of Quad Cities, Wheeler donned a hockey mask and a State U. college shirt. Armed with machine guns and taser-shooting gloves, he became the hero Wild Dog. The Quad Cities police were not happy about Wild Dog's vigilante crime-fighting methods, but he soon became a local hero.

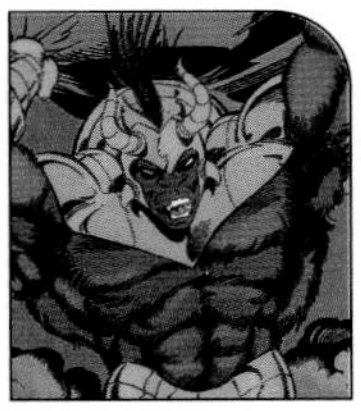

WILDEBEEST
DEBUT *The New Teen Titans* #36 (Oct. 1987)
BASE Science City, Russia
ALLIES New Titans, Cyborg **ENEMIES** Superboy-Prime
BACKGROUND The Wildebeest Society was a group of super-strong villains. The Teen Titan Jericho took control of the Society after he was possessed by a demon, and initiated the creation of human/animal hybrids as hosts for the group. The Society was destroyed, but one member, Baby Wildebeest, survived and joined the New Titans. Wildebeest was later murdered by Superboy of Earth Prime.

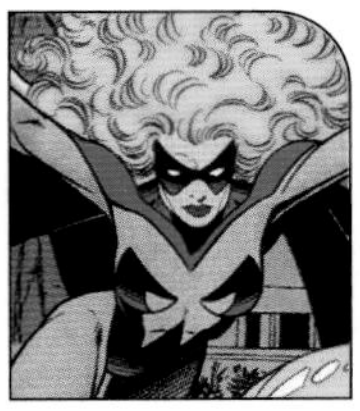

WINDFALL
DEBUT *Batman and the Outsiders* #9 (Apr. 1984)
REAL NAME Wendy Jones **BASE** Los Angeles, California
ALLIES The Outsiders, Suicide Squad **ENEMIES** Kobra
BACKGROUND Wendy Jones was a metahuman able to generate and control winds, from breezes to tornadoes. Unlike her sister, the water-wielding villain New Wave, Wendy fought for justice with the Outsiders. Duped into joining Strike Force Kobra, Windfall eventually realized her mistake and rejoined the Outsiders. She was later recruited to the Suicide Squad and died in action in the Middle East.

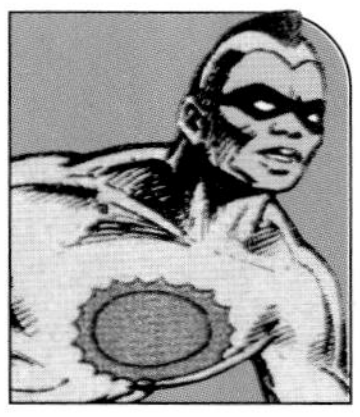

WING
DEBUT *Detective Comics* #20 (Oct. 1938)
ALLIES Crimson Avenger, Seven Soldiers of Victory **ENEMIES** Nebula Man
BACKGROUND Wing was a Chinese immigrant to the US in the 1930s, who worked for ace reporter Lee Travis, secretly the crime-fighting Crimson Avenger. Donning his own costume, Wing and Travis joined the All-Star Squadron during World War II, and Wing became the unofficial eighth member of the heroic team known as the Seven Soldiers of Victory. In a battle with the cosmic being Nebula Man, Wing sacrificed his life to save the Seven Soldiers, who were scattered across time.

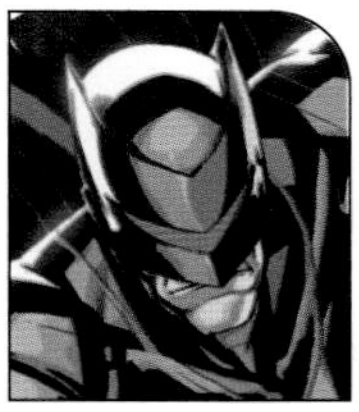

WINGMAN
DEBUT *Batman* #85 (Jun. 1951)
REAL NAME Benedict Rundstrom **BASE** Sweden
AFFILIATION Club of Heroes, Black Glove **ENEMIES** Batman
BACKGROUND When billionaire philanthropist John Mayhew assembled the Batman-inspired International Club of Heroes, Rundstrom—Wingman—was among their number. Years later, he was killed by an accomplice after joining the Black Glove criminal organization. After Rundstrom's death, the identity of Wingman was briefly assumed by Jason Todd (aka Robin/the Red Hood), then by Todd's father, Willis.

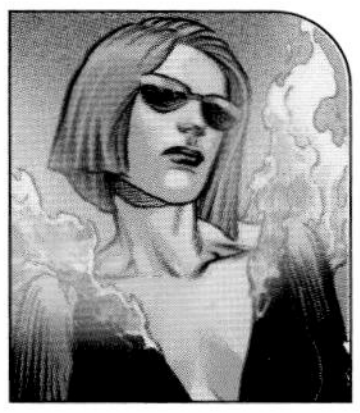

WITCHFIRE
DEBUT *JLA* #61 (Feb. 2002)
REAL NAME Rebecca Carstairs **BASE** San Francisco, California
ALLIES Power Company **ENEMIES** Nekron, Seven Deadly Sins
BACKGROUND As a youngster, Rebecca found a book of spells, inspiring her to dabble in magic. As an adult, she took the name Witchfire. After accidentally summoning a demon, she vowed to refine her abilities. She joined the Super Hero team Power Company, but discovered she was a homunculus, a magically created artificial being. She died at the hands of Hecate while visiting the Oblivion Bar.

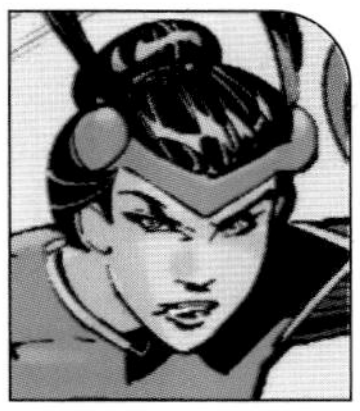

WONDER-WOMAN OF CHINA
DEBUT *New Super-Man* #1 (Sep. 2016)
REAL NAME Peng Dailan **BASE** Shanghai
AFFILIATION Justice League of China **ENEMIES** Fahai
BACKGROUND Long ago, the legendary creature Green Snake was trapped in stone by the turtle Fahai after achieving human form. Centuries later, she was freed by Dr. Omen of the Ministry of Self-Reliance, who gave her the name Peng Deilan. She became the Wonder-Woman of China, forming the Justice League of China with Super-Man, Bat-Man, and other heroes.

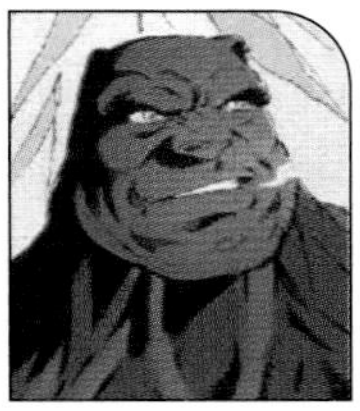

WYLDE
DEBUT *Outsiders: Alpha* #1 (Nov. 1993)
REAL NAME Charlie Wylde **BASE** Los Angeles
AFFILIATION Outsiders **ENEMIES** Roderick
BACKGROUND The bodyguard of millionaire Geoffrey Barron—inventor of the Technocrat armor—Charlie Wylde accompanied his boss to Markovia, where they were attacked by a bear. Mortally wounded, Wylde was merged with the bear by the mage Sebastian Faust. Wylde joined Faust's Outsiders, but struggled to control his bestial nature. Eventually he became all bear, and was left in the local zoo.

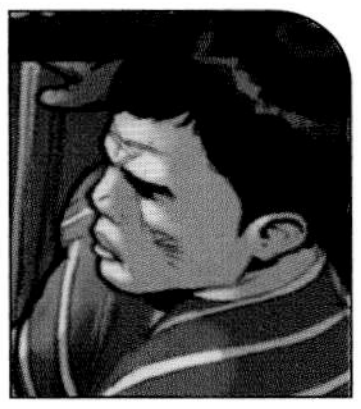

YO-YO
DEBUT *Flashpoint* (Vol. 2) #1 (Jul. 2011)
REAL NAME Chang Jie-Ru **EYES** Brown **HAIR** Black
ALLIES Suicide Squad, Harley Quinn **ENEMIES** Basilisk, Red Orchid
Chang Jie-Ru was a convict able to increase or decrease his body mass who joined the Suicide Squad to shorten his sentence. Yo-Yo chose to sacrifice his life by stretching his neck around his sister, the crime boss Red Orchid. The convict pleaded with Deadshot to detonate a nanobomb that was implanted beneath his skin. Deadshot triggered the bomb, and both Yo-Yo and Red Orchid were killed.

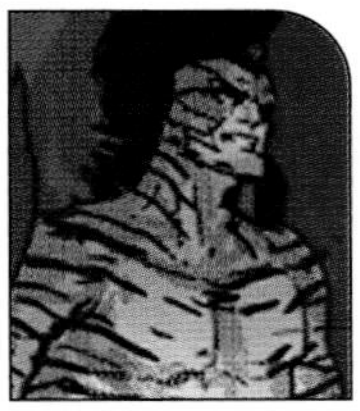

ZEBRA-MAN
DEBUT *Detective Comics* #275 (Jan. 1960)
REAL NAME Jacob Baker **BASE** Gotham City
ALLIES Kobra **ENEMIES** Batman, Outsiders **BACKGROUND** Inventor Jacob Baker transformed himself into Zebra-Man by bathing himself in rays from his magnetic force machine, granting him a striped appearance and magnetic powers, which he controlled via a special belt. Committing a series of robberies, he was apprehended by Batman. Later, would-be world conqueror Kobra duplicated Baker's process to create a second Zebra-Man for his Strike Force team.

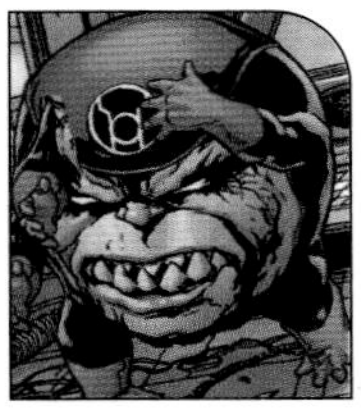

ZILIUS ZOX
DEBUT *Final Crisis: Rage of the Red Lanterns* #1 (Dec. 2008)
ALLIES Red Lanterns **ENEMIES** Sinestro
BACKGROUND The Red Lantern of Sector 3544 was Zilius Zox, a savage, hate-filled creature who pledged allegiance to Atrocitus and swore revenge against Sinestro and the Sinestro Corps. Zox notoriously murdered the Sinestro Corps Soldier of Sector 2332 by crushing him within his giant mouth and then seemingly swallowing parts of his body. He possessed superstrength and super-speed, and his Red Lantern Ring gave him the rage-fueled powers of flight and energy projection.

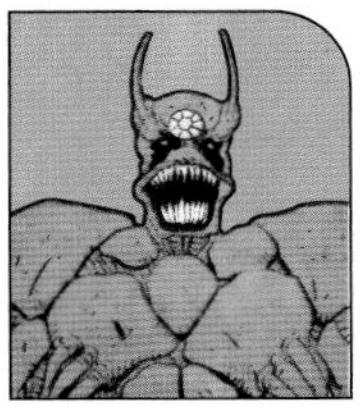

ZUGGERNAUT
DEBUT *Firestorm the Nuclear Man* #66 (Dec. 1987)
ENEMIES Firestorm, Soyuz
BACKGROUND Zuggernaut was a shape-shifting, symbiotic alien that crash-landed in Russia and then merged its monstrous body with a small-time criminal, Matvei Rodor. Zuggernaut tried to kill one of Rodor's enemies, a prosecutor named Soliony, but was thwarted by the American hero Firestorm. Zuggernaut returned to battle the Russian Super Hero team Soyuz, but was again defeated by Firestorm, who used the creature's own explosive energies to defeat it.

INDEX

ACKNOWLEDGMENTS

Dusty Abell, Dan Abnett, Jerry Acerno, Daniel Acuña, Vincenzo Acunzo, Art Adams, Neal Adams, Dan Adkins, Charlie Adlard, Jack Adler, Kalman Andrasofszky, Ron Adrian, Ian Akin, Christian Alamy, Gerry Alanguilan, Oclair Albert, Jeff Albrecht, Rafael Albuquerque, Juan Albarran, Oclair Albert, Alfredo Alcala, Enrique Alcatena, Pascal Alixe, Lee Allred, Laura Allred, Michael Allred, Bob Almond, Marlo Alquiza, Sal Amendola, Brad Anderson, Brent Anderson, Murphy Anderson, Mirka Andolfo, Kaare Andrews, Mark Andreyko, Ross Andru, Roge Antonia, Jim Aparo, Sergio Aragones, Renato Arlem, Paolo Armitano, Jason Armstrong, Ulises Arreola, Tom Artis, Stan Aschmeier, Mahmud Asrar, Michael Atiyeh, Derec Aucoin, Terry Austin, Brandon Badeaux, Mark Badger, Mark Bagley, Bernard Baily, Michael Bair, Kyle Baker, Jim Balent, Darryl Banks, Matt Banning, Carlo Barberi, Rain Baredo, David Baron, Dell Barras, Mike Barreiro, Eduardo Barreto, Al Barrionuevo, Eddy Barrows, Sy Barry, Hilary Barta, Sami Basri, Chris Batista, Eric Battle, John Beatty, Terry Beatty, David Beaty, C.C. Beck, Jordie Bellaire,Howard Bender, Scott Benefield, Julie Benson, Shawna Benson, Ed Benes, Mariah Benes, Joe Benitez, Ryan Benjamin, Joe Bennett, Lee Bermejo, Ramon Bernado, Ian Bertram, Simone Bianchi, Jack Binder, Jerry Bingham, J.J. Birch, Steve Bird, Simon Bisley, Stephen Bissette, BIT, Tex Blaisdell, Fernando Blanco, Bret Blevins, Greg Blocks, Blond, Will Blyberg, Jon Bogdanove, Brian Bolland, Henry Boltinoff, John Bolton, Philip Bond, Roger Bonet, Richard Bonk, Brett Booth, Alisson Borges, Geraldo Borges, Wayne Boring, Ron Boyd, Belardino Brabo, Ken Branch, Craig Brasfield, Brett Breeding, Jeff Brennan, Andrei Bressan, Norm Breyfogle, Mark Bright, June Brightman, June Brigman, Philippe Briones, Pat Broderick, Greg Brooks, Bob Brown, Daniel Brown, Garry Brown, Reilly Brown, Jimmy Broxton, Joe Brozowski, D. Bruce Berry, Al Bryant, Rick Bryant, Brian Buccellato, Rebecca Buchman, Mark Buckingham, Rich Buckler, Danny Bulanadi, Cullen Bunn, Rick Burchett, Chris Burnham, Ray Burnley, Jack Burnley, Sal Buscema, Buzz, Mitch Byrd, John Byrne, Stephen Byrne, Ralph Cabrera, Jim Calafiore, Talent Caldwell, Ben Caldwell, Dennis Calero, Ignacio Calero, Robert Campanella, Marc Campos, Giuseppe Camuncoli, Eric Canete, Zander Cannon, Greg Capullo, W.C. Carani, Nick Cardy, Sergio Cariello, Richard Case, John Cassaday, Marco Castiello, Anthony Castrillo, John Cebollero, Joe Certa, Gary Chaloner, Keith Champagne, Ernie Chan, Ron Chan, Bernard Chang, Kiki Chansamone, Jim Charalampidis,Travis Charest, Howard Chaykin, Michael Chen, Sean Chen, Jim Cheung, Cliff Chiang, Brian Ching, Michael Choi, Nick Choles, Bert Christman, John Tyler Christopher, Tom Chu, Ian Churchill, Vicente Cifuentes, Yidiray Cinar, Matthew Clark, Mike Clark, Scott Clark, Andy Clarke, Becky Cloonan, Martin Coccolo, Dave Cockrum, Andre Coelho, Olivier Coipel, Gene Colan, Jack Cole, Simon Coleby, Hector Collazo, Vince Colletta, Bill Collins, Mike Collins, Ernie Colon, Amanda Conner, Kevin Conrad, Will Conrad, Andrew Constant, Carlos D'Anda, Darwyn Cooke, Dave Cooper, Pete Costanza, Denys Cowan, Jeremy Cox, P. Craig Russell, Clayton Crain, Dennis Cramer, Reed Crandall, Saleem Crawford, Steve Crespo, Jake Crippen, Chris Cross, Charles Cuidera, Paris Cullins, Fernando Dagnino, Andrew Dalhouse, Federico Dallocchio, Rodolfo Damaggio, Tony S. Daniel, Alan Davis, Dan Davis, Ed Davis, Shane Davis, Sam De La Rosa, Randy Deburke, Mike DeCarlo, Nelson DeCastro, Marc Deering, Nuzio DeFilippis, Adam DeKraker, Luciana del Negro, Nick Derington, Carmine Di Giandomico, Jose Delbo, John Dell, Jesse Delperdang, J.M. DeMatteis, Mike Deodato Jr., Tom Derenick, Hi-Fi Design, Johnny Desjardins, Stephen DeStefano, Tony DeZuniga, Netho Diaz, Dick Dillin, Steve Dillon, Steve Ditko, Rachel Dodson, Terry Dodson, Derec Donovan, Colleen Doran, Evan Dorkin, Les Dorscheid, Alberto Dose, Bob Downs, Mike Dringenberg, Victor Drujiniu, Christian Duce, Armando Durruthy, Michal Dutkiewicz, Jan Duursema, Bob Dvorak, Kieron Dwyer, Tim Dzon, Dale Eaglesham, Scot Eaton, Neil Edwards, Martin Egeland, Lee Elias, Chris Eliopulos, Randy Elliott, Lee Elias, Gabe Eltaeb, Will Ely, Randy Emberlin, Tan Eng Huat, Steve Epting, Gary Erskine, Steve Erwin, Mike Esposito, Ric Estrada, George Evans, Nathan Eyring, Rich Faber, Jason Fabok, Nathan Fairbairn, Romulo Fajardo Jr., Mark Farmer, Wayne Faucher, Duncan Fegredo, Tom Feister, Norman Felchie, Jim Fern, Raúl Fernández, Javi Fernandez, Eber Ferreira, Julio Ferreira, Juan Ferreyra, Pascal Ferry, Nick Filardi, David Finch, Fabrizio Fiorentino, John Fischetti, Creig Flessel, Sandu Florea, John Floyd, Max Fiumara, John Ford, Travel Foreman, John Forte, Tom Fowler, Ramona Fradon, Francesco Francavilla, Gary Frank, Frank Frazetta, Fred Fredericks, George Freeman, Ron Frenz, Paul Fricke, Derek Fridolfs, Richard Friend, Danis Frietas, Jenny Frison, James Fry, Anderson Gabrych, Kerry Gammill, Veronica Gandini,Lee Garbett, German Garcia, Manuel Garcia, Alex Garner, Ron Garney, Brian Garvey, Alé Garza, Carlos Garzón, Phil Gascoine, Stefano Gaudiano, Drew Geraci, Mitch Gerads, Sunny Gho, Frank Giacoia, Vince Giarrano, Dave Gibbons, Ian Gibson, Joe Giella, Keith Giffen, Craig Gilmore, Dick Giordano, Sam Glanzman, Jonathan Glapion, Adam Glass, Patrick Gleason, Scott Godlewski, Frank Gomez, Fernando Gonzales, Adrian Gonzales, Neil Googe, Julius Gopez, Jason Gorder, Al Gordon, Chris Gordon, Sam Grainger, Jerry Grandenetti, Mick Gray, Dan Green, Timothy Green II, Sid Greene, Mike Grell, Al Grenet, Tom Grindberg, Mat Groom, Peter Gross, Tom Grummett, Ig Guara, Fred Guardineer, Renato Guedes, R.M. Guera, Luis Guerrero, Gianluca Gugliotta, Jackson Guice, Yvel Guichet, Andres Guinaldo, Paul Guinan, Mike Gustovich, J. H. Williams III, Gene Ha, Matt Haley, Jim Hall, Craig Hamilton, Cully Hamner, Scott Hampton, Scott Hanna, Ed Hannigan, Chad Hardin, Fred Harper, Ron Harris, Tony Harris, James Harvey, Irwin Hasen, Jeremy Haun, Mike Hawthorne, Rob Hayes, Fred Haynes, Doug Hazlewood, Daniel HDR, Russ Heath, Don Heck, Marc Hempel, Andrew Hennessy, Daniel Henriques, Scott Hepburn, Phil Hester, Everett E. Hibbard, Kyle Higgins, Bryan Edward Hill, Bryan Hitch, Rick Hoberg, James Hodgkins, Josh Hood, Ken Hooper, Dave Hoover, Sandra Hope, Alex Horley, Greg Horn, Jody Houser, Kyle Hotz ,Richard Howell, Corin Howell, Mike Huddleston, Jeff Huet, Adam Hughes, Dave Hunt, Rob Hunter, Victor Ibanez, Jamal Igle, Stuart Immonen, Carmine Infantino, Frazer Irving, Mark Irwin, Geof Isherwood, Chris Ivy, Jack Jadson, Mikel Janín, Dennis Janke, Klaus Janson, Alex Jay, Georges Jeanty, Dennis Jensen, Oscar Jimenez, Phil Jimenez, Jorge Jiménez, Jock, Dave Johnson, Drew Johnson, Staz Johnson, Jeff Johnson, Arvell Jones, Casey Jones, J.G. Jones, Kelley Jones, Robert Jones, Malcolm Jones III, Arnie Jorgensen, Ruy José, Tom Joyner, Dan Jurgens, Justiniano, John K. Snyder III, Barbara Kaalberg, John Kalisz, Michael Kaluta, Viktor Kalvachev, Bob Kane, Gil Kane, Kano, Rafael Kayanan, Stan Kaye, Joe Kelly, A.J. Kent, Dale Keown, Karl Kerschl, Karl Kesel, Jessica Kholinne, Jack Kirby, J.J. Kirby, Leonard Kirk, Tyler Kirkham, Jeff King, Tom King, Tyler Kirkham, Barry Kitson, George Klein, Scott Koblish, Irene Koh, Scott Kolins, Tony Kordos, Don Kramer, Peter Krause, Ray Kryssing, Adam Kubert, Andy Kubert, Joe Kubert, Aaron Kuder, Szymon Kudranski, Andy Kuhn, Alan Kupperberg, Michel Lacombe, José Ladrönn, David Lafuente, Harry Lampert, Greg Land, Justin Land, Stefano Landini, Andy Lanning, David Lapham, Serge Lapointe, Michael Lark, Greg LaRocque, Bud LaRosa, Salvador Larroca, Erik Larsen, Ken Lashley, Stanley Lau, Bob Layton, Bob Le Rose, Rob Lea, Garry Leach, Rob Lean, Jim Lee, Norman Lee, Paul Lee, Alvin Lee, Jae Lee, Alex Lei, Steve Leialoha, Rob Leigh, Jay Leisten, Jeff Lemire, Rick Leonardi, Bob Lewis, Mark Lewis, Steve Lieber, Rob Liefeld, Sonny Liew, Steve Lightle, Ron Lim, Mark Lipka, John Livesay, Victor Llamas, Beni Lobel, Kinsun Loh, Don Lomax, Alvaro Lopez, David Lopez, Aaron Lopresti, John Lowe, Jorge Lucas, José Luis Garcia-Lopez, Tula Lotay, Marissa Louise, Adriano Lucas, Emanuela Lupacchino, Daniel LuVisi, Greg Luzniak, Tom Lyle, Howard M. Shum, Mike Machlan, Dev Madan, Wilson Magalháes, Kevin Maguire, Rick Magyar, Larry Mahlstedt, Doug Mahnke, Alex Maleev, Marcelo Maiolo, Francis Manapul, Leonardo Manco, Tom Mandrake, Mike Manley, Clay Mann, Lou Manna, Guillem March, Pablo Marcos, Marvin Mariano, Bill Marimon, David Marquez, Álvaro Martínez, Cindy Martin, Cynthia Martin, Gary Martin, Laura Martin, Marcos Martin, Shawn Martinbrough, Kenny Martinez, Roy Allan Martinez, Marcos Marz, José Marzan Jr., Nathan Massengill, Jason Masters, Steve Mattsson, J.P. Mayer, Sheldon Mayer, Mike Mayhew, Rick Mays, David Mazzucchelli, Trevor McCarthy, Ray McCarthy, Aaron McClennan, Tom McCraw, John McCrea, Scott McDaniel, Luke McDonnell, Todd McFarlane, Tom McGraw, Ed McGuinness, Dave McKean, Mark McKenna, Mike McKone, Frank McLaughlin, Bob McLeod, Shawn McManus, Tom McWeeney, Lan Medina, Paco Medina, Linda Medley, Carlos Meglia, David Meikis, Adriana Melo, Jaime Mendoza, Jesús Merino, Mort Meskin, William Messner-Loebs, J.D. Mettler, Jonboy Meyers, Pop Mhan, Joshua Middleton, Grant Miehm, Rodolfo Migliari, Mike Mignola, Danny Miki, Al Milgrom, Frank Miller, Steve Mitchell, Lee Moder, Sheldon Moldoff, Romano Molenaar, Jorge Molina, Karl Moline, Shawn Moll, Steve Montano, Jim Mooney, Jerome Moore, Stuart Moore, Travis Moore, Dan Mora, Marcio Morais, Mark Morales, Rags Morales, David Moran,Ruben Moreira, Tomeu Morey, Gabriel Morrissette, Gray Morrow, Win Mortimer, Paul Mounts, Ibrahim Moustafa, Jeffrey Moy, Phil Moy, Sean Murphy, Brian Murray, Mayo Naito, Todd Nauck, Paul Neary, Rudy Nebres, Mark Nelson, Diogenes Neves, Fabiano Neves, Denis Neville, Don Newton, Dustin Nguyen, Tom Nguyen, Peter Nguyen, Art Nichols, Troy Nixey, Martin Nodell, Graham Nolan, Cary Nord, Irv Novick, Leo Nowak, Kevin Nowlan, John Nyberg, Michael O'Hare, Sonia Oback, Bob Oksner, Ben Oliver, Ariel Olivetti, Patrick Olliffe, Jerry Ordway, Joe Orlando, Steve Orlando, Guillermo Ortego, Ryan Ottley, Andy Owens, Richard Pace, Carlos Pacheco, Carlo Pagulayan, Mark Pajarillo, Tom Palmer, Jimmy Palmiotti, Peter Palmiotti, Dan Panosian, Eduardo Pansica, Pete Pantazis, George Papp, Yanick Paquette, Charles Paris, Jeff Parker, Ande Parks, Mike Parobeck, Francisco Paronzini, Sean Parsons, Fernando Pasarin, James Pascoe, Allen Passalaqua, Bruce D. Patterson, Chuck Patton, Jason Paz, Jason Pearson, Paul Pelletier, Mark Pennington, Andrew Pepoy, Benjamin Percy, Mike Perkins, Rich Perrotta, Frank Perry, Harry G. Peter, Brandon Peterson, Bob Petrecca, Hugo Petrus, Joe Phillips, Javier Piña, Wendy Pini, FCO Plascencia, Ivan Plascencia, Al Plastino, Kilian Plunkett, Keith Pollard, Adam Pollina, Alberto Ponticelli, Francis Portela, Howard Porter, Howie Post, Eric Powell, Joe Prado, Miguelanxo Prado, Hendry Prasetya, Bruno Premiani, Christopher Priest, Mark Propst, Steve Pugh, Javier Pulido, Jack Purcell, George Pérez, Joe Quesada, Dan Quintana, Wil Quintana, Frank Quitely, Mac Raboy, Pablo Raimondi, Elton Ramalho, Humberto Ramos, Rodney Ramos, Ron Randall, Khary Randolph, Tom Raney, Rich Rankin, Norm Rapmund, Fred Ray, Brian Reber, Bruno Redondo, Frank Redondo, Sal Regia, Ivan Reis, Rod Reis, Paul Renaud, Cliff Richards, Roy Richardson, Robin Riggs, Eduardo Risso, Paul Rivoche, Trina Robbins, Jeremy Roberts, Clem Robins, Andrew Robinson, Jerry Robinson, Roger Robinson, Kenneth Rocafort, Robson Rocha, Denis Rodier, Anibal Rodriguez, Carlos Rodriguez, Danny Rodriguez, Jasen Rodriguez, Rodin Rodriguez, Noel Rodriguez, Francisco Rodriguez De La Fuente, Marshall Rogers, Prentis Rollins, T.G. Rollins, John Romita Jr., William Rosado, John Rosenberger, Alex Ross, Dave Ross, Luke Ross, Riley Rossmo, Duncan Rouleau, Craig Rousseau, George Roussos, Stephane Roux, Jim Royal, Mike Royer, Josef Rubinstein, Steve Rude, Marco Rudy, Nei Ruffino, Felix Ruiz, Mark Russell, Vince Russell, Paul Ryan, Matt Ryan, Tony S. Daniel, Mike S. Miller, Bernard Sachs, Stephen Sadowski, Jesús Saís, Edgar Salazar, Tim Sale, Javier Saltares, Chris Samnee, Daniel Sampere, David Sampere, Alejandro Sanchez, José Sánchez, Alex Sanchez, Rafa Sandoval, Derlis Santacruz, Mateus Santolouco, Matt Santorelli, Marco Santucci, Clement Sauvé Jr., Alex Saviuk, Kurt Schaffenberger, Evan Shaner, Liam Sharp, Mitch Schauer, Christie Scheele, Otto Schmidt, Ira Schnapp, Mark Schultz, Damion Scott, Nicola Scott, Trevor Scott, Bart Sears, Tim Seeley, Stephen Segovia, Stjepan Šejić, Mike Sekowsky, Mike Sellers, Val Semeiks, Miguel Sepulveda, Buzz Setzer, Declan Shalvey, Eric Shanower, Hal Sharp, Liam Sharp, Kevin Sharpe, Howard Sherman, Pen Shumaker, Joe Shuster, Jon Sibal, Bill Sienkiewicz, R.B. Silva, Emanuel Simeon, Tom Simmons, Joe Simon, Dave Simons, Walter Simonson, Howard Simpson, Alex Sinclair, Paulo Siqueira, Jeremy Skipper, Steve Skroce, Louis Small Jr., Andy Smith, Bob Smith, Cam Smith, Dietrich Smith, Jeff Smith, Tod Smith, Peter Snejbjerg, Sno-Cone Studios, Ray Snyder, Scott Snyder, Ryan Sook, Andrea Sorrentino, Beth Sotelo, Chris Sotomayor, Aaron Sowd, Dexter Soy, Jack Sparling, Dan Spiegle, Dick Sprang, Frank Springer, Chris Sprouse, Alex Sollazzo, Claude St. Aubin, Cat Staggs, John Stanisci, Fiona Staples, Jim Starlin, Arne Starr, Leonard Starr, Rick Stasi, John Statema, Joe Staton, Ken Steacy, Marvin Stein, Brian Stelfreeze, N. Steven Harris, Dave Stevens, Cameron Stewart, Roger Stewart, John Stokes, Kevin Stokes, Karl Story, Larry Stroman, Larry Stucker, Robert Stull, Michael Suayan, Goran Sudzuka, Tom Sutton, Curt Swan, Ardian Syaf, Michael T. Gilbert, Marcio Takara, Sana Takeda, Bryan Talbot, Billy Tan, Philip Tan, Romeo Tanghal, Babs Tarr, Jordi Tarragona, Christopher Taylor, Tom Taylor, Ty Templeton, Jason Temujin Minor, Greg Theakston, Art Thibert, Stephen Thompson, Frank Thorne, John Timms, Marcus To, Peter Tomasi, Alex Toth, Julian Totino Tedesco, John Totleben, Tim Townsend, Jonas Trindade, Andy Troy, Tim Truman, Chaz Truog, Koi Turnbull, Dwayne Turner, Michael Turner, George Tuska, James Tynion IV, Angel Unzueta, Carlos Urbano, Alina Urusov, Juan Valasco, Ethan Van Sciver, Brad Vancata, Rick Veitch, Sal Velluto, Robert Venditti, Charles Vess, Al Vey, Carlos Villagran, Ricardo Villagran, José Villarrubia, Dexter Vines, Alessandro Vitti, Juan Vlasco, Trevor Von Eeden, Wade Von Grawbadger, Brennan Wagner, Matt Wagner, Ron Wagner, Brad Walker, Kev Walker, Chip Wallace, Steve Wands, John Watson, Lee Weeks, Joe Weems, Alan Weiss, Kevin J. West, Chris Weston, Doug Wheatley, Mark Wheatley, Dean White, Glenn Whitmore, Bob Wiacek, Mike Wieringo, Aron Wiesenfeld, Admira Wijaya, Anthony Williams, Freddie E. Williams II, Rob Williams, Scott Williams, J.H. Williams III, Joshua Williamson, Bill Willingham, G. Willow Wilson, Ryan Winn, Phil Winslade, Chuck Wojtkiewicz, Marv Wolfman, Michele Wolfman, Walden Wong, Wally Wood, Pete Woods, John Workman, Moe Worthman, Chris Wozniak, Bill Wray, Jason Wright, Berni Wrightson, Annie Wu, Xermanico, Kelly Yates, Tom Yeates, Steve Yeowell, Leinil Francis Yu, Patrick Zircher.

The publishers have made every effort to identify and acknowledge the artists whose work appears in this Encyclopedia.